Culture,
Leadership,
and
Organizations

The GLOBE Study of 62 Societies

62 GLOBE Societies

1. Albania
2. Argentina
3. Australia
4. Austria
5. Bolivia
6. Brazil
7. Canada (English speaking)
8. China
9. Colombia
10. Costa Rica
11. Czech Republic
12. Denmark
13. Ecuador
14. Egypt
15. El Salvador
16. England
17. Finland
18. France
19. Georgia
20. Germany-East (former GDR)
21. Germany-West (former FRG)
22. Greece
23. Guatemala
24. Hong Kong
25. Hungary
26. India
27. Indonesia
28. Iran
29. Ireland
30. Israel
31. Italy
32. Japan
33. Kazakhstan
34. Kuwait
35. Malaysia
36. Mexico
37. Morocco
38. Namibia
39. The Netherlands
40. New Zealand
41. Nigeria
42. The Philippines
43. Poland
44. Portugal
45. Qatar
46. Russia
47. Singapore
48. Slovenia
49. South Africa (Black Sample)
50. South Africa (White Sample)
51. South Korea
52. Spain
53. Sweden
54. Switzerland
55. Switzerland (French-Speaking)
56. Taiwan
57. Thailand
58. Turkey
59. United States
60. Venezuela
61. Zambia
62. Zimbabwe

Major GLOBE Collaborators

The GLOBE Coordinating Team[1]

Staffan Akerblom, Stockholm School of Economics, Switzerland

Felix Brodbeck, University of Munich, Germany

Jagdeep Chhokar, Indian Institute of Management—Ahmedabad, India

Marcus Dickson, Wayne State University, Michigan, USA

Peter Dorfman, New Mexico State University, USA

Paul Hanges, University of Maryland, USA

Mansour Javidan, University of Calgary, Canada

Enrique Ogliastri, Instituto Centroamericano de Administracion de Empresas, Costa Rica

Ruiz-Quintanilla, Antonio S. A., Aarhus School of Business, Denmark

Marius van Wyk, University of South Africa, South Africa

GLOBE Country Co-Investigators[2]

Abdalla, Ikhlas A., Arab Fund for Economic & Social Development (Qatar)

Adetoun, Bolanle Akande, Potchefstroom University (South Africa)

Adetoun, Babajide Samuel, Appropriate Development Associates (Nigeria)

Akande, Adebowal, Potchefstroom University (South Africa)

Agourram, Hafid, University of Quebec—Montreal (Morocco)

Akerblom, Staffan, Stockholm School of Economics (Sweden)

Akande, Bolanle Elizabeth, The Center for Sustainable Development and Gender Issues (Nigeria)

al-Homoud, Moudi, Kuwait University (Kuwait)

Altschul, Carlos, Universidad de Buenos Aires (Argentina)

Alvarez-Backus, Eden, Sony Electronics (Philippines)

Andrews, Julian, University of Alberta (Canada)

Arias, Maria Eugenia, The University of Melbourne (Costa Rica and El Salvadore)

Arif, Mirian Sofyan, University of Indonesia (Indonesia)

Ashkanasy, Neal, University of Queensland (Australia)

Asslani, Arben, Bellevue University (Albania)

Audia, Guiseppe, London Business School (Italy)

Bakacsi, Gyula, Budapest University of Economic Sciences (Hungary)

Bautista, Arnoldo, National Center of Investigation and Technological Development (Mexico)

Bao, Jimmy, Fudan University (China)

Bendova, Helena, Jihoceske University (Czech Republic)

Beveridge, David, Western Illinois University (Bolivia)

Bhagat, Rabi S., University of Memphis (USA)

Blacutt, Alejandro, Universidad Catolica Bolivian (Bolivia)

Bodega, Domenico, University of Luigi Bocconi (Italy)

Bodur, Muzaffer, Bogazici University (Turkey)

Booth, Simon, University of Reading (England)

Booysen, Annie E, University of South Africa (South Africa)

Bourantas, Dimitrios, Athens University of Economics and Business (Greece)

Brenk, Klas, Univerziti Ljubjana (Slovenia)

Brodbeck, Felix, Aston Business School (Germany)

Carl, Dale Everton, University of Calgary (Canada)

Castel, Philippe, Universite de Bourgogne (France)

Chang, Chieh-Chen, National Sun Yat-Sen University (Taiwan)

Chau, Sandy, Lingnam College (Hong Kong)

Cheung, Frenda, Hong Kong Polytechnic University (Hong Kong)

Chhokar, Jagdeep S., Indian Institute of Management—Ahmedabad (India)

Chiu, Jimmy, City University of Hong Kong (Hong Kong)

Cosgriff, Peter, Lincoln University (New Zealand)

Dastmalchian, Ali, University of Lethbridge (Iran)

Dela-Coleta, Jose Augusto, Centro Universitario do Triangulo (Brazil)

Dela-Coleta, Marilia Ferreira, Universidade Federal de Uberlandia (Brazil)

den Hartog, Deanne N., Erasmus Universiteit (Netherlands)

Deneire, Marc, University of Nancy 2 (France)

Donnelly-Cox, Gemma, University of Dublin—Trinity College (Ireland)

Dorfman, Peter W, New Mexico State University (Mexico)

Earley, Christopher, University of Indiana (China)

Elgamal, Mahmoud A. E., Kuwait University (Kuwait)

Erez, Miriam, Israel Institute of Technology (Israel)

Falkus, Sarah, University of Queensland (Australia)

Fearing, Mark, Lincoln University (New Zealand)

Field, Richard H. G., University of Alberta (Canada)

Fimmen, Carol, Western Illinois University (Bolivia)

Frese, Michael, University of Giessen (Germany)

Fu, Pingping, Chinese University of Hong Kong (China)

Grachev, Mikhail V., Western Ilinois Universssity (Russia)

Gutierrez, Celia, Complutense University (Spain)

Hartanto, Frans Mardi, Institut Technologi Bandung (Indonesia)

Hhashha, Mohamed Abou, Alexandria University (Egypt)

Holmberg, Ingalill, Stockholm School of Economics (Sweden)

Holzer, Marina, Altschul Consultores (Argentina)

Hoppe, Michael, Center for Creative Leadership (USA)

Howell, Jon P., New Mexico State University (Mexico)

Ibrieva, Elena, University of Nebraska—Lincoln (Kazakhstan)

Ickis, John C., INCAE (Costa Rica)

Ismail, Zakaria, Universiti Kebangsaan Malaysia (Malaysia)

Jarmuz, Slawomir, University of Opole (Poland)

Javidan, Mansour, University of Calgary (Iran)

Jesuino, Jorge Correia, Instituto Superior de Sciencias do Trabalho e da Empresa (Portugal)

Ji, Li, Hong Kong Baptist University (Singapore)

Jone, Kuen-Yung, Kaohsiung Medical College (Taiwan)

Jones, Geoffrey, University of Reading (England)

Jorbenadse, Revaz, Tbilisi State University (Georgia)
Kabasakal, Hayat, Bogazici University (Turkey)
Keating, Mary, University of Dublin—Trinity College (Ireland)
Keller, Andrea, University of Zurich (Switzerland [French-speaking])
Kennedy, Jeffrey C., Lincoln University (New Zealand)
Kim, Jay S., Ohio State University (South Korea)
Kipiani, Giorgi, Georgian Academy of Sciences (Georgia)
Kipping, Matthias, University of Reading (England)
Konrad, Edvard, Universiti Ljubljana (Slovenia)
Koopman, Paul L., Vrije Univeriteit-Amsterdam (Netherlands)
Kuan, Fuh-Yeong, Shu-Te Institute of Technology (Taiwan)
Kurc, Alexandre, University of Nancy 2 (France)
Lacassagne, Marie-Francoise Universite de Bourgogne, (France)
Lee, Sang M., University of Nebraska—Lincoln (Albania and (Kazakhstan)
Leeds, Christopher, University of Nancy 2 (France)
Leguizamon, Francisco, INCAE (Costa Rica)
Lindell, Martin, Swedish School of Economics and Business Administration (Finland)
Lobell, Jean, AcXEL International (Philippines)
Luthans, Fred, University of Nebraska—Lincoln (Albania and Kazakhstan)
Maczynski, Jerzy, University of Wroclaw (Poland)
Mansor, Norma, University of Malaysia (Malaysia)
Martin, Gillian, University of Dublin—Trinity College (Ireland)
Martin, Michael, University of Nebraska—Lincoln (Albania)
Martinez, Sandra M., Widener University (Mexico)
McMillen, Cecilia, University of San Francisco de Quito (Costa Rica, El Salvador, and Guatemala)
Messallam, Aly, Alexandria University (Egypt)
Misumi, Emiko, Institute for Group Dynamics (Japan)
Misumi, Jyuji, Institute for Group Dynamics (Japan)
Morsi, Nabil M., Alexandria University (Egypt)
Ngin, Phyllisis M., Melbourne Business School (Singapore)
O'Connell, Jeremiah, Bentley College (Spain)
Ogliastri, Enrique, Instituto Centroamericano de Administracion de Empresas, Costa Rica (Colombia)
Papalexandris, Nancy, Athens University of Economics and Business (Greece)
Peng, T. K., I-Shou University (Taiwan)
Preziosa, Maria Marta, Instituto para el Desrrollo de Ejecutivos en la Argentina (Argentina)
Prieto, Jose M., Complutense University (Spain)
Rakitsky, Boris V., Institute of Perspectives and Problems of the Country (Russia)
Reber, Gerhard, Johannes Kepler University (Austria)
Rogovsky, Nikolai, International Labor Organization (Russia)
Rozen, Amir, Israel Institute of Technology (Israel)
Sabadin, Argio, Universiti Ljubljana (Slovenia)
Sahaba, Majhoub, Groupe EFET (Morocco)
Siles, Marcelo, Michigan State University (Bolivia)
Salgado, Elvira, University of the Andes, Bogota (Colombia)
Salon de Bustamente, Colombia, Universidad de los Andes (Venezuela)
Santana-Melgoza, Carmen, Smith College (Mexico)
Sauers, Daniel A, Lincoln University (New Zealand)

Schramm-Nielson, Jette, Copenhagen Business School (Denmark)
Schultz, Majken, Copenhagen Business School (Denmark)
Shi, Zuqi, Fudan University (China)
Sigfrids, Camilla, Swedish School of Economics and Business Administration (Finland)
Song, Kye-Chung, Chungnam National University (South Korea)
Szabo, Erna, Johannes Kepler University (Austria)
Teo, Albert C., National University of Singapore (Singapore)
Thierry, Henk, University of Tilburg (Netherlands)
Tjakranegara, Jann Hidayat, Institut Technologi Bandung (Indonesia)
Trimi, Sylvana, University of Nebraska—Lincoln (Albania)
Tsui, Anne S., Hong Kong University of Science and Technology (China)
Ubolwanna, Pavakanum, Thammasat University (Thailand)
van Wyk, Marius W., University of South Africa (South Africa)
Vondrysova, Marie, University of South Bohemia (Czech Republic)
Weibler, Juergen, University of Hagen (Switzerland)
Wilderom, Celeste, Tilburg University (Netherlands)
Wu, Rongxian, Suzhou University (China)
Wunderer, Rolf, University of St. Gallen (Switzerland)
Yakob, Nik Rahiman Nik, Universiti Kebangsaan Malaysia (Malaysia)
Yang, Yongkang, Fudan University (China)
Yin, Zuoqiu, Fudan University (China)
Yoshida, Michio, Kumamoto University (Japan)
Zhou, Jian, Fudan University (China)

GLOBE Senior Research Associates[3]

Roy-Bhattacharya, Joydeep, Independent Literary Author, USA
Ram Aditya, Florida International University, USA
Mary Sully de Luque, Thunderbird University, Arizona, USA
Vipin Gupta, Grand Valley State University, Michigan, USA

End Notes

1. The Globe Coordinating Team served as an advisory group to the Principal Investigator, Robert J. House, with respect to policies and procedures for data collection and administration of GLOBE.

2. The Country Co-Investigators (CCIs) assisted in the formulation of the instruments used in this study, collected the data relevant to their countries and assisted in interpretation of the data. The countries they represented are in parenthesis following their names and their institutional affiliations.

3. The Senior Research Associates assisted Robert House in the administration of the GLOBE research program, provided advice to Country Co-Investigators, maintained GLOBE files and budget, provided status reports, and performed other administrative functions.

Culture, Leadership, and Organizations

The GLOBE Study of 62 Societies

Edited By

Robert J. House
University of Pennsylvania

Paul J. Hanges
University of Maryland

Mansour Javidan
University of Calgary

Peter W. Dorfman
New Mexico State University

Vipin Gupta
Grand Valley State University

SAGE Publications
International Educational and Professional Publisher
Thousand Oaks ■ London ■ New Delhi

For information:

Sage Publications, Inc.
2455 Teller Road
Thousand Oaks, California 91320
E-mail: order@sagepub.com

Sage Publications Ltd.
1 Oliver's Yard
55 City Road
London EC1Y 1SP
United Kingdom

Sage Publications India Pvt. Ltd.
B-42, Panchsheel Enclave
Post Box 4109
New Delhi 110 017 India

Printed in the United States of America

Library of Congress Cataloging-in-Publication Data

Culture, leadership, and organizations: The GLOBE study of 62 societies /
edited by Robert J. House . . . [et al.].
    p. cm.
Includes bibliographical references and index.
ISBN 0-7619-2401-9 (Cloth)
  1. Global Leadership and Organizational Behavior Effectiveness Research Program.
2. Leadership—Research. 3. Organizational behavior—Research.
4. Leadership—Cross-cultural studies. 5. Organizational behavior—Cross-cultural studies.
6. Social values—Cross-cultural studies. I. Title: GLOBE study of 62 societies.
II. House, Robert J. III. Global Leadership and Organizational Behavior Effectiveness
Research Program.
HD57.7 .L4323 2004 302.3′5—dc22   2003024360

This book is printed on acid-free paper.

05 06 07 10 9 8 7 6 5 4 3 2

Acquisitions Editor:	Al Bruckner
Editorial Assistant:	MaryAnn Vail
Copy Editor:	Edward Meidenbauer
Production Editor:	Diane S. Foster
Typesetter:	C&M Digitals (P) Ltd.
Proofreader:	Libby Larson and Kris Bergstad
Indexer:	Molly Hall
Cover Designer:	Ravi Balasuriya

CONTENTS

FOREWORD

A nthropologist Redfield (1948) defined *culture* as "shared understandings made manifest in act and artifact" (p. vii). This is consistent with the definition used by the GLOBE research project, which examines culture as practices and values. *Practices* are acts or "the way things are done in this culture," and *values* are artifacts because they are human made and, in this specific case, are judgments about "the way things should be done."

GLOBE measured practices and values exist at the levels of industry (financial services, food processing, telecommunications), organization (several in each industry), and society (62 cultures). Thus, the GLOBE researchers measured culture at different levels with both practices and values. Then they asked: How is culture related to societal, organizational, and leadership effectiveness?

The GLOBE research could be called the Manhattan Project of the study of the relationship of culture to conceptions of leadership. One hundred and seventy investigators from 62 cultures worked on this project. Twenty of them participated in writing this book. They tested 27 hypotheses that linked culture to interesting outcomes, with data from 17,300 managers in 951 organizations. They measured the variables with cultural sensitivity, developing instruments in consultation with members of the relevant cultures. By using focus groups, and by heavy dependence on the previous literature, the investigators developed instruments that tapped local meanings that were appropriate for each level of the data and also had equivalence across cultures.

Cross-cultural research is tricky and difficult. The researchers took full advantage of methodologies developed during the past 50 years to do their research in a sophisticated way. They did pilot tests, they used double translations, they checked the psychometric characteristics of their instruments, and they eliminated response biases. They used multiple measurements of the constructs. They checked reliabilities and construct validity with multitrait multimethod approaches. They started with huge numbers of items and dropped more than half. They checked their results against the work of Hofstede (e.g., their Power Distance practices measure correlated with Hofstede's Power Distance .61, $p < .01$, but Power Distance values did not correlate; the Gender Egalitarianism dimension, on the other hand, had no relation to Hofstede's Masculinity dimension), Schwartz (e.g., Uncertainty Avoidance values correlated .74 with Shalom Schwartz' Embeddedness), and Inglehart (see below). They measured organizational and societal culture with different forms of the instrument. They developed unobtrusive methods for the measurement of some of the constructs. They analyzed the data with multilevel confirmatory factor analysis and hierarchical linear modeling (similar to regression analysis except that it takes the level—i.e., industry, organization, society—into account). They addressed the reverse ecological fallacy and identified clusters of societies and patterns of outstanding leadership. They then linked the clusters of societies and the patterns of leadership, and examined how these clusters are related to interesting health, economic, and social indicators. They also tested how well their results could be generalized beyond the particular samples of managers, methods, or kinds of data analyses.

The investigators used an imaginative theoretical framework in which leader acceptance and effectiveness were the dependent variables and social culture and organizational practices were the independent variables. In between these sets of variables they included variables that may moderate the relationships between the independent and dependent variables, such as cultural theories of what is a good leader and organizational contingencies imposed by the fact that the data came from different industries.

The result is an encyclopedia of findings linking culture to societal functioning and leadership. Table after table give data that contrast cultures on such topics as the percent of the sample in each culture who dislike democracy to the percentages who consider a particular leadership attribute desirable. The findings can answer fascinating questions. In what cultures can a leader violate the societal norms and get away with it? What leader traits are universally desirable and what traits are undesirable? What is the ideal of the outstanding leader in Northern Europe or in the Middle East or in eight other clusters of cultures? What organizations from what countries can be successful (or unsuccessful) in mergers and acquisitions?

In carrying out this project they broke new ground by developing additional dimensions of societal cultural variation. For instance, they distinguished between *institutional* and *in-group* collectivism. The former reflects institutions that encourage collective rewards, collective distribution of rewards, and collective action. Institutional collectivism is a cultural pattern that can lead to leadership effectiveness. In-group collectivism involves pride and loyalty for the organization. It is also related negatively to divorce rates. They also added new dimensions of organizational culture, and showed that both practices and values are useful in distinguishing among different kinds of organizations. They found that organizational cultures reflect societal cultures.

Previous research, such as Hofstede's 1980 monumental study, had identified four dimensions of cultural variation—Power Distance, Individualism, Masculinity, and Uncertainty Avoidance. The GLOBE researchers used Future Orientation, Gender Equality, Assertiveness, Humane Orientation, In-group Collectivism, Institutional Collectivism, Performance Orientation, Power Distance, and Uncertainty Avoidance.

Here is a brief description of some of the empirical content of these dimensions. *Performance Orientation* is related to high religious diversity and a low concentration of the largest religion, indicating a culture that is nondogmatic with a creative orientation. Empirically this attribute of a culture helps economic accomplishments, but people in such cultures do not live as long as they do in some other cultures.

Assertiveness is related to natural resources such as oil or metals not being important in the country's exports. Societies high in this attribute do well in global competitiveness but exhibit low levels of psychological health.

Future Orientation is related to a large number of trademarks per capita. In countries high on this attribute people do not visit spontaneously, but call before they visit. Many people use English as a way to advance in their career. People enjoy economic prosperity, and there is scientific advancement, democracy, gender equality, and social health.

Humane Orientation is related to few retail outlets per capita. People who live in such cultures tend to use extended, warm greetings. Hospitality is very important. People show empathy and are very high in satisfaction.

Institutional Collectivism is an attribute that is especially high in Confucian Asia cultures. These are societies that are less segmented than in other parts of the world.

In-Group Collectivism is related to low divorce rates and poor due process, suggesting emphasis on the family.

Gender Egalitarianism is related to a high proportion of women earning an income. Women have access to resources. It is positively correlated with longevity.

Power Distance is related to a limited number of scientists per unit of gross national product. These are societies in which the rich differ from the poor, and thus economic growth often results in unemployment and, instead of helping the poor, makes their position even less satisfactory. Empirically, there is low societal health and little human development (e.g., education).

Uncertainty Avoidance is related to a high share of home corporations in national research and development. In such cultures there is an extensive, modern telecommunication system. There is scientific progress and the government supports economic activities.

One could develop fascinating hypotheses to explain such empirical relationships. Thousands of doctoral dissertations in the future will start with these findings.

Leadership was studied with six culturally implicit theories of leadership: Charismatic/Value-based, Team-Oriented, Participative, Autonomous, Humane, and Self-Protective leadership. In most cultures the first of these is considered most desirable. The second is desirable. The other leadership styles, except for the Self-Protective, are seen as acceptable. But whereas the first is universally desirable (of course, how could one not like a leader who inspires, is visionary, self-sacrifices, and is performance oriented?), the other patterns are often culturally contingent. To be ambitious, for instance, is "good" in some cultures and "bad" in other cultures.

The chapters in this volume contain impressive reviews of the literature corresponding to each of the dimensions of cultural variation. In the case of the collectivism construct, for instance, the authors traced the development of the concept over the course of 3,750 years! The findings of the project are presented in each of these dimension chapters. The findings are too numerous to mention. A few will be selected just to provide the flavor of what is to come.

The standard literature assumed that societal practices and values are positively correlated. In this study, often, they were negatively correlated. In short, the managers indicated that "the way we do things" is negatively related to "what would be the ideal way of doing things." This was especially strong in the case of Power Distance. In most cultures the managers said there was a lot of Power Distance and they would like very much less Power Distance. If Uncertainty Avoidance was high, the managers indicated that they would have liked less of it. In most male-oriented cultures many respondents would have liked less of it. In most cultures there was much collectivism and not enough emphasis on high performance.

The data suggest that for economic development the managers are correct in wanting less Power Distance, less male domination, and more high performance because that is the pattern that was found in the countries with high gross national product per capita. The results suggest that movements toward economic and gender equality as seen in Scandinavia, for instance, can be recommended.

For high prosperity one needs high Performance Orientation, Institutional Collectivism, and Uncertainty Avoidance, and little Power Distance and In-Group Collectivism. For human development, such as good health, the culture should be low in In-Group Collectivism and Power Distance. Life expectancy was positively correlated with Uncertainty Avoidance practices but negatively correlated with Uncertainty Avoidance values.

A major focus of the study was the identification of leadership styles associated with different cultural patterns. Here we find attributes that facilitate (e.g., decisiveness) and inhibit (e.g., irritable) outstanding leadership. Charismatic/Value-based leadership (leader is visionary, inspirational, self-sacrificing, performance oriented) is seen as most desirable everywhere. Team-Oriented (leader is collaborative, team integrator, diplomatic) and Participative (leader is not autocratic) leadership are generally desirable, but in some cultures they are not. In most cultures Autonomous and Humane (modest, compassionate) leadership are neither desirable nor undesirable. Self-Protective (leader is self-centered, status conscious, conflict inducer) leadership is undesirable. We find that Charismatic/Value-based leadership is particularly high in the Anglo cluster of countries and low in the Middle East. Team Oriented is high in Latin America and low in the Middle East. Humane is high in South Asia and low in Nordic Europe. Autonomous is high in East Europe and low in Latin America. Self-Protective is high in South Asia and the Middle East and low in Nordic Europe.

Performance Orientation is related to all culturally implied theories of leadership, except the Self-Protective. It is linked especially to charismatic leadership. Charismatic/Value-based leadership is high also where there is Gender Equality, Future Orientation, and Humane Orientation.

In-Group Collectivism values are positively related to the Charismatic/Value-based style and negatively related to the Self-Protective leadership style.

The Middle East is interesting because the Self-Protective kind of leadership is seen as less of a problem than in other parts of the world. In the Middle East also the Charismatic/Value-based and Team-Oriented leaderships were not given the high endorsement they received in other regions. Finally, in the Middle East there was a local cluster of desirable attributes for leadership, such as familial, humble, and faithful. It makes one wonder if in the rush to maximize economic development many cultures no longer emphasize the humane attributes of warm hospitality and empathy that one finds in that part of the world.

One of the ways to evaluate a new study is to look at the way the findings fit or do not fit existing knowledge. The specific findings generally fit well with what we know, but they provide also many new perspectives. For example, the researchers identified 10 clusters of countries (by using both cultural and climatic data): Latin America, Anglo, Latin Europe, Nordic Europe, Germanic Europe, Confucian Asia, Sub-Saharan Africa, Middle East, Southern Asia, and East Europe. This does not differ much from Samuel Huntington's (1996) typology in *The Clash of Civilizations and the Remaking of World Order.* Huntington identified these civilizations: Western, Latin American, African, Islamic, Sinic, Hindu, Orthodox, Buddhist, and Japanese. Huntington's major criterion was religion, so it is not surprising that the two sets of clusters are not identical. The clusters also fit the results of other researchers. For example, anthropologist Peter Murdock (1981) classified African cultures the way the present researchers classified their countries, with the countries North of the Sahara going into one group and those South of the Sahara going into another group.

Inglehart's data (1997) show that the major contrast in his measures is between the countries of Protestant Europe and the Muslim and African countries. That is also seen here, where the most differences are seen between Europe and the Middle East in practices and values as well as in leadership patterns. We can then argue that mergers and acquisitions that include countries from Europe and the Middle East will be most problematic.

In a book that contains thousands of findings one can easily find things to criticize. Three examples will suffice.

1. We know from the work of Osgood that most concepts are high or low in evaluation. If we look at the desirable leadership patterns, they consist mostly of positively evaluated attributes; the undesirable patterns consist mostly of negatively evaluated attributes.

2. How can one represent large countries like China, India, or the United States with a few samples? Would one not need a dozen samples? For India, for instance, would it not be nice to have samples from Ahmedabad, Mumbai, Delhi, Allahabad, Patna, Kolkata, Bhubaneswar, Srinagar, Hyderabad, Bangalore, Mysore, and Chennai to pick up the major cultures and languages of India?

3. Can we believe each statement? For instance, the observation that in Greece managers have a dim view of "leadership" may depend on the way leadership was translated. If they used *archon,* which is an acceptable translation, then the observation may be due to the fact that this term has the same linguistic root as *archondas,* a rather arrogant upper class person.

If one were to go over all the findings with such a fine-toothed comb one could raise many questions. But one lifetime would not suffice to do that. There is so much here.

In sum, this is a most exciting book for those interested in the relationship of culture and leadership.

—HARRY C. TRIANDIS

REFERENCES

Hofstede, G. (1980). *Culture's consequences: International differences in work-related values.* London: Sage.

Huntington, S. P. (1996). *The clash of civilizations and the remaking of world order.* New York: Simon & Schuster.

Inglehart, R. (1997). *Modernization and postmodernization: Cultural, economic, and political change in 43 societies.* Princeton, NJ: Princeton University Press.

Murdock, G. P. (1981). *Atlas of world cultures.* Pittsburgh: University of Pittsburgh Press.

Redfield, R. (1948). Introduction to B. Malinowski, *Magic, science, and religion.* Boston: Beacon Press.

PREFACE

The idea for GLOBE came to me in the summer of 1991. At that time a substantial amount of research had recently been published indicating the validity of the charismatic leadership paradigm. Leader charisma, as defined by Weber (1947), House (1976) and Bass (1985), had been found to be predictive of individual satisfaction in India (Pereira, 1987), mean academic performance scores of educational institutions in Singapore (Koh, Terborg, & Steers, 1991), performance of U.S. presidents (House, Spangler, & Woycke, 1991) and profit and cost performance in large grocery stores in the Netherlands (subsequently published in 1993, Koene, Pennings, & Schreuder, 1993). The wide variety of cultures in which these studies were conducted suggested to me that charismatic leader behavior may be universally acceptable and effective.

Consequently, I began thinking about conducting a cross-cultural study based on data to be collected from approximately 20 culturally diverse societies to test the cross-cultural generalizability of charismatic leadership in organizations. I began reading the organizational cultural literature to prepare for such a study. After reading a fair sampling of the organizational cultural literature I concluded that I was learning very little because the conceptualization and research methodology of the empirical work in this literature were not very rigorous.

I also read Hofstede's (1980) book and a small sample of the more general cross-cultural literature. After reading a number of studies concerning organizational culture and cross-cultural research, I decided to proceed with the development of the GLOBE research design without doing an exhaustive literature review. I judged that such a review would take me at least a year and that my knowledge as a social scientist would likely be sufficient for a preliminary research design. I also decided that I would rely on experienced cross-cultural social scientists to advise me concerning unique methodological problems associated with GLOBE. I spent most of the 1991–1992 academic year completing outstanding commitments and did some additional reading with respect to cross-cultural literature.

EVOLUTION OF GLOBE

In the summer of 1992, I was a visiting professor at the Vrie University of Amsterdam where I worked with Paul Koopman, Henk Thiery, and Celeste Wilderome. I drafted a preliminary research design and met with these scholars several times. During these meetings we generated a questionnaire item pool consisting of approximately 300 questions relevant to Hofstede's four dimensions of culture plus three additional dimensions: performance and humane and future orientation. During the autumn of 1992, I was a visiting professor at the European Institute for Business Administration. There

I worked with Phillip Podsakoff to further develop the questionnaire item pool. In addition to items relevant to organizational practices, Phil and I also generated items relevant to leader attributes and behavior. By the end of that semester, we had developed a total of approximately 735 items to measure cultural and leadership dimensions.

During the spring semester of 1993, I was a visiting professor at the Departments of Psychology and Management at the University of Maryland. While there I met Paul Hanges, who agreed to participate in GLOBE and assume major responsibility for data storage, maintenance, and analysis. I also met Marcus Dickson, who was to become Paul's Research Assistant with respect to GLOBE data maintenance and analysis. Paul and Marcus were in the Department of Psychology at the University of Maryland.

I also met and recruited Mike Agar and Jeff Thomas. Mike is an anthropologist and Jeff was a Ph.D. student in management. Jeff served as Mike's assistant and they jointly produced guides for anthropological interviewing, media data collection, and content analysis of interview and media information. These guides were combined to form the Qualitative Research Manual, which was designed to be a self-instruction guide for country co-investigators (CCIs). Several CCIs used this manual for guidance when doing qualitative research.

In the summer of 1993, I was a visiting professor at the University of Victoria, on Victoria Island in British Columbia, Canada. As of approximately mid-May of 1993, the GLOBE research design was completed and a questionnaire item pool of more than 700 items had been developed.

In May of 1993, the U.S. Department of Education announced a request for proposals under the auspices of the Dwight D. Eisenhower Leadership Education Program. The Department of Education would fund GLOBE and provided a budget of $300,000. In 1994 the grant was renewed with an additional funding of $325,000.

In August of 1993, I had begun recruiting CCIs with the objective of obtaining representation of 20 countries, rather evenly distributed throughout the major regions of the world.

By October of 1993, scholars from approximately 20 countries had agreed to participate. Also, approximately 10 countries had written to me, unsolicited, offering to participate. Naturally, I accepted these offers. Encouraged by such enthusiasm for GLOBE and the grant from the Department of Education, I increased my aspiration to include 40 countries in GLOBE. To ensure representation of least 40 countries in the final sample, after allowing for attrition, I continued to recruit additional countries until we reached 65. This number was reached by approximately January 1994.

To provide me with advice I recruited Michael Agar, Marcus Dickson, Paul Hanges, and Antonio Ruiz Quintanilla. We labeled this group as the *U.S. GLOBE Coordinating Team.* The title of the U.S. GLOBE Coordinating Team implied a strong U.S. bias. Consequently this group and I recruited six additional scholars: Mansour Javidan from Canada, Peter Dorfman from the U.S., Stephan Akerblom from Sweden, Felix Brodbeck from Germany, Enrique Ogliastri from Columbia, and Marius Van Wyck from South Africa. We labeled this group the *GLOBE Coordinating Team.* This group met at least once per year. Several problems were discussed and committees were established to make recommendations with respect to solutions to these problems.

In August of 1994, all CCIs were invited to attend a meeting in Calgary, Canada. Fifty-four CCIs representing 38 cultures attended the meeting. Problems were discussed and committee task forces were established to solve these problems. Finally, a definition of leadership was agreed upon at the Calgary meeting.

Leadership was defined as the ability to motivate, influence, and enable individuals to contribute to the objectives of organizations of which they are members. Data were collected from 62 countries during the interval between 1994 and 1997.

Upon collection of the data from the 62 societies, Paul Hanges and I prepared an outline for the present book. As the reader can see from the table of contents, the intent of the book was to be a seamless whole, not an anthology of articles written previously. It was obvious that writing the book was going to be a huge job, more than two people could complete in several years. Fortunately, Mansour Javidan, Peter Dorfman with the aid of his assistant, Renee Brown, and Vipin Gupta volunteered to participate as coeditors. We formed the GLOBE integrative team consisting of Paul Hanges, Mansour Javidan, Peter Dorfman, Vipin Gupta, and myself to work closely to create a seamless book. Over the past three years, the team had several week-long meetings in Philadelphia to help move things along. We have also had many hour long conference calls to resolve various issues.

LESSONS LEARNED

One of the major things we learned from the GLOBE experience is that managing a multination research program of the scope of GLOBE is more than a full-time endeavor, even with excellent help from office administrators, postdoctoral research fellows, and research assistants. Throughout 1994–1996, we have had four undergraduate research assistants who are of tremendous help and fun to be around. In the summer of 1995, one of the research assistants began counting the number of correspondence items that had been sent by GLOBE to CCIs or others. When she reached 15,000 messages she stopped counting! The 15,000 messages did not include the messages that were stored on my e-mail hard drive, nor did they include mass mailings or messages sent since July 1995. Dividing 15,000 by the number of working days it took to process them yields 33.3 messages per day. On this basis I estimate that since the beginning of the GLOBE program, we have processed *at least* 30,000 pieces of correspondence plus mass mailings and network-wide postings on the e-mail net. If we add the number of CCIs messages sent and include mass mailing and network-wide posting on the e-mail net, the number would be approximately 46,000 messages in 2 years and 10 months.

We also learned that it is extremely difficult to obtain funding for such a large program. We have submitted proposals to 27 potential funding agencies or foundations for Phase 3 of GLOBE and have only recently been successful. It appears that additional funding will have to be raised with grant proposals with smaller budgets. This is an extremely time-consuming effort. Each proposal needs to be modified to meet the requirements of the potential funder.

We also confirmed an earlier conviction: the value of persistence. It was necessary to be in contact with the CCIs continuously, to monitor their progress, to try to help them solve problems, to provide encouragement for some, to mildly cajole others. From 1993 through June of 1996, I worked about 12 hours per business day and about 6 hours on both weekend days when I was not traveling. Some of this time was of course devoted to teaching and institutional work at Wharton.

Throughout the data collection process it became apparent that several countries were not able to collect the data. In some cases this was due to lack of interest and in other cases lack of access to samples. As a consequence, country-investigating teams from five countries were replaced during the Phase 2 collection period. Three countries dropped out of GLOBE and were not replaced, bringing the total number of cultures studied to 62.

Almost all of the teams that dropped out of GLOBE and the teams that were replaced were headed by consultants or senior professors. The consultants found the research to be too demanding because of their need to continue their normal consulting function. Several of the senior professors who accepted responsibility for the GLOBE data collection delegated this responsibility to junior professors. These senior professors neglected the GLOBE research and consequently their teams were ineffective.

The lesson learned is that it is generally better to recruit less well-established scholars who have a great deal to gain from participation in such a research project than to recruit consultants or well-reputed scholars who have less to gain. If senior professors are recruited it is important to stress the importance of their total involvement in the conduct of the research and obtain their commitment for such participation as part of the recruiting process.

The original questionnaire items measuring cultural, organizational, and leadership variables were developed on the basis of Q-sorts, item evaluations, and psychometric analyses described above. These tasks took longer than expected. Consequently, the questionnaire scales were not ready for use at the time for which they were initially scheduled. Further, almost all of the country co-investigators found it much more difficult to gain access to samples than was originally expected. Consequently the schedule for data collection was changed several times. As a result, country co-investigators from two countries had obtained commitment dates from participating organizations for scale administration that were earlier than the time at which the scales were available. This caused embarrassment for some of the country co-investigators and concern about whether GLOBE would be successfully completed. The remaining teams were not embarrassed because they had not arranged for data collection to take place prior to the availability of the questionnaires.

The research design also called for the development of scales to measure strategic organizational contingency variables (size, strategy, technology, and organizational environment) as well as scales to measure unobtrusive measures and participant observations relevant to the core GLOBE dimensions. The development of these scales was not completed until December of 1995, approximately 6 months later than originally planned. This delay was due to the fact that the scales to measure unobtrusive measures and participant observations were much more difficult to develop than originally anticipated. The lesson learned is that cross-cultural research takes much longer than single-culture research and should be planned accordingly.

Another lesson learned is that it is important to maintain schedule flexibility and to explain the need for schedule changes clearly to all involved. It is important to develop among participating investigators a high tolerance for uncertainty because the need for schedule changes will be inevitable. Tolerating schedule changes was quite difficult for many of the countries, especially those with low scores on Hofstede's tolerance of uncertainty measures. Some CCIs rather strongly urged me to terminate relationships with CCI teams that were behind schedule. Had we done this there would be no GLOBE data at this time because only two countries met the original schedule deadlines. As will be explained below, this was due to many factors associated with the administration of GLOBE and not due to delinquency of CCIs.

It was originally planned to have four phases for the entire GLOBE research program. When it became apparent that we would not be funded for Phase 3, I recommended to the GLOBE Coordinating Committee that we integrate many of Phase 2 and Phase 3 research questions into Phase 2 in order to have a coherent research product and to take advantage of what might be accomplished with existing funds, given the momentum that had developed. The committee agreed. This change involved collecting some, but not much, additional data relevant to organizational demography and strategic contingencies. Some CCIs objected to this, reflecting either a low tolerance for change or a belief that it was unfair to ask them to put forth additional effort. The additional effort would be only marginally more than what was originally agreed on however, because the collection of demographic variables was specified as one of the CCI responsibilities in the initial recruiting letter and had been reaffirmed several times subsequently.

Despite the problems concerning schedule changes and some problems concerning uncertainty with respect to measurement instruments and research design, the country co-investigators were able to cope with the schedule changes and have thus far been able to obtain questionnaire responses from middle managers in each of 62 countries. In addition, we have been able to collect unobtrusive measurement data for the majority of the societies studied.

CONCLUSION

We have a very adequate dataset to replicate Hofstede's (1980) landmark study and extend that study to test hypotheses relevant to relationships among societal-level variables, organizational practices, and leader attributes and behavior. We also have sufficient data to replicate middle-management perceptions and unobtrusive measures. The original data collection target was December of 1995. Data collection was finalized about August of 1997. The data collection would have gone much more quickly, smoothly, and efficiently had the scales been developed earlier and had all country co-investigating teams been able to access samples earlier. However, to have accomplished such smooth and efficient data collection would have required a much longer schedule and would have delayed final data collection. Even if we had established a longer schedule we would certainly have met unanticipated problems.

My final conclusion is that we are in a position to make a major contribution to the organizational behavior and leadership literature. To date more than 90% of the organizational behavior literature reflects U.S.-based research and theory. Hopefully GLOBE will be able to liberate organizational behavior from the U.S. hegemony.

SPECIAL CONTRIBUTIONS OF THE EDITORIAL TEAM

All of the members of the editorial team, including Mary Sully de Luque, contributed to the final chapter of this book. However, Mansour Javidan wrote the final chapter that was reviewed by all members of the editorial team. The members of the editorial team worked long and hard for the last three years. Among other tasks, Peter Dorfman, with the aid of Renee Brown, performed copyediting duties; checked for continuity of terminology, data, and content; and ensured data consistency among chapters for conformity of presentation. Renee Brown and Mary Sully de Luque created the mechanism to keep track of chapter drafts, no small task given the multiple editing of each chapter by the editorial team members.

Peter Dorfman was responsible for reading the entire manuscript and ensuring that the general material on leadership processes was consistent across chapters. He worked to achieve uniformity and accuracy for data analysis and presentation for the culturally-endorsed leadership profiles. Peter also worked with Paul Hanges to develop the template for presentation of statistical analyses regarding the relationship of societal-cultural dimensions and leadership dimensions. Peter also developed the format for presenting these relationships in figure form used throughout the text. Both Renee and Peter regularly conferred with other editorial team members to assure that the revision of chapters followed a regular sequence to minimize or eliminate errors regarding text changes, omissions, and deletions.

Paul Hanges had the prime responsibility for developing the GLOBE scales. This involved everything from introducing the frame of reference in the organizational and societal culture scale items to analyzing the item evaluation reports conducted by CCIs and reviewing the translation-back translation reports, to planning and conducting the statistical analyses that were used to verify the psychometric properties of the GLOBE scales as well as their validity. He also was responsible for building the GLOBE database and for evaluating and determining the highly sophisticated statistical approach that we would use to test the GLOBE hypotheses. When current statistical procedures, such as the traditional response bias correction procedure, didn't fully address our questions, we relied on Paul to identify or develop new approaches that could more adequately address the goals of GLOBE. Paul was successful in this regard. See Appendix B: Response Bias Correction Procedure Used in GLOBE.

The tangible product of his work can be seen in the quality of the GLOBE scales and the statistical analyses conducted to test the GLOBE hypotheses. While his statistical contributions are very clear, it may not be also clear that his contributions extended beyond statistics. He helped distribute information among the GLOBE community by proposing, developing, and maintaining the first GLOBE Web site. The identification of universal leadership attributes were also a function of Paul's work on GLOBE and these attributes were really a side product of his efforts developing the leadership scales, referred to as CLT scales throughout this book. His contributions also extend to the intellectual discussions that we had regarding the meaning of the GLOBE scales and whether they had meaning beyond the opinions of the middle managers who completed the scales.

Mansour Javidan was the editor of all the chapters on cultural dimensions. He wrote the Performance Orientation chapter which became the model for all dimension chapters. He then worked very closely with the writers of each dimension chapter to make sure that the conceptualization, literature review, and interpretation of the findings were comprehensive and consistent across all dimension chapters. He went through up to five revisions with the writers of these chapters. The result is that Part 4 of the book, even though written by a large number of authors from different parts of the world, is a seamless and consistent piece. Mansour read the entire manuscript to make sure any connections between dimension chapters and others are properly addressed in all chapters of the book. He further designed the external dataset. He first developed a series of hypotheses to link external data with GLOBE cultural dimensions and worked with Markus Hauser to develop a large database of external data from various sources which were directly relevant to GLOBE. The database was made available to the authors of dimension chapters who used it to link their specific cultural dimensions to external data. As a result, we extended our original theoretical model to incorporate the relationship between culture and societal achievement, and performed an extensive empirical investigation of that relationship. Mansour has also played a helpful managerial role to ensure the progress of our book. Over the past three years, he helped the editorial team coordinate its activities and progress. He also has made many presentations and keynote speeches on GLOBE at a large number of conferences all over the world.

Vipin Gupta's rich knowledge of international and strategic management, and valuable research methodology skills have been great assets to the GLOBE Project. Vipin conducted extensive multidisciplinary literature searches finding theoretical and empirical evidence regarding GLOBE dimensions. Along with Paul Hanges, he formulated regional and climatic clusters of the societal cultures. He also provided data analysis for the sections on regional and climate clustering and on organizational culture scores. Vipin reviewed all of the empirical chapters to verify the statistical analyses and provide additional discussion regarding interpretations of the data. He also formulated and operationalized, with the help of Mary Sully de Luque, the unobtrusive and outcropping validation measures for the GLOBE societal cultural scales. He painstakingly checked the consistency of reported findings across different chapters, and between tables and text.

We would like to give special thanks to Mary Sully de Luque, who devoted tireless effort to this project during her 3 years as a Wharton Senior Fellow, despite being a loving and caring mother to a new born baby, Devin, who was born three months after Mary joined GLOBE. Mary, having worked for two U.S. senators, brought to bear a substantial amount of administrative ability as well as her scholarly contributions. During her tenure, Mary took charge of assembling the multiple parts of the GLOBE phase 3 project, corresponding with all Country Co-Investigators, facilitating the back-translation process, developing significant parts of the databases, analyzing preliminary data, evaluating appropriate statistical procedures, and generally maintaining the project. Additionally, and no less importantly, Mary became an intricate part of this book. She coauthored the measurement validation chapter, working countless hours on the content analysis required of this type of research. Her contribution as lead author on the Uncertainty Avoidance chapter was invaluable. In the final year of the project, Mary became the curator of the book chapters; a role Peter Dorfman suggested to sustain continuity in the process of multiple editing of the chapters. In retrospect, the success of any project of this magnitude requires the addition of this type of process. Clearly, Mary worked long and hard on this book and went far beyond the normal expectations of her position as a Post Doctoral Research Fellow. Without her participation, both scholarly and administrative, the completion of this book would not have been possible.

ACKNOWLEDGMENTS

We would like to thank many people who directly or indirectly contributed to development and completion of this book. Foremost, we would like to thank our spouses Tessa House, Carol Shouvlin Hanges, Soheila Yazdanbakhsh, Sharon Dorfman, Bhakti Gupta, and Edgard Luque for their patience and perseverance with this project. The support they provided was invaluable, especially through the final few years of the writing of this book. The first author would like to especially thank Joseph Frank Bernstein for continued financial support, and Donald Bigelow, of the Dwight D. Eisenhower Research Program at the U.S. Department of Education, and the National Science Foundation for grant funding of this research.

Special acknowledgments for organizations that assisted in this project go to University of Pennsylvania; University of Maryland; the University of Calgary; New Mexico State University; Grand Valley State University; Thunderbird, the American Graduate School of International Management; and the Industrial Management Institute of Iran. Specifically, we would like to thank the Department of Psychology at the University of Maryland for providing computer support for this project.

A project of this magnitude requires the participation and support of a multitude of people. We respectfully acknowledge the contribution of the many book coauthors and country co-investigators and the support of their institutions in providing the resources to accomplish this research. We would like to thank Michael Bond for providing his scholarly expertise and Habir Singh for his unwavering academic support. Numerous people contributed during various phases of this project; of these we would like to acknowledge the academic assistance of Harry Triandis; Major Paul Bliese; Katherine Klein; David Saunders, former Dean of Management at the University of Calgary; as well as the research assistance of James Zale, Gavaskar Balasingam, Louani Bascara, Bhairvee (Ravi) Shavdia, Karen Toll, Narda Quigley, Sandra Martinez, and Gian

Casimir. We would also like to thank Michael Grojean, Ellen Godfrey, Mina Sipe, Beng-Chong Lim, Lisa Nishii, and William Oakley for helping update and maintain the GLOBE database over the years. In addition, we would like to thank Marcus Dickson for all of his assistance during the many years of the GLOBE project. Special thanks go to Geri Grosso, Renee Brown, and Angela Smith who provided administrative assistance essential for this project.

We are also grateful to MaryAnn Vail and Diane Foster for their patience and assistance in bringing this book to fruition.

—ROBERT J. HOUSE

REFERENCES

Bass, B. M. (1985). *Leadership and performance beyond expectations.* New York: Free Press.

Hofstede, G. (1980). *Culture's consequences: International differences in work-related values.* Beverly Hills, CA: Sage.

House, R. J. (1976). A 1976 theory of charismatic leadership. In J. Hunt & L. Larson (Eds.), *Leadership: The cutting edge* (199–272). Carbondale: Southern Illinois University Press.

House, R. J., Spangler, D., & Woycke, J. (1991). Personality and charisma in the U.S. presidency: A psychological theory of leadership effectiveness. *Administrative Science Quarterly, 36,* 364–396.

Koene, H., Pennings, H., & Schreuder, M. (1993). Leadership, culture, and organizational effectiveness. In K. E. Clark, M. E. Clark, & D. P. Campbell (Eds.), *The impact of leadership* (pp. 230–241). Greensboro, NC: The Center for Creative Leadership.

Koh, W. L., Terborg, J. R., & Steers, R. M. (1991, August). *The impact of transformational leaders on organizational commitment, organizational citizenship behavior, teacher satisfaction and student performance in Singapore.* Paper presented at the meeting of the Academy of Management, Miami.

Pereira, D. (1987). *Factors associated with transformational leadership in an Indian engineering firm.* Paper presented at the meeting of the Administrative Science Association of Canada, Vancouver.

Weber, M. (1947). *The theory of social and economic organizations* (T. Parsons, Trans.) New York: Free Press. (Original work published 1924)

PART I

INTRODUCTION

ROBERT J. HOUSE

At the present time there is a greater need for effective international and cross-cultural communication, collaboration, and cooperation, not only for the effective practice of management but also for the betterment of the human condition. Ample evidence shows that cultures of the world are getting more and more interconnected and that the business world is becoming increasingly global. As economic borders come down, cultural barriers will most likely go up and present new challenges and opportunities in business. When cultures come into contact, they may converge on some aspects, but their idiosyncrasies will likely amplify. The information resulting from the GLOBE research program can be used as a guide when individuals from different cultures interact with each other. Although this book is primarily addressed to academicians, it contains a wealth of information relevant to the practices of leadership and organizations.

The first three chapters will be of interest to individuals engaged in cross-border interactions, be they buyers, sellers, or intermediaries. In Part I, contributing authors point out that what is expected of leaders, what leaders may and may not do, and the status and influence bestowed on leaders vary considerably as a result of cultural forces in the societies in which the leaders function. Readers in many Western nations might be surprised to learn that the extremely positive connotation associated with the word "leadership" is not universal, and some societies have a very skeptical view of leaders and leadership. Yet, the extent to which the meaning and enactment of leadership is culturally contingent is still relatively unknown. Although cultural differences figure predominantly in cross-cultural literature, some common management and leadership practices are also likely, given the current trend toward globalization of economies and an ever increasing number of multinational firms.

Chapter 1 presents an introduction to Project GLOBE. In Chapter 1, we illustrate the evidence relevant to the globalization of business during the past two decades and the consequent increased need for cross-cultural acumen of individuals who engage in cross-border interactions. We illustrate the importance of cross-cultural understanding on the part of people who engage in cross-border interactions with a hypothetical example of two firms considering merging. In this example, we illustrate variation in one dimension of cultures, namely the tendency to avoid uncertainty. We also illustrate variation in conceptions of leadership across cultures.

Chapter 2 presents a summary of selected major findings resulting from Project GLOBE and starts with a basic discussion of the construct of leadership. You might find it as intriguing as we did to discover the wide divergence of beliefs in the world about what constitutes effective leadership. Chapter 2 also presents a listing of the cultural attributes and a description of the leadership attributes studied. When these attributes are scaled into groups of related attributes, they are referred to as leadership *dimensions*. We will use this terminology throughout this book. Throughout the book, we present discussions of managerial implications of the GLOBE findings.

Chapter 3 presents a *nontechnical summary* of the major findings of the GLOBE research program. This chapter provides a concise summary of the findings from the GLOBE project. Only general information is provided here and care has been taken that the discussion not be too repetitive with discussions in upcoming chapters. The brief summary given in the chapter is intended to be selective, not comprehensive, with the information provided.

As discussed throughout this volume, a wealth of research examines the interrelationships among various conceptions of societal culture and industry and various forms of leadership, organizational behavior, structure, and culture. The fact that different industries impose different demands on organizations is obvious and well supported in the organizational strategy iterature. Clearly, we are much further along in our understanding of the cultural influence on these processes than we were 40 years ago. Yet much remains to be learned. This book is intended to increase our understanding of the effects of societal culture on leadership, organizational cultures, economic competitiveness of nations, and the human condition. Part I starts us on this fascinating journey.

1

ILLUSTRATIVE EXAMPLES OF GLOBE FINDINGS

ROBERT J. HOUSE

The 21st century may very well become known as the century of the "global world" (McFarland, Senen, & Childress, 1993). This prophetic statement appears to be well supported by recent evidence and experience. We present a review of this evidence later in this chapter.

In this book, we report the results of a 10-year research program, the Global Leadership and Organizational Behavior Effectiveness Research Program (GLOBE). The major purpose of Project GLOBE is to increase available knowledge that is relevant to cross-cultural interactions. The results are presented in the form of quantitative data based on responses of about 17,000 managers from 951 organizations functioning in 62 societies throughout the world. The questionnaire reports of managers were complemented by interview findings, focus group discussions, and formal content analyses of printed media.

The information presented in this book describes how each of 62 societies scores on nine major attributes of cultures and six major global leader behaviors. When quantified in the form of responses to questionnaires, these cultural attributes and leader behaviors are referred to as dimensions of culture or leadership. As we shall show, we found that there is wide variation in the values and practices relevant to the nine core dimensions of cultures and wide variation

in perceptions of effective and ineffective leader behaviors. We shall also show that there are a select set of cultural dimensions that are strongly associated with country competitiveness, country prosperity, individual prosperity (gross national product per capita) and the physical and psychological well-being of members of the societies we studied. This variation is associated with variation in the nine major attributes of the cultures we studied.

More specifically, we report empirical findings concerning the rankings of 62 societies (with at least three societies from each major geographical region of the world) with respect to nine attributes of their cultures. We also report the effects of these attributes on what is expected of leaders, and the effects of these attributes on organizational practices in each of the societies studied. The nine attributes are Future Orientation, Gender Egalitarianism, Assertiveness, Humane Orientation, In-Group Collectivism, Institutional Collectivism, Performance Orientation, Power Concentration versus Decentralization (frequently referred to as Power Distance in the cross-cultural literature), and Uncertainty Avoidance. When quantified these attributes are referred to as cultural dimensions. The rationale for the selection of these cultural dimensions, and their definitions are provided in the following chapter.

In this chapter we review the evidence relevant to the globalization of business during the past two decades and the consequent increased need for cross-cultural acumen of leaders and those who engage in cross-border interactions. We illustrate the importance of cross-cultural understanding on the part of people who engage in cross-border interactions with a hypothetical example of two firms considering merging. In this example we illustrate variation in one dimension of cultures, namely the tendency to avoid uncertainty. We also illustrate variation in conceptions of leadership across cultures.

INCREASED GLOBALIZATION OF BUSINESS

At the present time there is a greater need for effective international and cross-cultural communication, collaboration, and cooperation, not only for the effective practice of management but also for the betterment of the human condition. Ample evidence, reviewed below, shows that cultures of the world are getting more and more interconnected and that the business world is becoming increasingly global.

Consider the following facts. As of 1988, more than 70% of American industry was facing stiff foreign competition *within* the U.S. market (Choate & Linger, 1988). Very likely this percentage is higher at this time. During the year 2001, worldwide exports of merchandise were almost $6 trillion U.S. dollars. Despite a decline of 10% in 2001, Asian countries (Japan excluded) had an average annual growth rate of 11% for the last decade, leading the world in the expansion of international trade (World Trade Organization, 2003).

There are other aspects to globalization besides foreign customers and competitors. Travel and tourism accounted for 383 million jobs in 2002, almost 50% more than in 1997 (Ehrlich, 2002, p. 232). The number of Internet users surpassed 665 million in 2002 up from 544 million in 2001 and the global number of Internet users will top 1 billion by 2005. The U.S. leads the world with more than 160 million users. Internet usage is growing rapidly in China, which is expected to surpass Japan by late 2003 (Computer Industry Almanac, 2003).

In the 1990s, international flows of investment have increased by more than threefold and investment in developing countries has grown sixfold. Further, in 2001 China replaced the U.S. as the leading recipient of foreign investment at an estimated value of $52 billion (U.S. dollars). The globalization of financial markets is a major driver of international trade and investment. In 1993 non-U.S. corporations raised $200 billion U.S. dollars by selling their shares on U.S. stock exchanges. In the year 2000 the amount increased to $1 trillion U.S. dollars (The Bank of New York, 2002, 2003). During the past decade, the world experienced an unprecedented volume of cross-border mergers and acquisitions. In 2002 the largest individual cross-border merger and acquisition transaction was Hong Kong-based China Mobile's payment of $10.2 billion U.S. dollars for Anhui Mobile Communications in mainland China (Organisation for Economic Co-operation and Development, 2003).

Clearly we are living in an increasingly interconnected and complex world. A significant consequence of globalization is the reduced dominance of American corporations in the world markets. In 1963, 67 of the world's largest industrial corporations were U.S. based. In 2001, 38 American companies were on the top 100 list. In contrast, the European continent had 42 and Japan had 11 of the world's largest corporations. The United States is influential, but it is no longer the most dominant force in international business ("The World's 500 Largest Industrial Corporations," 2002).

The implication for corporations involved in international trade and cross-border mergers and acquisitions is that they are facing increasingly global employees, customers, suppliers, competitors, and creditors, best described by the following passage:

So I was visiting a businessman in downtown Jakarta the other day and I asked for directions to my next appointment. His exact instructions were: "Go to the building with the Armani Emporium upstairs—you know, just above the Hard Rock café—and then turn right at McDonald's." I just looked at him and laughed, "Where am I?" (Friedman, 1997, p. A15)

The Increased Importance of Sensitivity to Cultural Differences

The increasing connection among countries, and the globalization of corporations, does not mean that cultural differences are disappearing or diminishing. On the contrary, as economic borders come down, cultural barriers could go up, thus presenting new challenges and opportunities in business. When cultures come into contact, they may converge on some aspects, but their idiosyncrasies will likely amplify. McDonald's serves wine and salads with its burgers in France. In India, where beef products are taboo, it created a mutton burger: The Maharajah Mac. Middle Easterners prefer toothpaste that tastes spicy. The Japanese like herbs in their medicines.

Globalization opens many opportunities for business but it also creates major challenges. One of the most important challenges is acknowledging and appreciating cultural values, practices, and subtleties in different parts of the world. All experts in international business agree that to succeed in global business, managers need the flexibility to respond positively and effectively to practices and values that may be drastically different from what they are accustomed to. This requires the ability to be open to others' ideas and opinions. Being global is not just about where you do business. It is also about how you do it. As Percy Barnevick, the CEO of the Swedish firm ABB put it,

> Global managers have exceptionally open minds. They respect how different countries do things, and they have the imagination to appreciate why they do them that way. . . . Global managers are made, not born. (Ehrlich, 2002, p. 234)

But this is easier said than done. Managers who work in the international arena are steeped in their own culture. They have lived many years of their lives in their own countries, have been educated there, and have spent years working there. It is not easy for one to understand and accept practices and values that vary from one's own personal experiences. As an experienced executive search expert pointed out,

> Global business makes sense, but it is much more difficult to do it than talk about it. The American manager prides himself or herself on directness, frankness, being in-your-face, being accountable. But that's almost unique in the world. (Ehrlich, 2002, p. 235)

In fact, as the research reported in this book demonstrates, directness, frankness, and "being in-your-face" are offensive behaviors in many parts of the world including Asia, Latin America, and the Nordic European countries.

Alfred Zeien, the now retired CEO of Gillette, stated that globally literate leaders were his company's scarcest resource (Ehrlich, 2002). He is not alone. In a survey of Fortune 500 firms, having competent global leaders was rated as the most important factor for business success. In the same survey, 85% of executives stated that they do not think they have an adequate number of global leaders and more than 65% believe that their existing leaders need additional skills and knowledge before they can meet or exceed the challenge of global leadership (Gregersen, Morrison, & Black, 1998).

Differing Views and Conceptualizations of Leadership

Leadership is culturally contingent. That is, views of the importance and value of leadership vary across cultures. The GLOBE research program, as well as a substantial amount of other empirical research (House, Wright, & Aditya, 1997), has shown that the status and influence of leaders vary considerably as a result of the cultural forces in the countries or regions in which the leaders function. For instance, Americans, Arabs, Asians, English, Eastern Europeans, French, Germans, Latin Americans, and Russians tend to romanticize the concept of leadership and consider leadership in both political and organizational arenas to be important. In these cultures leaders are commemorated with statues, names of major avenues or boulevards, or names of buildings. Many people of German-speaking Switzerland, the Netherlands, and Scandinavia are skeptical about leaders and the concept of leadership for fear that they will accumulate and abuse power. In these countries it is difficult to find public commemoration of leaders.

An Illustration of Differences and Cultural Practices

Here we illustrate the importance of one of the cultural dimensions studied as part of the GLOBE research program. The dimension we highlight is the tendency to avoid uncertainty, however we note that the other eight dimensions have equally important implications.

Based on questionnaire responses from about 17,000 managers in 62 societies, our findings reveal that there is wide variation among societies on this dimension, ranging from 2.88 to 5.37 on a seven-point scale. Examples of societies that are very high on the tendency to avoid uncertainty are China, Singapore, and German-speaking and Scandinavian countries. Examples of societies that are very low on this tendency are the Latin American countries, and the Eastern European countries.

Now consider how individuals in high and low uncertainty avoidance cultures tend to behave. Most individuals in high uncertainty avoidance cultures have a strong tendency toward formalizing their interactions with others, documenting agreements in legal contracts, being orderly, keeping meticulous records, documenting conclusions drawn in meetings, formalizing policies and procedures, establishing and following rules, verifying verbal communications in writing, and taking moderate calculated risks.

In contrast, most individuals in low uncertainty avoidance cultures tend to exhibit the following traits and practices: they are more informal; rely on the word of others they trust rather than contractual arrangements; are less concerned with orderliness and the maintenance of records; do not document the conclusions drawn in meetings; rely on informal interactions and informal norms rather than formalized policies, procedures, and rules; and tend to be less calculating when taking risks.

If individuals from high and low uncertainty avoidance cultures are aware of their differences with respect to this cultural dimension, they will more likely know what to expect from each other, and possibly be able to negotiate mutually agreeable approaches to conflict resolution, problem solving, decision making, and management practices.

Consider for example two organizations that are considering merging. One of the major findings of the GLOBE research program is that operational and managerial practices tend to reflect the societal orientation in which they function. The organizations in high or low uncertainty avoidance cultures tend to reflect their respective societal orientation toward uncertainty. If one of the potential merging organizations is from a high uncertainty avoidance societal culture and the other from a societal culture that is low on uncertainty avoidance orientation, there are likely to be substantial differences in the way they function. If the decision makers in both of the firms know, in advance, the other organization's proclivity to be high or low on uncertainty avoidance, they can take actions to assess the potential problems that will be incurred after the merger, and on this basis they can determine whether the risk of the merger is too high. In such a merger, it is reasonably predictable that there will be large differences in formalization of roles in the form of job descriptions, accounting practices in terms of frequency of reporting, formalization, and specificity of accounting information.

There are also likely to be substantial differences in decision-making practices. In organizations that function in high uncertainty avoidance cultures the decision making is likely to be more formalized and analytical. In organizations that function in low uncertainty avoidance cultures, decision making is likely to be based more on intuition than formal analysis. There is likely to be disagreement among decision makers concerning the degree of documentation of decisions, specificity of reports, and record keeping. In each firm, it would be possible to establish task forces to investigate not only the differences in managerial and operational practices, but also the possible consequences of such differences. On this basis, decision makers would be better informed about what to expect following the completion of the merger. Problem-solving task forces could be established to resolve differences and work out mutually agreeable practices. Thus knowledge of the uncertainty avoidance orientation of each firm would be very useful for both premerger assessment of possible problems and postmerger problem solving and conflict resolution.

DIFFERENCES IN LEADERSHIP PRACTICES

The nine cultural dimensions studied in project GLOBE also have implications for leadership. Most interesting, in all cultures leader team orientation and the communication of vision, values, and confidence in followers are reported to be highly effective leader behaviors. There is some variation concerning Participative leadership ranging from 4.50 to 6.09 on a seven-point scale. There is also wide variation with respect to two major dimensions of leader behavior identified in the GLOBE program: Autonomous leadership and Self-Protective leadership. Autonomous leadership is characterized by a high degree of independence from superiors and a high degree of social distance from subordinates, a tendency to be aloof, and to work alone. Autonomous leadership is reported to slightly contribute toward organizational effectiveness in countries of Eastern Europe (except Hungary) and Germanic Europe (except the Netherlands), with countries' ratings ranging up to 4.63 on a seven-point scale measuring the effectiveness of this leader dimension. In contrast, Autonomous leadership is reported to be ineffective in Latin America (except Argentina), Middle Eastern (except Egypt), and Anglo countries, with average country scores ranging as low as 2.27 on this leadership dimension.

Self-Protective leadership is characterized by self-centeredness, elitism, status consciousness, narcissism, and a tendency to induce conflict with others. Leaders who engage in self-protective behavior were reported by managers in Albania, Taiwan, Egypt, Iran and Kuwait being slightly effective with average country ratings ranging up to 4.62 on a seven-point scale. In contrast, self-protective behavior was reported by managers to be an impediment to highly effective leadership in all other nations, especially France and Northern European countries, with scores as low as 2.55.

Knowing what is considered to be effective or ineffective in the cultures with which one interacts is likely to facilitate conflict resolution and improve the performance of interacting individuals. Individuals from different cultures often interact with each other as negotiators, managers, members of joint ventures, or expatriates working in foreign cultures. Again, we believe that knowledge of each group's culturally endorsed leader behaviors would be beneficial to all individuals involved in substantial intercultural interactions.

PLAN OF THIS BOOK

The book is structured in five sections. In Part I, we discuss the history of the GLOBE project and what it tries to accomplish. We also discuss the various conceptual models that led us to our hypotheses. In addition, we provide a nontechnical summary of the findings to inform the reader of what is to come in the proceeding chapters. In Part II, we review the prior literature on culture and organizational leadership as well as societal influence on organizational culture practices. We also consider contingencies such as the industrial sector of the organization, as a potential facilitator or inhibitor of the impact of societal culture on organizational culture. In Part III, the research methodology of the project is described. The research design used to collect the questionnaire data as well as the development and validation of the constructs measured in the questionnaires are discussed in this section. Additional archival data sets that we used in this project are examined. Lastly, in this section we discuss the statistical methodology used to analyze the data and explain the rationale. In Part IV, we discuss the empirical findings and we discuss how societal culture influences organizational culture, as well as how these two factors influence culturally endorsed implicit theories of leadership. Finally, in Part V, we discuss the implications for our work, both research implications and practical implications, of the GLOBE project.

REFERENCES

Choate, P., & Linger, J. (1988). Tailored trade: Dealing with the world as it is. *Harvard Business Review, 66*(1) 87–88.

Computer Industry Almanac. (2003). Retrieved June 25, 2003 from http://www.c-i-a.com/pr1202.htm

Ehrlich, H. J. (2002). The Wiley book of business quotations. New York: John Wiley.

Friedman, T. (1997, July 14). Jobs or trees? *The New York Times,* p. A15.

Gregersen, H. B., Morrison, A. J., & Black, J. S. (1998). Developing leaders for the global frontier. *Sloan Management Review, 40*(1) 21–32.

House, R. J., Wright, N., & Aditya, R. N. (1997). Cross cultural research on organizational leadership: A critical analysis and a proposed theory. In P. C. Earley & M. Erez (Eds.), *New perspectives on international industrial/organizational psychology* (pp. 535–625). San Francisco, CA: New Lexington Press.

Organisation for Economic Co-operation and Development. (2003). *Trends and recent developments in foreign direct investment.* Retrieved June 25, 2003 from http://www.oecd.org/pdf/M00042000/M00042212.pdf

The Bank of New York. (2002). *Depositary receipts (ADRs and GDRs): 2001 year-end market review.* New York: The Bank of New York.

The Bank of New York. (2003, January). *The ADR investor.* New York: The Bank of New York.

The world's 500 largest industrial corporations. (2002, July 22). *Fortune.*

McFarland, L. J., Senen, S., & Childress, J. R. (1993). *Twenty-first-century leadership.* New York: Leadership Press.

World Trade Organization. (2003, June). WTO *World tourism barometer, 1*(1), 1–14.

2

OVERVIEW OF GLOBE

ROBERT J. HOUSE

MANSOUR JAVIDAN

As stated in Chapter 1, GLOBE is an acronym for the *Global Leadership and Organizational Behavior Effectiveness Research Program.* The GLOBE research program consists of three phases, and possibly additional phases to follow. The three phases involved three related empirical studies, and Phases 1 and 2 are reported in this book. GLOBE Phase 1 was devoted to the development of research instruments and is reported in Chapter 8 by Hanges and Dickson. Phase 2 is devoted to the assessment of the nine core attributes of societal and organizational cultures. When quantified, these attributes are referred to as cultural dimensions. In Phase 2, we also ranked 62 cultures according to their societal dimensions and tested hypotheses about the relationship between these cultural dimensions and several important dependent variables described below. These rankings and tests of hypotheses are reported in Chapters 12 through 21 of this book. Phase 2 also investigates the interacting effect of societal cultural dimensions and industry (finance, food processing, and telecommunications) on organizational practices and culturally endorsed implicit theories of leadership.

The third phase of Project GLOBE is currently underway. In this phase, we are investigating the impact and effectiveness of specific leader behaviors and styles of CEOs on subordinates'

attitudes and performance. Phase 3 will identify the impact over 3 to 5 years of the leader behavior of CEOs on organizational effectiveness. Phase 3 will also include tests of the moderating effects of culture on relationships between organizational practices and organizational effectiveness.

MAJOR QUESTIONS CONCERNING THE EFFECTS OF CULTURES ON THE PRACTICE OF LEADERSHIP

We are just beginning to understand how culture influences leadership and organizational processes. Numerous research questions remain unanswered. What cultural attributes affect societies' susceptibility to leadership influence? To what extent do cultural forces influence the expectations that individuals have for leaders and their behavior? To what extent will leadership styles vary in accordance with culturally specific values and expectations? To what extent does culture moderate relationships among organizational processes, organizational form, and organizational effectiveness? What principles and laws of leadership and organizational processes transcend cultures? Can such principles be discovered and empirically verified? Although we do not have comprehensive answers to these questions,

9

progress has been made in several areas (see Dorfman, 2004; House, Wright, & Aditya, 1997 for an extensive review of relevant leadership literature).

GLOBE is a programmatic research effort designed to explore the fascinating and complex effects of culture on leadership, organizational effectiveness, economic competitiveness of societies, and the human condition of members of the societies studied. To address these issues we conducted an extensive quantitative and qualitative study of 62 cultures. The specific cultures studied will be described below.

Specific objectives of GLOBE include answering the following fundamental questions:

1. Are there leader behaviors, attributes, and organizational practices that are universally accepted and effective across cultures?

2. Are there leader behaviors, attributes, and organizational practices that are accepted and effective in only some cultures?

3. How do attributes of societal and organizational cultures influence whether specific leader behaviors will be accepted and effective?

4. How do attributes of societal and organizational cultures affect selected organizational practices?

5. How do attributes of societal cultures affect the economic, physical and psychological welfare of members of the societies studied?

6. What is the relationship between societal cultural variables and international competitiveness of the societies studied?

The Need for Cross-Cultural Leadership Theory and Research

Given the increasing globalization of industrial organizations and the growing interdependencies among nations, the need for a better understanding of cultural influences on leadership and organizational practices has never been greater. Leaders confront situations that are highly complex, constantly evolving, and difficult to interpret. Managers of global firms are facing unprecedented fierce and rapidly changing competition.

The 21st century may very well become known as the century of the "global world" (McFarland, Senen, & Childress, 1993). Although there is some controversy with respect to the effects of leaders on organizational effectiveness, we believe that effective organizational leadership is critical to the success of international operations. We also believe that the amount of influence, prestige, and privilege given to leaders varies widely by culture. In some cultures, there are severe constraints on what leaders can and cannot do. In other cultures, leaders are granted a substantial amount of power over followers and are given special privileges and high status.

Globalization of industrial organizations presents numerous organizational and leadership challenges. They include the design of multinational organizational structures, the identification and selection of leaders appropriate to the cultures in which they will be functioning, the management of organizations with culturally diverse employees, as well as cross-border negotiations, sales, and mergers and acquisitions. Unfortunately, the literature provides little in the way of guidance for leaders facing these challenges (House, Wright, & Aditya, 1997; House & Aditya, 1997). Cross-cultural research and the development of cross-cultural theory are needed to fill this knowledge gap.

There are compelling reasons for considering the role of societal and organizational culture in influencing leadership and organizational processes. What we need are theories of leadership and organizations that transcend cultures. However, there are inherent limitations in applying theories across widely varying cultures. What functions effectively in one culture may not in another culture. Cross-cultural research on leadership and organizations will help us test our knowledge in other cultures, identify boundary conditions for our theories, fine-tune existing theories by incorporating cultural variables, and identify potentially universal aspects of leadership (Berry & Dason, 1974; Dorfman, 2004).

Although research literature relevant to the above questions has increased substantially in the past 15 years, it is often atheoretical, fraught with methodological problems, and fragmented across a wide variety of publication outlets. More questions than answers persist regarding the culturally contingent aspects of leadership. Project GLOBE is designed to contribute theoretical developments and empirical findings to fill this knowledge deficiency.

THE GLOBE RESEARCH PROGRAM

GLOBE is a worldwide, multiphase, multimethod project intended to answer the questions raised above. The concept of a global research program concerned with leadership and organization practices was conceived in the summer of 1991. In the spring of 1993 a grant proposal was written that followed a substantial literature review and development of a pool of 735 questionnaire items. GLOBE was funded in October 1993, and the recruiting of GLOBE country co-investigators (referred to hereafter as CCIs) to collect data in 62 societies began.[1] One hundred seventy social scientists and management scholars from 62 cultures representing all major regions of the world are currently engaged in this long-term programmatic series of cross-cultural studies. Table 2.1 lists the countries in which cultures were studied as part of the GLOBE research reported in this book.

The CCIs, together with the principal investigators and research associates, comprise the members of the GLOBE community. The CCIs are responsible for leadership of the project in a specific culture in which they have expertise. Their activities include collecting quantitative and qualitative data, ensuring the accuracy of questionnaire translations, writing country-specific descriptions of their cultures, interpreting the results of quantitative data relevant to their culture, and contributing insights from their unique cultural perspectives to the ongoing GLOBE research. In most cases, CCIs are natives of the cultures from which they are collecting data and reside in that culture. Some of the CCIs have extensive experience in more than one culture. Most cultures have a research team of between two and five CCIs working on the project.

The initial activities of the project as a whole were coordinated by the GLOBE coordinating team (GCT), which consists of members from a variety of cultures. The members of this team are listed in the front of this book. More than 100 articles and book chapters have been written based on the GLOBE data that have been collected to date.

Independent Variables

The first significant question addressed by Project GLOBE concerns the differentiating attributes of societal and organizational cultures. To address this issue we developed 735 questionnaire items on the basis of prior literature and our own theorizing. Responses to these questions by middle managers in two pilot studies were analyzed by conventional psychometric procedures (e.g., item analysis, factor analysis, cluster analysis, generalizability analysis). These analyses resulted in the identification of nine major attributes of cultures and six global leader behaviors of culturally endorsed implicit theories of leadership (referred to as CLTs throughout the remainder of this book). These analyses are reported in greater detail in Chapter 8 by Hanges and Dickson.

When quantified, these cultural attributes are referred to as cultural *dimensions* and serve as the independent variables of Project GLOBE. The nine cultural dimensions we identified as independent variables are Uncertainty Avoidance, Power Distance, Institutional Collectivism, In-Group Collectivism, Gender Egalitarianism, Assertiveness, Future Orientation, Performance Orientation, and Humane Orientation. We developed original scales for each of these dimensions. There were two forms of questions for each dimension. The first of these two forms measured managerial reports of actual practices in their *organization* and managerial reports of what *shoule be* (values) in their organization. The second form measured managerial reports of practices and values in their *societies.* Thus we have 18 scales to measure the practices and values with respect to the core GLOBE dimensions of culture. A description of the two forms, and the levels of analysis at which they are applied, is presented below.

Following are the definitions of the core GLOBE cultural dimensions.

Uncertainty Avoidance is the extent to which members of an organization or society strive to avoid uncertainty by relying on established social norms, rituals, and bureaucratic practices.

Table 2.1   Countries Participating in GLOBE

Albania	Finland	Kazakhstan	South Africa (Black sample)
Argentina	France	Kuwait	South Africa (White sample)
Australia	Georgia	Malaysia	South Korea
Austria	Germany-East (former GDR)	Mexico	Spain
Bolivia	Germany-West (former FRG)	Morocco	Sweden
Brazil	Greece	Namibia	Switzerland
Canada (English-speaking)	Guatemala	The Netherlands	Switzerland (French-speaking)
China	Hong Kong	New Zealand	Taiwan
Colombia	Hungary	Nigeria	Thailand
Costa Rica	India	Philippines	Turkey
Czech Republic	Indonesia	Poland	United States
Denmark	Iran	Portugal	Venezuela
Ecuador	Ireland	Qatar	Zambia
Egypt	Israel	Russia	Zimbabwe
El Salvador	Italy	Singapore	
England	Japan	Slovenia	

People in high uncertainty avoidance cultures actively seek to decrease the probability of unpredictable future events that could adversely affect the operation of an organization or society and remedy the success of such adverse effects.

Power Distance is the degree to which members of an organization or society expect and agree that power should be stratified and concentrated at higher levels of an organization or government.

Collectivism I, *Institutional Collectivism,* is the degree to which organizational and societal institutional practices encourage and reward collective distribution of resources and collective action.

Collectivism II, *In-Group Collectivism,* is the degree to which individuals express pride, loyalty, and cohesiveness in their organizations or families.

Gender Egalitarianism is the degree to which an organization or a society minimizes gender role differences while promoting gender equality.

Assertiveness is the degree to which individuals in organizations or societies are assertive, confrontational, and aggressive in social relationships.

Future Orientation is the degree to which individuals in organizations or societies engage in future-oriented behaviors such as planning, investing in the future, and delaying individual or collective gratification.

Performance Orientation is the degree to which an organization or society encourages and rewards group members for performance improvement and excellence.

Humane Orientation is the degree to which individuals in organizations or societies encourage and reward individuals for being fair, altruistic, friendly, generous, caring, and kind to others.

We hypothesized that these dimensions significantly differentiate societies and organizations and can be used to address the questions raised above. The scores on the dimensions do indeed differentiate cultures as hypothesized. We found significant differentiation among cultures and significant respondent agreement within cultures for all dimensions. The analyses and findings are presented in Chapter 8 by Hanges and Dickson.

Origins of the Dimensions

The first six culture dimensions have their origins in the dimensions of culture identified by Hofstede (1980). The scales to measure the first three dimensions are designed to reflect the same constructs as Hofstede's (2001) dimensions labeled Uncertainty Avoidance, Power Distance, and Individualism.

Our measure of individualism and collectivism derives from a factor analysis of a set of items intended to measure collectivism in general. This factor analysis resulted in two dimensions: In-Group Collectivism and Institutional Collectivism. Institutional Collectivism may take the form of laws, social programs, or institutional practices designed to encourage collective behavior. The Institutional Collectivism dimension has not been studied in prior research. In-Group Collectivism has its roots in research conducted by Triandis (1995). This dimension reflects the degree to which people have pride and loyalty in their families and organizations.

On the basis of Hofstede's discussion of his masculinity dimension, we developed two dimensions labeled Gender Egalitarianism and Assertiveness. We found it necessary to develop our own measures reflecting these two variables because Hofstede's measure of masculinity, the MAS index, is confounded by many items that we judged to be irrelevant to the concept of masculinity. The MAS index lacks face validity, and is confounded by items that appear to measure multiple constructs. We will discuss this scale in more detail in Chapter 14.

Future Orientation is derived from Kluckhohn and Strodtbeck's (1961) Past, Present, Future Orientation dimension, which focuses on the temporal orientation of most people in the society. This dimension is conceptually, but only marginally, similar to the dimension called Confucian Work Dynamism by Hofstede and Bond (1988), and later referred to as Long-Term Orientation in Hofstede's second edition of *Culture's Consequences* (2001). We have serious reservations about the interpretation of the Confucian Work Dynamics as a measure of long-term orientation. We will discuss these reservations in more detail in Chapter 13.

Performance Orientation was derived from McClelland's (1961) work on need for achievement. McClelland's need for achievement is assumed to be a nonconscious motive and generally measured by the use of projective tests. Our measure of Performance Orientation differs from that of McClelland's measure of need for achievement in that it is measured by the use of closed-end questionnaire items. We will test the assumption that our measure of Performance Orientation predicts societal-level outcome variables such as economic performance.

Humane Orientation has its roots in Kluckhohn and Strodtbeck's (1961) dimension entitled Human Nature as Good versus Human Nature as Bad, as well as Putnam's (1993) work on the civic society and McClelland's (1985) conceptualization of the affiliative motive.

Uncertainty Avoidance has a long history of discussion in the organizational behavior literature but was most recently conceptualized by Cyert and March (1963) as an organizational attribute.

Power Distance was initially conceived of by Mulder (1971) as a measure of power differential between superiors and subordinates. Hofstede (1980) elevated the dimensions of power distance and uncertainty avoidance to the societal level of analysis.

Hofstede also included a measure he labeled masculinity. As stated above, we substituted the GLOBE measures of Gender Egalitarianism and Assertiveness, which we think better represents the theoretical construct of masculinity.

Our substitution avoids the confusion and interpretation difficulties of Hofstede's measure of masculinity.

Dependent Variables

A major question addressed by the GLOBE research program concerns the relationships between the nine core GLOBE cultural dimensions and several dependent variables. The dependent variables consisted of leadership dimensions derived from culturally endorsed implicit leadership theory (CLT), the Human Development Index, indices of economic prosperity (gross national product [GNP] per capita), measures of the psychological and physical welfare of members in each culture, as well as several additional variables related to the human condition. Javidan and Hauser describe these additional variables in detail in Chapter 7. Analyses of the relationship between the core GLOBE dimensions and dependent variables are presented in Chapters 12 through 21.

LEADER BEHAVIOR AND ATTRIBUTES

A major question addressed by GLOBE is the extent to which specific leader characteristics and actions are universally endorsed as contributing to effective leadership, and the extent to which these qualities and actions are linked to cultural characteristics. We identified 21 primary leader attributes or behaviors that are universally viewed as contributors to leadership effectiveness and 8 that are universally viewed as impediments to leader effectiveness. Furthermore, 35 specific leader attributes or behaviors are considered to be contributors in some cultures and impediments in other cultures. All of these findings are presented in Chapter 21.

Finally, we identified six *global* leader behaviors. These global leader behaviors (leadership dimensions) are briefly defined as follows:

Charismatic/Value-Based Leadership. A broadly defined leadership dimension that reflects ability to inspire, to motivate, and to expect high performance outcomes from others based on firmly held core values. The GLOBE Charismatic/Value-Based leadership dimension includes six leadership subscales labeled (a) visionary, (b) inspirational, (c) self-sacrifice, (d) integrity, (e) decisive and (f) performance oriented.

Team-Oriented Leadership. A leadership dimension that emphasizes effective team building and implementation of a common purpose or goal among team members. This leadership dimension includes five subscales labeled (a) collaborative team orientation, (b) team integrator, (c) diplomatic, (d) malevolent (reverse scored), and (e) administratively competent.

Participative Leadership. A leadership dimension that reflects the degree to which managers involve others in making and implementing decisions. The GLOBE CLT Participative leadership dimension includes two subscales labeled (a) nonparticipative and (b) autocratic (both reverse scored).

Humane-Oriented Leadership. A leadership dimension that reflects supportive and considerate leadership but also includes compassion and generosity. This leadership dimension includes two subscales labeled (a) modesty and (b) humane orientation.

Autonomous Leadership. A newly defined leadership dimension that refers to independent and individualistic leadership attributes. This dimension is measured by a single subscale labeled autonomous leadership, consisting of individualistic, independence, autonomous, and unique attributes.

Self-Protective Leadership. From a Western perspective, this newly defined leadership behavior focuses on ensuring the safety and security of the individual and group through status enhancement and face saving. This leadership dimension includes five subscales labeled (a) self-centered, (b) status conscious, (c) conflict inducer, (d) face saver, and (e) procedural.

Project GLOBE also addresses how organizational practices are influenced by societal cultural forces. We describe the research questions, hypotheses, and research design pertinent to the relationship between societal culture as well as both leadership and organizational aspects of GLOBE in Chapters 12 through 21.

QUALITATIVE RESEARCH

Project GLOBE also uses qualitative methods to provide richly descriptive and scientifically valid accounts of cultural influences on leadership and organizational processes. Qualitative aspects of Project GLOBE include measurement of societal culture, organizational culture, and leadership attributes and behaviors reported to enhance or impede effectiveness. Contemporaneous with the quantitative analysis, culture-specific qualitative research has been conducted extensively in 25 cultures and will be reported in a subsequent book in which each culture is described in detail in separate chapters (Chokkar, Brodbeck, & House, in press). Qualitative culture-specific interpretations of local behaviors, norms, and practices were developed through content analysis of data derived from interviews and focus groups, of published media.

CONSTRUCT DEFINITIONS OF LEADERSHIP AND CULTURE

Leadership has been a topic of study for social scientists for much of the 20th century, yet there is no universal consensus on the definition of leadership (Bass, 1990; Yukl, 2002). Scholars have advanced a wide variety of definitions. The core of almost all such definitions concerns influence—that is, how leaders influence others to help accomplish group or organizational objectives.

The variety of definitions is appropriate because the purpose of the research should drive the definition of leadership. Smith and Bond (1993) specifically note,

> If we wish to make statements about universal or etic aspects of social behavior, they need to be phrased in highly abstract ways. Conversely, if we wish to highlight the meaning of these generalizations in specific or emic ways, then we need to refer to more precisely specified events or behaviors. (p. 58)

We understand and expect that the evaluative and semantic interpretation of the term leadership and the ways in which leadership and

organizational processes are enacted are likely to vary across cultures. However, we also expect that some aspects of leadership will be universally endorsed as effective or ineffective.

In August of 1994, the first GLOBE research conference was held at the University of Calgary in Canada. Fifty-four researchers from 38 countries met to develop a collective understanding of the project and to initiate its implementation. The researchers spent considerable time generating a working definition of leadership that reflected their diverse viewpoints. A consensus emerged: The GLOBE definition of leadership is *the ability of an individual to influence, motivate, and enable others to contribute toward the effectiveness and success of the organizations of which they are members.*

As with leadership, there is no universally agreed-upon definition among social scientists for the term *culture*. Generally speaking, culture is used by social scientists to refer to a set of parameters of collectives that differentiate each collective in a meaningful way. The focus is on the "sharedness" of cultural indicators among members of the collective. The specific criteria used to differentiate cultures usually depend on the preferences of the investigator and the issues under investigation. The criteria tend to reflect the discipline of the investigator.

For Project GLOBE, culture is defined as *shared motives, values, beliefs, identities, and interpretations or meanings of significant events that result from common experiences of members of collectives that are transmitted across generations*. It is important to note that these are psychological attributes and that this definition can be applied at both the societal and organizational levels of analysis.

GLOBE OPERATIONAL DEFINITION OF CULTURE

The most parsimonious operationalizations of *societal* culture consist of commonly experienced language, ideological belief systems (including religion and political belief systems), ethnic heritage, and history. In a similar way, the most parsimonious operationalizations of *organizational* culture consist of commonly used nomenclature within an organization, shared organizational values, and organizational history. For purposes of GLOBE research, culture is operationally defined by the use of indicators reflecting two distinct kinds of cultural manifestations: (a) the commonality (agreement) among members of collectives with respect to the psychological attributes specified above; and (b) the commonality of observed and reported practices of entities such as families, schools, work organizations, economic and legal systems, and political institutions.

The core cultural dimensions specified above are measured in terms of two manifestations of cultures: *modal practices* and *modal values* of collectives. Modal practices are measured by the responses of middle managers to questionnaire items concerning "What Is," or "What Are," common behaviors, institutional practices, proscriptions, and prescriptions. This approach to the assessment of culture grows out of a psychological and behavioral tradition in which it is assumed that cultures should be studied as they are interpreted by their members (Segall, Lonner, & Berry, 1998) and that shared values are enacted in behaviors, policies, and practices.

Values are expressed in response to questionnaire items concerning judgments of "What Should Be," which are intended as a measure of the respondents' values concerning the practices reported by the respondents. These may be referred to as *contextualized values* as opposed to more abstract values such as values concerning justice; independence; freedom; and a world of order, beauty, and peace. Emphasis on values grows out of an anthropological tradition of culture assessment (Kluckhohn & Strodtbeck, 1961). GLOBE researchers tested the assumptions presented above and the results are presented in Chapters 12 through 19.

THE GLOBE CONCEPTUAL MODEL

The theory that guides the GLOBE research program is an integration of implicit leadership theory (Lord & Maher, 1991), value–belief theory of culture (Hofstede, 1980; Triandis, 1995), implicit motivation theory (McClelland, 1985), and structural contingency theory of organizational form and effectiveness (Donaldson, 1993; Hickson, Hinings, McMillan, & Schwitter,

1974). The key features of the first three theories are briefly outlined below. The integrated theory is then described. The acronym for GLOBE Culturally Endorsed Implicit Theory of Leadership is CLT and this acronym will be used throughout the book. Because tests of structural contingency theory are not reported in this book, this theory is not described here. For a more detailed description of the integrated theory, see House, Wright, and Aditya (1997).

Implicit Leadership Theory

According to this theory individuals have implicit beliefs, convictions, and assumptions concerning attributes and behaviors that distinguish leaders from followers, effective leaders from ineffective leaders, and moral leaders from evil leaders. These beliefs, convictions, and assumptions are referred to as individual implicit theories of leadership.

It is believed that implicit leadership theories held by individuals influence the way they view the importance of leadership, the values they attribute to leadership, and the values they place on selected leader behaviors and attributes. The following propositions express the major assertions of implicit leadership theory.

1. Leadership qualities are attributed to individuals, and those individuals are accepted as leaders on the basis of the degree of congruence between the leader behaviors they enact and the implicit leadership theory held by the attributers.

2. Implicit leadership theories constrain, moderate, and guide the exercise of leadership, the acceptance of leaders, the perception of leaders as influential, acceptable, and effective, and the degree to which leaders are granted status and privileges.

Substantial experimental evidence supports this theory (Hanges, Braverman, & Rentsch, 1991; Hanges et al., 1997; Lord & Maher, 1991; Sipe & Hanges, 1997). A major part of the GLOBE research program is designed to capture the CLTs of each society studied. We found that if aggregated to the societal level of analysis, responses to the leadership questionnaire reflect the culturally endorsed implicit theory of leadership of the societies studied. The evidence for this is that there is a high and significant within-society agreement with respect to questions concerning the effectiveness of leader attributes and behavior. Further, aggregated leadership scores were significantly different among the societies studied. Thus, each society studied was found to have a unique profile with respect to the culturally endorsed implicit theory of leadership.

Value–Belief Theory

According to value–belief theory (Hofstede, 2001; Triandis, 1995), the values and beliefs held by members of cultures influence the degree to which the behaviors of individuals, groups, and institutions within cultures are enacted, and the degree to which they are viewed as legitimate, acceptable, and effective. Collectively, the core GLOBE cultural dimensions described earlier reflect not only the dimensions of Hofstede's and Trandis's theories but also McClelland's theory of human motivation and economic development (McClelland, 1985). The humane, power distance, and performance orientation of cultures are conceptually analogous to the affiliative, power, and achievement motives in McClelland's theory of human motivation.

Implicit motivation theory is a theory of nonconscious motives originally advanced by McClelland, Atkinson, Clark, and Lowell (1953). In its most general form, the theory asserts that the essential nature of long-term and complex human motivation can be understood in terms of three implicit (nonconscious) motives: achievement, affiliation, and power (social influence). This theory also identifies three explicit (conscious) motives related to achievement, affiliation, and power that are predictive of short-term, noncomplex behavior. In contrast to behavioral intentions and conscious values, which are predictive of discrete task behaviors for short periods of time under constant situational forces (Ajzen & Fishbein, 1970), implicit motives are predictive of (a) motive arousal in the presence of particular stimuli; (b) spontaneous behavior in the absence of motive-arousal stimuli; and (c) long-term individual *global* behavior patterns, such as social relationship patterns, citizenship behavior, child-rearing practices, and leadership styles.

We will test the assumption that middle manager reports of explicit motives, if aggregated to the societal or organizational level, function in the same way that McClelland asserts implicit motives function. Whereas McClelland's theory is an individual theory of both nonconscious and conscious motivation, the GLOBE theory is a theory of motivation resulting from cultural forces. Cross-cultural tests of some of the major aspects of the integrated theory are reported in Chapters 12 through 21 of this volume.

THE INTEGRATED THEORY

The central proposition of the integrated theory is that the attributes and entities that differentiate a specified culture are predictive of organizational practices and leader attributes and behaviors that are most frequently enacted and most effective in that culture.

The integrated theory also consists of the following propositions, which are shown in the system diagram in Figure 2.1:

1. Societal cultural norms of shared values and practices affect leaders' behavior. Substantial empirical evidence supports this assertion (Dorfman, 2004; House, Wright, & Aditya, 1997; Schein, 1992; Schneider, 1987; Schneider, Goldstein, & Smith, 1995). First, founders and original members of organizations are immersed in their own societal culture. Consequently their leader behavior and management practices are likely to reflect behavior patterns favored in that culture. Subordinates of the original founder of an organization and subsequent leaders also use management practices that reflect the values shared by members of the culture. For example, founders and subsequent leaders establish selection criteria for hiring and promotions, serve as role models by setting personal examples, and socialize organizational members in a manner that reflects the broader culture in which they function. Further, dominant cultural norms induce global leader behavior patterns and organizational practices that are expected and viewed as legitimate.

The attributes and behaviors of leaders are also a reflection of prevailing organizational practices in their industries. Industrial practices

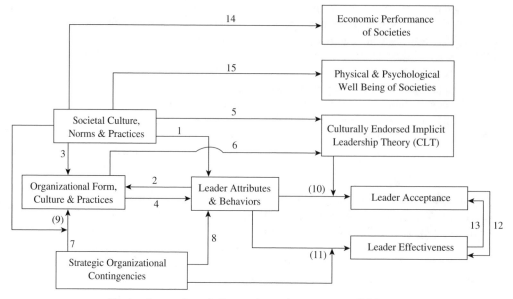

Numbers in parentheses indicate an interaction among two adjoining arrows.

Figure 2.1   Theoretical Model

are to a nontrivial extent indicative of societal cultural dimensions (e.g., Kopelman, Brief, & Guzzo, 1990).

2. Leadership affects organizational form, culture, and practice. Founders and subsequent leaders continue to influence and maintain the organizational culture (Bass, 1985; Miller & Droge, 1986; Schein, 1992; Thompson & Luthans, 1990; Yukl, 2002).

3. Societal cultural values and practices also affect organizational culture and practices. Although societal culture has a direct impact on organizational culture, over time, organizational cultures influence the broader societal culture. Collective meaning that results from the dominant cultural values, beliefs, assumptions, and implicit motives endorsed by societal culture results in common leadership and implicit organization theories held by members of the culture (House, Wright, & Aditya, 1997; Lord & Maher, 1991).

4. Organizational culture and practices also affect leaders' behavior. Over time, founders and subsequent leaders in organizations respond to the organizational culture and alter their behaviors and leader styles accordingly (Lombardo, 1983; Schein, 1992; Trice & Beyer, 1984).

5,6. Societal culture and organizational culture and practices influence the process by which people come to share implicit theories of leadership. Over time, CLT profiles are developed in each culture in response to both societal and organizational culture and practices. CLT profiles are composed of the six CLT leadership dimensions.

7. Strategic organizational contingencies (organizational environment, size, and technology) affect organizational form, culture, and practices. Organizational practices are largely directed toward meeting the requirements imposed by organizational contingencies (Burns & Stalker, 1961; Donaldson, 1993; Lawrence & Lorsch, 1967; Tushman, Newman, & Nadler, 1988).

8. Strategic organizational contingencies affect leader attributes and behavior. Leaders are selected to meet the requirements of organizational contingencies. They will then continue to adjust behavior on the basis of these contingencies.

9. Relationships between strategic organizational contingencies and organizational form, culture, and practices will be moderated by cultural forces. For example, in low uncertainty avoidance cultures we expect that forces toward formalization will be weaker, and therefore the relationship between such forces and organizational formalization practices will be lower. In low power distance cultures, we expect that forces toward centralization of decision making will be weaker, and therefore the relationship between such forces and decentralization and delegation practices will be lower. We specify such moderating effects in detail below when we discuss Phase 3 hypotheses.

10. Leader acceptance is a function of the interaction between CLTs and leader attributes and behaviors. Accordingly, leader attributes and behaviors that are congruent with CLTs will be more accepted than leader attributes and behaviors that are not congruent with CLTs.

11. Leader effectiveness is a function of the interaction between strategic organizational contingencies and leader attributes and behaviors. Leader attributes and behaviors that meet the requirements of strategic organizational contingencies will result in increased leader effectiveness.

12. Acceptance of the leader by followers facilitates leader effectiveness. Leaders who are not accepted by members of their organization will find it more difficult and arduous to influence these members than leaders who are accepted.

13. Leader effectiveness, over time, will increase leader acceptance. Effective leaders will, over time, demonstrate their competence by being effective. Demonstration of competence will change attitudes of some of the organizational members toward the leader and result in increased acceptance of the leader. Further, over time, followers who do not accept the leader will either be dismissed or will leave their organization voluntarily.

14. Societal cultural practices are related to economic competitiveness of nations. Societies that are high on power distance and low on uncertainty avoidance and performance orientation will be less competitive internationally, because these dimensions of culture are assumed to impede competitive performance.

15. Societal cultural practices are related to the physical and psychological well-being of their members. Cultures that are high on power distance and low on humane orientation practices will have members who are dissatisfied with life in general. Further, in such societies members will have less social support and less access to medical care.

In summary, the differentiating values and practices of each culture and the organizational contingencies faced by each organization will be predictive of the leader attributes and behaviors and organizational practices that are most frequently perceived as acceptable and most frequently enacted. Further, selected attributes of cultural practices will predict the economic competitiveness of nations and physical and psychological well-being of their members.

The theory is depicted in Figure 2.1 in the form of a systems model. The complexity of the model, however, mitigates being tested comprehensively. Rather, individual linkages or subsets of linkages can be tested, and the validity of the model can be inferred from such tests. House, Wright, and Aditya (1997) present a more detailed, fine-grained elaboration of the relationships depicted in Figure 2.1.

Two Fundamental Cross-Cultural Issues

Two central aspects of cultures are frequently discussed in cross-cultural literature: culturally generalizable and culturally specific aspects. Culturally generalizable phenomena are common to all cultures to some extent. A phenomenon is culturally generalizable if all cultures can be assessed in terms of a common metric and cultures can be compared in terms of such phenomena. In contrast, culturally specific phenomena occur in only a subset of cultures, and are not comparable across all cultures.

Project GLOBE uses a variety of methods to make cross-cultural comparisons. The primary sources of data used to measure the core GLOBE dimensions are questionnaire responses of middle managers in three selected industries: financial services, food processing, and telecommunications. Data were collected from approximately 17,000 managers in 951 organizations throughout the world. At least three cultures in each major region of the world are included in the sample (see Chapter 10 by Gupta and Hanges in this volume, for a description of the regions studied). When aggregated to the culture level of analysis, responses to the questionnaire provide measurement of the practices and values relevant to the nine core GLOBE dimensions.

The sampling strategy for the collection of questionnaire data "controls" for nation, industry, occupation broadly defined (managers), and organizational level broadly defined (middle management). The samples for Phase 2, in which hypotheses are tested, are described in more detail in Chapter 6 by House and Hanges. Sampling from middle managers permits us to make generalizations about the subcultures of middle managers in the three industries studied. This sampling strategy increases the internal validity of the study by ensuring that the units of analysis are well defined and internally homogeneous and therefore comparable.

Strictly speaking, we are studying the cultures of middle managers in 62 cultures. Thus, we must be cautious when making generalizations about national cultures. However, as we demonstrate in Chapter 9 by Gupta, Sully de Luque, and House, the core GLOBE societal practice and value dimensions are strongly and significantly correlated with unobtrusive measures that reflect the broader society. Also demonstrated in Chapter 9 is that the core GLOBE societal value measures are significantly correlated with independently collected indicators of societal values in the World Value Survey (Inglehart, Basanez, & Moreno, 1998). Thus we can conclude that both the GLOBE questionnaire responses reflect the broader culture in which the middle managers are embedded rather than the cultures of middle managers alone.

The term *construct* refers to the construction of conceptions or ideas by the investigator. A construct is a product of the investigator's creativity. The major constructs investigated in the GLOBE research program are the nine dimensions of cultures described previously. Examples of questionnaire items for

each dimension are presented in Chapters 12 through 19.

THE GLOBE QUESTIONNAIRE SCALES

In this section, we very briefly describe Phase 1 of Project GLOBE. Phase 1 is concerned with scale development and validation and is described in more detail in Chapter 8 by Hanges and Dickson. After briefly describing Phase 1, we will present an overview of the methodology and objectives for GLOBE Phase 2. The remainder of the book will then be devoted to literature reviews, and explication of the methodology of Phase 2, results, discussion, and conclusion.

Questionnaire Development and Validation

Two pilot studies were conducted. The first was designed to identify appropriate factor structures for the societal level, organizational level, and leadership questionnaires. The second study was designed to replicate the first study and determine whether the findings are stable. The two pilot studies and analyses of the data collected for Phase 2 all demonstrated that the scales had sound psychometric properties.

More specifically, the GLOBE scales are all unidimensional and demonstrate significant and nontrivial within-culture response agreement, between-culture differences, and respectable reliability of response consistency. Generalizability coefficients, which are joint measures of these psychometric properties, exceed .85 for all scales. These coefficients indicate that the scales can be meaningfully applied to measure leadership variables and cultural variables at the societal and organizational levels of analysis.

Statistical analyses reported in Chapter 8 by Hanges and Dickson also provide support for the construct validity of the culture scales, within the context of a nomological network. Further, correlations between unobtrusive measures and corresponding societal level organizational practice scales were all significant. Correlations between the societal values scales and independently gathered data relevant to each scale were also found to be significant. (Inglehart et al., 1998) The findings also demonstrated strong convergent and discriminate validity of the societal-level scales. These findings are reported in more detail in Chapter 9 by Gupta, Sully de Luque, and House.

Statistical analyses also indicated justification for grouping the items into scales relevant to nine core GLOBE values. Analyses also indicated justification for aggregating the scales to the organizational and societal levels of analysis. We demonstrate that for all culture dimension scales measuring *values,* and for most cultural dimension scales measuring *practices,* there are significant and substantial relationships between organizational practices and the societies in which they are embedded.

Finally, the generalizability coefficient which is a joint measure of the above properties is .85 or above for all scales. This coefficient is well above the minimum standard for such research. The development and validation of these dimensions is described in more detail in Chapter 8 by Hanges and Dickson.

The Leadership Questionnaire

The GLOBE Leader Attributes and Behavior Questionnaire includes 112 leader attributes and behaviors items. Leader attributes were rated 1 through 7 with 1 indicating "This behavior or characteristic greatly inhibits a person from being an outstanding leader" to a high of 7 indicating "This behavior or characteristic contributes greatly to a person being an outstanding leader." Examples of the Leader Behavior Questionnaire items are presented Table 2.2.

These items are based on a review of the leadership literature as well as findings relevant to leadership resulting from focus groups, interviews, and analysis of media. Factor analysis yielded 21 leadership subscales. A second order factor analysis of the 21 scales yielded four factors. Two of the factors were subdivided into two subscales each, thus yielding six global leader behavior dimensions. We will report statistical analysis relevant to these dimensions after describing the societal and organizational culture questionnaire. The 21 leadership subscales and the six global leader behavior dimensions are presented by Hanges

and Dickson (Chapter 8, this volume). The relationships between the six global leader behaviors and the nine cultural dimension scales are described in Chapter 21 by Dorfman, Hanges, and Brodbeck.

The Societal and Organizational Culture Questionnaires

Questionnaire items for the nine core GLOBE dimensions were written to elicit reports of current societal and organizational practices and respondents' values with respect to these practices. Questionnaire items were derived from a review of relevant literature, interviews, and focus groups conducted in several cultures, as well as extant organizational and culture theory. These items were designed to obtain data about both the societal and the organizational cultural variables. Respondents rated the items on a 7-point Likert-type scale. For some scales, the response indicators ranged from 1, indicating high agreement, to 7, indicating high disagreement. For other scales, the verbal anchors in the 7-point scale reflected the end points on a continuum (e.g., 1 = assertive, 7 = nonassertive). All culture scales, however, were 7-point scales. The items were written as "quartets" having isomorphic structures across the two levels of analysis (societal and organizational) and across the two culture manifestations (*As Is* and *Should Be*).

Table 2.3 contains an example of a quartet of parallel culture items showing essentially the same question in four forms: organization and society practices (questions with *As Is* response format) and organizational and societal values (questions with *Should Be* response format). Responses to *As Is* questions reveal the perceptions of middle managers concerning current practices in their societies and their organizations. Responses to *Should Be* questions reveal managers' values with respect to what they believe should be the practices in their societies or organizations.

To eliminate the problem of common source bias respondents were divided into two groups within each organization studied. The Alpha group responded to questions designed to capture the respondents' reports of the core GLOBE dimensions with respect to their

Table 2.2   Sample Items and Response Alternatives From the Culturally Endorsed Leadership Theory (CLT) Questionnaire

Definition of Leadership	Ability to influence, motivate and enable others to contribute to success of their organization.
Sample CLT Items	*Sensitive:* Aware of slight changes in moods of others. *Motivator:* Mobilizes, activates followers. *Evasive:* Refrains from making negative comments to maintain good relationships and save face. *Diplomatic:* Skilled at interpersonal relations, tactful. *Self-interested:* Pursues own best interests.
Response Alternatives	Inhibits or contributes to outstanding leadership 1. Greatly inhibits 2. Somewhat inhibits 3. Slightly inhibits 4. Has no impact 5. Contributes slightly 6. Contributes somewhat 7. Contributes greatly

organizations (hereafter referred to as the organizational level of analysis). The Beta group responded to questions designed to capture respondents' reports for societal-level dimensions described above (hereafter referred to as the societal level of analysis). This division eliminated the problem of common source variance: one group described organizations, the other societies. However, both Alpha and Beta groups responded to the leader attributes and behavior questionnaire. This questionnaire was designed to capture the CLTs of the cultures studied.

Samples

National borders may not be an adequate way to demarcate cultural boundaries, because many countries have large subcultures. The country samples also need to be relatively homogeneous within cultures to make valid comparisons and therefore contribute to the internal validity of the study. For multicultural countries, whenever possible, we sampled the subculture in which there is the greatest amount of commercial activity. When possible, we also sampled more than one subculture (indigenous and Caucasian subcultures in South Africa, French and German subcultures in Switzerland, and East and West subcultures in Germany).

The units of analysis for Phase 2 of Project GLOBE consist of cultural-level aggregated responses of samples of typical middle managers in three industries: food processing, financial services, and telecommunications services. The food-processing industry is a relatively stable industry. The telecommunications and financial industries may be stable or unstable, depending on country and economic conditions. By including these industries, we have obtained more than 17,000 middle manager questionnaire responses from 951 organizations. Some of the organizations in our sample function in stable environments whereas others function in dynamic environments with high- and low-technology industries.

Cultures in at least three countries in each of the following geographic regions are represented in the GLOBE sample: Africa, Southern Asia, Europe (Eastern, Southern, and Northern), Latin America, North America, the Middle East, and the Pacific Rim as indicated in Table 2.1.

Table 2.3   Example of Parallel Items for the Culture Scales

Organization As Is

The pay and bonus system in this organization is designed to maximize:

| 1 | 2 | 3 | 4 | 5 | 6 | 7 |

Individual Interests   Collective Interests

Organization Should Be

In this organization, the pay and bonus system *should* be designed to maximize:

| 1 | 2 | 3 | 4 | 5 | 6 | 7 |

Individual Interests   Collective Interests

Society As Is

The economic system in this society is designed to maximize:

| 1 | 2 | 3 | 4 | 5 | 6 | 7 |

Individual Interests   Collective Interests

Society Should Be

I believe that the economic system in this society *should* be designed to maximize:

| 1 | 2 | 3 | 4 | 5 | 6 | 7 |

Individual Interests   Collective Interests

PHASE 2 HYPOTHESES

The results of Pilot Studies 1 and 2 set the stage for Phase 2 by providing the requisite questionnaire scales to test hypotheses. A number of hypotheses were developed with respect to independent variables. Societal culture dimensions and organizational culture dimensions were used as independent variables. The dependent variables were CLTs, national prosperity, and welfare of the members of the cultures. Various propositions, hypotheses, and potential relationships regarding the independent and dependent variables are presented in chapters throughout the book. In addition, we ranked cultures and regions (referred to as culture clusters) on each of the nine core GLOBE cultural dimensions and the six CLT leadership dimensions.

Validation of the Societal-Level Scales in Phase 2

All instruments are subject to potential unknown biases. In addition to the traditional statistical procedure of standardization of scores used to eliminate response bias, we developed a new procedure to estimate and remove response bias for each country with respect to the core GLOBE dimensions and CLTs (see Chapter 8 by Hanges & Dickson, Chapter 21 by Dorfman et al., and Appendix C which describes in more detail how we treated response bias).

Phase 2: Universal and Culturally Contingent CLT dimensions

One of the objectives of GLOBE is to determine whether there are CLT dimensions that are universally endorsed and dimensions that are differentially endorsed across cultures. Recall that CLTs are culturally endorsed dimensions composed of perceived effective or ineffective leader attributes or behaviors about which members within each culture agree. Profiles of CLT dimensions reflect what is commonly referred to as "leadership styles" in the leadership literature.

Shaw (1990) suggests that much of the cross-cultural literature indicates differences in managerial beliefs, values, and style. He also suggests that these differences are a reflection of societal cultural differences. Dorfman (2004) and House, Wright, and Aditya (1997) have reviewed the relevant cross-cultural literature extensively. They find support for Shaw's suggestion in studies by O'Connell, Lord, and O'Connell (1990) and Gerstner and Day (1994).

Using the means of Phase 2 leader attribute questionnaire subscales from 61 countries, we performed a multilevel confirmatory factor analysis to reconfirm the factor analyses conducted in two prior pilot studies. The factor structure of the Phase 2 leadership attribute and behavior questionnaire confirmed findings of the two prior pilot studies. Second-order factor analysis of the resulting 112 leader behavior and attribute items produced four factors: (1) Team-Oriented Charismatic/Value-Based leadership (2) Humane-Oriented leadership (3), Participative-Self-Protective leadership and (4) Autonomous leadership. Assisted by prevailing theory, we divided Factor 1 into Charismatic/Value-Based leadership and Team-Oriented leadership to create two dimensions. We also divided Factor 4 into two dimensions: Self-Protective leadership and Participative leadership (the scores of the nonparticipative subscales were reversed to reflect Participative leadership).

These divisions preserved conceptual clarity while providing dimensions related to current leadership theory and prior empirical studies.

The 21 subscales are grouped into six higher-order leader behavior–attribute dimensions, which are presented in Chapter 8. As previously stated, we refer to the higher-order dimensions as *global* CLT dimensions because they represent classes of leader behavior rather than specific leader behaviors. We refer to the 21 first-order factors as primary CLT subscales. These subscales measure more-specific leader attributes and behaviors. Composite profiles of the six CLT dimensions represent what is generally referred to as leadership styles.

STRENGTHS OF THE GLOBE RESEARCH DESIGN

Project GLOBE differs from previous cross-cultural research in several ways. The primary strength of this research is that we have not made assumptions about how best to measure cultural phenomena. Rather, we use multiple measurement methods to empirically test which methods are most meaningful. This is most evident in the development of four sets of measures assessing culture: (a) those based on shared values of organizational or society members, (b) those based on reported current organizational and societal practices, (c) unobtrusive measures, and (d) those based on scales derived from the World Value Survey.

We developed new measures and collected original data for our independent variables rather than relying on measures developed at other times in other places from other samples. Because the organizational culture, societal culture, and leadership measures used in Phase 2 were completed by different respondents, we were able to eliminate the frequently encountered problem of common source bias. The psychometric properties of the GLOBE scales and tests of their validity exceed normal empirical research standards and are described in Chapter 8 by Hanges and Dickson.

CONTRIBUTIONS

The results of the GLOBE research program fill a substantial knowledge gap concerning the cross-cultural forces relevant to effective leadership, effective organizational practices, national prosperity, and the physical and psychological welfare of members of cultures. The research findings will be useful not only in resolving several important theoretical social science issues but also in answering a wide range of practical questions.

Practical Relevance

The quantitative findings presented in this book will provide substantial enlightenment concerning the processes by which culture influences leadership and organizational practices. Chapter 1 represents an illustration of how knowledge of the GLOBE core dimensions can be useful for practical purposes. In subsequent chapters, the reader will find a specification of universal and culturally contingent leader attributes and behaviors, as well as commonly enacted and most-favored leader behavior patterns and organizational practices found in the cultures studied. The reader will also be able to develop an understanding of the role of cultural influences on the reported effectiveness of leader behaviors and organizational practices. In addition, leader behaviors that are culturally offensive are identified and described (see Chapters 12 through 21).

Finally, we related our independent variables to objective dependent variables taken from independently collected archival data. The dependent variables are country prosperity (GNP per capita), scores on the Human Development Index, and indicators of the psychological and physical well-being of the members of the cultures studied. This information will be useful as content for leadership training and career development programs intended to prepare individuals who will manage and lead others in unfamiliar cultures.

The country scores on our independent variables will be useful for the adjustment and effective interaction of individuals who work with others from the cultures studied. More specifically, this information will be useful to expatriates, managers of diverse cultural and ethnic groups both domestic and abroad, individuals involved in the management of public and private international affairs, and those who

conduct negotiations with commercial and political organizations in other cultures.

Knowledge of the culturally endorsed implicit theories of leadership in each culture, and the reported most- and least-effective leader attributes and behaviors will be useful to those working with members of the cultures studied. Activities such as selecting, counseling, and training these individuals will be facilitated by the results of this study. Potential managers can benefit from information regarding the kinds of behaviors and organizational practices that are acceptable and effective and unacceptable and ineffective in the cultures studied. Recall that our sample of cultures includes at least three societies from each major region of the world. Further, recall that we collected data from three quite diverse industries; within each industry, organizations face substantially different problems, forms of competition, and demands from external sources. We found a high degree of correlation among the findings across the three industries. Also recall that our findings are supported by independently collected data. For these reasons, we believe that our findings are quite generalizable.

Information regarding the constraints imposed on leaders by cultural norms will be useful to decision makers who need to anticipate and respond to the actions of leaders of other cultures. Knowledge about cultural and organizational norms and practices can be used to inform the formulation of meaningful prescriptions for strategy and policy formulation, organizational improvement, human resource management practices, and the design of organization structures and incentive and control systems.

Beneficial Social and Economic Applications

The research program is expected to have several additional beneficial social and economic applications. Countries that share similar regional resources and backgrounds can make comparisons to determine similarities and differences among themselves and share ways to improve intercountry relationships, economic productivity, and quality of life for their citizens. The empirical findings have also led to increased intercultural communication among educators who normally would not have contact with each other. The GLOBE CCIs have been extremely active in practicing cross-cultural communications. GLOBE-related research has been presented in more than 250 conference papers and more than 100 working papers, chapters of books, or journal articles.

Many of the CCIs serve as university faculty members, social scientists, and consultants. Being indigenous to their cultures, many CCIs are influence and change agents within those cultures. We expect that the GLOBE findings will be useful to individuals functioning as change agents within their societies.

Ancillary Social Science Contributions

The resulting data can be used for multiple purposes beyond the hypotheses of the study. For example, the worldwide Phase 2 data can be used to compare countries with their trading partners or their major competitors with respect to cultural, organizational, or leadership practices. These comparisons can lead to strategies to improve trade or to facilitate harmonious and productive relationships across borders. We have already witnessed more than 50 research projects and papers presented at scholarly conferences in which cultural and managerial practices have been compared among subsets of the GLOBE participating nations.

Relationships between the independent variables of this study and economic prosperity have also been subjected to analysis. The societal-level data can be used in subsequent analyses of important issues such as the construction of econometric or sociological models. The data collected for our independent variables can be related to firm-level practices such as forms of production systems and organization, transfer of technology, pricing, risk taking when entering new markets, investment in research and development, and foreign investment practices. The measures of culture can also be related to national levels of saving, distribution of wealth and social privileges, consumption levels and patterns, issues of economic growth and development, regulatory practices, and national productivity and efficiency. Further, the GLOBE societal culture dimensions can be also be related to such outcomes as mortality rates, life expectancy rates, hygiene practices, preventative or remedial medical practices, stress levels, suicide rates, frequency of ethnic and border conflicts, indicators of social unrest, and violations of human rights. To date, cultural influences on such variables have largely been ignored.

Chapter 7 by Javidan and Hauser reports relationships between GLOBE societal level variables and economic prosperity of nations, the Human Development Index, and measures of the psychological and physical welfare of the members of cultures. The worldwide data has been used to determine relationships between societal level GLOBE dimensions and many indices of social and physical well-being.

The following chapter presents a nontechnical summary of the major research findings resulting from Phases 1 and 2 of the GLOBE research program.

APPENDIX: STRUCTURAL CONTINGENCY THEORY

Although a report of research findings relative to this theory is not included in this book because the results of Phase 3 are not yet available, we describe this theory for the sake of completeness. The central proposition of this theory is that there is a set of demands that are imposed on organizations that must be met for them to ensure survival and guarantee effectiveness. These demands are referred to as *organizational contingencies*. It is asserted that these contingencies influence organizational form and practice and that congruence between the demands of the contingencies and organizational form and practice is associated with organizational effectiveness. Although this is a popular theory, its empirical verification is limited to small sample studies of organizations in industrialized countries (Child, 1981). Hickson, Hinings, McMillan, and Schwitter (1974) have asserted that the propositions of structural contingency theory are universal and culturally transcendent. This assertion rests on the assumption that organizational contingencies impose demands on organizations that are so powerful and universal that it is imperative for all organizations to respond in essentially the same way to function effectively and thus survive in competitive environments. We refer to this assertion as the *task environment imperative.* Child (1981) has presented a serious challenge to this assertion.

ENDNOTE

1. We excluded the Czech Republic from the analysis because of pervasive response bias.

REFERENCES

Ajzen, L., & Fishbein, M. (1970). *Understanding attitudes and predicting social behavior.* Englewood Cliffs, NJ: Prentice Hall.

Bass, B. M. (1985). *Leadership and performance beyond expectations.* New York: Free Press.

Bass, B. M. (1990). *Bass & Stogdill's handbook of leadership: Theory, research, and managerial applications* (3rd ed.). New York: Free Press.

Berry, J. W, & Dasen, P. R. (1974). Introduction. In J. W. Berry & P. R Dasen (Eds.), *Culture and cognition* (pp. 1–20). London: Methuen.

Burns, T., & Stalker, G. M. (1961). *The management of innovation.* London: Tavistock.

Child, J. (1981). Culture, contingency, and capitalism in the cross-national study of organization. In L. L. Cummings (Ed.), *Research in organizational behavior* (pp. 303–356). Greenwich, CT: JAI.

Chokkar, J., Brodbeck, F., & House, R. J. (Eds.). (in press). *Cultures of the world: A GLOBE anthology.* Thousand Oaks: Sage.

Cyert, R., & March, J. (1963). *A behavioral theory of the firm.* Englewood Cliffs, NJ: Prentice Hall.

Donaldson, L. (1993). *Anti-management theories of organization: A critique of paradigm proliferation.* Cambridge, UK: Cambridge University Press.

Dorfman, P. W. (2004). International and cross-cultural leadership research. In B. J. Punnett & O. Shenkar (Eds.), *Handbook for international management research* (2nd ed., pp. 265–355). Ann Arbor, MI: University of Michigan.

Gerstner, C. R., & Day, D. V. (1994). Cross-cultural comparison of leadership prototypes. *Leadership Quarterly, 5*(2), 121–134.

Hanges, P. J., Braverman, E. P., & Rentsch, J. R. (1991). Changes in raters' impressions of subordinates: A catastrophe model. *Journal of Applied Psychology, 76,* 878–888.

Hanges, P. J., Lord, R. G., Day, D. V., Sipe, W. P., Smith, W. C., & Brown, D. J. (1997, April). Leadership and gender bias: Dynamic measures and nonlinear modeling. In R. G. Lord (Chair), *Dynamic systems, leadership perceptions, and gender effects.* Symposium presented at the 12th Annual Conference of the Society for Industrial and Organizational Psychology, St. Louis, MO.

Hickson, D. J., Hinings, C. R., McMillan, J., & Schwitter, J. P. (1974). The culture-free context of organization structure: A tri-national comparison. *Sociology 8,* 59–80.

Hofstede, G. (1980). *Culture's consequences: International differences in work-related values.* London: Sage.

Hofstede, G. (2001). *Culture's consequences: International differences in work related values* (2nd ed.). Thousand Oaks, CA: Sage.

Hofstede, G., & Bond, M. H. (1988). The Confucius connection: From cultural roots to economic growth. *Organizational Dynamics, 16,* 4–21.

House, R. J., & Aditya, R. N. (1997). The social scientific study of leadership: Quo vadis? *Journal of Management, 23*(3), 409–473.

House, R. J., Wright, N. S., & Aditya, R. N. (1997). Cross-cultural research on organizational leadership: A critical analysis and a proposed theory. In P. C. Earley & M. Erez (Eds.), *New perspectives in international industrial organizational psychology* (pp. 535–625). San Francisco: New Lexington.

Inglehart, R., Basanez, M., & Moreno, A. (1998). *Human values and beliefs: A cross-cultural sourcebook—Political, religious, sexual, and economic norms in 43 societies.* Ann Arbor: University of Michigan Press.

Kluckhohn, F. R., & Strodtbeck, F. L. (1961). *Variations in value orientations.* New York: HarperCollins.

Kopelman, R. E., Brief, A. P., & Guzzo, R. A. (1990). *The role of climate and culture in productivity.* In B. Schneider (Ed.), *Organizational climate and culture* (pp. 282–318). San Francisco: Jossey-Bass.

Lawrence, P. R., & Lorsch, J. W. (1967). *Organization and environment.* Cambridge, MA: Harvard University Press.

Lombardo, M. M. (1983). I felt it as soon as I walked in. *Issues and Observations, 3*(4), 7–8.

Lord, R., & Maher, K. J. (1991). *Leadership and information processing: Linking perceptions and performance.* Boston: Unwin-Everyman.

McClelland, D. C. (1961). *The achieving society.* Princeton, NJ: Van Nostrand.

McClelland, D. C. (1985). *Human motivation.* Glenview, IL: Scott, Foresman.

McClelland, D. C., Atkinson, J. W., Clark, R. A., & Lowell, E. L. (Eds.). (1953). *The achievement motive.* Norwalk, CT: Appleton-Century-Crofts.

McFarland, L. J., Senen, S., & Childress, J. R. (1993). *Twenty-first-century leadership.* New York: Leadership Press.

Miller, D., & Droge, C. (1986). Psychological and traditional determinants of structure. *Administrative Science Quarterly, 31*(4), 539–560.

Mulder, M. (1971). Power equalization through participation. *Administrative Science Quarterly, 16,* 31–38.

O'Connell, M. S., Lord, R. G., & O'Connell, M. K. (1990, August). *Differences in Japanese and American leadership prototypes: Implications for cross-cultural training.* Paper presented at the meeting of the Academy of Management, San Francisco.

Putnam, R. D. (1993). *Making democracy work.* Princeton, NJ: Princeton University Press.

Schein, E. H. (1992). *Organizational culture and leadership: A dynamic view* (2nd ed.). San Francisco: Jossey-Bass.

Schneider, B. (1987). The people make the place. *Personnel Psychology, 40,* 437–454.

Schneider, B., Goldstein, H. W., & Smith, D. B. (1995). The ASA Framework: An update. *Personnel Psychology, 48,* 747–783.

Segall, M. H., Lonner, W. J., & Berry, J. W. (1998). Cross-cultural psychology as a scholarly discipline: On the flowering of culture in behavioral research. *American Psychologist, 53,* 1101–1110.

Shaw, J. B. (1990). A cognitive categorization model for the study of intercultural management. *Academy of Management Review, 15*(4), 626–645.

Sipe, W. P., & Hanges, P. J. (1997, April). Reframing the glass ceiling: A catastrophe model of changes in the perception of women as leaders. In R. G. Lord (Chair), *Dynamic systems, leadership perceptions, and gender effects.* Symposium presented at the 12th Annual Conference of the Society for Industrial and Organizational Psychology, St. Louis, MO.

Smith, P. B., & Bond, M. H. (1993). *Social psychology across cultures: Analysis and perspectives.* London: Harvester Wheatsheaf.

Thompson, K. R., & Luthans, F. (1990). Organizational culture: A behavioral perspective. In B. Schneider (Ed.), *Organizational climate and culture* (pp. 319–344). San Francisco: Jossey-Bass.

Triandis, H. C. (1995). *Individualism and collectivism.* Boulder, CO: Westview Press.

Trice, H. M., & Beyer, J. M. (1984). *The cultures of work organizations.* Englewood Cliffs, NJ: Prentice Hall.

Tushman, M. L., Newman, W. H., & Nadler, D. A. (1988). Executive leadership and organizational evolution: Managing incremental and discontinuous change. In R. H. Kilman & T. J. Covin (Eds.), *Corporate transformation: Revitalizing organizations for a competitive world* (pp. 102–130). San Francisco: Jossey-Bass.

Yukl, G. A. (2002). *Leadership in organizations* (5th ed.). Englewood Cliffs, NJ: Prentice Hall.

3

A Nontechnical Summary of GLOBE Findings

Mansour Javidan

Robert J. House

Peter W. Dorfman

This chapter provides a brief summary of the findings in the upcoming chapters of this book. To gain a complete understanding of the concepts, findings, and interpretations, the reader needs to consult the upcoming chapters. Only general information is provided here and care has been taken not to repeat the same information from the upcoming chapters. Furthermore, we do not intend to provide a comprehensive summary due to the volume of work involved. Rather, only selective information is provided.

As stated in Chapter 2, GLOBE is a multimethod, multiphase research program designed to conceptualize, operationalize, test, and validate a cross-level integrated theory of the relationship among culture and societal, organizational, and leadership effectiveness. In this book, we report on the parts of the integrated theory that focus on the relationship among culture, leadership, and societal effectiveness. We do not report the relationship between culture and organizational effectiveness. This topic is the focus of the third phase of the GLOBE research program, which is currently under way.

During the mid-1990s, in Phases 1 and 2, a large multinational team of 170 researchers and their support groups throughout the world collected data from more than 17,000 middle managers in 951 organizations in telecommunications, food processing, and finance industries in 62 societies. This book reports the findings of the first two phases of Project GLOBE. More than 25% of the respondents were female. The only significant difference between female and male respondents was in regard to Gender Egalitarianism values and practices, and the importance of several leadership dimensions.

As stated in Chapter 2, culture is conceptualized in terms of nine cultural attributes that, when quantified, are referred to as dimensions. GLOBE measures both cultural *practices* (the way things are) and *values* (the way things should be) at the organizational and societal levels of analysis. Table 3.1 provides a brief description of each dimension and a sample questionnaire item for each dimension. Each

Table 3.1   Culture Construct Definitions and Sample Questionnaire Items

Culture Construct Definitions	Specific Questionnaire Item
Power Distance: The degree to which members of a collective expect power to be distributed equally.	Followers are (should be) expected to obey their leaders without question.
Uncertainty Avoidance: The extent to which a society, organization, or group relies on social norms, rules, and procedures to alleviate unpredictability of future events.	Most people lead (should lead) highly structured lives with few unexpected events.
Humane Orientation: The degree to which a collective encourages and rewards individuals for being fair, altruistic, generous, caring, and kind to others.	People are generally (should be generally) very tolerant of mistakes.
Collectivism I (Institutional Collectivism): The degree to which organizational and societal institutional practices encourage and reward collective distribution of resources and collective action.	Leaders encourage (should encourage) group loyalty even if individual goals suffer.
Collectivism II (In-Group Collectivism): The degree to which individuals express pride, loyalty, and cohesiveness in their organizations or families.	Employees feel (should feel) great loyalty toward this organization.
Assertiveness: The degree to which individuals are assertive, confrontational, and aggressive in their relationships with others.	People are (should be) generally dominant in their relationships with each other.
Gender Egalitarianism: The degree to which a collective minimizes gender inequality.	Boys are encouraged (should be encouraged) more than girls to attain a higher education. (Scored inversely.)
Future Orientation: The extent to which individuals engage in future-oriented behaviors such as delaying gratification, planning, and investing in the future.	More people live (should live) for the present rather than for the future. (Scored inversely.)
Performance Orientation: The degree to which a collective encourages and rewards group members for performance improvement and excellence.	Students are encouraged (should be encouraged) to strive for continuously improved performance.

item was measured using a scale ranging from 1 to 7. GLOBE dimensions of societal culture have been validated through the use of unobtrusive measures and independently collected data from the World Values Survey (Inglehart, Basanez, & Moreno, 1998). Table 3.2 shows the descriptive statistics for GLOBE cultural dimensions. Appendix A provides the correlation coefficients among all the cultural values and practices. The following are several of the more interesting findings by the GLOBE research program.

SOCIETAL CULTURES

- The means for the nine cultural practices scores range from 3.37 (Gender Egalitarianism) to

Table 3.2 Means and Standard Deviations for GLOBE Cultural Practices and Values Descriptive Statistics

GLOBE Cultural Dimensions Practices and Values	Minimum	Maximum	Mean	Standard Deviation
Uncertainty Avoidance practices	2.88	5.37	4.16	.60
Future Orientation practices	2.88	5.07	3.85	.46
Power Distance practices	3.89	5.80	5.17	.41
Institutional Collectivism practices	3.25	5.22	4.25	.42
Humane Orientation practices	3.18	5.23	4.09	.47
Performance Orientation practices	3.20	4.94	4.10	.41
In-Group Collectivism practices	3.53	6.36	5.13	.73
Gender Egalitarianism practices	2.50	4.08	3.37	.37
Assertiveness practices	3.38	4.89	4.14	.37
Uncertainty Avoidance values	3.16	5.61	4.62	.61
Future Orientation values	4.33	6.20	5.49	.41
Power Distance values	2.04	3.65	2.75	.35
Institutional Collectivism values	3.83	5.65	4.73	.49
Humane Orientation values	4.49	6.09	5.42	.25
Performance Orientation values	4.92	6.58	5.94	.34
In-Group Collectivism values	4.94	6.52	5.66	.35
Gender Egalitarianism values	3.18	5.17	4.51	.48
Assertiveness values	2.66	5.56	3.82	.65

$N = 61$ societal cultures

5.17 (Power Distance). Most GLOBE societies are reported to be somewhat male oriented and to experience high levels of power distance.

- The means for six of the cultural practices scores, namely, Uncertainty Avoidance, Future Orientation, Institutional Collectivism, Humane Orientation, Performance Orientation, and Assertiveness are around 4, which is the mid-point of the scale.
- The means for two cultural practices scores, namely, Power Distance and In-Group Collectivism, are above 5 on the 7-point scale. GLOBE societies are generally reported to experience

relatively high levels of power distance and are generally in-group oriented.

- The mean score of Gender Egalitarianism practices is the lowest among all practice dimensions (3.37) indicating that GLOBE societies are reported to be male oriented.
- The means for the nine cultural values scores range from 2.75 (Power Distance) to 5.94 (Performance Orientation). Most GLOBE societies prefer lower levels of power differentiation and higher levels of performance orientation.
- The largest range of societal scores for cultural practices among GLOBE societies is

related to In-Group Collectivism. The highest reported country score on this dimension was 6.36 (Philippines) and the lowest reported country score was 3.53 (Denmark) for a difference of 2.83.

- The smallest range of societal scores for cultural practices among GLOBE societies is related to Assertiveness. The highest reported country score on this dimension was 4.89 (Albania) and the lowest reported country score was 3.38 (Sweden) for a difference of 1.51.

- Interestingly, the opposite is true for the GLOBE range of scores for cultural values. The lowest range relates to In-Group Collectivism (1.58) and the largest range relates to Assertiveness (2.90). In other words, GLOBE societies are reported to be rather close in their Assertiveness practices, but very different in terms of Assertiveness values. In contrast, they are reported to be very different in terms of In-Group Collectivism practices

but very close on their In-Group Collectivism values.

- The mean scores for values are lower than those for practices in the case of two dimensions: Power Distance (−2.42) and Assertiveness (−0.32). For all the other dimensions, the mean values scores are higher than the mean practices scores.

- Only for one dimension, Gender Egalitarianism, the correlation between the reported values and practices scores is significant and positive. For seven other dimensions, it is significant and negative. It is insignificant for In-Group Collectivism.

- Ten cultural clusters were identified: Latin America, Anglo, Latin Europe (Italy, Portugal, Spain, France, Switzerland [French-speaking], Israel), Nordic Europe, Germanic Europe, Confucian Asia, Sub-Saharan Africa, Middle East, Southern Asia, and Eastern Europe. The cultural profiles of these clusters are reported in Figures 3.1 to 3.10.

(Text continues on page 37)

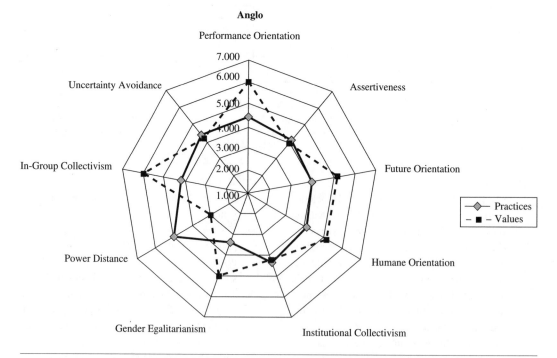

Figure 3.1   Cultural Dimension Scores for the Anglo Societal Cluster

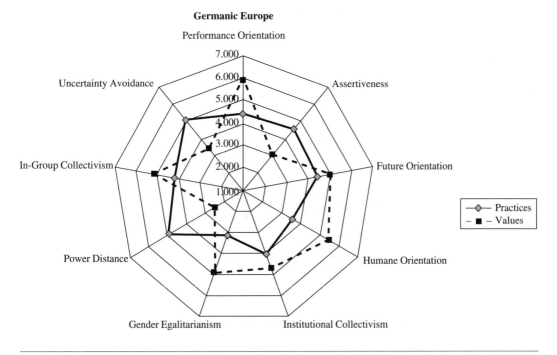

Figure 3.2   Cultural Dimension Scores for the Germanic Europe Societal Cluster

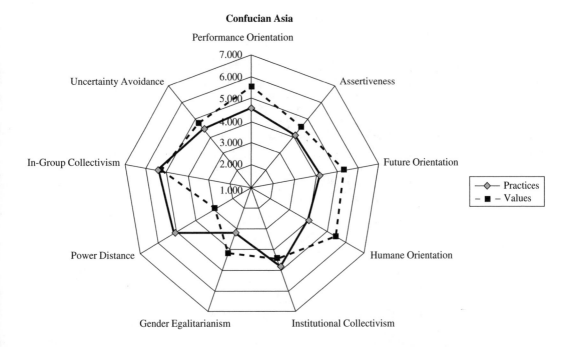

Figure 3.3   Cultural Dimension Scores for the Confucian Asia Societal Cluster

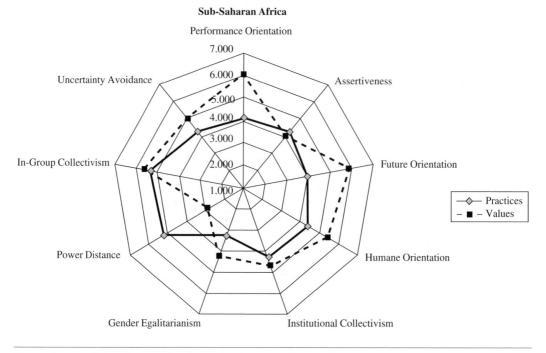

Figure 3.4   Cultural Dimension Scores for the Sub-Saharan Africa Societal Cluster

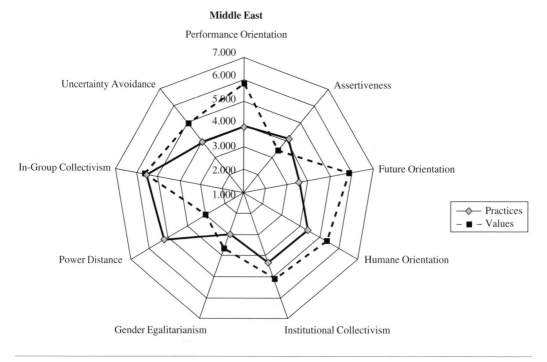

Figure 3.5   Cultural Dimension Scores for the Middle East Societal Cluster

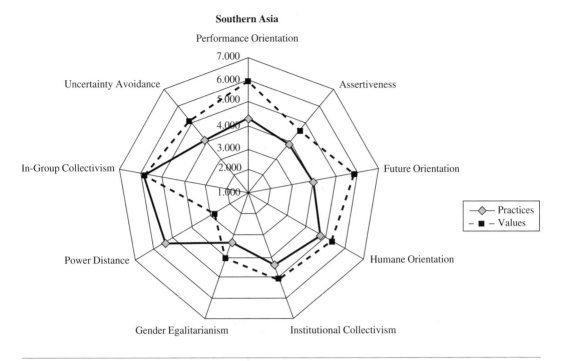

Figure 3.6 Cultural Dimension Scores for the Southern Asia Societal Cluster

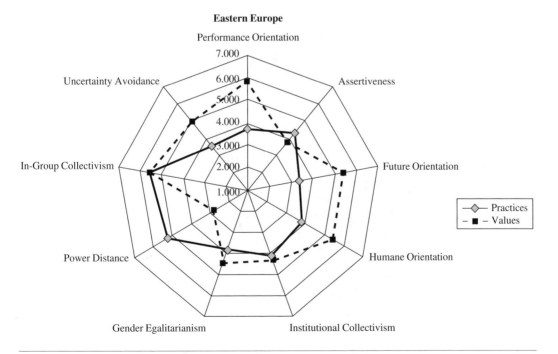

Figure 3.7 Cultural Dimension Scores for the Eastern Europe Societal Cluster

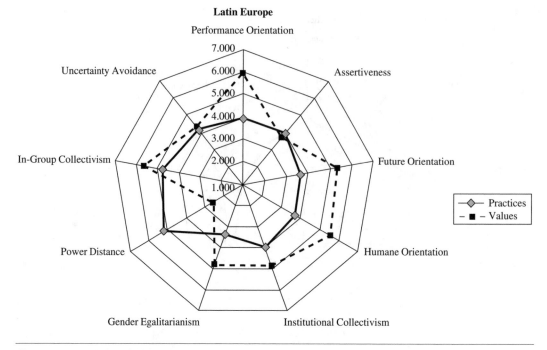

Figure 3.8   Cultural Dimension Scores for the Latin Europe Societal Cluster

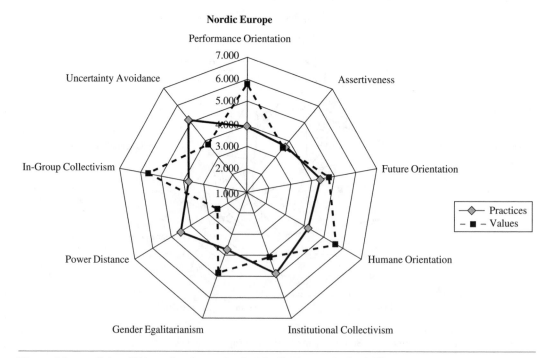

Figure 3.9   Cultural Dimension Scores for the Nordic Europe Societal Cluster

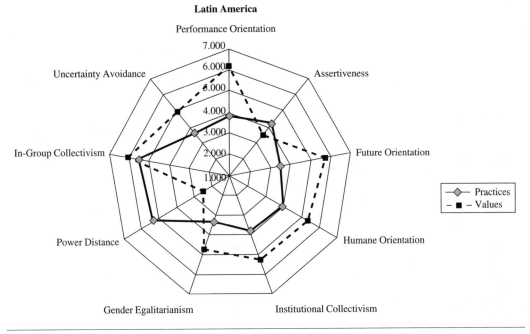

Figure 3.10 Cultural Dimension Scores for the Latin America Societal Cluster

SOCIETAL CULTURE AND ORGANIZATIONAL CULTURE

- Organizational cultures reflect the societies in which they are embedded. For example, organizations with high performance orientation are found in societies with high performance orientation.
- The absolute difference between values and practices are larger for societies than for organizations.

CULTURE AND SOCIETAL EFFECTIVENESS

Societal effectiveness is conceptualized in terms of *economic health, success with science and technology, the human condition,* and *societal values.* The data for the above aspects of societal effectiveness were obtained from the Human Development Report (United Nations Development Program, 1998), The Global Competitiveness Report (1998), The World Development Indicators (2000), and the World Values Survey.

Economic Health is defined in terms of economic prosperity, economic productivity, government support for economic prosperity, societal

support for economic competitiveness, and the Competitiveness Index. *Success with science and technology* consists of success in applied science, and success in basic science. The *human condition* consists of societal health, human health, life expectancy, general satisfaction, psychological health, and Human Development Index. *Societal values* refer to values toward family and friends, achievement, political ideology, religion, and gender equality. Following are some of the major findings with respect to culture and societal effectiveness: Tables 3.3 to 3.6 provide summaries of the findings.

- Societal Performance Orientation, Future Orientation, and Uncertainty Avoidance practice scores are positively and significantly related to most measures of economic health, namely, economic prosperity, government and public support for competitiveness and prosperity, and competitiveness rankings (Table 3.3).
- The societal Institutional Collectivism practice score is positively and significantly correlated with three out of five measures of economic health. In contrast, In-Group Collectivism is negatively and significantly related with three measures of economic health, namely, economic

Table 3.3   Cultural Practices and Economic Health+

Cultural Practices	Economic Prosperity	Economic Productivity	Government Support for Prosperity	Societal Support for Competitiveness	World Competitiveness Index
Performance Orientation	.29* n = 57		.50** n = 40	.58** n = 40	.61** n = 41
Future Orientation	.54** n = 57		.63** n = 40	.48** n = 40	.62** n = 41
Gender Egalitarianism					
Assertiveness					
Institutional Collectivism	.33* n = 57		.36* n = 40		.40** n = 41
In-Group Collectivism	−.78** n = 57		−.67** n = 40		−.45** n = 41
Power Distance	−.53** n = 57		−.65** n = 40	−.47** n = 40	−.53** n = 41
Humane Orientation					
Uncertainty Avoidance	.60** n = 57		.74** n = 40	.44** n = 40	.60** n = 41

+ Only significant coefficients are reported, n = GLOBE subsample.

* Correlation is significant at the 0.05 level (2-tailed).

** Correlation is significant at the 0.01 level (2-tailed).

prosperity, government support for prosperity, and competitiveness ranking (Table 3.3).

- The Societal Power Distance practice score is negatively and significantly related to all measures of economic health except productivity (Table 3.3).

- Economic prosperity and the World Competitiveness Index are positively and significantly related to four cultural practices dimensions: Performance Orientation, Future Orientation, Institutional Collectivism, and Uncertainty Avoidance. They are both negatively and significantly related to In-Group Collectivism and Power Distance practice scores (Table 3.3).

- Government and societal support for prosperity and competitiveness are both positively and significantly related to three cultural practice dimensions: Performance Orientation, Future

Orientation, and Uncertainty Avoidance. They are both negatively and significantly related to Power Distance practice scores (Table 3.3).

- No cultural practice or value dimension is related to economic productivity (Tables 3.3 and 3.4).

- Economic prosperity and competitive rankings are both negatively correlated with Performance Orientation, Future Orientation, Institutional Collectivism, and Uncertainty Avoidance value scores (Table 3.4).

- Societal health and general satisfaction are positively and significantly correlated with practice scores of Performance Orientation, Future Orientation, and Uncertainty Avoidance. They are negatively and significantly related with In-Group Collectivism and Power Distance practices (Table 3.5).

Table 3.4   Cultural Values and Economic Health+

Cultural Values	Economic Prosperity	Economic Productivity	Government Support for Prosperity	Societal Support for Competitiveness	World Competitiveness Index
Performance Orientation	−.28* n = 57				−.44** n = 42
Future Orientation	−.62** n = 57		−.57** n = 40		−.41** n = 41
Gender Egalitarianism	.36** n = 57				
Assertiveness					
Institutional Collectivism	−.48** n = 57		−.46** n = 40		−.47** n = 41
In-Group Collectivism	−.30* n = 57				
Power Distance				.47** n = 40	.38* n = 41
Humane Orientation					
Uncertainty Avoidance	−.80** n = 57		−.75** n = 40		−.49** n = 41

+ Only significant coefficients are reported, n = GLOBE subsample.

* Correlation is significant at the 0.05 level (2-tailed).

** Correlation is significant at the 0.01 level (2-tailed).

- The Human Development Index (HDI) and life expectancy are negatively and significantly related to practice scores on In-Group Collectivism, Power Distance, and Humane Orientation. HDI is positively correlated with Gender Egalitarianism (Table 3.5).
- Societal health, general satisfaction, and HDI are all negatively correlated with Future Orientation and Uncertainty Avoidance values scores (Table 3.6).
- No cultural practice or value dimension is related to psychological health (Tables 3.5 and 3.6).

CULTURE AND LEADERSHIP

Leadership attributes are measured through a questionnaire containing 112 leadership items.

Each item is defined and measured on a scale ranging from 1 to 7. A score of 1 means that the attribute greatly inhibits outstanding leadership and a score of 7 means that the attribute contributes greatly to outstanding leadership.

- GLOBE identified 22 leadership attributes that are universally desirable. Ninety-five percent of the societal average scores for these attributes were larger than 5 on a 7-point scale, and the worldwide grand mean score exceeded 6 on a 7-point scale. "Decisiveness" and "foresight" are examples of such attributes.
- Eight leadership attributes were identified as universally undesirable. Ninety-five percent of the societal average scores for these attributes were less than 3 on a 7-point scale, and the worldwide grand mean score was lower than 3

Table 3.5   Cultural Practices and Human Condition+

Cultural Practices	Societal Health	Human Health	Life Expectancy	General Satisfaction	Psychological Health	Human Development Index (HDI)
Performance Orientation	.53** n = 40			.40* n = 37		
Future Orientation	.70** n = 40			.56** n = 38		
Gender Egalitarianism						.29* n = 56
Assertiveness						
Institutional Collectivism						
In-Group Collectivism	−.60** n = 40		−.45** n = 56	−.69** n = 38		−.56** n = 56
Power Distance	−.62** n = 40		−.33** n = 56	−.48** n = 38		−.36** n = 56
Humane Orientation			−.35** n = 56			−.37** n = 56
Uncertainty Avoidance	.76** n = 40		.28* n = 56	.63** n = 38		.28* n = 56

+ Only significant coefficients are reported, n = GLOBE subsample.

* Correlation is significant at the 0.05 level (2-tailed).

** Correlation is significant at the 0.01 level (2-tailed).

on a 7-point scale. "Irritable" and "ruthless" are examples of such attributes.

- Many leadership attributes are culturally contingent. They are desirable in some cultures and undesirable in others. "Ambitious" is an example with a societal score ranging from 2.85 to 6.73. "Elitist" is another example with a societal score range of 1.61 to 5.00. In some cultures the concept of leadership is romanticized and leaders are given exceptional privileges and status and are held in great esteem.

- During focus interviews, it was reported that in some cultures like the Netherlands or Switzerland, the concept of leadership is denigrated and members of the cultures are highly suspicious of individuals who are in positions of authority for fear that they will acquire and abuse power. In these cultures, substantial constraints are placed on what individuals in positions of authority can and cannot do, and such individuals are given no special treatment, status, or privileges.

- We were able to empirically establish that there are culturally based shared conceptions of leadership, referred to as *culturally endorsed implicit theories of leadership* (CLT). That is, members of cultures share common observations and values concerning what constitutes effective and ineffective leadership. Leadership attributes were statistically grouped into 21 "first-order" primary factors (henceforth called

Table 3.6   Cultural Values and Human Condition+

Cultural Values	Societal Health	Human Health	Life Expectancy	General Satisfaction	Psychological Health	Human Development Index (HDI)
Performance Orientation			−.30* n = 56			
Future Orientation	−.54** n = 40		−.49** n = 56	−0.45** n = 38		−.50** n = 56
Gender Egalitarianism			.28* n = 56	.59** n = 38		.43** n = 56
Assertiveness						
Institutional Collectivism	−.33* n = 40					
In-Group Collectivism	−.39* n = 40					
Power Distance						
Humane Orientation						
Uncertainty Avoidance	−.74* n = 40		−.44** n = 56	−.66** n = 38		−.59** n = 56

+ Only significant coefficients are reported, n = GLOBE subsample.

* Correlation is significant at the 0.05 level (2-tailed).

** Correlation is significant at the 0.01 level (2-tailed).

primary leadership dimensions) that were then consolidated into six "second-order" *global* leadership dimensions. Combined, they represent the culturally endorsed leadership theory dimensions (CLTs).

- The six *global* CLT leadership dimensions are: (a) Charismatic/Value-Based leadership, (b) Team Oriented leadership, (c) Participative leadership, (d) Autonomous leadership, (e) Humane-Oriented leadership, and (f) Self-Protective leadership.
- Charismatic/Value-Based leadership is generally reported to contribute to outstanding leadership. The range of mean societal scores among GLOBE countries is 4.5 to 6.5 on a 7-point scale.

- Team Oriented leadership is generally reported to contribute to outstanding leadership. The range of mean societal scores among GLOBE countries is 4.7 to 6.2 on a 7-point scale.
- Participative leadership is generally reported to contribute to outstanding leadership, although there are meaningful differences among countries and clusters. The range of mean societal scores among GLOBE countries is 4.5 to 6.1 on a 7-point scale.
- Humane-Oriented leadership is reported to be neutral in some societies and to moderately contribute to outstanding leadership in others. The range of mean societal scores is 3.8 to 5.6 on a 7-point scale.

- Autonomous leadership is reported to range from impeding outstanding leadership to slightly facilitating outstanding leadership. The range of mean societal scores is 2.3 to 4.7 on a 7-point scale.
- Self-Protective leadership is generally reported to impede outstanding leadership. The range of mean societal scores among GLOBE countries is 2.5 to 4.6 on a 7-point scale.

LEADERSHIP PROFILES OF CULTURAL CLUSTERS

- Cluster scores on the culturally endorsed leadership theory (CLT) dimensions are provided in Figures 3.11 to 3.16. Charismatic/Value-Based leadership receives the highest reported score in the Anglo cluster (6.05) and the lowest score in the Middle East cluster (5.35).
- Team Oriented leadership receives the highest reported score in the Latin American cluster (5.96) and the lowest score in the Middle East cluster (5.47).
- Participative leadership receives the highest reported score in Germanic Europe cluster (5.86) and the lowest score in the Middle East cluster (4.97).
- Humane-Oriented leadership receives the highest reported score in Southern Asia (5.38) and the lowest score in Nordic Europe (4.42).
- Autonomous leadership receives the highest reported score in Eastern Europe (4.20) and the lowest score in Latin America (3.51).
- Self-Protective leadership receives the highest reported score in Southern Asia (3.83) and the lowest score in Nordic Europe (2.72).

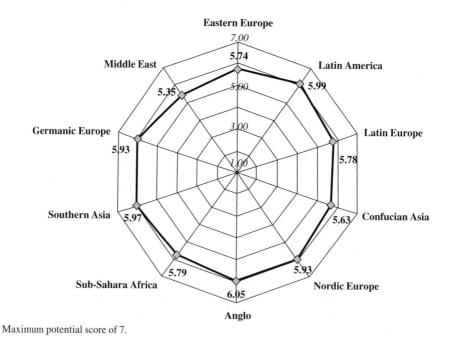

Maximum potential score of 7.

Figure 3.11 Charismatic/Value-Based Leadership Dimension Scores for Each Culture Cluster

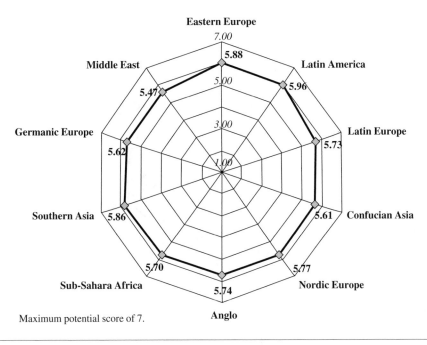

Figure 3.12   Team Oriented Leadership Dimension Scores for Each Culture Cluster

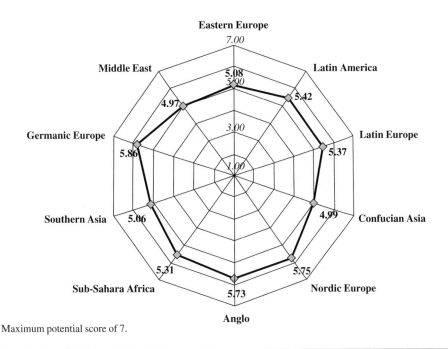

Figure 3.13   Participative Leadership Dimension Scores for Each Culture Cluster

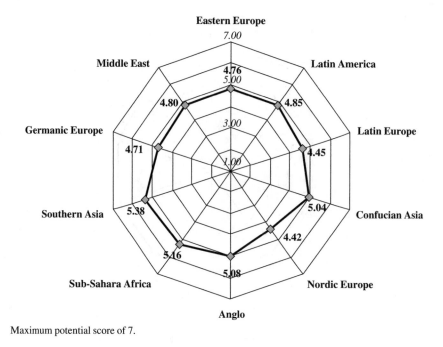

Maximum potential score of 7.

Figure 3.14   Humane-Oriented Leadership Dimension Scores for Each Culture Cluster

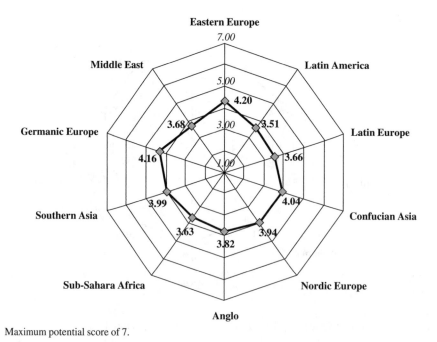

Maximum potential score of 7.

Figure 3.15   Autonomous Leadership Dimension Scores for Each Culture Cluster

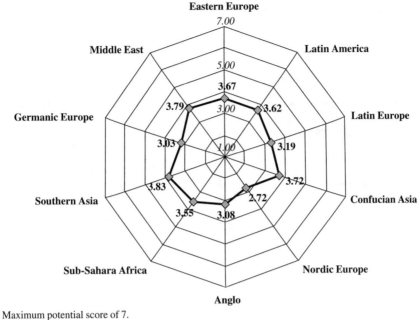

Maximum potential score of 7.

Figure 3.16   Self-Protective Leadership Dimension Scores for Each Culture Cluster

CULTURE DIMENSIONS AND LEADERSHIP CLTS

- In general, cultural dimension values, not practices, are related to CLT leadership dimensions. Both values and leadership CLTs represent desired end states: one reflects culture, the other leadership attributes.
- Figures 3.17 to 3.22 summarize the relationship between cultural dimensions and CLT dimensions. They show the relative contribution of each cultural dimension toward each CLT dimension.
- Performance Orientation (values) is the only cultural dimension that at the organizational level is a significant predictor of all six global CLT dimensions. It is positively correlated with five and negatively correlated with one, Self-Protective leadership.
- Uncertainty Avoidance (values) is a positive predictor of Self-Protective leadership, Team-Oriented leadership, and Humane-Oriented leadership. It is a negative predictor of Participative leadership.
- Future Orientation and Humane Orientation (values) are both positive predictors of

Humane Oriented, Team-Oriented, and Charismatic/Value-Based leadership.
- In-Group Collectivism (values) is a positive predictor of Charismatic/Value-Based and Team-Oriented leadership and a negative predictor of Self-Protective leadership.
- Gender Egalitarianism (values) is a positive predictor of Participative and Charismatic/Value-Based leadership, and a negative predictor of Self-Protective leadership.
- Institutional Collectivism (values) is a negative predictor of Autonomous leadership.
- Power Distance (values) is a positive predictor of Self-Protective leadership and a negative predictor of Charismatic/Value-Based and Participative leadership.

In this chapter, we have provided a preview of what the reader can expect to see in the upcoming chapters. The chapter is not intended to be comprehensive. Rather, it is a brief collection of findings that reflect what is in the rest of the book, although the charts and tables in this chapter are not repeated in the upcoming chapters.

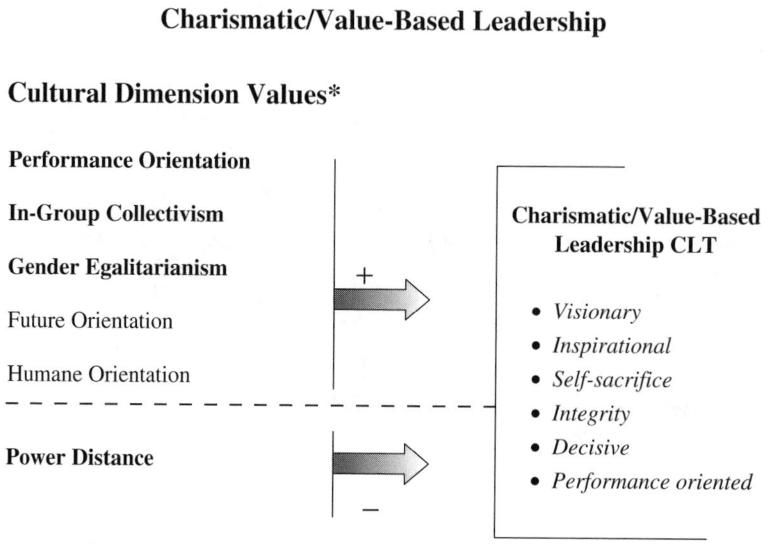

Charismatic/Value-Based Leadership

Cultural Dimension Values*

Performance Orientation

In-Group Collectivism

Gender Egalitarianism

Future Orientation

Humane Orientation

Power Distance

+

−

Charismatic/Value-Based Leadership CLT

- *Visionary*
- *Inspirational*
- *Self-sacrifice*
- *Integrity*
- *Decisive*
- *Performance oriented*

Figure 3.17   Cultural Value Drivers of the Charismatic Value-Based CLT Leadership Dimension

NOTES: This figure summarizes information from Chapters 12–19 and 21–22. As such, it combines results from both the single and multiple HLM statistical tests linking cultural values to leadership dimensions.

* The most important cultural dimensions for this leadership CLT are bolded.

Team-Oriented Leadership

Cultural Dimension Values*

Uncertainty Avoidance

In-Group Collectivism

Humane Orientation

Performance Orientation

Future Orientation

[No dimensions were negatively related.]

+

−

Team Oriented Leadership CLT

- *Collaborative team orientation*
- *Team integration*
- *Diplomatic*
- *Malevolent (reverse-scored)*
- *Administratively competent*

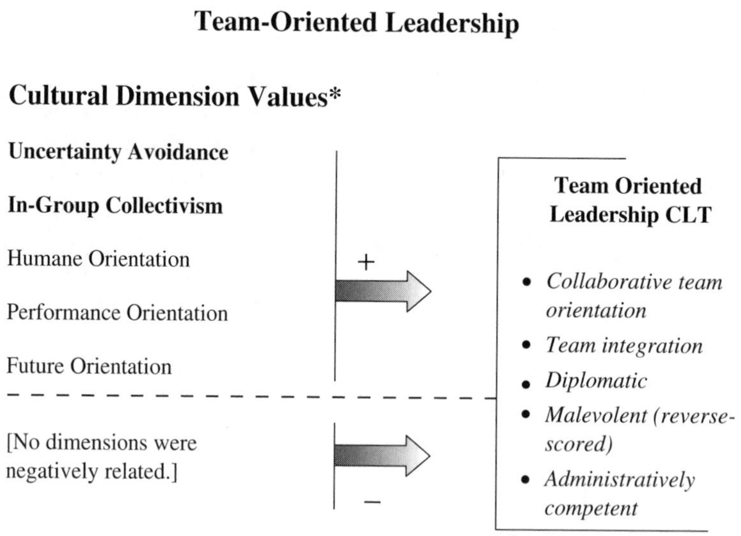

Figure 3.18   Cultural Value Drivers of the Team Oriented CLT Leadership Dimension

NOTES: This figure summarizes information from Chapters 12–19 and 21–22. As such, it combines results from both the single and multiple HLM statistical tests linking cultural values to leadership dimensions.

* The most important cultural dimensions for this leadership CLT are bolded.

Participative Leadership

Cultural Dimension Values*

Performance Orientation

Gender Egalitarianism

Humane Orientation

$+$

⟶

Participative Leadership CLT

- *Participative*
- *Autocratic (reverse-scored)*

Uncertainty Avoidance

Power Distance

Assertiveness

$-$

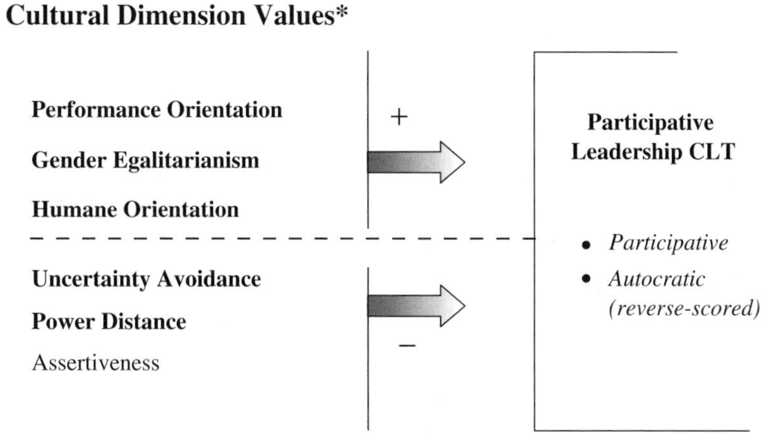

Figure 3.19   Cultural Value Drivers of the Participative CLT Leadership Dimension

NOTES: This figure summarizes information from Chapters 12–19 and 21–22. As such, it combines results from both the single and multiple HLM statistical tests linking cultural values to leadership dimensions.

* The most important cultural dimensions for this leadership CLT are bolded.

Humane Oriented Leadership

Cultural Dimension Values*

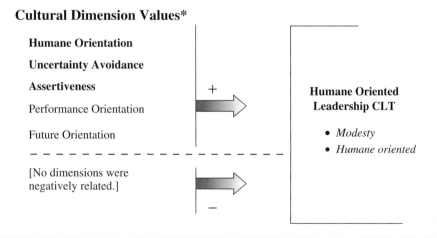

Humane Orientation

Uncertainty Avoidance

Assertiveness

Performance Orientation

Future Orientation

$+$

Humane Oriented Leadership CLT

- *Modesty*
- *Humane oriented*

[No dimensions were negatively related.]

$-$

Figure 3.20   Cultural Value Drivers of the Humane Oriented CLT Leadership Dimension

NOTES: This figure summarizes information from Chapters 12–19 and 21–22. As such, it combines results from both the single and multiple HLM statistical tests linking cultural values to leadership dimensions.

* The most important cultural dimensions for this leadership CLT are bolded.

Autonomous Leadership

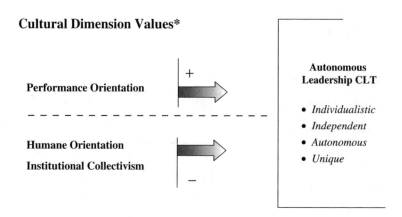

Figure 3.21   Cultural Value Drivers of the Autonomous CLT Leadership Dimension

NOTES: This figure summarizes information from Chapters 12–19 and 21–22. As such, it combines results from both the single and multiple HLM statistical tests linking cultural values to leadership dimensions.

* The most important cultural dimensions for this leadership CLT are bolded.

Self-Protective Leadership

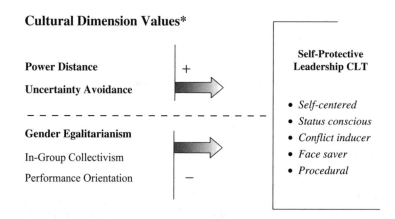

Figure 3.22   Cultural Value Drivers of the Self-Protective CLT Leadership Dimension

NOTES: This figure summarizes information from Chapters 12–19 and 21–22. As such, it combines results from both the single and multiple HLM statistical tests linking cultural values to leadership dimensions.

* The most important cultural dimensions for this leadership CLT are bolded.

REFERENCES

Inglehart, R., Basanez, M., & Moreno, A. (1998). *Human values and beliefs: A cross-cultural sourcebook.* Ann Arbor: University of Michigan Press.

The World Bank. (2000). *World development indicators.* Washington, DC: Author.

World Economic Forum. (1998). *The global competiveness report.* Geneva, Switzerland: Author.

United Nations Development Program. (1998). *Human development report.* New York: Oxford University Press.

PART II

PRIOR LITERATURE

PETER W. DORFMAN

Part II provides the foundation for GLOBE's investigation of the influence of societal culture on leadership and organizational behavior. This section reviews various literature related to commonly asked research questions and findings that provide the necessary context to interpret GLOBE results. Chapter 4 by Dorfman and House starts with a basic discussion of leadership and provides an introduction to the significant role of culture's influence on leadership processes. A major assertion throughout this book is that there appears to be a wide divergence of beliefs in the world about what constitutes effective leadership. As pointed out in the Part I introductory chapters, what is expected of leaders, what leaders may and may not do, and the status and influence bestowed on leaders vary considerably as a result of cultural forces in the countries or regions in which the leaders function. Readers in many Western nations might be surprised to learn that the extremely positive connotation associated with the word *leadership* is not universal, and some societies have a very skeptical view of leaders and leadership. Yet, the extent to which the meaning and enactment of leadership is culturally contingent is still relatively unknown. Although cultural differences figure predominantly in cross-cultural literature, some common management and leadership practices are also likely given the current trend toward globalization of economies and an ever-increasing number of multinational firms. Empirical evidence for cultural universality as well as cultural specificity is discussed extensively in Chapters 4 and 21. Chapter 4 also provides information related to cross-cultural differences related to the origin of leaders within a society, preferred leader behaviors, distinct role demands placed on leaders, and differential impact of commonly enacted leader behaviors.

Chapter 5, by Dickson, BeShears, and Gupta, provides the foundation for investigating the relationships among societal culture, industry sectors (e.g., financial versus telecommunication), and organizational structures. As discussed throughout this volume, a wealth of research examines the interrelationships between various conceptions of societal culture and industry, and various forms of organizational behavior, structure, and culture. The fact that different industries impose different demands on organizations is obvious and well supported in the organizational strategy literature (Gordon, 1991). Specific organizational practices necessary for survival may lead organizations to monitor and carefully control employees' behavior. The vast majority of research on society-organization linkages, and on industry–organization linkages as well, however, has focused on the measurement and description of relationships, without specifying the mechanisms by which the influence is enacted. For instance, the level and degree of governmental regulation, development of the industry within a society, and national economic system are just a few of the many factors that affect the ways in which a given industry is enacted in a given society. In recent years, organizational researchers have fortunately begun to identify potential explanatory mechanisms to understand these relationships more thoroughly. Theoretical models that are discussed in this chapter include: Cultural immersion, social network, resource dependency, and institutional theory. The chapter concludes with the premise that truly understanding when and how these mechanisms affect an industry requires both culturally generalizable and culturally specific perspectives. The culturally generalizable approach is necessary to identify which general principles are commonly more active than others, whereas the culturally specific perspective tells us about the mechanisms active in specific situations.

Thus, the information in Part II provides ample evidence that cultural forces influence many aspects of leadership, industry, and organizational phenomena. And clearly, we are much further along in our understanding of the cultural influence on these processes than we were 38 years ago when Haire, Ghiselli, and Porter (1966) published their seminal study. Yet much remains to be learned. These chapters set the stage for understanding the potential interaction between leadership and societal culture, industry sectors, and organizational cultures.

REFERENCES

Gordon, G. G. (1991). Industry determinants of organizational culture. *Academy of Management Review, 16,* 396–415.

Haire, M., Ghiselli, E. E., & Porter, L. (1966). *Managerial thinking: An international study.* New York: John Wiley.

4

Cultural Influences on Organizational Leadership

Literature Review, Theoretical Rationale, and GLOBE Project Goals

Peter W. Dorfman

Robert J. House

Leadership is an enigma—a puzzle within a puzzle. It has an "I know it when I see it" feel, yet there is no single, comprehensive definition that encompasses all divergent views about leadership. Capturing the essence of effective leadership has been an elusive goal sought by scholars throughout history, but like the blind men examining different parts of the elephant, researchers report truth about the discrete elements of leadership, yet have difficulty finding a common frame or gestalt regarding the concept. The enigma of leadership is even more fascinating, complex, and daunting if looked at through a cross-cultural lens. Examples of the variety of views about leadership found around the world were presented in this volume's overview (Chapter 2) by House and Javidan. Now consider some findings from the cross-cultural research literature pertaining to effective leadership:

- Leadership styles emphasizing participation, which are commonly accepted in the individualistic West, are of questionable effectiveness in the collectivistic East (Dorfman, 2004).
- Asian managers place heavy emphasis on paternalistic leadership (Redding, 1990) and group maintenance activities (Bass, Burger, Doktor, & Barrett, 1979).
- Charismatic leaders may display a highly assertive manner, as in the case of John F. Kennedy or Martin Luther King, Jr., or a quiet, nonassertive manner, as in the case of Mahatma Gandhi, Nelson Mandela, and Mother Teresa (House, Wright, & Aditya, 1997).
- A leader who "Listens carefully to what you say" is seen as more rewarding in the U.S. than in China. The converse is true regarding "leadership that praises you to others, but not you directly" (Jones, Rozelle, & Chang, 1990).

AUTHORS' NOTE: Phases 1 and 2 of the GLOBE research program were funded by the Dwight D. Eisenhower Leadership Education Program of the Department of Education of the United States. Funds to support data collection in three African countries were provided by a grant from the Reginald Jones Center for Strategic Leadership.

- The Malaysian leader is expected to behave in a manner that is humble, modest, and dignified (House et al., 1999).
- In India, there is a preference for leadership that is proactive, morally principled, ideological, bold, and assertive, in contrast to reactive, pragmatic, instrumental, quiet, and nurturing (Chhokar, in press).
- The combination of family and tribal norms and bureaucratic organizational structures fosters authoritarian management practices that may be characterized as a "sheikocracy" leadership style in Arabian countries (Al-Kubaisy, 1985).

These examples speak to the multifaceted question "to what extent is leadership culturally contingent"? For many years the academic literature barely touched on this issue, yet expatriate managers working in multinational companies hardly need to be reminded of the wide variety of *management* practices found around the world. Laurent (1983), and more recently Trompenaars (1993), document the astonishing diversity of organizational practices worldwide, of which many are acceptable and considered effective in one country but ineffective in a neighboring country. For instance, supervisors are expected to have precise answers to subordinates' questions in Japan, but less so in the United States. As another example, the effectiveness of working alone or in a group is perceived very differently around the world and this will certainly influence the quality and aptitude of virtual teams found in multinational organizations (Davis & Bryant, 2003). An inescapable conclusion is that acceptable management practices found in one country are hardly guaranteed to work in a different country.

Although fascinating in its own right, does the diversity of management practices worldwide constitute a management problem? We believe it does, given the interrelatedness of the world economy. Consider the management dilemma posed within the European Union. To the extent that management practices in Europe are said to stop at national boundaries, the emergence of a generic "Euromanager" in the European Union becomes problematic (Brodbeck et al., 2000). Training a knowledgeable, globally competent manager is an obvious problem for multinational European companies: What management practices should the Euromanager use, and for which subordinates, colleagues, and supervisors? The multicultural reality is not just an abstract phenomenon to ponder; real people in those companies are searching for more effective management practices. Titus Lokananta, for example, is an Indonesian Cantonese holding a German passport, managing a Mexican multinational corporation producing Gummy Bears in the Czech Republic (Millman, 2000).

Should we, however, conclude that cultural differences are so vast that finding common management practices among countries are the exception rather than the rule and will ever remain so? Not necessarily. Companies are forced to share information, resources, and training in a global world economy. The best business schools educate managers from all over the world in the latest management techniques. Using academic jargon, the issue of common versus unique business and management practices is framed using contrasting perspectives embodied in the terms *cultural universals* versus *cultural specifics*. The former are thought to be found from the process of cultural convergence whereas the latter from maintaining cultural divergence. Perhaps not surprisingly, empirical research supports both views. For example, in their event management leadership research program Smith and Peterson (1988) found both commonalities and differences across cultures in the manner by which managers handled relatively routine events in their work. All managers preferred to rely on their own experience and training if appointing a new subordinate, relative to other influences such as consultation with others or using formal rules and procedures. However, there were major differences in countries in the degree to which managers used formal company rules and procedures in contrast to more informal networks, and these differences covary with national cultural values (Smith, 2003; Smith, Dugan, & Trompenaars, 1996). As another example, Hazucha and colleagues (Hazucha, Hezlett, Bontems-Wackens, & Ronnqvist, 1999) found a good deal of similarity among European countries regarding the importance of core management competencies for a Euromanager. Yet there were significant differences among countries in the perceived attainment of these skills.

Should we also expect that leadership processes, like management practices, be similarly influenced by culture? The apparent answer is yes—substantial empirical evidence (see House et al., 1997) indicates that leader attributes, behavior, status, and influence vary considerably as a result of culturally unique forces in the countries or regions in which the leaders function. But, as the colloquial saying goes "the devil is in the details," and current cross-cultural theory is inadequate to clarify and expand on the diverse cultural universals and cultural specifics that have been elucidated in cross-cultural research. Some researchers currently subscribe to the philosophy that the primary impact of cultures depends on the level of analysis used in the research program. That is, some view the basic functions of leadership as having universal importance and applicability, but the specific ways in which leadership functions are enacted are strongly affected by cultural variation (Chemers, 1997; Smith & Peterson, 1988). The GLOBE project will test this fundamental assumption. From a practical viewpoint, because the meaning of specific leadership actions and behaviors are influenced by the cultural context (Smith, 1997), we need more information to help leaders practice everyday leadership, such as information on participation, direction, coaching, and motivation.

There is also a scientific rationale, in addition to practical applications, for conducting cross-cultural research. From a scientific and theoretical perspective, compelling reasons exist for considering the role of culture in influencing leadership processes. Conventional practice labels theories that transcend cultures as "transcultural," "culture free," "cultural universal," or "etic processes." However, we should realize the inherent limitations in transferring theories across cultures (Chemers, 1997; Poortinga & Malpass, 1986): what works in one culture may not *necessarily* work in another. Research that supports cultural diversity is generally referred to as "cultural specific," "culturally unique," or "emic processes." Through cross-cultural research, we may determine which aspects of a leadership theory are culturally universal and which are culturally unique. As Triandis (1993) suggests, leadership researchers will be able to fine-tune theories by investigating

cultural variations as parameters of the theory. Cross-cultural research may also help uncover new theoretical relationships by forcing the researcher to consider a much broader range of noncultural variables (Chemers, 1983). For instance, models promoting participative leadership may be valid for relatively sophisticated employees in developed countries, but less valid for employees in less-developed countries where egalitarianism may not be highly valued. Cultural variations may therefore highlight relationships between theoretical constructs and specify important theoretical boundary conditions. The GLOBE research program was designed to further theory development by devising an empirically based theory of cross-cultural leadership in addition to helping managerial leaders by specifying the how, why, what, and where of cultural impacts on leadership processes.

Before embarking on a discussion of our current state of knowledge regarding the influence of culture on leadership, it may be worthwhile to consider the degree to which cultural influence is expected to play a significant role in the future given today's global world. We ask the question, are cultural influences a transient phenomenon in a fast changing global economy? Academics often frame this question as a discussion of the "culture convergence hypothesis."

CULTURAL CONVERGENCE: HOW FAR WILL IT GO?

Are cultural differences here to stay, or will forces of globalization blur differences among nations and organizations? It is often suggested that there is a substantial amount of cross-national convergence of management practices, values, and beliefs (Boyacigiller, Kleinberg, Phillips, & Sackmann, 1996). This occurs as a result of interactions among organizations engaged in cross-border trading, and widespread proliferation of management education programs that reflect Western assumptions, values, and practices. Some scholars subscribe to the most extreme form of the cultural convergence thesis: convergence of management principles and practices throughout the industrial world is thought to be deterministic and inevitable, even if it takes decades, generations, or centuries (Farmer & Richman, 1965).

It is difficult to assess the extent of international convergence that may be taking place with regard to leadership practices because of the lack of historical baseline data; however, there are a limited number of studies that support the convergence hypothesis. Ralston, Gustafson, Elsass, Cheung, and Terpstra (1992) found that responses of Hong Kong managers reflected more Western values than did responses of Chinese managers, and more Eastern values compared with responses of American managers. This suggests cultural convergence as a result of more exposure of the Hong Kong managers to both western and eastern societies. Also, management practices in multiple industries in Korea (Amsden, 1990) and Taiwan (Wade, 1990) have become more similar to Japanese management in the 1980s. In a recent study, convergence between Japanese and Korean management styles was found to be a result of increased globalization rather than simple growth by the firm (Lee, Roehl, & Choe, 2000). As another example, an ethnographic study by Martinez (2000) documents the tremendous influence of the United States as a source of managerial models and practices for Mexican entrepreneurs as they struggle to improve organizational performance.

It also appears that management practices may be converging toward other than U.S.-style management (Alpander, 1973; Beechler & Yang, 1994; Craig, Douglas, & Grein, 1992). American authors have also proposed American adoption of Japanese management practices typical of Japanese organizations during the 1980s (Ouchi, 1981; Pascale & Athos, 1981). In sum, we are relatively confident that there is no evidence of a single model of management practices or of cultural values toward which all nations are converging. It is most likely that there is some convergence toward U.S. practices, some toward Western European practices, and some toward Japanese practices.

Although some convergence is likely taking place with respect to management practices, there is also a great deal of stability with respect to the more fundamental aspects of both cultural practices and psychological commonalities

within cultural entities. Studies in many geographic regions show consistent results between earlier and subsequent studies even though as many as 20 years may have elapsed between the time the two studies were conducted. Hofstede's rankings of countries by cultural dimensions, which are based on data collected between 1967 and 1973, have been replicated by several studies of selected countries conducted in the late 1980s and 1990s (Hoppe, 1993). What little evidence exists suggests that change in fundamental cultural values such as those studied by Hofstede (1980) appear to be very slow, and likely quite resistant to convergence forces (Hofstede, 2001). Indeed, maintaining cultural uniqueness is sometimes viewed very positively. Europeans have been particularly sensitive to the diversity of management systems that exist across contemporary Europe, and the perseverance of such differences is often seen as a desirable outcome (Brodbeck et al., 2000). Thus, cultural diversity of employees found worldwide in multinational organizations presents a substantial challenge with respect to the design of multinational organizations and the design of effective leadership styles.

VARIED PERSPECTIVES OF LEADERSHIP

As noted in the overview (Chapter 2) by House and Javidan, leadership has been a topic of study for social scientists for much of the 20th century, yet there is no consensual agreed-on definition of leadership (Bass, 1990; Yukl, 2002). Perhaps surprisingly, the word *leadership* is a relatively new addition to the English language; it appeared approximately 200 years ago in writings about political influence in the British Parliament. However, from Egyptian hieroglyphics, we know that symbols for "leader" existed as long as 5,000 years ago (Bass, 1990). Simply put, leaders have existed in all cultures throughout history. The practice and philosophy of leaders and leadership can be gleaned from writings as diverse in content, philosophy, and time as those found in Greek classics such as Homer's *Iliad*, the Old and New Testaments, essays about Confucius in China, and Machiavelli's rules and principles written in the 16th century for obtaining and holding power in Italy.

A seemingly endless variety of definitions of leadership have been developed, perhaps as many as there are persons who attempted to define the construct, as Stogdill (1974) wryly noted many years ago. Definitions usually contain the constructs most interesting to specific researchers, as seen in the varying central themes of leadership traits, behaviors, role relationships, interaction patterns, change, or sense making. Sometimes the constructs are defined in terms of a central process as Schein does when evoking the notion of leadership creating evolutionary change (e.g., Schein, 1992). In contrast, Yukl (2002) argues for a broad conception of leadership that encompasses the determination of the group or organization's objectives, organization of work activities, motivation of followers, facilitation of cooperative relationships and teamwork, and enlistment of support from people outside the group or organization. Global leadership, a new term reflecting the importance of the global economy, is defined as "influence across national and cultural boundaries" (Mobley & Dorfman, 2003). Thus, although definitions may vary, almost all have at their core the concepts of influence and setting objectives: Leaders influence others to help accomplish group or organizational objectives.

The variety of definitions is appropriate, as the degree of specificity of the definition of leadership should be driven by the purposes of the research (Smith & Bond, 1993). The goals of the GLOBE Project involve determining which aspects of leadership and organizational practices are comparable across cultures, while also identifying and specifying culture-specific differences in leadership and organizational practices. We also recognize and even expect that the evaluative and semantic interpretation of the term *leadership,* and the ways in which leadership and organizational processes are enacted, are likely to vary across cultures. But we also expect that some aspects of leadership will be universally endorsed. In keeping with the scope of this chapter, we address the phenomena of organizational leadership and not leadership in general.

We might begin by asking whether the concept of leadership itself is defined and conceptualized differently across cultures. No definitive answer to this question presently exists, but

there is evidence that evaluative interpretations of leadership vary across cultures. For instance, Americans are generally enamored with the notion of leadership and place a premium on leaders. For most Americans, the term leadership evokes a positive connotation—it is a desirable characteristic and highly praised. Organizational success is often attributed solely, if not mistakenly, to the chief executive (Meindl, 1990). Leaders considered to have made a major contribution to society are often not only revered but also often emulated, especially in societies with highly stratified distributions of power. Qualitative research by the second author of this chapter disclosed a proliferation of public commemorations of macho-like military leaders in France, England, the United States, and Russia, and a marked absence of such commemorations in Australia, Canada, Ireland, the Netherlands, New Zealand, and the German regions of Switzerland. Hofstede (1980) found France to be the eighth highest scoring country on Power Distance. He reported no data on Russia. The remainder of these latter countries was found by Hofstede to be ranked 25th or lower on Power Distance in his 40-country study.

But positive semantic evaluations of leadership are not universal. For example, Europeans seem less enthusiastic about leadership than do Americans. As Serge Moscovici writes,

> when we Europeans say leader, we think, as if by conditioned reflex, of Hitler . . . no one would forget the havoc the leadership principle wreaked in Germany's history and in ours. . . . In short, everything seems to indicate that leadership is an unintended and undesirable consequence of democracy, or a "perverse effect" as we say in France. (Graumann & Moscovici, 1986, pp. 241–242)

In Holland, consensus and egalitarian values are held in high esteem (Hofstede, 1993), and anecdotal evidence suggests that the Dutch believe that the concept of leadership is overvalued. Other nations also seem to downplay the importance of leadership. CEOs of large successful Japanese corporations, for example, credit subordinates for organizational accomplishments while deemphasizing their own role as contributors to organizational success (Bass & Yokochi, 1991).

Nations can exhibit a profound backlash against leaders who represent countercultural values. Statues of high-level communist leaders in Moscow and Budapest were retired to "cemeteries of statues," preserving them for posterity but keeping them out of public view. The Irish Republican Army destroyed Lord Nelson's statue in Dublin and the Irish government never replaced it because of its pro-British symbolism. Institutions, streets, and cities were converted to their pre-Communist names in almost all former Soviet Union nations: former Leningrad is once again St. Petersburg and Stalingrad is now Volgograd. The former Karl Marx Institute of Economics in Budapest is now the Hungarian Institute of Economics.

WESTERN-DOMINATED LEADERSHIP RESEARCH

Most of the leadership research during the past half-century was conducted in the United States, Canada, and Western Europe (Yukl, 2002). The same description applies to the researchers who conducted these studies because they have been primarily trained in the West. Perhaps as a result, almost all prevailing theories of leadership and most empirical evidence is North American in character, that is individualistic rather than collectivistic; emphasizing U.S. assumptions of rationality rather than ascetics, religion, or superstition; stated in terms of individual rather than group incentives; stressing follower responsibilities rather than rights; assuming hedonistic rather than altruistic motivation; and assuming centrality of work and democratic value orientation (House, 1995, pp. 443–444). Hofstede (1993) makes a similar point: "In a global perspective, US management theories contain several idiosyncrasies not necessarily shared by management elsewhere" (p. 81). Hofstede mentions three such idiosyncrasies: A stress on market processes, a stress on the individual, and a focus on managers rather than workers. Cross-cultural psychological, sociological, and anthropological research shows that many cultures do not share these assumptions. As a result, many scholars have noted the obvious "need for a better understanding of the way in which leadership is enacted in various cultures and a need for an empirically grounded theory to explain differential leader behavior and effectiveness across cultures" (House, 1995, pp. 443–444; see also Bass, 1990; Boyacigiller & Adler, 1991; Dorfman, 2004; Dorfman & Ronen, 1991).

THE GLOBE DEFINITION OF LEADERSHIP

As previously discussed in the overview (Chapter 2), in August 1994 the first GLOBE research conference was held at the University of Calgary in Canada. Fifty-four researchers from 38 countries gathered to develop a collective understanding of the project and to initiate its implementation. At this meeting, GLOBE researchers generated a working definition of *leadership* reflecting diverse viewpoints. A consensus emerged for a universal definition of organizational leadership: *the ability of an individual to influence, motivate, and enable others to contribute toward the effectiveness and success of the organizations of which they are members.* Note that this is a definition of *organizational* leadership, not leadership in general.

The GLOBE project uses the concept of implicit leadership theory (ILT) as a critical explanatory mechanism by which culture influences leadership processes. Leadership prototypes within ILT are profiles of presumed effective or preferred leader attributes or behaviors (Lord & Maher, 1991). Using prototypes in this manner is a natural development of the social information processing literature (Croker, Fiske, & Taylor, 1984; Rosch, 1975). Models developed from this literature can illustrate how cultures shape the basic ways people collect, store, organize, and process information about leaders. Shaw (1990) argues that much of the cross-national literature indicating differences in managerial beliefs, values, and styles can be interpreted as showing culturally influenced differences in leader prototypes. Prototypes may include leader behaviors, values, attitudes, and personality traits. At this point we are not certain whether there are universally endorsed prototypes of effective leaders, or even universal characteristics of effective leaders. Project GLOBE intends to answer this question. The cross-cultural research literature examining prototypes will be explored in more detail later in this chapter and in Chapter 21.

VARIED PERSPECTIVES ON CULTURE

As with *leadership,* there is no consensually agreed-on definition among social scientists for the term *culture,* a term used by social scientists to refer to a set of parameters of collectives that differentiate the collectives from each other in meaningful ways. The focus is on the "sharedness" of cultural indicators among members of the collective. Culture is variously defined in terms of several commonly shared processes: shared ways of thinking, feeling, and reacting; shared meanings and identities; shared socially constructed environments; common ways in which technologies are used; and commonly experienced events including the history, language, and religion of their members. As discussed in the overview chapter, Project GLOBE defines culture as "shared motives, values, beliefs, identities, and interpretations or meanings of significant events that result from common experiences of members of collectives and are transmitted across age generations." This definition can apply for both societies and organizations, and may be investigated at the societal and organizational levels of analysis.

PRIOR EMPIRICAL RESEARCH:
CULTURE AND LEADERSHIP

We now turn to a review of the empirical cross-cultural leadership literature and specifically concentrate on general topics of interest and, for the most part, studies conducted after the 1990 review of cross-cultural leadership research that appeared in *Bass and Stogdill's Handbook of Leadership Research* (Bass, 1990). Certain conclusions from the Bass review, however, are worth noting. Specifically, many studies were concerned with the effects of differences in cultural or subcultural units on managerial behaviors, attitudes, preferences, and motivations. National boundaries were used to specify cultural units in almost all of these studies, consistent

with the experiential definition of culture. The method of analysis for almost all of the studies in the Bass review was the group mean comparison based on aggregation of individual responses.

Two major trends in the cross-cultural leadership literature were evident from the Bass review. First, substantial research has been conducted to examine the applicability of Western leadership theory in multiple national settings. Second, a great deal of effort has been made to compare the leadership styles and requirements of small groups of nations. Usually, the comparisons are made among the U.S., Western European, Latin American, and Asian nations. Consequently, more is known about leadership in these regions than is known about leadership in Southern Asian, African, Arab, and Eastern European countries.

The Bass review also reveals a number of shortcomings in the cross-cultural leadership research literature. First, there is a lack of theoretical cohesiveness among the studies cited. Whereas some investigators draw from well-established theories of leadership, many merely describe national differences and draw on rather atheoretical and unsystematic intellectual frameworks. Second, Bass found that there was a dearth of studies based on more than three or four countries. Third, many studies make use of existing standardized U.S. instruments that may not fully capture non-Western or non-U.S. conceptualizations of leadership.

The good news is that since the Bass 1990 review, cross-cultural leadership theory and research have improved immeasurably. More recent studies frequently are grounded in theory, based on more than a comparison of two or three countries, use sophisticated quantitative analysis, provide in-depth qualitative descriptions, and often use perspectives from researchers in non-Western countries. Subsequent to the review by Bass (1990), extensive reviews of the cross-cultural leadership literature can be found in Chemers (1997); Dorfman (1996, 2004); House, Wright, and Aditya (1997); and Peterson and Hunt (1997).

Conducting cross-cultural research is, by its very nature, difficult to conceptualize and conduct. As a result, far more questions than answers still exist regarding the culturally contingent aspects of leadership; teams of cross-national researchers find that cultural differences are real and affect everyday decisions and interactions among team members (Dorfman, Hanges, & Dickson, 1998). The following review must, by necessity, be selective and focused on research that paints a picture of what we currently know about the influence of culture on leadership processes and, perhaps more importantly, what we do not know about these processes that the GLOBE project was designed to study.

LEADERSHIP TOPICS STUDIED WITHIN A CROSS-CULTURAL LEADERSHIP FRAMEWORK

We first summarize major topics that emerged from our literature review. Part of our review considers non-Western conceptualizations and studies of leadership processes that often have escaped notice. We then describe the multiple goals and practical applications of the GLOBE Project and finish with a list of future projects. In the remainder of this section, we describe findings relevant to the most frequent topics addressed in the cross-cultural leadership literature. For heuristic purposes, the review is arranged roughly in an order that mirrors the variables presented within the GLOBE integrated leadership model presented in the overview chapter (see Figure 1 in Chapter 2).

Origin of Leaders

Ascriptions of achievement provide normal routes for an individual's rise to leadership and vary in a predictable manner according to one's culture. Other influential factors such as differences in education, class, occupation, ownership, and technical expertise are also determinants to filling leadership roles in different countries (Boyd, 1974; Harbron, 1965; Lee & Schwendiman, 1982; McClelland, 1961). A leader's origin also influences his or her behavior if working as an expatriate. For example, managers of Pakistani origin working in England exhibited a substantial effect of origin not shared by British managers (Shackleton & Ali, 1990). However, the effect of origin did not overwhelm the context of expatriate managers.

Location of residence, in addition to national origin, often has a powerful effect on individuals (Huo & Randall, 1991).

Modernization

Differential expectations of, and preferences for, specific leader behaviors will vary according to the degree of societal modernization. Merit is more often expected to be the basis of performance evaluation and compensation in modernized nations. Leaders in countries where cultural norms are more tradition-bound often take factors other than merit into account if deciding on salary increases (Bass et al., 1979; Ryterbrand & Thiagarajan, 1968; Ulin, 1976). They are also more likely to find bribery to be acceptable, and are more likely to relegate women to lower-status positions (Davis, Ming, & Brosnan, 1986). On the other hand, leaders from modern societies tend to focus more on issues of merit, orderliness, punctuality, intended rationality, and progress (Bass et al., 1979; Inkeles, 1966).

Unique Role Demands of Leaders

The differential role demands placed on leaders may vary according to demographic composition of organizations, national or regional political systems, or the strategic requirements of the leader's organizations (Anzizu & Nuenos, 1984; Bass, 1990; Heller, 1958). Organizational management practices in China, India, and Hong Kong are often based on kinship relationships—that is, hiring relatives is often the norm rather than the exception—a system used in many large-scale enterprises in these countries as well. Large Indian firms practice many of these same behaviors, such as obedience to elders based on deference to the wisdom of experience (Chowdry & Tarneja, 1961). This is a tendency that persists today. Five of the largest business organizations in India—Reliance (managed by the Ambani family), Birla, Goenka, Kirloskar, and Tata—remain family-managed. In Mexico, the large family owned and operated business structures called *grupos* are examples in point. The importance of strong family ties and paternalistic management practices are emphasized, and these businesses retain their management characteristics even after expansion to larger organizational entities (Dorfman & Howell, 1997). Samsung and Hyundai Motor Company, Korean *chaebols,* also fit this same model of family-centered conglomerates in which leadership succession is family dominated (Steers, Shinn, & Ungson, 1989).

Antecedents to Preferred Leader Behavior

Several antecedents to preferred leader behavior are addressed in the cross-cultural leadership literature. Religious beliefs and the cultural norms expressed by the dominant elite are often predecessors to leadership positions. Also, preferences for certain leader behaviors have been shown to be associated with the dominant norms of cultural entities (Redding & Casey, 1975; Stening & Wong, 1983), gender egalitarianism (Paris, 2003), and religious or ideological values such as Confucianism (Hofstede & Bond, 1988), Catholicism (Pelletier, 1966), and the Protestant work ethic of saving, sacrifice, hard work, and investment (Weber, 1930). McClelland (1961) and Boyd (1974) noted the role that landed gentry played in the development of leadership traits in Confucian China and Victorian England. Specifically, leaders in both countries were expected to possess good manners, good physical conditioning, and classical training. Interviews conducted in France by the second author of this chapter indicate that French leaders are generally well educated and expected to be "cultivated"—that is, classically educated. It is likely that the dominant elite serve as role models for aspiring leaders, especially if the elite are respected and trusted.

Leader Prototypes

As introduced earlier in this chapter, leadership prototypes are profiles of presumed typical or preferred leader attributes or behaviors (Lord & Maher, 1991). Prototypes may include leader behaviors, values, attitudes, and personality traits. To cite one amusing example, executive recruiters reported that the following attributes were among the more unusual characteristics they were asked to look for: Over 6 feet tall, 10 handicap or lower in golf, fiddle player and

storyteller, no one wearing eyeglasses, and one who has run a marathon (Ritchie, 1999). Several relatively small-scale studies have demonstrated that leadership prototypes vary across cultures.

An initial study by O'Connell, Lord, and O'Connell (1990) supports the argument that societal culture plays a strong role in the content of organizational leadership prototypes. Japanese and American leadership prototypes differed in significant respects. Gerstner and Day (1994) provide additional evidence that leadership prototypes vary across cultures. As expected, attributes that were seen as most characteristic of business leaders varied across countries. The Gerstner and Day (1994) study and the O'Connell and colleagues (1990) study are useful exemplars of research examining leadership prototypes, but findings are limited by small samples and other methodological issues. More recently, Den Hartog and colleagues (1999), using a subset of the GLOBE data presented in this book, tested the hypothesis that specific aspects of transformational/charismatic leadership are strongly and universally endorsed across cultures. Brodbeck and colleagues (2000), also using a subset of the GLOBE data, tested the assumption that leadership concepts are culturally endorsed and leadership prototype dimensions are highly correlated with cultural dimensions found within Europe. In-depth discussions of prior research on ILT, rationale for using ILT as a main construct for GLOBE, and research results linking culture to leadership prototypes are presented in Chapter 21.

Preferences for Leadership Styles

Followers differ by nation in their preferences and acceptance for intensity and kind of communication with leaders (Earley, 1984), task versus person orientation (Blake & Mouton, 1970; Misumi, 1974; Scandura, Von Glinow, & Lowe, 1999), and responses to organizational development efforts (Deyo, 1978). They also differ regarding preferences for close versus general supervision, democratic versus autocratic leader behavior, importance of morality (Hui & Tan, 1999), and emphasis placed on interaction facilitation (Gibson, 1995). A prevailing difference, which will be supported by the GLOBE project, is subordinates' preference of leadership styles that vary along the differing degrees of participatory practices (Bass, 1990; Bass et al., 1979; Osland, Monteze, & Hunter, 1998; Torres, 2000).

Leadership Behavior Patterns

Modal leader behavior patterns differ widely across countries in their emphasis on individualistic versus team orientation; particularism versus universalism (Dorfman, 1998; Dorfman & Howell, 1988; Smith et al., 1996); performance versus maintenance orientation (Shenkar, Ronen, Shefy, & Chow, 1998; Smith, Misumi, Tayeb, Peterson, & Bond, 1989; Smith, Peterson, Misumi, & Bond, 1992); authoritarian versus democratic orientation (Al-Hajjeh, 1984; Stening & Wong, 1983); paternalism (Redding & Casey, 1975); reliance on personal abilities, subordinates, or rules (Smith & Peterson, 1995); leader influence processes (Rahim, Kim, & Kim, 1994; Schmidt & Yeh, 1992); and consensual decision making and service orientation (Bass et al., 1979).

Behavioral Impact of Leadership

Finally, there have been many studies investigating the effects of culture on the generally accepted dependent variables in the discipline of organizational behavior. Scholars have examined the effect of cultural influences on employee attitudes such as job satisfaction, motivation, job performance, and other criteria such as general welfare. Most studies conducted by leadership researchers in different parts of the world reflect an awareness and understanding of leadership research conducted in America and other Western countries (Smith & Peterson, 1988). Keeping with the behavioral tradition within the leadership literature, much of the empirical cross-cultural research in the past 30 years has been ethnocentric (research designed and tested in one culture and replicated in another culture) rather than truly comparative (designed to test similarities and differences across two or more cultures) (Adler, 1984). Consistencies and differences have been found among cultures. As one

example, Dorfman and colleagues (1997) found evidence for the universal effectiveness of three popular contingency leadership behaviors (leader supportiveness, contingent reward, and charismatic leadership) and also found culturally unique influences for three other leadership behaviors (participativeness, directiveness, and contingent punishment). Although their study was limited to five countries in the Pacific Rim, including the United States and Mexico, it reinforces the often stated belief that the "individualistic" United States is different from more "collectivistic" countries. Differences were most notably apparent by the unique effects of participation and contingent punishment having positive impacts only in the United States.

What follows is a summary of cross-cultural leadership studies with respect to commonly studied behavioral aspects of leadership. Task-oriented and relationship-oriented leadership dimensions, which were originally conceptualized in the United States, appear to be important leadership behaviors in many cultures (Bond & Hwang, 1986; Chemers, 1997; Misumi, 1985; Sinha, 1980). In general, cross-cultural studies support the importance of considerate leadership in increasing subordinates' satisfaction. The universality of leader supportiveness should not be surprising because supportive leaders show concern for followers and are considerate and available to listen to follower's problems. Exceptions to this general finding, however, can be found and are particularly informative in pointing out cultural differences. As one example, leadership effectiveness in the Middle East, given the strong role of Islam in the Arabic world, led to leadership effectiveness *not* being related to the supervisor's level of consideration, but rather to the supervisor's strong directive behavior (Scandura, Von Glinow, & Lowe, 1999).

Results concerning task-oriented leadership are complex and defy simple explanation (Bass, 1990). Korman's (1966) review of studies in the U.S. concludes that there is a lack of consistent results for task-oriented leadership. Not surprisingly, cross-cultural studies examining the impact of directive behaviors on employees also show conflicting and not easily interpretable results (Anderson, 1983; Kakar, 1971; Kennis, 1977; Yukl, 2002).

Participatory and charismatic leadership styles have also been studied in cross-cultural contexts, with the former showing major differences among cultures and the latter having more universally positive effects. In the Dorfman and colleagues (1997) study, participatory leadership had positive correlations with satisfaction with one's supervisor for all nations, but when controlling for simultaneous effects of several different leadership behaviors, the United States was the single culture in which participative leadership had a positive influence on employee performance. The actual *level* of participation for the United States was also the highest in all sampled countries. We might also note that the Vroom and Jago (1988) model of participatory decision making should be a useful theoretic approach to examine leadership differences across cultures. In one exploratory study, Jago and colleagues (1993) found that German, Austrian, and Swiss managers were the most participative; Polish and Czech managers the most autocratic; and the U.S. and French managers between the extremes. Two other findings were particularly interesting. First, unlike managers of other nations, Polish managers were more likely to be participative only on trivial matters and not on important issues. Second, there were differences across countries in scenarios in which subordinate conflict was likely—for example, the U.S. and Polish managers were likely to become autocratic in conflict-producing situations. The researchers developed predictions of participation based on Hofstede's power distance scores and results were generally supportive for the prediction that participation scores would be higher for lower power distance cultures (Jago et al., 1993). We suspect that further understanding about participatory leadership will be even more important for multinationals as societies move toward more egalitarian practices and because power sharing is critical within virtual teams that span time and geographic boundaries (Davis & Bryant, 2003).

Not surprisingly, strong empirical evidence supports the importance of charismatic leadership in the West, and growing evidence suggests that it is also important in non-Western societies. Despite substantive and legitimate criticism, including definition and measurement problems (Hunt, 1991; Smith & Peterson, 1988; Yukl,

2002), charismatic theories fare quite well under empirical scrutiny. Numerous studies using a variety of methods (including field studies, case histories, management games, interviews, and laboratory experiments) and samples (including middle- and lower-level managers, top-level corporate leaders, educational, and national leaders) attest to the significant and robust impact of charismatic and transformational leadership (Bass, 1997). Furthermore, Bass (1991) notes confirming cross-cultural evidence for the proposition that there is a hierarchy of leadership effectiveness among various leadership styles—transformational leaders are more effective than those practicing transactional leadership, who, in turn, are more effective than *laissez-faire* leaders (who are not effective). This hierarchy of relationships was found for field grade officers in Germany and Canada; New Zealand professionals and administrators; senior managers in Italy and Sweden; and middle-level managers in Japan, Belgium, Canada, Spain, Saudi Arabia, and India (Bass, 1991; Bass & Avolio, 1993; Bass, Waldman, Avolio, & Bebb, 1987; Bass & Yokochi, 1991; Howell & Avolio, 1993). These studies generally support a near universalistic position regarding the potential impact of charismatic and transformational leadership across cultures.

On a less supportive note, a methodologically sophisticated study examining the effects of charismatic leadership on individuals at multiple organizational levels found little support for the Shamir, House, and Arthur's self-concept-based charismatic theory (Shamir, Zakay, Breinin, & Popper, 1998). Clearly, much remains to be learned about the process by which charismatic leadership affects followers. Certainly, if considered from a cross-cultural perspective, one can entertain a hypothesis that the enactment of charismatic leadership and transformational leadership will likely be culture specific. In addition, it would be wise not to forget that individuals in societies previously dominated by charismatic dictators generally view autocratic charismatic leadership as undesirable. Interviews and focus groups conducted as an early part of the GLOBE research program revealed strong reservations, suspicions, and distaste for authoritarian charismatic leadership among German, Mexican, Portuguese, and

Spanish managers, and rather widespread distrust of managers in general in many of the countries of the former Soviet Union. Similar negative feelings about Saddam Hussein quickly emerged in Iraq after the overthrow of his regime, although some segments of Iraq's population have remained supportive of him due to prior tribal, family, ideological, and religious affiliations. This distaste for charismatic leadership, and distrust of management, is likely the result of historical association with despotic charismatic leadership to which these nations were subjected.

Although it might be stating the obvious, because cultures vary in degree of internal homogeneity, the effects of particular leadership styles are likely to vary within the society. Triandis (1994) noted that even within individualistic cultures there are those who are more individualistic than others (labeled "idiocentric") and those who are more group or collectivist oriented (labeled "allocentric"). The same holds true for collectivist societies; some individuals may be relatively idiocentric even if the majority are allocentric. Identification with the dominant societal values of one's culture may be a particularly important variable that influences the relationship between leaders' behavior and subordinate outcomes. For instance, Dorfman and Howell (1988) found no *overall* relationships between Mexican and Taiwanese employees' cultural values and the following dependent variables: work satisfaction, satisfaction with superiors, organizational commitment, and performance. Yet, the impact of directive leadership and selected reward and punishment practices were significantly higher for those who identified with the dominant cultural values (e.g., high power distance) than for employees who did not. This study clarifies one of the limitations of interpreting countries as monolithic cultures and shows the effect of differential degrees of socialization within countries. As a personal reflection, the first author strongly suggests that simple replication of prior behavioral studies without a comprehensive theoretical rationale should be avoided. Hopefully, the GLOBE theoretical rationale presented in Chapter 2 will lead to productive research studies with both theoretical and practical payoffs.

NON-WESTERN CONCEPTUALIZATIONS OF LEADERSHIP

What types of leadership theories have been advanced in non-Western countries? Few long-term leadership research programs exist outside the West, but some non-Western scholars have advanced particularistic views of leadership cognizant of their indigenous cultures. Research programs by two non-Western theorists stand out in importance. The first is Misumi's research in Japan over the past 40 years and the second is Sinha's research in India.

Misumi's performance–maintenance (PM) theory of leadership (1985) identifies four types of leaders classified by their focus on two basic leadership functions labeled Performance and Maintenance. The Performance (P) function reflects two aspects: a leader's planning, guiding, and developing work procedures; and pressure on subordinates to work hard and get the work done. The Maintenance (M) function reflects the leader's promoting of group stability and social processes. These central leadership functions in the PM theory are similar to the "task-oriented" and "support-oriented" leadership functions previously addressed in Western theories of leadership. Misumi's results suggest that for effective leadership in Japan, supervisors must emphasize Performance-oriented (P) and Maintenance-oriented (M) factors *together*. Current studies now indicate that the Performance factor (P) should be separated into a Planning factor and a Pressure factor. However, as pointed out by Smith (1997), although Misumi's theory superficially resembles U.S. theories in terms of the kinds of variables studied, it parts company in several important respects. First, leaders must always perform both functions, and second, the specific behaviors associated with each function will vary according to context. Furthermore, tests of Misumi's PM theory conducted in nations other than Japan provide evidence regarding the issue of culture-free versus culture-specific leadership (Peterson, Brannen, & Smith, 1994; Peterson, Smith, & Peng, 1995; Peterson, Smith, & Tayeb, 1993). Misumi's PM leadership instrument was adapted for use in China, but researchers found it necessary to add an additional leadership factor, labeled "C" for character and morals, to adequately characterize Chinese leadership (Ling & Fang, 2003; Wang, 1994).

Similar to Misumi's research in Japan, early efforts to study leadership in India were influenced by conceptual links to Western social scientists. However, research results were often inconsistent and at odds with prevailing beliefs about the nature of effective leadership in Indian organizations. Research data often supported the interpretation that democratic, participative, and considerate leaders were most effective, whereas managers and workers often voiced a preference for paternalistic and nurturing leaders who are also authoritarian and assertive (Kakar, 1971; Sinha, 1994). To reconcile these inconsistent beliefs about effective leadership, Sinha (1980, 1984) developed a Nurturant-task oriented model (NT) that incorporated a combination of leadership styles. The model suggests that an ideal leader in India is both nurturant and task oriented. According to the theory, a nurturant-task-oriented (NT) leader needs to show affection, care for subordinates, and commit toward their growth. However, the leader's nurturance is contingent on the subordinate's task accomplishment—the leader becomes a benevolent source of support provided that the subordinate respects and obeys the supervisor, works hard, and is highly productive. In short, the leader is paternalistic and authoritative. At this point in the relationship, however, the leader can encourage the subordinate to be more independent and to actively participate with the leader in decision making. Still, this relationship is very much like the Japanese management-familyism system in which the supervisor benevolently guides the subordinate who, in turn, must reciprocate with complete obedience and absolute loyalty (Whitehill & Takezawa, 1968).

Sinha (1980, 1984) presents research evidence that the effectiveness of NT is affected by a number of contingency variables such as the subordinate's desire for a dependency relationship and acceptance of a hierarchical relationship. Triandis (1994) speculates that even in cultures not typically appreciative of democratic relationships, participatory leadership can be effective given worker training to accept, expect, and appreciate such styles. We might also speculate that a form of the NT model would hold for other high power distance and collectivist

cultures that value hierarchical and personalized relationships. It is likely not a coincidence that Sinha's NT leader resembles Misumi's PM leader in Japan, the "benevolent/paternalistic" leader in Iran (Ayman & Chemers, 1983), the paternalistic *patron* in Mexico (Bass, 1990), or the family-dominated leaders of Korean *chaebols* (Steers, Shin, & Ungson, 1989). The importance of both the Misumi and Sinha research programs is that they emphasize the importance of context as determining which processes of leadership are considered effective and which are not (Smith, 1997).

As a final consideration of non-Western conceptualizations of leadership, it is interesting to consider leadership styles in countries very different from the West such as in the Arabic world of the Middle East. The pervasive influence of the Islamic religion is a key to understanding the Arab world and, presumably, leadership in the Arab world (Hagan, 1995). In Arabic, the word for leadership is *al kiyada,* which refers to officers in the military or high-ranking members of the government. Historically, a leader is a great hero who leads warriors into battle, and therefore not unexpectedly, the concept of leadership is rooted in traditional military concepts of leadership (Scandura et al., 1999). Modern Arab management practices have been influenced by Islamic religion, tribal and family traditions, the legacy of colonial bureaucracies, and contact with Western nations (Ali, 1990). Tribal traditions influence all aspects of life and, as a consequence, managers are expected to act as fathers—viewing their role in a highly personalized manner characterized by providing and caring for employees and favoring individuals within the family and tribe over outsiders. The legacy of a highly structured bureaucracy left by the ruling Ottoman Empire and European nations is superimposed on these Islamic family–tribal traditions.

The combination of family and tribal norms in addition to bureaucratic organizational structures fosters authoritarian management practices that may be characterized as a "sheikocracy" leadership style (Al-Kubaisy, 1985). This style is characterized by a patriarchal approach to managing that includes strong hierarchical authority, subordination of efficiency to human relations and personal connections, and sporadic conformity to rules and regulations contingent on the personality and power of those who make them.

Leadership studies in the Middle East are almost nonexistent due to the inherent difficulty of conducting organizational research there. However, a few research studies shed some light on leadership this area of the world. Scandura and colleagues (1999) found striking differences in effective leadership styles between a U.S. managerial sample and a sample of managers from the Middle East (Jordan and Saudi Arabia). Although they used the fairly old concept of leadership as being composed of two leadership styles (initiating structure and consideration), the results were dramatic. Whereas the people-oriented style (i.e., consideration) was related to job satisfaction and leader effectiveness for the U.S. sample, the task-oriented style (i.e., initiating-structure) was not. Exactly opposite results were found for the Middle East sample. They conclude that strong and decisive leadership is expected from an Arab person, hence the effectiveness of setting high goals and standards of performance characteristic of initiating structure, whereas a considerate leader might be perceived as being weak and indecisive. Scandura and Dorfman, in a series of *Leadership Quarterly* letters (Scandura & Dorfman, in press), discuss culture and charismatic leadership, particularly as they relate to the Middle East. Of course given the current world situation, we need to know a great deal more than we do about leadership in this part of the world.

THREE COMPETING PROPOSITIONS: CULTURAL CONGRUENCE, CULTURAL DIFFERENCE, AND NEAR UNIVERSALITY OF LEADER BEHAVIORS

The discussion thus far suggests three contrasting propositions testable within Project GLOBE. The propositions differ in the extent to which effective leadership is characterized by the congruence, or lack of congruence, between endemic cultural forces and specific styles, behaviors, and images associated with leaders. The three propositions are labeled: cultural congruence, cultural difference, and near universality. Each of these propositions enjoys some empirical support, but they have not been explicitly tested to date.

Nevertheless, the contrasts have significant theoretical and practical significance.

The Cultural Congruence Proposition

This proposition asserts that cultural forces affect the kind of leader behavior that is usually accepted, enacted, and effective within a collective. Accordingly, behavior that is consistent with collective values will be more acceptable and effective than behavior that represents conflicting values. This hypothesis is taken as an article of faith among culture theorists. The available empirical evidence supports this hypothesis (House, Wright, & Aditya, 1997); however, a rigorous test of this proposition is important for both practical and theoretical reasons.

Following are several examples illustrating the cultural congruence proposition. Nations in Hofstede's sample that have high power distance and collectivism scores experience a tendency toward behaviors that are consistent with high scores on these dimensions. For instance, the heavy emphasis placed by Asian managers on paternalism (Dorfman & Howell, 1988; Farmer & Richman, 1965) and group maintenance activities (Bass et al., 1979; Bolon & Crain, 1985; Ivancevich et al., 1986) is consistent with countries that are highly collective. Hofstede's uncertainty avoidance scores are associated with less risky entry into foreign markets and more full disclosure of accounting information. Achievement motivation reflected in grammar school books was found to be predictive of entrepreneurial behavior 25 years later (McClelland, 1961). In individualistic societies, people prefer individual rather than group-based compensation practices and exhibit greater willingness to take risks (Erez, 1997). These empirical findings support the congruence proposition.

A corollary of the cultural congruence proposition is that violation of cultural norms by leaders or managers will result in dissatisfaction, conflict, and resistance on the part of followers or subordinates and, at times, lower performance of leaders, their work units, and their subordinates. Anecdotal examples from the literature on expatriate adjustment illustrate lower productivity and satisfaction if collective norms and expatriate values conflict (Lindsay & Dempsey, 1985; Weiss & Bloom, 1990).

The Cultural Difference Proposition

Juxtaposed to the cultural congruence proposition is the cultural difference proposition. According to this proposition, increased task performance of followers, organizations, and institutions in societies will be induced by the introduction of selected values, techniques, and behavior patterns that are different from those commonly valued in the society. The rationale for this hypothesis is that by being different with respect to some behaviors, leaders introduce more changes of the kind required for innovation and performance improvement.

Several examples of minority groups leading the way to industrialization, business development, and entrepreneurship illustrate this hypothesis. Some examples include the Methodists in England, the Protestant Huguenots in France prior to the Edict of Nantes, and Cubans in the United States who fled from Cuban communism. These groups and their leaders acted and behaved in ways that were largely outside the cultural norms of the larger societies but were effective in business development. The incredible success of the mainland Chinese entrepreneurs in Southeast Asia presents an equally fascinating case study of entrepreneurs who are different from the culture in which they live (Redding, 1990). However, as argued by Smith (1997), the success of such leaders is due in part to the congruence between the kinds of ethnically homogeneous businesses created and requisite networks of region-of-origin and family connections. In contrast, the proposition of successful leadership through induction of practices that are different from the model cultural practices is still viable if we consider leaders as shapers of change rather than simply embodiments of the status quo. For instance, a central feature of charismatic leadership is the envisioning of change and an innovative vision to which followers should aspire. Sinha (1995) argues that a successful Indian leader may have to buck the normally relationship-oriented culture by placing greater emphasis on task performance, which will eventually change the leadership style from being more directive to more participative.

Thus, it appears that leaders can initiate change by being different with respect to some leader behaviors. No research has been conducted to determine the precise leader behaviors associated with such improvement. We hypothesize that the leader behaviors associated with breakthrough improvements in organizations and societies are often those associated with the introduction of constructive change, such as articulating a vision of a different way of life and communicating high performance expectations and confidence in followers.

The Near Universality of Leader Behaviors Proposition

This proposition asserts that there are some leader behaviors that are universally, or near universally, accepted and effective. Despite wide-ranging differences in cultural norms across countries studied, there is some support for this proposition. Bass and colleagues (1979) found that managers from 12 culturally diverse countries indicated a desire to get work done while using less authority. Similarly, Smith and Peterson (1995) found that managers in 30 countries reported satisfaction with events for which they were delegated substantial discretion. Transformational leadership has been found to be more acceptable and effective in Canada (Howell & Avolio, 1993; Howell & Frost, 1989), India (Pereira, 1987), Japan (Bass, 1997), the Netherlands (Koene, Pennings, & Schreuder, 1991), and Singapore (Koh, Terborg, & Steers, 1991), as well as the United States (Bass & Avolio, 1993).

Bass (1997) argues that the three components of transformational leadership are near universal: charisma, intellectual stimulation of followers, and individualized consideration toward followers. Bass (personal communication, June 15, 1996) reports that

> Although some fine tuning may be required, on all continents people's ideal leader is transformational, not transactional. . . . Transformational leadership is more effective than contingent reward which in turn is more effective than managing by exception. Laissez faire leadership is contraindicated.

Bass also argues that leaders can learn to become more transformational in formal training programs. This assertion remains to be empirically demonstrated. It should be noted that the Bass measures operationalize leader behaviors (and attributions) as rather general items such as "inspires loyalty to him or her," or "is a model for me to follow." It is likely that these behaviors (or attribution process) will be enacted differentially in a culture-specific manner. For example, as noted by House and colleagues (1997), transformational leadership may be enacted in a highly assertive manner (as in the cases of John F. Kennedy, Martin Luther King, Jr., Theodore Roosevelt, or Winston Churchill) or in a quiet, non-aggressive manner (as in the cases of Mahatma Gandhi, Nelson Mandela, or Mother Teresa). In all of these cases, however, charismatic qualities are evident. These individuals articulated an ideological message, set personal examples of the values inherent in their message, conveyed a sense of strong confidence in themselves and in their followers, and were in turn highly respected and trusted by their followers.

Several specific hypotheses relating culture to leadership processes will be advanced in chapters throughout this book. One such hypothesis, given the previous discussion of universality, might take the position that charismatic/value-based leadership and integrity attributes will be universally endorsed as contributors to outstanding leadership. Although not specifically predicted as a hypothesis, we expect that most respondents will view some attributes such as "malevolent" and "dictatorial" as universal impediments to outstanding leadership. Most interesting from a cross-cultural viewpoint are the attributes that in some societies may be considered to enhance outstanding leadership and in other societies considered to impede outstanding leadership.

Conclusion: Cultural Influences on Leadership and GLOBE Goals

The above review of empirical research clearly shows that cultural forces influence many aspects of the leadership phenomena. These include: prototypical requisites for leadership positions; privileges, power, and influence granted to leaders;

degree to which leadership roles are filled by ascription or achievement; modal leader behavior patterns; preferences for and expectations of leaders; and follower and subordinate reactions to different kinds of leader behavior. In addition, culturally defined antecedents to preferred leader behaviors have been revealed through research, including dominant norms, dominant elites, ideological and religious values, modernization, unique role demands, and historical experiences with leaders.

Although we are much further along in our understanding of the cultural influence on leadership processes than we were almost 40 years ago when Haire and colleagues (1966) conducted their seminal study, much remains to be learned. It seems likely that the meaning and importance of leadership vary across cultures, and actions and behaviors are context specific, but a more precise understanding of the subtle nuances and precise mechanisms by which culture works await further research—hence Project GLOBE. Hopefully, the first few chapters of the book have made it clear that the GLOBE project should be seen as a journey. The ultimate destination is to validate a cross-level integrated theory specifying the relationship among culture and societal, organizational, and leadership effectiveness. This chapter has concentrated on the relationship among culture, leadership, and organizational effectiveness. Although the GLOBE project is also concerned with societal effectiveness, the present chapter has not reviewed this literature.

We have learned a great deal during this current phase of Project GLOBE with regard to the relationships between culture and leadership. The remaining chapters of the book will provide information with respect to

- Identifying leader characteristics that are universally accepted and considered effective across cultures.
- Specifying leadership attributes considered effective in some cultures, but not others.
- Testing the hypothesis that organizations mirror the societies in which they are embedded.
- Extending the conceptualization of implicit leadership theory (ILT) to culturally endorsed implicit leadership theory (CLT).

- Grouping leadership attributes into meaningful combinations to form primary and global CLT leadership dimensions.
- Determining which dimensions of culture are related to culturally endorsed CLT leadership dimensions.
- Generating profiles of CLT leadership dimensions considered effective for specific cultures and culture clusters.
- Determining which cultural dimensions considered together have a maximal influence on CLT leadership dimensions.
- Discussing the importance of our findings for leaders in multicultural environments.

The Project GLOBE journey is far from over. On our way to validating the integrated theory, additional GLOBE projects, some proposed and some underway, are intended to

- Validate relationships as specified in multiple propositions within the integrated model presented in Chapter 2.
- Expand the model as suggested by research findings. This has already occurred during our research and will be an ongoing endeavor.
- Provide a rich ethnographic description of managerial leadership and organizational processes for countries participating in GLOBE. Culture specific chapters will be published as a companion volume to this book.
- Examine the effect of violating cultural norms relevant to leadership and organizational practices.
- Determine the extent to which leadership universals are enacted in a culturally specific or universal manner.
- Identify leader behaviors and organizational practices that are universal and those that are culturally specific.
- Determine if the effectiveness of specific leadership behaviors are invariant to culturally endorsed (CLT) leadership prototypes (i.e., can one lead democratically in a high power distance culture with strong authoritarian norms?).

We hope that the information presented in this book will challenge readers to develop new theories, hypothesize relationships that we have not considered, and conduct research related to the influence of culture on leadership.

Let the journey continue through the enigmatic landscape of leadership.

SUMMARY: ANTICIPATED THEORETICAL AND PRACTICAL CONTRIBUTIONS OF PROJECT GLOBE

The GLOBE research program is directed toward filling a substantial knowledge gap concerning the cross-cultural forces relevant to effective leadership and organizational practices.

It is designed to contribute to the development of empirically based cross-cultural leadership and organizational theory by investigating the roles of societal and organizational values and institutionalized practices, organizational contingency variables, and implicit leadership theories as antecedents to cross-cultural variance in leader behavior, leader influence, leader effectiveness, and organizational practices and performance. GLOBE research is also designed to contribute to organizational theory and practice by exploring relationships among societal and organizational cultural variables and organizational effectiveness and by conducting cross-cultural tests of structural contingency theory. The research findings will be useful for resolving several important theoretical social science issues and for a wide variety of practical purposes.

GLOBE results should also lead to improvements in the practice of leadership. Each leadership profile from geographic areas around the world contains a description of the attributes perceived as facilitating or impeding outstanding leadership. We also include information specifying culturally endorsed values and common practices in the societies and organizations studied. Both kinds of information should have substantial practical value for leaders who practice management in the cultures studied or who interact with individuals from these cultures. This information can also supply effective and valuable case content for leadership training and career development programs, and for the design of management and leadership education programs to prepare individuals who will manage and lead personnel in cultures other than their own.

REFERENCES

Adler, N. J. (1984). Understanding the ways of understanding: Cross-cultural management methodology reviewed. *Advances in International Comparative Management, 1,* 31–67.

Al-Hajjeh, A. A. (1984). Managerial leadership and work-related values of American and Middle Eastern nationals: A cross-cultural study. *Dissertation Abstracts International, 45*(6-A).

Ali, A. J. (1990). Management theory in a transitional society: The Arab's experience. *International Studies of Management and Organization, 20*(7), 7–35.

Al-Kubaisy, A. (1985). A model in the administrative development of Arab Gulf countries. *The Arab Gulf, 17*(2), 29–48.

Alpander, G. G. (1973). Drift to authoritarianism: The changing managerial styles of the U.S. executive overseas. *Journal of International Business Studies, 4*(2), 1–14.

Amsden, A. H. (1990). *Asia's next giant: South Korea and late industrialization.* New York: Oxford University Press.

Anderson, L. R. (1983). Management of the mixed-cultural work group. *Organizational Behavior and Human Performance, 31,* 303–330.

Anzizu, J. M., & Nuenos, P. (1984). *Leadership under sociopolitical change: Business enterprise in Spain.* Paper presented at the 75th Anniversary Colloquium, Harvard Business School, Boston.

Ayman, R., & Chemers, M. M. (1983). Relationship of supervisory behavior ratings to work group effectiveness and subordinate satisfaction among Iranian managers. *Journal of Applied Psychology, 68*(2), 338–341.

Bass, B. M. (1990). *Bass & Stogdill's handbook of leadership: Theory, research, and managerial applications* (3rd ed.). New York: Free Press.

Bass, B. M. (1991, August). *Is there universality in the Full Range model of leadership?* Paper presented at the National Academy of Management Annual Meeting, Miami.

Bass, B. M. (1997). Does the transactional–transformational leadership paradigm transcend organizational and national boundaries? *American Psychologist, 52*(2), 130–139.

Bass, B. M., & Avolio, B. J. (1993). Transformational leadership: A response to critiques. In M. M. Chemers & R. Ayman (Eds.), *Leadership theory and research* (pp. 49–80). San Diego: Academic.

Bass, B. M., Burger, P. C., Doktor, R., & Barrett, G. V. (1979). *Assessment of managers: An international comparison.* New York: Free Press.

Bass, B. M., Waldman, D. A., Avolio, B. J., & Bebb, M. (1987). Transformational leadership and the falling dominoes effect. *Group and Organizational Studies, 12,* 73–87.

Bass, B. M., & Yokochi, J. (1991, Winter/Spring). Charisma among senior executives and the special case of Japanese CEO's. *Consulting Psychology Bulletin, 1,* 31–38.

Beechler, S., & Yang, J. Z. (1994). The transfer of Japanese-style management to American subsidiaries: Contingencies, constraints, and competencies. *Journal of International Business Studies, 3,* 467–491.

Blake, R. R., & Mouton, J. S. (1970). The fifth achievement. *Journal of Applied Behavioral Science, 6*(4), 413–426.

Bolon, D. S., & Crain, C. R. (1985). *Decision sequence: A recurring theme in comparing American and Japanese management.* Paper presented at meeting of the Academy of Management, San Diego, CA.

Bond, M., & Hwang, K. K. (1986). The social psychology of the Chinese people. In M. H. Bond (Ed.), *The psychology of the Chinese people* (pp. 213–266.). Hong Kong: Oxford University Press.

Boyacigiller, N., & Adler, N. (1991). The parochial dinosaur: Organizational science in a global context. *Academy of Management Review, 16,* 262–290.

Boyacigiller, N. A., Kleinberg, M. J., Phillips, M. E., & Sackmann, S. A. (1996). Conceptualizing culture. In B. J. Punnett & O. Shenkar (Eds.), *Handbook for international management research* (pp. 157–208). Cambridge, MA: Blackwell.

Boyd, D. P. (1974). Research note: The educational background of a selected group of England's leaders. *Sociology, 8,* 305–312.

Brodbeck, F. C., Frese, M., Akerblom, S., Audia, G., Bakacsi, G., Bendova, H., et al. (2000). Cultural variation of leadership prototypes across 22 European countries. *Journal of Occupational and Organizational Psychology, 73,* 1–29.

Chemers, M. M. (1983). Leadership theory and research: A systems-process integration.

In P. B. Paulus (Ed.), *Basic group processes* (pp. 9–39). New York: Springer-Verlag.

Chemers, M. M. (1997). *An integrative theory of leadership.* London: Lawrence Erlbaum.

Chhokar, J. S. (in press). Leadership and culture in India: The GLOBE research project. In J. Chhokar, F. Brodbeck, & R. J. House (Eds.), *Managerial cultures of the world: GLOBE in-depth studies of the cultures of 25 countries* (Vol. 2). Thousand Oaks, CA: Sage.

Chowdry, K., & Tarneja, R. (1961). *Developing better managers: An eight-nation study.* New York: National Industrial Conference Board.

Craig, C. S., Douglas, S. P., & Grein, A. (1992). Patterns of convergence and divergence among industrialized nations: 1960–1988. *Journal of International Business Studies, 4,* 773–787.

Croker, J., Fiske, S. T., & Taylor, S. E. (1984). Schematic bases of belief change. In J. R. Eisen (Ed.), *Attitudinal judgment* (pp. 197–226). New York: Springer-Verlag.

Davis, D. D., & Bryant, J. L. (2003). Influence at a distance: Leadership in global virtual teams. In W. H. Mobley & P. W. Dorfman (Eds.), *Advances in global leadership* (Vol. 3, pp. 303–340). Oxford: JAI.

Davis, H. J., Ming, L. W., & Brosnan, T. F. (1986, August). *The Farmer-Richman model: A bibliographic essay emphasizing applicability to Singapore and Indonesia.* Paper presented at the Academy of Management, Chicago.

Den Hartog, D., House, R. J., Hanges, P. J., Ruiz-Quintanilla, S. A., & Dorfman, P. W., & GLOBE Associates. (1999). Culture specific and cross culturally generalizable implicit leadership theories: Are attributes of charismatic/transformational leadership universally endorsed? *Leadership Quarterly, 10*(2), 219–256.

Deyo, F. C. (1978). The cultural patterning of organizational development: A comparative case study of Thailand and Chinese industrial enterprises. *Human Organization, 37,* 68–72.

Dorfman, P. W. (1996). International and cross-cultural leadership research. In B. J. Punnett & O. Shenkar (Eds.), *Handbook for international management research* (pp. 267–349). Oxford: Blackwell.

Dorfman, P. W. (1998). Implications of vertical and horizontal individualism and collectivism for leadership effectiveness. In L. C. Change & R. B. Peterson (Eds.), *Advances in international comparative management* (Vol. 12, pp. 53–65). Greenwich, CT: JAI.

Dorfman, P. W. (2004). International and cross-cultural leadership research. In B. J. Punnett & O. Shenkar (Eds.), *Handbook for international management research* (2nd ed., pp. 267–349). Ann Arbor: University of Michigan Press.

Dorfman, P. W., Hanges, P. J., & Dickson, M. W. (1998). *Challenges in cross-cultural research: The GLOBE Project—A mini-United Nations or the champion Chicago Bulls?* Paper presented at the International Conference of Applied Psychology, San Francisco.

Dorfman, P. W., & Howell, J. P. (1988). Dimensions of national culture and effective leadership patterns. In R. N. Farmer & E. G. McGoun (Eds.), *Advances in international comparative management* (Vol. 3, pp. 127–150). London: JAI Press.

Dorfman, P. W., & Howell, J. P. (1997). Managerial leadership in the United States and Mexico: Distant neighbors or close cousins? In C. S. Granrose & S. Oskamp (Eds.), *Cross cultural work groups.* Thousand Oaks, CA: Sage.

Dorfman, P. W., Howell, J. P., Hibino, S., Lee, J. K., Tate, U., & Bautista, A. (1997). Leadership in Western and Asian countries: Commonalities and differences in effective leadership processes across cultures. *Leadership Quarterly, 8*(3), 233–274.

Dorfman, P. W., & Ronen, S. (1991, August). *The universality of leadership theories: Challenges and paradoxes.* Paper presented at the National Academy of Management annual meeting, Miami.

Earley, P. C. (1984). Social interaction: The frequency, use of, and valuation in the United States, England, and Ghana. *Journal of Cross-Cultural Psychology, 15,* 477–485.

Erez, M. (1997). A culture-based model of work motivation. In P. C. Earley & M. Erez (Eds.), *New perspectives on international industrial/ organizational psychology* (pp. 193–242). San Francisco: New Lexington Press.

Farmer, R. N., & Richman, B. M. (1965). *Comparative management and economic progress.* Homewood, IL: Irwin.

Gerstner, C. R., & Day, D. V. (1994). Cross-cultural comparison of leadership prototypes. *Leadership Quarterly, 5*(2), 121–134.

Gibson, C. (1995). An investigation of gender differences in leadership across four countries. *Journal of International Business Studies, 26*(2), 255–279.

Graumann, C. F., & Moscovici, S. (1986). *Changing conceptions of leadership.* New York: Springer-Verlag.

Hagan, C. M. (1995). *Comparative management: Africa, the Middle East, and India.* (Working Paper). Boca Raton, FL: Florida Atlantic University.

Haire, M., Ghiselli, E. E., & Porter, L. (1966). *Managerial thinking: An international study.* New York: John Wiley.

Harbron, J. D. (1965). The dilemma of an elite group: The industrialist in Latin America. *Inter-American Economic Affairs, 19,* 43–62.

Hazucha, J. F., Hezlett, S. A., Bontems-Wackens, S., & Ronnqvist. (1999). *In search of the Euro-manager: Management competencies in France, Germany, Italy, and the United States* (Vol. 1, pp. 267–290). Stamford, CT: JAI.

Heller, T. (1958). Changing authority patterns: A cultural perspective. *Academy of Management Review, 10,* 488–495.

Hofstede, G. (1980). *Culture's consequences: International differences in work-related values.* Beverly Hills, CA: Sage.

Hofstede, G. (1993). Cultural constraints in management theories. *Academy of Management Executive, 7*(1), 81–94.

Hofstede, G. (2001). *Culture's consequences: Comparing values, behaviors, institutions, and organizations across nations.* Thousand Oaks, CA: Sage.

Hofstede, G., & Bond, M. H. (1988). The Confucius connection: From cultural roots to economic growth. *Organizational Dynamics, 16,* 4–21.

Hoppe, M. (1993). The effects of national culture on the theory and practice of managing R&D professionals abroad. *R&D Management, 23*(4), 313–325.

House, R. J. (1995). Leadership in the 21st century: A speculative inquiry. In A. Howard (Ed.), *The changing nature of work.* San Francisco: Jossey Bass.

House, R. J., Hanges, P. J., Ruiz-Quintanilla, S. A., Dorfman, P. W., Javidan, M., Dickson, M., et al. (1999). Cultural influences on leadership and organizations: Project GLOBE. In W. F. Mobley, M. J. Gessner, & V. Arnold (Eds.), *Advances in global leadership* (Vol. 1, pp. 171–233). Greenwich, CT: JAI.

House, R. J., Wright, N. S., & Aditya, R. N. (1997). Cross-cultural research on organizational leadership: A critical analysis and a proposed theory.

In P. C. Earley & M. Erez (Eds.), *New perspectives in international industrial/organizational psychology* (pp. 535–625). San Francisco: New Lexington Press.

Howell, J. P., & Avolio, B. J. (1993). Transformational leadership, transactional leadership, locus of control and support for innovation. *Journal of Applied Psychology, 78,* 891–902.

Howell, J. M., & Frost, P. J. (1989). A laboratory study of charismatic leadership. *Organizational Behavior and Human Decision Processes, 43*(2), 243–269.

Hui, C. H., & Tan, G. C. (1999). The moral component of effective leadership: The Chinese case. In W. Mobley, M. J. Gessner, & V. Arnold (Eds.), *Advances in global leadership* (Vol. 1, pp. 249–266). Stamford, CT: JAI Press.

Hunt, J. G. (1991). *Leadership: A new synthesis.* Newbury Park, CA: Sage.

Huo, P. Y., & Randall, D. M. (1991). Exploring subcultural differences in Hofstede's survey: The case of the Chinese. *Asia Pacific Journal of Management, 8,* 159–173.

Inkeles, A. (1966). The modernization of man. In M. Weiner (Ed.), *Modernization: The dynamics of growth* (pp. 138–150). New York: Basic Books.

Ivancevich, J. M., Schweiger, D. M., & Ragan, J. W. (1986). *Employee stress, health, and attitudes: A comparison of American, Indian and Japanese managers.* Paper presented at the Academy of Management, Chicago.

Jago, A. G., Reber, G., Bohnisch, W., Maczynski, J., Zavrel, J., & Dudorkin, J. (1993, November). *Culture's consequences? A seven nation study of participation.* Paper presented at the Proceedings of the 24th annual meeting of the Decision Sciences Institute, Washington, DC.

Jones, A. P., Rozelle, R. M., & Chang, W. C. (1990). Perceived punishment and reward values of supervisor actions in a Chinese sample. *Psychological Studies, 35,* 1–10.

Kakar, S. (1971). Authority patterns and subordinate behavior in Indian organizations. *Administrative Science Quarterly, 16,* 298–307.

Kennis, I. (1977). A cross-cultural study of personality and leadership. *Group and Organizational Studies, 2*(1), 49–60.

Koene, H., Pennings, H., & Schreuder, M. (1991). Leadership, culture, and organizational effectiveness. In K. E. Clark, M. E. Clark, &

D. P. Campbell (Eds.), *The impact of leadership.* Greensboro, NC: Center for Creative Leadership.

Koh, W. L., Terborg, J. R., & Steers, R. M. (1991). *The impact of transformational leaders on organizational commitment, organizational citizenship behavior, teacher satisfaction and student performance in Singapore.* Paper presented at the Academy of Management, Miami, FL.

Korman, A. K. (1966). Consideration, initiating structure and organizational criteria. *Personnel Psychology, 18,* 349–360.

Laurent, A. (1983). The cultural diversity of Western conceptions of management. *International Studies of Management and Organization, 13*(2), 75–96.

Lee, J. K., Roehl, T., & Choe, S. (2000). What makes management style similar and distinct across borders? Growth, experience and culture in Korean and Japanese firms. *Journal of International Business Studies, 31*(4), 631–652.

Lee, S. M., & Schwendiman, G. (1982). *Japanese management: Cultural and environmental considerations.* New York: Praeger.

Lindsay, C. P., & Dempsey, B. L. (1985). Experiences in training Chinese business people to use U.S. management techniques. *Journal of Applied Behavioral Science, 21,* 65–78.

Ling, W. Q., & Fang, L. (2003). The Chinese leadership theory. In W. H. Mobley & P. W. Dorfman (Eds.), *Advances in global leadership* (Vol. 3, pp. 183–204). Oxford: JAI.

Lord, R. G., & Maher, K. J. (1991). *Leadership and information processing: Linking perceptions and performance* (Vol. 1). Cambridge, MA: Unwin Hyman.

Martinez, S. M. (2000). *An ethnographic study of the Mexican entrepreneur: A configuration of themes and roles impacting managerial leadership in an emerging economy* Unpublished doctoral dissertation, New Mexico State University, Las Cruces.

McClelland, D. C. (1961). *The achieving society.* Princeton, NJ: Van Nostrand.

Meindl, J. R. (1990). On leadership: An alternative to the conventional wisdom. In B. A. Staw (Ed.), *Research in organizational behavior* (Vol. 12, pp. 159–203). New York: JAI.

Millman, J. (May 9, 2000). Trade wins: The world's new tiger on the export scene isn't Asian; it's Mexico. *Wall Street Journal,* p. A1.

Misumi, J. (1974, July). *Action research on the development of leadership, decision-making processes and organizational performance in a Japanese shipyard.* Paper presented at the International Congress of Applied Psychology, Liege, Belgium.

Misumi, J. (1985). *The behavioral science of leadership: An interdisciplinary Japanese research program.* Ann Arbor: University of Michigan Press.

Mobley, W. H., & Dorfman, P. W. (Eds.). (2003). *Advances in global leadership* (Vol. 3). Oxford: JAI.

O'Connell, M. S., Lord, R. G., & O'Connell, M. K. (1990). *Differences in Japanese and American leadership prototypes: Implications for cross-cultural training.* Paper presented at the Meeting of the Academy of Management, San Francisco, CA.

Osland, J. S., Monteze, M. S., & Hunter, L. (1998). A comparative study of managerial styles among female executives in Nicaragua and Costa Rica. *International Studies of Management and Organization, 28*(2), 54–73.

Ouchi, W. (1981). *Theory Z: How American business can meet the Japanese challenge.* Reading, MA: Addison-Wesley.

Paris, L. (2003). *The effect of gender and culture on implicit leadership theories: A cross-cultural study.* Unpublished doctoral dissertation, New Mexico State University, Las Cruces.

Pascale, R. T., & Athos, A. G. (1981). *The art of Japanese management.* New York: Simon & Schuster.

Pelletier, G. (1966). Business management in French Canada. *Business Quarterly—Canada Management Journal, 31*(3), 56–62.

Pereira, D. (1987). *Factors associated with transformational leadership in an Indian engineering firm.* Paper presented at the Administrative Science Association of Canada, Vancouver.

Peterson, M. F., Brannen, M. Y., & Smith, P. B. (1994). Japanese and U.S. leadership: Issues in current research. In S. B. Prasad (Ed.), *Advances in international comparative management: A research annual* (Vol. 9, pp. 57–82). Greenwich, CT: JAI.

Peterson, M. F., & Hunt, J. G. (1997). Overview: International and cross-cultural leadership research (Part II). *Leadership Quarterly, 8*(4), 339–342.

Peterson, M. F., Smith, P. B., & Peng, T. K. (1995). Japanese and American supervisors of a U.S. workforce: An intercultural analysis of behavior meanings. In S. El-Badry, H. Lopez-Cepero, & T. Hoppe (Eds.), *Navigating the Japanese market: Business and socio-economic perspectives* (pp. 229–249). Austin, TX: IC2 Institute.

Peterson, M. F., Smith, P. B., & Tayeb, M. H. (1993). Development and use of English versions of Japanese PM leadership measures in electronics plants. *Journal of Organizational Behavior, 14*(3), 251–267.

Poortinga, Y. H., & Malpass, R. S. (1986). Making inferences from cross-cultural data. In W. J. Lonner & J. W. Berry (Eds.), *Field methods in cross-cultural research* (pp. 12–46). Beverly Hills, CA: Sage.

Rahim, A. M., Kim, N. H., & Kim, J. S. (1994). Bases of leader power, subordinate compliance, and satisfaction with supervision: A cross-cultural study of managers in the U.S. and S. Korea. *The International Journal of Organizational Analysis, 2*(2), 136–154.

Ralston, D. A., Gustafson, D. J., Elsass, P. M., Cheung, F. M., & Terpstra, R. H. (1992). Eastern values: A comparison of managers in the United States, Hong Kong, and the People's Republic of China. *Journal of Applied Psychology, 77,* 664–671.

Redding, S. G. (1990). *The spirit of Chinese capitalism.* New York: deGruyter.

Redding, S. G., & Casey, T. W. (1975, August). *Managerial beliefs among Asian managers.* Paper presented at the Annual Meeting of the Academy of Management, New Orleans.

Ritchie, R. J. (1999). Reconciling I/O psychology and executive perspectives on global leadership competencies. In W. Mobley, M. J. Gessner, & V. Arnold (Eds.), *Advances in global leadership* (Vol. 1, pp. 115–125). Greenwich, CT: JAI.

Rosch, E. (1975). Universals and cultural specifics in human categorization. In R. Brislin & S. Bochner & W. Lonner (Eds.), *Cross-cultural perspectives in learning* (pp. 177–206). Beverly Hills, CA: Sage.

Ryterbrand, E. C., & Thiagarajan, K. M. (1968). *Managerial attitudes toward salaries as a function of social and economic development* (Technical Report No. 24). Rochester, NY: University of Rochester, Management Research Center.

Scandura, T. A., & Dorfman, P. (in press). Leadership research in a post-GLOBE world. *Leadership Quarterly Letters.*

Scandura, T. A., Von Glinow, M. A., & Lowe, K. B. (1999). When East meets West: Leadership "best practices" in the United States and the Middle East. In W. Mobley, M. J. Gessner, & V. Arnold (Eds.), *Advances in global leadership* (Vol. 1, pp. 235–248). Greenwich, CT: JAI.

Schein, E. H. (1992). *Organizational culture and leadership: A dynamic view* (2nd ed.). San Francisco: Jossey-Bass.

Schmidt, S. M., & Yeh, R. S. (1992). The structure of leader influence: A cross-national comparison. *Journal of Cross-Cultural Psychology, 23*(2), 251–264.

Shackleton, V. J., & Ali, A. H. (1990). Work-related values of managers: A test of the Hofstede model. *Journal of Cross-Cultural Psychology, 21*(1), 109–118.

Shamir, B., Zakay, E., Breinin, E., & Popper, M. (1998). Correlates of charismatic leader behavior in military units: Subordinates' attitudes, unit characteristics, and superiors' appraisals of leader performance. *Academy of Management Journal, 41*(4), 387–409.

Shaw, J. B. (1990). A cognitive categorization model for the study of intercultural management. *Academy of Management Review, 15*(4), 626–645.

Shenkar, O., Ronen, S., Shefy, E., & Chow, I. H. (1998). The role structure of Chinese managers. *Human Relations, 51*(1), 51–72.

Sinha, J. B. P. (1980). *The nurturant task leader.* New Delhi: Concept.

Sinha, J. B. P. (1984). A model of effective leadership styles in India. *International Studies of Management and Organization, 14*(3), 86–98.

Sinha, J. B. P. (1994). Cultural imbeddedness and the developmental role of industrial organizations in India. In H. C. Triandis, M. D. Dunette, & L. M. Hough (Eds.), *Handbook of industrial and organizational psychology* (2nd ed., Vol. 4, pp. 727–764). Palo Alto, CA: Consulting Psychologists Press.

Sinha, J. B. P. (1995). *The cultural context of leadership and power.* Thousand Oaks, CA: Sage.

Smith, P. B. (1997). Cross-cultural leadership: A path to the goal? In P. C. Earley & M. Erez (Eds.), *New perspectives on international industrial/ organizational psychology* (pp. 626–639). San Francisco: New Lexington Press.

Smith, P. B. (2003). Leaders' sources of guidance and the challenge of working across cultures. In

W. Mobley & P. Dorfman (Eds.), *Advances in global leadership* (Vol. 3, pp. 167–182). Oxford: JAI.

Smith, P. B., & Bond, M. H. (1993). *Social psychology across cultures: Analysis and perspectives.* London: Harvester Wheatsheaf.

Smith, P. B., Dugan, S., & Trompenaars, F. (1996). National culture and the values of organizational employees: A dimensional analysis across 43 nations. *Journal of Cross-Cultural Psychology, 27*(2), 231–264.

Smith, P. B., Misumi, J., Tayeb, M. H., Peterson, M. F., & Bond, M. H. (1989). On the generality of leadership style across cultures. *Journal of Occupational Psychology, 30,* 526–537.

Smith, P. B., & Peterson, M. F. (1988). *Leadership, organizations and culture: An event management model.* Newbury Park, CA: Sage.

Smith, P. B., & Peterson, M. F. (1995, August). *Beyond value comparisons: Sources used to give meaning to management events in 30 countries.* Paper presented at the Academy of Management Annual Meeting, Vancouver, Canada.

Smith, P. B., Peterson, M. F., Misumi, J., & Bond, M. H. (1992). A cross-cultural test of Japanese PM leadership theory. *Applied Psychology: An International Review, 42*(1), 5–19.

Steers, R. M., Shinn, Y. K., & Ungson, G. R. (1989). *The Chaebol: Korea's new industrial might.* New York: Harper.

Stening, B. W., & Wong, P. S. (1983). Australian managers' leadership beliefs. *Psychological Reports, 53,* 274–278.

Stogdill, R. M. (1974). *Handbook of leadership: A survey of the literature.* New York: Free Press.

Torres, C. (2000). Leadership style norms among Americans and Brazilians: Assessing differences using Jackson's return potential model. *The Sciences and Engineering, 60,* 8–13.

Triandis, H. C. (1993). *The contingency model in cross-cultural perspective.* San Diego: Academic.

Triandis, H. C. (1994). Cross cultural industrial psychology. In H. C. Triandis, M. D. Dunette, & L. M. Hough (Eds.), *Handbook of industrial and organizational psychology* (2nd ed., Vol. 4, pp. 104–172). Palo Alto, CA: Consulting Psychologists Press.

Trompenaars, F. (1993). *Riding the waves of culture: Understanding cultural diversity in business.* London: Breatley.

Ulin, R. D. (1976). African leadership: National goals and the values of Botswana University students. *Comparative Education, 12,* 145–155.

Vroom, V. H., & Jago, A. (1988). *The new leadership: Managing participation in organizations.* Englewood Cliffs, NJ: Prentice Hall.

Wade, R. (1990). *Governing the market: The role of government in East Asian industrialization.* Princeton, NJ: Princeton University Press.

Wang, Z. M. (1994). Culture, economic reform and the role of industrial and organizational psychology in China. In H. C. Triandis, M. D. Dunette, & L. M. Hough (Eds.), *Handbook of industrial and organizational psychology* (2nd ed., Vol. 4, pp. 689–725). Palo Alto, CA: Consulting Psychologists Press.

Weber, M. (1930). *The Protestant ethic and the spirit of capitalism.* London: Allen & Unwin.

Weiss, J. W., & Bloom, S. (1990). Managing in China: Expatriate experiences and training. *Business Horizons, 33,* 23–29.

Whitehill, A. M., & Takezawa, S. (1968). *The other worker.* Honolulu: East-West Center Press.

Yukl, G. A. (2002). *Leadership in organizations* (5th ed.). Upper Saddle River, NJ: Prentice Hall.

5

THE IMPACT OF SOCIETAL CULTURE AND INDUSTRY ON ORGANIZATIONAL CULTURE

Theoretical Explanations

MARCUS W. DICKSON

RENEE S. BESHEARS

VIPIN GUPTA

Because national culture and industry are integral parts of the environment in which organizations function, organizational culture by implication should be influenced both by the broader societal culture and by the industry in which they operate. As has been noted throughout this volume, a wealth of research examines the interrelationships among various conceptions of societal culture and industry and various forms of organizational behavior, structure, and culture, and we do not purport to present an exhaustive review of that literature here. However, the vast majority of the writing on society-organization linkages, and on industry-organization linkages as well, has focused on the measurement and description of relationships, without specifying the mechanisms by which the influence is enacted. Fortunately, in the past decade, organizational

researchers have begun to understand the need to identify potential explanatory mechanisms to more thoroughly understand the phenomenon of interest. For example, Earley and Erez (1997) in their edited book *New Perspectives on International Industrial/Organizational Psychology* describe a variety of findings, including Lawler's (1986) research showing that quality control circles were generally quite successful in Japan, but that their success was much less consistent in the United States. Earley and Erez go on to note that "What have been missing from I/O research literature are the theoretical frameworks people can bring to bear in explaining such patterns, not simply describing them" (p. 3).

In this chapter, we briefly present several potential mechanisms by which society-level variables and industry-level variables might have their impact on organizational culture.[1] We provide brief descriptions of the theories and present examples to better convey the proposed mechanism in action. Finally, we propose possible conditions under which each of the mechanisms is more or less likely to be active than the others. First, however, we briefly outline GLOBE's assumptions about the measurement and dimensionality of culture as it is enacted at the society and organization levels.

GLOBE's Cultural Dimensions: Values and Practices

Throughout this volume, members of the GLOBE Project presume that it is useful to conceive of cultural dimensions operating at both the society and organization levels of analysis. GLOBE questionnaire items are largely constructed around "quartets" in which the same concept is addressed in terms of both practices and values at both the societal and organizational levels (Hanges & Dickson, Chapter 8, this volume). Thus, a deliberate choice was made in the GLOBE Project to treat cultural dimensions as homologous across levels of analysis.

Other cross-cultural scholars have advocated different approaches to this issue. Hofstede, for example, argues that societies are differentiated by values whereas organizations are differentiated by practices, and that a different set of dimensions of practice will be more useful for differentiating organizations than the set of dimensions of values that best differentiate societies (e.g., Hofstede, Neuijen, Ohayv, & Sanders, 1990; Hofstede & Peterson, 2000). Given the unique opportunity to collect data from a large number of organizations from a large number of countries from every region of the world, GLOBE investigators chose to address this question empirically. By collecting data on both practices and values at both the society and organization levels of analysis and by using advanced modeling techniques to test the relationships among and between these dimensions and levels, we believed that we would be able to provide a more definitive answer to the question of whether both values and practices differ meaningfully at both the society and organization levels. Indeed, Hanges and Dickson (Chapter 8, this volume) present

evidence suggesting that: (a) values and practices both serve to differentiate between societies and organizations; (b) the values and practices each account for unique variance; (c) the values and practices scales interact; and (d) the dimension of values and practices can be meaningfully applied at both levels.

Unlike the field of personality, in which many researchers have concluded that a specific taxonomy of dimensions (the five-factor model) is sufficient and the most parsimonious, we do not believe that cultural researchers have yet reached the point in this field of research where we can say which taxonomy of cultural dimensions is most parsimonious. We thus look forward to further explorations of the dimensionality of culture, and the assessment of systematic variation in practices and values across levels of culture, in the hope of reaching such a taxonomy. Prior to that future date, however, we turn now to our proposals for mechanisms by which societal culture can have its impact on the homologous dimensions of organizational culture.

Levels of Impact on Organizational Culture

There are, of course, myriad factors that affect the creation and evolution of organizational cultures: The presence or absence of competitors; local, regional, national, and global economic conditions; the nature of the business (manufacturing or service or other types of ventures); the nature of the available labor supply, and so forth. Many of these factors are highly idiosyncratic and are likely to have unique effects on specific kinds of organizations. However, some factors are likely to have similar effects on a variety of organizations, and thus are likely to be more systematic in their impact. We are especially interested in these types of effects, and we broadly categorize them three ways: effects in which the nature of the societal culture has an impact on the nature of the organization; effects in which the nature of the global industry has an impact on the nature of the organization; and effects in which the nature of the industry as it is manifested in a given society has an impact on the nature of the organization. We will hereafter in this chapter refer to these types of effects as *society effects, industry effects,* and *society-by-industry interaction effects,* respectively.

Society Effects

As noted previously, a wealth of literature indicates that organizations reflect a variety of aspects of the societies in which they exist. For example, Shane, Venkataraman, and MacMillan (1995) found that differences between societies on uncertainty avoidance, power distance, and individualism were related to preferred championing behavior in organizations in those societies. Hayes and Prakasam (1989) found that societal differences in power distance predicted the type of consultant–client relationship preferred in those societies; firms in countries characterized by high power distance preferred relationships that were more directive and less collaborative. Indeed, Tata and Prasad (1992) present a model describing the potential negative outcomes that can accrue to an organization that strays from the expectation to match society and industry norms.

Thus, it seems clear that societal characteristics can and do influence the characteristics of the organizations within the society. In looking for such effects, therefore, one should expect to see (a) similarities among all (or certainly most) organizations within the society, and (b) a clear origin at the societal level for the organization-level similarities.

Industry Effects

The fact that different industries impose different demands on organizations is obvious and well supported in the organizational strategy literature (Gordon, 1991). Dickson, Aditya, and Chhokar (2000) argue that "The nature of the industry influences organizational culture through the constraints it places on the behavior of all persons in the organization" (p. 454). Further, specific organizational practices may be essential if an organization hopes to survive in the industry (Burns & Stalker, 1961; Lawrence & Lorsch, 1967). In addition, Gordon (1991) cites Gagliardi (1986) in making similar points, when he notes that "industry-driven assumptions lead to value systems that are consistent with these assumptions, and these value

systems prevent the company from developing strategies, structures, or processes that would conflict with these assumptions and be 'antagonistic' to the culture" (p. 398). Gordon goes on to argue that differences in organizational culture largely have their basis in differences in industries. In support of this argument, Reynolds (1986) conducted a study using 14 cultural dimensions derived from the dimensions most commonly used in the organizational culture literature. In surveying respondents from three international advanced technology industrial firms, 14 restaurants in an international fast-food chain, and a computer software and custom software firm, Reynolds found statistically significant differences for 12 of the 14 cultural dimensions. These results suggest a strong industry impact on organizational culture across these three industries.

Analogous to societal effects, in looking for industry effects, one should expect to see (a) similarities among most organizations within a given industry across cultures and (b) clear evidence that the origin for the organization-level similarities resides at the industry level of analysis.

Unfortunately, there is less empirical evidence for an effect of industry that is consistent across societies than there is for societal effects operating on organizational culture. Although this does not mean that such an effect does not exist, we can only speculate as to the size of such effects based on the extant literature. As argued in the next section of the paper, we expect the effect of *industry* to primarily be carried through society–industry interactions.

Society-by-Industry Interaction Effects

Anyone who has traveled internationally will recognize that similar industries all over the world are enacted differently in different countries. Utilities are an obvious example, with some countries having government-run monopolies, others having nongovernmental monopolies, others having state or province or regional monopolies, and still others having varying forms and levels of competition. Thus, the telecommunications industry may exist in virtually every society, but country-level differences in how the industry functions are significant. Level and degree of governmental regulation, development of the industry within a society, and national economic system are just a few of the other factors that can affect the ways in which a given industry is enacted in a given society.[2]

An interesting example of this type of effect is provided by Soeters and Schreuder (1988) in their examination of Dutch and U.S. accounting firms. They found that there were national differences in the firms' practices, in that the U.S. firms were all lower on uncertainty avoidance than the Dutch firms, but all of the accounting firms in both societies had uncertainty avoidance scores that were lower than even the lowest scoring country in Hofstede's (1980) study, suggesting that there was an industry effect that differed in its magnitude between societies. Tata and Prasad (1992) provide another, nonempirical, example of this type of interaction. They propose a model of organizational design for effectiveness that incorporates a consideration of the effects of the market, the current technology, the industrial environment, and the societal culture. More importantly, they discuss the interactions of the market, the technology, and the industry with the societal culture as having an impact on the design of an effective organization.

EXPLANATORY MECHANISMS

We now turn to descriptions of the several mechanisms by which we believe industry and society effects occur. Although there are myriad potential explanations, some more macro and some more micro, we have identified several specific theoretical models that we believe help to explain the influence process among society, industry, industry within society, and organization levels of analysis. Specifically, we will refer to:

- Cultural immersion theory
- Social network theory
- Resource dependency theory
- Institutional theory
- Other potential mechanisms, at micro, meso, and macro levels.

Cultural Immersion Theory

Most people live their entire lives within a single societal culture—they become immersed in that culture and may in many ways forget that other cultures perceive and experience the world differently. In the language of cognitive psychology, they develop "shared schemas" or common patterns of thinking, responding, and interpreting stimuli they encounter.

One outcome of this process is that, if people from a given society share schemas, then the organizations within that society are likely to have structures and cultures that reflect those schemas. We believe that this process is likely to lead to both a direct effect of societal culture on organizational culture, and an effect mediated by organizational founder or leader characteristics.

Direct Effect of Society on the Organization

As noted above, the normative prescriptions and behavioral expectations that characterize a given culture are likely to lead to patterns of thought and behavior that are highly routinized. Researchers approaching the study of culture from a cognitive psychological perspective (e.g., Erez & Earley, 1993; Lord & Maher, 1991; Smith & Peterson, 1988; Smith, Peterson, & Wang, 1996) describe a process whereby sociocultural events activate particular cultural meaning systems within a cognitive network, and within a given culture certain ways of thinking and certain response patterns to stimuli (such as schemas) are activated more often than others as a result of cultural expectations. As a consequence, over time these schema become readily available and more easily activated than alternatives. In other words, "the more often a particular pattern is activated in a connectionist network, the more efficient its activation is in the future" (Hanges, Lord, & Dickson, 2000, p. 143). Eventually, people will no longer be consciously aware of the fact that there are other ways of perceiving the world or of responding to situations—the culturally congruent schema have become chronic, and as Hanges, Lord, and Dickson (2000) note, it is difficult to get people off of the familiar path to consider less familiar (and thus less cognitively available) alternative responses. In this way, a direct societal effect is created, in that the shared expectations of the society lead directly to patterns of behavior practices and values that characterize organizations within that society.

For example, Lee and Barnett (1997, p. 398), following earlier theorizing such as that by Emery and Trist (1965), view organizations as "open systems influenced by the environment." They operationalized organizational culture in terms of perceived distances between pairs of concepts such as happiness, seniority, success, the self, one's job, supervisor, money and the names of the countries. They observed significant differences among organizational cultures of a Taiwanese-owned, a Japanese-owned, and an American-owned bank located in their respective countries, but found little difference between the Taiwanese-owned bank and an American-owned bank located in Taiwan. These findings highlight the influence of national culture more than that of leader's values in determining organizational culture. In addition, Meschi and Roger (1994) report a strong linear relationship between perceived distance separating national cultures and that separating organizational cultures ($r = .71$).

Further, a great deal of the more atheoretical literature on society effects seems to imply this process, though it is rarely explicitly described. For example, Schuler and Rogovsky (1998) tested for society effects on the generally accepted methods of managing human resources. They found that Hofstede's (1980) four dimensions of culture were associated with specific compensation practices, though they did not focus on the mechanisms by which that might occur. Similarly, Jang (1997) found that the network structure of shared public relations firms was influenced by the differences in national cultures (as well as the companies' business types), such that American companies were more centralized than Japanese firms. Again, however, the explanation for why this might be is implied more than stated, with the implication being that this is reflective of the larger culture: that is, that this mode of operations "makes sense" to the people in those cultures. As a last of a great many potential examples, Harrison (1993) tested the influence of societal culture and managerial personality on the relation between reliance on accounting performance measures in the evaluative style of superiors. Using data from Singapore and Australia (representing high power distance and low individualism, and low power distance and high individualism cultures, respectively),

Harrison found that culture did influence this relationship but that managerial personality did not. Again, however, the fact that the societal-level sharing of values is treated as sufficient explanation for the pattern of characteristics at the organizational level implies a cultural immersion explanation.

Effect Mediated by Founders or Leaders

When the founder of an organization decides who to bring in as initial key players in the organization and how to structure the organization, he or she typically makes decisions on the basis of what "makes sense" to them. Organizational leaders later in the organizational life cycle operate in a similar manner. In so doing, they hire people who share their own values, and they create organizational structures that reflect those values (Giberson & Resick, 2001). Schneider's (1987; Schneider, Goldstein, & Smith, 1995) Attraction-Selection-Attrition (ASA) model states this explicitly, and argues that an eventual outcome of this process (along with organizational socialization) is increasing homogeneity within organizations on a variety of dimensions, including personality (Schneider, Smith, Taylor, & Fleenor, 1998) and values and cultural perceptions (Haudek, 2001). The ASA model is addressed in more detail below.

We suggest that the values systems that the founders and leaders hold and the schemas that have become chronic are likely to be reflective of the values and shared schemas of the larger society (Hanges, Lord, & Dickson, 2000; Lord, Brown, & Freiberg, 1999), although of course there is variation among organizational founders and leaders in the hierarchy of those values (Locke, 1991). Similarly, the degree to which common behavioral patterns and cultural schemas have become chronic for specific founders may be somewhat individualized, but are likely to also reflect the societal culture. Thus, the cultural immersion process has, in addition to the direct effect described above, an effect on organizational culture and structure that is mediated by the values of founders and other organizational leaders. In other words, the culture affects the founder or leader directly, and the founder or leader then affects the organization directly.

Schein's (1992) description of the creation of organizations culture fits with the perspective that leaders have direct effects on organizational culture and structure. He argues that organizational leaders select people who reflect their own values and assumptions, and put into place organizational structures and features that reflect their values and assumptions, and it is these structures and features that encourage the development of certain types of culture. In addition, Hambrick and Mason (1984) identified several hypotheses about the demographics of top management teams and how those demographics would relate to organizational structure and performance. Miller and Droege (1986) and Miller, Kets de Vries, and Toulouse (1982) found a relationship between specific leader personality components (such as need for achievement and locus of control) and gross measures of organization structure (such as centralization and formalization).

To summarize the preceding discussion, societal culture influences perceptions and values of societal members, and because leaders are members of societal cultures they are thus affected to varying degrees by their societal cultures. It is also well established that organizational founders and leaders affect their organizations' structures and cultures. Thus, there is significant evidence for both the direct influence of societal culture on organizational culture, and the influence of societal culture on organizational culture mediated by the values of founders or leaders.

Social Network Theory

Social network theory approaches the issues raised in this chapter from the assumption that organizations are influenced by the social networks in which they are embedded and that these social networks constrain the behaviors and choices of various actors within the networks. According to this theory, these constraints are either based on cohesion or structural equivalence mechanisms (Burt, 1987), which are described below.

Cohesion research suggests that direct interaction with others results in socially constructed perceptions (Ibarra & Andrews, 1993). The multiplicity and density of interaction within a cohesive network provide an effective channel for building and transmitting shared perceptions and cues. The organizations participating in a cohesive network interact intensively on learning and innovative activities, and help one another select and develop shared best practices. The influence mechanism in such a network tends to be cooperative, and there is greater use of direct, dyadic ties for interorganizational influence. Further, in a cohesive network, non-business as well as business organizations can transmit social culture to various member organizations. The cohesive relationships also define the group boundaries, which tend to be stronger within an identifiable social geographic area than across geographical boundaries, thus suggesting society effects. From this perspective, bounded information and contact within the group tend to generate shared values and practices among organizations within a society. In a cohesive group, the members tend to demonstrate strong behavioral conformity and coordinated patterns of behavior (Levine & Moreland, 1990). Cohesion allows the group to punish deviation and reward behaviors consistent with group norms (Guzzo & Dickson, 1996; Guzzo & Shea, 1992). Further, cohesion can facilitate reputation enhancement, thus leading to enhanced perceptions of credibility and reliability. A natural outcome of this process is the "bandwagon-effect" in which people and organizations "follow the crowd," such as adopting popular organizational innovations or reading and relying on best-selling business press books whether they are appropriate to the organizational context or not. As such, cohesion can be a powerful source of society effects on organizational culture.

A structural equivalence perspective, on the other hand, can often lead to similar predictions as a cohesion perspective, but through different explanatory mechanisms. From this perspective, an actor (whether an individual or an organization) may play a similar role in a social network as another actor. She or he may provide similar input to the network while maintaining similar relationships with other network members. These two similar actors may be seen, to some extent, as interchangeable with each other as they fill the same role within the network. In other words, they are structurally equivalent. The point is that if one actor adopts an innovation that could serve to differentiate it from the other actor (making the two nonequivalent), the nonadopter faces pressures to quickly adopt the innovation to reduce the possibility of a negative comparison with the adopting actor (Burt, 1983). To illustrate, if two graduate students work with the same professors on similar research and one learns a new data analytic technique, the other is pressured to learn the new technique as well. Similarly, if two companies produce similar products for a target market and one introduces a new feature to their products, the other is pressured to adopt that new feature as quickly as possible.

Structural equivalence research thus suggests that the actors sharing similar patterns of role relationships with others face common role constraints and opportunities, and therefore tend to have similar behaviors associated with management of those role constraints and opportunities. Structural equivalence generates competition among organizations because their roles are substitutable due to similarity in their relationships and interaction patterns (Burt, 1987). The intense competition may limit the ability of the firms to adopt new social innovations, or alternatively add to the willingness of the firms to be more organic, flexible, and responsive, so that they can differentiate from one another. In either case, a structural equivalence perspective would lend itself to explanation and prediction of what we refer to as industry effects.

In addition to competition effects, structural equivalence may also generate other kinds of social influences. Structurally equivalent actors may influence each other via indirect ties to similar others, such as customers and vendors, and thereby adopt similar values and practices. Because similar environmental conditions induce similarity among organizations, this process may be termed as ecological influence (Cartwright, 1965). In addition, structural equivalence may also operate through social information processing and social comparison channels, whereby the organizations compare with and benchmark against firms with equivalent roles. Again, some degree of similarity in values and practices can emerge as a result of such social comparison, resulting in knowledge spillovers and organizational learning. Alternatively, the similar network relationships may generate similar socialization effects, support service conditions, demand and

supply conditions, and other shared experiences, all generating industry effects that partially share experiences and behaviors common across the society. Thus, a combination of cohesion at the society level and structural equivalence at the industry level can contribute to interactive society and industry effects.

At the international level, the social network theory predicts some degree of fragmentation in the cohesion network (organizations forming subgroups) because it is difficult for each organization to interact with every other member of the network (Berelson & Steiner, 1964). Within each subgroup there would be intensive interaction among organizations with similar values and practices. These strong sustained ties generate *cliques*: densely connected subgroups of reciprocated ties within a social network (Doreian, 1979). The clique-type behavior can be particularly strong among organizations belonging to traditional societies. In these cases, society as well as industry effects can be quite weak because there may be different patterns of organizational behaviors depending on the clique to which the firms belong.

In summation, firms within each industry tend to have considerable interaction with each other, and so tend to have similar characteristics, because of social cohesion and social influence. Social cohesion effects tend to be weaker for organizations across industries than for organizations within industries. Further, for industries across societies, social cohesion is complemented by structural equivalence, which can also generate similar organizational cultures across different societies for firms facing similar network characteristics. The degree of cohesion and structural equivalence varies for each industry and society, presumably leading to society–industry interaction effects. One of the interesting implications of this process is that effects that appear to be at the societal level may in reality be driven by interorganizational interaction rather than by a cross-level effect of the society.

Resource Dependency Theory

Resource dependency theory is rooted in the need for organizations to control necessary resources (Pfeffer, 1981; Pfeffer & Salancik, 1978). It focuses on how the organizations adopt practices and values, and introduce them to their network partners so as to gain access to and best use those resources that will reduce their dependence on critical contingencies or will otherwise improve their competitive position. Dependency theorists view the organization as being embedded within larger interorganizational and societal networks and cultural systems. This environment not only influences the organization's input and output markets, but its beliefs, norms, and historical traditions. To prosper in their environment, organizations must strive to achieve social legitimacy in addition to technological and operational efficiency (Abernathy & Chua, 1996). Thus, resource dependency theory research focuses on (a) the nature of environmental uncertainty and complexity and the impact of this uncertainty on the strategic imperatives the organization must meet and (b) the organization's subsequent efforts to develop an appropriate organizational structure.

Bartol and Martin's (1988, 1989, 1990) dependency theory is largely a more narrowly focused, microlevel version of resource dependency theory. Dependency theory builds on two basic assumptions about managerial behavior: (a) managers are dependent, to varying degrees, upon their subordinates; and (b) managers use pay and other valued resources to manage their dependence upon their subordinates (Klein et al., 2000). Dependency theory and resource dependency theory are largely homologous: They propose that similar dynamics occur between managers and subordinates within organizations as well as among organizations and their suppliers, vendors, and consumers. Thus, individual managers make decisions based on dependencies and threats to dependency relationships in much the same way as organizations and organizational subunits do.

Some examples of dependency relationships and expected outcomes might facilitate understanding of the resource dependency model. First, countries that have formalized relationships as trading partners are likely to become more similar to each other in terms of their behaviors and structures, even if the deeply held values driving those behaviors do not coalesce (see Chapter 20, this volume, by Brodbeck et al.). Thus, we see Canadian, Mexican, and American organizations making strategic shifts to enhance their trade relationships as a result of the North American Free Trade Agreement, and we see similar shifts among the nations of the European Union. As new trade regulations promoting trade across these national borders have taken effect, and trade has indeed increased, organizations in these countries find that they have grown more dependent upon organizations in other countries either because of supply or sales relationships. Thus, dependency effects become evident.

The changes in the health care industry in the United States provide a vivid example of dependency theory within a single industry and country. Health care providers in the United States are dependent on insurance companies for payment, and insurance companies are for-profit enterprises. When the American insurance industry began to promote managed care and the use of health maintenance organizations as a means of reducing costs, most health care providers (both individuals and organizations) were compelled to participate in the system or lose access to patients and the accompanying revenue stream. Health care providers thus went along with managed care reforms despite the fact that many concerns about compromises in quality of care were raised from the beginning (cf. *Patient Right to Know Act of 1996,* 1996; *Views of Healthcare Providers,* 1993).

Although there is a fair amount of research from a dependency theory perspective, we see the bulk of dependency theory's arguments as being incorporated in institutional theory. We thus now turn to institutional theory and will focus in much more detail on that perspective.

Institutional Theory

Institutional theory is in some ways similar to dependency theory, but focuses primarily on the organization's institutional environment rather than on tangible resources exclusively. This environment consists of the elaboration of rules, practices, symbols, beliefs, and normative requirements to which individual organizations must conform to receive support and legitimacy (DiMaggio & Powell, 1983; Meyer & Rowan, 1977). Institutional theory can best be explained as a theory of legitimacy-seeking. Organizations respond to pressures from society and other organizations to behave in a way that is deemed legitimate. Scott and Meyer (1991), for example, argue that institutional agencies (e.g., governmental agencies, laws, courts, professional organizations, interest groups, public opinion, or other sources of perceived legitimacy) have "the power to formulate or influence rules and regulations or to promulgate norms and standards governing [organizational] practice" (p. 317). They go on to argue that organizational decision makers may not critically evaluate organizational practices that have become institutionalized, but instead view such practices as valued ends in themselves. Of course, one difficulty in providing examples of such processes is that what appears to an outsider to be an example of institutionalization of a practice appears to insiders to be a valued practice, and so it is often difficult to find agreement on what would constitute the influence of institutional pressures. Nonetheless, we point first to extreme examples, such as the maintenance until 1945 of a British Civil Service position with the task of standing on the Cliffs of Dover with a spyglass, watching for Napoleon. There had actually been several efforts made to eliminate this position over the years (especially after Napoleon died), but these efforts had always been resisted, with a variety of explanations given for why the position should be maintained (Townsend, 1970). We would interpret this as an example of an institutionalized practice.

Tolbert and Zucker (1983) use an institutional theory explanation to explain the diffusion of civil service structures in city governments in the early part of the 20th century in the United States. They found that, when states legislatures passed laws mandating that cities adopt civil service structures, large numbers of cities did so very quickly, making the diffusion of the structure sudden and rapid. In states that did not mandate the implementation of civil service structures for city governments, however, diffusion was more gradual, only increasing in rapidity when the form became perceived as more legitimate. The end result of this process is that, whereas prior to 1900 there was significant debate about civil service (i.e., whether it changed city government from a political organization into a corporation), by the 1920s there was little conflict, and by the 1930s it was accepted as given.

A wide variety of organizational strategies and practices, including personnel selection (Meyer & Rowan, 1991) and training (Scott & Meyer, 1991), have been examined from this perspective. Institutional theorists conclude that managers perceive these human resource strategies as valued ends in themselves, above and beyond their practical utility. For example, Goodstein (1994, pp. 353–355) has documented that employers face substantial institutional pressures to adopt work–family programs such as on-site child care, flextime, job sharing, and voluntary part-time employment, and Klein, Berman, and Dickson's (2000) research suggests that law firms are more likely to allow attorneys to work part-time for societally valued reasons (e.g., caring for a new child) than for other, more personalized reasons.

Isomorphism

The primary principle in institutional theory is isomorphism; organizations are pressured to become isomorphic with, or conform to, a set of institutionalized beliefs and processes. DiMaggio and Powell (1983) identify three types of isomorphism: *coercive isomorphism, mimetic isomorphism,* and *normative isomorphism.*

Coercive isomorphism is a response to formal and informal pressures exerted on organizations by other organizations on which they are dependent and by the larger cultural expectations of the society in which they exist (including such things as political, legal, cultural, historical, and regional conditions). The two aspects of coercive isomorphism seem to operate at different levels. The influence of other organizations parallels dependency theory, and seems to us more likely to be a mechanism for society-by-industry interaction effects. For example, a major manufacturing company with many suppliers dependent upon it can essentially dictate structural, accounting, scheduling, and many other aspects of those suppliers' business functioning. We see examples of this in the United States in the automotive parts and materials industry, in which many organizations have been compelled to adapt themselves to integrate more effectively with the major auto makers (Wrigley, 1997). In addition, this process could also explain the acceptance of the managed care movement by

U.S. health care providers, again showing the similarity of prediction between resource dependency theory and institutional theory.

Coercive isomorphism also includes the pressures put on an organization to conform to the cultural norms of the society in which they operate. This type of influence seems clearly to be operating at the society effects level. This type of influence is evident in different pay structures, which may reflect cultural differences in power distance, uncertainty avoidance, and individuality. In addition, the work–family accommodation issues cited above (Goodstein, 1994; Klein, et al., 2000) would likely be examples of this form of isomorphism, in that generalized society-level cultural expectations probably drive these organizational practices. This form of isomorphism seems likely to us to contribute to society effects, industry effects, and society-by-industry interaction effects on organizational values and practices. Interestingly, the more recent movements in resistance to managed care can be thought of in this context: Health care providers eventually grew weary of being compelled to provide what they perceived as substandard care (i.e., not meeting the legitimate expectations of the broader society) and, so as to restore perceptions of legitimacy, have in some cases left the managed care system and in others have attempted to band together to resist the pressures of managed care from the insurance industry.

Mimetic isomorphism generally involves a transformation that takes place in the face of uncertainty, if an organization models itself after another, more successful, organization. Organizations usually mimic other organizations that are either in their field and perceived as more legitimate, outside their field (and perceived as legitimate) but similar in complexity, or those organizations that are perceived as being "on the cutting edge" (DiMaggio & Powell, 1983). If organizations mimic other organizations in the same field, an industrial culture tends to emerge in which organizations within a given industry behave similarly in the manner that is perceived as most successful. If organizations mimic other organizations similar in complexity or organizations seen as being on the cutting edge the influence of national culture may emerge. For example, highly bureaucratic

organizations may be more commonplace in societies in which bureaucratic governments exist, or in cultures in which power distance and uncertainty avoidance are high. What is perceived as being cutting edge may also reflect overall societal or national cultural values. Some cultures may be more apt to follow trends and fads than others, and this would influence the degree to which organizations adopt these practices.

It follows from the description above that mimetic isomorphism would primarily be active at the society and the society-by-industry interaction effect levels. We would trace the basis for this argument back to Katz and Kahn (1966). According to Katz and Kahn, people are overwhelmed with information and of necessity develop systems by which they can filter incoming information. The probable outcome of such filtration is that events that occur and data generated within the boundaries of their system become much more salient than events and information generated elsewhere. Dickson, Aditya, and Chhokar (2000) argue that for most people the most cognitively available comparators (i.e., the sources of information most likely to be within the filtration system) are organizations within their own society and industry. This occurs because most people are significantly less knowledgeable about organizations in other countries or even in other industries within their own country. Of course, some people have broad knowledge of other societies and industries than their own, but even for these few individuals, the level of perceived similarity of organizations within their own national borders may lead them to more easily attend to and recall, and thus be influenced by, organizations "closer to home" (Festinger, 1954).

Finally, educational or professional pressures to conform to a set of rules and norms characterize normative isomorphism. Educational or training programs and professional societies or associations influence professionals operating within organizations. This type of pressure can be powerful if these professional entities push for state-sanctioned actions, such as licensing or certification. On a less severe level, normative isomorphism can dictate how certain organization members will speak, behave or dress (Ouchi, 1980). This type of isomorphism can again operate at the different levels, either national or industrial. The degree to which normative influences will affect organizations will depend upon the number of professionals from the same field that exist within a particular society or industry. For example, medical doctors who comprise a large portion of the workforce influence the health care industry. Their high involvement in associations and societies can pressure organizations to adopt certain practices that the profession as a whole deems most appropriate, such as continuing education or licensing. This type of influence can be tempered, however, by the broader societal culture. Although the professional associations exert pressures on organizations, the norms of the national or societal culture will be operating within the professional societies.

Complexities of Isomorphic Pressures

Although institutional theory and isomorphism can operate at different cultural levels, as we have noted above, it is most likely that the influences at each level interact with one another so that ultimately we see society-by-industry interaction effects as a result of isomorphic pressure. Although industries may operate in similar ways regardless of the country in which they exist, it is impossible to completely override the cultural norms that exist within a particular society. Because culture essentially exists within the minds of people and is manifested in behavior, organizational members will adopt norms and standards that are most familiar to them.

Whereas different types of isomorphism may operate at various levels of cultural influence (national or societal versus industrial), specific cultural dimensions may drive organizational isomorphism differentially. For example, in a high power distance societal culture, the most prevalent form of institutional influence may be coercive isomorphism, specifically the dependency aspect of coercive isomorphism. Because societies high in power distance perceive the wielding of influence and domination as appropriate behavior, organizations will fall into either a powerful or a dependent position relative to other specific organizations. However, whether they are dependent or dominant will depend upon the comparator, and the organizational behavior

is likely to vary from organizational relationship to relationship. This inconsistency of behavior patterns does not imply that the culture is unclear or unstable, but rather that the culture includes the idea that organizations engage differentially with other organizations on the basis of their relative dominance.

In societies high in uncertainty avoidance, on the other hand, there may also be a commonality of coercive isomorphism, but more so in response to the values of the greater society. Institutional theory would predict that organizations that are viewed as legitimate by the greater society are going to prosper, whereas organizations that do not adopt and reflect the societal culture's values will not.

Even more complex, there may be a three-way interaction between the cultural dimension, the type of isomorphism, and the level of cultural influence. The previous description of organizations high in power distance provides an example. Although the dependency portion of coercive isomorphism may be operating if power distance is high, the cultural influence may stem from the specific industry within which the organization operates. Thus, although the cultural influence might be expected to be great due to high power distance, the specific cultural effect may be dependent upon what is viewed as legitimate within the industry. For example, the power distance norm may generally be enacted in a given society through the lack of superiors consulting subordinates when making decisions. This approach is likely to be acceptable and workable in industries in which leadership arises through demonstrated expertise at lower levels in the hierarchy (e.g., financial services). However, it may not be workable in a dynamic and technology-driven industry such as telecommunications, in which upper-level managers may have little if any understanding of the technologies they supervise, yielding a situation in which it is imperative for the manager to seek opinions and suggestions from lower-level employees. In such a case, we would expect other manifestations of the power distance norm to emerge in that industry. We thus see that, although institutional theory can provide a framework to interpret and predict the transmission of cultural values and establishment of common organizational behavioral patterns, it is neither a simple process nor a simplistic explanation.

Comparing Institutional Theory to Resource Dependency Theory and Cultural Immersion Theory

Finally, it is important to make two distinctions in the relationship between institutional theory and other approaches outlined thus far. First, some authors suggest that cultural immersion is the process by which institutional theory and isomorphic processes have their effects. However, we have treated institutional theory and cultural immersion theory as separate sources of influence. The reason for this is that we see isomorphic pressures within institutional theory as largely, though not exclusively, operating at a conscious level of awareness. That is, organizational actors make conscious choices based on the various perceived pressures to conform. Cultural immersion, on the other hand, seems to operate below a level of conscious awareness: Schemas and behavioral patterns become chronic not because people choose to make them so, but because they are activated so regularly that over time they become easier to retrieve and harder to ignore, in a process involving neuronal interconnections rather than conscious choice (Bechtel & Abrahamsen, 1996; Smith, 1996; Strauss & Quinn, 1997).

Second, we see dependency theory's emphasis on influence through pressure based on the threat of loss of resources to be largely incorporated into the coercive isomorphism process. Although it is clear that these two theories are not identical and did not develop along similar conceptual paths, research supports both of them, and for the sake of parsimony and concision we, for the most part, view dependency theory (and the more micro resource dependency theory) as special cases subsumed under institutional theory's coercive isomorphism process.

ADDITIONAL MECHANISMS OF INFLUENCE

There are a variety of other potential mechanisms that could be contributing to the transmission of cultural values from the society and industry levels to the organizational level. From a microlevel perspective, Holland's research (cf. Holland, 1996) is well known for demonstrating that different types of work (which largely translates into different industries) attract and are best suited for different types of people (e.g., Oleski & Subich, 1996). This point about person–job fit has been shown to hold true in several societies (e.g., Farh, Leong, & Law, 1998), though questions have been raised about the cross-cultural applicability of Holland's Vocational Preference Inventory measure (e.g., Leong, Austin, Sekaran, & Komarraju, 1998). Thus, if the people within an industry worldwide are similar to each other in certain ways and are different from people in other industries, the behavior of organizations in those industries are likely to reflect the characteristics of the people in them, thus creating an industry-level effect. Similarly, to the extent that industries vary by society, there may be differential attraction and fit across countries, leading to country-by-industry interaction effects.

From a mesolevel perspective, Schneider's (1987; Schneider, Goldstein, & Smith, 1995) Attraction-Selection-Attrition (ASA) model extends Holland's concepts to demonstrate that individuals are differentially attracted to organizations based on their perceived fit with that organization, that organizations differentially select employees based on perceived fit. Accordingly, those employees who find that they do not fit with the values and structures of the organization experience attrition (either voluntary or involuntary). As noted above, the net result of the ASA process is increasing homogeneity within organizations around both personality (Schneider, Smith, Taylor, & Fleenor, 1998) and perceptions of organizational culture (Haudek, 2001). Thus, organizations and individuals are both active in assessing the cultural values congruence of each other, and organizations come over time to have strongly shared perceptions about the environment in which they operate.

From a macrolevel perspective, global and national regulation of work in general and industries in specific serve to limit the behavior of individuals and organizations. For example, national regulations governing workplace safety lead to specific modifications in work structures for organizations regardless of industry, though, of course, industries will be differentially affected by different types of regulations. Nations also regulate specific industries, leading to influence only on organizations within those industries and their suppliers. Global and international regulations also affect organizational behavior, as illustrated by the destruction of European and North American livestock possibly infected with foot and mouth disease.

Thus, there are a variety of theoretical explanatory mechanisms for the transmission of cultural values from societal and industry levels to the level of the organization. Indeed, each may contribute to the process in some form, and some may actually describe similar processes from differing perspectives and points of view. Our goal thus far has been to provide some rationale for expecting such effects, and some reasonable explanations for how these cross-level effects might occur, rather than attempting to competitively rule in favor of one approach at the expense of others.

Concluding Examples and Research Agenda

As a conclusion to this chapter, we turn to several examples that we believe follow from the processes we have described, and which might be addressed more thoroughly in future research. In some cases, we provide evidence in support of our propositions, and in others will rely on the interest and expertise of future researchers for testing.

ISO 9000 and QS 9000

Our examples of possible influence patterns are based on the widespread adoption of the International Organization for Standardization's ISO 9000 certification in the manufacturing industry, particularly in the United States but also in Europe and elsewhere (for information on the standardization sponsored by the International Organization for Standardization see www.iso.ch). This type of rigorous documentation was originally viewed as an avenue for increased awareness of quality issues. At the time ISO 9000 (and QS 9000, referring specifically to the automotive industry) took hold, quality was becoming the primary focus of the American

automobile industry. Institutional theory tells us that the United States automotive industry was affected by the industrial influence of the Japanese automotive industry. More specifically, the automakers in the United States were undergoing a mimetic isomorphism, striving to become more similar to the Japanese automakers that were viewed by the larger society as more successful and therefore more legitimate (society effect coercive isomorphism). Because the U.S. automotive industry supports many suppliers, these suppliers were pressured to emphasize quality as well. To comply with the automotive standard, which the "Big Three" U.S. automobile manufacturers created in 1994, suppliers must have written procedures for every plant operation, appropriate testing of their products for quality assurance, and a printed quality manual, as mandated by QS 9000 (Wrigley, 1997).

Competition, of course, is one of the factors encouraging all auto suppliers to comply with QS 9000. Those who do not comply will not get another chance to compete, according to the automakers. The dependence of the suppliers on the large automotive organizations (industry effect coercive isomorphism) essentially forced them to become more quality-conscious, despite the fact that many organizations have struggled with the implementation of ISO or QS 9000 (Guilhon, Martin, & Weill, 1998). Thus, the ISO 9000 (QS 9000) certification program is thriving because of the institutional belief systems in the United States's manufacturing arena. More specifically, this seems to be because of the complex interactions between isomorphism and the level of cultural influence.

Continuing with ISO 9000 certification as an example, we can consider other perspectives on the mechanisms to explain why organizations in various circumstances would choose to participate in the certification process. In a society high on uncertainty avoidance, for example, organizations may want as much certainty as possible about the credentials of and processes used by their suppliers, leading those supply organizations to adopt ISO 9000 because of the legitimacy such certification provides in the eyes of customers. In a high power distance society, however, it may be more common for organizations to enforce their preferences on suppliers dependent on the organization, and so suppliers may choose

ISO 9000 certification because their primary customer instituted a policy that all suppliers must be ISO 9000 compliant.

Convergence of Expected Outcomes

Finally, one of the primary points that we want to make in this section is that many of the theoretical perspectives presented lead to similar expected outcomes, though perhaps through differing processes. For example, as we noted above, predictions building from dependency theory and institutional theory are inevitably going to be similar, given that they each focus, at least in part, on relationships between organizations in which one organization is dependent upon, and thus influenced by, another. Cultural immersion theory, institutional theory, and social networks theory all lead to the conclusion that organizations with whom other organizations have frequent contact and who are seen as highly effective by other organizations will be emulated by those other organizations. The level of conscious awareness of the process by the individuals involved and the focus on action at the individual or organizational level may differ, but the ultimate outcome expected is quite similar. This is perhaps one reason why there has not been a wealth of research on identifying which specific mechanisms are actually in play—the outcomes are often similar, regardless of the mechanism, and so there is little to be gained by teasing apart the processes by which the outcome occurs. Nonetheless, we believe that it *does* matter whether organizations consciously choose to emulate or acquiesce to other organizations or do so based on decisions of individuals influenced at nonconscious levels, and that it *does* matter whether the decision is made out of a desire for enhanced performance or a fear of losing business. Thus, as Brodbeck and colleagues (Chapter 20, this volume) point out, even though the same behaviors may ultimately occur at the societal level, the reasons behind them may differ. It is important to understand those reasons if we are to truly understand organizational and individual behavior and values. We cannot simply ignore the black box because the outcomes predicted by the different theoretical approaches are likely to be similar.

Having discussed these potential mechanisms by which societal culture influences organizational culture, we conclude with the argument that to truly understand when and how these mechanisms have their effects requires both culturally generalizable and culturally specific perspectives. The culturally generalizable approach is necessary to identify whether one or more of the general principles we have outlined here are in general more commonly active than are others, whereas the culturally specific perspective tells us about the mechanisms active in specific situations. In addition, taking both the "outsider" and "insider" senses leads us to conclude that sometimes important aspects of a culture are not evident to insiders, but those aspects of culture may not be interpretable by outsiders. For these reasons, in GLOBE we have taken both perspectives. This book presents our attempts to uncover general principles and cross-cultural findings. The companion volume (edited by Chhokar, Brodbeck, and House) allows GLOBE country teams for each culture, made up of both cultural insiders and outsiders, to present their interpretations of their target culture and to articulate how a wide variety of factors, including those identified in this chapter, play out in that specific context. We believe that the interplay between outsider and insider makes GLOBE unique in its approach and explanatory power for addressing these important issues.

ENDNOTES

1. Following the GLOBE approach outlined throughout this volume, we consider culture at both the societal and organizational levels to include both common practices and shared values.

2. Of course, the influence that societal culture may exert on industry-level variables of a country only serves to make the situation more complicated (e.g., McClelland, 1961).

REFERENCES

Abernathy, M. A., & Chua, W. F. (1996). A field study of control system "redesign": The impact of institutional processes on strategic choice. *Contemporary Accounting Research, 13,* 569–595.

Bartol, K. M., & Martin, D. C. (1988). Influences on managerial pay allocations: A dependency perspective. *Personnel Psychology, 41,* 361–378.

Bartol, K. M., & Martin, D. C. (1989). Effects of dependence, dependency threats, and pay secrecy on managerial pay allocations. *Journal of Applied Psychology, 74,* 105–113.

Bartol, K. M., & Martin, D. C. (1990). When politics pays: Factors influencing managerial compensation decisions. *Personnel Psychology, 43,* 599–614.

Bechtel, W., & Abrahamsen, A. (1996). *Connectionism and the mind: An introduction to parallel processing in networks.* Cambridge, MA: Blackwell.

Berelson, B., & Steiner, G. (1964). *Human behavior: An inventory of scientific findings.* New York: Harcourt, Brace, and World.

Burns, T., & Stalker, G. M. (1961). *The management of innovation.* London: Tavistock Publications Ltd.

Burt, R. S. (1983). *Toward a structural theory of action.* New York: Academic.

Burt, R. S. (1987). Structural contagion and innovation: Cohesion vs. structural equivalence. *American Journal of Sociology, 92,* 1287–1335.

Cartwright, D. (1965). Influence, leadership, control. In J. G. March (Ed.), *Handbook of organizations* (pp. 1–47). Chicago: Rand McNally.

Dickson, M. W., Aditya, R. N., & Chhokar, J. S. (2000). Definition and interpretation in cross-cultural organizational culture research: Some pointers from the GLOBE research program. In N. Ashkanasy, C. Wilderom, & M. Petersen (Eds.), *Handbook of organizational culture and climate,* (pp. 447–464). Thousand Oaks, CA: Sage.

DiMaggio, P. J., & Powell, W. W. (1983). The iron cage revisited: Institutional isomorphism and collective rationality in organizational fields. *American Sociological Review, 48,* 147–160.

Doreian, P. (1979). *Mathematics and the study of social relations.* London: Weidenfeld & Nicolson.

Earley, P. C., & Erez, M. (1997). Introduction. In P. C. Earley & M. Erez (Eds.), *New perspectives on international industrial/organizational psychology* (pp. 1–10). San Francisco: New Lexington Press.

Emery, F. E., & Trist, E. L. (1965). The causal texture of organizational environments. *Human Relations, 18,* 21–32.

Erez, M., & Earley, P. C. (1993). *Culture, self-identity, and work.* New York: Oxford University Press.

Farh, J., Leong, F. T. L., & Law, K. S. (1998). Cross-cultural validity of Holland's model in Hong Kong. *Journal of Vocational Behavior, 52,* 425–440.

Festinger, L. (1954). A theory of social comparison processes. *Human Relations, 7,* 117–140.

Gagliardi, P. (1986). The creation and change of organizational cultures: A conceptual framework. *Organization Studies, 7,* 117–134.

Giberson, T. R., & Resick, C. (2001, April). Transferring leader values: Using ASA to understand organizational culture creation. In M. W. Dickson (Chair), *The attraction-selection-attrition model: Current research and theory.* Symposium conducted at the meeting of the Society for Industrial/Organizational Psychology, San Diego, CA.

Goodstein, J. D. (1994). Institutional pressures and strategic responsiveness: Employer involvement in work-family issues. *Academy of Management Journal, 37,* 350–382.

Gordon, G. G. (1991). Industry determinants of organizational culture. *Academy of Management Review, 16,* 396–415.

Guilhon, A., Martin, J., & Weill, M. (1998). Quality approaches in small or medium-sized enterprises: Methodology and survey results. *Total Quality Management, 9*(8), 689–701.

Guzzo, R. A., & Dickson, M. W. (1996). Teams in organizations: Recent research on performance and effectiveness. *Annual Review of Psychology, 47,* 307–338.

Guzzo, R. A., & Shea, G. P. (1992). Group performance and intergroup relations in organizations. In M. D. Dunnette & L. M. Hough (Eds.), *Handbook of industrial and organizational psychology* (Vol. 1, pp. 269–313). Palo Alto, CA: Consulting Psychologists Press.

Hambrick, D. C., & Mason, P. A. (1984). Upper echelons: The organization as a reflection of its top managers. *Academy of Management Review, 9,* 193–206.

Hanges, P. J., Lord, R. G., & Dickson, M. W. (2000). An information processing perspective on leadership and culture: A case for connectionist architecture. *Applied Psychology: An International Review, 49,* 133–161.

Harrison, G. L. (1993). Reliance on accounting performance measures in superior evaluative style: The influence of national culture and personality. *Accounting, Organizations and Society, 18*(4), 319–339.

Haudek, G. (2001, April). A culture variance test of the ASA homogeneity hypothesis. In M. W. Dickson (Chair), *The attraction-selection-attrition model: Current research and theory.*

Symposium conducted at the meeting of the Society for Industrial/Organizational Psychology, San Diego, CA.

Hayes, J., & Prakasam, R. (1989). Culture: The efficacy of different modes of consultation. *Leadership and Organization Development Journal, 10,* 24–32.

Hofstede, G. (1980). *Culture's consequences: International differences in work-related values.* Beverly Hills, CA: Sage.

Hofstede, G., Neuijen, B., Ohayv, D. D., & Sanders, G. (1990). Measuring organizational cultures: A qualitative and quantitative study across twenty cases. *Administrative Science Quarterly, 35,* 286–316.

Hofstede, G., & Peterson, M. F. (2000). Culture: National values and organizational practices. In N. Ashkanasy, C. Wilderom, & M. Petersen (Eds.), *Handbook of organizational culture and climate* (pp. 401–415). Thousand Oaks, CA: Sage.

Holland, J. L. (1996). Integrating career theory and practice: The current situation and some potential remedies. In M. L. Savickas & W. B. Walsh (Eds.), *Handbook of career counseling theory and practice* (p. 1–11). Palo Alto, CA: Davies-Black Publishing.

Ibarra, H., & Andrews, S. B. (1993). Power, social influence, and sense making: Effects of network centrality and proximity on employee perceptions. *Administrative Science Quarterly, 38,* 277–303.

Jang, H. (1997). Cultural differences in an interorganizational network: Shared public relations firms among Japanese and American companies. *Public Relations Review, 23*(4), 327–341.

Katz, D., & Kahn, R. L. (1966). *The social psychology of organizations.* New York: John Wiley & Sons.

Klein, K. J., Berman, L. M., & Dickson, M. W. (2000). May I work part-time? An exploration of predicted employer responses to employee requests for part-time work. *Journal of Vocational Behavior, 57,* 85–101.

Lawler, E. E., III. (1986). *High-involvement management: Participative strategies for improving organizational performance.* San Francisco: Jossey-Bass.

Lawrence, P. J., & Lorsch, J. W. (1967). *Organization and environment.* Boston: Harvard Business School, Division of Research.

Lee, M., & Barnett, G. A. (1997). A symbols-and-meaning approach to the organizational cultures of banks in the United States, Japan, and Taiwan. *Communication Research, 24*(4), 394–412.

Leong, F. T. L., Austin, J. T., Sekaran, U., & Komarraju, M. (1998). An evaluation of the cross-cultural validity of Holland's theory: Career choices by workers in India. *Journal of Vocational Behavior, 52,* 441–455.

Levine, J. M., & Moreland, R. L. (1990). Progress in small group research. In M. R. Rosenzweig & L. W. Porter (Eds.), *Annual review of psychology* (Vol. 41, pp. 585–634). Palo Alto: Annual Reviews.

Locke, E. A. (1991). The motivation sequence, the motivation hub, and the motivation core. *Organizational Behavior and Human Decision Processes, 50,* 288–299.

Lord, R. G., Brown, D. J., & Freiberg, S. M. (1999). Understanding the dynamics of leadership: The interaction of self-concepts in the leader/follower relationship. *Organizational Behavior and Human Decision Processes, 78,* 167–203.

Lord, R. G., & Maher, K. J. (1991). *Leadership and information processing: Linking perceptions and performance.* Boston: Unwin Hyman.

McClelland, D. C. (1961). *The achieving society.* Princeton, NJ: Van Nostrand.

Meschi, P., & Roger, A. (1994). Cultural context and social effectiveness in international joint ventures. *Management International Review, 34*(3), 197–215.

Meyer, J. W., & Rowan, B. (1977). Institutional organizations: Formal structure as myth and ceremony. *American Journal of Sociology, 83,* 340–363.

Meyer, J. W., & Rowan, B. (1991). Institutional organizations: Formal structure as myth and ceremony. In W. W. Powell & P. J. DiMaggio (Eds.), *The new institutionalism in organizational analysis* (pp. 41–62). Chicago: The University of Chicago Press.

Miller, D., & Droege, C. (1986). Psychological and traditional determinants of structure. *Administrative Science Quarterly, 31,* 539–560.

Miller, D., Kets de Vries, M. F., & Toulouse, J. (1982). Top executive locus of control and its relationship to strategy-making, structure, and environment. *Academy of Management Journal, 25,* 237–253.

Oleski, D., & Subich, L. M. (1996). Congruence and career change in employed adults. *Journal Of Vocational Behavior, 49,* 221–229.

Ouchi, W. G. (1980). Market, bureaucracies and clans. *Administrative Science Quarterly, 25,* 124–141.

Patient Right to Know Act of 1996, 104th Cong., 2d Sess. (1996) (testimony of Mark E. Rust).

Pfeffer, J. (1981). *Power in organizations.* Marshfield, MA: Pitman.

Pfeffer, J., & Salancik, G. R. (1978). *The external control of organizations: A resource dependence perspective.* New York: Harper & Row.

Reynolds, P. D. (1986). Organizational culture as related to industry, position, and performance: A preliminary report. *Journal of Management Studies, 23*(3), 333–345.

Schein, E. H. (1992). *Organizational culture and leadership* (2nd ed.). San Francisco: Jossey-Bass.

Schneider, B. (1987). The people make the place. *Personnel Psychology, 40,* 437–453.

Schneider, B., Goldstein, H. W., & Smith, D. B. (1995). The ASA framework: An update. *Personnel Psychology, 48,* 747–773.

Schneider, B., Smith, D. B., Taylor, S., & Fleenor, J. (1998). Personality and organizations: A test of the homogeneity of personality hypothesis. *Journal of Applied Psychology, 83,* 462–470.

Schuler, R. S., & Rogovsky, N. (1998). Understanding compensation practice variations across firms: The impact of national culture. *Journal of International Business Studies, 29*(1), 159–177.

Scott, W. R., & Meyer, J. W. (1991). The rise of training programs in firms and agencies: An institutional perspective. In L. L. Cummings & B. M. Staw (Eds.), *Research in organizational behavior* (Vol. 13, pp. 297–326). Greenwich, CT: JAI Press.

Shane, S., Venkataraman, S., & MacMillan, I. (1995). Cultural differences in innovation championing strategies. *Journal of Management, 21*(5), 931–952.

Smith, E. R. (1996). What do connectionism and social psychology offer each other? *Journal of Personality and Social Psychology, 70,* 893–912.

Smith, P. B., & Peterson, M. F. (1988). *Leadership, organizations, and culture: An event management model.* Newbury Park, CA: Sage.

Smith, P. B., Peterson, M. F., & Wang, Z. M. (1996). The manager as mediator of alternative meanings: A pilot study from China, the USA, and U.K. *Journal of International Business Studies, 27*(1), 115–137.

Soeters, J., & Schreuder, H. (1988). The interaction between national and organizational cultures in accounting firms. *Accounting, Organizations and Society, 13,* 75–85.

Strauss, C., & Quinn, N. (1997). *A cognitive theory of cultural meaning.* New York: Cambridge University Press.

Tata, J., & Prasad, S. (1992). Optimum production process, national culture, and organization design. *European Business Review, 92*(1), VII.

Tolbert, P. S., & Zucker, L. G. (1983). Institutional sources of change in the formal structure of organizations: The diffusion of civil service reform, 1880–1935. *Administrative Science Quarterly, 28,* 22–39.

Townsend, R. (1970). *Up the organization: How to stop the corporation from stifling people and strangling profits.* New York: Fawcett Books.

Views of Healthcare Providers, 103rd Cong., 1st Sess. (1993) (testimony of James S. Todd).

Wrigley, A. (1997, December 16). Although only about 12% of tier 1 suppliers to the big three automakers were QS 9000 certified at the beginning of 1997, the vast majority are QS 9000 certified as of the end of 1997. *American Metal Market Metal Technology Quarterly,* 2A.

PART III

RESEARCH METHODOLOGY

PAUL J. HANGES

The chapters in this section focus on the various research methodologies that we use in Project GLOBE to measure our constructs and test our hypotheses. As will be discussed in these chapters, we used both qualitative and quantitative methods to develop the GLOBE scales as well as to assess the nature of the constructs that were measured by these scales. Although we collected original data to test our hypotheses, we also used archival data to help us more completely understand the generalizability of these measured constructs.

House and Hanges in Chapter 6 discuss the research design followed in Project GLOBE. As part of this project, responses from questionnaires were obtained from 17,370 middle managers (i.e., 1,943 Phase 1 respondents and 15,427 Phase 2 respondents) who worked in 951 organizations. These middle managers came from a total of 62 societies. They completed questions asking them about their organization's culture, their society's culture, and their beliefs about the effectiveness of various attributes for outstanding leaders. In addition to questionnaire methodology, the GLOBE project reported in this book used archival data, media analyses, individual and focus group interviews, and unobtrusive measures in an integrative approach to understand and measure cultures and leadership.

The process used to develop these scales is described in Chapter 8 by Hanges and Dickson.

Following the GLOBE conceptual model, we developed *societal* culture items for the nine core GLOBE dimensions and then constructed parallel *organizational* items for these same nine dimensions. Further, for both the organizational and societal culture dimension scales, we wrote items that independently measured two manifestations of culture (i.e., *practices* and *values*). Thus, the GLOBE culture items were written as "quartets." That is, we tried to maintain an isomorphic structure to our culture items so that for each GLOBE dimension we had four scales that differed in terms of the targeted level of analysis (i.e., societal or organizational) and the targeted cultural manifestation (i.e., practices or values).

In generating leadership items, our focus was on developing a comprehensive list of leader attributes and behaviors rather than on simply using a priori leadership scales. Although we did, however, refer to the existing leadership literature when creating our leadership items, we did not limit ourselves to these extant theories or concepts. Items were rated on a seven-point scale that ranged from a low of "This behavior or characteristic greatly inhibits a person from being an outstanding leader" to a high of "This behavior or characteristic contributes greatly to a person being an outstanding leader." The initial stages of this project, which took about 2½ years to complete, focused on the development of these three types of scales (i.e., societal, organizational, and leadership).

Psychometric properties of the GLOBE scales were assessed and documented in Chapter 7. We found that our scales, on average, exceeded professional standards with regard to properties such as dimensionality, interitem reliability, interrater agreement, and aggregatability. This chapter also discusses and computes measures to deal with potential cultural response bias contamination. It also summarizes the initial work that provides evidence for the construct validity of the GLOBE scales. Construct validity provides important information about the nature of the constructs measured by the GLOBE scales as well as possible boundary conditions of these scales.

To further demonstrate construct validity, evidence presented in Chapter 8 supports the generalizability of the GLOBE constructs. Some of this research required obtaining archival data to develop alternative nonquestionnaire-based measures of the GLOBE societal cultural constructs. This work is fully described by Gupta, Sully de Luque, and House in Chapter 9. These authors provide strong evidence for convergent and discriminant validity. Further, Javidan and Hauser in Chapter 7 also used archival data to assess the implications of the GLOBE scale scores.

In Chapter 10, Gupta and Hanges describe the process of grouping the GLOBE societies into a smaller cluster of societies we label a *culture cluster*. These culture clusters are based on an assessment of commonly used indicators such as language, history, religion, and geography. Gupta and Hanges empirically demonstrate the validity of these clusters using the GLOBE societal culture dimensions. These authors also report on a second type of grouping in which the GLOBE societies were sorted in clusters on the basis of similarity in physical climate experienced by people in those societies. Both societal clustering procedures are used and discussed in the chapters appearing in Part IV of this book.

Last, Hanges, Dickson, and Sipe in Chapter 11 explain the rationale underlying the statistical techniques we used to test the GLOBE hypotheses. It is important to reiterate that the GLOBE data is multilevel in structure with possible analysis at four different levels: individual, organizational, industry, and societal. That is, individuals work within organizations, which in turn are found within three industries (financial, food processing, and telecommunication). Industries in turn are found within societal cultures. The GLOBE project, like the Hofstede (1980) study that preceded it, uses societal culture rather than individuals as units of analysis. We also use organizational culture as units of analysis. Thus, unlike the Hofstede study, the research design used in GLOBE allowed exploration of our hypotheses at multiple levels of analysis.

It should be noted that we make no assumptions that relationships among variables at the ecological level (organizations and societies) also are valid at the individual level. Nevertheless, we are fortunate to be able to determine the extent to which relationships hold at multiple levels—Leung and Bond (1989) refer to these as "strong etic relationships." Although we do not dwell on the intracultural analyses, these results provide additional evidence to the validity of our overall findings described at the societal level.

Taken together, the information provided in Chapters 7, 8, 9, and Appendix C provide empirical support for the assertion that the constructs measured by the GLOBE scales generalize beyond the sample from which the data were obtained (i.e., middle manager from one of three industries), the method used to collect these data (i.e., self-report), and the "sets of operations" applied on these data (i.e., aggregation). The findings reflect the broader societal and organizational cultures under study.

REFERENCES

Boring, E. G. (1945). The use of operational definitions in science. *Psychological Review, 52,* 243–245.

Bridgman, P. W. (1927). *The logic of modern physics.* New York: Macmillan.

Hofstede, G. (1980). *Culture's consequences: International differences in work-related values.* London: Sage.

Hofstede, G. (2001). *Culture's consequences: Comparing values, behaviors, institutions and organizations across nations* (2nd ed.). Thousand Oaks, CA: Sage.

Leung, K., & Bond, M. H. (1989). On the empirical identification of dimensions for cross-cultural comparisons. *Journal of Cross-Cultural Psychology, 20,* 133–151.

Messick, S. (1981). Constructs and their vicissitudes in educational and psychological measurement. *Psychological Bulletin, 89,* 575–588.

Robinson, W. S. (1950). Ecological correlations and the behavior of individuals. *American Sociological Review, 15,* 351–357.

Shadish, W. R., Cook, D. T., & Campbell, T. D. (2002). *Experimental and quasi-experimental designs for generalized causal inference.* Boston, MA: Houghton Mifflin.

United Nations Development Program. (1998). *Human development report.* New York: Oxford University Press.

van de Vijver, F., & Leung, K. (1997). *Methods and data analysis for cross-cultural research.* Thousand Oaks, CA: Sage.

World Economic Forum. (1998). *The global competitiveness report.* Geneva, Switzerland: Author.

6

RESEARCH DESIGN

ROBERT J. HOUSE

PAUL J. HANGES

As indicated earlier, GLOBE is a long-term, multiphase, multimethod research program. This chapter describes the research design used in Project GLOBE. The conceptual model driving the GLOBE project was shown in Chapter 2 by House and Javidan. Given its complexity, all the relationships and propositions specified in the model cannot possibly be tested in one study. Thus, GLOBE was designed to assess the model's propositions over a series of research phases. In particular, there are currently three phases of the GLOBE project. The first phase focused on the development and validation of a set of scales that were needed to test the constructs specified in the conceptual model. Items were written to assess 9 dimensions of societal culture, 9 dimensions of organizational culture, and 21 primary leadership scales. The psychometric properties of these scales were assessed in two pilot studies and a complete description of the scale development and validation process is in Chapter 8 by Hanges and Dickson.

The second phase focused on empirically testing some of the propositions specified in the GLOBE conceptual model. More precisely, using the culture and leadership scales developed during Phase 1, we tested the propositions discussed by House and Javidan in Chapter 2 that concerned the relationships between societal and organizational culture on dimensions of culturally endorsed leadership (i.e., Propositions 3, 5, and 6). Further, we tested Propositions 14 and 15, which concerned the relationship among societal culture, economic prosperity, and the human condition (see Chapter 7 by Javidan and Hauser for a description of the process used to develop these measures). The information provided in this book reflects the more quantitatively oriented aspects of these first two phases. A second book (Chokkar, Brodbeck, & House, in press) includes the qualitative oriented aspects of the first two phases of Project GLOBE and describes country-specific information.

The third phase of GLOBE is currently being conducted. This phase tests the portion of the conceptual model concerned with the relationships among actual (observed) leadership behavior of CEOs, culturally endorsed implicit theories of leadership (CLT), leadership acceptance, leadership effectiveness, and organization effectiveness.

In the next section of this chapter, we discuss in detail the sampling rationale and strategy used to collect the Phase 2 GLOBE data. Next, we discuss the questionnaire and archival datasets used to test the GLOBE propositions. Finally, we discuss the implications of the GLOBE research design for handling a number of common problems found in the cross-cultural literature.

SAMPLING DESIGN

We used a stratified sampling strategy in which four different strata (i.e., individuals, organizations, industries, and societies) were included. In particular, the GLOBE Phase 2 sampling strategy required that data from each society met the following criteria: (a) respondents had to be middle managers, (b) multiple respondents had to be obtained from organizations, (c) two or more organizations had to be obtained from two of three types of industries (financial, food processing, and telecommunication), and (d) at least two industries had to be obtained for each society. Half of the respondents from a given organization completed one version of the GLOBE culture and leadership questionnaire (labeled *version Alpha*). The other half completed a second version of the GLOBE culture and leadership questionnaire (labeled *version Beta*). By administering these questionnaires to separate samples of middle managers from the same organization or society, we minimized or even eliminated common source response bias concerning societal and organizational phenomena.

Sampling of Individuals

A total of 17,370 middle managers from 951 organizations in three industries completed the culture and leadership questionnaires in both Phases 1 and 2 of GLOBE. Specifically, 1,943 respondents participated in the Phase 1 pilot studies and 15,427 respondents participated in Phase 2. As reported in Chapter 8 by Hanges and Dickson, the number of respondents by country ranged from 27 to 1,790 with an average per country of 251 respondents. More than 90% of our societies had sample sizes of 75 respondents or greater.[1]

In addition to culture and leadership items, the Phase 2 questionnaires also contained several demographic questions. Although most of the samples included demographic information, some did not. The reasons for this varied. Several of our country co-investigators (CCIs) did not include this demographic information in their version of the questionnaire. The decision was a conscious omission on the part of the CCIs in that they believed that asking demographic information would substantially lessen the response rate, something akin to asking about personal income in questionnaires in the United States. In other cases, respondents did not complete the demographic section of the questionnaire. A complete set of demographic data was collected from more than 8,000 respondents. We can use this subsample to estimate some of the characteristics of the GLOBE respondents. In particular, approximately 74.8% of our respondents were men. Further, all respondents indicated that they had an average full-time work experience of 19.2 years, of which an average of 10.5 years were spent as managers. They indicated that they had worked for their current organizations an average of 12.2 years. Finally, 51.4% indicated that they had worked for a multinational corporation, 44.0% indicated that they belonged to professional associations, and 43.8% indicated that they participate in industrial or trade association activities.

Sampling of Organizations and Industries

The Phase 2 data were obtained from middle managers employed in 951 separate organizations. Only corporations headquartered in the host cultures were included in our sample. Therefore, we deliberately excluded from our sample foreign multinational corporations. Multinational corporations were excluded because their members would be from multiple cultures and their responses would not be indicative of the societal culture in which these organizations functioned. We specified this sample requirement because respondents from these organizations would most likely, with very few exceptions, be almost completely from the societal culture in which these organizations functioned.

Finally, only organizations from one of three industries (food processing, financial services, and telecommunications services) were included in the GLOBE sample. We limited our organizations to these three industries because, after polling the CCIs involved in the initial phases of the project, we determined that these industries were present in all countries of the world. Further, we chose these industries because they systematically differed from one another and these differences have important implications for organizational culture. In particular, the food-processing industry is a relatively stable industry whereas the telecommunications and financial industries may be stable or unstable depending on country and economic conditions. As discussed by Brodbeck, Hanges, Dickson, Gupta, and Dorfman in Chapter 20, a review of both the qualitative and quantitative literature concerning these three industries verified that these industries systematically differed in meaningful ways. Thus, organizations within these industries were expected to use different organizational practices to successfully adapt to their different types of environments.

Sampling of Societal Cultures

A total of 62 societal cultures were included in the GLOBE sample. It should be noted that the original sampling strategy did not include all of the final participating societies. Indeed, the original sampling strategy only specified that data from 20 countries would be collected. These original 20 countries represented a convenience sample in that Robert House knew social scientists living in these countries. Once CCIs in these original countries were identified and after the first pilot study was started, the sampling strategy was modified to include an additional 20 countries. The additional recruitment of countries went very quickly and by the end of the first pilot study, CCIs from a total of 40 countries were actively participating in GLOBE. The addition of the second 20 countries fortuitously allowed us to replicate Pilot Study 1 with an independent sample of countries.

Given the ease of recruiting these 40 countries, we modified the sampling strategy again. Specifically, this modification focused on collecting data from additional countries to ensure that Project GLOBE had data from at least three countries in each of the major geographic regions of the world. A total of 62 societies

were finally included in the GLOBE sample. These societies come from North and South Africa, Asia, Europe (Eastern, Central, and Northern), Latin America, North America, the Middle East, and the Pacific Rim. The final sample size of 62 societies included at least 3 countries from each major region of the world. See Chapter 10 by Gupta and Hanges for a detailed description of these regions.

It should be noted that the reader may want to substitute the term *country* or *nation* rather than the label *society* or *societal culture* that we use in Project GLOBE. We use the term *societal culture* to recognize the complexity of the culture concept and because we occasionally sampled two subcultures from a single nation. It was recognized that national borders may not be an adequate way to demarcate cultural boundaries because many countries have large subcultures. It is impossible to obtain representative samples within each nation of such multicultural nations such as China, India, or the United States. Nonetheless, the samples drawn from such countries need to be comparable with respect to the dominant forces that shape cultures, such as ecological factors, history, language, and religion. The country samples also need to be relatively homogeneous within cultures with regard to their reports of the construct being measured. For multicultural countries, whenever possible we sampled the subculture in which there is the greatest amount of commercial activity. We sampled two subcultures in South Africa, Switzerland, and Germany. These subcultures were indigenous and Caucasian subcultures in South Africa, French and German subcultures in Switzerland, and East and West subcultures in Germany.

Summary

By following our sampling strategy, we created a "nested structure" in the Phase 2 database. In other words, multiple middle managers were sampled from organizations (i.e., "individuals were *nested* within organizations"). Further, only domestic organizations were sampled, thus organizations were *nested* within societies. The consequence of having a nested structure in a database is that it produces covariation among the responses that need to be accounted for in the data analytic procedures. As discussed in Chapter 11 by Hanges, Dickson, and Sipe, we used a number of the statistical techniques, such as hierarchical linear modeling, to test the GLOBE Phase 2 propositions.

GLOBE Measures

To test the GLOBE propositions, we collected original data in a field study using questionnaires as well as accessing archival data to develop additional measures. The archival data served two purposes. First, we used the data as a mechanism for construct validation of the culture dimension scales. Second, we were able to determine the relationships between the culture dimensions and important economic and human condition variables.

The following sections will describe the GLOBE culture and leadership questionnaire that was used to collect original information from the middle managers. After this, we will also briefly describe the archival data sources.

Culture and Leadership Questionnaire

As described in Chapter 8 by Hanges and Dickson, the Phase 2 GLOBE culture and leadership questionnaire contained items that measured organizational culture, societal culture, and culturally endorsed leadership attributes. Item generation for the culture scales was accomplished by Robert House with substantial help from Paul Koopman, Henk Thierry, and Celeste Wilderom of the Netherlands and Phillip Podsakoff of the United States. The initial item pool contained 753 items, of which 382 were leadership items and 371 were societal and organizational culture items.

In generating the leadership items, our focus was on developing a comprehensive list of leader attributes and behaviors rather than on developing a priori leadership scales. The initial pool of leadership items was based on leader behaviors and attributes described in several extant leadership theories. The theories are described in House and Aditya (1997). These leadership items consisted of behavioral and attribute descriptors. Items were rated on a seven-point

scale that ranged from a low of "This behavior or characteristic greatly inhibits a person from being an outstanding leader" (response score = 1) to a high of "This behavior or characteristic contributes greatly to a person being an outstanding leader" (response score = 7).

Organizational and societal culture items were written for the nine core GLOBE dimensions, described above, at both the societal and the organizational levels. We also wrote the items to reflect two culture manifestations: societal practices reported "As Is" and values reported in terms of what "Should Be." These two culture manifestations correspond to Schein's (1992) concepts of artifacts and espoused values as levels of culture. Specifically, Schein argues that both artifacts and espoused values are important elements of culture. Artifacts are the "visible products of the group" (p. 17) and the organizational practices and processes that make these visible products and behavior routine. In contrast, espoused values are "someone's sense of what ought to be as distinct from what is" (p. 19). The GLOBE culture items were written as "quartets" having isomorphic structures across the two levels of analysis (societal and organizational) and across these two culture manifestations (practices and values).

The basic structure of the items comprising quartets is identical, but the frame of reference varied according to the particular cultural manifestation and levels of analysis being assessed. Items were derived from a review of relevant literature and interviews and focus groups held in several countries, as well as from extant organizational and culture theory. Psychometric analyses indicated justification for grouping the items into scales relevant to nine core GLOBE dimensions of societies and organizations.

Versions Alpha and Beta

Two versions of the GLOBE questionnaire were developed. Independent samples of middle managers completed one of two questionnaires. Half of the respondents in each organization completed the *organizational* culture questionnaire (version Alpha), and the other half completed the *societal* culture questionnaire (version Beta). On version Alpha of the questionnaire, there were 75 questions asking about organizational culture. On version Beta of the questionnaire, there were 78 questions asking about societal culture. Both versions of the questionnaire contained the same 112 leadership attributes questions. These two different versions of the questionnaire enabled us to collect *independent* assessments of organizational and societal culture. This process eliminates common source method variance when determining relationships between organizational and societal variables. Further, for the hierarchical linear modeling (HLM) analyses comparing societal culture with leadership, we compared the societal culture scores from the middle manager sample that completed version Beta with the CLT dimension scores from the middle manager sample that completed version Alpha. We found that the culture and leadership scales, on average, exceeded professional standards with regard to properties such as unidimensionality, reliability, and aggregatability. A complete description of the questionnaire development and scale validation process is discussed in Chapter 8 by Hanges and Dickson.

Archival Databases

To further demonstrate construct validity and generalizability of the GLOBE scales, archival data was used to develop alternative, non-questionnaire-based measures of the GLOBE societal cultural constructs. Some of this work is described by Gupta, Sully de Luque, and House in Chapter 9. These authors report strong relationships between scales assessing the same construct but measured using different methods (i.e., convergent validity) versus the relationships found if comparing different traits measured with either the same method or across different methods (i.e., discriminant validity).

In addition, Javidan and Hauser in Chapter 7 also used archival data to assess the implications of the GLOBE scale scores. However, rather than create alternative measures of the same cultural constructs, Javidan and Hauser used this additional archival data to assess additional societal level constructs. More specifically, using data resources such as the *United Nations' Report on Human Development* (United Nations Development Program, 1998) and other economic reports, these authors obtained

measures of a society's economic health; the society's success in science and technology; the overall quality of the living in a society; and societal values surrounding service to community, tolerance of diversity, and the nature of work. Javidan and Hauser develop several hypotheses concerning relationships between these societal level constructs and the GLOBE scales.

Unit of Analysis

The units of analysis for Project GLOBE consisted of cultural-level aggregated responses of middle managers. There are several issues that need to be recognized with regard to this unit of analysis as well as the nested structure in the GLOBE data. First, when developing the research strategy for the GLOBE project, we were quite aware of the general "levels of analysis" problem that bedevils many cross-cultural research projects. Inappropriately assuming that cultural-level characterizations and relationships apply to individuals within these cultures is commonly labeled the "ecological fallacy" error (Robinson, 1950). The "reverse ecological fallacy," described by Hofstede (2001), is said to occur if one compares cultures on measures created for use at the individual level. The point he is making is that cultures are not simply "king-sized individuals" and cannot be understood simply on the basis of the internal logic of individuals. The GLOBE team was well aware of both potential problems of ecological fallacy and reverse ecological fallacy when designing our study. Indeed, as described in Chapter 8, we carefully constructed our scales so that they measured constructs at the targeted level of analysis (organizational or societal, not individual). Also we empirically assessed the extent to which we were successful in developing scales assessing constructs at the desired level.

Further, van de Vijver and Leung (1997) discuss how hierarchical linear modeling (HLM) is an ideal statistical procedure for testing hypotheses with data containing a multilevel structure. As Hanges, Dickson, and Sipe indicate in Chapter 11, HLM can be thought of as analogous to regression analysis except that it inherently takes levels of analysis issues into account. Therefore, HLM can "address the separate and joint effects of variables at different levels on the dependent measure" (p. 126, van de Vijver & Leung, 1997). Hofstede (2001) also suggests that critical insights can be obtained by studying the same database simultaneously at different levels of analysis. To our knowledge, project GLOBE is the first large-scale cross-cultural and cross-organizational project to take advantage of multilevel models and to use HLM in hypothesis testing.

As a second important issue, we should discuss the potential boundary conditions for the GLOBE scales. Consider that the GLOBE societal and organizational cultural *practices* and *values* scale scores originate from self-report responses of individual middle managers. One possible boundary condition is whether the GLOBE scale constructs generalize beyond the constraints of the methods (i.e., self-report methodology) and sample (i.e., middle managers that come from one of three industries) that were used to collect the original GLOBE data.

There are researchers and methodologists that hold a measurement philosophy in which constructs are believed to be completely bounded by the methods by which they are measured. This measurement philosophy, called *operationalism*, was extremely influential during the 1940s and 1950s. Operationalism was first proposed by Bridgman (1927), a Nobel prize-winning physicist, but made famous in the social sciences by B. F. Skinner and others. According to Bridgman, a construct is "nothing more than a set of operations." In other words, concepts such as intelligence, motivation, and even culture are synonymous with the way they are measured. For example, Boring's (1929) definition of intelligence (i.e., "intelligence is what tests test") is a classic illustration of the belief that constructs are bounded by the way they are measured.

In contrast to this measurement philosophy, it is now believed that constructs can extend beyond their measurement methodology (Cook & Campbell, 1979; Messick, 1981; Shadish, Cook, & Campbell, 2002). However, this belief is not taken on faith but must be empirically demonstrated. Thus, the question of whether the GLOBE constructs extend beyond a "set of operations" (e.g., aggregation of individual responses) or the characteristics of the sample (e.g., middle managers from one of three industries studied) is an excellent one. This question clearly requires some attention.

As described in Chapter 8 by Hanges and Dickson, our societal culture scales meaningfully correlate with other researchers' self-report measures in which the data were collected from populations different from middle managers. Further, as discussed by Gupta, Sully de Luque, and House in Chapter 9, the GLOBE societal culture scales showed significant positive relationships with alternative culture measures that were developed using archival sources. This comparison revealed that there are stronger relationships between scales assessing the same construct but measured using different methods (convergent validity) versus the relationships found if comparing different traits measured with either the same method or across different methods (discriminant validity). Further, the results comparing the measures of economic and the human condition variables developed by Javidan and Hauser and the GLOBE societal culture scales, discussed in Chapters 12–19, also provides evidence that the generalizability of the GLOBE constructs extend beyond the boundaries of the methodology used to collect them.

Finally, we have evidence of strong correspondence between the questionnaire and the qualitative data (interviews, focus groups, media analyses) concerning the CLTs. Although not reported in this book, these results are discussed in the forthcoming Chokkar, Brodbeck, and House (in press) GLOBE book.

In addition to this evidence, there is more direct evidence that our aggregated societal culture scale extends beyond just aggregated individual reports of cultural practices and values. This direct evidence comes from the HLM statistical analyses. As reported in Appendix C by Hanges, Sipe, and Godfrey, these additional analyses found that the aggregated culture scales added significant variance in the prediction of the CLTs over and beyond that accounted for by individual level variation. The fact that the aggregated HLM coefficients at the ecological level of analysis provide information beyond individual level results is interpreted as direct evidence that there is a *context effect* (Bliese, 2000) in our data (i.e., the results obtained at the society level are not simply a reflection of the average individual level results).

Taken together, this information provides empirical support for the assertion that the constructs measured by the GLOBE scales generalize beyond the sample from which the data were obtained (middle manager from one of three industries), the method used to collect these data (self-report), and the sets of operations applied on these data (aggregation). The findings reflect the broader societal and organizational cultures under study.

UNIQUE STRENGTHS OF THE GLOBE RESEARCH DESIGN

Project GLOBE differs from previous cross-cultural research in several ways. We use multiple measurement methods to empirically validate the hypothesized relationships in our integrated model. This is most evident in the development of our questionnaire measures assessing culture: (a) based on self-reports of shared *values* of organizational or society members, (b) based on self-reports of current organizational and societal *practices,* and (c) unobtrusive measures as well as the Work Values Survey (Inglehart, Basanez, & Moreno, 1998). In addition, we developed measures of leader attributes that differentiate cultures in terms of perceived effectiveness.

We developed new measures and collected original data to test our hypotheses and answer research questions, rather than relying on measures developed at other times in other places from other samples. Because different people completed the organizational culture, societal culture, and leadership measures used in Phase 2, we were able to eliminate the frequently encountered problem of common source bias. By use of multiple indicators of societal culture, we were able to minimize, if not eliminate, common method variance.

ENDNOTE

1. We made the difficult decision to keep data from societies with less than 75 respondents. We did so particularly because these samples came from relatively underdeveloped and unstudied societies (e.g., Namibia, Zimbabwe).

REFERENCES

Bliese, P. D. (2000). Within-group agreement, non-independence, and reliability: Implications for data aggregation and analysis. In K. J. Klein & S. W. J. Kozlowski (Eds.), *Multilevel theory, research, and methods in organizations: Foundations, extensions, and new directions* (pp. 349–381). San Francisco, CA: Jossey-Bass.

Boring, E. G. (1929). *A history of experimental psychology.* New York: Century.

Bridgman, P. (1927). *The logic of modern physics.* New York: MacMillan.

Chokkar, J., Brodbeck, F., & House, R. J. (Eds.). (in press). *Cultures of the world: A GLOBE anthology.* Thousand Oaks: Sage.

Cook, T. D., & Campbell, D. T. (1979). *Quasi-experimentation: Design and analysis issues for field settings.* Chicago: Rand-McNally.

Hofstede, G. (2001). *Culture's consequences: International differences in work-related values* (2nd ed.). Beverly Hills, CA: Sage.

House, R. J., & Aditya, R. (1997). The social scientific study of leadership: Quo vadis? *Journal of Management, 23*(3), 409–473.

Inglehart, R., Basanez, M., & Moreno, A. (1998). *Human values and beliefs: A cross-cultural sourcebook.* Ann Arbor: University of Michigan.

Messick, S. (1981). Constructs and their vicissitudes in educational and psychological measurement. *Psychological Bulletin, 89,* 575–588.

Robinson, W. S. (1950). Ecological correlations and the behavior of individuals. *American Sociological Review, 15,* 351–357.

Schein, E. (1992). *Organizational culture and leadership* (2nd ed.). San Francisco: Jossey-Bass.

Shadish, W. R., Cook, T. D., & Campbell, D. T. (2002). *Experimental and quasi-experimental designs for generalized causal inference.* Boston, MA: Houghton-Mifflin.

United Nations Development Program. (1998). *Human development report.* New York: Oxford University Press.

van de Vijer, F., & Leung, K. (1997). *Methods and data analysis for cross-cultural research.* London: Sage.

7

THE LINKAGE BETWEEN GLOBE FINDINGS AND OTHER CROSS-CULTURAL INFORMATION

MANSOUR JAVIDAN

MARKUS HAUSER

Throughout mankind's history, geography, ethnicity, and political boundaries have helped create distinctions and differences among different peoples. Over time, societies have evolved into groups of people with distinguishable characteristics that help set them apart from other human communities. It is only in the later part of the 20th century that advances in technology and improvements in telecommunication and transportation have enabled societies to quickly and easily learn about and from others. Marco Polo, the great Italian world traveler, would have marveled at the speed and ease with which his adventures can be replicated today.

One of the consequences of stronger connections among different cultures is increasing interest in two fundamental questions: First, in what way are human communities different or similar? Secondly, why? Psychologists, sociologists, economists, management scholars, as well as many researchers from other disciplines have been attempting to find the answers to these two questions. GLOBE is one such endeavor. Its intent is to explore the cultural values and practices in a wide variety of countries, and to identify their

impact on organizational practices and leadership attributes.

Like many other research programs in the field of cross-cultural studies, GLOBE is focused on specific aspects of societal culture—the values and practices of societal members. Because human societies are complex, multifaceted, and multidimensional entities, the results of cross-cultural studies would benefit from linking with other lines of cross-cultural research. The fundamental goal of cross-cultural research is to find the answers to the two basic questions posited above. Connecting the various streams of research and understanding will help to produce a richer picture of the nature of the differences and similarities among different nations, geographies, and ethnicities.

It is for this reason that an effort has been made to relate the GLOBE findings to other types of cross-national information. The upcoming chapters of this book will show how the different societies in the GLOBE sample compare on values and practices relating to nine important cultural dimensions: Performance orientation, power distance, future orientation, gender egalitarianism, assertiveness, humane orientation, institutional collectivism, in-group collectivism, and uncertainty avoidance. In this chapter, we compare these results with other types of cross-national data to provide a richer description of our findings and enhance our confidence in the results.

In selecting the appropriate types of archival data, two important criteria were adopted: First, the statistics and data had to be relevant and significant to an understanding of cross-cultural issues. There is no shortage of cross-national work, but not all cross-national research is relevant to the fundamental questions asked by GLOBE researchers. Knowing the average height of the population in different societies may be interesting but does not make any contribution to the theoretical framework driving the GLOBE project or to the better understanding of its findings. Secondly, the source of the information and its quality had to be credible. Not every piece of cross-cultural work is of high scholarly quality. To be acceptable for inclusion, the additional data had to be collected by qualified sources and had to have passed strict scholarly screening before appearing in the public domain.

On the basis of the above two criteria, we identified two types of cross-national data. The first type of data is the specific information that is conceptually related to each of GLOBE's cultural dimensions and is found in the extant literature in many academic fields. For example, Chapter 12 by Javidan on Performance Orientation relates the GLOBE findings to McClelland's cross-cultural work on need for achievement. Chapter 17 by Carl, Gupta, and Javidan relates power distance to government corruption, and the chapter on future orientation relates this core GLOBE dimension to saving rates in different countries.

The second type of information, and one that is presented in this chapter, is collected through general comparative cross-national studies. There is an overwhelming amount of public information about countries. To simply use every single piece of data is unfeasible and not particularly useful. To address this issue, it was decided to create a unique database that includes comparative information directly relevant to GLOBE cultural dimensions and is structured in a way that can be related to GLOBE core dimensions. In Chapters 12 to 19, each of the GLOBE cultural dimensions will be related to the archival data presented in this chapter.

The theoretical logic underpinning our selection of specific archival data lies in the role of culture. The perspective guiding GLOBE is that culture is a set of basic and shared practices and values that evolve over time and help human communities find solutions to problems of external adaptation (how to survive) and internal integration (how to stay together) (Schein, 1992). As stated in Chapter 2 by House and Javidan, culture is a set of values relating to what is desirable and undesirable in a community of people, and a set of formal or informal practices to support those values. It reflects the modal collective agreement on meanings and interpretations. Such agreements turn into social influences by producing "a set of compelling behavioural, affective, and attitudinal orientations and values for the members" (House, Wright, & Aditya, 1997, p. 538). These social influences evolve over a long period of time on the basis of the society's history, geography, and religion, and its experiences in successfully or unsuccessfully adapting to external pressures and solving internal problems (Shein, 1992). To the extent that different communities face different types of survival challenges, their collective learnings in the form of culture may be different. This is the process of cultural evolution.

In selecting the relevant types of archival data, we identified the behavioral manifestations and cultural artifacts that reflect a society's attempts to address its challenges of external adaptation and internal integration. We focused on the tools that different societies use to address the issues of external adaptation and internal integration, as well as the outcomes of their efforts.

Technology is a critical tool in any society's arsenal of weapons to deal with its external adaptation challenges. Internal integration challenges are addressed by the way a society deals with three important units: the individual as the most basic unit, the family as the way individuals are socialized into their society, and the government as the guardian of collective values and action.

The outcome of the society's efforts to deal with its external adaptation and internal integration challenges is reflected in the general well being of the society and its members. This is reflected in its economic performance and prosperity as well as the extent of societal and human health and quality of life.

As suggested earlier, culture evolves over time as the community learns the ways to deal with its external adaptation and internal integration challenges. We would thus expect a direct connection between cultural dimensions and the various elements and outcomes of the society's attempts to deal with its challenges. To guide the search for the relevant archival data, a series of hypotheses were generated as to the type of information that theoretically should be correlated with each GLOBE dimension. Each dimension chapter will present the relevant literature and the exact nature of the relationship between a particular type of data and each cultural dimension. The following are the hypotheses that were generated to link cultural practices and external data.

1. Societies that are highly performance oriented (Chapter 12) tend to:
   A. Be more economically prosperous and competitively successful
   B. Have a stronger social support for competitiveness
   C. Enjoy higher levels of human development.

2. Societies that are highly future oriented (Chapter 13) tend to
   A. Be more economically productive
   B. Enjoy higher levels of societal health
   C. Have higher rates of national savings.

3. Societies that are high on gender egalitarianism (Chapter 14) tend to
   A. Be economically more prosperous
   B. Enjoy higher levels of human development
   C. Enjoy higher levels of psychological health.

4. Societies that are high on assertiveness (Chapter 15) tend to
   A. Perform better in terms of global competitiveness
   B. Be more economically prosperous
   C. Exhibit lower levels of psychological health.

5. Societies that are more collectively oriented (Chapter 16) tend to
   A. Enjoy higher levels of societal health
   B. Enjoy higher levels of human health
   C. Enjoy higher levels of human development.

6. Societies that are lower on power distance (Chapter 17) tend to
   A. Be more economically prosperous and competitively successful
   B. Enjoy higher levels of societal health
   C. Enjoy higher levels of human development.

7. Societies that are more humane oriented (Chapter 18) tend to
   A. Have better human conditions
   B. Be more economically prosperous
   C. Enjoy higher levels of satisfaction.

8. Societies that are high on uncertainty avoidance (Chapter 19) tend to
   A. Enjoy healthier state of mind
   B. Enjoy stronger scientific progress
   C. Have governments that support economic activities.

As for the sources of data, the United Nations and the World Bank are highly reputable providers of cross-national data. They produce extensive information on economic performance and demographic features of different countries. The World Economic Forum (WEF) and International Institute for Management Development (IMD) in Switzerland both produce annual reports on competitiveness of different countries. Because the Global Competitiveness report by WEF shares a larger number of countries with GLOBE, we decided to use their findings.

A comprehensive source of information on societal values is the *World Values Survey,* which continues to expand its database of values in different countries. The reports produced by the above sources consist of a very large number of items on each country. A method had to be adopted for selecting a parsimonious number of items that were most relevant to GLOBE cultural dimensions. The solution was to follow the traditional process of data reduction: The different types of data from these sources were first clustered into conceptual groupings. For example, it was hypothesized that the number of telephone lines in use per 1,000 inhabitants, electricity consumption per capita, and paper consumption per 1,000 people are all related to the construct of economic prosperity.

In the second step, factor analysis was conducted to verify the unidimensionality of each conceptual grouping. For example, all the items hypothesized to relate to economic prosperity were factor-analyzed to empirically verify that they are indeed elements of the same construct. In this way, two important benefits were achieved: (a) The huge pool of data was reduced to a small and manageable number of factors and (b) factors were generated that are more powerful and robust indicators of the concepts of interest. For example, a factor like *economic prosperity* is a richer indicator than any one of its individual items such as number of phone lines.

In conducting this process, an important assumption was made: Not every piece of archival data is relevant to every GLOBE dimension. For example, societal health was expected to relate to humane orientation but not necessarily to uncertainty avoidance. Nevertheless, it was decided to produce a standard and consistent dataset to ensure consistency, comparability, and ease of interpretation among the different cultural dimension chapters.

In the following pages, we present the sources of information and explain the factors and their respective items created through the data reduction process. Table 7.1 shows the different sources and types of archival data used in the upcoming chapters of the book. A brief description of each report will follow.

THE HUMAN DEVELOPMENT REPORT

The *Human Development Report* is an annual report that has been produced by the United Nations Development Program (1998) since 1990. The decision to produce such a report was based on the belief that although consumption is a reliable measure of economic health, it is not necessarily a good measure of human development. Economic growth and higher consumption are not an end in themselves but are a means to human development.

Human development was defined as "a process of enlarging people's choices, achieved by expanding human capabilities and functioning" (United Nations Development Program, 1998, p. 14). The three critical elements of human development are long and healthy lives, a reasonable standard of living, and knowledge. Although income is an important driver of well-being, it is not the only one. A measure has been designed called the Human Development Index (HDI) that is a specific measure of a country's achievement in the three areas of human development: longevity (measured by life expectancy), knowledge (measured by educational attainment), and standard of living (measured by adjusted income).

Table 7.1   Sources and Types of Archival Data Used in the Upcoming Chapters

Report	Publisher	Type of Data
The Human Development Report (HDR)	The United Nations Development Program	Human Development Index and other economic data
The Global Competitiveness Report (GCR)	The World Economic Forum	Country competitiveness rankings
The World Competitiveness Yearbook (WCY)	IMD (International Institute for Management Development)	Country competitiveness rankings
The World Development Indicators (WDI)	The World Bank	A wide range of data on countries
The World Values Survey (WVS)	The University of Michigan	Societal values

HDI is a simple average of the life expectancy index, educational attainment index (a combination of adult literacy and elementary school enrollment), and real gross domestic product per capita. The 1998 *Human Development Report* includes data from 174 countries. Table 7.2 shows the GLOBE countries' HDI values and rankings.

Table 7.2   Human Development Index for GLOBE Countries

Country	HDI Value	HDI Rank
Canada	0.980	1
France	0.946	2
United States	0.943	4
Finland	0.942	6
Netherlands	0.941	7
Japan	0.940	8
New Zealand	0.939	9
Sweden	0.936	10
Spain	0.935	11
Austria	0.933	13
United Kingdom	0.932	14
Australia	0.932	15
Switzerland	0.930	16
Ireland	0.930	17
Denmark	0.928	18
Germany	0.925	19
Greece	0.924	20
Italy	0.922	21
Israel	0.913	22
Hong Kong, China	0.909	25
Singapore	0.896	28
Korea, Republic of	0.894	30
Portugal	0.892	33
Costa Rica	0.889	34
Argentina	0.888	36
Slovenia	0.887	37
Czech Republic	0.884	39
Venezuela	0.860	46

Country	HDI Value	HDI Rank
Hungary	0.857	47
Mexico	0.855	49
Poland	0.851	52
Colombia	0.850	53
Kuwait	0.848	54
Qatar	0.840	57
Thailand	0.838	59
Malaysia	0.834	60
Brazil	0.809	62
Turkey	0.782	69
Russian Federation	0.769	72
Ecuador	0.767	73
Iran, Islamic Republic of	0.758	78
South Africa	0.717	89
Kazakhstan	0.695	93
Indonesia	0.679	96
Philippines	0.677	98
Albania	0.656	105
China	0.650	106
Namibia	0.644	107
Georgia, Republic of	0.633	108
Guatemala	0.615	111
Egypt	0.612	112
El Salvador	0.604	114
Bolivia	0.593	116
Morocco	0.557	125
Zimbabwe	0.507	130
India	0.451	139
Nigeria	0.391	142
Zambia	0.378	146

NOTE: HDI = Human Development Index. From *Human Development Report*, United Nations Development Program, 1998.

GLOBAL COMPETITIVENESS RANKINGS BY THE WORLD ECONOMIC FORUM

The first annual ranking of various countries was produced by the World Economic Forum in 1979. The report compares the participating countries in terms of the factors that help improve the prospects of long-term economic prosperity and standards of living. The report is compiled on the basis of two types of data. The quantitative data are measures of a country's technological capacity, infrastructure, and economic performance. The data are accessed from published sources. The survey data are compiled from the World Economic Forum's annual *Executive Opinion Survey*. The 1998 survey collected responses from more than 3,000 executives. The combination of the quantitative and survey data is categorized into eight "factors of competitiveness" (World Economic Forum, 1998, p. 78). The following is a brief description of each factor:

Openness: The degree of openness to foreign trade and investment, financial flows, exchange rate policy, and ease of exporting.

Government: The role of the state in the economy—the burden of government expenditures, marginal tax rates, fiscal deficits, rates of public savings, and the overall competence of the public service.

Finance: The level of competition in financial markets, the perceived stability and solvency of financial institutions, levels of national savings and investment, and credit ratings given by outside observers.

Infrastructure: The quality of roads, railways, ports, and telecommunications. Cost of air transportation and the overall infrastructure investment.

Technology: Extent of computer usage, the spread of new technologies, the level and quality of research and development, and the overall ability of the economy to absorb new technologies.

Management: Overall management quality, marketing, employee training and motivation practices, compensation schemes, and the quality of internal control systems.

Labor: The efficiency and competitiveness of the domestic labor markets, labor costs relative to international norms and labor market efficiency, education and skill levels, and the extent of distortionary labor taxes.

Institutions: The extent of business competition, the quality of legal institutions and practices, the extent of corruption and vulnerability to organized crime.

Once the data collection and standardization are completed, an index is created for each one of the above eight categories. Each country receives a score and a ranking on each category. The overall competitiveness index is calculated as the weighted average of the eight factor indices. Every participating country is then graded and ranked on the overall competitiveness index. The 1998 *Global Competitiveness Report* (World Economic Forum, 1998) covered 53 countries. Table 7.3 shows the competitiveness rankings for GLOBE countries.

Table 7.3 Competitiveness Rankings of GLOBE Countries

Country	1998 WEF Ranking
Argentina	36
Australia	14
Austria	20
Belgium	27
Brazil	46
Canada	5
China Mainland	28
Chile	18
Colombia	47
Czech Republic	35
Denmark	16
Egypt	38
Finland	15
France	22
Germany	24
Greece	44

Country	1998 WEF Ranking
Hong Kong SAR	2
Hungary	43
Iceland	30
India	50
Indonesia	31
Ireland	11
Israel	29
Italy	41
Japan	12
Korea	19
Luxembourg	10
Malaysia	17
Mexico	32
Netherlands	7
New Zealand	13
Norway	9
Peru	37
Philippines	33
Poland	49
Portugal	26
Russia	52
Singapore	1
Slovakia	48
South Africa	42
Spain	25
Sweden	23
Switzerland	8
Taiwan	6
Thailand	21
Turkey	40
United Kingdom	4
United States	3
Ukraine	53
Venezuela	45
Vietnam	39
Zimbabwe	51

NOTE: WEF = World Economic Forum. From *Global Competitiveness Report*, World Economic Forum, 1998.

WORLD DEVELOPMENT INDICATORS

The *World Development Indicators* is an annual publication of the World Bank. It uses data collection efforts of several multilateral organizations and provides a range of indicators on member countries of the United Nations. A brief listing of the type of indicators included in the year 2000 publication is given below:

- *World View:* Size of the economy, gender differences, long-term structural change.
- *People:* Population, labor force structure, unemployment, wages and productivity, education efficiency, health expenditure, reproductive health, and mortality.
- *Environment:* Rural and urban environment and land use, deforestation, energy efficiency, traffic and congestion, and air and water pollution.
- *Economy:* Growth of output and merchandise trade, structure of output, exports, demand and consumption, central government finances, and external debt.
- *States and markets:* Credit, investment, expenditure, stock markets, tax policies, defense expenditures, state-owned enterprises, and science and technology.
- *Global links:* Regional trade blocs, tariff barriers, global financial flows, aid dependency, foreign labor and population, and travel and tourism.

THE WORLD VALUES SURVEY

The *World Values Survey* is a project initiated by Ronald Inglehart at the University of Michigan. It is intended to better understand the values and beliefs of people in different societies and political systems and to provide a sound basis for further research in the field of social science. The database is continually expanded and revised. New countries and questions are periodically added. The latest database consists of representative samples from 71 countries. The number of participants ranges from a low of 304 to a high of 4,147. During the period from 1988–1993, the participants were asked more than 350 questions about a large variety of topics. The 1999 version has 237 items. A brief listing of the topics is provided below:

- *Ecology:* Values toward the environment, nuclear energy, and animal rights.
- *Economy:* Values toward social welfare, third world development, management and ownership of business organizations, income equality, technological development, the state of the country's economy, and individual freedom.
- *Education:* Values toward scientific advances, educational and cultural organizations, and confidence in the educational system.
- *Emotions:* Feelings and emotions, and values toward voluntary work.
- *Family:* Importance of family, relationships with partners and parents, values toward marriage and children, and trust in family.
- *Gender and sexuality:* Views toward women's groups, sexual freedom, women, and homosexuality.
- *Government and politics:* Views toward politics and political parties, political attitudes toward the society and country's goals, and confidence in the various organs of the society.
- *Health:* Views toward the state of health and health voluntary organizations.
- *Individual:* Views toward free choice, individual development, responsibility, and self-confidence.
- *Leisure and friends:* Importance of friends, views toward leisure and sports.
- *Morality:* Views toward abortion, cheating, drugs, and lying.
- *Religion:* Importance of religion, meaning of life, views toward the church, belief in good and evil, and views toward God.
- *Society and nation:* Views toward youth work organizations, tolerance of people who are different, confidence in social security systems, trust in different types of groups and individuals.
- *Work:* Importance of work, types of voluntary work, important aspects of a job, and reasons for working.

The results of this survey are provided in a variety of formats. A valuable and comprehensive source is *Human Values and Beliefs: A Cross-Cultural Sourcebook* (Inglehart, Basanez, & Moreno, 1998). The program's Web site address is http://wvs.isr.umich.edu/

CREATING THE RELEVANT ARCHIVAL DATA FACTORS

As explained earlier in this chapter, a two-stage data reduction process was used to create unidimensional factors consisting of the data reported by the various sources. The process for data reduction was as follows: First, in collaboration with Robert House, we identified the items that in their judgment were relevant to GLOBE dimensions. We then grouped these items into conceptually related clusters. The result was four conceptual factors: *Economic Health, Success in Science and Technology, Human Condition,* and *Societal Attitudes.*

Then, we conducted factor analyses of the items in each of the four conceptual factors. This step produced several nonorthogonal rotated subfactors for each one of the four general factors. With two exceptions, Cronbach's alphas are over 0.70. A brief description of the various factors and subfactors will follow.

Economic Health

The GLOBE measure of a country's economic health is a composite measure using a variety of economic indicators. It includes data related to the country's prosperity, productivity, and competitiveness. It also reflects the extent of government support for economic prosperity and the general societal support for economic competitiveness of the country. Table 7.4 shows the specific items from the various sources that generated each subfactor.

Success in Science and Technology

A country's accomplishments in regard to science and technology are a strong indicator of its present and future success and prosperity. We identified two overall measures to assess the participating countries: 1. Their success in applied science, which refers to the country's performance in terms of commercializing and exploiting technology. 2. A country's ability to invest in basic science. These two measures are related but quite different. Basic science tends to require greater investment and a longer time

(Text continues on page 112)

Table 7.4   Economic Health

Economic Prosperity

(A higher score on this scale means a more prosperous country) (Alpha = .949)

- Telephone lines (Number of main lines in use per 1,000 inhabitants) (WCY)
- Cellular mobile telephone subscribers (Number of subscribers per 1,000 inhabitants) (WCY)
- Electricity consumption per capita, 1995 (HDR)
- Personal computers per 1,000 people (HDR)
- Fax machines per 1,000 people, 1995 (HDR)
- Paper consumption per 1,000 people (HDR)

Economic Productivity

(A higher score on this item means a more productive country)

- Value added per worker in manufacturing (WDI)

Public Sector Support for Economic Prosperity

(A higher score on this scale means the public sector is more supportive) (Alpha = .933)

- Public service (1 = The public service is exposed to political interference, 10 = The public service is not exposed to political Interference) (WCY)
- Bribing and corruption (1 = Bribing and corruption exist in the public sphere, 10 = Bribing and corruption does not exist in the public sphere) (WCY)
- Financial resources (1 = Lack of sufficient financial resources constrains technological development, 10 = Lack of sufficient financial resources does not constrain technological development) (WCY)
- Development and application of technology (1 = Development and application of technology is constrained by the legal environment, 10 = Development and application of technology is not constrained by the legal environment) (WCY)
- Competition laws (1 = Competition laws do not prevent unfair competition in your country, 10 = Competition laws prevent unfair competition in your country) (WCY)
- Economic literacy (1 = Economic literacy is generally low among the population, 10 = Economic literacy is generally high among the population) (WCY)
- Industrial relations (1 = Labor relations are generally hostile, 10 = Labor relations are generally productive) (WCY)

Societal Support for Economic Competitiveness

(A higher score means the society is more supportive) (Alpha = .825)

- Restructuring of the economy (1 = Restructuring the domestic economy is not adapted for long-term competitiveness, 10 = Restructuring the domestic economy is adapted for long-term competitiveness) (WCY)
- Political system (1 = The political system is not well adapted to today's economic challenges, 10 = The political system is well adapted to today's economic challenges) (WCY)
- Labor regulations (1 = Labor regulations [hiring and firing practices, minimum wages, . . .] are too restrictive, 10 = Labor regulations are flexible enough) (WCY)

(Continued)

Table 7.4 (Continued)

- Infrastructure maintenance and development (1 = Infrastructure maintenance and development is not adequately planned and financed, 10 = Infrastructure maintenance and development is adequately planned and financed) (WCY)
- Values of the society (1 = Values of the society [hard work, innovation] do not support competitiveness, 10 = Values of the society support competitiveness) (WCY)

Competitiveness Index (GCR)

(The higher number means a more competitive country)

These rankings are produced based on the competitiveness index calculated for each country.

NOTE: GCR = Global Competitiveness Rankings by World Economic Forum (1998); HDR = *Human Development Report* (United Nations Development Program, 1998); WVS = *World Values Survey,* 1994, WCY = *World Competitiveness Yearbook* (IMD, 1999). WDI = World Development Indicators (World Bank, 2000).

frame. It also needs a strong university-based scientific capability. Applied science, in contrast, tends to be shorter-term oriented, and is heavily dependent on the corporate sector. Table 7.5 shows the specific factors and items used to measure each category.

Table 7.5   Success in Science and Technology

Success in Applied Science

- Patents granted to residents (Average annual number of patents granted to residents) (WCY)
- Change in patents granted to residents (Annual compound percentage change) (WCY)
- Securing patents abroad (Number of patents secured abroad by country residents) (WCY)
- Business expenditure on research and design, in millions of U.S. dollars (WCY)
- Total research and design personnel nationwide, full-time work equivalent (WCY)

Success in Basic Science

(A higher score means more success) (Alpha = .750)

- Company–university cooperation (1 = Technology transfer between companies and universities is insufficient, 10 = Technology transfer between companies and universities is sufficient) (WCY)
- Basic research (1 = Basic research does not enhance long-term economic and technological development, 10 = Basic research enhances long-term economic and technological development) (WCY)
- Science and technology and youth (1 = Science and technology does not arouse the interest of

---

NOTE: GCR = *Global Competitiveness Report* (World Economic Forum, 1998); HDR = *Human Development Report* (United Nations Development Program, 1998); WVS = *World Values Survey,* 1994; WCY = *World Competitiveness Yearbook* (IMD, 1999).

Human Condition

Although economic success is a strong indicator of a country's quality of life, it is not an all-encompassing measure. Human condition is a broad measure of the living conditions in different countries. It provides a detailed look at such issues as justice and security, access to health care, life expectancy, level of satisfaction and happiness with life, psychological health, and satisfaction with work.

We identified six general categories to assess human condition: Societal health is a measure of quality of life, justice, and alcohol and drug abuse. Human health is a measure of access to doctors and nurses. Life expectancy is the average life span of the population. General satisfaction reflects general state happiness and satisfaction. Psychological health relates to people's state of emotions. The Human Development Index was explained earlier. The factors are presented in Table 7.6

Table 7.6 Human Condition

Societal Health

(A higher score means a healthier society) (Alpha = .863)

- Justice (1 = Justice is not fairly administered in society, 10 = Justice is fairly administered in society) (WCY)
- Personal security and private property (1 = Personal security and private property are not adequately protected, 10 = Personal security and private property are adequately protected) (WCY)
- Quality of life (1 = Quality of life in your country is not high, 10 = Quality of life in your country is high) (WCY)
- Alcohol and drug abuse (1 = Alcohol and drugs abuse pose a serious problem at the work place, 10 = Alcohol and drugs abuse do not pose a serious problem at the work place) (WCY)

Human Health

(A higher score reflects healthier individuals) (Alpha = .724)

- Doctors per capita
- Nurses per capita
- Infant survival per 1,000

Life Expectancy

(A higher score on this item means longer life expectancy)
This statistic is provided in the *Human Development Report* (United Nations Development Program, 1998).

General Satisfaction

(A higher score on this scale means greater satisfaction) (WVS) (Alpha = .880)

V10. Taking all things together, would you say you are . . . 1) Very happy, 2) Quite Happy, 3) Not Very happy, 4) Not at all happy, 5) Don't know (percentage who are very happy and quite happy)

(Continued)

Table 7.6 (Continued)

V11. All in all, how would you describe your state of health these days? Would you say it is very good, good, fair, poor, or very poor? (percentage of "very good" or "good")

V65. All things considered, how satisfied are you with your life as a whole these days? (Ten-point scale: 1 = Dissatisfied and 10 = Satisfied); (percentage of "satisfied"—codes 7 to 10.)

V82. During the past few weeks, did you ever feel "Pleased about having accomplished something"? (percentage of "yes")

V165. How satisfied are you with the way the people now in national office are handling the country's affairs? (percentage of "fairly satisfied" and "very satisfied").

V213. How widespread do you think bribe taking and corruption is in this country? (percentage of "a few public officials are engaged in it" and "almost no public officials are engaged in it").

Psychological Health*

(A lower score means a higher level of psychological health) (WVS) (Alpha = .850)

V85. During the past few weeks, did you ever feel "So restless you couldn't sit long in a chair"? (percentage of "yes")

V87. During the past few weeks, did you ever feel . . . "Very lonely or remote from other people"? (percentage of "yes")

V89. During the past few weeks, did you ever feel . . . "Bored"? (percentage of "yes")

V91. During the past few weeks, did you ever feel . . . "Depressed or very unhappy"? (percentage of "yes")

Human Development Index

(A higher score means higher quality of life) (HDR)

This statistic is provided in the *Human Development Report* (United Nations Development Program, 1998).

NOTE: GCR = *Global Competitiveness Report* (World Economic Forum, 1998); HDR = *Human Development Report* (United Nations Development Program, 1998); WVS = *World Values Survey,* 1994; WCY = *World Competitiveness Yearbook* (IMD, 1999)

* The items in this scale are from the 1993 version of WVS. They were not included in the later version of the survey.

Societal Attitudes

Another category distinguishing countries from each other is that of societal attitudes. It reflects attitudes toward family, friends and others, achievement, and political matters among others. We created six major categories: *Family and friends* refers to strength of family ties and respect for family and friends. *Others* refers to attitudes toward other people. *Achievement* reflects the views toward results orientation, initiative, and hard work. *Political ideology* is a set of attitudes toward democracy, involvement, and the role of government. *Religion* consists of views about religious devotion and dogma. *Gender equality* reflects the attitudes toward men and women. Table 7.7 below shows the factors and their individual items.

Table 7.7   Societal Attitudes

FAMILY AND FRIENDS (WVS)

Strength of Family Ties

(A higher score means stronger ties) (Alpha = .82)

V70. One of my main goals in life has been to make my parents proud (percentage of "agree" and "strongly agree")

V4. How important is family in your life? (percentage of "rather important" and "very important")

V13. What are the parents' responsibilities to children? (percentage of "parents' duty is to do their best for their children even at the expense of their own well-being")

Respect for Family and Friends

(A higher score means higher respect) (Alpha = .76)

V12. Regardless of what the qualities and faults of one's parents are, one must always love and respect them (percentage of "agree")

V71. I make a lot of effort to live up to what my friends expect (percentage of "agree" and "strongly agree")

V219. Do you live with your parents? (percentage of "yes")

ACHIEVEMENT (WVS)

Achieving Results

(A higher score means greater importance) (Alpha = .76)

V66. How much freedom of choice and control do you feel you have over the way your life turns out? (1 = not at all, 10 = a great deal) (percentage of selecting "7" to "10")

V67. I always continue to work on a task until I am satisfied with the results (percentage of "agree" and "strongly agree")

V73. Regardless of whether you are actually looking for a job, which would you, personally, place first if you were looking for a job? (percentage of "doing an important job which gives you a feeling of accomplishment")

Initiative

(A higher score means greater importance) (Alpha = .90)

V80. Which aspects of a job are important to you? (percentage of "an opportunity to use initiative")

V83. Which aspects of a job are important to you? (percentage of "a responsible job")

POLITICAL IDEOLOGY (WVS)

Disdain for Democracy

(A higher score means more negative views) (Alpha = .90)

V160. In democracy, the economic system runs badly (percentage of "agree" and "strongly agree")

V161. Democracies are indecisive and have too much squabbling (percentage of "agree" and "strongly agree")

V162. Democracies aren't good at maintaining order (percentage of "agree" and "strongly agree")

(Continued)

Table 7.7 (Continued)

Passiveness

(A higher score means greater passiveness) (Alpha = .80)

V118. Have you ever, or would you ever, sign a petition? (percentage of "would never do")
V119. Have you ever, or would you ever, join in a boycott? (percentage of "would never do")
V120. Have you ever, or would you ever, attend lawful demonstrations? (percentage of "would never do")
V121. Have you ever, or would you ever, join unofficial strikes? (percentage of "would never do")

Lack of Voice

(A higher score means less voice) (Alpha = .85)

V104. What should be the most important goal of the country? (reverse of percentage of "seeing that people have a say in how things are done in their jobs and communities")
V106. What should be the most important goal of the country? (reverse of percentage of "giving people more say in important government decisions" and "protecting freedom of speech")

Dislike for Democracy

(A higher score means more negative views) (Alpha = .95)

V157. How good is having a democratic system? (percentage of "bad" and "very bad")
V163. Democracy may have its problems but it's better than any other form of government (percentage of "disagree" and "strongly disagree").

Role of Government

(A higher score means a more active role for the government) (Alpha = .72)

V126. 1 = Private ownership of business and industry should be increased, 10 = Government ownership of business and industry should be increased (percentage of selecting "7" to "10")
V127. 1 = Government should take more responsibility to ensure that everyone is provided for, 10 = People should take more responsibility to take care of themselves (percentage of selecting "1" to "4").

Stability

(A higher score means more emphasis on stability) (Alpha = .77)

V106. Which one is most important? (percentage of "maintaining order in the nation")
V108. Which one is most important? (percentage of "a stable economy")

RELIGION (WVS)

Religious Devotion

(A higher score means stronger devotion) (Alpha = .93)

V9. How important is religion in your life? (percentage of "rather important" and "very important")
V178. Which statement is close to your point of view? (percentage of "There are absolutely clear guidelines about good and evil. These always apply to everyone, whatever the circumstances")
V181. Apart from weddings, funerals, and christenings, about how often do you attend religious services these days? (percentage of "only on special holy days" to "more than once a week")

V182. Independently of whether you go to church or not, would you say you are (percentage of "a religious person")

V190. How important is God in your life? 1 = not at all important. 10 = very important (percentage of "7" to "10").

Religious Dogma

(A higher score means stronger dogma) (Alpha = .96)

V185. Do you believe people have a soul? (percentage of "yes")
V186. Do you believe the Devil exists? (percentage of "yes")
V187. Do you believe in hell? (percentage of "yes")
V188. Do you believe in heaven? (percentage of "yes")

GENDER EQUALITY (WVS)

(A higher score means higher equality) (Alpha = .91)

V19. What should children be encouraged to learn at home? (percentage of "tolerance and respect for others")
V61. When jobs are scarce, men should have more right to a job than women (percentage of "disagree")
V93. Do you think that a woman has to have children to be fulfilled? (percentage of "not necessary")
V101. On the whole, men make better political leaders than women do (percentage of "disagree" and "strongly disagree")
V103. A university education is more important for a boy than for a girl (percentage of "disagree" and "strongly disagree")

NOTE: GCR = *Global Competitiveness Report* (World Economic Forum, 1998); HDR = *Human Development Report* (United Nations Development Program, 1998); WVS = *World Values Survey,* 1999.

THE IMPACT OF NATIONAL WEALTH

In the second edition of his book *Culture's Consequences,* Hofstede (2001) consistently tested for the moderating effect of wealth when computing correlations between his cultural dimensions and many types of secondary data. His rationale was that economic wealth can confound such relationships. For example, he argued that increasing affluence causes higher levels of individualism in society. So, in correlating cultural dimensions with any other type of data, his concern was that a spurious correlation may be found caused by the impact of wealth rather than culture, or that the relationship may be significant at some income levels but insignificant at other levels.

In his review of Hofstede's book, Smith (2002) cautioned against such an approach, arguing that national wealth could be an integral part of a country's culture. It is not necessarily an extraneous variable that can be easily taken out. Moderating for wealth may deprive us of a better understanding of the complex dynamics of culture formation and maintenance.

The issue raised by these authors is important and they both make an important case. GLOBE is sympathetic to both points and takes a rigorous approach to the issue. In subsequent chapters, we will show correlations between each cultural dimension and many of the archival variables discussed earlier here. GLOBE takes the view that gross national product per capita (GNP/capita) is a reflection of a society's natural resources as well as its effectiveness in managing its external adaptation and internal integration challenges (Schein, 1992). As a result, it is plausible that it would be correlated with many aspects of its culture. But the relationship is not just a simple unidirectional one; although wealth can be accumulated as a result of a society's success, it can also help facilitate its further success. National wealth has a reinforcing effect that can help facilitate the relationship between culture and other national features. A performance-oriented society can prosper and as a result can better educate its people who will contribute more to their societies. The relationships among wealth, national culture,

Table 7.8 Correlations Between Cultural Dimensions and GNP per Capita (1998)

GLOBE Cultural Dimension		GNP per Capita
Uncertainty Avoidance	Values	−.82**
	Practices	.66**
Future Orientation	Values	−.65**
	Practices	.54**
Institutional Collectivism	Values	−.37**
	Practices	.13
Humane Orientation	Values	.28*
	Practices	−.36**
Performance Orientation	Values	−.17
	Practices	.32**
In-Group Collectivism	Values	−.38**
	Practices	−.76**
Power Distance	Values	−.12
	Practices	−.39**
Assertiveness	Values	−.12
	Practices	−.02
Gender Egalitarianism	Values	.44**
	Practices	.00

* Correlation is significant at the 0.05 level (2-tailed).
** Correlation is significant at the 0.01 level (2-tailed).
$N = 61$

and other archival variables are so intertwined that they cannot be easily isolated, and cause and effect relationships, although intuitively appealing, are hard to verify empirically. Therefore, we decided to follow a three-step process:

1. We calculated the correlations between all cultural dimensions and GNP/capita to identify the cultural dimensions that are significantly correlated. The results are shown in Table 7.8. Six out of nine values and six out of nine practices are significantly correlated with GNP/capita. This is strong evidence for our premise that GNP/capita is an integral part of a society's culture.

2. We calculated the correlations between all archival variables and GNP/capita to identify the archival variables that are significantly correlated. The results are shown in Table 7.9. Sixteen out of 21 variables are significantly correlated with GNP/capita, suggesting that the archival variables of interest to us are generally relevant and consequential because they are related to national wealth.

3. From the above two steps, it is clear that wealth, national culture, and archival variables are in many ways interconnected. It is tempting at this stage to calculate the correlations between cultural dimensions and archival variables while partialling out GNP/capita. The problem with this approach is that the results are not symmetric. If the correlation is still significant after controlling for GNP/capita, we can

Table 7.9   Correlations Between GNP per Capita and Archival Variables

Archival Variables	GNP per capita (1998)
Economic prosperity	.90** n = 58
Economic productivity	.15 n = 41
Public sector support for economic prosperity	.75** n = 41
Societal support for economic competitiveness	.29 n = 41
Competitiveness index (WEF, 1998)	.69** n = 42
Success in science and technology	.33* n = 41
Success in basic science	.63** n = 41
General satisfaction	.68** n = 39
Strength of family ties	−.49** n = 39
Respect for family and friends	−.67** n = 39
Achieving results	.30 n = 39
Initiative	.06 n = 39
Disdain for democracy	−.41* n = 26
Passiveness	−.39* n = 38
Lack of voice	−.72** n = 39
Dislike for democracy	−.33 n = 27
Role of government	−.79** n = 39
Stability	−.52** n = 39

(Continued)

Table 7.9 (Continued)

Archival Variables	GNP per capita (1998)
Religious devotion	−.43** n = 39
Religious dogma	−.44** n = 37
Gender equality	.62** n = 39

* Correlation is significant at the 0.05 level (2-tailed).

** Correlation is significant at the 0.01 level (2-tailed).

interpret it to mean that the two are related even if we hold GNP/capita constant. But if the relationship is not significant, it does not necessarily mean that the relationship is spurious. Due to the intercorrelations between the variables, partialling out GNP/capita does not control just for wealth. Given that wealth is a part and parcel of a country's culture, partialling it out takes many other aspects of the culture out of the relationship and we do not really know how to interpret the results. As a possible solution, we conducted a regression analysis with the archival data as the dependent variable. Three independent variables were entered in three separate steps: The specific cultural dimension, GNP/capita, and their interaction. The purpose of this procedure is to verify Hofstede's (2001) approach, in which he compared the correlation coefficients between his cultural dimensions and his variables of interest in wealthy countries and in poor countries. Such an approach is based on the assumption that GNP/capita has an interaction effect with the cultural dimension. Our results showed that in more than 300 such regressions, only nine cases of significant interaction effects were observed, leading to the conclusion that they are random occurrences. We therefore, have no evidence for a significant moderating effect for GNP/capita.

To conclude, at the start of this chapter, we suggested that the fundamental purpose of cross-cultural research is to find the answers to two questions: How are human communities different or similar, and why? In Chapters 12 to

19 of this book, we address these two questions in terms of a variety of cultural dimensions. Each chapter focuses on one cultural dimension such as performance orientation. To answer the first question, the chapter will present the GLOBE project results related to the particular cultural dimension. To answer the second question, the chapter provides a detailed analysis of the relationship between GLOBE findings and the other types of cross-cultural findings described in this chapter.

It is important to note that the analyses reported in the forthcoming chapters are cross-sectional and correlational and can only postulate possible relationships, falling short of reaching causal conclusions. We should also be cognizant of the potential deficiencies in correlating different types of cross-national data and their implications for interpreting the results. The data refer to complex concepts and are collected in different time frames using different methodologies. Despite the potential shortcoming, the reported analyses will provide a richer and fuller understanding of the similarities and differences among cultures and their possible correlates.

REFERENCES

Hofstede, G. (2001). *Culture's consequences* (2nd ed.). Thousand Oaks, CA: Sage.

House, R. J., Wright, N. S., & Aditya, R. N. (1997). Cross-cultural research on organizational leadership: A critical analysis and a proposed theory. In P. C. Earley & M. Erez (Eds.), *New perspectives in international industrial organizational psychology* (pp. 535–625). San Francisco: New Lexington.

International Institute for Management Development. (1999). *The world competitiveness yearbook.* Lausanne, Switzerland: Author.

Inglehart, R., Basanez, M., & Moreno, A. (1998). *Human values and beliefs: A cross-cultural sourcebook.* Ann Arbor: University of Michigan Press.

Schein, E. H. (1992). *Organizational culture and leadership* (2nd ed.). San Francisco: Jossey-Bass.

Smith, P. B. (2002, January). Culture's consequences: Something old and something new. *Human Relations, 55*(1), 119–137.

The World Bank. (2000) *World development indicators.* Washington DC: Author.

World Economic Forum. (1979). *Report on international competitiveness.* Geneva, Switzerland: Author.

World Economic Forum. (1998). *The global competitiveness report.* Geneva, Switzerland: Author.

United Nations Development Program. (1998). *Human development report.* New York: Oxford University Press.

8

THE DEVELOPMENT AND VALIDATION OF THE GLOBE CULTURE AND LEADERSHIP SCALES

PAUL J. HANGES

MARCUS W. DICKSON

As discussed previously, the GLOBE Project was designed to explore the relationship among organizational and societal culture, and the content of culturally endorsed implicit leadership theory (CLT) belief systems. Several hypotheses outlined in earlier chapters of this book specified how certain aspects of culture might affect the content of these belief systems. In the present chapter, we describe the procedure followed to develop the set of self-report scales that were used to test these hypotheses. These scales were developed by following a multistage process in which a more qualitative evaluation of the items (e.g., item review, Q-sorting, translation, and back translation) was followed by a more quantitative assessment of scales properties (e.g., multilevel confirmatory factor analysis, correlational analysis, etc.). Although somewhat dry, this chapter describes the evolution in our thinking about organizational culture, societal culture,

and CLT leadership dimensions. As we collected preliminary data and tested our theories, we refined and sharpened our construct definitions, and consequently modified our scales. To aid the reader, we have attempted to balance the need for detail with the need for clarity. Those wishing greater detail about the societal culture and leadership scales are referred to Hanges, House, Dickson, Dorfman, and GLOBE (2003). Further analysis of the organizational culture scales can be found in Dickson (1997).

PHASE 1: QUESTIONNAIRE SCALE DEVELOPMENT

The first step in developing the GLOBE scales was choosing the general approach that we would follow when developing these scales. At the broadest level, there are two general approaches: the *empirical* (criterion-referenced) approach and the

AUTHORS' NOTE: The work reported in this chapter was partially funded by the National Science Foundation under Grant No. 9711143.

theory-driven (construct-oriented) approach (Nunnally & Bernstein, 1994). The critical difference between these approaches is the time when the construct measured by a scale is specified: either before (i.e., theory-driven approach) or after (i.e., empirical approach) the scale is developed.

More specifically, the empirical approach relies on the statistical analysis of participants' responses to a wide variety of items. Statistical analyses such as exploratory factor analyses or correlational analyses might be performed to identify items that highly covary, or regression analyses might be performed to identify items that uniquely contribute to the prediction of some dependent variable. Typically the items used in these empirically derived scales were originally written for purposes other than the one at hand. After the items comprising a scale are identified, the researcher tries to determine the construct underlying the scale. Examples of empirically derived scales can be found in the personnel selection literature (e.g., biodata instruments) (Cascio, 1998), the personality literature (e.g., the Minnesota Multi-Phasic Personality Inventory) (Nunnally & Bernstein, 1994), and even the cross-cultural literature (e.g., Hofstede's culture scales) (Hofstede, 2001).

Although empirically developed scales usually successfully correlate with other variables and this approach can potentially identify new constructs (Nunnally & Bernstein, 1994), several problems with scales developed in this manner have been noted. For example, it is very difficult to determine the actual construct measured by empirically developed scales. Indeed, it is quite possible that multiple unintended constructs are also measured by such scales. The consequence of this construct ambiguity is that it is very difficult to interpret the nomological network (i.e., pattern of empirical relationships) obtained with the scale. Indeed, obtained relationships might be due to the construct of interest or might be due to the unintended constructs also measured by the scale (Messick, 1981). Another problem is that because the items were not originally written to measure the construct of interest, it is possible that certain biases in the items cannot be directly corrected. Indeed, these biases might result in a mislabeling of the underlying construct or could potentially confound the results of any study that

uses the scale. Although statistical corrections might minimize the impact of these biases, it cannot eliminate all of these biases.[1] Another problem with empirically derived scales is that the properties of the scales can be unstable if the dataset used to generate the scale is small (Nunnally & Bernstein, 1994). Indeed, a substantial sample size may be required to develop empirically derived scales with stable properties. Finally, empirically derived scales have an increased probability of lacking desirable psychometric properties (e.g., they might be multidimensional and exhibit poor internal reliability). Indeed, despite their correlations with other variables, many of the critiques against Hofstede culture scales are a direct outcome of the empirical approach used to create them (cf. Roberts & Boyacigiller, 1984; Smith, 2002).

The other approach to scale development is the theory-driven (construct-oriented) approach. With this approach, a target construct is specified before any items are written. Depending upon the care taken by the scale developer, not only is the nature of the construct specified but its boundary conditions, target population, and any potential biases (e.g., cultural response bias) that could affect the scale are also specified (Nunnally & Bernstein, 1994). Statistical analyses (e.g., confirmatory factor analysis, reliability and generalizability analysis) are then performed to confirm the a priori structure of the scale. Scales that are constructed following this approach tend to exhibit acceptable levels of face-validity and, more importantly, have desirable psychometric properties (e.g., unidimensionality). The consequence of constructing scales in this manner is the relatively unambiguous interpretation of any empirical relations obtained with this scale as well as the possibility of new insights by allowing more complex statistical analyses (e.g., item response theory) to be conducted.

Although several examples of theory-driven scales can be identified, a good example from the cross-cultural literature is Shalom Schwartz' development of his values survey. Before developing his survey, Schwartz reviewed the empirical, philosophical, and religious literature from various cultures and identified several values that he believed to be universally relevant (Smith & Schwartz, 1997). These values were then grouped into 10 categories and he developed a theory of the interrelations among these value categories (Schwartz, 1992, 1994). On the basis of his theory as well as prior work by other researchers (e.g., Rokeach, 1973), Schwartz developed his survey. Consistent with the theory-driven approach to scale development, Schwartz specified several potential biases that could limit the value of his scale (e.g., having items only assessing Western societies values; cultural response bias) and took steps to minimize the influence of these factors (Smith & Schwartz, 1997). The advantages provided by Schwartz' values survey to the cross-cultural literature is a clear example of the utility of developing scales according to the theory-driven approach. Thus, it was this approach that we attempted to follow when developing the GLOBE scales.

Construct Specification

As indicated previously, we first specified the general nature of the constructs that we wanted to measure before writing any items or developing any of the GLOBE scales. This critical step, which unfortunately is frequently overlooked, determines how the items should be written as well as the kinds of statistical analyses that need to be performed to assess the adequacy of the scales (Kozlowski & Klein, 2000). We propose that organizational culture, societal culture, and culturally endorsed implicit leadership theory are what multilevel researchers call *convergent–emergent constructs* (Kozlowski & Klein, 2000). These constructs are *convergent* because the responses from people within organizations or societies are believed to center about a single value usually represented by scale means. They are called *emergent* because even though the origin of these constructs are a function of the cognition, affect, and personality of the survey respondents, the properties of these constructs are actually manifested at the aggregate- or group- (e.g., organization or society) level of analysis.

Thus, by conceptualizing the GLOBE constructs as convergent–emergent, we are implicitly hypothesizing that respondents within organizations or societies will exhibit some similarity in their perceptions of organizational or societal culture as well as their perceptions of the CLTs.

Some assessment of the actual convergence among people within an organization or a society is clearly required to demonstrate that the GLOBE scales were designed appropriately. Further, the convergent–emergent conceptualization of the GLOBE constructs suggests that the GLOBE scales need to be designed so that they operate at an appropriate level of analysis. In other words, the psychometric properties of GLOBE scales should emerge at either the organizational or societal level of analysis (depending on the desired focus of the scale). Therefore, some empirical verification that the GLOBE scales are operating at their targeted level of analysis is also required. It should be noted that the GLOBE scales were designed to assess variation at a particular level of analysis and so it should not be surprising if different psychometric properties are found if researchers use these scales at different levels than the one they were designed for. Clearly, because the GLOBE scales were designed to assess convergent–emergent constructs, they were not designed to assess individual variation within organizations or societies and should not be used for this purpose. We test these assumptions and hypotheses as part of our scale development and validation process.

Dimension Specification and Item Generation

Now that the general nature of the GLOBE constructs have been identified (i.e., convergent–emergent constructs), the next task was to specify the exact cultural and leadership dimensions that would be used to differentiate organizations and societies and to write items that assessed these dimensions. As indicated by House and Javidan in Chapter 2 of this book, we originally identified seven cultural dimensions that might influence the type of behaviors and attributes desired of leadership in a society. These dimensions were: (a) Uncertainty Avoidance; (b) Power Distance; (c) Individualism and Collectivism; (d) Gender Egalitarianism; (e) Future Orientation; (f) Performance Orientation; and (g) Humane Orientation.

A total of 371 culture items were originally written. Most of these items were derived through interviews and focus groups held in several countries. To ensure that the content domain of the

Table 8.1   Example of Culture Item Quartets Across Organizational and Societal Levels and the Two
Culture Manifestations

Organizational Cultural *Practices* (As Is)

The pay and bonus system in this organization *is* designed to maximize:

Individual Interests						Collective Interests
1	2	3	4	5	6	7

Organizational Cultural *Values* (Should Be)

In this organization, the pay and bonus system *should be* designed to maximize:

Individual Interests						Collective Interests
1	2	3	4	5	6	7

Societal Cultural *Practices* (As Is)

The economic system in this society *is* designed to maximize:

Individual Interests						Collective Interests
1	2	3	4	5	6	7

Societal Cultural *Values* (Should Be)

I believe that the economic system in this society *should be* designed to maximize:

Individual Interests						Collective Interests
1	2	3	4	5	6	7

---

culture construct was adequately covered, we categorized the GLOBE culture items into those assessing more tangible attributes of culture (e.g., current policies and practices) and those assessing more intangible attributes (e.g., cultural norms and values). This categorization helped identify problems in having too many or too few items assessing tangible or intangible aspects of culture in our organizational and societal culture scales. Indeed, we wrote new items so that our culture scales followed a "parallel quartet" structure. That is, we wrote four versions of each culture item so that both the tangible (i.e., cultural practices) and intangible (i.e., cultural values) aspects of culture were assessed across the two levels of analysis considered in the GLOBE project (i.e., organizational culture and societal culture). The items assessing the cultural practices of an organization or society focused respondents' attention on how things *are* (referred to as "As Is" items), whereas the items

assessing the cultural values of an organization or society focused respondents' attention on how things *should be* (referred to as "Should Be" items). The importance of specifying the appropriate frame of reference for questionnaire items has been emphasized in both the levels of analysis (e.g., Klein, Conn, Smith, & Sorra, 2001; Klein, Dansereau, & Hall, 1994; Payne, Fineman, & Wall, 1976; Schneider, 1990; Schriesheim, 1979; Yammarino, 1990) and the cross-cultural (e.g., Dickson, Aditya, & Chhokar, 2000; Hanges, Lord, & Dickson, 2000) literature. Thus, the basic structure of our items comprising parallel quartets was identical, but the frame of reference was varied according to the particular cultural manifestation and level of analysis being assessed. Table 8.1 contains an example of a quartet of parallel culture items, showing essentially the same question in four forms: Organization Cultural Practices (As Is); Organization Cultural Values (Should Be);

Societal Cultural Practices (As Is); and Societal Cultural Values (Should Be).

With respect to the leadership items, 382 items were originally written. Consistent with the way implicit leadership theory of individuals has been measured in previous research (e.g., Foti & Lord, 1987; Lord, Foti, & DeVader, 1984; Lord & Maher, 1991a, 1991b), the GLOBE leadership items consisted of behavioral and trait descriptors (e.g., autocratic, benevolent, nurturing, and visionary) along with a brief definition of these descriptors. The items were written to reflect a variety of traits, skills, abilities, and personality characteristics potentially relevant to leadership emergence and effectiveness. In generating the items, our focus was on developing a comprehensive list of leader attributes and behaviors rather than on solely using a priori leadership scales. However, the initial pool of leadership items was partially based on several extant leadership theories, and thus included leader behaviors and attributes described in established leadership theories. Items were rated on a seven-point scale that ranged from a low of "This behavior or characteristic greatly inhibits a person from being an outstanding leader" to a high of "This behavior or characteristic contributes greatly to a person being an outstanding leader." The definition of leadership provided to our respondents along with several examples of leadership items and the response scale used for these items are shown in Tables 8.1 and 8.2.[2]

Item Review Process

The societal and organizational culture items were screened for appropriateness by use of three procedures: Q-sorting, item evaluation, and translation and back translation. Leadership items were screened by item evaluation and conceptual equivalence of the back translation. The Q-sorting procedure consisted of sorting the culture items into theoretical categories represented by the a priori dimensions of culture described above, first by seven PhD students in the Department of Psychology at the University of Maryland and subsequently by country co-investigators (CCIs) representing 38 countries. The sorters were not told the particular cultural dimension that each item was intended to measure. Items that were categorized by 80% of the

sorters into the categories for which they were theoretically intended were retained for further analysis. There were no dimensions of societal or organizational culture for which a majority of items failed to meet this criterion. Thus, a sufficient number of items were retained for the measurement of each dimension.

In addition to this sorting task, CCIs provided Item Evaluation Reports in which they noted any items containing words or phrases that were ambiguous or could not be adequately translated in the target country's native language. CCIs also identified questions that might be culturally inappropriate. Most of the items that were problematic were dropped from further consideration. In some cases, we were able to rewrite items to eliminate potential problems but retain the intent and dimensionality of the original item.

Finally, the cross-cultural literature indicates that a systematic bias may occur if respondents complete a survey that is not in their native language (Brislin, 1986). To prevent this, the questionnaires were translated into several languages. CCIs were responsible for having the survey translated from English into their native language. This was done by the CCI, by some other person fluent in both languages, or most often by a professional translator. The translation was then independently translated again, from the native language of the culture back to English. This back-translation was then sent to the authors of this chapter, who compared the original English version of the survey with the back-translation to verify the accuracy of the translation. A pragmatic approach (Brislin, 1976, 1986) was taken in evaluating the adequacy of the back-translations. In other words, we were more concerned with the accuracy with which the *concepts* were translated rather than the exact words being used in the translations. When discrepancies between the original survey and the back-translations were encountered, the CCI was notified and the discrepancy was discussed. If necessary, revisions in the translation were made.

As a result of editing or deleting items as a result of the Q-sorting, item evaluation, and translation and back-translation processes, the item pools were reduced by approximately 50%. One benefit of subjecting our items to this multistep evaluation process is that the items that

Table 8.2   Sample CLT Questionnaire Items and Response Alternatives

GLOBE's Definition of Leadership	*Ability to influence, motivate, and enable others to contribute to success of their organization.*
Sample CLT Items	*Sensitive:* Aware of slight changes in moods of others. *Motivator:* Mobilizes, activates followers. *Evasive:* Refrains from making negative comments to maintain good relationships and save face. *Diplomatic:* Skilled at interpersonal relations, tactful. *Self-interested:* Pursues own best interests.
Response Alternatives	1 = This behavior or characteristic *greatly inhibits* a person from being an outstanding leader. 2 = This behavior or characteristic *somewhat inhibits* a person from being an outstanding leader. 3 = This behavior or characteristic *slightly inhibits* a person from being an outstanding leader. 4 = This behavior or characteristic *has no impact* on whether a person is an outstanding leader. 5 = This behavior or characteristic *contributes slightly* to a person being an outstanding leader. 6 = This behavior or characteristic *contributes somewhat* to a person being an outstanding leader. 7 = This behavior or characteristic *contributes greatly* to a person being an outstanding leader.

survived are very likely to exhibit measurement equivalence across countries. In other words, the ability of sorters who came from different world cultures to agree on the allocation of items indicates that these sorters had similar interpretations of the items as well as the theoretical dimensions underlying the items. Further, the fact that the remaining items also survived an explicit evaluation for cultural inconsistencies and the translation and back-translation process strongly suggests commonalty of meaning of the questionnaire items and scales across cultures.

Pilot Studies

Two empirical pilot studies were conducted to assess the psychometric properties of the resulting a priori culture scales and to empirically develop leadership scales.

Pilot Study 1

The CCIs in 28 countries (see Table 8.3 for these countries) distributed the survey of retained items to individuals in their respective countries who had full-time working experience as a white-collar employee or manager. Because the survey was lengthy, it was divided into two parallel versions, *A* and *B*. Each version contained approximately half of the leadership items and half of the organizational and societal culture items. A total of 877 individuals completed the first pilot study survey.

Several different statistical analyses were performed to assess the psychometric properties of the scales. Specifically, we conducted a series of exploratory factor analyses, reliability analyses, and aggregation analyses (e.g., $r_{wg(J)}$ analyses, intraclass correlations [ICC(1)], one-way analyses of variance) on our scales. It should be noted that because we wanted these scales to measure organizational or societal level and not individual level variation, we performed these analyses on the means of the country item responses for each scale. We refined our scales on the basis of these analyses while trying to maintain, whenever possible, the isomorphic quartet structure of the culture scales described above. These statistical analyses, if considered together, provide useful information about the construct validity of the culture scales.

Separate factor analyses of each of the culture scales indicated that they were all unidimensional. A first-order exploratory factor analysis of the leader attributes items yielded 16 unidimensional factors that describe *specific* leader attributes and behaviors.

The $r_{wg(J)}$ analyses (James, Demaree, & Wolf, 1984, 1993), demonstrated that aggregation of the organizational and societal culture scales is appropriate (average $r_{wg(J)} = .73$, $n = 54$).[3] Intraclass correlation coefficients [ICC(1)] and one-way analyses of variance (Bliese, 2000; McGraw & Wong, 1996; Shrout & Fleiss, 1979) for each of the scales indicated statistically significant within-culture agreement and between-culture differences. The societal culture scales exhibited low to moderate correlations with each other. Thus, they provide independent and unique information about societal cultures.

The leadership subscales substantially differed in their relationship to one another. The absolute correlation among the leadership subscales ranged from a low of .00 (e.g., Status-Conscious with Calmness) to a high of .86 (Status-Conscious with Procedural). Overall, 20% of the interrelationships were statistically significant. A second-order factor analysis of the 16 leadership factors yielded 4 unidimensional factors that describe *classes* of leader behaviors that represent *global* leader behavior patterns.

To summarize, at the end of Pilot Study 1, we developed 16 factorially derived leadership subscales at the societal level of analysis that represent specific leader behaviors. These subscales could be further classified into four second-order factorially derived leadership dimensions that represent global leader behavior patterns. We have seven organizational culture practices (As Is) scales, seven organizational culture values (Should Be) scales, seven societal culture practices (As Is) scales, and seven societal culture values (Should Be) scales.

Pilot Study 2

The purpose of the second pilot study was to replicate the psychometric analyses of the scales in a different sample, and assess the robustness of the psychometric properties of our scales. Data for Pilot Study 2 came from 15 countries that did not participate in the previous pilot study (see Table 8.3). In general, the psychometric properties of all of the scales were confirmed by replication process. A total of 1,066 individuals completed one of the three versions (organizational culture items, societal culture items, and leadership items) of the Pilot Study 2 questionnaires. Our results not only confirmed the psychometric properties of the leadership subscales and the culture scales,[4] but they also verified through aggregation tests that we were justified in aggregating these scales to their target level of analysis.

PHASE 2: FINAL SAMPLE AND CONFIRMATION OF MEASUREMENT SCALES

Phase 2 of GLOBE was designed to formally test the hypotheses concerning culture and leadership. In the present chapter, we use these data to provide further evidence concerning the psychometric properties of the GLOBE scales. It should be noted that additional items were written during Phase 1 of GLOBE on the basis of the results of the pilot studies as well as focus groups and interviews conducted by the CCIs. We added several leadership attribute items as well as some culture items to the questionnaire. These new leadership items were written to ensure that our 16 original leadership subscales were not biased by including only western leadership behaviors. Further, we wrote several items that described autocratic, self-aggrandizing, manipulative, and punitive behaviors because it was suggested in the interviews and focus groups that some societies might view these behaviors as enhancing leader effectiveness. The Phase 2 data were used to identify additional leadership scales among these items with the final result being an expansion of the original 16 leadership subscales to 21 subscales. See Table 8.4 for a listing of these leadership subscales.

We also added several items to develop an alternative measure of the cultural dimension of collectivism. These items were added because it became clear that the collectivism culture scales derived from the pilot studies

Table 8.3   GLOBE Participating Countries for Pilot Studies 1 and 2 and Phase 2

Participating Countries	Pilot Study 1	Pilot Study 2	Phase 2
Albania			*
Argentina	*		*
Australia	*		
Austria	*		*
Belgium	*		*
Bolivia		*	*
Brazil	*		*
Canada (English-speaking)	*		*
China		*	*
Colombia	*		*
Costa Rica		*	*
Czech Republic			*
Denmark			*
Ecuador		*	*
Egypt	*		*
El Salvador		*	*
England	*		*
Finland	*		*
France	*		*
Georgia, Republic of			*
Germany (Former West)	*		*
Germany (Former East)			*
Greece	*		*
Guatemala		*	*
Hong Kong	*		*
Hungary	*		*
India		*	*
Indonesia		*	*
Iran	*		*
Ireland			*
Israel	*		*
Italy		*	*
Japan			*

(Continued)

Table 8.3 (Continued)

Participating Countries	Pilot Study 1	Pilot Study 2	Phase 2
Kazakhstan			*
Kuwait		*	*
Malaysia			*
Mexico	*		*
Morocco			*
Namibia			*
Netherlands	*		*
New Zealand	*		*
Nigeria	*		*
Norway		*	
Philippines	*		*
Poland	*		*
Portugal	*		*
Puerto Rico	*		
Qatar			*
Russia		*	*
Singapore	*		*
Slovenia			*
South Africa (Black sample)			*
South Africa (White sample)	*		*
South Korea			*
Spain	*		*
Sweden	*		*
Switzerland	*		*
Taiwan	*	*	*
Thailand		*	*
Turkey		*	*
United States of America			*
Venezuela	*		*
Zambia			*
Zimbabwe			*

NOTE: Countries identified with a * indicate that they provided data for the specified data collection period. Countries marked with a * for Pilot Study 1 provided qualitative item information or survey data, or both.

Table 8.4   Leadership Prototype Scales: First Order Factors and Leader Attribute Items

Administratively Competent
- Orderly
- Administratively Skilled
- Organized
- Good Administrator

Autocratic
- Autocratic
- Dictatorial
- Bossy
- Elitist

Autonomous
- Individualistic
- Independent
- Autonomous
- Unique

Charismatic I: Visionary
- Foresight
- Prepared
- Anticipatory
- Plans Ahead

Charismatic II: Inspirational
- Enthusiastic
- Positive
- Morale Booster
- Motive Arouser

Charismatic III: Self-Sacrificial
- Risk Taker
- Self-Sacrificial
- Convincing

Conflict Inducer
- Normative
- Secretive
- Intragroup Competitor

Decisive
- Willful
- Decisive
- Logical
- Intuitive

Diplomatic
- Diplomatic
- Worldly
- Win–Win Problem Solver
- Effective Bargainer

Face Saver
- Indirect
- Avoids Negatives
- Evasive

Humane Orientation
- Generous
- Compassionate

Integrity
- Honest
- Sincere
- Just
- Trustworthy

Malevolent
- Hostile
- Dishonest
- Vindictive
- Irritable

Modesty
- Modest
- Self-Effacing
- Patient

Nonparticipative
- Nondelegator
- Micromanager
- Nonegalitarian
- Individually Oriented

Performance Oriented
- Improvement-Oriented
- Excellence-Oriented
- Performance-Oriented

Procedural
- Ritualistic
- Formal
- Habitual
- Procedural

Self-Centered
- Self-Centered
- Nonparticipative
- Loner
- Asocial

Status Consciousness
- Status-Conscious
- Class-Conscious

Team I: Collaborative Team Orientation
- Group-Oriented
- Collaborative
- Loyal
- Consultative

Team II: Team Integrator
- Communicative
- Team Builder
- Informed
- Integrator

did not include items relevant to collectivistic in-group phenomena. The new items were adapted from Triandis's (1995) work on collectivism so that they conformed to our multiple manifestation (i.e., practices and values) and the multiple levels of analysis conceptualization of culture. The additional items focused on collectivistic in-group phenomena such as group pride, loyalty, and cohesiveness. In addition, the original Individualism–Collectivism scale placed Individualism and Collectivism at two ends of one continuum, but research appearing in press at that time (i.e., Gelfand, Triandis, & Chan, 1996) indicated that individualism and collectivism might be independent dimensions. The new collectivism items were added to the Pilot Study 2 survey and an exploratory factor analysis on the Pilot Study 2 data confirmed that our original collectivism scales and the new Triandis-based collectivism scales measured separate aspects of collectivism. We confirmed the two collectivism scales by factor analytically deriving two dimensions of Collectivism: Institutional Collectivism (the original Individualism–Collectivism scales) and In-Group Collectivism (consisting of items relevant to family and organization and based on Triandis' scales).

Thus, at the beginning of Phase 2, we confirmed scales measuring eight cultural practices (As Is) and eight cultural values (Should Be) scales at both the organizational and societal levels of analysis with which to measure the seven original culture dimensions plus the new Collectivism scale based on Triandis (1995).

Samples

The analyses reported in this book are based on 17,370 middle managers from 62 different societies and cultures (see Table 8.3). The number of respondents by country ranged from 27 to 1,790 with an average per country of 251 respondents. The middle managers represent a total of 951 different local (i.e., nonmultinational) organizations from one of three industries: food processing, financial services, and telecommunications services. These three industries were selected because we believed that they were present in most, if not all, countries in the world, and because we believed that these industries systematically differed from one another. As discussed by Brodbeck, Hanges, Dickson, Gupta, and Dorfman in Chapter 20, a review of both the qualitative and quantitative literature on these three industries show that they differ in the types of environmental realms that they experience and so by sampling organizations within these industries we have obtained a fair number of dynamic organizations and high-technology organizations in the overall sample. Our design strategy consisted of obtaining responses of middle managers in two of the three target industries in each country studied.[5] This yielded samples from approximately 40 countries in each of the target industries. Regardless of the industry that was sampled, half of the respondents from a given organization completed the organizational culture items and the leadership attribute items (i.e., Questionnaire Form Alpha) and the other half completed the societal culture items as well as the leadership attribute items (i.e., Questionnaire Form Beta). The society-level means of the leadership item responses for Form Alpha respondents were not significantly different from those for Form Beta respondents. Thus, the individual leadership scale scores for the two samples were combined to produce means on the leadership scales for all cultures. As a result of the independent assessment of the organizational and societal variables, and because the mean leadership scale responses in each sample in each culture were not different, the responses are relatively free of common source response bias.

Statistical Analyses

A variety of statistical analyses were conducted to determine the psychometric properties of our scales. First, we used James and colleagues' (1984; James, Demaree, Wolf, 1993) $r_{wg(J)}$ and ICC(1) to determine whether aggregation was justified. The James and colleagues' $r_{wg(J)}$ measure compares the observed variance within each organization or society to the variance expected if there is no within-organization or within-society agreement. Stronger support for the convergent nature of the construct measured by the scale is obtained as $r_{wg(J)}$ approaches 1. The ICC(1) statistic also provides information on the appropriateness of aggregation with this statistic comparing the variance between organizations or societies with the variance within organizations or societies. Evidence for the convergent nature of the construct measured by a scale is obtained as the ICC(1) becomes larger than zero. Second, we used Muthen's (1990, 1994) multilevel confirmatory factor analyses protocol to confirm the factor structure of our scales. This procedure tests the proposed multilevel factor structure by simultaneously fitting the hypothesized factor structure on both the between-society level variance–covariance matrix and the within-society level variance–covariance matrix (see Dyer, Sipe, & Hanges, 1997; Hanges, Dyer, & Sipe, 1999, for more detailed discussions of this analysis and its ability to test for a multilevel factor structure).[6] Finally, we assessed the reliability of our scales with respect to two random error sources. First, we calculated the internal consistency of our scales at the organizational and societal level to assess the extent to which our scales were free from error caused by item variability. Second, we calculated ICC(2) (Shrout & Fleiss, 1979) to assess the extent to which our scales were generalizable across different respondents in an organization or society (i.e., interrater reliability).

Results for Phase 2

The consequence of adding items and conducting additional factor analyses resulted in expanding the original 16 leadership subscales to 21 subscales. These additional basic factors represent both positive and negative elements of leadership (viewed from a conventional Western perspective).

Aggregation Verification

Overall, these results support aggregation. The average $r_{wg(J)}s$ for the organizational and societal cultural practices (As Is) scales are .69 and .85, respectively. The average $r_{wg(J)}s$ for the organizational and societal cultural values (Should Be) scales were both .80. Finally, the average $r_{wg(J)}$ for the leadership attribute subscales was .78. See Hanges, House, and colleagues (2003) for more details, if desired.

We also calculated ICC(1) for these scales and these values are shown in Table 8.5. It should be noted that the average ICC(1) reported in the organizational literature is .12 (James, 1982) with the typical values ranging from .05 to .20 (Bliese, 2000). The average ICC(1) for the GLOBE organizational cultural practices (As Is) scales is .22, whereas the average ICC(1) for the organizational cultural values (Should Be) scales is .27. The average ICC(1) for the society cultural practices (As Is) culture scales is .25, whereas the average ICC(1) for the society cultural values (Should Be) scales is .27. The average ICC(1) for the leadership attribute subscales is .18. Given the value of ICC(1) typically found in the organizational research, the aggregation of the GLOBE scales to their targeted levels of analysis is strongly supported.[7] In summary, the Phase 2 data again support the appropriateness of aggregating these scales to the organizational and societal level of analysis.

Multilevel Confirmatory Factor Analysis

Overall, the results of the Muthen multilevel confirmatory factor analysis replicated the factor structure of the culture scales. We primarily used the comparative fit index (CFI) to assess the fit of the factor structure to our data. The average CFI for the organizational cultural practices (As Is) and organizational cultural values (Should Be) scales were .93 and .94, respectively. The average CFI for the societal cultural practices (As Is) and societal cultural values (Should Be) scales were .89 and .95, respectively. The low CFIs were primarily a function of the Gender Egalitarianism cultural practices (As Is) and Gender Egalitarianism cultural values (Should Be) scales, at both the societal and organizational levels of analysis. Using exploratory maximum likelihood factor analysis on the group level variance–covariance matrix, we discovered that these scales could be separated into two unidimensional factors. These two factors appeared to be meaningful with the first factor consisting of items assessing the assertiveness of an organization or society and the second factor reflecting the degree of equality between men and women in an organization or society. When these two scales were treated separately, the internal consistency of these subscales was substantially improved. We therefore decided to treat these two subfactors of Gender Egalitarianism separately for future analyses.

The average CFI for the leadership attribute subscales was .92. This result indicated substantial support for our leadership subscales. However, for three of our scales (i.e., Charismatic I: Visionary, Self-centered, and Decisive), the CFIs were lower than desired (i.e., CFI = .86, .85, and .78, respectively). We examined these three scales and discovered that the low fit indices were primarily a function of a different (and much weaker) factor structure operating at the within-society level of analysis. Because these scales were created to measure culturally endorsed (i.e., emergent–convergent) constructs, we changed the pooled within-society factor structure. We discovered that the goodness of fit of these scales improved to acceptable levels if a two-factor within-society structure was imposed. Thus, we interpreted these results as supporting the between-society factor structure of the leadership and culture scales. For the three scales that required a different factor structure at the within-society level of analysis, the multilevel

Table 8.5 ICC(1), Internal Consistency, and ICC(2) Results for Organizational and Societal Culture Scales and the CLT Subscales: Phase 2 Data

GLOBE Cultural Dimension Scales

	ORGANIZATIONAL			SOCIETAL	
PRACTICES (AS IS)	ICC(1)	Internal Consistency	ICC(2)	ICC(1)	Internal Consistency	ICC(2)
Performance Orientation	.23	.68	.93	.27	.72	.87
Assertiveness	.23	.60	.93	.31	.75	.91
Future Orientation	.18	.57	.91	.17	.80	.92
Humane Orientation	.15	.78	.89	.21	.88	.91
Collectivism I: Institutional Collectivism	.17	.44	.90	.23	.67	.93
Collectivism II: In-Group Collectivism	.19	.70	.91	.29	.77	.98
Gender Egalitarianism	.33	.46	.96	.36	.66	.90
Power Distance	.20	.55	.92	.19	.80	.91
Uncertainty Avoidance	.28	.67	.95	.36	.88	.96

GLOBE Cultural Dimension Scales

	ORGANIZATIONAL			SOCIETAL	
VALUES (SHOULD BE)	ICC(1)	Internal Consistency	ICC(2)	ICC(1)	Internal Consistency	ICC(2)
Performance Orientation	.27	.61	.94	.15	.90	.89
Assertiveness	.31	.50	.95	.29	.53	.95
Future Orientation	.17	.52	.90	.20	.76	.92
Humane Orientation	.21	.61	.92	.10	.70	.84
Collectivism I: Institutional Collectivism	.23	.43	.93	.30	.77	.95
Collectivism II: In-Group Collectivism	.29	.63	.95	.13	.66	.87
Gender Egalitarianism	.36	.65	.96	.28	.88	.95
Power Distance	.19	.45	.91	.14	.74	.88
Uncertainty Avoidance	.36	.60	.96	.38	.85	.96

FIRST ORDER LEADERSHIP SCALES	ICC(1)	INTERNAL CONSISTENCY	ICC(2)
Administratively Competent	.16	.85	.89
Autocratic	.20	.79	.92
Autonomous	.13	.59	.87
Charismatic I: Visionary	.18	.92	.91
Charismatic II: Inspirational	.19	.93	.91
Charismatic III: Self-sacrificial	.14	.52	.88
Conflict Inducer	.23	.71	.93
Decisive	.20	.68	.92
Diplomatic	.13	.64	.87
Face Saver	.25	.79	.94
Humane Orientation	.16	.66	.90
Integrity	.15	.87	.89
Malevolent	.15	.88	.89
Modest	.17	.61	.90
Nonparticipative	.19	.71	.91
Performance Oriented	.15	.82	.89
Procedural	.29	.85	.95
Self-Centered	.14	.75	.88
Status Consciousness	.23	.76	.93
Team I: Collaborative Team Orientation	.12	.76	.86
Team II: Team Integrator	.24	.82	.93

factor analysis confirmed the earlier discussion that the properties of scales measuring emergent–convergent constructs operate at a particular level of analysis.[8]

Reliability

As indicated earlier, we assessed the reliability of our scales with respect to two random error sources. First, we calculated the internal consistency of our scales at the organizational or societal level of analysis to assess the degree to which our scales were free from error caused by item variability. To calculate these internal consistency estimates, we first aggregated the items comprising each scale to the organizational or societal level of analysis and computed Cronbach's alpha on the basis of these averaged item responses. Table 8.5 shows the internal consistency estimates for our scales. The average Cronbach alpha for the organizational cultural practices (As Is) and the organizational cultural values (Should Be) scales were 0.61 and 0.55, respectively. The average Cronbach alpha for the society cultural practices (As Is) and society cultural values (Should Be) scales were .77 and .75, respectively. Finally, the average internal consistency for the 21 leadership attribute subscales was .75. Although there were a few organizational culture scales that had lower Cronbach alphas than desired, the majority of our scales exhibited adequate internal consistency.[9]

Second, we explored the extent to which our scales exhibited interrater reliability. In particular, we assumed that an average of 45 responses[10] per organization or society were available[11] and computed ICC(2) (Shrout & Fleiss, 1979) for our scales to assess the extent to which our scales exhibited interrater reliability. The ICC(2)s for our scales are also shown in Table 8.5. As shown in this table, even with an assumed average of 45 responses per organization or society, the interrater reliability of our scales was quite sizable. The average ICC(2) for the organizational cultural practices (As Is) and cultural values (Should Be) scales were .92 and .94, respectively. The average ICC(2) for the societal cultural practices (As Is) and cultural values (Should Be) scales were .93 and .95, respectively. The average ICC(2) for the leadership attribute subscales was .90. In summary, these results strongly suggest that by averaging the responses of at least 45 respondents, our scales exhibited sufficient reliability to differentiate organizations and societies on our culture and leadership scales.

Global Leadership Scales

As we expected based on the pilot studies, there were significant interrelationships among the leadership attribute scales. Thus, we conducted a second-order maximum likelihood exploratory factor analysis. Using a number of criteria to determine the number of factors to extract (i.e., meaningfulness of the factor structure; all retained factors account for more variance than a single item; in other words, the eigenvalue of a retained factor is greater than one, etc.), we settled on a six-factor solution. The factors that were identified are (a) Charismatic/Value-Based leadership, (b) Team-Oriented leadership, (c) Autonomous leadership, (d) Humane-Oriented leadership, (e) Participative leadership, and (f) Self-Protective leadership. We refer to the 6 second-order factors as CLT leadership dimensions and to the 21 subscales as basic CLT leadership dimensions.[12] The six global leadership dimensions are found in Table 8.6. The internal consistency reliability and interrater reliability for these CLT leadership dimensions (computed by using the linear composite reliability formula provided in Nunnally and Bernstein, 1994) are also shown in this table. As seen in the table, the reliability of the scales designed to measure these global CLT dimensions are very acceptable (i.e., average internal consistency reliability = .84; average interrater reliability = .95).

Construct Validation

The aforementioned results provide strong evidence that the GLOBE scales were constructed properly, that they measured variation at the desired level of analysis, and that they could be used to reliably make distinctions between organizations or societies. Although these results document the psychometric properties of our scales, it should also be noted that these results also provide some initial information about the construct validity of our scales. In this section, we more closely examine the construct validity

Table 8.6   Global Culturally Endorsed Implicit Leadership (CLT) Dimensions

1. *Charismatic/Value-Based*, 4.5–6.5
   (Internal Consistency: .95)
   (Interrater reliability: .98)
   *Charismatic I: Visionary
   *Charismatic II: Inspirational
   *Charismatic III: Self-sacrifice
   *Integrity
   *Decisive
   *Performance oriented

2. *Team Oriented*, 4.8–6.2
   (Internal Consistency: .93)
   (Interrater reliability: .96)
   *Team I: Collaborative Team Orientation
   *Team II: Team Integrator
   *Diplomatic
   *Malevolent (reverse scored)
   *Administratively competent

3. *Self-Protective*, 2.6–4.6
   (Internal Consistency: .93)
   (Interrater reliability: .98)
   *Self-centered
   *Status consciousness
   *Conflict inducer
   *Face saver
   *Procedural

4. *Participative*, 4.5–6.1
   (Internal Consistency: .85)
   (Interrater reliability: .95)
   *Autocratic (reverse scored)
   *Nonparticipative (reverse scored)

5. *Humane Oriented,* 3.8–5.6
   (Internal Consistency: .76)
   (Interrater reliability: .93)
   *Modest
   *Humane orientation

6. *Autonomous*, 2.3–4.7
   (Internal Consistency: .59)
   (Interrater reliability: .87)
   *Autonomous

NOTE: The numbered, italicized topics are Global CLT leadership dimensions. They comprise first-order leadership attribute (CLT) scales. Numbers following Global CLT names represent the range of country-level mean values on a seven-point scale ranging from 1 (greatly inhibits) to 7 (contributes greatly) to outstanding leadership. Internal consistency reliability for the Global CLTs were obtained by using the internal consistency of the first-order leadership attribute scales (Table 8.4) and applying Nunnally and Bernstein's (1994) formula for unit-weighted linear composite scores. Interrater reliability estimates were obtained in a similar fashion except that the ICC(2) estimates were used instead of the internal consistency estimates for these first-order leadership attribute scales.

of our scales by building a nomological network with respect to our measures of culture and leadership. To accomplish this, we examined the relationships of our scales and measures with other measures of similar concepts previously investigated by well-recognized cross-cultural researchers. Specifically, we examined the correlations among five of our culture scales and scales developed by Hofstede (1980) and Schwartz (1994). In addition, we examined the relationship of our culture scales with unobtrusive measures developed by GLOBE (Chapter 9, by Gupta, Sully de Luque, & House, this volume). Before describing the results of our attempt to build a nomological network, we first touch on the troublesome issue of response bias if conducting cross-cultural survey research.

Cultural Response Bias

The cross-cultural literature has noted that people from different cultures sometimes exhibit different response patterns when completing questionnaires (Triandis, 1994). For example, in Asian cultures, people tend to avoid the extreme ends of a scale (to avoid diverging from the group) whereas in Mediterranean cultures, people tend to avoid the midpoint of a scale (to avoid appearing noncommittal) (Hui & Triandis, 1989; Stening & Everett, 1984). The presence of these culturally based response patterns is believed to bias subsequent cross-cultural comparisons based on self-report data because these response patterns are not a function of the intended construct of interest. Thus, several cross-cultural researchers have argued that interpretation of the rank order of cultures based on average scale scores is problematic. These researchers argue that some correction is needed to minimize the influence of this bias.

Although a multimethod approach is probably the optimal manner to minimize the influence of this bias (Triandis, 1994), a statistical standardization correction procedure has been developed that is believed to remove cultural-response biases from the original "uncorrected" questionnaire responses (van de Vijver & Leung, 1997). In the GLOBE project, we performed this statistical correction procedure and correlated our original scales with these "response bias corrected" scales to ascertain the extent to which response bias was a problem with our scales. Further, we developed an extension of this procedure to help interpret the rank ordering of the countries on the basis of this correction. This extension of the traditional response bias correction procedure and its ability to identify specific societies that exhibit substantial response bias is discussed in Appendix B.

Following Triandis' (1994) description of the current statistical correction procedure used in the cross-cultural literature, we calculated each individual's mean and standard deviation across all items in the survey. It is critical when computing these means and standard deviations that the items measure a wide range of constructs. Only if this is true will an individual's mean and standard deviation reflect response bias tendencies as opposed to responses to some meaningful construct. After computing these values, an individual's corrected item scores are computed by subtracting that individual's average response from the actual response for that item and dividing this difference by that individual's standard deviation. Corrected scale scores were then created by combining the appropriate corrected items and these corrected scale scores were then aggregated to the society level of analysis.

To assess the extent to which the uncorrected scale scores were subject to cultural-response bias, we correlated the corrected scale scores that were aggregated to the society level of analysis with the aggregated uncorrected scale scores. We first correlated the corrected and uncorrected societal culture scales. These correlations revealed a substantial degree of agreement between the

scales (i.e., range of correlations for the societal cultural practices (As Is) scales: .93 to .98; average correlation for societal cultural practices (As Is) scales: .95; range of correlations for the societal cultural values (Should Be) scales: .86 to .98; average correlation for the societal cultural values (Should Be) scales: .93). The magnitude of these correlations implies that cultural-response bias plays a small role in our culture scales.

We also correlated the corrected and uncorrected first- and second-order leadership attribute scales. Once again, a substantial level of agreement existed between the corrected and uncorrected first-order (range of correlations: .85 to .99; average correlation: .93) and second-order (range of correlations: .87 to .98; average correlation: .95) leadership scales. This magnitude of these correlations once again implies that cultural-response bias plays a small role in our leadership scales.

Nomological Network:
Correlation of GLOBE's and
Hofstede's (1980) Culture Scales

As we noted previously, three of the culture dimensions that we measured are direct descendants of the culture dimensions identified by Hofstede (1980). Specifically, we developed scales to measure Uncertainty Avoidance, Power Distance, and Individualism–Collectivism, with an additional scale to measure collectivism on the basis of Triandis' work. (Our Gender Egalitarianism scale was not intended to reflect the same construct as Hofstede's Masculinity scale, though there are some similarities between our Assertiveness scales and Hofstede's Masculinity scale.) Although this construct similarity between some of the GLOBE cultural dimensions and Hofstede's dimensions enables quick identification of hypotheses concerning which scales will exhibit convergent validity, it is important to remember that Hofstede's scales do not differentiate cultural practices from cultural values. Thus, before generating hypotheses about which GLOBE culture scales will converge with Hofstede's scales, it is important to examine Hofstede's scales to ascertain which cultural manifestation (i.e., practices or values) is being measured.

With respect to power distance, Hofstede's scale appears to be focusing on organizational cultural practices. Specifically, two of the three items in Hofstede's Power Distance scale used in the IBM study assess cultural practices (i.e., As Is) whereas the remaining item appears to be a values-based question asking about the type of manager preferred by the respondents (p. 101). This mixing of cultural practices and values within one scale causes some problems in generating specific hypotheses about which GLOBE scales will correspond to Hofstede's measures. However, given that two of the three items appear to measure practices, we decided that this scale primarily assesses cultural practices.

With respect to uncertainty avoidance, Hofstede's scale included three items, the first of which is clearly a values item: "Company rules should not be broken even when the employee thinks it is in the company's best interest" (p. 164). The second item assesses a behavioral intention or expectation (i.e., the length of time that an employee intends to remain with his or her current employer), whereas the third item assesses an outcome (i.e., the frequency that a respondent experiences feeling nervous or tense at work). Unfortunately, these last two items do not seem to fit clearly into either a practices or values framework. This scale clearly lacks face validity with respect to the construct it is intended to measure and the label assigned to it. Interestingly, Hofstede himself noted that this scale was perhaps not the best measure of the construct, given that it was created from existing items and that the concept was not well defined at the time of the scale's development (1980, p. 163). Given that there is a single item that clearly measures cultural values, we conclude that Hofstede's uncertainty avoidance scale possibly corresponds with GLOBE's Uncertainty Avoidance cultural values (Should Be) scale, but only modestly.

Hofstede's individualism scale and his Masculinity scale appear to be assessing cultural values, rather than cultural practices. Further, because Hofstede's individualism scale places individualism and collectivism on a single dimension, we expect that this scale should meaningfully relate to our Collectivism I: Institutional Collectivism values measure of this construct.

In summary, on the basis of this analysis we expected the following convergence:

- Hofstede's Power Distance scale should be positively related to GLOBE's Power Distance cultural practices (As Is) scale.
- Hofstede's Uncertainty Avoidance scale should be modestly positively related to GLOBE's Uncertainty Avoidance cultural values (Should Be) scale.
- Hofstede's Individualism scale should be negatively correlated to GLOBE's Collectivism I: Institutional Collectivism cultural values (Should Be) scale.

We did not generate a specific hypothesis for the Masculinity scale because the GLOBE scales were not designed to directly build on Hofstede's work. Rather, the GLOBE scales were an attempt to refine the concept into two separate, distinctive, and meaningful dimensions. Although we do not have a specific hypothesis, we explored the relationships between the Hofstede Masculinity and GLOBE Gender Egalitarianism and Assertiveness scales. In general, we expect that convergence will occur on the GLOBE cultural values scales of this construct.

We tested our hypotheses by using the country scale scores reported in Hofstede's (1980) book, as well as later updates to these country rankings (Hofstede, 2001), and correlating the country-level scores with the country-level scores from the GLOBE project. These findings related to convergent validity are reported in Table 8.7.

Consistent with our predictions, there was a significant positive correlation between the Hofstede Power Distance scale and our societal Power Distance cultural practices (As Is) scale ($r(41) = .61, p < .01$). Further, Hofstede's Power Distance scale did not significantly correlate with the GLOBE societal Power Distance cultural values (Should Be) scale ($r(41) = .03, p > .05$).

Also consistent with our predictions, there was a significant positive correlation between Hofstede's Uncertainty Avoidance scale and the GLOBE Uncertainty Avoidance cultural values (Should Be) ($r(41) = .32, p < .05$) scale. Somewhat surprising, however, was the significant negative correlation between Hofstede's Uncertainty Avoidance scale and the GLOBE cultural practices scale of this dimension

Table 8.7   Convergent Validity Coefficients Between GLOBE Scales and Hofstede Scales

GLOBE Scales		Hofstede Scales
		Power Distance
Power Distance	Practices (As Is)	0.61**
	Values (Should Be)	−0.03
		Uncertainty Avoidance
Uncertainty Avoidance	Practices (As Is)	−0.61**
	Values (Should Be)	0.32**
		Individualism
Institutional Collectivism	Practices (As Is)	0.15
	Values (Should Be)	−0.55 **
In-Group Collectivism	Practices (As Is)	−0.82**
	Values (Should Be)	−0.20
		Masculinity
Gender Egalitarianism	Practices (As Is)	−0.16
	Values (Should Be)	0.11
Assertiveness	Practices (As Is)	0.42**
	Values (Should Be)	−0.12

** $= p < .01$

($r(41) = .61, p < .01$). The negative correlation between these two scales is consistent with the general GLOBE finding that the cultural practice scales are negatively correlated with the cultural values scales.

As we predicted, the Hofstede Individualism scale was significantly negatively related to our societal Collectivism I: Institutional Collectivism cultural values (Should Be) scale ($r(41) =− .55, p < .01$) and not to our societal Collectivism I: Institutional Collectivism cultural practices (As Is) scale ($r(41) = .15, p > .05$). With respect to the GLOBE Collectivism II: In-Group Collectivism construct, the results in Table 8.6 show that Hofstede's Individualism scale significantly negatively correlates with the GLOBE practices measure. Once again, this negative correlation is consistent with the general

GLOBE finding that the cultural practice scales are negatively correlated with the cultural values scales.

Finally, with respect to the Hofstede Masculinity scale, the only significant relationship was with GLOBE's societal Assertiveness cultural practices (As Is) scale ($r(40) = .42, p < .01$).

In summary, there was evidence of convergence between the two sets of scales on many but not all dimensions. It is important to keep in mind, however, that contrary to Hofstede's research, the GLOBE project scales were developed and psychometrically tested for construct validity as the project progressed from inception. In addition, GLOBE set out to assess both the more objective as well as subjective aspects of similar dimensions of culture. Indeed, as we have shown, the Hofstede (1980) measures combine these two aspects of culture. The GLOBE scales measure these two aspects of culture separately and, as shown in the correlations with Hofstede's measures, the patterns of relationships differ depending upon which aspect of culture was being measured. Thus, one contribution of the present culture measures is that, for each dimension of culture assessed, both the practices and values aspects of culture are measured separately.

Nomological Network:
Correlation of GLOBE Scales
With the Schwartz Value Survey

In 1994, Schwartz extended his individual-level taxonomy of human values to the society level to identify dimensions that differentiate cultures. Following Kluckhohn's (1951) and Rokeach's (1973) conceptualization of culture, Schwartz defined human values as desirable goals that people use as guiding principles in their lives (Schwartz, 1992, 1994). An individual's priorities among a set of values is a function of that individual's unique experiences as well as the experiences shared by everyone in a given society. Schwartz developed a values survey that can be used to identify a set of values that can differentiate individuals from one another (Schwartz & Bilsky, 1987) or that can differentiate societies from one another. With respect to the societal application of Schwartz's survey, seven dimensions were identified that differentiate societies. His seven ecological dimensions are Embeddedness (previously labeled Conservatism), Intellectual Autonomy, Affective Autonomy, Hierarchy, Egalitarianism, Mastery, and Harmony (Schwartz, 1994, 2001; Schwartz & Melech, 2000). Brief descriptions of these constructs are provided in Table 8.8.

On the basis of Schwartz's society-level values taxonomy, we expected stronger relationships between Schwartz's scales and the GLOBE societal cultural values (Should Be) scales. In general, we do not expect the GLOBE cultural practices (As Is) scales will correlate with Schwartz's dimensions because his scales are clearly assessing cultural values. On the basis of the apparent conceptual overlap

between some of the GLOBE scales and some of the Schwartz scales, we expected several specific scales to be correlated. Specifically, we predicted that

- Schwartz's Embeddedness scale would be positively related to the GLOBE societal Uncertainty Avoidance and Collectivism cultural values (Should Be) scales
- Schwartz's Intellectual Autonomy scale would be negatively related to the GLOBE societal Uncertainty Avoidance and Collectivism cultural values (Should Be) scales
- Schwartz's Hierarchy dimension would be positively related to the GLOBE societal Power Distance cultural values (Should Be) scale
- Schwartz's Egalitarianism dimension would be positively related to the GLOBE societal Gender Egalitarianism cultural values (Should Be) scale but negatively related to the GLOBE societal Assertiveness cultural values (Should Be) scale
- Schwartz's Mastery dimension would be positively related to the GLOBE societal Performance Orientation cultural values (Should Be) scale

Schwartz (2001) collected mean ratings on his seven dimensions for 64 different countries. These means were provided by averaging ratings provided by schoolteachers who were sampled from each culture. Schoolteachers were selected because they, to a substantial extent, convey societal values across generations. Using the Phase 2 GLOBE data, Sagiv and Gupta (2002) found 48 countries in common with the Schwartz list. These researchers correlated the societal-level GLOBE scale scores with the Schwartz data. Overall, they found good agreement between the GLOBE cultural values scales and the Schwartz scales. The correlations from their study that correspond to the aforementioned hypotheses are reproduced in Table 8.8.

As shown in this table, most of our hypotheses received some support. More specifically, as predicted, Schwartz's Embeddedness dimension was significantly positively related to the GLOBE Uncertainty Avoidance cultural values scale. Schwartz's Intellectual Autonomy dimension was significantly negatively related to the GLOBE Uncertainty Avoidance cultural values scale. Schwartz's Hierarchy dimension was significantly positively related to the GLOBE Power Distance cultural values scale. Schwartz's Egalitarian Commitment dimension was significantly positively related to our societal Gender Egalitarianism cultural values measure and negatively related to our societal Gender Assertiveness cultural values scale.

It should be noted, however, that not all of our hypotheses were supported. Schwartz's Embeddedness dimension was not significantly related to either of the GLOBE Collectivism values scales. Schwartz's Intellectual Autonomy dimension was not significantly related to either of the GLOBE Collectivism values scales. Finally, Schwartz's Mastery dimension was not significantly related to the GLOBE Performance Orientation cultural values scale.

The pattern of the correlations obtained with Schwartz's scales provides additional convergent validity evidence for our scales. The correlations between Schwartz's scales and our scales indicate the generalizability of the constructs measured by the GLOBE scales given the different development approach taken by Schwartz to develop his scales as well as the different sample (i.e., schoolteachers) used for his country means.

Nomological Network: Correlation of GLOBE Scales With Unobtrusive Measures

Although the previous analyses provided additional information about the construct validity of the GLOBE scales, it is important to realize that this evidence all concerned constructs assessed using survey methodology. Some of the construct validity evidence may be attributable to the common use of surveys across the Hofstede, Schwartz, and GLOBE studies. Thus, further evidence on the construct validity of the GLOBE measures would be obtained if we find meaningful relationships between our scales and nonsurvey measures of these culture constructs. In an attempt to assess the convergence of culture constructs independent of survey methodology, a set of unobtrusive measures (i.e., measures that use naturally occurring data) was developed. Use of unobtrusive measures has the advantage of being free from the reactive sources of error that can affect other measurement approaches (Brewer & Hunter, 1989).

Gupta, Sully de Luque, and House in Chapter 9 describe GLOBE's development of a set of unobtrusive measures for the GLOBE culture practices dimensions. As discussed in that chapter, the unobtrusive measures are based on a content analysis of archival data to generate measures of societal cultural practices. Gupta and colleagues report that the intercorrelations of the unobtrusive measures and the GLOBE culture practices scales range from a low of .51 for the societal Humane Orientation cultural practices (As Is) scale to a high of .65 for societal Gender Egalitarianism cultural practices (As Is) scale (Gupta et al., Chapter 9, this volume). In other words, these results show that the GLOBE survey responses provided by middle managers in three industries correspond to archival sources concerning societal practices. This reinforces the conclusion that the construct validity evidence for our scales is not bounded by survey measurement methodology. Further, the GLOBE society practices measures and the unobtrusive measures that did not correspond to the GLOBE measures had lower correlations than those that did correspond to the GLOBE measures.

Nomological Network: Correlation of GLOBE Scales With World Values Survey Data

The construct validity of the GLOBE's societal value scales was assessed by developing new culture scales using the data obtained from Inglehart, Basanez, and Moreno's (1998) World Values Surveys (WVS) project. The WVS data consists of responses from approximately 350 questions of human values (Inglehart et al., 1998) ranging from issues involving family to issues regarding work to topics concerning political and social matters. Nine separate culture dimensions that were conceptually consistent with the GLOBE cultural values dimensions were developed. Information about the development of these new scales using the WVS data is provided in Chapter 9. Project GLOBE and the WVS data had a total of 39 societies in common.

Gupta and colleagues argue that examining the WVS data can be used to test the construct

Table 8.8   Convergent Validity Coefficients Between GLOBE Scales and Schwartz's Scales

GLOBE Values Scale	*Schwartz Values Scale*
	Embeddedness Cultural emphasis on the maintenance of status quo, minimization of disruptions to traditional order (social order, family security, respect for tradition)
Uncertainty Avoidance	.74**
Institutional Collectivism	.14
In-Group Collectivism	.15
	Intellectual Autonomy Cultural emphasis on the promotion and protection of individual pursuit of intellectual directions
Uncertainty Avoidance	−.61**
Institutional Collectivism	−.13
In-Group Collectivism	−.14
	Hierarchy Cultural emphasis on the legitimacy of hierarchical and differential allocation of financial and social resources
Power Distance	.33*
	Egalitarianism Cultural emphasis on the transcendence of selfish interests, voluntary cooperation, and concern for the welfare of others
Gender Egalitarianism	.65**
Assertiveness	−.44**
	Mastery Cultural emphasis on active efforts to modify the social and natural environment through action
Performance Orientation	.12

NOTE: We have no hypotheses about Schwartz's Harmony scale, which refers to the importance of being in tune with the natural and social world.

** $p < .01$.

validity of the GLOBE culture scales. In particular, they argue that this comparison would be meaningful because the two projects had several methodological differences. For example, unlike the GLOBE sample, which was limited to middle managers from three types of industries, the WVS data came from all adult citizens (18 years or older) from each society. Inglehart and colleagues (1998) attempted to create representative samples for each society in their sample. Another difference is that unlike the GLOBE scales which were collected using self-report questionnaires, the WVS data were collected using face-to-face interviews. Further, the response format used in the WVS varied across questions. Some questions asked for categorical information whereas others asked for respondents to answer using an ordinal-level scale. Finally, the rationale for conducting these two studies differed. The WVS data was collected to explore intergeneration differences in the social, political, and economic values. As discussed earlier in this book, the GLOBE surveys were designed specifically for measuring societal cultural values and practices constructs. It is for these methodological reasons that Gupta and colleagues argue a meaningful analysis of the convergent and discriminant validity of the GLOBE cultural values scales could be conducted using the WVS data.

Comparing the correlations between the GLOBE scales and the new scales that measure the same culture construct, the convergent validities were all statistically significant, ranging from 0.38 to 0.88 with the average of 0.59. Comparing the correlations between the GLOBE scales and the WVS scales that measure different culture constructs, the average discriminant validity was 0.24 and this average coefficient was significantly less than the average convergent coefficient of 0.59. In other words, these results show that the GLOBE survey responses provided by middle managers in three industries correspond to interview responses provided by a representative sample of individuals that were independently collected. These results provide evidence for the construct validity of the GLOBE cultural values scales. See Chapter 9 by Gupta and colleagues for a more detailed discussion of these results.

Nomological Network: Sensitivity of GLOBE Scales to Industry Effects

As discussed earlier in this book, the GLOBE conceptual model indicates that the industrial sector to which an organization belongs and the common kinds of pressures (e.g., the rate of technological change and the general level of environmental turbulence) encountered by organizations in an industrial sector should influence the kinds of practices adopted in that organization. In contrast to organizational practices, however, the practices adopted on a society-wide basis should be relatively unaffected by the contingencies experienced by organizations in a particular industrial sector. Unless a society is dominated by a single industry, broader factors (e.g., shared language, historical trends, and environmental conditions) influence societal cultural practices. Indeed, the GLOBE

conceptual model indicates that societal cultural practices should also influence the cultural practices of an organization.

Given this rationale, additional information for the construct validity of the GLOBE culture scales can be obtained by demonstrating that an objective characteristic (i.e., industrial sector of an organization) affects the organizational cultural practices scales but not the societal cultural practices scales. To assess the hypothesis that the industrial sector affects the GLOBE practices scales, we separated the GLOBE data by industry and correlated the rank order of the societies across the three industries using the organizational and societal cultural practices scales. Our hypothesis about the industry effect on the cultural practices scales would be supported if the organizational cultural practices scales exhibited low correlations with (i.e., low reliability due to sensitivity to industry differences) across the three industries but the societal cultural practices scales showed high correlations (i.e., high reliability due to insensitivity to industry differences).

Consistent with expectations, the organizational cultural practices scales were found to have a low average correlation of 0.38 (i.e., average financial–food correlation = 0.41; average financial–telecommunication correlation = 0.33; average food–telecommunication correlation = 0.39) whereas the societal cultural practices scales had an average correlation of 0.73 (i.e., average financial–food correlation = 0.88; average financial–telecommunication correlation = 0.62; average food–telecommunication correlation = 0.68). Thus, even though the organizational and societal practices scales were composed of similar items that only differed in the level of focus of the question (i.e., organization versus society), industry differences substantially affected the organizational but not the societal cultural practices scales. These findings provide additional evidence for the construct validity of our scales.[13]

Nomological Network: Construct Validity of the CLT Scales

The construct validity of the GLOBE CLT leadership dimensions cannot be directly assessed by a psychometric analysis of the

GLOBE data as it was with our culture dimension scales. Given the nature of our research design investigating implicit leadership theory, instead we can provide an indirect assessment of the meaningfulness of global CLT leadership dimensions by examining the relationship of our dimensions to prior leadership literature. Of the six global CLT leadership dimensions, four are closely related to prior leadership constructs found in the extant leadership literature. The GLOBE Charismatic/Value-Based CLT dimension contains three subscales that embody current aspects of charismatic leadership: developing a vision, inspiring others, and engaging in self-sacrificial behaviors. Integrity and decisiveness, also found in the Charismatic/Value-Based CLT dimension, have been linked to effective leadership and are consistent with charismatic leadership theory. Our second major CLT dimension, Team Oriented, reflects a current interest in the leadership of teams found in contemporary leadership textbooks (e.g., Yukl, 2002). This dimension includes several subscales related to the successful leadership of teams: collaborative team orientation and team integration. It also contains two scales that concern administrative and diplomatic skills that would be consistent with team effectiveness. The Humane Oriented CLT leadership dimension may be considered directly related to "leadership consideration," a major leadership behavior identified in the classic leadership Ohio State and Michigan studies (Bass, 1990). Our fourth major CLT dimension, Participative leadership, also has a long and important tradition within the leadership literature.

In contrast to the previously mentioned CLT dimensions that might be expected given the leadership literature, we found two dimensions that are probably not typically associated with leadership, at least within the "Western–oriented" leadership literature. The first dimension, Autonomous, reflects an individualistic, independent, and unique aspect of leadership. Our second unexpected CLT dimension, Self-Protective, would likely be viewed negatively from a Western perspective, and has not been previously part of the leadership literature. Nevertheless, aspects of this dimension can easily be identified within an "Eastern" leadership

perspective, as face saver and status consciousness may be important if viewed from a non-Western perspective.

CONCLUSIONS

In summary, as part of the GLOBE project, we have developed scales that assess organizational and societal culture and culturally shared implicit theories of leadership. These scales were found to be aggregatable, reliable, and unidimensional. Evidence for construct validity of the culture scales was provided from several sources.

We do, of course, recognize that there are limitations to our research. First, we have intentionally chosen to focus on perceptions of *organizational* leadership, rather than political or moral leadership. Implicit leadership theory predicts that the behaviors seen as effective for organizational leaders will be different from the behaviors seen as effective for other types of leaders (Lord & Maher, 1991b; Hanges, Lord, & Dickson, 2000) or from effective followers (Leslie and Van Velsor, 1998), and thus our measures may be less applicable to follower perceptions or nonbusiness leadership arenas. We suspect that many of our findings will be found to be generalizable to other domains. This speculation remains to be tested empirically.

A second limitation of the research presented here is that it is monomethod: All scale data presented were collected using questionnaires. However, the correlations of the scales with unobtrusive measures suggest that this potential issue is not a major concern here. Further, the data are not subject to common source bias as is often the case in monomethod research, as the societal culture and leadership items were completed by different people.

A third limitation is that we only have preliminary information about the construct validity evidence of the leadership scales. Unlike the societal culture scales, there are no a priori cross-cultural implicit leadership scales that were available to correlate with our scales. Clearly, further validation of these scales is needed. In a forthcoming anthology, chapters from different societies are presented in which descriptions of culturally endorsed leadership theories are developed by using alternative methodologies (e.g., media analyses, focus group discussions). These authors compare the leadership profiles generated by these alternative methods with the profiles provided by our scales. The overall result of approximately 25 country specific chapters provides evidence of construct validity of our leadership scales.

Finally, it cannot be repeated often enough: These scales were primarily designed to measure convergent–emergent constructs. That is, our primary goal when developing these scales was to differentiate *between* organizational and societal cultures. They were not specifically designed to measure differences *within* cultures or between individuals. Thus, our scales are most immediately useful to cross-cultural rather than intracultural researchers.

ENDNOTES

1. An illustration of this problem can be found in the team literature with the concept of group potency (Guzzo, Yost, Campbell, & Shea, 1993). Group potency refers to the belief of team members that their team has the competencies to successfully complete its tasks. Early studies attempting to measure group potency borrowed items from the individual focused self-efficacy literature. Specifically, they asked each team member to rate his or her own individual task competence. Individual responses to these items were then aggregated to the team level of analysis and these average self-efficacy measures were believed to be a good indicator of group potency. Unfortunately, subsequent research indicated that this assumption was invalid (Yost, 1993). Indeed, it is possible to have a team comprised of individuals who have very healthy beliefs of their own capabilities (i.e., strong average self-efficacy scores) but who have no confidence in the capabilities of the other team members (i.e., low group potency) (Yost, 1993). This example illustrates that the bias caused by using the wrong type of item (individualized self-efficacy items) cannot be eliminated even though the data was properly manipulated (i.e., aggregated to the team level of analysis).

2. It became clear fairly early in the GLOBE project, that the term *leader* activated different concepts in respondents across our societies. For example, in contemporary Germany, the term *Führer* ("leader") is used to describe one certain politician in German history closely associated with the Holocaust (i.e., Adolf Hitler), and thus *Führer* is generally perceived negatively. Rather, business leaders in Germany are generally called *Führungskraft, Führungsperson,* or *Manager.* Interestingly, in contemporary Austria, the German word *Führer* seemed not to have the same association with the Holocaust. In order to have all our respondents describe the behaviors and trait descriptors of business leaders, the country co-investigators decided that it was necessary to develop a general definition of leadership. Our jointly agreed-on definition is shown in Table 8.1, and this definition appeared at the beginning of the leadership items section of the survey. It was hoped that this definition oriented our respondents to a common leader concept without biasing their responses by inadvertently suggesting that certain types of behaviors or traits are more desirable than others.

3. Research has shown that $r_{wg(J)}$ can produce values less than zero or greater than 1 (Lindell & Brandt, 1997). We recoded any of these "out of bound" values to zero before computing our average $r_{wg(J)}$s, as recommended by James, Demaree, and Wolfe (1993).

4. It should be noted that the Pilot Study 2 confirmatory factor analyses were performed on the total variance–covariance matrices (i.e., total or pancultural level of analysis) instead of the organizational or societal level of analysis. We performed the analyses at this level because aggregating the scales to the societal level of analysis would result in too few observations (i.e., 12 to 13) to permit use of confirmatory factor analytic procedures. Performing the confirmatory factor analysis on total variance–covariance matrices provides a conservative test of the dimensionality of our scales (Muthen, 1989). As indicated by Kreft and De Leeuw (1998), the total variance–covariance matrix (i.e., the pancultural matrix) contains both between-group level as well as the within-group level information. The more within-group information contained in our total variance–covariance matrices, the less likely it is that the between-group factor structure obtained in Pilot Study 1 would be replicated. However, if the dimensionality of the scales were replicated in Pilot Study 2, then support for the invariance of the scale could be declared.

5. Although obtaining samples from at least two industries in each society was our goal, four of the societies (i.e., Denmark, El Salvador, Namibia, and Venezuela) provided data from only one industry.

6. Cross-cultural researchers typically test the equivalence of a scale by performing a multigroup confirmatory factor analysis in which the equivalence of a within-society factor structure is compared across multiple societies. Lack of measurement equivalence is declared if different factor structures are found across societies. We did not perform our confirmatory factor analysis in this manner because the convergent–emergent nature of our constructs directly implies that the similarity of any within-group factor structure is not the critical issue. The important issue for scales measuring convergent–emergent constructs is the appropriateness of a factor structure that accounts for between organization or societal variation.

It should be noted, however, that Muthen's multilevel confirmatory factor analysis provides some information about the equivalence of the within-group factor structure. In this statistical procedure, the within variance–covariance matrix is estimated by pooling the within-society matrices from each society and imposing a factor structure on this pooled within-group matrix. Within-society measurement equivalence is declared with this procedure if (a) the imposed factor structure adequately fits the pooled within-society matrix or (b) any lack of fit can be eliminated by modifying this common within-society factor structure. Lack of fit caused by measurement nonequivalence cannot be eliminated by modifying the factor structure applied on the pooled within-society variance–covariance matrix. However, it should be recognized that the most direct assessment of measurement equivalence as it is traditionally conceived in the cross-cultural literature would be to test for societal differences in the within-society factor structure. Unfortunately, the multilevel confirmatory factor analysis procedure cannot test for these interactions.

7. It is important to remember when examining ICC(1) values that it indicates the percentage of total scale score variance attributable to between organization–society differences. It is not surprising therefore, that given all the differences that can occur between people within organizations or societies, ICC(1)'s in the 5–20% range indicate fairly powerful effects of the overall organization or society.

8. It should be noted that imposing a different factor structure at the within-society level of analysis

for these three scales does not mean that these scales lack measurement equivalence across societies. Rather, as noted in Endnote 4, lack of fit caused by measurement nonequivalence cannot be eliminated by modifying the factor structure imposed on the pooled within-society variance–covariance matrix. Rather, evidence for measurement equivalence across societies for these scales is provided because the same two-factor structure was imposed on the pooled within-society covariance matrix and the fit of the model exceeded accepted standards.

9. Although the low internal consistency for some of our organizational culture scales was disappointing, we decided to keep these scales in our study. The literature on criterion-referenced tests has documented the utility of scales exhibiting little, if any, internal consistency (e.g., Nunnally & Bernstein, 1994). All of our scales exhibited some level of internal consistency. Thus, even the organizational culture scales exhibiting low internal consistency might prove to be useful for predicting when certain leadership attributes are culturally endorsed. Clearly, these results suggest that the constructs measured by these scales are slightly broader at the organizational level of analysis. Future research should add items to these scales to improve the coverage of the content domain at the organizational level of analysis.

10. Generalizability analyses conducted on Pilot Study 2 data indicated that we needed an average of 45 respondents per organization or society to have reliable scaling of our organizations or societies. Our CCIs used this number of respondents as the desired minimum sample size from each organization for Phase 2 data collection. However, it is important to note that the Pilot Study 2 data only permitted societal level comparisons and so this target number of respondents overestimated the actual number needed to achieve reliable organizational level data. As shown in Table 8.4, the organizational level scales exhibited acceptable levels of reliability even though we did not have an average of 45 respondents per organization.

11. It should be noted that we had more than an average of 45 respondents for our society-level scales. Thus, the ICC(2) estimates reported in Table 8.4 are conservative estimates for the society-level culture and leadership scales.

12. We performed the following steps to create the six global CLT dimensions. First, all of the first-order CLT scales were standardized. Standardization

equalized the variance of the first-order scales and enabled us to create six unit-weighted composite scores by simply adding the first-order CLT scales specified in Table 8.5 for each global leadership dimension. Without this standardization, the summation of the first-order CLT scales would have created differentially weighted composite scores in which the first-order scales with larger variances would have more influence on the composite (i.e., have a greater weight) than scales with smaller variances. Second, we computed the mean and variance for our six global CLT dimensions by following the linear composite formulas specified in Nunnally and Bernstein (1994). Specifically, these formulas indicate that the mean of a unit-weighted linear composite is the sum of the means of the unstandardized first-order scales used to create that composite. The standard deviation of a linear composite is obtained by adding the variance of the unstandardized scales and twice the covariances among these scales and taking the square root of this sum. Third, we multiplied the global CLT dimension by the calculated standard deviation and added the calculated mean to create unstandardized, unit-weighted global CLT dimensions. Finally, we divided these global CLT dimensions by the number of scales used to create them so that the range of the global CLT dimensions was on the original 1 to 7 scale.

13. Although one might develop a similar hypothesis for the organizational and societal cultural values scales, it should be remembered that the data collection strategy used in GLOBE probably minimizes the effect of industry on the organizational cultural values scales. Specifically, the CCIs identified organizations that represented one of the three specified industries and were representative of their societal culture. The CCIs were specifically instructed that they could not include multinational corporations. Thus, the strategy used to identify the organizations in GLOBE probably increased the overlap between organizational and societal cultural values. Indeed, the results showed that the average correlation for the organizational cultural values scales was 0.74 (i.e., average financial–food correlation = 0.80; average financial–telecommunication correlation = 0.70; average food–telecommunication correlation = 0.74) whereas it was 0.77 for the societal cultural values scales (i.e., average financial–food correlation = 0.79; average financial–telecommunication correlation = 0.76; average food–telecommunication

correlation = 0.77). While these results are in the hypothesized direction (i.e., average correlation for the organizational cultural values scales is smaller than the average correlation for the societal cultural values scales), the magnitude of this effect is substantially reduced.

REFERENCES

Bass, B. M. (1990). *Bass and Stogdill's handbook of leadership: Theory, research, and managerial applications* (3rd ed.). New York: Free Press.

Bliese, P. D. (2000). Within-group agreement, non-independence, and reliability: Implications for data aggregation and analysis. In K. J. Klein & S. W. J. Kozlowski (Eds.), *Multilevel theory, research, and methods in organizations: Foundations, extensions, and new directions* (pp. 349–381). San Francisco, CA: Jossey-Bass.

Brewer, J., & Hunter, A. (1989). *Multimethod research: A synthesis of styles.* Newbury Park, CA: Sage.

Brislin, R. W. (Ed.). (1976). *Translation: Application and research.* New York: John Wiley/Halsted.

Brislin, R. W. (1986). The wording and translation of research instruments. In W. J. Lohner & J. W. Berry (Eds.), *Field methods in cross-cultural research* (pp. 137–164). Beverly Hills, CA: Sage.

Cascio, W. F. (1998). *Applied psychology in human resource management* (5th ed.). Englewood Cliffs, NJ: Prentice Hall.

Dickson, M. (1997). *Universality and variation in organizationally cognitive prototypes of effective leadership.* Unpublished doctoral dissertation, Department of Psychology, University of Maryland.

Dickson, M. W., Aditya, R. N., & Chhokar, J. S. (2000). Definition and interpretation in cross-cultural organizational culture research: Some pointers from the GLOBE research program. In N. Ashkanasy, C. Wilderom, & M. Petersen (Eds.), *Handbook of organizational culture and climate* (pp. 447–464). Thousand Oaks, CA: Sage.

Dyer, N., Sipe, W. P., & Hanges, P. J. (1997). Multilevel confirmatory factor analysis: Demonstration of Muthen's technique. *Academy of Management Best Paper Proceedings,* 391–394.

Foti, R. J., & Lord, R. G. (1987). Prototypes and scripts: The effects of alternative methods of processing information. *Organizational Behavior and Human Decision Processes, 39,* 318–341.

Gelfand, M. J., Triandis, H. C., & Chan, K. S. (1996). Individualism versus collectivism or versus authoritarianism? *European Journal of Social Psychology, 26,* 397–410.

Guzzo, R. A., Yost, P. R., Campbell, R. J., & Shea, G. P. (1993). Potency in groups: Articulating a construct. *British Journal of Social Psychology, 32,* 87–106.

Hanges, P. J., Dyer, N., & Sipe, W. P. (1999, April). Multilevel confirmatory factor analysis: Demonstration of Muthen's technique. In S. Palmer, G. Ziets, & P. Bliese (Chairs), *Advances in multilevel research: New techniques and methodological issues.* Symposium conducted at the meeting of the Society of Industrial and Organizational Psychology, Atlanta, GA.

Hanges, P. J., House, R. J., Dickson, M. W., Dorfman, P. W., & GLOBE. (2003). *The development and validation of scales to measure societal and organizational culture.* Manuscript submitted for publication.

Hanges, P. J., Lord, R. G., & Dickson, M. W. (2000). An information-processing perspective on leadership and culture: A case for connectionist architecture. *Applied Psychology: An International Review, 49,* 133–161.

Hofstede, G. (1980). *Culture's consequences: International differences in work-related values.* London: Sage.

Hofstede, G. (2001). *Culture's consequences: Comparing values, behaviors, institutions and organizations across nations* (2nd ed.). Thousand Oaks, CA: Sage.

Hui, C. C., & Triandis, H. C. (1989). Effects of culture and response format on extreme response style. *Journal of Cross-Cultural Psychology, 20,* 296–309.

Inglehart, R., Basanez, M., & Moreno, A. (1998). *Human values and beliefs: A cross-cultural sourcebook.* Ann Arbor: University of Michigan.

James, L. R. (1982). Aggregation bias in estimates of perceptual agreement. *Journal of Applied Psychology, 76,* 219–229.

James, L. R., Demaree, R. G., & Wolf, G. (1984). Estimating within-group interrater reliability with and without response bias. *Journal of Applied Psychology, 69,* 85–98.

James, L. R., Demaree, R. G., & Wolf, G. (1993). $R_{wg(J)}$: An assessment of within group interrater agreement. *Journal of Applied Psychology, 79,* 306–309.

Klein, K. J., Conn, A. L., Smith, D. B., & Sorra, J. S. (2001). Is everyone in agreement? Exploring the determinants of within-group agreement in survey responses. *Journal of Applied Psychology, 86,* 3–16.

Klein, K. J., Dansereau, F., & Hall, R. J. (1994). Levels issues in theory development, data collection, and analysis. *Academy of Management Review, 24,* 308–324.

Kluckhohn, C. (1951). The study of culture. In D. Lerner & H. D. Lasswell (Eds.), *The policy sciences* (pp. 86–101). Stanford, CA: Stanford University Press.

Kozlowski, S. W. J., & Klein, K. J. (2000). A multilevel approach to theory and research in organizations: Contextual, temporal, and emergent processes. In K. J. Klein & S. W. J. Kozlowski (Eds.), *Multilevel theory, research, and methods in organizations: Foundations, extensions, and new directions* (pp. 3–90). San Francisco, CA: Jossey-Bass.

Kreft, I., & De Leeuw, J. (1998). *Introducing multilevel modeling.* Thousand Oaks, CA: Sage.

Leslie, J. B., & Van Velsor, E. (1998). *A cross-national comparison of effective leadership and teamwork: Toward a global workforce.* Greensboro, NC: Center for Creative Leadership.

Lindell, M. K., & Brandt, C. J. (1997). Measuring interrater agreement for ratings of a single target. *Applied Psychological Measurement, 21,* 271–278.

Lord, R. G., Foti, R., & DeVader, C. (1984). A test of leadership categorization theory: Internal structure, information processing, and leadership perceptions. *Organizational Behavior and Human Performance, 34,* 343–378.

Lord, R. G., & Maher, K. J. (1991a). Cognitive theory in industrial and organizational psychology. In M. D. Dunnette & L. M. Hough (Eds.), *Handbook of industrial and organizational psychology* (2nd ed., Vol. 2, pp. 1–62). Palo Alto, CA: Consulting Psychologists Press.

Lord, R., & Maher, K. J. (1991b). *Leadership and information processing: Linking perceptions and performance.* Boston: Unwin-Hyman.

Messick, S. (1981). Constructs and their vicissitudes in educational and psychological measurement. *Psychological Bulletin, 89,* 575–588.

McGraw, K. O., & Wong, S. P. (1996). Forming inferences about some intraclass correlation coefficients. *Psychological Methods, 1,* 30–46.

Muthen, B. O. (1989, June). *Latent variable modeling in heterogeneous populations.* Presidential address to the Psychometric Society, Princeton, New Jersey.

Muthen, B. O. (1990, June). *Mean and covariance structure analysis of hierarchical data.* Paper presented at the Psychometric Society, Princeton, New Jersey.

Muthen, B. O. (1994). Multilevel covariance structure analysis. *Sociological methods & research, 22,* 376–398.

Nunnally, J. C., & Bernstein, I. H. (1994). *Psychometric theory* (3rd ed.). New York: McGraw-Hill.

Payne, R. L., Fineman, S., & Wall, T. D. (1976). Organizational climate and job satisfaction: A conceptual synthesis. *Organizational Behavior and Human Performance, 16,* 45–62.

Roberts, K., & Boyacigiller, N. (1984). Cross-national organizational research: The grasp of the blind man. In B. M. Staw & L. L. Cummings (Eds.), *Research in organizational behavior* (Vol. 6, pp. 423–475). Greenwich CT: JAI.

Rokeach, M. (1973). *The nature of human values.* New York: Free Press.

Sagiv, L., & Gupta, V. (2002, August) Schwartz theory of cultural dimensions of values. In V. Gupta & R. J. House (Chairs), *Reconciling the findings of five cross-cultural research programs: Hofstede, Trompenaars, World Values Survey, Schwartz and GLOBE.* Symposium conducted at the meeting of the Academy of Management, Denver, CO.

Schneider, B. (1990). The climate for service: An application of the climate construct. In B. Schneider (Ed.), *Organizational climate and culture* (pp. 393–412). San Francisco: Jossey-Bass.

Schriesheim, C. A. (1979). The similarity of individual directed and group directed leader behavior descriptions. *Academy of Management Journal, 22,* 345–355.

Schwartz, S. (1992). Universals in the content and structure of values: Theoretical advances and empirical tests in 20 countries. In M. Zanna (Ed.), *Advances in experimental social psychology* (Vol. 25, pp. 1–65). New York: Academic.

Schwartz, S. (1994). Beyond individualism-collectivism: New cultural dimensions of values. In U. Kim, H. C. Triandis, C. Kagitçibasi, S. C. Choi, & G. Yoon (Eds.), *Individualism and collectivism: Theory, method and applications* (pp. 85–119). London: Sage.

Schwartz, S. (2001, April). *Antecedents and consequences of national variation on three cultural dimensions.* Keynote address at the meeting of Institute for Research on Intercultural Cooperation, Tilburg, The Netherlands.

Schwartz, S., & Bilsky, W. (1987). Toward a universal psychological structure of human values. *Journal of Personality and Social Psychology, 53,* 550–562.

Schwartz, S., & Melech, G. (2000). National differences in micro and macro worry: Social, economic, and cultural explanations. In E. Diener & E. Suh (Eds.), *Subjective well-being across cultures and nations* (219–256). Boston: MIT Press.

Shrout, P. E., & Fleiss, J. L. (1979). Intraclass correlations: Uses in assessing rater reliability. *Psychological Bulletin, 86,* 420–428.

Smith, P. B. (2002). Culture's consequences: Something old and something new. *Human Relations, 55,* 119–124.

Smith, P. B., & Schwartz, S. H. (1997). Values. In J. Berry, M. Segall, & C. Kagitçibasi (Eds.), *Handbook of cross-cultural psychology* (Vol. 3, pp. 77–118). Boston, MA: Allyn & Bacon.

Stening, B. W., & Everett, J. E. (1984). Response styles in a cross-cultural managerial study. *Journal of Social Psychology, 122,* 151–156.

Triandis, H. C. (1994). Cross-cultural industrial and organizational psychology. In H. C. Triandis, M. D. Dunnette, & L. M. Hough (Eds.), *Handbook of industrial and organizational psychology* (2nd ed., Vol. 4, pp. 103–172). Palo Alto, CA: Consulting Psychologists Press.

Triandis, H. C. (1995). *Individualism and collectivism.* Boulder, CO: Westview.

van de Vijver, F., & Leung, K. (1997). *Methods and data analysis for cross-cultural research.* Thousand Oaks, CA: Sage.

Yammarino, F. J. (1990). Individual- and group-directed leader behavior descriptions. *Educational and Psychological Measurement, 50,* 739–759.

Yost, P. R. (1993). *Individual versus group performance: I can't but we can.* Unpublished master's thesis, University of Maryland, College Park.

Yukl, G. A. (2002). *Leadership in organizations* (5th ed.). Upper Saddle River, NJ: Prentice Hall.

9

Multisource Constuct Validity of GLOBE Scales

Vipin Gupta

Mary Sully de Luque

Robert J. House

In this chapter we assess the construct validity of the GLOBE societal-level cultural scales through the use of measures derived from independent sources. Recall that the GLOBE cultural scales were constructed using questionnaire responses of the middle-level managers aggregated to the societal and organizational levels of analysis. The use of independent measures allows us to assess the degree to which the GLOBE societal level scales are meaningful indicators of the constructs they are intended to measure.

A notable theme in assessing construct validity is the use of multiple methods because some of the variance in scales may be a function of the measures. In this chapter, we apply tests of convergent and discriminant validity to the GLOBE dimensions (Rossi, Wright & Anderson, 1983)[1]. For the first part of this chapter, we rely on archival data obtained from secondary studies

of societal practices to clarify the thematic content of the GLOBE societal cultural practices scales. Then, we apply the identified thematic content to formulate unobtrusive measures of societal level GLOBE practice constructs by performing a content analysis of 1998 Culturgrams to assess the construct validity of the GLOBE cultural practice scales.[2] Following conventional procedures, the content analysis we conducted is guided by a priori hypotheses (Krippendorf, 1980). In the second part of this chapter, we develop scales from the World Values Survey (WVS) data to create validation measures to test the construct validity of the GLOBE societal value scales. Two of the four World Value Surveys (Inglehart, Basanez, & Moreno, 1998) conducted during 1990–1993 and 1995–1997 coincide with the administration of the GLOBE questionnaires, which were administered between 1995 and 1997.

AUTHORS' NOTE: The authors wish to thank Klaus Krippendorff for his review and helpful comments on the early part of this study. In addition, we gratefully acknowledge the dedicated support provided by Sally Chan, James Zale, Danielle Rizk, Tom Spies, and Julia Kang at various times during the preparation of this manuscript. Without their assistance this research would not have been possible. We are grateful to Paul Hanges for his invaluable guidance, suggestions, and reviews of this chapter.

We begin the discussion in the first part of the chapter by examining the validity of the GLOBE societal-cultural practice constructs using unobtrusive measures derived from a content analysis of Culturgrams. In the second part of the chapter, we then examine the validity of the GLOBE societal cultural value constructs using questionnaire scales derived from the WVS.

DEVELOPING UNOBTRUSIVE MEASURES OF THE GLOBE SOCIETAL CULTURAL PRACTICES SCALES

Unobtrusive measures commonly refer to data collected in a way that avoids obtrusive interaction between the investigator and the subjects being studied (Webb, Campbell, Schwartz, & Sechrest, 1966, 2000). They are often referred to as nonreactive measures (Sechrest & Belew, 1983) because they do not require respondents to participate in the research process. For example, in an often-cited classic study, a museum had new floor tiles installed in front of each exhibit. After a period of time, the wear-and-tear of the tiles was measured as an unobtrusive measure of patron traffic and interest in each exhibit (Melton, 1933).

Archival Data and Objective Correlates

We began by using published quantitative data to gain insights into the meaning of GLOBE dimensions and enrich their conceptual definitions. There is an abundance of information routinely gathered by businesses, governments, and various organizations that can be accessed and analyzed by researchers. For example, by examining the degree to which GLOBE survey data correlates with available archival data, one could determine if earned income or literacy of women is related to the survey-based GLOBE measure of gender egalitarianism. The use of these findings will hopefully explicate the meaning of GLOBE data beyond that which was previously understood or assumed.

The most prominent sources for international quantitative archival data are multilateral agencies that are part of the United Nations system, such as the World Bank. These agencies systematically collate a wide variety of data from various national sources and try to provide these in a comparable format for policy and academic analysis. In addition, several researchers and research organizations publish reference data on civil liberties, corruption, climate, and other variables (Parker, 1997). We obtained such archival data from several well-recognized cross-cultural sources: Kurian (1997), Sullivan (1991), UNESCO (1997), the World Bank (1997), and Parker (1997). Selected items that showed significant correlations with the GLOBE aggregated society practices data are given in Table 9.1.

Content Analysis

Content analysis is designed to measure the presence or absence of specific concepts within various recorded texts (or other symbolic material) to make inferences about the phenomenon of interest (Shapiro & Markoff, 1997). Using the descriptions of the core GLOBE societal dimensions presented in this volume, we conducted a content analysis of the cultural dimensions in the societies described in the Culturgrams that were included in the GLOBE sample. The objective of the content analysis was to support or disconfirm the validity of the GLOBE societal-level practices measures.

Our goal of content analysis is to examine the universality of GLOBE practices dimensions by drawing probabilistic inferences from strategically selected text. As such, our research design was guided by qualitative analysis of text, driven by a priori criteria, to be coded into quantified scores, allowing for comparison with the core GLOBE dimensions. Once again, the purpose of this content analysis is to establish or disconfirm the validity of GLOBE societal-level practices measures.

Research Design

There is no universally agreed upon method for conducting content analysis (Weber, 1990). In designing our content analysis, we combined the recommendations of three scholars (Carley, 1994; Krippendorff, 1980; Weber, 1990)[3].

Table 9.1   Correlation of Archival Data with Aggregated Society Practice Scale Scores[1]

Construct	Item	Correlation
Performance Orientation	High religious diversity	.47***
	Low concentration of largest religion	.55***
	Low share of government funding in national R&D *–indicating nondogmatic creativity orientation, free market competition, and low government intervention*	.36*
Assertiveness	Low dominance of natural resources in exports *–indicating passive encounter with the environment*	.42**
Future Orientation	High number of trademarks per capita *–indicating investments in long-term intellectual property*	.58***
Humane Orientation	High marriage rates	.40**
	Few retail outlets per capita *–indicating low access to products, especially low socioeconomic status of the cultures (reverse scored)*	.55***
Institutional Collectivism	Earlier time zone *–indicating eastern and southeastern location where societal collectivism is predominant*	.54***
In-Group Collectivism	Low divorce rates	.60***
	Poor due process *–indicating an emphasis on sustaining the family*	.62***
Gender Egalitarianism	High proportion of women in earned income	.43**
	High male–female societal equality *–indicating low discrimination against women and women's contribution to workforce*	.46***
Power Distance	Limited number of scientists per $ of GNP	.56***
	Unequal distribution of income and private consumption expenditure (Gini index) *–indicating social inequity and suppression of intellectual inquiry*	.41**
Uncertainty Avoidance	High share of home corporations in national R&D	.51***
	High share of machine and transport equipment in trade	.47***
	High use of fax machines per capita *–indicating high emphasis on information processing, information availability, and need for security*	.53***

NOTE: N varies from 40–54. ***$p < 0.001$. **$p < 0.01$. *$p < 0.05$.

[1] There is no effect of GNP, per capita income, population size of country, or year of independence on the correlations between the unobtrusive measures and their isomorphic-questionnaire-based measures. However, selected subsamples such as more or less wealthy countries, indicated differences in correlations suggesting boundary conditions for some of the unobtrusive measures.

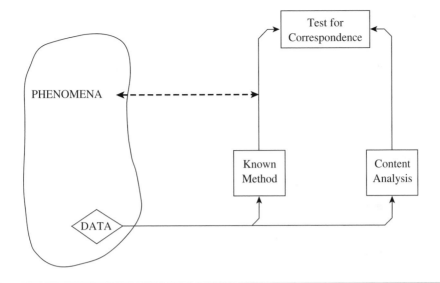

Figure 9.1   Content analysis design to compare different methods

SOURCE: Based on Krippendorf, K. (1980). *Content Analysis: An Introduction to Its Methodology. Thousand Oaks, CA: Sage.*

Applying the Framework for Content Analysis

In our content analytic study, we sought to identify and code societal-level textual indicators of the nine GLOBE cultural practices dimensions, in an effort to assess the validity of the GLOBE dimension measures. Selected for this study is a content analysis design to compare different methods, in which "two or more methods are applied to the same data or to different data obtained from the same situation to test whether the two methods yield comparable results" (Krippendorff, 1980, pp. 51). This design shows that different research methods that purport to be measuring the same construct result in similar findings. Figure 9.1 shows this design.

Searching for Suitable Data

As stated above, we selected 1998 Culturgrams reports as our data text source for content analyses of the core GLOBE practice scales. These reports are published by the David M. Kennedy Center for International Studies at Brigham Young University, and provide comparable and consistent, four page descriptions of cultures of 170 societies around the world.

These descriptions include daily customs and lifestyle, historical highlights, and the political and economic structure of each culture.

In 1998, Culturgrams were bound in two volumes. Volume 1 covered North and South America, and Western and Eastern Europe. Volume 2 covered the Middle East, Asia, Africa, and Pacific areas. Culturgram reports did not exist for two of the countries covered in the GLOBE study: Qatar and Kuwait. We investigated the history of these nations and found that Qatar's culture is most similar to United Arab Emirates, and Kuwait's culture is most similar to Saudi Arabia. Therefore, we chose to use the United Arab Emirates' report as a proxy for Qatar, and the Saudi Arabia report as a proxy for Kuwait[4].

Searching for Contextual Knowledge

In content analysis, both establishing empirical links connecting the qualitative data to the GLOBE cultural practice dimensions and making inferences on the basis of the data are fundamental. We refer to this as the *construct–inference link* (Krippendorff, 1980).

To achieve this construct–inference link, we reviewed Culturgrams from a sample of ten non-GLOBE societies. Krippendorff (1980) suggests involving experts who are familiar with the theoretical linkages between the data and the concepts of study in this search for contextual knowledge. Thus, two members of the research team inspected the text data, each developing construct-inference examples independently. From this we identified culturally relevant concepts related to each of the nine GLOBE constructs.[5]

Strategy Development and Definition of Measures

Developing Strategies

Several strategies for conducting content analyses have been suggested (Roberts, 1997). We chose *conceptual analysis* for our investigation. Conceptual analysis, or thematic analysis (Stone, 1997), commonly focuses on the detection of specific words or concepts, as well as the identification of patterns or themes in the text. Carley (1994) defines a concept "as a single idea regardless of whether it is represented by a single word or phrase" (p. 726).

Two ways of analyzing concepts have been noted in the research: explicit concept analysis and implicit concept analysis (Carley, 1994). Actual words and phrases that appear in the text represent explicit concepts. Implied words and phrases that occur in the text indicate implicit concepts. By using explicit concepts alone, researchers may overlook more indirect nuances in their sources of content analysis data. Implicit analysis allows greater ability to extract deep meaning from the text. Thus, we used both implicit and explicit concept analysis in our research.

Examining embedded concepts within the text proved to be an important advantage in this analysis. For example, "visiting one another" was identified as an important indicator of the Humane Orientation dimension. In the Culturgram text, the implicit messages regarding visiting included such considerations as (a) whether the importance of visiting was the primary variable mentioned in the section on the topic, implying a more humane culture, (b) whether the author was emphatic about the importance of visiting, implying a more humane culture, (c) whether visiting was a warm and sincere gesture (more humane) or was an expected ritualistic act (more impersonal and therefore not counted as humane), and (d) whether other implicit or explicit concepts throughout the text contradicted or diminished the importance of visiting.

Examining implicit concepts allowed for nonobvious concepts to surface. In addition, when analyzing concepts for Institutional Collectivism, the macro or societal level was a central feature of this dimension. Implicit concepts indicating Institutional Collectivism in the Culturgram text included such phenomena as group-oriented activities that were encouraged or sponsored by formal organizations such as government agencies, foundations, or educational institutions. Examples of unobtrusive indicators of Institutional Collectivism include high numbers of sponsored team sports, social clubs, or recreational centers, all of which imply a form of institutional collectivism other than families.

These examples illustrate that making implicit concepts explicit and then quantifying these concepts is important because it results in the construction of a translation rule. These rules established our confidence in the coding and ensured coding consistency throughout the text (Carley, 1994). Translation rules guide coders to record various concepts in a precise manner. The coders would discuss the concepts—in this case the cultural activity related to the identified themes—and develop instructions (or rules) on how to note the occurrence of the concept. Other important elements of this stage of the content-analysis process are defining measurements[6] and defining categories[7].

The unobtrusive items for each of the GLOBE society practices are presented in Table 9.2.

Coding for Unobtrusive Indicators

The next step in the content analysis process involved the actual coding of the text. Coding rules were specified and manual coding began. Manual coding was essential for this analysis in that much of the coding extracted implicit information. Extensive training in identifying unobtrusive indicators was provided for the coders to assure that they made appropriate qualitative judgments about the contents of

Table 9.2   Content Analysis Measures of GLOBE Society Practices Constructs

Scale	Content analysis measures
Performance Orientation	People tend to emphasize all-round economic accomplishments.
	The society maintains a diversity of religion.
Assertiveness	People have forceful and expressive behaviors.
	People exhibit a toughness in their behavior.
	Dominant behavior is characteristic.
Future Orientation	People tend to arrange social and family visits in advance, and avoid spontaneous visits.
	Most people seek to learn and use English as an important language for communication in the modern world.
Humane Orientation	Warm greetings are of the essence.
	Hospitality and visiting are very important and highly cherished.
	People show empathy in their interactions with others.
Institutional Collectivism	Societal-level collective behaviors are important.
	The culture engages in more team-associated activities.
	Highly prominent subgroups or segmentation do not exist in the culture.
In-Group Collectivism	The father usually plays the role of the family head.
	Most people lack access to the opportunities for personal advancement.
Gender Egalitarianism	Most women have access to resources that allow them to pursue personal goals as freely as men.
	It is proper for women to have a job.
Power Distance	Economic growth tends to go hand-in-hand with the unemployment, poverty, and stratification of society by income.
	People derive little enjoyment from their work
Uncertainty Avoidance	Medical facilities are effective in keeping the society essentially healthy and disease-free, indicating reliability and breadth of home research initiatives.
	The nation strives for an extensive and modern telecommunications system, indicating a growing information technology capability.

the Culturgram text. All unobtrusive indicators were rated on a 5-point scale, with 5 representing high scores on the indicators. Using this type of scale required conceptualizing the source material on a continuum (Krippendorff, 1980), with the final dimension scores consisting of the overall averages of the dimension indicators. Two experts, each of whom had a PhD in management, coded all societies independently.

This enhanced the reliability of the study because it promoted reproducibility of the findings through the use of multiple raters.

From the Culturgrams, a sample of 10 countries not in the GLOBE sample was coded on each of the nine GLOBE practice dimensions. The average initial results were compared across the 10 societies on all unobtrusive indicators. In both the first and second rounds

Table 9.3   Interrater Correlation and Internal Consistency Reliability Estimates for Unobtrusive Measures

Unobtrusive Measures	Interrater correlation	Reliability estimate*
Performance Orientation	.83**	.90
Assertiveness	.74**	.86
Future Orientation	.92**	.96
Humane Orientation	.69**	.81
Institutional Collectivism	.55**	.70
In-Group Collectivism	1.00**	1.00
Gender Egalitarianism	.91**	.95
Power Distance	.88**	.93
Uncertainty Avoidance	.95**	.97

* Based on the Spearman-Brown Prophecy formula (Nunnally & Bernstein, 1994). ** $p < 0.01$.

of preliminary coding based on cultures not in the GLOBE study, items with lower coding agreement between coders were discussed, other discrepancies were sorted out, and recoding was conducted until an acceptable level of agreement was achieved.

This rigor in coding the sample texts clarified coding rules and weaved information into the classification process (Weber, 1990). After the coders reached an acceptable level of agreement, the reliability of the coding and the validity of the scales could be measured.

Assessing Quality and Accuracy

In this study, reliability was assessed as the consistency with which multiple raters coded the Culturgram texts. Table 9.3 gives the interrater correlation for each of the nine unobtrusive measurement scales. The scale score for each dimension consists of scores from two raters. The average interrater correlation was 0.70 across nine unobtrusive measure scales, which is within the accepted reliability range (Nunnally & Bernstein, 1994). In addition, using the Spearman-Brown Prophecy formula we produced reliability estimates for each of the average unobtrusive scores. These consist

of the averaging of rater responses and are also provided in Table 9.3.

One way to assess validity of unobtrusive measures is to determine if the measured data are related to other analyses of the construct in ways predicted by the theory (Bowen and Bowen, 1999). Two primary aspects of validity are convergent validity and discriminant validity (Campbell & Fiske, 1959; Weber, 1990). For this part of our study, convergent validity is represented as the agreement, or correlation, between the unobtrusive measures and the corresponding GLOBE measures to assess societal-level cultural practices through text analysis and survey questionnaire responses, respectively. A dimension has discriminant validity if it is relatively distinct from other criteria variables. Validity may best be clarified through the use of a multitrait–multimethod matrix (Campbell & Fiske, 1959). For this study, the multiple traits consisted of the nine cultural dimensions. The two methods consisted of the questionnaire-based method (GLOBE societal-level practice scales) and the content-coding method (unobtrusive measures of culture). Table 9.4 provides the complete multitrait–multimethod matrix. Table 9.5 provides a summary of this information.

Table 9.4   The Multitrait-Multimethod Matrix of Societal Practice Measures

		Unobtrusive Variables									GLOBE Variables							
	A_1	B_1	C_1	D_1	E_1	F_1	G_1	H_1	I_1	A_2	B_2	C_2	D_2	E_2	F_2	G_2	H_2	I_2
Method 1																		
A_1*	(.90)																	
B_1	.10	(.86)																
C_1	.56**	.01	(.96)															
D_1	.19	−.20	.19	(.81)														
E_1	.10	−.29*	.13	.44**	(.70)													
F_1	−.33*	−.09	−.47**	−.08	−.05	(1.0)												
G_1	.23	.13	−.38**	.18	.08	.55**	(.95)											
H_1	−.50**	−.05	−.72**	−.07	−.08	.64**	−.32*	(.93)										
I_1	.56**	1	.72**	.11	.01	−.56**	.39**	−.70**	(.97)									
Method 2																		
A_2	**.56***	−.06	.31*	.13	.10	.04	−.03	−.26*	.35**	(.72)								
B_2	.15	**.59***	0	.07	−.12	.26*	.03	.15	.09	.05	(.75)							
C_2	.63**	.11	**.62***	.26*	.12	−.13	.15	−.46**	.47**	.62**	.08	(.80)						
D_2	−.13	−.04	−.25	**.51***	.03	.17	−.23	.08	−.30*	.25**	−.42**	.07	(.88)					
E_2	.30*	.20	.27*	−.06	**.58***	−.11	.02	−.22	.26*	.42**	−.38**	.47**	.41**	(.67)				
F_2	−.47**	−.17	−.59**	−.21	−.17	**.58***	−.44**	.61**	−.62**	−.11	.13	−.40**	.27**	.11	(.77)			
G_2	.10	.04	.10	.10	.03	−.27*	**.65***	.01	.04	−.30*	−.10	−.07	−.14*	−.03	−.23	(.66)		
H_2	−.49**	−.09	−.43**	−.26**	−.21	.37**	−.26*	**.62***	−.36**	−.33*	.21	−.44**	−.15*	−.30*	.61**	−.32*	(.80)	
I_2	.51**	.15	.54**	.22	.08	.30*	.29*	−.60**	**.60***	.58**	−.08	.75**	.01	.38**	−.59**	−.06	−.48**	(.88)

NOTE: Letters A, B, C, D, E, F, G, H, and I refer to statuses on the dimensions of culture. Subscripts 1 and 2 refer to the 2 methods used in this study. Method 1 refers to the Unobtrusive items and Method 2 refers to the GLOBE items. Validity coefficients are the diagonal set of boldface numbers; reliability coefficients are the numbers in parentheses along the principal diagonal. For this study, the reliability coefficient for the unobtrusive items was calculated by aggregating two raters to form the scores for the dimensions, then using the Spearman-Brown Prophecy formula. A = Performance Orientation. B = Assertiveness. C = Future Orientation. D = Humane Orientation. E = Institutional Collectivism. F = In-Group Collectivism. G = Gender Egalitarianism. H = Power Distance. I = Uncertainty Avoidance. * $p < 0.05$ ** $p < 0.01$

159

Convergent Validity

Convergent validity exists if the coefficients in the validity diagonal are high and statistically significant (Campbell & Fiske, 1959). As shown in the first column of Table 9.5, the convergent coefficients in the validity diagonal range from 0.51 to 0.65, and all of them are significant at $p < 0.01$, confirming convergent validity for each of the nine constructs. These convergent validities are also shown in column 1, Table 9.5.

Discriminant Validity

Discriminant validity exists if (a) the validity coefficients are higher than values lying in their column and row in the same heterotrait–heteromethod triangle, (b) the validity coefficients are higher than all coefficients in the heterotrait–monomethod triangles, and (c) the same pattern of trait interrelationships is seen in all triangles (Campbell & Fiske, 1959). These conditions are very restrictive because they seek to test not only discriminant validity, but also to test whether the results are generalizable to other methods. Therefore, these conditions have been rarely applied in practice. Using a more practical approach appropriate for the task of testing discriminant validity, we adopted three modified conditions for testing the discriminant validity of the constructs using the matrix:

Condition 1: First, in the heterotrait–heteromethod (HTHM) triangles, we computed the average HTHM absolute correlation of each GLOBE measure with the nine unobtrusive measures, as given in column 2a, Table 9.5. These discriminant correlations (G,U) range from 0.09 to 0.41, with an average of 0.23. Similarly, we computed the average absolute HTHM correlation of each unobtrusive measure with the nine GLOBE variables, as given in column 2b, Table 9.5. These discriminant correlations (G,U) range from 0.11 to 0.35, with an average of 0.23. For discriminant validity, the convergent coefficient in the validity diagonal, as given in column 1, Table 9.5, should exceed both of these two HTHM correlations. This condition holds true for all nine measures.

Condition 2: Second, in the heterotrait-monomethod (HTMM) triangles, we computed average HTMM absolute correlations of each unobtrusive measure with the other eight unobtrusive measures, as given in column 3,

Table 9.5. These discriminant coefficients (U) ranged from 0.12 to 0.40, with an average of 0.29. Similarly, we computed average HTMM absolute correlations of each GLOBE measure with the other eight GLOBE measures, as given in column 4, Table 9.5. These discriminant coefficients (G) ranged from 0.16 to 0.37, with an average of 0.29. For discriminant validity, the convergent coefficient in the validity diagonal, as shown in column 1, Table 9.5, should exceed both of these HTMM correlations. This condition holds true for all nine measures.

Condition 3: Third, the reliability of each unobtrusive measure (column 5, Table 9.5) and each GLOBE variable (column 6, Table 9.5) should exceed the respective HTMM discriminant coefficients. This condition holds true for all nine unobtrusive measures as well as nine GLOBE variables.

Thus, we conclude that the GLOBE societal practice constructs have convergent as well as discriminant validity.

Summary and Limitations of Unobtrusive Measures and Archival Data

We examined several major issues in Part I of this chapter pertaining to the construct validity of the GLOBE culture scales. The first issue addressed was interpretive in nature. By correlating several archival indices, collected independently from the GLOBE research program, we were able to identify patterns of behavior associated with each GLOBE societal-level practice dimension and thus gain a better understanding of these dimensions. The findings confirm that the GLOBE scales do indeed capture information that goes beyond the literal interpretation of the GLOBE practices measures. The content analysis of the Culturgrams further supported and helped clarify the interpretations of the GLOBE measures. The correlations of the unobtrusive measures with the societal-level practice scores demonstrate an impressive association between these scores.

The second issue addressed related to sampling, questioning whether the responses of the middle-level managers from the GLOBE sample yield valid data concerning the general characteristics of the society as a whole. The correlations of the Culturgram scores with

Table 9.5 Multitrait-Multimethod Matrix of Societal Practice Measures

GLOBE Cultural Dimensions	1 Convergent $(G,U)^a$	2a Discriminant $(G,U)^b$	2b Discriminant $(U,G)^c$	3 Coefficients Discriminant $(U)^d$	4 Discriminant $(G)^e$	5 Reliability $(U)^f$	6 Reliability $(G)^g$
Performance Orientation	0.56	0.16	0.35	0.32	0.33	0.90	0.72
Assertiveness	0.59	0.11	0.11	0.12	0.18	0.86	0.75
Future Orientation	0.62	0.29	0.32	0.40	0.36	0.96	0.80
Humane Orientation	0.51	0.15	0.16	0.18	0.22	0.81	0.88
Institutional Collectivism	0.58	0.18	0.11	0.15	0.31	0.70	0.67
In-Group Collectivism	0.58	0.41	0.21	0.35	0.31	1.00	0.77
Gender Egalitarianism	0.65	0.09	0.18	0.28	0.16	0.95	0.66
Power Distance	0.62	0.31	0.26	0.39	0.36	0.93	0.80
Uncertainty Avoidance	0.60	0.34	0.34	0.40	0.37	0.97	0.88
Average	0.59	0.23	0.23	0.29	0.29	0.90	0.77

NOTES: Summary conditions for construct validity: 1> 2(a), 2(b), 3, & 4; 5>3; 6>4.

a G,U (Convergent coefficient) = Correlation of the GLOBE measure with the unobtrusive measure.

b G,U (Discriminant coefficient) = Average absolute correlation of a GLOBE measure with the nine unobtrusive measures.

c U,G (Discriminant coefficient) = Average absolute correlation of an unobtrusive measure with the nine GLOBE measures.

d U (Discriminant coefficient) = Average absolute correlation of an unobtrusive measure with other eight unobtrusive measures.

e G (Discriminant coefficient) = Average absolute correlation of a GLOBE measure with other eight GLOBE measures.

f U (Reliability) = Reliability of an unobtrusive measure.

g G (Reliability) = Reliability of a GLOBE measure.

161

the GLOBE practice scores demonstrate that the managerial responses reflect the society in which the respondents are embedded, not merely the cultures of middle managers.

Each research method used to study culture has its strengths and limitations. A general issue associated with the study of culture is the inherent multilayered complexity of the subject matter. As a result, the research methods used must balance depth and sensitivity with breadth; in this manner, researchers can detect both fine cultural nuances and develop a sense of the overall cultural context. Clearly, assessing the culture dimensions independently, in isolation from the other dimensions, may lead to premature conclusions and mistaken assumptions of culture. Examining the dimensions in tandem, however, may provide an enhanced appraisal of cultures studied.

With respect to the use of unobtrusive measures as a research method, two issues surface as to how intervening variables may affect the relationships between the unobtrusive measures and the GLOBE scores. The first issue addresses whether intervening variables may exist when the unobtrusive measure is a good measure of the construct in question. The second issue focuses on what happens when the unobtrusive measure itself is not capturing everything it should and, as a result, is not fully reflective of the construct. For instance, a study of recycling behavior across cultures using post hoc behavior data could overlook the fact that in some societies there tends to be considerable in-home recycling, such as use of empty bottles and cans for storage purposes. By focusing on specific manifestations of recycling behavior, it might be difficult to obtain a true and appropriate appraisal of environmental and waste sensitivity, which may be considered a proxy for future orientation. Clearly, considerable time and effort must be spent to ensure that the unobtrusive measures used are appropriate indicators of the constructs being examined.

Another limitation of unobtrusive measures relates to selective recording of data. Researchers with various interests, biases, and experiences may focus on certain objects and relationships. For instance, female observers of men may document different features of communication, gestures, and clothing than male observers

of women, and vice versa (Kellehear, 2001). Accordingly, unobtrusive measures are best used in conjunction with other variables.

With respect to the use of archival data or data from questionnaires, interviews, and census reports for cultural analysis, other limitations are notable. Archival data are often gathered for alternative purposes, which then define the scope of samples and the choice of variables. These data can help infer relationships among variables within and across cultures. However, the specific inferences derived from secondary analysis may not be relevant for each subgroup within or across cultures.

QUESTIONNAIRE VALIDATION MEASURES FOR GLOBE SOCIETAL VALUE SCALES

The construct validity of the GLOBE's societal value scales based on "Should Be" response formats was assessed by correlating the GLOBE societal-level value scales with other indices created from the World Values Surveys (WVS) (Inglehart, Basanez, & Moreno, 1998). We used selected questionnaire items of the WVS, described below as "outcropping measures." In this section, we seek to assess the validity of the nine GLOBE societal cultural value dimensions.

The World Values Survey includes responses across societies covering a range of economic, political, and cultural issues, from approximately 350 questions relevant to human values (Inglehart et al., 1998). Questions in the WVS range from questions involving self and family, to issues regarding work and jobs, to topics concerning political and social matters. The World Values Surveys were administered to respondents in more than 70 societies, of which 39 overlap with the 62 societies in the GLOBE sample. The WVS raw data are publicly available. For these reasons, we considered the WVS data to be adequate data from which we could construct scales relevant to the GLOBE societal-level value scales listed in Chapter 2 of this volume.

The World Values Survey Methodology

The WVS survey methodology for measuring values differs substantively from that of GLOBE in five major ways. First, the sampling universe of the World Values Surveys consisted of all adult citizens, ages 18 and older. Representative samples were used in most cases. To accomplish this, a random selection of locations was made in each society, and then individuals were sampled in each location. The available World Values Survey data also contain weights to make the samples replicate the national population parameters more closely[8]. Project GLOBE uses a more concentrated sample of middle-level managers from three industries (food processing, financial services, and telecommunication).

Second, the data collection method varied from that of Project GLOBE. The World Values Surveys were carried out through face-to-face interviews. GLOBE surveys were given to the respondents to complete, in some cases in the presence of the investigator and some cases not. A third difference between the two research projects was that the timeframe for data collection differed substantially for each. The WVS data have been collected at four different times: in the early 1980s, in the early 1990s, in the late 1990s, and in the early 2000s. All the nations sampled in the early 1980s were sampled again in one of the two 1990s questionnaire administrations[9]. We elected to use the combined data from the two 1990s samples for the purposes of validation because Inglehart & Baker (2000) showed that although there were some shifts in the values of societies over the two 1990s questionnaire administrations, those shifts were not drastic. GLOBE data, in contrast, were collected over a single period of time, between 1995 and 1997.

A fourth difference between the two projects was that unlike the survey instrument used for data collection in Project GLOBE, the WVS instrument contains items in a variety of nonstandardized formats. Both nominal and ordinal scales were used in the WVS data collection; some questions have yes–no answers, whereas others have a 3-point, 5-point, 7-point, or 10-point response format. For the purposes of the GLOBE study, we took an average of the responses of each item for each society. In some questions, the respondent had to choose a first and second preference from a group of four items. We assigned a score of 2 to the first preference, a score of 1 to the second preference, and a score of 0 to the remaining items, for each

respondent. Thus, all aggregates assumed the underlying construct to be nominal. Because the values covered by the WVS concerned a broad array of human beliefs, we expected substantial differences in the variances among the items. Therefore, we standardized all the items to a mean of 0 and a standard deviation of 1, so that an equal weight was given to all items used. The GLOBE instrument contained items in a standard 7-point response format. To construct the WVS cultural scales that reflected GLOBE societal-level values scales, we used a simple aggregated mean of items selected to correspond to the GLOBE scales.

A fifth and final difference between the two survey sources concerns the purpose of the surveys. The World Values Surveys were intended to test the intergeneration differences in the social, political, and economic values, arising as a result of the processes of postindustrialism. The GLOBE surveys were designed specifically to develop and measure middle managers' reports of selected societal cultural values and practices and other related cultural and leadership constructs.

Given the substantive differences of these sources, we determined that the WVS data could be used as a source to establish convergent and discriminant validity of GLOBE's societal value scales. Consistent with our tests of unobtrusive measures, we used the validation procedures recommended by Campbell and Fiske (1959).

Hypotheses for the Development of the Outcropping Measures of the GLOBE Societal Value Dimensions

We created hypotheses for the development of WVS scales for the nine GLOBE societal value dimensions. These value dimensions are defined in Chapter 2 and are discussed in detail in Chapters 12 through 19. The theoretical connections outlined in the following sections describe the inference linkages between the GLOBE societal value dimensions and the selected WVS questionnaire items. The indirect and implicit inference linkages concerning the WVS items are based on "outcroppings" associated with the core GLOBE value dimensions. Outcroppings are implicit and usually unexpected effects of theoretical formulations.

The concept of "outcroppings" can be illustrated with the following example:

> Complexity Theory, as an (unexpected) outcropping of Chaos Theory in physics, has shown many levels of proof that suggest that "reverse entropy" (or "Centropy" as J. J. Hurtak calls it) also exists. Centropy would be the natural tendency for simple things to become more complex, hence the name "complexity theory." (Wilcock, 1999)

In this example, the original chaos theory gave rise to an additional insight, which was not expected by physicists at the time of formulation of chaos theory. The outcropping of complexity theory serves to provide new insights and to further validate chaos theory.

In this section, we review several outcroppings associated with the GLOBE societal level value dimensions. We use selected items from the WVS that we believe have inferential linkages to the GLOBE value dimensions as a source of illustrating outcroppings of the GLOBE value dimensions. These linkages were not originally anticipated when the GLOBE value dimensions were formulated.

The GLOBE Societal Value Dimensions of Culture

Performance Orientation Values and Choice in Work

The Performance Orientation value dimension reflects the extent to which a society is reported to encourage and reward performance excellence and improvement. This dimension is described in more detail in Chapter 12 by Javidan. Performance Orientation values encourage a preference for challenge and being in control of one'sm destiny. An outcropping of the Performance Orientation dimension, although not explicitly stated, implies a norm of preference for having jobs in which people control what they do and when they do it. Extending the logic a bit further, it is likely that performance-oriented cultures place a high value on work choice. The WVS included one item for freedom of choice to work and one item that refers to motivation of people to work. Given the arguments regarding performance orientation, we advance the following hypothesis:

Hypothesis 1: The societal value of performance orientation is associated with norms that encourage a preference to choose one's work or job

Assertiveness Values and Political Involvement

The Assertiveness value dimension is associated with the following preferences, among others: strong expression, articulation, and communication of one's thoughts, feelings, beliefs, and rights, both in political and social forums (see Chapter 15 by Den Hartog). An outcropping of the conceptualization of assertiveness is that assertiveness-oriented societies will have a high degree of political activism among their members (Lange & Jakubowski, 1976). The GLOBE construct of Assertiveness implies, but does not specifically postulate, that in assertiveness-oriented cultures individuals throughout the socioeconomic ladder are aware of the value of participation in politics. In addition, the norm of assertiveness enables and encourages individuals in these cultures to express themselves politically. Thus, political assertiveness is an outcropping of the GLOBE construct of Assertiveness.

From the above comments, it is suggested that greater political involvement is more frequently found in assertive cultures. The WVS included several items regarding societal political involvement. Given the arguments regarding assertiveness, we advance the following hypothesis:

Hypothesis 2: Societal norms of assertiveness are associated with greater political activity on the part of societal members

Future Orientation Values and Spiritual Orientation

The GLOBE Future Orientation value dimension is described and discussed in Chapter 13 by Ashkanasy, Gupta, Mayfield, and Trevor-Roberts. It is related to the concept of short-term versus long-term orientation. It is also associated with the distinction between materialistic versus spiritual orientation (Cervantes & Ramirez, 1992). Spiritual orientation is an outcropping of GLOBE's conceptualization of future orientation. In future-oriented cultures, the material and spiritual realms are more integrated (Cross, 2001). This integration is also an outcropping of the GLOBE definition of future orientation because it was not expected at the time the Future Orientation dimension was formulated.

From the above comments, it is clear that spiritual orientation is expected to be more frequently found in cultures that score high on future orientation. Thus we advance the following hypothesis:

Hypothesis 3: Societies that score high on the value of future orientation will be characterized by strong spiritual orientation among their members

Humane Orientation Values and Public Morality

The Humane Orientation value construct is discussed in Chapter 18 by Kabasakal and Bodur. The norms of societies valuing humane orientation are concerned with improvement of the human condition. One of the distinguishing norms of humane-oriented societies is public morality (Kurtz, 2001). Public morality is expressed through laws and norms that emphasize and reinforce moral behavior.

Thus we would expect a sense of public morality to be stronger and more frequently found in humane-oriented cultures. We identified three items in the WVS concerning public morality. The above discussion suggests the following hypothesis:

Hypothesis 4: Societies that are reported to value humane orientation will be characterized by norms that encourage and reinforce a sense of public morality

Institutional Collectivism Values and Societal Respect

The Institutional Collectivism value construct reflects inducements and rewards for collective behavior and norms, rather than incentives and rewards for the enactment of individual freedom and autonomy (see Chapter 16 by Gelfand, Bhawuk, Nishii, and Bechtold). Institutional collectivism emphasizes shared objectives, interchangeable interests, and respect for socially legitimated institutions (Chatman, Polzer, Barsade, & Neale, 1998).

In organizations, institutional collectivism likely takes the form of strong team orientation and development. To the extent possible, tasks are likely to be based on group rather than individual performance. Personal independence has low priority in institutionally oriented collective societies (Ryff, 1989). The notion of autonomous individuals, living free of society while living in that society, is contrary to the norms of societies that embrace institutional collectivism (Shweder & Bourne, 1984).

Societies characterized by lower institutional collectivism tend to embrace a preoccupation with self-reliance and independent personality (Bellah, Madsen, Sullivan, Swindler, & Tipton, 1985). A common guiding principle in Asian societies that score high on institutional collectivism is that "The nail that sticks out gets pounded down"; in the Netherlands, a common idiom is, "The head that rises above the ditch gets shot off."

From the above comments, we conclude that a high degree of respect for legitimated societal institutions is more frequently found in institutionally collective cultures. The WVS included one item regarding a high priority on respect for legitimated societal institutions. On the basis of the above discussion regarding institutional collectivism, we advance the following hypothesis:

Hypothesis 5. Societies reported to value institutional collectivism have members who place a high priority on societal respect

In-Group Collectivism Values and Pride in Family and Nation

The In-Group Collectivism value dimension encompasses how individuals relate to an in-group as an autonomous unit and how individuals attend to responsibilities concerning their in-group (see Chapter 16). In-group collectivism norms reflect both pride in membership of group members and general affective identification toward family, group, community, and nation (Triandis, Bontempto, Villareal, Asai, & Lucca, 1988).

In strong in-group collectivistic societies, there is an emphasis on collaboration, cohesiveness, and harmony. Responsibility and identification with the group begins with the immediate group, and then gradually extends externally. Put differently, in-group collectivism represents a strong sense of group identity and may extend to the national level (Triandis, Bontempto, Villareal, Asai, & Lucca, 1988).

From the above comments, it is inferred that a sense of pride in family, groups, and nation is more frequently found in in-group collectivistic societies. The WVS included several items regarding a sense of pride in family, groups, and nation. On the basis of the literature reviewed above we advance the following hypothesis:

Hypothesis 6: High reported societal value of in-group collectivism is associated with a sense of pride in family, groups, and nation

Gender Egalitarianism Values, Gender Parity, and Unity in Diversity

The Gender Egalitarianism value dimension reflects the degree to which men and women perform common tasks and are treated equally with respect to status, privilege, and rewards (see Chapter 14 by Emrich, Denmark, and Den Hartog). Further, greater gender egalitarian societies tend to advocate the notion of unity in diversity. This notion is conceptualized as unity without uniformity and diversity without fragmentation. Such societies are less likely to promote cultural hegemony, thus allowing the encouragement of ethnic diversity. To members of egalitarian societies, a diverse community represents a rich source of ideas and techniques. Members of societies characterized by higher gender egalitarianism not only tolerate diversity, but emphasize understanding, respect, and the nurturing of diversity in their communities through sustained committed efforts (Martin, 1993).

From the above comments, it is suggested that a sense of gender parity and unity in diversity are more frequently found in societies reported to be characterized by gender egalitarianism. The WVS included several items indicating both a sense of gender parity and a sense of unity in diversity. Given the above arguments involving gender egalitarianism, we advance the following hypothesis:

Hypothesis 7a: Societies reported to value gender egalitarianism are associated with a strong sense of gender parity
Hypothesis 7b: Societies reported to value gender egalitarianism are associated with a strong sense of unity in diversity

Power Distance Values and Monopolistic Orientation

The Power Distance value dimension reflects the extent to which members of a culture expect and agree that power should be shared unequally (see Chapter 17 by Carl, Gupta, and Javidan). One manifestation of the value placed on power distance concerns monopolistic orientation. In high power distance societies, power holders are granted greater status, privileges, and material rewards than those without power. In high power distance societies one would theoretically expect there to be higher acceptance of monopolistic practices by power holders. We refer to such acceptance as monopolistic orientation. A monopolistic market is comprised of several niches, in each of which the supply of goods and services is concentrated in hands of single enterprise. In such markets, monopolistic enterprise seeks to restrict market entry on the part of potential competitors through differentiation on the basis of one or more characteristics—including advertising claims and consumer perceptions of quality and convenience—not all of which are necessarily real and many of which are usually imagined and ingrained through creative communication and reinforcement. In societies in which monopolistic power is not valued, there tend to be more frequent and concerted attacks on the powerbase of the monopolistic niches.

We speculate that monopolistic orientation can be used as an indicator of the value placed on power distance in a society. In other words, monopolistic orientation is likely to be more frequently found in high power distance cultures. The WVS included several items regarding monopolistic orientation. Given the arguments involving power distance, we advance the following hypothesis:

Hypothesis 8: In societies reported to value high power distance, there will be greater monopolistic orientation

Uncertainty Avoidance Values and Sociotechnical Orientation

The Uncertainty Avoidance value construct focuses on the extent to which people seek orderliness, consistency, structure, formalized procedures, and laws to deal with naturally occurring uncertainty as well as important events in their daily lives (see Chapter 19 by de Luque and Javidan). It is linked to the use of procedures, such as standardized decision rules, that can minimize the need to predict uncertain events in the future (Cyert & March, 1963).

Sociotechnical theory (Emory & Trist, 1960) suggests approaches for managing uncertainty. The exploitation of proven technologies tends to be greater in high uncertainty avoidance cultures (Nakata & Sivakumar, 1996). Thus, for instance, high uncertainty avoidance customs foster mass availability of information technologies. People in cultures reported to be high on uncertainty avoidance are theoretically expected to have a heightened sense of concern with the need for effective communication and coordination. Therefore, they are also expected to be willing to invest in reliable technological support systems to effectively access social information and support. For example, the GLOBE societal-level Uncertainty Avoidance practices dimension is positively and significantly correlated with information processing technologies such as fax machines, Internet connections, computers, and telephones. These correlations all control for population size in the societies studied. All of these technical devices serve to reduce uncertainty by facilitating information processing and transmission.

Technological support systems reflect an institutionalized form of knowledge diffusion, because such systems incorporate the collective social knowledge about solutions to societal problems. In societies characterized by uncertainty avoidance values, positive outcomes tend to be less attributed to people's abilities and more to technology and investments in social organization (Chandler, Sharma, & Wolf, 1983; Yan & Gaier, 1994).

It follows from the discussion above that societies may manage uncertainty by using both social and technical approaches. The WVS included several items regarding sociotechnical orientation. Given the arguments involving uncertainty avoidance, we suggest that a sociotechnical orientation should be related to uncertainty avoidance as stated in the following hypothesis:

Hypothesis 9: The reported societal value of uncertainty avoidance is associated with sociotechnical orientation

Data and Operational Scales

The data for constructing outcropping measure scales are taken from the Wave 2 and Wave 3 of the WVS (for details concerning the WVS, see Chapter 7 by Javidan and Hauser, this volume). Comparable data were available for a total of 39 societies with Project GLOBE. The World Value Surveys are intended to measure culture as a system of "beliefs, values, knowledge, and skills that have been internalized by the people of a given society" (Inglehart, 1997, p. 15).

Guided by the above hypotheses, the items in the World Values Surveys were Q-sorted into ten categories: one category for each of the nine GLOBE cultural constructs, and a nonapplicable category (for a detailed description of Q-sort methods, see McKeown, 1988). Two raters, each with a PhD in management, classified items from the WVS into the GLOBE dimensions. First, one researcher developed themes based on a literature search to find theoretical and empirical evidence about the themes. He then carefully read through the WVS and, on the basis of his knowledge of culture and international management, identified several themes that he believed to be related to the GLOBE societal-level value dimensions.

Before initially selecting items to be considered for the Q-sort, an additional researcher proficient in political science and social psychology assisted in discussing and identifying appropriate themes for values at the societal level. Furthermore, to ensure we were adequately selecting value-focused items, an external reviewer helped define concepts for the values dimensions and assisted in the analytic evaluation of items. Having verified that the themes were associated with relevant cultural dimensions, a second person coded the items from the WVS that she inferred reflected the themes.

The WVS questionnaire items were not used for validation purposes if the coders could not unambiguously determine their meaning and intent. For instance, the WVS item that states the importance of "seeing that people have more say in how things are done at their jobs and in their communities" could have been theoretically related to our definition of political involvement (a correlate of Assertiveness) or theoretically related to our definition of sociotechnical governance (a correlate of Uncertainty Avoidance). Such items were excluded if the distinctiveness of an item could not be determined.

Close attention was given to interpreting the GLOBE societal value constructs for content. For instance, the scale of Sociotechnical Orientation used to validate the construct of Uncertainty Avoidance values was assessed using only items that suggested social and technical approaches for managing uncertainty. The final selection of the items was based on measures with convincing face validity as corroborated by the GLOBE principal investigator. The scale score for each dimension is composed of scores from the two raters. As a result of this item identification process, we obtained a conservative interrater agreement ranging from 0.75 to 1.00. Of the nine GLOBE value validation scales plus the "nonapplicable" category, we had an average interrater agreement of 0.82. Table 9.6 provides the items for the nine outcropping measures scales. We assessed the unidimensionality of these scales by conducting a principal components factor analysis. The factor loadings for these scales are shown in Table 9.6. The Cronbach alpha reliability coefficient of all the scales exceeds the standard of 0.70.

At first glance, several of the items selected for validation of the GLOBE values scales may not appear to directly affect the dimension of interest. However, for all items we developed either direct or indirect inference linkages, which may have been explicit or implicit, thus making these items relevant to the dimensions through the rationale described earlier.

Findings

The test of construct validity can be done using the multitrait–multimethod matrix (Campbell & Fiske, 1959). The nine cultural constructs represent different traits. The two methods of measurement, GLOBE variables and items from the WVS, represent different sources. The rater scores from the WVS were correlated with the GLOBE societal level values scores for the

sample of countries common in both studies. Table 9.7 provides the multitrait–multimethod matrix. The correlations between constructs measured by a single method are termed as the heterotrait–monomethod triangles. Of the two triangles, the first represents the selected WVS measures and the second the GLOBE variables. In addition, the heteromethod block is composed of the validity diagonal (bold values in the table), and two heterotrait–heteromethod triangles.

The matrix can be grouped into three partitions: diagonals, triangles, and blocks. There are two heterotrait–monomethod triangles, which give correlations among measures that share the same method of measurement, one for the questionnaire-based method, and the other for the unobtrusive measurement method (Campbell & Fiske, 1959). The diagonals of these triangles contain the estimates of the reliability of each measure in the matrix and are termed reliability diagonals (monotrait–monomethod). In addition, the matrix also contains a square heteromethod block, which gives correlations between constructs measured by two different methods. This square block can be partitioned into a validity diagonal (bold values in the table), and two heterotrait–heteromethod triangles (Campbell & Fiske, 1959). The coefficients in the validity diagonal represent correlations between the measures of the same trait using different methods (i.e., the GLOBE questionnaire method and outcropping measurement method). Because the two methods are intended to measure the same concept or trait, the coefficients in the validity diagonal are expected to be strongly correlated, and are termed as monotrait–heteromethod correlations. Further, because the coefficients in the two heterotrait–heteromethod triangles share neither method nor trait, those coefficients are expected to be very low (Campbell & Fiske, 1959).

The coefficients in the validity diagonal represent correlation between each GLOBE variable and the corresponding outcropping measures. Convergent validity exists when the coefficients in the validity diagonal are high and statistically significant. The correlation between the hypothesized pairs ranges from 0.38 to 0.88, and are all statistically significant at $p < 0.05$ for each of the nine validity coefficients.

Discriminant validity is achieved if several criteria are met. First, the coefficients in the

Table 9.6 Operational Scales for the Outcropping Measures to Compare With GLOBE Values Scales

	Factor Loadings
1. Choice in Work (alpha = 0.76)	

V66. Feel much freedom of choice and control over the way life turns out	.81
V124. Our present society must be valiantly defended against all subversive forces	.82
V172. In this country, people in need are poor because of laziness and lack of will power	−.84

V152. The political system as it is today is going on very well	.90
V165. Dissatisfied with the way the people now in national office are handling the country's affairs	−.94
V166. Generally speaking, this country is run for the benefit of all the people, as opposed to a few big interests looking out for themselves	.90

3. Spiritual Orientation (alpha = 0.95) (reverse scored)

V9. Low importance of religion in life	−.93
V22. Religious faith is not an especially important quality for children to learn at home	−.88
V18. Not brought up religiously at home	−.78
V182. Not religious	−.90
V183. Don't believe in God	−.94
V184. Don't believe in life after death	−.85
V191. Don't find comfort and strength from religion	−.85

V192. Claiming government benefits to which one is not entitled is generally justifiable	−.85
V193. Avoiding a fare on public transport is generally justifiable	−.90
V194. Cheating on taxes if one has a chance is generally justifiable	−.87

5. Societal Respect (alpha = 1.00) (reverse scored)

V78. In general, it is not important to have a job that is respected by people	−1.00

V4. Family is not very important in life	−.81
V13. Parents have a life of their own and should not be asked to sacrifice their own well-being for the sake of their children	−.79
V205. Not at all proud of my nationality	−.88

(Continued)

Table 9.6 (Continued)

7a. Gender Parity (alpha = 0.92) (reverse scored)

	Factor Loadings
V61. When jobs are scarce, men should have more rights to a job than women	−.92
V101. On the whole, men make better political leaders than women do	−.95
V103. A university education is more important for a boy than for a girl	−.92

V52. Accept people of a different race as neighbors	.93
V56. Accept neighbors from salient communities, such as Muslims in the United States	.85
V57. Accept immigrants and foreign workers as neighbors	.95

V104105a. The goal of a high level of economic growth should be given top priority over the next 10 years in this nation	.81
V108109b. Progress toward a less impersonal and more humane society should be given top priority in this nation	−.86
V125. We need larger income differences as incentives for individual effort	.63
V128. Competition is harmful and brings out the worst in people, as opposed to stimulating people to work hard and develop new ideas	−.72

9. Sociotechnical Orientation (alpha = 0.82)

V63. Even when jobs are scarce, employers should not give more priority to home nationals over immigrants	−.67
V73/74-1. A good income so that there are no worries about money is an important factor for people looking for a job	.72
V113. Against a change in the way of life to more emphasis on the development of technology	−.83
V126. Government ownership of business and industry should be increased, as opposed to private ownership	.70
V127. People should take more responsibility for providing for themselves rather than having the government provide for everyone	−.73
V131. One should not be cautious about making major changes because you never achieve much in life unless you act boldly	−.72

heterotrait–heteromethod triangles are not as high as those in the validity diagonal. In addition, the coefficients in the heterotrait–monomethod triangles are also less than the coefficients in the validity diagonal. Last, the reliability of the measures exceeds the coefficients in the heterotrait–monomethod triangles (Campbell & Fiske, 1959).

Using heterotrait-heteromethod triangles, one may compute the average absolute correlation of

Table 9.7   The Multitrait-Multimethod Matrix of Societal Value Measures

	Outcropping Measures										GLOBE Variables								
	A_1	B_1	C_1	D_1	E_1	F_1	G_1	H_1	I_1	(J)	A_2	B_2	C_2	D_2	E_2	F_2	G_2	H_2	I_2
Outcropping Measures																			
A_1*	(.76)									.32*									
B_1	.37**	(.90)								.08									
C_1	.19	−.05	(.95)							.06									
D_1	.56**	.22	.21	(.81)						.26*									
E_1	−.17	−.06	.24	.12	(1.00)					−.23									
F_1	.34**	.10	.69**	.34**	.24*	(.76)				.09									
G_1	.48**	.23	−.13	.29*	−.31**	.15	(.92)			.50**									
H_1	−.33**	−.07	.10	−.19	.09	.01	−.45**	(.75)		−.24									
I_1	−.43**	−.22	.15	−.25*	.45	.05	−.73**	.38**	(.82)	−.34*									
GLOBE																			
A_2	**.38***	−.01	.38	.59**	.21	.41*	.27	−.32	−.03	.36*	(.90)								
B_2	.19	**.39***	−.15	.00	−.02	.07	−.22	.03	.23	−.20	−.06	(.53)							
C_2	.13	−.33	**.59***	.49	.34*	.56**	−.19	−.19	.39*	−.01	.69**	.03	(.76)						
D_2	.25	−.07	.24	**.70***	−.04	.26	.24	−.38*	−.12	.38*	.61**	−.12	.38**	(.70)					
E_2	.08	−.07	.42**	.16	**.51***	.30	.00	−.22	.23	.15	.43**	−.22	.50**	.07	(.77)				
F_2	.26	−.25	.44**	.35*	.17	**.60***	.18	−.21	.14	.23	.70	−.02	.66**	.27*	.36**	(.66)			
G_2	.25	−.12	.23	.26	−.07	.25	**.67***	−.35	−.57**	.51**	.28*	−.29*	−.16	.28*	.00	.21	(.88)		
H_2	−.19	.18	−.22	−.48**	−.16	−.18	−.33*	**.60***	.09	−.27	−.61**	.29*	−.36**	−.62**	−.37**	−.42**	−.51**	(.74)	
I_2	.00	−.19	.34**	.08	.43**	.44**	−.58**	.27	**.88***	−.29	.25	.19	.64**	.02	.45**	.35**	−.49**	.04	(.85)

NOTE: Letters A, B, C, D, E, F, G, H, and I refer to statuses on the dimensions of culture. Subscripts 1 and 2 to refer to the 2 methods used in this study. Method 1 refers to the Outcropping Measure items and Method 2 refers to the GLOBE items. Validity coefficients are the diagonal set of boldface numbers; reliability coefficients are the numbers in parentheses along principal diagonal. For criteria variable, $N = 73$; for GLOBE, $N = 62$; for multitrait-multimethod, $N = 39$. Gender Parity Scale used as Validation Measure for Gender Egalitarianism.

*A = Performance Orientation. B = Assertiveness. C = Future Orientation. D = Humane Orientation. E = Institutional Collectivism. F = In-Group Collectivism.

G = Gender Egalitarianism. H = Power Distance. I = Uncertainty Avoidance. (J) = Unity in Diversity. * $p < 0.05$ ** $p < 0.01$

each outcropping measure (W) with the nine GLOBE variables (G). This average is labeled as the discriminant coefficient (W,G). Similarly, we compute the average absolute correlation of each GLOBE variable with the nine outcropping measures. This average is labeled as the discriminant coefficient (G,W). Table 9.8 shows that for each of the nine variables, both types of discriminant coefficients are smaller than the validity diagonal coefficients. The overall average discriminant coefficient is 0.24 for both (G,W) and (W,G), which is significantly less than the average convergent coefficient validity (i.e., diagonal coefficient) of 0.59.

Similarly, using heterotrait–monomethod triangles, the discriminant coefficient (G) was computed as the average correlation of each GLOBE measure with the other eight GLOBE measures; and a discriminant coefficient (W) as the average correlation of each outcropping measure with the other eight outcropping measures. The overall average discriminant coefficient (G) is 0.33, and overall average criteria discriminant coefficient (W) is 0.26, both of which are also significantly less than the average convergent coefficient shown in the first column of Table 9.8.

Last, the reliability of both GLOBE measures and outcropping measures exceeds the discriminant coefficient computed from heterotrait–monomethod triangles. Thus, we conclude that the GLOBE societal value constructs have convergent as well as discriminant validity.

Using the construct validation procedure, we established the convergent as well as discriminant validity of the GLOBE societal value constructs. In addition, we showed that the outcropping measures indeed capture the domain of meaning theoretically intended by the GLOBE societal value constructs.

Our findings must be viewed in the light of potential limitations of the outcropping measures. These measures capture a part of the overall domain of meaning intended by the respective value constructs. The potential domain of meaning of each value construct is quite broad-based. For instance, the value of uncertainty avoidance would be related to a range of indicators associated with the need for security, as well as other indicators that might help resolve the uncertainty about unknown, or

help minimize the costs of unexpected change. Sociotechnical orientation is one way in which members of a society can manage uncertainty collectively. Several other approaches for managing uncertainty may exist, and the significance of sociotechnical orientation may itself vary for the sampled societies as well as for the nonsampled societies. Further, the relevance of sociotechnical orientation for managing uncertainty might grow or fall over the years across any given set of societies. Therefore, it would be important to confirm that the outcropping measures are indeed relevant for the societies in the target sample before using them independently or as tests of convergent validity in other cross-cultural studies. Because we did not have evidence of the relevance of the outcropping measures for each society studied, we may have made a conservative error. Despite this possibility, we were able to demonstrate both convergent and discriminant validity of the GLOBE scales using the outcropping measures.

In addition, it would be fruitful to examine data from the ongoing fourth wave of the World Values Survey, which expands the sample of societies and also provides more updated information, and reaffirm the findings on the basis of the second and third waves of the survey. Data from other independent cross-cultural studies may also be used for further validation, and for refining the domain of meaning that should be empirically associated with the GLOBE societal value constructs. Last, because the coders were able to identify only a single item from the WVS measures for the Institutional Collectivism construct, it may be advisable to identify an alternative theme, or use an alternative data source. Despite these conservative limitations, we were able to demonstrate convergent and discriminant validity of the GLOBE societal scales.

CONCLUSIONS

In conclusion, we found that GLOBE measures of cultural practices and values can be validated by the use of independent measures from other sources. The aggregated reports of middle-level managers concerning societal values and practices correlated, as predicted, with a range of theoretically predicted national level variables.

Table 9.8 Multitrait-Multimethod Matrix Summary for Societal Value Measures

GLOBE Cultural Dimensions	1 Convergent $(G,W)^a$	2a Discriminant $(G,W)^b$	2b Discriminant $(W,G)^c$	3 Discriminant $(W)^d$	4 Discriminant $(G)^e$	5 Reliability $(W)^f$	6 Reliability $(G)^g$
				Coefficients			
Performance Orientation	0.38	0.28	0.17	0.36	0.45	0.76	0.90
Assertiveness	0.39	0.11	0.15	0.17	0.15	0.90	0.53
Future Orientation	0.59	0.33	0.30	0.22	0.43	0.95	0.76
Humane Orientation	0.70	0.20	0.30	0.27	0.30	0.81	0.70
Institutional Collectivism	0.51	0.19	0.18	0.21	0.30	1.00	0.77
In-Group Collectivism	0.60	0.25	0.31	0.24	0.37	0.76	0.66
Gender Egalitarianism	0.67	0.26	0.25	0.35	0.28	0.92	0.88
Power Distance	0.60	0.23	0.25	0.20	0.40	0.75	0.74
Uncertainty Avoidance	0.88	0.29	0.23	0.33	0.30	0.82	0.85
Average	0.59	0.24	0.24	0.26	0.33	0.85	0.75

NOTES: Summary Conditions for Construct Validity: 1 > 2(a), 2(b), 3, & 4; 5 > 3; 6 > 4

[a] G,W (Convergent coefficient) = Correlation of the GLOBE measure with the outcropping measure.

[b] G,W (Discriminant coefficient) = Average absolute correlation of a GLOBE measure with the nine outcropping measures.

[c] W,G (Discriminant coefficient) = Average absolute correlation of an outcropping measure with the nine GLOBE measures.

[d] W (Discriminant coefficient) = Average absolute correlation of an outcropping measure with other eight outcropping measures.

[e] G (Discriminant coefficient) = Average absolute correlation of a GLOBE measure with other eight GLOBE measures.

[f] W (Reliability) = Reliability of an unobtrusive measure.

[g] G (Reliability) = Reliability of a GLOBE measure.

Thus, the triangulation of traditional survey, questionnaire validation, and unobtrusive methods provide a valid and balanced perspective of societal culture unavailable by each perspective alone. In addition, these alternative data sources helped to uncover cultural values and practices of societies not included in the GLOBE or the WVS questionnaire responses. Further, the unobtrusive and outcropping measures can be used to identify and outcropping changes in cultural values and practices, thereby helping the creation of indices of cultural change. These indices could be used to make appropriate adjustments in the GLOBE cultural values and practices scores for future use. Such adjustments would allow more reliable assessment of the contemporary cultural values and practices, and help develop effective strategic and policy decisions rooted in cultural trends.

ENDNOTES

1. Construct validity may be assessed through testing the convergent hypothesis and the discriminant hypothesis (Rossi, Wright, & Anderson, 1983). The convergent hypothesis is that items within the domain of meaning, although derived from different methods, correlate together because they all reflect the same underlying construct or 'true' score. The discriminant hypothesis is that items from one domain will not correlate with items from another domain (Rossi, Wright, & Anderson, 1983, pp. 100–101). Each construct is intended to measure a common *domain of meaning*. The degree to which researchers have representatively sampled from that domain of meaning connotes *content validity* of the scale.

2. We selected Culturgrams reports (1999) as our data text source in our content analyses because they include descriptions of daily customs and life in societies. These reports provide comparable and consistent, four page descriptions of cultures of 170 societies around the world.

3. We discuss these under the following topic headings: (a) applying the framework for content analysis, (b) searching for suitable data, (c) searching for contextual knowledge, (d) developing a strategy and defining measurements, (e) coding for unobtrusive indicators, and (f) assessing quality and accuracy.

4. Each Culturgram follows a standard format with sections of information that include a map indicating the continental location and principal cities; a descriptive background of the major historical, political, and social events of the country; a depiction of the topography and climate; some general characteristics of the people; a description of population demography; a review of the languages spoken, especially noting the prevalence of English spoken; a statistical percentage itemization of types of religion; an overview of general attitudes; and considerations of appearance. Other sections incorporated in these four-page reports are: examination of common customs and courtesies; description of traditional greetings and gestures; information regarding visiting, eating, and lifestyle habits; and review of beliefs about family, dating, and marriage. In addition, these texts comprise information on analysis of social and economic issues; diet and recreation; major holidays; instructive details regarding commerce, society, government, the economy, education, transportation, and communication, as well as a discussion of health-related risks to citizens and visitors in the country. Last, each Culturgram report contains information for travelers to each country, as well as useful addresses to obtain further details.

5. The following is an illustration of our process of developing a rationale for constructs. The construct of uncertainty avoidance is related to reliability, durability, and breadth of concepts. The medical sector is one of the critical domains predicated on reliable and stabilizing domestic initiatives. This is so because many diseases tend to be climate and society-specific and are subject to mutation over time. Thus, durable and broad-based home research is essential to developing preventive and curative solutions. On the basis of this inference clarification process, the item "medical facilities are effective in keeping the society essentially healthy and disease-free" was formed to represent uncertainty avoidance.

After this process of linking the GLOBE societal practice construct to the inferences, the project director reviewed the final constructs. It was determined that six of the nine dimension constructs demonstrated more than adequate face validity, but three of the nine dimension constructs lacked convincing face validity. At this point, the research team secured feedback from other experts to reformulate the construct-inference process for the three problematic GLOBE dimensions of humane orientation, assertiveness, and societal collectivism. Numerous meetings were held before the team agreed on the construct-inference definitions for these dimensions of culture.

6. Concurrent with developing strategies for content analysis, it is important to formulate the units

of analysis, which is sometimes called *unitizing* (Krippendorff, 1980). In our content analysis, the sampling unit was the four-page Culturgram report for each country that corresponded with the GLOBE project countries. The context units define the segment of the text to be examined in order to characterize a recording unit. These units set physical limits on the contextual information that may comprise the recoding units. Context units do not need to be independent, and may overlap and contain many recording units. In our study, the context units were sections of the text into which the Culturgram were divided. These sections of the texts described aspects of the culture such as history, general attitudes, family, and economy. For example, the Humane Orientation culture dimension evaluates such issues as concern for others, friendliness, sensitivity toward others, and generosity.

By contrast, recording units are seldom defined in terms of physical boundaries. The division between recording units is reached through a descriptive effort (Krippendorff, 1980). In this content analysis, the recording units were the theoretically driven ideas relating to the nine cultural dimensions. To illustrate, the Denmark Culturgram section on general attitudes included the statements "Danes are known for their tolerance of other people and diverse points of view. They admire individuals with a friendly attitude, a sense of humor, intelligence, sociability, personal stamina, integrity and an open mind. . . . A love for understatement, rather than exaggeration, prevails" (p. 78). Thus, recording units in this section could be coded higher on Humane Orientation, given the reference to friendliness and tolerance, and lower on Assertiveness Orientation, given the reference to nonassertive behavior. After designating these units, we then defined and delineated the actual coding of the units. Referential units were used in this analysis. Referential units indicate how a unit is represented, defining the ideas to which an expression refers. The referential unit denotes a similar expression in different ways, often defined by specific notions, events, persons, acts, or objects, (Krippendorff, 1980). For example, the Performance Orientation item, "The society maintains a diversity of religions" was coded in terms of the dominant religion, as well as openness to other religions such as in terms of state laws (secular or not), and recent growth of new religious ideologies in the society.

7. It was necessary in this content analysis to take note of issues pertaining to the definition of categories. Two basic decisions are suggested when developing category definitions: whether the categories should be (a) mutually exclusive and (b) broad or narrow (Weber, 1990). Mutually exclusive categories were required in this analysis to ensure that our variables were not confounded. Recording units needed to be classified in a single category. Simultaneous classification in two or more categories would have resulted in violation of fundamental statistical assumptions and would have rendered unreliable results (Weber, 1990). This decision process is illustrated below.

When coding for Power Distance the item "Economic growth tends to go hand-in-hand with the unemployment, poverty, and stratification of society by income," we identified referent units relating to the effects of unequal distribution of income and private consumption expenditure in the society. Evidence of unemployment and poverty were found in the text regarding the economy, and occasionally these indications were embedded in the discussion, which required a thoughtful reading for implicit information. To assess the stratification of society by income, we looked for references to gaps between rich and poor that were specific in the text and generally uncomplicated to code. A second decision in the development of category definitions involved how broad or narrow the categories would be. Decisions were made to code some concepts very specifically and some more broadly. For example, the In-Group Collectivism item "Most people lack access to the opportunities for personal advancement" reflects a social system in which intellectual autonomy is not facilitated. The Human Development Index value for each country was used as a narrowly defined category to assess the collectivism category. In contrast, the concept of Uncertainty Avoidance was defined broadly. This concept is related to the use of information technologies, supporting ample feedback, and building capabilities for information technology usage. It should be noted that all initial decisions regarding strategy development and measurement defining issues were dependent on the information available in Culturgrams as identified at the time of exploratory analysis of non-GLOBE sample societies.

8. We chose not to use their weight system because of the subjectivity involved in the choice of parameters used for weighting.

9. The data for the early 2000s cycle were not publicly available as we conducted this research.

REFERENCES

Bellah, R. N., Madsen, R., Sullivan, W. M., Swindler, A., & Tipton, S. M. (1985). *Habits of the heart: Individualism and commitment in American life.* Berkeley: University of California Press.

Bowen, W. M., & Bowen, C. C. (1999). Typologies, indexing, content analysis, meta-analysis, and scaling as measurement techniques. In G. J. Miller & M. L. Whicker (Eds.), *Handbook of research methods in public administration* (pp. 51–86). New York: Marcel Dekker.

Brigham Young University. (1999). *Culturgrams* (1998–1999 ed., 2 volumes). Provo, UT: Brigham Young University.

Campbell, D. T., & Fiske, D. W. (1959). Convergent and discriminate validation by the multitrait-multimethod matrix. *Psychological Bulletin, 56*(2), 81–105.

Carley, K. (1994). Content analysis. In R. E. Asher (Ed.), *The encyclopedia of language and linguistics* (Vol. 2, pp. 725–730). Edinburgh: Pergamon Press.

Cervantes, J. M., & Ramirez, O. (1992). Spirituality and family dynamics in psychotherapy with Latino children. In L. A. Vargas & J. D. Koss-Chioino (Eds.), *Working with culture* (pp. 103–128). San Francisco: Jossey-Bass.

Chandler, T. A., Sharma, D. D., & Wolf, F. M. (1983). Gender differences in achievement and affiliation attributions: A five nation study. *Journal of Cross-Cultural Psychology, 14,* 241–256.

Chatman, J. A., Polzer, J. T., Barsade, S. G., & Neale, M. A. (1998). Being different yet feeling similar: The influence of demographic composition and organizational culture on work processes and outcomes. *Administrative Science Quarterly, 43,* 749–780.

Cross, T. (2001). Spirituality and mental health: A Native American perspective. *Focal Point, 15*(2), 37–38.

Cyert, R. M., & March, J. G. (1963) *A behavioral theory of the firm.* Englewood Cliffs, NJ: Prentice Hall.

Emery, F. E., & Trist, E. L. (1960). Socio-technical systems. In C. W. Churchman & M. Verhulst (Eds.), *Management sciences, models and techniques* (pp. 83–97). London: Pergamon.

Inglehart, R. (1997). *Modernization and postmodernization: Cultural, economic and political change in 43 societies.* Princeton, NJ: Princeton University Press.

Inglehart, R. & Baker, W. E. (2000). Modernization, cultural change, and the persistence of traditional values, *American Sociological Review, 65,* 19-51.

Inglehart, R., Basanez, M., & Moreno, A. (1998). *Human values and beliefs: A cross-cultural sourcebook.* Ann Arbor: University of Michigan.

Kellehear, A. (2001). *Unobtrusive methods: An introduction.* Retrieved from http://www.allen-unwin.com/Academic/unobtrus.pdf

Krippendorff, K. (1980). *Content analysis: An introduction to its methodology.* Beverly Hills, CA: Sage.

Kurian, G. T. (1997). *The illustrated book of world rankings.* Armonk, NY: Sharpe Reference.

Kurtz, P. (2001). Two competing moralities. *Free Inquiry Magazine, 21*(3). Retrieved from http://www.secularhumanism.org/library/fi/kurtz_22_4.htm

Lange, A., & Jakubowski, P. (1976). *Responsible assertive behavior.* Champaign, IL: Research Press.

Martin, P. Y. (1993). Feminist practice in organizations: Implications for management. In S. Fagenson (Ed.), *Women in management: Trends, perspectives and challenges* (pp. 274–296). Newbury Park, CA: Sage.

McKeown, B. (1988). *Q methodology.* Newbury Park, CA: Sage.

Melton, A. (1933). Some behavior characteristics of museum visitors. *Psychological Bulletin, 30,* 720–721.

Nakata, C., & Sivakumar, K. (1996). National culture and new product development: An integrative review. *Journal of Marketing, 60,* 61–72.

Nunnally, J. C., & Bernstein, I. H. (1994). *Psychometric theory* (3rd ed.). New York: McGraw Hill.

Parker, P. M. (1997). *National cultures of the world: A statistical reference.* Westport, CT: Greenwood Press.

Roberts, C. W. (1997). *Text analysis for the social sciences: Methods for drawing inferences from texts and transcripts.* Mahwah, NJ: Lawrence Erlbaum.

Rossi P. H., Wright, J. D., & Anderson, A. B. (Eds.). (1983). *The handbook of survey research.* New York: Academic Press.

Ryff, C. D. (1989). Happiness is everything or is it? Explorations on the meaning of psychological well-being. *Journal of Personality and Social Psychology, 57,* 1069–1081.

Sechrest, L., & Belew, J. (1983). Nonreactive measures of social attitudes. *Applied Social Psychology Annual, 4,* 23–63.

Shapiro, G., & Markoff, J. (1997). A matter of definition. In C. W. Roberts (Ed.), *Text analysis for the social sciences: Methods for drawing statistical inferences from texts and transcripts.* Mahwah, NJ: Lawrence Erlbaum.

Shweder, R. A., & Bourne, E. J. (1984). Does the concept of the person vary cross-culturally? In R. A. Shweder & R. A. LeVine (Eds.), *Culture theory: Essays on mind, self, and emotion* (pp. 158–199). New York: Cambridge University Press.

Stone, P. J. (1997). Thematic text analysis: New agendas for analyzing text content. In C. W. Roberts (Ed.), *Text analysis for the social sciences: Methods for drawing statistical inferences from texts and transcripts* (pp. 171–189). Mahwah, NJ: Lawrence Erlbaum.

Sullivan, M. J., III. (1991). *Measuring global values: The ranking of 162 countries.* New York: Greenwood Press.

Triandis, H. C., Bontempo, R., Villareal, M. J., Asai, M., & Lucca, N. (1988). Individualism and collectivism: Cross-cultural perspectives on self-in-group relationships. *Journal of Personality and Social Psychology, 54,* 323–338.

United Nations Education, Science and Culture Organization. (1997). *Statistical yearbook.* New York: Author.

Webb, E., Campbell, D. T., Schwartz, R. D., & Sechrest, L. (1966). *Unobtrusive measures: Nonreactive research in the social sciences.* Chicago: Rand McNally.

Webb, E., Campbell, D. T., Schwartz, R. D., & Sechrest, L. (2000). *Unobtrusive measures.* Thousand Oaks, CA: Sage

Weber, R. P. (1990). *Basic content analysis* (2nd ed.). Newbury Park, CA: Sage.

Wilcock, D. (1999, March 8). *Convergence.* Retrieved from http://www.dprins.demon.nl/convergence/9913.html

World Bank. (1997). *World development indicators 1997 CD-ROM.* Washington, DC: United Nations.

Yan, W. F., & Gaier, E. L. (1994). Causal attributions for college success and failure: An Asia-American comparison. *Journal of Cross-Cultural Psychology, 25,* 146–158.

10

REGIONAL AND CLIMATE CLUSTERING OF SOCIETAL CULTURES

VIPIN GUPTA

PAUL J. HANGES

In this chapter, we establish two types of clustering of GLOBE societies: (a) regional clusters and (b) physical climate clusters. These clusters are used in the following chapters to analyze variations in specific cultural and leadership dimensions.

PART A: REGIONAL CLUSTERING OF SOCIETAL CULTURES

This part of the chapter discusses the conceptual and empirical process by which we grouped the 61 GLOBE societal cultures into a set of ten *regional clusters*.[1] We had multiple goals in mind when we developed these clusters. First, we wanted to understand the similarities and differences among the GLOBE societies using a more holistic approach rather than focusing on

similarities and differences among these societies one dimension at a time. For each cluster, we developed profiles using all GLOBE cultural dimensions (nine scales for cultural *practices* and nine scales for cultural *values*). These profiles can be thought of as unifying themes linking societal cultures together within distinct regions of the world. In our view, these profiles provide a convenient way of summarizing intercultural similarities as well as intercultural differences. Second, we expected these societal clusters would provide a useful tool for exploring the extent to which each cultural cluster is associated with specific leadership attributes. As indicated previously in this volume, we expected distinct leadership prototypes (i.e., CLTs—culturally endorsed leadership theory) will be associated with effective leadership across different cultures. In Chapter 21, we

AUTHORS' NOTE: Peter Dorfman put in long hours on editing and commenting on the various versions of this chapter, but politely refused the offer to be a coauthor. We also thank Felix Brodbeck and Michele Gelfand for their very helpful comments on an earlier draft of this chapter, and Bhakti Gupta for her assistance in preparing figures for this chapter.

present the CLTs for each societal cluster and show how specific leadership prototypes are empirically linked to GLOBE cultural dimensions. That is, we consider these cultural clusters to be helpful for summarizing the culturally endorsed leadership prototypes that prevail in the societies associated with specific cultural clusters. Third, the GLOBE data provides an opportunity to empirically validate the appropriateness of societal clusters, particularly clustering procedures that are based on cultural values and practices, in contrast to clusters based on concrete variables such as language, geography, and modernity. Grouping countries (cultures or societies) on the basis of constructs such as work goals, values, or beliefs has proved difficult to validate. The vast database of the GLOBE project provides a unique opportunity to not only develop clusters, but also to empirically assess the adequacy of our clustering scheme.

The fourth and fifth reasons for clustering societies concern the practical and theoretical benefits that should result from an adequate clustering of societies. In terms of practical benefits, clusters provide a useful framework for managing the complexities of multicultural operations. Multinational corporations have the difficult job of operating in nations that have different sets of cultural expectations, beliefs, and values. Likewise, clusters may provide useful information for working with diverse nationalities or cultures within a specific country. Practices, policies, and procedures that work quite effectively in one culture may dramatically fail or produce counterproductive behavior in another culture. Information relevant to clusters should assist the selection and cultural training of managers who work in global environments. In addition, cluster information can help managers understand the viability of policies, practices, technologies, and human resources as they are applied across cultural boundaries. Finally, societal clusters may also help regional managers determine limits and boundaries for moving human resources and products across societies.

Cluster-based information can assist in theory development. Judicious sampling within and across societal clusters can test potential boundary conditions for management theories

and interventions. Clusters may be used to guide the sampling strategy for cross-cultural research to ensure that an adequate sampling of cultural variability is included in the samples. Researchers can also test the generalizability of empirical findings obtained in one culture to other cultures. Thus, clusters provide us with important information regarding societal variation and are a coherent and convenient way to summarize intercultural similarity as well as intercultural differences. Both the practical and theoretical implications for clustering are presented in more detail later in this chapter.

The information in this chapter follows the same order we used to construct the GLOBE clusters. First, we reviewed the extant literature to determine the criteria other scholars have used to cluster societies. To better understand the dominating cultural forces responsible for societal development, we conducted historical and cultural analyses of their influence on different regions around the world. We integrated the extant literature on previous clustering attempts with this in-depth review of historical and cultural forces to establish our 10 regional clusters. The thesis that these societal clusters reflect greater differences in cultural practices and values across societies from different clusters than societies within the same cluster was tested using discriminant analysis. Through this analysis we confirmed the viability of our regional clusters.

Forces Influencing Regional Clustering

Scholars have used three major forces to group countries into similar clusters: (a) geographic proximity (Furnham, Kirkcaldy, & Lynn, 1994), (b) mass migrations and ethnic social capital (Portes & Zhou, 1994), and (c) religious and linguistic commonality (Cattell, 1950). Of these three forces, geography has long been identified as having a major influence on culture. For example, Hofstede (1980) reported geographical latitude to be the single largest factor explaining intersocietal variation in cultural dimensions such as power distance. Geography can influence culture because the physical topography of a region can limit the interactions among people, the nature of the physical climate in a region can influence the goals of people living in that region, and the economic prosperity of a region can be affected by its physical geography. Mass migrations often extend the social capital—the cohesive interrelationships and networks developed to facilitate social action—from one society to places far beyond its original geographical boundaries (Portes & Zhou, 1994). For instance, mass migrations from the United Kingdom during the second half of the past millennium have been a critical factor in the creation of an ethnic Saxon culture across geographically distant nations such as Australia, South Africa, and the United States (Ronen & Shenkar, 1985). Within the same geographic region and level of economic development, religion and language distinguish societal clusters. For example, one can differentiate between religious–linguistic societal clusters of Germanic (Germans) and Latin Europe (Romans). The shared religious and linguistic institutions may generate similar paradigms of metaphysical philosophies of science that guide beliefs, behaviors, and values in each society (Berry, Poortinga, Segall, & Dasen, 1992; Smith & Bond, 1994).

Although geographical, ethnic, and religious–linguistic forces contribute to the formation of societal clusters, economic forces may sometimes cut across these factors and therefore reduce their influence among these clusters. The economic view holds that cultural differences are minimal in economically developed societies, which tend to share common management models to realize economic efficiency (Hyden, 1983). Furthermore, cultural patterns in developing countries reflect idiosyncratic and nonuniversalistic influences, but economic development generates a global convergence in the values and behaviors from developed societies to developing ones (Dunlap, Harbison, Kerr, & Myers, 1975).

To mitigate some of these influences in emerging markets and facilitate a universal global culture, several multilateral institutions such as the International Monetary Fund have sponsored management workshops that are based on the belief that diffusion of Western management models would contribute to economic development (Kerrigan & Luke, 1987). The economic view thus implies that grouping of societies into cultural clusters may be artifactual.

Indeed, researchers espousing this view believe that societal clusters really reflect differing levels of economic development and once these differences have been taken into account, these researchers believe that societies will not meaningfully cluster.

Nevertheless, contrasting evidence suggests cultures tend to be quite different even among societies at similar levels of economic development. Thus, Trepo (1973) reported how the transfer of management by objectives (MBO) from the United States to France was unsuccessful. In particular, it was difficult to reconcile the significance of hierarchy in French culture with joint participation of supervisor and subordinate to reach decisions regarding the subordinate's performance. Trompenaars (1993) and Hofstede (1980) provide many additional examples that support the differentiation of cultures even among countries of similar economic development.

In summary, several factors contribute to shared cultures among people of different societies. Economic forces may moderate some of these factors, but it may be difficult to change fundamental characteristics of beliefs and behaviors of people within different societies. In such cases, one may find distinct cultures of societies at any level of economic development, and also cutting across different degrees of modernity. In addition to these factors, several researchers have indicated that social and psychological variables such as attitudes, values, and work goals can be used to cluster societies (e.g., Haire, Ghiselli, & Porter, 1966; Ronen & Shenkar, 1985). In the next section of this chapter, we review the previous empirical attempts to cluster societies.

Empirical Studies on the Clustering of Societies

There has been approximately a half-century of effort to identify clusters of societies using the analysis of international-level data (Cattell, 1950). One of the most well-known and most-referenced clustering of societies was proposed by Ronen and Shenkar (1985). Their research is a good example on how work-related values and attitudes can be used to group countries together in a meaningful way. We will save the discussion of this study until last because of its direct relevance to the GLOBE project. The earliest impetus to clustering research can be traced to the pioneering works of Toynbee (1947) and Cattell (1950). Toynbee identified 21 distinct living or extinct cultural patterns across civilizations. Of the 21 patterns that he identified, only five clusters are still surviving: Western, Orthodox Christian, Islamic, Hindu, and Far Eastern. Cattell (1950) analyzed about 80 variables to construct 12 factor dimensions that measured various psychological, sociological, demographic, and economic characteristics of the societies within his sample. His societal clusters included (a) Catholic Homeland, (b) Catholic Colonial (including Latin American countries), (c) Eastern European, (d) Nordic, (e) Islamic, (f) East Baltic, (g) Hamitic (including Arab societies), and (h) Oriental (India and China). In his study, the larger developed nations, such as France, Germany, the United Kingdom, the United States, the Soviet Union, and Japan, could not be clustered with any of these and emerged as independent units in the analysis. In a review paper, Woliver and Cattell (1981) noted that 12–20 factors are necessary for full cluster descriptions, and termed these as "syntality" factors. In contrast to the individual culture dimensions, which indicate how societies differ from one another, syntality factors identify commonalities among clustering of societies. Cattell used secondary data on the organized behaviors of the group as a whole (e.g., the number of treaties a group makes, the group's gross national product, the frequency of a group's involvement in war, and the group's plan for welfare) as variables that loaded on his syntality factors.

Most more recent work on clustering has included psychological variables such as employee attitudes and goals, or management practices variables such as perceived roles and management styles, rather than socioeconomic data to cluster countries. Using 3,641 respondents in 14 countries, Haire, Ghiselli, and Porter (1966) surveyed Maslow need satisfaction, attitude toward democratic managerial practices, and cognitive descriptions of the managerial role. The resulting societal clusters showed strong economic patterns and religion–language subpatterns within each economic grouping. Later, Sirota and Greenwood (1971) surveyed 13,000 sales,

technical, and service personnel in 25 nations, and collected data on 14 work goals. The economic and religion–language patterns were still reflected in the resulting clusters; however, some anomalies surfaced as Latin American nations were mapped together with Sweden and Israel. Brazil, Japan, and India did not group in a meaningful interpretable way with other societies.

In another study, Ronen and Kraut (1977) studied the importance of 15 work goals using a sample of 4,000 technicians in 15 nations. Though the number of nations in the sample was small, the clusters had strong religion–language basis. Hofstede's (1976) study, which involved 315 middle-level managers representing 26 nationalities on a set of 12 scales measuring personal and interpersonal values, indicated that the national groupings on the basis of values could be interpreted in terms of religion, language, and geography. Hofstede (1980) replicated these results using a survey of IBM managers from a much larger sample of nationalities and found that Japan was isolated from the Far Eastern cluster of nations, indicating some moderating role of economic factors.

More recently, Furnham, Kirkcaldy, and Lynn (1994) surveyed 12,000 students from 41 countries from 5 continents (South America, North America, Europe, Africa, and Asia-Pacific). Results of this study highlighted distinct Western and Eastern cultures. For example, Schwartz (1999) reported the findings for grade-school teacher samples from 44 nations and university student samples from 40 nations, whereby nations were plotted along with the structure of seven value types on a two-dimensional graph. For both samples, there emerged a distinct East Europe cluster, a West Europe cluster, an English-speaking cluster, a Far East cluster, an Islamic cluster, and a Latin America cluster.

Separately, Inglehart and Baker (2000) plotted 65 societies on two-dimensions of cross-cultural variations using data from the 1990–1991 and 1995–1998 World Values Surveys. The first dimension was Traditional/Secular-Rational authority and the second was Survival/Self-Expression. They identified a Protestant Europe cluster, an English-speaking cluster, a Latin America cluster, an African cluster, a South Asia cluster, a Catholic Europe cluster, an Orthodox cluster within a broader ex-Communist cluster, and a Confucian cluster.

Other studies have examined the similarities and differences among European countries with respect to culture and leadership attributes. Smith, Dugan, and Trompenaars (1996) analyzed data on personal values and behavioral intentions of 10,000 managers and employees from 43 nations. They concluded that a fundamental divide exists between Eastern and Western Europe, and noted that the footprint of history that appears to leave the sharpest imprint at present is not the legacy of the Roman Empire, but that of the Soviet Union. Western European countries tend to value *achieved* status: that is, social standing and prestige reflecting the ability of an individual to acquire an established position in society as a result of individual accomplishments. In contrast, Eastern European countries tend to value *ascribed* status: that is, social standing or prestige that is the result of inheritance or hereditary factors. Smith (1997) analyzed a subset of these data that excluded Central and East European countries. The North European countries in the Anglo and Nordic cluster and Germany valued participation, equality, and utilitarian involvement. The South European countries included in the Latin European and the Near East cluster, along with Austria valued reliance on supervisors, hierarchy, and loyal involvement. Zander (1997) also found different leadership style preferences between Northern and Southern European countries: Those in the north preferred coaching and those in the south preferred directing.

Brodbeck and colleagues (2000) recently analyzed the GLOBE database for leadership prototypes of 22 European nations and found 6 basic clusters and 2 meta-clusters: Anglo, Nordic, and Germanic countries in the first metacluster of Northern and Western Europe; and Latin European, Arab (Near East), and Central and Eastern European countries in the second metacluster of Southern and Eastern Europe. The former group favored interpersonal directness and proximity far more than the latter.

In a study of 15 countries representative of Western Europe, Tixier (1994) compared different management and communication styles across Europe and found several exceptions to the "usually accepted cultural clusters of northern European, southern European, Latin, Anglo-Saxon, Nordic, and Germanic countries" (Tixier, 1994, p. 8). Still, the Northern European model, with its Germanic and Nordic variants, was clearly differentiated from the Southern European model on the basis of Latin (Catholic) traditions. In Northern Europe, the Germanic model was distinguished by comanagement or codetermination. Responsibilities were clearly and precisely defined in a military way, and there was little scope for individuals to use personal discretion, as is frequently the case in Latin European countries. The Nordic model shares democratic and participatory spirit with the Germanic model, but is also highly egalitarian. Each person seeks opinions from others and must justify all proposals and accept counterproposals. The Latin European model, in contrast, inclines people to tightly control information, secrets, and power, and also endorses hierarchy.

Perhaps the most referenced and enduring research findings regarding the empirical clustering of societies in the organizational literature was that proposed by Ronen and Shenkar (1985). Their pioneering work used previously published data that was subsequently subjected to a statistical procedure known as "smallest space analysis" (Guttman, 1968). The results of the cluster analysis procedure were presented in the form of a figure that grouped countries together in terms of their similarity on work-related variables. For instance, Latin American and Latin European countries were closely related to each other as were the Germanic and Nordic countries. They also proposed Arabic, Near Eastern, Anglo, and Far Eastern clusters. Brazil, Japan, India, and Israel were considered independents and remained separate from other identifiable clusters. Their results provide a useful example and structure for understanding the relationship between these worker attitudes and values and country groupings. They paid particular attention to studies containing the kind of data used in the present GLOBE project (including work-related values and attitudes of respondents within each society) and it is for this reason that we have saved the discussion of the Ronen and Shenkar study until last. However, Ronen and Shenkar (1985) had to rely on prior studies that were rather limited in the number and sample of societies. Further, these studies did not have a sufficient representation of societies from Eastern Europe, Africa, and Asia. Because

GLOBE provides data from a large number of organizations in societies with significant regional differentiation, we are in a position to replicate and extend Ronen and Shenkar's (1985) clustering of societies. Further, we can empirically validate our proposed clustering scheme as well as others previously proposed.

In sum, the prior empirical studies suggest that religion–language, geography, and ethnicity, and work-related values and attitudes are relevant factors in the clustering of societies. Economic development may also be associated with significant changes in the society's work culture, and push it apart from other societies that do not have a similar level of economic development (as in the case of Latin America and Latin Europe). Still, as we should expect, societies that share similar religion–language, geography, and ethnicity tend to look alike in regards to fundamental characteristics. It should be noted, however, that intercultural similarities may hide significant within-society heterogeneity. For instance, Ronen and Shenkar (1985) note:

> Many countries are not homogenous: they consist of various populations. They may differ according to language (French and Flemish in Belgium; French, German, and Italian in Switzerland, etc.); according to climate and differing proximity to other countries (e.g. Northern and Southern Italy); or according to urban/rural and other differences. (p. 441)

GLOBE researchers remained cognizant of intraculture variability particularly with respect to countries such as South Africa, where vastly different societal cultures exist within the same country. We have identified our societal clusters by considering the history of the societies under consideration as well as the religious, linguistic, and economic similarities. Further, the development of the GLOBE societal clusters were informed by the results of the aforementioned empirical studies.

Developing Regional Clusters of GLOBE Societies

The process and results of the GLOBE societal culture clustering for major geographical regions in the world are presented below.

Our overall goal was to adequately cluster 61 societies participating in the GLOBE study. As indicated by the previous review of the "clustering literature," there is no perfect or widely accepted clustering of countries. This is probably desirable given the different purposes for undertaking this effort. Different societal clusters may be equally valid given the uses for which the process was developed. GLOBE researchers used the results of previous empirical studies, other factors such as common language, geography, and religion, and, perhaps most importantly, historical accounts when constructing the final GLOBE clusters.

Table 10.1 presents a list of countries organized in societal clusters by our proposed schema. As a result of our analysis, we propose that 61 GLOBE societies can be grouped into 10 distinct clusters. For ease of discussion, these ten clusters are described as belonging to the following geographic regions of the world: Europe, the Americas, Africa, and Asia. What follows is a discussion of the rationale for proposing these specific clusters.

Europe

We propose that European societies should be grouped into Anglo, Latin Europe, Nordic Europe, Germanic Europe, and Eastern Europe clusters. The rationale for this grouping is explained below.

Anglo Cluster

Anglo Cluster includes England (and societies dominated by the English), Australia, South Africa (White sample), Canada, New Zealand, Ireland, and the United States of America. This cluster is based on several factors including ethnic and linguistic similarities, and migration patterns originating centuries ago from areas now identified as Northern Europe. As Stenton (1971) noted, during the Roman Empire several Germanic people had migrated to Britain since at least the 3rd century A.D. Rome withdrew its army from Britain in A.D. 410. In the ensuing struggle for power, Germanic Oisc gained kingship in the latter half of the 5th century, bequeathing the name of the *Oiscingas* on the Kentish (British) royal household. During this period, as supported by archeological evidence and recorded in the Chronicles of Anglo Saxons (Swanton, 2000), there were significant migrations—craftsmen, warriors, and others—from Jutland (northern Denmark), Angeln (as the border region of Denmark and Germany was called), and Saxony (Germany), in addition to Frisians from the Netherlands and Franks from northern France and Central Germany, especially to the eastern half of Britain (Swanton, 2000). Over time, the boundaries between the Angles and Saxons, the two dominant groups of migrants, blurred to give rise to Anglo-Saxon (English) culture in Britain, which had perceptible influence on the local Celtic culture, language, and institutions (for further references, see Williamson, 1999). Over the second millennium, Anglo culture diffused to Ireland, the United States, Canada, South Africa, Australia, and New Zealand, as the English migrants penetrated these societies. We therefore propose that the following GLOBE societies be grouped into the Anglo cluster: United Kingdom, United States, Canada, South Africa (White sample), Ireland, Australia, and New Zealand. This clustering of countries is consistent with the findings of Ronan and Shenkar (1985).

Latin Europe Cluster

The Latin Europe cluster consists of the regions influenced by Roman culture (Latourette, 1965, Chapter 8). As Latourette (1965) emphasizes,

> the Catholic Reformation had its mainsprings and its most cogent expressions in what might be called Latin Europe—the countries in Western Europe which had been most extensively incorporated in the Roman Empire. To be more precise, Protestantism became the prevailing religion among the Germanic peoples who, with one exception, had not settled within the former confines of the Roman Empire. The exception—Great Britain—was more apparent than real, for here the Anglo-Saxon and then the Scandinavian invaders had never been under Roman rule and they had wiped out all cultural traces of the Roman occupation. (Retrieved from http://www.religion-online.org/cgi-bin/relsearchd. dll/showchapter?chapter_id=579)

Martin Luther (1483–1546) taught that Roman Catholicism teaches Salvation from Original Sin through faith alone, and that Original Sin could not be overcome by one's own actions or merits. Under Roman Catholicism, one could only have faith that God would grant salvation, and that such salvation was possible only through sacraments performed by a priest, and that true priest must take a vow of celibacy (Ozment, 1986). Luther promoted use of vernacular instead of Latin, and empowerment of the laity to have a direct relationship with God. In 1529, the Germanic reforms were termed as Protestant, when Reformed delegates in Germany issued a Protestatio. The Latin Europe cluster, which rejected the German-minded empowering spirit of the Protestant reforms, includes Italy, Portugal, Spain, France, Switzerland (French speaking), and Israel.

With the exception of Israel and French-speaking Switzerland, this clustering of countries is consistent with the findings of Ronen and Shenkar (1985). We conceptualized the Latin Europe cluster to be based on more than embracing the Catholic religion, as indicated by Israel's inclusion as part of this cluster. Although many Jews converted to Catholicism due to religious repression by the church, others migrated to Eastern Europe to escape from such repression. These migrants, who later founded Israel, retained their social and business ties with the Latin European region and are therefore included as part of the Latin Europe cluster.

Nordic Europe Cluster

The cluster of Nordic Europe is related to the historical concept of Scandinavia. According to the Random House Encyclopaedia, Scandinavia is the "region of northern Europe consisting of the kingdoms of Sweden, Norway and Denmark; culturally and historically Finland and Iceland are often considered part of this area" (quoted at http://www.faqs.org/faqs/nordic-faq/part2_NORDEN/preamble.html). *Scandinavia* was first a geographical term referring to the Scandinavian peninsula—Sweden and Norway. This was the island of "Scandinauia" that Roman historian Pliny the Elder identified in 67 C.E. to be situated in the sea at the edge of the world, north of Germania (Pliny, 1991). Later, political unions, territorial expansion, and cultural interactions stretched the peninsular concept to include Denmark, Finland and Iceland. In Nordic languages, the word *Scandinavien* means the countries that were the ancient land of the Norsemen, an ethnic concept that includes Denmark, Norway, and Sweden (and sometimes Iceland), but excludes Finland, which forms a part of Scandinavia only on a broader cultural basis (Einola & Turgeon, 2000).

The term "Nordic countries" itself originated from French "Pays Nordiques," and initially referred to the "northern" countries in general and could be applied even to nations such as Canada. Subsequently, the term Nordic became established to refer exclusively to the five Scandinavian countries, with their model of welfare state and common history, culture, and religion, and similar languages (Einola & Turgeon, 2000). The Nordic language term *Norden* (*Pohjola* or *Pohjoismaat* in Finnish) also refers to these five Scandinavian countries, which since 1956 have cooperated in the Nordic Council. The Nordic Council recognizes the dating of the formal cooperation among the nations of the region to 1397, when Margrete, the queen of Denmark and Norway, was crowned the queen of Sweden (Einola & Turgeon, 2000). Accordingly, we propose to group the following GLOBE societies into the Nordic Europe cluster: Finland, Sweden, and Denmark. This clustering of societies is consistent with the findings of Ronen and Shenkar (1985).

Germanic Europe Cluster

The Germanic Europe cluster consists of societies that continue to use the German language. Language, however, is not the primary reason for their clustering. The distinctive Germanic culture can be traced to at least 5400 B.C. (Schake, 1998). Tacitus (A.D. 55–117), who was Roman, published a pamphlet *Germenia* on the people of Germany, and described these people as possessing a love of freedom and fighting. Even after the Germanic people were converted to Roman Catholicism, they continued to practice traditional religious practices and beliefs. Subsequently, during the postmedieval times, the Protestant form of Christianity evolved as a distinct Germanic interpretation of life. Though former East Germany was under the communist regime of Eastern Europe for about 40 years, traditional German values such as orderliness, straight forwardness, honesty, and loyalty remained an integral part of the East German society. The traditional cultural leaders, including poets, novelists, philosophers, and religious leaders also continued to play a major role in public life and in social welfare. As such, the cultural patterns remained largely stable, facilitating reintegration with the West later (see also Sowards, 1996, for additional explanations). We propose that the following GLOBE societies be included in the Germanic Europe cluster: the Netherlands, Austria, Switzerland, former West Germany, and former East Germany. This clustering is again consistent with the findings of Ronen and Shenkar (1985), except for Switzerland, which is an additional nation in our study.

Eastern Europe Cluster

The most common explanation of the Eastern Europe cluster is based on Soviet hegemony. The Soviet factor, though obviously important, does not reflect other relevant forces, such as geography and pre-Soviet history. Sowards (1996) has recommended an alternative formulation of the Eastern European region:

> Since 1945, it has been deceptively easy to define Eastern Europe in terms of Soviet Communist domination. By this method, Eastern Europe is synonymous with the "satellites" set up by Stalin after the Second World War—it is the region on the far side of the Iron Curtain. Now that the Iron Curtain has disappeared, it is easier to see the flaws in this approach, but for students of the area it always offered problems. For example, Greece was frequently excised from the area, on the grounds that it was not a Communist country, and lumped into something called the "Mediterranean." But to assert that Greece and Spain share more in their historical backgrounds than do Greece and Romania, one has to forget a great deal of Greek history. (Retrieved from http://www.lib.msu.edu/ sowards/balkan/lecture2.html)

McNeill (1964) also highlighted that the history of Eastern Europe has been shaped by an exceptional form of a fundamentally Asian culture, that of the steppe nomad (found in the vast tracts of land in southeastern Europe and Asia). The "great war captains" continuously created the "steppe empire" in the region to pull together separate pastoral groups, and constantly imposed controls over the land, labor, produce, and freedom of movement of the region's peasant families. The presence of mountains and forests provided social stability and promoted group cohesiveness. As such, the societies in the Balkans and Central Europe, Eastern Europe, and Central Asia share significant similarities. We propose that the following GLOBE societies be included in the Eastern Europe[2] cluster: Hungary, Russia, Kazakhstan, Albania, Poland, Greece, Slovenia, and Georgia. This cluster of countries has not been adequately sampled in prior studies and so it is not surprising that this cluster really has not emerged in the prior research. Thus, this is a newly proposed clustering of societies.

The Americas

Whereas the United States and Canada have been included in the Anglo cluster discussed above, the other GLOBE societies in the Americas share a distinct Latin culture, as explained below.

Latin America Cluster

Catholicism has a dominant influence on the societies in the Americas, with the exception of the United States and Canada. In addition, these societies "share a common Roman law heritage, a common Iberian colonial past, and present-day patterns of social organization" (Rosenn, 1988, p. 128). There also tends to be an emphasis on Spanish and Portuguese languages. The culture is characterized by the values of personalism, particularism, and paternalism (Osland, De Franco, & Osland, 1999). First, personalism refers to *simpatica,* or a sense of connection and avoiding direct affronts to personal dignity (Albert, 1996). At the workplace, supervisors are expected to attend family functions of the employees, and have a regard for what would happen to the family if a poorly performing employee were fired. Second, particularism refers to the legitimacy of using personal connections for one's particular benefits. This concept is

supported by the tradition of civil law from Spain and Portugal. The civil law, in contrast to the precedent-based common law in Anglo nations, is founded on general deductive principles. As such, the rules are subject to constant reinterpretation depending on particular facts. In fact, there exists a Brazilian saying, "For friends, everything; for strangers, nothing; and for enemies, the law" (Rosenn, 1988, p. 143). Finally, Latin American paternalism derives its roots from the Iberian monarchy, the Catholic Church, and the extended patriarchal family. The family's boundaries are guided by *compadrazgo* (i.e., coparenting), in which a child's godparents move beyond friendship to formalize a closer bond to the family in the baptismal ceremony. There is a fairly low level of trust of those who are not part of their family or close friends. We propose that the following GLOBE societies be classified into the Latin America cluster: Costa Rica, Venezuela, Ecuador, Mexico, El Salvador, Columbia, Guatemala, Bolivia, Brazil, and Argentina. This cluster of countries corresponds to the prior research showing a Latin American societal culture distinguishable from that of the rest of the world. Therefore, unlike Ronen and Shenkar (1985), we include Brazil as part of this cluster, rather than as an independent nation.

Africa

We propose that African societies be classified into two clusters: Middle East and Sub-Saharan Africa.

Middle East Cluster

The most prominent basis of Middle East culture lies in the Near Eastern civilization of North Africa and West Asia that has existed since at least pre-Sumerian times in the 4th and 3rd millennia B.C. The Arab conquest of Africa's northern rim began within years after the death of the Prophet Muhammad more than 1,300 years ago. The North African region encompasses the Great Sahara Desert and Nile River Valley (Danowitz, Nassef, & Goodman, 1995), and includes Mauritania, Western Sahara, Morocco, Algeria, Tunisia, Libya, and Egypt. The culture of this Northern Rim came to be shaped by Islamic moral and legal code (the Koran and the *Sharia*), the Arabic language (the key to understanding Islamic scriptures), and the geographic features the Nile River and the Sahara Desert. In these societies, the scope of government and law was limited, for Islam alone had the total regulatory force. A clear distinction existed between what was legal and what was moral (such as in dress code), and moral inappropriateness was strongly criticized and punished as a crime against Islam and the society. The pan-regional influence of Islam was solidified under the Ottoman Turk Empire of medieval times and subsequent European imperialism (Karsh & Karsh, 1999). Anderson (1995) emphasizes:

> European imperialism came relatively late to the Middle East and North Africa and was characterized by a preoccupation with the geostrategic— as opposed to economic—value of the region. To ensure low-cost access to the region and to guarantee their global strategic interests, the European powers first attempted to identify and support compliant local political authorities in protectorates of varying degrees of formality. When the regional political system collapsed with the demise of the Ottoman Empire in the First World War, the European powers reconfigured the political and economic landscape of the region, inventing new states and imposing European-style administrations, thereby creating a regional system that would secure European political interests. (p. 29)

We propose that the following GLOBE societies be included in the Middle East cluster: Qatar, Morocco, Turkey, Egypt, and Kuwait. The clustering of these nations is consistent with the Arabic cluster of Ronen and Shenkar (1985), though our study sampled only one nation (Kuwait) included in their Arabic cluster. Further, we departed from Ronen and Shenkar (1985) by including Turkey as part of this cluster. We placed Turkey in the Middle East cluster due to the strong historical and cultural links dating to the Ottoman period connecting Turkey with the other societies in the Middle East.

Sub-Saharan Africa Cluster

The Sub-Saharan African societies did not experience the kind of homogenization northern African societies experienced with respect to domains such as religion, language, and customs. Further, due to limited interethnic marriages and interaction, there exists a vast diversity in ethnicity, religion, language, and customs in the southern and central African Rim. Historically, this rim was difficult to access and was economically rather isolated from Egypt and other countries that formed the core of Arab civilization. The Arab societies looked toward the southern African region primarily for slave trading, thereby further isolating those societies. Subsequently, although facilitating Christian missionary efforts to set up schools and social interest groups in the region, the British also persisted in their "divide and rule" policy by empowering and coercing indigenous chiefs to regulate local affairs to promote British commercial and economic interests in the colonies. The history of slavery and distrust remains strongly entrenched in the psyche of the indigenous southerners. Stead (1996) notes that since the introduction of slavery in the Cape Colony (dating back to 1658), the divisions among White, Black, Indian, and Colored people (persons of mixed racial ancestry) emerged and deepened as non-White people were denied many human rights. Racial separation was greatly exacerbated after 1948 when the National Party came to power in South Africa and pursued its policy of apartheid, or separateness. Racial segregation remains to be bridged socially and mentally throughout the region, even after formal abolition of apartheid during the 1990s.

A distinctive philosophical concept in Sub-Saharan Africa cluster is *Ubuntu,* which refers to humaneness that individuals and groups display for one another (Mbigi & Maree, 1995). Ubuntu is the "foundation for the basic values that manifest themselves in the ways" Sub-Saharan African people believe and behave toward each other and everyone else they encounter (Mangaliso, 2001, p. 24). The concept is summed up in the phrase *umntu ngumntu ngabanye* (a person is a person through others), which implies that the relationship and recognition by others is at the core of a person's identity. Consequently, the Sub-Saharan African cluster is characterized by the norms of reciprocity, suppression of self-interest, the virtue of symbiosis, and human interdependence (Mangaliso, 2001). We propose that the following GLOBE societies be included in the Sub-Saharan Africa cluster: Namibia, Zambia, Zimbabwe, Nigeria, and South Africa (Black sample). It should be noted that prior empirical work has not really identified this cluster before. However, for the reasons stated above, we believe that there is justification for believing that these societies will cluster together.

Asia

Prior empirical research has identified a single Asian cluster (e.g., Ronen & Shenkar, 1985). However, in their discussion, Ronen and Shenkar suggest that this single cluster may be artifactual in that prior empirical research did not have an adequate sampling of these societies. In GLOBE, we hypothesize that the Asian societies (excluding Central Asia and Middle East) can be grouped into two different clusters: Confucian and Southern Asian. These two clusters have quite distinct worldviews. The teachings and works of Confucius, and later Buddha, had a distinct historical influence on the Confucian cluster; whereas those in the Southern Asian cluster shared Brahmanism and Buddhist, Islamic, and Christian influences. Historically, China and India have had distinct spheres of influence in Confucian Asian and Southern Asian societies respectively. Huxley (1997) in his review of ancient legal systems, for instance, suggests that during the third and second centuries before the Common Era (B.C.E) there flourished three distinct schools of natural law originating from India, China, and the Hellenistic world, thus recognizing that the distinctiveness of the Indian and Chinese cultures dates back to these historical times.

Southern Asia Cluster

Radioactive dating of archeological materials indicates a continuous development of cultural sequence in the Greater Indus Valley, covering eastern Iran, southeastern Turkmenistan, Baluchistan, Afghanistan, Pakistan, and western India, since at least 5,000 B.C. (Thapar & Moghul, 1996). More than 1,200 of the 1,600 known settlements of the valley were on the Saraswati river (now dry), with the rest distributed mainly on its key tributaries such as the Indus. Archeologically attested historical evidence shows India's strong cultural influence in Southeast Asian nations, dating to the first millennium A.D. (Vallibhotama & Saraya, 1996). The early kingdoms in Southeast Asia were organized along the Indian societal lines; that is, using Buddhist or Brahmin officials as their advisors.

> The local rulers, who came into contact with the foreigners mainly through trade, felt attracted to certain elements of Indian civilization, which they subsequently adopted and adapted to their own needs . . . As far as "Sinization" is concerned, this was quite a different process. It was confined to northern Viet Nam . . . . (Vallibhotama & Saraya, 1994, p. 417)

A distinct cultural feature of the region, spanning from ancient Persia to the modern Philippines, was the rather peaceful and interactive coexistence of diversity over long periods. As Levi-Strauss (1951) noted, people of widely differing religious beliefs coexisted peacefully in spite of these differences. For instance, the southern Asians have shown over history their ability to live together despite different beliefs. In the region, one frequently finds Islamic mosques next to Hindu temples with families of gods and goddesses, and Buddhist pagodas or Christian churches or Sikh Gurudwaras with images of their teachers. These "complementary forms of faith seem irreconcilable yet they co-exist peaceably" (Levi-Strauss, 1951). The region historically shared common Vedic culture, and later absorbed Islamic and British influences within its boundaries.

In the societies of the region, there were continuous efforts to realize a rich interaction and balance among spirituality, psychology, philosophy, morality, politics, economics, and society. The societies in the Southern Asia cluster, in particular Iran, also shared strong and sustained interactions with the Arab cluster. Several of these societies, especially Malaysia and Indonesia, have enjoyed considerable migration of Chinese over the second millennium A.D. and have maintained strong economic links with China, South Korea, Taiwan, and Japan over the recent decades. Further, due to their peculiar colonial situation under the Portuguese culture, Mexican-American influences have been quite prominent in the Philippines. In regard to the Philippines, Inglehart, Petterson, and Puranen (1994) note that although geographically close to China and Taiwan, she was not historically shaped by the Confucian model and is culturally closer to the South Asian societies and Latin American societies, with whom the Philippines shares a history of Hispanic colonization. On the whole, despite the diversity of external influences, an interesting feature shared by all Southern Asian societies is their propensity to successfully assimilate external and modern influences with their indigenous cultures (see Gupta, Surie, & Chhokar, 2002, for additional references and evidence). We propose that the following GLOBE societies be included in the Southern Asia cluster: Iran, India, Indonesia, Philippines, Malaysia, and Thailand.

Confucian Asia Cluster

The Confucian cluster is defined by the strong historical influence of China and Confucian ideology. Japan, though geographically isolated from China, has had rich cultural interactions with China. Even currently, Japan shares close affinity with the Chinese culture. As Lowe (1998) noted,

> Hofstede's results also differentiate between East Asian societies on his "etic" dimensions with, for example, Japan showing a unique cultural profile, predicting differences in structure and behaviour with its immediate "Confucian" neighbours. The differences in structure may be reliably attributed to differing institutional environments, but what all these Confucian societies do appear to have structurally in common is a reliance upon "networks" which are co-ordinated through the mechanism of trust, and this common structure can be more reliably attributed to common cultural influences. (p. 328)

Using the extensive World Values Survey, Inglehart and Carballo (1997) also identify coherent value system patterns of secularism deriving from common societal objectives in the Confucian cluster. Brett (1997) observed that the Confucian influence extended to those Eastern societies located within the China cultural orbit namely Korea, Japan, Hong Kong, Taiwan and Singapore, not to mention overseas Chinese communities everywhere. In China, itself, Confucianism has provided the indispensable mainstay of a system of education that is more than two thousand years old. (Retrieved from http://department.monm.edu/classics/Speel_Festschrift/brett.htm)

Some distinctive Confucian teachings included the emphasis on learning through a hierarchical, family modeled institution, which taught principles such as diligence, self-sacrifice, and delayed gratification. The Confucian model of a family included the firm but compassionate father, the loyal child who can never fully repay a deep debt to the parents, and the ancestors who are to be respected and worshipped (Wei-ming, 1996). Therefore, we propose the following GLOBE societies be grouped into the Confucian cluster: Taiwan, Singapore, Hong Kong, South Korea, China, and Japan. Table 10.1 and Figure 10.1 provide a display of the ten regional clusters of societies.

EMPIRICAL TEST OF SOCIETAL CLUSTERS

We statistically tested the empirical validity of the proposed clustering presented in Table 10.1. Discriminant analysis is a statistical technique that develops a linear function from a set of variables (i.e., societal culture dimensions in the present study) believed to be important in differentiating group membership (i.e., the hypothesized societal clusters) of the data observations (i.e., GLOBE societies). We therefore use this technique to test the hypotheses that our hypothesized GLOBE societal clustering, as summarized in Table 10.1, is supported by our data. We will use this technique to statistically test the extent to which our classification is supported by the data.

Because discriminant analysis builds a linear function by using the empirical data, we randomly split our data at the individual level into two halves (i.e., developmental sample and holdout sample). The developmental sample consisted of all the GLOBE societies and was used to build the linear function connecting

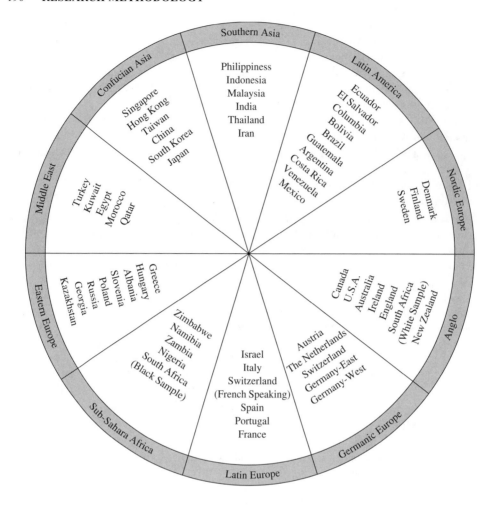

Figure 10.1   Country Clusters According to GLOBE

the GLOBE culture dimensions to the societal clusters. Although the holdout sample consisted of different respondents, it also contained data for all the GLOBE societies and this sample was used to test the robustness of our discriminant analysis. We used the societal practices (As Is) and societal values (Should Be) scores on nine GLOBE cultural scales as the variables used to predict the group membership of our societies in our discriminant analysis. The nine GLOBE cultural dimensions are: (a) Performance Orientation, (b) Assertiveness, (c) Future Orientation, (d) Humane Orientation, (e) Institutional

Collectivism, (f) In-Group Collectivism, (g) Gender Egalitarianism, (h) Power Distance, and (i) Uncertainty Avoidance.

In the developmental sample (i.e., the sample used to develop the linear discriminant function), five discriminant functions captured 92.8% of the variation among the GLOBE societal clusters. For this sample, 59 of the 61 societies were classified accurately into the hypothesized clusters (see Table 10.1), yielding 96.7% classification reliability of the discriminant functions. Post hoc analysis revealed that only two countries were not classified as predicted: Costa

Table 10.1   GLOBE Society Cluster Samples

Anglo	Latin Europe	Nordic Europe	Germanic Europe
Australia	France	Denmark	Austria
Canada	Israel	Finland	Germany (Former
England	Italy	Sweden	East)
Ireland	Portugal		Germany (Former
New Zealand	Spain		West)
South Africa	Switzerland		Netherlands
(White sample)	(French-speaking)		Switzerland
United States			

Eastern Europe	Latin America	Sub-Saharan Africa	Middle East
Albania	Argentina	Namibia	Egypt
Georgia	Bolivia	Nigeria	Kuwait
Greece	Brazil	South Africa	Morocco
Hungary	Colombia	(Black sample)	Qatar
Kazakhstan	Costa Rica	Zambia	Turkey
Poland	Ecuador	Zimbabwe	
Russia	El Salvador		
Slovenia	Guatemala		
	Mexico		
	Venezuela		

Southern Asia	Confucian Asia
India	China
Indonesia	Hong Kong
Iran	Japan
Malaysia	Singapore
Philippines	South Korea
Thailand	Taiwan

Rica and Guatemala. It turns out that in the developmental sample, both of these countries had a greater likelihood of being classified into the Latin Europe cluster than into the originally hypothesized Latin America cluster.

Although the results of the discriminant functions on the development sample yielded strong supportive results for the GLOBE societal clustering, it is important to assess the robustness of this result because the linear functions developed by the discriminant analysis might overfit the developmental data and thus, the adequacy of the reclustering accuracy could be inflated. Thus, we examined the adequacy of the discriminant analysis linear functions to classify the GLOBE societies in the holdout sample. We achieved the following results using this technique. In the holdout sample, 36 of the 61 societies were classified as predicted,

amounting to 59% accuracy rate for the discriminant functions. Post hoc analyses revealed some reasons for this drop in accuracy. Specifically, Table 10.2 provides summary data on the average probability of classification of societies into their hypothesized cluster, and the average probability of classification into the best alternative cluster. As can be seen in this table, for societies in 8 of the 10 clusters, the average probability of classification into their hypothesized cluster exceeded 0.75. The two exceptions were the Germanic Europe (0.50) and Sub-Saharan Africa (0.53) clusters. Germanic European societies had a large 0.40 probability of being classified into the Nordic Europe cluster. Sub-Saharan African societies had 0.16 probability of classification into the Middle East cluster. Thus, geographical proximity and associated cultural interactions may be a

Table 10.2   Average Discriminant Probability of Classification of Societies Into Clusters

Hypothesized Cluster	Average Probability of Classification Into Hypothesized Cluster	Average Probability of Classification Into the Next Alternative Cluster
Anglo	0.99 (Anglo)	0.01 (Latin Europe)
Latin Europe	0.78 (Latin Europe)	0.13 (Anglo)
Nordic Europe	1.00 (Nordic Europe)	0.00
Germanic Europe	0.50 (Germanic Europe)	0.40 (Nordic Europe)
Eastern Europe	0.87 (Eastern Europe)	0.13 (Confucian Asia)
Latin America	0.75 (Latin America)	0.16 (Latin Europe)
Sub-Saharan Africa	0.53 (Sub-Saharan Africa)	0.16 (Middle East)
Middle East	0.90 (Middle East)	0.10 (Confucian Asia)
Southern Asia	0.83 (Southern Asia)	0.08 (Middle East) 0.08 (Confucian Asia)
Confucian Asia	0.83 (Confucian Asia)	0.17 (Sub-Saharan Africa)

key factor influencing the misclassifications. Indeed, when we combine the Germanic Europe cluster with the Nordic Europe cluster and the Sub-Saharan Africa cluster with the Middle East cluster, the overall predictive accuracy of the original discriminant function for the hold-out sample is 69% (42 of 61 societies predicted correctly).

Thus, it appears that there is good support for the GLOBE societal clusters. However, the cultural separation of the Germanic Europe and the Nordic Europe clusters as well as the Sub-Saharan Africa and the Middle East clusters is not as great as the differences among the other clusters. Given that the prior empirical research has repeatedly found that the Germanic Europe and the Nordic Europe clusters could be separated, and because of considerable differences in the history of Sub-Saharan Africa and the Middle East, we decided to stay with our original 10 societal clusters with the caveat that some of these clusters are not as differentiable as others. Future research will determine whether all 10 of the GLOBE societal clusters are appropriate as distinct entities.

Societal Values and Practices

To further compare each cluster's characteristics (on the culture dimension scales), we aggregated societal values scores and societal practices scores of each society to the cluster level. Each cluster's societal values and practices averages are shown using radar graphs in Figures 10.2 to 10.10. Table 10.3 categorizes the societal clusters into high, medium, and low groupings based on mean societal practices (As Is) scale on each dimension. Table 10.4 categorizes clusters using mean societal values (Should Be) into high, medium, and low clusters on each dimension. There were statistically significant differences in mean societal scores of clusters in high and low categories. The medium category had moderate levels of mean societal scores.

As shown in Tables 10.3 and 10.4, and Figures 10.2 to 10.10, there are significant differences across various clusters. The Meta-Western region (Nordic Europe, Germanic Europe, Latin Europe, Anglo, and Latin America clusters), and the Meta-Eastern region (Eastern

(Text continues on page 199)

Table 10.3   Cultural Clusters Classified on Societal Culture Practices (As Is) Scores

Cultural Dimension	High-Score Clusters	Mid-Score Clusters	Low-Score Clusters	Cluster-Average Range
Performance Orientation	Confucian Asia Germanic Europe Anglo	Southern Asia Sub-Saharan Africa Latin Europe Nordic Europe Middle East	Latin America Eastern Europe	3.73–4.58
Assertiveness	Germanic Europe Eastern Europe	Sub-Saharan Africa Latin America Anglo Middle East Confucian Asia Latin Europe Southern Asia	Nordic Europe	3.66–4.55
Future Orientation	Germanic Europe Nordic Europe	Confucian Asia Anglo Southern Asia Sub-Saharan Africa Latin Europe	Middle East Latin America Eastern Europe	3.38–4.40
Humane Orientation	Southern Asia Sub-Saharan Africa	Middle East Anglo Nordic Europe Latin America Confucian Asia Eastern Europe	Latin Europe Germanic Europe	3.55–4.71
Institutional Collectivism	Nordic Europe Confucian Asia	Anglo Southern Asia Sub-Saharan Africa Middle East Eastern Europe	Germanic Europe Latin Europe Latin America	3.86–4.88
In-Group Collectivism	Southern Asia Middle East Eastern Europe Latin America Confucian Asia	Sub-Saharan Africa Latin Europe	Anglo Germanic Europe Nordic Europe	3.75–5.87
Gender Egalitarianism	Eastern Europe Nordic Europe	Latin America Anglo Latin Europe Sub-Saharan Africa Southern Asia Confucian Asia Germanic Europe	Middle East	2.95–3.84
Power Distance		Southern Asia Latin America Eastern Europe Sub-Saharan Africa Middle East Latin Europe Confucian Asia Anglo Germanic Europe	Nordic Europe	4.54–5.39
Uncertainty Avoidance	Nordic Europe Germanic Europe	Confucian Asia Anglo Sub-Saharan Africa Latin Europe Southern Asia	Middle East Latin America Eastern Europe	3.56–5.19

NOTE: Means of high-score clusters are significantly higher ($p < 0.05$) than the rest, means of low-score clusters are significantly lower ($p < 0.05$) than the rest, and means of mid-score clusters are not significantly different from the rest ($p > 0.05$).

Table 10.4   Cultural Clusters Classified on Societal Culture Values (Should Be) Scores

Cultural Dimension	High-Score Clusters	Mid-Score Clusters	Low-Score Clusters	Cluster Average Range
Performance Orientation	Latin America	Sub-Saharan Africa Anglo Southern Asia Latin Europe Germanic Europe Nordic Europe Eastern Europe Middle East	Confucian Asia	5.53–6.24
Assertiveness	Southern Asia Confucian Asia	Sub-Saharan Africa Anglo Eastern Europe Latin Europe Nordic Europe Latin America	Middle East Germanic Europe	3.07–4.65
Future Orientation	Sub-Saharan Africa Southern Asia Middle East Latin America	Eastern Europe Latin Europe Anglo Confucian Asia	Germanic Europe Nordic Europe	4.76–5.87
Humane Orientation		All 10 Clusters		5.31–5.64
Institutional Collectivism	Latin America Middle East Southern Asia	Latin Europe Germanic Europe Sub-Saharan Africa Confucian Asia	Eastern Europe Anglo Nordic Europe	4.08–5.32
In-Group Collectivism	Latin America Anglo	Southern Asia Latin Europe Nordic Europe Sub-Saharan Africa Middle East Eastern Europe	Confucian Asia Germanic Europe	5.16–6.06
Gender Egalitarianism	Germanic Europe Anglo Nordic Europe Latin Europe Latin America	Eastern Europe Sub-Saharan Africa	Confucian Asia Southern Asia Middle East	3.65–4.91
Power Distance	Middle East	Confucian Asia Sub-Saharan Africa Anglo Eastern Europe Southern Asia Nordic Europe Latin Europe Germanic Europe	Latin America	2.51–3.03
Uncertainty Avoidance	Southern Asia Middle East Sub-Saharan Africa Latin America Eastern Europe	Confucian Asia Latin Europe	Anglo Nordic Europe Germanic Europe	3.46–5.16

NOTE: Means of high-score clusters are significantly higher ($p < 0.05$) than the rest, means of low-score clusters are significantly lower ($p < 0.05$) than the rest, and means of mid-score clusters are not significantly different from the rest ($p > 0.05$).

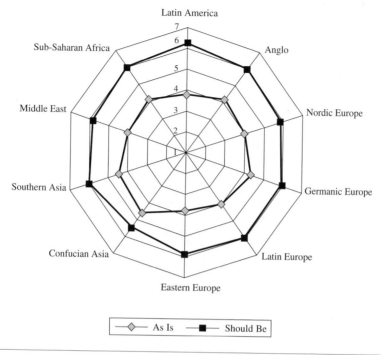

Figure 10.2   Societal Cluster Scores for Performance Orientation

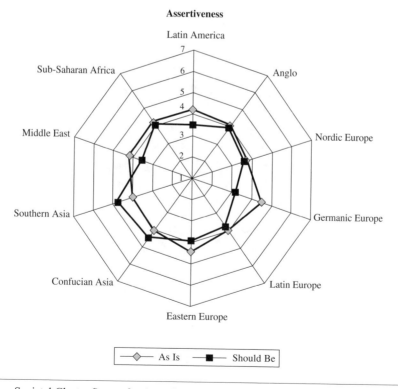

Figure 10.3   Societal Cluster Scores for Assertiveness

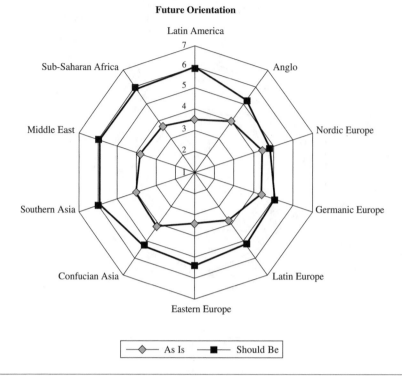

Figure 10.4   Societal Cluster Scores for Future Orientation

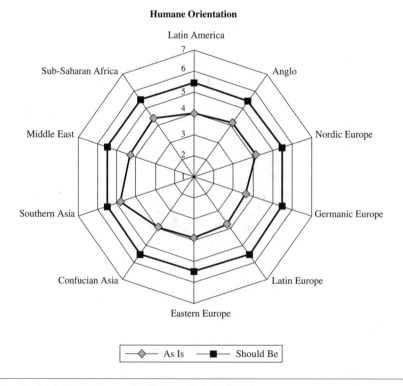

Figure 10.5   Societal Cluster Scores for Humane Orientation

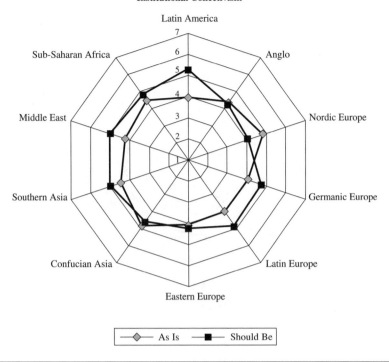

Figure 10.6 Societal Cluster Scores for Institutional Collectivism

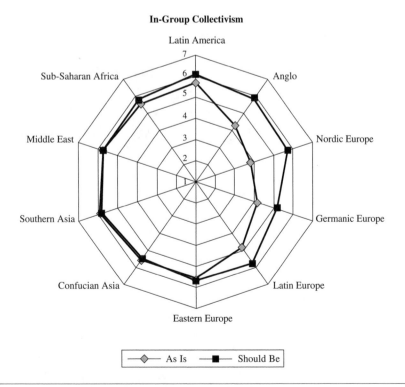

Figure 10.7 Societal Cluster Scores for In-Group Collectivism

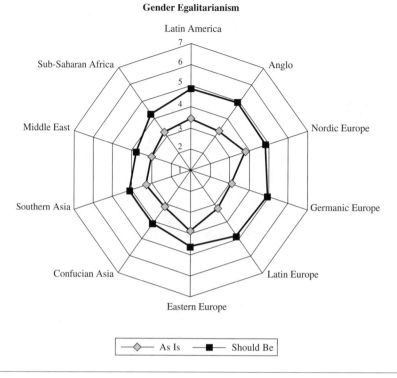

Figure 10.8   Societal Cluster Scores for Gender Egalitarianism

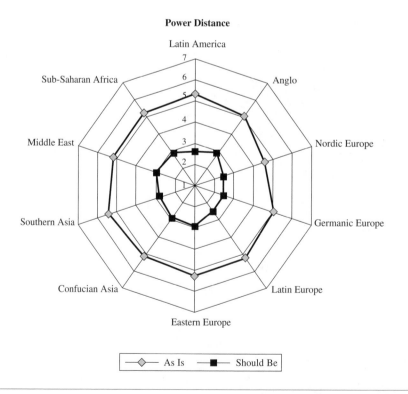

Figure 10.9   Societal Cluster Scores for Power Distance

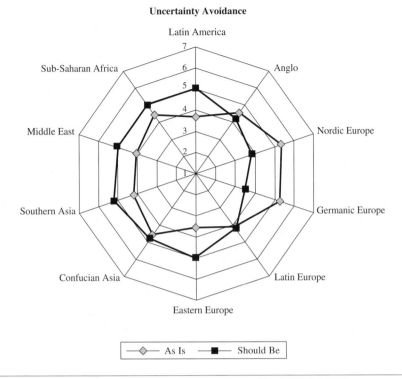

Uncertainty Avoidance

Legend: ◇ As Is — ■ Should Be

Figure 10.10 Societal Cluster Scores for Uncertainty Avoidance

Europe, Confucian Asia, Southern Asia, Middle East, and Sub-Saharan Africa clusters) are noticeably different from each other.

Within the Western region, the Germanic Europe cluster shows high practices scores for Performance Orientation, Uncertainty Avoidance, Future Orientation, and Assertiveness, but low practices scores for Humane Orientation, Institutional Collectivism, and In-Group Collectivism. Put differently, societies in the Germanic Europe cluster rely on more assertive, and individualistic approaches, which are futuristic, well-defined, result oriented, and often harsh, reflecting the technocratic orientation of the Germanic societies, considered to be "a reaction against the Hitler era. The very word 'leader' is 'Führer' in German with all that that denotes" (de Vries, 2000, retrieved from http://matilde.emeraldinsight.com/vl=8159516/cl=63/nw=1/rpsv/now/archive/june2000/spotlight.htm). The Nordic Europecluster, which is culturally most similar to the Germanic Europe cluster, shows strong practices scores for Uncertainty Avoidance and Future Orientation, and weak practices scores for In-Group Collectivism. However, it also has

weak practices scores for Power Distance and Assertiveness, and strong practices scores for Institutional Collectivism and Gender Egalitarianism. Smiley (1999), for instance, notes that Nordics tend to be modest, punctual, honest, and high-minded, and rich people generally dress, eat, and travel in the same style as the prosperous middle class, all of which reflect underplaying of assertive, familial, and masculine authority and emphasis on certainty, social unity, and cooperation.

The Latin Europe cluster is distinguished by weak practices scores for Institutional Collectivism and Humane Orientation, indicating the affective autonomy orientation of Latin European societies. Latin America is characterized by high practices scores for In-Group Collectivism, and low scores for Performance Orientation, Uncertainty Avoidance, Future Orientation, and Institutional Collectivism. In other words, Latin American societies tend to enact life as it comes, taking its unpredictability as a fact of life, and not overly worrying about results. There is less concern with institutional collective goals than with family bonds. Finally,

Anglo practices scores tend to be higher for Performance Orientation, but lower for In-Group Collectivism. These traits indicate high goal orientation of Anglo societies, where rewards tend to be based on merit and achievement goals take precedence over the family bonds.

The respondents in the five Western clusters perceive their societal practices as lower in In-Group Collectivism, Humane Orientation, and Power Distance, but higher in Uncertainty Avoidance and Future Orientation. In contrast to the Eastern region, they scored stronger in values for Gender Egalitarianism, but scored weaker in values for Uncertainty Avoidance, Future Orientation, Power Distance, and Assertiveness. These characteristics are typical of industrialized—structured and predictable—societies, but ones that rely on rationalism not authority. The respondents in the five Eastern clusters perceive their societal practices to be high in Humane Orientation and In-Group Collectivism, and are less concerned with Gender Egalitarianism. Respondents in these societies report higher values and practices of Power Distance; and although they report significantly lower practices of Uncertainty Avoidance and Future Orientation, they report stronger values of Uncertainty Avoidance and Future Orientation.

Within the Eastern clusters, Eastern Europe, with its strong links to the rest of Europe, is distinguished by the practices of higher Gender Egalitarianism and In-Group Collectivism, but lower Performance Orientation, Uncertainty Avoidance, and Future Orientation. In contrast, the Confucian Asia societal cluster is characterized by practices of higher Performance Orientation, Institutional Collectivism, and In-Group Collectivism. The goals are collective and family-oriented, and rewards are significant for performance toward meeting collective goals.

Southern Asian societies report significantly higher practices of In-Group Collectivism and Humane Orientation. These practices reflect a deep community orientation, which is the hallmark of these societies. Middle Eastern societies report lower Uncertainty Avoidance, Future Orientation, and Gender Egalitarianism in their practices than did other clusters, but greater practices of In-Group Collectivism. The Middle East cluster represents societies that believe the future unfolds with the will of Allah

and must not be approached using instrumental means. Instead, the family forms the basis for insurance against future contingencies, and looks toward the male members for primary protection and support. Finally, managers in the Sub-Saharan Africa societies report stronger practices of Humane Orientation. This attribute highlights the humanistic model of these societies that live a difficult and rural kind of life.

Metaconfiguration of Clusters

We used Multidimensional Scaling Procedure to assess the degree of overall distance among the 10 cultural clusters, across the nine values and the nine practices dimensions of societal culture. Based on several alternate measures of computing average distance in societal culture dimensions, we identified a metaconfiguration of the distances in the cultural practices and values of the 10 cultural clusters. This metaconfiguration of GLOBE cultural clusters is given in Figure 10.11.

The vertical North–South axis of the metaconfiguration separates the five Western clusters from the five Eastern clusters. Four quadrants are identifiable. Quadrant I consists of Middle East, Sub-Saharan Africa, and Eastern Europe clusters. Quadrant II consists of Latin America and Latin Europe clusters. Quadrant III consists of Anglo, Germanic Europe, and Nordic Europe clusters. Quadrant IV consists of Confucian Asia and Southern Asia clusters. Anglo and Sub-Saharan Africa clusters appear in the center of the configuration. As seen from Tables 10.3 and 10.4, Anglo and Sub-Saharan Africa clusters have mid-level scores on most of the *practices* and *values* dimensions of GLOBE.

We also examined the extent to which individual's values and practices in their societal culture are influenced by societal clusters, as distinguished from the independent society (i.e., nation). Table 10.5 presents *eta squares* of the society and cluster effects on individual values and practices in their societal culture. Eta square measures the proportion of variance accounted by the fixed societal or cluster effects. The results indicate that societal cluster effects account for more than two-thirds of the intersociety differences in values as well as practices of Uncertainty Avoidance, Future

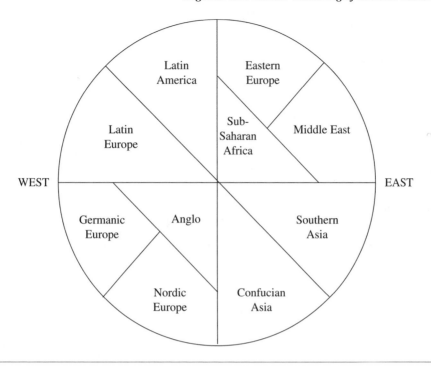

Figure 10.11   Metaconfiguration of GLOBE Societal Cultures

Orientation, and Institutional Collectivism. In other words, the clusters captured shared societal attributes of the kind of goals pursued (individual or collective), the frame of the goals (short-term or futuristic), and the structure of the goals (rule-based or uncertainty-oriented). These societal attributes also discriminate among several clusters. Tables 10.3 and 10.4, for instance, indicated that managers in Latin American societies report lower practices, but higher values, for collective goals, futuristic orientation, and rule-based structures. In contrast, Nordic European societies report lower practices and higher values for individual goals, shorter-term orientation, and uncertainty-oriented structure.

Cluster effects for Power Distance and Humane Orientation values account for only a quarter of the intersocietal variations. As shown in Table 10.4, the range for the cluster means on these two dimensions is very low. On the whole, cluster effects account for 54% of the intersocietal variation in values and 65% of the intersocietal variation in practices. Thus the majority of societal effects on an individual's values and practices are explained by the cluster factor.

This suggests that the societal cluster is an appropriate and relevant unit of analysis, and that the GLOBE cluster classifications are reliable indicators of reports of worldwide cultural attributes. Next, we further explore the practical (i.e., managerial implications) and theoretical advantages of our clustering of societies.

Managerial Implications

Human resource staffing: The use of regional clusters should be of great help for the selection and training of managers who work in global environments. To the extent that regional clusters capture important cultural distinctions both within and among clusters, the process of selecting managers to work in multicultural environments should be simpler. Rather than developing a separate selection procedure for 60-plus countries, it is obvious that fewer procedures would be necessary. Criteria can be developed for use in countries within a specific cluster. In addition, where validity studies would be extremely difficult to carry out due to limited samples in particular countries, the sample size can be increased dramatically by

Table 10.5   Percentage of Variance in Individual Values (Should Be) and Practices (As Is) About Societal
Cultures, Accounted by Society and Cluster Effects

GLOBE Cultural Dimensions	Society Effect	Cluster Effect	Cluster and Society
Societal Should Be			
Performance Orientation	0.15	0.05	32%
Uncertainty Avoidance	0.39	0.33	86%
Future Orientation	0.21	0.15	71%
Humane Orientation	0.11	0.03	25%
Institutional Collectivism	0.31	0.21	68%
In-Group Collectivism	0.14	0.07	53%
Gender Egalitarianism	0.30	0.18	62%
Assertiveness	0.31	0.15	49%
Power Distance	0.14	0.04	27%
Overall	**0.21**	**0.11**	**54%**
Societal As Is			
Performance Orientation	0.14	0.08	58%
Uncertainty Avoidance	0.36	0.29	80%
Future Orientation	0.21	0.14	66%
Humane Orientation	0.19	0.10	55%
Institutional Collectivism	0.24	0.16	65%
In-Group Collectivism	0.56	0.48	86%
Gender Egalitarianism	0.17	0.09	53%
Assertiveness	0.18	0.10	57%
Power Distance	0.18	0.06	32%
Overall	**0.22**	**0.15**	**65%**

NOTE: Percentage of variances in table are eta^2 obtained from a multivariate analysis of variance. All eta^2 were significant at $p = 0.001$.

using a grouping of country samples within regional clusters.

Human resource training: Interpersonal conflict based on cultural misunderstanding is likely to occur in multicultural environments in which managers must deal with people of vastly different backgrounds. By grouping countries with similar backgrounds, a limited set of training programs can be developed to assist managers in acquiring the skills necessary for effective leadership. For instance, if a particular multinational firm promotes delegation and participatory management among managers, training should be provided for employees who originate in high power distance cultures. Managers and employees alike from these cultures will likely have much less experience with a participatory, value-based, or team-oriented management philosophy.

Effective management: Regional clusters have implications for managers operating within cultures. Culture dimension scores provide managers with an initial assessment of the culture and hints on how to behave in that culture. Using a behavioral perspective of culture, the shared constraints of members of a certain group limit the behavior of group members (see Bond & Smith, 1996). The event-management leadership research by Smith and colleagues illustrates this point. In their 25-country study, Smith and Peterson (1994) asked managers how much they relied upon eight sources of meaning (e.g., formal organization rules, national norms) for eight categories of events (e.g., handling poor subordinate performance). Results indicated that event management processes were related to cultural dimensions. For instance, managers in collectivist, high power distance countries (e.g., Iran, Korea, and the Philippines) showed an aversion to using subordinates as a source of guidance. This type of information should assist managers when operating in common cultures. As another example using the results of this GLOBE project, effective managerial leadership requires an understanding of the desired leadership attributes from each culture. As an obvious example, leaders that originate from Humane Orientation societal cultures are expected to embody humane personality attributes and behave accordingly.

Reducing expatriate failures: The rate of expatriate failure is a subject of considerable debate. Irrespective of the precise percentage of failures, all agree that the human and financial costs associated with personnel who do not succeed are great. GLOBE researchers speculate that expatriate failure rates should be associated with the cultural distance between the home and host country. It is reasonable to expect that failure rates should be less for managers moving within a particular regional cluster and greater for managers moving across cultures. As a second,

related hypothesis, the greater the cultural distance between societal clusters, the higher the likelihood of failure. These, of course are empirical questions that can be tested and have both practical and theoretical implications.

IMPLICATIONS FOR THEORY BUILDING

Clustering countries in the GLOBE project can play an important role in organizational theory development. As discussed below, the GLOBE taxonomy of cultures can assist researchers in several ways.

Sampling cultures for cross-cultural studies: It is hard to overemphasize the importance of adequate sampling for cross-cultural studies (van de Vijver & Leung, 1997). A major issue for cross-cultural research concerns selection of countries that are required to test a specific theory. As noted by van de Vijver and Leung (1997), sampling may take the form of systematic, random, or convenience sampling, with the last least preferred. The GLOBE cultural groupings provide researchers with a guide to systematically sample respondents on the basis of specific variables of interest. The GLOBE clusters may be used as a guide to ensure that an adequate sampling of cultural variability is included in the samples. It may be possible to select fewer country samples if the researcher is confident that the country selection represents a significant range of cultural variables and variability on each cultural variable. The sampling issue is critical to ruling out explanations other than culture, a problem inherent in cross-cultural research.

Ruling out rival explanations: How should researchers avoid the trap of blindly inferring that cross-national differences are the result of cultural differences? Although it may seem obvious, it is critical to pay careful attention to initially developing a rigorous research design that minimizes the potential for alternative explanations (Brett, 1997, p. 373). Careful selection of cross-national samples is crucial to ruling out explanations alternative to culture. As Campbell (1986) and van de Vijver and Leung (1997) argue, rival explanations to cross-cultural findings can be greatly reduced as the number of countries in a cross-cultural study increase. This assumes that there is a compelling theoretical framework and the cultures can be ordered along a theoretically relevant dimension. Yet, the difficulty of conducting a research study increases concomitantly as the number of countries sampled increases. Using the GLOBE societal clusters, a researcher can selectively pick countries that represent critical cultural differences. For instance, one might select two countries from three clusters that represent the range of cultures on a specific cultural dimension such as Institutional Collectivism. Differences among these six countries could provide a wealth of information by a priori hypothesizing the existence of greater across-culture variability than within-cluster variability. Results such as this would strengthen the argument that culture, rather than some other social-institutional variable contributes to the findings.

Using societal clusters as a blocking technique may isolate specific aspects of social systems that are potential causal mechanisms not easily detected by examining results from studies using multiple countries not grouped in a coherent way. For instance, consider the case in which there are consistent results within societal clusters but different findings between two societal clusters. Assume that multiple religious, legal, and political systems are found among countries within each societal cluster and these are the same in both societal clusters (e.g., Latin American and Latin European). Also assume that the two societal clusters differ on one particular cultural dimension such as Power Distance. In this case the institutional factors of religion, legal, and political systems are less likely and the cultural dimensions more likely to contribute to the results. Conversely, there may be situations in which a researcher can formulate and test hypotheses that pit a cultural explanation against a religious explanation as the primary determining factor that influences results.

Validating and "fine-tuning" leadership theories: At a basic level, leadership researchers will be able to determine if leadership theories and empirical findings that are valid in one culture also generalize to other cultures. In addition, researchers will be able to specify boundary conditions and "fine-tune" theories by

investigating cultural variations as parameters of the theory. As Triandis (1993) notes,

> As we develop a better understanding of cross-cultural leadership, we will develop theorems of the form: If a culture is high in X, theory Y works as expected; if a culture is low in X, theory Y must be modified as follows. (p. 169)

As one example, the congruence hypothesis based on implicit leadership theory (Lord, 2000) asserts that leadership effectiveness should be related to the degree of fit between the leader's behavior and the implicit leadership theory held by followers. For the GLOBE project, we labeled implicit leadership theories held by members of a particular culture *culturally endorsed leadership theories* (CLTs). The grouping of societies will enable more sensitive testing of this theory as the researcher can not only test differences within countries, but test the consistency of findings within and across cultural groupings.

Developing regional, not global theories: Alan Rugman (2001) argues that the era of globalization is dead. Instead, a set of regional trading blocks dominate the world economy. Numerous examples abound including the North American Free Trade Agreement (NAFTA), the European Union (EU), and Asia-Pacific Economic Cooperation (APEC). The GLOBE societal clusters mirror some, but not all of these trading blocks. For instance, GLOBE countries within the Latin European, Germanic Europe, and Nordic Europe clusters comprise many of the countries found within the burgeoning European Union. Most GLOBE countries within the Confucian Asia and Southern Asia clusters are also members of APEC. We might hypothesize that while these trading blocks are natural from geographic perspective, common cultural similarities are strong contributors to these bonds. If so, it is likely that researchers will discover common organizational patterns within these regional blocks. Contrast this position with that of many cross-cultural researchers who embrace the view that management styles stop at national borders. The quote "there are truths on this side of the Pyrenees that are falsehoods on the other" embodies this position (Pascal, 1995, p. 294). In contrast, we might find that regional differences rule. This would have enormous implications for developing more parsimonious leadership and organizational behavior theories.

Cross-cultural replication using qualitative research. Reliability is a problem inherent in all research and may be particularly important in qualitative research. For example, qualitative research methods frequently use in-depth interviews with relatively small sample sizes. An important issue concerns the reliability, and hence validity, of findings in qualitative studies using interpretive methods with small sample sizes. Indigenous culture-specific results from qualitative research should be similar to results from societies within the same societal cluster in contrast to societies from more distant clusters. That is, increased credibility of findings can be inferred if similar results are apparent in cultures that belong to a particular societal cluster, but not in dissimilar clusters. Replication within societal clusters provides a triangulation check that may be used for different research paradigms, but might be particularly useful for qualitative research.

Insights, parsimony, and ease of communication: Our experience has been that it is easier to gain insights to macro cultural influences on organizational behavior by viewing the "big picture" rather than presenting data for more than 60 countries. For instance, common language, geography, and the level of development (Chemers, 1997) stood out as primary factors that determined the Ronen and Shenkar (1985) grouping of countries. From a practical perspective, by grouping societal cultures into a set of "like-minded" clusters, we can demonstrate differences among societal clusters on several cultural dimensions that have managerial implications for the entire set of countries comprising this cluster. Hofstede (1980, p. 48) accomplished something like this in empirically grouping countries based on high–low scores on his culture dimensions. The resulting figures from Hofstede's research that compares countries on two culture dimensions simultaneously are reproduced in numerous textbooks and journal articles. They capture the essence of country differences in an easy to understand format. We take

this approach a step further by a priori developing societal clusters, validating the grouping of cultures within the cluster, and then empirically examining differences among clusters.

As a practical matter, it becomes increasingly difficult to make sense of the cross-cultural data and communicate findings if the number of countries exceeds more than a handful. As an example, consider the difficulty of not only identifying which cultural dimensions account for differences, but also describing country-by-country differences on these dimensions. For instance, assume that you have a sample of four countries, two from Anglo cultures (the United States and Australia) and two from Confucian Asia cultures (Japan and China). We can expect that each group of two similar countries varies from the other group on cultural dimensions such as collectivism and power distance. Now increase the sample to 20 or 40 countries. Although we may find a relationship between a specific cultural dimension and the phenomenon of interest (e.g., participative leadership style), conveying the rank order of 40 specific countries on this dimension becomes a terribly difficult task. It is much easier to discuss how one particular country (e.g., South Korea) is in the Confucian Asia cluster, which scored higher on Power Distance and Collectivism than did the Anglo cluster. We can then predict that this country, and other countries within this cluster, is likely to place low importance on participative leadership.

PART B: CLIMATIC CLUSTERING OF SOCIETAL CULTURES

A second method to classify societal cultures is to use physical climates as a basis for clustering. Hofstede (1980) identified physical climate as the primary force influencing societal cultures. Unfortunately, due to a variety of methodological problems, there have been very limited tests of the strength and the direction of the relationship between physical climates and societal cultures.

Managers may benefit considerably from understanding how cultural regions may be grouped according to the climatic feature shared by them. Common climatic groupings can be useful in organizing joint research and development programs, and in facilitating cross-cultural knowledge exchange about climate-specific technological solutions. Thus, humidity resistant technologies can be shared among the cultural clusters that share similar humid climates. In addition, once such technologies are perfected, and their transfer and training process fine-tuned, they can be adopted cost-effectively even in less-humid cultural clusters for enhanced product quality.

Physical climate consists of an array of important variables, such as temperature, rainfall, humidity, altitude, and pressure. However, societal and human factors play an important role in how the climatic endowments are used. Pollution, global warming, and deforestation have substantive effects on the climate of the nations and regions, as well as the whole planet. Climate clusters can allow one to investigate the influence of these societal interventions.

We first review prior efforts to classify societies using physical climate conditions and propose a climatic classification of 61 GLOBE societies. Then, we review research on the relationship between physical climate and societal behavior and investigate the views of the two opposing research camps—one that holds physical climate to be an important defining influence on societal culture, and the other that does not.

We found evidence for the interrelationship between physical climate and culture. The significance of this interrelationship between physical climate and cultural dimensions is presented in greater depth in the specific dimension chapters (12–19).

Climatic Clustering of Societies

Scholarly interest in the clustering of physical climates dates to antiquity. In the Greek period, philosophers identified three climate zones, termed *klimata* (Aristotle, 334 B.C./1969 in *Meteorologica*). These were: (a) a torrid (or tropical-equator) zone, distinguished by its extreme heat; (b) a temperate zone, distinguished by its moderate temperature; and (c) a frigid (or polar) zone, distinguished by its extreme cold. The temperate climate of the Mediterranean was posited as a major strength for the Greek Empire (Strabo, 9–5 B.C./1917–1932).

In the 19th century, following Darwin's evolutionary theory of species, considerable interest emerged in studying regionally varying vegetation patterns as adaptive responses to natural climate (Oliver, 1996). Several classifications of climate were offered. Two of the contributions are particularly notable for our purposes. First, Koeppen (1936) defined vegetation zones in terms of mean temperatures, and then subdivided them into several precipitation classes. The warm and moist climates were in the low latitudes (tropics), warm and dry climates were in subtropics, temperate and moist climates were in mid to high latitudes, and finally, cold and dry climates were in the polar and subpolar regions. Second, in an influential update, Russian climatologist Alisov (1956) focused on the mechanisms of energy balance at the earth's surface. Because the bodies of water heat and cool more slowly than do the landmasses, the interiors of large continents have more extreme temperatures than do the coastal areas. The wind movements also generate the flow of warm ocean currents away from the equator and cold ocean currents away from the poles.

By examining the climatic literature, researchers have suggested the following seven major clusters of world climates:

1. Tropical humid and monsoon climate, or simply *tropical humid climate,* is generally found between 15° north and south of the equator. Temperatures are high, with small annual ranges. There is plentiful precipitation, though there may be a short dry season, usually in the winters.

2. Tropical wet and dry climate, also known as *savanna climate,* is also found between 15° north and south of the equator. It has distinct wet and dry seasons, with most of the precipitation occurring in the summer. Temperatures are high throughout the year, but tend to vary significantly across different months of the year.

3. Tropical and subtropical desert and steppe climate, or simply *desert climate,* is generally found between 15° and 30° north and south latitude. It tends to have very low and unreliable precipitation. Thus, for example, a location with

Table 10.6   Climatic Regions and GLOBE Societies

Tropical Humid:

Costa Rica, Ecuador, Columbia, Philippines, Singapore, Indonesia, Malaysia, India

Tropical Wet and Dry (Savanna):

Guatemala, El Salvador, Venezuela, Thailand, Nigeria, Zambia, Zimbabwe

Desert:

Egypt, Israel, Kazakhstan, Kuwait, Namibia, Turkey, Qatar, South Africa (Black Sample), South Africa (White Sample), Mexico, Iran

Subtropical Humid:

Bolivia, Brazil, Argentina, Hong Kong, Taiwan

Subtropical Wet and Dry (Mediterranean):

Albania, Greece, Italy, Portugal, Slovenia, Spain, Morocco

Marine West Coast (Maritime):

Denmark, France, Germany (former East), Germany (former West), Ireland, New Zealand, Netherlands, Switzerland, Switzerland (French Speaking), United Kingdom

Continental:

Austria, Finland, Hungary, Japan, Korea, Sweden, Poland, Canada, Russia, China, Georgia, United States, Australia

---

NOTE: The above classification is tentative. Most societies cut across several climatic areas. One could, for instance, alternatively classify Bolivia into the Tropical Humid climate, Brazil into the Savanna climate, Iran into the Continental climate, and Georgia into the Mediterranean climate. A more sophisticated approach to climate classification is beyond the scope of this chapter.

a 10-year mean of 5 centimeters might have received 50 centimeters in one year as a result of an unusual intrusion of moist air, followed by 9 years with no measurable precipitation. Daily temperature variations are usually extreme.

4. Subtropical humid climate is typically found on the eastern sides of the continents between 20° and 35° north and south latitude. It tends to have a uniform distribution of precipitation throughout the year, with summers somewhat wetter than winters.

5. Subtropical wet and dry climate, also known as *the Mediterranean climate,* is characteristic of the western sides of the continents, which are between 30° and 45° latitude north and south. It tends to show the unusual combination of hot, dry summers and cool, wet winters. Annual temperature ranges are generally smaller than in humid tropical climates, and the atmosphere tends to be drier.

6. Marine West Coast climate, also known as *the maritime climate,* generally lies on the western sides of the continents between 35° and 50° latitude north and south. There is significant precipitation throughout the year, though monthly amounts vary as a function of the storm systems. The temperature tends to have few extremes. Winters are mild and summers are cool because of the moderating influences of the ocean.

7. Continental climate is typically found between 30° and 60° latitude, which has large landmasses. Summers tend to be hot and winters cold, with below freezing temperature means from one to several months, because of the lack of any moderating influences of the ocean. Winter precipitation frequently occurs in the form of snow. There are both significant yearly and daily variations in weather.

Table 10.6 lists the GLOBE societies in each of the above seven climatic regions.

Of the several attributes distinguishing between the above climatic regions, seven stand out for their prominence (Oliver, 1996; Parker, 1995). These include: (a) square of absolute latitude, as a measure of solar radiation; (b) mean temperature (celsius); (c) rain (mm/month), as a measure of the amount of precipitation; (d) rain days (per month), as a measure of the frequency of precipitation; (e) atmospheric pressure (millibars/square cm) in January; (f) atmospheric pressure (millibars/square cm) in July; (g) humidity (percentage).

Table 10.6 shows the average climatic statistics for the seven clusters.

Consistent with the predictions of Greek scholars and Koeppen, seven climatic clusters accounted for about 84% of the intersociety variation in absolute latitude, and more than 50% variation in temperature, rainfall, and rain days. Thus, the climatic clustering of 61 GLOBE discriminates among societies by the amount of solar radiation as well as by the mean temperature and the amount and frequency of rain precipitation.

Relationship Between Physical Climate and Societal Culture Dimensions

Many scholars have suggested that physical climate is an important factor influencing culture (Diamond, 1997; Hausmann, 2001; Hofstede, 1980; Huntington, 1915; Landes, 1998; Montesquieu, 1748/1989; Sachs, 2001). Indeed, physical climate hypothesis has been nearly as popular for explaining societal behaviors as the competing hypotheses of religion (Weber, 1904/1930) and history-shaped institutions (North, 1990).

In one of the early studies, Montesquieu (1748/1989) articulated how physical climate shapes a range of sociocultural behaviors, including work ethic, religious beliefs, aggression, combativeness, mortality, fertility, obesity, sexism, and industrial development (agriculture, trade, and commerce). Several of these sociocultural behaviors can be seen as unobtrusive manifestations of the societal culture dimensions, such as Performance Orientation (work ethic), Assertiveness (aggression, combativeness), and Gender Egalitarianism (sexism). The climatic explanation for cultural behaviors gained much popularity among the European intellectuals of the 18th and 19th centuries, who invoked the climatic logic to posit and rationalize a divine determinism of the superiority of Christian Europe (see Herder, 1791/1868; Ritter, 1865).

In the early 20th century, Huntington (1915) became a strong proponent of the so-called climate hypothesis, positing that most of the variances in social and economic behaviors can be explained in terms of the differences in physical climates. He concluded suboptimal climate contributed to the low level of development in the tropical world in terms of physical, mental, and socioeconomic attributes of people in Asia. In his view, the relationship between climate and efficiency depended on climate both directly and indirectly "through race, diet, parasitic diseases, hygiene, sanitation and social and political customs" (Huntington, William, & Valkenburg, 1933, p. 124).

Subsequent scholars particularly emphasized the thesis that climate influences labor productivity levels. Specifically, an equivalent amount of physical effort is more productive in temperate and polar regions than it is in equatorial regions, where greater heat demands higher amount of effort for a given level of performance (Parker, 1995). Year-round heat in tropical regions encourages the proliferation of insects and parasites, which results in faster transmission of diseases (Landes, 1998). In contrast, winter is less supportive of insect and parasite population and enables the people in colder regions to enjoy healthier lives. Using data from the World Health Organization, Landes (1998) observed that in Sub-Saharan Africa many people harbor not one parasite, but several, and hence are too sick to work. However, others show that tropical diseases cause about a fourth of human deaths in comparison to respiratory diseases, most of which are not as important in humid tropics as in cooler regions (Porter & Sheppard, 1998). One may speculate that the climatic influences on labor productivity and health may be relevant for societal culture dimensions such as power distance. In conditions where the labor productivity is low, people may be more willing to allow some control of labor for its effective organization, and thus societies could evidence higher levels of power distance.

More recently, Diamond (1997) also asserted that environment molds history. He proposed that all of the important differences between human

Table 10.7 Mean Attributes of Climatic Regions, Using GLOBE Society Sample

Climatic Regions	Latitude	Temperature	Rainfall	Humidity	Rain Days	Atmospheric Pressure July	Atmospheric Pressure January	N
Tropical Humid	7.5	23.1	157.0	72.4	12.6	1011.0	1013.6	8
Savanna	14.3	22.6	139.7	68.1	10.3	1014.4	1013.1	7
Desert	30.6	17.8	35.5	58.5	4.8	1007.2	1017.0	11
Subtropical Humid	23.8	19.2	126.4	76.2	10.4	1011.2	1012.4	5
Mediterranean	39.9	17.1	62.3	66.4	8.0	1013.6	1018.3	7
Maritime	49.6	10.1	69.2	76.3	14.2	1013.4	1014.6	10
Continental	45.8	9.3	81.9	68.1	11.9	1011.0	1017.9	13
Grand Average	32.6	16.0	89.3	68.8	10.3	1011.4	1015.7	61

societies, and all of the differences that led some societies to prosper and progress and others to lag behind, were due to the nature of each society's local environment and its geographical location. In his view, culture (termed "proximate factor") itself is determined by the climate (termed "ultimate factor"), and has a relatively minor role in understanding societies' historical practices. In particular, he emphasized the significance of the East–West geographical layout of Eurasia, and the North–South layout in Africa and the Americas. He posited that because climate changes little with longitude but quite rapidly with latitude, the Eurasian nations enjoyed fairly uniform climatic conditions. Hence, agricultural innovations developed in one region could diffuse and be shared by several societies, generating a large pool of common plant and animal varieties available throughout the region. In contrast, the diffusion of the new varieties in the Americas or in Africa was limited because of significant variation in climates, and so the technological growth was local and economic growth slow. One may speculate that the greater feasibility of cross-societal exchange and higher returns on technology development in Eurasia would be associated with several societal culture dimensions, such as future orientation and uncertainty avoidance.

Sachs (2001), on the other hand, asserted that the temperate climates supported greater population over the past centuries and thus facilitated more rapid advances in temperate climate technologies than in tropical climate technologies. Further, "Since technologies in the critical areas of agriculture, health, and related areas could diffuse within ecological zones, but not across ecological zones, economic development spread through the temperate zones but not through the tropical regions" (Sachs, 2001, p. 12). Acemoglu, Johnson, and Robinson (2002) elaborated that there has been a gradual drift over the course of history to development of more advanced technologies in the temperate climates. More specifically, the tropical areas offered a favorable environment for early civilizations, reflected in terms of the tropical origin of humans and lower-required calorie intake in the warmer areas. However, appropriate technologies developed more rapidly in the temperate areas and made temperate societies more productive. These technologies, which included the heavy plow, systems of crop rotation, domesticated animals, and high productivity European crops such as wheat and rice, had comparatively limited influence in the tropical areas. One may speculate that the advanced technologies, such as the heavy plow and high productivity crops, would be relevant for societal culture dimensions such as in-group collectivism. Availability of advanced technologies can reduce the need for relying on the family and group effort and help inculcate more independent values and practices.

Hausmann (2001) summarized several developmental liabilities for the societies that are tropical, landlocked and far from the coast. First, the average income of the tropical nations currently is about a third of the income of temperate-zone societies. Except for Singapore and Brunei, none of the tropical nations is in the top 30 richest nations of the world. Over the past few decades, the economic growth rates in the tropical nations have been one and a half percentage points lower than that in the temperate nations (Hausmann, 2001). Second, coastal nations with their entire population within 100 kilometers of the sea tend to grow 0.6 percent faster per year than the nations whose population is farther than 100 kilometers from the sea. The cost of shipping goods a kilometer over the sea is a seventh of the cost of shipping over the land (Hausmann, 2001). The lack of access to cheap shipping impedes the ability of these nations' economies to take-off because the societies in early stages of development tend to have an advantage in bulky, low-value-added goods for which cost of shipping is important for gaining economies of scale. Third, because landlocked nations' transported goods need to cross other nations' borders, they have particularly high transportation costs. The median landlocked country pays up to 50% more in transportation costs than the median coastal nation (Hausmann, 2001). The cost of shipping a standard container from the United States to a landlocked African nation can be up to four times the cost of shipping the same to a coastal African nation. The coordination of infrastructure expenditures among the landlocked nations can be a big impediment. The landlocked Paraguay, for instance, suffered from low agricultural productivity until the Mercosur agreement in the mid-1990s enabled barge transportation through Brazil and Argentina

(Hausmann, 2001). The coastal versus landlocked factor, which is an important variable in climate determination, could potentially be significant for several societal culture dimensions such as institutional collectivism and humane orientation. In noncoastal, landlocked regions, a more collective spirit could emerge, and also there may be more concern about the humane condition because the attention of people is focused primarily on the internal society and proximate neighbors, as opposed to trading exchange with the larger world.

Climate–Culture Relationship Hypothesis

In summary, physical climate may shape several socioeconomic behaviors, which we expect will be associated with the nine GLOBE societal culture dimensions. Interestingly, there are two different and contrasting views on the relationship between physical climate and societal culture dimensions.

According to Landes (1998), positive physical climate shapes development-supporting societal culture dimensions. He notes that better climate is the first and foremost factor accounting for the wealth of Europe (and the West) in comparison with the poverty of the other nations. In his view, such climatic conditions as better soils, better topography, better natural vegetation, better health, and better nutrition, have played a critical role in technological and economic progress in Europe.

In contrast, Hofstede (1980) holds that the adverse physical climate shapes development-supporting societal culture dimensions. Hofstede used geographical latitude of capital cities as a proxy for climate and found that 43 percent of the variation in the cultural dimension of power distance is accounted by climatic factors. In his research, tropical countries, with the exception of Israel, tended to be higher on power distance, compared with the higher latitude countries. He proposed that in the colder zone, the adverse climate created survival challenges for the traditional societies. They needed to develop appropriate technology for surviving the tough cold conditions. Such technology could not be developed and applied without urbanization, mass literacy, social mobility, and emergence of a middle class. Further, a representative government was needed to encourage the use

of technology, and such democracy inevitably meant a culture of questioning authority—or lack of power distance. In contrast, the stable conditions in the tropical zone facilitated agriculture in rural communities. There was no need for education of the lower classes: they could farm and live a self-sustained life. Accordingly, military or autocratic rulers gained power, and enforced a culture of dependency and lack of questioning of authority.

Taking into account these contrasting perspectives, GLOBE proposes that it is misleading to attribute a zero-sum relationship to the climatic variables. Under extreme conditions, the physical climate variables may have a significant influence on the socioeconomic behaviors and GLOBE societal culture dimensions. On the other hand, under moderate conditions, the physical climate variables may not have any significant role in socioeconomic behaviors, and religion and historically developed institutions could instead be more pertinent shapers of societal culture dimensions.

There exists substantial prior research evidence supporting the above extreme climate hypothesis. Those interested in exploring this evidence in greater depth should refer to Parker (1995). Parker lists 3,000-odd references on research that has evaluated the link between climate and physiological effects (acclimation and physical comfort, allergies, diet and nutrition, disease and illness, hormones, metabolism and thermoregulation), psychological effects (affective disorders, aggression, cognition, mood and personality, mental illnesses, and stress), sociological effects (accidents, culture, crime, birth and death rates, migration), and economic effects (food, housing, clothing, health care, agriculture, manufacturing, tourism, and savings). Of the seven climatic attributes, extremity of thermoclimate (temperature) has a particularly important influence on the societal behaviors.

On the one hand, extreme cold in the polar regions has an important influence on human behaviors. Here, people show more frequent symptoms of seasonal affective disorders, depression, and suicidal intent and occurrences (Lamberg, 1994; Lewy, Wehr, Goodwin, Newsome, & Markey, 1980). In these regions, the mood disorders rise during the fall and winter months, and peak toward the end of winter. Specifically, human body compensates for external temperatures lower than 37 degrees Celsius, the normal body temperature, by inducing overeating and weight gain for enhanced hormonal secretion (Parker, 1995). A small part of the brain, the pineal body, monitors the amount and quality of light received by the human eyes. With reduced light, the pineal body secretes extra hormonal chemical melatonin, which controls sleep and puts the body into a hibernating mode for the winter months, thereby generating mood disorders and aversion to work (Lewy et. al, 1980). In the United States, the prevalence of winter affective disorder rises dramatically from Florida to Maine and from southern California to Oregon, in tandem with declining hours of daylight (Lamberg, 1994).

Similarly, extreme heat also has an important influence on societal behaviors. In Southern Asia, for instance, rural communities have adopted behaviors that enable them to adapt to the hot and humid tropical climate efficiently. They tend to rest during the peak hot hours and work during the cooler mornings and evenings. Srinanda (1997) notes that the Southern Asian farmers

> adopted numerous time-tested techniques in soil management, crop combinations, irrigation and drainage and general land use practices to minimize the adverse effects of excesses of heat and moisture or seasonal moisture deficits, the impact of high rainfall intensities or strong winds. (p. 226)

Incremental learning and use of time-tested techniques could be a key factor inducing people, for instance, to avoid uncertainty, and to rely on family and groups, and thus be relevant for several societal culture dimensions.

In extreme climates, social development may occur both as a reaction to the extreme conditions, as well as to mitigate the adverse effects of those extreme conditions. Van de Vliert, Huang, and Levine (2002), for instance, offer a thermal demands–resources theory to explain why societal development is more necessary and more useful in less comfortable—colder or hotter—climatic environments. According to their theory, basic human need for thermal comfort, nutritional comfort, and healthiness make life in extreme-temperature (colder or hotter) climates more demanding than in moderate climates. In societies with higher levels of socioeconomic development, up to 50% of income is spent on

climate-related products, including housing, clothing, food, and household energy; the figure goes up to 90% in societies with lower levels of socioeconomic development (Parker, 2000).

On the other hand, in moderate climates, societal development would be expected to be rather independent of the constraining influences of the climatic attributes such as thermoclimate. Van de Vliert and colleagues (2002), for instance, studied 33,584 voluntary workers' reasons for helping in a sample of 33 nations. They found that an individual volunteer's self-serving and altruistic motivations were unrelated with comfortable climates (i.e., moderate-temperature climates), but were related with uncomfortably colder or hotter climates. On the whole, physical climate may be expected to shape distinctive patterns of cultural behaviors in each physical climate cluster, depending on the specific climatic variables that are salient in that cluster. Yet, the effect of physical climate is not likely to be determinative; people may adapt to the effects of physical climate and may enact cultural behaviors that lack any relationship with the physical climate.

In summary, GLOBE proposes that

Hypothesis 1: The physical climate accounts for small variance in societal culture and leaves overwhelming flexibility for societies to shape their societal cultures.

Testing of GLOBE Hypothesis on Climatic–Culture

We evaluate the relationship between seven physical climatic clusters and ten regional clusters developed in Part A of this chapter, and examine if the physical climates can provide a rival explanation of the emergence of regional clusters. We thus examine the hypothesis that the GLOBE societies would show an ability to carve out their distinctive cultural values and practices and would not be overwhelmingly constrained by physical climatic conditions.

We use an Unordered Two-Way Frequency table to analyze the degree of association between the 7 physical climate clusters and 10 regional clusters. The null hypothesis of independence between the two categorical variables is tested by the Pearson chi square statistic: aggregated squared differences between the observed

Table 10.8   Chi Square Test for the Dominant Relationship Between Climatic Regions and Cultural Clusters, Using GLOBE Sample

Cultural cluster	Highest Pearson Chi Square Statistic Component	Climatic Cluster for Highest Statistic
Eastern Europe	3.11	Continental
Latin America	4.90	Tropical
Confucian Asia	2.22	Continental
Latin Europe	2.70	Subtropical
Nordic Europe and Germanic Europe	10.53	Maritime
Anglo	3.28	Maritime
Sub-Saharan Africa and Middle East	9.80	Desert
Southern Asia	8.17	Tropical
Total of Highest Components	44.71** $(df = 8)$	
Total of Other Components	34.59* $(df = 20)$	
Total Chi Square statistic	79.30** $(df = 28)$	

* $p < 0.5$.

** $p < .01$.

and expected frequencies/agregated expected frequencies.

For a valid test of independence, the expected value in each cell should be at least 1. Therefore, we collapsed tropical humid and tropical wet and dry regions into a composite tropical group; and subtropical humid and subtropical wet and dry regions into a composite subtropical group. In using latitude as a basis for developing a common tropical grouping and a common subtropical grouping, we were guided by the literature that latitude is the most important factor in determining physical climates and also our finding that latitude accounts for greatest variation in the seven physical climate regions.

We also collapsed the cultural clusters of Nordic Europe and Germanic Europe into a composite Northern Europe group; and the cultural clusters of Sub-Saharan Africa and Middle East into a composite Greater Africa group. In choosing the cultural clusters to combine, we were guided by the literature that Northern Europe and Greater Africa have distinctive cultures, and the finding of Part A that there is considerable

overlap in the cultures of Nordic and Germanic societies, and of Sub-Saharan Africa and Middle East societies.

The chi square for the relationship between cultural and climate clusters was significant: 79.30 ($p < .01$, $df = 28$). We computed the maximum chi square component for each of the cultural clusters, as shown in Table 10.8. The physical climate region associated with the maximum chi square component of a cultural cluster indicates the type of climate typically associated with a given type of culture.

As shown in Table 10.8, the Latin American and Southern Asian societies tend to be in tropical climates, Sub-Saharan Africa and Middle East societies in desert climates, Latin European societies in subtropical climates, Anglo and Nordic Europe and Germanic Europe societies in maritime climates, and Eastern European and Confucian Asian societies in continental climates. These eight components account for 44.71 of the total 79.30 ($p < .01$). After taking into account these strongest culture–climate components, there is much weaker, though still

Table 10.9   General Linear Multivariate Analysis: Physical Climate and Societal Culture

General Linear Model	Wilks' Lambda	F	Hypothesis df	Error df	Significance	Eta Squared
Fixed Factor: Climate Region *Variable Factor:* Societal Culture Practice Dimensions	.11	2.37	54.00	239.15	.00	.31
Fixed Factor: Climate Region *Variable Factor:* Societal Culture Practice Dimensions	.08	2.87	54.00	239.15	.00	.35
Fixed Factor: Cultural Cluster *Variable Factor:* Physical Climate Attributes	.01	5.05	63.00	259.55	.00	.47

significant, evidence ($p < .05$) for the relationship between culture and climate.

To analyze this residual relationship, we reexamined our assumption that the Sub-Saharan Africa and Middle East clusters are characterized by one dominant climate. We conducted a chi square analysis using only 10 Greater Africa societies, of which 3 were from tropical climate (all in Sub-Saharan Africa culture), 6 were from desert climate, and 1 was from Mediterranean climate. The societies in Sub-Saharan Africa cluster were associated with tropical climate, whereas those in Middle East cluster had a dominant association with desert climate.

Similarly, we reexamined the assumption that the Nordic and Germanic clusters are characterized by one dominant climate. We conducted a chi square analysis using only 8 Northern European societies, of which 5 were from maritime climate (only 1 in Nordic), and 3 were from continental climate (only 1 in Germanic). The findings indicated that the societies in the Germanic cluster are associated with maritime climate, and those in the Nordic cluster are associated with continental climate.

Thus, in summary, tropical climate is prominent in Latin American, Southern Asian, and Sub-Saharan African societies. Latin European societies tend to have subtropical climate, and

Middle Eastern societies have desert climate. Anglo and Germanic societies have maritime climate. Nordic, Eastern Europe, and Confucian Asian societies generally have continental climate.

Put differently, different climatic conditions are indeed associated with alternative cultural clusters. Now we investigate if the climatic conditions, as evident in the GLOBE sample of societies, overwhelm the ability of the societies to shape their societal cultures. The results of the Multivariate General Linear Analysis are shown in Table 10.9.

As shown in Table 10.9, the physical climatic region accounts for 31% of the variation in cultural practices and 35% of the variation in cultural values. On the other hand, cultural cluster accounts for 47% of the variation in climatic attributes. Thus, only about a third of the variation in cultural practices and values may be attributed to the differences in physical climates. Further, there is about as much variation in physical climate attributes within each cultural cluster, as there is between different cultural clusters. On the whole, on the basis of the analysis of the GLOBE sample, these findings confirm Hypothesis 1 that the societies enjoy considerable flexibility in shaping their cultures. Physical climates do not preclude or dominate the influence of other factors, such as religion and institutional history, as manifested in and captured by the cultural clusters.

Managerial and Theoretical Implications of Climatic Clusters

Our findings carry several important managerial and theoretical implications as listed below.

First, our study highlights that the geographical climate may be a basis for the design of organizational centers. The organization design of the firms may put the cultural regions dominated by tropical influences—Latin America, Sub-Saharan Africa, and Southern Asia—into one climate coordination center. Similarly, the cultural regions dominated by continental influences—Nordic Europe, Eastern Europe, and Confucian Asia—might be put into another climate coordination center. Such climate coordination centers can allow the firms to share their climate-specific know-how across divisions and more effectively invest in climate-related products and technologies. Ford Motors, for instance, experienced tropical dust-related problems in its Brazilian assembly line operations, and the dust-resistant technologies developed by it proved to be a quite attractive feature in the high-end vehicles for the affluent temperate climates (Saloner, Shepard, & Podolny, 2001, p. 342).

Second, it is often believed that certain climates are more effective in developmental terms, either because they provide stronger incentives for hard work ("adverse climate thesis") or because they support greater capability for hard work ("positive climate thesis"). Alternatively, observed climatic influences on development may simply reflect limited incomes of certain societies. Higher-income nations can afford to invest in technologies and purchase products that allow them to sustain productivity and enjoy comforts without the debilitating effects of their climate. The climatic clustering can allow one to test these contrasting views and develop a better understanding of how to strategically manage climatic and cultural endowments and their interactions.

Third, our study demonstrates that under certain conditions, physical climate attributes and cultural dimensions may be closely related. Including both types of variables in the analysis can help better tease out rival and complementary

effects of historical forces and climatic forces on societal behavior.

CONCLUSIONS

This chapter describes the process and methods used to create the GLOBE clustering of societies and the tests used to validate the clusters. In Part A, we noted the significance of the similarities of religion, language, ethnicity, and level of modernity, and that of geographic proximity, described in previous research. An in-depth analysis of the historical and political forces influencing world cultures indicated that societies could be grouped into 10 major clusters. Empirical support for the GLOBE clustering to distinguish among societies in terms of the cultural practices and values espoused by people within those societies was obtained. Further, these clusters explain the majority of society-level influences on individual values. In Part B, we identified key climatic attributes, and developed a climatic clustering of the GLOBE societies. We found that each cultural region is associated with a dominant climatic cluster. On the whole, the societies showed a capacity to develop practices and values that eschew climatic determinism. The relevance of both regional as well as physical climate clusters for understanding variances in cultural dimensions are discussed in more detail in Chapters 12–19.

ENDNOTES

1. We excluded the Czech Republic from the analysis because of pervasive response bias.

2. A more appropriate label for this cluster might be Central and Eastern Europe, but we use Eastern Europe for the sake of parsimony.

REFERENCES

Acemoglu, D., Johnson, S., & Robinson, J. A. (2002). Reversal of fortune: Geography and institutions in the making of the modern world income distribution. *The Quarterly Journal of Economics, 117*(4), 1231–1294.

Albert, R. D. (1996). A framework and model for understanding Latin American and Latino/Hispanic cultural patterns. In D. Landis & R. Bhagat (Eds.), *Handbook of intercultural training* (2nd ed., pp. 327–348). Thousand Oaks, CA: Sage.

Alisov, B. P. (1956). *Climate of the USSR.* Moscow: Moscow State University publications.

Anderson, L. (1995). Peace and democracy in the Middle East: The constraints of soft budgets. *Journal of International Affairs, 49*(1), 25–44.

Aristotle. (1969). *Meteorologica* (H. D. Lee, Trans.). Cambridge, MA: Harvard University Press. (Original work dates to 334 B.C.)

Berry, J. W., Poortinga, Y. H., Segall, M. H., & Dasen, P. R. (1992). *Cross-cultural psychology: Research and applications.* NY: Cambridge University Press.

Bond, M. H., & Smith, P. B. (1996). Cross-cultural social and organizational psychology. *Annual Review of Psychology, 47,* 205–235.

Brett, C. (1997). The importance of learning in the Ancient East: As illuminated by Confucian aphorisms. In T. J. Sienkewicz & J. E. Betts (Eds.), *Festschrift in honor of Charles Speel* (Part IV, chap. 1). Retrieved from http://department.onm.edu/classics/Speel_Festschrift/brett.htm

Brodbeck, F. C., Frese, M., Ackerblom, S., Audia, G., Bakacsi, G., Bendova, H., et al. (2000). Cultural variation of leadership prototypes across 22 European countries. *Journal of Occupational and Organizational Psychology, 73,*1–29.

Campbell, J. D. (1986). Similarity and uniqueness: The effects of attribute type, relevance, and individual differences in self-esteem and depression. *Journal of Personality and Social Psychology, 50,* 281–294.

Cattell, R. (1950). The principal culture patterns discoverable in the syntax dimensions of existing nations. *Journal of Social Psychology, 32,* 215–253.

Chemers, M. M. (1997). *An integrative theory of leadership.* Mahwah, NJ: Lawrence Erlbaum.

Danowitz, A. K., Nassef, Y., & Goodman, S. E. (1995). Cyberspace across the Sahara: Computing in North Africa. *Communications of the ACM, 38*(12), 23–28.

Diamond, J. M. (1997). Guns, germs, and steel: The fates of human societies, New York: W. W. Norton.

Dunlap, J. F., Harbison, F. H., Kerr, H. C., & Myers, C. (1975). Industrialism and industrial man reconsidered. Princeton, NJ: Princeton University Press.

Einola, K., & Turgeon, N. (2000). *Scandinavian television markets: A regional perspective* (Working Paper No. 2000–05). Montreal: CETAI-HEC.

Furnham, A., Kirkcaldy, B. D., & Lynn, R. (1994). National attitudes, competitive, money and work: First, second and third world differences. *Human Relations, 47, 1,* 119–132.

Gupta, V., Surie, G., & Chhokar, J. (2002). Cultural worldviews and their foundations: The case of Southern Asia. In B. Pattanayak & V. Gupta (Eds.), *Creating performing organizations: International perspectives for Indian management* (pp. 440-465). New Delhi: Sage.

Guttman, L. (1968). A general normative technique for finding the smallest coordinate space for a configuration of points. *Psychometrika, 33,* 469–506.

Haire, M., Ghiselli, E., & Porter, L. (1966). *Managerial thinking: An international study.* New York: Wiley.

Hausmann, R. (2001). Prisoners of geography. *Foreign Policy, 122,* 44–53.

Herder, J. G. (1868). *Reflections on the philosophy of the history of mankind.* Chicago: University of Chicago Press. (Original work published 1791)

Hofstede, G. (1976). Nationality and espoused values of managers. *Journal of Applied Psychology, 61*(2), 148–155.

Hofstede, G. (1980). *Culture's consequences: International differences in work-related values.* Beverly Hills, CA: Sage.

Huntington, E. (1915). *Civilization and climate.* New Haven: Yale University Press.

Huntington, E., William, F. E., & Valkenburg, S. (1933). Economic and social geography. New York: John Wiley.

Huxley, A. (1997). Golden yoke, silken text. *The Yale Law Journal, 6*(106), 1885–1951.

Hyden, G. (1983). *No shortcuts to progress: African development management in perspective.* Berkeley: University of California Press.

Inglehart, R., & Baker, W. E. (2000). Modernization, cultural change, and the persistence of traditional values. *American Sociological Review, 65,* 19–51.

Inglehart, R., & Carballo, M. (1997). Does Latin America exist? (And is there a Confucian culture?): A global analysis of cross-cultural differences. *Political Science & Politics, 30*(1), 34–46.

Inglehart, R., Petterson, T., & Puranen, B. (1994). *Global coordination of the World Values Surveys: A proposal to the ban of Sweden Tercentenary Foundation.* Available from http://wvs.isr.umich.edu/papers/global.htm

Karsh, E., & Karsh, I. (1999). *Empires of the sand: The struggle for mastery in the Middle East, 1789–1923.* Boston, MA: Harvard University Press.

Kerrigan, J. E., & Luke, J. (1987). *Management training strategies for developing countries.* Boulder, CO: Lynne Rienner.

Koeppen, W. (1936). *Handbuch der Klimatologie* [Handbook of climatology]. Berlin: Verlagsbuchhandlung.

Lamberg, L. (1994). *Body rhythms: Chronobiology and peak performance.* New York: William Morrow.

Landes, D. S. (1998). The wealth and poverty of nations: Why some are so rich and some so poor. New York: W.W. Norton.

Latourette, K. S. (1965). *Christianity through the ages.* New York: Harper & Row.

Levi-Strauss, C. (1951). Foreword to documents on South Asia. *International Social Science Bulletin, III*(4).

Lewy, A. J., Wehr, T. A., Goodwin, F. K., Newsome, D. A., & Markey, S. P. (1980). Light suppresses melatonin secretion in humans. *Science, 210* (4475), 1267–1269.

Lord, R. G. (2000). Leadership. In A. E. Kazdin (Ed.), *Encyclopedia of psychology* (Vol. 3, pp. 775–786). Washington, DC: American Psychological Association.

Lowe, S. (1998). Culture and network institutions in Hong Kong: A hierarchy of perspectives. A response to Wilkinson. 'Culture institutions and business in East Asia.' *Organization Studies, 19*(2), 321–343.

Mangaliso, M. P. (2001). Building competitive advantage from Ubuntu: Management lessons from South Africa. *Academy of Management Executive, 15*(3), 23–33.

Mbigi, L., & Maree, J. (1995). *Ubuntu: The spirit of African transformational management.* Randburg, South Africa: Knowledge Resources (Pty) Ltd.

McNeill, W. H. (1964). *Europe's steppe frontier, 1500–1800.* Chicago: University of Chicago Press.

Montesquieu, C. (1989). *The spirit of laws* (A. M. Cohler, B. C. Miller, & H. S. Stone, Trans.). New York: Cambridge University Press. (Original work published 1748)

North, D. C. (1990). Institutions, institutional change and economic performance. New York: Cambridge University Press.

Oliver, J. E. (1996). Climatic zones. In S. H. Schneider (Ed.), *Encyclopedia of climate and weather* (Vol. 1., pp. 141–145). New York: Oxford University Press.

Osland, J. S., De Franco, S., & Osland, A. (1999). Organizational implications of Latin American culture: Lessons for the expatriate manager. *Journal of Management Inquiry,* 8(2), 219–234.

Ozment, S. E. (1986). *The age of reform 1250–1550: An intellectual and religious history of late medieval and reformation Europe.* New Haven: Yale University Press.

Parker, P. M. (1995). *Climatic effects on individual, social and economic behavior: A physioeconomic review of research across disciplines.* Westport, CT: Greenwood.

Parker, P. M. (2000). *Physioeconomics: The basis for long-run economic growth.* Cambridge: MIT Press.

Pascal, B. (1995). *Pensees 1623–62* (A. J. Krailsheimer, Trans.). New York: Penguin Books.

Pliny the Elder. (1991). *Natural history: A selection* (J. F. Healy, Trans.). New York: Penguin Books.

Porter, P., & Sheppard, E. (1998). *A world of difference: Society, nature, development.* New York: Guilford Press.

Portes, A., & Zhou, M. (1994). Should immigrants assimilate? *Public Interest, 116,* 18–33.

Ritter, K. (1865). Comparative geography (W. Gage, Trans.). Philadelphia: Lippincott.

Ronen, S., & Kraut, A. (1977). Similarities among countries based on employee work values and attitudes. *Columbia Journal of World Business, 12,* 89–96.

Ronen, S., & Shenkar, O. (1985). Clustering countries on attitudinal dimensions: A review and synthesis. *Academy of Management Review, 10*(3), 435–454.

Rosenn, K. S. (1988). A comparison of Latin American and North American legal traditions. In L. A. Tavis (Ed.), *Multinational managers and host government interactions* (pp. 127–152). South Bend, IN: University of Notre Dame Press.

Rugman, A. (2001). *The end of globalization: Why global strategy is a myth & how to profit from the realities of regional markets.* New York: AMACOM.

Sachs, J. D. (2001). *Tropical underdevelopment* (NBER Working Paper No. 8119). Cambridge, MA: NBER.

Saloner, G., Shepard, A., & Podolny, J. (2001). *Strategic management.* New York: John Wiley.

Schake, L. M. (1998). The Schakes of La Charette: 1855–1996. Available from http://www.rootsweb. com/~mowarren/schake/part1b.html

Schwartz, S. H. (1999). A theory of cultural values and some implications for work. *Applied*

Psychology: An International Review, 48(1), 23–47.

Sirota, D., & Greenwood, M. (1971). Understand your overseas work force. *Harvard Business Review, 19,* 53–60.

Smiley, X. (1999, January 23). Survey: The Nordic countries: Happy family? *The Economist, 350*(8103), N3–N6.

Smith, P. B. (1997). Leadership in Europe: Euro-management or the footprint of history? *European Journal of Work and Organizational Psychology, 6,* 375–386.

Smith, P. B., & Bond, M. (1994). *Social psychology across cultures.* Boston: Allyn & Bacon.

Smith, P. B., Dugan, S., & Trompenaars, F. (1996). National culture and the values of organizational employees. *Journal of Cross-Cultural Psychology, 27,* 231–264.

Smith, P. B. & Peterson, M. F. (1994). Leadership as event-management: A cross-cultural survey based upon middle managers from 25 nations. In *Cross-cultural studies of event management.* Symposium conducted at the 23rd International Congress of Applied Psychology, Madrid, Spain.

Sowards, S. W. (1996). *Twenty-five lectures on modern Balkan history (The Balkans in The Age of Nationalism).* Available from http://www.lib.msu.edu/sowards/balkan/index.htm

Srinanda, K. U. (1997). Climate and societies in Southeast Asia. In M. Yoshino, M. Domroes, A. Douguedroit, J. Paszynski, & L. Nkemdirim (Eds.), *Climate and societies: A climatological perspective* (pp. 203–233). The Netherlands: Kluwer Academic.

Stead, G. B. (1996). Career development of black South African adolescents: A developmental-contextual perspective. *Journal of Counseling and Development, 74*(3), 270-275.

Stenton, F. M. (1971). Anglo-Saxon England. *The Oxford history of England* (3rd ed.). Oxford: Clarendon Press.

Strabo. (1917-1932). *The geography of Strabo: Vols. 1-8* (H. L. Jones. Trans.). Cambridge: Harvard University Press. (Original work dates to 9–5 B.C.)

Swanton, M. (Trans.). (2000). *The Anglo-Saxon chronicles.* London: Phoenix Press.

Thapar, B. K., & Moghul, M. R. (1996). The Indus Valley (3000–1500 B.C.). In A. H. Dani & J. P. Mohen (Eds.), *History of humanity: Vol. II.*

From the third millennium to the seventh century BC (pp. 246–265). Geneva: UNESCO.

Tixier, M. (1994). Management and communication styles in Europe: Can they be compared and matched? *Employee Relations, 16*(1), 8–26.

Toynbee, A. (1947). *A study of history.* New York: Oxford University Press.

Trepo, G. (1973, Autumn). Management style a la Francaise. *European Business,* 71–79.

Triandis, H. C. (1993). Collectivism and individualism as cultural syndromes. *Cross-Cultural Research, 27,* 155–180.

Trompenaars, F. (1993). *Riding the waves of culture: Understanding cultural diversity in business.* London: Economist Books.

Vallibhotama, S., & Saraya, D. (1996). South-east Asia from AD 300 to 700. In J. Herrmann & E. Zurcher (Eds.), *History of humanity: Vol. III. From the seventh century BC to the seventh century AD.* Geneva: UNESCO.

van de Vijver, F., & Leung, K. (1997). *Methods and data analysis for cross-cultural research.* Thousand Oaks, CA: Sage.

Van de Vliert, E., Huang, X., & Levine, R. V. (2002). *National wealth and thermal climate as predictors of motives for volunteer work.* Unpublished paper, University of Groningen, The Netherlands.

de Vries, M. K. (2000). Spotlight on Manfred Kets de Vries. In *Emerald Now,* available from http://www.emeraldinsight.com/now/archive/june2000/spotlight.htm

Weber, M. (1930) The protestant ethic and the spirit of capitalism. New York: Harper Collins Academic. (Original work published 1904)

Wei-ming, T. (ed.) (1996). *Confucian traditions in East Asian modernity.* Cambridge, MA: Harvard University Press.

Williamson, R. (1999). *Who were the Anglo Saxons?* Available from http://www.regia.org/Saxon1.htm.

Woliver, R., & Cattell, R. (1981). Reoccurring national patterns from 30 years of multivariate cross-cultural studies. *International Journal of Psychology, 14,* 171–198.

Zander, L. (1997). *The licence to lead: An 18 country study of the relationship between employees' preferences regarding interpersonal leadership and national culture.* Sweden: Stockholm School of Economics.

11

Rationale for GLOBE Statistical Analyses

Societal Rankings and Test of Hypotheses

Paul J. Hanges

Marcus W. Dickson

Mina T. Sipe

In this chapter, we discuss the rationale underlying the statistical procedures used to analyze and help interpret two aspects of the GLOBE data. First, we discuss the logic underlying the methodology used to band countries together on the basis of similar rank ordering on the nine cultural practices and values dimensions. Second, we discuss the methodology used to test the hypotheses concerning the relationships among societal culture, organizational culture, and culturally endorsed implicit leadership theory (i.e., CLT leadership dimensions).

It should be noted that the purpose of this chapter is only to describe the logic underlying these statistical procedures. We leave the presentation, interpretation, and discussion of results to the authors of the various chapters that follow. Our intent is to provide a framework to aid the reader's understanding and interpretation of the GLOBE statistical analyses.

Ranking of GLOBE Societies and the Application of Test Banding

The rank ordering of the GLOBE societies on the societal cultural dimensions is a deceptively easy procedure to complete. For any given culture scale, the societies are simply placed in descending order depending on the societal practice or value. However, whereas the actual process of ranking the societies is straightforward, we have found that the meaning of differences in the rank order of societies can be easily over-interpreted. More precisely, there is a tendency to concentrate on the relative position of the societies and ignore the scale values used

AUTHORS' NOTE: We would like to thank Paul Bleise, Katherine Klein, and Robert Ployhart for their very helpful comments on an earlier draft of this material. We would also like to thank David Hofmann for his helpful comments on hierarchical linear modeling.

to generate these rankings. Thus, all differences in the relative position of societies are interpreted as meaningful even though the magnitude of the societal difference with regard to the actual scale values is sometimes trivial. In an attempt to address this problem, we used a technique discussed in the psychometric and personnel selection literature known as *test banding* (Cascio, Outtz, Zedeck, & Goldstein, 1991; Guion, 1998; Hanges, Grojean, & Smith, 2000; Zedeck, Cascio, Goldstein, & Outtz, 1996). This procedure groups test scores into bands in which the scores within a particular band are considered as being not meaningfully different. The rationale for such banding lies with the concept of measurement unreliability. In other words, the premise for using test banding in the present context is that there is an imperfect relationship between the obtained scale score for a society on a particular cultural dimension and that society's population value (i.e., the scale score obtained if all society members complete the survey) on that cultural dimension. The primary factor contributing to this imperfect relationship is the presence of random error. Random error can result in two or more societies appearing different on the obtained cultural scale scores (and thus being ranked differently) even though these societies are in actuality essentially equivalent on the construct of interest. Test banding was thus developed to identify a range of scores that cannot be distinguished from the top score in a band. It should be noted, however, that using this banding procedure for the GLOBE scales assumes that the influence of systematic biases such as construct misspecification, biased sampling of construct domain, and question-construction problems are minimal.

The width of a test band is a function of the confidence level that the researcher requires before declaring that two societies truly differ and by the *standard error of the difference* (SED) of some measure (Cascio et al., 1991; Guion, 1998; Zedeck et al., 1996). The SED is calculated by the following formula (Gulliksen, 1950):

$$SED = S_x \sqrt{2} \sqrt{(1 - r_{xx'})} \qquad (11.1)$$

In this equation, S_x represents the standard deviation of the GLOBE societies on some culture

scale and r_{xx} represents the reliability of this scale. For our ranking of societies, we used generalizability theory as our reliability estimate to estimate our bands because generalizability theory combines the information about the scale's internal consistency and interrater reliability (Hanges & Dickson, Chapter 8). The SEDs for our societal cultural and CLT scales are shown in Table 11.1.

The actual size of the test band is determined by multiplying the SED by some standardized normal distance (C):

$$Bandwidth = C \times SED \qquad (11.2)$$

For a 95% confidence around the test band, C is set to 1.96 (Hanges et al., 2000).

Once the width of a test band for a particular scale is determined, we applied the test band concept in the following manner. For a particular cultural dimension, the GLOBE societies were placed in rank order. One bandwidth was then subtracted from the scale score of the society holding the top position in the rankings. All societies that fall within the top band are considered to be equivalent even though their relative positions in the rankings differ. The remaining bands are derived by taking the scale score for the highest ranked society that did not fall within the first band and subtracting one bandwidth from that score, and so on.

For example, as shown in Sully de Luque and Javidan's chapter on uncertainty avoidance (Chapter 19), Thailand is the top-ranked society in terms of societal Uncertainty Avoidance values whereas Greece is in the 17th position on this dimension (see Table 19.8). The differences in the rank position of these two societies may give the impression that they meaningfully differ on the degree to which Uncertainty Avoidance values are espoused. However, as shown in Table 19.8, both of these countries fall within the same band. In other words, in contrast to the conclusion one would reach by just examining the rankings, Greece cannot be reliably differentiated from Thailand in terms of societal Uncertainty Avoidance values. As this example illustrates, the test banding procedure provides useful additional information to help the reader appropriately interpret differences among the GLOBE societies.[1]

Table 11.1   SED Information for the Societal Culture Scales

Societal Culture Dimension Scale	SED	
	Practices	Values
Power Distance	.27	.19
Uncertainty Avoidance	.32	.30
Institutional Collectivism	.32	.29
In-Group Collectivism	.50	.28
Gender Egalitarianism	.32	.27
Assertiveness	.32	.59
Humane Orientation	.26	.18
Performance Orientation	.32	.17
Future Orientation	.31	.26

In conclusion, the banding methodology was used to minimize the possibility that society rank orderings will be over-interpreted. For ease of presentation as well as to help us to efficiently convey information about societies that cluster at the top, middle, or bottom range of a cultural dimension, we used the fixed band methodology to identify a group of societies that could not be distinguished from the top-scoring society in a particular band. Finally, as noted by Hanges and Dickson in Chapter 8, we examined the influence of response bias on our rank ordering of the GLOBE societies and found that the relative position of our societies was substantially robust. As outlined in Appendix B, only three countries (i.e., Czech Republic, France, and Morocco) consistently exhibited significant shifts in their rank position if response bias corrected scale scores were used to rank the societies. Two other countries (i.e., Qatar and Taiwan) exhibited a significant change in their rank position for only cultural practices scale scores. Thus, except for these exceptions, the rank ordering and banding of the GLOBE societies appears to be relatively robust to response bias.

STATISTICAL ANALYSES TESTING MAIN GLOBE HYPOTHESES

Several specific hypotheses concerning the relationship among organizational culture, societal culture, and the CLT leadership dimensions were specified by House and Javidan in Chapter 2. In this section, we answer the following question: What is the most appropriate statistical analytic procedure for testing the GLOBE hypotheses? To answer this question, we had to consider the nature of the variables contained in the GLOBE conceptual model, the nature of the hypotheses being tested, and the structure of the GLOBE database.

As indicated in earlier chapters of this book, the model driving the GLOBE project included variables believed to operate at different levels of analysis. To be more specific, this model indicated that both organizational and societal cultures would uniquely influence the attributes contained in middle managers' CLT profiles (Dickson, BeShears, & Gupta, Chapter 5). Conceptual models that include variables operating at different levels of analysis have been referred to as multilevel (Kozlowski & Klein, 2000), cross-level (Rousseau, 1985), meso (House, Rousseau, & Thomas, 1995), or mixed-determinant (Klein, Dansereau, & Hall, 1994) models or theories in the scientific literature. Consistent with the multilevel model driving the GLOBE project, we developed scales that measured these constructs at the appropriate level of analysis (Hanges & Dickson, Chapter 8). Clearly, the statistical technique used to test the GLOBE conceptual model and hypotheses requires that it is able to handle relationships operating at multiple levels of analysis.

Beyond the multilevel nature of the conceptual model, scales, and hypotheses, the structure of the GLOBE database produced several constraints that need to be considered when choosing a statistical methodology. To be more specific, the responses in the GLOBE database came from middle managers employed in one of three industries (i.e., the financial, food service, and telecommunications industries) throughout the world. The primary sampling strategy used by the GLOBE country co-investigators was to gain access to multiple organizations from at least two of these three industries in each society and to distribute the GLOBE questionnaires to as many middle managers in each organization as possible.

This sampling strategy produced what is called a *nested structure* in the GLOBE database. In other words, the middle managers are nested within organizations because multiple middle managers were sampled from each organization. Further, organizations are nested within societies because multiple organizations were sampled from each society. The consequence of having this nested structure is that it produces covariation among the responses of middle managers. This covariation among respondents is not surprising given that we were asking middle managers from the same organization and society questions about their organization's and society's culture. Covariation among respondents creates problems for traditional statistical analyses, such as ordinary least squares regression analyses, because independence of observations is a critical assumption for these procedures (Bryk & Raudenbush, 1987; Hofmann, Griffin, & Gavin, 2000). The statistical technique used in Project GLOBE to analyze the conceptual model thus had to be

able to handle constructs operating at multiple levels in a database with a nested structure.

Historically, researchers have used one of two statistical approaches to testing conceptual models that have variables at different levels of analysis or data that has a nested structure (Bryk & Raudenbush, 1987; Hofmann, 1997; Hofmann et al., 2000). The first traditional statistical approach, which we will refer to as the *aggregated* approach, involved averaging both the independent and dependent variables to some higher level of analysis (e.g., scale values from individuals from the same organization are averaged to obtain an organizational mean score). Both of these variables would be aggregated even if only one truly operated at the group level. Statistical analyses were then performed on the aggregated data and the degrees of freedom associated with these analyses were a function of the number of groups sampled (Hofmann, 1997). The second traditional approach, which we will refer to as the *disaggregated* approach, required assigning the average group score on the higher-level construct (e.g., organizational culture) to each individual group member. Statistical analyses were then performed using the entire database (i.e., all middle managers) (James & Williams, 2000; Kreft & Leeuw, 1998).

Both of these approaches have limitations for testing the GLOBE multilevel conceptual model. For example, the aggregated approach cannot assess models in which more than one level of analysis is operating (Hofmann, 1997), whereas the disaggregated approach has been criticized for ignoring the nested structure of data (Goldstein, 1995; Hox, 1995) and is most appropriately used if the dependent variable in the analysis operates at the individual level of analysis (James & Williams, 2000). Because a conceptual model that has multiple independent and dependent variables that operate at different levels of analysis is being tested in Project GLOBE, neither of these two traditional approaches are optimal approaches for testing our hypotheses.

One statistical technique that has been discussed in the organizational literature as an effective tool for analyzing multilevel conceptual models and nested data is *hierarchical linear modeling* (HLM) (Hofmann, 1997; Hofmann et al., 2000). Although HLM is somewhat new to the organizational literature, it actually has been used in other fields (such as agricultural and physical sciences) for quite some time, although it is typically not referred to as HLM in these fields. HLM has been referred to as *multilevel linear models* in the sociological research (Goldstein, 1995), *mixed effects* and *random effects models* in the biometrics literature, *random coefficient regression models* in the econometrics literature, and as *covariance components models* in the statistical literature (Bryk & Raudenbush, 1987).

HLM can be thought of as a multistep process designed to test relationships between independent and dependent variables at multiple levels. We will use an example to help explain how we used this analytic procedure in GLOBE. A possible hypothesis that we might want to test is whether middle managers in high humane orientation organizations and societies share the perception that being "participative" is an effective attribute for leaders. Using this example, it should be noted that there are three levels of variation implicitly specified in this hypothesis. Differences among multiple middle managers from the same organization contribute to individual-level variation in the dependent variable. Differences among the average response across the various organizations represent organizational-level variation, and finally, differences in the average response across the various societies represent societal-level variation. We will consider all three of these levels in our analysis of our data.

Although there is probably some individual-level variation in perceptions of middle managers concerning the effectiveness of participative leadership, it should be noted that our hypothesis did not specify any particular individual-level predictors of this variation. Thus, in the first step of the HLM analysis, we use the following equation:

$$Participative_{ijk} = \pi_{0jk} + e_{ijk} \qquad (11.3)$$

In this equation, "$Participative_{ijk}$" represents a particular middle manager's rating on the Participative CLT dimension. This middle manager comes from organization j, which is embedded in society k. The intercept (π_{0jk}) in this equation is the unadjusted mean participative leadership rating for organization j in society k and e_{ijk} represents random level variation in responses among the middle managers. As shown in this equation, there are no predictors of individual-level variation on participative leadership ratings.

The second step of HLM considers organizational-level variation in the dependent variable. In contrast to the individual level, our hypothesis specified two predictors of organizational-level variation. So, we used the intercepts (π_{0jk}) obtained for each organization from the prior step (i.e., unadjusted mean participative leadership ratings for a particular organization) as the dependent variable and predicted this variable by using the aggregated organizational-level Humane Orientation practices (As Is) and values (Should Be) scales. More specifically:

$$\pi_{0jk} = \beta_{00k} + \beta_{01k} (ORG\_AS\_IS)_{jk} + \beta_{02k} (ORG\_SHOULD\_BE)_{jk} + r_{0jk}$$

$$(11.4)$$

In this equation, π_{0jk} represents the intercept obtained from the prior HLM step (Equation 11.3), β_{00k} represents the unadjusted mean participative leadership rating for society k, "ORG_AS_IS" represents the group-mean centered[2] (organizational score is subtracted from the societal average) Humane Orientation practices for organization j and "ORG_SHOULD_BE" represents the group-mean-centered Humane Orientation values score for organization j. Further, β_{01k} and β_{02k} represent the organizational-level HLM coefficients for these two predictors in society k, respectively. If one or both of these HLM coefficients are significant, there is support for the hypothesis that organizational-level culture is predictive of participative leadership. Finally, r_{0jk} represents organizational-level error.

The third step of the HLM analysis considers societal-level variation in the dependent variable. As with the step 2 of HLM, our hypothesis specified two predictors of this societal-level variation. Thus, we used the societal intercepts (β_{00k}) from the prior step (i.e., aggregated societal participative leadership ratings) as the dependent variable and predicted societal-level differences by using aggregated societal-level Humane Orientation cultural practices (As Is) and values (Should Be) scales. More specifically:

$$\beta_{00k} = \gamma_{000} + \gamma_{001} \ (SOC\_AS\_IS)_k + \gamma_{002}$$
$$(SOC\_SHOULD\_BE)_k + U_{00k}$$

$$(11.5)$$

In this equation, γ_{000} represents the unadjusted average participative leadership rating for the entire data set, "SOC_AS_IS" represents the average score on societal Humane Orientation practices, "SOC_SHOULD_BE" represents the average score on societal Humane Orientation values. Further, γ_{001} and γ_{002} represent the societal-level HLM coefficients for these two predictors, respectively. If one or both of these HLM coefficients are significant, there is support for the hypothesis that societal-level culture is predictive of participative leadership. Finally, U_{00k} represents societal-level error.

In this example, we assumed that the researcher was only interested in assessing whether organizational or societal culture predicted the extent to which participation was a component of a group's CLTs. This type of analysis is referred to as a *random intercepts* model (Bryk & Raudenbush, 1987; Kreft & Leeuw, 1998). In random intercept models, only the means of the dependent variable (i.e., the intercepts in Equations 11.4 and 11.5) are allowed to vary across organizations or societies and the focus of such models is to predict this group-level variation. We used a random intercept model when testing the GLOBE hypotheses concerning the relationship between CLTs and culture.

It is incorrect, however, to believe that all HLM analyses are limited to random intercept models. For example, a researcher might inquire whether the relationship between organizational Humane Orientation cultural practices and the Participative CLT varies over societies. Perhaps there are some societies for which this organizational cultural practice is a stronger determinant of the Participative CLT. More concisely, we wonder whether the β_{01k} in Equation 11.4 varies across societies. This question is addressed by conducting a *random slopes* HLM model (Bryk & Raudenbush, 1987; Kreft & Leeuw, 1998). In random slope models, some societal-level

cultural variable is used as a predictor of the organizational cultural practice–CLT leadership dimension slope (β_{01k}). The goal of this model can roughly be thought of as similar to the goal of traditional moderated multiple regression analysis in which some variable (e.g., societal Humane Orientation cultural practices) is believed to moderate the relationship between two other variables (e.g., the organizational cultural practices–CLT dimension relationship). We used a random slope HLM model in the Brodbeck, Hanges, Dickson, Gupta, and Dorfman chapter to test the GLOBE hypotheses concerning a possible society-by-industry interaction on organizational cultural practices.

In summary, HLM was developed to enable empirical validation of multilevel conceptual models and analysis of large databases containing a nested structure. This technique overcomes some deficiencies of the previous analytic approaches[3] and is an increasingly popular technique in the social sciences. In the GLOBE project, we specified a three-level HLM (i.e., individual, organizational, and societal levels of analyses) and used a random intercept model to test the hypotheses that cultural variables predict CLT leadership dimensions (discussed in Chapters 12–19) but a random slope model to test the effect of society and industry on organizational culture (discussed in Chapter 20). However, before we discuss the specific models used to test these hypotheses, there are two issues that need clarification.

Issue 1: Method Used to Center Data

As shown in the prior example, HLM uses group-level variables to predict variation in intercepts and slopes of lower-level equations. It is important to note, therefore, that the proper interpretation of an HLM analysis depends on the scale properties of the predictors used in these lower-level equations. For example, an intercept is defined as the value of the dependent variable when a predictor in the equation is set to zero (Cohen & Cohen, 1983). If the predictor has a meaningful zero point, then a researcher can directly interpret the value of the intercept and easily derive hypotheses identifying group-level predictors associated with between-group differences in the intercept. On the other hand, if the predictor does not have a meaningful zero point (as is true with most measures used in the social sciences), the researcher may want to transform the predictor in some way to make the intercept more meaningful. In HLM, researchers affect the meaning of the intercept by centering their predictors.

There are several options available for centering data in HLM (i.e., grand-mean centering, raw-metric scaling, group-mean centering) (Bryk & Raudenbush, 1987; Kreft & Leeuw, 1998), and each of these options have different implications for the nature of the hypotheses being tested by HLM (Bryk & Raudenbush, 1987; Hofmann et al., 2000). The option that we eventually selected for GLOBE analysis is to *group-mean center* the predictors in the analysis. If predictors are group-mean centered, the intercepts of the equation in the three levels of our HLM example are interpreted as the unadjusted mean of the dependent variable for organizations, societies, or the entire sample (Hofmann & Gavin, 1998). Thus, a random intercept HLM analysis with group-mean centering can be thought of as conceptually related to the traditional aggregated level analysis because group-level variables are used to predict dependent variable group means (i.e., intercepts). In addition, group-mean centering divides the dependent variable's variance into three separate portions (i.e., that due to individual-, organizational-, and societal-level variation) (Hofmann et al., 2000). Thus, group-mean centering enables researchers to a priori specify the level of analysis at which a specific predictor should influence the dependent variable (e.g., organizational culture predictors should account for organizational variation in leadership scales) (Hofmann & Gavin, 1998).

In addition to group-mean centered, predictors can also be *grand-mean centered.* With grand-mean centering, the average score on some predictor for the entire database is removed from all scores on that predictor. With grand-mean centering, the value of the intercept for a particular group is interpreted as the mean for that group after the influence of the predictors included in the equation has been removed (i.e., the intercept is now interpreted as the adjusted group mean). In addition, with grand-mean centering, the HLM analyses can be basically

thought of as performing a hierarchical analysis in which the significance of some higher group-level predictor (e.g., societal culture) reflects the unique contribution of this predictor over the contribution of all lower-level predictors (e.g., organizational culture) (Hofmann, 1997; Hofmann et al., 2000). Thus, the particular centering method used in the HLM analysis is very important.

In Project GLOBE, we used group-mean centering in our HLM analyses. We decided to use this centering approach for two reasons. First, we were interested in the effects of culture on CLT leadership dimensions at both the organizational and societal levels of analysis. Thus, we developed specific hypotheses concerning the relationship between organizational culture and CLT leadership dimensions and societal culture and CLT leadership dimensions. As indicated above, group-mean centering allows us to partition the dependent variable's variance to these different levels of analyses. Second, and more importantly, our conceptual model indicated that in addition to affecting CLT leadership dimensions, societal culture also affected organizational culture. We wanted to follow the traditional logic used in data analytic procedures in which the significance of exogenous variables (i.e., variables whose causes are not established in the model being tested) are first established and then the influence of the exogenous variables are controlled for before testing the significance of any endogenous variables (i.e., variables whose causes are outlined in the model being tested) (Pedhazur & Schmelkin, 1991). Although group-mean centering does not perform this statistical control, we decided that it would be inappropriate to use grand-mean centering because use of that centering approach would control for an endogenous variable in the GLOBE model (i.e., organizational culture) before testing the influence of an exogenous variable (i.e., societal culture). Considering all factors together we therefore used group-mean centering in our analyses.

Issue 2: Assessment of Predictor Importance

After determining that a predictor exhibits a significant relationship with the dependent

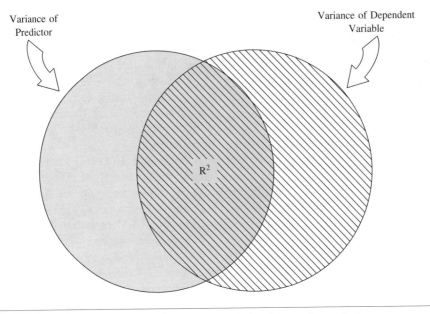

Figure 11.1   Venn diagram illustrating R^2 in typical single-level regression analysis

variable, researchers typically want to assess the strength of the connection between these two variables. In regression analysis, the usual way of assessing the contribution of a predictor to an equation is to calculate R^2 or the "amount of variance explained" or shared in the dependent variable by a particular predictor or set of predictors. Figure 11.1 shows a Venn diagram illustrating R^2 as it is typically conceptualized in ordinary least squares regression with one predictor (also known as *simple regression*). The circle on the left of this figure represents the variance of a predictor whereas the circle on the right represents the variance of the dependent variable. The overlapping portion of these two circles represents the relationship between these two variables. As the magnitude of the relationship increases, the amount of overlap of these two circles increases. The percentage of the dependent variable variance contained in the overlapping region, labeled R^2, is interpreted as the percentage of dependent variable variance explained by the predictor.

Similar to simple regression analysis, R^2 can also be estimated when performing HLM analyses. However, because HLM assesses the predictability of the dependent variable across different levels of analysis, the calculation and

interpretation of R^2 is slightly more complex. Figure 11.2 presents a Venn diagram illustrating how to interpret R^2 when a HLM analysis is conducted. The biggest circle in this figure represents the dependent variable's variance. Continuing with the example used earlier in this chapter, the dependent variable is the Participative leadership CLT scale and, as shown in Figure 11.2, the variance of this variable cuts across three levels of analyses (i.e., individual, organizational, and societal). In Figure 11.2, it appears that approximately 30% of the dependent variable's variance is at the individual level, 50% is at the organizational level, and 20% is at the societal level.

As outlined in Equation 11.3 and discussed earlier in this chapter, the GLOBE model does not specify any individual-level predictors of the CLT leadership dimensions. This is because we were primarily interested in the shared aspects of CLT profiles in Project GLOBE and not differences among individuals within organizations and societies. Indeed, as discussed by Hanges and Dickson in Chapter 8 the constructs underlying the CLT leadership scales were conceptualized as convergent–emergent constructs. Thus, the individual-level portion of the dependent

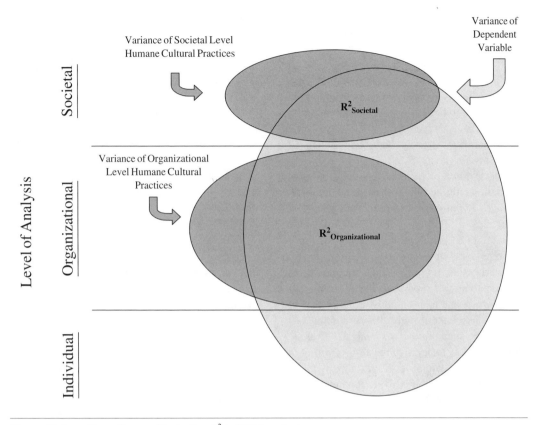

Figure 11.2 Venn diagram illustrating R^2 in HLM analysis

variable's variance can be thought of as error variance caused by random as well as systematic differences among respondents. Though individual-level predictors could have been identified (see the discussion of gender differences by Emrich, Denmark, and Den Hartog in Chapter 14), the GLOBE hypotheses outlined by House and Javidan in Chapter 2 were not concerned with individual-level variation. Whereas this level had to be included in the HLM analyses so that unbiased significance tests can be obtained for the GLOBE hypotheses regarding the organizational and societal predictors (e.g., Bliese & Hanges, 2002; Kenny & Judd, 1986), the individual level of analysis will not be included in any estimates of explained variance in the present book.

At the organizational level, we hypothesized that Humane Orientation organizational cultural practices would predict differences in average

organizational Participative CLT ratings (see Equation 11.4). The large oval in Figure 11.2 represents the variance associated with this organizational-level predictor, and the region of this circle that overlaps with the dependent variable is the R^2 for this organizational-level predictor. It is important to note that the variance of this predictor only exists at the organizational level of analysis. Thus, the overlapping portion of the predictor and dependent variable (labeled R^2 Organizational) only occurs at the organizational level of analysis. This indicates that R^2-organizational is a level-specific measure in that it only indicates the percentage of organizational-level variance in the Participative CLT leadership rating explained by the Humane Orientation cultural practices scale. In Figure 11.2, the circle for Humane Orientation organizational cultural practices overlaps with approximately 60 percent of the variance of the dependent variable that exists *at the organizational level* (i.e., R^2-organizational-0.60). Another way to think of R^2-organizational is that it is a sample-weighted estimate of the R^2 that would have been obtained if the dependent and independent variables were averaged to the organizational level of analysis (i.e., a traditional aggregated multilevel analysis) and a simple regression analysis were performed provided that the influence of society had been statistically removed in this analysis.

Last, to complete this example, Humane Orientation cultural practices at the societal level were also hypothesized to predict societal-level differences in Participative CLT ratings (see Equation 11.5). The circle at the top of Figure 11.2 represents this societal-level predictor and the overlapping region of this circle with the dependent variable represents the R^2 for this predictor. Once again, it should be noted that the variance associated with this predictor only exists at the societal level of analysis. Thus, R^2-societal is a level-specific measure reflecting the proportion of societal-level Participative CLT rating variance explained by Humane Orientation societal cultural practices. In Figure 11.2, it looks as if approximately 80% of the dependent variable's *societal-level variance* (i.e., the top third of the dependent variable's circle) is shared with this societal-level predictor (i.e., R^2-societal = 0.80). Another way to think of this R^2 is that it is a sample-weighted estimate of the variance that would have been explained if the dependent and independent variables were averaged to the societal level of analysis (i.e., traditional aggregated multilevel analysis) and a simple regression analysis were performed.

These two measures of explained variance can add up to greater than 100% because they are level-specific measures that are focused on variance of the dependent variable operating at different levels. Comparing these two level-specific measures for a given predictor provides information about the level at which the predictor has its greatest effect on the dependent variable. In the present example, it appears that Humane Orientation cultural practices measured at the societal level have a slightly greater relationship with Participative CLT ratings (i.e., R^2-societal) than do Humane Orientation cultural practices measured at the organizational level (i.e., R^2-organizational).

Although Figure 11.2 provides a useful conceptual picture of R^2 in HLM, the amount of variance accounted for by a predictor at a particular level of analysis is actually computed by using the following formula:

$$R^2_{level2} = \frac{(\sigma^2_{null} - \sigma^2_{mod1})}{\sigma^2_{null}}$$

(11.6)

In this formula, σ^2_{null} represents the variance of the dependent variable at a particular level in the null HLM model (i.e., a no-predictor model in which the total variance of the dependent variable is only split into portions operating at different levels of analysis) and σ^2_{mod1} represents the variance of the dependent variable at that same level in the model after some predictor has been entered into the equation.[4]

We used a random intercept model with group-mean centered predictors when we examined the influence of organizational and societal culture on CLT leadership dimensions. In these analyses, which are reported in Part IV, we used Equation 11.6 to estimate the amount of CLT dimension variance accounted for by the cultural dimensions at the organizational- and societal-level of analysis.

It should be noted, however, that Bryk and Raudenbush (1987) and Klein and Kozlowski (2000) have warned about the misleading impression that could potentially result if only these level-specific R^2 measures were examined. These authors argue that although a predictor might explain a substantial portion of variance at a particular level (e.g., 75% of organizational variation in the dependent variable explained), this predictor could still be trivial because only a negligible amount of the dependent variable's total variance exists at that level (e.g., only 1.5% of the dependent variable's entire variance is at the organizational level). Thus, these authors recommend that a predictor needs to explain a nontrivial portion of level-specific *and* total variation in the dependent variable to be considered important.

The total explained variance for a set of predictors is calculated by multiplying the level-specific R^2 for a particular level by the proportion of total dependent variable variance that exists at that level (i.e., ICC_{level}) and adding these products across all levels of analysis. More concisely,

$$R^2_{Total} = \sum R^2_{level} (ICC_{level}) \qquad (11.7)$$

Continuing with the example in Figure 11.2, Humane Orientation cultural practices accounts for 46% of the total variance in Participative CLT ratings (i.e., R^2-societal (.80)* $ICC_{societal}$ (.20) + R^2-organizational (.60)* $ICC_{organizational}$ (.50) = .46). In this example, Humane Orientation cultural practices are clearly a nontrivial predictor of Participative CLT ratings. In summary, examining both the amount of explained variance at a particular level of analysis as well as the amount of total explained variance is a useful strategy to minimize the chances of misleading oneself about the importance of the HLM results (Klein & Kozlowski, 2000; Lance & James, 1999). The HLMs reported in Part IV primarily report the R^2 total for each analysis.

In summary, we have discussed HLM as well as our rationale for using group-mean centering. We also reviewed how to interpret the importance of predictors in random intercept models. In the next section of this chapter, we specify the exact HLM models that were used to test the GLOBE conceptual model. There are two separate aspects of the conceptual model that were tested via HLM. First, HLM was used to test the hypotheses connecting the nine culture dimensions with the six CLT leadership dimensions. Second, HLM was used to test the hypotheses concerning the effect of the society and industry variables on organizational culture. As noted at the beginning of this chapter, we do not discuss the results of any analyses in this chapter. Rather, the purpose of this discussion is to provide a framework to help the reader interpret the empirical results discussed in Part IV.

Specification of Random Intercept HLM models in Project GLOBE: Test of Culture-CLT Hypotheses

We conducted a series of HLM analyses to test the hypotheses concerning the effect of organizational and societal culture on the CLT leadership dimensions. The six higher-order CLT dimensions were used as dependent variables and the nine cultural practices and nine cultural values measures were used as independent variables in these analyses. We tested these hypotheses by performing two kinds of analyses. First, we ran a dimension-specific HLM analysis in which the culture scales for only one dimension were used to predict each CLT leadership dimension (e.g., organizational and societal Humane Orientation cultural practices and values scales predicting Participative CLT dimension ratings). This type of analysis provides useful information about the connection between each cultural dimension and the six CLT dimensions. The results of these analyses are discussed in the chapters focusing on the cultural dimensions in Part IV.

Second, we also tested our hypotheses using a more competitive approach that included all hypothesized organizational and societal cultural predictors in our HLM analyses to assess which cultural predictors, if any, uniquely predicted each CLT dimension. It is possible that some of the findings obtained in the dimension-specific analyses will not be supported in the competitive analyses because of the interrelationships among the GLOBE cultural dimensions. Thus, the competitive analyses can be thought of as producing a parsimonious model connecting the various cultural dimensions with the CLT scales. The results of the competitive analyses are discussed in Chapter 21.

Regardless of whether the GLOBE hypotheses were being tested in a dimension-specific or competitive manner, all of these HLM analyses can be technically described as *random-intercept* models in which three levels (i.e., individual, organizational, and societal) of analysis were specified and the cultural predictors were group-mean centered. As specified by House and Hanges in Chapter 6, different middle managers completed the two GLOBE questionnaires. We used Form Alpha responses to obtain the organizational culture and CLT data for our analyses.

It should be noted that we only included data from organizations that had 7 or more respondents. This cutoff was chosen so that we had an average of 45 middle managers responding to the organizational culture scales per organization. Previous analyses revealed that this average sample size was needed to provide reliable organizational level data (Hanges & Dickson, Chapter 8). We used the responses to Form Beta to obtain the societal culture data for our analyses.

Finally, we also performed several additional analyses to ensure that we interpreted our results correctly. First, we reran all of our HLM analyses using the response bias corrected scores discussed in Chapter 8. More than 80% of all the results either remained the same or became stronger when using the response bias corrected scores.[5] Thus, the culture-CLT relationships that are reported in the next several chapters are robust with respect to response biases. Second, we also ran a series of contextual analyses to assess whether any organizational culture–CLT relationships were truly a function of organizational-level covariation between these constructs and not due to the fact that the same individuals completed both the organizational culture and CLT scales (i.e., organizational-level results not due to individual-level covariation). Specifically, contextual analysis examines whether the organizational-level culture–CLT relationship is significantly different from the individual-level group-mean centered relationship between the culture and CLT scales. If the contextual analysis finds that the organizational-level culture–CLT relationships are significantly different from the individual-level relationships, then evidence exists that the relationships are truly operating at the organizational level. Appendix C contains a more detailed description and results of this analysis. As can be seen in Appendix C, there is substantial evidence that our organizational culture–CLT relationships were a function of organizational-level covariation.[6]

To summarize, we used the organizational culture scales that were validated at the organizational level to assess organizational-level culture–CLT effects, and we used the societal culture scales that were developed and validated at the societal level to assess societal-level culture–CLT leadership dimension effects. Thus, we measured our variables and tested our hypotheses in a way consistent with the levels specified within the GLOBE multilevel conceptual model.

Test of Society and Industry Effects on Organizational Culture: Specification of Random Slope HLM Models in Project GLOBE

In addition to testing the relationship between culture and CLT leadership dimensions, we also tested the GLOBE hypothesis that societal cultural and organizational contingencies affected organizational cultural practices. As discussed by Dickson and colleagues (Chapter 5) and Brodbeck and colleagues (Chapter 20), we hypothesized that organizations might adopt practices consistent with their broader societal culture. We also hypothesized that different industries might have different organizational cultural practices and that the effect of industry might interact with organizational characteristics (e.g., company size, management style) or with societal cultural values. To test the industry-organizational cultural practice relationships moderated by organizational or societal characteristics hypothesis, we performed a series of random slope HLM models. As with the aforementioned HLM analyses, three levels of analysis (i.e., individual, organizational, and societal) were specified in these random slope models. However, unlike the random intercept models, two orthogonally coded variables representing the main effect of industry were included in all of these analyses. Comparisons among these models in terms of their relative fit to the data indicate the presence or absence of interaction effects.

More technically, we used the nine organizational cultural practice scales as the dependent variables in this analysis. For each organizational cultural practice scale, we computed three HLM models. The first model served as a baseline model, and it simply assessed how much dependent-variable variance was operating at the societal, organizational, or industry level of analysis. To put it more technically, the coefficients associated with the industry main effect in this baseline model were treated as *fixed* effects. That is, we forced the main effect for industry to be constant across all organizations in all societies. Thus, this model assumed that the effect of industry on organizational cultural practices was not moderated by other factors. The fit of this model to the empirical data served as a standard that we compared to our next two models.

In the second model, we tested whether the effect of industry on organizational cultural practices interacted with some organizational characteristic. We tested for this interaction by treating the coefficients for the two orthogonally coded industry variables as random factors at the organizational level of analysis. In other words, we allowed the industry coefficients to differ across organizations. If the fit of this second model was significantly better than the fit of the baseline model, then there is evidence that the effect of industry on organizational cultural practices was moderated by some organizational-level characteristic. Additional tests would have to be run to identify the specific organizational characteristic causing the interaction.[7]

The third and final model that we ran assessed whether the effect of industry on organizational cultural practices was moderated by societal-level factors (e.g., societal culture values). This was tested by treating the coefficients for the two orthogonally coded industry variables as random factors at the society level of analysis. If the fit of this third model was significantly better than the fit of the baseline model, then there is evidence that the effect of industry on organizational cultural practices was moderated by some societal-level characteristic. Additional tests would have to be run to identify the specific societal characteristic causing the interaction. Results of these analyses are reported in Chapter 20 by Brodbeck and colleagues.

SUMMARY AND CONCLUSION

In this chapter, we have described the procedure used to rank order the societies participating in the GLOBE Project on the nine cultural practices and values dimensions. To facilitate interpretation of which societies truly differ from each other on a given dimension, we incorporated test banding. We then presented our rationale for using hierarchical linear modeling to test the main GLOBE hypotheses, and described our specific application of HLM to the GLOBE data.

Almost all of the statistical analyses reported in this book were performed using two-tailed tests. Two-tailed statistical tests are useful for testing hypothesized as well as detecting unexpected statistical relationships while maintaining a desired error-rate level for these statistical tests. We used two-tailed tests because of the relative novelty of the CLT leadership construct and the fact that Project GLOBE is the first large-scale, cross-cultural empirical study exploring organizational and societal correlates of culturally endorsed beliefs about leadership. The only time that a one-tailed test was used was when we verified the HLM analyses by using the response-bias corrected scales.

With the background in statistical methodology and rationale presented in this chapter, we trust that the reader will be well prepared to appropriately and accurately interpret the results presented by our colleagues in the dimension-specific chapters that follow.

ENDNOTES

1. This approach to banding is what Cascio and colleagues (1991) refer to as the "fixed banding" approach. There are other approaches (Zedeck et al., 1996) and the reader could even use the SED information provided in Table 11.1 to obtain more detailed banding information than we can provide by using the fixed band methodology. For example, the reader could develop bands around each of the GLOBE societies (i.e., society-specific bands) to gain a more refined understanding of how the various societies differ from one another. By using the SED reported for each scale (e.g., SED of 0.30 for the Societal Uncertainty Avoidance cultural values scale) and choosing a particular confidence level (e.g., 95% confidence level is associated with a C of 1.96), the scale's bandwidth for each dimension can be determined (i.e., societal Uncertainty Avoidance cultural values is approximately 0.59). Adding this bandwidth to Greece's scale score yields the top value for this society's band (i.e., 5.68). Subtracting this bandwidth from the average scale score for Greece yields the bottom value for this society's band (i.e., 4.50). Comparing this band (i.e., 4.50–5.68) with the other societies in Sully de Luque et al's (this volume) Table 19.8 reveals that the value placed on Uncertainty Avoidance in Greece is significantly greater than the value placed on Uncertainty Avoidance in either Italy or Portugal or in any of the societies listed in the

C, D, and E bands of this table. Using the bands in this way will yield detailed information about the relative position of each of our GLOBE societies.

2. There are several options for scaling data (i.e., grand-mean centering, raw-metric scaling, group-mean centering) (Bryk & Raudenbush, 1987; Kreft & Leeuw, 1998). The particular centering method used has implications for the type of hypothesis being tested by the HLM analyses. We will discuss the reason for our choice of group-mean centering in a later section of this chapter.

3. Of course, HLM is not without its own problems (see James & Williams, 2000).

4. Although R^2 can be computed and interpreted when conducting HLM analyses, it is important to realize that there are circumstances in which this statistic is ill-defined. For example, there are times when Equation 11.6 will produce negative R^2 estimates for predictors. Kreft and De Leeuw (1998) indicate that R^2 estimates are meaningful only if random intercept models with group-mean-centered predictors are being tested.

5. Because the purpose of these additional analyses was to determine whether response bias affected our HLM analyses, we conducted these analyses using one-tailed tests. In other words, we only considered the HLMs to replicate if the coefficients for a response bias corrected predictor were significant and in the same direction as the coefficients associated with that predictor in the original HLM analysis.

6. We did not need to perform a contextual analysis for the societal-level culture–CLT relationships because the societal culture data and the CLT data came from different respondents in this study. Thus, any obtained relationships between societal culture and the CLT dimensions could only result from societal-level covariation.

7. Specifically, the organizational characteristic believed to cause the interaction would be identified by entering the measured variable into a new HLM model. This new model would consist of the main effect due to industry and the measured organizational characteristic as well as the industry–organizational characteristics interaction. If the fit of this new model is equal to the fit the organizational-level "random slope" HLM model described in the text of this chapter, then there is support for the belief that the measured organizational characteristic (or some variable highly correlated with it) was responsible for the organizational-level interaction with industry.

REFERENCES

Bliese, P. D., & Hanges, P. J. (2002). *Being both too liberal and too conservative: The perils of treating grouped data as though it is independent.* Manuscript submitted for publication.

Bryk, A. S., & Raudenbush, S. W. (1987). *Hierarchical linear models.* Newbury Park, CA: Sage.

Cascio, W. F., Outtz, J., Zedeck, S., & Goldstein, I. L. (1991). Statistical implications of six methods of test score use in personnel selection. *Human Performance, 4,* 233–264.

Cohen, J., & Cohen, P. (1983). *Applied multiple regression/correlation analysis for the behavioral sciences* (2nd ed.). Hillsdale, NJ: Lawrence Erlbaum.

Goldstein, H. (1995). *Multilevel statistical models* (2nd ed.). London: John Wiley.

Guion, R. M. (1998). *Assessment, measurement, and prediction for personnel decisions.* Mahwah, NJ: Lawrence Erlbaum.

Gulliksen, H. (1950). *Theory of mental tests.* New York: John Wiley.

Hanges, P. J., Grojean, M. W., & Smith, D. B. (2000). Bounding the concept of test banding: Reaffirming the traditional approach. *Human Performance, 13,* 181–198.

Hofmann, D. A. (1997). An overview of the logic and rationale of hierarchical linear models. *Journal of Management, 23,* 723–744.

Hofmann, D. A., & Gavin, M. B. (1998). Centering decisions in hierarchical linear models. *Journal of Management, 24,* 623–641.

Hofmann, D. A., Griffin, M. A., & Gavin, M. B. (2000). The application of hierarchical linear modeling to organizational research. In K. J. Klein & S. W. J. Koslowski (Eds.), *Multilevel theory, research, and methods in organizations* (pp. 467–511). San Francisco: Jossey-Bass.

House, R. J., Rousseau, D. M., & Thomas, D. (1995). The MESO paradigm: A framework for the integration of micro and macro organizational behavior. In L. L. Cummings & B. M. Staw (Eds.), *Research in organizational behavior* (pp. 71–114). Greenwich CT: JAI.

Hox, J. J. (1995). *Applied multilevel analysis.* Amsterdam: TT-Publikaties.

James, L. R., & Williams, L. J. (2000). The cross-level operator in regression, ANCOVA, and contextual analysis. In K. J. Klein & S. W. J. Koslowski (Eds.), *Multilevel theory, research, and methods* in organizations: Foundations, extensions, and new directions (pp. 382–424). San Francisco: Jossey-Bass.

Kenny, D. A., & Judd, C. M. (1986). Consequences of violating the independence assumption in analysis of variance. *Psychological Bulletin, 99*, 422–431.

Klein, K. J., Dansereau, F., & Hall, R. J. (1994). Levels issues in theory development, data collection, and analysis. *Academy of Management Review, 19*, 195–229.

Klein, K. J., & Kozlowski, S. W. J. (2000). From micro to meso: Critical steps in conceptualizing and conducting multilevel research. *Organizational Research Methods, 3,* 211–236.

Kozlowski, S. W. J., & Klein, K. J. (2000). A multilevel approach to theory and research in organizations: Contextual, temporal, and emergent processes. In K. J. Klein & S. W. J. Kozlowski (Eds.), *Multilevel theory, research, and methods in organizations* (pp. 3–90). San Francisco, CA: Jossey-Bass.

Kreft, I., & Leeuw, J. D. (1998). *Introducing multilevel modeling.* Thousand Oaks, CA: Sage.

Lance, C. E., & James, L. R. (1999). V^2: A proportional variance accounted for index for some cross-level and person-situation research designs. *Organizational Research Methods, 2,* 395–418.

Pedhazur, E. J., & Schmelkin, L. P. (1991). *Measurement, design, and analysis: An integrated approach.* Hillsdale, NJ: Lawrence Erlbaum.

Rousseau, D. M. (1985). Issues of level in organizational research: Multilevel and cross-level perspectives. In L. L. Cummings & B. Staw (Eds.), *Research in organizational behavior* (pp. 1-37). Greenwich, CT: JAI.

Zedeck, S., Cascio, W. F., Goldstein, I. L., & Outtz, J. (1996). Sliding bands: An alternative to top-down selection. In R. S. Barrett (Ed.), *Fair employment strategies in human resource management* (pp. 222–234). Westport, CT: Quorum Books.

PART IV

EMPIRICAL FINDINGS

MANSOUR JAVIDAN

The chapters in this part of the book provide the findings concerning each of the nine GLOBE cultural dimensions. The rationale for the selection of these chapters was provided by House and Javidan in Chapter 2. In Chapters 12 through 19, the reader will find the following:

- An explanation of the construct of each cultural dimension and its roots
- GLOBE's definition of each cultural dimension and how it relates to the existing literature
- An explanation of the scales used to measure the construct at the societal and organizational levels
- The overall and industry-specific findings concerning each cultural dimension
- Rankings of the societies for each cultural dimension
- The relationship between the GLOBE findings and a variety of social and economic indicators
- A comparison of the GLOBE findings with the findings of other researchers
- The relationship between societal values and practices and organizational values and practices with respect to each cultural dimension
- An examination of each cultural dimension at the organizational and societal level of analysis as a predictor of culturally endorsed leadership theory (CLT) dimensions.

The cultural findings reported in these chapters are based on the reports of the middle managers from three industries: food processing, telecommunications, and financial services in 62 societies. The psychometric properties of GLOBE scales were discussed in Chapter 8 by Hanges and Dickson.

The reported findings are based on the average scores of the respondents in each society. An important question in all of these Chapters is the extent to which the aggregated survey scores can be generalized to represent the societies under study. As explained in chapter 9 by Gupta, Sully de Luque, and House, the GLOBE cultural practices and values are validated against a series of unobtrusive measures and independently collected World Values Survey (Inglehardt, Basanez, & Moreno, 1998) data to ensure that the constructs measured by the GLOBE societal scales generalize beyond the middle-manager population. Furthermore, in Appendix C, Hanges, Sipe, and Godfrey show that survey findings represent more than the aggregates of individual-level relationships.

Despite these important attempts, the reader still needs to take caution in generalizing our findings at the society level. Societal cultures are too complex to be measured in their entirety in any single study. It is difficult, if not impossible, to claim that one has fully understood and measured a societal culture for several reasons: First, it is impossible to identify a truly random sample in many societies. Second, each culture consists of a variety of subcultures that may differ on some aspects and be similar on others. Third, strictly speaking, to make generalizable statements about a phenomenon like culture, we need more than one study and one sample. Given the paucity of such studies, any cross-cultural researcher needs to be cautious in making such claims.

The above limitations and constraints make any well-designed cross-cultural research program a truly daunting task, but one that is critical. Cross-cultural researchers need to be extremely diligent in their research design and interpretation of their findings. We at GLOBE have taken unprecedented steps in terms of our research design and, as will be apparent in the following chapters, have taken a strict approach in interpreting our findings. The reader will find the wording in these chapters to be deliberate, meticulous, and accurate. We believe this is warranted to reflect the care in the research program and to communicate our findings clearly.

RESPONSE BIAS

Each dimension chapter provides the rank order of the 62 GLOBE societies in terms of their societal cultural practices and values scale scores. The rank ordering of the 62 societies on the basis of the six CLT dimension scores is presented in Chapter 21 by Dorfman, Hanges, and Brodbeck. When interpreting the rank order of societies, it is important to note that people from different cultures sometimes exhibit different response patterns when completing questionnaires. The presence of these culturally based response patterns is believed to bias subsequent cross-cultural comparisons based on self-report data because these response patterns are not a function of the intended construct of interest. A statistical standardization correction procedure has been developed in the cross-cultural literature that is believed to remove cultural-response biases from the original "uncorrected" questionnaire responses (van de Vijver & Leung, 1997).

In the GLOBE project, we performed this statistical correction procedure and correlated our original scales with these "response-bias-corrected" scales to ascertain the extent to which response bias was a problem with our scales. Further, we developed an extension of this procedure to help interpret the rank ordering of the societies on the basis of this correction. This extension of the traditional response bias correction procedure and its ability to identify specific societies that exhibit substantial response bias is discussed in Appendix B. This appendix also includes society rankings using adjusted scores corrected for cultural response bias.

BANDS

In addition to the concern about response bias, we also need to caution the reader about not over-interpreting differences in the rank order of societies. There is a tendency to concentrate on the relative position of the societies and ignore the scale values used to generate these rankings. Thus, all differences in the relative position of societies are interpreted as meaningful even though the magnitude of the societal difference with regard to the actual scale values is sometimes trivial. In an attempt to address this problem, Hanges, Dickson, and Sipe in Chapter 11 used a technique discussed in the psychometric and personnel selection literature known as test banding. This procedure groups societal scores into bands in which the scores within a particular band are considered as being not meaningfully different. Thus, this banding methodology identifies a range of scores that cannot be distinguished from the top score in a band.

QUARTETS

Separate culture items were written for the nine core GLOBE dimensions at both the societal and the organizational levels. In addition to these two levels of analysis, we wrote separate culture items to reflect cultural practices (*As Is* response format) versus values (*Should Be* response format). The items were written as "quartets" having isomorphic structures across the two levels of analysis (societal and organizational) and across the two culture manifestations (practices and values). The basic structure of the items comprising quartets is identical, but the frame of reference is varied according to the particular cultural manifestation and levels of analysis being assessed. The specific way that these are measured is explained in the dimension chapters.

Confidence Intervals

Finally, we report correlations throughout the chapters in this section. Although we report whether the correlations are significantly different from zero, we do not report the confidence intervals associated with these correlations. The confidence intervals provide the best estimate of the population correlation between two variables. To help give the reader a feel for the magnitude of our estimation accuracy, Appendix D gives confidence intervals for various correlations.

References

Inglehart, R., Basanez, M., & Moreno, A. (1998). *Human values and beliefs: A cross-cultural sourcebook.* Ann Arbor: University of Michigan Press.

van de Vijver, F., & Leung, K. (1997). *Methods and data analysis for cross-cultural research.* Thousand Oaks, CA: Sage.

12

PERFORMANCE ORIENTATION

MANSOUR JAVIDAN

Performance orientation reflects the extent to which a community encourages and rewards innovation, high standards, and performance improvement. Despite its intuitive appeal, the concept of performance orientation has not received much attention in the literature. For instance, even the best-known cross-cultural study, conducted by Hofstede (1980, 2001; Hofstede et al., 1990) did not conceptualize or measure it as an independent cultural dimension. Arguably, the most influential and renowned treatment of performance orientation was Max Weber's classic analysis in *The Protestant Ethic and the Spirit of Capitalism* (1904/1930, 1904/1998). Weber's thesis, based on his analysis of the history and doctrine of Catholic and Protestant religions, is that the fundamental difference between the two lies in their approach to work and performance in this world. He argued that Catholicism focused on "good works" as the exclusive path to salvation. Praying, confession, and giving to charity were the things that Catholics were required to do to ensure eternal peace. Consequently, the attention of a typical Catholic was distracted from the earthly activities and focused on doing good. Spending time and energy on earthly activities was nothing but a waste of the opportunity to prepare for the eternal world.

In contrast, the Protestant doctrine introduced the idea of work as a *calling*. Martin Luther (1483-1546) emphasized the notion that doing worldly work is not a distraction from godly life. Indeed, any type of ordinary work, in Luther's mind, was a religiously sanctioned step toward salvation. He believed that every individual was capable of and accountable for working toward his or her own salvation, and therefore, the intermediation of monks and monasteries was unnecessary. Luther further believed that performing day-to-day activities in a disciplined and proper manner was a requirement for salvation.

The notion of work as a calling was further expanded, elaborated, and radicalized by John Calvin (1509-1564), whose doctrine of predestination required that every aspect of one's ordinary life activities be a step toward manifestation of God's glory and perfection. To Calvin, the one and only purpose for the world's existence is the glorification of God. Every individual is responsible to help in this regard by doing his or her absolute best in performing daily duties and activities. The fulfillment of daily activities is not in the interest of the flesh, but for the glory of God:

> Let us every one proceed according to our small ability, and prosecute the journey we have begun. No man will be so unhappy but that he may

every day make some progress, however small. Therefore, let us not cease to strive, that we may be incessantly advancing in the way of the Lord, nor let us despair on account of smallness of our success; for however our success may not correspond to our wishes, yet our labor is not lost, when this day surpasses the preceding one; provided that with sincere simplicity we keep our end in view, and press forward to the goal, not practicing self-adulation, nor indulging our own evil propensities, but perpetually exerting our endeavors after increasing degrees of amelioration, till we shall have arrived at a perfection of goodness, which indeed, we seek and pursue as long as we live.... (Calvin, I, pp. 775–776, excerpt in McClelland, 1961, p. 49)

Weber thus chronicled a historical evolution of religious and social views toward work, from the medieval notion that work in this world is a distraction from the godly life to the Protestant ethic, which saw work as a fundamental requirement for being convinced of being among the elect and for satisfying God's requirements. The most fundamental consequence of this change is the increased emphasis on improving the social and human lot, and greater attention to performance improvement as a religious calling. The societies that practiced Calvinist doctrine viewed their religious mandate as one of constantly striving to improve their economic and social conditions. To them, performance orientation was a gift and a duty from God.

Several decades later, David C. McClelland, the noted American psychologist, and his colleagues (1955, 1958, 1961) introduced the concept of need for achievement, which is defined as the need to do better all the time (1987, p. 228). He argued that individuals with high need for achievement (*nAch*) tend to achieve pleasure from progressive improvement, like to work on tasks with moderate probabilities of success because they represent a challenge, take personal responsibility for their actions, seek frequent feedback, search for information on how to do things better, and are generally innovative.

McClelland (1961) set out to propose a psychological perspective on Weber's chronicle of the Protestant Reformation. Weber's hypothesis was that the Protestant values of self-reliance

and hard work led to the evolution of the spirit of modern and rational capitalism. McClelland proposed a more detailed process in which the Protestant values led to greater emphasis among parents on teaching their children to have high standards and to value independence. Such emphasis in turn resulted in higher need for achievement among sons, who then became active entrepreneurs and generated higher rates of economic growth. Winterbottom (1953) showed that mothers of 8- to 11-year-old boys with high nAch tended to set high performance expectations for them at an earlier age. Rosen and D'Andrade (1959) also showed that parents of sons with high nAch tended to set higher standards for them than those of the sons with lower need for achievement. Other data show that Protestant parents tend to put more emphasis on the importance of knowledge, independence, self-reliance, planning, and achieving (McClelland, Rindlisbacher, & deCharms, 1955; Rosen, 1959; Veroff, Atkinson, Feld, & Gruin, 1960).

Several studies have compared the motives for having children in a variety of countries (Bulatao, 1979; Darroch, Meyer, & Singarimbun, 1981; Fawcett, 1983; Hoffman, 1987; Kagitçibasi, 1982). They have identified two sets of values attributed to having children: economic and psychological. In many less developed countries, children are seen as the source of support for parents in old age. They are expected to be obedient and to take care of their parents when they are in need. Iranians refer to their children as the "cane for the hand in the old age." In contrast, American and German parents dismiss such a notion.

In societies in which support for the parents is a paramount virtue, obedience rather than autonomy is highly valued. Family-interest rather than self-interest of the child is the priority. Close parental supervision is a sign of love and affection rather than unwelcome intrusion. Such family surroundings and practices are not conducive for development of the child's sense of self-identity and self-confidence. Children's identity is part of that of the family. They are socialized to be followers and to accept the wishes of those in positions of authority, such as parents and older siblings. Self-reliance, self-confidence, innovativeness, and the will to achieve new things and break tradition are frowned on.

To McClelland, the critical outcome of the Protestant doctrine and the spirit of reform was its impact on individuals' need for achievement. Parents became supportive of the children's self-confidence and self-reliance and encouraged them to set higher standards for their success and to work hard toward achieving their goals. Social and economic success then provided the feedback necessary to institutionalize higher levels of nAch at the family and societal level:

> If people had to set standards for their behavior based on their personal revelations rather than on church authority, they tended to be more achievement oriented and more interested in personally figuring out what was best for them to do. (McClelland, 1987, p. 259)

The Protestant ethic is not the only religion to foster hard work and worldly performance. In a study of cultural values in many countries, Hofstede and Bond (1988) supported Kahn's (1979) hypothesis that one of the main reasons for the impressive economic growth and prosperity of Southeast Asian countries during the period 1965–1985 was the Confucian or neo-Confucian cultural roots of the region.

Kong Fu Zu, who was renamed Confucius by the Jesuit missionaries, was an influential civil servant and social philosopher in China around 500 B.C. He preached many rules and procedures for daily life in his country. Among the key principles of the Confucian teachings were his emphasis on hard work, acquisition of new skills, patience and perseverance, and thrift (Hofstede and Bond, 1988). These values are very similar to the Puritan principles enunciated by Benjamin Franklin, which heavily influenced Max Weber's writings.

Kahn (1979) and Hofstede and Bond (1988) argued that Confucian principles of perseverance, working hard, and learning new skills have been instrumental in helping shape and drive the economic progress in the Southeast Asian region. So, although they explored a different part of the world, a different time period, and a different religious environment, they reached conclusions similar to those of Weber's (1904/1930, 1904/1998) in the sense that cultural values of performance orientation exist more strongly among some peoples than others, and are a critical force in shaping and influencing their social and economic behavior.

Further evidence for a broader interpretation of the Protestant ethic was found by Fyans, Salili, Maehr, and Desai (1983), who explored the possibility that there may be a universal definition of achievement. On the basis of Duda's (1980, 1981) argument for a cross-cultural perspective in defining achievement, they used Maehr's (1974) theoretical definition, which consists of personal responsibility, standards of excellence, and challenge. They factor analyzed the data collected by Osgood, Miron, and May (1975) from 15- to 18-year-old male students from 30 different language communities.

The authors identified a universal factor of achievement consisting of such concepts as knowledge, progress, masculinity, success, work, freedom, and courage. They concluded that there is a universally accepted definition of the concept of achievement. Their results led them to the conclusion, similar to McClelland's (1961), that the Protestant ethic is a special case of a universal achievement ethic, focusing on individual responsibility, hard work, knowledge, and challenge. But they also pointed out that despite such universality in definition, cultures are quite different in terms of the way they actually manifest the concept. They showed a wide range in the 30 different language communities' scores on this factor. They found that high-scoring cultures tend to focus on the future, achievement, taking initiative, and independent competence. The low-scoring cultures tend to focus on tradition, family, affiliation, and social ties. Other authors have shown that some societies have very strong paternalistic values, which may be in conflict with performance orientation (James, Chen, & Cropanzano, 1996; Kanungo & Aycan, 1997). In such societies as Turkey, Pakistan, and Taiwan, people in positions of authority are expected to act like parents and to take care of their employees and their families. They are expected to have a holistic view of employees rather than a narrow, task-based view.

Schwartz and Bilsky (1987) proposed a theoretical structure of societal values consisting of seven motivational domains. One of the domains in this structure is "achievement," which they defined as "personal success through demonstrated competence" (1987, p. 880). They compared two samples in Israel and Germany and empirically confirmed the existence of this domain. They further showed that the achievement domain is opposed to the "prosocial" domain, which is a reflection of the society's humane orientation. Their conclusion was that pursuit of achievement in a society is in conflict with the promotion of social welfare. They later confirmed the existence of the achievement value domain and its opposition to the prosocial value in a comparative study of five nations: Australia, Finland, Hong Kong, Spain, and the United States (Schwartz & Bilsky, 1990).

Further support for the universality of achievement need was produced by Haire, Ghiselli, and Porter (1966) who, in a study of managers in 12 countries, showed that self-actualization and autonomy are the most important and least-satisfied need categories in all the participating countries. Managers across different cultures voiced a universal desire to control their own future and to realize their potential. They also expressed universal dissatisfaction about the opportunity to do so.

Similarly, Bass, Burger, Doktor, and Barrett (1979) asked managers in 12 countries to rank order a variety of goals. They found that self-actualization was ranked as the most important goal. Managers across the participating countries reported that pursuing the opportunity and the independence to achieve one's potential is the most important driving force in their minds. Bigoness and Hofstede (1989) collected data on work goals from 13 different countries at two points in time, 14 years apart. They found that job challenge and job freedom were universally ranked as the top two work goals across the sample. Similar results were reported by Sirota and Greenwood (1971), who surveyed 13,000 employees of a company in 25 countries about their work goals: Individual achievement and job-related accomplishments were universally ranked as the most important goals.

Cultural Variation

Despite the universal acceptance of job-related accomplishment as an important work goal, there is some evidence that different societies use different criteria for measuring accomplishment. In a cross-national study of managers, Laurant (1986) found that people from different countries define career success in different ways. Eighty-eight percent of Americans identified "achieving results" as the most important reason for career success. French managers, however, selected different criteria. The majority of French managers (88%) selected "having high potential" as the most important criterion, whereas 89% of British managers voted for "skills in interpersonal relations and communications."

Parsons and Shils (1951) argued that societies differ in the way they confer status upon their members. They suggested two fundamentally different sets of criteria, which they called *achievement* and *ascription*. Achievement-oriented societies tend to accord status on the basis of accomplishments. People are usually evaluated on the basis of how they perform their current duties and produce results.

Ascribing cultures confer status mostly on the basis of who the individual is. Such characteristics as age, gender, social and family connections, education, alma mater, and profession are important criteria for social status. In these societies, status is generally separate from one's current duties. It is bestowed upon the individual, not upon the task or the individual's accomplishments.

Achievement and ascription cultures are fundamentally different. In the United States, the idea that anyone can become President is a strong reflection of achievement orientation, whereas in France, becoming President without attending the right *grande école* and without the right connections is impossible (Schneider & Barsoux, 1997). In Japan, historically, promotion to higher positions has been based on seniority, gender, and age, although this seems to be changing toward achievement rather than ascribed status.

In societies in which seniority and age are major requirements, it is usually unacceptable to have people report to bosses who are younger than they are. An extreme and unfortunate case of such a culture was excerpted from the *Economist* by Schneider and Barsoux:

> . . . an American oil company set up a drilling operation on a Pacific island and hired local labor. Within a week, all the foremen were found lined up on the floor, their throats cut. Only afterwards did they understand that hiring younger men as foremen to boss older workers was not acceptable in a society where age indicates status. (1997, p. 9)

The two types of culture also differ in terms of their perspective on feedback and evaluation. Those in achievement cultures tend to desire and value feedback because it helps them find out how well they are doing (McClelland, 1961; Schneider & Barsoux, 1997). On the other hand, those in ascribing cultures tend to frown on the notion of evaluation because they see it as an evaluation of who the person is rather than of how he or she is doing. As one French manager explained, "The French get offended by positive or negative feedback. If you question my job, you are questioning my honor, my value, and my very being" (Schneider & Barsoux, 1997, p. 141).

Trompenaars and Hampden-Turner (1998) produced empirical support for the existence of the two types of cultures. In a study of 30,000 respondents, mostly managers, from 47 countries, they showed that people from countries like the United States, Norway, and Australia believe in getting the job done even at the expense of individual freedom, and that respect does not depend on family background. In contrast, the respondents from Oman and Argentina prefer individual freedom even at the expense of getting the job done, and believe in family background as the key determinant of social respect.

As mentioned earlier in this chapter, the seminal cross-cultural study by Hofstede (1980, 2001) did not directly assess performance orientation, but one of his cultural dimensions intersects with our GLOBE construct. He viewed performance or achievement orientation as a part of a broader cultural dimension that he called *masculinity/femininity*. As he described it,

There is a common trend among the vast majority of societies, both traditional and modern, as to the distribution of gender roles apart from procreation: Men must be more concerned with economic and other achievements and women must be more concerned with taking care of people in general and children in particular. (2001, p. 280)

Hofstede (2001) interpreted his masculinity dimension as embodying such attributes as challenge and job recognition, advancement, importance of money, importance of students' performance at school, stress on equity, and the ideal value of performance. However, his interpretation of the dimension also included two other distinct attributes, namely the extent of assertiveness and gender egalitarianism. As a result, Hofstede's notion of performance or achievement orientation is intermingled with other cultural attributes and is not directly measured.

COMPARISON OF HIGH VERSUS LOW PERFORMANCE-ORIENTED SOCIETIES

Culture is a set of basic and shared practices and values that help human communities find solutions to problems of external adaptation—how to survive—and internal integration—how to stay together (Schein, 1992). Performance orientation is an important dimension of a community's culture. It relates to the issues of both external adaptation and internal integration. It is an internally consistent set of practices and values that have an impact on the way a society defines success in adapting to external challenges, and the way the society manages interrelationships among its people.

The medieval Catholic view toward external adaptation was one of total submission. Nature, represented by God's emissaries and monasteries, was in full control. The masses could not survive in a religious sense without the overpowering presence of the Church. The Protestant Reformation ushered in an era of self-confidence and power among the masses. Not only were they believed to have the power to survive and succeed, but they were also required to stand on their own and to do their best.

Performance Orientation and External Adaptation

A key element of performance orientation as a cultural dimension is the nature of the individual's relationship with the outside world (Kluckhohn & Strodtbeck, 1961; Schein, 1992). Some societies view this relationship as one of subjugation, others see it as one of harmony, and still others view it as one of dominance. The Moslem phrase *Insh'allah* (God willing) is an example of subjugation (Schneider & Barsoux, 1997). The Chinese view of the need for help from *feng shui* masters in designing buildings is a reflection of the value of harmony with nature (Schneider & Barsoux, 1997). The phrase "may the best man win" is an example of the value of control, dominance, and competitiveness.

The ancient Greeks viewed the world as being dominated by godlike powers such as Apollo (God of truth) or Athena (God of justice) who were constantly in conflict. Humans were powerless. Their destiny was in the hands of the gods, so their survival depended on their ability to achieve harmony with the gods (Trompenaars & Hampden-Turner, 1998).

The cultural value of harmony with nature is best described in the words of Chief Seattle of the Duwamish and Squamish tribes in the letter he wrote to the President of the United States in 1852:

> . . . the earth does not belong to man, man belongs to earth. . . . Man did not weave the web of life, he is merely a strand in it. Whatever he does to the web, he does to himself. . . . The shining water that moves in the streams and rivers is not just water, but the blood of our ancestors. . . . How can you buy or sell the sky? The land? The idea is strange to us. If you don't own. . . how can you buy. . .? (Campbell, 1988, p. 3)

Trompenaars and Hampden-Turner (1998) used Rotter's (1966) scale to identify the extent to which societies varied in terms of their internal or external locus of control. In their survey of 30,000 respondents, they found that people in several Arab countries see no value in attempting to control natural forces. They also found that most of the people from Norway, Israel, and the United States believe that what happens to an individual is their own doing, whereas most of the people from Venezuela, China, and Nepal believe otherwise.

The internal locus of control (Rotter, 1966) and belief in individual responsibility is associated with such important societal values and practices as collective self-confidence, ambition, energy, thirst for learning and betterment, high standards of performance, and ambitious expectations (Hofstede & Bond, 1988; McClelland, 1961). People from societies with belief in individual responsibility value knowledge and vigorously pursue improvement. They are persistent and industrious in pursuing their goals (Fyans et al., 1983) and are willing to expend the effort needed to get the job done.

These practices are in turn manifested in the form of strong competitiveness. They generate the desire to dominate rather than be dominated. The wish to be better than others and to defeat rivals is driven by self-confidence and ambition. Japanese executives have been criticized in the past for their extreme obsession with destroying their competitors, even at the expense of their own companies (Omae, 1982).

Another aspect of performance orientation in relation to external adaptation is a society's perspective on time (Hall, 1959; Kluckhohn & Strodtbeck, 1961; Trompenaars & Hampden-Turner, 1998). Societies that are rated highly on this dimension seem to view time as limited and sequential. They see it as a valuable and nonrenewable commodity. As a result, they tend to have a sense of urgency in meeting their challenges and making decisions. The societies that are rated lower on this dimension tend to view time as a circular and perpetual resource and, as a result, do not feel much urgency in getting things done. Time is to be savored and not rushed.

Performance Orientation and Internal Integration

Human communities over time tend to develop a series of assumptions, practices, and values that influence the nature of interrelationships within the community (Schein, 1992). These assumptions help determine desirable and undesirable behavior among the members and thus help sustain the community over time.

Table 12.1   Higher Performance Orientation Societies Versus Lower Performance Orientation Societies

Societies That Score Higher on Performance Orientation, Tend to:	*Societies That Score Lower on Performance Orientation, Tend to:*
• Value training and development • Emphasize results more than people • Reward performance • Value assertiveness, competitiveness, and materialism • Expect demanding targets • Believe that individuals are in control • Have a "can-do" attitude • Value and reward individual achievement • Have performance appraisal systems that emphasize achieving results • View feedback as necessary for improvement • Value taking initiative • Value bonuses and financial rewards • Believe that anyone can succeed if he or she tries hard enough • Believe that schooling and education are critical for success • Value what you do more than who you are • Attach little importance to age in promotional decisions • Value being direct, explicit, and to the point in communications • Have a monochronic approach to time • Have a sense of urgency	• Value societal and family relationships • Emphasize loyalty and belongingness • Have high respect for quality of life • Emphasize seniority and experience • Value harmony with the environment rather than control • Have performance appraisal systems that emphasize integrity, loyalty, and cooperative spirit • View feedback and appraisal as judgmental and discomforting • View assertiveness as socially unacceptable • Regard being motivated by money as inappropriate • View merit pay as potentially destructive to harmony • Value "attending the right school" as an important success criterion • Emphasize tradition • Have high value for sympathy • Associate competition with defeat and punishment • Value who you are more than what you do • Pay particular attention to age in promotional decisions • Value ambiguity and subtlety in language and communications • Have a polychronic approach to time • Have a low sense of urgency

In contrast to less performance-oriented societies, highly performance-oriented societies tend to value those individuals and groups that produce results and accomplish their assignments (Parsons & Shils, 1951; Trompenaars & Hampden-Turner, 1998). As a result of focusing on achievement, they tend to value tasks more than social relationships.

Another element of performance orientation is the use of language (Hall, 1960). Highly performance-oriented societies tend to use low-context language (Hall, 1959), emphasizing the need to be direct, clear, and explicit. Less performance-oriented cultures tend to use high-context language, which is less direct, more ambiguous, and more subtle. What is not said is as important as what is said (Schneider & Barsoux, 1997).

The above descriptions present a picture of what it means to be a performance-oriented society. Table 12.1 provides a summary comparison of a typical society that has a strong culture of performance orientation and a society with a weak performance orientation. One needs to be cognizant, however, that societal culture is far too complex to be presented in black and white. Extreme cases are presented here to help explain the concept, but it should also be clear that most cultures do not neatly fit into the extremes in any typology stereotype. Although the table shows cultural attributes that tend to cluster together, it does not rule out the fact that not all these attributes go together at all times. Societies usually have differing mixes of the extreme cases presented in the table.

GLOBE Measures
OF PERFORMANCE ORIENTATION

Four GLOBE Performance Orientation scales were developed to assess this construct. Two scales reflect Performance Orientation *practices* and two scales reflect Performance Orientation *values*. As with all culture dimension scales in the GLOBE project, practices and values are measured for societies and organizations within societies. The participants' assessment of the extent to which a society engages in Performance Orientation practices is one of our *As Is* measures. This scale is a composite of three items that assess societal cultural practices (see Table 12.2 for a sample item). The questions relate to the society's current practices regarding innovation, improvement, and reward systems. In essence, they measure the extent to which a society is perceived to encourage and reward performance improvement.

Similarly, four questionnaire items were used to measure existing practices in organizations

that constitute a second *As Is* measure (see Table 12.4 for a sample item). The questions relate to the extent to which organizations facilitate and reward improved performance, and the extent to which individuals set challenging goals for themselves.

All questionnaire items, including those presented as sample items in Tables 12.2 through 12.5, met exacting statistical standards as described by Hanges and Dickson in Chapter 8. The construct validity of these scales was confirmed across all GLOBE societies.

The previously described scales assessed societal and organizational practices (As Is); two additional scales were developed to assess each respondent's values (Should Be). Tables 12.3 and 12.5 show questionnaire items that measure participants' expressed views on the way things "Should Be" in their societies and organizations. From here on we refer to *Should Be* measures as *values* in contrast to *As Is* measures, which indicate *practices*.

To sum up, the GLOBE scales measure the extent to which a society or an organization encourages the practice of rewarding performance improvement and setting challenging goals, and the extent to which the respondents value these practices.

It may be useful at this point to review the conceptualization and measurement of performance orientation by Trompenaars (1993). In a survey of 15,000 managers in 53 countries, he conceptualized performance orientation as a contrast to social relations. He asked each respondent to select one of the following two statements:

1. A company is a system designed to perform functions and tasks in an efficient way.

Table 12.2   Performance Orientation: Society Practices – Sample Item

In this society, students are encouraged to strive for continuously improved performance. (reverse scored)						
Strongly agree			Neither agree nor disagree			Strongly disagree
1	2	3	4	5	6	7

Table 12.3   Performance Orientation: Society Values – Sample Item

I believe that teen-aged students *should be* encouraged to strive for continuously improved performance. (reverse scored)						
Strongly agree			Neither agree nor disagree			Strongly disagree
1	2	3	4	5	6	7

Table 12.4   Performance Orientation: Organization Practices – Sample Item

In this organization, employees are encouraged to strive for continuously improved performance. (reverse scored)						
Strongly agree			Neither agree nor disagree			Strongly disagree
1	2	3	4	5	6	7

Table 12.5   Performance Orientation: Organization Values – Sample Item

In this organization, employees *should be* encouraged to strive for continuously improved performance. (reverse scored)						
Strongly agree			Neither agree nor disagree			Strongly disagree
1	2	3	4	5	6	7

People are hired to fulfill these functions with the help of machines and other equipment. They are paid for the tasks they perform. (Performance)

2. A company is a large group of people working together. The people have social relations with other people and with the organization. The functioning is dependent upon these relations. (Social relations)

Trompenaars and Hampden-Turner (1998) measured the extent to which each society uses performance or other criteria for granting status by the percentage of respondents who disagreed with the following two statements:

1. The most important thing in life is to think and act in the ways that best suit the way you really are, even if you do not get things done. (1 = strongly agree; 5 = strongly disagree)

2. The respect a person gets is highly dependent on his or her family background. (1 = strongly agree; 5 = strongly disagree)

The first item reflects the two extreme points of a societal value that the appropriate behavior is one that truly represents the individual's freedom versus the one that produces results. The second question deals with a particular way that a society ascribes value to its members, namely their family background. To the extent that the respondent disagrees with either of these questions, he or she holds a performance-oriented perspective.

GLOBE's measures are different from these in the sense that they focus on a community's values and practices on whether or not innovation

Table 12.6   Grand Mean for Performance Orientation

Variable	Mean	Standard Deviation	Minimum	Maximum	Valid N
Performance Orientation practices	4.10	.41	3.20	4.94	61
Performance Orientation values	5.94	.34	4.92	6.58	61

and improvement should be rewarded. The one GLOBE item that is similar to Trompenaars and Hampden-Turner's (1998) is an item that measures the extent to which rewards should be based on performance or other factors.

To summarize, the GLOBE scales of Performance Orientation seem to be the only direct measure of this concept in terms of practices and values. They clearly and explicitly contrast societies and organizations on the extent to which they facilitate and reward their people for wanting to meet higher standards and achieve higher goals.

GLOBE FINDINGS
ON PERFORMANCE ORIENTATION

Table 12.6 shows the grand means of society practices and society values scales for Performance Orientation across all GLOBE societies. Compared to the other cultural dimensions measured, the society practices score has a midlevel average rating of 4.10 with a range of 3.20 to 4.94.

The society values average score for Performance Orientation, at 5.94 with a range of 4.92 to 6.58 is the highest of all GLOBE scales. Compared with the other GLOBE cultural dimensions of Uncertainty Avoidance, Future Orientation, Power Distance, Humane Orientation, Collectivism, and Assertiveness, Performance Orientation is the most cherished. The middle manager responses indicate that people from all over the world are seeking a society that strongly encourages and rewards innovation, challenging goals, and improvement. This is a particularly important finding because despite such importance, the concept

has received little attention from other cross-cultural authors.

Table 12.6 shows that there is a substantial and significant difference between the average scores for the current perceived level of societal Performance Orientation and the desired level. Respondents' aspirations about how much their societies should focus on performance are far beyond their perceptions of the level of their societies' current practices. They tend to be rather harsh in their assessment of how much Performance Orientation is practiced in their countries as compared to how much Performance Orientation should be practiced. For instance, the highest score on practices is for Switzerland at 4.94 out of a range of 1 to 7, which is not very high. In contrast, the highest score for values is 6.58, for El Salvador.

Two possible explanations are plausible. First, there might be a human need to belong to a high performance-oriented and successful society. It may be satisfying for humans, no matter what culture they are from, to be associated with success and achievement. This is reflected in the fact that societies with the highest Performance Orientation values scores are from all parts of the world. They represent Asia, Europe, South America, North America, and Africa. It may be a basic human need to excel and to succeed, and to have high performance standards (McClelland, 1961). Another possible explanation is the issue of social desirability in responding to these questions. This point has been addressed in Chapters 8 and 9.

Overall Scores and Industry Scores

In each society, data were collected from at least one of the following industries: Food

Table 12.7   Performance Orientation Correlation Matrix-Society Practices*

Performance Orientation	Food Industry Score	Finance Industry Score	Telecommunication Industry Score
Overall score	.92** $n = 44$	.97** $n = 54$	.80** $n = 31$
Food industry score		.86** $n = 40$	.63** $n = 21$
Finance industry score			.67** $n = 29$

* Sample sizes are different because not all three industries were selected in each country.

** $p < .01$ (2-tailed).

Table 12.8   Performance Orientation Industry Correlation Matrix-Society Values

Performance Orientation	Food Industry Score	Finance Industry Score	Telecommunication Industry Score
Overall score	.92** $n = 44$	.93** $n = 54$	.88** $n = 31$
Food industry score		.79** $n = 40$	.72** $n = 21$
Finance industry score			.71** $n = 29$

** $p < .01$ (2-tailed).

processing, finance, and telecommunications. Table 12.7 shows the correlation between the overall societal practices score for each society and the scores for the participating industries. As seen in this table, all correlations are significant.

The values scores are also highly correlated, as shown in Table 12.8. These findings increase our confidence in the generalizability of the results in the sense that they are not industry specific. They represent three very different industries with varied histories and dynamics. What they do share is their national heritage. Our findings seem to represent general societal practices and values rather than those driven by the forces in a specific industry.

The Correlation Between Overall Practices and Values Scores

The society scores on values scales have a modest, but significant -0.28 ($p < 0.05$ $N = 61$) correlation with the scores on practices scales. In other words, the two constructs are minimally related such that people's aspirations are not strongly related to their current assessments.

The lack of a strong relationship is borne out by Tables 12.9 and 12.10, which show the

Table 12.9   Performance Orientation: Society Practices*

Band					
A		B		C	
Country	Score	Country	Score	Country	Score
Switzerland	4.94	Egypt	4.27	Namibia	3.67
Singapore	4.90	Switzerland[c]	4.25	Slovenia	3.66
Hong Kong	4.80	Germany[d]	4.25	Argentina	3.65
Albania	4.81	India	4.25	Bolivia	3.61
New Zealand	4.72	Zimbabwe	4.24	Portugal	3.60
South Africa[a]	4.66	Denmark	4.22	Italy	3.58
Iran	4.58	Japan	4.22	Kazakhstan	3.57
Taiwan	4.56	Ecuador	4.20	Qatar	3.45
South Korea	4.55	Zambia	4.16	Hungary	3.43
Canada[b]	4.49	Costa Rica	4.12	Russia	3.39
USA	4.49	South Africa[e]	4.11	Venezuela	3.32
Philippines	4.47	France	4.11	Greece	3.20
China	4.45	Mexico	4.10		
Austria	4.44	Germany[f]	4.09		
Indonesia	4.41	England	4.08		
Australia	4.36	Israel	4.08		
Ireland	4.36	Brazil	4.04		
Malaysia	4.34	Spain	4.01		
Netherlands	4.32	Morocco	3.99		
		Kuwait	3.95		
		Colombia	3.94		
		Thailand	3.93		
		Nigeria	3.92		
		Poland	3.89		
		Georgia	3.88		
		Turkey	3.83		
		Finland	3.81		
		Guatemala	3.81		
		Sweden	3.72		
		El Salvador	3.72		

NOTES: Our response bias correction procedure identified response bias in some countries for this scale (see endnotes).

* Higher scores indicate greater performance orientation.

a South Africa (Black sample)
b Canada (English-speaking)
c Switzerland (French-speaking)
d Germany (West): Former FRG
e South Africa (White sample)
f Germany (East): Former GDR

individual country scores on each scale (a detailed explanation of the scores and the bands is provided in Chapter 8 by Hanges and Dickson).[1] For example, among the societies with high practices scores, the Philippines has a high values score, Taiwan has a low values score, and New Zealand has an average values score. Canada and the United States have

Table 12.10   Performance Orientation: Society Values*

Band									
A		*B*		*C*		*D*		*E*	
Country	*Score*	*Country*	*Score*	*Country*	*Score*	*Country*	*Score*	*Country*	*Score*
El Salvador	6.58	South Africa[a]	6.23	Switzerland	5.82	Russia	5.54	Japan	5.17
Zimbabwe	6.45	Mexico	6.16	Greece	5.81	Netherlands	5.49	South Africa[f]	4.92
Colombia	6.42	Canada[b]	6.15	Spain	5.80	Kazakhstan	5.41		
Slovenia	6.41	Guatemala	6.14	Sweden	5.80	Turkey	5.39		
Namibia	6.40	USA	6.14	Morocco	5.76	South Korea	5.25		
Portugal	6.40	Brazil	6.13	Israel	5.75				
Venezuela	6.35	Poland	6.12	Thailand	5.74				
Argentina	6.35	Finland	6.11	Taiwan	5.74				
Ecuador	6.32	Austria	6.10	Indonesia	5.73				
Philippines	6.31	Germany[c]	6.09	Singapore	5.72				
Nigeria	6.27	Iran	6.08	Georgia	5.69				
Zambia	6.24	Italy	6.07	China	5.67				
		Bolivia	6.05	France	5.65				
		India	6.05	Hong Kong	5.64				
		Malaysia	6.04	Albania	5.63				
		Kuwait	6.03	Denmark	5.61				
		Germany[d]	6.01						
		Switzerland[e]	5.98						
		Ireland	5.98						
		Qatar	5.96						
		Hungary	5.96						
		New Zealand	5.90						
		Costa Rica	5.90						
		Egypt	5.90						
		England	5.90						
		Australia	5.89						

NOTES: Our response bias correction procedure identified response bias in some countries for this scale (see endnotes).

* Higher scores indicate greater performance orientation.

a South Africa (White sample)
b Canada (English-speaking)
c Germany (East): Former GDR
d Germany (West): Former FRG
e Switzerland (French-speaking)
f South Africa (Black sample)

midlevel values scores but represent high practices scores. South Africa (Black sample) has a relatively low values score, but a high practices score. This finding further supports the argument, made earlier, that it is a fundamental human attribute to desire a highly performance-oriented society independent of the current level of societal practices.

The weak correlation between practices and values measures is exhibited across all three industries. As can be seen from Table 12.11, no discernable relationship exists between the participants' assessment of their society's current level of Performance Orientation and their views on its value across industries. However, there is a small negative relationship between

Table 12.11   Performance Orientation Industry Correlation Matrix-Society Values and Society Practices

Industry Score	Overall Score— Practices	Food Industry Score— Practices	Finance Industry Score— Practices	Telecommunication Industry Score— Practices
Overall score values	−.28* n = 61			
Food industry score values		−.17 n = 44		
Finance industry score values			−.26 n = 54	
Telecommunication industry score values				−.32 n = 31

* Correlation is significant at the .05 level (2-tailed).

overall practices and values scores ($r = .308$, $p < .05$).

GLOBE PERFORMANCE ORIENTATION AND OTHER ECONOMIC AND SOCIAL INDICATORS

In this section, we compare and contrast the GLOBE findings on Performance Orientation with those of other major cross-cultural and comparative studies focusing on different countries' social and economic performance. As explained in Chapter 7 by Javidan and Hauser, four major ongoing reports produce the relevant data: The IMD's Global Competitiveness Ranking, the United Nations' Human Development Report, and the World Values Survey. The findings of these studies are grouped into four categories: Economic health, success in science and technology, human condition, and societal values.

Performance Orientation and Economic Health

What is the relationship between Performance Orientation and economic health? Do the more performance-oriented societies enjoy healthier economies? Will societies with higher aspirations for Performance Orientation exhibit higher economic prosperity? You may recall that in the first section of Chapter 7, we proposed a series of hypotheses. The following are those relating to Performance Orientation. Societies that score high on performance orientation practices tend to:

a. Be more economically prosperous and competitively successful

b. Have stronger societal support for competitiveness

c. Enjoy higher levels of human development

Table 12.12 provides the answers to these questions. It shows the correlation coefficients between the two GLOBE dimensions of Performance Orientation practices and values, and the various elements of economic health. As explained in Chapter 7, these are *economic prosperity,* which refers to consumption and growth; *economic productivity,* which refers to a supportive labor environment and growth in productivity; *government support for prosperity,* reflecting the extent to which the government and the political body are supportive of

Table 12.12 Relationship Between Performance Orientation and Economic Health

Performance Orientation	Economic Prosperity	Economic Productivity	Government Support for Prosperity	Societal Support for Competitiveness	World Competitiveness Index
Society values	−.28* $n = 57$	.16 $n = 40$	−.22 $n = 40$	.08 $n = 40$	−.44** $n = 42$
Society practices	.29* $n = 57$	−.26 $n = 40$	.50** $n = 40$	.58** $n = 40$	.61** $n = 41$

* Correlation is significant at the .05 level (2-tailed).

** Correlation is significant at the .01 level (2-tailed).

economic progress; and finally, *societal support for competitiveness,* which is a measure of the general social attitude toward and support for business competitiveness.

In addition to these measures, we also examined the relationship between GLOBE findings and the World Competitiveness Index produced by IMD.

The table shows that respondents' aspirations in terms of how much a society should value performance is not positively related to the society's economic performance.

*Economic Productivity,
National Competitiveness, Economic
Prosperity, and GLOBE Findings on
Performance Orientation Practices*

As shown in Table 12.12 above, respondents' views on their societies' current level of Performance Orientation are significantly related to their countries' level of economic prosperity and national competitiveness. In other words, Hypothesis *a* is supported—performance-oriented societies are more economically prosperous. These findings are consistent with the notion suggested by Weber (1904/1930, 1904/1998), Rostow (1952), and Parsons (1951): Societal practices that encourage achievement orientation are key to economic and business success. As McClelland (1961) eloquently stated in his book, *The Achieving Society:*

In conclusion, if we look back over the diverse findings reported in this chapter, they confirm our general hypothesis to a surprising extent,

considering the many sources of error that could affect our measures. A concern for achievement as expressed in imaginative literature—folk tales and stories for children—is associated in modern times with a more rapid rate of economic development. The generalization is confirmed not only for Western, free-enterprise democracies like England and the United States but also for Communist countries like Russia, Bulgaria, or Hungary, or primitive tribes that are just beginning to make contact with modern technological society. It holds in the main whether the society is developed or underdeveloped, poor or rich, industrial or agricultural, free or totalitarian. In other words, there is a strong suggestion here that men with high achievement motives will find a way to economic achievement given fairly wide variations in opportunity and social structure. What people want, they somehow manage to get, in the main and on the average, though . . . other factors can modify the speed with which they get it. (p. 105)

This view is not, however, universally shared. Trompenaars and Hampden-Turner (1998) compared societies in terms of their orientation toward ascription or achievement. They argued that "there is no evidence that either orientation belongs to a 'higher' level of development, as modernization theorists used to claim" (p. 110). They also criticized the notion that Protestant countries are more economically successful than Catholic countries:

A second glance at the scores shows that there are growing difficulties with the thesis that an achievement orientation is the key to economic success. In the first place, Protestant cultures are no longer growing faster than Catholic or Buddhist ones. Catholic Belgium, for example, has a slightly higher GDP per capita than the more Protestant Netherlands. Catholic France and Italy have been growing faster than the UK or parts of the Protestant Scandinavia. (p. 110)

Two points need to be made in response to the authors' criticism. First, they do not provide any evidence on the validity of their research instruments and there are serious questions as to whether specific items match the construct of interest. For example, their measure of a society's achievement orientation is the percentage of respondents who disagree with the statement: "The most important thing in life is to think and act in the ways that best suit the way you really are, even if you do not get things done."

It is not clear at all that, in the respondents' minds, this item refers to achievement orientation. It could easily be interpreted to mean individualism and individual freedom. Having said that, we correlated the authors' results on this item with measures of economic health used by GLOBE and found strong and significant correlation with three of the four scales: economic prosperity (correlation = .573, $p < .001$), public support for economic prosperity (correlation = .547, $p < .001$), and societal support for economic prosperity (correlation = .367, $p < .05$). So, contrary to their claim about lack of a relationship, their purported measure of achievement orientation is in fact related to economic success.

The second point related to their criticism is in regard to the authors' comment about the distinction between Catholic and Protestant countries. As we have stated earlier in this chapter, the Protestant Reformation may simply be a specific case of change in societal values leading to self-confidence and higher achievement motivation and performance orientation, but is certainly not the only one. Hofstede and Bond (1988) showed that Confucian Dynamism was strongly correlated with economic growth among 22 nations between 1965 and 1985. Their description of Confucian Dynamism has much in common with McClelland's need for achievement and GLOBE's Performance Orientation, lending support for the argument that no particular religion or philosophy has a monopoly on achievement.

A few other researchers have also shown results that do not support the culture-economic performance linkage. In a study of 41 countries, Lynn (1991) found no relationship between work ethic, achievement motivation, or improvement orientation and economic growth. Furnham, Kirkcaldy, and Lynn (1996) studied a sample of 42,000 students in 42 countries and showed that work ethic, achievement motivation, and improvement orientation were negatively correlated to gross domestic product and had no significant relationship with economic growth. An important point about their study is that their measures seem to be a combination of values, societal practices, and individual practices and, as such, may be confounded. Combining values and practices tends to complicate the interpretation of findings due to the fact that, as we have shown here, they are not necessarily related. Furthermore, earlier in this section we showed that values were not related to most economic variables.

In summary, the economic prosperity and competitiveness of a society is a complex and multidimensional concept. It evolves over time as a result of many forces and drivers. It is strongly dependent on the nation's economic productivity because a paramount goal in any society is to produce rising standards of living for its citizenry (Porter, 1990). Our findings point to the conclusion that cultural practices are an important correlate of economic productivity and prosperity. Along with other variables (Porter, 1990), cultures with high Performance Orientation practices scores foster leaders who value and reward hard work, ambition, high standards, and performance improvement. They lead to the formation of corporations that are ambitious, hard working, competitive, and successful. The success of the private sector, in turn, drives the overall prosperity of the economy and the population.

Government and Societal Support for Economic Prosperity and GLOBE Findings on Performance Orientation

As shown in Table 12.12, Performance Orientation practices scores are significantly related to the level of societal support for economic success, confirming Hypothesis *b*— Performance oriented societies have stronger social support for competitiveness. The relationship is significant even after controlling for gross national product (GNP) per capita. Societies that are reported to be more performance oriented are associated with more advanced political systems, more flexible labor regulations, and higher general levels of economic literacy among the population. Their competition laws are more supportive of business competitiveness and their labor-relations environments are less hostile. Their public service is less intrusive and less influenced by political interference.

For much of the 20th century, the world of politics was the battleground for two fundamentally different political ideologies (Macpherson, 1966): The liberal ideology, which was based on rationality, self-interest, and property rights; and the socialist ideology, which was most concerned with the treatment of labor and distribution of wealth. The foundation for the liberal ideology is the equity norm, which focuses on equal opportunity for all to contribute and to gain, and to be rewarded according to their contributions (Deutsch, 1975). The foundation for the socialist ideology is the protection of human well-being. The two value systems result in two different approaches to the role of government and the nature of distribution of wealth and resources in the society. With the collapse of the communist ideology, liberalism has emerged as the winning value system for most of the world.

The picture emerging from our findings is consistent with the writings of many authors who have explored the role of government from different perspectives (Hirsch, 1991; Hofstede & Bond, 1988; Jessop, 1991; McClelland, 1987; Onis, 1995; Porter, 1990; Swanson, 1967). Swanson showed that the Protestant Reformation was more successful in those European communities where governments tended to be more democratic and less centralized. McClelland (1987) suggested that "an open, competitive structure in which self-reliance is rewarded, as in the democratically ruled cities at the time of the Reformation, seems to be an important source of encouragement for developing achievement motivation" (p. 461).

Jessop (1991) and Hirsch (1991) argued that due to changes in customer demand and technology and the increasing mobility of the workforce, the role of the state is to facilitate and encourage flexibility and reinvigoration by promoting innovation, small business, technological development, and competition. Onis (1995) suggested that such state intervention policies as subsidized loans, price ceilings, and protectionism are dysfunctional due to the state's inability to manage influence processes and the uncontrollable power of bureaucrats and politicians. Finally, Porter (1990), in his study of 10 major trading countries, concluded that the political and legal environment in a society plays a critical role in its competitiveness among other nations. He suggested that the government's proper role is

> to encourage—or even push—companies to raise their aspirations to higher levels of competitive performance. . . . Government policies that succeed are those that create an environment in which companies can gain competitive advantage. . . . Government has critical responsibilities for fundamentals like the primary and secondary education systems, basic national infrastructure, and research in areas of broad national concern. (pp. 87–88)

Our findings provide large-scale empirical support for Porter's and other authors' arguments, although it is important to remember that we showed a significant *negative* correlation between scores of Performance Orientation values and practices at the society level (and no significant relationships at the industry level). In other words, the societies with low Performance Orientation practices scores tend to aspire to higher levels than those that report high practices. This is easily understandable and probably reflects a universal finding for all GLOBE cultural dimensions that have socially desirable characteristics: the less one has, the more one desires.

Our findings also show that governments do not act in a vacuum. Governments operate in a milieu of national cultural values and practices. Government policies and actions are derived from and are reflections of societal values. They, in turn, act to reinforce and sustain those values. The fact that Canadian tax rates are higher than those in the United States is a

Table 12.13   Relationship Between Performance Orientation and Human Condition

Performance Orientation	Societal Health	Human Health	Life Expectancy	General Satisfaction	Psychological Health	Human Development Index (HDI)
Society values	−.30 $n = 40$	−.06 $n = 56$	−.30* $n = 56$	.11 $n = 37$	.05 $n = 27$	−.24 $n = 56$
Society practices	.53** $n = 40$	.12 $n = 56$	.10 $n = 56$	.51* $n = 37$	−.23 $n = 27$	.09 $n = 56$

** Correlation is significant at the .01 level (2-tailed).

* Correlation is significant at the .05 level (2-tailed).

reflection of a Canadian value system, which favors a stronger government role in the society than that favored by the Americans. Governments tend to shy away from policies that are fundamentally against national sentiments. Porter's admonitions on the role of government are all logical, in the economist's tradition of the rational man, but they fail to take into consideration the critical role of national value systems.

Intrusiveness and pervasiveness of government regulations, which usually lead to cumbersome and complicated regulatory frameworks, may be caused by deep-rooted societal values that prefer more structure, less uncertainty, and a bigger government. Rationalizing the regulatory framework may involve more than a change in laws. It may warrant a fundamental change in the society's value system.

Many variables play a role in achieving economic progress and prosperity. Economists have made a convincing case for the importance of such variables as investment, infrastructure, and domestic competition, but our findings point to an even more fundamental requirement. There may be a cultural reason for the fact that some societies are more successful in creating and sustaining the economic attributes that are needed for national success. In the absence of cultural attributes such as ambition, high standards, and hard work, societies may be less predisposed to accumulate the economic ammunition for growth, or may be less inclined to use that ammunition even if it may be available.

Performance Orientation and Human Condition

Economic health is only one aspect of a society's well-being. Another dimension is the general health of the populace and the society. What is termed *human condition* here refers to the general quality of life and the state of mind of the people in a particular society.

In this section, we examine the relationship between GLOBE findings on Performance Orientation and six different dimensions of human condition. As explained in Chapter 7, *societal health* refers to the quality of life, safety, and security in a society. *Human health* reflects physical health of the populace. *General satisfaction* measures the extent to which people are happy and satisfied. *Psychological health* refers to emotional well-being. The data we use are from the World Values Survey (Inglehart, Basanez, & Moreno, 1998). The other measure of the human condition is the Human Development Index, prepared by the United Nations, which reflects life expectancy, adult literacy, and standard of living.

Table 12.13 shows that the aggregated reports of societal Performance Orientation values have only one significant correlation with the above six dimensions: Life expectancy. The table also shows that reported Performance Orientation practices do not produce significant correlations with four of the six dimensions. They are significantly correlated only with societal health and general satisfaction, but not the other four remaining dimensions related to human condition. These findings strongly suggest that people in societies whose practices stress innovation, accomplishment, and improvement tend to enjoy a more civil society. They benefit from the rule of the law and private property and a higher quality of life. They generally feel happier, healthier, and more satisfied with life. They do not, however, necessarily enjoy longer lives. They also do not score any higher on the United Nations Human Development Index. In other words, Hypothesis *c* (Performance oriented societies enjoy higher levels of human development) is not confirmed. These findings are consistent with those by Furnham et al. (1996), whose study of 42,000 students in 42 countries showed that work ethic and achievement motivation were not significantly related to the Human Development Index (HDI).

One possible way of understanding these results is that cultures with high Performance Orientation practices scores have demanding requirements and expectations of their members. As such, they are associated with a variety of behavioral manifestations and cultural artifacts. What these findings show is that higher levels of economic and societal health, and a more positive state of mind, are the more visible manifestations of such cultural practices. On the other hand, societies that are reported to being performance oriented are not necessarily associated with longer lives, greater psychological health, or a more humanistic atmosphere, as measured by HDI. It seems that the emphasis on hard work and continuous improvement, although generating a positive state of mind, may in fact take a toll in terms of psychological well-being. On the other hand, the societies that are reported to be less performance oriented and less economically successful may indeed enjoy a more stress-free lifestyle that would help improve psychological well-being and life expectancy.

An interesting issue is the relationship between HDI and economic health. The HDI was created by the United Nations in 1990 on the premise that economic prosperity is not an end in itself, but a means to a more humane society. It was designed as a measure of the extent to which societies have been able to improve life expectancy, adult literacy, and economic conditions. Our analysis shows that the HDI values are significantly related to economic prosperity, public support for economic prosperity, and competitiveness rankings. The findings can be interpreted in three ways. One is to conclude that this relationship is caused only by the fact that gross domestic product per capita numbers are included in both variables. A second interpretation is that those countries that improve their literacy rates and life expectancy tend to reap the benefits in terms of a more competitive and more prosperous society. An alternative interpretation is that those societies that are competitive and prosperous tend to do a better job of taking care of their people.

Perhaps a surprising finding is that there is no relationship between economic productivity and HDI values. In other words, better living conditions are not associated with a more productive workforce. Societal support for productivity and economic productivity do not seem to be connected to what the society does to help improve the living conditions of its people.

Political Ideology

Table 12.14 shows no relationship between Performance Orientation practices and the extent of socialist thinking in political ideology. In contrast, those societies with higher Performance Orientation practices scores tend to show a more positive view toward democracy and prefer a less active role for the government. They believe that democracies run well and are good at maintaining order. They also prefer a strong role for the private ownership of business and a greater reliance on individual rather than government responsibility for individual well-being. It is difficult to reach any causal directional conclusions. One possible interpretation is that the popularity of democratic systems has enabled societies to become performance oriented. On the other hand, it could be argued that high performance oriented societies have been economically successful and have built middle classes that have nurtured democratic views.

Religion

Our analysis of the relationship between reported Performance Orientation practices and

Table 12.14   Relationship Between Performance Orientation and Political Ideology

Performance Orientation	Disdain for Democracy	Role of Government
Society values	.34 n = 24	.04 n = 37
Society practices	−.50* n = 24	−.35* n = 37

* Correlation is significant at the .05 level (2-tailed).

religion showed no significant results. Such lack of relationship between religiousness and Performance Orientation practices warrants attention. As we described earlier in this chapter, religion, in the form of the Protestant ethic, may have played an important role in creating greater interest in worldly success. With the passage of time, the connection between religiousness and Performance Orientation may have diminished. Confucian Dynamism (Hofstede & Bond, 1988) or the Protestant ethic may have had an early impact as a trigger toward hard work and accomplishment, but these values may now be in place without their religious undertone. The explanation for this may lie in the nature of how cultures evolve. Cultural values come to being in response to particular external adaptation or internal integration challenges because they help the human community solve such challenges. The community's success with the cultural values provides the feedback necessary for institutionalization of the cultural values. But over time, the connection between the initial reason for the creation of the value and the practicing of the value tends to diminish and fade and the cultural value becomes "mental programming of the mind" (Hofstede, 1980). Further, as GLOBE's unobtrusive measures show, high Performance Orientation practices scores tend to be related to lack of dominance of a single religion. The societies with stronger reported Performance Orientation practices tend to draw from a diversity of religious ideologies, and are not dogmatic about religions.

On the other hand, the data also show that being highly dedicated to religion and the eternal world does not take away the desire for success and achievement. Although medieval Catholicism may have prevented people from paying attention to worldly affairs, today's Catholic countries may not see worldly success and eternal peace as being at odds or mutually exclusive. A possible explanation is that cross-cultural communication and contact has created a new set of external adaptation problems: How to succeed in the global village. It is possible that nonreligious societies have learned from the religious ones to work hard and to set high standards of performance just to be able to keep up in the global arena. So, over time, the more religious societies and the less religious societies may have been converging and becoming more similar in their views toward performance orientation, although for very different reasons.

To summarize, the following are the key findings from the comparison of the GLOBE Performance Orientation cultural dimension and those in other published comparative reports.

Societies that score higher on Performance Orientation practices

- are economically more successful and globally more competitive
- enjoy a more positive attitude toward life and live in a more civil society
- prefer a strong role for private ownership of business
- prefer individual accountability for their own well-being

In contrast, societies that score higher on Performance Orientation practices do not

- enjoy healthier or longer lives
- score higher on the United Nations' Human Development Index
- have stronger religious practices

Societies that score higher on Performance Orientation values

- experience weak economic prosperity
- are less competitive
- have lower life expectancy

In contrast, societies that score higher on Performance Orientation values do not

- enjoy government or societal support for economic success
- benefit from a civil society with high levels of health and life expectancy
- score higher on the United Nations' Human Development Index
- represent any particular political ideology

As is clear from the above list, reported Performance Orientation values do not show strong associations with such other measures as economic productivity or societal health. This is consistent with their lack of strong relationship with reported Performance Orientation practices.

PERFORMANCE ORIENTATION AND SOCIETY DEMOGRAPHICS

To explore the impact of societal demographics, we examined the relationship between Performance Orientation and two variables: Physical climate and geographic region. We categorized the GLOBE societies in terms of their climate. As discussed in Chapter 10 by Gupta and Hanges, we created seven categories of climate: Tropical humid, tropical wet and dry (savanna), desert, subtropical humid, subtropical wet and dry (Mediterranean), marine west coast, and continental.

Huntington (1924) was one of the first scholars to focus on the relationship between physical climate and achievement:

Climate influences health and energy, and these in turn influence civilization. . . . On an average the

men of genius in the North Sea countries would be more energetic than those of other regions because they would enjoy better health. . . . They would be continually stimulated by their cool, bracing climate, and would feel like working hard all the year, whereas their southern and eastern colleagues in either hot weather or cold would be subject to periods of depression which are a regular feature of the less favored parts of Europe. (p. 233)

Woytinsky and Woytinsky (1953) summarized Huntington's ideal climate as "mean temperature of approximately 40°F in winter and 64°F in summer, relative humidity of about 60% at noon and high enough at night that dew is precipitated, and variability of weather with frequent but not extreme changes" (p. 29).

McClelland (1961) found that climate did in fact have an impact on the need for achievement. He found that cultures with high nAch scores generally live in relatively dry and moderate climates and those with low scores tended to be in tropical climates. Toynbee's (1947) explanation was that nations' success depends on the level of challenge they face. Those societies in which the challenge from the physical environment is "just right" tend to rise and succeed. Those that face too small (tropical) or too great (arid) a challenge tend to underperform.

The GLOBE clustering of climates was explained in Chapter 10. We conducted analyses of variance (ANOVAs) tests to determine if there exist climatic differences in the reported practices and values of societal Performance Orientation. We found weak evidence of climatic differences in the societal practices ($F[6, 54 = 2.10]$, $p < .07$) and societal values ($F[6, 54 = 2.02]$, $p < .08$) concerning Performance Orientation. Further analysis (not shown) found that climatic differences account for 25% of the variation in societal Performance Orientation practices scores, whereas 75% represent idiosyncratic societal differences. With respect to societal Performance Orientation values, 13% of the variation was explained by climatic differences, whereas 87% represented unique societal differences. In other words, climatic differences have a modest but nontrivial significant effect on societal Performance Orientation culture. Table 12.15 shows the scores for each climate cluster.

Table 12.15   Climate and Performance Orientation

Climate	Society Practices			Society Values		
	Mean	N	Standard Deviation	Mean	N	Standard Deviation
Tropical Humid Costa Rica Ecuador Colombia Philippines Singapore Indonesia Malaysia India	4.33	8	0.29	6.06	8	0.27
Tropical Wet and Dry El Salvador Venezuela Guatemala Thailand Nigeria Zambia Zimbabwe	3.87	7	0.30	6.25	7	0.27
Desert Egypt Israel Kazakhstan Kuwait Namibia Turkey Qatar Iran South Africa (White sample) South Africa (Black sample) Mexico	4.02	11	0.39	5.84	11	0.44
Subtropical Wet and Dry Albania Greece Italy Portugal Slovenia Spain Morocco	3.84	7	0.51	5.98	7	0.31
Subtropical Humid Bolivia Brazil Argentina Hong Kong Taiwan	4.13	5	0.53	5.98	5	0.30

Climate	Society Practices			Society Values		
	Mean	N	Standard Deviation	Mean	N	Standard Deviation
Marine West Coast Denmark France Germany (East and West) Ireland New Zealand Netherlands Switzerland Switzerland (French-speaking) United Kingdom	4.33	10	0.28	5.84	10	0.20
Continental Austria Finland Hungary Japan Korea Sweden Poland Georgia Canada U.S. Russia China Australia	4.09	13	0.42	5.81	13	0.34

Another element of society demographics is geographic region, which showed a significant relationship with GLOBE measures of Performance Orientation practices and values. As discussed in Chapter 8 by Hanges and Dickson, there are significant differences in values and practices for every cultural dimension among the 62 societal cultures (e.g., recall that we use the term *societal cultures* rather than nations). Further, GLOBE societies are grouped into 10 clusters of geographical regions. One-way ANOVA tests revealed significant cross-regional differences in Performance Orientation societal practices ($F[9, 51 = 5.37]$, $p < .01$) as well as in the societal values scores ($F[9, 51 = 2.87]$, $p < 0.01$). Further analysis showed that regional differences account for 58% of the variation in Performance Orientation societal

practices scores, whereas 42% represent idiosyncratic societal differences. With respect to societal Performance Orientation values, 32% of the variation was explained by regional differences, whereas 68% represented unique societal differences. In other words, there is extensive regional commonality among societies with respect to Performance Orientation values and practices.

Table 12.16 shows the mean GLOBE scores on the two dimensions for each geographic region. The highest practices score belongs to Confucian Asia clusters (4.58) and the lowest average score belongs to Eastern Europe (3.73). The range for values scores was from 5.53 (Confucian Asia) to 6.24 (Latin America).

The findings point to the conclusion that people in different geographic areas rate their

Table 12.16   Geographic Region and Performance Orientation

Geographic Region	Society Practices			Society Values		
	Mean	N	Standard Deviation	Mean	N	Standard Deviation
Nordic Europe Finland Sweden Denmark	3.92	3	0.27	5.84	3	0.26
Eastern Europe Albania Kazakhstan Hungary Poland Russia Slovenia Greece Georgia	3.73	8	0.50	5.82	8	0.33
Latin America Argentina Bolivia Brazil Colombia Costa Rica Ecuador El Salvador Guatemala Mexico Venezuela	3.85	10	0.28	6.24	10	0.20
Middle East Egypt Kuwait Morocco Qatar Turkey	3.90	5	0.30	5.81	5	0.25
Latin Europe Italy Portugal Spain France Switzerland (French-speaking) Israel	3.94	6	0.28	5.94	6	0.27
Germanic Europe Austria Germany (Former West) Germany (Former East) The Netherlands Switzerland	4.41	5	0.32	5.90	5	0.26

Geographic Region	Society Practices			Society Values		
	Mean	N	Standard Deviation	Mean	N	Standard Deviation
Sub-Saharan Africa Namibia Nigeria South Africa (Black sample) Zambia Zimbabwe	4.13	5	0.37	6.05	5	0.64
Confucian Asia Taiwan Singapore Hong Kong South Korea China Japan	4.58	6	0.25	5.53	6	0.25
Southern Asia India Indonesia Malaysia Philippines Thailand Iran	4.33	6	0.23	5.99	6	0.22
Anglo Australia Canada New Zealand U.S. South Africa (White sample) England Ireland	4.37	7	0.22	6.03	7	0.14

societies differently in terms of how important performance is, and in their aspirations about how important it should be. It is noteworthy that the Confucian Asia cluster is among the highest scoring groups, lending support to Hofstede and Bond's (1988) argument for the role of cultural undertones in building strong performance-oriented societies.

To summarize, our findings lead to three important conclusions: First, respondents' aspirations in terms of Performance Orientation are somewhat dependent on geography and climate. It appears that although people all over the world want a society that is more interested in getting better results and improving its performance, those in different regions and climates do have differing aspirations.

Second, geography and climate also have a role to play in how people assess their societies' current Performance Orientation practices. People in different geographic and climate clusters have differing assessments of their societies' current practices. These differences seem to be associated with the dominant religion, language, and cultural heritage of the cluster. It appears that geographic proximity

Table 12.17   Performance Orientation and McClelland's Need for Achievement

McClelland Need for Achievement	Performance Orientation	
	Society Practices	Society Values
Society scores	−.12 (N = 27)	.04 (N = 27)

facilitates cross-cultural communication and the spread of values. The only exception is the Anglo countries, which are not physically close, but whose similarity can be explained through colonial heritage and immigration (Ronen & Shenkar, 1985).

Third, using the information in Table 12.16, we compared the differences between the clusters' scores on practices and values. The average difference for the five geographic clusters with the lowest score on practices (Eastern Europe, Latin America, Latin Europe, Nordic Europe, and Middle East) is 2.12. The average difference for the three clusters with the highest scores on practices (Confucian Asia, Anglo, and Germanic Europe) is 1.38. In other words, those clusters with lower practices scores tend to value Performance Orientation higher, presumably because they want to catch up. On the other hand, those clusters with higher practices scores are more complacent. This finding is consistent with the arguments by McClelland (1961) and Furnham (1990) that a society's ambition and achievement orientation diminishes with its success.

COMPARISON OF GLOBE FINDINGS WITH RELEVANT LITERATURE

Limited cross-cultural research exists on the topic of performance orientation. One of the first writings on this topic was by McClelland (1958, 1961), who content-analyzed and coded the stories that students read in elementary schools in different countries. He assigned each society a grade for the way the stories emphasize need for achievement. Table 12.17 shows the correlation between McClelland's society scores on need for achievement reported in his later work (McClelland, 1987) and GLOBE's

scores on Performance Orientation for the countries that are in common between the two samples. Neither correlation is significant.

As stated earlier, Trompenaars (1993), in a survey of 15,000 managers in 53 countries, conceptualized performance orientation in contrast to social relations. He asked each respondent to select one of the following two statements:

1. A company is a system designed to perform functions and tasks in an efficient way. People are hired to fulfill these functions with the help of machines and other equipment. They are paid for the tasks they perform. (performance)

2. A company is a large group of people working together. The people have social relations with other people and with the organization. The functioning is dependent upon these relations. (social relations)

The only significant correlation with GLOBE scores on Performance Orientation is between Trompenaars's percentage of people who selected item 1 and the GLOBE scores on society values, but its direction is contrary to expectation. It is negative. In another study, Trompenaars and Hampden-Turner (1998) explored the notion of ascribed versus achieved status. They measured the extent to which a society uses performance or other criteria for granting status by the percentage of respondents who disagreed with the following two statements:

3. The most important thing in life is to think and act in the ways that best suit the way you really are, even if you do not get things done. (1 = strongly agree; 5 = strongly disagree).

4. The respect a person gets is highly dependent on his or her family background. (1 = strongly agree; 5 = strongly disagree).

The first item reflects the two extreme points of a societal value that the appropriate behavior is one that truly represents the individual's preferences versus the one that produces results. The second question deals with a particular way that a society ascribes value to its members, namely their family background. To the extent that the respondent disagrees with either of these questions, he or she is purported to hold a performance-oriented perspective.

We correlated the GLOBE Performance Orientation societal practice scale scores with the individual items and the average of the two items in Trompenaars and Hampden-Turner's study for the 37 countries that were in common. There are no significant correlations with GLOBE results. We also correlated the responses to the aggregated GLOBE Performance Orientation items with the scores reported by Trompenaars, Trompenaars and Hampden-Turner, and McClelland. Except for three items, all the other correlations were insignificant. The three significant correlations are:

- Trompenaars 3 (The most important thing in life is to think and act in the ways that best suit the way you really are, even if you do not get things done) and the GLOBE item, "In this society, major rewards are based on only performance effectiveness," or are based on "Factors other than performance effectiveness." Pearson correlation: 0.32 ($p < .05$).
- Trompenaars 3 (The most important thing in life is to think and act in the ways that best suit the way you really are, even if you do not get things done) and the GLOBE item, "I believe that people should set challenging goals for themselves." Pearson correlation: .39 ($p < .05$).
- There is a significant relationship between the GLOBE item ("I believe that people should set challenging goals for themselves") and Trompenaars's percentage selecting performance (A company is a system designed to perform functions and tasks in an efficient way. People are hired to fulfill these functions with the help of machines and other equipment. They are paid for the tasks they perform). The Pearson correlation is $-.534$ ($p < .01$).

From the inconsistent results described above, it appears that the construct of performance orientation at a cross-cultural level is neither well defined nor well developed. It has been conceptualized by various authors in different ways. It seems that the previous work has focused on the concept in contrast to other things, whereas GLOBE is taking a different approach. GLOBE's conceptualization of performance orientation is different from those of other researchers in the sense that its measures focus on drive for performance improvement and challenging goals. It examines the responses on a continuum of low to high performance orientation. Other researchers have taken an indirect approach to performance orientation. Trompenaars and Hampden-Turner (1998) explored it in contrast to being oneself or the person's background and family connection. Trompenaars (1993) examined it in contrast to maintenance of social relations. McClelland, (1958, 1961) measured it in terms of projections based on children's stories. Although none of these approaches are necessarily superior or inferior, the GLOBE measurement approach has the advantage of relying on informed reports of a society's performance orientation or lack of it. Furthermore, these measures are independently validated by unobtrusive measures.

PERFORMANCE ORIENTATION AS A DIMENSION OF ORGANIZATIONAL CULTURE

An organization is a group of individuals who are expected to work together as a community. As such, they need a set of values to help manage the interactions among the members and to help succeed in dealing with the challenges they face (Schwartz & Bilsky, 1990; Schein, 1992). Where do these values come from? Among the several potential sources, the societal culture plays an important role for two reasons. First, the success of the organization in external adaptation requires closeness to the contextual culture. To succeed, the organization needs to assimilate, or at a minimum, respect and appreciate its broader environment. Second, the employees working in the organization are members of the society and have been socialized into its values and assumptions. It is only natural to expect them to bring those same values into their dealings within the organization.

Kreder and Zeller (1988) compared 27 German and 13 U.S. companies in terms of the extent to which their control mechanisms were task or employee oriented. They found that the U.S. companies were more task-oriented, using formalized planning systems and meticulous monitoring mechanisms. The German companies, however, were more employee-oriented, with greater participation and concern for employees' personal problems.

Hofstede, Neuijen, Ohayv, and Sanders (1990) factor-analyzed 54 items relating to organizational practices in 20 organizational units of 10 organizations in Denmark and the Netherlands. They identified six factors, two of which related to performance orientation. They called them *results orientation* versus *process orientation,* which opposes concern for the ends with that of the means, and *results orientation* versus *employee orientation,* which opposes a concern for people to a concern for getting the job done.

The Relationship Between Societal and Organizational Practices and Societal and Organizational Values

As indicated in Chapter 2 by House and Javidan, the GLOBE theoretical model postulates that societal practices and values affect organizational practices and values. Two hierarchical linear models (HLMs) were conducted to test these hypotheses for organizational Performance Orientation practices and values. We tested the GLOBE hypothesis regarding the effect of societal culture on organizational culture by conducting HLM analyses in which organizational GLOBE Performance Orientation was predicted by GLOBE societal Performance Orientation. These analyses supported our hypotheses that societal Performance Orientation practices have a significant and strong positive relationship with organizational Performance Orientation practices ($p < .01$). We found a similar significant and even stronger relationship between societal Performance Orientation values and organizational Performance Orientation values

($p < .01$). Both analyses support a principal proposition in the GLOBE theoretical model (i.e., Proposition 3, Figure 2.1, Chapter 2, by House & Javidan): organizational cultural values and practices are significantly related to societal values and practices.[2] Further, the finding that societal values are associated with and likely predictors of organizational values supports the argument that performance orientation is a deeply held value related to a fundamental human need for achievement (McClelland, 1961) and for enhancing one's self-concept (Shamir, 1991).

Performance Oriented as a Leadership Characteristic

As explained in Chapter 8 (Hanges & Dickson), one of the confirmed first-order factors for leadership is *performance oriented.* It refers to the extent a leader stresses continuous improvement and has high standards of performance. Table 12.18 shows the three items that were confirmed as the components of the first-order leadership factor called *performance orientation.*

The construct of performance orientation has not been directly studied in the leadership literature. The earliest work related to this concept was the leadership studies conducted at Ohio State University in the United States, where a leader's role was classified as *consideration* versus *initiating structure* (Fleishman, 1953; Halpin & Winer, 1957; Hempill & Coons, 1957). Similarly, a major research program was conducted at the University of Michigan that characterized leader behavior in terms of task-oriented behavior, relations-oriented behavior, and participative leadership (Katz & Kahn, 1952; Katz, Maccoby, & Morse, 1950).

The consideration or relations-oriented dimension relates to those behaviors that are primarily concerned with building and sustaining relationships with people, increasing teamwork, and building identification with the organization (Yukl, 1998). Examples are friendliness, showing concern, and being interested in the well-being of subordinates.

Initiating structure or task-oriented behavior reflects those behaviors that are important in

Table 12.18   Performance Orientation as a Leadership Characteristic: Leader Attribute Item Components

	1 *Greatly* *Inhibits* *Leadership* *Effectiveness*	*2* *Somewhat* *Inhibits*	*3* *Slightly* *Inhibits*	*4* *No* *Impact*	*5* *Contributes* *Slightly*	*6* *Contributes* *Somewhat*	*7* *Contributes* *Greatly to* *Leadership* *Effectiveness*
Improvement Oriented	Seeks continuous performance improvement						
Excellence Oriented	Strives for excellence in performance of self and subordinates						
Performance Oriented	Sets high standards of performance						

getting the task completed, improving efficiency, and increasing reliability. Examples are setting goals, defining subordinates' roles, and explaining the way the work is done.

Although the two dimensions were originally thought to be independent, later research has shown it to be otherwise. In a meta-analysis of the research conducted after 1968, Fisher and Edwards (1988) showed a clear relationship between considerate leadership and employee productivity. They showed that the correlation between considerate leadership and job performance ranged from .27 to .45. Schriesheim, House, and Kerr (1976) showed that the correlation between consideration and initiating structure had a mean of .52, casting further doubt on the expected independence of the two concepts.

The interdependence between the two concepts was addressed by Blake and Mouton (1964), who developed the managerial grid and proposed that effective leaders are high on both concern for people and concern for production. Although their model has received little research support, Misumi and Peterson (1985), in a 30-year research program in Japan, identified two types of leadership behavior, which they called the performance-maintenance (PM) theory of leadership. As stated earlier, they suggested that the two dimensions are not independent, but interdependent. The Maintenance function facilitates the Performance function. They showed that leaders who are high on both

dimensions are consistently more effective in Japan.

A more recent genre of leadership theory is the neo-charismatic school of thought (House & Aditya, 1997), which postulates that effective leaders not only combine task-oriented and employees-oriented behaviors, but they also show specific skills and mind-set relating to, among other things, setting ambitious goals and communicating high expectations of their subordinates (House, 1977). They achieve ambitious goals by building their subordinates' self-confidence and by intellectually challenging them (Bass, 1985).

GLOBE's empirically derived construct of *leadership* Performance Orientation directly relates to this notion of ambition and challenge. It reflects the leader's excellence orientation and constant pursuit of improvement. It is not concerned with task orientation or employee orientation per se. It goes beyond these categories and focuses on the extent to which the attribute of excellence orientation is seen to lead to effectiveness.

Table 12.19 shows the overall and industry averages across all GLOBE societies. On a 7-point scale, the average is around 6.00, which is very high, reflecting the participants' belief that performance orientation is a highly effective characteristic for leaders. The universal view seems to be that those who set high standards and pursue continuous excellence are effective leaders.

Table 12.19   Grand Mean for Performance Orientation as a Leadership Characteristic

Variable	Mean	Standard Deviation	Minimum	Maximum	Valid N
Performance Oriented, telecommunications industry	6.03	0.36	5.02	6.67	31
Performance Oriented, finance industry	6.02	0.46	3.87	6.66	55
Performance Oriented, food industry	6.04	0.32	5.06	6.62	44
Performance Oriented, overall country score	6.02	0.37	4.51	6.64	61

The reason for such high demand for excellence-oriented leaders may be related to human motivation and self-concept (Shamir, 1991). Self-concept is one's sense of one's own competence, power, achievement, and abilities. Shamir, House, and Arthur (1993) suggested that people are intrinsically motivated to enhance their self-concept. Performance-oriented leaders elevate their subordinates' self-concept by acting as a role models, convincing them that the standards are indeed very high but achievable, showing confidence in them, supporting and rewarding their accomplishments, giving them autonomy, and intellectually challenging them. This argument is supported by Haire et al. (1966), who showed that among managers in 12 countries, autonomy and self-actualization are the most-important and yet least-satisfied need categories. Javidan and Carl (1998), in a study of a large group of Canadian executives, showed that leaders who set high targets and ambitious goals tend to elevate their subordinates' self-confidence and self-actualization.

Although there is universal agreement across countries and industries on the value of leader performance orientation, there is still, as shown in Table 12.20 below, a range of views on its importance. Countries like Ecuador rate this leadership dimension very high with an average of 6.64. The lowest score belongs to Qatar at 4.51, which is still positive although not as strong as those in the *A* band (a detailed explanation of scores and bands is provided in Chapter 11).

As shown in Table 12.19, the mean scores on this dimension were almost identical across the three industries participating in the study. Table 12.21 shows the correlation coefficients for the scores in the three industries. The scores are significantly correlated across all three industries.

SOCIETY DEMOGRAPHICS AND LEADERSHIP PERFORMANCE ORIENTATION

To explore the impact of society demographics, we examined the relationship between the GLOBE Performance Oriented leadership scores and two variables: Physical climate and geographic region. We categorized the GLOBE countries in terms of their climate and found no significant difference in leadership scores across the different climate types ($p = .25$).

Geographic region showed a significant ($p < .01$) relationship. Clusters explained 44.3% of the societal level differences in performance-oriented leadership. Table 12.22 shows that performance-oriented leadership is considered most effective in the Anglo cluster at 6.33, and least effective in the Middle East culture at 5.48. Chapter 21 (Dorfman, Hanges, & Brodbeck)

(Text continues on page 272)

Table 12.20   Performance Orientation as a Leadership Characteristic-Individual Country Scores

Band							
A		B		C		D	
Country	*Score*	*Country*	*Score*	*Country*	*Score*	*Country*	*Score*
Ecuador	6.64	Italy	6.18	Taiwan	5.67	South Korea	5.18
Philippines	6.56	Portugal	6.18	China	5.64	Morocco	5.10
U.S.	6.46	Zimbabwe	6.16	Albania	5.62	France	5.10
Canada[a]	6.43	Namibia	6.16	Iran	5.56	Qatar	4.51
Colombia	6.39	Hungary	6.15	South Africa[f]	5.47		
Ireland	6.38	Costa Rica	6.15				
England	6.38	Mexico	6.14				
Brazil	6.36	Singapore	6.11				
Indonesia	6.36	Malaysia	6.11				
Australia	6.35	Germany[c]	6.11				
Israel	6.34	Zambia	6.10				
Germany[b]	6.33	Guatemala	6.09				
New Zealand	6.31	Kuwait	6.08				
Spain	6.23	Switzerland	6.08				
Austria	6.23	Denmark	6.05				
El Salvador	6.22	Venezuela	6.05				
Argentina	6.20	Finland	6.04				
		Bolivia	6.04				
		South Africa[d]	6.01				
		Nigeria	6.00				
		Thailand	5.98				
		Kazakhstan	5.97				
		Sweden	5.96				
		India	5.96				
		Netherlands	5.95				
		Georgia	5.94				
		Russia	5.92				
		Turkey	5.91				
		Poland	5.87				
		Switzerland[e]	5.87				
		Hong Kong	5.82				
		Greece	5.82				
		Egypt	5.79				
		Slovenia	5.76				
		Japan	5.73				

a Canada (English-speaking)
b Germany (East): Former GDR
c Germany (West): Former FRG
d South Africa (White sample)
e Switzerland (French-speaking)
f South Africa (Black sample)

Table 12.21   Performance Orientation as a Leadership Characteristic-Correlation Matrix

	Food Industry Score	Finance Industry Score	Telecommunication Industry Score
Overall Score	0.96** $n = 44$	0.96** $n = 55$	0.72** $n = 31$
Food Industry Score		0.86** $n = 41$	0.91** $n = 21$
Finance Industry Score			0.57** $n = 29$

** Correlation coefficients are significant at the 0.01 level (2-tailed).

Table 12.22   Geographic Region and Leadership-Performance Orientation

	Performance Orientation as a Leadership Attribute		
Geographic Region	Mean	N	Standard Deviation
Nordic Europe Finland Sweden Denmark	6.02	3	0.05
Eastern Europe Albania Kazakhstan Hungary Poland Russia Slovenia Greece Georgia	5.88	8	0.16
Latin America Argentina Bolivia Brazil Colombia Costa Rica Ecuador El Salvador Guatemala Mexico Venezuela	6.23	10	0.19
Middle East Egypt Kuwait	5.48	5	0.66

Geographic Region	Performance Orientation as a Leadership Attribute		
	Mean	*N*	*Standard Deviation*
Morocco Qatar Turkey			
Latin Europe Israel Italy Portugal Spain France Switzerland (French-speaking)	5.99	6	0.47
Germanic Europe Austria Germany (Former West) Germany (Former East) The Netherlands Switzerland	6.14	5	0.15
Sub-Saharan Africa Namibia Nigeria South Africa (Black sample) Zambia Zimbabwe	5.98	5	0.29
Confucian Asia Taiwan Singapore Hong Kong South Korea China Japan	5.69	6	0.30
Southern Asia India Indonesia Malaysia Philippines Thailand Iran	6.20	6	0.23
Anglo Australia Canada New Zealand U.S. South Africa (White sample) England Ireland	6.33	7	0.15

shows significant relationships between societal clusters and the Charismatic/Value-Based culturally endorsed leadership (CLT), in which one essential aspect of this CLT is Performance Orientation.

THE RELATIONSHIP BETWEEN PERFORMANCE ORIENTATION AS A SOCIETAL DIMENSION AND PERFORMANCE ORIENTED AS A LEADERSHIP CHARACTERISTIC

Table 12.23 shows the relationship between the overall society practices and society values scores and performance oriented leadership, as well as the scores for each industry. The values scores are significantly and positively correlated with performance oriented leadership. The practices scores are not related to performance oriented leadership. We should remind the reader that performance oriented leadership is the first-order factor for the second-order factor labeled Charismatic/Value-Based leadership. (For more information,

please see the next section and Chapter 8 by Hanges & Dickson).

To summarize our findings, it is clear that the GLOBE respondents throughout the world see leaders who have high standards and are determined to seek continuous improvement as highly effective. This desire is so strong and universal that it is independent of the societies' Performance Orientation practices. We explain such high expectations in terms of the construct of self-concept (Shamir et al., 1993), which is the mental image that an individual has of him- or herself. It is one's sense of one's own competence, power, achievement, and abilities. Leaders who are demanding and excellence oriented elevate their followers' self-concept. The experience of working for such leaders helps build the followers' self-confidence and self-worth because being associated with such leaders provides constant feedback of real or perceived success and improvement, thus making the subordinates feel they are capable of achieving better results. To demand high performance orientation from leaders seems to satisfy one's need for a positive and enhanced self-concept.

Table 12.23 Performance Orientation as a Societal Dimension and Performance Oriented as a Leadership Characteristic-Correlation Matrix

	Society Practices	Society Values	Food Practices	Food Values	Telecom Practices	Telecom Values	Finance Practices	Finance Values
Performance Oriented— Overall	.09	.46**						
Performance Oriented— Food			.04	.51**				
Performance Oriented— Telecom					−.20	.70**		
Performance Oriented— Finance							.24	.32*

* Significant at 0.05 level.

** Significant at 0.01 level (2-tailed).

INTERPRETATION OF HLMS USING PERFORMANCE ORIENTATION TO PREDICT CULTURALLY ENDORSED LEADERSHIP

As indicated by the conceptual GLOBE model, culture is believed to have its effect on the content of CLTs at multiple levels of analysis. More specifically, we hypothesized that the leader attributes perceived to be effective would be a function of (a) societal cultural practices (as measured by the societal practices cultural scales); (b) societal cultural values (as measured by the societal values scales); (c) organizational cultural practices (as measured by the organizational practices scales), and (d) organizational cultural values (as measured by the organizational values scales).

In the present chapter we have discussed the results of statistical analyses examining the extent to which one particular cultural dimension (Performance Orientation) has an effect on CLTs. Specifically, we examine the extent to which the content of CLTs varies as a function of Performance Orientation values and practices in (a) societies and (b) organizations within societies.

We tested for the relationship between culture and the six GLOBE CLT leadership dimensions by using hierarchical linear modeling (HLM). An overview of HLM analyses and a detailed discussion of how we conducted these analyses as well as how to interpret the R^2 information in HLM is provided in Chapter 11 by Hanges, Dickson, and Sipe. In this next section, we discuss the results of the HLM analyses exploring the relationship between organizational and societal culture and the content of CLTs.

HLM Analysis: Organizational and Societal Variation

In the present analysis we examine the simultaneous predictive power of organizational and society Performance Orientation values and practices on six CLTs. Competitive tests of all culture dimensions and CLTs are presented in Chapter 21 by Dorfman and colleagues.[3] In general, we expect that societal and organizational values will be more strongly related to

CLT leadership dimensions than societal and organizational practices. As indicated previously, our notions of values and CLT leadership dimensions represent idealized concepts of how the world *Should Be* in contrast to practices that represent the world *As Is*. As you read through the results discussed below, it may be helpful to view Figure 12.1 for a visual summary. The figure, however, shows only results regarding cultural values, not practices. (All HLM coefficients are presented in Table 21.10 of Chapter 21 by Dorfman et al.)

Performance Orientation was found to be a better predictor for some of the CLTs (e.g., Charismatic/Value-Based leadership) than for others (e.g., Self-Protective leadership).

When organizational level and societal level Performance Orientation values and practices were considered, significant relationships were found with the following dimensions:

- *Charismatic/Value-Based leadership.* Performance Orientation cultural values scores were significantly related to the Charismatic/Value-Based leadership dimension and explained a total of 28.0% of the organizational and societal variance for this dimension. Approximately 60% of this variance was associated with forces operating at the organizational level of analysis. The remaining portion of the explained variance (40%) was associated with forces operating at the societal level of analysis.

Specifically, the organizational Performance Orientation cultural values scores were positively related ($p < .01$) to the Charismatic/Value-Based leadership dimension. Charismatic/Value-Based leadership is more likely to be a part of a shared leadership belief system in organizations with high Performance Orientation values scores.

The societal Performance Orientation cultural values scores were positively related ($p < .01$) to the Charismatic/Value-Based leadership dimension. Charismatic/Value-Based leadership is more likely to be a part of the shared leadership belief system in societies with high Performance Orientation values scores.

- *Team-Oriented leadership.* Performance Orientation cultural values scores were

Performance Orientation Cultural Dimension

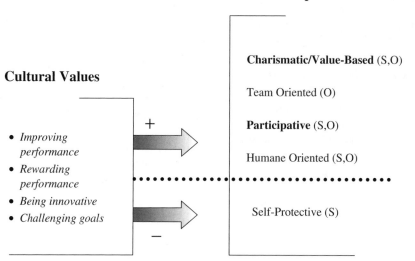

Figure 12.1   Performance Orientation Cultural Values as Drivers for CLT Leadership Dimensions

* Only statistically significant relationships are shown ($p < .05$; see Table 21.10, Chapter 21 by Dorfman et al.). The most important leadership CLT relationships are in bold (i.e., relationship is significant at both society and organization levels of analyses or highest HLM coefficient within each level of analysis).

O = Organizational level

S = Societal level

significantly related to the Team-Oriented leadership dimension and explained a total of 10.4% of the organizational and societal variance. All of the explained variance was associated with forces operating at the organizational level of analysis. The organizational Performance Orientation cultural values scores were positively related ($p < .01$) to the Team-Oriented leadership dimension. Team-Oriented leadership is more likely to be a part of a shared leadership belief system in organizations with high Performance Orientation values scores.

• *Participative leadership.* Performance Orientation cultural values scores were significantly related to the Participative leadership dimension and explained a total of 8.3% of the organizational and societal variance. Approximately 30.2% of this variance was associated with forces operating at the organizational level of analysis. The remaining portion of the explained variance (69.8%) was

associated with forces operating at the societal level of analysis.

The organizational Performance Orientation cultural values scores were positively related ($p < .01$) to the Participative leadership dimension. Participative leadership is more likely to be a part of a shared leadership belief system in organizations with high Performance Orientation values scores. The societal Performance Orientation cultural practices scores were positively related ($p < .05$) to the Participative leadership dimension. Participative leadership is more likely to be a part of the shared leadership belief system in societies with high Performance Orientation values scores.

• *Humane-Oriented leadership.* Performance Orientation cultural practices and values scores were significantly related to the Humane-Oriented leadership dimension and explained a total of 13.6% of the organizational and societal variance. Approximately 46.5% of this variance was associated with forces operating at the organizational level of analysis. The remaining portion of the explained variance (53.5%) was associated with forces operating at the societal level of analysis.

The organizational Performance Orientation cultural values scores were positively related ($p < .01$) to the Humane-Oriented leadership dimension. Humane-Oriented leadership is more likely to be a part of a shared leadership belief system in organizations with high Performance Orientation values scores. The societal Performance Orientation cultural practices scores were positively related ($p < .01$) to the Humane-Oriented leadership dimension. Humane-Oriented leadership is more likely to be a part of the shared leadership belief system in societies with high Performance Orientation practices scores.

• *Autonomous leadership.* Performance Orientation cultural values scores were significantly related to the Autonomous leadership dimension but explained a total of just 1.2% of the organizational and societal variance. All of the explained variance was associated with forces operating at the organizational level of analysis. The organizational Performance Orientation cultural values scores were positively related ($p < .01$) to the Autonomous leadership dimension. Autonomous leadership is more likely to be a part of a shared leadership belief system in organizations with high Performance Orientation values scores.

• *Self-Protective leadership.* Performance Orientation cultural practice and values scores were significantly related to the Self-Protective leadership dimension but explained a total of just 0.3% of the organizational and societal variance. All of the explained variance was associated with forces operating at the organizational level of analysis. The organizational Performance Orientation cultural values scores were negatively related ($p < .01$) to the Self-Protective leadership dimension. Self-Protective leadership is less likely to be a part of a shared leadership belief system in organizations with high Performance Orientation values scores.

In summary, our results show that Performance Orientation cultural practices and values are significantly related to all six of our CLT dimensions. However, some of these relationships were stronger than others. In particular, Charismatic/Value-Based leadership, Humane-Oriented leadership, and Team-Oriented leadership exhibited stronger relationships with Performance Orientation culture than did Autonomous leadership or Self-Protective leadership.

What Does It All Mean?

Overall, consistent with Project GLOBE's conceptual model, our analyses indicate that the kind of leadership viewed as effective is a reflection of the extent to which an organization and society practice and value Performance Orientation. When organizations were viewed as valuing Performance Orientation, the CLT endorsed at the organizational level was more likely to be composed of Charismatic/Value-Based, Participative, Humane-Oriented, Team-Oriented, and Autonomous leadership styles. However, Self-Protective leadership was less likely to be a component of the CLTs of these organizations.

When societies were viewed as valuing Performance Orientation, the CLT endorsed at the societal level was more likely to be composed of Charismatic/Value-Based and Participative leadership styles. We also found that societal Performance Orientation practices were associated with the content of the CLTs. In particular, those societies that were viewed as having Performance Orientation practices were more likely to have Humane-Oriented leadership as a component of their CLT.

By far, there were more significant relationships with Performance Orientation values and the CLTs than there were with Performance Orientation practices at both the organizational and societal levels of analysis. This is an important finding. When individuals think about effective leader behaviors, they are more influenced by the value they place on the desired future than their perception of current realities. The concept of leadership has an idealistic undertone based on the leader's impact on their self-concept and ambitions (Shamir et al., 1993). Our results, therefore, suggest that leaders are seen as the society's instruments for change. They are seen as the embodiment of the ideal state of affairs. Our findings also suggest how big the challenge facing the leaders is. They have to work under conditions and cultural practices that are not very conducive or supportive, but they are assessed to a significant extent on their ability to fulfill the expectations of their followers.

Charismatic/Value-Based leadership has significant associations with Performance Orientation at both organizational and societal levels of analysis. It is the reported most-effective attribute of leaders in societies that value performance. Performance-oriented societies are in pursuit of excellence. They desire innovation, challenge, and ambition. Their reported effective leader behavior is one that is Charismatic/Value-Based: A visionary, inspirational, decisive, and performance-oriented leadership with high integrity and willingness to accept self-sacrifice to achieve their vision. House (1977), Burns (1978), and Bass (1985) have suggested that charismatic leaders tend to articulate ideological goals that are deeply rooted in values and aspirations of the group (Yukl, 1998). They communicate high expectations and express confidence in their subordinates. Because almost all societies in our study scored very high on society Performance Orientation values, it appears that charismatic leadership is a universally endorsed instrument for satisfaction of human ideals.

Participative leadership also was positively associated with Performance Orientation cultural values at both the organizational and societal levels. The existing literature on the benefits of participative leadership is not conclusive: "In summary, after 40 years of research on participation, we are left with the conclusion that participative leadership sometimes results in higher satisfaction, effort, and performance, and at other times it does not" (Yukl, 1998, p. 126).

From our results, it appears that despite the lack of conclusive evidence for its effectiveness, Participative leadership is consistently reported to be effective by organizations and societies reported to value performance excellence highly. Respondents report as effective leaders those who not only provide a vision, but also empower individuals to help achieve it; leaders who are willing to trust others and allow them the opportunity to think and decide for themselves and to influence the leader's decisions (Yukl, 1998).

SUMMARY AND CONCLUSIONS

Performance Orientation is an important cultural dimension that has not been sufficiently examined in past theoretical or empirical research. The few researchers who have discussed it have usually explored it in contrast to other societal values such as ascription (Parsons & Shils, 1951). GLOBE focused on Performance Orientation as a distinct cultural dimension. We defined it as the extent to which a human community encourages and rewards setting challenging goals, innovation, and performance improvement. Its importance is due to its impact on the way the community addresses challenges of external adaptation and internal integration.

Societies whose respondents report strong Performance Orientation tend to have specific distinguishing characteristics. They value education and learning, emphasize results, set high performance targets, value taking initiative, and prefer explicit and direct communications. In contrast, societies whose respondents report low Performance Orientation are reported to value social and family relations, loyalty, tradition, and seniority, and use subtle and indirect language.

Societal culture influences and regulates human behavior in the society. Cultural values and practices help identify socially acceptable and unacceptable behavior. Two specific arenas for the impact of these values are organizational culture and effective leadership attributes. Organizations are a micro version of the society in which they operate. They are populated by individuals who have grown up in the host culture, and their success in external adaptation and internal integration depends on their ability to assimilate their broader environment. In this chapter we have demonstrated that organizations are reported to reflect the culture (practices and values) in the society in which they are embedded.

Not only are organizations reflective of societal values and practices, societal cultures also influence the nature of leadership. Leaders have to deal with followers who are part of the broader societal and the narrower organizational cultures. The followers' criteria for assessing their leaders' performance are in all likelihood influenced by their societal and organizational practices. Therefore, although there may be other mediating variables, we hypothesized that Performance Orientation, as a specific dimension of societal culture, has an impact on organizational practices and values and the society's effective leadership attributes. We found this to be true.

At the organizational level, Performance Orientation relates to the extent to which the organization is focused on ambitious and challenging goals and results and is driven by competition and winning through innovation and performance improvement. At the leadership level, Performance Orientation reflects the leader's excellence orientation and constant pursuit of improvement. It relates to the extent to which leaders set ambitious goals, communicate high expectations for their subordinates, build their subordinates' self-confidence, and intellectually challenge them. GLOBE's conceptualization of performance oriented leadership is different from the traditional taxonomy of task orientation versus consideration. However, it is related to leadership theories that stress goal setting and performance improvement such as those found in the more recent theories of charismatic and transformational leadership.

The chapter examined the historical and religious roots of the concept of performance orientation. Although the most well-known writing on the topic is Weber's (1904/1930, 1904/1998) analysis of the evolution of the Protestant ethic and its distinction from Catholicism, others have shown that the Protestant religion is not the only one that encourages performance orientation. Various authors seem to point to the conclusion that several religious schools in different parts of the world have emphasized the importance of hard work and achievement. Some have even viewed it as the path to salvation.

Over time, religious practices have led parents in many communities to instill high standards of performance, a high level of work ethic, strong self-confidence and self-reliance, and a strong desire for improvement in their children. Families have been a fertile ground for socializing children in the society's values and practices.

GLOBE's measures of the construct at the societal and organizational levels are different from the existing scales in the literature. They do not compare the extent to which a society values performance as against other variables such as family connections. Rather, they directly assess the extent to which a community is reported to encourage and reward setting challenging goals, innovation, and performance improvement. Not surprisingly, we did not find strong relations between GLOBE's measures and the other measures of performance orientation.

Our results show that reports of societal values of Performance Orientation are only weakly related to reports of societal practices. For the most part, regardless of the extent of their current practices, respondents in all societies studied report a desire for high standards of performance. At the same time, we showed that reports of societal values have little relation with other available data on societies. There was little connection to the societies' economic and social health. Societies in which Performance Orientation is reported to be highly valued do not necessarily enjoy a greater economic prosperity, or a public attitude or government sector that encourages more competitiveness. They also do not enjoy a higher level of societal, human, or psychological health, and their life expectancy is not any higher.

On the other hand, reported societal Performance Orientation practices are highly correlated with important measures of economic health and tend to enjoy higher levels of economic prosperity. They are supported by a public attitude that encourages competitiveness, and a public sector that facilitates prosperity. They are also more competitive in global markets. However, we also showed that strong Performance Orientation practices are not associated with better human or psychological health, higher life expectancy, or higher ratings on the United Nations Human Development Index.

Geography was shown to have a particularly strong impact on the society's level of reported Performance Orientation practices, but a weaker effect on values. Physical proximity seems to facilitate transmission and communication of practices and values. The only exception is the Anglo cluster, which, despite geographic dispersion, shows strong cultural similarity, probably due to the countries' colonial heritage.

Our findings also showed that Performance Orientation as a leadership attribute is viewed very positively. Its average score was 6.00 where the maximum scale score was 7. There seems to be a universal demand for leaders who set high standards and encourage performance. Even though there were significant differences among geographic regions as to the importance of Performance Orientation to effective leadership, the range of scores was 5.48 to 6.33, indicating a strong desire for this attribute in all regions.

The GLOBE model postulates that societal and organizational cultures have an impact on the content of the society's culturally endorsed leadership theories (CLTs). Our HLM analyses confirmed this. Two specific CLTs received particularly strong endorsement at both organizational and societal levels: Charismatic/Value-Based leadership and Participative leadership. Societies and organizations that value Performance Orientation seem to look to charismatic leaders who paint a picture of an ambitious and enticing future, but leave it to the people to build it.

ENDNOTES

1. Our response bias correction procedure identified response bias in some countries for this scale. We recomputed the predicted response bias corrected scale score for each country:

Practices: France, 4.43 (moves from band B to band A); Indonesia, 4.14 (moves from band A to band B); Morocco, 4.31 (moves from band B to band A); Philippines, 4.21 (moves from band A to band B); Qatar, 3.76 (moves from band C to band B); and Taiwan, 4.27 (moves from band A to band B).

Values: Ecuador, 5.95 (moves from band A to band B); France, 6.10 (moves from band C to band B); Morocco, 6.12 (moves from band C to band B); and New Zealand, 6.24 (moves from band B to band A).

For a complete discussion of this procedure and all response bias corrected scores, see Appendix C.

2. As reported in Chapter 20 by Brodbeck, Hanges, Dickson, Gupta, and Dorfman, we found that all the cultural dimensions of organizational cultural values and practices significantly differed across societies. Although important, this prior analysis did not identify the particular aspect of societal differences that was related to organizational culture. In the present chapter, we found that societal and organizational Performance Orientation practices were significantly related (R^2 Total = 3.5%, R^2 Societal = 39.2%, $p < .01$). We found even stronger results for societal and organizational Performance Orientation values (R^2 Total = 11.2%, R^2 Societal = 57.5%, $p < .01$). As discussed in Chapter 11 by Hanges, Dickson, and Sipe, the R^2 Total considers all levels of analysis (i.e., individual, organizational, and societal) whereas the R^2 Societal isolates the societal level portion of the dependent variable and indicates the percentage of variance accounted for by the predictor at only this level. Whereas we have primarily taken the conservative approach and reported the R^2 Total in GLOBE, several scholars suggest that R^2 Societal provides a more accurate description of aggregated relationships. For further discussion, see the paper by Lance and James (1999).

3. Results between the single HLM and multiple HLM tests will likely differ somewhat. The differences between the results of the multiple HLMs and single HLMs are conceptually similar to the differences between a multiple regression analysis and a correlation coefficient. Table 21.10 in Chapter 21 by Dorfman et al. presents both single and multiple HLM coefficients. In addition, the relationships for all culture dimension values are summarized in Chapter 3.

REFERENCES

Bass, B. M. (1985). *Leadership and performance beyond expectations.* New York: Free Press.

Bass, B. M., Burger, P. C., Doktor, R., & Barrett, G. V. (1979). *Assessment of managers.* New York: Free Press.

Bigoness, W. J., & Hofstede, G. (1989, August). *A cross-national study of managerial Values: A quasi-longitudinal investigation.* Paper presented at the annual meeting of the Academy of management, Washington, D.C.

Blake, R. R., & Mouton, J. S. (1964). *The managerial grid.* Houston, TX: Gulf Publishing.

Bulatao, R. A. (1979). *On the nature of the transition in the value of children* (Report No. 60-AP). Honolulu: East-West Center Publishers.

Burns, J. M. (1978). *Leadership*. New York: Harper & Row.

Campbell, J. (1988). *The power of myth*. New York: Doubleday.

Darroch, R. K., Meyer, P. A., & Singarimbun, M. (1981). *Two are not enough: The value of children to Javanese and Sudanese parents* (Report No. 60-D). Honolulu: East-West Center Publishers.

Deutsch, M. (1975). Equity, equality, and need: What determines which values will be used as the basis of distributive justice? *Journal of Social Issues, 31,* 137–149.

Duda, J. L. (1980). Achievement motivation among Navajo students: A conceptual analysis with preliminary data. *Ethos, 8,* 316–337.

Duda, J. L. (1981). *A cross-cultural analysis of achievement motivation in sports and the classroom.* Unpublished doctoral dissertation, University of Illinois at Urbana-Champaign.

Fawcett, J. T. (1983). Perceptions of the value of children: Satisfactions and costs. In R. A. Bulatao, R. D. Lee, P. E. Hollerbach, & J. Bongarrts (Eds.), *Determinants of fertility in developing countries: Vol. I.* Washington, DC: National Assembly Press.

Fisher, B. M., & Edwards, J. E. (1988). Consideration, initiating structure and their relationships with leader effectiveness: A meta-analysis. In *Best paper proceedings* (pp. 201–205). Anaheim, CA: Academy of Management.

Fleishman, E. A. (1953). The description of supervisory behavior. *Personnel Psychology, 37,* 1–6.

Furnham, A. (1990). *The Protestant work ethic.* London: Routledge.

Furnham, A., Kirkcaldy, B., & Lynn, R. (1996). National attitudes to competitiveness, money and work amongst young people: First, second, and third world differences. *Human Relations, 47,* 119–132.

Fyans, Jr., L. J., Salili, F., Maehr, M. L., & Desai, K. A. (1983). A cross-cultural exploration into the meaning of achievement. *Journal Of Personality and Social Psychology, 44*(5), 1000–1013.

Haire, M., Ghiselli, E. E., & Porter, L. W. (1966). *Managerial thinking: An international study.* New York: John Wiley.

Hall, E. T. (1959). *The silent language.* New York: Anchor.

Hall, E. T. (1960, May/June). The silent language of overseas business. *Harvard Business Review, 38*(3), 87–95.

Halpin, A. W., & Winer, B. J. (1957). A factorial study of the leader behavior descriptions. In R. M. Stogdill & A. E. Coons (Eds.), *Leader behavior: Its description and measurement* (pp. 39–51). Columbus, OH: Ohio State University, Bureau of Business Research.

Hempill, J. K., & Coons, A. E. (1957). Development of the leader behavior description questionnaire. In R. M. Stogdill & A. E. Coons (Eds.), *Leader behavior: Its description and measurement* (pp. 6–33). Columbus, OH: Bureau of Business Research, Ohio State University.

Hirsch, J. (1991). From the Fordist to the post Fordist state. In B. Jessop (Ed.), *The politics of flexibility: Restructuring state and industry in Britain, Germany, and Scandinavia* (pp. 67–81). Hants, UK: Edward Elgar.

Hoffman, L. W. (1987). The value of children to parents and child rearing patterns. In C. Kagitçibasi (Ed.), *Growth and progress in cross-cultural psychology* (pp. 159–170). Lisse: Swetz and Zeitlinger.

Hofstede, G. (1980). *Culture's consequences: International differences in work-related values.* Beverly Hills, CA: Sage.

Hofstede, G. (1998). *Masculinity and femininity: The taboo dimensions of national cultures.* Thousand Oaks, CA: Sage.

Hofstede, G. (2001). *Culture's consequences: Comparing values, behaviors, institutions, and organizations across nations* (2nd ed.). Thousand Oaks, CA: Sage.

Hofstede, G., & Bond, M. H. (1988). The Confucian connection: From cultural roots to economic growth. *Organization Dynamics,* 5–21.

Hofstede, G., Neuijen, B., Ohayv, D. D., & Sanders, G. (1990). Measuring organizational cultures: A qualitative and quantitative study across twenty studies. *Administrative Science Quarterly, 35,* 286–316.

House, R. J. (1977). A 1976 theory of charismatic leadership. In J. G. Hunt & L. L. Larson (Eds.), *Leadership: The cutting edge* (pp. 189–209). Carbondale: Southern Illinois University Press.

House, R. J., & Aditya, R. N. (1997). The social scientific study of leadership: Quo vadis? *Journal of Management, 23*(3), 409–473.

Huntington, E. (1924). *The character of races.* New York: Scribners.

Inglehart, R., Basanez, M., & Moreno, A. (1998). *Human values and beliefs: A cross-cultural sourcebook.* Ann Arbor: University of Michigan Press.

James, K., Chen, D. L., & Cropanzano, R. (1996). Culture and leadership among Taiwanese and U.S. workers: Do values influence leadership ideals? In M. N. Ruderman, M. W. Hughes-James, & S. E. Jackson (Eds.), *Selected research on work team diversity* (pp. 33–52). Greensboro, NC: Center for Creative Leadership.

Javidan, M., & Carl, D. (1998). *Motivational consequences of charismatic leadership: An empirical investigation.* Paper presented at the meeting of the Decision Sciences Institute, Las Vegas, NV.

Jessop, B. (1991). The welfare state in the transition from Fordism to post-Fordism. In B. Jessop (Ed.), *The politics of flexibility: Restructuring state and industry in Britain, Germany, and Scandinavia* (pp. 82–105). Hants, UK: Edward Elgar.

Kagitçibasi, C. (1982). *The changing value of children in Turkey* (Report No. 60-E). Honolulu: East-West Center Publishers.

Kahn, H. (1979). *World economic development: 1979 and beyond.* Boulder, CO: Groom Helm.

Kanungo, R. N., & Aycan, Z. (1997, June). *Organizational culture and human resource practices from a cross-cultural perspective.* Paper presented at the Canadian Psychological Association Annual Conference, Toronto.

Katz, D., & Kahn, R. L. (1952). Some recent findings in human relations research. In E. Swanson, T. Newcomb, & E. Hartley (Eds.), *Readings in social psychology.* New York: Holt, Rinehart & Winston.

Katz, D., Maccoby, N., & Morse, N. C. (1950). *Productivity, supervision, and morale in an office situation.* Ann Arbor: University of Michigan, Institute for Social Research.

Kluckhohn, F. R., & Strodtbeck, F. L. (1961). *Variations in value orientations.* New York: Harper & Row.

Kreder, M., & Zeller, M. (1988). Control in German and U.S. companies. *Management International Review, 28*(3), 58–66.

Lance, C. E., & James, L. R. (1999). A proportional variance accounted for some cross-level and person-situation research designs. *Organizational Research Methods, 2,* 395–418.

Laurant, A. (1986). The cross-cultural puzzle of global human resource management. *Human Resource Management, 25*(1), 91–102.

Lynn, R. (1991). *The secret of the miracle economy.* London: SAU.

Macpherson, C. B. (1966). *The real world of democracy.* New York: Oxford University Press.

Maehr, M. L. (1974). Culture and achievement motivation. *American Psychologist, 29,* 887–896.

McClelland, D. C. (1955). Some social consequences of achievement motivation. In M. R. Jones (Ed.), *Nebraska Symposium on Motivation: 1955* (pp. 41–64). Lincoln: University of Nebraska Press.

McClelland, D. C. (1958). Methods of measuring human motivation. In J. W. Atkinson (Ed.), *Motives in fantasy, action, and society* (pp. 7–42). Princeton, NJ: Van Nostrand.

McClelland, D. C. (1961). *The achieving society.* Princeton, NJ: Van Nostrand.

McClelland, D. C. (1987). *Human motivation.* Cambridge, UK: Cambridge University Press.

McClelland, D. C., Rindlisbacher, A., & deCharms, R. C. (1955). Religious and other sources of parental attitudes toward independence training. In D. C. McClelland (Ed.), *Studies in motivation* (pp. 389–400) New York: Appleton-Century-Crofts.

Misumi, J., & Peterson, M. F. (1985). The performance-maintenance (PM) theory of leadership: Review of a Japanese research program. *Administrative Science Quarterly, 30,* 198–223.

Omae, K. (1982). *The mind of the strategist: The art of Japanese business.* New York: McGraw-Hill.

Onis, Z. (1995). The limits of neo liberalism: Toward a reformulation of development theory. *Journal of Economic Issues, 29*(1), 97–119.

Osgood, C. E., Miron, M., & May, W. (1975). *Cross-cultural universals of affective meaning.* Urbana: University of Illinois Press.

Parsons, T. (1951). *The social system.* Glencoe, IL: Free Press.

Parsons, T., & Shils, E. A. (1951). *Towards a general theory of action.* Cambridge, MA: Harvard University Press.

Porter, M. (1990, March/April). The competitive advantage of nations. *Harvard Business Review,* 73–93.

Ronen, S., & Shenkar, O. (1985). Clustering countries on attitudinal dimensions: A review and synthesis. *Academy of Management Review,* 10(3), 435–454.

Rosen, B. C. (1959). Race, ethnicity and the achievement syndrome. *American Sociological Review,* 24, 47–60.

Rosen, B. C., & D'Andrade, R. G. (1959). The psychosocial origins of achievement motivation. *Sociometry, 22,* 185–218.

Rostow, W. W. (1952). *The process of economic growth.* New York: Norton.

Rotter, J. B. (1966). Generalized expectations for internal versus external control of reinforcement. *Psychological Monograph, 609,* 1–28.

Shamir, B. (1991). Meaning, self, and motivation in organizations. *Organization Studies, 12,* 405–424.

Shamir, B., House, R. J., & Arthur, M. B. (1993). The motivational effects of charismatic leadership: A self-concept based theory. *Organization Science, 4,* 1–17.

Schein, E. H. (1992). *Organizational culture and leadership* (2nd ed.). San Francisco: Jossey-Bass.

Schneider, S. C., & Barsoux, J. L. (1997). *Managing across cultures,* London: Prentice Hall.

Schriesheim, C. A., House, R. J., & Kerr, S. (1976). Leader initiating structure: A reconciliation of discrepant research results and some empirical tests. *Organizational Behavior and Human Performance, 15,* 297–321.

Schwartz, S. H., & Bilsky, W. (1987). Toward a universal psychological structure of human values. *Journal of Personality and Social Psychology, 53*(3), 550–562.

Schwartz, S. H., & Bilsky, W. (1990). Toward a theory of the universal content and structure of values: Extensions and cross-cultural replications. *Journal of Personality and Social Psychology, 58*(5), 878–891.

Sirota, D., & Greenwood, M. J. (1971). Understanding your overseas work force. *Harvard Business Review, 49*(1), 53–60.

Swanson, G. E. (1967). *Religion and regime.* Ann Arbor: University of Michigan Press.

Trompenaars, F. (1993). *Riding the waves of culture,* London: Nicholas Brealey.

Trompenaars, F., & Hampden-Turner, C. (1998). *Riding the waves of culture* (2nd ed.). New York: McGraw-Hill.

Toynbee, A. J. (1947). *A study of history* (Vols. 1–6, abridged; D. C. Somervell, Ed.). New York: Oxford University Press.

Veroff, J., Atkinson, J. W., Feld, S., & Gurin, G. (1960). The use of thematic apperception to assess motivation in a nationwide interview study. *Psychological Monograph.*

Weber, M. (1930). *The Protestant ethic and the spirit of capitalism* (T. Parsons, Trans.). New York: Scribner. (Original work published 1904)

Weber, M. (1998). *The Protestant ethic and the spirit of capitalism* (2nd ed.). Los Angeles: Roxbury. (Original work published 1904)

Winterbottom, M. R. (1953). *The relation of childhood training in independence to achievement motivation.* Unpublished doctoral dissertation, Ann Arbor, University of Michigan.

Woytinsky, W. S., & Woytinsky, E. S. (1953). *World population and production.* New York: Twentieth Century Fund.

Yukl, G. (1998). *Leadership in organizations.* Upper Saddle River, NJ: Prentice Hall.

13

FUTURE ORIENTATION

NEAL ASHKANASY

VIPIN GUPTA

MELINDA S. MAYFIELD

EDWIN TREVOR-ROBERTS

The concept of future orientation has been widely discussed in the literature, and has been operationalized and interpreted in a variety of ways (Seijts, 1998). Future orientation has been identified as a dimension of the more general construct, time orientation, that relates to the subjective experience of time (Trommsdorff, 1983). It has been identified consistently as a basic value orientation of all cultures (Kluckhohn & Strodtbeck, 1961). Cultural future orientation is the degree to which a collectivity encourages and rewards future-oriented behaviors such as planning and delaying gratification (House et al., 1999). In this chapter, we first provide a historical and philosophical overview of the future orientation construct, and a review of disciplinary research conducted in the past few decades. We then discuss correlates of the constructs at the societal, organizational, and individual levels of analysis. In the second part of the chapter, we describe results of the GLOBE 62-society study of future orientation. We provide rankings of societies on GLOBE's measures of future orientation, discuss relationships of GLOBE's measures with other measures that exist in the literature, and present some key societal correlates of GLOBE's measures. We also describe GLOBE's measures of future orientation at the organizational level. Lastly, we discuss the relationship of GLOBE's measures of future orientation with reports of effective leadership at different levels of analysis.

HISTORICAL AND PHILOSOPHICAL OVERVIEW

Historical View of Future Orientation

Although the construct of future orientation received growing attention from 20th century scholars, it has been an important characteristic of cultural systems for a long time. In this

AUTHORS' NOTE: The authors would like to acknowledge the contributions to this chapter of Research Assistants Louise Earnshaw and Alison Wallace.

section, we briefly review how the construct was represented in ancient civilizations.

Ancient societies tended to use concepts of time shaped by agriculture, such as "planting time"—when it was time to plant the crop, or "harvesting time"—when it was time to harvest the crop (Malinowski, 1926–1927). Time was generally not used as a force to govern social and personal life. For instance, children were suckled when they cried rather than at a regular time. In the ancient Greek civilization, a *Chronus* concept of time evolved (Leach, 1961). *Chronus* implied a significant event in time and possibly derived from the word *Cronus,* which represented the god of the harvest. Greeks used the concept of *Chronus* as a point of reference to place other less significant events. In modern times, the concept of *Chronus* has been extended beyond its original reference to the harvest time, and is evident in discussions that refer to the birth of the Christ, two World Wars, the end of the Cold War, and the terrorist attack on the United States on September 11, 2001. At the individual level, the *Chronus* concept is reflected in the date of one's birth, graduation, or marriage. In the Roman period, the *week* was used as a measure of time, though it referred not to a quarter of a lunar month, but to the time between food markets (Sorokin & Merton, 1990). Consequently, Roman society had several weeks that did not consist of seven days.

The concept of time appeared to be more sophisticated in Eastern civilizations. Both India and China relied on astrological and astronomical time, which was based on the shifts in seasons, phases of the moon, the position of the sun, the length of shadows, and the direction of winds. In ancient Vedic India, the life of individuals, at least in principle, was governed by the system of *ashrama,* based on different episodes or events in life (Ariarajah, 1986). Individual life was divided into four phases: student, householder, hermitage, and detachment, each of 21 years (25 years according to some accounts). This division was intended to help individuals achieve all the objectives to lead a perfectly satisfied life and to achieve spiritual communion by systematically moving from learning to working phase, then to the servicing and meditation phases. In each phase of life, specific goals were set to be accomplished, though the goals varied by the individual's social class and aspirations and potential. The student phase included childhood (spent with parents) and adolescence (spent with a teacher). As a student, an individual learned the responsibilities of living in a community from a teacher. After the end of 21 years, the individual was ready to leave the school and become a householder by marrying and accomplishing the goal of acquiring material wealth and nurturing progeny, as well as learning to exercise restraint and moderation. The householder life stage was informed by what the student learned during the student phase. During the hermitage phase, the individual began withdrawing from routine social activities, increasingly giving responsibility to the children and offering support and assistances services. Finally, in the detachment phase, the individual was to learn how to relate to the world in a spirit of renunciation, thereby realizing the ultimate goal of spiritual communion.

In ancient China, orientation toward time and future was intertwined with a circular concept of time, which embraced past, present, and future generations and included a belief that the dead can influence succeeding generations (Teather & Chow, 2000). Chinese philosophy viewed times as "either advantageous or disadvantageous" (Yi, 1750/1998). Tools such as *feng shui* were used to identify selectively advantageous times for specified events for a particular individual family or community, or for the nation as a whole. Advantageous times, once gone, were seen as repeating themselves in the future; therefore, patience was deemed an important virtue for success in life. In this sense, the Chinese concept of time appeared as cyclical, with its structure composed of the recurring cycles of the seasons, of the phases of the moon and planets, and the associated rituals in one's life (Hu, 1995). Embedded within this cyclical concept of time, however, was a deeper—transformational—worldview of time (Tu, 1991). The transformational effects of time were seen as an interactive function of several human and nonhuman factors; current human actions were seen to be only one of the factors influencing realization of goals.

A more sophisticated concept of time began emerging in the Western world only around the

17th century when public clocks were put in most cities and market towns of Western Europe. Though in the early years timekeeping was imprecise, the advent of the industrial revolution resulted in a new worldview that "required worker discipline if machine and man were to be integrated" (Thrift, 1990, p. 114). The growth of railroads was a major turning point in forging a discipline for precision time-keeping and for pacing life according to time. Further, concepts of time and future orientation merged, as time became associated with the idea of progress, innovation, and an orientation toward achieving goals (Teather & Chow, 2000). The past, on the other hand, was characterized as "tradition-bound," "backward," and "out of date." The thrust of future orientation was to "save" time, which took the properties of a commodity and was deemed equivalent to money (Becker, 1965).

With the advent of globalization a renewed interest in understanding the concept of time and its relationship with orientation toward the future has emerged. Fundamental to this new perspective was a differentiation between physical, or linear time, and social, or episodic and cyclical time. In terms of social time, several elements with a bearing on future orientation have been identified, such as "enduring" time, which is slow and of long duration, or "erratic" time under situations of uncertainty (Gurvitch, 1964). Gurvitch observed that in ancient Western societies, enduring time guided the life of the peasant classes, and erratic time governed the life of the ruling classes. Similarly, in modern societies, "just-in-time" has become particularly relevant for the stable environments, and "Internet time" for the high velocity environments.

Philosophical View of Future Orientation

The significance of time as a central process in analyzing and understanding aspects of human nature has a long and controversial history among social and physical scientists. In Kant's (1781/1965) philosophy, time conception is an "innate ability" that colors the way people experience the world. Several early philosophers, notably John Stuart Mill (1843/1986), David Hume (1739/1987), and Jeremy

Bentham (1789/1970), observed a tendency of individuals to undervalue future outcomes by spending time on dysfunctional activities such as hedonistic pleasure, and suggested societal mechanisms for restraining individual dysfunctional action. However, hardcore behaviorists, including Watson (1913) and Skinner (1937), rejected inclusion of a subjective concept of time in the scientific study of behavior. They instead focused on the influence of past-learned contingencies on current behavior, and showed disinterest in possible feedback of imagined or expected future environments. On the other hand, the social psychologists, particularly Kurt Lewin (1942), showed their concern about characterizing behavior just in terms of past experiences. They instead suggested classifying time in terms of three categories (past orientation, present orientation, and future orientation), and laid foundations for the subsequent psychological, managerial, and cross-cultural research on future-time orientation.

Fresh philosophical interest in the concept of future orientation as a distinguishing and essential characteristic of cultures has emerged during recent times. For illustrative purposes, one such force is the concept of spiritual orientation, with a thrust on spiritual fulfillment, self-expression, and emotional well-being, which is a key element of postmodern societies (Inglehart, 1997). Spiritual orientation refers to a sense of purpose and being, a sense of future, a sense of a higher power guiding and shaping existence (Cross, 2001). The industrialized, capitalist cultures have tended to be short-term and materialistic, which separated the material and the spiritual sphere without any integration (Hofstede, 2001).

However, the new and emerging service economy is showing a strong concern for virtue, with a pragmatic integration of morals and practice, as evidenced by the downfall of the Enron Corporation, the accounting firm Arthur Andersen, and the WorldCom Corporation. The emphasis is more on long-term orientation, with a greater integration of the material and the spiritual spheres. As opposed to the exclusive materialism of the past, the emphasis is on a more inclusive focus on spiritual fulfillment and self-expression. The thrust of this new viewpoint is that the spirit and soul are not limited by time and space. Spiritual inclusiveness is fueled by many forces including the aging of the baby-boomer generation, which is beginning to contemplate death, increasing fears of job security, and the waning influence of institutions (such as churches and extended families) that once provided spiritual support (Brandt, 1995).

Summary

From historical and present, as well as emerging standpoints, future orientation emerges as a key factor guiding human behavior. Therefore, it is important to explore the concept of future orientation in more detail, and to analyze GLOBE findings related to this concept.

Concept of Future Orientation

Time perspective is a process of differentiating personal and social experiences into temporal frames, thereby giving order, coherence, and meaning to those experiences, events, and objects (Fraisse, 1963; Frank, 1939; Lewin, 1942). There are three broad categories of temporal frames: Past, present and future (Kluckhohn & Strodtbeck, 1961; Lewin, 1942). These temporal frames help in encoding, storing, and recalling not just perceived, but also expected, targeted (goals), contingent, and imagined experiences and scenarios (Keough, Zimbardo, & Boyd, 1999). Some individuals and collectives tend to use specific temporal frames extensively, whereas others use them very sparingly. Thus, cultures become differentiated in their future orientation.

Cultures with low future orientation, or high present orientation, show the capability to enjoy the moment and be spontaneous. They are free of past worries or future anxieties, but at the same time may seek hedonistic pleasures. They may show incapacity or unwillingness to plan a sequence to realize their desired goals, and may not appreciate the warning signals that their current behavior negatively influences realization of their goals in the future (Keough et al., 1999).

In contrast, cultures with high future orientation have a strong capability and willingness to imagine future contingencies, formulate future goal states, and seek to achieve goals and develop

strategies for meeting their future aspirations. However, they may lack a solid appreciation of situational realities because of a neglect of their present personal and social relationships and interactions (Keough et al., 1999). In summary, as a result, future-oriented individuals and cultures have a capacity to enrich their lives and maintain self-control, whereas present-oriented individuals and cultures strive to simplify their lives and rely more on others.

Finally, the concept of past orientation shares considerable similarities with the concept of future orientation because individuals and collectives with high past orientation also show a high capacity and willingness to correct their current behavior. Past-oriented individuals and collectives do so by recalling and showing appreciation for prior learning, memories, obligations, and traditions (Keough et al., 1999). Therefore, they prefer to sustain their favorable past experiences and seek to plan for maintaining the status quo if favorable experiences dominate in their past. Similarly, they may prefer not to repeat their unfavorable past experiences, and thus make all-around efforts to develop and realize a new vision and state of the future, grounded in some ideals of the past, once the sequence of events disjoining the present from the past has transpired. In stable environments, past orientation may result in repetition of past behaviors in the present, as well as in the future, and the schism with the concept of future orientation is empirically easier to identify. More generally, past-oriented individuals and collectives believe that plans should be evaluated in terms of their fit with the customs and traditions of society and that innovation and change are legitimated only according to past experience. By contrast, future-oriented individuals and collectives seek to evaluate plans primarily in terms of anticipated future benefits, going beyond their traditions.

Based on the above, the GLOBE definition of Future Orientation is the extent to which members of a society or an organization believe that their current actions will influence their future, focus on investment in their future, believe that they will have a future that matters, believe in planning for developing their future, and look far into the future for assessing the effects of their current actions.

Next we review the construct of future orientation at three levels of analysis—societal, organizational, and individual—using cross-cultural, managerial, and psychological disciplinary perspectives. Then we will discuss how Future Orientation is measured as part of Project GLOBE.

Societal-Level Future Orientation: The Cross-Cultural Perspective

Several cross-cultural studies have noted the importance of future orientation at the societal level. Here we describe four major cross-cultural studies on future orientation: (a) Kluckhohn and Strodtbeck (1961), (b) Hofstede and Bond (1988), (c) Trompenaars and Hampden-Turner (1998), and (d) Hall (1960). Each of these studies uses a different operationalization of the construct of future orientation, and thus highlight multifaceted dimensions of this construct.

Kluckhohn and Strodtbeck Study: In a pioneering cross-cultural study, Kluckhohn and Strodtbeck (1961) demonstrated that time orientation is an important value orientation that differentiates cultures. In their landmark work, Kluckhohn and Strodtbeck studied five communities in the Southwestern United States: Spanish-American, Mormon, Texan, Zuni, and Rimrock Navaho. They found that the three dimensions generated from time orientation (past-present, past-future, and present-future) were effective in differentiating between the cultures. The past-present dimension divided the five communities into two distinct groups. The first, made up of Navaho and Zuni, had no special preference for past or present orientation; the other (Spanish-American, Texan, and Mormon) strongly favored the present time position over the past. The past-future dimension showed four major divisions. The Zuni (who were moderately inclined toward the past), the Navaho (who were indifferent between the past and future), and the Spanish-Americans (who moderately favored the future) formed three distinct groups. The fourth group contained the Texans and the Mormons, who had a strong preference for the future. Finally, the present-future dimension distinguished the groups only

in the degree of how strongly each prefered the present. The Spanish-Americans strongly favored the present over the future, the Navaho and the Zuni moderately favored the present, and Texans and Mormons were indifferent between the present and the future.

The way societies deal with conceptions of past, present, and future is one of their basic value orientations. Past-oriented societies use the past to anticipate the future; present-oriented societies resolve current problems without regard to long-term implications; and future-oriented societies focus on the long-term implications of past and present actions (Kluckhohn & Strodtbeck, 1961). Bluedorn (2000) describes this as the trichotomy of time (the past, present, and future), but adds that some individuals and societies have difficulty in determining where the boundary of the present exists in relation to the past and the future.

Hofstede and Bond Study: Before describing Hofstede and Bond's study, it would be useful to understand the background for it. During the 1970s and 1980s, scholars became increasingly interested in understanding societal differences in future orientation (Agarwal, 1993; Matthews & Ornauer, 1976). A widespread interest in future orientation emanated from the rise of Japanese competitive dominance in the international markets and the apparent shift in the locus of economic growth and monetary leadership to the Orient. Japanese development was followed by the rapid growth of several East Asian nations, particularly the four dragons—Hong Kong, Singapore, South Korea, and Taiwan. During the 1980s, development extended beyond Japan and the four dragons, to encompass Southeast Asian countries, especially Malaysia, Thailand, and Indonesia. Though ethnically a minority in the community, immigrant Chinese families controlled most of the business and economic operations in these Southeast Asian countries. Scholars identified the material success of overseas Chinese businesses with their reliance on the Confucian ethic. The Confucian ethic was worldly in its prescriptions, focused on the quality of relationships that a person should try to maintain, and the social and civic duties of a person for living a healthy social life and creating a healthy civic society.

In the meantime, opening and liberalization saw China emerging as the fastest growing nation on the international landscape. Scholars postulated that a high savings rate in East Asia and Japan was actually a product of the Confucian ethic, which promoted a long-term orientation.

Hofstede and Bond (1988) developed a measure of Confucian Dynamism, and showed that their measure of Confucian Dynamism was positively correlated with the economic growth rate of nations. Predictably, East Asian and Japanese societies scored high on the Confucian Dynamism Index, whereas Anglo societies scored low. These findings were subsequently replicated by Ralston, Gustafson, Elsass, Cheung, and Terpstra (1992) in a study of practicing managers in the United States, Hong Kong, and the People's Republic of China. In Hofstede and Bond's study some non-Confucian countries, such as Brazil and India, also scored fairly high on the Confucian Dynamism Index.

Hofstede (2001, p. 355) observed that the Confucian Dynamism Index captures only some aspects of the Confucian ethic and excludes others, such as filial piety, and therefore needs to be relabeled. He emphasized that the core feature of the Confucian Dynamism Index is its assessment of a society's persistence with the value of thrift; therefore, in his view, the index was really a measure of long-term orientation, not of Confucian ethic. To support his assertion, Hofstede (2001) reported that the index is positively correlated with the percentage of respondents in a society selecting "thrift" as a quality that children can be encouraged to learn at home ($r = .70$, $p < .01$). On the other hand, the index was negatively correlated with the percentage of respondents rating "leisure time" as important in their life. The data for these two correlations came from the World Values Survey (Inglehart, Basanez, & Moreno, 1998).

However, only 13 nations overlapped between the Confucian Dynamism Index scores sample and the World Values Survey sample; therefore, the correlations are not creditable by themselves. Perhaps, not surprisingly, Hofstede (2001) also found and reported that the Confucian Dynamism Index did not show any correlation with the percentage of students in a society identifying "thrifty" as a real psychological trait of a person ($r = .11$), and was correlated only with the percentage of students identifying "persistence" as a real trait ($r = 0.61$; $p < .05$). Data on the students came from Williams, Satterwhite, and Saiz's (1998) study, and included 12 overlapping nations.

Nevertheless, Franke, Hofstede, and Bond (1991) postulated that although Confucian Dynamism encompasses a wider set of values than future orientation alone, long-term orientation lies at its heart. Hofstede and Bond (1988) reported that Confucian Dynamism explained differences in national economic growth rates between countries, whereas Takyi-Asiedu (1993) emphasized that Confucian Dynamism is linked to entrepreneurship. Hofstede and Bond (1988, p. 16) concluded that Confucian Dynamism is, in essence, a "dynamic, future oriented mentality," as opposed to a static or tradition-oriented mind-set. More recently, Hofstede, Van Deusen, Mueller, Charles, and The Business Goals Network (2002) reported that business tycoons in Anglo, Latin American, and Latin European countries are perceived by MBA students from those nations as focused more on "this year's profits." In contrast, business tycoons in India, China, and Hong Kong tend to put greater priority on "profits ten years from now." The Confucian Dynamism Index showed a multiple correlation of 0.62 with "this year's profits" (negative) and "profits ten years from now" (positive).

On the basis of the available evidence, Hofstede (2001) reinterpreted the meaning of his Confucian Work Dynamic construct and labeled it *Long-Term Orientation*. He reported that the Confucian Dynamism Index is positively correlated with Read's (1993) measure of "marginal propensity to save," defined as the change in real per capita gross domestic saving from 1970 to 1990, in percentages of the sum of the changes in private consumption plus domestic saving over the same period. Therefore, in Hofstede's view, a long-term orientation is critical for a high propensity to save, whereas a short-term orientation results in a propensity to spend and enjoy leisure in the present.

However, although a high rate of savings has indeed been a distinguishing feature of the economic growth model of Confucian societies, it does not imply that the high savings rate in these societies arises from long-term orientation. A high savings rate may, for instance, be accounted for by the comparatively high costs of consumption in most Confucian societies, along with high taxes on consumption and poor availability of social security for the elderly, which forces people to save a higher proportion of their incomes.

Further, although "persistence" and "thrift" positively loaded on the Confucian Dynamism Index, the index also included other items that have little association with the concept of long-term orientation. Other positively loaded items included "ordering relationships by status and observing this order" and "having a sense of shame." In addition, there were four negatively loaded items: "Personal steadiness and stability," "protecting your face," "respect for tradition," and "reciprocation of greetings, favors, and gifts." Is it appropriate to identify "respect for tradition" as inversely related with long-term or future orientation? The answer is not necessarily affirmative. Larwood, Falbe, Kriger, and Meising (1995), in fact, showed that a positive relationship exists between past and future orientation (see also Cottle, 1967; Trompenaars & Hampden-Turner, 1998). Future orientation involves taking a long-term perspective that includes recognition of how history and tradition define opportunities and capabilities for the future. Low future orientation, on the other hand, induces societies to emphasize only their immediate concerns.

In addition, postwar success of Japan and East Asian societies may be an outcome of factors other than a Confucian work ethic. Ouchi (1981), for instance, emphasized the role of historical context in shaping Japanese future orientation. Because little of Japan is suited for agriculture, the planting and harvesting of rice can only be accomplished with the cooperation of 20 or more people. Thus, Ouchi asserted, the Japanese have had to develop the capacity to work together in harmony, and this accounts for the societal value that individual considerations are outweighed by concerns for group welfare. This allowed Japanese organizations to emphasize collective responsibility, lifetime employment, and slow evaluation and promotion processes.

In contrast, the United States is largely arable: A single family can produce enough food to survive. Thus, historically, neighbors were distant, leading Americans to value independence and individuality. As a result, American organizations emphasized short-term employment, rapid evaluation and promotion, and individual responsibility.

Also, some evidence suggests that Confucian societies may not really be especially long-term oriented and that Anglo societies may not really be that much more short-term oriented. The Japanese, for instance, are skeptical of anyone's ability to forecast the future in specific terms and believe that 5 years is too long a time for meaningful plans (Lauenstein, 1985). The Japanese are acutely aware that plans can go awry because of unanticipated events (Lauenstein, 1985). Moreover, they reject the possibility of developing "sustainable" competitive advantage, and believe that any advantage is necessarily "transient."

> Their approach is almost uniformly to identify a promising area in which to invest, to find a way to achieve some temporary advantage on the basis of which to establish themselves in the market, and then to rely on unremitting effort to make further progress. (Lauenstein, 1985, p. 79)

Thus, Confucian Dynamism in Japan reflects a state of open-ended improvisational readiness, as opposed to a positive regard for the future and planning for the future. More generally, the Confucian philosophy holds that what goes up will eventually go down: This encourages people to persist with what is working well until the times are good, and with what is not working well until the times turn around. On the other hand, although Anglo societies may lack Confucian Dynamism, they still demonstrate agility that is oriented toward the future, which is backed by a strong endorsement of visionary leadership (House, Wright, & Aditya, 1997). In Anglo societies, the leadership vision offers not just long-term goals, but also the direction through which such goals may be accomplished.

With the economic meltdown of Japan and several other Confucian societies over the 1990s, the issue of whether Anglo cultures are indeed short-term oriented and Confucian cultures are long-term oriented has been debated widely in the literature (Laverty,

1996). Recent scholarly work (see, for instance, Davis & Steil, 2001) emphasizes that Anglo societies tend to have more efficient markets. Under efficient markets, one does not expect organizations to maximize short-term profits at the cost of long-term benefits. Therefore, it is not appropriate to characterize Anglo societies as short-term. On the other hand, lower efficiency of markets in most Confucian societies makes it difficult to validate the commonly held belief that those societies are more long-term oriented.

Trompenaars and Hampden-Turner Study: More recently, Trompenaars and Hampden-Turner (1998) presented data, based on a questionnaire item from Cottle (1967), to show that long- versus short-term time horizons differentiated among 42 national cultures. *Time horizon* refers to the length of the planning horizon. Although their data showed Confucian cultures to be clustered at the long-term end of the scale and Anglo cultures to be at the short-term end, their findings were quite different from those of Hofstede's (2001). For example, in Trompenaars and Hampden-Turner's study Pakistan was ranked higher than all the Confucian societies except Hong Kong in terms of a long-term time horizon. In Hofstede's (2001) study, Pakistan was ranked the least among 23 societies for which the Confucian Dynamism scores were reported. Trompenaars and Hampden-Turner measured time horizon as an average of the time horizon for past, present, and future. They reported that societies with a higher time horizon for the past also tend to have a higher time horizon for the present and for the future. The concept of time horizon, however, should not be confused with the concept of future orientation, though they appear to be similar on the surface. In many cases, a long-term time horizon may be consistent with a lack of future orientation when the long term is just a ballooning of a fundamentally short-range vision. Das (1987) emphasizes that executives with shorter future orientations often merely extend their short-term visualizations to the longer term instead of actually being able to perceive a distant time horizon.

Another important dimension of time is polychronicity (Bluedorn, 2000). Polychronicity is the propensity of individuals and societies to be involved in many tasks at once (also termed parallel processing) rather than sequentially (sometimes called synchronicity; see Trompenaars & Hampden-Turner, 1998). In sequential cultures, time is seen as either a series of sequential events occurring at regular intervals or as cyclical with repetitive patterns, both of which can be worked out in advance (Trompenaars & Hampden-Turner, 1998). In polychronous cultures, time is seen as requiring several activities to be performed in parallel, which is often more difficult to plan in advance.

Hall's Study: Hall (1960) highlighted how societal orientation toward time influences standards of temporal precision. The concept of time as linear and monochronic creates a sense of urgency because time is seen as a commodity or a resource to be saved, spent, or wasted, as seen in North America and Northern Europe (Hall, 1960). On the other hand, if time is conceived as expansive, ongoing, and unlimited, the sense of urgency is reduced, as is common in Latin America and the Middle East (Hall, 1960). Thus, in Latin America and the Middle East it is generally acceptable to take more time for completing a contract than is scheduled and to arrive several hours late to a scheduled meeting. In North America and Northern Europe one is expected to be on time for meetings and for work. Although the effects of future orientation on the sense of urgency have not been analyzed, Schneider (1989) predicted that more future-oriented societies would view time with greater urgency. This prediction remains to be tested.

Organizational-Level Future Orientation: The Managerial Perspective

Future orientation is the fundamental decision variable for all organizations because it represents the problem of allocation of resources over time, or what is termed the problem of *intertemporal choice* (Laverty, 1996). Organizational managers have to decide, for instance, whether to exploit prior capabilities or explore new product and market opportunities even if they are disruptive to their current performance; whether to invest in incremental learning and improvements or in radical experimentations and innovations;

and whether to train their workforce and preventively maintain their machinery. In all these instances, organizations choose between maximizing their current profits, which may suboptimize future profits, and developing a balance that would enhance overall profitability over both the short and long terms.

Numerous researchers such as Bluedorn (2000), Hofstede (2001), Lim and Seers (1993), Ouchi (1981), Quinn and McGrath (1985), Schriber and Gutek (1987), and Trompenaars and Hampden-Turner (1998) have emphasized the importance of the future orientation construct for organizations. Future orientation in an organizational setting involves preparing the organization to meet future environmental changes (Brommer & De La Porte, 1992) and is, therefore, an essential leadership attribute. Indeed, future orientation is the basis of formal organizational strategy that, by definition, involves the planned future actions of a firm (Trompenaars & Hampden-Turner, 1998).

Schriber and Gutek (1987) posit that the norms of time in organizations affect the scheduling and coordination of people and tasks, how organizations treat stakeholders, and how they view the firm's strategy for the future. Webber (1972), in discussing the relation between the past and future, suggested that the concern of organizational managers with the past should be in the service of a better and more fruitful future. Managers should be concerned about where the organization is going because nothing is more important than the organization's future. In this respect, Das (1986) underlined the importance of future orientation among executives in relation to the strategic planning needed to prepare their organizations for continued growth in complex environments. Moore (1963) emphasized that for predicting the future, organizations need "to make appropriate and timely adaptations to the inevitable" (p. 97).

Long-range planning was introduced in the 1950s as a method for extrapolating an organization's past into the future (Ansoff, 1988). Long-range planning is based on the assumption that the future environment will develop in a logically incremental manner. This planning is uniquely suited for making incremental strategic development explicit, guided, and coordinated among different parts of an organization.

Cultural attitudes toward uncertainty have a significant influence on the organization's future orientation. In societies that find it difficult to deal with uncertainty, organizations tend to focus on short-term, operational plans. Horovitz (1980) found that French firms focus more on shorter-term plans in comparison to British firms, whereas German firms lie in between. Interestingly, France scores higher on Hofstede's uncertainty avoidance index than the British, whereas Germany lies in between. However, Hofstede's measure of uncertainty avoidance lacks face validity and may well be a measure of stress rather than uncertainty avoidance.

The future orientation of organizational managers is also related to their flexibility (Tendam, 1987). Flexibility of managers, in turn, contributes to the organization's flexibility. Tendam suggests that flexibility is the ability of an organization to adapt to changing environments and to pursue new goals. An inflexible organization that is unable to adapt to the changing environment will not be likely to make above-normal profits or even survive. Tendam states that three aspects of an organization's culture determine its flexibility: A strong vitality, a future orientation, and a sense of mission and direction. Thus, a future-oriented organization has the ability to be flexible and respond to today's competitive and high-tech environment. One measure of flexibility or agility is speed. Onken (1999) demonstrated that the constructs of polychronic culture (which connotes a sense of urgency and decisiveness in performing multiple tasks) and speed are correlated in an organizational context ($r = 0.44$, $p < 0.05$). In another study of top management teams, Eisenhardt (1989) also found that simultaneous consideration of multiple alternatives led to faster decisions in a high-velocity environment.

The future orientation of organizations is also associated with better performance. Schriber and Gutek (1987) identified 13 temporal dimensions of organizational culture, including future orientation. Lim and Seers (1993), in using 5 of these dimensions, found that, among others, future orientation was a positive predictor of organizational performance, at least among manufacturing organizations in the southern United States. They concluded that an organization's time norms have an impact on the managerial values that govern work processes and behaviors. Brommer and De La Porte (1992) suggest that a firm's orientation to the future aligns the organization to face an uncertain future environment, thereby enhancing its competitive advantage and performance prospects. On the other hand, Onken (1999) found another dimension of time, polychronicity (the emphasis on parallel processing), had a moderately positive effect on the performance indicators of return on assets and return on sales.

An interesting paradox of the construct of future orientation is that changing the temporal dimension of an organization's culture may be extremely difficult because time orientation is one of culture's most fundamental values, as well as being ingrained at the individual level of analysis (Bluedorn, 2000). This is a significant challenge for leaders who attempt to change an organization's time orientation. Although not impossible, any attempt to change a value or belief is difficult, and the embedded nature of future orientation makes this even more challenging (House et al., 1997; Schein, 1985).

Each societal culture may have its own way to support future orientation in organizations. For instance, studies on India and Southeast and East Asia show a process of strategic planning quite distinct from the rational approach dominant in the West. Haley and Tan (1999) observe that, "Strategic planning in South and Southeast Asia has developed into a process which is ad-hoc and reactive, highly personalized, idiosyncratic to the leader, and which uses relatively limited environmental scanning" (p. 96). The firms following such strategic planning approaches have also been immensely successful; for instance, Singapore International Airlines, which follows a similar approach, is regularly named as the best-run airline in the world.

More generally, Schneider (1989) identified five elements of strategic planning (scanning, selecting, interpreting, validating, and prioritizing) and suggested that each element may vary across organizations. In terms of scanning, organizations may be active or reactive

(Keegan, 1983), focused or broad (Daft & Weick, 1984), narrow or comprehensive (Fredrickson, 1984), and formal or informal (Stubbart, 1982). They may also differ in terms of resources directed at the scanning function and in their ability to absorb what they have scanned (Cohen & Levinthal, 1990).

With regard to selecting, organizations may be guided by rational–objective or subjective–personal sources (Mintzberg, 1975), detailed and well-documented written reports or verbally communicated and personally observed information (Kotter, 1982), industry–academic experts or colleagues–friends (Kobrin, Basek, Blank, & La Palombara, 1980), and quantitative or qualitative approaches (Mintzberg, 1975). When interpreting new information, organizations may frame the selected information in terms of threat or opportunity (Dutton & Jackson, 1987); costs or benefits (Tversky & Kahneman, 1974); and they may try to fit the new information intuitively with a rather philosophical mission or rational–analytically with more concrete objectives.

Validating the relevance of interpreted rules may occur through a variety of systems in different societal and organizational cultures. Some illustrative systems include authoritarianism (as in Southern Asia), religious scriptures (as in the Middle East), bureaucratic procedure (as in Latin Europe), historical precedent (as in Nordic cultures), political coalitions (as in Germanic cultures), achievement goals (as in Anglo cultures), and consensus (as in Confucian cultures). Thus, in Japan (a Confucian society) extensive face-to-face interaction is encouraged and multiple perspectives are sought (Yoshino, 1976). The main goal is to develop a peripheral vision to discern subtle changes and to gather 75% of strategic information through surveillance as opposed to search processes (Keegan, 1983). In the United States (an Anglo society) the focus is on specialized task-related knowledge (Kagono, Nonaka, Sakakibara, & Okumura, 1985). In Sweden (a Nordic society) informal personal views allow confirmation of historical precedents and social relevance (Hedlund & Aman, 1984). Finally, in France (a Latin European society) theoretical discussion of bureaucratic rules guides the plans of the organization (Crozier, 1964).

Similarly, prioritizing planning issues also varies as a function of organizational contingencies and perceptions related to strategic significance, urgency, and probability of success. A strategically critical issue may be prioritized at the top, whereas an uncertain issue may warrant breaking up into smaller steps and putting commitment on hold until further information is available (Schneider, 1989).

The relationship of future orientation to different elements of strategic planning at the organizational level remains to be investigated.

Individual-Level Future Orientation: The Psychological Perspective

Early psychologists (Lewin, 1926; Piaget, 1952) suggested that an extended future time perspective was an important component of "normal" cognitive development of individuals and that its presence would lead to adaptive personality functioning. These psychologists proposed a prescriptive view of future time orientation, emphasizing the factors that would help an individual develop a future time orientation. Numerous scholars have since studied the concept of future orientation (Cottle & Klineberg, 1974; Fraisse, 1963; Hoornaert, 1973; Kastenbaum, 1961, 1964; Nuttin, 1964; Pervin, 1989; Wallace & Rabin, 1960; Zaleski, Chlewinski, & Lens, 1994). Scholars variously define future orientation as a general concern for future events (Kastenbaum, 1961), a general inclination to organize for the future (Wallace, 1956), and a general capacity to anticipate the future (Gjesme, 1983a). Nurmi (1991) suggests that the concept of future orientation also relates to the way that people give meaning to their lives and the environment. Indeed, it is this capacity to reflect continuously on assumptions and expectations about the future that differentiates humans from other life forms (Novaky, Hideg, & Kappeter, 1994).

Some scholars prefer to describe future orientation in terms of a specific context. In specific terms, future orientation refers to representation or conceptualization of a particular life domain, such as professional career or social relations, in terms of time (Peetsma, 1993). On the other hand, a general future orientation is characterized by an *extension* perspective, indicating a representation of events or objects in the more remote and distant, as opposed to in the near, future (see Gjesme, 1975; Winnubst, 1975). An important characteristic of specific future orientation is the value of a certain event, object, or life domain in the future. The relevance expressed by a person with respect to a certain event, object, or life domain in the future defines the motivational role of future orientation (Frank, 1939; Peetsma, 1993).

The concept of future orientation is an integral part of the concept of *attitude* and is interpreted as an attitude toward a specific event, object, or life domain perceived in terms of time (Peetsma, 1993). The concept of future time orientation includes four components: Affective, cognitive, motivational, and investment (Peetsma, 1993; Rosenberg & Hovland, 1960; Seginer & Schlesinger, 1998; Trommsdorff, 1983). The affective component refers to an optimistic or pessimistic view of the future generally, and of specific events, objects, and life domains. The cognitive component refers to knowledge or expectations about the future and of the social realities that may influence the future. The cognitive aspect deals with the psychological experience of time and can be viewed as an individual's ability to perceive the world beyond its present physical state, which, as Toda (1983) argues, is necessary to provide a reliable context for planning one's future behavior. The motivational component relates to the anticipated value a person places on the future outcomes of his or her present behavior, and acts as a motivational force. Finally, the investment component relates to the manifestation of the motivational intentions, in terms of the impulse (onset), intensity (depth), and perseverance (duration) of behaviors toward realizing the desired future state (Peetsma, 1993).

Several scholars have emphasized the facilitative role of future orientation for achievement orientation (Gjesme, 1979, 1981; Raynor, 1969, 1974; Sagie, Elizur, & Yamauchi, 1996). Raynor and Entin (1982) concluded on the basis of a review of several studies that individuals with higher future orientation also tend to have higher levels of achievement motivation. They described the link between future orientation and achievement motivation in terms of the "step-path" theory of action: Future-oriented individuals transform future time into discrete subgoals, and thereby bring the "future into the present." They thus become more persistent over a period of time, resulting in high achievement motivation. Individuals who are more future-oriented are likely to engage in any given activity not just because of the value they place on the end goals of the activity, but also because the immediate outcomes of the activity are expected to be the means to some future goals. If success in present tasks is necessary to continue to future tasks, then more future-oriented people may also strive to work harder on the current tasks (Raynor, 1969, 1974). Not only does future orientation involve seeking opportunities for desired states, but it also involves avoiding undesired states (Seginer & Schlesinger, 1998). Future-oriented people engage in more planning and are more cautious in initiating new tasks, as they seek stronger and positive linkages between their current tasks and desired states over a distant future. On the other hand, less future-oriented individuals lack impulse control (Klineberg, 1968) and the ability to make appropriate linkages between present actions and future outcomes, resulting in low achievement motivation. Research also suggests that procrastination—the avoidance of a specific task or work that needs to be accomplished—is related to a tendency to engage in short-term pleasurable activities (Ferrari & Emmons, 1995), and less future-oriented procrastinators find the process of goal setting less satisfying than their future-oriented, non-procrastinating peers (Lasane & Jones, 1999). Thus, less future-oriented individuals tend to demonstrate a "temporal myopia" by neglecting future rewards in favor of present rewards (Lay & Schouwenburg, 1993).

A high future orientation is also associated with perceptions of the future as being open-ended, as opposed to being limited (Lang & Carstensen, 2002). Such perceptions influence the selection of goals by individuals. A perception of the future as open-ended, expansive, and filled with opportunities encourages people to prioritize goals that optimize the future, which often include the acquisition of knowledge, seeking contacts, or even taking some risks that could be useful in the more distant future. Such

a perception of time tends to be particularly prominent among young people and is related to the goals of receiving social acceptance, becoming financially independent, and pursuing career interests (Lang & Carstensen, 2002). On the other hand, a limited perception of the future encourages an emphasis on emotionally meaningful goals, which are associated with achieving immediate benefits (Lang & Carstensen, 2002).

Carstensen (1993) interprets the relationship between future time orientation and goal selection in terms of socioemotional selectivity theory. The research done on this theory suggests that when an individual with limited future time orientation pursues instrumental goals, such as learning new skills from others, he or she is likely to feel impatient, disappointed, or irritated. Similarly, when an individual with an expansive future time orientation is forced by a situation to prioritize emotionally meaningful immediate goals, he or she may be unable to invest in knowledge-enhancing social contacts and information exchanges, thus resulting in a lower quality of relationships and lower psychological health (Lang & Carstensen, 2002).

The influence of societal variables on an individual's future orientation is quite complex. In general, society provides the building blocks on which individuals develop their orientation to the future (Nurmi, 1991). Sundberg, Poole, and Tyler (1983) postulate that the cognitive structure of an individual's future orientation is determined by the internalization of social pressures and common expectations of future events. Trempala and Malmberg (1998) confirm that individuals' future orientation is mediated by their perception of the society in which they live as opposed to societal culture directly affecting their future orientation. Their data suggest that the perceived changes in economic prospects and educational opportunities affect adolescents' orientation to the future, rather than ideological changes in themselves. Culture has a limited direct influence on adolescents' expectations about the future. Thus, it seems that a culture effect is mediated through individual experience. This partially explains why there is such variation in future orientation at the individual level as well as at the societal level.

CORRELATES OF FUTURE ORIENTATION

Correlates of Societal-Level Future Orientation

Time orientation is fundamental to a culture (Bluedorn, 2000), and there are many factors that contribute to the time orientation of a society. These, however, can be broadly grouped into six categories: Attitudes toward socialization, socioeconomic condition, political stability, education, gender roles, and religion.

Socialization: Socialization by national, community, and family institutions plays an important role in future time orientation of the members of a society. Many societies define a "futuristic" image and entrust responsibility for socializing individuals to media and education. For instance, before the break up of the Soviet Union, communist Russia idealized the image of "the new Soviet man" (Horowitz, 1989) representing members who were to create and adapt to a new society. Future orientation was directed toward facilitating the development of traits and behaviors such as compliance, patriotism, and adherence to communist ideology, as well as of interpersonal values such as politeness, self-discipline, and individual modesty (Shouval, Kav Venaki, Bronfenbrenner, Devereux, & Kiely, 1986). A centralized and compulsory curriculum was developed for schools, along with a system of academic training for educators and pedagogic coaching for parents (Horowitz, 1989). However, this future-oriented image was partly discredited after the dissolution of the Soviet Union, and an alternative image of people focused on emotionally meaningful immediate goals was also legitimated.

A different experience characterized the Jews, who historically preserved their tradition for generations and thus evidenced a past orientation. The family life of Ethiopian Jews, for instance, was organized around the extended family in a hierarchical structure, usually headed by an elder male, with defined gender roles (Roer-Strier & Rosenthal, 2001). The socialization goals focused on the community, with an emphasis on an individual's ability to cope with hardship and other stressful events in life. The image of an ideal man in the traditional Jewish society was one of a hardworking person oriented toward showing respect for elders, preserving traditions, and maintaining self-restraint and self-control (Roer-Strier & Rosenthal, 2001). However, after the formation of Israel an alternative image of "New Israelis" evolved, with children expected to grow into adults who are strong, healthy, independent, proud, living in their own land, and adhering to the ideology of fraternity. Toward this end, children were reared separately on *kibbutzim* (collective settlements), learning new values from educated professionals and spending very limited time with their parents to maintain distance from the past orientation (Roer-Strier & Rosenthal, 2001). Over time, as the new values filtered into Israeli society, the rearing role of *kibbutzim* has become less prominent.

Socioeconomic Condition: The level of future orientation of cultures also relates to the socioeconomic situation of the society (Trommsdorff, 1983). For example, for nomadic societies a very short future orientation is quite functional as the critical factors affecting their life, such as food and water, occur in the near future. Long-term expectations for disadvantaged groups are often pessimistic, so it is unhealthy for individuals to dwell on them. In a study of a socially and economically deprived group of Native Americans a more extended future orientation was associated with maladaptive social behavior, whereas a shorter time perspective was related to adaptive behavior (cf. Graves, 1972, cited in Trommsdorff). This finding parallels similar findings by Zaleski et al. (1994), who found that youth in socially deprived situations focus on current survival rather than the future.

Political Stability: The level of political stability of a culture has also been suggested as an influence on the future orientation of collective members (Novaky et al., 1994; Trempala & Malmberg, 1998). Trempala and Malmberg suggest that the way adolescents perceive changes to political stability affects their orientation to the future. For example, members of a politically unstable society with little chance of achieving stability in the near future can only realistically expect to deal with immediate problems and expectancies. Thus, unpredictable and difficult environments in emerging and transitional economies can preclude future-oriented time perspective (Triandis, 1984). Short-term concerns may predominate, and change may be guided primarily by past experiences, hindering attempts toward strategic long-term planning. On the other hand, more predictable environments in industrialized markets support planning (Jaeger & Kanungo, 1990). People in these environments give less regard to past social and organizational traditions and make decisions based on the merits for the future.

Education: Abstract thinking is a necessary condition for an individual to structure the future (Trommsdorff, 1983); therefore, Trommsdorff suggests that educational level may alter perceptions of the future. This is supported by Novaky and colleagues (1994) who, in a study of future orientation in Hungary, found that level of schooling has an impact on proclivity to engage in activities likely to be important for the future. For example, respondents with lower levels of education tended to emphasize work and not to do anything for their future. Respondents with secondary schooling or higher strove to do something for the future and emphasized the importance of both further study and work, as well as the education of their children. Thus, the general level of education in a culture affects the future orientation of collective members.

Gender Roles: Cultural expectations of gender roles influence the future orientation of individuals and this, in turn, affects societal values and expectations (Nurmi, 1991). For example, Sundberg and colleagues (1983) showed that Indian adolescents had greater gender difference in future orientation than their American or Australian peers, and concluded that this was reflected in the way that values related to future orientation are passed on to children.

Religion: The dominant religion in a society also determines the future orientation of societal members (Doob, 1971). We discussed earlier the relationship between Confucianism and future orientation as postulated by Hofstede and Bond (1988). Previously, Weber (1958) identified a similar link between the Protestant religion and a range of wealth-creating behaviors, including frugality and hard work. To Weber, wealth creation in a Protestant society was driven by a calling from God, that inspired people to dream of a prosperous future for themselves and to work hard independently and confidently to realize that dream.

Gaddis (1997) describes how members of the Judeo-Christian and Islamic religions believe in the concept of a sovereign God and humans who are not able to comprehend, let alone influence, the future. Catholic religious beliefs include the view that sacrifice is helpful to salvation, being charitable to others is a virtue, and people should endure the wrongs that have been done against them. The consequences of these beliefs are that Catholics often believe that problems or events are meant to be and cannot be altered (Wing Sue & Sue, 1990). Similarly, Islamic religious beliefs put an emphasis on partnership and mutual help, as opposed to planning for the future. For instance, Islamic banking, based on the Koran (the Islamic holy book) forbids *riba*—the charging of interest. It rejects time value for money, and instead upholds the concept of *halal*—or the purity in which investors derive their income from profits on investments in which they participate and share the risks with the borrowers. Currently, due to a limited development of Islamic banking products, nearly 80% of Islamic funds are invested in short-term commodity trades, whereas a Western bank brings together a buyer and a seller of commodities at a predetermined markup (Barakat & Sarver, 1997).

However, religion may not constrain the development of future orientation and, similarly, lack of future orientation may emerge across all religions. Cahill (1998) ascribes the development of future orientation in several societies following a Judeo-Christian tradition to a change in philosophy from a cyclical view to a linear view of the cosmos that facilitates and accepts continuous change. Similarly, although Weber's analysis ascribes a future-oriented characteristic to Protestant cultures of the 19th and early 20th centuries, most postwar discourse has attributed a shorter-term orientation to many Protestant societies focused on consumption (Hofstede, 2001).

Further, religion may have a complex relationship with future orientation. For instance, time plays a fundamentally important role in Hinduism and Buddhism (Agarwal, 1993). The principles of Hinduism and Buddhism do not encourage hard work focused exclusively on the pursuit of material wealth because these societies judge individual worth less by material achievement than by spiritual orientation, accomplishments, and realizations (Hofstede, 2001). Consequently, planning gains a paramount significance in the Hinduism and Buddhism context because planning is seen as essential to integrate the dualities of materialism and spiritualism.

Correlates of Organizational-Level Future Orientation

Although societal future orientation is a major factor influencing an organization's future orientation, an additional range of strategic contingencies and forces may have an independent influence. Below, we discuss four such forces: Competitive environment and technology, organizational structure and size, institutional systems, and leadership behavior.

Competitive Environment and Technology: The environment in which an organization competes may influence its future orientation. Judge and Spitzfaden (1995) suggested that in high technology industries the management of strategic time horizons is crucial to a firm's survival. Onken's (1999) questionnaire-based study confirmed that in hypercompetitive industries characterized by high velocity and increased pace of technological advancement speed is critical for the firms just to survive in that industry. Each firm must emphasize speed or be vulnerable to failure. In contrast, in nonhypercompetitive industries, the firms may use speed to realize competitive advantages over their competitors. In such industries, firms that are faster in their decision making tend to perform better than those that are not. For enhancing speed within a given time, D'Aveni (1994) emphasized the importance of firms undertaking multiple strategies and implementing them quickly. Because future orientation can aid in integrating and executing multiple strategies, it may be expected to correlate with survival under hypercompetitive markets and superior performance under more stable and predictable markets.

Organizational Structure and Size: Organizations that have a more future-oriented culture are likely to have an organic structure (Onken, 1999). According to Burns and Stalker (1961), an organic structure is rather flexible and fluid and is capable of dealing with unstable conditions through a network of relationships and a shared perception of goals. In comparison, less future-oriented cultures are likely to have a mechanistic structure that buffers the organizational units from environmental contingencies, changes, and uncertainties, and allows them to perform their routine and specialized tasks. Similarly, organizational ecologists suggest that smaller and entrepreneurial organizations, being more organic, tend to be more future oriented and are guided by a vision of the future. On the other hand, larger organizations rely more on bureaucratic and routine procedures and may be less future oriented. Although larger organizations may have greater resources for planning, they may value exploitation of prior capabilities more than exploring new opportunities for betterment of the future (Hannan & Freeman, 1984).

Institutional Systems: Several elements of national institutions have been identified to contribute to, or inhibit, the development of organizational future orientation. Some notable elements are highlighted below:

A. *Planning and Control Tools:* Many firms evaluate projects involving capital investments, and research and development, using discount techniques such as net present value (future profits discounted by the expected minimum rate of return). The formal discount techniques are based on measurable benefits and ignore intangible benefits such as learning and reputation. Therefore, organizations that use such techniques are likely to become more biased toward applied research and against long-term investments (Hayes & Abernathy, 1980).

B. *Multidivisional Structure:* As organizations grow and diversify, many of them adopt a multidivisional form (M-form) of organizational structure (Chandler, 1962). The M-form helps corporate headquarters evaluate the performance of divisions. However, because divisional activities are difficult to compare and because the top managers lack specialized knowledge about the divisional activities, the headquarters are forced to rely primarily on quarterly accounting reports for information on divisional performance. Divisional managers, therefore, have fewer incentives to make long-term investments because such efforts are not reflected in the accounting reports and are therefore not rewarded (Loescher, 1984).

C. *Managerial Mobility:* Many institutional systems encourage managers to make investments that offer rather quick paybacks, resulting in a less future-oriented organizational culture. A system characterized by a high level of managerial mobility allows the managers to exit the firm before the final success of the project is known and thus benefit from a reputation associated with the temporary success of the projects they initiated (Rumelt, 1987).

D. *Institutional Investors:* Institutional investors, such as pensions and mutual funds, and professional investment managers may discourage organizational future orientation (Johnson & Kaplan, 1987). Organizations focused on future returns that are difficult to quantify and validate may experience decreases in current profits and be unable to pay short-term dividends. Professional investment managers and institutional investors dislike such stocks, and so the futuristic organizations whose stocks are dominantly held by such investors may suffer substantial declines in their stock values. Lack of substantive knowledge about the organization's view of future returns further discourages institutional and professional investment managers from investing in the companies focused on novel futuristic projects. Consequently, institutional investors may focus more on the short-term profits and induce the organizations to have limited future orientation (Johnson & Kaplan, 1987).

E. *Patient Capital:* The nature of the relationships between capital markets and the organizations may also influence organizational future orientation. According to Porter (1992), organizations tend to become short-term oriented if the "funds supplied by external capital providers move rapidly from company to company usually based on perceptions of opportunities for near-term appreciation" (p. 69). Such "impatient" capital results in a breakdown in the relationship between the investors and the organizations, thus adding to the cost of capital of the organization and making long-term investments less attractive. In contrast, if the capital is "patient" and "dedicated," the owners gain better appreciation of the firm's capabilities and long-term prospects and organizational future orientation is promoted (Porter, 1992).

F. *Intellectual Property Rights:* Institutions that have effective systems for protecting and enforcing intellectual property rights strongly motivate the members of their organizations to invest in research and developmental projects that can be patented, copyrighted, or trademarked. On the other hand, weak systems for protecting intellectual property rights discourage future-oriented investments (North, 1990).

Leadership Behavior: In addition to the competitive, structural, and institutional factors, leadership also plays an important role in organizational future orientation. An important function of leadership is envisioning the future, providing long-term direction, and articulating it to followers (Bryman, 1996; Kouzes & Posner, 1996; Yukl, 1998). Thoms and Greenberger (1995) suggest that the ability to create a vision is partially dependent on the future-time perspective of the leader: A leader who is focused on future orientation is already interested in directing energy toward the future. Such proactive thinking about the future increases in line with the leader's hierarchical level and amount of responsibility. The future-oriented concept of *vision* is particularly associated with charismatic leadership (Bass, 1998). Bass notes that the key characteristic of charismatic leadership is the ability to develop a vision for the future and to communicate the vision to followers.

Correlates of Individual-Level Future Orientation

In the field of psychology, hundreds of articles have been published over the past three decades examining the correlates of future orientation. The correlates of individual-level future orientation may be classified into two types: general (Gjesme, 1983b) and contextual (Oner, 2000). The general correlates of future orientation focus on the adaptive and motivational effects of future orientation. The contextual correlates of future orientation focus on the role of individual interpretations, culture, and situational factors (Oner, 2000; Trommsdorff, 1983). The study of contextual correlates is guided by a view that people everywhere are oriented toward the past, the present, and the future. Yet there are differences in the meaning, manifestation, and value placed on these three orientations, specifically on future orientation, that can be better appreciated by referring to the specific context of people's behaviors (Sundberg et al., 1983). Individual future orientation is not simply a reflection of societal future orientation, but is guided by an individual's interpretation of the cultural future orientation.

General Correlates

Upbringing: Upbringing is a key factor influencing the capacity to be coherent and to organize events in anticipation of the future (Lomranz, Shmotkin, & Katznelson, 1983). Nurmi (1991) has noted that most of the development of individual future orientation occurs in family settings during adolescence, although Benson (1994) shows that some future-oriented processes and behaviors occur in infants as young as 9 months. Sundberg and colleagues (1983) found that in Anglo-American cultures adolescents focused on their personal happiness, future family, and leisure activities, whereas adolescents from more traditional societies expressed greater interest in their parent's family, the health of others, and societal topics

in general. Adolescents' interests and attitudes toward various life domains differ among societies with different future orientations, and this is ultimately reflected in the values and practices they adopt as adults.

Age: An individual's future orientation is related to his or her perceptions of remaining time to live, which is generally a function of the individual's age. According to Carstensen's (1993) socioemotional selectivity theory, an individual's perceptions of future orientation influence his or her priority of specific goal contents. In later adulthood, personal networks intended to support improved social functioning tend to reduce in size. Older people seek to maintain emotionally close social partners while increasingly excluding more peripheral social partners (Lang & Carstensen, 1994). Age differences in goal selection are related to an individual's perception of future time. If younger people perceive their time to be limited, such as by imagining a geographical move, they also prefer familiar social partners. On the other hand, if older people perceive their time to be expansive, such as by imagining advanced medical care, they tend to seek new relationships (Fung, Carstensen, & Lutz, 1999).

Deprivation: Scholars have suggested that deprivation of various types, such as socioeconomic comforts and positive experiences, may mitigate the development of an individual's future-time perspective (Agarwal, Tripathi, & Srivastava, 1983). Individuals socialized in lower socioeconomic classes may consequently have a lower future orientation, whereas those socialized in higher socioeconomic classes are likely to have a higher future orientation.

Several studies in the United States (Mehta, Rohila, Sundberg, & Tyler, 1972; Nurmi, 1987; O'Rand & Ellis, 1974; Trommsdorff & Lamm, 1975) have shown that adolescents with a relatively high socioeconomic status extend their horizons farther into the future compared with young people from a low socioeconomic background. Adolescents with a high socioeconomic status tend to plan their future more than youths with a relatively low socioeconomic position (e.g., Cameron, Desai, Bahador, & Dremel, 1977–1978). Nurmi (1987) found this to be true especially for hopes concerning vocational interests. Boocock (1978) found that American adolescents from high-status homes make major life-course transitions at a later age than their low-status peers. Poole and Cooney (1987) and Trommsdorff, Lamm, and Schmidt (1979) found that future working life is more emphasized in the thinking of lower-class adolescents, whereas middle-class adolescents tend to be more interested in education, career, and leisure activities.

Adaptive Capacity: Several studies on the general correlates of future orientation focus on its adaptive aspects. Extended future orientation helps develop adaptive capacity among individuals by encouraging behaviors such as learning, savings, relationship building, marriage, and childrearing (Alvos, Gregson, & Ross, 1993; Barndt & Johnson, 1955; Davids, Kidder, & Reich, 1962; Klineberg, 1967; Mischel, 1974; Murrell & Mingrone, 1994; Stein, Sarbin, & Kulik, 1968; Teahan, 1958; Volder & Lens, 1982). Optimism is another personal characteristic related to future orientation (Marko & Savickas, 1998). A low orientation toward the future can be disruptive to an individual's optimism about his or her future and adversely influence his or her feelings of control and general mental health (Cohen, 1967; Keough et al., 1999). Thus, individuals with higher future orientation have been found to show a greater delay of gratification (Davids & Falkof, 1975) and a lower psychopathology (Wallace, 1956). For instance, students with a strong future focus are more academically successful and hold fewer irrational beliefs (Blinn & Pike, 1989; Poole & Cooney, 1987). Morris (1992) found that adolescent leaders hold a confident view of the self and also have a propensity to seek long-term rather than short-term goals.

Incentive and Motivating: The concept of time perspective is also interpreted as a motivating factor in human behavior (Frank, 1939). Negative future time perspectives, or low future orientation, are identified as a key source of lack of motivation (Nuttin, 1964). Future orientation gives people the incentive to perform and achieve and to strive for certain goals. Human motivation is one of the most prominent concerns in all social sciences research, because greater motivation is critical to higher performance and other outcomes desired by individuals. Gjesme (1975) showed that individuals who were strongly oriented toward the future were more motivated by a future goal than were individuals less oriented toward the future. Future-oriented individuals modified the psychological distance between present and future by perceiving the future distance in time nearer than individuals low in future orientation. Further, more future-oriented individuals were better influenced by persuasive communications advocating a distant goal, whereas less future-oriented individuals were better influenced by a more immediate goal message (Strathman, Gleicher, Boninger, & Edwards, 1994).

Contextual Correlates

Investment: The concept of motivation manifests itself in specific concrete "investment" behaviors that reflect underlying motivation. More future-oriented individuals tend to generate greater investments. Extensive research has linked the concept of future orientation positively with achievement orientation manifested, for instance, in greater academic success. Students with greater future orientation tend to invest greater effort in their classes, show greater intensity to work in the classroom, and evidence more perseverance in doing their homework (Peetsma, 2000; Roede, 1989).

Delay of Gratification: Delay of gratification is the ability to defer an immediately available reward for the sake of a delayed larger reward (Nadler, 1975). More future-oriented people show a better ability to delay gratification and a stronger sense of self-identity and career orientation. Agarwal and colleagues (1983) show that individuals who are highly future oriented as well as reflective were better able to tolerate delay of gratification. In a study of the predictors of high job turnover, Griffeth and Hom, (1988) found that participants with a lower ability to delay gratification were more prone to terminate employment and were also more likely to have an external locus of control. Individual willingness to delay gratification may be a function of societal cultural influences. Gallimore, Weiss, and Finney's (1974) study asked Hawaiian and Japanese American adolescents to indicate what they would do with a $1,500 windfall. The Hawaiians indicated they were more prone to immediate expenditure than the Japanese Americans, and were more likely to share with family and others. The Japanese Americans, on the other hand, were more prepared to allocate the money to education. However, MacKinnon-Slaney's (1994) study suggests that the support for significant others (such as employers financing the study, partners caring for the family) can nurture the ability to delay gratification and encourage pursuit of higher education among adults, even in societies not acculturated to a future-oriented belief in higher education.

Psychological Health: Numerous studies have investigated and generally confirmed Lewin's (1951) thesis relating future orientation as a characteristic of psychologically well-developed and healthy individuals, and conversely relating lower future orientation with a lower quality of psychological health (Novaky et al., 1994; Sundberg et al., 1983; Zimbardo & Boyd, 1999). Future orientation of individuals has been shown to facilitate performance of health maintenance and illness prevention behaviors. Less future-oriented individuals, on the other hand, show greater tendency to ignore the potential future risks that health-compromising behaviors can bring (Keough et al., 1999). Keough and colleagues demonstrated that greater future orientation is associated with lower use of alcohol, tobacco, and drugs, whereas a lower future orientation is associated with a greater abuse of alcohol, tobacco, and drugs. Similarly, more future-oriented people are more likely to delay their first sexual act and are likely to have fewer sexual partners once they initiate sexual activity, as compared with those with lower future orientation. Consequently, more future orientation is associated with low-HIV risk behavior (Rothspan & Read, 1996).

Societal Health: One of the most important measures of societal health linked to future orientation is the development of an individual's relationships. More future-oriented individuals show a stronger ability and willingness to form and sustain new relationships and thus demonstrate a stronger societal fit. However, future-oriented individuals may also be more sensitive to reflecting on whether the relationships they are forming could be sustained, and thus show dissatisfaction in cultures and situations in which relationships have a low probability of being sustained. For instance, in Turkey, a high concern for future commitment in opposite-sex relationships has been found to negatively influence relationship satisfaction (Oner, 2000). Individuals with greater concern for future commitment are more likely to show emotions such as jealousy and possessiveness and be less satisfied in their relationships (Oner, 2000). Such dissatisfaction effect in individuals concerned with future commitment is associated with low levels of self-esteem (Oner, 2000). Further, because future-oriented individuals seek permanent relationships, they are circumspect in initiating relationships and in their ongoing relationships, yet they may feel inexperienced and lonely and not enjoy the temporary relationships in which they are involved. Some experience with temporary relationships may help individuals with high future orientation to be less cautious about starting new relationships and develop meaningful, steady relationships (Oner, 2000).

SUMMARY OF CONCEPTUAL OVERVIEW

In this overview of the literature on future orientation, we have discussed the construct from three perspectives: (a) cross-cultural (at the societal level), (b) managerial (at the organizational level), and (c) psychological (at the individual level).

At the societal level, research has consistently linked time perceptions and attitudes to important outcomes, including economic success (e.g., Franke et al., 1991; Hofstede, 2001), although the links are often complex and difficult to interpret. Future orientation appears to be developed during childhood and adolescence, but the impact of society, culture, and geographic factors interact to determine adult attitudes. These, in turn, are derived from socioeconomic and political conditions, education, gender roles, and religion. Socioeconomic conditions influence future orientation because under socially and economically disadvantaged conditions, a shorter future orientation may be functional. Political stability ensures that societies, organizations, and leaders can confidently look beyond their immediate future. Level of education affects members' ability to think abstractly, which is necessary for organizations, societies, and leaders to structure the future. Gender roles influence future orientation through families and groups. Spirituality in religion is inherently oriented to the future, so the dominant religion and spirituality might contribute significantly to a culture's future orientation.

The societal effects carry over to organizations and individuals. Although there has been a dearth of research dealing directly with the effect of future orientation on organizational outcomes, findings to date have shown that long-term orientation is associated with a more strategic perspective. Organizations having a long-term orientation have also been shown to be more adaptive and flexible, and thus better able to cope with change in today's turbulent environment. In this case, the future orientation of organizations and their leaders is determined by the nature of the competitive environment and technology, the future orientation of the individuals involved in strategic planning, and the nature of leadership. For instance, industries focused on technologies may encourage members in societies and organizations to be more focused on long-term investments. Industries focused on price-sensitive competition, on the other hand, may precipitate a concern toward immediate survival and short-term profitability. Similarly, the definition of charismatic leadership is based on a concept of vision that implies a long-term view of the world, and substantial evidence shows that such leadership has a positive influence on independent measures of both organizational and work-group performance (Antonakis & House, 2002; Fiol, Harris, & House, 1999).

On the basis of the above analysis, Table 13.1 provides a summary comparison in terms of "typical" strong versus weak cultural future orientation. The extreme cases are presented to help explain the concept, but it should also be clear that cultures do not neatly fit into stereotypes. Although the table shows cultural attributes that tend to cluster together, it does not rule out the fact that not all of these attributes may go together at all times. Thus, societies can be expected to have differing mixes of the extreme cases presented in Table 13.1.

GLOBE MEASURES OF FUTURE ORIENTATION

Project GLOBE uses two constructs to portray a society's level of future orientation: Questionnaire items with an *As Is* response format pertain to respondents' assessment of the extent to which a society actually engages in future orientation practices. We refer to this as Future Orientation *practices*. Questionnaire items with a *Should Be* response format pertain to respondents' assessment of the extent to which a society should engage in future orientation practices; we refer to this as Future Orientation *values*.

Separate questionnaire scales were developed to measure each construct at the societal level and at the organizational level within a society. Therefore, a total of four scales were created to measure each construct of interest—two scales measured practices and two scales measured values. Separate questionnaires were administered to two groups of managers. The first group responded to questions concerning their organizational practices and values. The dimensions are measured as composites of quantitative items asked directly from the participating managers.

Tables 13.2a and 13.2b show sample questionnaire items relating to participants' views on the societal practices and values. Tables 13.3a and 13.3b show sample items measuring the participant's views on the organizational practices and values. The soundness of the psychometric properties of these scales was confirmed across all societies sampled in the GLOBE project.

Table 13.1   Higher Future Orientation Societies Versus Lower Future Orientation Societies

Societies That Score Higher on Future Orientation, Tend to:	*Societies That Score Lower on Future Orientation, Tend to:*
• Achieve economic success	• Have lower levels of economic success
• Have a propensity to save for the future	• Have a propensity to spend now, rather than to save for the future
• Have individuals who are psychologically healthy and socially well adjusted	• Have individuals who are psychologically unhealthy and socially maladjusted
• Have individuals who are more intrinsically motivated	• Have individuals who are less intrinsically motivated
• Have organizations with a longer strategic orientation	• Have organizations with a shorter strategic orientation
• Have flexible and adaptive organizations and managers	• Have inflexible and maladaptive organizations and managers
• View materialistic success and spiritual fulfillment as an integrated whole	• See materialistic success and spiritual fulfillment as dualities, requiring trade-offs
• Value the deferment of gratification, placing a higher priority on long-term success	• Value instant gratification and place higher priorities on immediate rewards
• Emphasize visionary leadership that is capable of seeing patterns in the face of chaos and uncertainty	• Emphasize leadership that focuses on repetition of reproducible and routine sequences

Table 13.2a   Future Orientation: Society Practices (As Is)

1. In this society, the accepted norm is to: (reverse scored)

Plan for the future						Accept the status quo
1	2	3	4	5	6	7

2. In this society, people place more emphasis on:

Solving current problems						Planning for the future
1	2	3	4	5	6	7

Table 13.2b   Future Orientation: Society Values (Should Be)

1. I believe that the accepted norm in this society *should be* to: (reverse scored)

Plan for the future						Accept the status quo
1	2	3	4	5	6	7

2. I believe that people who are successful *should:* (reverse scored)

Plan ahead						Take life events as they occur
1	2	3	4	5	6	7

Table 13.3a   Future Orientation: Organization Practices (As Is)

1. The way to be successful in this organization is to: (reverse scored)

   Plan ahead

   Take events as they occur

   | 1 | 2 | 3 | 4 | 5 | 6 | 7 |

2. In this organization, the accepted norm is to: (reverse scored)

   Plan for the future

   Accept the status quo

   | 1 | 2 | 3 | 4 | 5 | 6 | 7 |

Table 13.3b   Future Orientation: Organization Values (Should Be)

1. In this organization, the accepted norm *should be* to: (reverse scored)

   Plan for the future

   Accept the status quo

   | 1 | 2 | 3 | 4 | 5 | 6 | 7 |

2. In this organization, people *should:*

   Worry about current crises

   Plan for the future

   | 1 | 2 | 3 | 4 | 5 | 6 | 7 |

Table 13.4   Grand Mean for GLOBE Societal Future Orientation

Variable	Mean	Standard Deviation	Minimum	Maximum	Valid N
Future Orientation practices	3.85	0.46	2.88	5.07	61
Future Orientation values	5.48	0.41	4.33	6.20	61

n = 61 cultures

GLOBE FINDINGS ON SOCIETAL FUTURE ORIENTATION

Overall Scores on Future Orientation[1]

Table 13.4 shows the grand means of GLOBE societal practices and societal values scales for Future Orientation across all GLOBE societies. The average of societal Future Orientation practices across 61 societies is 3.85, and the range is 2.88–5.07. The mean value of 3.85 falls just below the midpoint of 4.0 on a scale of 1 to 7. Thus, in general, most societies are reported to have moderate levels of Future Orientation practices. In other words, the sampled societies of the world currently give near equal priorities to the futuristic concerns (by planning and living for the future) and the immediate issues (acting with limited or no planning, accepting the status quo, and solving current problems). The average score for Future Orientation practices is the second lowest,

Table 13.5   Future Orientation: Society Practices*

Band							
A		B		C		D	
Country	*Score*	*Country*	*Score*	*Country*	*Score*	*Country*	*Score*
Singapore	5.07	Sweden	4.39	El Salvador	3.80	Poland	3.11
Switzerland	4.73	Japan	4.29	Qatar	3.78	Argentina	3.08
South Africa[a]	4.64	England	4.28	Zimbabwe	3.77	Russia	2.88
Netherlands	4.61	French-speaking		China	3.75		
Malaysia	4.58	Switzerland	4.27	Turkey	3.74		
Austria	4.46	Germany[c]	4.27	Ecuador	3.74		
Denmark	4.44	Finland	4.24	Portugal	3.71		
Canada[b]	4.44	India	4.19	Iran	3.70		
		Philippines	4.15	Zambia	3.62		
		U.S.	4.15	Bolivia	3.61		
		South Africa[d]	4.13	Costa Rica	3.60		
		Nigeria	4.09	Slovenia	3.59		
		Australia	4.09	Kazakhstan	3.57		
		Hong Kong	4.03	Spain	3.51		
		Ireland	3.98	Namibia	3.49		
		South Korea	3.97	France	3.48		
		Taiwan	3.96	New Zealand	3.47		
		Germany[e]	3.95	Thailand	3.43		
		Mexico	3.87	Georgia	3.41		
		Egypt	3.86	Greece	3.40		
		Indonesia	3.86	Venezuela	3.35		
		Albania	3.86	Colombia	3.27		
		Israel	3.85	Kuwait	3.26		
		Brazil	3.81	Morocco	3.26		
				Italy	3.25		
				Guatemala	3.24		
				Hungary	3.21		

a South Africa (Black Sample)
b Canada (English-speaking)
c Germany (West): Former FRG
d South Africa (White Sample)
e Germany (East): Former GDR

* Higher scores indicate greater future orientation

Our response bias correction procedure identified response bias in some countries for this scale (see endnotes).

among the nine GLOBE practices dimensions of culture, next only to Gender Egalitarianism practices, which has the lowest average score.

The average of societal Future Orientation values, across 61 societies, is substantially higher at 5.48, with a range of 4.33–6.20. In all GLOBE societies, the respondents prefer a more strategic and long-term perspective of their problems and the available opportunities. The mean of 5.48 on Future Orientation values is third highest among the nine GLOBE value dimensions, next to Performance Orientation values (5.94) and In-Group Collectivism values (5.66).

Table 13.5 lists the scores of individual societies on the GLOBE Future Orientation societal practices scale. The scores ranged from 2.88 (Russia) to 5.07 (Singapore) with a standard deviation of 0.46. These findings are consistent with prior research. Comparative international studies, for instance, have shown that journalism in Russia has "lagged behind" that of other nations in the sense that its dominant temporal constructions were less focused on the future throughout the 20th century (Ekecrantz, 2001). Singapore, on the other hand, practices a governance system in which "the government always opts for what works for the country in the longer term rather than for what will please the people in the short term" (*Principles of Governance*, 2001). The decisions and actions are legitimated on the basis of their implications for the society in the long run, free from the vicissitudes of popular opinion (Subramaniam, 2001).

The practices scale results are grouped into four bands. (See Chapter 11 by Hanges, Dickson, and Sipe for a further explanation of the bands.) Each band represents a group of societies that do not differ significantly from one another in terms of Future Orientation practices. Interestingly, contrary to the predictions of Hofstede and Bond (1988), there is no evidence of Confucian societies scoring highest on the Future Orientation practices or Anglo societies scoring the least. Confucian societies are scattered across three of the four bands: A (Singapore), B (Japan), and C (China). Three Anglo societies, on the other hand, are in Bands A (Canada) and B (United States and United Kingdom). Many Eastern Europe and Latin America societies score low on Future Orientation practices, which may partly indicate the turbulent and transitional conditions in those societies during the 1990s. Many Northern European societies, on the other hand, score quite high on future orientation practices, which may partly be attributable to their political stability and socioeconomic status.

Table 13.6 shows the scores of individual societies on the GLOBE Future Orientation society values scale. The scores ranged from 4.33 (Denmark) to 6.20 (Thailand). Surprisingly, most industrialized and higher-income countries have comparatively low scores on Future Orientation values and fall into bands B, C, and D. In contrast, emerging and lower-income societies score high on Future Orientation values and are mostly placed in bands A and B. These findings contradict the popular view in the literature, reviewed earlier, that lower socioeconomic status encourages a focus on immediate concerns for survival, whereas higher socioeconomic status allows savings and investments for the future.

There could be two possible explanations for this surprising finding. First, industrialized and higher-income nations may associate future orientation with capitalistic materialism and value immediate gratification that is made feasible by the focus on accumulating material wealth. On the other hand, emerging and lower-income societies nations may value the need for spiritual strength to look beyond their current material deprivations. Interestingly, Thailand, which scores highest on the Future Orientation values scale, also has a distinctively strong emphasis on Buddhism—a religion known to strongly integrate spiritual and material needs (Swearer, 1997). Buddhism, along with monarchy and nation, defines the very identity of the Thai people and is a core pillar of their society (Eng, 1997).

Second, industrialized and higher-income nations may like to enjoy the present more because they already have accumulated substantial wealth and material resources. The emerging and lower-income nations may see a stronger need for taking a long-term perspective and sacrificing for the future because they must cope with scarce and limited resources.

Comparing Tables 13.5 and 13.6, respondents in all except one society value Future Orientation more than they actually practice it. The sole exception is Denmark, whose aggregated practices rating is 4.44 and values rating is 4.33. Denmark in fact, as noted earlier, has also scored a lower rating for Future Orientation values than any other country in the GLOBE sample. Denmark's low values score for Future Orientation is reflected in the nature of Danish media. Denmark stands apart as the only nation in the world that gives history, with very wide time frames, a prominent position in the media (Ekecrantz, 2001). Danish media regularly contain stories about or references to history, not necessarily as a background for today's events, but as anecdotes that appear to serve little more than entertainment value (Ekecrantz, 2001).

Table 13.6   Future Orientation: Society Values*

Band							
A		*B*		*C*		*D*	
Country	*Score*	*Country*	*Score*	*Country*	*Score*	*Country*	*Score*
Thailand	6.20	Colombia	5.68	Australia	5.15	Denmark	4.33
Namibia	6.12	South Africa[a]	5.66	Austria	5.11		
Zimbabwe	6.07	Bolivia	5.63	Finland	5.07		
Nigeria	6.04	Spain	5.63	Netherlands	5.07		
El Salvador	5.98	India	5.60	England	5.06		
Ecuador	5.94	Georgia	5.55	Kazakhstan	5.05		
Philippines	5.93	New Zealand	5.54	France	4.96		
Qatar	5.92	Singapore	5.51	Sweden	4.89		
Italy	5.91	Hong Kong	5.50	Germany[e]	4.85		
Guatemala	5.91	Russia	5.48	French-speaking			
Zambia	5.90	Portugal	5.43	Switzerland	4.80		
Malaysia	5.89	Slovenia	5.42	Switzerland	4.79		
Mexico	5.86	Albania	5.42	China	4.73		
Morocco	5.85	Canada[b]	5.35				
Iran	5.84	U.S.	5.31				
Turkey	5.83	Japan	5.25				
Egypt	5.80	Israel	5.25				
Venezuela	5.79	Germany[c]	5.23				
Argentina	5.78	Ireland	5.22				
Kuwait	5.74	Poland	5.20				
Indonesia	5.70	Costa Rica	5.20				
Hungary	5.70	Taiwan	5.20				
South Korea	5.69	South Africa[d]	5.20				
Brazil	5.69	Greece	5.19				

a South Africa (White Sample)
b Canada (English-speaking)
c Germany (East): Former GDR
d South Africa (Black Sample)
e Germany (West): Former FRG

* Higher scores indicate greater future orientation

Our response bias correction procedure identified response bias in some countries for this scale (see endnotes).

The Correlation Between Overall Practices and Values Scores

Societal scores on the Future Orientation values scale are negatively correlated ($r = -.41$, $p < .01$, $N = 61$) with the scores on the Future Orientation practices scale. The negative correlations indicate that the lower the practices score, the higher the reported value of Future Orientation. A prototypical example is former East German society, whose reported practices score is 3.95 and values score is 5.20. Conversely, the societies that place a lower value on Future Orientation are likely to report stronger practices of Future Orientation. A prototypical example is Switzerland, whose aggregated reports of Future Orientation practices is 4.73 (band A) and values is 4.79 (band C).

These data suggest that a negative correlation between practices and values of Future Orientation does not reflect a dislike of Future Orientation in the societies with stronger practices of Future Orientation. On the contrary, societies reporting weaker practices of Future Orientation have stronger aspirations for Future Orientation. It may be that societies lacking

Table 13.7a   Descriptive Statistics for GLOBE Industry-Level Societal Future Orientation

Variable	N	Minimum	Maximum	Mean	Standard Deviation
Finance Future Orientation practices	55	2.98	5.07	3.89	0.48
Finance Future Orientation values	55	4.14	6.19	5.50	0.45
Food Future Orientation practices	45	3.11	5.06	3.90	0.47
Food Future Orientation values	45	4.63	6.15	5.46	0.38
Telecom Future Orientation practices	32	2.06	4.67	3.81	0.55
Telecom Future Orientation values	32	4.61	6.63	5.45	0.44

Future Orientation practices suffer most from the uncertainty and unpredictability of not addressing the longer-term fundamental issues. Therefore, such societies are most conscious of the need for moving toward a more strategic and spiritually fulfilling perspective.

Overall Scores and Industry Scores

In each society, GLOBE data were collected from one or more of three industries: food processing, financial services, and telecommunications. Table 13.7a provides the means of societal Future Orientation practices and values for each of the industries across all the sampled societies.

The means of societal Future Orientation practices and values are not significantly different across the three industries ($p > .10$). However, the telecommunications sector has substantially lower minimum (2.06 in Thailand) and lower maximum (4.67 in Switzerland) practices scores than the other two sectors. The telecommunications sector also has a higher standard deviation on the Future Orientation practices scores. Further, the telecommunications sector has substantially higher maximum Future Orientation values scores (6.63 in Thailand), whereas the finance sector has substantially lower minimum Future Orientation values scores (4.14 in Denmark).

In the telecommunications industry, traditional reliance on government control contributed to weaker Future Orientation practices scores in such societies as Thailand. In Thailand, the few private firms that entered the telecom sector have become monopolies in their niches and have just adopted the monopolistic practices of the public sector, with few incentives for efficiency (Blasko, 1998). Because strategic planning is critical to development of technology in the telecom sector, the respondents in the telecom sector, including those from Thailand, place a higher value on Future Orientation.

Table 13.7b shows the correlation between the overall societal Future Orientation practices score for each society and the scores for the participating industries. As seen in this table, all correlations are significant, though correlations involving telecom industry practices of Future Orientation are of smaller size than the correlations between the food and finance sectors.

The Future Orientation values scores are also highly correlated across industries, as shown in Table 13.7c. In terms of values, the telecom industry's pattern is quite similar to the other two industries. Thus, there appears to be more cross-industry convergence in Future Orientation with respect to values than with respect to practices.

The Correlation Between Overall Practices and Value Scores

Industry scores on the Future Orientation values scales show a negative correlation with industry scores on the Future Orientation practices scales, as can be seen in Table 13.7d. The correlation is of moderate size and significance for the finance (-0.33, $p < 0.05$) and food

Table 13.7b   Future Orientation Correlation Matrix: Society Practices

Future Orientation	Food Industry Score	Finance Industry Score	Telecommunication Industry Score
Overall score	.94** $n = 45$	.95** $n = 55$	.75** $n = 32$
Food industry score		.91** $n = 41$	.52** $n = 22$
Finance industry score			.45* $n = 30$

** $p < .01.$ *$p < .05.$

Table 13.7c   Future Orientation Correlation Matrix: Society Values

Future Orientation	Food Industry Score	Finance Industry Score	Telecommunication Industry Score
Overall score	.91** $n = 45$	.95** $n = 55$	.92** $n = 32$
Food industry score		.75** $n = 41$	.81** $n = 22$
Finance industry score			.80** $n = 30$

** $p < .01.$

Table 13.7d   Future Orientation: Industry Correlation Matrix (Society Values and Practices)

Future Orientation	Overall Score Practices	Food Industry Score Practices	Finance Industry Score Practices	Telecommunication Industry Score Practices
Overall score values	−.41* $n = 61$			
Food industry score values		−.39* $n = 45$		
Finance industry score values			−.33* $n = 55$	
Telecommunication industry score values				−.68** $n = 32$

** $p < .01.$ *$p < .05.$

Table 13.8 Correlations of Societal Future Orientation With Other Cultural Dimensions of Society

GLOBE Societal Culture Construct	Correlation With Future Orientation Practices	Correlation With Future Orientation Values
Uncertainty Avoidance practices	.76**	−.57**
Uncertainty Avoidance values	−.53**	.67**
Power Distance practices	−.52**	.60**
Power Distance values	—	—
Institutional Collectivism practices	.46**	−.25*
Institutional Collectivism values	−.30*	.48**
In-group Collectivism practices	−.44**	.62**
In-group Collectivism values	−.42**	.51**
Performance Orientation practices	.63**	—
Performance Orientation values	—	.41**
Gender Egalitarianism practices	—	—
Gender Egalitarianism values	—	−.36**
Assertiveness practices	—	—
Assertiveness values	—	—
Humane Orientation practices	—	.26*
Humane Orientation values	—	—

* Significant at $p < .05$. **Significant at $p < .01$.

(−.39, $p < .05$) sectors, but is quite strong (−.68, $p < .01$) for the telecommunications sector. These findings indicate that the societies in which the telecom industry was traditionally governed by short-term practices, due to such factors as protective government regulation, are now acutely aware of the need to reform and adopt more strategic approaches for infrastructure improvement and development.

The Correlation With Other Globe Society Culture Dimensions

In this section we review the relationships between managerial responses to the GLOBE societal-level Future Orientation practices scale and responses to other scales. The correlations of societal Future Orientation practices and values scores with the other eight dimensions of culture assessed in the GLOBE program are presented in Table 13.8.

Future Orientation Practices and Other GLOBE Dimensions

Managerial responses to the GLOBE questionnaire reveal that Future Orientation practices are positively correlated with the practices of Uncertainty Avoidance, Institutional Collectivism, and Performance Orientation, but are negatively correlated with the practices of Power Distance and In-Group Collectivism. Indeed, several societies with relatively high scores on the GLOBE Future Orientation practices scale are reported to have well-developed collective institutions. Such institutions likely encourage members to consider collective interests in making decisions about how to manage information, technology, and knowledge, and in reducing uncertainty. Such a mind-set allows the members to look far into the future to assess the effects of their current actions because the future uncertainties and risks are lowered. Performance criteria can be specified more clearly and rewards can be given on the basis of these criteria. There is a limited role given to power under these conditions, and the members generally do not rely on families for absorbing uncertainties or meeting unanticipated contingencies. Uncertainties and contingencies, even if they arise, could possibly be met through adaptive, entrepreneurial planning. Denmark and the Netherlands are examples of GLOBE societies that fit the prototype of high practices scores of Future Orientation, Uncertainty Avoidance, Institutional Collectivism, and Performance Orientation, but low practices scores of Power Distance and In-Group Collectivism. Gupta, Macmillan, and Surie (in press) report that in Nordic and Germanic societies, such as the Scandinavian countries and the Netherlands, entrepreneurial leadership tends to be more effective. Entrepreneurial leadership manages change and uncertainty through a discovery driven planning mind-set, through painting a scenario, dismantling power structures, and empowerment of the members for collective gain.

Further, as seen from Table 13.8, Future Orientation practices scores are negatively correlated with the values of Uncertainty Avoidance, Institutional Collectivism, and In-Group Collectivism. In societies with strong future oriented practices, the leaders may have confidence in the abilities of their members and in the collective safety net of their institutions, and may expect their members to be more innovative and tolerant of change. These leaders may also prefer the members to develop their own personal potential, and to have freedom to satisfy their own aspirations, and do not value a strong institutional or in-group collectivism. Japan and South Africa (Black sample) are examples of societies that fit the prototype of low values scores of Uncertainty Avoidance, Institutional Collectivism, and In-Group Collectivism, but high practices scores of Future

Orientation. In Japan, for instance, there has been a strong recognition of the need to develop a more innovative orientation and to overcome the traditional mind-set of imitative learning within groups.

Future Orientation Values and Other GLOBE Dimensions

Table 13.8 also shows that Future Orientation values are positively correlated with the values of Uncertainty Avoidance, Institutional Collectivism, In-Group Collectivism, and Performance Orientation, but are negatively correlated with the values of Gender Egalitarianism. Aspirations for higher future orientation may reflect an understanding that most uncertainties can be managed through techniques such as scenario planning, and their negative effects minimized through lowering of uncertainty via better information, knowledge, and technology. Collective safety nets of the institutions and of the families and relationships may be additional vehicles valued in these societies. However, such societies may also seek a more traditional role for women. Prior research suggests that women may put less effort into advancing professionally because they put lower value on status and salary and more value on their families (Van Vianen & Fischer, 2002). Consequently, women may be expected to provide a family safety net in societies that value future orientation.

Guatemala and Ecuador are societies that fit the prototype of high values scores of Future Orientation, Uncertainty Avoidance, Institutional Collectivism, In-Group Collectivism, and Performance Orientation, but low values scores of Gender Egalitarianism. In general, many Latin American societies identify their female population as a "vulnerable group" with only a limited capacity to engage in future planning. Barrig and Beckman (2001) observe that the convulsive political situations in nations such as Ecuador, coupled with the continuing lack of stable legal systems in nations such as Guatemala, make social participation, especially of women, largely a myth.

In addition, Table 13.8 indicates that Future Orientation values are positively correlated with the practices of Power Distance, In-Group

Table 13.9   Spearman's Rank Correlation Among Different Measures of Future Orientation

	GLOBE Values	*Hofstede (2001)*	*Spector et al. (2001)*	*Matthews & Ornauer (1976)*	*Trompenaars & Hampden-Turner (1998)*
GLOBE Practices	−.40** *n* = 61	.03 *n* = 27	.28 *n* = 14	.55 *n* = 8	.07 *n* = 30
GLOBE Values		−.06 *n* = 27	.25 *n* = 14	−.29 *n* = 8	−.47** *n* = 30
Hofstede (2001)			.40 *n* = 15	.11 *n* = 9	.19 *n* = 24
Spector et al. (2001)				N/A	.17 *n* = 11

** *p* < .01.

Collectivism, and Humane Orientation, but negatively correlated with the practices of Uncertainty Avoidance and Institutional Collectivism. Indeed, societies that value future orientation are often very humane, caring, and generous in their practices, and many maintain strong family bonds. Several of them rely heavily on authoritarian and paternalistic power, with a considerable gulf among different strata of the society and among different members of the family. Thailand and Morocco are illustrative societies in the GLOBE sample that fit the prototype of high values scores of Future Orientation and high practices scores of Power Distance, In-Group Collectivism, and Humane Orientation, but low practices scores of Uncertainty Avoidance and Institutional Collectivism. In these societies, people may aspire toward future orientation to transform the authoritarian, kinship-oriented, and fragmented institutional fabric in their cultures. Morocco, for instance, lies at the outer rim of the Arab world and has traditionally experienced considerable ethnic fragmentation and tension. In recent years, it has made steady progress toward democratization, adopting the principle of ethnic pluralism in governance, although the dominant societal practices remain authoritarian and bureaucratic, as in most other Arab states (Ibrahim, 1998).

COMPARISON OF GLOBE FINDINGS WITH PREVIOUS STUDIES

It is interesting to compare the findings of GLOBE to other cross-cultural studies that have investigated the same or similar variables. Two such studies based on questionnaire data similar to the GLOBE study are those conducted by Hofstede (2001) and by Spector and colleagues (2001). Other studies that have produced comparable data are by Matthews and Ornauer (1976) and Trompenaars and Hampden-Turner (1998). In Table 13.9, we present Spearman's rank correlations between the GLOBE scores and the scores obtained from the earlier studies. Tables 13.10a and 13.10b provide correlations between the GLOBE scores and the scores from two other major cross-cultural studies: Schwartz (1999) and Inglehart and Baker (2000).

The Matthews and Ornauer Study

In a study of attitudes toward the future (presented as "the Year 2000"), Matthews and Ornauer (1976) asked respondents to indicate the extent to which they agreed with the single statement that the future is so uncertain we

Table 13.10a GLOBE Future Orientation and Schwartz's Measures

Schwartz Scales	GLOBE Future Orientation Society Practices	GLOBE Future Orientation Society Values
Autonomy-Embedded	.07	−.50**
Embeddedness	−.08	.50**
Intellectual Autonomy	−.03	−.46**
Affective Autonomy	.13	−.43**

NOTE: We thank Shalom Schwartz and Lilach Sagiv for providing the above correlations.

$N = 48$

** Correlation significant at $p < 0.01$.

Table 13.10b GLOBE Future Orientation and Inglehart's Modernization and Postmodernization Dimensions

Inglehart & Baker	GLOBE Future Orientation Society Practices	GLOBE Future Orientation Society Values
Traditional: Secular authority	.28 $N = 36$	−.70** $N = 36$
Survival: Self-expression values	.61** $N = 37$	−.69** $N = 37$

** Correlation is significant at $p < 0.01$.

can only take one year at a time, with response on an Agree-Neutral-Disagree scale. We have analyzed their results on a 1–3 scale in which 1 = Agree and 3 = Disagree. Matthews and Ornauer surveyed only 11 countries, 8 of which overlap with the GLOBE sample. However, neither the GLOBE Future Orientation practices nor values scale was related to the belief that the future is uncertain ($p > 0.10$). We might speculate that in societies that view the future as amenable to planning, future-oriented practices may be greater. Such societies may also value more spontaneous behaviors, rejecting overanalysis and overplanning, which may preclude the capacity to take advantage of unpredicted trends and events.

The Trompenaars and Hampden-Turner Study

Trompenaars and Hampden-Turner (1998) asked respondents to indicate their past, present, and future horizons by using a 1–7 scale, in which 1 = seconds and 7 = years. They computed a long-term horizon index by averaging the scores for the length of past, present, and future horizons reported in each society. Their data include 30 nations that are common with the GLOBE study. As reported in Table 13.9, their long-term horizon index is significantly and negatively correlated with GLOBE's Future Orientation values scale (rho = − .47, $p < .05$), though the correlation with GLOBE's Future Orientation practices scale is not significant (rho = .07, $p > .10$). Some societies that place a higher value on future orientation may have a short-term horizon. Similarly, some societies that place a lower value on future orientation may have a long-term horizon.

The Hofstede and Spector and Colleagues Studies

Hofstede (2001) reinterpreted the Confucian Dynamism scale discussed earlier in this chapter as a measure of long-term orientation. The original Confucian Dynamism scale was based on Chinese Cultural Connection questionnaire surveys administered in 23 nations (Hofstede & Bond, 1988). Hofstede (2001) added scores for 11 additional nations using data from the European Media and Marketing Survey 1997, which contained four questions from the Confucian Dynamism scale. Of these four questions, only two—"thrift" and "respect for tradition"—were correlated in the expected negative direction ($r = .64$, $p < .01$, $n = 11$), and interpreted by Hofstede (2001) as measures of long-term orientation. These measures are subject to multiple interpretations and lack face validity. Hofstede (2001) also estimated comparable scores for 7 additional nations on the basis of observations and descriptive information. Consequently, in total, comparable GLOBE data are available for a subsample of 27 nations. As shown in Table 13.9, neither GLOBE Future Orientation practices (rho = .03) nor GLOBE Future Orientation values (rho = .06) scales show any relationship with Hofstede's presumed Long Term Orientation scale. Data on the Confucian Dynamism scale were also collected by Spector and colleagues (2001), who also referred to the scale as long-term orientation. The correlation of Spector and colleagues' scores with the GLOBE Future Orientation practices scale (rho = .28, $p > .10$) and GLOBE Future Orientation values scale (rho = .25, $p > .10$) is also small and insignificant. These findings suggest a need for caution in interpreting the Confucian Dynamism scale as a proxy for long-term orientation, and indicate that such interpretation may not be appropriate.

The Schwartz Study

Schwartz (1999) identified three fundamental values distinguishing all cultures: (a) autonomy versus embeddedness, (b) hierarchy versus egalitarianism, and (c) mastery versus harmony. Of these, the first is very pertinent to the cultural concept of Future Orientation.

In embedded cultures people are perceived as entities bounded in the collectivity: They find meaning in life by participating in the group and identifying with its goals. Values of social order, family security, respect for tradition, and obedience are emphasized. On the other hand, in autonomous cultures, individuals are perceived as autonomous, nonbounded entities who find meaning in life through their uniqueness. Two types of autonomy are distinguished in Schwartz's framework. First, intellectual autonomy, in which individuals are encouraged to follow their own ideas and intellectual directions, emphasizes creativity, curiosity, and broadmindedness. Second, affective autonomy, in which people are encouraged to find positive experiences for themselves, with an emphasis on variety, excitement, and pleasure in life.

Cultures embedded in relationships may take a more long-term view of their efforts—relations generally encourage a quid pro quo kind of behavior that is ongoing in nature. On the other hand, autonomous cultures may have a more short-term focus, with more contractual kinds of behavior (see Granovetter, 1985). Indeed, as reported in Table 13.10a, GLOBE's Future Orientation values scale is negatively related to Schwartz's autonomy-embedded scale ($r = .50$, $p < .01$). Further, GLOBE's Future Orientation values correlates negatively with affective and intellectual autonomy ($r = .43$ and $-.46$, $p < .01$) and positively with Schwartz's embeddedness scale ($r = .50$, $p < .01$). However, GLOBE's Future Orientation practices scale is not correlated with any of these measures. Thus, the value of future orientation shares the belief in quid pro quo and long-term interaction inherent in embeddedness, as opposed to contractual transience and spot relationships associated with autonomy.

The Inglehart and Baker Study

Inglehart and Baker (2000, p. 21) identify two dimensions in which cultures become differentiated as a result of the differences in their development. The first, termed *traditional versus secular-rational authority,* is "linked with early industrialization and the rise of the working class" and reflects the process of modernization. The second, termed *survival versus self-expression values,* "reflects the changes linked with the affluent conditions of advanced industrial society and with the rise of the service and knowledge sectors" and captures the dynamics of postmodernization.

A traditional worldview, prominent in preindustrial and premodern societies, reflects an emphasis on obedience to traditional authority, particularly deference to God, that goes with deference to the family and the nation. On the other hand, in a secular worldview prominent in industrial and modern societies, authority is legitimated by rational–legal norms linked with an emphasis on economic accumulation and individual achievement. The survival and self-expression values dimension reflects how unprecedented levels of wealth and the emergence of welfare states in a postindustrial society give rise to a shift from scarcity norms emphasizing hard work and self-denial, to postmodern values emphasizing the quality of life, subjective well-being, and related postmaterialist priorities of self-expression. According to Inglehart and Baker (2000), the societal development process is associated with an increased probability of a shift first from traditional to secular–rational authority, and second, from survival to self-expression values. Consequently, the societies ahead on secular–rational and self-expression dimensions are likely to be more future oriented.

As reported in Table 13.10b, the GLOBE societal Future Orientation practices scale is positively correlated to both the traditional–secular–rational authority scale ($r = .28, p > .10$) and the survival–self-expression scale ($r = .61, p < .01$), though the correlation is significant only with the latter. Societies reported to be future oriented are more likely to encourage individuals to express themselves and to lead a high quality of life. In contrast, the GLOBE societal Future Orientation values scale is negatively and significantly correlated to both the traditional–secular–rational authority scale ($r =- .70, p < .01$) and the survival–self-expression scale ($r = .69, p < .01$). In societies that rely on traditional authority and survival values, the respondents are more likely to endorse the value of future orientation—possibly to seek a higher quality of life.

Summary

The GLOBE study appears to be the first to have clearly identified future orientation as a societal cross-cultural dimension within a comprehensive theoretical framework. As we noted earlier, the Hofstede (2001) scale is really a measure of Confucian Dynamism, and future orientation is only a presumed facet of this measure, while the Trompenaars and Hampden-Turner (1998) scale is a measure of time horizon, as opposed to future-oriented behavior. The correlations with the scales developed by Schwartz (1999) and Inglehart and Baker (2000) to capture the fundamental values and shifts in these values further underline the significance of GLOBE's Future Orientation scale.

ECONOMIC AND SOCIAL CORRELATES OF GLOBE SOCIETAL FUTURE ORIENTATION

In this section, we compare and contrast the GLOBE findings on societal Future Orientation with those of other major cross-cultural and comparative studies focusing on different countries' social and economic performance. As explained in Chapter 7 by Javidan and Hauser, four major ongoing reports provided the relevant data: the IMD's Global Competitiveness Ranking, the World Economic Forum's Competitiveness Ranking, the United Nations Human Development Report, and the World Values Survey. The findings of these studies are grouped into eight categories: economic health, human condition, scientific advancement, family and friends, political ideology, spiritual attitudes, gender attitudes, and national savings.

Table 13.11a   Relationship Between Future Orientation and Economic Health

Future Orientation	Economic Prosperity	Government Support for Prosperity	Societal Support for Competitiveness	World Competitiveness Index
Societal values	−.62** *n* = 57	.57** *n* = 40	−.16 *n* = 40	−.41** *n* = 41
Societal practices	.54** *n* = 57	.63** *n* = 40	.48** *n* = 40	.62** *n* = 41

** *p* < .01.

These categories of data will be examined to test hypotheses that future-oriented societies tend to (a) be more economically prosperous, (b) enjoy higher levels of societal health, (c) be more scientifically advanced, (d) have looser ties with family and friends, (e) have more open and progressive political ideology, (f) have more spiritually oriented attitudes, (g) have favorable gender attitudes, and (h) have higher rates of national savings.

Future Orientation and Economic Health

What is the relationship between future orientation and economic health? Do the more future-oriented societies enjoy healthier economies? What about the societies with higher aspirations for future orientation?

Table 13.11a provides the answers to these questions. It shows the correlation coefficients between the two GLOBE dimensions of Future Orientation, practices and values, and the various elements of economic health. These are economic prosperity, which refers to consumption and growth; government support for prosperity, reflecting the extent to which the government and the political body are supportive of economic progress; and societal support for competitiveness, a measure of the general social attitude toward and support for business competitiveness. In addition to these measures, we also examined the relationship between GLOBE findings and a well-known measure of global competitiveness, the World Economic Forum's Global Competitiveness Index.

These results show significant positive relationships between the economic indicators and the GLOBE practices measures, and negative relationships with GLOBE values measures of Future Orientation. Economic prosperity, for example, is positively associated with GLOBE Future Orientation scale scores in practice ($r = .54$, $p < .01$), and negatively correlated with Future Orientation values scores ($r = − .62$, $p < .01$). There are three possible explanations for this finding. First, the negative sign associated with the values score and prosperity may just be an artifact of the negative correlations that we noted earlier between values and practices indices of Future Orientation as measured in Project GLOBE. Thus, cultures that have shorter-term practices are less prosperous, and therefore aspire for a longer-term perspective that would be conducive to higher prosperity. Second, in some societies, value expression alone may not guarantee the implementation of the planning practices or progress on the economic front.

Third, GLOBE's practices and values scales may partly capture different aspects of the Future Orientation construct. Gupta, Sully de Luque, and House show in Chapter 9 that GLOBE's Future Orientation practices scale scores are correlated with the unobtrusive and other external measures dealing with advanced planning and investments in intellectual properties. In contrast, GLOBE's Future Orientation values scale is correlated with the World Values Survey indicators dealing with spiritual orientation. In societies that value future orientation

Table 13.11b Relationship Between Future Orientation and Human Condition

Future Orientation	Societal Health	Human Health	Life Expectancy	General Satisfaction	Human Development Index
Societal values	−.54* n = 40	−.14 n = 56	−.49** n = 56	−.45** n = 38	−.50** n = 56
Society practices	.70** n = 40	.14 n = 56	.20** n = 56	.56** n = 38	.20 n = 56

* Correlation is significant at the .05 level (2-tailed).

** Correlation is significant at the .01 level (2-tailed).

there is a greater emphasis on supporting both spiritual as well as material growth, whereas in societies that practice future orientation there tends to be an emphasis on material growth only. If the practices of future orientation do not support spiritual growth, then planning may not be widely practiced even though the people may be quite aware of the value of a futuristic perspective. On the other hand, in societies whose members place lower values on future orientation, the thrust toward spiritual orientation tends to be low. Under this situation, it is potentially feasible for the societies to practice planning for material prosperity. (For a more detailed discussion, see Chapter 9)

Our results provide a qualified support for the first hypothesis. Although Future Orientation practices are aligned with societal economic success, Future Orientation values are inversely related to societal economic success. In other words, low level of societal economic success appears to contribute to a support for delay in gratification, and thus values of future orientation.

Future Orientation and Human Condition

Economic health is only one aspect of a society's well-being. Another dimension is the general health of the populace of the society. What is termed *human condition* here refers to the general quality of life in a particular society.

In this section, we examine the relationship between GLOBE findings on Future Orientation and five different dimensions of human condition. *Societal health* refers to the quality of life, safety, and security in a society. *Human health* reflects the physical health of the populace. *Life expectancy* reflects expected years of life at birth. *General satisfaction* measures the extent of peoples' happiness with their lives; this term comes from the World Values Survey. The Human Development Index, prepared by the United Nations, is a measure of longevity, education, and standard of living.

As shown in Table 13.11b, a pattern of significant correlations provides a qualified support for the second major hypothesis: Countries that have highly future-oriented practices tend to enjoy higher levels of societal health. Specifically, GLOBE Future Orientation practices are positively associated with all five of the measures of human condition, and the correlation with two measures is significant: Societal health and general satisfaction. GLOBE Future Orientation values, on the other hand, are associated negatively with all five of the measures, and the correlation with four measures is significant: Societal health, life expectancy, general satisfaction, and human development. These findings are similar to those found for economic health. It is possible that the managerial reports of Future Orientation values reflect an expression of deprivation, frustration, or dissatisfaction with the status quo of Future Orientation practices.

Table 13.11c   Future Orientation and Success in Science and Technology

	Future Orientation Values	*Future Orientation Practices*
Success in basic science	−.62** N = 40	.54** N = 40

** Correlation is significant at the .01 level (2-tailed).

Table 13.11d   Future Orientation and Family and Friends

	Future Orientation Values	*Future Orientation Practices*
Strength of family ties	.49** N = 38	−.19 N = 38
Respect for family and friends	.61** N = 38	−.48* N = 38

* Correlation is significant at the .05 level (2-tailed).

** Correlation is significant at the .01 level (2-tailed).

Future Orientation and Scientific Advancement

One of the important rationales for future-oriented culture is to help societies develop a capacity to invest and succeed in basic science and technology. *Success in basic science* is a measure that reflects university–corporate cooperation and arousal of the interest of youth in science and technology.

As shown in Table 13.11c, the success in basic science measures is positively related to the GLOBE Future Orientation practices scale ($r = .54$, $p < .01$), but negatively related to the GLOBE Future Orientation values scale ($r = −.62$, $p < .01$). This finding confirms the hypothesis that societies may value future orientation to transform their weak capacities in basic science, and not just to transform their societal and economic conditions.

Future Orientation and Family and Friends

Another dimension of interest is family values and friendship. We examined the relationship between GLOBE's Future Orientation construct and two measures of family and friendship values. *Strength of family ties* refers to the bonds with family members. *Respect for family and friends* refers to a positive attitude toward in-group relationships.

As shown in Table 13.11d, both measures of family and friendship values are positively and significantly related with GLOBE's Future Orientation values scale. In contrast, both measures have a negative relationship with GLOBE's Future Orientation practices scale, though the correlation is significant only for the *respect for family and friends* measure ($−.48$, $p < .05$). Our literature review indicated that future-oriented people are likely to focus on developing new relationships and, in the process, may be diverted from respecting their existing relationships. On the other hand, as the relationship with Trompenaars and Hampden-Turner's measure indicated earlier, GLOBE's Future Orientation values scale is associated with a shorter time horizon. The societies in which people value future orientation may thus be focused on bonding with their existing circle of friends and family members.

Thus, we find a broad support for the fourth hypothesis: More future-oriented practices do facilitate looser ties with family and friends.

Table 13.11e Future Orientation and Political Ideology

Political Ideology	Future Orientation Values	Future Orientation Practices
Disdain for democracy	.22 N = 26	−.53** N = 26
Passiveness	.53** N = 37	−.38* N = 37
Lack of voice	.43** N = 38	−.42** N = 38
Dislike for democracy	.28 N = 27	−.39* N = 27
Role of government	.53** N = 38	−.52* N = 38
Stability	.22 N = 38	−.33* N = 38

* Correlation is significant at the .05 level (2-tailed).

** Correlation is significant at the .01 level (2-tailed).

Future Orientation and Political Ideology

The next domain of interest is political ideology. We use six measures of political ideology: Disdain for democracy, passiveness, lack of voice, dislike for democracy, role of government, and stability.

As shown in Table 13.11e, all six measures of political ideology are negatively and significantly associated with GLOBE's Future Orientation practices scale. People in societies with stronger future-oriented practices are less likely to be passive and to reject democracy, and are more likely to express their voice. They are also less likely to support a strong role for the government, and more likely to reject stability in favor of development. In essence, societies with stronger future-oriented practices may encourage stronger opportunities for people to be involved and engaged in the political and governance process.

In contrast, the GLOBE's Future Orientation values scale score is positively associated with all six measures of political ideology, and the correlation is significant for three measures: Passiveness, lack of voice, and role of government. In societies in which people value more future orientation, people are less likely to express their voice and be politically active, and the government is more likely to play an important role in the governance process. As noted earlier, Singapore is an illustration of such a society.

We thus find support for the fifth hypothesis: More Future Orientation practices are associated with more active political ideology at the mass level, whereas more Future Orientation values are associated with more active political ideology at the government level.

Future Orientation and Spiritual Attitudes

As discussed previously, the concept of future orientation has gained prominence with the rise of an interest in the spiritual aspects of religion. A long-term orientation is expected to support an integration of the material and the spirit and allow people to discover more meaning and fulfillment in their life.

We use two measures of spiritual attitudes. *Religious devotion* refers to being devoted to

Table 13.11f Future Orientation and Spiritual Attitudes

Spiritual Attitudes	Future Orientation Values	Future Orientation Practices
Religious devotion	.64** N = 38	−.13 N = 38
Religious dogma	.56** N = 37	−.01 N = 37

** Correlation is significant at the .01 level (2-tailed).

Table 13.11g Future Orientation and Gender Equality

	Future Orientation Values	Future Orientation Practices
Gender equality	−.44** N = 38	.40* N = 38

 * Correlation is significant at the .05 level (2-tailed).

** Correlation is significant at the .01 level (2-tailed).

soul-searching and purifying rituals. *Religious dogma* refers to belief in the matters of spirit. As shown in Table 13.11f, the GLOBE Future Orientation values scale is positively and significantly associated with both measures of spiritual attitudes. In contrast, the GLOBE Future Orientation practices scale does not show any correlation with either of the measures.

These findings support the sixth hypothesis that more future-oriented aspirations are associated with spiritually oriented attitudes.

Future Orientation and Gender Attitudes

Gender is another factor of interest in relation to GLOBE's cultural dimension of Future Orientation. Table 13.11g correlates Future Orientation practices and values scales with a measure of gender equality. The correlation is positive for Future Orientation practices (.40, $p < .05$), but negative for Future Orientation values (−.44, $p < .01$). As noted previously, societies with higher Future Orientation values

scores also tend to be less economically and socially prosperous. Consequently, the empowerment of women may become particularly difficult in such societies. On the other hand, the findings also suggest that if societies adopt future-oriented practices, they likely recognize the need and benefits of empowering women and make stronger efforts toward realization of gender egalitarianism.

The findings thus appear to be consistent with the hypothesis that future orientation practices are conducive to positive attitudes toward gender.

Future Orientation and National Savings

As noted earlier, Hofstede (2001) has identified a national propensity to save as an important validation indicator for the construct of long-term or future orientation, and several scholars, such as Edwards (1995), have identified social attitudes as one important determinant of thrift. One may expect future orientation

Table 13.11h Relationship Between Future Orientation and National Savings Rate (as percentage of Gross Domestic Product)

National Savings Rate	Future Orientation Societal Values	Future Orientation Societal Practices
Gross Domestic Savings	−.16 $n = 55$	.39** $n = 55$
Genuine Domestic Savings	−.23 $n = 55$	.42** $n = 5$

** $p < .01$. * $p < .05$.

to contribute to individuals' taking a long-term view of their behavior and to be willing to save for improving their future.

Using the World Development Indicators (World Bank, 2000), we extracted savings data in terms of two indices: Gross domestic savings and genuine domestic savings. Genuine domestic savings was calculated by correcting for capital consumption of assets, education, natural resources, and environmental depletion (CO_2 emissions). The results are shown in Table 13.11h.

The results shown in Table 13.11h indicate that there is a positive correlation between Future Orientation practices scores and both measures of national savings. On the other hand, there is no significant correlation between Future Orientation values and either measure of national savings. Societies that are reported to aspire toward more future orientation would not necessarily save a lot due to limited economic resources and possibly because of a spiritual faith that God will provide good fortune in their future.

Summary

In summary, the GLOBE societal Future Orientation practices scale is positively correlated with economic health, societal health, scientific advancement, democratic political ideology, gender equality, and national savings; whereas the GLOBE societal Future Orientation values scale is negatively related with all these constructs except national savings, with which it is not related. Further, the GLOBE societal

Future Orientation practices scale is negatively related to family and friends, whereas the GLOBE societal Future Orientation values scale is positively related to this construct. Also, whereas the GLOBE societal Future Orientation practices scale is not related to spiritual orientation, the GLOBE societal Future Orientation values scale is positively related to spiritual orientation.

FUTURE ORIENTATION AND GEOGRAPHICAL CLUSTERS

To explore the impact of geographical clusters, we examined the relationship between Future Orientation and two variables: Physical climate and regional clusters.

Future Orientation and Physical Climate

A key attribute of physical climate is "climatic stability," which refers to the constancy and predictability of climate and weather, and is higher on average in the tropics (Molles, 2001). Similarly, in the tropics the climates tend to be "benign" and are less disturbing to populations (Molles, 2001). Consequently, in the tropics, more specialists are supported, because the availability of the specific resources is more predictable given the climatic stability. On the other hand, more generalist orientation becomes critical for survival in the nontropical societies, because the society cannot depend on a specific array of resources, and so the people need to be more flexible in their use of resources

Table 13.12a   Physical Climate and Future Orientation

Climatic Region	N	Society Practices			Society Values		
		Mean	SD	SE	Mean	SD	SE
Tropical humid	8	4.06	0.57	0.20	5.68	0.25	0.09
Tropical wet and dry (savanna)	7	3.61	0.30	0.11	5.99	0.13	0.05
Desert	11	3.81	0.36	0.11	5.66	0.34	0.10
Subtropical humid	5	3.70	0.38	0.17	5.56	0.23	0.10
Mediterranean	7	3.51	0.23	0.09	5.55	0.26	0.10
Marine west coast (maritime)	10	4.15	0.43	0.14	4.98	0.32	0.10
Continental	13	3.87	0.55	0.15	5.27	0.29	0.08

NOTE: *SD* = Standard deviation of the mean estimate. 95% confidence interval = Mean ± 1.96* Standard Error (*SE*).

(Molles, 2001). Further, higher solar input favors higher rates of photosynthesis in the tropics, which increases the productivity of the plant resources and, hence, of the formation of plant-based minerals and other resources. With more total resources and more diversity in resources, more total opportunities exist and more diversity in these opportunities exist. As a result of these factors, future orientation becomes less costly and more beneficial for the people in tropical societies. The opportunity cost of resources would be lowered so that delay in the gratification of any specific kind of resource or even total resources should be perceived less costly and demanding on the people. On the other hand, future orientation would be perceived as costly for the people in nontropical societies because limited resource availability should make the opportunity cost of those resources high. Therefore, we hypothesize that the values of future orientation will be significantly lower in the nontropical societies than in the tropical societies. As described in Chapter 10, Gupta & Hanges sorted participating GLOBE societies into seven clusters on the basis of climate: tropical humid, tropical wet and dry (savanna), subtropical humid, subtropical wet and dry (Mediterranean), desert, marine west coast (maritime), and continental. An analysis of variance (not shown) indicated that climatic clusters account for 20% of the between-society differences in GLOBE Future Orientation practices ($p > .05$), and 57% of the between-society differences in GLOBE Future Orientation values ($p < .01$). The differences in societal Future Orientation practices are not significantly related to the physical climates of those societies. However, the differences in values of societal Future Orientation are significantly related to physical climates.

Table 13.12a shows the grand mean scores for Future Orientation values and practices for each climatic region. We used Analysis of Variance Contrast tests to assess if the means in a climatic cluster are significantly higher or lower compared with all other climatic clusters. Societal values of Future Orientation are significantly low in maritime climates (mean = 4.98, contrast = $-$ .61, $p < .01$) and in continental climates (mean = 5.27, contrast = .29, $p < .01$); and are significantly high in savanna climates (mean = 5.99, contrast = .51, $p < .01$).

The above findings are broadly consistent with our hypothesis that nontropical societies tend to favor a lower future orientation due to a higher perceived opportunity cost of resources. The lower Future Orientation values ratings for maritime and continental climates indicate

Table 13.12b   Geographic Region and Future Orientation

Culture Cluster Region	N	Society Practices			Society Values		
		Mean	SD	SE	Mean	SD	SE
Latin America	10	3.54	0.28	0.09	5.75	0.22	0.07
Anglo	7	4.08	0.31	0.12	5.33	0.21	0.08
Nordic Europe	3	4.36	0.11	0.06	4.76	0.38	0.22
Germanic Europe	5	4.40	0.31	0.14	5.01	0.19	0.08
Latin Europe	6	3.68	0.35	0.14	5.33	0.41	0.17
Eastern Europe	8	3.38	0.31	0.11	5.38	0.21	0.08
Confucian Asia	6	4.18	0.47	0.19	5.31	0.34	0.14
Southern Asia	6	3.98	0.41	0.17	5.86	0.21	0.08
Sub-Saharan Africa	5	3.92	0.46	0.21	5.87	0.38	0.17
Middle East	5	3.58	0.30	0.13	5.83	0.06	0.03

NOTE: *SD* = Standard deviation of the mean estimate. 95% Confidence interval = Mean ±1.96* Standard Error (*SE*).

higher aspirations for consumption, and may reflect respondents' desire to enjoy the present. In tropical wet and dry (i.e., savanna) climates, stronger planning orientation is valued.

Future Orientation and Regional Clusters

As discussed in Chapter 8 by Hanges and Dickson, there are significant differences in values and practices for every cultural dimension among the 62 societal cultures studied. Gupta and Hanges in Chapter 10 have also categorized GLOBE societies into 10 cultural or regional clusters: Eastern Europe, Latin America, Latin Europe, Nordic Europe, Germanic Europe, Anglo, Middle East, Southern Asia, Sub-Saharan Africa, and Confucian Asia. An analysis of variance (ANOVA) revealed that cultural clusters accounted for 66% of the between-society differences in Future Orientation practices ($p < .01$), and 71% of the between-society differences in Future Orientation values ($p < .01$).

Table 13.12b shows the grand mean scores of Future Orientation values and practices for each geographical region. We used the Analysis of Variance Contrast test to assess whether the means in a cultural cluster are significantly higher or lower compared with all other cultural clusters. Future Orientation practices scores are significantly higher in Germanic Europe (*contrast* = .54, $p < .01$) and Nordic Europe (*contrast* = .49, $p < .05$); they are significantly lower in Eastern Europe (*contrast* = .58, $p < .01$), Latin America (*contrast* =− .41, $p < .01$) and the Middle East (*contrast* = .36, $p < .05$).

Future Orientation societal values scores are significantly higher in sub-Saharan Africa (*contrast* = .47, $p < .01$), Southern Asia (*contrast* = .46, $p < .01$), the Middle East (*contrast* = .43, $p < .01$), and Latin America (*contrast* = .33, $p < .01$); they are significantly lower in Nordic Europe (*contrast* = .75, $p < .01$) and Germanic Europe (−.48).

Respondents' reports of strong practices and weak values for Future Orientation in the

Nordic and Germanic Europe clusters could be partly explained by their reliance on "professional bureaucracy" (Mintzberg, 1979; Weber, 1958). Professional bureaucratic work culture in Nordic and Germanic Europe involves an emphasis on the skills and knowledge of operating professionals to function. Professionals are formally trained and granted considerable autonomy over their own work (Weber, 1958). They work rather independently of their teams, with whom they coordinate through well-planned standardized rules and systems. Despite these well-planned standards, professional aspirations are usually too complex to be fully codified through formal and advance planning; a sense of instant discretionary decision making grounded in professional know-how is always valued for enjoying the present (Mintzberg, 1979).

In contrast, weak practices and strong values scores for Future Orientation in the Middle East and Latin America clusters are indicative of their peculiar approach to relationships. In these societies, people value efforts and plans to develop family-like relational bonding and believe that these family-like relationships provide an insurance against any future contingencies and, thus, are less likely to practice planning for the future. Moreover, Middle Eastern and Latin American societies have a multifocus or polychronic orientation toward the future (Sharda & Miller, 2001). They would like to keep future well-being in mind, but in practice are highly responsive to situational demands. They may, for instance, sit for several hours chatting with friends of friends just to strengthen the bonds with their friends.

Furthermore, a high priority on spiritual orientation and a holistic view toward matter and spirit could account for high values scores of Future Orientation in the Sub-Saharan Africa and Southern Asia clusters. Finally, traditional reliance on government planning could explain low practices scores for Future Orientation in the Eastern Europe cluster. Also, the turbulent post-Soviet environment has possibly contributed to difficulties in practicing future planning, making people less confident of their abilities to shape their future through advance planning and deliberated decisions.

Interestingly, the Future Orientation societal practices and values scores for the Confucian

Asia and Anglo clusters are not significantly higher or lower than those for the other clusters and are similar to the international average. This finding casts concerns on trying to measure the construct of Future Orientation using the Confucian Dynamism scale (Hofstede, 2001).

GLOBE FINDINGS ON ORGANIZATIONAL FUTURE ORIENTATION

GLOBE used a different set of questions to measure *organizational* culture. This questionnaire was administered to a different set of respondents than those who completed the societal culture questionnaire. To compute organizational scores on Future Orientation we used data from only those organizations having at least seven respondents in the GLOBE sample. Table 13.13 gives the summary statistics for organizational Future Orientation for a sample of 276 organizations. Below, we discuss the GLOBE findings with respect to organizational practices organizational values, interindustry differences, and interorganizational variability.

Organizational Practices: As shown in Table 13.13, the mean Future Orientation organizational practices score is 4.61, which is higher than the mean of Future Orientation societal practices score of 3.85 (see Table 13.4). Respondents perceive their organizations to be more future oriented in practice than their societies.

Organizational Values: As shown in Table 13.13, the mean Future Orientation organizational values score is 5.66, which is only marginally higher than the mean Future Orientation societal values score of 5.48 (see Table 13.4).

Interindustry Differences: As shown in Table 13.13, the means of Future Orientation organizational practices in the three industries—financial, food processing, and telecommunications—are not significantly different from one another.

Interorganizational Variability: Finally, as is evident from Table 13.13, standard deviations of organizational Future Orientation scores are

Table 13.13 Descriptive Statistics for GLOBE Organizational Future Orientation

Variable	N	Min	Max	Mean	Standard Deviation
Overall Future Orientation practices	276	2.67	6.24	4.61	0.66
Overall Future Orientation values	276	4.28	6.78	5.66	0.45
Finance Future Orientation practices	130	2.67	6.24	4.60	0.67
Finance Future Orientation values	130	4.31	6.67	5.63	0.44
Food Future Orientation practices	91	2.67	6.21	4.73	0.65
Food Future Orientation values	91	4.73	6.78	5.73	0.39
Telecom Future Orientation practices	53	3.00	5.50	4.39	0.63
Telecom Future Orientation values	53	4.28	6.78	5.61	0.58

much higher for the reported practices than for values. This is true for the overall as well as industry-specific scores. The respondents to the organizational questionnaire share a strong consensus on the value of Future Orientation, but they vary substantially more in their reports of Future Orientation practices. The differences in ability to use Future Orientation effectively could have significant influence on the differences in competitive advantage of the organizations, especially in light of the high value given to Future Orientation by the sampled organizations. Further research is needed to investigate barriers to future planning in many organizations around the world, and to disseminate the best practices in this regard. Increased uncertainty and volatility in the environments, because of globalization and crisis-like situations, could be partly responsible for the difficulties in using traditional approaches to planning.

The Relationship Between Societal and Organizational Practices and Societal and Organizational Values

As indicated in Chapter 2 by House and Javidan, the GLOBE theoretical model also postulates that societal practices and values affect organizational practices and values. We conducted two hierarchical linear models (HLMs) to test these hypotheses for organizational Future Orientation practices and values. We tested the GLOBE hypothesis regarding the effect of societal culture on organizational culture by conducting HLM analyses in which organizational Future Orientation was predicted by societal Future Orientation. These analyses supported our hypotheses that societal Future Orientation practices have a significant and strong positive relationship with organizational Future Orientation practices ($p < .01$). We found a similar significant and strong relationship between societal Future Orientation values and organizational Future Orientation values ($p < .01$). Both analyses support a principal proposition in the GLOBE theoretical model (i.e., Proposition 3, Figure 2.1, Chapter 2, by House & Javidan): Societal cultural values and practices affect organizational cultural values and practices.[2]

GLOBE FINDINGS ON FUTURE ORIENTATION AND VISIONARY LEADERSHIP

As explained in Chapter 4 by Dorfman and House, GLOBE empirically identified 21 first-order scales to measure leadership attributes and behaviors that are reported to contribute to

Table 13.14   Charismatic I: Factor Components of Visionary as a Leadership Characteristic

Leadership Attributes	1 Greatly Inhibits Leadership Effectiveness	2 Somewhat Inhibits	3 Slightly Inhibits	4 No Impact	5 Contributes Slightly	6 Contributes Somewhat	7 Contributes Greatly to Leadership Effectiveness
Inspirational	Inspires emotions, beliefs, values, and behaviors of others; inspires others to be motivated to work hard						
Anticipatory	Anticipates, attempts to forecast events; considers what will happen in the future						
Prepared	Is ready for future events						
Intellectually stimulating	Encourages others to think and use their minds; challenges beliefs, stereotypes and attitudes of others						
Foresight	Anticipates possible future events						
Plans ahead	Anticipates and prepares in advance						
Able to anticipate	Able to anticipate future needs successfully						
Visionary	Has a vision and imagination of the future						
Future-oriented	Makes plans and takes actions based on future goals						

effective leadership. One of the scales is *Charismatic I: Visionary,* or simply *Visionary Leadership.* This scale consists of nine items, shown in Table 13.14, and reflects visionary leaders' readiness for future events, their emphasis on anticipating future events, and their capability to do so successfully with experience, their imaginativeness and vision, their goal-based planning and action behavior, and their ability to inspire and motivate others to work hard. This leadership scale is one of six others that comprise the global leadership dimension labeled Charismatic/Value-Based and will be discussed later.

Society Scores on Visionary Leadership

Table 13.15 shows the scores on Visionary Leadership for the 61 societies in the GLOBE sample. The societies are grouped into four bands, with band A consisting of significantly higher scores, and band D consisting of significantly lower scores.

Some notable societies on the top end of band A include Canada, the United States, the Philippines, Israel, and Ireland. Visionary leadership directed at transformational initiatives has been widely identified to be strongly effective in the United States and the Canadian context (Bass, 1998). The Philippines experienced a substantial exposure to the American model of leadership during the 20th century, which could account for its high emphasis on visionary leadership. Both Israeli and Irish people live by a strong emphasis on building a unique identity for their nations, which may translate into a high endorsement of visionary leadership.

Some less expected societies at the top include Ecuador (with the highest mean of 6.50), Colombia, and Iran. In these societies, deregulation, trade liberalization, privatization, and globalization have resulted in slow progress by comparable regional and international standards. Yet, strong charismatic leaders have been able to offer an alternative vision to people in

Table 13.15   Charismatic I: Visionary Leadership (Society Scores)

Band							
A		B		C		D	
Country	Score	Country	Score	Country	Score	Country	Score
Ecuador	6.50	Singapore	6.17	Taiwan	5.66	France	5.06
Philippines	6.46	Switzerland	6.17	Japan	5.63	Morocco	4.84
Israel	6.45	Namibia	6.16	Egypt	5.52	Qatar	4.62
Canada[a]	6.36	Argentina	6.15	South Africa[f]	5.39		
Colombia	6.36	South Africa[b]	6.15				
Iran	6.35	Brazil	6.15				
Ireland	6.33	Austria	6.13				
Netherlands	6.30	Switzerland	6.12				
Finland	6.29	Portugal	6.11				
U.S.	6.28	Zambia	6.10				
Hungary	6.27	Switzerland[c]	6.10				
Zimbabwe	6.27	Thailand	6.09				
Turkey	6.25	Russia	6.07				
Italy	6.24	Costa Rica	6.06				
Australia	6.24	Guatemala	6.06				
New Zealand	6.23	Sweden	6.05				
Indonesia	6.23	Poland	6.03				
Kuwait	6.22	India	6.02				
El Salvador	6.21	Malaysia	6.01				
England	6.21	Slovenia	6.00				
Bolivia	6.20	Germany[d]	5.99				
Denmark	6.20	Albania	5.97				
Greece	6.19	Spain	5.91				
		Nigeria	5.89				
		Kazakhstan	5.88				
		Germany[e]	5.86				
		China	5.85				
		Georgia	5.82				
		Mexico	5.78				
		Hong Kong	5.76				
		South Korea	5.76				
		Venezuela	5.74				

a Canada (English-speaking)
b South Africa (White Sample)
c Switzerland (French-speaking)
d Germany (West): Former FRG
e Germany (East): Former GDR
f South Africa (Black Sample)

these societies. For instance, the Ayatollah Ruhollah Khomeini, spiritual leader of Iran from 1979 to 1989, is believed by many to have displayed a charismatic vision in single-handedly leading a popular revolution that overthrew the U.S.-supported monarch, Mohammed Reza Shah, who had been ruling Iran since 1953 (Shirley, 1994).

Table 13.16   Grand Mean for Charismatic I: Visionary as a Leadership Characteristic

Variable	Mean	Standard Deviation	Minimum	Maximum	Valid N
Charismatic I: Visionary overall societal score	6.02	0.36	4.62	6.50	61
Charismatic I: Visionary finance industry	6.03	0.42	4.03	6.49	56
Charismatic I: Visionary food industry	6.04	0.32	4.71	6.55	45
Charismatic I: Visionary telecommunications industry	6.06	0.33	5.02	6.45	32

At the bottom, there are three societies in band D. Qatar has the lowest score of 4.62, followed by Morocco (4.84) and France (5.06). In Qatar, for several decades nearly four fifths of the workforce has consisted of expatriates, which may make the enactment of visionary leadership quite difficult (Ali, 1995). Similarly, several scholars have underlined French distrust of visionary leaders, and their emphasis on bureaucratic rules that minimize the possibilities of any person imposing his or her view of the future (see, for instance, Crozier, 1964).

We may also note that even the societies in band D report the effectiveness of Visionary Leadership at above the midpoint of 4.0, reflecting the universal reported effectiveness of visionary leadership.

Overall Scores and Industry Scores on Visionary Leadership

Table 13.16 shows the overall and industry averages across all societies sampled. On a 7-point scale, the average is 6.02, which is very high, reflecting the participants' belief that Visionary Leadership is a highly effective leader behavior. The universal view among the GLOBE sample is that charismatic visionary leaders are effective leaders.

Table 13.16 also shows that the mean scores for the Visionary Leadership dimension are almost identical across the three industries in the GLOBE sample, ranging from 6.03 (finance sector) to 6.06 (telecommunications sector). Further, as can be seen from Table 13.17, the correlations between the three industries and the overall score are both significant and large.

Societal Demographics and Visionary Leadership

To explore the impact of societal demographics, we examined the relationship between Visionary Leadership and two variables: Physical climate and regional clusters. Although we found no significant differences in Visionary Leadership scores across different climate types ($p > .10$), regional clusters did explain a significant 32.7% ($F = 2.75$, $p < .05$) of the between-society differences in Visionary Leadership.

Table 13.18 presents grand means for Visionary Leadership across the 10 regional clusters. The Analysis of Variance Contrast tests indicated that Visionary Leadership is endorsed significantly more strongly in the Anglo cluster at 6.26 (contrast = .27, $p < .05$), and significantly less strongly in the Middle East cluster at 5.49 (contrast = .57, $p < .01$).

Indeed, Anglo societies are known for their visionary leadership, possibly as a transformational framework for directing short-term profit oriented behaviors and to allow for individual autonomy (Bass, 1998). On the other hand, Khadra (1990) observes that in the Middle East

Table 13.17 Industry Correlation: Charismatic I: Visionary Leadership

Visionary Leadership	Food Industry Score	Finance Industry Score	Telecommunication Industry Score
Overall score	.94** n = 45	.96** n = 56	.72* n = 32
Food industry score		.84** n = 42	.79** = 22
Finance industry score			.56** n = 30

* p < .05.

** p < .01.

Table 13.18 Regional Clusters and Visionary Leadership

Geographical Region	N	Mean	SD
Eastern Europe	8	6.03	0.15
Latin America	10	6.12	0.23
Latin Europe	6	5.98	0.48
Confucian Asia	6	5.80	0.20
Nordic Europe	3	6.18	0.12
Anglo	7	6.26	0.07
Sub-Saharan Africa	5	5.96	0.35
Southern Asia	6	6.20	0.18
Germanic Europe	5	6.08	0.17
Middle East	5	5.49	0.75

the commonly effective form of leadership is the "caliphal model" based on an authoritarian leadership.

Societal and Organizational Future Orientation Culture and Visionary Leadership

Because the concept of visionary leadership is rooted in anticipation of the future, development of goals and plans, and inspiring behaviors that go beyond the stereotypes, visionary leadership should theoretically be more effective if a societal culture is future oriented.

Table 13.19 shows the correlation between GLOBE Future Orientation society practices and society values scales and the Visionary Leadership scale. Both correlations are near zero and are nonsignificant, suggesting that leaders who are able to anticipate the future,

Table 13.19 Correlation Between Future Orientation and Charismatic I: Visionary Leadership

	Society Practices	*Society Values*	*Organizational Practices*	*Organizational Values*
Charismatic I: Visionary	.08 $N = 61$	−.01 $N = 61$	−.09 $N = 271$	.35** $N = 271$

** Correlation significant at $p < .01$.

plan ahead, have foresight, and are well prepared for the future may be effective in societies with a varying range of societal Future Orientation practices and values. Visionary leadership may offer a framework within which spontaneous behaviors may be enacted successfully and rewards ensured (in less future-oriented societies), as well as a framework for long-term planning and goal-oriented behavior (in more future-oriented societies).

Within the organizational context, visionary leadership may be particularly relevant for nurturing a future-oriented culture in organizations, as described in the earlier review section on the correlates of organizational Future Orientation. To test this hypothesis, we aggregated reported Visionary Leadership scores across respondents for each organization separately. For a sample of 271 organizations, data were available for both the Visionary Leadership scale as well as for GLOBE's organizational Future Orientation values and practices scales.

As reported in Table 13.19, the Visionary Leadership scale had no correlation with the organizational Future Orientation practices scale ($r = -.09$). However, the correlation with the organizational Future Orientation values scale is both positive and significant ($r = .35$, $p < .01$). The respondents who value more Future Orientation in their organizations also tend to believe in the effectiveness of Visionary Leadership. Thus, one possible way in which Visionary Leadership can be promoted in organizations may be through a strategic institutionalization of a culture of future orientation.

Next, we examine how future orientation at the society and organizational levels influences alternative forms of culturally implicit theories of leadership (CLTs).

GLOBE FUTURE ORIENTATION AND CULTURALLY ENDORSED LEADERSHIP

Below we examine relationships between Future Orientation scores and the six CLTS. Competitive tests of all culture dimensions and CLTs are presented in Chapter 21 by Dorfman and colleagues. In general, we expect that societal and organizational values will be more strongly related to CLT leadership dimensions than societal and organizational practices. As indicated previously, our notions of values and CLT leadership dimensions represent idealized concepts of how the world *"Should Be"* in contrast to practices that represent the world *"As Is."* As you read through the results discussed below, it may be helpful to view Figure 13.1 for a visual summary. The figure, however, only shows results regarding cultural values, not practices. (All HLM coefficients are presented in Table 21.10 of Chapter 21 by Dorfman et al.)[3]

We tested for the relationship between culture and the CLT leadership dimensions by using hierarchical linear modeling (HLM). An overview of HLM analyses and a detailed discussion of how we conducted these analyses, as well as how to interpret the R^2 information in HLM, is provided in Chapter 11 by Hanges, Dickson, and Sipe. In this next section, we discuss the results of the HLM analyses exploring the relationship between organizational and societal culture and the content of CLTs.

In the present analyses we examine the simultaneous associations of organizational and societal GLOBE Future Orientation scores in a single analysis. The total amount of organizational and societal variance explained by Future Orientation scales ranged from 0–19.2%. Future Orientation values or practices were found to be more

Future Orientation Cultural Dimension

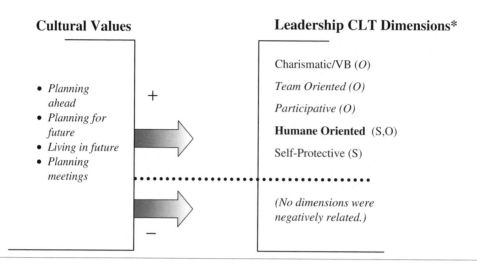

Figure 13.1   Future Orientation Cultural Values as Drivers for CLT Leadership Dimensions

NOTES: * Only statistically significant relationships are shown (p < .05; see Table 21.10, Chapter 21 by Dorfman et al.). The most important leadership CLT relationships are bolded (i.e., relationship is significant at both society and organization levels of analyses or highest HLM coefficient within each level of analysis).

O = Organizational level

S = Societal level

strongly associated with some of the CLTs (e.g., Team-Oriented leadership) than for others (e.g., Autonomous leadership). More specifically,

• *Charismatic/Value-Based leadership.* Future Orientation cultural practices and values scores were significantly related to the Charismatic/Value-Based leadership dimension and explained a total of 6.7% of the organizational and societal variance for this dimension. All of this explained variance was associated with forces operating at the organizational level of analysis. The organizational Future Orientation cultural values scores were positively related (*p* < .01) to the Charismatic/Value-Based leadership dimension. Charismatic/Value-Based leadership is more likely to be a part of a shared leadership belief system in organizations reported to espouse Future Orientation values.

• *Team-Oriented leadership.* Future Orientation cultural practices and values scores were significantly related to the Team-Oriented

leadership dimension and explained a total of 19.2% of the organizational and societal variance for this dimension. Approximately 37.7% of this total explained variance was associated with forces operating at the organizational level of analysis. The remaining portion of the explained variance (62.3%) was associated with forces operating at the societal level of analysis.

The organizational Future Orientation cultural values scores were positively related (*p* < .01) to the Team-Oriented leadership dimension. That is, Team-Oriented leadership is more likely to be a part of a shared leadership belief system in organizations reported to espouse Future Orientation values. The societal Future Orientation cultural practices scores were negatively related (*p* < .05) to the Team-Oriented leadership dimension. Team-Oriented leadership is less likely to be a part of the shared leadership belief system in societies reported to espouse Future Orientation practices.

• *Participative leadership.* Future Orientation cultural practices and values scores were significantly related to the Participative leadership dimension, but explained a total of just 1% of the organizational and societal variance for this dimension. All of this explained variance was associated with forces operating at the organizational level of analysis. The organizational Future Orientation cultural values scores were positively related ($p < .05$) to the Participative leadership dimension. In contrast, the organizational Future Orientation cultural practices scores were negatively related ($p < .05$) to the Participative leadership dimension.

• *Humane-Oriented leadership.* Future Orientation cultural practices and values scores were significantly related to the Humane-Oriented leadership dimension and explained a total of 10.2% of the organizational and societal variance for this dimension. Approximately 42.8% of this total explained variance was associated with forces operating at the organizational level of analysis. The remaining 57.2% of the explained variance was associated with forces operating at the societal level of analysis. Both the organizational and societal Future Orientation cultural values scores were positively related ($p < .01$) to the Humane-Oriented leadership dimension. Humane-Oriented leadership is more likely to be a part of a shared leadership belief system in organizations and societies reported to espouse Future Orientation values.

• *Autonomous leadership.* Future Orientation cultural practices and values scores were not significantly related to the Autonomous leadership dimension at either the organizational or societal level of analysis.

• *Self-Protective leadership.* Future Orientation cultural practices and values were significantly related to the Self-Protective leadership dimension and explained a total of 19.1% of the organizational and societal variance for this dimension. All of this variance was associated with forces operating at the societal level of analysis. The societal Future Orientation cultural values scores were positively related ($p < .05$) to this CLT dimension. Self-Protective leadership is more likely to be a part of the shared leadership

belief system in societies reported to espouse Future Orientation values.

Summary

Overall, our analyses support the notion that the kind of leadership viewed as effective in organizations is a reflection of the extent to which the organization and society as a whole value future orientation. When organizations were viewed as valuing Future Orientation, the CLT endorsed at the organizational level is more likely to be composed of Participative, Humane-Oriented, Team-Oriented, and Charismatic/Value-Based leadership styles. When societies were viewed as valuing Future Orientation, the CLT endorsed at the societal level is more likely to be composed of Self-Protective and Humane-Oriented leadership styles. We also found that current organizational and societal Future Orientation practices were associated with the content of the CLTs. When organizations report low Future Orientation practices, the CLT endorsed at the organizational level of analysis is more likely to include Participative leadership. When societies report low Future Orientation practices, the CLT is more likely to include Team-Oriented leadership styles. By far, there were more significant relationships with Future Orientation values and the CLTs than there were with Future Orientation practices at both the organizational and societal levels of analysis. This is understandable because both the CLT and the core GLOBE value dimensions describe valued behaviors and desired states of affairs.

SUMMARY AND CONCLUSIONS

In this chapter, we reviewed the literature on future orientation as a societal and organizational culture characteristic and its individual level manifestations. We also presented a comprehensive analysis of the Future Orientation culture data collected as a component of the GLOBE project, including the relationship of Future Orientation as a societal and organizational characteristic with key dimensions of leadership.

An important finding of the study is that, irrespective of practice, Future Orientation is almost universally valued. Across the entire study, on a 7-point scale, the GLOBE measure of Future Orientation as a societal value scored 5.48, whereas the Future Orientation in practices score was 3.85. The respondents in each society in the GLOBE sample, with the sole exception of Denmark, value more Future Orientation than they report actually practicing. Also very important, in this chapter we have demonstrated that organizations reflect the culture (practices and values) in the society in which they are embedded. Societies that are future oriented likely have organizations within them that are also future oriented.

We found a strong negative correlation between Future Orientation practices and values. The respondents in societies with weaker practices of Future Orientation have stronger aspirations for Future Orientation. It may be that the societies lacking future oriented practices suffer most from the uncertainty and unpredictability of not addressing the longer-term fundamental issues. Therefore, respondents in such societies are most conscious of the need for moving toward a more strategic perspective.

Surprisingly, most industrialized and higher-income countries have comparatively low scores on Future Orientation values. In contrast, emerging and lower-income markets score high on Future Orientation values. These findings contradict the popular view in the literature that lower socioeconomic status encourages a focus on immediate concerns for survival, whereas higher socioeconomic status allows savings and investments for the future. It is likely that industrialized and higher-income nations enjoy the present more and are not overly concerned about a future orientation because they have already accumulated substantial wealth and material resources. The emerging and lower-income nations may, on the other hand, see a stronger need for taking a long-term perspective and sacrificing for the future because they must cope with scarce and limited resources.

The means of societal Future Orientation practices and values are not significantly different across the three industries sampled in the GLOBE project (food processing, financial services, and telecommunications). Still, traditional stability in the market structure and lack of visionary leadership under government

control may have contributed to perceptibly weaker Future Orientation practices reported by the telecommunications sector in some societies such as Thailand. The negative correlation between practices and values of societal Future Orientation is very prominent for the telecommunications sample. The societies in which this industry was traditionally governed by short-term practices, due to such factors as protective government regulation, appear to be acutely aware of the need to reform and to adopt more strategic approaches for infrastructure improvement and development. The GLOBE data show a strong cross-industry convergence in Future Orientation values and practices.

Several societies with relatively high scores on the GLOBE Future Orientation practices scale are reported to have well-developed collective institutions. In these societies, the leaders have confidence in the abilities of their members and in the collective safety net of their institutions, and they expect their members to be more innovative and tolerant of change. As illustrated by the case of some Nordic and Germanic societies in the GLOBE sample, under these conditions more entrepreneurial leadership may be promoted and power structures may be dismantled.

Similarly, the societies with stronger aspirations for Future Orientation also value collective safety nets of the institutions and of families and relationships, and seek to lower the uncertainty in their environments. Here the role of women in supporting families becomes even more salient. As illustrated by the case of many Latin American societies in the GLOBE sample, the women in such societies may become a vulnerable group engaged primarily in microfamily issues, with limited capacity or opportunity to participate in macrolevel strategic planning. Further, in some societies, such as in the Middle East, people may aspire toward future orientation to reform the authoritarian, kinship-oriented, and fragmented institutional fabric in their cultures.

Interestingly, neither GLOBE Future Orientation practices (rho = .03) nor GLOBE Future Orientation values (rho =− .06) scales show any relationship with Hofstede's Confucian Dynamism scale. Also, contrary to the predictions of Hofstede and Bond (1998), there is no evidence of Confucian societies scoring highest on Future Orientation practices, or Anglo societies scoring the least. China, for instance, scores less than Canada, the United States, and the United Kingdom on reported Future Orientation practices.

Still, the GLOBE Future Orientation values scale does appear to capture the belief in quid pro quo and long-term interaction inherent in Schwartz's cultural embeddedness scale, as opposed to contractual transience and spot relationships associated with Schwartz's cultural autonomy scale (1999). Further, the societies that are reported to be future oriented are actually more likely to encourage individuals to express themselves and to lead a high quality of life, as evidenced by a strong positive correlation of GLOBE societal Future Orientation practices scale with Inglehart and Baker's (2000) survival versus self-expression scale ($r = .61$, $p < .01$). Conversely, in societies that depend more on traditional authority or on survival motivation, the value of future orientation becomes more salient.

The societies reported to have stronger practices of future orientation tend to show better economic and societal health, more scientific advancement, more democratic political ideals, more empowered gender status, and greater domestic savings. Under such conditions, family and friends may play a less prominent role in the life of people. On the other hand, the aspirations for future orientation are stronger in societies that have weak economic and societal health, less scientific advancement, less democratic political ideals, and less empowered gender status. These aspirations for future orientation are interrelated with a strong emphasis on family and friends and on spiritual orientation. Family, friends and spiritual orientation may offer critical support under weak economic, societal, scientific, political, and gender conditions.

Physical climate plays an important role in defining the societal values of Future Orientation. Societies in the relatively unpredictable nontropical maritime and continental climates tend to report lower values of Future Orientation, whereas respondents from the societies in more predictable tropical wet and dry (i.e., savanna) climates report greater preference for Future Orientation.

The analysis of regions showed that most Nordic and Germanic societies report strong practices, but weak values, of Future Orientation. These findings may be attributable to high levels of political stability and socioeconomic status, and a great emphasis on professional bureaucracy in the Northern European region. The Northern European societies tend to have well laid-out procedures for long-term planning. At the same time, improvising by professionals to deal with emergent opportunities is well respected and valued. In contrast, most Latin American and Middle Eastern societies report strong values, but weak practices, of Future Orientation. In these societies, people value long-term relationships but often believe that the relationships can help one deal with any unplanned future contingencies, and people are therefore less likely to plan ahead.

Societies in Sub-Saharan Africa and Southern Asia stand out for their high value on Future Orientation, possibly reflecting the high priority they set on spiritual orientation and a holistic view favoring matter that is integrated with spirit on a long-term basis. On the other hand, Eastern Europe is distinctive in its low reported Future Orientation practices, which may partly indicate the turbulent and transitional conditions in that region during the 1990s.

Consistent with other related findings, societal practices and values of future orientation for the Confucian Asia and Anglo clusters are not significantly higher or lower than the other clusters, and are similar to the international average. This finding casts doubt the effectiveness of measuring the construct of future orientation using the Confucian Dynamism scale (Hofstede, 2001).

At the organizational level, practices are reported to be more future oriented within organizations than throughout societies. In addition, the respondents who report their societies to have Future Orientation practices are also likely to report their organizations as practicing future orientation. Similarly, the Future Orientation values at the organizational level are strongly and directly correlated with the Future Orientation values at the societal level ($r = .52$, $p < .01$), although the values for future orientation are reported to be equally strong for both organizations as well as societies. The reported future orientation of organizations does not vary by industry.

The organizations sampled in the GLOBE program share a strong consensus on the *value* of Future Orientation, but they vary substantially more in their abilities to currently *practice* it. It is probable that differences in ability to effectively use future orientation could have significant influence on the differences in competitive advantage of the organizations, especially in light of the high value given to Future Orientation by the sampled organizations.

The organizations that report stronger values of Future Orientation are more likely to endorse the effectiveness of Visionary Leadership, though the reported organizational practices of Future Orientation are not associated with the endorsement of Visionary Leadership. Similarly, visionary leaders who are able to anticipate the future, plan ahead, have foresight, and are well-prepared for the future may be effective in societies with varying ranges of societal Future Orientation practices and values.

Visionary Leadership is endorsed significantly more strongly in the Anglo cluster at 6.26 (contrast = .27, $p < .05$), and significantly less strongly in Middle East cluster at 5.49 (contrast = .57, $p < .01$). Anglo societies are known for their visionary leadership, possibly as a transformational framework for directing short-term profit-oriented behaviors and to allow for individual autonomy. Israel and Ireland also report high scores on Visionary Leadership: Both Israeli and Irish people live by a strong vision of promoting a unique identity for their nations, which may translate into a high endorsement of visionary leadership.

On the other hand, in the Middle East, authoritarian leadership is commonly more effective. In Qatar, for instance, nearly four fifths of the workforce has been composed of other countries' expatriates for several decades, which may make the enactment of visionary leadership quite difficult (Ali, 1995). France also stands out for its low endorsement of visionary leadership. The French often distrust visionary leaders and emphasize bureaucratic rules that minimize the possibilities of any person pushing his or her idiosyncratic view of the future.

We also examined in depth the relationships between Future Orientation and dimensions of leadership identified in the GLOBE study. We chose to emphasize the relationships of CLT leadership dimensions with cultural values rather than practices for reasons discussed previously. Both cultural values and CLT leadership dimensions reflect idealized constructs rather than actual cultural practices or leadership behaviors. When organizations are viewed as valuing Future Orientation, the CLT endorsed at the organizational level is more likely to be composed of Participative, Humane-Oriented, Team-Oriented, and Charismatic/Value-Based leadership styles. Interestingly, societal Future Orientation values are also associated with preferences for a more Self-Protective leadership. Viewed in its totality, this cultural dimension was related to five of the six CLT leadership dimensions, and was second only to Performance Orientation in its importance to idealized leadership styles.

ENDNOTES

1. Our response bias correction procedure identified response bias in some countries for this scale. We recomputed the predicted response bias corrected scale score for each country. Response bias corrected scores are:

Practices: France, 3.74 (no change in band); Qatar, 4.08 (moves from band C to band B); and Taiwan, 3.65 (moves from band B to band C).

Values: Ecuador, 5.62 (moves from band A to band B); France, 5.35 (moves from band C to band B); Morocco, 6.33 (no change in band); and New Zealand, 5.90 (moves from band B to band A).

For a complete discussion of this procedure and all response bias corrected scores, see Appendix C, this volume.

2. As reported in Chapter 20 by Brodbeck, Hanges, Dickson, Gupta, and Dorfman, we found that all the cultural dimensions of organizational cultural values and practices significantly differed across societies. Although important, this prior analysis did not identify the particular aspect of societal differences that was related to organizational culture. In the present chapter, we found that societal and organizational Future Orientation practices were significantly related (R^2 Total = 3.9%, R^2 Societal = 42.5%, $p < .01$). We also found strong results for societal and organizational Future Orientation values (R^2 Total = 4.6%, R^2 Societal = 32.9%, $p < .01$). As discussed in Chapter 11

by Hanges, Dickson, and Sipe, the R^2 Total considers all levels of analysis (i.e., individual, organizational, and societal) whereas the R^2 Societal isolates the societal-level portion of the dependent variable and indicates the percentage of variance accounted for by the predictor at only this level. Although we have primarily taken the conservative approach and reported the R^2 Total in GLOBE, several scholars suggest that R^2 Societal provides a more accurate description of aggregated relationships. For further discussion, see the paper by Lance and James (1999).

3. Results between the single HLM and multiple HLM tests will likely differ somewhat. The differences between the results of the multiple HLMs and single HLMs are conceptually similar to the differences between a multiple regression analysis and a correlation coefficient. Table 21.10 in Chapter 21 by Dorfman and colleagues presents both single and multiple HLM coefficients. In addition, the relationships for all culture dimension values are summarized in Chapter 3.

REFERENCES

Agarwal, A. (1993). Time, memory, and knowledge representation: The Indian perspective. In J. Altarriba (Ed.), *Cognition and culture: A cross-cultural approach to psychology* (pp. 45–55). Amsterdam: Elsevier Science.

Agarwal, A., Tripathi, K. K., & Srivastava, M. (1983). Social roots and psychological implications of time perspective. *International Journal of Psychology, 18*(5), 367–380.

Ali, A. J. (1995). Cultural discontinuity and Arab management thought. *International Studies of Management & Organization, 25*(3), 7–30.

Alvos, L., Gregson, R. A. M., & Ross, M. W. (1993). Future time perspective in current and previous injecting drug users. *Drug and Alcohol Dependence, 31*(2), 193–197.

Ansoff, H. I. (1988). *The new corporate strategy.* New York: John Wiley.

Antonakis, J., & House, R. J. (2002). An analysis of the full-range leadership theory: The way forward. In B. J. Avolio & F. J. Yammarino (Eds.), *Transformational and charismatic leadership: The road ahead* (pp. 3–33). New York: JAI/ Elsevier Science.

Ariaraja, S. W. (1986). Hindu spirituality: An invitation to dialogue? *Ecumenical Review, 38*(1), 75–81.

Barakat, M., & Sarver, E. (1997, January 30). Western banks taking 1st steps into Islam's "no interest" world. *American Banker, 162*(20), 9.

Barndt, R. J., & Johnson, D. M. (1955). Time orientation in delinquents. *Journal of Abnormal and Social Psychology, 51,* 343–345.

Barrig, M., & Beckman, E. (2001). Latin American feminism. *NACLS Report on the Americas, 34*(5), 29–36.

Bass, B. M. (1998). *Transformational leadership: Industrial, military, and educational impact.* Mahwah, NJ: Lawrence Erlbaum.

Becker, G. (1965). A theory of the allocation of time. *The Economic Journal, 75,* 493–517.

Benson, J. B. (1994). The origins of future orientation in the everyday lives of infants and toddlers. In M. M. Haith, J. B. Benson, R. R. Roberts, & B. Pennington (Eds.), *The development of future-oriented processes* (pp. 375–407). Chicago: University of Chicago Press.

Bentham, J. (1970). *An introduction to the principles of morals and legislation.* London: Methuen. (Original work published 1789)

Blasko, J. C. (1998). Overcoming the legal and historical obstacles to privatization: The telecommunications sector in Thailand. *Case Western Reserve Journal of International Law, 30*(2/3), 507–539.

Blinn, L. M., & Pike, G. (1989). Future time perspective: Adolescents' predictions of their interpersonal lives in the future. *Adolescence, 24*(94), 289–301.

Bluedorn, A. C. (2000). Time and organizational culture. In N. M. Ashkanasy, C. P. Wilderom, & M. F. Peterson (Eds.), *Handbook of organizational culture and climate* (pp. 117–128). Thousand Oaks, CA: Sage.

Boocock, S. S. (1978). The social organization of the classroom. *Annual Review of Sociology, 4,* 1–28.

Brandt, R. B. (1995). *Morality, utilitarianism and rights.* Cambridge, UK: Cambridge University Press.

Brommer, M., & De La Porte, R. (1992). A context for envisioning the future. *National Productivity Review, 11,* 549–552.

Bryman, A. (1996). Leadership in organizations. In S. Clegg, C. Hardy, & W. Nord (Eds.), *Handbook of organization studies* (pp. 276–292). London: Sage.

Burns, T., & Stalker, G. M. (1961). *The management of innovation* (1st ed.). London: Tavistock.

Cahill, T. (1998). *The gifts of the Jews.* New York: Doubleday.

Cameron, P., Desai, K. G., Bahador, D., & Dremel, G. (1977–1978). Temporality across the life-span. *International Journal of Aging and Human Development, 8,* 229–259.

Carstensen, L. L. (1993). Motivation for social contact across the life span: A theory of socioemotional selectivity. *Nebraska Symposium on Motivation, 40,* 209–254.

Chandler, A. D., Jr. (1962). *Strategy and structure: Chapters in the history of the industrial enterprise.* Cambridge: MIT Press.

Cohen, J. (1967). *Psychological time and health and disease.* Springfield, IL: Charles C Thomas.

Cohen, W. M., & Levinthal, D. A. (1990). Absorptive capacity: A new perspective on learning and innovation. *Administrative Science Quarterly, 35,*128–152.

Cottle, T. (1967). The Circles Test: An investigation of perception of temporal relatedness and dominance. *Journal of Projective Technique and Personality Assessments, 31,* 58–71.

Cottle, T. J., & Klineberg, S. L. (1974). *The present of things future.* New York: Free Press.

Cross, T. (2001). Spirituality and mental health: A Native American perspective. *Focal Point, 15*(2), 37–38.

Crozier, M. (1964). *The bureaucratic phenomenon.* Chicago: Chicago University Press.

Daft, R. E., & Weick, K. E. (1984). Towards a model of organizations as interpretation systems. *Academy of Management Review, 9,* 284–295.

Das, T. K. (1986). *The subjective side of strategy making: Future orientations and perceptions of executives.* New York: Praeger.

Das, T. K. (1987). Strategic planning and individual temporal orientation. *Strategic Management Journal, 8,* 203–209.

D'Aveni, R. A. (1994). *Hyper-competition.* New York: Free Press.

Davis, E. P., & Steil, B. (2001). *Institutional investors.* Cambridge: MIT Press.

Davids, A., & Falkof, B. B. (1975). Juvenile delinquents then and now: Comparison of findings from 1959 and 1974. *Journal of Abnormal Psychology, 84,* 161–164.

Davids, A., Kidder, C., & Reich, M. (1962). Time orientation in male and female juvenile delinquents. *Journal of Abnormal and Social Psychology, 64,* 239–240.

Doob, L. W. (1971). *The patterning of time.* New Haven, CT: Yale University Press.

Dutton, J. E., & Jackson, S. E. (1987). Categorizing strategic issues: Links to organizational action. *Academy of Management Review, 12,* 76–90.

Edwards, S. (1995). *Why are saving rates so different across countries? An international comparative analysis* (Working Paper No. 5097). Cambridge, MA: NBER.

Eisenhardt, K. M. (1989). Making fast strategic decisions in high-velocity environments. *Academy of Management Journal, 32,* 543–576.

Ekecrantz, J. (2001, August). *Postmodern times? A comparative study of temporal constructions.* Paper presented at the 15th Nordic Conference on Media and Communication Research, Reykjavík, Iceland.

Eng, P. (1997). Thai democracy: The people speak. *Washington Quarterly, 20*(4), 169–189.

Ferrari, J. R., & Emmons, R. A. (1995). Methods of procrastination and their relation to self-control and self-reinforcement: An exploratory study. *Journal of Social Behavior and Personality, 10*(1), 135–142.

Fiol, C. M., Harris, D., & House, R. J. (1999). Charismatic leadership: Strategies for affecting social change. *Leadership Quarterly, 10,* 449–482.

Fraisse, P. (1963). *The psychology of time* (J. Leith, Trans.). Westport, CT: Greenwood.

Frank, L. K. (1939). Time perspectives. *Journal of Social Philosophy, 4,* 293–312.

Franke, R. H., Hofstede, G., & Bond, M. H. (1991). Cultural roots of economic performance: A research note. *Strategic Management Journal, 12,* 165–173.

Fredrickson, J. W. (1984). The comprehensiveness of strategic decision processes: Extension, observations, future directions. *Academy of Management Journal, 27,* 445–466.

Fung, H. H., Carstensen, L. L., & Lutz, A. M. (1999). Influence of time on social preferences: Implications for life-span development. *Psychology and Aging, 14,* 595–604.

Gaddis, J. L. (1997). *We now know: Rethinking cold war history.* Oxford, UK: Clarendon Press.

Gallimore, R., Weiss, L. B., Finney R., & Tharp, R. G. (1974). Cultural differences in delay of gratification: A problem of behavior classification. *Journal of Personality & Social Psychology, 30,* 72–80.

Gjesme, T. (1975). Slope of gradients of performance as a function of achievement motive, goal distance in time, and future time orientation. *The Journal of Psychology, 91,* 143–160.

Gjesme, T. (1979). Future orientation as a function of achievement motives, ability, delay of gratification, and sex. *Journal of Psychology, 101,* 173–188.

Gjesme, T. (1981). Is there any future in achievement motivation? *Motivation and Emotion, 5,*115–138.

Gjesme, T. (1983a). Introduction: An inquiry into the concept of future orientation. *International Journal of Psychology, 18,* 347–350.

Gjesme, T. (1983b). On the concept of future time orientation: Considerations of some functions' and measurements' implications. *International Journal of Psychology, 18,* 443–461.

Granovetter, M. (1985). Economic action and social structure: The problem of embeddedness. *American Journal of Sociology, 91,* 481–510.

Graves, T. D. (1972). *Urban Indian personality and the "culture of poverty."* Unpublished manuscript, University of California, Los Angeles.

Griffeth, R. W., & Hom, P. W. (1988). A comparison of different conceptualizations of perceived alternatives in turnover research. *Journal of Organizational Behavior, 9,* 103–111.

Gupta, V., Macmillan, I. C., & Surie, G. (in press). Entrepreneurial leadership: Developing and validating a cross-cultural construct. *Journal of Business Venturing.*

Gurvitch, G. (1964). *The spectrum of social time.* Dordrecht, The Netherlands: D. Reidel.

Haley, G., & Tan, C.-T. (1999). East vs. West: Strategic marketing management meets the Asian networks. *Journal of Business and Industrial Marketing 14*(2), 91–101.

Hall, E. T. (1960). The silent language in overseas business. *Harvard Business Review, 38,* 87–96.

Hannan, M. T., & Freeman, J. (1984). Structural inertia and organizational change. *American Sociological Review, 49,*149–164.

Hayes, R. H., & Abernathy, W. J. (1980). Managing our way to economic decline. *Harvard Business Review, 58*(4), 67–77.

Hedlund, G., & Aman, P. (1984). *Managing relationships with foreign subsidiaries: Organization and control in Swedish MNCs.* Västervik, Stockholm: Sveriges Mekanförbund.

Hofstede, G., & Bond, M. H. (1988). The Confucius connection: From cultural roots to economic growth. *Organizational Dynamics, 16*(4), 4–21.

Hofstede, G. (2001). *Culture's consequences: Comparing values, behaviors, institutions and organizations across nations.* Thousand Oaks, CA: Sage.

Hofstede, G., van Deusen, C., Mueller, C., Charles, T., & The Business Goals Network. (2002). What goals do business leaders pursue? A study in fifteen countries. *Journal of International Business Studies, 33*(4), 785–803.

Hoornaert, J. (1973). Time perspective: Theoretical and methodological considerations. *Psychologica Belgica, 13,* 265–294.

Horovitz, J. H. (1980). *Top management control in Europe.* London: Macmillan.

Horowitz, R. T. (1989). *The Soviet man in an open society.* New York: University Press of America.

House, R. J., Hanges, P. J., Ruiz-Quintanilla, S. A., Dorfman, P. W., Javidan, M., Dickson, M., Gupta, V., et al. (1999). Cultural influences on leadership and organizations: Project GLOBE. In W. Mobley, J. Gessner, & V. Arnold (Eds.), *Advances in global leadership, 1* (pp. 171–234). Greenwich, CT: JAI.

House, R. J., Wright, N. S., & Aditya, R. N. (1997). Cross-cultural research on organizational leadership: A critical analysis and a proposed theory. In C. Earley & M. Erez (Eds.), *New perspectives on international industrial/organizational psychology* (pp. 535–635). San Francisco: New Lexington.

Hu, C. T. (1995). Historical time pressure: An analysis of Min Pau (1905–1908). In C. C. Huang & E. Zurcher (Eds.), *Time and space in Chinese culture* (pp. 329–60). Leiden, The Netherlands: Brill.

Hume, D. (1987). *A treatise on human nature* (2nd ed.). Oxford: Clarendon Press. (Original work published 1739)

Ibrahim, S. E. (1998). Ethnic conflict and state-building in the Arab world. *International Social Science Journal, 50*(156), 229–242.

Inglehart, R. (1997). *Modernization and postmodernization: Cultural, economic and political change in 43 societies.* Princeton, NJ: Princeton University Press.

Inglehart, R., & Baker, W. E. (2000). Modernization, cultural change, and the persistence of traditional values. *American Sociological Review, 65*(1), 19–51.

Inglehart, R., Basanez, M., & Moreno, A. (1998). *Human values and beliefs: A cross-cultural source-book.* Ann Arbor: University of Michigan Press.

Jaeger, A., & Kanungo, R. (1990). Introduction: The need for indigenous management in developing countries. In A. Jaeger & R. Kanungo (Eds.), *Management in developing countries* (pp. 1–23). New York: Routledge.

Johnson, H. T., & Kaplan, R. S. (1987). *Relevance lost.* Boston: Harvard Business School Press.

Judge, W. Q., & Spitzfaden, M. (1995). The management of strategic time horizons within biotechnology firms: The impact of cognitive complexity on time horizon diversity. *Journal of Management Inquiry, 4*(2), 179–196.

Kagono, T., Nonaka, I., Sakakibara, K., & Okumura, A. (1985). *Strategic vs. evolutionary management: A U.S.-Japan comparison of strategy and management.* Amsterdam: North-Holland.

Kant, I. (1965). *Critique of pure reason.* London: Macmillan. (Original work published 1781)

Kastenbaum, R. (1961). The dimensions of future time perspective: An experimental analysis. *Journal of General Psychology, 65,* 203–218.

Kastenbaum, R. (1964). Cognitive and personal futurity in later life. *Journal of Individual Psychology, 19,* 216–219.

Keegan, W. J. (1983). Strategic market planning: The Japanese approach. *International Marketing Review, 1,* 1–15.

Keough, K. A., Zimbardo, P. G., & Boyd, J. N. (1999). Who's smoking, drinking, and using drugs? Time perspective as a predictor of substance use. *Basic and Applied Social Psychology, 21*(2), 149–164.

Khadra, B. (1990). The prophetic-caliphal model of leadership: An empirical study. *International Studies of Management and Organization, 20,* 37–51.

Klineberg, S. L. (1967). Changes in outlook on the future between childhood and adolescence. *Journal of Personality and Social Psychology, 7,* 185–193.

Klineberg, S. L. (1968). Future time perspective and the preference for delayed reward. *Journal of Personality and Social Psychology, 8,* 253–257.

Kluckhohn, F. R., & Strodtbeck, F. L. (1961). *Variations in value orientations.* Evanston, IL: Row, Peterson.

Kobrin, S., Basek, J., Blank, S., & La Palombara, J. (1980). The assessment and evaluation of noneconomic environments by American firms. *Journal of International Business Studies, 11,* 32–47.

Kotter, J. P. (1982). *The general managers.* New York: Free Press.

Kouzes, J. M., & Posner, B. Z. (1996). Envisioning your future: Imagining ideal scenarios. *The Futurist, 30*(3), 14–20.

Lance, C. E., & James, L. R. (1999). A proportional variance accounted for index for some cross-level and person-situation research designs. *Organizational Research Methods, 2,* 395–418.

Lang, F. R., & Carstensen, L. L. (1994). Close emotional relationships in late life: Further support for proactive aging in the social domain. *Psychology and Aging, 9,* 315–324.

Lang, F. R., & Carstensen, L. L. (2002). Time counts: Future time perspective, goals, and social relationships. *Psychology and Aging, 17*(1), 125–139.

Larwood, L., Falbe, C. M., Kriger, M., & Miesing, P. (1995). Structure and meaning of organizational vision. *Academy of Management Journal, 38,* 740–769.

Lasane, T. P., & Jones, J. M. (1999). Temporal orientation and academic goal-setting: The mediating properties of a motivational self. *Journal of Social Behavior and Personality, 14,* 31–44.

Lauenstein, M. C. (1985). SMR Forum: Diversification—The hidden explanation of success. *Sloan Management Review, 27*(1), 49–55.

Laverty, K. J. (1996). Economic "short-termism": The debate, the unresolved issues, and the implications for management practice and research. *Academy of Management Review, 27,* 825–860.

Lay, C. H., & Schouwenburg, H. C. (1993). Trait procrastination, time management, and academic behavior. *Journal of Social Behavior and Personality, 8*(4), 647–662.

Leach, E. R. (1961). Two essays concerning the symbolic representation of time. In *Rethinking anthropology* (pp. 124–136). London: Athlone Press.

Lewin, K. (1926). Intention, will and need. In D. Rapaport (Ed.), *Organization and pathology of thought* (pp. 95–151). New York: Columbia University Press.

Lewin, K. (1942). Time perspective and morale. In G. Watson (Ed.), *Civilian morale* (pp. 48–70). Boston: Houghton Mifflin.

Lewin, K. (1951). *Field theory in social science.* New York: Harper & Brothers.

Lim, Y. M., & Seers, A. (1993). Time dimensions of work: Relationships with perceived organizational performance. *Journal of Business and Psychology, 8*(1), 91–102.

Loescher, S. M. (1984). Bureaucratic measurement, shuttling stock shares, and shortened time horizons: Implications for economic growth. *Quarterly Review of Economics and Business, 24,* 8–23.

Lomranz, J., Shmotkin, D., & Katznelson, D. B. (1983). Coherence as a measure of future time perspective in children and its relationship to delay of gratification and social class. *International Journal of Psychology, 18*(5), 407–413.

MacKinnon-Slaney, F. (1994). The adult persistence in learning model. *Journal of Counseling and Development, 72*(3), 268–275.

Malinowski, B. (1926–1927). Lunar and seasonal calendar in the Trobriands. *Journal of the Anthropological Institute of Great Britain and Ireland, 56–57,* 203–215.

Marko, K. W., & Savickas, M. L. (1998). Effectiveness of a career time perspective intervention. *Journal of Vocational Behavior, 52,* 106–119.

Matthews, D., & Ornauer, H. (1976). The year 2000 questionnaire and the marginals of 11 nations. In H. Ornauer, H. Wiberg, A. Sicigski, & J. Galtang (Eds.), *Images of the world in the year 2000* (pp. 637–702). Atlantic Highlands, NJ: Humanities Press.

Mehta, P. H., Rohila, P. K., Sundberg, N. D., & Tyler, L. E. (1972). Future time perspective of adolescents in India and the United States. *Journal of Cross-Cultural Psychology, 3,* 293–302.

Mill, J. S. (1986). *A system of logic.* New York: Classworks. (Original work published 1843)

Mintzberg, H. (1975). The manager's job: Folklore and fact. *Harvard Business Review, 53*(4), 49–61.

Mintzberg, H. (1979). *The structuring of organizations.* Englewood Cliffs, NJ: Prentice Hall.

Mischel, W. (1974). Processes in delay of gratification. In W. Mischel & L. Berkowitz (Eds.), *Advances in experimental social psychology* (pp. 249–288). San Diego, CA: Academic Press.

Molles, M. C. (2001). *Ecology: Concepts and applications* (2nd ed.). New York: McGraw-Hill.

Moore, W. (1963). *Man, time and society.* New York: Wiley.

Morris, G. B. (1992). Adolescent leaders: Rational thinking, future beliefs, temporal perspectives and other correlates. *Adolescence, 27*(105), 173–181.

Murrell, A. J., & Mingrone, M. (1994). Correlates of temporal perspective. *Perceptual and Motor Skills, 78,* 1331–1334.

Nadler, A. (1975). Delay of gratification: Review and suggestions for future research. *Catalog of selected documents in psychology, 5*(2), 79.

North, D. C. (1990). *Institutions, institutional change and economic performance.* Cambridge, UK: Cambridge University Press.

Novaky, E., Hideg, E., & Kappeter, I. (1994). Future orientation in Hungarian society. *Futures, 26*(7), 759–770.

Nurmi, J. (1987). Age, sex, social class, and quality of family interaction as determinants of adolescents' future orientation: A developmental task interpretation. *Adolescence, 22,* 977–991.

Nurmi, J. (1991). How do adolescents see their future? A review of the development of future orientation and planning. *Developmental Review, 11,* 1–59.

Nuttin, J. (1964). The future time perspective in human motivation and learning. *Acta Psychologica, 23,* 60–82.

O'Rand, A., & Ellis, R. A. (1974). Social class and social time perspective. *Social Forces, 53,* 53–62.

Oner, B. (2000). Future time orientation and relationships with the opposite sex. *The Journal of Psychology, 134,* 306–314.

Onken, M. H. (1999). Temporal elements of organizational culture and impact on firm performance. *Journal of Managerial Psychology, 14*(3/4), 231–244.

Ouchi, W. (1981). *How American business can meet the Japanese challenge.* Reading, MA: Addison-Wesley.

Peetsma, T. T. D. (1993, August 31- September 5). *Future time perspective as an attitude: The validation of a concept.* Paper presented at the 5th Conference of the European Association for Research on Learning and Instruction (EARLI), Aix-en-Provence, France.

Peetsma, T. T. D. (2000). Future time perspective as a predictor of school investment. *Scandinavian Journal of Educational Research, 44*(2), 177–192.

Pervin, L. A. (Ed.). (1989). *Goal concepts in personality and social psychology.* Hillsdale, NJ: Lawrence Erlbaum.

Piaget, J. (1952). *The origins of intelligence in children.* New York: International Universities Press.

Poole, M. E., & Cooney, G. H. (1987). Orientations to the future: A comparison of adolescents in Australia and Singapore. *Journal of Youth and Adolescence, 16*(2), 129–151.

Porter, M. E. (1992). Capital disadvantage: America's failing capital investment system. *Harvard Business Review, 70*(5), 65–82.

Principles of governance. (2001). Retrieved January 3, 2001, from the Singapore government website http://www1.moe.edu.sg/ne/About_NE/Govern ance/governance& - 9 5;principles.htm

Quinn, R. E., & McGrath, M. R. (1985). The transformation of organizational cultures: A competing values perspective. In P. J. Frost, L. F. Moore, M. R. Louis, C. C. Lundberg, & J. Martin (Eds.), *Organizational culture* (pp. 315–334). Beverly Hills, CA: Sage.

Ralston, D. A., Gustafson, D. J., Elsass, P. M., Cheung, F., & Terpstra, R. H. (1992). Eastern values: A comparison of managers in the United States, Hong Kong, and the People's Republic of China. *Journal of Applied Psychology, 77*, 64–671.

Raynor, J. O. (1969). Future orientation and motivation of immediate activity: An elaboration of the theory of achievement motivation. *Psychological Review, 76*, 606–610.

Raynor, J. O. (1974). Future orientation in the study of achievement motivation. In J. W. Atkinson & J. O Raynor (Eds.), *Motivation and achievement* (pp. 219–236). Washington, DC: Winston.

Raynor, J. O., & Entin, E. E. (1982). *Motivation, career striving, and aging.* Washington, DC: Hemisphere.

Read, R. (1993). *Politics and policies of national economic growth.* Unpublished doctoral dissertation, Stanford University, CA.

Roede, E. (1989). *Explaining student investment: An investigation of high school students' retrospective causal accounts of their investment in school.* Amsterdam: Stichting Centrum voor Onderwijsonderzoek van de Universiteit van Amsterdam.

Roer-Strier, D., & Rosenthal, M. K. (2001). Socialization in changing cultural contexts: A search for images of the "adaptive adult." *Social Work, 46*, 215–228.

Rosenberg, M. J., & Hovland, C. I. (1960). Cognitive, affective, and behavioral components of attitudes. In C. I. Hovland & M. J. Rosenberg (Eds.), *Attitude organization and change* (pp. 1–14). New Haven, CT: Yale University Press.

Rothspan, S., & Read, S. J. (1996). Present versus future time perspective and HIV risk among heterosexual college students. *Health Psychology, 15*, 131–134.

Rumelt, R. P. (1987). Theory, strategy, and entrepreneurship. In D. J. Teece (Ed.), *The competitive challenge* (pp.137–158). New York: Harper & Row.

Sagie, A., Elizur, D., & Yamauchi, H. (1996). The structure and strength of achievement motivation: A cross-cultural comparison. *Journal of Organizational Behavior, 17*, 431–444.

Schein, E. H. (1985). *Organizational culture and leadership.* San Francisco: Jossey-Bass.

Schneider, S. C. (1989). Strategy formulation: The impact of national culture. *Organization Studies, 10*, 149–168.

Schriber, J. B., & Gutek, B. A. (1987). Some time dimensions of work: Measurement of an underlying aspect of organizational culture. *Journal of Applied Psychology, 72*(4), 642–650.

Schwartz, S. H. (1999). A theory of cultural values and some implications for work. *Applied Psychology: An International Review, 48*, 23–47.

Seginer, R., & Schlesinger, R. (1998). Adolescents' future orientation in time and place: The case of the Israeli kibbutz. *International Journal of Behavioral Development, 22*, 151–167.

Seijts, G. H. (1998). The importance of future time perspective in theories of work motivation. *The Journal of Psychology, 132*, 154–168.

Sharda, B. D., & Miller, G. A. (2001). Culture and organizational structure in the Middle East: A comparative analysis of Iran, Jordan and the USA. *International Review of Sociology, 11*(3), 309–324.

Shirley, E. G. (1994, Fall). The Iran policy trap. *Foreign Affairs, 96*, 75–93.

Shouval, R., Kav Venaki, S., Bronfenbrenner, U., Devereux, E. C., & Kiely, E. (1986). Anomalous reactions to social pressure of Israeli and Soviet children raised in family versus collective settings. In T. R. Horowitz (Ed.), *Between two worlds: Children from the Soviet Union in Israel* (pp. 67–90). New York: University Press of America.

Skinner, B. F. (1937). Two types of conditioned reflex: A reply to Konorski and Miller. *Journal of General Psychology, 16*, 272–279.

Sorokin, P., & Merton, R. (1990). Social time: A methodological and functional analysis. In

Hassard, J. (Ed.), *The sociology of time* (pp. 56–66). Basingstoke, UK: Macmillan.

Spector, P. E., Cooper, C. L., Sparks, K., Bernin, P., Büssing, A., Dewe, P., et al. (2001). An international study of the psychometric properties of the Hofstede Values Survey Module 1994. *Applied Psychology: An International Review, 50,* 269–281.

Stein, K. B., Sarbin, T. R., & Kulik, J. A. (1968). Future time perspective: Its relation to the socialization process and the delinquent role. *Journal of Consulting and Clinical Psychology, 32,* 257–264.

Strathman, A., Gleicher, F., Boninger, D. S., & Edwards, C. S. (1994). The consideration of future consequences: Weighing immediate and distant outcomes of behavior. *Journal of Personality and Social Psychology, 66,* 742–752.

Stubbart, C. (1982). Are environment scanning units effective? *Long Range Planning, 15*(3), 139–145.

Subramaniam, S. (2001). The dual narrative of "good governance": Lessons for understanding political and cultural change in Malaysia And Singapore. *Contemporary Southeast Asia: A Journal of International and Strategic Affairs, 23*(1), 65–80.

Sundberg, N. D., Poole, M. E., & Tyler, L. E. (1983). Adolescents' expectations of future events—A cross-cultural study of Australians, Americans, and Indians. *International Journal of Psychology, 18,* 415–427.

Swearer, D. K. (1997). The worldliness of Buddhism. *Wilson Quarterly, 21*(2), 81–93.

Takyi-Asiedu, A. (1993). Some socio-cultural factors retarding entrepreneurial activity in Sub-Saharan Africa. *Journal of Business Venturing, 8,* 91–98.

Teahan, J. E. (1958). Future time perspective, optimism, and academic achievement. *Journal of Abnormal and Social Psychology, 57,* 379–380.

Teather, E. K., & Chow, C. S. (2000). The geographer and the feng shui practitioner: So close and yet so far apart? *Australian Geographer, 31*(3), 309–332.

Tendam, H. W. (1987). Managerial flexibility: A strategic asset. *Leadership & Organization Development Journal, 8*(2), 11–16.

Thoms, M. A., & Greenberger, D. B. (1995). The relationship between leadership and time orientation. *Journal of Management Inquiry, 4,* 272–292.

Thrift, N. (1990). The making of capitalist time consciousness. In J. Hassard. (Ed.), *The sociology of Time* (pp. 105–129). Basingstoke, UK: Macmillan.

Toda, M. (1983). Future time perspective and human cognition: An evolutional view. *International Journal of Psychology, 18*(5), 351–365.

Trempala, J., & Malmberg, L. (1998). The anticipated transition to adulthood: Effects of culture and individual experience on Polish and Finnish adolescents' future orientations. *Journal of Psychology, 132,* 255–267.

Triandis, H. C. (1984). Toward a psychological theory of economic growth. *International Journal of Psychology, 19,* 79–95.

Trommsdorff, G. (1983). Future orientation and socialization. *International Journal of Psychology, 18,* 381–406.

Trommsdorff, G., & Lamm, H. (1975). An analysis of future orientation and some of its social determinants. In J. T. Fraser & H. Lawrence (Eds.), *The study of time II* (pp. 343–361). New York: Springer.

Trommsdorff, G., Lamm, H., & Schmidt, R. W. (1979). A longitudinal study of adolescents' future orientation (time perspective). *Journal of Youth and Adolescence, 8,* 131–147.

Trompenaars, F., & Hampden-Turner, C. (1998). *Riding the waves of culture: Understanding cultural diversity in global business* (2nd ed.). New York: McGraw-Hill.

Tu, W. M. (1991). The continuity of being: Chinese visions of nature. In J. B. Callicott & R. T. Ames (Eds.), *Nature in Asian traditions of thought: Essays in environmental philosophy* (pp. 67–78). New Delhi: Sri Satguru Publications.

Tversky, A., & Kahneman, D. (1974). Judgment under uncertainty: Heuristics and biases. *Science, 185,* 1124–1131.

Van Vianen, A. E., & Fischer, A. H. (2002). Illuminating the glass ceiling: The role of organizational culture preferences. *Journal of Occupational and Organizational Psychology, 75,* 315–337.

Volder, M. M. de, & Lens, W. (1982). Academic achievement and future time perspective as a cognitive-motivational concept. *Journal of Personality and Social Psychology, 42,* 566–571.

Wallace, M. (1956). Future time perspective in schizophrenia. *Journal of Abnormal and Social Psychology, 52,* 240–245.

Wallace, M., & Rabin, A. I. (1960). Temporal experience. *Psychological Bulletin, 57* (3), 213–236.

Watson, J. B. (1913). Psychology as the behaviorist views it. *Psychological Review, 20,* 158–177.

Webber, M. J. (1972). *Impact of uncertainty on location.* Cambridge: MIT Press.

Weber, M. (1958). *The Protestant ethic and the spirit of capitalism.* New York: Scribner's Press.

Williams, J. E., Satterwhite, R. C., & Saiz, J. L. (1998). *The importance of psychological traits: A cross-cultural study.* New York: Plenum.

Wing Sue, D., & Sue, D. (1990). Counseling American Indians. In *Counseling the culturally different: Theory and practice* (pp. 175–188). New York: John Wiley.

Winnbust, J. A. M. (1975). *Het Westerse Tijds-syndroom: Conceptuele integratie en eerste aanzet tot construct-validatie van eeen reeks molaire tijdsvariabelen in de psychologie* [The Western Time Syndrome: Conceptual integration and first attempt to construct validation of a series of molar time variables in psychology]. Nijmegen, The Netherlands: Stichting Studentenpers Nijmegen.

World Bank. (2000). *Towards a measure of genuine savings.* Retrieved September 2000 from http://www.worldbank.org/data/wdi2000/pdfs/tab3_15.pdf

Yi, C. H. (1998). *Yi Chung-Hwan's t'aengniji: The Korean classic for choosing settlements* (University of Sydney East Asian Series No. 12; I. C. Yoon, Ed. & Trans.). Sydney, Australia: Wild Peony. (Original work published c. 1750)

Yoshino, M. Y. (1976). *Japan's multinational enterprises.* Honolulu: Hawaii University Press.

Yukl, G. (1998). *Leadership in organizations* (4th ed.). Upper Saddle River, NJ: Prentice Hall.

Zaleski, Z., Chlewinski, Z., & Lens, W. (1994). Importance of and optimism-pessimism in predicting solution to world problems: An intercultural study. In Z. Zaleski (Ed.), *Psychology of future orientation* (pp. 207–228). Lublin, Poland: Towarzystwo Naukowe KUL.

Zimbardo, P. G., & Boyd, J. N. (1999). Putting time in perspective: A valid, reliable individual-differences metric. *Journal of Personality and Social Psychology, 77,* 1271–1288.

14

CROSS-CULTURAL DIFFERENCES IN GENDER EGALITARIANISM

Implications for Societies, Organizations, and Leaders

CYNTHIA G. EMRICH

FLORENCE L. DENMARK

DEANNE N. DEN HARTOG

INTRODUCTION

"Societies that are relatively unconcerned with demarcating men from women are less common than those concerned with affirming men's masculinity; but comparatively egalitarian societies have existed in every major region of the world." (Coltrane, 1992).

Human beings are complex, social creatures capable of assuming multiple roles at any given time and over the course of their lives. One of the most fundamental ways in which societies differ is in the extent to which each prescribes and proscribes different roles for women and men (Hofstede, 1980, 1998). Some societies are more gender egalitarian and seek to "minimize

gender role differences" (House et al., 1999), whereas other societies are more gender differentiated and seek to maximize such differences. In this chapter, we explore the nature, antecedents, and implications of cross-cultural differences in gender egalitarianism, or the division of roles between women and men. We then present findings on gender egalitarianism from Project GLOBE. Finally, we discuss the implications of these cross-cultural differences in gender egalitarianism for societies, organizations, and leaders.

In *Culture's Consequences*, Hofstede (1980) identified four norms that varied systematically across cultures and reflected "a basic and enduring anthropological fact about a national

AUTHORS' NOTE: We would like to thank Erica Heitner for her assistance in the preparation of this chapter.

society: that society's specific answer to a general problem with which any human society has to cope" (Hofstede, 1998, p. 10). Hofstede's masculinity/femininity dimension addressed the problem of the "duality of female versus male" (p. 11). Perhaps because societies' answers to this problem are both widely debated and wide-ranging in impact, Hofstede (1998) characterized masculinity/femininity as the "taboo dimension of national cultures." He observed that the taboo placed on this dimension was greatest among masculine countries, presumably because of "concerns that lead to stress on political correctness in writing about gender and to vigilance against sexual harassment" (p. 209). In reality, the problem of the duality of female and male is twofold in nature. A society must decide both whether to emphasize and reward behaviors that are stereotypically masculine versus feminine and how to allocate social roles between the genders. We consider these two problems in turn.

The first problem associated with the duality of female and male involves a society's general preoccupation with the "assertiveness" (a stereotypically masculine trait) versus the "nurturance" (a stereotypically feminine trait) of its members (Hofstede, 1980, p. 278). Some societies emphasize and reward the pursuit of recognition and advancement, whereas others emphasize and reward cooperation and caring. As such, societies can be ordered along a continuum, ranging from highly assertive to highly nurturing, to reflect the behaviors and traits that they value in their members.

The second problem associated with the duality of the sexes involves a society's beliefs about the way in which social roles should be allocated between women and men. Some societies prescribe differentiated roles, whereas other societies prescribe overlapping or egalitarian roles. Some societies compel men to work outside the home and women to work inside the home (visible roles), whereas others encourage men and women to participate equally in both venues. In addition, some societies encourage men to engage in "ego" roles and women to engage in "social" roles in the home and in the community, whereas others encourage men and women to engage equally in both emotional roles. In the next section, we discuss in some

detail the development and nature of Hofstede's masculinity/femininity dimension to underscore the differences between it and the measure of Gender Egalitarianism developed in Project GLOBE. Ultimately, we argue that masculinity/ femininity (Hofstede, 1980, 1998, 2001) confounds assertiveness, gender egalitarianism, humane orientation, and achievement orientation, thereby yielding findings that are difficult to interpret.

HOFSTEDE'S MASCULINITY/FEMININITY DIMENSION OF SOCIETAL CULTURE

Conceptually, masculinity/femininity (Hofstede, 1980, 1998, 2001) appears to encompass at least two distinct aspects of societal culture. The first aspect reflects differences among societies in the extent to which each emphasizes and rewards "tough" or "masculine" values such as assertiveness, success, and competition versus "tender" or "feminine" values such as nurturance and solidarity. The emphasis that societies place on masculine versus feminine values manifests itself in a variety of ways. For example, "masculine" cultures have been shown to score higher in achievement motivation and in acceptance of a "machismo style" of management (Triandis, 1994), and to value individual achievement over solidarity, confrontation over cooperation, and independent thought over honoring moral obligations (Doney, Cannon, & Mullen, 1998).

A second aspect of masculinity/femininity (Hofstede, 1980, 1998, 2001) reflects differences among societies in their beliefs about the behavior that is appropriate for males versus females. In more masculine cultures, males are expected to be assertive and tough, whereas females are expected to be modest and tender. In more feminine cultures, both females and males are expected to be modest and tender. These expectations are presumably conveyed through powerful socialization agents such as families, peers, schools, the media, and so forth (Hofstede, 1980). Although cultures do vary in their socialization of males and females, Hofstede (1980) and others (e.g., Coltrane, 1992; Williams & Best, 1982, 1990b) assert that the most common socialization pattern is one in which males are expected to be assertive, but females are expected to be nurturing. Several studies have confirmed this pattern of socialization. In one 45-nation study (Barry, Bacon, & Child, 1957), for example, males were higher on self-reliance, achievement, and independence, whereas females were higher on nurturance, responsibility, and obedience. This pattern emerged in all 45 nations. More recently, scholars have discovered "virtually perfect" correspondence between "sex differences in socialization emphases and sex differences in behavior" (Segall, Dasen, Berry, & Poortinga, 1990, p. 250). These expectations shape not only the behavior of males and females, but their opportunities as well:

> Organizations in masculine societies provide unequal opportunities for men and women to advance in the managerial echelon and stress work centrality over family life, independence over dependence, decision over intuition, assertiveness over consideration, results over process, equity over equality and an adversarial over a mutual style of conflict resolution and negotiation. (Erez, 1994, p. 573)

Development of the Masculinity/Femininity Index

Masculinity/femininity was measured originally by surveying a sample of IBM employees in 40 countries in the late 1960s and early 1970s (Hofstede, 1980). Additional data were collected in the early 1970s that replicated the original findings. The survey itself contains questions related to 14 "work goals" such as earnings, challenge, cooperation, and employment security. Respondents were asked to consider these work goals and then, "Try to think of . . . which would be important to you in an ideal job; disregard the extent to which they are contained in your present job. How important is (each work goal)" (Hofstede, 2001, p. 256). Respondents rated each of the 14 work goals on a 5-point scale, with "1" being "of utmost importance to me" and "5" being of "very little or no importance." Hofstede (1980) identified two clusters in his analysis of respondents' ratings: individualism/collectivism (see Gelfand, Bhawuk, Nishii, & Bechtold, Chapter 16) and

masculinity/femininity (Hofstede, 1980, 1991). For the masculinity pole of this dimension, greatest importance was attached to the work goals of earnings, recognition, advancement, and challenge. In contrast, for the femininity pole, greatest importance was attached to having a good working relationship with one's manager, cooperation among peers, living in a desirable area, and employment security.

Hofstede (1980) chose the masculinity/ femininity label for this dimension, because it was the only one on which men and women in the IBM sample scored differently. Men in this sample attached greatest importance to work goals such as earning and advancement (hence, "masculinity"), whereas women attached greatest importance to goals such as cooperation and a good working relationship with manager (hence, "femininity"). Hofstede (1991) concluded, "The importance of earnings and advancement corresponds to the masculine, assertive, and competitive social role. The importance of relations with the manager and with colleagues corresponds to the feminine, caring, and social-environment role" (p. 82).

Replicating the Masculinity/Femininity Dimension

One criticism of Hofstede's (1980) original study was that the cultural dimensions were derived exclusively from the responses of IBM employees. In response, several scholars have conducted follow-up studies to gauge the extent to which similar dimensions and findings would emerge if markedly different samples of respondents were surveyed. For example, Hoppe (1998) noted that very few of Hofstede's (1980) respondents held leadership positions at IBM, and so he conducted a comprehensive follow-up study of 1,500 higher-level managers from 19 countries (Hoppe, 1990, 1993, 1998). These respondents were alumni of an international study center called the Salzburg Seminar. On average, there were more women in Hoppe's (19%) than in Hofstede's (9%) sample, and Hoppe's respondents were older and more highly educated. The masculinity/ femininity scores obtained in this follow-up study were correlated ($r = .36, p > .05$) with Hofstede's study (1980). They were more highly correlated ($r = .83, p < .01$), however, with a reformulated version of Hofstede's index (1998, 2001). In Hofstede's original formulation, four work values comprised the masculinity/femininity dimension: advancement and earning for masculinity and security and cooperation for femininity. The reformulated index retains advancement (masculinity) and cooperation (femininity) but replaces the other two goals with two new items. For masculinity, the new item measures individuals' beliefs in a just world by gauging the extent to which they agree with this statement: "When people have failed in life it is often their own fault." For femininity, the new item measures the extent to which individuals agree that "Most people can be trusted." Although this reformulated index yielded stronger correlations between respondents at IBM and the Salzburg Seminar, the gender differences that initially prompted Hofstede to label the dimension masculinity/femininity failed to replicate in the latter sample. Specifically, the men and women at the Salzburg Seminar created nearly identical rank orderings of Hofstede's 14 work goals (rho = 0.96, $p < .01$).

A more recent study of male airline pilots from 19 countries also failed to replicate Hofstede's (1980) masculinity/femininity index (Merritt, 2000). One possible explanation for this finding is that these male pilots ranked "employment security"—a feminine work value— so highly due to the volatility in the aviation industry. Further, the fact that male pilots are employed in a relatively financially rewarding occupation may account for their relatively low rankings of "earnings"—a masculine work value (Merritt, 2000). Taken together, the results from Hoppe's (1998) and Merritt's (2000) studies suggest limitations in the generalizability of the masculinity/femininity dimension.

Other Criticism of the Masculinity/Femininity Dimension

Masculinity/femininity, like individualism/ collectivism, affects the way that individuals function in their social environments. Hofstede and Vunderink (1994), noted, however, that though the individualism/collectivism dimension has been largely accepted by scholars, the same is not true for the masculinity/femininity dimension, which has received far more criticism. They argue

that both dimensions were presaged by the early anthropological work of Inkeles and Levinson (1954/1969, 1954/1997), and that the original research data confirmed that both dimensions reflected important aspects of societal culture. Hofstede and Vunderink (1994) have argued, too, that some scholars' inappropriate interpretation of findings related to the masculinity/femininity dimension are partly to blame for the confusion surrounding it: "In quite a few cases, differences in psychological functioning across cultures that conceptually clearly relate to the *mas/fem* distinction have indiscriminately been attributed to individualism/collectivism: Masculinity at the individualist pole and femininity at the collectivist pole" (p. 330). Another criticism is that masculinity/femininity does not yield as "intuitive" a clustering as do other dimensions. For example, individualism/collectivism typically yields clear contrasts between the Western and Asian cultures, whereas masculinity/femininity does not. The latter "bundles countries that are not engaged in common institutional dialogues, as is the case for Asian countries versus the West" (Hofstede & Vunderink, 1994, p. 330).

Masculinity/femininity has also been criticized as overemphasizing conventional gender roles that may be less valid for self-description (Bem, 1975; Fagenson, 1990; Martin, 1987) given declining differences in the socialization of males and females in many countries (Segall et al., 1990). The nonsignificant sex differences in Hoppe's (1998) aforementioned study suggest that this criticism may be a valid one. To this criticism, Hofstede and Vunderink (1994) responded that masculinity/femininity is a dimension of national culture, and

> . . . [is] not meant to describe individuals, but dominant patterns of socialization ("mental programming") in nations; these dominant patterns will affect different individuals to different degrees, and some components of a national culture pattern may be found in one individual, while other complementary components will be found in other individuals within the same society. (p. 331)

Correlates of Masculinity/Femininity

In Hofstede's (1980) original study, masculinity/femininity was not significantly correlated with the other three dimensions of societal culture, with one exception. When Hofstede distinguished between wealthier and poorer countries, masculinity/femininity and uncertainty avoidance were positively correlated ($r = .43$, $p < .05$) in the wealthier countries, but negatively correlated ($r = .21, p > .05$) in the poorer countries (Hofstede, 1980). Moreover, the combination of these two dimensions was the best predictor of McClelland's (1961) "need for achievement." Presumably, societal norms for masculinity and uncertainty avoidance influence individuals' values with regard to potential motivators. Masculinity/femininity reflects the opposition of ego needs versus affiliation needs, respectively, whereas uncertainty avoidance reflects the opposition of success motivation (low uncertainty avoidance) versus fear motivation (high uncertainty avoidance).

Masculinity/femininity has been significantly correlated with numerous societal-level measures. For example, more masculine societies were found to be less permissive than more feminine cultures (Hofstede, 1991). Governments in more masculine societies were more likely to sacrifice the environment in pursuit of economic growth (Hofstede, 1991). Masculinity/femininity has been significantly correlated with various viewpoints as well (Hofstede, 1980, 1991). For example, respondents from more masculine societies more strongly endorse viewpoints such as "individuals make better decisions than groups," "it is better to work for a large corporation than a small one," and "employees will avoid work if they can."

Finally, Hofstede's (1980, 1998, 2001) masculinity/femininity dimension has been significantly correlated with various value dimensions, although not always in directions that make intuitive sense. As one might expect, masculinity/femininity was positively correlated with "mastery," or the self-assertion to control one's social and physical environments in a 23-nation study (Schwartz, 1994). But masculinity/femininity was also positively correlated with "human-heartedness" or the social awareness and need to be courteous to others in another, 22-nation study (Chinese Culture Connection, 1987). The correlation with mastery makes intuitive sense. The correlation

with human-heartedness, in contrast, is somewhat puzzling, especially given that items that load positively on this measure seem to reflect more feminine values such as "kindness," "patience," and "courtesy."

To summarize, Hofstede's (1980) original study represents a milestone in the research on national cultures. However, the findings to date are mixed with regard to the reliability and validity of his masculinity/femininity dimension. Conceptually, this dimension appears to encompass at least two distinct subdimensions: specifically, the extent to which societies foster and reward stereotypically masculine versus feminine behavior among members in general and the extent to which they advocate differentiated versus egalitarian roles for women and men more specifically. To further complicate matters, stereotypical masculine behaviors include success striving and assertiveness, whereas stereotypical feminine behaviors include nurturance and gender egalitarianism. As a result, Hofstede's masculinity/femininity measure confounds at least four dimensions of societal culture and possibly others. Consequently, it is very difficult to interpret the masculinity/femininity measure itself and its correlations with other measures. For the purposes of Project GLOBE, we chose to empirically investigate cultural dimensions of Performance Orientation (see Javidan, Chapter 12) in lieu of success striving, Humane Orientation (Kabasakal & Bodur, Chapter 18) in lieu of nurturance, as well as Assertiveness (Den Hartog, Chapter 15) and Gender Egalitarianism as two distinct cultural dimensions. The results of Project GLOBE empirically confirm the conceptual division of these constructs.

Project GLOBE's Gender Egalitarianism measure constitutes the focus of this chapter. At its core, this measure reflects societies' beliefs about whether members' biological sex should determine the roles that they play in their homes, business organizations, and communities. Societies with greater gender egalitarianism rely less on biological sex to determine the allocation of roles between the sexes. Henceforth, then, we refer to societies that seek to minimize differences between the roles of females and males in homes, organizations, and communities as gender egalitarian. In principle and in practice, any distinction among societies with respect to this dimension is continuous rather than dichotomous in nature. Thus, gender egalitarianism is a relative term, with any given society being more or less egalitarian than other societies in the same study. In the next section, we discuss the larger context of the Gender Egalitarianism construct and its relevance to individuals, organizations, and societies.

The Larger Context of Gender Egalitarianism

Scholars from multiple perspectives recognize the universality of the division of roles between the sexes. Some anthropologists regard the duality of female and male as one of the most fundamental dualities in the human existence—a duality that dictates reproduction and, hence, the perpetuation of societies (Braidotti, 1994; Gilmore, 1996; Linke, 1992; Roschrhomberg, 1994). Women not only bear children, but also feed and nurture them. Hence, the responsibility for nurturing people generally, and children, more specifically, falls on women. Men, on the other hand, are placed in charge of economic matters.

From a psychological perspective, sex ranks alongside age as a "universal dimension for differentiating people" (Fiske & Taylor, 1991, p. 121). Psychological differentiation of the sexes occurs by assigning distinct and nonoverlapping personality traits to females and males. The duality of male assertiveness and female nurturance is a common stereotypic portrait. Studies have found that women are considered more communal and expressive than men, whereas men are deemed more competent, agentic, and instrumental than women (Denmark, Rabinowitz, & Sechzer, 2000).

From a biological perspective, only childbearing and child begetting constitute absolute sex differences. All other differences are statistical with, for example, the average man being taller, stronger, and heavier than the average woman, and the average woman having greater finger dexterity, longer life-expectancy, and faster metabolism than the average man

(Hofstede, 1980, p. 262). These absolute and statistical biological differences shape, in part, societal norms regarding the behavior, activities, and occupations that are deemed suitable for each gender.

Of course, history offers numerous examples of women who managed to circumvent the prevailing cultural norms of their societies to pursue careers that were prohibited to them. For example, the Brontë sisters ("Acton, Currer, and Ellis Bell"), Mary Ann Evans ("George Eliot"), and Amantine Aurore Dudevant ("George Sand") assumed male noms de plume to pursue celebrated literary careers (Jordan & Patten, 1995; Walton, 2000). In medicine, Dr. Mary Putnam Jacobi initially wrote anonymously for the prestigious *New York Medical Record*. Over time, however, she made fewer concessions to the limits placed on her by the male-dominated medical profession and pioneered the use of survey data in medical research (Wells, 2001). Though notable, women such as these constitute exceptions (McElvaine, 2000). Moreover, societal norms regarding appropriate roles for females and males affect not only their career choices and success (Heilman, 1995; Stroh, Brett, & Reilly, 1992; Walker & Fennell, 1986), but also their mental and physical health (Girard, 1993; Peterson & Smith, 1997; Piccinelli & Simon, 1997), mortality (Kattler & Williamson, 1988; Pampel & Park, 1986; Pattnayak & Shai, 1995), parent–child relationships (Coltrane, 1988, 1992; Katz & Konnor, 1981; Mead, 1949), and a host of other outcomes that dictate the nature and quality of human life. Our focus in this chapter is on the cultural norms that shape the roles and, hence, lives of females and males in societies around the globe.

Gender egalitarianism can best be explored in the context of its attitudinal domain and its behavioral manifestations. Figure 14.1 depicts the two components of Gender Egalitarianism as conceptualized and measured in Project GLOBE. Its attitudinal domain relates to the fundamental values, beliefs, and attitudes held by members of a society with regard to gender stereotypes and gender-role ideology. The behavioral manifestations are actions and behaviors observed in a society in relation to gender egalitarianism—for example, gender discrimination and gender equality.

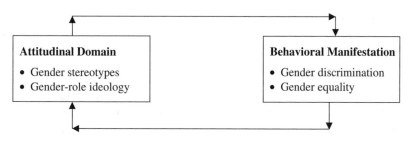

Figure 14.1   The Two Components of Gender Egalitarianism

The Attitudinal Domain

Studies of gender stereotypes examine the cognitive structures that guide the way people attend to, encode, and retrieve information about females and males in their social environments (e.g., Heilman, Block, & Martell, 1995). These cognitive structures guide information processing, because they serve as powerful expectations about the behavior, qualities, and abilities of females and males. There are substantial cross-cultural similarities in gender stereotypes (Best et al., 1977; Best & Williams, 1993; Williams & Best, 1982). Children as young as 5 years of age, in both Western countries such as France, Norway, and the United States as well as non-Western countries such as Malaysia, Nigeria, and Peru hold distinct stereotypes of women versus men. For example, children in these countries viewed women as weak, gentle, meek, and emotional, but viewed men as aggressive, strong, and dominant. Evidence suggests that gender stereotypes only strengthen with age, with 8-year-old children holding stereotypes of women and men that are even more "sex-typed" and consistent cross-culturally. Results obtained with college-age students are similar to those obtained with children. In one 25-nation study (Williams & Best, 1990a), for example, students characterized men as active, strong, aggressive, adult, autonomous, and achievement-oriented, but characterized women as passive, weak, nurturing, child-like, deferential, and affiliation-oriented. In addition, traits ascribed to men were judged to be more favorable, active, and strong than were traits ascribed to women, although there were substantial cross-cultural differences.

Although no cross-cultural studies have attempted to relate these differences to our concept of Gender Egalitarianism, we would expect greater convergence in judgments of the favorableness, activity, and strength of traits ascribed to women compared with those ascribed to men in more gender-egalitarian societies.

A second associated concept to consider is gender-role ideology, which "refers to an individual's beliefs about proper role relationships between women and men" (Best & Williams, 1993, p. 222). Individuals' gender-role ideologies vary along a continuum of "traditional" to "modern." Traditional ideologies view men as more "important" (p. 222) than women and advocate relationships in which men dominate and control women. In contrast, modern ideologies view men and women as equals and advocate egalitarian relationships between them. Based on this definition of gender-role ideology, it seems likely that it is associated with our concept of Gender Egalitarianism. One cross-cultural study (Williams & Best, 1990b) supports this notion: The more similarly women and men were perceived to be, the greater women's participation in higher education and in the labor force. This study also revealed a positive association between development or modernization and gender-role ideology, with men's and women's roles perceived more similarly in more economically and socially developed countries. Presumably, the blurring of gender roles generates a more egalitarian cultural climate in which "traditional patriarchal patterns of female seclusion and male dominance are replaced by women's greater civil equality and political participation" (Segall et al., 1990,

p. 255). In this way, gender-role ideologies and gender egalitarianism are linked in theory and in reality.

Behavioral Manifestations

A third concept associated with gender egalitarianism is gender discrimination. Both gender stereotypes and gender-role ideologies reflect individuals' internalized beliefs regarding the behavior, qualities, roles, and abilities of females and males and, as such, comprise the attitudinal domain of gender egalitarianism. By contrast, gender discrimination constitutes an external act (i.e., a behavioral manifestation) that prevents members of one sex from gaining the recognition, occupations, positions, and status accorded to equally qualified members of the opposite sex. These concepts are associated, because it seems likely that gender stereotypes and gender-role ideologies play key roles in gender discrimination. The Supreme Court of the United States gave legal standing to this argument when it ruled that gender stereotyping was a precursor to gender discrimination and, as such, constituted a violation of women's civil rights:

> In the specific context of stereotyping, an employer who acts on the basis of a belief that a woman cannot be aggressive, or that she must not be, has acted on the basis of gender. . . . We are beyond the day when an employer could evaluate employees by assuming or insisting that they matched the stereotype associated with their group. . . . An employer who objects to aggressiveness in women but whose positions require this trait places women in an intolerable Catch 22: out of a job if they behave aggressively and out of a job if they don't. (*Price Waterhouse v. Hopkins*, 1989, pp. 1790–1791)

Gender egalitarianism and the concepts of gender stereotypes, gender-role ideology, and gender discrimination are interwoven because beliefs about what females and males can and should do reinforce a society's preferences regarding the allocation of roles between them. In the case cited above, gender stereotypes that depicted, and even demanded, passivity in women led Price Waterhouse to deny Ann Hopkins, an aggressive and achievement-oriented woman,

partnership in its firm. In this way, gender stereotypes, and the discrimination they fostered, served to reinforce societal norms regarding appropriate roles for women and men in the American workplace.[1]

The final concept to consider is gender equality (Hendrix, 1994). Studies of gender equality focus on the degree to which women and men are represented equally in the labor force and in positions of authority (e.g., Blackburn, Jarman, & Siltanen, 1993; Charles, 1992; Clark & Anker, 1993; Jacobs & Lim, 1992; Kukreja, 1992; Moore & Shackman, 1996; Nuss & Majka, 1983; Wright, Baxter, & Birkelund, 1995). Studies of gender equality also examine women's and men's relative contributions to child rearing and housework (e.g., Berk & Berk, 1979; Chafetz & Hagan, 1996; Coverman & Sheley, 1986; Hochschild, 1989; Reskin & Padavic, 1994; South & Spitze, 1994; Szalai, 1972). Thus, the concept of gender equality, like gender discrimination, constitutes a behavioral manifestation of societies' beliefs about the appropriate allocation of roles between the sexes, or gender egalitarianism. The more that a society seeks to minimize differences in the roles allocated to the sexes, the more equality we would expect to find in women's and men's participation in the labor force, positions of authority, child rearing, and housework. The more that a society seeks to maximize differences in the roles allocated to the sexes, the more inequality we would expect to find in women's and men's participation in these same areas.

To summarize, we began this section with a discussion of different perspectives—anthropological, psychological, and biological—on the duality between the sexes. We moved next to a consideration of the two key components of gender egalitarianism: its attitudinal domain and behavioral manifestations. By taking into consideration the larger context of gender egalitarianism, it is possible to anticipate its causes and consequences. As a cultural norm, gender egalitarianism reflects individuals' stereotypes and ideologies regarding females and males. These beliefs play a key role in gender discrimination, an act that promotes gender inequality in homes, workplaces, and communities. In this way, the relationships among gender stereotypes and gender-role ideology on the one hand and gender discrimination and gender inequality on the other comprise a recurrent feedback loop. Specifically, gender stereotypes and ideologies about what is possible or appropriate for females and males limit their social roles, thereby affecting their participation in the labor force and their contributions to their families. Gender inequality in the home, workplace, and society shapes, in turn, individuals' gender stereotypes and ideologies, bringing us full circle. The concept of gender egalitarianism grounds this feedback loop in powerful and overarching cultural norms about the division of roles between the sexes. These norms, though not explicit in Figure 14.1, are the focus of this chapter. Next, we consider past research on the causes of cross-cultural differences in gender egalitarianism and explore its relevance to individuals, organizations, and societies.

COMPARISON OF HIGH VERSUS LOW GENDER EGALITARIANISM SOCIETIES

The principal goal of social-scientific research is to disentangle the causes and consequences of important social phenomena. In practice, this goal is often very difficult to achieve. For example, Hofstede (1980) attempted to explain why Scandinavian countries scored so highly on a feminine (vs. masculine) trait scale relative to the other countries in his sample. He speculated that cultural norms promoting overlapping or egalitarian roles for women and men might be rooted in the days when Viking men were away from their villages for long periods of time. When these men were away, Scandinavian societies presumably had no choice but to allow and even encourage women to assume traditionally masculine roles. However, Hofstede suggested an alternative explanation when he questioned whether Viking men traveled "so far and so long . . . because they had women who were able to manage the home front?" (1980, p. 206). Here, Hofstede confronted the classic "Which came first?" dilemma. Did the men's absences necessitate a more gender-egalitarian culture, or did minimized gender-role differences make it possible for the men to sally forth in the first place?

Confounded explanations such as these may never be resolved to our satisfaction. Nonetheless, we devote this section to a discussion of the potential causes of cross-cultural differences in gender egalitarianism. It has been suggested that "our reasoning about sex roles and inequality has been woefully oversimplistic," and that "we need to at least think about multiple causes and feedback relations as we try to develop our theories further" (Hendrix & Hossain, 1988, p. 452). With this critique and recommendation in mind, we cover a number of potential causes of gender egalitarianism. The majority of these have not been examined in the context of gender egalitarianism per se, but in the context of associated constructs such as gender stratification, gender ideology, and gender equality. In this section, we attempt to make the case for a causal relationship between these potential cultural drivers and gender egalitarianism specifically (see Table 14.1).

Table 14.1   Cultural Drivers of Gender Egalitarianism

- Parental investment
- Climate or geographic latitude
- Religion
- Economic development
- Social structure and resource control
- Mode of production
- Political system

Parental Investment

Earlier, we noted that the only absolute differences between the sexes are that men beget children whereas women bear children. Not surprisingly, this difference has a profound impact on gender-role differences, even as we begin the 21st century. The theory invoked most frequently to explain the impact of biological differences on women's and men's social roles is parental investment theory (Trivers, 1972). According to this theory, parental investment is defined as "any investment that enhances the offspring's chances of survival at the cost of the parent's ability to invest in other offspring" (p. 139). Among mammals, females are more limited than males in the number of offspring that they can produce; therefore, their parental investment is necessarily greater:

> In mammals the female is uniquely adapted to care for the young, and the male is not necessarily joined to the mother-offspring unit. In most mammals the parents do not remain together after copulation, and the male contributes no parental investment except the sperm. (Katz & Konnor, 1981, p. 159)

The balance between the parental investments of women and men varies across cultures. In the past 20 years, scholars have focused on men's participation in child rearing as a potential explanation of cross-cultural differences in the division of roles between the sexes (Coltrane, 1988, 1992; Katz & Konnor, 1981).

For example, numerous explanations have been proposed to account for women's limited public authority in most countries. Common to virtually all of these explanations "is the notion that women's primary responsibility for child rearing, while culturally conditioned, constrains their ability to exercise public power" (Coltrane, 1988, p. 1061). Earlier, we argued that gender stereotypes, gender-role ideologies, gender discrimination, and gender inequality combine to form a recurrent feedback loop. Coltrane (1988, 1992) and others (e.g., Chodorow, 1978; Mead, 1949; Parsons, 1964; Slater & Slater, 1965) have argued similarly that the "sexual division of labor in child rearing" (Coltrane, 1988, p. 1061) reinforces gender-role stereotypes and ideologies by exposing children to women and men in their traditional roles of caretakers and providers, respectively. Through exposure to women and men in traditional gender roles, children come to internalize these in the form of stereotypes and ideologies. In this way, gender roles are passed down through successive generations.

This argument has led some to speculate that, by increasing men's parental investment (Trivers, 1972) or involvement in child rearing, it might be possible to increase the public prestige and authority of women. Greater paternal investment in child rearing may not only give women more time to pursue nontraditional social roles, it may also expose children to more women and men in nontraditional social roles. In this way, increased paternal investment may help to create a new set of beliefs about the roles that are possible and appropriate for women and men. In a sample of 90 nonindustrial societies (Coltrane, 1988), the more active men's involvement in child rearing, the greater women's decision making and authority in their communities. Thus, the greater men's role in child rearing in a society and the closer their proximity to their young children, the more affectionate their relationships with their children and the greater the public prestige of women in that society. This relationship held even after controlling for several factors that were believed to influence women's status such as a male social structure, external warfare, and societal complexity.

A more recent study of 92 nonindustrial societies (Coltrane, 1992) demonstrated a strong and consistent relationship between men's parental investment and key measures of women's prestige in the home and in society, thereby replicating the results reported above (Coltrane, 1988). Results showed that men's parental investment was negatively correlated with women's deference to men, husbands' dominance over their wives, and an ideology of women's inferiority. The closer men's proximity to their children, the more active their role in caring for their children: the more affectionate their relationships with their children, the more egalitarian the treatment of and beliefs about women in that society. These results pinpoint potential mediators of the earlier-reported (Coltrane, 1988) relationship between men's parental investment and women's status. Specifically, the quality of men's relationships with their children may affect the way they treat and view women (Coltrane, 1992), which, in turn, may affect women's access to decision making and to positions of authority in society (Coltrane, 1988).

Climate or Geographical Latitude

The ambient temperature of a society, as measured by its geographical latitude or distance from the equator, may be another key determinant of gender egalitarianism. As Hofstede (1980) noted, ambient temperature "clearly comes first. . . . In more moderate climates, survival presupposes the mastery of complex skills by both men and women, which makes extreme inequality between the sexes unlikely" (p. 203). In other words, both women and men must attain similar complex skills in less-hospitable climates to ensure survival. In fact, the relationship between Hofstede's masculinity/femininity dimension and geographical latitude was significant in his original survey (1980): Nations closer to the equator had more masculine cultures, whereas nations closer to the poles had more feminine cultures. This relationship was moderated, however, by national wealth. Specifically, the relationship between geographical latitude and masculinity/femininity was stronger among poor than among wealthy countries (Hofstede, 1980, p. 203). Presumably, the greater struggle for existence (Darwin, 1859/1958) in poor rather than in rich countries increased the salience of biological determinants of gender roles.

More recent investigations have provided additional insight into the role of ambient temperature in gender roles (Peterson & Smith, 1997; Van de Vliert, 1998; Van de Vliert, Schwartz, Huismans, Hofstede, & Daan, 1999; Van de Vliert & Van Yperen, 1996). In each of these studies, Triver's (1972) parental investment theory plays a key explanatory role, because a society's ambient temperature is theorized to affect the degree to which both parents must invest in offspring if the offspring are to survive. In tropical, hunter–gatherer societies, women could gather nearby vegetation year-round and thereby "adequately feed themselves and their children without male provisioning" (Miller, 1994, p. 228). In societies that lie closer to the poles, however, females depend on males to provide meat during the winter, a time when vegetation is dormant. The greater need for male provisioning in colder climates ensures that males will have both greater investment in as well as closer proximity to their offspring. Simply put, it is more demanding to meet basic needs of food, safety, and security in cold climates than in warm climates (Van de Vliert & Van Yperen, 1996). To raise children in cold climates, then, requires cooperation between men and women. This type of "cross-gender exchange, complementary division of labor, and maintenance of mixed-gender interest groups could result in more egalitarian interactive behavior" (Coltrane, 1992, p. 94).

Several scholars have examined the relationship between extreme ambient temperature and Hofstede's masculinity/femininity dimension of societal culture (Peterson & Smith, 1997; Van de Vliert, 1998; Van de Vliert et al., 1999). For example, Van de Vliert and his colleagues (1999) found a positive relationship between ambient temperature and cultural masculinity in 53 countries: The greater the mean ambient temperature of a society's capital, the more masculine its culture. This relationship was significant even after controlling for such factors as population size, population density, economy, and democracy. This and other studies (Hofstede, 1980; Peterson & Smith, 1997; Van de Vliert, 1998) suggest that extreme ambient temperature is a key antecedent of "the culturally programmed tendency of a society's male inhabitants to manifest masculinity" (Van de Vliert, 1998, p. 128). On the basis of Triver's (1972) parental investment theory, it seems likely that ambient temperature also plays a role in the culturally programmed tendency to assign females and males distinct, gender-differentiated roles in homes, organizations, and communities.

The fundamental conclusion of this section is that there is a higher level of cultural masculinity in warmer than in colder climates. Parental investment theory (Trivers, 1972) seems to provide a powerful explanatory hypothesis for this phenomenon. An alternative hypothesis—based on resource dependency theory—would claim that men are granted more status in colder climates because their dexterity and physical attributes are more important to the survival of the family. To date, however, the data most clearly favor Trivers' parental investment theory.

Religion

Scholars continue to debate the potential causal role of religion in gender egalitarianism and related constructs. Monotheism—or the belief in one god—has been linked to the low status of females in societies (Stover & Hope, 1984). The low status of females and monotheistic beliefs are theoretically linked by the fact that virtually all monotheistic cultures worship a male, rather than a female, god (Paxton, 1997). In contrast, polytheistic cultures worship a variety of gods, which often includes both male and female figures. Some have argued that the superior status accorded to males in monotheistic religions causes female's low status. However, some sociologists—for example, Durkheim—have argued the reverse: That "monotheism is a reflection of the causally prior low status of women" (Gray, 1987, p. 1121; see also Verweij, Ester, & Nauta, 1997).

To further complicate matters, obtained correlations between monotheism and gender equality are mixed. In one cross-cultural study, women's status and monotheism were negatively correlated such that women were accorded lower status in monotheistic societies (Stover & Hope, 1984). However, Gray (1987) reanalyzed these findings to examine the possibility that only a subset of geocultural regions was responsible for this correlation:

> Most societies in the Circum-Mediterranean region exhibit both active high gods [i.e., monotheism] and low female status. Societies in the Insular Pacific region usually lack high gods and award high status to women. The societies in these two regions are so uniform that they alone might account for the statistically significant relation between gender bias and monotheism. (p. 1125)

Gray discovered, in fact, that monotheism predicted low status for women in the African, Circum-Mediterranean, East Eurasian, and South American regions of the world but predicted high status for women in the Insular Pacific and North American regions of the world. Thus, monotheism's effect on women's status was not a uniform one worldwide.

Up to this point, our focus has been on the role of religion generally in concepts related to gender egalitarianism—specifically, women's status and prestige, as well as beliefs about women's roles in society. However, the presence or absence of "high gods" (Gray, 1987) or overall religiosity of a culture does not tell the full story, because different religions hold different beliefs about appropriate gender roles in society. In one study, for example, Paxton (1997) examined the relationship between varying dominant religions (i.e., Protestant, Islam, Roman Catholic, and Other) and the representation of women in national legislatures. Drawing linkages between an ideology of women's inferiority in matters of politics and administration and specific religious ideologies, Paxton argued that, although there was variation among Protestant religions, they were generally less patriarchal than the Catholic or Islamic religions. This difference may be due to the fact that religious leaders in both Catholicism and Islam are uniformly male, whereas other religions permit women to hold leadership positions. Geographical region was also a significant predictor of women's representation in national legislatures (Paxton, 1997). Their representation was lowest in the Middle East, Southern Africa, South America, and Asia. The introduction of religion into the equation significantly reduced the predictive power of geographical region. As predicted, Catholicism was negatively associated with women's representation in national legislatures; however, Islam was not. One of the regional variables that remained significant even after the introduction of the religious ideology variables was that of the Middle East, which lead Paxton to speculate that "the interpretation of Muslim doctrine may be more severe in the Middle East" (p. 461). This is true in many countries in the Middle East where religious groups hold political power. Perhaps Islam is more strictly interpreted in the Middle East than in other regions because it is the center of Islamic orthodoxy.

The relationship between religion and gender egalitarianism becomes further complicated by the argument that a society's norms concerning masculinity/femininity affect its religious mentality rather than the reverse (Verweij et al., 1997). Building on prior research and theory (Hofstede, 1991), Verweij and his colleagues argued that a society's gender-role distinctions affect the cognitions and attitudes of its members:

> In masculine countries, God—represented in a male image as Father, King, Shepherd—is felt to be more important in people's everyday lives than in feminine countries. In a feminine culture, relations are more important than distinctions and positions, and therefore in the domain of religion a hierarchical God, or a more outspoken male or female representation of God, is less acceptable than a more nondescript, individualized image of God. (p. 312)

Thus, according to Verweij and his colleagues, the culturally programmed tendency to prescribe differentiated gender roles precedes a society's religious beliefs, thoughts, and practices. Data from the 1990 European Values Survey of 16 Western, industrialized nations is consistent with this prediction. Nations' masculinity/femininity scores constituted "one of the most important single society characteristics explaining cross-national differences in secularization" (Verweij et al., 1997, p. 322), such that the more feminine a nation's culture, the less religiously oriented and orthodox its members.

In summary, scholars continue to debate both the nature and causality of the relationship between religion and constructs related to gender egalitarianism. Nonetheless, there is sufficient empirical evidence and sound theory to regard societies' religious beliefs, thought, and behavior as potentially key antecedents of their tendencies to use members' biological sex to determine their social roles.

Economic Development

Nations vary in the nature and health of their economies. Several past studies have examined the link between various economic indicators and the status and roles of women in societies. Although it is difficult to argue conclusively that economic factors play a causal role in gender egalitarianism and related concepts, it is perhaps easier to argue than the reverse. Moreover, past scholars have typically argued that economic factors play a causal role, and we do so here as well (e.g., Menard, 1990; Moore & Shackman, 1996; Nuss & Majka, 1983; Shen & Williamson, 1999; Sigelman & Tsai, 1985).

The underlying, causal assumption of most past research in this area is that an "acceleration of economic development is accompanied by inevitable improvement in other spheres of society" (Nuss & Majka, 1983, p. 30). According to this modernization perspective (Moore & Shackman, 1996), economic development creates new opportunities for women and other marginalized groups because it both increases available jobs and changes the social and cultural climate. Although theoretically and intuitively compelling, there is mixed evidence for the impact of economic development on women's roles and status in societies (e.g., Smelser, 1970 vs. Boserup, 1970).

One 162-nation study, for example, examined the relationship between national economic development and the integration of women into the labor force (Nuss & Majka, 1983). Gross National Product (GNP), or the value of all products and services produced by a nation, served as the measure of national economic development, and crude labor force participation rates of women served as a measure of their integration into the labor force. There was no overall linear or curvilinear relationship between GNP and women's labor force participation. Instead, higher per capita GNP was associated with increases in women's participation only in traditionally female occupations in the clerical and communication sectors of nations' economies. From these findings, Nuss and Majka (1983) concluded that, "a division of labor between women and men is a global phenomenon. . . . Economic development has no predictive value for the integration of women into the essential sectors of the economy. . . . The same is true for important occupations" (p. 44).

More recently, a study of 32 developing nations found that higher levels of direct investment in a nation led to a "feminization of the tertiary" or service sector of the economy (Kukreja, 1992). Thus, economic development did not create new roles for women in these countries. Instead, it "pushed" them into performing more of the same types of services they had performed in the past. Although women now received financial remuneration for these services, their roles in the labor force were limited, nevertheless, to those traditionally deemed suitable for them.

Given the mixed findings from the modernization perspective, researchers examined it and an alternative, economic competition perspective in one study of 100 nations from all regions of the world (Moore & Shackman, 1996). This alternative perspective argues that gender inequality persists or even increases with growth in industrialization because it stimulates competition between women who are relatively powerless and men who wish to retain their power. The findings from this study supported the economic competition perspective rather than the modernization perspective: GNP had a negative impact on women's participation in administrative occupations, but no impact on women's representation in parliament. Therefore, economic development was associated with either a negative change or no change in women's representation in traditionally male positions in commerce and in politics, respectively.

In summary, the impact of a nation's wealth or economic development on gender equality in the labor force is more equivocal than originally envisioned. One reason may be the types of measures used. GNP is a confounded measure of economic development because of the influence of population size. Regardless, evidence gathered to date suggests that economic development does not create new roles for women but, instead, simply provides more venues— "pink-collar ghettos" (Nuss & Majka, 1983, p. 42)—for them to engage in their traditional, service-oriented roles.

Social Structure and Resource Control

The conflict over scarce resources constitutes one of the most basic struggles in human existence. In many societies, men form strong fraternal interest groups that link "coresident, related men" (Coltrane, 1992) to maintain control over scarce resources and to enhance their power and prestige:

> In a system of patrilineage, not only is descent reckoned through the male line, but there is a tendency for inheritance to flow disproportionately to men. . . . Patrilocality requires women to move near their husband's kin groups at marriage and is commonly seen as enabling men to appropriate women's labor and products while it enhances the authority of senior men. (Coltrane, 1992, p. 93)

According to resource theory (McDonald, 1980; Safilios-Rothschild, 1970), strong fraternal interest groups—created and reinforced by patrilineal descent and patrilocality—promote traditional gender ideologies and gender inequality in societies, because they limit women's ability to "contribute valued resources to the marriage" (Warner, Lee, & Lee, 1986, p. 121). The rationale for this assertion is that

women have relatively few valued resources to contribute to their marriages when they are prevented from both inheriting their families' wealth and living close enough to draw on their support, status, and power. By contrast, the presence of matrilineal descent and matrilocality are theorized to promote more modern gender ideologies and gender equality in societies, because women have more economic and familial resources and, hence, power at their disposal.

There are relatively few societies that trace individuals' lineages and the like through the maternal line, however, just as there are relatively few truly gender egalitarian societies (Coltrane, 1992). Furthermore, as with other potential antecedents of gender egalitarianism, it is difficult to claim unequivocally a causal relationship between a society's structure or resource control and its allocation of roles between the sexes. It seems reasonable to conceptualize societal structure as playing a causal role in gender egalitarianism, nonetheless, because the manner in which a society traces members' ancestries and transfers wealth from one generation to the next is both enduring and highly institutionalized. Thus, this societal aspect likely takes temporal and, hence, causal precedence over other more changeable aspects of societies. With a causal relationship in mind, then, we review several key studies of the relationship between societal structure and various concepts related to gender egalitarianism.

A study of 100 nonindustrialized societies was conducted to identify the "circumstances or conditions under which wives may have greater or lesser decision-making authority in marriage" (Warner et al., 1986, p. 122). The researchers examined women's access to material resources, as operationalized by lineage and locality, and to social resources in two family structures: nuclear and extended. Following on Whytes's (1978) earlier work, it was hypothesized that the presence of multiple adults of both sexes in extended families promotes greater role differentiation between the sexes. If a wife is not able to care for the children in an extended family, then this responsibility need not fall to the husband. A grandmother, aunt, or sister can assume responsibility for the children. In contrast, if the wife is not able to care for the children in a nuclear family, the husband must care for them himself. In Warner and colleague's study, five coders read ethnographic material on more than 100 societies and then rated each on the degree to which wives exercised decision-making authority over their own and family members' behavior, including that of their husbands. Wives had a high degree of power in 46.3% of societies with a nuclear family structure, but in only 29.2% of societies with an extended family structure. In addition, wives had a high degree of power in 70% of societies with matrilineal descent and matrilocality, but in only 32.5% of societies with patrilineal descent and patrilocality. Together, these two findings suggest that access to material resources alone could not account for cross-cultural differences in gender egalitarianism. Social resources in the form of an interdependency and exchange of traditional husband and wife roles also played a key explanatory role.

A second study of 93 nonindustrial societies (Coltrane, 1992) confirmed the dual importance of resource control and male–female interdependence in gender egalitarianism: Women's control of property was negatively correlated with men's displays of manliness, women's deference to men, and husbands' domination of their wives. The more control women had over property, inheritances, and the proceeds from productive labor, the less "belligerence and bravado" (pp. 102–103) men displayed. However, it was only when women both controlled property and shared child rearing responsibilities with men that they were "likely to avoid the harassment and humiliation that comes from being simultaneously feared and denigrated by men" (p. 105).

Two additional studies examined the issue of social structure and resource control, one in the religious domain (Welch, 1982) and the other in the political domain (Welch, 1983). The tenets of resource theory found mixed support in the study of women's religious roles. As predicted, greater "kin power" (e.g., matrilocality) was positively associated with women's selection into the shaman role. However, counter to prediction, greater "property control" (e.g., matrilineage) was negatively associated with women's selection into the shaman role (Welch, 1982). A second study (Welch, 1983) examined the utility of resource theory for explaining the

extent and nature of women's representation in formalized political roles. Contrary to the predictions of resource theory, women's kinship power, property control, and labor value were not significant predictors of women's access to formalized political roles. Consistent with resource theory, women's solidarity was a significant predictor. Thus, predictions associated with resource theory were only partially supported in this study of women's political participation. Despite mixed findings, this study offers an important contribution to the literature in its demonstration of the pivotal role that psychological resources such as women's solidarity can play in promoting gender equality in societies by "transform[ing] a collectivity and prepar[ing] it for various types of socio-political action" (Welch, 1983, p. 69).

To summarize, the social structures put in place to control scarce resources appear to play a key role in the division of roles between the sexes. Women are shown greater deference by men, exert greater decision-making authority, and are more likely to gain access to key religious and political roles when they have greater control over critical economic, social, and psychological resources.

Mode of Production

In a seminal treatise, Sacks (1979) theorized that women's control over the means of production determines their status in societies (see also Hendrix & Hossain, 1988). In this treatise, women's control of production is considered the key mediator in the relationship between mode of production (defined below) and women's social status. Hendrix and Hossain (1988) empirically tested Sack's (1979) causal model in a worldwide sample of 93 tribal and historical societies. In this study, they operationalized mode of production as a combination of two variables: Type of descent system (i.e., matrilineal, patrilineal, or both) and level of social stratification (i.e., recognizing neither class nor wealth distinctions vs. recognizing one but not the other). By combining these two variables, Hendrix and Hossain created a trichotomy of mode of production: The communal mode, the kin corporate mode, and the class mode. Their dependent variable reflected three areas of women's social status: Power and political participation, equality or inequality in sex standards, and invidious stereotypes of women. The results failed to support Sacks's contention that women's control of production mediated the relationship between mode of production and women's social status. Instead, control of production and mode of production emerged as separate antecedents of cross-cultural differences in the social status of women. Women's power and prestige declined as the mode of production became more sophisticated (Hendrix & Hossain, 1988). For this reason, we consider mode of production separate from social structure and resource control (see previous section) as a potential antecedent of gender egalitarianism.

One operationalization of mode of production is a simple dichotomy between agricultural versus all other modes (Becker & Posner, 1993). In one study of "primitive" societies, Becker and Posner examined the relationship between this dichotomized mode of production variable and a measure of the "fixed schedule of compensation, called bloodwealth . . . for killing a human being" (p. 426). Of particular interest was the ratio of the restitution demanded of those who kill a man versus those who kill a woman. If a society's bloodwealth ratio equaled one, equal value was placed on men's and women's lives. A ratio of greater than 1.00 indicated that greater value was placed on men's lives, whereas a ratio of less than 1.00 indicated that greater value was placed on women's lives. The average bloodwealth ratio across the 34 societies studied equaled 1.07, indicating that "men are, on average, only 7% more valuable than women" (p. 429). Of central interest, though, the greater a society's reliance on an agricultural mode of production, the more likely it was to place equal or, even, greater value on the lives of women relative to the lives of men.

To summarize this section, mode of production is significantly related to gender egalitarianism such that greater sophistication in modes of production (Hendrix & Hossain, 1988) or a reliance on nonagricultural (Becker & Posner, 1993) modes of production is linked to the low status and value of women in a society. It is less clear, however, whether mode of production plays a causal role in women's status.

Political Systems

Scholars have argued that proportional representation systems may increase the percentage of female officeholders because citizens cast ballots for parties rather than for individual candidates (Lovenduski & Hills, 1981; Lovenduski & Norris, 1989; Paxton, 1997; Rule, 1987). Party ballots presumably reduce the salience of a candidate's sex, thereby reducing the perceived risk of nominating a female candidate in a proportional representation system. In a simple plurality system such as the United States,' citizens cast votes for candidates rather than parties, thereby increasing the salience of sex, race, and other individual-level characteristics.

One study examined the association between countries' political systems and women's representation in national legislatures (Paxton, 1997). The study covered two time periods—1975 and 1988—in approximately 107 nations from all geographical regions of the world. As predicted, there was a greater percentage of women elected in countries that featured a proportional representation system rather than a simple plurality system, in both time periods. These findings suggest that women may indeed be seen as less risky candidates in a proportional representation system, because the party list may serve as a buffer that decreases the salience of their gender in the minds of voters (Paxton, 1997). In this way, the nature of a society's political system may play a role in gender egalitarianism.

Societies' political systems may also play a role in gender egalitarianism by either facilitating or hindering the rise of women's and other opposition movements (Clark & Carvalho, 1996). In Clark and Carvalho's (1996) 66-nation study, a political regime that tolerated opposition was the single greatest predictor of the occurrence of a women's movement ($r = .61$). Political openness remained the strongest predictor even after controlling for numerous measures of women's labor force participation, percentage of eligible children in secondary school, degree of industrialization, and several additional measures thought to be related to the rise of women's movements in societies. Again, the rise of women's movements is critical to this discussion

Table 14.2   Higher Gender Egalitarianism Societies Versus Lower Gender Egalitarianism Societies

Societies That Score Higher on Gender Egalitarianism Tend to:	Societies That Score Lower on Gender Egalitarianism Tend to:
• Have more women in positions of authority	• Have fewer women in positions of authority
• Accord women a higher status in society	• Accord women a lower status in society
• Afford women a greater role in community decision making	• Afford women no or a smaller role in community decision making
• Have a higher percentage of women participating in the labor force	• Have a lower percentage of women participating in the labor force
• Have less occupational sex segregation	• Have more occupational sex segregation
• Have higher female literacy rates	• Have lower female literacy rates
• Have similar levels of education of females and males	• Have a lower level of education of females relative to males

of cultural drivers of gender egalitarianism because, as noted earlier, the solidarity created through such movements provides a key psychological resource in women's attempts to assume leadership positions in societies (Welch, 1983).

In short, both the nature and openness of a nation's political system may play important and potentially causal roles in women's success in attaining leadership roles traditionally reserved for men. Altogether, we have identified seven potential antecedents of cross-cultural differences in gender egalitarianism: Parental investment, climate, economic development, social structure and resource control, mode of production, religion, and political system.

Summary of Cultural Drivers of Gender Egalitarianism

From the preceding discussion, one gains a sense of the complex nature of gender egalitarianism and related constructs. Gender egalitarianism is complex in the sheer number and range of antecedents that drive cross-cultural differences in the division of roles between the sexes. It is complex, too, in that studies within a particular area sometimes yield contradictory findings. Even so, portraits begin to emerge of societies that seek to minimize gender-role differences as opposed to those that seek to maximize these differences. Although necessarily

tentative and general, the portraits presented in Table 14.2 reflect the pervasive effects of cultural norms regarding gender egalitarianism on males, females, and nations (see also House et al., 1999). We devote the next two sections of this chapter to describing the measurement of the Gender Egalitarianism dimension in Project GLOBE and to exploring the relationship between it and key political, economic, religious, and social indicators.

GLOBE Measures of Gender Egalitarianism

In GLOBE, Gender Egalitarianism was measured at both the societal and organizational levels. At the societal level, participating managers completed two scales: One that assessed their perceptions of the current (*As Is*, or *practices*) degree of Gender Egalitarianism in their societies, and another that assessed their perceptions of the ideal (*Should Be*, or *values*) degree of Gender Egalitarianism in their societies. Managers also completed two scales—*practices* and *values*—that assessed their perceptions of the degree of Gender Egalitarianism in their organizations. Thus, Gender Egalitarianism was measured using four scales, each with three to five quantitative items that survived the statistical procedures described by Hanges and

Table 14.3   Sample Items From the Gender Egalitarianism Scale-Societal Practices (As Is)

1-17. In this society, boys *are* encouraged more than girls to attain a higher education:						
Strongly agree			Neither agree nor disagree			Strongly disagree
1	2	3	4	5	6	7
1-36. In this society, who *is* more likely to serve in a position of high office?						
Men						Women
1	2	3	4	5	6	7

Table 14.4   Sample Items From the Gender Egalitarianism Scale-Societal Values (Should Be)

3-17. I believe that boys *should be* encouraged to attain a higher education more than girls:						
Strongly agree			Neither agree nor disagree			Strongly disagree
1	2	3	4	5	6	7
3-39. I believe that opportunities for leadership positions *should be:*						
More available for men than for women			Equally available for men and women			More available for women than for men
1	2	3	4	5	6	7

Dickson in Chapter 8. Each item was measured on a 7-point scale. All four scales were validated in all societies involved in the GLOBE project to ensure the comparability of the Gender Egalitarianism measures cross-culturally. When interpreting results involving *As Is* and *Should Be* scales, we henceforth use the terms *practices* and *values*, respectively, to emphasize that participating managers' *As Is* responses reflect their perceptions of current practices, whereas their *Should Be* responses reflect their underlying values with regard to an ideal society on this dimension.

Table 14.3 contains sample items from the societal practices scale that was developed to measure participating managers' perceptions of current Gender Egalitarianism practices in their societies. Items are worded exactly as administered, with emphases added to highlight the focus on practices.

Table 14.4 contains sample items from the societal values scale. These items are worded exactly as administered, with emphases added to highlight the focus on values.

Table 14.5 contains a sample item from the organizational Gender Egalitarianism practices scale. This item is worded exactly as administered, with emphasis added to highlight the focus on practices.

Table 14.6 contains a sample item from the organizational Gender Egalitarianism values scale. This item is worded exactly as administered, with emphasis added to highlight the focus on values.

Much cross-cultural research has been conducted using Hofstede's masculinity/femininity dimensions. As noted earlier in this chapter, however, Hofstede's original dimension encompasses at least two GLOBE dimensions—particularly, Aggressiveness and Gender Egalitarianism. Later in this chapter we compare the current findings on Gender Egalitarianism with Hofstede's (1998, 2001) most recent findings on masculinity/femininity.

GLOBE FINDINGS ON GENDER EGALITARIANISM

Mean scores for the GLOBE Gender Egalitarianism scales must be interpreted differently from mean scores for other GLOBE cultural scales.

Table 14.5   Sample Item From the Gender Egalitarianism Scale-Organizational Practices (As Is)

1-17. In this organization, men *are* encouraged to participate in professional development activities more than women.

			Strongly agree			Neither agree nor disagree			Strongly disagree
			1	2	3	4	5	6	7

Table 14.6   Sample Item From the Gender Egalitarianism Scale-Organizational Values (Should Be)

3-17. In this organization, men *should be* encouraged to participate in professional development activities more than women.

			Strongly agree			Neither agree nor disagree			Strongly disagree
			1	2	3	4	5	6	7

All GLOBE cultural items were measured on 7-point scales, and all are constructed such that 7 is the conceptual maximum response, with the exception of Gender Egalitarianism. Its conceptual maximum for most items is 4, or the midpoint of the scale. For these items, a score of 1 indicates strong male domination—for example, "strong" agreement that leadership opportunities are (in the case of practices) or should be (in the case of values) more available for men than for women, whereas a score of 4 on this same item indicates that leadership opportunities are or should be equally available for men and women. A score of 7 indicates a belief that there is or should be, in contrast, preferential treatment of women who seek positions of leadership. Whether this reflects a belief that women are better suited to lead or a desire to redress past discrimination is uncertain. Regardless, a score of 4 represents equal treatment of men and women or maximum gender egalitarianism for this item. This midpoint as the conceptual maximum is also true for the majority of items that comprise the Gender Egalitarianism scales. There are a couple of exceptions to this rule, however. One example is the item that addresses opportunities for boys versus girls to attain a higher education. For this item, a score of 1 indicates "strong" agreement that boys are (in the case of practices) or should be (in the case of values) encouraged more than girls to attain a higher

education. A score of 4 indicates indifference ("neither agree nor disagree"), but a score of 7 indicates "strong" disagreement that boys should be favored in this regard. Thus, for this item, the most gender egalitarian response is not one in which the respondent indicates essentially no opinion but, instead, one in which the respondent registers strong disagreement.

The interpretive complexity of the items used to measure Gender Egalitarianism relative to the other cultural dimensions in GLOBE reflects its ongoing evolution. The response scales for Gender Egalitarianism items were originally written to reflect Hofstede's masculinity/femininity dimension: that is, to differentiate societies in terms of the degree to which they were masculine or feminine. This rationale is reflected in the original GLOBE name for this dimension: Gender Differentiation. But as we discussed in Chapter 8 (by Hanges & Dickson), analyses performed on data from the two pilot studies quickly clarified that our Gender Differentiation items did not measure a single cultural construct but two conceptually distinct, albeit correlated, ones. The Hofstede masculinity/femininity scale correlated with the subset of GLOBE cultural items that were subsequently labeled Assertiveness, whereas the Schwartz egalitarianism scale correlated with the subset of GLOBE cultural items that were subsequently labeled Gender Egalitarianism.

Table 14.7   Grand Means for Gender Egalitarianism

Variable	Mean	Standard Deviation	Minimum	Maximum	Valid N
Gender Egalitarianism society practices	3.37	0.37	2.50	4.08	61
Gender Egalitarianism society values	4.51	0.48	3.18	5.17	61

Thus, our understanding of the Gender Egalitarianism dimension evolved over time, and we would argue that it will and should continue to evolve over the course of future studies. One recommendation for future studies would be to construct items that use the full 7-point response scale, with 7 reflecting the greatest degree of Gender Egalitarianism.

Societal Practices

Across all societies surveyed in GLOBE ($N = 61$), the mean ($M = 3.37$) and standard deviation scores ($SD = 0.37$) for Gender Egalitarianism societal *practices* are lower than for all other cultural dimensions. The mean scores for all other cultural dimensions range from 3.85 to 5.17, which results in a grand mean of 4.25 for all dimensions for all GLOBE countries.

The maximum societal practices score is 4.08. This score does not differ significantly from the midpoint (4.00). Thus, no society in GLOBE is perceived to be female dominated to the point of, for example, encouraging girls, more so than boys, to attain a higher education or of having more women than men in positions of high office. When interpreted in the context of the specific items that comprise the Gender Egalitarianism measure, the mean score of 3.37 indicates a modest, cross-cultural reliance on biological sex in the allocation of roles between females and males.

Interestingly, the standard deviation of 0.37 for Gender Egalitarianism societal practices is tied with Assertiveness for the lowest standard deviation score among the GLOBE societal culture dimensions. Because standard deviation is an indication of variability, the lower score for Gender Egalitarianism indicates greater agreement among respondents in their perceptions of current gender egalitarian practices in their societies than in their perceptions of current practices associated with any other cultural dimensions, with the exception of Assertiveness.

Societal Values

GLOBE respondents indicate that their societies should be ($M = 4.51$) less male dominated than they are now ($M = 3.37$). This can be interpreted to mean that GLOBE respondents generally prefer their societies not to favor men in attainment of higher of education or leadership positions.

Summary of Societal Practices and Values

Table 14.7 contains the summary statistics for both of the Gender Egalitarianism societal-level scales. Taken together, these two measures revealed a paradoxical world in which individuals indicate that biological sex dictates, in part, the roles that are appropriate for females and males, despite believing that biological sex should not dictate these roles. However, these results must be interpreted with caution because it is unclear whether managers responded in socially desirable ways when reporting how society should be with regard to gender egalitarianism. In addition, the results may be affected by the current composition of managers in these societies. Those groups who benefit most from gender egalitarian practices may endorse such practices, whereas those groups who perceive themselves as either unaffected or harmed by gender egalitarian practices may

Table 14.8   Gender Egalitarianism Correlation Matrix-Societal Practices

Gender Egalitarianism	Food Industry Score	Finance Industry Score	Telecommunication Industry Score
Overall score	.94** N = 45	.95** N = 55	.78** N = 32
Food industry score		.87** N = 41	.74** N = 22
Finance industry score			.53** N = 30

** All correlation coefficients significant at $p < .01$ level (2-tailed).

Table 14.9   Gender Egalitarianism Industry Correlation Matrix-Societal Values

Gender Egalitarianism	Food Industry Score	Finance Industry Score	Telecommunication Industry Score
Overall score	.93** N = 45	.97** N = 55	.96** N = 32
Food industry score		.84** N = 41	.83** N = 22
Finance industry score			.89** N = 30

** All correlation coefficients significant at $p < .01$ level (2-tailed).

report a desire for a less gender egalitarian society. However, if the societal values measures accurately reflect managers' attitudes and if these managers are in positions to effect change, we may begin to see a movement in many societies toward greater gender egalitarianism. For example, we may begin to see girls and boys encouraged more equally to attain a higher education and to see more women in leadership positions.

Overall Scores and Industry Scores. As noted earlier, GLOBE society co-investigators gathered societal culture data in three industries: Food, finance, and telecommunications. Table 14.8 below lists the correlation coefficients for the

overall societal practices score for each society and the scores for the participating industries, collapsing across all societies surveyed. As seen in this table, all coefficients are significant, thereby indicating consistency across industries in managers' perceptions of their societies' current practices with respect to gender egalitarianism.

Table 14.9 lists the correlation coefficients for the overall societal values score for each society and the scores for the participating industries, collapsing across all societies surveyed. Again, all coefficients are significant, indicating that the managers' perceptions of how gender egalitarian their societies should be are generally consistent across industries. In other words, all managers surveyed report similar feelings about how their societies should divide roles between women and men, regardless of the industry in which they work.

The Correlation Between Overall Practices and Values Scores. Managers' perceptions of their societies' practices and values with respect to Gender Egalitarianism are significantly correlated ($r = .32$, $p < .05$). This coefficient constitutes a medium-sized effect (Cohen, 1988). Thus, the more gender egalitarian a society's current practices, the more gender egalitarian a manager's values. Of course, this coefficient does not provide insight into the discrepancy (D) between practices and values in a society. As noted earlier, managers overall express a desire for their societies to be more gender egalitarian than they are currently ($D = 1.14$). Managers from Zambia and the Philippines are most prototypical in this respect. Their data points fall closest to the regression line, reflecting their desire for their societies to be somewhat more gender egalitarian than they are now ($Ds = 1.45$ and $.94$, respectively). Less prototypical are managers from Qatar, who express a desire for their society to be slightly less gender egalitarian than it is currently ($D = .25$).

Tables 14.10a and 14.10b contain Gender Egalitarianism practices for both sets of scores, and countries are sorted into "bands." Countries in band A score higher on Gender Egalitarianism than do countries in band B, which in turn score higher on Gender Egalitarianism than do countries in B and C, and so forth. Within a given band—for example, Hungary and Hong Kong in band A (see Table 14.10a)—there are no significant differences in countries' scores on Gender Egalitarianism. Across different bands—for example, Hungary in band A and New Zealand in band B—society scores differ significantly.

Overall Scores and Industry Scores. Although overall scores on the societal level practices and values scales are significantly correlated ($r = .32$, $p < .05$), industry scores on these two scales are not significantly correlated except for the food industry, as displayed in Table 14.11. Thus, within financial and telecom industries, the participating managers' assessments of their societies' current practices are unrelated to their values with regard to Gender Egalitarianism.

GLOBE GENDER EGALITARIANISM AND OTHER ECONOMIC AND SOCIAL INDICATORS

In this section, we will compare and contrast the GLOBE findings on Gender Egalitarianism with those of other major cross-cultural and comparative studies that focused on key economic and social indicators. As Javidan and Hauser explained in Chapter 7, data for these indicators were taken from the following five reports: *The Human Development Report*, the *Global Competitiveness Report*, the *World Competitiveness Yearbook*, the *World Development Indicators*, and the *World Values Survey*. Key indicators from these studies are grouped and then examined in the following two categories: Economic Health and Human Condition.

Gender Egalitarianism and Economic Health

In our review of the literature, we discovered that the relationship between economic development and the status and roles of women in societies was more equivocal than scholars originally envisioned. The modernization perspective had dominated much of past research, with its assumption that economic development creates opportunities for women to take on nontraditional roles in society in general and in the labor force in particular (Moore & Shackman, 1996). However, evidence gathered to date suggests that economic development may instead propel women into performing their traditional (service) roles for pay in what some have termed "pink-collar ghettos" (Nuss & Majka, 1983, p. 42), a finding that is consistent with the economic competition perspective. Although past research is equivocal with respect to the relationship between economic health and the division of roles between women and men, we nonetheless hypothesize the following:

- *Hypothesis 14.1:* Societies that are more gender egalitarian would be more prosperous economically.

Table 14.10a   Gender Egalitarianism: Society Practices (As Is)*

Band					
A		B		C	
Country	*Score*	*Country*	*Score*	*Country*	*Score*
Hungary	4.08	Switzerland[c]	3.42	Kuwait	2.58
Russia	4.07	Australia	3.40	South Korea	2.50
Poland	4.02	Finland	3.35		
Slovenia	3.96	Thailand	3.35		
Denmark	3.93	U.S.	3.34		
Namibia	3.88	Brazil	3.31		
Kazakhstan	3.84	South Africa[d]	3.27		
Sweden	3.84	Indonesia	3.26		
Albania	3.71	Italy	3.24		
Canada[a]	3.70	New Zealand	3.22		
Singapore	3.70	Ireland	3.21		
Colombia	3.67	Japan	3.19		
England	3.67	Israel	3.19		
Portugal	3.66	Taiwan	3.18		
South Africa[b]	3.66	El Salvador	3.16		
Philippines	3.64	Germany[e]	3.10		
France	3.64	Austria	3.09		
Mexico	3.64	Ecuador	3.07		
Qatar	3.63	Germany[f]	3.06		
Venezuela	3.62	China	3.05		
Costa Rica	3.56	Zimbabwe	3.04		
Georgia	3.55	Guatemala	3.02		
Bolivia	3.55	Nigeria	3.01		
Malaysia	3.51	Spain	3.01		
Netherlands	3.50	Iran	2.99		
Argentina	3.49	Switzerland	2.97		
Greece	3.48	India	2.90		
Hong Kong	3.47	Turkey	2.89		
		Zambia	2.86		
		Morocco	2.84		
		Egypt	2.81		

NOTE:

a Canada (English-speaking)
b Switzerland (French-speaking)
c South Africa (Black Sample)
d South Africa (White Sample)
e Germany (West): Former FRG
f Germany (East): Former GDR

* Lower scores indicate greater male domination.
Our response bias correction procedure identified response bias in some countries for this scale (see endnotes).

We examined this hypothesis by computing the correlations among Gender Egalitarianism practices and values, three indicators of economic health, two indicators of support for economic progress, and an indicator of global competitiveness. Javidan and Hauser provide an in-depth discussion of these measures in Chapter 7, and so we provide only brief definitions here. The first indicator of economic health is *economic prosperity,* which reflects the

Table 14.10b   Gender Egalitarianism: Society Values (Should Be)*

Band							
A		B		C		D	
Country	*Score*	*Country*	*Score*	*Country*	*Score*	*Country*	*Score*
England	5.17	South Africa[e]	4.60	Taiwan	4.06	Kuwait	3.45
Sweden	5.15	Ecuador	4.59	Indonesia	3.89	Qatar	3.38
Ireland	5.14	Philippines	4.58	Malaysia	3.78	Egypt	3.18
Portugal	5.13	Guatemala	4.53	Iran	3.75		
Canada[a]	5.11	Poland	4.52	Morocco	3.74		
Denmark	5.08	India	4.51	Georgia	3.73		
U.S.	5.06	Singapore	4.51	China	3.68		
Australia	5.02	Turkey	4.50				
Colombia	5.00	Zimbabwe	4.46				
Brazil	4.99	France	4.40				
Netherlands	4.99	Hong Kong	4.35				
Argentina	4.98	Japan	4.33				
Switzerland	4.92	Zambia	4.31				
Germany[b]	4.90	South Africa[f]	4.26				
Germany[c]	4.89	Namibia	4.25				
Greece	4.89	Finland	4.24				
Italy	4.88	Nigeria	4.24				
Austria	4.83	New Zealand	4.23				
Slovenia	4.83	South Korea	4.22				
Spain	4.82	Albania	4.19				
Venezuela	4.82	Russia	4.18				
Bolivia	4.75	Thailand	4.16				
Kazakhstan	4.75						
Mexico	4.73						
Israel	4.71						
Switzerland[d]	4.69						
El Salvador	4.66						
Costa Rica	4.64						
Hungary	4.63						

NOTE:

a Canada (English-speaking)
b Germany (East): Former GDR
c Germany (West): Former FRG
d Switzerland (French-speaking)
e South Africa (White Sample)
f South Africa (Black Sample)

* Lower scores indicate greater male domination.
Our response bias correction procedure identified response bias in some countries for this scale (see endnotes).

level of consumption and growth in a society. The second is *economic productivity,* which reflects the favorableness of the labor environment and gains in worker productivity. The third indicator, *GNP per capita,* represents the Gross National Product per person in a society. Participating managers' perceptions of their societies' practices with regard to Gender Egalitarianism are not correlated with any of these three indicators. It is possible that the low standard deviation associated with this measure limits the potential to uncover links between it and these measures. In contrast, managers' values positively correlate with all three indicators,

Table 14.11   Gender Egalitarianism Industry Correlation Matrix

Gender Egalitarianism	Overall Score Practices	Food Industry Score Practices	Finance Industry Score Practices	Telecommunication Industry Score Practices
Overall score values	.32* $N = 61$			
Food industry score values		.31* $N = 45$		
Finance industry score values			.20 $N = 55$	
Telecommunication industry score values				.29 $N = 32$

* Correlation significant at $p < .05$ level (2-tailed).

indicating that the more gender egalitarian a society's values, the healthier its economy. Two additional indicators reflect the support for economic progress in a society. The first indicator, *government support for prosperity,* reflects the extent to which government programs and regulations facilitate economic progress. *Societal support for competitiveness,* the second indicator, reflects society members' attitudes toward economic progress. Neither Gender Egalitarianism measure is significantly correlated with these support measures. Finally, the *world competitiveness index*—a measure of the extent to which various factors such as a society's domestic economy, government, and infrastructure support economic competitiveness—is also uncorrelated with the two measures of Gender Egalitarianism.

To summarize, the findings in this section provide partial support for Hypothesis 14.1. The three significant and positive correlations are consistent with the modernization perspective discussed earlier (Moore & Shackman, 1996). This perspective contends that economic growth creates new opportunities and roles for women, thereby minimizing gender-role differences. Of course, the correlational nature of the present findings precludes any conclusions about the direction or, even, presence of a causal relationship between a society's economic

health and a desire to minimize gender-role differences. The modernization perspective assumes that economic growth causes a cultural shift in attitudes and practices surrounding the participation of women and other disadvantaged groups in the labor force. The reverse causal explanation is that a cultural shift in gender egalitarianism fuels economic growth by prompting a society to capitalize more fully on the talents of all members. In light of the present findings, this latter explanation seems less plausible than the modernization perspective's one, because economic health is positively correlated with egalitarian values, but not practices, in Project GLOBE. The notion that a cultural shift in gender egalitarianism precedes economic development would be more plausible if current practices were also positively correlated with the various measures of economic health.

Gender Egalitarianism and Human Condition

Indicators of economic health reflect one aspect of overall well-being in any society. Another important aspect is the general health of a society's members. Consistent with Hauser and Javidan's terminology in this volume, we use the term *human condition* here to describe

Table 14.12 Relationship Between Gender Egalitarianism and Economic Health

Gender Egalitarianism	Economic Prosperity	Economic Productivity	GNP per Capita	Government Support for Prosperity	Societal Support for Competitiveness	World Competitiveness Index
Society practices	.10 N = 57	−.10 N = 40	−.00 N = .61	−.07 N = 40	.16 N = 40	.06 N = 41
Society values	.36** N = 57	.30 N = 40	.44** N = .61	.19 N = 40	−.10 N = 40	.06 N = 41

* Correlation significant at *p* < .05 level (2-tailed).

** Correlation significant at *p* < .01 level (2-tailed).

Table 14.13 Relationship Between Gender Egalitarianism and Human Condition

Gender Egalitarianism	Societal Health	Human Health	Life Expectancy	Psychological Health	General Satisfaction	Human Development Index (HDI)
Society practices	−.22 N = 40	.21 N = 56	.21 N = 56	÷ 15 N = 27	÷ 11 N = 38	.29* N = 56
Society values	.18 N = 40	.15 N = 56	.28* N = 56	÷ 14 N = 27	.59** N = 38	.43** N = 56

* Correlation significant at *p* < .05 level (2-tailed).

** Correlation is significant at *p* < .01 level (2-tailed).

the general quality of life in a society. We explore six indicators in this section: Societal health, human health, life expectancy, psychological health, general satisfaction, and the 1998 Human Development Index to test the following correlational hypotheses:

- *Hypotheses 14.2 and 14.3.* Societies that are more gender egalitarian would enjoy higher levels of human development and psychological health.

In Table 14.13 we find a pattern of correlations similar to those found between the Gender Egalitarianism measures and various indicators of countries' economic health. Specifically, participating managers' values with regard to

Gender Egalitarianism are more consistently and strongly correlated with various human condition indicators than are their perceptions of the current practices in their societies. Specifically, managers' perceptions of current practices in their societies significantly correlate with only one of the indicators—the 1998 Human Development Index. Thus, the more gender egalitarian a society's current practices, the greater its members' longevity, knowledge, and standard of living. Managers' values are more strongly correlated, however, with the 1998 Human Development Index. These same values are also significantly and positively correlated with two other indicators of human condition—life expectancy and general satisfaction. These correlations indicate that the more gender

Table 14.14   Relationship Between Gender Egalitarianism and Political Ideology

Gender Egalitarianism	Disdain for Democracy	Dislike of Democracy	Role of Government	Passiveness	Lack of Voice	Stability
Society practices	.59** N = 26	.44* N = 27	−.01 N = 38	.08 N = 37	−.08 N = 38	.06 N = 38
Society values	−.00 N = 26	−.30 N = 27	−.60** N = 38	−.41* N = 37	−.62** N = 38	−.56** N = 38

* Correlation significant at *p* < .05 level (2-tailed).

** Correlation is significant at *p* < .01 level (2-tailed).

egalitarian a society's values, the longer its members' life expectancies, and the happier and more satisfied their lives.

To summarize, managers' values with regard to Gender Egalitarianism are more strongly and consistently associated with key indicators of human condition than are managers' perceptions of their societies' practices. The more gender egalitarian a manager's values, the greater the longevity in their societies, the more knowledgeable and satisfied their societies' members, and the greater their standard of living. This pattern of findings suggests that modernization more generally, rather than economic modernization specifically (Moore & Shackman, 1996), may serve to minimize gender-role differences. As discussed in the previous section on economic health, however, the causal chain of events may run in reverse such that minimized gender-role differences may prompt positive changes in the overall well-being of a society's members. Again, however, the fact that managers' values with regard to Gender Egalitarianism are more strongly and consistently related to the various measures of human condition than are their perceptions of current practices renders this latter explanation less convincing than the one offered in the modernization perspective (Moore & Shackman, 1996).

Religion and Political Ideology

Earlier, we reviewed several studies that presented a conflicting account of the relationship between religion and concepts related to gender egalitarianism. Gender Egalitarianism practices and values scores are not significantly correlated with the strength of religious devotion or dogma in the societies sampled in the GLOBE project (*p* > .10).

In contrast to the results associated with religious ideology, the Gender Egalitarianism measures are significantly correlated with several measures of societies' political ideologies. In Table 14.14, we find that the members of societies with more Gender Egalitarian practices express both greater disdain for and dislike of democracy. At first glance, these correlations seem counterintuitive. Earlier in the chapter, though, we described a study that examined the impact of countries' political systems on women's representation in national legislatures (Paxton, 1997). Paxton and others (e.g., Lovenduski & Hills, 1981; Lovenduski & Norris, 1989; Rule, 1987) argued that simple plurality systems such as the United States' pose an obstacle to female officeholding, because the focus on individual candidates (rather than parties) makes candidate gender salient in the minds of voters. To the extent that voters stereotype women as less politically astute or able than men, or embrace more traditional gender-role ideologies that place women in the home rather than in political office, increasing the salience of women candidates' gender would decrease their representation in national legislatures. Consistent with this argument, Paxton (1997) found greater percentages of women legislators in nations with proportional representation systems in which voters cast ballots for parties rather than for individual candidates. Extending this line of reasoning, the positive correlations between current Gender Egalitarian practices in societies and members' disdain and dislike for democracy may reflect distrust of the individual or personality-centered democracy—typified by the United States—which has been shown to restrict women's opportunities in the political arena.

Gender Egalitarian values are not significantly correlated with disdain for or dislike of democracy, but they are correlated with the other four indicators of political ideology. Thus, there is no overlap or consistency in the pattern of results obtained with the practices versus values measures of Gender Egalitarianism. Managers' values regarding the division of roles between women and men are negatively correlated with the role of government, passiveness, lack of voice, and stability (see Table 14.14). The role of government indicator reflects the extent to which a society's members believe that government should regulate industry and ensure the welfare of its citizens. Higher scores on this measure indicate a desire for a more active government, and so the obtained negative correlation here indicates that members of societies with more Gender Egalitarian values would prefer less active governments. They would prefer their governments to stay out of the business of business, and for people to take responsibility for themselves. The earlier discussion of the relationship between Gender Egalitarian values and countries' economic health may provide insight into this finding. In that section, we discovered that the more gender egalitarian a society's values, the greater its economic prosperity, productivity, and GNP per capita. Therefore, if members of societies with more egalitarian values express a preference for less government, they may do so simply because they perceive a lesser need for government to intervene to ensure their economic health.

The negative correlations between Gender Egalitarianism values and three additional indicators of political ideology—passiveness, lack of voice, and stability—can be construed as a portrait of empowerment. Members of societies that embrace more gender egalitarian values are less passive, indicating a greater willingness to join boycotts and attend lawful demonstrations. They are also stronger proponents of voice, attaching greater importance to freedom of speech and the rights of individuals to have a say in their governments and communities. Finally, members of societies that embrace more gender egalitarian values attach less importance to order and stability, indicating a greater acceptance of change. Earlier, we argued the societies that seek to minimize gender-role differences enable both women and men to engage in activities that were once prohibited to them. This greater personal freedom, accompanied by greater economic health, may account for the greater activity, voice, and openness-to-change among members of societies that espouse more gender-egalitarian values.

To summarize, the following are the key findings from the comparison of Gender Egalitarianism and key indicators from archival sources:

Significant correlations indicate that societies that scored higher on Gender Egalitarianism practices

- Achieve greater longevity, knowledge, and standards of living for their members (*Human Development Report*)
- Express greater disdain for and dislike of democracy

Nonsignificant correlations indicate that societies that scored higher on Gender Egalitarianism practices

- Are neither more nor less economically prosperous or productive
- Experience neither more nor less governmental or societal support for economic growth
- Are neither more nor less competitive globally (*World Competitiveness Yearbook*)
- Enjoy neither better nor worse societal, human, or psychological health
- Experience neither shorter nor longer life expectancies

- Experience neither more nor less general satisfaction among members
- Are neither more nor less dogmatic or devoted to religious ideologies

Significant correlations indicate that societies that scored higher on Gender Egalitarianism values

- Enjoy greater economic prosperity and GNP per capita
- Experience longer life expectancies
- Experience greater general satisfaction among members
- Achieve greater longevity, knowledge, and standards of living for their members *(Human Development Report)*
- Prefer a lesser role for government
- Have members who are more active, vocal, and open to change

Nonsignificant correlations indicate that societies that scored higher on Gender Egalitarianism values

- Have neither more nor less governmental or societal support for economic growth
- Are neither more nor less competitive globally *(World Competitiveness Yearbook)*
- Enjoy neither better nor worse societal, human, or psychological health
- Express neither more nor less disdain for or dislike of democracy
- Are neither more nor less dogmatic or devoted to religious ideologies

From these lists, it is clear that the values measure of Gender Egalitarianism is more consistently linked with key indicators of social and economic indicators than is the practices measure. As noted earlier, the standard deviation for Gender Egalitarian practices was the lowest among the various societal practices measures in GLOBE. This low standard deviation may account, in part, for the relatively low number of significant correlations between the various indicators and Gender Egalitarian practices versus values.

GENDER EGALITARIANISM AND SOCIETY DEMOGRAPHICS

As discussed in Chapter 8 by Hanges and Dickson, there are significant differences in values and practices for every cultural dimension among the 62 societal cultures (i.e., recall that we use the term societal cultures rather than nations). In this section, we examine Gender Egalitarianism in the context of three key demographic characteristics of countries: Climate, ambient temperature, and geographic region.

Climate

Hofstede (1980) noted that climate constituted an antecedent, rather than a consequence or mere correlate, of masculinity/femininity because it "clearly comes first" (p. 203). Hofstede and his colleagues (Hofstede, 1980; Van de Vliert et al., 1999) argued that, because both men and women must master complex survival skills in cold climates, inequality between them is less likely in countries that lie closer to the poles. We categorized GLOBE countries into the following seven climates: Tropical humid, tropical wet and dry, desert, subtropical wet and dry, subtropical humid, marine west coast, and continental. We conducted an analysis of variance (ANOVA) to determine whether there were significant cross-climate differences in the two measures of Gender Egalitarianism.

The results for the societal practices measure are not significant: $F(6, 54) = 0.66$, $p > .10$. Managers' perceptions of their societies' current practices with respect to the division of roles between the sexes do not vary as a function of their countries' climates. A different picture emerges from the results of the societal values measure of Gender Egalitarianism. Here, managers' values vary significantly as a function of their countries' climates: $F(6, 54) = 2.32$, $p < .05$.

The mean scores on Gender Egalitarianism values are similar to those obtained by Hofstede and his colleagues (Hofstede, 1980; Van de Vliert et al., 1999). Managers from Denmark, Ireland, New Zealand, and other countries that enjoy a marine west coast climate ($M = 4.84$)

Table 14.15   Gender Egalitarianism and Climate

	Society Practices			Society Values		
Climate	*Mean*	*N*	*Standard Deviation*	*Mean*	*N*	*Standard Deviation*

Tropical Humid
  Colombia
  Costa Rica
  Ecuador
  India
  Indonesia
  Malaysia
  Philippines
  Singapore
	3.41	8	0.30	4.44	8	0.40

Tropical Wet and Dry
  El Salvador
  Guatemala
  Nigeria
  Thailand
  Venezuela
  Zambia
  Zimbabwe
	3.15	7	0.25	4.45	7	0.24

Desert
  Egypt
  Iran
  Israel
  Kazakhstan
  Kuwait
  Mexico
  Namibia
  Qatar
  South Africa
    (White sample)
  South Africa
    (Black sample)
  Turkey
	3.31	11	0.45	4.14	11	0.59

Subtropical Wet and Dry
  Albania
  Greece
  Italy
  Morocco
  Portugal
  Slovenia
  Spain
	3.42	7	0.0	4.64	7	0.49

Subtropical Humid
  Argentina
  Bolivia
  Brazil
  Hong Kong
  Taiwan
	3.40	5	0.15	4.63	5	0.41

	Society Practices			Society Values		
Climate	*Mean*	*N*	*Standard Deviation*	*Mean*	*N*	*Standard Deviation*
Marine West Coast Denmark France Germany (former East) Germany (former West) Ireland Netherlands New Zealand Switzerland Switzerland (French Speaking) United Kingdom	3.37	10	0.31	4.84	10	0.31
Continental Australia Austria Canada China Finland Georgia Hungary Japan Poland Russia South Korea Sweden United States	3.48	13	0.47	4.51	13	0.50

expressed the most Gender Egalitarian values. In contrast, managers from Iran, Qatar, and Turkey, which experience a desert climate ($M = 4.14$), expressed the least Egalitarian values. Table 14.15 provides summary statistics for all seven climates.

Ambient Temperature

Earlier in the chapter we noted that ambient temperature has been identified as a key antecedent of cross-cultural differences in masculinity (Hofstede, 1980; Peterson & Smith, 1997; Van de Vliert, 1998; Van de Vliert et al., 1999; Van de Vliert & Van Yperen, 1996). Past studies have demonstrated that the lower a society's average daytime temperature, the more

feminine its culture. Parental investment theory (Trivers, 1972) has been invoked as a potential explanation for this relationship, with scholars noting that the colder and less hospitable the climate, the greater the need for both women and men to invest in their offspring (e.g., Van de Vliert & Van Yperen, 1996). This greater need for cooperation between men and women is thought to result in a more egalitarian division of roles between the sexes (Coltrane, 1992, p. 94).

To examine this possibility, we correlated Gender Egalitarianism practices and values scores with recent measures of the average ambient or daytime temperature (in Fahrenheit) in countries' capital cities. Consistent with past research in this area and parental investment

Table 14.16   Relationship Between Gender Egalitarianism and Ambient Temperature

	Gender Egalitarianism Society Practices	Gender Egalitarianism Society Values
Ambient temperature	−.27* N = 61	−.43* N = 61

* Correlation significant at *p* < .05 level (2-tailed).

** Correlation significant at *p* < .01 level (2-tailed).

theory (Trivers, 1972), ambient temperature is significantly and negatively correlated with both Gender Egalitarianism practices and values (see Table 14.16). Thus, the lower a society's average daytime temperature, the more gender egalitarian the society.

Geographic Region

Another key demographic characteristic is a society's geographic region. Geographic region is a broader demographic measure than is ambient temperature, because countries within the same geographic region often not only share similar climates, but also similar histories, religions, and peoples compared with countries in different geographic regions. In GLOBE, we classified each society into one of the following 10 culture clusters: Eastern Europe, Latin America, Latin Europe, Confucian Asia, Nordic Europe, Anglo, Sub-Saharan Africa, Southern Asia, Germanic Europe, and Middle East. The results of separate one-way analyses of variance (ANOVA) for both Gender Egalitarianism practices ($F[9,51] = 4.39$, $p < .01$) and values ($F[9,51] = 9.59$, $p < .01$) yield significant cross-regional differences.

The nature of these differences can be seen in Table 14.17. The Eastern Europe ($M = 3.84$) cluster scored highest on Gender Egalitarianism practices, followed by the Nordic Europe ($M = 3.71$) cluster. In contrast, the Middle East ($M = 2.95$), Confucian Asia ($M = 3.18$), and Germanic Europe ($M = 3.14$) clusters scored lowest on this same scale. Managers in every culture cluster reported that they would like their societies to be more gender egalitarian than they are currently.

Nonetheless, there were significant cross-regional differences in Gender Egalitarianism values. The Germanic Europe ($M = 4.91$) and Anglo ($M = 4.91$) clusters scored highest on this scale, whereas the Middle East ($M = 3.65$) cluster scored lowest. Interestingly, although the Eastern Europe cluster scored highest on Gender Egalitarianism practices, they fell midrange relative to the other clusters' Gender Egalitarianism values scores. In contrast, the Germanic Europe cluster scored among the lowest on Gender Egalitarianism practices but scored the highest on Gender Egalitarianism values. Thus, when talking about potential cross-regional differences in gender egalitarianism, it is critical to distinguish between practices and values with regard to women's and men's roles in society.

GENDER EGALITARIANISM AND OTHER GENDER-RELATED MEASURES

In the introduction to this chapter, we noted that gender egalitarianism is related to several concepts, including masculinity/femininity, gender-role stereotypes, gender-role ideology, gender discrimination, and gender equality. In this section, we examine the relationship between GLOBE's measures of Gender Egalitarianism and several of these concepts.

Hofstede's Masculinity/ Femininity Dimension

Hofstede (1980) developed the masculinity/ femininity dimension of societal culture by asking managers in his IBM sample to rate the

Table 14.17   Gender Egalitarianism and Geographic Region

Geographic Region	Society Practices			Society Values		
	Mean	N	Standard Deviation	Mean	N	Standard Deviation
Nordic Europe Finland Sweden Denmark	3.71	3	0.31	4.82	3	0.51
Eastern Europe Albania Kazakhstan Hungary Poland Russia Slovenia Greece Georgia	3.84	8	0.23	4.46	8	0.40
Latin America Argentina Bolivia Brazil Colombia Costa Rica Ecuador El Salvador Guatemala Mexico Venezuela	3.41	10	0.25	4.77	10	0.17
Middle East Egypt Kuwait Morocco Qatar Turkey	2.95	5	0.40	3.65	5	0.52
Latin Europe Italy Portugal Spain France Switzerland (French- speaking) Israel	3.36	6	0.26	4.77	6	0.24
Germanic Europe Austria Germany (former West) Germany (former East) The Netherlands Switzerland	3.14	5	0.21	4.91	5	0.06

(Continued)

Table 14.17 (Continued)

Geographic Region	Society Practices			Society Values		
	Mean	N	Standard Deviation	Mean	N	Standard Deviation
Sub-Saharan Africa Namibia Nigeria South Africa (Black Sample) Zambia Zimbabwe	3.29	5	0.45	4.30	5	0.09
Confucian Asia Taiwan Singapore Hong Kong South Korea China Japan	3.18	6	0.41	4.19	6	0.29
Southern Asia India Indonesia Iran Malaysia Philippines Taiwan	3.28	6	0.29	4.10	6	0.36
Anglo Australia Canada New Zealand U.S. South Africa (White sample) England Ireland	3.40	7	0.20	4.91	7	0.36

importance of 14 work goals to an "imaginary ideal job" (1998, p. 7). These goals included "challenge, (living in a) desirable area, earnings, cooperation (with colleagues), training, (fringe) benefits, recognition, physical (working) conditions, freedom, (job) security, (career) advancement, use of skills, (relationship with) manager, and personal time (for personal or family life)" (p. 7). When Hofstede factor analyzed managers' ratings, he discovered two dimensions: one that he labeled individualism/collectivism, and another that he labeled masculinity/femininity. According to Hofstede, masculinity was reflected through goals that enhanced a manager's ego (i.e., "ego roles") without regard for personal relationships—for example, "earnings," "advancement," and "use of skills." In contrast, femininity was reflected through goals that emphasized social aspects of work such as "(relationship with) manager" and "cooperation (with colleagues)"—hence Hofstede's term "social goals."

Hofstede adopted the masculinity/femininity label for two reasons. First, he argued that past research on work goals had demonstrated consistent differences between the women's and men's work goals, with women emphasizing social goals associated with building strong and caring relationships and men emphasizing ego goals or personal achievement. Second, he found that masculinity/femininity was the only dimension of societal culture that yielded significant and consistent differences between women and men respondents in the IBM sample (Hofstede, 1980, 1998, 2001).

In an earlier section, we explained that Hofstede's masculinity/femininity dimension was divided into two separate dimensions in GLOBE: Assertiveness (see Den Hartog, Chapter 15) and Gender Egalitarianism. Despite this separation, we expected to discover a significant, albeit imperfect, correlation between Hofstede's (1998, 2001) society scores for masculinity/femininity and GLOBE's society scores for Gender Egalitarianism practices and values. To test this prediction, we computed the correlations among these measures for the 47 countries included in both research projects. Contrary to our prediction, Hofstede's masculinity/femininity scores are uncorrelated with scores on both Gender Egalitarianism scales. The correlation between Hofstede's dimension and Gender Egalitarianism practices occurs in the predicted direction, however, with the more feminine societies tending also to engage in more gender egalitarian practices ($r = -.17$, $p > .10$). This coefficient approaches, but does not achieve, significance, and so it should be interpreted cautiously. In contrast, the correlation between masculinity/femininity and Gender Egalitarianism values is essentially zero ($r = -.02$, $p > .10$). The absence of any link between these two measures is particularly unexpected given that managers were instructed to think in terms of an "ideal" when completing both—the ideal imaginary job for Hofstede's masculinity/femininity measure and ideal societal practices for GLOBE's Gender Egalitarianism values measure. Thus, we had greater reason to predict a significant correlation between Hofstede's measure and values, rather than practices, with regard to the division of

roles between men and women. This did not prove to be the case, however. Earlier in this chapter, we asserted that Hofstede's measure of masculinity/femininity confounds assertiveness, gender egalitarianism, humane orientation, and achievement orientation, thereby yielding findings that are difficult to interpret. To the extent that this assertion is true, there may simply be too much variance in masculinity/femininity that is unrelated to Gender Egalitarianism to uncover any variance that is shared between the two measures.

Gender Stereotypes and Gender-Role Ideologies

Earlier in the chapter we introduced a two-component model to illustrate the larger context of Gender Egalitarianism (refer back to Figure 14.1). The first component—the attitudinal domain—reflects the fundamental values, beliefs, and attitudes that members of a society hold with regard to gender stereotypes and gender-role ideologies. Gender stereotypes and gender-role ideologies represent parallel constructs, because stereotypes about the psychological attributes of women and men and ideologies about the roles that women and men can and should play in society are both grounded in a powerful feedback loop (Best & Williams, 1993). Throughout this chapter, we have argued that this feedback loop occurs within the larger context of societal norms regarding the division of roles between the sexes. In this section, we examine gender stereotypes and gender-role ideologies separately as potential key correlates of these societal norms.

Gender Stereotypes. In our earlier discussion of gender stereotypes, we briefly described a 25-nation study in which university students completed a 300-item adjective checklist (Williams & Best, 1990a). For each adjective or trait, students indicated whether it was "more frequently associated with men than with women, more frequently associated with women than with men, or not differentially associated with the two sexes" (p. 21). They then asked the students to rate these same traits

Table 14.18 Relationship Between Gender Egalitarianism, Gender Stereotypes, and Gender-Role Ideologies

Gender Egalitarianism	Favorability of Female Traits+	Activity of Female Traits+	Strength of Female Traits+	Male's Gender-Role Ideologies+	Female's Gender-Role Ideologies+
Society practices	−.04 N = 22	.05 N = 22	−.03 N = .22	−.06 N = 14	.18 N = 14
Society values	−.58** N = 22	−.12 N = 22	÷ 53** N = .22	.41 N = 14	.52* N = 14

+ Measure calculated by subtracting ratings of female traits from ratings of male traits; thus, a lower score indicates more positive stereotypes of females.

++ Higher scores indicate more modern gender-role ideologies.

 * Correlation significant at $p < .05$ level (2-tailed).

** Correlation significant at $p < .01$ level (2-tailed).

on the following three dimensions: Favorability, activity, and strength. These ratings revealed that male-stereotyped traits such as "adult" and "achievement-oriented" were rated more positively on these three dimensions than were female-stereotyped traits such as "child-like" and "affiliation-oriented," although there were cross-cultural differences. Based on the conceptual model outlined earlier (see Figure 14.1), we proposed that this gender gap would be smaller in societies whose practices and values are more (vs. less) gender egalitarian.

Correlation analyses reveal that the measure of Gender Egalitarianism values is, in fact, strongly and negatively correlated with the gaps or mean differences in both the perceived favorability ($r = .58, p < .01$) and strength ($r = .53, p < .01$) of traits ascribed to males versus females (see Table 14.18). No significant correlation was found for the activity dimension, however. Thus, as predicted, the more gender egalitarian a society's values, the more favorably and strongly its university students perceived "female" (relative to "male") traits to be in Williams and Best's study. In contrast, Gender Egalitarian practices scores are unrelated to students' perceptions of the favorability, activity, and strength of these same traits (rs

ranging from −.04 to .05). Thus, the model proposed earlier (see Figure 14.1) receives partial support: The more egalitarian a society's values (but not practices), the more favorable members' stereotypes of females relative to their stereotypes of males.

Gender-Role Ideologies. The second facet of the attitudinal domain of gender egalitarianism is gender-role ideologies (see Figure 14.1). As noted earlier, individuals' gender-role ideologies vary along a continuum of "traditional" to "modern" (Best & Williams, 1993). Traditional ideologies view men as more important than women and advocate relationships in which men dominate and control women. In contrast, modern ideologies view men and women as equals and advocate egalitarian relationships between them. For this reason, we hypothesized a significant and positive relationship between GLOBE's measures of Gender Egalitarianism and the modernity of gender-role ideologies.

In a 14-nation study of gender-role ideologies, approximately 100 university students completed a 30-item survey of gender-role relationships, using a 7-point scale (Williams & Best, 1990b). The higher their overall ratings, the more modern their gender-role ideologies.

These ratings were computed separately for men and women. Across countries, women ($M = 4.75$) espoused more modern ideologies than did men ($M = 4.41$). Most relevant to our investigation, correlational analyses yield partial support for the hypothesized positive relationship between Williams and Best's (1990b) measures of gender-role ideologies and GLOBE's measures of Gender Egalitarianism. The correlation coefficients associated with managers' perceptions of current practices and both men's and women's gender-role ideologies are nonsignificant (see Table 14.18). In contrast, the coefficients associated with managers' values and both men's and women's gender-role ideologies constitute "medium-to-large" and "large" effects (Cohen, 1988), respectively, although the former does not achieve statistical significance. With only 14 countries represented in Williams and Best's study, the power to detect significant correlations with their measures and the GLOBE measures of Gender Egalitarianism is necessarily quite low. Therefore, Cohen's effect sizes labels may provide the most meaningful gauge of the links between these measures. These links suggest that members of societies in which gender egalitarianism is highly valued espouse greater equality of women and men.

Similar to gender stereotypes, then, gender-role ideologies were more closely related to managers' values regarding the division of roles between women and men than to their beliefs about current practices in this area. This follows the overall pattern of stronger and more consistent relationships between Gender Egalitarianism values and several key economic, social, and other indicators reported earlier. As noted earlier, gender-role ideologies reflect individuals' "beliefs about *proper* [emphasis added] role relationships between women and men" (Williams & Best, 1990b, p. 87). This emphasis on ideological preferences is echoed most closely in GLOBE's conceptualization of Gender Egalitarianism as a value, or conviction, regarding the ideal roles of women and men in a society. In contrast, the conceptual link between gender-role ideologies and Gender Egalitarianism practices may be more tenuous in that an individual may trumpet the virtues of a society in which women and

men are treated equally but recognize that women and men are not, in fact, treated equally. From a purely statistical standpoint, the weaker correlations between various measures and Gender Egalitarianism practices (vs. values) may stem from the relatively low standard deviation associated with managers' perceptions of current practices. As noted earlier, the standard deviation for Gender Egalitarianism practices ($SD = 0.37$) is the lowest among the nine GLOBE dimensions (SDs ranging from 0.37 to 0.73). This low standard deviation may account for the dearth of significant relationships for this measure compared with the values measure ($SD = 0.48$).

To summarize, we argued earlier that gender egalitarianism reflects and affects individuals' ideologies and stereotypes regarding women and men. We referred to this as the attitudinal domain of the gender egalitarianism construct. The results from the previous two sections provide moderate support for this argument. Stereotypes of women are more favorable and strong in societies in which managers report a desire to minimize gender-role differences. Moreover, gender-role ideologies advocate greater importance, rights, and freedom for women in these same societies. Taken together, then, we find strong convergent validity between GLOBE's measure of Gender Egalitarianism values, and both gender stereotypes and gender-role ideologies.

Women's Participation in the Economy, Government, and Politics

In the conceptual model outlined in Figure 14.1 we proposed that attitudes regarding the appropriate roles of women and men manifest themselves behaviorally in the form of gender discrimination and equality. According to this argument, the more gender egalitarian a society, the greater women's participation in the economy, government, and politics. We examined this general thesis by computing the correlations between GLOBE's practices and values measures of Gender Egalitarianism and four archival measures of women's participation in various aspects of societies (see Table 14.19). The first archival measure is the rate of women's economic

Table 14.19   Gender Egalitarianism and Women's Participation in the Economy, Government, and Politics

Gender Egalitarianism	Women's Economic Activity	Women's Purchasing Power	Percentage of Women in Government	First Year Women in Legislature
Society practices	.34** N = 59	.33** N = 57	.28* N = 54	−.03 N = 54
Society values	.13 N = 59	.24 N = 57	.37** N = 54	−.46** N = 28

* Correlation significant at $p < .05$ level (2-tailed).

** Correlation significant at $p < .01$ level (2-tailed).

activity, which is calculated as the percentage of women in the labor force divided by the percentage of the society's total population of women age 15 years and older. Consistent with the earlier hypothesized model, women's economic activity is significantly and positively correlated with managers' perceptions of the Gender Egalitarianism of their societies' practices, but not their societies' values. The second archival measure is the affluence or purchasing power of women relative to men in a society. Not surprisingly, women's purchasing power is strongly and positively correlated with their rate of participation in the labor force. Moreover, this power is positively correlated with managers' perceptions of both current Gender Egalitarianism practices and values regarding the division of roles between women and men, although the latter correlation does not achieve statistical significance. The third archival measure is the percentage of women employed at all levels of government. This measure is positively correlated with both GLOBE measures of Gender Egalitarianism: The more Gender Egalitarian a society's practices and values, the greater the percentage of women employed by the government. The final archival measure is the year when the first woman was appointed or elected to a nation's legislative body. Interestingly, this measure is negatively correlated with societies' values, but not practices, with regard to the division of roles between women and men. The more

Gender Egalitarian a society's values, the earlier a woman was appointed or elected to its legislative body. Taken together, these correlations between GLOBE measures of Gender Egalitarianism and various indicators of women's participation in key sectors of society provide support for the conceptual model proposed in Figure 14.1. In this model, individuals' attitudes regarding what is possible or appropriate for women and men delimit their social roles, thereby affecting their participation in the labor force, and in society overall. The results from this section confirm that the more Gender Egalitarian a society's values in some instances, or practices in others, the greater various indicators of gender equality such as women's participation and representation in the labor force, government, and politics. These results provide support not only for the conceptual model outlined earlier, but also for the validity of Gender Egalitarianism as operationalized in the GLOBE project.

GENDER EGALITARIANISM AS A DIMENSION OF ORGANIZATIONAL CULTURE

Organizational culture is the glue that binds organization members together in pursuit of a common goal. Scholars have argued that an organization's culture reflects the fundamental beliefs and values of its founder or, in some cases, a transformational CEO who assumes leadership at a critical point in the organization's history (Schein, 1983). Other scholars have noted, however, that an organization's culture must also reflect the fundamental beliefs and values of the larger society in which it operates because, as Freud is often quoted, "that which comes first is primary" (Adler, 1991; Schneider, 1988). Placed in the context of a discussion of culture, Freud's axiom acknowledges that people typically identify more closely with their societies' cultures than with their organizations' cultures. For this reason, collisions between societal and organizational cultures are often dramatic and noteworthy. A prime example is the collision that occurred between the Disney Corporation, with its taboo against alcoholic beverages in its family-oriented theme parks, and the French culture in which wine is often served in family settings. Predictably, Disney, not France, modified its culture to ensure the survival of its then-floundering Euro Disney theme park.

THE RELATIONSHIP BETWEEN SOCIETAL AND ORGANIZATIONAL PRACTICES AND SOCIETAL AND ORGANIZATIONAL VALUES

In this section, we report the findings on the relationship between societal and organizational Gender Egalitarianism *practices* and *values* with regard to the division of roles between women and men. As House and Javidan indicated in Chapter 2, GLOBE's conceptual model postulates that organizational practices and values reflect, in part, the practices and values of the societies in which they operate, and so we expected to find a link between the societal and organizational measures of Gender Egalitarianism. We used hierarchical linear modeling (HLM) to test for this link in the model. Specifically, we conducted two HLMs to test these hypotheses for organizational Gender Egalitarianism practices and values. We tested the GLOBE hypothesis regarding the effect of societal culture on organizational culture by conducting HLM analyses in which organizational Gender Egalitarianism was predicted by societal Gender Egalitarianism. These analyses supported our hypotheses that societal Gender

Egalitarianism practices have a significant and strong positive relationship with organizational Gender Egalitarianism practices ($p < .01$). We found a similar significant and even stronger relationship between societal Gender Egalitarianism values and organizational Gender Egalitarianism values ($p < .01$). Both analyses support a principal proposition in the GLOBE theoretical model (i.e., Proposition 3, Figure 2.1, Chapter 2, by House and Javidan): Societal cultural values and practices affect organizational cultural values and practices.[3]

To summarize, societal Gender Egalitarianism practices predicted organizational practices, and societal Gender Egalitarianism values predicted organizational values. Thus, the results from the two HLM analyses provide support for the general hypothesis that organizations' cultures are, to some degree, a function of their societies' cultures regarding the division of roles between women and men.

INTERPRETATION OF HLMs USING GLOBE GENDER EGALITARIANISM TO PREDICT CULTURALLY ENDORSED LEADERSHIP

In the GLOBE conceptual model (House et al., 1999), culturally endorsed leadership theories (CLTs) are determined, in part, by cultural practices and values with regard to Gender Egalitarianism, at both the societal and organizational levels. For this reason, we hypothesized that managers' implicit theories about the attributes associated with effective leadership would be related to the practices and values measures of Gender Egalitarianism at both the societal and organizational levels. This chapter presents relationships between one culture dimension (Gender Egalitarianism) and the six CLTS. Competitive tests of all culture dimensions and CLTs are presented in Chapter 21 by Dorfman and colleagues.[4] In general, we expect that societal and organizational values will be more strongly related to CLT leadership dimensions than societal and organizational practices. As you read through the results discussed below, it may be helpful to view Figure 14.2 for a visual summary. The figure, however, only shows

Gender Equalitarianism Cultural Dimension

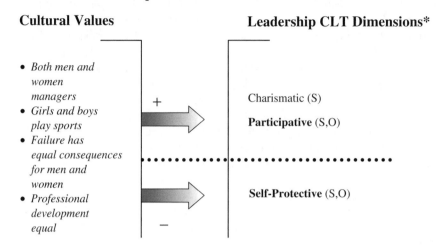

Figure 14.2   Gender Egalitarianism Cultural Values as Drivers for CLT Leadership Dimensions

* Only statistically significant relationships are shown ($p < .05$; see Table 21.10, Chapter 21 by Dorfman et al.). The most important leadership CLT relationships are bolded (i.e., relationship is significant at both society and organization levels of analyses or highest HLM coefficient within each level of analysis).

O = Organizational level

S = Societal level

results regarding cultural values, not practices (all HLM coefficients are presented in Table 21.10 of Chapter 21 by Dorfman et al.) We tested these hypotheses by using HLM analyses. Specific relationships are discussed below, but as predicted, societal and organizational values were more strongly related to most CLT leadership dimensions than were societal and organizational practices. The total amount of organizational and societal variance explained by Gender Egalitarianism ranges from 0 to 41.4%. Gender Egalitarianism explains the greatest proportion of variance in Self-Protective and Participative leadership. It was not significantly related to Autonomous leadership.

More specifically, when organizational-level and societal-level Gender Egalitarianism values and practices were considered, significant relationships were found with the following:

• *Charismatic/Value-Based leadership.* Gender Egalitarianism cultural values scores were significantly related to the Charismatic/ Value-Based leadership dimension and explained a total of 21.7% of the organizational and societal variance for this dimension. All of the explained variance was associated with forces operating at the societal level of analysis. The societal Gender Egalitarianism cultural values scores were positively related ($p < .01$) to the Charismatic/Value-Based leadership dimension. Charismatic/Value-Based leadership is more likely to be a part of the shared leadership belief system in societies with high Gender Egalitarianism *values* scores.

• *Team-Oriented leadership.* Gender Egalitarianism practices scores were significantly related to the Team-Oriented leadership dimension but explained a total of just 09% of the organizational and societal variance for this dimension. All of the explained variance was associated with forces operating at the organizational level of analysis. The organizational Gender Egalitarianism cultural practices scores were positively related ($p < .01$) to the Team-Oriented leadership dimension. Team-Oriented leadership is more likely to be a part of the shared leadership belief system in organizations reported to have Gender Egalitarianism practices.

• *Participative leadership.* Gender Egalitarianism cultural values scores were significantly related to the Participative leadership dimension and explained a total of 41.4% of the organizational and societal variance for this dimension. Approximately 4.2% of this explained variance was associated with forces operating at the organizational level of analysis. The majority of the explained variance (95.8%) was associated with forces operating at the societal level of analysis.

The organizational Gender Egalitarianism cultural values scores were positively related ($p < .01$) to the Participative leadership dimension. Participative leadership is more likely to be part of the shared leadership belief system in organizations reported to espouse Gender Egalitarianism values.

The societal Gender Egalitarianism values scores were positively related ($p < .01$) to the Participative leadership dimension. Participative leadership is more likely to be a part of the shared leadership belief system in societies reported to espouse Gender Egalitarianism values.

• *Humane-Oriented leadership.* Gender Egalitarianism cultural practices scores were significantly related to the Humane-Oriented leadership dimension but explained a total of just 2.0% of organizational and societal variance for this dimension. All of the explained variance was associated with forces operating at the organizational level of analysis. The organizational Gender Egalitarianism cultural practices scores were positively related ($p < .05$) to the Humane-Oriented leadership dimension. Humane-Oriented leadership is more likely to be a part of the shared leadership belief system in organizations reported to have Gender Egalitarianism practices.

• *Autonomous leadership.* Gender Egalitarianism cultural practices and values scores were not significantly related to the Autonomous leadership dimension.

• *Self-Protective leadership.* Gender Egalitarianism cultural values scores were significantly negatively related to the Self-Protective leadership dimension and explained a total of 44.0% of the organizational and societal variance for this dimension. Approximately 3.8% of the explained variance was associated with forces operating at the organizational level of analysis. The remaining portion of the explained variance (96.2%) was associated with forces operating at the societal level of analysis.

The organizational Gender Egalitarianism cultural values scores were negatively related ($p < .01$) to the Self-Protective leadership dimension. Self-Protective leadership is less likely to be a part of a shared leadership belief system in organizations reported to espouse Gender Egalitarianism values.

The societal Gender Egalitarianism cultural values scores were negatively related ($p < .01$) to the Self-Protective leadership dimension. Self-Protective leadership is less likely to be a part of the shared leadership belief system in societies reported to espouse Gender Egalitarianism values.

To summarize, the results from the HLM analyses indicate that societal values with regard to the division of roles between men and women drove beliefs about the attributes that contribute to effective leadership. The more Gender Egalitarian a society's values, the more strongly its managers endorsed Participative and Charismatic/Value-Based leader attributes and the more strongly they shunned Self-Protective leader attributes. The results associated with the organizational-level scales are consistent for Gender Egalitarian organizational values. The more managers described their organization as having these types of values, the more strongly they endorsed Participative leadership attributes and shunned Self-Protective leadership attributes. The more Gender Egalitarian managers' perceptions of their organizations' current *practices*, the more strongly they endorsed Team-Oriented leadership. In addition to finding greater consistency in the results obtained with the societal (vs. organizational) measures of Gender Egalitarianism, we also found greater strength in the societal measures. In this case, though, it was the values rather than the practices that predicted managers' implicit theories of leadership. Taken together, the findings from this section support the argument that societal and organizational culture values influence the desired level of Charismatic/Value-Based and Participative leadership in a positive manner, whereas they negatively influence the level of Self-Protective leadership attributes.

GENDER DIFFERENCES ON CLT LEADERSHIP RATINGS AND CULTURAL DIMENSION VALUES AND PRACTICES

Given the discussion of gender differences throughout the chapter, it is likely that males and females have different perceptions of what is valued in a society. Indeed, the popular press and the academic literature on gender and leadership (cf. Eagly & Johannesen-Schmidt, 2001; Heilman, 2001; Schein 1983) indicate that male and female managers view leadership roles quite differently, with men viewing hierarchical and competitive interpersonal behaviors as components of the leadership role and women viewing collaborative and consensus building behaviors as components of this role.

To test the possibility that gender differences would be found in GLOBE data, we conducted supplemental statistical analyses exploring differences between men and women in terms of how they rated CLT attributes considered important for outstanding leadership as well as how they rated societal Gender Egalitarianism practices and values. These analyses involved several steps. The first step was to identify the gender of GLOBE respondents; however, several countries did not provide demographic information for any respondents in their samples, or their samples consisted entirely of men. In the first case, the lack of demographic information was a conscious omission as the investigators had reason to believe that asking demographic information would substantially lessen the response rate, something akin to asking about personal income in questionnaires in the United States. Only those samples for which the respondents' gender could be identified were included in this analysis. Also, these

supplemental analyses were limited to societal culture samples in which both men and women were surveyed. Although the absence of female managers is perhaps telling in itself, it should be noted that gender bias is only one possible explanation for why a particular sample does not include female respondents.

In addition to these considerations, a statistical issue further limited the sample available for this supplemental analysis. Because gender is a dichotomous variable, relationships between gender and other variables such as leadership perceptions reflect not only actual mean rating differences by men and women, but also differential proportions of men and women respondents in the samples across societies. As pointed out by a number of statisticians (e.g., Cohen & Cohen, 1983; Nunnally & Bernstein, 1993), the maximum relationship possible between a dichotomous variable and a continuous variable decreases as the relative proportions of men and women vary from .50. If the different societies varied dramatically in the percentage of women included in their samples, any significant gender-by-culture interaction could simply reflect the differential proportions of men and women across the GLOBE-sampled cultures. Because we are interested in capturing only those gender differences that are conceptually meaningful, we included countries only if the percentage of female and male respondents was roughly equal. We identified 30 societies that met the aforementioned criteria. The full sample consisted of 5,645 males (73.7%) and 2,012 females (26.3%). Approximately one half of the societal samples could not be included in this analysis because they did not meet all the criteria.

A series of hierarchical linear models (see Chapter 11 by Hanges, Dickson, & Sipe) were conducted to test whether men and women rated the CLT leadership dimensions differently. These analyses revealed significant gender differences for four of the six CLT dimensions. Specifically, women rated Charismatic/Value-Based leadership (t (30) = 2.19, $p < .05$), Participative leadership (t (30) = 4.31, $p < .01$), and Team-Oriented leadership (t (30) = 3.78, $p < .01$) significantly higher than did men. In contrast, men rated Self-Protective leadership (t (30) = 3.74, $p < .01$) significantly higher than did women. It should be noted, however, that although these results are statistically significant, the total variance accounted for by gender was small (i.e., 0.2% for Charismatic/Valued-Based; 0.9% for Participative; 0.5% for Team-Oriented; and 0.7% for Self-Protective).[5] Finally, there are no significant gender differences for Humane-Oriented (t (30) = 0.30, $p > .05$) or Autonomous (t (30) = 1.16, $p > .05$) leadership.

Although the prior HLM analyses are informative, it should be noted that these analyses looked for a constant gender relationship on the CLT dimensions across countries. It may be that gender differences interact with societal culture such that certain societies would be more prone to socialize men and women to differentiated leadership roles. In other words, it is possible that the gender effect differs across societal cultures. We therefore performed an additional analysis to determine whether the gender effect on the CLT leadership dimensions differed across cultures. The HLM analyses indicated that there were significant interactions between gender and societal culture for five of the six CLT dimensions. Only the Humane-Oriented CLT dimension failed to show a significant gender by culture interaction (t (30) = 27.32, $p > .05$).

More specifically, gender differences on the Charismatic/Value-Based CLT dimension significantly differed across societal cultures (t (30) = 45.39, $p < .05$). For example, the gender differences for this leadership dimension were minimal for Sweden but fairly substantial for Guatemala. The gender effect also significantly differed for Participative (t (30) = 69.66, $p < .01$), Team-Oriented (t (30) = 52.00, $p < .01$), Self-Protective (R^2(30) = 67.76, $p < .05$), and Autonomous (R^2 (30) = 49.66, $p < .05$) CLT leadership dimensions. Although we could rank societies in terms of the magnitude of their gender differences on these CLT scores, it would be more meaningful to identify one or more societal-level construct that might be causing these interactions. Although identifying such constructs is beyond the scope of this chapter, interested readers should read Paris (2003) for a more complete exploration of these cultural moderators. She found that women and men rated the various

CLT dimensions more similarly the more gender egalitarian their societies.

In addition to gender differences on CLT dimensions, it is also possible that men and women might hold different perceptions of their societies' cultural practices and values. The gender role literature suggests that people's beliefs about the capabilities of males and females are a function of how males and females are socialized in a society. The socialization process emphasizes certain behaviors in children, and these gender-differentiated experiences will convey different "meta-messages" about gender-appropriate behaviors. These meta-messages are hypothesized to influence the self-concept, personal goals, and cognitive heuristics used by individuals in that society. Thus, males and females will likely differentially describe the practices and values of their societal cultures if they have experienced different socialization experiences in that society. We explored this possibility with the GLOBE data. Before discussing the results, however, it should be noted that societal culture was measured only on Form B of the GLOBE survey. Thus, the sample size for the gender differences on culture is approximately one-half of the sample size available for the prior analyses.

In general, the HLMs did not find gender differences when societal cultural practices were examined. However, perhaps not surprisingly, societal Gender Egalitarianism cultural practices were rated significantly differently, on average, by men and women (t (16) = 2.98, $p < .01$). Women described their societies as having slightly more gender egalitarian practices than did men. Although statistically significant, this effect did not account for a substantial portion of societal Gender Egalitarianism practices ($t = 0.2$%). Interestingly, the HLMs also revealed that gender differences did not differ across societies (t (16) = 0.00, $p > .05$). Overall, gender did not appear to affect ratings of societal Gender Egalitarianism practices.

Similar results were obtained for societal Gender Egalitarianism values. Significant gender differences were found for societal Gender Egalitarianism values (t (16) = 2.93, $p < .05$). Women described their societies as having more Gender Egalitarianism values than did men. This gender effect accounted for 2.3% of the total variance in societal Gender Egalitarianism.[6] Moreover, this gender effect differed as a function of societal culture (t (16) = 63.36, $p < .05$).

The only other societal culture variable that exhibited a significant gender effect was societal Humane Orientation cultural dimension values (t (16) = 2.91, $p < .01$). Men described their societies as valuing Humane Orientation more than did women. Although statistically significant, this effect did not account for a substantial portion of the variance ($R^2 = 0.0\%$).

In summary, we found few significant gender differences when comparing men's and women's ratings on all cultural practices and values, with the exception of one dimension. Not surprisingly, we found that societal Gender Egalitarianism cultural practices and values were sensitive to gender differences. The effect of gender was stronger for cultural values than it was for cultural practices.

SUMMARY AND CONCLUSIONS

We began this chapter by defining the construct of gender egalitarianism as the way in which societies divide roles between women and men. The more gender egalitarian a society, the less it relies on biology to determine women's and men's social roles. This construct varies along a continuum in that societies can be rated as more or less gender egalitarian relative to other societies in the same study. More gender egalitarian societies believe that men and women are suited for similar roles, whereas less gender egalitarian societies believe that men and women should assume different roles.

We proposed a two-component model of gender egalitarianism that included an attitudinal domain and behavioral manifestations. The attitudinal domain included the concepts of gender stereotypes and gender-role ideology. These concepts reflect individuals' beliefs about the qualities of women and men, and the roles that they should assume, respectively. When individuals' actions are consistent with their beliefs in these areas, we see the behavioral manifestations of gender egalitarianism— specifically, gender discrimination and gender

equality. The more gender egalitarian a society, the less gender discrimination and inequality one would expect to find in key venues. The relationship between the attitudinal domain and the behavioral manifestations of gender egalitarianism comprises a recurrent feedback loop: Beliefs about what is possible or appropriate for women and men affect their treatment and roles in homes, workplaces, and societies. Any gender discrimination and inequality that results serves to reinforce individuals' stereotypes and ideologies, bringing us full circle.

We next reviewed prior research linking various concepts associated with gender egalitarianism and potential "cultural drivers." This review underscored the difficulty of disentangling individual causes of gender egalitarianism such as religion and political systems and parental investment in children. Past research has documented empirically a strong positive relationship between men's parental investment and women's status in homes and societies. Similarly, parental investment has been identified as a key mediator of the relationship between ambient temperature and gender equality: Colder climates require men to invest more heavily in their offspring, thereby promoting greater mixed-gender exchange and gender equality.

Past research presented a less straightforward picture of the link between other cultural drivers and concepts related to gender egalitarianism. For example, the link between a society's religion and the status of women was equivocal. Monotheism did not have the same impact on women's status across cultures. In addition, the overall religiosity of a culture could not account for the division of roles between the sexes. It may be that the differential status of men and women within religious life may be reflected in their differential status in society overall. In the Catholic and Islamic faiths, religious leaders are almost always men, whereas in other faiths leadership positions are divided more equally between men and women. It also has been argued, however, that beliefs about appropriate roles for women and men might cause religious attitudes rather than the reverse.

The past literature on the link between nations' economic health and women's status and roles is equally complex. The modernization perspective proposes that economic growth creates additional work opportunities for women and other disadvantaged groups, whereas the economic competition perspective holds that gender inequality persists despite economic development because women do not possess sufficient power to capitalize on this development. Findings from past research are most consistent with the economic competition perspective: Although economic growth is associated with a rise in women's labor force participation, they tend to cluster in occupations traditionally deemed suitable for women—notably in service and in communication. Thus, economic growth seems simply to provide new venues—"pink-collar ghettos"—for women to pursue stereotypically female roles.

The ways in which resources are controlled are also related to women's status and power in societies. Specifically, the intergenerational transfer of wealth is an institutionalized practice that affects the division of roles between men and women. Women were ascribed much higher power and status in those few societies with matrilineal descent and locality than in the many societies with patrilineal descent and locality. In one study, women fared better only if they had some control over property and shared parental responsibility with men.

Political systems were the last cultural driving force that we reviewed. Women were more likely to attain political offices in societies that favored a proportional representation system simply because the partisan nature of elections may serve to decrease the salience of their biological sex. In addition, women made greater gains in societies that tolerated the formation of political opposition groups—a finding that was the first to pinpoint women's solidarity as a powerful resource for women to gain greater equality in their societies.

The GLOBE project surveyed 62 societies on nine cultural dimensions, including Gender Egalitarianism. This dimension was measured by surveying workplace managers regarding their perceptions of current practices and values with regard to the division of roles between females and males. Overall findings suggested that societies currently rely to some extent on biological sex to allocate appropriate roles to members, despite the fact that most managers reported that this practice was not an ideal one. If managers' espoused values accurately reflect their deeply held values and they are in positions to effect social change, then we may begin to see a movement in many countries toward increased gender egalitarianism.

In addition, we explored the relationships between GLOBE's measure of Gender Egalitarianism and other social and economic indicators in these 62 societies and discovered several significant correlations. Specifically, members of societies whose practices are currently more gender egalitarian achieved greater longevity, knowledge, and standards of living. These members also expressed greater disdain for democracy. A potential explanation for this finding is that members whose societies are currently more gender egalitarian may distrust democracy because the simple plurality system of what may be the most visible and, hence, prototypical democracy in the world, the United States, has been linked to greater gender inequality in political representation. This type of inequality would be incompatible with gender-egalitarian practices.

Societies in which managers espoused more gender-egalitarian values were more prosperous economically. People living in these societies had longer life expectancies and experienced greater overall satisfaction with their lives. They also acquired greater levels of knowledge and enjoyed higher standards of living. Members of societies that embraced more gender-egalitarian values expressed a desire for less government. Although this finding seemed counterintuitive initially, it eventually wove together in our minds with two additional findings associated with this measure. First, as already noted, members of societies with stronger gender-egalitarian ideals enjoyed greater economic prosperity, knowledge, longevity, satisfaction, and so forth. Consequently, these individuals may feel sufficiently empowered that they desire less governmental "interference" in their lives. A sense of empowerment emerges from the findings associated with various indicators of individuals' political ideologies as well. The more gender egalitarian a society's values, the more active, vocal, and open to change were its members. If members feel that they can safeguard their own well-being and effect change when necessary, they may have less desire for and tolerance of "big government."

Our investigation of the relationship between gender egalitarianism and society demographics explored climate, ambient temperature, and geographic region. Findings indicated that societies with maritime climates such as Denmark and New Zealand were most gender egalitarian whereas those with desert climates such as Iran and Qatar were least gender egalitarian. This is consistent with the finding that the lower a society's average daytime temperature, the more gender egalitarian its practices and values. With regard to geographic region, the Eastern Europe and Nordic Europe clusters reported the highest current levels of gender egalitarianism, whereas the Middle East, Confucian Asia, and Germanic Europe clusters reported the lowest. In terms of ideal levels of gender egalitarianism, however, the Germanic Europe cluster reported the highest levels, followed closely by the Anglo cluster. The Middle East cluster reported the lowest ideal gender egalitarianism.

We devoted the next section to an examination of the relationships between gender egalitarianism and various measures that were theorized to be conceptually related. Contrary to our expectations, GLOBE's measures of Gender Egalitarianism were unrelated to Hofstede's (1980, 1998, 2001) measure of masculinity/femininity. A potential explanation for this finding is that masculinity/femininity confounds too many societal norms to share sufficient, unique variance with a measure designed specifically to reflect beliefs about the division of roles between women and men. We did, however, find support for the notion that gender egalitarianism represents a powerful and overarching cultural norm that grounds the feedback loop between individuals' gender stereotypes and ideologies on the one hand, and gender inequality and discrimination on the other. Stereotypes of women were more positive in societies that embraced gender egalitarian values. Moreover, greater gender equality was not only advocated in these societies in the form of more modern gender-role ideologies, but also achieved to a greater degree in labor forces, governments, and national politics.

We also examined Gender Egalitarianism as a dimension of organizational culture. An organization's culture can serve as the social glue that compels members of an organization to work collaboratively toward a single goal. Scholars have argued that organizational culture constitutes a microcosm of the larger society. A comparison of societal and organizational levels of Gender Egalitarianism revealed that organizational cultures reflect the culture (practices and values) in the society in which they are embedded. Societal values and practices predicted organizational values and practices regarding the allocation of roles between women and men.

An additional analysis focused on the extent to which culturally endorsed implicit theories of leadership reflect, in part, organizational and societal norms with regard to Gender Egalitarianism. The most consistent findings to emerge from these analyses were that more gender egalitarian organizations and societies endorsed charismatic leader attributes such as "foresight," "enthusiastic," and "self-sacrificial" and participative leader attributes such as "egalitarian," "delegator," and "collectively oriented." These same organizations and societies shunned self-protective leader attributes such as "self-centered," "status-conscious," "secretive," "evasive," and "formal." These results have important practical implications for leaders: Individuals whose organizations and societies seek to minimize gender-role differences must work to cultivate charismatic and participative qualities and to extinguish self-protective qualities if they wish to be perceived as effective leaders of their organizations and societies.

For the final set of analyses, we found that there were significant differences between male and female respondents regarding the rated importance of CLT leadership dimensions, with men and women perceiving a greater contribution of Charismatic/Value-Based, Participative, and Team-Oriented attributes to outstanding leadership. In contrast, women perceived Self-Protective leadership attributes to be more detrimental to outstanding leadership than did men. Finally, as might be expected, gender effects differed significantly across societal cultures. One plausible explanation lies in our finding that gender differences in ratings of various CLT dimensions increased with the level of gender inequality across societies.

In conclusion, GLOBE's measures proved useful for collecting and analyzing a wealth of cross-cultural data. By gathering information regarding gender egalitarianism across 61 societies and investigating its relationship with social, economic, and demographic factors, we were able to identify the characteristics of societies that seek to minimize gender-role differences versus those that seek to maximize such differences. To the extent that managers such as those who participated in this study are in positions to influence cultural norms, they may be able to serve as change agents by fostering gender-egalitarian practices and values in their organizations and societies, thereby increasing the levels of prosperity and well-being in both realms.

ENDNOTES

1. The case of *Ann Hopkins v. Price Waterhouse* provides an interesting case in point of Hofstede's (1998) claim that masculinity/femininity (in Project GLOBE, Assertiveness and Gender Egalitarianism) constitutes the "taboo" dimension of societal culture. Very briefly, the case was one in which a woman, Ann Hopkins, charged Price Waterhouse with gender discrimination after having been denied partnership twice despite very positive work performance. Susan Fiske, a social psychologist, served as an expert witness in this case. In her testimony, Fiske cited empirical research on conditions that facilitate gender stereotyping, indications and consequences of gender stereotyping, and ways to prevent it (Loftus, 1991). As part of its appeal of a lower court ruling in Ms. Hopkins's favor, Price Waterhouse challenged the scholarly integrity of Fiske, specifically, and of social-scientific research, generally. An appellate court again ruled in Ms. Hopkins's favor, and so Price Waterhouse made one final appeal to the Supreme Court of the United States. In response to Price Waterhouse's attack on social-scientific research, the American Psychological Association (APA) convened a panel of scholars (Fiske, Borgida, Deaux, & Heilman) and one attorney (Bersoff) to construct and file an amicus curiae (friend of the court) brief with the Supreme Court. This APA brief outlined the current state of sex stereotyping and sex discrimination research as it pertained to the facts of the *Price Waterhouse v. Hopkins* case. The Supreme Court's decision relied heavily on the brief, as evidenced by extensive references to the brief in the written opinion. The panel's task did not end with the Court's ruling, however. Two scholars (Barrett & Morris) criticized the panel's methods, conclusions, and motives, thereby prompting a spirited and, at times, acrimonious debate in the scholarly literature (Barrett & Morris, 1993a, 1993b; Fiske, Bersoff, Borgida, Deaux, & Heilman, 1991, 1993a, 1993b). One wonders whether this debate—the fact that it occurred at all and was so contentious once begun—stemmed, in part, from the taboo nature of issues surrounding gender egalitarianism.

2. Our response bias correction procedure identified response bias in some countries for this scale. We recomputed the predicted response bias corrected-scale score for each country. Response bias corrected scores are:

Practices: Morocco, 3.08 (no change in band); Qatar, 3.86 (no change in band); and Taiwan, 2.92 (no change in band).

Values: Finland, 4.47 (no change in band); France, 4.71 (moves from band B to band A); Morocco, 4.07 (no change in band).

For a complete discussion of this procedure and all response bias corrected scores, see Appendix B of this volume.

3. As reported in Chapter 20 by Brodbeck, Hanges, Dickson, Gupta, and Dorfman, we found that all the cultural dimensions of organizational cultural values and practices significantly differed across societies. Although important, this prior analysis did not identify the particular aspect of societal differences that was related to organizational culture. In the present chapter, we found that societal and organizational Gender Egalitarianism practices were significantly related (R^2 Total = 6.2%, R^2 Societal = 34.4%, $p < .01$). We found even stronger results for societal and organizational Gender Egalitarianism values (R^2 Total = 32.7%, R^2 Societal = 90.8%, $p < .01$). As discussed in Chapter 11 by Hanges, Dickson, and Sipe, the R^2 Total considers all levels of analysis (i.e., individual, organizational, and societal) whereas the R^2 Societal isolates the societal level portion of the dependent variable and indicates the percentage of variance accounted for by the predictor at only this level.

Although we have primarily taken the conservative approach and reported the R^2 Total in GLOBE, a number of scholars suggest that R^2 Societal provides a more accurate description of aggregated relationships. For further discussion, see the paper by Lance and James (1999).

4. Results between the single HLM and multiple HLM tests will likely differ somewhat. The differences between the results of the multiple HLMs and single HLMs are conceptually similar to the differences between a multiple regression analysis and a correlation coefficient. Table 21.10 in Chapter 21 by Dorfman et al. presents both single and multiple HLM coefficients. In addition, the relationships for all culture dimension values are summarized in Chapter 3.

5. Gender differences accounted for 0.2%, 1.1%, 0.6%, 0.9% of variance at the individual level of analysis in the Charismatic/Value-Based, Participative, Team-Oriented, and Self-Protective CLT leadership dimensions, respectively. See Chapter 11 by Hanges, Dickson, and Sipe for a discussion of these different explained variances.

6. The individual level, explained variance for gender on this variable was 3.1%. See Chapter 11 by Hanges, Dickson, and Sipe for a discussion of this explained variance term.

References

Adler, N. J. (1991). *International dimensions of organizational behavior* (pp. 58–60). Boston: PWS-Kent.

Barrett, G. V., & Morris, S. B. (1993a). The American Psychological Association's amicus curiae brief in *Price Waterhouse v. Hopkins*: The values of science versus the values of the law. *Law and Human Behavior, 17,* 201–215.

Barrett, G. V., & Morris, S. B. (1993b). Sex stereotyping in *Price Waterhouse v. Hopkins*. *American Psychologist, 48,* 54–55.

Barry, H., Bacon, M. K., & Child, I. L. (1957). A cross-cultural survey of some sex differences in socialization. *Journal of Abnormal and Social Psychology, 55,* 327–332.

Becker, G. S., & Posner, R. A. (1993). Cross-cultural differences in family and sexual life. *Rationality and Society, 5,* 421–431.

Bem, S. L. (1975). Sex role adaptability: One consequence of psychological androgyny. *Journal of Personality and Social Psychology, 31,* 634–643.

Berk, R., & Berk, S. F. (1979). *Labor and leisure at home.* Beverly Hills, CA: Sage.

Best, D. L., & Williams, J. E. (1993). A cross-cultural viewpoint. In A. E. Beall & R. J. Sternberg (Eds.), *The psychology of gender* (pp. 215–248). New York: Guilford Press.

Best, D. L., Williams, J. E., Cloud, J. M., Davis, S. W., Robertson, L. S., Edwards, J. R., Giles, H., & Fowles, J. (1977). Development of sex trait stereotypes among young children in the U.S., England and Ireland. *Child Development, 43,* 1375–1384.

Blackburn, R. M., Jarman, J., & Siltanen, J. (1993). The analysis of occupational gender segregation over time and place: Considerations of measurement and some new evidence. *Work Employment and Society, 7,* 335–362.

Boserup, E. (1970). *Woman's role in economic development.* London: Allen & Unwin.

Braidotti, R. (1994). *Nomadic subjects.* New York: Columbia University Press.

Chafetz, J. S., & Hagan, J. (1996). The gender division of labor and family change in industrial societies: A theoretical accounting. *Journal of Comparative Family Studies, 27,* 187–219.

Charles, M. (1992). Cross-national variation in occupational sex segregation. *American Sociological Review, 57,* 483–502.

Chinese Culture Connection. (1987). Chinese values and the search for culture-free dimensions of culture. *Journal of Cross-Cultural Psychology, 18,* 143–164.

Chodorow, N. (1978). *The reproduction of mothering.* Berkeley: University of California Press.

Clark, R., & Carvalho, J. (1996). Female revolt revisited. *International Review of Modern Sociology, 26,* 27–42.

Clark, R. L., & Anker, R. (1993). Cross-national analysis of labor force participation of older men and women. *Economic Development and Cultural Change, 41,* 489–512.

Cohen, J. (1988). *Statistical power analysis for the behavioral sciences* (2nd ed.). Hillsdale, NJ: Lawrence Erlbaum.

Cohen, J., & Cohen, P. (1983). *Applied multiple regression/correlation analysis for the behavioral sciences* (2nd ed.). Hillsdale, NJ: Lawrence Erlbaum.

Coltrane, S. (1988). Father–child relationships and the status of women: A cross-cultural study. *American Journal of Sociology, 93,* 1060–1095.

Coltrane, S. (1992). The micropolitics of gender in nonindustrial societies. *Gender and Society, 6,* 86–107.

Coverman, S., & Sheley, J. F. (1986). Men's housework and child-care time, 1965–1975. *Journal of Marriage and Family, 48,* 413–422.

Darwin, C. (1958). *The origin of species by natural selection or the presentation of favoured races in the struggle for life.* New York: Mentnor. (Original work published in 1859)

Denmark, F., Rabinowitz, V., & Sechzer, J. (2000). *Engendering psychology.* Boston: Allyn & Bacon.

Doney, P. M., Cannon, J. P., & Mullen, M. R. (1998). Understanding the influence of national culture on the development of trust. *Academy of Management Review, 23,* 601–620.

Eagly, A. H., & Johannesen-Schmidt, M. C. (2001). The leadership styles of women and men. *Journal of Social Issues, 57,* 781–787.

Erez, M. (1994). Toward a model of cross-cultural industrial and organizational psychology. In H. C. Triandis, M. D. Dunnette, & L. M. Hough (Eds.), *Handbook of industrial and organizational psychology* (2nd ed., Vol. 4, pp. 559–607). Palo Alto, CA: Consulting Psychologists Press.

Fagenson, E. A. (1990). Perceived masculine and feminine attributes examined as a function of individuals' sex and level in the organizational power hierarchy: A test of four theoretical perspectives. *Journal of Applied Psychology, 75,* 204–211.

Fiske, S. T., Bersoff, D. N., Borgida, E., Deaux, K., & Heilman, M. E. (1991). Social science research on trial: Use of sex stereotyping research in *Price Waterhouse v. Hopkins. American Psychologist, 46,* 1049–1060.

Fiske, S. T., Bersoff, D. N., Borgida, E., Deaux, K., & Heilman, M. E. (1993a). Accuracy and objectivity on behalf of the APA. *American Psychologist, 48,* 55–56.

Fiske, S. T., Bersoff, D. N., Borgida, E., Deaux, K., & Heilman, M. E. (1993b). What constitutes a scientific review? A majority retort to Barrett and Morris. *Law and Human Behavior, 17,* 217–233.

Fiske, S. T., & Taylor, S. E. (1991). *Social cognition* (2nd ed.). New York: McGraw-Hill.

Gilmore, D. D. (1996). Above and below: Toward a social geometry of gender. *American Anthropologist, 98,* 54–67.

Girard, C. (1993). Age, gender, and suicide: A cross-national analysis. *American Sociological Review, 58,* 553–574.

Gray, J. P. (1987). Do women have higher social status in hunting societies without high gods? *Social Forces, 65,* 1121–1131.

Heilman, M. E. (1995). Sex stereotypes and their effects in the workplace: What we know and what we don't know. *Journal of Social Behavior and Personality, 10,* 3–26.

Heilman, M. E. (2001). Description and prescription: How gender stereotypes prevent women's ascent up the organizational ladder. *Journal of Social Issues, 57,* 657–674.

Heilman, M. E., Block, C. J., & Martell, R. F. (1995). Sex stereotypes: Do they influence perceptions of managers? *Journal of Social Behavior and Personality, 10,* 237–252.

Hendrix, L. (1994). What is sexual inequality? On the definition and range of variation. *Cross-Cultural Research, 28,* 287–307.

Hendrix, L., & Hossain, Z. (1988). Women's status and mode of production: A cross-cultural test. *Signs, 13,* 437–453.

Hochschild, A. (1989). *The second shift.* New York: Viking.

Hofstede, G. (1980). *Culture's consequences: International differences in work-related values.* Beverly Hills, CA: Sage.

Hofstede, G. (1991). *Cultures and organizations: Software of the mind.* London: McGraw-Hill.

Hofstede, G. (1998). *Masculinity and femininity: The taboo dimension of national cultures.* Thousand Oaks, CA: Sage.

Hofstede, G. (2001). *Culture's consequences: Comparing values, behaviors, institutions, and organizations across nations* (2nd ed.). Thousand Oaks, CA: Sage.

Hofstede, G., & Vunderink, M. (1994). A case study in masculinity/femininity differences: American students in the Netherlands vs. local students. In A. M. Bouvy, F. J. R. van de Vijver, P. Boski, & P. Schmitz (Eds.), *Journeys into cross-cultural psychology* (pp. 329–347). Lisse, The Netherlands: Swets & Zeitlinger.

Hoppe, M. H. (1990). *A comparative study of society elite: International differences in work-related values and learning and their implications for management training and development.* Unpublished doctoral dissertation, University of North Carolina at Chapel Hill.

Hoppe, M. H. (1993). The effects of national culture on the theory and practices of managing research-and-development professionals abroad. *R & D Management, 23,* 313–325.

Hoppe, M. H. (1998). Validating the masculinity/femininity dimension on elites from 19 countries. In G. Hofstede (Ed.), *Masculinity and femininity: The taboo dimension of national cultures* (pp. 29–43). Thousand Oaks, CA: Sage.

House, R. J., Hanges, P. J., Ruiz-Quintanilla, S. A., Dorfman, P. W., Javidan, M., Dickson, M. W., et al. (1999). Cultural influences on leadership and organizations: Project GLOBE. In W. H. Mobley, M. J. Gessner, & V. Arnold (Eds.), *Advances in global leadership* (pp. 171–233). Greenwich, CT: JAI.

Inkeles, A., & Levinson, D. J. (1969). National character: The study of modal personality and sociocultural systems. In G. Lindzey & E. Aronson (Eds.), *Handbook of social psychology* (Vol. 4, pp. 418–506). New York: McGraw-Hill. (Original work published 1954)

Inkeles, A., & Levinson, D. J. (1997). National character: The study of modal personality and sociocultural systems. In A. Inkeles, *National character: A psycho-social perspective.* New Brunswick, NJ: Transaction. (Original work published 1954)

Jacobs, J. A., & Lim, S. T. (1992). Trends in occupational and industrial sex segregation in 56 countries, 1960–1980. *Work and Occupations, 19,* 450–486.

Jordan, J. O., & Patten, R. L. (1995). *Nineteenth-century British publishing and reading practices.* Cambridge, UK: Cambridge University Press.

Kattler, D., & Williamson, J. B. (1988). Welfare state development and life expectancy among the aged: A cross-national analysis. *Journal of Aging Studies, 2,* 13–24.

Katz, M. M., & Konnor, M. J. (1981). The role of the father: An anthropological perspective. In M. E. Lamb (Ed.), *The role of the father in child development* (2nd ed., pp. 155–185). New York: John Wiley.

Kukreja, S. (1992). The political economy of the feminization of the tertiary in developing countries: Some cross-national findings. *International Review of Modern Sociology, 22,* 79–97.

Lance, C. E., & James, L. R. (1999). A proportional variance accounted for index for some cross-level and person-situation research designs. *Organizational Research Methods, 2,* 395–418.

Linke, U. (1992). Manhood, femaleness, and power: A cultural analysis of prehistoric images of reproduction. *Comparative Studies in Society and History, 34,* 579–620.

Loftus, E. F. (1991). Resolving legal questions with psychological data. *American Psychologist, 46,* 1046–1048.

Lovenduski, J., & Hills, J. (1981). *The politics of the second electorate: Women and public participation.* London: Routledge & Kegan Paul.

Lovenduski, J., & Norris, P. (1989). Selecting women candidates: Obstacles to the feminization of the House of Commons. *European Journal of Political Research, 17,* 533–562.

Martin, C. L. (1987). A ratio measure of sex stereotyping. *Journal of Personality and Social Psychology, 52,* 489–499.

McClelland, D. C. (1961). *The achieving society.* Princeton, NJ: Van Nostrand Rheinhold.

McDonald, G. W. (1980). Family power: The assessment of a decade of theory and research. *Journal of Marriage and the Family, 42,* 841–854.

McElvaine, R. S. (2000). *Eve's seed: Biology, the sexes and the course of history.* New York: McGraw-Hill.

Mead, M. (1949). *Male and female.* New York: William Morrow.

Menard, S. (1990). Cross-national models of fertility, family planning, and development: Testing for reciprocal effects. *Studies in Comparative International Development, 25,* 60–90.

Merritt, A. (2000). Culture in the cockpit: Do Hofstede's dimensions replicate? *Journal of Cross-Cultural Psychology, 31,* 283–301.

Miller, E. M. (1994). Paternal provisioning versus mate seeking in human populations. *Personality and Individual Differences, 17,* 227–255.

Moore, G., & Shackman, G. (1996). Gender and authority: A cross-national study. *Social Science Quarterly, 77,* 274–288.

Nunnally, J. C., & Bernsrein, I. H. (1994). *Psychometric theory* (3rd ed.). New York: McGraw-Hill.

Nuss, S., & Majka, L. (1983). The economic integration of women: A cross-national investigation. *Work and Occupations: An International Sociological Journal, 10,* 29–48.

Pampel, F. C., & Park, S. (1986). Cross-national patterns and determinants of female retirement. *American Journal of Sociology, 91,* 932–955.

Paris, L. (2003). *The effect of gender and culture on implicit leadership theories: A cross-cultural study.* Unpublished doctoral dissertation. New Mexico State University, Las Cruces, NM.

Parsons, T. (1964). *Social structure and personality.* New York: Free Press.

Pattnayak, S. R., & Shai, D. (1995). Mortality rates as indicators of cross-cultural development: Regional variations in the Third World. *Journal of Developing Societies, 11,* 252–262.

Paxton, P. (1997). Women in national legislatures: A cross-national analysis. *Social Science Research, 26,* 442–464.

Peterson, M. F., & Smith, P. B. (1997). Does national culture or ambient temperature explain cross-national differences in role stress? No sweat! *Academy of Management Journal, 40,* 930–946.

Piccinelli, M., & Simon, G. (1997). Gender and cross-cultural differences in somatic symptoms associated with emotional distress: An international study in primary care. *Psychological Medicine, 27,* 433–444.

Price Waterhouse v. Hopkins, 490 U.S. 288 (1989).

Reskin, B., & Padavic, I. (1994). *Women and men at work.* Thousand Oaks, CA: Pine Forge Press.

Roschrhomberg, I. (1994). Hierarchical opposition and the concept of Um-Yang (Yin-Yang): A reevaluation of values in the light of the symbolism of Korean rituals for the dead. *Anthropos, 89,* 471–491.

Rule, W. (1987). Electoral systems, contextual factors and women's opportunity for election to parliament in twenty-three democracies. *The Western Political Quarterly, 40,* 477–498.

Sacks, K. (1979). *Sisters and wives: The past and future of sexual inequality.* Westport, CT: Greenwood.

Safilios-Rothschild, C. (1970). The study of family power structure: A review, 1960–1969. *Journal of Marriage and the Family, 32,* 345–352.

Schein, E. H. (1983). The role of the founder in creating organizational culture. *Organizational Dynamics, 12,* 13–28.

Schneider, S. C. (1988, Summer). National vs. corporate culture: Implications for human resource management. *Human Resource Management,* p. 239.

Schwartz, S. H. (1994). Beyond individualism and collectivism: New cultural dimensions of values. In U. Kim, H. C. Triandis, C. Kagitçibasi, S. C. Choi, & G. Yoon (Eds.), *Individualism and collectivism: Theory, method, and applications* (pp. 85–199). Thousand Oaks, CA: Sage.

Segall, M. H., Dasen, P. R., Berry, J. W., & Poortinga, Y. H. (1990). *Human behavior in global perspective: An introduction to cross-cultural psychology.* New York: Pergamon.

Shen, C., & Williamson, J. B. (1999). Maternal mortality, women's status, and economic dependency in less developed countries: A cross-national analysis. *Social Science & Medicine, 49,* 197–214.

Sigelman, L., & Tsai, Y. (1985). Urbanism and women's labor force status: A cross-national study. *International Journal of Comparative Sociology, 26,* 109–118.

Slater, P., & Slater, D. (1965). Maternal ambivalence and narcissism. *Merrill-Palmer Quarterly, 11,* 241–259.

Smelser, N. (1970). Mechanisms of change and adjustment. In J. Finkle & R. Gable (Eds.), *Political development and social change.* New York: John Wiley.

South, S. J., & Spitze, G. (1994). Housework in marital and nonmarital households. *American Sociological Review, 59,* 327–347.

Stover, R. G., & Hope, C. A. (1984). Monotheism and gender status: A cross-societal study. *Social Forces, 63,* 335–348.

Stroh, L. K., Brett, J. M., & Reilly, A. H. (1992). All the right stuff: A comparison of female and male managers' career progression. *Journal of Applied Psychology, 77,* 251–260.

Szalai, A. (1972). *The use of time: Daily activities of urban and suburban populations in twelve countries.* The Hague: Mouton.

Triandis, H. C. (1994). Cross-cultural industrial and organizational psychology. In H. C. Triandis, M. D. Dunnette, & L. M. Hough (Eds.), *Handbook of industrial and organizational psychology* (2nd ed., Vol. 4, pp. 103–172). Palo Alto, CA: Consulting Psychologists Press.

Trivers, R. L. (1972). Parental investment and sexual selection. In B. Campbell (Ed.), *Sexual selection and the descent of man, 1871–1971.* Chicago: Aldine.

Van de Vliert, E. (1998). Gender role gaps, competitiveness, and temperature. In G. Hofstede

(Ed.), *Masculinity and femininity: The taboo dimensions of national cultures* (pp. 117–129). Thousand Oaks, CA: Sage.

Van de Vliert, E., Schwartz, S. H., Huismans, S. E., Hofstede, G., & Daan, S. (1999). Temperature, cultural masculinity and domestic political violence: A cross-national study. *Journal of Cross-Cultural Psychology, 30,* 291–314.

Van de Vliert, E., & Van Yperen, N. W. (1996). Why cross-national differences in role overload? Don't overlook ambient temperature! *Academy of Management Journal, 39,* 986–1004.

Verweij, J., Ester, P., & Nauta, R. (1997). Secularization as an economic and cultural phenomenon: A cross-national analysis. *Journal for the Scientific Study of Religion, 36,* 309–324.

Walker, H. A., & Fennell, M. L. (1986). Gender differences in role differentiation and organizational task performance. *Annual Review of Sociology, 12,* 255–275.

Walton, W. (2000). *Eve's proud descendants: Four women writers and republican politics in nineteenth-century France.* Stanford, CA: Stanford University Press.

Warner, R. L., Lee, G. R., & Lee, J. (1986). Social organization, spousal resources, and marital power: A cross-cultural study. *Journal of Marriage and the Family, 48,* 121–128.

Welch, M. R. (1982). Female exclusion from religious roles: A cross-cultural test of competing explanations. *Social Forces, 61,* 79–98.

Welch, M. R. (1983). Women and political leadership roles: A cross-cultural study. *International Journal of Sociology of the Family, 13,* 57–77.

Wells, S. (2001). *Out of the dead house: Nineteenth-century women physicians and writing of medicine.* Madison: University of Wisconsin Press.

Whyte, M. K. (1978). *The status of women in preindustrial societies.* Princeton, NJ: Princeton University Press.

Williams, J. E., & Best, D. L. (1982). *Measuring sex stereotypes: A thirty nation study.* Beverly Hills, CA: Sage.

Williams, J. E., & Best, D. L. (1990a). *Measuring sex stereotypes: A multination study.* Newbury Park, CA: Sage.

Williams, J. E., & Best, D. L. (1990b). *Sex and psyche: Gender and self viewed cross-culturally.* Newbury Park, CA: Sage.

Wright, E. O., Baxter, J., & Birkelund, G. E. (1995). The gender gap in workplace authority: A cross-national study. *American Sociological Review, 60,* 407–435.

15

ASSERTIVENESS

DEANNE N. DEN HARTOG

"Blessed are the meek: for they shall inherit the earth" (Matt. 5:5).

This quote from the Bible reflects belief in nonaggressive, nonassertive values to guide behavior. According to the Bible, these beliefs will, in the end, be rewarded. However, it is not clear that this is indeed an assumption shared within and between cultures in these times.

One of the GLOBE dimensions of societal and organizational values and practices is the Assertiveness cultural dimension. Broadly speaking, cultural assertiveness reflects beliefs as to whether people are or should be encouraged to be assertive, aggressive, and tough, or nonassertive, nonaggressive, and tender in social relationships. The results of Project GLOBE show that assertiveness is an important aspect of a society's culture, but it has received relatively little attention in the cross-cultural literature. This chapter will present the GLOBE findings concerning assertiveness as a dimension of culture. It will present a review of relevant literature, a description of Project GLOBE's approach to the study of assertiveness in 62 societies, and the findings resulting from Project GLOBE's research program concerning assertiveness. These findings show that assertiveness, as a

cultural set of GLOBE-defined practices and values, is significantly related to findings by other researchers concerning a wide variety of social and economic indicators as well as indicators of psychological well-being and physical health of the members of cultures. Finally, in this chapter I will also examine reported assertiveness practices and values as they relate to culturally endorsed implicit leadership theories (CLTs).

LITERATURE ON THE CONCEPT OF ASSERTIVENESS

The GLOBE questionnaire scale that taps the cultural dimension of assertiveness asks whether people in their society, in general, practice, or should be encouraged to practice, assertive or nonassertive behavior. Assertiveness in Project GLOBE is defined as the degree to which individuals in organizations or societies are assertive, tough, dominant, and aggressive in social relationships (House et al., 1999). An assertive attitude is often seen in business. For instance, "Just do it," the famous Nike slogan, implies valuing such an assertive attitude. Webster's dictionary defines *assertive* as "positive or confident in a persistent way." It also mentions "aggressive" as a synonym. According to Webster's dictionary, *aggressive* negatively implies "a bold and energetic pursuit of one's ends," connoting in derogatory usage a ruthless desire to dominate. It also defines aggressiveness, in a favorable sense, as being "enterprising, or taking initiative."

Although *assertive* and *aggressive* are sometimes seen as similar, there are also different views. Assertiveness is sometimes conceptualized as the midpoint on a continuum between nonassertive and aggressive behavior (Rakos, 1991). In such views the two are similar, but assertiveness is less extreme than aggressiveness; however, other literature explicitly contrasts aggressiveness and assertiveness. For instance, Loeber and Hay (1997) define aggression as "a category of behavior that causes or threatens physical harm to others" (p. 373). Aggression is often mentioned together with violence, hostility, and antisocial behavior. Many attempts to distinguish between assertion and aggression have invoked the notion of "social acceptability" (Rakos, 1991). Aggression is often seen as having different intentions. In that case, aggression is seen as behavior with a coercive content, intended to dominate, humiliate, or blame others rather than as behavior intended to assert oneself or stand up for one's own personal rights. When compared to assertiveness, aggressive behavior can be seen as taking a different linguistic form, such as using threats, imperatives, or verbal disparagement rather than confidently expressing one's opinion (Crawford, 1995; Hollandsworth, 1977). Aggression and assertion are also contrasted in terms of their proposed effects on others. In such views, aggressive behavior leads to harm and strained relationships whereas assertion should result in a minimization of negative emotions or even to stronger relationships (e.g., Lange & Jabukoski, 1976). Thus, aggressive behavior is not always seen as synonymous with assertive behavior and, when contrasted, is often seen in a less positive light.

Judging from the frequent use of terms such as "cut-throat competition" or "aggressive marketing strategies," having such an "aggressive" attitude in the Western business world seems to have a relatively positive connotation. Aggressive then implies being tough, fast, and forceful as opposed to weak and vulnerable. According to Hofstede (1980, 1991, 2001) the word *aggressive* carries a positive connotation only in what he calls "masculine" countries.

In his seminal work on societal culture, Hofstede (1980, 2001) described differences among societies in the modal desirability of selected work goals. He developed a scale titled the MAS index (which taps the culture dimension labeled *masculinity vs. femininity*). In almost every country that Hofstede studied, he found that men favored a select set of job attributes more than women (Hofstede, 1980, 1991). For the masculine pole of his MAS scale, high importance was attached to "earnings," "recognition," "advancement," and "challenge." For the opposite feminine pole, high importance was attached to having a good working relationship with one's direct supervisor, "cooperation," "living area," and "employment security." According to Hofstede, the higher the aggregated country or culture score on the masculine items, and the lower the aggregated responses on feminine items, the more a society can be seen as a "macho," or masculine-oriented, society.

Also, according to Hofstede, masculinity implies dominant values in a society that stresses assertiveness and being tough, the acquisition of money and material objects, and *not* caring for others, the quality of life, or people. Hofstede's measure of masculinity (the MAS index), however, does not include any indicators of assertiveness, toughness, aggressiveness, or dominance. Thus, the scale can be seen as lacking face validity with respect to directly measuring assertiveness or aggressiveness as a dimension of culture. (See Chapter 14 on Gender Egalitarianism by Emrich, Denmark, and Den Hartog for more detail on Hofstede's MAS index.)

Beyond Hofstede's well-known masculinity dimension, which we will show differs substantially from the GLOBE Assertiveness dimension, assertiveness has—to our knowledge—rarely been studied as a dimension of culture in its own right. Assertiveness has, however, received ample attention in the psychological literature. In this literature, assertiveness was defined as a set of social skills or a style of responding amenable to training (e.g., Crawford, 1995) or as a facet of personality (e.g., Rathus, 1973). Without trying to be exhaustive, we will first discuss some of the literature on assertiveness as a style of responding, and assertiveness as a personality trait. As assertiveness is often described as a primarily masculine characteristic, we will also very briefly review some findings from research on gender roles and stereotyping in the workplace. Next, Assertiveness is examined as an attribute or dimension of national culture. After that the GLOBE measures and findings concerning Assertiveness as a dimension of culture are presented.

A PSYCHOLOGICAL PERSPECTIVE

Assertiveness as a Style of Responding: The Assertiveness-Training Hype

As stated, in much of the psychological and behavioral literature, assertiveness became defined as a set of social and communicative skills amenable to training. The label "assertive" for a specific category of interpersonal behaviors and the focus of attention on the use of assertiveness training to alleviate interpersonal problems originates in the work of Wolpe (1958). This approach was based on Salter's (1949) *Conditioned Reflex Therapy*, the first approach to apply behaviorism to clinical problems involving communication. Salter applied a conditioning model to verbal and nonverbal behaviors, such as the ability to say what one feels, to contradict and disagree, and to speak directly through the frequent use of "I statements" (Crawford, 1995). An example of how assertiveness is defined in the psychological literature is the following: "Assertion basically involves asking for what one wants, refusing what one doesn't want, and expressing positive and negative messages to others" (Booream & Flowers, 1978, p. 15).

Assertive behavior is explicitly contrasted to passive behavior (Crawford, 1995). Such passive behavior is attributed to those who fail to express their true thoughts and feelings, allow themselves to be dominated or humiliated by others, and who comply with requests or demands of others even if they themselves do not want to (Lange & Jakubowski, 1976).

Assertiveness and assertiveness training as a behavior therapy technique became popular among a large segment of the United States population in the early to mid-70s. Books, articles, and workshops aimed at the mass market claimed that a lack of assertiveness causes problems for people and offered techniques for becoming more assertive. As stated, assertiveness was seen as a style of (communicative) behavior, amenable to training. As Rakos (1991) noted, the self-improvement literature often simplified the concept of assertion to "saying no" and "getting your own way" (Smith, 1975) or to "standing up for your rights" and "get(ting) where and what you want" (Baer, 1976). Many of the mass-market books were aimed specifically at women buyers. Virtually all such popular books claimed women were especially in need of assertiveness training and "blamed" gender socialization for this. According to Crawford (1995), authors drew heavily on stereotypes of female passivity. Only rarely did they provide research evidence, other than paper-and-pencil inventories completed by college students, that women as a group have trouble asserting themselves.

Assumptions Underlying Assertiveness Training

As Crawford (1995, p. 56) noted, underlying the behavioral literature on assertiveness was a set of values and assumptions about "healthy" and "adaptive" interpersonal behavior that remained implicit and unexamined. An individualistic ethic made assertion seem like everyone's right. In this body of literature on assertiveness, individual perceptions, feelings, and beliefs are valued above the maintenance and process of social relationships, and the ideal relationship is one of parallel self-fulfillment (Crawford, 1995). According to Shoemaker and Satterfield (1977) the implied philosophy of social relationships in assertiveness is one of benign self-interest. The individualism of the assertive philosophy is also evident in the language of assertiveness techniques. Clients are taught to use "I–me" messages: "From this perspective, learning specific conversational techniques in order that one's own opinions and decisions should prevail is a route to self-fulfillment" (Crawford, 1995, p. 57). The popular assertiveness literature encourages people to dispense with reasons or justifications for their feelings or behaviors, implying that individuals should be the sole judges of their own actions (Crawford, 1995).

Besides individualism, the notion of assertive behavior also reflects rationality and pragmatism (Rakos, 1991). Rationality plays a role in determining the appropriate expression of emotion, a key element in assertive behavior. For instance, Wolpe (1982) defines assertive behavior as "the appropriate expression of any emotion other than anxiety toward another person" (p. 118). The ability to produce such an appropriate response requires the accurate discrimination of situational cues, decision-making skills, and the emission of acceptable social behavior, all of which are produced by rational rather than emotional processes. Rationality is involved in our deductive inference, information processing and decision making, the way in which we judge and comprehend behavior of others, in explanations for events that happen to us, and in the further understanding of our environment (Irani, 1986; Rakos, 1991).

Pragmatism—the notion that what works is much more important than dogmatism or ideology—also underlies assertiveness training. Assertiveness training emphasizes that assertive behavior is only one option for coping with difficult or problematic circumstances, and in many instances it may not be the preferred one. In other words, there is no ideological mandate always to respond assertively. "Such pragmatism is, of course, highly adaptive in our modern world, with its shifting value systems, complex and ambiguous situations, and increasing cultural and social heterogeneity" (Rakos, 1991, p. 5).

Over the years, literally hundreds of studies were done on assertiveness and assertiveness training. Some of these studies describe the definition and variety of assertive speech, for instance, asking what would constitute an appropriate assertive response. Others describe programs for assertiveness training, evaluate their outcomes, or discuss which types of people can benefit most from such training. Yet other studies report the development, reliability, and validity of paper-and-pencil tests for measuring levels of assertiveness in prospective clients (Crawford, 1995). The true hype of assertiveness training seems to have passed. It is now used in a far more limited manner as a behavioral therapy technique

that can help alleviate specific problems, and fewer studies are devoted to it. Rakos (1991) holds the decline in interest in assertiveness training is probably due to the complex nature of assertiveness. For example, consideration of the social and cultural context is an essential foundation of a functionally useful assertive response. In other words, the functionality of assertive behavior to obtain desired outcomes, as well as whether certain actions will be seen as assertive or nonassertive, depends on the situation.

An example of such a situational constraint has to do with gender of both "asserters" and observers. Research shows that the social consequences of assertive behavior differ for men and women. For instance, Kelly, Kern, Kirkley, Patterson, and Keane (1980) showed that assertive women were seen as more competent but less likable than nonassertive women, a distinction that was not made for assertive men. Following up on this, Crawford (1988) designed a study testing the evaluation of assertive behavior. She developed scenarios in which a woman or man behaved assertively. Raters then rated the models. The results showed that raters judged the models on social competence and likeability. Assertiveness was evaluated differently depending on the sex of the assertive model and the age of the research participant. Assertive women models received the lowest likeability ratings of all from older male participants. Such gender differences are the focus of Chapter 14 of this volume, which describes GLOBE's measures and findings on Gender Egalitarianism.

Obviously, culture is another important situational influence that determines whether responding assertively is valued and which types of responses are appropriate. "At least some of the differences in assertiveness among cultural groups are fundamentally due to cognitive variables stemming from cultural values and norms" (Rakos, 1991, p. 14). However, the issue as to whether one culture is more or less assertive than another may be complex. For instance, Sue, Ino, and Sue (1983) found that whereas the self-reports of general assertiveness behavior for Chinese Americans were less than assertive behavior reported by European Americans, actual assertiveness behaviors did not differ.

As stated, the literature on assertiveness training is strongly U.S.-dominated, and the concept seems linked to culture. As was described in earlier chapters, other cultures do not share the same assumptions. For instance, Hofstede (1993, p. 81) noted that United States management theories contain several idiosyncrasies not necessarily shared by management elsewhere; for example, "a stress on market processes, a stress on the individual, and a focus on managers rather than workers." The same seems to hold in the area of assertiveness. As Furnham (1979) notes,

> the concept of assertiveness is culture bound, and particularly North American. In many other cultures, asserting oneself in the way that is normative in North America and parts of Europe is neither encouraged nor tolerated. Humility, subservience, and tolerance are valued above assertiveness in many other cultures, especially for women. (p. 522)

For instance, an employee voicing disagreement to his or her boss is an accepted and positively evaluated manner of expressing oneself in some cultures, but may be unacceptable in others. Whether and how such assertive responding is done and how it is valued depends on societal norms regarding such behavior. Such norms describe the degree to which people in organizations or societies are (or should be) assertive in social relationships.

Assertiveness as a Personality Trait

In addition to the body of psychological assertiveness literature that focuses on assertiveness as a style of responding, there is also a body of literature that has examined assertiveness as a more stable personality trait. According to this perspective, some people are inherently more assertive than others.

In the field of personality research, evidence is accumulating that most personality measures can be reduced to a five-factor model, which is now labeled the "Big Five" (Goldberg, 1990). The dimensions composing this model are neuroticism, extraversion or surgency, openness to experience, agreeableness, and conscientiousness. Interestingly, the five-factor structure has been found to generalize across many cultures (McCrae & Costa, 1997). In this Big Five model, assertiveness can be seen as part of *extraversion*. Extroverts tend to be sociable and gregarious, but also surgent, dominant, and ambitious as well as assertive, active, and adventurous.

According to Watson and Clark (1997), extroverts are more likely to take on leadership roles. Extraversion has also been found to be associated with job performance and career success. For instance, in the United States, dominance and sociability differentiated between successful and unsuccessful executives, with dominant executives being more successful (Rawls & Rawls, 1968). Also, extraversion predicted salary and job level in a United Kingdom study (Melamed, 1996a, 1996b). In their meta-analytical study, Barrick and Mount (1991) found that extraversion was a valid predictor of job performance for two occupational groups: managers and sales people. In these groups, traits such as being assertive, active, and sociable were significantly (but only moderately) associated with more effective performance. Several longitudinal studies also confirm this link between success and extraversion. For instance, assessment center ratings of expressive social skills predicted later managerial promotions (Howard & Bray, 1994), and childhood ratings of shyness were negatively associated with adult occupational status (Caspi, Elder, & Bem, 1988). Also, positive relationships of high extraversion with extrinsic career success (a variable describing a combination of income, promotions, and occupational status) were found (Judge, Higgins, Thoresen, & Barrick, 1999). Interestingly in this study, both measures taken in childhood and adulthood predicted later career success.

Nonassertiveness (in terms of being tender and nondominant) can be linked to the Big Five factor of *agreeableness*. Agreeable people are cooperative (trusting, caring) and likable (good natured, gentle); they are also softhearted and tolerant. The meta-analysis by Barrick and Mount (1991) suggests agreeableness is not an important predictor of job performance. Moreover, in the previously mentioned longitudinal study by Judge and colleagues (1999) agreeableness negatively predicted extrinsic career success. Similarly, affability (the degree to which an individual is nurturing, nonaggressive, supportive, and sympathetic) was negatively related to management potential (Howard & Bray, 1988).

To summarize, literature shows that in terms of personality, high rather than low levels of assertiveness are linked to effectiveness and success. However, such studies are predominantly based on United States samples and, to a lesser extent, samples from the United Kingdom. Whether these results are similar in other cultures remains to be seen. Assertiveness is also often seen as a "masculine" rather than "feminine" trait. The next section briefly reviews some of the research on assertiveness and gender. More detailed information on real and perceived gender differences in society is presented in Chapter 14 by Emrich, Denmark, and Den Hartog.

Assertiveness and Stereotypes

Hofstede (2001) notes that assertiveness seems to be a trait or behavior that people associate more with men than with women (see chapter 14, this volume). Segall, Dasen, Berry, and Poortinga (1990) state that

> risking oversimplification, we can summarize the picture of sex-differences in behavior that is presented by anthropology and cross-cultural psychology as showing males to be more self-assertive, achieving, and dominant and females to be more socially responsive, passive, and submissive. (p. 250)

Such characteristics refer to sex-trait *stereotypes* and do not imply actual differences between the sexes. The real differences in behavior between genders seem to be less pronounced than the *beliefs* about those behavioral differences (e.g., Segall et al., 1990). For instance, as seen in Chapter 14, this volume, Williams and Best (1982) found some general agreement across countries in differentially attributing traits to men or women. Traits related to assertiveness such as dominance, aggression, autonomy, achievement, and endurance were ascribed to men and traits related to nonassertiveness such as deference, nurturance, and abasement to women. Williams and Best (1989) also found that the self-perceptions of men and women were less stereotypical in more economically and

socially developed countries. In such countries, higher proportions of women attend university and are gainfully employed, the ideology regarding the status of women is more egalitarian, and women and men perceive themselves to be more similar. Interestingly, in most of the 25 countries Williams and Best studied, women were more liberal than the men. Such differences have also been found in other studies (e.g., Kalin, Heusser, & Edmonds, 1982; Scher, Nevo, & Beit-Hallahmi, 1979).

Besides gender, assertiveness is also associated with the stereotype of successful managers. Successful managers are seen as assertive, dominant, and frank. Different studies also found a strong concurrence between the ratings of men and successful managers and a weak one between ratings of women and successful managers. Successful managers were viewed as more similar to men than to women on attributes considered critical to effective work performance, such as ambition, assertiveness, leadership ability, self-confidence, and forcefulness (e.g., Brenner, Tomkiewicz, & Schein, 1989; Heilman, Block, Martell, & Simon, 1989; Schein, 1973). A recent international replication by Schein (2001) found that this pattern still held to a large extent, especially among male respondents in the five countries included in the study (China, Japan, Great Britain, Germany, and the United States). Fagenson (1990) assessed the effects of both gender and the position one holds in the organizational hierarchy and found that there was no relation between individuals' sex and possession of "masculine" characteristics, such as assertiveness. Instead, masculinity was found to be related to the individuals' perceived power and their position in the organizational hierarchy. Individuals in upper levels were reported to be more masculine than those in the lower levels, and men and women in the organization's upper tier saw themselves similarly with respect to masculine attributes. Therefore, Fagenson holds labeling attributes such as assertiveness as masculine is a misnomer that may cause confusion. More accurate labels might be "powerful" or "successful" attributes.

Taken together, the findings from these and many other studies in this area suggest that— at least in the United States—assertiveness is an important attribute associated with being successful in a managerial position. Also, it is often associated more with men than women, although the differences are in part stereotypical rather than true. The actual differences seem less pronounced. Men may indeed exhibit (slightly) more assertive behavior than women, although this is likely be confounded with the fact that men more often hold positions of power in the organizational (and societal) hierarchy.

Assertiveness as a Dimension of Culture

The concept of assertiveness, as stated, originates (in part) from Hofstede's culture dimension of masculinity versus femininity. In masculine societies men are supposed to be assertive and tough and women are expected to be modest and tender. In contrast, femininity pertains to societies in which social gender roles overlap (Hofstede, 1980, 1998, 2001). As stated, this dimension conceptually appears to encompass several distinct aspects (including gender differences, success striving, and assertiveness). See Chapter 14 by Emrich, Denmark, and Den Hartog for a review of the work on masculinity.

According to Hofstede (2001), high MAS means high assertiveness or ambitiousness (p. 164). Although assertiveness is seen as part of the masculinity dimension, the MAS index used to measure it does not include items that specifically target assertiveness and aggressiveness in relationships. Assertiveness as a culture dimension originates partly in Hofstede's masculinity dimension, but also differs from it substantially. Below, we describe the Assertiveness construct as used in the GLOBE study and review some of the other work on national cultures that is reflected in the construct.

To our knowledge, there are no studies focusing on assertiveness as a cultural dimension. One study undertaken in several European nations does investigate assertiveness as a so-called "national characteristic" that may differ across cultures (Peabody, 1985). Peabody was interested in the question of whether different nationalities have different (stereotypical) perceived psychological characteristics. He used pairs of trait-adjectives to describe such "national characteristics," with examples such as conceited versus modest, self-controlled versus impulsive, and severe versus lenient. Judges

were asked to indicate where someone from a certain nationality was likely to be located on a pair of traits (e.g., an Englishman is likely to be [more or less] "passive" vs. [more or less] "forceful"). Different groups of judges compared self-judgments (judging a target having one's own nationality) and judgments by others (judging a target that has a different nationality than one's own).

Peabody found three factors: One he labeled *self-assertiveness versus unassertiveness*, and the other two he labeled a general *evaluative* dimension and a dimension describing *tight versus loose control over impulse expression*. Items in his final scale for assertiveness were aggressive versus peaceful, passive versus forceful, conceited versus modest, self-confident versus unassured, bold versus timid, and active versus inactive. The national characteristics were perceived to be similar by both residents of a specific country and people with other nationalities. Thus, there were differences between nationality targets on the assertive versus unassertive dimension. For instance, judges in his study agree that the English are relatively nonassertive, whereas the Germans and Americans are seen as highly assertive. Thus, the stereotypical view of Germans and Americans is that they are assertive. As stated, GLOBE sees Assertiveness not only as a behavior, trait, or even a stereotypical national characteristic, but also as a relevant dimension of national cultures that reflects shared societal beliefs about whether people are or should be assertive and tough-minded, or unassertive and tender in their social relationships. To our knowledge, assertiveness has not been studied as a separate cultural dimension in this manner.

As noted earlier, culture can be seen as a set of relatively stable, basic, and shared practices and values that help human social groups or societies find solutions to two fundamental problems. The first is how to survive, grow, and adapt to the environment (external adaptation). The second is the problem of internal integration that permits daily functioning and ensures the capacity or ability to adapt and survive (Schein, 1992). Assertiveness is an important dimension of a community's culture that relates both to the issues of external adaptation and especially to internal integration. It is an internally consistent set of practices and values regarding the way in which people are seen to and ought to behave in social relationships in a community.

The Role of Assertiveness in External Adaptation and Internal Integration

An interesting element of assertiveness as a cultural dimension pertains to the nature of the relationship of individuals, groups, and societies with the outside world (Kluckhohn & Strodtbeck, 1961; Schein, 1992). As was noted in Chapter 12 by Javidan on Performance Orientation as a cultural dimension, some societies view this relationship as one of subjugation, others see it as one of harmony, and still others view it as one of dominance. Assertive societies will tend to take the view of dominance. This view reflects the assumption that nature can be controlled and manipulated, a pragmatic orientation toward the nature of reality, and a belief in human perfectibility. Kluckhohn and Strodtbeck (1961) refer to this as the "doing" orientation. "It is taken for granted that the proper thing to do for people is to take charge and actively control their environment" (Schein, 1992, p. 127). At the other extreme is a "being" orientation, which correlates closely with the assumption that nature is powerful and humanity is subservient to it. This orientation implies a kind of fatalism: Because one cannot influence nature, one must be accepting and enjoy what one has (Schein, 1992). Societies that are high on a "doing" orientation probably also have (and value) more assertive behaviors than societies that have a "being" orientation.

To our knowledge, there is no direct research evidence on assertiveness as a cultural dimension (with the exception of the study on stereotypical national characteristics by Peabody described above). However, several other studies are directly relevant to assertiveness as a cultural dimension. For instance, in line with Kluckhohn and Strodtbeck, Trompenaars and Hampden-Turner (1997) hold

> societies which conduct business have developed two major orientations towards nature. They either believe they can and should control nature by imposing their will upon it, as in the ancient biblical injunction "multiply and subdue the earth"; or they believe that man is part of nature and must go along with its laws, directions and forces. (p. 141)

In line with this, they contrast inner-directed (or internal) versus outer-directed (or external) oriented cultures. They link this distinction to Rotter's work on internal versus external locus of control. In Rotter's U.S.-based work, having an internal locus of control was related to having more success than having an external locus of control.

However, Trompenaars and Hampden-Turner (1997) show there are large differences in the degree to which people from different countries feel one has control over nature or is controlled by nature (or in general by forces outside one's own control). For instance, if asked to choose between the statements "what happens to them is their own doing" and "sometimes I feel that I do not have enough control over the directions my life is taking," 82% of United States managers choose the former (implying they believe they control their own destiny) versus only 40% of Russian and 39% of Chinese managers. Thus, vast differences exist in this belief in internal control. Assertiveness reflects such an internal orientation.

Trompenaars and Hampden-Turner describe cultures emphasizing internal control as having a dominating attitude bordering on aggressiveness toward nature and a discomfort if the environment seems out of control. In contrast, in external cultures one finds a flexible attitude, a willingness to compromise and keep the peace as well as a comfort with "natural" cycles and shifts. In internal cultures, conflict and resistance mean one has convictions, whereas in external cultures, harmony and responsiveness are seen as sensible. In internal cultures the focus is on the self and one's own group or organization, whereas in external cultures the focus is on the "other": that is, the customer, partner, or colleague. Regarding doing business, Trompenaars and Hampden-Turner (1997) hold that in internal cultures, "playing hardball" is legitimate to test the resilience of an opponent and, in contrast, softness, persistence, politeness, and patience are needed to succeed in external cultures.

In line with the "doing" or internal orientation, societies that are highly assertive believe in the value of competition and competitiveness. "Eat or be eaten," "control your destiny," "try to be a winner," and "win-some, lose-some" are examples of statements associated with such a competitive mind-set. Most people from the United States fervently believe in competition according to Kohn (1986). It is believed to be needed for economic prosperity and essential for achievement in sports, science, arts, and other areas. In the U.S., competition is seen as "a fundamental aspect of human nature; people live in a dog-eat-dog world; people need to compete to survive and prosper" (Bonta, 1997, p. 121). Similarly, as noted in Chapter 12 by Javidan, Japanese executives have been criticized in the past for their extreme obsession with destroying their competitors, even at the expense of their own companies.

Shared views in society on how to deal with competition and cooperation are manifestations of human cultures. Bonta (1997) reviewed the literature on nonviolent or peaceful societies and showed that, for most of these societies, the defining elements in their beliefs are a strong opposition to competition and strong support for cooperation. For example, Bonta (1997) describes the differences in rituals in competition-versus cooperation-oriented societies. In Western societies, competitive activities such as ritualized sports and elections for leadership positions "promote social cohesion and civic pride in the virtues of competition, 'manliness' and aggressiveness" (p. 313). In contrast, the rituals of peaceful societies (e.g., chanting and healing ceremonies) "help integrate the society, protect them from hostile outside forces, and focus people on worldviews of opposition to competition, a need for harmony, and the virtue of non-violence" (p. 313).

The peaceful, or nonviolent, societies Bonta describes include the Amish and Balinese, as well as several aboriginal and native tribes from different continents. In such peaceful societies, competition is clearly linked to aggression and violence. Children are not taught competitive games. They learn by example, observing only cooperative and peaceful behavior and no aggressive or competitive behavior. Bonta holds that in many of these societies, people feel uncertain about the intentions of others, which forces them to constantly reaffirm their mutual commitments to cooperative, peaceful relationships. Anger and aggression are negatively valued, whereas, generally, nurturance and cooperation are positively valued. Many such societies also de-emphasize individual achievement as this, to them, is closely linked to competitiveness and hence aggressiveness. Bonta also noted that although these societies are cooperative and egalitarian, they are not necessarily collectivistic. Bonta found substantial variation in degrees of collective sharing of resources. He also noted that the cooperative behavior and belief in peacefulness is not merely a reflection of economic organization. Rather, the peacefulness they achieve is due to their very strong beliefs in their need to be peaceful, and the psychological strategies they use to reinforce and strengthen those shared beliefs and attitudes in daily practices (Bonta, 1997). For example, it would be acceptable for a baseball game in Japan to end in a tie; however, in the United States baseball games are extended until there are clear winners and losers regardless of the length of the game.

Assertiveness is also linked to the preferred use of language in society. As described above, assertiveness can be seen as a style of responding that implies making one's wants known to others and in no uncertain terms. In many Western cultures, this is expected or at least asserted to be accomplished most efficiently by being direct and unambiguous. Indeed, Holtgraves (1997) found a negative relationship between assertiveness (as an individual-level trait) and indirect language use in the United States. Also, such conversational indirectness was found to correlate negatively with social desirability. Thus, in the United States, saying what one means in a direct manner, even in terms of "brutal honesty" and "tough love," is valued (Holtgraves, 1997). This is not the case in many non-Western cultures. Many cultures value a less-direct manner of responding. Thus, in assertive societies people will tend to use what is also referred to as *low-context* language, which is speech that is direct, clear, and explicit (Hall, 1959; Schneider & Barsoux, 1997). In contrast, less-assertive cultures tend to use *high-context* language, which is less direct, more ambiguous, and more subtle (Schneider & Barsoux, 1997). In such cultures, directions and messages are implied rather than explicitly expressed. It is expected that the person receiving the implicit message will infer the meaning of the message or "read between the lines."

High-context language or indirectness in communication can be linked to face management (e.g., Brown & Levinson, 1987; Holtgraves, 1992). As Holtgraves explained, people

> are motivated to collectively manage the face (or public identity) of each other and they do this by phrasing their remarks politely. A primary linguistic mechanism for politeness and face management is indirectness. Thus, the face threat of a speech act is lessened when it is performed indirectly. (Holtgraves, 1997, p. 633)

Although face management in some form or another is probably important in many cultures, people from collectivistic cultures are generally more concerned with face management than people from individualistic countries (Ting-Toomey, 1988). Some empirical support for the idea of cultural differences in this area exists. In Holtgraves's (1997) research, for instance, Koreans were found to be more indirect than U.S. Americans.

Besides a preference for directness versus indirectness in communication, societal norms can also influence the amount of emotion one typically shows in public within a certain society. Trompenaars and Hampden-Turner (1997) contrast *neutral* and *affective* cultures. In affective cultures, showing one's emotions—in laughter, gesture, as well as heated debate—is the norm. For instance, in Latin American and Southern European countries (such as Spain and Italy) people openly show emotions. In more neutral cultures, people tend to keep their emotions in check. In such cultures, keeping a subdued manner, maintaining self-possessed conduct, and not openly showing emotion is the norm. For instance, in Scandinavian and many Asian countries, people tend to show less emotion in public. In highly assertive and direct societies, communication is also likely to be more emotionally expressive.

As described by Carl and Gupta in Chapter 17 on Power Distance, within all societies there are status and power differentials. Assertiveness is one of the aspects of culture that relates to how status is typically accorded in society.

Whereas some societies accord status to people on the basis of their achievements, others ascribe it to people on the basis of age, gender, social class, profession, or other criteria (Trompenaars & Hampden-Turner, 1997). Achieved status refers to what one has done or personally accomplished. Ascribed status refers to earning status based on socioeconomic status, family lineage, age, profession, or family connections. Given the emphasis on competition, highly assertive societies should theoretically be expected to accord status based on achievements rather than ascribe it based on attributes such as age, profession, or family connections.

Doney, Cannon, and Mullen (1998) link societal norms and values to trust-building processes within society. In more assertive societies, trust-building processes will mostly be based on either calculations of the intentions of others or on estimates of their capabilities to fulfill their commitments. The perception that others are opportunistic and seek to maximize their self-interests stimulates a calculative trust-building process. Trust can be based on the calculated risks and costs involved in trusting or not trusting others. Cultural assertiveness influences the likelihood that people will act opportunistically, as well as the costs associated with such behavior. Doney and colleagues note that evidence from anthropology, psychology, and political science confirms a cultural pattern of assertiveness and aggressiveness that is consistent with a tendency toward opportunism. The so-called "tough" values in such assertive and masculine societies (e.g., visible achievement and making money) suggest that in such societies the potential rewards for opportunistic behavior may well exceed their costs.

The second trust-building process likely in societies stressing assertiveness involves others' capabilities. Individuals differ in their competence, ability, or expertise. Trustees' capabilities will, in the eyes of a trustor, influence their ability to keep their promises, and trust is based on a trustee's perceived capability to keep such promises. Societal norms and values supporting assertive behavior, individual initiative, and wealth creation should influence the importance placed on individual capabilities. For instance, in highly assertive cultures, "super-achievers" are likely to be respected, and a norm for excelling

Table 15.1   Higher Assertiveness Societies Versus Lower Assertiveness Societies

Societies That Score Higher on Assertiveness, Tend to:	Societies That Score Lower on Assertiveness, Tend to:
• Value assertive, dominant, and tough behavior for everyone in society	• View assertiveness as socially unacceptable and value modesty and tenderness
• Have sympathy for the strong	• Have sympathy for the weak
• Value competition	• Value cooperation
• Believe that anyone can succeed if he or she tries hard enough	• Associate competition with defeat and punishment
• Value success and progress	• Value people and warm relationships
• Value direct and unambiguous communication	• Speak indirectly and emphasize "face-saving"
• Value being explicit and to the point in communications	• Value ambiguity and subtlety in language and communications
• Value expressiveness and revealing thoughts and feelings	• Value detached and self-possessed conduct
• Have relatively positive connotations for the term *aggression* (e.g., aggression helps to win)	• Have far more negative connotations with the term *aggression* (e.g., aggression leads only to negative outcomes)
• Have a just-world belief	• Have an unjust-world belief
• Try to have control over the environment	• Value harmony with the environment rather than control
• Stress equity, competition, and performance	• Stress equality, solidarity, and quality of life
• Have a "can-do" attitude	• Emphasize tradition, seniority, and experience
• Emphasize results over relationships	• Emphasize integrity, loyalty, and cooperative spirit
• Value taking initiative	
• Reward performance	• View "merit pay" as potentially destructive to harmony
• Expect demanding and challenging targets	
• Believe that individuals are in control	• Value who you are more than what you do
• Value what you do more than who you are	• Build trust on the basis of predictability
• Build trust on the basis of capabilities or calculation	• Think of others as inherently worthy of trust
• Act and think of others as opportunistic	

is supported. This also holds in cultures that Hofstede (1980) labeled "masculine." Individual brilliance is admired and the "stars" are idolized (Doney et al., 1998; Kale, 1991; Kale & Barnes, 1992). In such circumstances, one's capability seems a reasonable base on which to form trust. In contrast, in cultures emphasizing norms for solidarity, service, and cooperation and that have a high social pressure to honor moral obligations, other forms of trust-building should prevail. For instance, in such societies people may be more likely to base trust on others' predictability rather than their capabilities (Doney et al., 1998).

What Does It Mean to Be a High or Low Assertiveness-Oriented Society?

The above descriptions present a picture of what it means to be assertive. Table 15.1 provides a summary comparison of a typical society that has a strongly assertive culture and a society that is low on assertiveness. However, one must keep in mind that societal culture is obviously far too complex to be presented in terms of a single dimension or in simple black and white terms. The extreme cases presented here are meant to help explain the concept of the GLOBE

Assertiveness dimension and some expected correlates, but it should also be clear that cultures do not neatly fit into stereotypes. Although the table shows cultural attributes that conceptually should tend to cluster together, it does not rule out the fact that not all these attributes cohere at all times. Societies usually have differing mixes of the extreme cases presented in this table (and in the other tables of this volume).

THE GLOBE MEASURES
OF ASSERTIVENESS

Comparison of High Versus Low Assertiveness Societies

As mentioned, Hofstede (1980, 2001) explicitly links his tough–tender dimension in terms of values to sex roles and gender equality (or inequality), even though his MAS index has no items explicitly tapping assertive attributes or behaviors. On the basis of the results of the two pilot studies reported in Chapter 8 by Hanges and Dickson, the GLOBE research design separates the three underlying dimensions that comprise Hofstede's MAS index and masculinity–femininity dimension, namely: Performance Orientation, Assertiveness, and Gender Egalitarianism. This separation has intuitive appeal, as these three variables may or may not be associated with each other in any particular culture. For instance, gender role differences in a society may be minimal (e.g., girls and boys are equally encouraged to attain higher education) and at the same time individuals in such a society may stress the necessity to be assertive, dominant, or aggressive in relationships with others. On the other hand, gender roles may be differentiated (e.g., it is easier and more accepted for men to attain higher-level positions than for women to do so) and at the same time the need to be submissive and nonassertive in business relationships *within* organizations is stressed, such as in Japanese culture. This is a first major difference between the GLOBE measures of Assertiveness and Gender Egalitarianism and Hofstede's MAS index.

The GLOBE conceptualization of Assertiveness also differs from Hofstede's concept of masculinity on several other grounds. The poles of the GLOBE assertiveness scales are claimed to represent high versus low Assertiveness. In contrast, Hofstede places one concept (masculinity) at one extreme of the dimension and another (femininity) at the other. As seen earlier, at the individual level masculine and feminine characteristics are not necessarily at opposite ends of a single dimension and people can have both types of traits. Such masculine and feminine traits are often found to be separate and even unrelated dimensions (Fagenson, 1990). Although we are clearly talking about different levels of analysis and different constructs, we feel the same may hold for "masculine" versus "feminine" values in society. In Project GLOBE, such feminine values are reflected more in the Humane Orientation cultural dimension (see Chapter 18 by Kabasakal & Bodur). This separation is conceptually appealing and also allows us to test the relationship between the Assertiveness cultural dimension and the Humane Orientation cultural dimension.

As stated, Hofstede's MAS index items measure success drive and materialism. In Project GLOBE, such a drive to excel and perform highly is measured explicitly in the measure for Performance Orientation (see Chapter 12 by Javidan). Also, the GLOBE items measuring Assertiveness do not explicitly emphasize the individualistic component of Hofstede's masculinity dimension. However, due to the shared emphasis of these three constructs on competition, dominance over the environment, and personal initiative we do expect a positive relationship among Assertiveness, Performance Orientation, and Individualism.

A caveat is in order. If indeed Hofstede's observation holds that within virtually all societies men tend to hold more "masculine" values—including the subset of those that have to do with Assertiveness—the sex distribution of respondents may influence results. As GLOBE respondents are all middle managers, women are likely to be underrepresented. The GLOBE sample included 25.2% female and 74.8% male middle managers. Whereas Hofstede (2001) does report gender differences on the masculinity dimension, Hoppe (1998) failed to find a significant difference in the responses of men and women with respect to Hofstede's dimensions.

The results may also be influenced by the fact that middle managers have a certain position in the organizational hierarchy. Their view on matters may differ from that of the shop floor or higher organizational levels. The views of other groups in society may also differ. However, as will be seen in Chapters 17 through 19 there is reason to believe that the middle manager reports of the societal dimensions in Project GLOBE are relatively representative of the society in which they are embedded. Clearly, more research is needed to clarify these issues further.

The GLOBE scales

Two constructs were created to measure a society's level of Assertiveness: Society *As Is* refers to the participants' assessment of the extent to which a society engages in Assertiveness practices, and society *Should Be* refers to the extent to which a society exhibits Assertiveness values. It is measured as a composite of quantitative items directly asked from the participating managers. Tables 15.2a an 15.2b and 15.3a and 15.3b show sample questionnaire items that survived rigorous statistical procedures (see Hanges & Dickson, chapter 8). The scales were confirmed across all the societies in the GLOBE study. As these are new scales, no cross-cultural work has been done on the concept of assertiveness as a societal culture dimension in the way it was conceptualized and operationalized in project GLOBE.

The two questionnaire items in Table 15.2a are sample items that measure respondents' *As Is* responses. These reflect the current societal practices.

Table 15.2b shows sample items of the societal scales for the managers' expressed views of how assertive people in the society *Should Be* in social relationships. The responses to these items reflect the respondents' values with respect to Assertiveness practices.

All scales range from 1 to 7. As was also described in previous chapters, Project GLOBE measures both societal and organizational cultures. Responding managers filled out either the questionnaire measuring societal culture or the questionnaire measuring organizational culture. Sample items for the organizational culture items measuring Assertiveness can be

Table 15.2a   Assertiveness: Society Practices (As Is)

1. In this society, people are generally: (reverse scored)						
Assertive						Nonassertive
1	2	3	4	5	6	7
2. In this society, people are generally: (reverse scored)						
Tough						Tender
1	2	3	4	5	6	7

Table 15.2b   Assertiveness: Society Values (Should Be)

1. In this society, people *should be* encouraged to be: (reverse scored)						
Assertive						Nonassertive
1	2	3	4	5	6	7
2. In this society, people *should be* encouraged to be: (reverse scored)						
Tough						Tender
1	2	3	4	5	6	7

Table 15.3a   Assertiveness: Organization Practices (As Is)

1. In this organization, people are generally: (reverse scored)

Assertive						Nonassertive
1	2	3	4	5	6	7

2. In this organization, people are generally: (reverse scored)

Tough						Tender
1	2	3	4	5	6	7

Table 15.3b   Assertiveness: Organization Values (Should Be)

1. In this organization, people *should be* encouraged to be: (reverse scored)

Dominant						Nondominant
1	2	3	4	5	6	7

2. In this organization, people *should be* encouraged to be: (reverse scored)

Tough						Tender
1	2	3	4	5	6	7

found in Tables 15.3a (practices) and 15.3b (values). By having separate samples of managers independently complete these two parts of the questionnaire we eliminate the possibility of common source bias when relating societal and organizational scores to each other. A more detailed description of the method used in the study can be found in Chapter 8, this volume.

The Findings: The Overall and Industry Scores on Societal Assertiveness

Table 15.4 shows the grand means of society practices and society values scales for Assertiveness across all countries represented in the GLOBE study.

Compared to the other cultural dimensions measured, the society practices score has a midlevel average rating of 4.13. Scores range from 3.38 (Sweden) to 4.89 (Albania). The means for the Assertiveness values scale range from 2.66 (Turkey) to 5.56 (Japan). The individual country scores will be described in more detail below. As explained in earlier chapters, in each country, data were collected from at least two of three industries: food processing, finance, and telecommunications. Table 15.5 shows the correlation between the societal Assertiveness practices and values scales for each participating industry as well as overall. As seen in this table, there is a significantly negative correlation ($r = - .26$, $p < .05$) between overall scores for Assertiveness practices and Assertiveness values. Similar negative correlations are found in the separate industries; however, for the subsamples in the food and telecommunications industry this correlation is not significant for the telecommunication industry and only marginally significant for the food industry (see Table 15.5).

People's aspirations regarding Assertiveness in society are modestly (and negatively) related to their assessments of current levels of Assertiveness. Table 15.6 shows the individual country scores on the *practices* scale and Table 15.7 shows the individual country scores on the *values* scale.[1]

In many cultures, people see their country as having a fair amount of assertiveness and they want *less* of it. This was also concluded from

Table 15.4   Grand Mean Across Countries for Societal Assertiveness

Variable	Mean	Standard Deviation	Minimum	Maximum	Valid N
Assertiveness practices	4.14	0.37	3.38	4.89	61
Assertiveness values	3.82	0.63	2.66	5.56	61

Table 15.5   Correlation Societal Assertiveness Practices and Values

Industry Score	Overall Score—Practices	Food Industry Score—Practices	Finance Industry Score—Practices	Telecommunication Industry Score— Practices
Overall score values	−.26* $N = 61$			
Food industry score values		−.26+ $N = 45$		
Finance industry score values			−.28* $N = 55$	
Telecommunications industry score values				−.21 $N = 32$

* Significant at $p < .05$ (2-tailed).

+ Significant at $p < .10$ (2-tailed).

the negative correlation between Assertiveness practices and values. For instance, Austria scores 4.62 out of a range of 1 to 7 on Assertiveness practices (band A), whereas the score for Assertiveness values is only 2.81 (band C) (see Tables 15.6 and 15.7).

A similar pattern is found for many other countries. For instance, Greece, former East Germany, and Turkey are also in the highest practices and lowest values bands (or group of countries). A similar but somewhat less-prominent pattern of wanting less Assertiveness is found for most other countries (respondents in 40 of 61 societies studied want less Assertiveness than is currently found in their societies). However, in 21 cultures, including most Asian countries, people indicate they want

more Assertiveness than they currently have. Many of these countries have relatively low levels of present Assertiveness. For instance, China has a relatively low societal practices score on Assertiveness (3.76) and a much higher societal values score (5.44), as does Japan (3.59 on practices and 5.56 on values). This pattern of scoring lower on practices and higher on values is found for several other Asian countries, including Indonesia, Singapore, Hong Kong, the Philippines, India, and Malaysia. Other such countries include Zimbabwe, Zambia, Iran, and Slovenia. As can be seen in Tables 15.6 and 15.7, all but 3 (Hong Kong, Georgia, and Singapore) of the 29 cultures that are in the practices A band (this band represents the highest scoring societies

Table 15.6   Assertiveness: Society Practices*

| Band | | | | | |
| A | | B | | C | |
Country	Score	Country	Score	Country	Score
Albania	4.89	France	4.13	Switzerland[f]	3.47
Nigeria	4.79	Qatar	4.11	New Zealand	3.42
Hungary	4.79	Ecuador	4.09	Sweden	3.38
Germany[a]	4.73	Zambia	4.07		
Hong Kong	4.67	Italy	4.07		
Austria	4.62	Zimbabwe	4.06		
El Salvador	4.62	Poland	4.06		
South Africa[b]	4.60	Canada[e]	4.05		
Greece	4.58	Iran	4.04		
Germany[c]	4.55	Philippines	4.01		
U.S.	4.55	Slovenia	4.00		
Turkey	4.53	Ireland	3.92		
Morocco	4.52	Taiwan	3.92		
Switzerland	4.51	Namibia	3.91		
Kazakhstan	4.46	Egypt	3.91		
Mexico	4.45	Guatemala	3.89		
Spain	4.42	Malaysia	3.87		
South Korea	4.40	Indonesia	3.86		
South Africa[d]	4.36	Finland	3.81		
Venezuela	4.33	Denmark	3.80		
Netherlands	4.32	Bolivia	3.79		
Australia	4.28	China	3.76		
Israel	4.23	Costa Rica	3.75		
Argentina	4.22	India	3.73		
Brazil	4.20	Russia	3.68		
Colombia	4.20	Portugal	3.65		
Georgia	4.18	Thailand	3.64		
Singapore	4.17	Kuwait	3.63		
England	4.15	Japan	3.59		

a Germany (East): Former GDR
b South Africa (White Sample)
c Germany (West): Former FRG
d South Africa (Black Sample)
e Canada (English-speaking)
f Switzerland (French-speaking)

* Higher scores indicate greater assertiveness.

Our response bias correction procedure identified response bias in some countries for this scale (see endnote 1).

on current Assertiveness practices) express a desire for *less* Assertiveness than they currently perceive in practice. In contrast, all 12 cultures except Albania in the values A band (highest scoring on desired Assertiveness) want more Assertiveness than they practice. In other words, societies scoring relatively high on current Assertiveness practices want less and

societies scoring relatively low want more Assertiveness.

In summary, the pattern found in the majority of countries shows the desire for less Assertiveness, perhaps reflecting the wish to belong to a relatively nonthreatening, nonaggressive society. However, as stated, a third of the countries seem to want more Assertiveness,

Table 15.7   Assertiveness: Society Values*

Band					
A		B		C	
Country	*Score*	*Country*	*Score*	*Country*	*Score*
Japan	5.56	Zambia	4.38	Germany[f]	3.09
China	5.44	Georgia	4.35	Netherlands	3.02
Philippines	5.14	U.S.	4.32	Greece	2.96
Iran	4.99	Canada[a]	4.15	Brazil	2.91
Hong Kong	4.81	Costa Rica	4.05	Russia	2.83
Malaysia	4.81	Spain	4.00	Austria	2.81
India	4.76	Ireland	3.99	Turkey	2.66
Indonesia	4.72	Namibia	3.91		
Zimbabwe	4.60	Poland	3.90		
Slovenia	4.59	Kazakhstan	3.84		
Albania	4.41	Italy	3.82		
Singapore	4.41	South Africa[b]	3.82		
		Australia	3.81		
		Qatar	3.80		
		Mexico	3.79		
		Switzerland[c]	3.78		
		Israel	3.76		
		Kuwait	3.76		
		South Korea	3.75		
		Bolivia	3.73		
		England	3.70		
		South Africa[d]	3.69		
		Finland	3.68		
		Ecuador	3.65		
		Guatemala	3.64		
		El Salvador	3.62		
		Sweden	3.61		
		Portugal	3.58		
		New Zealand	3.54		
		Thailand	3.48		
		Morocco	3.44		
		Colombia	3.43		
		Denmark	3.39		
		France	3.38		
		Hungary	3.35		
		Venezuela	3.33		
		Egypt	3.28		
		Taiwan	3.28		
		Argentina	3.25		
		Nigeria	3.23		
		Germany[e]	3.23		
		Switzerland	3.21		

a Canada (English-speaking)
b South Africa (Black Sample)
c Switzerland (French-speaking)
d South Africa (White Sample)
e Germany (East): Former GDR
f Germany (West): Former FRG

* Higher scores indicate greater assertiveness.
Our response bias correction procedure identified response bias in some countries for this scale (see endnote 1).

and many Asian countries, especially, stress assertiveness in this regard. Later in the chapter we will examine regional differences in assertiveness in more detail. It seems societies scoring high on Assertiveness tend to strive for less, and societies scoring low on Assertiveness express a desire for more. These results indicate that in contrast to some other culture dimensions, Assertiveness is not universally desirable or undesirable. A possible explanation is that too much Assertiveness may be felt to be a threat to internal integration. Too much competition, dominance, and aggression would create an unsafe, untrusting environment, which would hinder people from achieving required levels of cooperation to complete tasks. On the other hand, too little Assertiveness may be a threat to external adaptation and survival. As such, too little Assertiveness may be experienced as weakness. In most environments a certain level of competition and dominance is needed to survive. Such issues need to be further explored in future studies.

A few things need to be kept in mind. As pointed out by Hanges and Dickson in Chapter 8, sample characteristics and response biases may influence the indicated levels of actual and desired Assertiveness. Respondents were all middle managers. This group may not represent the society as a whole regarding Assertiveness. On average, managers may well be more assertive and tough than nonmanagers in the population. The items referring to Assertiveness may therefore be more favorably interpreted by managers than by other people in the managers' society. Also, in many societies managers are predominantly male, and women in managerial roles may need to exhibit more assertive leadership behaviors than women in general. Surprisingly, as discussed in the chapter on Gender Egalitarianism by Emrich and colleagues, we did not find significant differences between men and women in terms of how they rated Assertiveness values and practices. On the other hand, unobtrusive measures presented in Chapter 9 (by Gupta, Sully de Luque, & House) and other indicators of construct validity throughout the book suggest that the responses of the middle managers reflect the society in which they are embedded and not the culture of middle managers exclusively.

Clearly, additional research in this area needs to be conducted.

Also, as stated in the introduction to this section, another problem in this type of research is that respondents in some cultures might be reluctant to choose extreme scores on either side of the scale when reporting their observations about their societies' level of Assertiveness. As seen above, the means on the GLOBE Assertiveness practices scales range from 3.38 to 4.89. The same degree of reluctance may not exist in reporting their aspirations and ambitions because the questionnaire items call for hypothetical responses. The means for the assertiveness values scale range from 2.66 to 5.56. In other words, the observed differences between practices and values may be a consequence of response propensities rather than real differences. Also, response tendencies may be larger in some cultures than in others. However, as will be shown later, the GLOBE Assertiveness dimension measures discriminate between countries and geographic regions, thus indicating that if there is a response tendency bias in some cultures, it is not so strong that it overwhelms cultural differences. Also, as can be seen in Appendix B (this volume), tests for response bias for the Assertiveness values and practices measures reveal that such bias was indicated in a small number of societies (including the Czech Republic, Morocco, Qatar, and Taiwan). With the exception of these societies there were no societal-level practices or values dimensions exhibiting response bias across several dimensions.

GLOBE ASSERTIVENESS AND HOFSTEDE'S (1980) MASCULINITY SCALE

As we noted previously, Assertiveness originates in the masculinity–femininity culture dimension identified by Hofstede (1980). As was described above, Hofstede asked respondents to rate the importance of work goals, such as earnings, recognition, advancement to higher-level jobs, and challenge (for the masculine pole) and a good working relationship with one's supervisor, cooperation, a desirable living area, and employment security (for the feminine pole). Nothing in his MAS scale dealt explicitly or even implicitly with assertiveness. In contrast, the GLOBE items focus on whether people in a society are or should be assertive, dominant, and tough or nonassertive, nonaggressive, and tender. It is, of course, interesting to test whether these new GLOBE Assertiveness scales have significant associations with the Hofstede (1980) masculinity scale. This was tested using the society-level scale scores reported in Hofstede's book (1980, as well as later updates to these country rankings). Those culture-level scores were correlated with the cultural-level scores from the GLOBE project.

The Hofstede masculinity scale significantly correlated with the GLOBE Assertiveness practices scale ($r = .37, p < .05$). In other words, societies scoring high in Assertiveness practices are also more likely to be higher on the Hofstede masculinity scale. However, Hofstede's masculinity scale scores did not correlate significantly with the GLOBE Assertiveness values scale ($r = .17, p > .10$). In other words, preferences for more assertiveness in societies (as measured by the GLOBE Assertiveness values scale) are *not* related to Hofstede's measure of masculinity. This raises a further question concerning what was being measured by Hofstede's measure of masculinity, which purportedly measures values and not practices.

Hanges and Dickson (in Chapter 8) point out that a lack of correlations is not necessarily surprising given that GLOBE scales were not constructed to build directly on Hofstede's work. The measures are quite different, and Hofstede's items do not explicitly address the question of Assertiveness in values. In fact, as stated earlier, there are no items in the Hofstede MAS scale that deal exclusively with assertiveness. Rather, Hofstede's MAS scale is similar to his individualism scale in that it assesses the importance of the selected aspects of work. Therefore, the significant correlation between the Hofstede MAS scale and the GLOBE Assertiveness practices scale can be seen as surprising. The likely explanation seems to be that GLOBE's scale assesses assertive behavior patterns, and people in societies that are more assertive are indeed more likely to value the types of work goals and opportunities Hofstede identified as masculine.

This tentative explanation supports the idea that masculinity and assertiveness at the cultural level are indeed related and seems worthy of future exploration.

The relationships with the other GLOBE dimensions are of interest because assertiveness has not yet truly been studied as a societal or cultural attribute. Knowledge of these relationships will also shed more light on the differences between the GLOBE Assertiveness and Hofstede's masculinity dimension. Given that both the GLOBE Assertiveness and Gender Egalitarianism cultural dimensions originate in Hofstede's masculinity–femininity dimension (see Chapter 14 by Emrich, Denmark, and Den Hartog), the relationship between these two is also of particular interest. A negative relationship between Assertiveness and Gender Egalitarianism is expected. As described in Chapter 14, assertiveness has been associated with men as well as "masculine" societies. According to Hofstede (1980), male-dominated societies should also be low on gender egalitarianism.

Similarly, respondents who scored high on Assertiveness practices report that people are generally assertive, dominant, and tough rather than nondominant and tender. Respondents scoring high on Assertiveness values means they feel people in society should be encouraged to be tougher and more dominant. It therefore seems likely that high levels of both current and aspired Assertiveness are related to valuing more Power Distance in society.

Another relationship that is interesting to test is the relationship between Assertiveness and the Performance Orientation dimension, especially when comparing our results to Hofstede's masculinity dimension. Hofstede explicitly links masculinity to striving for success and valuing challenging work and material wealth. He holds that in masculine societies, individuals strive for personal success and material gain and in feminine societies for a welfare-oriented society (Hofstede, 1991). Thus, as—according to Hofstede—assertiveness is one of the key features of such masculine societies, a positive relationship between Assertiveness and success striving is expected. As stated earlier, on the basis of a masculine society's stress on competition and individualism, a modest positive correlation with Individualism is also expected.

Also interesting in terms of the comparison to Hofstede's masculinity dimension is, of course, GLOBE's Humane Orientation dimension (see Chapter 18 by Kabasakal & Bodur). Bajdo and Dickson (2001) take humane orientation as an indication of femininity. If femininity and masculinity can be seen as "opposite ends of a continuum," a significant negative relationship between Assertiveness and Humane Orientation can be expected. However, the Chinese Culture Connection (1987) reported a positive correlation between the MAS index and their measure of human-heartedness (which deals with social awareness, kindness, and being courteous to others; see also Chapter 14 by Emrich, Denmark, & Den Hartog). Correlations of the societal-level Assertiveness scales with the other GLOBE dimensions are reported in Table 15.8. (see also Appendix A).

As Table 15.8 shows, the results support only some of the expectations. The hypothesized relationship between Assertiveness and Gender Egalitarianism is partially supported. Assertiveness practices are not correlated with Gender Egalitarianism (practices or values). However, the correlation between GLOBE's Assertiveness values and Gender Egalitarianism values ($r = -.28$) is negative. This makes sense because striving for *more* assertiveness is related to striving for *less* gender equality or, in other words, for more "male-oriented" values.

This general pattern does not always hold, though. For example, according to its middle managers, behavior in social relationships in Sweden tends to be tender and nonassertive (lowest rank). Swedish managers also indicate they want slightly more Assertiveness. Also, Sweden is a country where equality between men and women is relatively high. Swedish managers indicate that they strongly feel that such equality should be advanced even further (Akerblom & Holmberg, in press). In other words, in this specific case, Assertiveness and Gender Egalitarianism are in the same direction regarding practices, but not necessarily values.

Interestingly, as reported in Chapter 14 by Emrich and colleagues, Gender Egalitarianism practices and values correlate significantly and positively ($r = .32$). In other words, in contrast with the negative correlation between Assertiveness practices and values, societies with higher levels of existing egalitarianism want even more. The pattern of correlations between Assertiveness and Gender Egalitarianism supports treating the two as separate dimensions rather than integrating them into a single dimension (which is what Hofstede's masculinity–femininity dimension suggests).

As stated, Hofstede (1980) links masculinity to a performance-oriented society. Thus, positive relationships between the Assertiveness and Performance Orientation dimensions were hypothesized. Only the relationship between GLOBE Assertiveness values and Performance Orientation practices was found to be significant ($r = .36$). The relationship between the measures for Assertiveness and Power Distance also presents partial support for our expectations. A significantly positive relationship between societal Assertiveness values and Power Distance values was found ($r = .29$). Striving for more assertiveness seems to be accompanied by valuing power distance in society.

As can be seen in Table 15.8, the relationship between the GLOBE measures of Assertiveness and Humane Orientation is not as straightforward as expected. In line with expectations, the GLOBE Humane Orientation practices scale correlates negatively with the Assertiveness practices scale. Thus, in line with expectations, societies whose aggregated reports indicate a high current Humane Orientation also report less assertiveness and aggressiveness in social relationships ($r = -.42$). However, the Assertiveness practices measure correlates significantly positively with the Humane Orientation values measure ($r = .35$), and the Assertiveness values measure correlates positively with the Humane Orientation practices measure (.45).

GLOBE's Assertiveness practices scale also correlates significantly negatively with the measure for Institutional Collectivism practices ($r = -.42$). This measure for Collectivism refers to collective interests and work (see also Chapter 16 by Gelfand, Bhawuk, Nishii, & Bechtold). Thus, in line with expectations, societies reported to be assertive, or "tough,"

Table 15.8   Correlations of Assertiveness With Other GLOBE Scales

GLOBE Cultural Dimensions Scales	Assertiveness Practices	Assertiveness Values
Gender Egalitarianism practices	÷ 0.8	−.01
Gender Egalitarianism values	.18	−.28*
Performance Orientation practices	.06	.36**
Performance Orientation values	÷ 01	−.02
Future Orientation practices	.07	.17
Future Orientation values	.09	.09
Institutional Collectivism practices	÷ 42**	.37**
Institutional Collectivism values	.12	−.21
In-Group Collectivism practices	.08	.28*
In-Group Collectivism values	÷ 24	.01
Humane Orientation practices	÷ 42**	.45**
Humane Orientation values	.35**	−.11
Power Distance practices	.16	−.05
Power Distance values	−.11	.29*
Uncertainty Avoidance practices	−.07	.07
Uncertainty Avoidance values	.04	.20

$N = 61$.

$* p < .05.$

$** p < .01$ (2-tailed).

also indicate lower current levels of social solidarity. In other words, in such societies a more individualistic approach is taken. However, Assertiveness values are positively correlated with the practices of both forms of Collectivism (.37 for Institutional Collectivism and .28 for In-Group Collectivism). In other words, societies that scored high on these forms of collectivism tend to strive for more Assertiveness.

The patterns show that the relations between the culture dimensions are complicated and not as straightforward as one might expect. Some of the relationships we find support Hofstede's work on the masculinity dimension, others run against it. Often the practices and values show different patterns of relationships.

GLOBE ASSERTIVENESS AND OTHER ECONOMIC AND SOCIAL INDICATORS

In this section, we compare and contrast the findings on GLOBE Assertiveness measures with those of other major cross-cultural and comparative studies focusing on different countries' social and economic performance. As explained in chapter 7 by Javidan and Hauser, four major ongoing reports produce the relevant data: the World Competitiveness

Yearbook, the United Nations Human Development Report, the World Development Indicators, and the World Values Survey. The findings of these studies are grouped into two categories: economic health and the human condition.

Assertiveness and Economic Health

Is there a relationship between Assertiveness as a societal culture dimension and economic health? Are societies with high Assertiveness practices or values scores more competitive? Do such societies enjoy healthier economies? Triandis (1994, p.129) holds that the rapid increases in standard of living among the high masculinity countries (in Hofstede's terms) suggests that masculinity may be relevant to economic development. Similarly, this may be the case for assertiveness. In other words, a positive relationship between Assertiveness practices and economic health is expected. Accordingly, in Chapter 7 of this volume, the following hypotheses were proposed: Cultures that score higher on Assertiveness tend to perform better in terms of global competitiveness and be more economically prosperous.

Table 15.9 shows the correlation coefficients between the two GLOBE measures of Assertiveness (practices and values), and the various elements of economic health and global competitiveness. These measures are described in more detail in Chapter 7 by Javidan and Hauser.

Table 15.9 shows that peoples' aspirations in terms of how much a society should value assertiveness, as well as their perceptions of how much a society practices assertiveness, are not substantially related to the country's economic performance. Of the 14 presented coefficients, only one is significant (in the expected direction). A significantly positive correlation is found between GLOBE Assertiveness values and success in science and technology. Thus, although the one relationship that is found is in the expected direction, it does not present strong evidence in support of our hypotheses. Therefore, one can conclude that no (or only very limited) support was found for the expected positive relationships between GLOBE Assertiveness and societal economic

health. Most of these indicators are available for only 40 of the GLOBE-sampled countries; therefore, some caution is needed in interpreting these results.

Assertiveness and Human Condition

As stated in Chapter 7 by Javidan and Hauser, economic health is only one aspect of a society's well-being. Another dimension is the general health of the populace and the society. The term *human condition* used here refers to the general quality of life and the state of mind of the people in a particular country. In this section, we examine the relationship between GLOBE findings on assertiveness and different dimensions of the human condition.

In many countries, our respondents indicate that they strive for less assertiveness, aggressiveness, and dominance in interpersonal relationships within their society than they currently experience. In Chapter 7 by Javidan and Hauser, the following hypothesis concerning the relationship between the GLOBE measure of Assertiveness and the human condition was proposed: Societies that score higher on Assertiveness tend to exhibit lower levels of human health. As stated, several variables associated with human health were examined (see Chapter 7 for a detailed description of these measures). Table 15.10 reports the relationships between GLOBE Assertiveness and these measures. Table 15.10 shows that none of the measures of human health are significantly related with either the Assertiveness practices scale or values scale.

Two of these indicators are available for only 38 or 40 of the GLOBE countries; therefore, some caution is needed in interpreting these results. The specific subset of countries available may mask possible effects. Further research in this area is required. For instance, the results of a study reported by Arrindell and colleagues (1997) suggest that the relationships between assertiveness and well-being may be somewhat more complicated. They found a significant negative interaction between Hofstede's masculinity and national wealth in predicting national subjective well-being (SWB) levels: In the poorer countries, masculinity correlated positively with SWB,

Table 15.9   Relationship Between Assertiveness and Economic Health

Assertiveness	Economic Prosperity	Economic Productivity	GNP per Capita	Government Support for Prosperity	Societal for Support Competitiveness	World Competitiveness Index	Success in Science and Technology
Society practices	−.08 N = 57	.11 N = 40	−.02 N = .61	÷ 12 N = 40	.02 N = 40	−.05 N = 41	÷ 13 N = 40
Society values	−.02 N = 57	−.16 N = 40	−.12 N = 61	÷ 03 N = 40	.29 N = 40	.14 N = 41	.34* N = 40

* Correlation significant at $p < .05$ level (2-tailed).

Table 15.10   Relationship Between Assertiveness and Human Condition

Assertiveness	Societal Health	Human Health	Life Expectancy	General Satisfaction	Human Development Index
Society practices	−.04 N = 40	−.20 N = 56	−.05 N = 56	−.02 N = 38	−.05 N = 56
Society values	.08 N = 40	.14 N = 56	−.15 N = 56	−.03 N = 38	−.21 N = 56

* Correlation significant at $p < .05$ level (2-tailed).
** Correlation significant at $p < .01$ level (2-tailed).

whereas a negative association was observed for the subset of richer countries. Relatively speaking, feminine-rich countries reported the highest SWB levels. Further research, taking national wealth into account, may be useful to unravel whether such patterns of interaction also exist for Assertiveness and societal health.

Religious Values and Political Ideology

We also examined the relationship between Assertiveness and societal values, religion, and political ideology. For instance, the results presented in Table 15.11 show no significant relationship between Assertiveness practices and measures of religious values and political ideology in societies. Again, the number of countries for which these data are available is limited (between 26 and 38).

How do these variables relate to assertive values in society? Only one of the relationships of such variables with GLOBE Assertiveness values is significant. Assertiveness values in society are positively correlated with having respect for family and friends, which may be an indicator of the positive relationship found with collectivism practices.

As presented by Hanges and Dickson in Chapter 8, the GLOBE Assertiveness values

Table 15.11   Relationship Between Assertiveness, Religious Values, and Political Ideology

Assertiveness	Respect for Family and Friends	Strength of Family Ties	Disdain for Democracy	Dislike of Democracy	Role of Government	Lack of Voice	Stability
Society practices	−.07 N = 38	.10 N = 38	−.34 N = 26	−.20 N = 27	.01 N = 38	.03 N = 38	1 N = 38
Society values	.36* N = 38	0 N = 38	− .08 N = 26	−.10 N = 27	.24 N = 38	.20 N = 38	.20 N = 38

* Correlation significant at *p* < .05 level (2-tailed).

** Correlation significant at *p* < .01 level (2-tailed).

Assertiveness	Achieving Results	Passiveness	Initiative	Religious Devotion	Religious Dogma	Gender Equality
Society practices	−.01 N = 38	.28 N = 37	.15 N = 38	.28 N = 38	.19 N = 37	−.08 N = 38
Society values	−.09 N = 38	−.05 N = 37	−.15 N = 38	−.01 N = 38	.21 N = 37	−.21 N = 38

* Correlation significant at *p* < .05 level (2-tailed).

** Correlation is significant at *p* < .01 level (2-tailed).

scale was also expected and found to relate significantly negatively to Schwartz's (1994) egalitarian commitment values dimension ($r = -.53$ $p < .01$). This dimension describes the transcendence of selfish interests and voluntary commitment to promote the welfare of others.

Summary

The following are the key learnings from the comparison of Assertiveness findings and findings in independently published reports. Those societies that score higher on Assertiveness values show the following characteristics (significant correlation coefficients):

- They have more success in science and technology
- They have more respect for family and friends
- They are lower on egalitarian commitment

ASSERTIVENESS, CLIMATE, AND COUNTRY DEMOGRAPHICS

Climate

The available literature suggests that climate may be an interesting variable to study in relation to assertiveness. In both laboratory and field studies, a relationship between individual temperature and aggression has been established (Van de Vliert, Schwartz, Huismans, Hofstede, & Daan, 1999). Such studies often focus on spontaneous, affect-based individual-level aggression.

A study by Schwartz (1968) examined the association between ambient temperature and organized political violence in 51 nations. Schwartz reported a curvilinear association between mean annual temperature and the frequency of coups, guerilla wars, and terrorism.

Such violence occurred more frequently in warm (M = 24°C/76°F) than in cold (M = 17°C/62°F) or hot (M = 30°C/86°F) countries. In a replication of this study, Van de Vliert and colleagues (1999) controlled for population size and density, socioeconomical development, and political democracy. The resultsm of their study using 136 countries show that, indeed, countries with moderate climates suffer much more from domestic political violence than colder countries, and slightly more than hotter countries.

Van de Vliert and colleagues (1999) introduce cultural masculinity as a possible mediator between temperature and aggression. Following Hofstede, they describe high cultural masculinity as characterizing societies in which men are expected to be dominant, assertive, tough, and focused on material success, whereas women are expected to be subordinate, modest, tender, and concerned with quality of life. In contrast, low masculinity (or cultural femininity) is found in cultures in which both men and women are expected to be subordinate, modest, tender, and concerned with quality of life. The explanation they provide for the proposed relevance of masculinity derives from paternal investment theory (e.g., Bjorklund & Kipp, 1996; Coltrane, 1988; Miller, 1994; Van de Vliert et al., 1999). This evolutionary social psychological theory derives from the biological construct of differential parental care. According to this theory it is more arduous for families to meet basic needs for safety, food, and security in colder climates. Therefore, more parental investment in the family is needed for survival of mother and offspring. Both paternal and maternal investment in the family is characterized by sacrifice, delay of gratification, and the evolution of cooperative attitudes and behaviors. Such symmetrical parental roles produce normative pressure on husbands to share responsibility for caring for children with their wives.

The emphasis on cooperative behavior in the nuclear family would likely generalize to other societal behavior, influencing people to make cooperative rather than competitive choices when dealing with others. Greater parental investment in the family in colder climates would then produce, according to this theory, cultures that are lower in masculinity

and show less violent behavior (Van de Vliert et al., 1999).

In contrast, in warmer climates, greater male investment in mate seeking leads to immediate gratification and increases the number of offspring. This more likely produces dominant and contentious attitudes and behaviors toward women and rivals in men. Asymmetrical parental roles are likely to emerge under such conditions, with men not needing to show much concern for offspring and women expected to invest in child-rearing and provisioning (e.g., Miller, 1994). Thus, it can be expected that societies in warmer regions would tend to evolve toward greater cultural masculinity, with men socialized to deal with interpersonal problems through aggressive competition rather than integrative cooperation (e.g., Van de Vliert, 1998).

> In sum, Paternal Investment Theory can explain why culturally more masculine societies, characterized by more dominance and violence, evolve in warmer climates. In more masculine compared with less masculine societies, issues of conflict are more likely to be managed through fight rather than flight and through aggression rather than negotiation. (Van de Vliert et al., 1999, p. 301)

Van de Vliert and his coauthors also suggest that similar to cold countries, it is harder to ensure survival in very hot countries than it is in moderately warm countries, leading to an increased need for paternal investment in survival of the family. Thus, they propose an inverted U-shaped association between temperature and cultural masculinity. They also propose a linear relationship between masculinity and domestic political violence, thus producing an overall curvilinear relationship between temperature and violence.

In a GLOBE subsample of 53 countries for which a MAS score was available, national differences on the cultural masculinity dimension were found to account for the curvilinear temperature–violence association, suggesting that culture mediates this association (Van de Vliert et al., 1999). Assertiveness and MAS are obviously different (as described and tested); however, it is interesting to see whether similar relationships are also found between climate and Assertiveness as measured in the GLOBE study.

As was indicated in Chapter 10 (Gupta & Hanges), the GLOBE societal cultures were categorized in terms of their climate. We created seven categories of climate: tropical humid, tropical wet and dry, desert, subtropical humid, subtropical wet and dry (Mediterranean), marine west coast (maritime), and continental. One-way ANOVA tests were conducted to determine whether climatic differences are found in the practices and values of societal Assertiveness. No significant differences are found for practices ($F6, 54 = .66, p > .10$) mean scores across different climate types, but weak cross-climatic differences exist in values ($F6, 54 = 1.98, p < .10$) mean scores of societal Assertiveness. Further analysis showed that climatic differences account for 18% of the variation in societal Assertiveness values scores, whereas 82% represent idiosyncratic societal differences.

The climatic means of societal practices and values of Assertiveness are given in Table 15.12. The means for practices ranged from 3.96 (tropical humid) to 4.30 (Mediterranean); however, these differences did not reach statistical significance. With respect to the values scale, tropical humid climate region (mean = 4.37, contrast = 0.62, $p < .01$) had a significantly higher average; and maritime climate region (mean = 3.43, contrast = –.43, $p < .05$) had a significantly lower average. To summarize, in our sample, climate has a very weak influence on the values measure of societal Assertiveness. Specifically, respondents in societies with a maritime climate tended to value softer, nonassertive approaches, whereas respondents in the humid tropics seem to aspire for more assertiveness within their society.

Table 15.12   Climate Clusters and GLOBE Societal Assertiveness

Climate Clusters	N	Societal Assertiveness Values		Societal Assertiveness Practices	
		Mean	Standard Deviation	Mean	Standard Deviation
Tropical Humid Colombia Costa Rica Ecuador India Indonesia Malaysia Philippines Singapore	8	4.37	0.60	3.96	0.18
Tropical Wet and Dry El Salvador Guatemala Nigeria Thailand Venezuela Zimbabwe Zambia	7	3.75	0.53	4.20	0.41
Desert Egypt Iran Israel Kazakhstan Kuwait Mexico Namibia	11	3.75	0.55	4.20	0.31

Climate Clusters	N	Societal Assertiveness Values		Societal Assertiveness Practices	
		Mean	Standard Deviation	Mean	Standard Deviation
Qatar South Africa[a] South Africa[b] Turkey					
Subtropical Humid Argentina Bolivia Brazil Hong Kong Taiwan	5	3.60	0.74	4.16	0.34
Mediterranean Albania Greece Italy Morocco Portugal Slovenia Spain	7	3.83	0.56	4.30	0.42
Maritime Denmark France Germany[c] Germany[d] Ireland Netherlands New Zealand Switzerland Switzerland[e] United Kingdom	10	3.43	0.32	4.10	0.45
Continental Australia Austria Canada[f] China Finland Georgia Hungary Japan Poland Russia South Korea Sweden U.S.	13	3.97	0.83	4.09	0.43

a South Africa (White Sample)
b South Africa (Black Sample)
c Germany (East): Former GDR
d Germany (West): Former FRG
e Switzerland (French-speaking)
f Canada (English-speaking)

In the climate analysis presented above, the countries were classified into different climates rather than examining temperature the way the aforementioned study by Van de Vliert and colleagues (1999) did. As they did find a significant relationship between temperature and the MAS index, further exploration of the relationship between temperature and Assertiveness was of interest. Fifty-four of the GLOBE countries are also in the analyses presented by Van de Vliert and coauthors (1999), excluding Georgia, Kazakhstan, and Qatar. Using the data on temperatures presented by Van de Vliert and colleagues (pp. 308–311), we calculated a correlation between temperature and the two societal Assertiveness scores. Assertiveness practices did not correlate with temperature ($r = -.06$). The correlation between societal Assertiveness values and average daytime temperature of the country's capital city was significant at the 5% level ($r = .28$) for these 54 societies. However, for the full sample of 61 cultures, using data explained in Chapter 10 by Gupta and Hanges, the correlation of values with temperature measure is not significant at the .05 level, but only at the .10 level ($r = .22$, $p < 0.10$). Also, the Assertiveness values score is significantly positively correlated with average rainfall ($r = .36$, $p < .01$, $N = 61$). Thus, although the specific countries and data sets used in the calculation seem to influence the strength of the relationships that are found, on the whole Assertiveness values are to some degree related to climate, whereas practices are not.

Following the Van de Vliert and colleagues (1999) study, we also assessed the relationship between Assertiveness and domestic political violence (DPV). They used the most recent 30-year period for which violence scores were available (1948–1977). The index was based on the logarithm of an additive combination of two indicators, namely the number of political riots and armed attacks (see Van de Vliert and colleagues for a more detailed description of the origins of this measure and the data on DPV). Assertiveness practices did not correlate significantly with DPV ($r = .15$); however, the correlation between societal Assertiveness values and DPV was significant at the .05 level ($r = .27$). The correlation between DPV and temperature ($r = .34$) was also significant at the .05 level. Thus, Assertiveness values are related to DPV.

Van de Vliert and colleagues (1999) also investigated the possible mediating role of masculinity in the relationship between temperature and DPV. They investigated curvilinear relationships between the variables and controlled for several possible confounding variables (e.g., population size and democracy). We did not perform similar analyses here as they are beyond the scope of this chapter. However, the positive correlation between GLOBE Assertiveness values and both rainfall and DPV seem interesting topics for further exploration. Along with the negative correlation between Assertiveness values and Gender Egalitarianism values, these data may help further develop ideas described by Van De Vliert and colleagues (1999).

Geographical Regions

As discussed in Chapter 8 by Hanges and Dickson, there are significant differences in values and practices for every cultural dimension among the 62 societal cultures (recall that we use the term societal cultures rather than nations). To explore further the possible impact of country demographics, the relationship between the GLOBE Assertiveness measure and geographic region was examined. As discussed in Chapter 10, GLOBE societies were grouped into 10 regional clusters. One-way analyses of variance show that significant cross-regional differences exist in the societal practices ($F9, 51 = 2.41$, $p < 0.05$) as well as in the societal values ($F9, 51 = 5.40$, $p < 0.01$) of societal Assertiveness. Further analysis showed that regional differences account for 30% of the variation in societal Assertiveness practices scores, whereas 70% represent idiosyncratic societal differences. With respect to societal Assertiveness values scores, 49% of the variation was explained by regional differences, whereas 51% represented unique societal differences. In other words, a substantial amount of variance in both societal Assertiveness practices and values is accounted for by differences in geographical regions.

Table 15.13 shows the mean scores on Assertiveness values and practices for each geographic region. The highest practices scores are found for the Germanic Europe (4.55, contrast = .48, *p* < .01) and Eastern Europe clusters (4.33, contrast = .24, *p* < .10). The lowest average practices scores are found for the Nordic Europe (3.66, contrast =– .50, *p* < .05) and Southern Asia clusters (3.86, contrast =– .28, *p* < .10). The Southern Asia (4.65, contrast = .92, *p* < .01) and Confucian Asia (4.54, contrast = .80, *p* < .01) clusters have the highest scores on Assertiveness values. The lowest values score is found for the Germanic Europe (3.07, contrast =– .81, *p* < .01) and Middle East clusters (3.39, contrast =– .47, *p* < .05).

It is noteworthy that in all regions but two (and these two score highest on Assertiveness values), people tend to strive for less assertiveness. Only in the Southern Asia and Confucian Asia clusters did people indicate they wanted more assertiveness, dominance, and aggression in their relationships with one another; these are two of the lowest-scoring regions with respect to current GLOBE Assertiveness practices.

Table 15.13   GLOBE Societal Assertiveness and Geographic Region

Geographic Region	*N*	Societal Assertiveness Values		Societal Assertiveness Practices	
		Mean	*Standard Deviation*	*Mean*	*Standard Deviation*
Nordic Europe Finland Sweden Denmark	3	3.56	0.15	3.66	0.25
Eastern Europe Albania Kazakhstan Hungary Poland Russia Slovenia Greece Georgia	8	3.78	0.67	4.33	0.42
Latin America Argentina Bolivia Brazil Colombia Costa Rica Ecuador El Salvador Guatemala Mexico Venezuela	10	3.54	0.32	4.15	0.28
Middle East Egypt Kuwait Morocco Qatar Turkey	5	3.39	0.46	4.14	0.39

(Continued)

Table 15.13 (Continued)

Geographic Region	N	Societal Assertiveness Values		Societal Assertiveness Practices	
		Mean	Standard Deviation	Mean	Standard Deviation
Latin Europe Italy Portugal Spain France Switzerland[a] Israel	6	3.72	0.21	3.99	0.36
Germanic Europe Austria Germany[b] Germany[c] Netherlands Switzerland	5	3.07	0.17	4.55	0.15
Sub-Saharan Africa Namibia Nigeria South Africa[d] Zambia Zimbabwe	5	3.99	0.53	4.24	0.35
Confucian Asia Taiwan Singapore Hong Kong South Korea China Japan	6	4.54	0.91	4.09	0.41
Southern Asia India Indonesia Iran Malaysia Philippines Taiwan	6	4.65	0.59	3.86	0.15
Anglo Australia Canada[e] New Zealand U.S. South Africa[f] England Ireland	7	3.89	0.28	4.14	0.40

a Switzerland (French-speaking)
b Germany (West): Former FRG
c Germany (East): Former GDR
d South Africa (Black Sample)
e Canada (English-speaking)
f South Africa (White Sample)

Summary

We found that climate types seem to be related to societal Assertiveness. For instance, in tropical humid societies, Assertiveness seems to be valued more than in the maritime societies. Greater rainfall was associated with stronger societal values of Assertiveness. We also found that cultures reported in the GLOBE survey as having a strong preference for assertiveness have more domestic political violence. This pattern does not hold for current levels of Assertiveness practices. In this study, we found Assertiveness practices to be unrelated to rainfall or to violence. Further research is needed in this area. Regional differences are important to people's practices and aspirations in terms of assertiveness: In some regions people want more assertiveness and in others people want less. Especially salient is Asia in that respect. This region consistently shows a desire for more assertiveness, whereas in other regions there is a desire for less assertiveness.

ASSERTIVENESS AS A DIMENSION OF ORGANIZATIONAL CULTURE: BACKGROUND

Schein (1992) defines organizational culture as

> a pattern of basic assumptions—invented, discovered or developed by a given group as it learns to cope with their problems of external adaptation and internal integration—that has worked well enough to be considered valuable and, therefore, to be taught to new members as the correct way to perceive, think, and feel in relation to those problems. (p. 9)

Deal and Kennedy (1982) simply define organizational culture as "the way we do things around here" (p. 4). Many different ways of operationalizing and measuring organizational culture are found in the literature (see, e.g., Denison, 1996).

Deal and Kennedy (1982) discuss an example of a model of organizational culture in which assertiveness may play a role. On the basis of their analysis of company cultures they describe four generic cultures: The tough-guy-macho culture, the work-hard/play-hard culture,

the bet-your-company rule, and the process culture. The tough-guy-macho culture seems most relevant to Assertiveness. According to Deal and Kennedy (1982), "tough" is the byword in this tough-guy-macho culture. "The need to make a quick decision and to accept the risk that very soon it may be proven wrong requires a tough attitude" (p. 109). There is strong internal competition. "Every meeting can become a war game where the most junior person in the room has to best the most senior person in order to win respect. If the junior person doesn't fight, he or she will be dismissed out of hand as a lightweight. A comer is the one who's aggressive whether right, wrong or indifferent" (p. 110). Chance and competition play a large role in tough-guy-macho cultures. This culture rewards risk-taking individualists, the kind of people for whom there is no reward in being part of a team and who strive to become a star. Deal and Kennedy state that "tough guys" will generally score points off each other, are studiously "in fashion" all the time, live wherever the "in" place is, and like competitive one-on-one sports.

The aggressive, tough, and competitive way people deal with others in the tough-guy-macho culture described by Deal and Kennedy (1982) gives one example of how the Assertiveness dimension, as measured in GLOBE, may be of interest in organizational cultures. Interestingly, regarding Gender Egalitarianism, according to Deal and Kennedy the tough-guy-macho culture probably discriminates least against women of any of the four types they propose. As they say, "after all, a star is a star" (p. 111).

As the results presented above indicate, current and aspired levels of Assertiveness are relevant to understand the ways people interact in a society. An interesting question is whether this dimension is also relevant for organizational cultures. As with the GLOBE societal questionnaire, the GLOBE organizational culture questionnaire includes questions asking respondents to report whether organizational practices or values are tough rather than tender, dominant rather than nondominant, and aggressive. The items ask for reflections on observations and values concerning the nature of relationships within the context of the organization.

THE RELATIONSHIP BETWEEN SOCIETAL AND ORGANIZATIONAL PRACTICES AND SOCIETAL AND ORGANIZATIONAL VALUES

As indicated in Chapter 2 by House and Javidan, the GLOBE theoretical model postulates that societal practices and values affect organizational practices and values. Two hierarchical linear models (HLMs) were conducted to test these hypotheses for organizational Assertiveness practices and values. We tested the GLOBE hypothesis regarding the effect of societal culture on organizational culture by conducting HLM analyses in which organizational Assertiveness was predicted by societal Assertiveness. These analyses did not support our hypotheses that societal Assertiveness practices have a significant and strong positive relationship with organizational Assertiveness practices ($p > .05$). However, we found a significant relationship between societal Assertiveness values and organizational Assertiveness values ($p < .01$). Therefore, for this culture dimension, only the analysis for Assertiveness values supports the principal proposition in the GLOBE theoretical model (i.e., Proposition 3, Figure 2.1, Chapter 2): societal cultural values and practices affect organizational cultural values and practices.[2]

Table 15.14 shows the grand means of organizational practices and organizational values scales for Assertiveness across all identifiable responding organizations in the GLOBE study.

The organizational practices score has a midlevel average rating of 4.11. Scores range from 3.16 to 5.88. Compared with other cultural dimensions measured, the organizational values scores have a low average rating of 3.96. Further, there is a huge interorganizational variation in the preferred assertiveness levels, ranging from 1.71 to 6.50.

Table 15.15 shows the correlation between the organizational Assertiveness practices and values scales. As seen in this Table, there is a significant *positive* correlation ($r = 0.38$, $p < 0.01$) between overall scores for Assertiveness practices and Assertiveness values.

One-way ANOVA tests were conducted to determine whether industry differences are found in the practices and values of organizational Assertiveness. No significant differences are found for practices ($F2, 271 = .07$, $p > .10$) mean scores across three industries. Similarly no significant differences are found for values ($F2, 271 = .48$, $p > .10$) mean scores across industries.

Table 15.14 Grand Mean Scores for Assertiveness in Organizations

Variable	Mean	Standard Deviation	Minimum	Maximum	Valid N
Assertiveness practices	4.11	0.48	3.16	5.77	276
Assertiveness values	3.96	0.73	1.71	6.50	276

Additional one-way ANOVA tests were conducted to determine if regional differences are found in organizational Assertiveness. Significant differences are found for practices ($F9, 266 = 6.97$, $p < .01$) mean scores across regional cultures. Similarly, significant differences are found for values ($F9, 266 = 9.01$, $p < .01$) mean scores across regional cultures. Further analysis showed that regional differences account for 19% of the variation in organizational

Assertiveness practices scores, and for 23% of the variation in organizational GLOBE assertiveness values scores.

Table 15.16 reports mean practices and values scores of organizational Assertiveness in different regions. Assertiveness practices are rated significantly higher in the Southern Asia (4.39; contrast = .33, $p < .01$) and Anglo (4.37; contrast = .31, $p < .01$) clusters. Assertiveness practices are rated as lower in the Middle East

Table 15.15   Correlation of Assertiveness Practices and Values in Organizations

Overall	Assertiveness values
Assertiveness practices	.38**

$N = 276$.

** $p < .01$ (2-tailed).

Table 15.16   GLOBE Organizational Assertiveness and Geographical Region

Geographic Region	N	Organizational Assertivenesss Values		Organizational Assertiveness Practices	
		Mean	Standard Deviation	Mean	Standard Deviation
Nordic Europe	26	3.77	0.23	3.74	0.23
Eastern Europe	36	3.98	0.53	4.07	0.34
Latin America	37	4.00	0.86	3.99	0.39
Middle East	22	3.24	0.61	3.99	0.55
Latin Europe	11	4.31	0.27	4.16	0.29
Germanic Europe	27	3.43	0.61	3.89	0.42
Sub-Saharan Africa	10	3.56	0.71	4.22	0.31
Confucian Asia	28	4.35	0.72	4.09	0.35
Southern Aisa	46	4.17	0.97	4.39	0.57
Anglo	33	4.36	0.34	4.37	0.35

(3.99) and Latin America clusters (3.99), but these are not significantly different from the rest of the regional clusters. Assertiveness values are rated significantly higher in the Anglo (4.36; contrast = .49, $p < .01$), Confucian Asia (4.35; contrast = .47, $p < .01$), and Latin Europe (4.31; contrast = .43, $p < .05$) clusters, and lower in the Middle East (3.24; contrast = .75, $p < .01$) and Germanic Europe (3.43; contrast = .54, $p < .01$) clusters.

In summary, Anglo organizations stand out for their reported positive proclivity toward assertiveness. The higher practices and values

of Assertiveness in Anglo organizations appear to be consistent with a high emphasis on assertiveness found in the Anglo business literature.

ASSERTIVENESS AS A PREDICTOR OF CULTURALLY ENDORSED LEADERSHIP THEORIES

One of the most interesting questions that the GLOBE project can answer concerns the relationship between perceived leader attributes and culture. Culture dimensions such as those studied in GLOBE yield many hypotheses regarding cross-cultural differences in leadership behaviors and attributes. For instance, cultures rated high in Assertiveness are probably more tolerant of strong, directive leaders than cultures rated low, in which a preference for more consultative, considerate leaders seems likely.

Hofstede (1991) also speculates that masculine and feminine societies create different management hero types, the masculine manager being assertive, decisive, and aggressive:

> He is a lonely decision-maker looking for facts rather than a group discussion leader. It does not hurt if he is slightly macho. . . . The manager in a feminine country is less visible, intuitive rather than decisive, and accustomed to seeking consensus. (p. 94)

One would expect that leaders would be expected to be tough, autonomous, and strong in cultures emphasizing assertiveness and dominance in social relationships.

As stated earlier in this volume, we identified 21 basic leadership factors (created from 112 items) that were later grouped into 6 global leadership dimensions by conducting first-order and second-order factor analyses, respectively. We identified six underlying dimensions of global leadership patterns that are viewed by managers as contributors or impediments to outstanding leadership (see Chapter 8 by Hanges & Dickson). These six leadership dimensions are: Charismatic/Value-Based leadership, Team-Oriented leadership, Participative leadership, Humane-Oriented leadership, Autonomous leadership, and Self-Protective leadership.

Interpretation of HLM Using GLOBE Assertiveness to Predict Culturally Endorsed Leadership

In this section of this chapter we present relationships between one culture dimension (Assertiveness) and the six CLTs. Competitive tests of all culture dimensions and CLTs are presented in Chapter 21 by Dorfman and coauthors.[3] In general, we expect that societal and organizational values will be more strongly related to CLT leadership dimensions than societal and

organizational practices. As indicated previously, our notions of values and CLT leadership dimensions represent idealized concepts of how the world "Should Be" in contrast to practices that represent the world "As Is." As you read through the results discussed below, it may be helpful to view Figure 15.1 for a visual summary. The figure, however, only shows results regarding cultural values, not practices. (All HLM coefficients are presented in Table 21.10 of Chapter 21 by Dorfman, Hanges, & Brodbeck.)

As described earlier in this volume, culture is believed to have its effect on the content of CLTs at multiple levels of analysis. Leader attributes perceived to be effective might be a function of (a) societal cultural practices as measured by the societal practices culture scales, (b) societal cultural values as measured by the societal values scales, (c) organizational cultural practices as measured by the organizational practices scales, and (d) organizational cultural values as measured by the organizational values scales. In the present chapter we discuss the results of statistical analyses examining the extent to which the cultural dimension of Assertiveness has an effect on CLTs. Specifically, we examine the extent to which the content of CLTs varies as a function of Assertiveness values and practices in societies and organizations within societies.

We tested for the relationship between culture and the CLT leadership dimensions by using hierarchical linear modeling (HLM). Although this statistical technique is somewhat new to the organizational literature, it actually has been used in other fields for quite some time. HLM can be thought of as a multistep process designed to test the significance of relationships between independent and dependent variables at multiple levels of analyses. An overview of HLM analyses and a detailed discussion of how these analyses were conducted is provided in Chapter 11 by Hanges, Dickson, and Sipe, and in Appendix C by Hanges, Sipe, and Godfrey.

HLM Analysis: Organizational and Societal Variation

In this analysis we examine the simultaneous associative relationships of organizational and

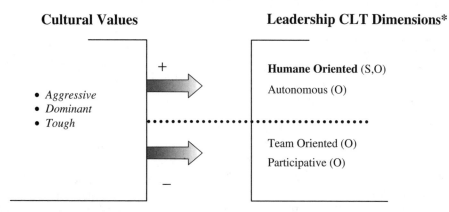

Figure 15.1   Assertiveness Cultural Values as Drivers for CLT Leadership Dimensions

* Only statistically significant relationships are shown ($p < .05$; see Table 21.10, Chapter 21 by Dorfman et al.). The most important leadership CLT relationships are bolded (i.e., relationship is significant at both society and organization levels of analyses or highest HLM coefficient within each level of analysis).

O = Organizational level

S = Societal level

societal Assertiveness values and practices and CLTs. The total amount of organizational and societal variance explained by Assertiveness ranged from 0 to 18.9%. Assertiveness was found to be a better predictor for some of the CLTs (e.g., Humane-Oriented leadership) than for others (e.g., Self-Protective leadership). More specifically, when organizational level and societal level Assertiveness values and practices were considered, significant relationships were found with

• *Charismatic/Value-Based leadership.* Assertiveness cultural practices scores were significantly related to the Charismatic/Value-Based leadership dimension but explained a total of just 2.0% of the organizational and societal variance for this dimension. All of the explained variance was associated with forces operating at the organizational level of analysis. The organizational Assertiveness cultural *practices* scores were negatively related ($p < .01$) to the Charismatic/Value-Based leadership dimension. Charismatic/Value-Based leadership is less likely to be a part of the shared leadership belief system in organizations reported to have Assertiveness practices.

• *Team-Oriented leadership.* Assertiveness practices and values scores were significantly related to the Team-Oriented leadership dimension and explained a total of 7.4% of the organizational and societal variance for this dimension. All of the explained variance was associated with forces operating at the organizational level of analysis. The organizational Assertiveness cultural practices scores were negatively related ($p < .01$) to the Team-Oriented leadership dimension, as were the organizational Assertiveness cultural values scores ($p < .01$). Team-Oriented leadership is less likely to be a part of the shared leadership belief system in organizations reported to have Assertiveness practices and values.

• *Participative leadership.* Assertiveness cultural practices and values scores were significantly related to the Participative leadership dimension but explained a total of just 2.1% of the organizational and societal variance for this dimension. All of the explained variance was associated with forces operating at the organizational level of analysis. The organizational Assertiveness cultural practices scores were negatively related ($p < .01$) to the Participative leadership dimension, as were the organizational Assertiveness cultural values scores ($p < .05$). Participative leadership is less likely to be a part of the shared leadership belief system in organizations reported to have Assertiveness practices and it is less likely to be a part of the shared leadership belief system in organizations reported to espouse Assertiveness values.

- *Humane-Oriented leadership.* Assertiveness cultural practices and values scores were significantly related to the Humane-Oriented leadership dimension and explained a total of 18.9% of the organizational and societal variance for this dimension. Approximately 65.4% of the explained variance was associated with forces operating at the organizational level of analysis. The remaining portion of the explained variance (34.6%) was associated with forces operating at the societal level of analysis.

Both the organizational Assertiveness cultural practices scores ($p < .01$) and the organizational Assertiveness cultural values scores ($p < .01$) were positively related to the Humane-Oriented leadership dimension. Humane-Oriented leadership is more likely to be a part of the shared leadership belief system in organizations reported to have Assertiveness practices and values.

The societal Assertiveness cultural values scores were positively related ($p < .01$) to the Humane-Oriented leadership dimension. Humane-Oriented leadership is more likely to be a part of the shared leadership belief systems in societies reported to espouse Assertiveness values.

- *Autonomous leadership.* Assertiveness cultural practices and values scores were significantly related to the Autonomous leadership dimension and explained a total of 5.9% of the organizational and societal variance for this dimension. All of this explained variance was associated with forces operating at the organizational level of analysis. Both the organizational Assertiveness cultural practices scores ($p < .05$) and the organizational Assertiveness cultural values scores ($p < .01$) were positively related to the Autonomous leadership dimension. Autonomous leadership is more likely to be a part of a shared

leadership belief system in organizations reported to have Assertiveness practices and values.

- *Self-Protective leadership.* Assertiveness cultural practices and values scores were not significantly related to the Self-Protective leadership dimension.

CLT Summary

Our results show that at the organizational level of analysis Assertiveness is negatively related to Team-Oriented (values and practices), Participative (values and practices), and Charismatic/Value-Based (practices) leadership, and positively related to Autonomous (values and practices) and Humane-Oriented (values and practices) leadership. Therefore, in almost all cases the results are consistent for both values and practices. When organizations were viewed as valuing and practicing Assertiveness, it was more likely that an Autonomous and Humane-Oriented leadership style would be a part of the organization's CLT. Also, it was less likely that Participative and Team-Oriented leadership would be part of the organization's CLT if organizations were viewed as valuing and practicing Assertiveness. Some of these findings are in line with expectations. For instance, at the organizational level, we find that the more that Assertiveness is valued and practiced in the organization the less likely it is that Participative leadership is part of the organization's CLT. The positive relationship of Assertiveness with the Humane-Oriented CLT leadership dimension is likely due to the need for leaders to provide social support in a highly assertive and likely threatening environment. This seems consistent with the path-goal theory of leadership (e.g., House, 1971, 1996). Overall, our analyses also indicate that the kind of leadership viewed as effective in part reflects the extent to which a society values Assertiveness. At the societal level, only the positive relationship with Humane-Oriented leadership was significant. Societies reported to value Assertiveness were found to endorse Humane-Oriented leadership; in other words, the CLT endorsed at the societal level of analysis would more likely include Humane-Oriented leadership. This again indicates that the relationship among masculine and feminine practices, values, and leadership dimensions is not as straightforward as suggested by Hofstede's (1980) masculinity–femininity dimension. This was also confirmed by the pattern of correlations between the Assertiveness and Humane Orientation societal culture measures presented earlier.

If you look at the overall picture (including the other culture dimensions presented in the other chapters), values seem to predict more variance in CLTs than practices. What people think about their effective leaders seems to be somewhat more influenced by their values than by the practices they perceive. Given the fact that people were asked to think of effective leaders, this is not surprising. Both the values and the CLTs have a "should be" component. They are a reflection of a desired rather than an actual reality. It would be interesting to test whether actual leader behavior is predicted more by the practices than the values.

Finally, we found that the coefficients for Assertiveness were stronger at the organizational level than at the societal level of analysis. Organizational Assertiveness had a stronger relationship with Team-Oriented and Participative leadership (all negative), and Humane-Oriented and Autonomous leadership (both positive) as compared to societal Assertiveness. Again, given the fact we were asking respondents to make judgments about organizational leadership, this is not surprising.

SUMMARY AND CONCLUSIONS

The GLOBE culture dimension questionnaire on Assertiveness asks whether there are differences among societies in the extent to which people in those societies generally practice or value assertiveness, aggressiveness, dominance, and toughness or nonassertiveness and tenderness. In this chapter we have demonstrated that organizations reflect Assertiveness cultural values, but not practices, in the society in which they are embedded.

As stated, this dimension originates in Hofstede's (1980) masculinity construct, and Hofstede's MAS scale indeed correlated significantly and positively with the GLOBE

Assertiveness practices scale. However, it did not correlate significantly with the GLOBE Assertiveness values scale. Thus, the Hofstede masculinity index seems to reflect assertive practices rather than values. Hence, the GLOBE Assertiveness dimension differs from the Hofstede masculinity dimension. One crucial difference is that Hofstede's masculinity dimension confounds gender inequality with success striving—constructs that in our view are not necessarily correlated. Further, his MAS scale included no items relevant to assertiveness. For instance, a society could at the same time be highly assertive but not very achievement or performance oriented. The GLOBE study measures these separately. In our view, the pattern of correlations between these constructs supports separating these constructs as well as separating values and practices.

We found that the GLOBE Assertiveness practices measure was not correlated with Gender Egalitarianism (practices or values). However, Assertiveness values and Gender Egalitarianism values are negatively correlated, meaning that preferring more assertiveness is related to preferring less gender equality or more male-oriented values. The significant relationship of Assertiveness values we found with the current practices of Performance Orientation is also of interest. Hofstede (1980, 1991, 2001) explicitly links masculinity to striving for success, progress, and material wealth. Thus, a positive relationship between Assertiveness and the Performance Orientation dimension would have been plausible but was found only for Assertiveness values in relation to practices, not aspirations of Performance Orientation.

The Assertiveness values scale was positively related to the Power Distance values measure. In addition, Assertiveness practices correlated negatively with Institutional Collectivism practices, and Assertiveness values were positively related with both Institutional and In-Group Collectivism practices scales.

The most intriguing results may be those related to the GLOBE Humane Orientation culture dimension. If this orientation can be taken as an indication of femininity, as measured by Hofstede, one might expect negative relationships of this measure with GLOBE Assertiveness and Hofstede's masculinity. Humane Orientation and Assertiveness practices, as measured in project GLOBE, were indeed negatively correlated at the societal level. However, Humane Orientation values were positively related to Assertiveness practices. Furthermore, when societies are reported to value Assertiveness, the CLT endorsed at the societal level of analysis more likely includes Humane-Oriented leadership. In contrast, at the organizational level, practicing and valuing Assertiveness the CLT less likely included Humane-Oriented leadership. This relationship again indicates that the relationship among masculine and feminine practices, values, and leadership dimensions is not as straightforward as suggested by Hofstede's (1980) masculinity–femininity dimension. Further research in this area is needed.

Few relationships were found with external data. For instance, Assertiveness values were positively related to "success in science and technology" and "respect for family and friends." As presented in Chapter 8 by Hanges and Dickson, the GLOBE Assertiveness values scale was also expected and found to relate significantly negatively to Schwartz's (1994) egalitarian commitment. The more societies value assertiveness, the less such a commitment to voluntarily helping others and transcending selfish interests is stressed.

Van de Vliert and colleagues (1999) found significant relationship between Hofstede's masculinity index and domestic political violence (DPV) over the most recent 30-year period for which violence scores were available (1948–1977). We also assessed the relationship between Assertiveness and the DPV data over this period. Assertiveness practices did not correlate significantly with DPV; however, the correlation between societal Assertiveness values and DPV was positive and significant. Comparing Assertiveness in climate types did not yield significant differences; however, Van de Vliert and colleagues (1999) found a significant relationship between Hofstede's MAS index and temperature. We calculated a correlation between temperature and the two GLOBE societal Assertiveness scores and found that GLOBE Assertiveness practices did not correlate with temperature, whereas Assertiveness values were weakly correlated with temperature. These findings held when we used the temperature data of Van de Vliert

and colleagues and only included the countries they included. Clearly, more research is needed on this issue.

The findings presented in this chapter also point to the conclusion that people in different geographic areas rate their societies differently in terms of how assertive they should be, in contrast to the current state of assertiveness within their society. That is, there are regional differences as to the actual difference between these two measures. In all regions but two (and these two score highest on Assertiveness values), people tend to strive for less assertiveness. Only the Southern Asia and Confucian Asia clusters' respondents indicate they want more assertiveness, dominance, and aggression in their relationships with others. It is, therefore, not surprising that in the sample as a whole Assertiveness practices and Assertiveness values correlate negatively. Overall, in most regions (with the notable exception of Asia), less Assertiveness is reported as desired.

We also reported on Assertiveness values and practices at the organizational level. Whereas a negative correlation between Assertiveness practices and values is found at the societal level, a positive correlation is found at the organizational level. Although no industry differences were found, there is a large variation between organizations, and, again, regional differences are found. Aggregated responses from Anglo organizations, especially, tend to score high on Assertiveness, which seems consistent with the emphasis in Anglo literature and media on individualism and aggressive attitudes needed to succeed in business.

Another interesting part of GLOBE Project concerns the relationship between perceived leader attributes and culture. The relationship between societal level Assertiveness and Humane-Oriented leadership was mentioned above. The relationships at the organizational level are stronger and in line with expectations. For instance, we found that the less that organizations practice and value Assertiveness, the more likely it is that the endorsed societal-level CLT includes Participative leadership. That is, organizations whose managers scored relatively high on actual or desired Assertiveness (dominance and toughness) prefer less Participative leaders. This also holds for Team-Oriented leadership. In contrast, in organizations valuing and practicing Assertiveness, it was more likely that the Humane-Oriented and Autonomous leadership styles were part of the CLT.

In this chapter we presented our ideas and the picture of findings regarding Assertiveness as a culture dimension. The pattern we found is intriguing and in some cases puzzling. More research is needed to fully understand the pattern of relationships unearthed here. However, in our view, the findings do support GLOBE's Assertiveness cultural dimension as an interesting and valuable, but also truly complex, dimension of national and organizational cultures.

ENDNOTES

1. Our response bias correction procedure identified response bias in some countries for this scale. We recomputed the predicted response bias corrected scale score for each country. Response bias corrected scores are:

Practices: Denmark, 4.04 (no change in band); Finland, 4.05 (no change in band); France, 4.44 (moves from band B to band A); Qatar, 4.39 (moves from band B to band A); and Nigeria, 4.53 (no change in band).

Values: Finland, 3.91 (no change in band); Japan, 5.84 (no change in band); Morocco, 3.68 (no change in band); and Taiwan, 2.91 (moves from band B to band C).

For a complete discussion of this procedure and all response bias corrected scores, see Appendix B.

2. As reported in Chapter 20 by Brodbeck, Hanges, Dickson, Gupta, and Dorfman, we found that all the cultural dimensions of organizational cultural values and practices significantly differed across societies. Although important, this prior analysis did not identify the particular aspect of societal differences that was related to organizational culture. In the present chapter, we found that societal and organizational Assertiveness practices were not significantly related ($p > .05$). However, we found strong results for societal and organizational Assertiveness values (R^2 Total = 29.6%, R^2 Societal = 92.6%, $p < .01$). As discussed in Chapter 11 by Hanges, Dickson, and Sipe, the R^2 Total considers all levels of analysis (i.e., individual, organizational, and societal), whereas the R^2 Societal isolates the societal level portion of the dependent variable and indicates the percentage of variance accounted for by the predictor at only this level. Whereas we have primarily taken the conservative approach and reported the R^2 Total in GLOBE, several scholars suggest that R^2 Societal provides a more accurate description of aggregated relationships. For further discussion, see the paper by Lance and James (1999).

3. Results between the single HLM and multiple HLM tests will likely differ somewhat. The differences between the results of the multiple HLMs and single HLMs are conceptually similar to the differences between a multiple regression analysis and a correlation coefficient. Table 21.10 in Chapter 21 by Dorfman et al. presents both single and multiple HLM coefficients. In addition, the relationships for all culture dimension values are summarized in Chapter 3.

REFERENCES

Akerblom, S. & Holmberg, I. (in press). "Primus inter pares": Leadership and culture in Sweden. In R. J. House & J. Chhokar (Eds.), *Cultures of the world: A GLOBE anthology of in-depth descriptions of the cultures of 14 countries* (Vol. 1). Thousand Oaks, CA: Sage.

Arrindell, W. A., Hatzichristou, C., Wensink, J., Rosenberg, E., van Twillert, B., Stedema, J., & Meijer, D. (1997). Dimensions of national culture as predictors of cross-national differences in subjective well-being. *Personality and Individual Differences, 23*(1), 37–53.

Baer, J. (1976). *How to be an assertive (not aggressive) woman in life, in love and the job.* New York: Signet.

Bajdo, L. M., & Dickson, M. W. (2001). Perceptions of organizational culture and women's advancement in organizations: A cross-cultural examination. *Sex Roles, 45*(5–6), 399–414.

Barrick, M. R., & Mount, M. K. (1991). The Big Five personality and job performance: A meta-analysis. *Personnel Psychology, 44,* 1–26.

Bjorklund, D. F., & Kipp, K. (1996). Parental investment theory and gender differences in the evolution of inhibition mechanisms. *Psychological Bulletin, 120,* 163–188.

Bonta, B. D. (1997). Cooperation and competition in peaceful societies. *Psychological Bulletin, 121,* 299–320.

Booream, C. D., & Flowers, J. V. (1978). A procedural model for training of assertive behavior. In J. M. Whitely & J. V. Flowers (Eds.), *Approaches to assertion training* (pp. 15–46). Monterey, CA: Brooks/Cole.

Brenner, O. C., Tomkiewicz, J., & Schein, V. E. (1989). The relationship between sex role stereotypes and requisite management characteristics revisited. *Academy of Management Journal, 32,* 662–669.

Brown, P., & Levinson, S. (1987). *Politeness: Some universals in language usage.* Cambridge, UK: Cambridge University Press.

Caspi, A., Elder, G. H., & Bem, D. J. (1988). Moving away from the world: Life-course patterns of shy children. *Development Psychology, 24,* 824–831.

Chinese Culture Connection. (1987). Chinese values and the search for culture-free dimensions of culture. *Journal of Cross-Cultural Psychology, 18*(2), 143–164.

Coltrane, S. (1988). Father-child relationships and the status of women: A cross-cultural study. *American Journal of Sociology, 93,* 1060–1095.

Crawford, M. (1988). Gender, age and the social evaluation of assertion. *Behavior Modification, 12,* 549–564.

Crawford, M. (1995). *Talking difference: On gender and language.* London: Sage

Deal, T. E., & Kennedy, A. A. (1982). *Corporate cultures: The rites and rituals of corporate life.* Reading, MA: Addison-Wesley.

Denison, D. R. (1996). What *is* the difference between organizational culture and organizational climate? A native's point of view on a decade of paradigm wars. *Academy of Management Review, 21*(3), 619–654.

Doney, P. M., Cannon, J. P., & Mullen, M. R. (1998). Understanding the influence of national culture on the development of trust. *Academy of Management Review, 23(3), 601–620.*

Fagenson, E. A. (1990). Perceived masculine and feminine attributes examined as a function of individuals' sex and level in the organizational power hierarchy: A test of four theoretical perspectives. *Journal of Applied Psychology, 75,* 204–211.

Furnham, A. (1979). Assertiveness in three cultures: Multidimensionality and cultural differences. *Journal of Clinical Psychology, 35,* 522–527.

Goldberg, L. R. (1990). An alternative "description of personality": The Big Five factor structure. *Journal of Personality and Social Psychology, 59,* 1216–1229.

Hall, E. T. (1959). *The silent language.* Garden City, NY: Anchor Press.

Heilman, M. E., Block, C. J., Martell, R. F., & Simon, M. C. (1989). Has anything changed? Current characterizations of men, women, and managers. *Journal of Applied Psychology, 74,* 935–942.

Hofstede, G. (1980). *Culture's consequences: International differences in work related values.* Beverly Hills, CA: Sage.

Hofstede, G. (1991). *Cultures and organizations: Software of the mind.* London: HarperCollins.

Hofstede, G. (1993). Cultural constraints in management theories. *Academy of Management Executive, 7(1),* 81–94.

Hofstede, G. (1998). *Masculinity and femininity: The taboo dimension of national cultures.* Thousand Oaks, CA: Sage.

Hofstede, G. (2001). *Culture's consequences: Comparing values, behaviors, institutions and organizations across nations* (2nd ed., rev.). Thousand Oaks, CA: Sage.

Hollandsworth, J. G. (1977). Differentiating assertion and aggression: Some behavioral guidelines. *Behavior Therapy, 8,* 347–352.

Holtgraves, T. (1992). The linguistic realization of face management: Implications for language production and comprehension, person perception and cross-cultural communication. *Social Psychology Quarterly, 55,* 141–159.

Holtgraves, T. (1997). Styles of language use: Individual and cultural variability in conversational indirectness. *Journal of Personality and Social Psychology, 73,* 624–637.

Hoppe, M. H. (1998). Validating the masculinity/femininity dimension on elites from 19 countries. In G. H. Hofstede (Ed.), *Masculinity and femininity: The taboo dimension of national cultures* (pp. 29–43). Thousand Oaks, CA: Sage.

House, R. J. (1971). Path-goal theory of leadership effectiveness. *Administrative Science Quarterly, 16,* 321–338.

House, R. J. (1996). Path-goal theory of leadership: Lessons, legacy and a reformulated theory. *Leadership Quarterly 7*(3), 323–352.

House, R. J., Hanges, P. J., Ruiz-Quintanilla, S. A., Dorfman, P. W., Javidan, M., Dickson, M., et al. (1999). Cultural influences on leadership and organizations: Project GLOBE. In W. Mobley (Ed.), *Advances in global leadership* (Vol. 1, pp. 171–233). Greenwich, CT: JAI.

Howard, A., & Bray, D. W. (1988). *Managerial lives in transition: Advancing age and changing times.* New York: Guilford.

Howard, A., & Bray, D. W. (1994). Predictions of managerial success over time: Lessons from the management progress study. In K. E. Clark & M. B. Clark (Eds.), *Measures of leadership* (pp. 113–130). West Orange, NJ: Leadership Library of America.

Irani, K. D. (1986). Introduction: Modes of rationality. In M. Tamny & K. D. Irani (Eds.), *Rationality in thought and action* (pp. 1–18). New York: Greenwood.

Judge, T. A., Higgins, C. A., Thoresen, C. J., & Barrick, M. R. (1999). The Big Five personality traits, general mental ability, and career success across the life span. *Personnel Psychology, 53,* 621–652.

Kale, S. H. (1991). Culture-specific marketing communications: An analytical approach. *International Marketing Review, 8,* 18–30.

Kale, S. H., & Barnes, J. W. (1992). Understanding the domain of cross-national buyer-seller interactions. *Journal of International Business Studies, 23,* 101–132.

Kalin, R., Heusser, C., & Edmonds, J. (1982). Cross-national equivalence of a sex-role ideology scale. *Journal of Social Psychology, 116,* 141–142.

Kelly, J. A., Kern, J. M., Kirkley, B. G., Patterson, J. N., & Keane, T. M. (1980). Reactions to assertive versus unassertive behavior: Differential effects for males and females and implications for assertiveness training. *Behavior Therapy, 11,* 670–682.

Kluckhohn, F., & Strodtbeck, F. L. (1961). Variations in value orientations. Westport, CT: Greenwood.

Kohn, A. (1986). *No-contest: The case against competition.* Boston: Houghton Mifflin.

Lance, C. E., & James, L. R. (1999). A proportional variance accounted for index for some cross-level and person-situation research designs. *Organizational Research Methods, 2,* 395–418.

Lange, A. J., & Jabuwkoski, P. (1976). *Responsible assertion: A model for personal growth.* Champaign, IL: Research Press.

Loeber, R., & Hay, D. (1997). Key issues in the development of aggression and violence from childhood to early adulthood. *Annual Review of Psychology, 48,* 371–410.

McCrae, R. R., & Costa, P. T., Jr. (1997). Personality trait structure as a human universal. *American Psychologist, 52,* 509–516.

Melamed, T. (1996a). Career success: An assessment of a gender specific model. *Journal of Occupational and Organizational Psychology, 69,* 217–242.

Melamed, T. (1996b). Validation of a stage model of career success. *Applied Psychology: An International Review, 45,* 35–65.

Miller, E. M. (1994). Paternal provisioning versus mate seeking in human populations. *Personality and Individual Differences, 17,* 227–255.

Peabody, D. (1985). *National characteristics.* Cambridge, UK: Cambridge University Press.

Rakos, R. F. (1991). *Assertive behavior: Theory, research and training.* London: Routledge.

Rathus, S. A. (1973). A 30-item schedule for assessing assertive behavior. *Behavior Therapy, 4,* 398–406.

Rawls, D. J., & Rawls, J. R. (1968). Personality characteristics and personal history data of successful and less successful executives. *Psychological Reports, 23,* 1032–1034.

Salter, A. (1949). *Conditioned reflex therapy.* New York: Farrar, Straus, & Giroux.

Schein, E. H. (1992). *Organizational culture and leadership* (2nd ed.). San Francisco: Jossey-Bass.

Schein, V. E. (1973). The relationship between sex role stereotypes and requisite management characteristics. *Journal of Applied Psychology, 57,* 330–335.

Schein, V. E. (2001). A global look at psychological barriers to women's progress in management. *Journal of Social Issues, 57,* 675–688.

Scher, D., Nevo, B., & Beit-Hallahmi, B. (1979). Beliefs about equal rights for men and women among Israeli and American students. *Journal of Social Psychology, 109,* 11–15.

Schneider, S. C., & Barsoux, J. L. (1997). *Managing across cultures.* London: Prentice Hall Europe.

Schwartz, D. C. (1968). On the ecology of political violence: "The long hot summer" as a hypothesis. *The American Behavioral Scientist, 11,* 24–28.

Schwartz, S. H. (1994). Cultural dimensions of values: Towards an understanding of national differences. In U. Kim, H. C. Triandis, C. Kagitçibasi, S. C. Choi, & G. Yoon (Eds.), *Individualism and collectivism: Theoretical and methodological issues* (pp. 85–119). Thousand Oaks, CA: Sage.

Segall, M. H., Dasen, P. R., Berry, J. W., & Poortinga, Y. H. (1990). *Human behavior in global perspective: An introduction to cross-cultural psychology.* New York: Pergamon.

Shoemaker, M., & Satterfield, D. O. (1977). Assertion training: An identity crisis that's coming on strong. In R. E. Alberti (Ed.), *Assertiveness: Innovations, applications, issues* (pp. 49–58). San Luis Obispo, CA: Impact.

Smith, M. J. (1975). *When I say no, I feel guilty.* New York: Bantam.

Sue, D., Ino, S., & Sue, D. M. (1983). Nonassertiveness of Asian Americans: An inaccurate assumption? *Journal of Counseling Psychology, 30,* 581–588.

Ting-Toomey, S. (1988). Intercultural conflict styles. In Y. Kim & W. Gudykunst (Eds.), *Theories in intercultural communication.* Newbury Park, CA: Sage.

Triandis, H. C. (1994). Cross-cultural industrial and organizational psychology. In H. C. Triandis, Dunnette & Hough (Eds.), *Handbook of industrial and organizational psychology* (2nd ed., Vol. 4, pp. 103–172). Palo Alto, CA: Consulting Psychologists Press.

Trompenaars, F., & Hampden-Turner, C. (1997). *Riding the waves of culture: Understanding cultural diversity in business* (2nd ed.). London: Nicholas-Brealey.

Van de Vliert, E. (1998). Gender role gaps, competitiveness, and masculinity. In G. Hofstede (Ed.), *Masculinity and femininity: The taboo dimension of national cultures* (pp. 117–129). Thousand Oaks, CA: Sage.

Van de Vliert, E., Schwartz, S. H., Huismans, S. E., Hofstede, G., & Daan, S. (1999). Temperature, cultural masculinity, and domestic political violence: A cross-national study. *Journal of Cross-Cultural Psychology, 30,* 291–314.

Watson, D., & Clark, L. A. (1997). Extraversion and its positive emotional core. In R. Hogan, J. Johnson, & S. Briggs (Eds.), *Handbook of personality psychology* (pp. 767–793). San Diego, CA: Academic Press.

Williams, J. E., & Best, D. L. (1982). *Measuring sex stereotypes: A thirty-nation study.* Beverly Hills, CA: Sage.

Williams, J. E., & Best, D. L. (1989). *Sex and psyche: Self-concept viewed cross-culturally.* Newbury Park, CA: Sage.

Wolpe, J. (1958). *Psychotherapy by reciprocal inhibition.* Stanford, CA: Stanford University Press.

Wolpe, J. (1982). *The practice of behavior therapy* (3rd ed.). New York : Pergamon.

16

Individualism and Collectivism

Michele J. Gelfand

Dharm P. S. Bhawuk

Lisa Hisae Nishii

David J. Bechtold

The constructs of individualism and collectivism have been widely discussed in the literature and have attained the status of paradigm in cross-cultural psychology (Segall & Kagitçibasi, 1997). In a discipline once defined by its methodology rather than by its coherent content (Kim, 1994), the influx of theory and research on individualism and collectivism has been a welcome Kuhnian shift in thinking. In just the past 25 years, more than 1,400 articles on individualism and collectivism have been published, and numerous books have been devoted exclusively to the constructs (Kim, Triandis, Kagitçibasi, Choi, & Yoon, 1994; Smith & Bond, 1993; Triandis, 1995). In this chapter, we first provide a historical overview of the constructs, and then a review of disciplinary research conducted in the past few decades. We then discuss correlates of the constructs at the societal, organizational, and individual levels of analysis. Our review is necessarily selective, as theory and research in this area are extensive and warrant a volume unto themselves. For other excellent reviews of these constructs, see Erez and Early (1993); Earley and Gibson (1998); Hofstede (1980, 2001); Kagitcibasi (1997); Kim and colleagues (1994); Markus, Kitayama, and Heiman (1997); Oyserman, Coon, and Kemmelmeier (2002); Schwartz (1994); Smith and Schwartz (1997); and Triandis (1995). In the second part of the chapter, we describe the results of the GLOBE 62-nation study of individualism and collectivism. We provide rankings of nations on GLOBE's measures of individualism and collectivism, discuss relationships of GLOBE measures with other measures that exist in the literature, and describe several societal correlates of GLOBE's measures.

AUTHORS' NOTE: The first two authors thank their mentor, Harry Triandis, for introducing us to the constructs of individualism and collectivism and for his friendship, tutelage, and support throughout the years.

Lastly, we discuss the relationship of GLOBE's measures of individualism and collectivism with perceptions of effective leadership at multiple levels of analysis.

HISTORICAL OVERVIEW

Early Philosophers and Individualism and Collectivism

Although the constructs of individualism and collectivism received much empirical attention in the 20th century, they have been manifested in cultural institutions for thousands of years. In this section, we briefly review how the constructs were represented in legal and religious institutions in ancient civilizations.

Legal Institutions. In the ancient civilizations of the Middle East and the Mediterranean, a review of the evolution of laws illustrates the shifting emphases of individualism and collectivism throughout the ages. Specifically, as discussed below, attributes of cultures first changed from being highly individualistic to becoming collectivist, as individuals became members of tribes and, ultimately, nations. Further, as these nations became more complex the system of laws evolved, emphasizing the need for rational systems of justice and individual rights, both of which are attributes of modern-day individualism (Triandis, 1995).

The first stage in the evolution of law in the Middle East was based on the notion of personal revenge. However, as these ancient tribes grew into nations, the need to protect the rights and safety of the group soon took precedence over the preference of individuals to act on their own behalf. This was codified in the laws of Hammurabi, the king of Babylonia (1792–1750 BC), who is credited with establishing some of the world's first written laws, wherein collective concerns replaced preferences of individuals

Unlike laws that exist in most countries today, these laws did not protect the rights of the individual, but rather described universal codes of behavior and punishment. Among other changes, the codes replaced the more individualistic notion of equivalent retaliation with a system of monetary fines. More generally, the Code of Hammurabi identified the need for individuals to maintain positive relations with others or else they would have to face heavy sanctions (Durant, 1935). The recognition of individuals as being interdependent and as having duties and obligations to other group members are defining attributes of the cultural construct that we now call *collectivism*.

It is important to note that the Code of Hammurabi was not the only legal expression of the collectivist cultural construct in the ancient Middle East. Written codes of conduct that centered on creating group standards of behavior were also part of the law of the Hebrews, most notably in the book of the Law of Moses (Kagan, 1966). Unlike the Code of Hammurabi, the Ten Commandments were clerical laws. Nevertheless, their purpose was also to establish standards for individual behavior to protect the group, rather than to allow individual preferences to determine what is right and what is wrong (Durant, 1935).

As cultures later developed, the more individualistic notion of rational principles and individual rights became more prevalent within legal systems. In Athens, Greece, and in Rome the practice of presenting individual cases before other individuals or formally appointed judges was part of the procedural codes. In the Law of Cincius (204 BC), legal representation was viewed as the most effective way to present the facts of a particular case. Importantly, this system was seen as superior to interpretations of right and wrong based on codes of normative behavior alone, the latter of which was common in earlier centuries and was more akin to collectivism (Durant, 1939).

Religious Institutions. The constructs of individualism and collectivism were also manifested in religious institutions throughout the centuries. In the West, concerns with group identity and in-group and out-group distinctions, both attributes of collectivism, can be seen in religious philosophies and practices. The ancient Hebrews' religion was based on the strong ethnic identity of the Jews (Durant, 1935) and was predicated on the belief that the Jews were the "chosen ones" of God. Other religious groups also viewed their religions as a form of group identity as contrasted to other groups. For example, in the Koran of the Moslems it is stated—"Believers, take neither the Jews nor the Christians for your friends" (Dawood, 1956). Likewise, within the Christian tradition, for individuals to be saved, they had to embrace the Christian God as the only one true God, and thus the establishment of a group identity came with conversion.

Religions in the East were much more focused on duties and obligations within hierarchical structures, which is associated with some forms of modern-day collectivism. In India, and in ancient Japan, caste systems were also developed, and group identity was even further reinforced with a legal system that held entire families responsible for individual members' actions (Durant, 1935). Likewise, in China philosophies reinforced the importance of group identity, conformity, and long-term relationships. Individual talent and skill were not as important as being responsible to the whole (Griffith, 1963).

Perhaps the most famous Chinese philosopher who espoused aspects of modern-day collectivism was Confucius. Similar to other Chinese philosophers, Confucius emphasized the importance of conformity to one's environment. Confucius also stressed the importance of obligations that individuals have within their family, within the nation, and within the world at large. Specifically, individuals were required to respect their fathers and elder brothers to maintain family harmony. This prepared the individual to respect the structures of the state, which were needed to maintain national harmony. National harmony would, in turn, create a world in harmony and peace (Yutang, 1938). Throughout his writings, Confucius criticized peoples need to be individuals and emphasized the importance of subjugating personal wants and desires for the greater good of the group (Streep, 1995). This philosophy, although 4,000 years old, is still prevalent in much of Eastern Asia today.

In sum, notions of modern-day individualism and collectivism can be seen in ancient legal and religious institutions. Below, we turn to a discussion of how the constructs of individualism and collectivism have been central in the evolution of political theory in the past several centuries.

Political Philosophers of the 18th and 19th Century and Individualism and Collectivism

In the late 18th century, the nature of the relationship of the individual to the state was at the center of much philosophical thought and debate (See Gelfand, Triandis, & Chan, 1996). Conceptions of individualism were generally synonymous with liberalism and included the ideas of maximum freedom of the individual, voluntary groups that individuals could join or leave as they pleased, and equal participation of individuals in group activities (*Encyclopedia Britannica,* 1953, p. 256a). As a moral-political philosophy, liberalism places a great importance on the freedom of individuals to use reason to make personal choices, and to have rights that protect these freedoms (Kim, 1994). Across societies, the importance of the freedom of individuals was also reflected in the American Revolution (all humans are created equal, and pursuit of happiness is their fundamental right) and the French Revolution (liberty, equality, fraternity).

At the same time, other philosophers, such as Jean Jacques Rousseau, emphasized the importance of the collective over any particular individual. For instance, in his *Social Contract* Rousseau argued that the individual is free only by submitting to the general will. The general will was conceived as the common core of opinion that remains after private wills cancel each other out. Rousseau argued that the general will, which can be ascertained by majority voting, is "always right and tends to the public advantage" (*Encyclopedia Britannica,* 1953, p. 256a).

Within the 19th century, the meaning of the term *individualism* was also significantly elaborated on in political thought by the French intellectual Alexis de Toqueville, who observed that individualism permeated the new society of the United States (Bellah, Madsen, Sullivan, Swidler, & Tipton, 1985). De Tocqueville used the term individualism in connection with democracy in American society, and contrasted the competitive American social structure with the structures found in Europe.

Lastly, within the 20th century, political philosophers such as Dewey (1930), Dumont (1986), and later Kateb (1992) also discussed ideas related to individualism. For example,

Dewey (1930) distinguished what he referred to as "old" individualism (which included the liberation from legal and religious restrictions) from the "new" individualism (which focused on self-cultivation). Dumont (1986) argued that individualism was a consequence of Protestantism (i.e., humans do not have to go to church to communicate with God), political developments (emphasis on equality and liberty), and economic developments (e.g., affluence). In more recent years, philosophers have explored the possibility that there are positive attributes of both individualism and collectivism (Taylor, 1989).

In sum, the constructs of individualism and collectivism have been central in discussions of political philosophy in the past few centuries. Next, we turn to the empirical assessment of individualism and collectivism at the societal, organizational, and individual levels of analysis.

OVERVIEW OF EMPIRICAL RESEARCH ON INDIVIDUALISM AND COLLECTIVISM

Individualism and Collectivism at the Societal Level

Within the 20th century there was extensive discussion of the constructs of individualism and collectivism in sociology (Durkheim, 1933; Parsons, 1949; Riesman, Denny, & Glazer, 1950), anthropology (Kluckhohn, 1956; Mead, 1961; Redfield, 1956), and psychology (Chinese Culture Connection, 1987; Hofstede, 1980, 2001; Markus & Kitayama, 1991; Schwartz, 1994; Triandis, 1995). Across each of these disciplines, scholars have been concerned with the nature of the relationship between the individual and the group, which is broadly referred to as *individualism and collectivism*. This theme has also been referred to as self-emphasis and collectivity (Parsons, 1949), *Gesellschaft* and *Gemeinschaft* (Toennies, 1957), mechanical and organic solidarity (Durkheim, 1933), individualism and collaterality (Kluckhohn & Strodtbeck, 1961), and agency and community (Bakan, 1966). Although there are subtle differences in the meanings of these terms, they all relate

to a theme that contrasts the extent to which people are autonomous individuals or embedded in their groups (Hofstede, 1980; Markus & Kitayama, 1991; Schwartz, 1994; Triandis, 1989). Below, we review major empirical projects on individualism and collectivism.

Kluckhohn and Strodtbeck. Kluckhohn and Strodtbeck (1961) conducted one of the first ethnographic comparative studies on value orientations in five small communities with distinct cultures in the Southwestern United States of America. They proposed a five-part typology of universal human value orientations. Most pertinent to our discussion, they argued that social relationships might be *lineal* (people do what authorities say), *collateral* (people do what peers say), or *individualistic* (people do what they themselves think is right). Other dimensions discussed by Kluckhohn and Strodtbeck included the relationship between humans and nature, the nature of time, the nature of activities, and the nature of human beings.

Importantly, in their view, these five principles varied from culture to culture, but only in their pattern; that is, the principles consisted of component parts that were themselves universals. In support of their value theory, Kluckhohn and Strodtbeck provided an analysis of these value orientations in five communities in the United States, including a Texan homestead community, a Mormon village, a Spanish-American village, a decentralized Navaho Indian band, and a highly centralized pueblo of Zuni. As such, they were of the first to advance theory and analysis of the individualism and collectivism constructs in the social sciences.

Hofstede. Hofstede (1980) used data from a morale survey of IBM employees from 40 countries to uncover cultural dimensions. On the basis of a factor analysis of the sum of all of the responses in each culture, Hofstede (1980) named one of the factors *individualism versus collectivism,* which he defined as follows:

> Individualism pertains to societies in which the ties between individuals are loose; everyone is expected to look after himself or herself and his or her immediate family. Collectivism as its opposite pertains to societies in which people from birth

onwards are integrated into strong, cohesive in-groups, which throughout people's lifetime continue to protect them in exchange for unquestioning loyalty. (51)

This bipolar factor was derived from a post hoc analysis and consisted of six items that related to differences in preferences for work goals. The individualistic pole of the dimension was associated with preferences for sufficient time for personal or family life, considerable freedom on the job, and having challenging work. By contrast, the collectivist pole of the dimension was associated with preferences for training opportunities, having good physical work conditions, and being able to use skills on the job. Hofstede (2001) argued that the positive loading on Personal Time (.86), Freedom (.49), and Challenge (.46) "stress the actors' independence from the organization," whereas the negative loading on Use of Skills (−.63), Physical Conditions (−.69), and Training (−.82) "stress what the organization does for the individual" (p. 214). Thus, for Hofstede, the positive loading represented individualism and the negative loading reflected collectivism, a point to which we will return below. It is also important to note that his analysis reflects factor loadings *across* societies. Indeed, this scale did not have high internal consistency at the individual level of analysis.

Hofstede's results (1980) showed that the United States, Australia, England, and the Netherlands were the most individualistic cultures he studied, whereas most East Asian, African, and Latin American cultures were collectivist. In Hofstede's analysis, individualism was highly inversely correlated with power distance ($r = .67$; Hofstede, 1980, p. 221). In addition, Hofstede correlated scores on individualism with a host of other social indicators (some of which are discussed below), providing further post hoc convergent validity for this factor.

The importance of Hofstede's (1980) study for cross-cultural research cannot be underestimated, as it was the first large-scale empirical project to put these abstract constructs on the empirical map. As such, it provided a "conceptual roof" under which existing studies could fall, as compared to the atheoretical stance that had previously characterized the cross-cultural

literature in management. Further, it also provided a ranking of nations in many regions of the world on the constructs, which have since been used for descriptive and prescriptive purposes.

Nevertheless, numerous questions were raised regarding the reliability, validity, generalizability, and robustness of Hofstede's findings (Erez & Earley, 1993; Schwartz, 1994; Smith & Schwartz, 1997). Scholars have also questioned whether Hofstede's (1980) findings were generalizable and robust. First, questions were raised regarding the validity of the specific items that were derived post hoc in Hofstede's (1980) culture-level factor analysis. For example, it is not clear why concerns with training opportunities and good physical work conditions were core aspects of collectivism. In this respect, the collectivistic pole of this scale lacks face validity. For example, on the basis of the content of the items, the factor could well have been labeled "individual freedom versus individual development." Alternatively, the factors could be seen as similar to Herzberg and colleagues' (Herzberg, Mausner, & Snyderman, 1959) intrinsic (work-related) and extrinsic (nonwork-related) factors (see Hofstede, 2001). Second, questions regarding measurement also abounded: Would the same dimensions be found using a sample that was not from IBM? Are individualism and power distance conceptually and empirically distinct, especially given the fact that they are so highly negatively related (see Hofstede, 1980)? Do the measurements on which the dimensions were based have different meanings across cultures? Would the results be the same if the measures were used in non-Western contexts? And finally, would the results replicate across time and with different samples? Studies that have addressed these issues are discussed below.

Furthermore, questions regarding the appropriate levels of analysis for the constructs have been raised since the original publication. As later noted by Hofstede (1994, 2001) and others (Triandis, 2002), despite an explicit discussion of levels of analysis in his 1980 study, confusion about the constructs has abounded since his original work, as some authors have applied his bipolar dimensions to distinguish the personalities of individuals within societies. Indeed, to clarify this confusion, Hofstede (1994) later reiterated that his analysis was, in his words,

> sociological and not psychological. It does not compare different personalities, but different societal contexts within which children grow up and develop their personalities. It is not about individuals, but about the constraints within which, in different countries, a psychology of relatedness should be developed. (Hofstede, 1994, p. x)

As discussed in later sections below, the nature of the construct may vary at the individual level of analysis, and Hofstede (1997) and others have warned against confusing such issues in theory and research on individualism and collectivism, as well as other dimensions of cultures.

The Chinese Culture Connection. As discussed in Chapter 4 of this volume, to address the possibility that Hofstede's (1980) questionnaire items were biased by Western values and assumptions, Bond and members of the Chinese Culture Connection (1987) developed a Chinese Value Survey that was based on Eastern, rather than Western, values. Specifically, they used a research strategy that consisted of administering a questionnaire developed by Chinese scholars to samples of 50 male and 50 female university students in 23 national cultures. A culture-level analysis revealed four dimensions of values: Integration, Human-Heartedness, Moral Discipline, and Confucian Work Dynamism. Chinese Culture Connection (1987) correlated nation-level scores on these dimensions with scores from Hofstede's 1980 study. Not surprisingly, scores on moral discipline, which includes a focus on moderation, purity, and having few desires, was negatively correlated with Hofstede's individualism index ($r = -.54$).

Somewhat more surprisingly, the Individualism scores positively correlated with Power Distance ($r = .55$) in the Chinese Culture Connection results. Scores on Integration were also positively associated with Individualism ($r = .65$) and negatively correlated with Power Distance ($r = -.58$). At first, this seems counterintuitive, yet an examination of the poles of this dimension helps to elucidate why this pattern may have been found. Specifically, the pole of

the integration factor related to Individualism included tolerance and trustworthiness, whereas the pole related to Collectivism included filial piety, chastity in women, and patriotism. Nevertheless, some items loading on the positive pole of Integration (e.g., noncompetitiveness, contentedness with one's position in life, being conservative)—and thus correlated with Individualism—are hard to explain. Scores of another factor, namely Human Heartedness, were not correlated with Individualism, but were negatively related to Hofstede's masculinity index. Again, the pattern of this correlation is counterintuitive, as the pole of this dimension that was related to high masculinity (a focus on success striving and materialism) included items such as patience and kindness, which one would have expected to correlate with the feminine pole of Hofstede's dimension.

In sum, data from the Chinese Culture Connection provide mixed results regarding the generalizability of Hofstede's (1980) individualism to the Eastern value survey that was constructed. Although moral discipline was correlated with individualism in the expected direction, other findings do not provide evidence of convergent validity for the individualism construct. It is important to note, however, that the Chinese Culture Connection survey was composed of very different items and was conducted within only 23 countries around the world. For more information about the masculinity scale see Chapter 14 by Emrich, Denmark, and Den Hartog.

Triandis and Colleagues. Triandis and his colleagues also provided converging evidence for the existence of the individualistic–collectivistic (IC) constructs at the culture level and have greatly elaborated on the meaning of the constructs. First, to probe the meaning of the constructs further, Triandis and colleagues polled a sample of social scientists in many nations as to their understanding of individualism and collectivism (Hui & Triandis, 1986). They found general consensus and, based on their results, developed more items to further investigate the constructs. In a later series of studies, Triandis and colleagues (1986) examined the structure of these items at the culture level in nine countries. Their culture-level analysis revealed four factors, two of which were reflective of individualism (*Self-Reliance with Hedonism* and *Separation from In-Groups*) and two of which were reflective of collectivism (*Family Integrity* and *Interdependence with Sociability*). They found Hofstede's (1980) nation scores on individualism and collectivism were correlated only with scores on Family Integrity, which is to be expected as a manifestation of collectivism ($r = .78$). More recently, Triandis, McCusker, and colleagues (1993) used the Leung-Bond procedure and extracted multiple universal and culture-specific independent dimensions of individualism and collectivism across cultures. Thus, unlike previous analyses, Triandis and colleagues have found evidence of the multidimensionality of the constructs at the culture level while at the same time confirming the overlap of some of the dimensions with Hofstede's (1980) original work.

Consistent with this perspective, Triandis argued that there are a large number of collectivist and individualist patterns (Triandis, 1994, 1995) and that not all collectivist cultures are identical, nor are all individualist cultures identical. Within this complexity, however, he argued that there are at least four defining features of the constructs, and that cultures are probably similar on the main defining features of the constructs. The four defining features are

1. *Definition of the self:* In collectivist cultures, the self is generally viewed as interdependent with others, which is accompanied by the sharing of resources. In individualistic cultures, the self is generally viewed as autonomous and independent of groups, and decisions regarding whether or not to share resources are made individually (Markus & Kitayama, 1991; Reykowski, 1994).

2. *The structure of goals:* In collectivist cultures, goals tend to be compatible with in-group goals. In individualistic cultures, individual goals tend not to be correlated with in-group goals (Schwartz, 1992, 1994; Triandis, 1988, 1990; Wagner & Moch, 1986).

3. *Emphasis on duties and obligations versus personal preferences:* In collectivist cultures, the determinants of social behavior are primarily duties and obligations, whereas in individualist

cultures, they are primarily attitudes, values, beliefs, personal needs, perceived rights, and contracts (Bontempo & Rivero, 1992; Davidson, Jaccard, Triandis, Morales, & Diaz-Guerrero, 1976; Miller, 1994).

4. *Emphasis on relatedness versus rationality:* In collectivist cultures, people tend to emphasize unconditional relatedness within groups, whereas in individualistic cultures people tend to emphasize rationality. Relatedness refers to giving priority to relationships and taking into account the needs of others, even if such relationships are not advantageous. Rationality refers to the careful computation of the costs and benefits of relationships (Kim et al., 1994).[1]

Apart from similarity on these core attributes, Triandis suggested that individualistic and collectivist cultures also differ on additional *culture-specific* elements of the constructs. In this respect, he suggested that the constructs must be defined polythetically as is done in other sciences (Triandis, 1994). For instance, in zoology each phylum contains many combinations of attributes, but only a few attributes are characteristic of all of the species within that phylum. Thus, the defining feature of the category *birds* may be wings and feathers, whereas yellow beaks and carnivorous are attributes that differentiate among various species of birds. Accordingly, collectivism is specified by some common defining attributes, but collectivism in Japan, for example, would require several more culture-specific attributes, and collectivism in an Israeli kibbutz would require some other combination of culture-specific attributes. Thus, Triandis was one of the first researchers to argue that individualism and collectivism should not be seen in pure dichotomies, but rather require additional theoretical refinement to understand specific cultures. We will return to these differences later when discussing the influence of individualism and collectivism within organizational contexts.

Horizontal and Vertical Collectivism. Triandis (1994, 1995) proposed that the most important attributes that distinguish among different kinds of individualism and collectivism are the relative emphases on *horizontal* and *vertical* social relationships. Horizontal patterns assume that one self is more or less like every other self. By contrast, vertical patterns consist of hierarchies, and one self is rather different from other selves. The ways in which these relative emphases combine with individualism and collectivism produce four distinct patterns, namely horizontal individualism (HI), vertical individualism (VI), horizontal collectivism (HC), and vertical collectivism (VC; Triandis & Gelfand, 1998).

More specifically, he argued that in horizontal individualistic (HI) cultures, such as Sweden and Australia, people want to be unique and distinct from groups and are high in self-reliance, but they are not especially interested in becoming distinguished or in having high status. In vertical individualistic (VI) cultures, such as the United States and France, people often want to become distinguished and acquire status, and they do this in individual competitions with others. In horizontal collectivist (HC) cultures, such as the Israeli kibbutz and Eskimo cultures, people see themselves as similar to others and emphasize common goals with others, interdependence, and sociability, but they do not submit easily to authorities. In vertical collectivist cultures (VC), such as India and China, people emphasize the integrity of the in-group, are willing to sacrifice their personal goals for the sake of in-group goals, and support competitions between their in-groups and out-groups. If in-group authorities want them to act in ways that benefit the in-group but are extremely distasteful to them, they submit to the will of these authorities.[2] Although this theory has not yet been tested at the culture level, it has received support at the individual level (Chen, Meindl, & Hunt, 1997; Singelis, Triandis, Bhawuk, & Gelfand, 1995; Triandis & Bhawuk, 1997; Triandis, Chen, & Chan, 1998; Triandis & Gelfand, 1998).

In sum, Triandis and his colleagues have further refined the constructs of individualism and collectivism and have elaborated on the notion that cultures can be further differentiated within this broad dimension. In addition, Triandis and colleagues (Hui, 1988; Triandis, Bhawuk, Iwao, & Sinha, 1995; Triandis, Bontempo, Villareal, Asai, & Lucca, 1988) have done considerable theoretical and empirical work on individualism and collectivism as a personality attribute at the individual level (referred to as *idiocentrism* and *allocentrism,* respectively) that will be described at length in sections below.

Schwartz and Colleagues. In another landmark study, Schwartz and colleagues (Schwartz, 1992, 1994; Schwartz & Bilsky, 1990) examined the structure of values among more than 44,000 teachers and students in 54 countries. Participants in each of the countries were asked to respond to a 56-item value instrument. Notably, Schwartz and his colleagues developed an a priori theory regarding the dynamics of value differences across nations. Specifically, they argued, and confirmed, that cultural value dimensions would reflect core solutions that emerge as nations attempt to cope with societal problems. Such problems include the following:

1. *Relations between individual and groups:* The extent to which people are autonomous as opposed to being embedded in groups, reflecting an emphasis on *autonomy versus conservation.*

2. *Assuring responsible social behavior:* How to motivate people to consider others' welfare and coordinate with them, reflecting an emphasis on *hierarchy versus egalitarianism.*

3. *The role of humankind in the natural and social world:* Is it more important to submit, to fit, or to exploit the environment, reflecting an emphasis on *mastery versus harmony.*

The results of a multidimensional scaling study provided evidence of these cultural value dimensions, which were based on a circumplex of seven basic value types. Most pertinent to this discussion, the first dimension in the circumplex was closely related to individualism and collectivism. At one pole were cultural values that Schwartz (1994) labeled *conservatism,* which he defined as

those values likely to be important in societies based on close-knit harmonious relations, in which the interests of the person are not viewed as distinct from those of the group. All of these values emphasize maintenance of the status quo, propriety, and avoidance of actions or inclinations of individuals that might disturb the traditional order. These are sociocentric values, appropriate in settings where the self lacks autonomous significance but has meaning as part of the collectivity (Miller, 1984). Cultures that emphasize Conservatism values are primarily concerned with security, conformity, and tradition. (p. 101)

The other end of this dimension included values related to what Schwartz labeled *intellectual and affective autonomy,* which were defined as

those values likely to be important in societies that view the person as an autonomous entity entitled to pursue his or her individual interests and desires. Two related aspects of autonomy appear to be distinguishable: a more intellectual emphasis on self-direction and a more affective emphasis on stimulation and hedonism.(p. 102)

Schwartz (1994) also predicted and confirmed the relationship of these values to other values in the circumplex. For example, as predicted, autonomy values were correlated with egalitarian commitment and with mastery values, whereas conservation values were correlated with hierarchy values. As expected, autonomy and conservation were negatively correlated ($r = .89$). Further analysis revealed that nation-level scores on Schwartz's values were also related to Hofstede's 1980 nation-level scores. Specifically, Hofstede's individualism dimension was positively correlated with Schwartz's autonomy value type (intellectual and affective) and negatively correlated with the conservation value type. In addition, Hofstede's individualism dimension was also correlated with the egalitarian commitment value type, suggesting a close relationship between autonomy and egalitarianism.

Schwartz and colleagues' research is notable in several ways. First, it is based on a universal theory of human values. It not only predicts a priori the nature of value dimensions, such as autonomy (individualism) and conservation (collectivism), but also describes the dynamics among these values and other values in the circumplex. Second, the project has been generally replicated at both the culture and individual levels of analysis, a point to which we will return in the section on individual-level individualism and collectivism. Finally, Schwartz

used sound measurement techniques and was concerned with equivalence of measurement issues, a problem that has been associated with previous research (Hofstede, 1980) on individualism and collectivism.

Smith, Dugan, and Trompenaars. Lastly, one other large-scale societal level study on individualism and collectivism was conducted by Smith, Dugan, and Trompenaars (1996). This study is based on Trompenaars's (1985, 1993) value survey of more than 11,000 employees from 58 countries. His original value questionnaire was designed to capture five dimensions proposed by Parsons and Shils (1951), namely, universalism and particularism, achievement and ascription, individualism and collectivism, affectivity and neutrality, and specificity and diffuseness. He also measured two other dimensions: a personality variable, internal and external locus of control (Rotter, 1966); and different orientations to time (Hall, 1959). Items used in the questionnaire presented scenarios and asked respondents how they would act in a given situation.

Smith and colleagues (1996) analyzed this database and found that the modal values of employees varied substantially across cultures. Using multidimensional scaling, they found two interpretable dimensions, conservatism versus egalitarian commitment (label adopted from Schwartz discussed above) and utilitarian involvement versus loyal involvement. These dimensions were significantly related to Hofstede's (1980) individualism and power distance dimensions. For example, collectivism was associated with a preference for closer work relations and higher involvement with one's company. Collectivism was also associated with particularism and a preference for ascription over achievement. Further they found that individualism was associated with modernity, which was measured by per capita gross national product, literacy rate, and life expectancy.

Summary

There has been a long tradition of research on individualism and collectivism at the societal level. Although different scholars have used different methods, samples, and sometimes different terminology, there is a general similarity in the nature of the constructs at the societal level. Disagreement exists on the degree to which the constructs are *broad* versus *specific,* which often results in differences in expectations regarding whether the constructs are *multidimensional* (Triandis, 1995) or *unidimensional* (Hofstede, 1980; Schwartz, 1994) at the societal level of analysis. In addition, disagreement exists regarding how closely individualism and collectivism are related to issues of power and hierarchy, with Schwartz and Hofstede arguing they are highly related, and Triandis and colleagues arguing that measures of such constructs may be orthogonal. At the same time, the literature has several omissions, which are the focus of the GLOBE study. First, most scholars have focused on individualism and collectivism as *value* dimensions and, as will be discussed in later sections, Project GLOBE adds to this tradition by examining both *values* and *practices* at the societal level. Second, much of the research on individualism and collectivism at the societal level has used items framed at the individual level of analysis. However, from a levels-of-analysis perspective this is problematic, as discussed by Hanges and Dickson in Chapter 8 of this volume. GLOBE adds to the literature by developing items that explicitly refer to the particular levels of analysis. Finally, GLOBE adds to this endeavor by taking a multilevel approach to individualism and collectivism. In this spirit, we next turn to the nature of the constructs at the organizational level of analysis.

Individualism and Collectivism at the Organizational Level

Organizational culture has been a central research issue in the organizational sciences over the past few decades. At this level of analysis, culture is construed as organizational members' shared beliefs and assumptions (Aycan et al., 2000; Schein, 1992). Although there has not been much empirical research on individualism and collectivism at the organizational level of analysis, theoretically speaking, we may draw on Triandis's (1995) four societal defining attributes to help illuminate the ways in which individualistic and collectivist organizational cultures are different.

In general, organizations that have individualistic cultures would have members who consider themselves as largely independent of the organization. Employees would also assume that they are hired because of their unique skills and abilities, rather than because of their relationships or social background. In such cultures, members would expect the organization to offer them something they need, and would be willing to leave the organization if their needs or goals were better served elsewhere. More generally, personal attitudes would be important determinants of organizational behaviors in individualistic organizational cultures. Furthermore, managers would assume that they need to compensate employees in a manner that is rationally consistent with their capabilities and performance, and would believe that individuals' hard work and successful performance is instrumental for attaining rewards. As an example, in the organizations within the United States the need for rational exchanges between an organization and its members begins with the process of recruitment and selection and continues until employees are terminated. Throughout all of these activities, an underlying notion of fairness, which is based on the notion of equity, must prevail. Indeed, in the United States, organizations are accountable to external regulatory agencies, such as federal and state governments, that define the rational procedures that ensure fairness in organizations.

By contrast, organizations that have collectivist cultures would have members who view themselves as highly interdependent with the organization. Generally speaking, the sharing of employees' identity with the organization would be so strong that the organization would become a part of members' self-identity. Employees would assume that their relationships and duties and obligations, not merely their unique attributes, are central in employment decisions. Further, managers would assume that employees are willing to make personal sacrifices in their goals and desires in order to fulfill obligations toward others in the organization. In return for their personal sacrifices, employees would expect the organization would stand by their side even in hard economic times. Employees would also expect to be compensated in a manner that provides the greatest benefit to all members in the group, rather than on a purely individual basis. In addition, employees would be less focused on their own attitudes toward the job and more focused on their duties and obligations to the organization. Thus, employees would view the nature of their relationship with the organization as one that is less a matter of rational exchanges and more a matter of long-term relational exchanges.

Some support for these tenets can be found in research at the organizational level of analysis. In a large-scale study of organizations in Denmark and the Netherlands, Hofstede, Neuijen, Ohayv, and Sanders (1991) found two dimensions that differentiated organizations that are relevant to the current discussion. The first dimension was the degree to which organizations are *parochial* versus *professional*. In parochial organizations, employees strongly identify with their organization and believe that organizational norms apply to their behavior at home as well as on the job. They also believe that their social background is an important determinant of hiring practices. By contrast, employees in professional organizations identify primarily with their job and consider their home-life to be private. In these organizational cultures, employees believe that job competence, not social background, is an important determinant of hiring practices.[3] The other relevant dimension was labeled *employee oriented* versus *job oriented*. In employee-oriented organizations, organizations take responsibility for employee welfare, important decisions are made by groups, and people feel their personal problems are to be solved by the organization. By contrast, in job-oriented organizations people perceive that the organization is interested only in the work they perform and not in their personal or family welfare. In such organizations, employees report that decisions tend to be made by individuals, rather than groups. Although neither of these dimensions were labeled as collectivist versus individualistic, they clearly have overlap with components of the constructs.

In a more recent study, Chatman, Polzer, Barsade, and Neale (1998) explicitly argued that

organizational cultures can be differentiated on the degree to which they are collectivist versus individualistic. They defined collectivist organizational cultures as those that emphasize *shared objectives, interchangeable interests,* and *commonalties* among members. By contrast, individualistic organizational cultures are those that emphasize individuals' *unique attributes* and *emphasize differences* among employees. Chatman and colleagues argued that organizational membership is a very salient category for members of collectivist organizational cultures, as compared to individualistic organizational cultures.

Importantly, although organizational individualism and collectivism is distinct from societal individualism and collectivism, the two levels are expected to be interrelated. According to the model of culture-fit (Kanungo & Jaeger, 1990), societal-level culture affects organizational work culture by shaping shared managerial assumptions about the nature of employees and how the organization needs to be structured for such employees. In addition, Kanungo, Aycan, and Sinha (1999) also argue that managerial assumptions about the nature of the task are also influenced by institutional characteristics, such as ownership status (public vs. private), industry (service vs. manufacturing), and resource availability (human and technological resources). Thus, according to Kanungo and his colleagues, internal organizational culture is shaped by the larger societal context in which it is embedded.

In some indirect support of some of these tenets, Aycan and colleagues (2000) found that across numerous countries, managers who perceived the sociocultural context to be high on collectivism (i.e., high on loyalty toward their community) were likely to assume that employees within their organizations had high obligations toward others. This included the notion that individuals should act in accordance with group needs and should compromise their own wishes for the benefit of helping the group (see also Aycan, Kanungo, & Sinha, 1999).

Along the same lines, Kim (1994) argued that in many Asian cultures organizations are erected in ways to sustain societal values and norms. As compared to individualistic cultures, which construct institutions to reflect the importance of individual rights, collectivist cultures construct institutions as extensions of the family to reflect the importance of the fulfillment of obligations (Kim, 1994). Similarly, Kashima and Callan (1994) argued that in Japan, managers explicitly design organizations through the use of metaphors that are familiar in the larger cultural context (i.e., the Japanese *ie,* or "household"). In this way, organizations consciously create collectivist organizational practices to be consonant with prevailing sociocultural contexts. In Japan, historically this has included the development of long-term relationships with employees from recruitment to retirement. It has also included family-like practices such as morning exercises, singing of company songs on special occasions, and assistance in helping employees find spouses. Within such organizations, employees make sacrifices for the company by putting in service hours or unclaimed overtime hours (Kashima & Callan, 1994).

Although there is not as much research on individualism and collectivism at the organizational level, there is increasing evidence that the constructs operate at this level of analysis and that they are influenced by the larger sociocultural context. Research by GLOBE, discussed in later sections, adds to this endeavor in several ways. First, GLOBE explicitly developed measures to assess individualism and collectivism at the organizational level of analysis and used organizational referents in its scales. Second, GLOBE explicitly examined the relationship between societal and organizational individualism and collectivism, furthering a multilevel perspective on the constructs.

Individualism and Collectivism at the Individual Level

In addition to examining individualism and collectivism and related constructs at the societal and organizational levels, many scholars have examined such distinctions at the individual level. In contrast to dimensions that differentiate nations or cultures, research at the individual level of analysis capitalizes on intracultural variability and examines dimensions that are derived from individual differences. As Triandis (1995) and Smith and Schwartz (1997) note, these levels of analysis are statistically independent

and, as such, the nature of the dimensions can vary at different levels of analysis.

Triandis and his colleagues were among the first to investigate the constructs at the individual level of analysis. To clearly differentiate their discussions from societal-level individualism and collectivism they adapted different terminology at this level, namely *idiocentrism* and *allocentrism,* respectively (Triandis, Leung, Villareal, & Clack, 1985). This terminology allows for the fact that there can be idiocentrics within collectivist cultures and allocentrics within individualistic cultures. Since this study was conducted, research at this level has demonstrated that in the United States, idiocentrism and allocentrism are orthogonal at the individual level (Gelfand et al., 1996), and individuals have access to both idiocentric elements and allocentric elements (Trafimow, Triandis, & Goto, 1991).[4]

Several scholars have found evidence for such individual differences within numerous nations. Hui (1988) devised the individualism and collectivism scale (INDCOL) and used it to reliably assess an individual's level of individualism and collectivism in the Hong Kong Chinese context. Later studies at the individual level illustrated that there are similar factor structures of individualism and collectivism within the United States, Japan, and Puerto Rico (Triandis et al., 1988). Likewise, Schwartz and Bilsky (1990) found that dimensions of values at the individual level were similar across many nations. Similar to the culture level, they found that values at the individual level are organized according to *openness to change versus conservation* dimension. This dimension was found in more than 90% of their 97 samples (Smith & Schwartz, 1997). Providing further converging evidence of the constructs at the individual level, Oishi, Schimmack, Diener, and Suh (1998) recently found correlations between Triandis's scales of idiocentrism and allocentrism and Schwartz's value measures. For example, vertical allocentrism was positively correlated with tradition and conformity values, vertical idiocentrism was positively correlated with power and achievement, horizontal allocentrism was positively correlated with benevolence, and horizontal idiocentrism was positively correlated with achievement and self-direction.

In more recent years, there has been an explosion of measures that have been developed to assess individualism and collectivism at the individual level (e.g., Bierbrauer, Meyer, & Wolfradt, 1994; Oyserman, 1993; Singelis, 1994; Wagner & Moch, 1986; Yamaguchi, 1994). Because of this proliferation of measures, there is some confusion at this level of analysis, as scholars develop measures that assess different aspects of the construct, using different methodologies, and often do not make reference to other measurements in the literature. On the other hand, such a varied approach to measurement at this level of analysis is perhaps not surprising. As Triandis (1995) has warned, the constructs are highly broad, multidimensional, and can take on different culture-specific (or emic) attributes in different cultural contexts. Nevertheless, in the future it would be useful to conduct construct validation studies that include numerous measures cited in the literature.

Despite this confusion, research does illustrate numerous demographic and social correlates of individualism and collectivism within cultures. Comparing across urban and rural locales within Estonia, Realo, Allik, and Vadi (1997) found that collectivism is higher in rural locations and individualism is higher in urban locations, a finding that has also been replicated in Sri Lanka (Freeman, 1997). With respect to race, in the United States, as compared to European Americans, persons of color have scored higher on collectivism (defined as an orientation toward the welfare of one's larger community) and familism (defined as an orientation toward the welfare of one's immediate family; Gaines et al., 1997; but see Oyserman et al., 2002, for a contrasting analysis). With respect to gender, Kashima et al. (1995) found no difference between men and women in Korea, Japan, Australia, mainland United States, and Hawaii on individualism (i.e., independence and agency) and collectivism (i.e., concern for welfare of collectives). Gender differences were found, however, for a separate construct: Emotional relatedness. More recent research also suggests that, at least within the United States, men may be more likely than women to define the self in terms of collectivities (Gabriel & Gardner, 1999).

In addition, Smith and Schwartz (1997) review data that illustrate numerous social background differences that are associated with individualism and collectivism, including age, education, and socioeconomic status. Specifically, younger and more educated individuals tend to be more individualistic than older and less educated individuals across numerous nations (Smith & Schwartz, 1997). With respect to social class, research on individualism and collectivism within cultures has generally been consistent with Hofstede's original findings at the societal level (discussed above): High socioeconomic classes tend to be more individualistic, whereas lower socioeconomic classes tend to be more collectivist (Marshall, 1997; Triandis, 1994). Interestingly, Marshall found that social class accounted for more variance in individualism and collectivism than country of origin in a comparison of Indonesia and New Zealand. Finally, Huismans and Schwartz (1992) examined the relationship between values and overall religiousness, and found that some components of Schwartz's dimension of *conservation* (i.e., tradition) are correlated with overall religiosity and, further, that this correlation was even stronger among Israeli Jews.

OVERALL SUMMARY

The constructs of individualism and collectivism have received attention at numerous levels of analysis. Not surprisingly, as with other areas within psychology and organizational behavior, there is often confusion regarding levels of analysis (see also Klein, Dansereau, & Hall, 1994). First, there is the question of whether the dimensions are similar at different levels of analysis. As stated previously, because such analyses are statistically independent, they are not necessarily similar. At the same time, it is also likely that there is conceptual similarity across levels of analysis for the constructs of individualism and collectivism (Schwartz, 1994). Second, there is the question of when it is appropriate to use a culture level of analysis versus an organizational or individual level of analysis in cross-cultural research. Schwartz argues cogently that this depends on the type of question asked:

If it is about relations of individual differences in value priorities to variation on other individual attributes, individual level value dimensions should be used, even when individuals from different cultural groups are studied. If the question is about relations of cultural differences in prevailing values to variation across cultures on other variables, culture-level dimensions should be used, even if these other variables are frequencies of individual behavior. (Smith & Schwartz, 1997)

Third, there is the question of the dimensionality of the constructs. Although research is inconclusive, several studies indicate that individualism and collectivism are multidimensional constructs at the societal, organizational, and individual levels. Taking all of these complexities into account, it is not surprising that the literature can be confusing and conflicting with respect to research findings (Earley & Gibson, 1998).

Before discussing the results of the GLOBE multilevel study of culture, we first discuss implications of individualism and collectivism for societies, organizations, and leadership.

CORRELATES OF INDIVIDUALISM AND COLLECTIVISM AT THE SOCIETAL LEVEL OF ANALYSIS

In this section, we review correlates of individualism and collectivism at the societal level of analysis. We discuss the relationship of the constructs to ecological factors, distribution of wealth, health, pace of life, family systems, language and communication, and social interaction patterns. We explicitly label this section "correlates" as it is often difficult to discern whether other variables are antecedents or consequences of societal individualism and collectivism.

Ecology

Numerous cross-cultural scholars have posited that cultural syndromes, such as individualism and collectivism, develop as adaptations to the ecological context (Berry, 1976; Berry, Poortinga, Segall, & Dasen, 1992; Berry, Trimble, & Olmedo, 1986). In a classic study, Barry, Child, and Bacon (1959) illustrated that in hunting and gathering ecologies, wherein self-reliance and freedom are crucial for survival, there is more emphasis on individualism. By contrast, in agricultural ecologies, wherein conformity and obedience are crucial for survival, there is more emphasis on collectivism. Triandis (1989) further argued that as societies move toward industrialization, there is a consequent shift back toward an emphasis on individualism. In this respect, the particular ecologies in which societies are situated create differential adaptations in the form of individualism and collectivism (Berry, 1994).

Distribution of Wealth

Hofstede (1980) found a positive correlation between individualism and wealth, with industrialized wealthy countries scoring higher on individualism than developing countries. Although this relationship has generally been unquestioned, the causality between the two constructs is still debated. In other words, does individualism lead to wealth or does wealth lead to individualism? In a later paper, Hofstede (1997) addressed this issue of causality and argued that an increase in national wealth causes an increase in individualism in a culture, and not vice versa. In this view, individualism is thought to increase as the discretionary capital that is available to people increases. That is, as people become more affluent, they have more freedom to "do their own thing" and, therefore, "financial independence leads to social independence" (Triandis, 1994, p. 165).

At the same time, others have questioned the positive relationship between individualism and wealth altogether. In a recent analysis, Bhawuk, Bechtold, and Munusami (2003) took a historical view of national wealth figures, and concluded that collectivism had been associated with wealth in the past. Using statistics presented by Kennedy (1987), they illustrate that India and China, as well as other countries considered to be part of the Third World today, had higher levels of manufacturing output than European countries during the 18th century. Implicit in this analysis is the idea that in the 18th century collectivism, and not individualism, was positively correlated with national wealth. As a result, Bhawuk and Bechtold (in preparation) conclude that claiming that collectivism is not suited for economic development is rather myopic and misleading.

Consistent with this analysis, if one examines economic indicators besides gross national product (GNP), it appears that collectivism, not individualism, is more predictive of wealth. For example, data from the Chinese Culture Connection (1987) illustrate that across 22 Asian nations Confucian Dynamism scores are highly correlated with average gross national growth ($r = .70, p < .001$). Likewise, Schwartz (1994) reported that larger household sizes, which were also correlated with scores on his conservation value dimension, also predicted national wealth.

Lastly, adding further complexity to this picture, Schwartz (1994) has argued that the association between individualism and wealth has changed over time since Hofstede's (1980) original analysis. Specifically, Schwartz (1994) illustrated that the associations of GNP with his more recent nation-level scores on conservation versus autonomy dimension is considerably weakened, accounting for half as much variance in his 1990 data, as compared with Hofstede's 1970s data. Although methodological and conceptual differences in the assessment of individualism are an obvious culprit, it is also possible that there has been a historical weakening of this association (Schwartz, 1994).

Collectively, these findings put into question the assertion that individualism is a necessary requirement for the acquisition of national wealth, and further reinforces the assertion that there is no simple relationship between individualism and collectivism and economic health. We will return to this point when examining Project GLOBE results in later sections.

Pace of Life

Pace of life refers to the speed, rate, and relative rapidity of activities within and across cultures (Levine & Norenzayan, 1999). In a more recent study, Levine and Norenzayan (1999) argued that individualistic cultures have a faster pace of life than collectivist cultures. This is based on the notion that individualistic cultures focus on achievement, which requires a greater concern with time. By contrast, collectivist cultures focus on the well-being of the collective, which requires less of an emphasis on time. In support of this, they found that societal collectivism was negatively associated with walking speed, the speed of postal requests, and with the accuracy of clocks across 31 countries. However, these relationships were nonsignificant after the effects of economic well-being (i.e., gross domestic product) were controlled, illustrating that economic factors play an important role in pace of life.

Health

Another indication of the well-being of nations relates to the health of its citizens. Research has illustrated that whether a culture is individualistic or collectivist has some health related correlates. Triandis et al. (1988) found that heart-attack rates were lower in collectivist cultures than individualistic cultures. Specifically, heart-attack rates were the lowest in Japan (1.8 per 1,000) and among the Trappist monks (1 per 1,000), whereas they were the highest among U.S. European American populations (9.8 per 1,000). The Japanese in Hawaii had a heart-attack rate of 3.8 per 1,000, which further supported the idea that as people acculturate and become more individualistic they are likely to have more heart attacks (Marmot & Syme, 1976).

Some research has focused on the relationship between individualism and collectivism and subjective well-being. At the societal level of analysis, Diener, Diener, and Diener (1995) found that individualism is positively correlated with this indicator of health, even after other variables (i.e., income) are controlled. Yet at the individual level of analysis, a different picture has emerged. Sinha and Verma (1994) found a positive association between allocentrism and psychological well-being, which was also moderated by social support. Under high social-support conditions, allocentrism was correlated with psychological well-being as well as with cheerfulness, optimism, playfulness, and a lack of frustration, but under no-social-support conditions the variables were not correlated.

On related points, because social support is higher in collectivist cultures, levels of alienation are expected to be higher in individualistic cultures (Sinha, 1988). In particular, Triandis and colleagues have argued that collectivist cultures tend to provide stronger social support through their extended family structure, and the family is the primary support group for all purposes. By contrast, in individualist cultures people have to develop their own support groups, and such support groups may be more temporary, causing greater alienation (Triandis, 1995; Triandis et al., 1990). This was supported in a study in India conducted by Sinha (1988) that found that the level of alienation increased as people migrated from rural to urban centers and left their social support groups behind in the village.

Family Systems

From an ecocultural perspective, adaptations to differential ecological environments result in differential emphases within families in individualistic and collectivist cultures. Not surprisingly, individualism is often associated with nuclear family structures, whereas collectivism is associated with extended family structures (Triandis, 1989). In support of this, in a 16-culture study, Georgas and colleagues (2001) found that members of individualistic cultures lived farther away from grandparents, aunts, uncles, and cousins; visited cousins less frequently; and telephoned aunts, uncles, and cousins less frequently than members of collectivist cultures.

Research has also shown that individualism and collectivism are related to marital processes. In a study of college students across 11 cultures, Levine, Sato, Hashimoto, and Verma (1995) found that love was assigned much more importance in marriage decisions in individualistic cultures, as compared to collectivist cultures. Evidence also shows that individualism and collectivism are related to societal divorce rates. In a study across 26 nations, Lester (1996) found that individualism scores, as reported by Hofstede (1980), were significantly related to divorce rates ($r = .40$), even after controlling for GNP per capita. Likewise, within particular groups such as Jewish Americans, allocentric orientation has been related to lower divorce rates (Brodbar-Nemzer, 1986).

Language and Communication

Research has illustrated that members of individualistic cultures tend to be direct and forthright in their communication, whereas members of collectivist cultures tend to be more indirect in their communication (Holtgraves, 1997). This results from the desire in collectivist cultures to save face and the need to attend to contextual factors, versus the desire in individualistic cultures to express inner opinions and views. Furthermore, in a number of studies, Gudykunst and his colleagues have found that people in collectivist cultures have greater self-disclosure, more perceived similarity, more shared networks, and greater confidence in members of the in-group than in members of the out-group, as compared to people in individualistic cultures (Gudykunst et al., 1992; Gudykunst, Gao, & Franklyn-Stokes, 1992). In addition, these authors have generally found that members of individualistic cultures have a greater ability to modify their self-presentations, and they are also more sensitive to others' expressive behaviors. By contrast, in collectivist cultures, people pay more attention to the status of the person with whom they are interacting (for other research on culture and language, see Kashima & Kashima, 1998, 1999).

Social Interactions Patterns

Research has shown that patterns of social interaction vary in individualistic and collectivist cultures. Generally speaking, individuals are more likely to engage in activities alone in individualistic cultures, whereas individuals are more likely to engage in group activities in collectivist cultures (Brandt, 1974; Choi, 1996). Brandt, for example, found that individuals in the United States tended to ski alone, whereas individuals in Korea tended to ski in groups (Triandis, 1994). This is also consistent with Wheeler, Reis, and Bond (1989), who found that Chinese had fewer social interactions than Americans, yet these interactions were longer, were more intimate, and were more likely to be in groups. It is also consistent with Putnam's (2000) book *Bowling Alone,* which describes the steady decline of civic activity within the United States. Along similar lines, at the individual level of analysis, Kashima et al. (1995) found that allocentrism is related to the degree to which friendship groups are cohesive across a number of countries. Lastly, research has also shown support for the notion that in-group and out-group distinctions are greater in social interactions in collectivist cultures. For example, Triandis et al. (1990) found that, compared to Americans, Chinese show a greater tendency to fight with or to avoid members of out-groups, and a greater tendency to give them orders to do something and to criticize them.

Summary

Societal level individualism and collectivism is related to a host of other societal phenomena, including ecology, economic activity, pace of life, health, family systems, language and communication, and social interaction patterns. A summary of the implications of individualism and collectivism for societies can be found in Table 16.1.

IMPLICATIONS OF INDIVIDUALISM AND COLLECTIVISM FOR ORGANIZATIONS

The above discussion focused on the linkage between societal-level individualism and collectivism on societal-level phenomenon. In this section, we turn our attention to the dynamics within organizations that are collectivist and individualistic in orientation. Although we focus on a different level of analysis in this section, it is important to recognize that societal-level individualism and collectivism are reflected in how managers form assumptions about their internal work culture (Kanungo & Jaeger, 1990) as discussed previously. Because organizational cultures are created by managers to reflect societal emphases on individualism and collectivism, the research cited in this section primarily focuses on cross-cultural (rather than within-culture) comparisons of the dynamics in work organizations.

Human Resource Management Practices

Human resource management (HRM) practices vary in individualistic and collectivist cultures, with an emphasis on independence and rationality in the former, and an emphasis on interdependence and obligations in the latter. Such emphases are manifested in selection, performance appraisal, job-design, and termination processes in organizations (Erez & Earley, 1993).

More specifically, HRM practices in organizations in individualistic cultures generally reflect shared assumptions of the need for systems that promote rational exchanges between members and the organization. First, selection is based on a rational calculation of the degree to which the applicant has knowledge, skills, and abilities that fit with the needs of the organization, as identified through job analyses. Indeed, the area of personnel selection testing, which has developed primarily in the United States, is based on rational decision-making models that are used to predict the performance of prospective applicants (Muchinsky, 2000). Once individuals have joined an organization, the ideal situation would be to have jobs designed such that individuals have autonomy and variety in order to ensure that individuals can experience meaningfulness and responsibility (Erez, 1994). Further, compensation in individualistic cultures is generally based on an equity model in which individuals are rewarded in direct relationship to their contribution to the success of the task (Erez, 1994). Likewise, promotions are based more on merit than on other factors such as seniority, tenure, age, and personal connections (Redding, Norman, & Schlander, 1994). Not surprisingly, employees in such cultures are more motivated by reward contingent on performance.

Dorfman and colleagues (1997), for example, found that in the United States contingent rewards were positively related to subordinates' performance and attitudes. Lastly, the decision to withdraw from an organization is often based on cost–benefit calculations regarding one's satisfaction on the job, the expected utility of a job search, and the costs of quitting (Mobley, 1977). If the organization decides to terminate an employee, the decision must be based on a

Table 16.1   Higher Individualism–Collectivism Societies Versus Lower Individualism–Collectivism Societies

Features of Cultures That Score High on Collectivism	Features of Cultures That Score High on Individualism
• Individuals are integrated into strong cohesive groups	• Individuals look after themselves or their immediate families
• The self is viewed as interdependent with groups	• The self is viewed as autonomous and independent of groups
• Group goals take precedence over individual goals	• Individual goals take precedence over group goals
• Duties and obligations are important determinants of social behavior	• Attitudes and personal needs are important determinants of behavior
• People emphasize relatedness with groups	• People emphasize rationality
• Ecologies are agricultural, and countries are often developing	• Ecologies are hunting and gathering, or industrial and wealthy
• There is a slower pace of life	• There is a faster pace of life
• There are lower heart-attack rates	• There are higher heart-attack rates
• There is lower subjective well-being	• There is higher subjective well-being
• There are more extended family structures	• There are more nuclear family structures
• Love is assigned less weight in marriage decisions	• Love is assigned greater weight in marriage decisions
• There are lower divorce rates	• There are higher divorce rates
• Communication is indirect	• Communication is direct
• Individuals are likely to engage in group activities	• Individuals are likely to engage in activities alone
• Individuals have fewer social interactions, but interactions tend to be longer and more intimate	• Individuals have more social interactions, but interactions tend to be shorter and less intimate
• Individuals make greater distinctions between in-groups and out-groups	• Individuals make fewer distinctions between in-groups and out-groups

NOTE: Although this table presents two extremes, it is important to recognize that these constructs represent a continuum and that, furthermore, there is also within-culture variation.

rational determination and must be supplemented with evidence that illustrates that the termination is based on specific job performance issues (Bhawuk, Bechtold, & Jones, 1998).

By contrast, human resource management practices in organizations that have a collectivist orientation are less likely to focus on rational exchanges between members and the organization. Rather, long-term relational commitments are generally established, and these relational commitments serve as guides for

behavior. Selection in such organizations can be significantly influenced by the relations that applicants have with other members within the organization or with institutions with whom the organization has contact. For example, Triandis and Vassiliou (1972) found that employers in Greece gave more weight to recommendations of friends and relatives when making hiring decisions, as compared with employers in the United States. As such, hiring the "most qualified" person in collectivist cultures can involve hiring a person with the best contacts and relationships with the organization. Furthermore, because individual differences are not as important as a determinant for selection, it is likely that training takes on much more importance in collectivist cultures (Triandis, 2002; see also Kashima & Callan, 1994). Unlike in individualistic cultures, jobs are likely to be designed around cohesive work groups so as to maximize the social and the technical aspects of the job (Erez, 1994). Such design systems would focus on team autonomy, team responsibility, and would try to maximize team-experienced meaningfulness (Erez, 1994).

In terms of compensation, considerations of what is equitable for the group, as well as seniority and personal needs are also important (Erez, 1994). Consistent with these notions, Podsakoff, Dorfman, Howell, and Todor (1986) found that contingent reward was not related to employee performance in the Mexican cultural context. Similarly, Aycan and colleagues (1999) found that Indian managers reported having less autonomy in their jobs and lower contingent reward for their performance (a rational strategy) than Canadian managers. Lastly, decisions to leave an organization would be heavily influenced by the opinions of one's in-group, in addition to market considerations (Wasti, 2000). Forced terminations are rare and are considered a last resort in these organizations. In this respect, it is likely that poor performance is more frequently tolerated and that it is the quality of the relationship between the individual and the organization that would have any effect on downsizing decisions (Bhawuk, Bechtold, & Jones, 1998).

Although this discussion has been focused on cross-cultural differences, there is also support for these notions at the individual level. Ramamoorthy and Carroll (1998) found that levels of individualist and collectivist orientations of job seekers within the United States predicted their reactions toward alternative human resource management practices. Specifically, they found that job seekers who were higher on collectivism measures were less likely to prefer the use of selection tests for hiring, less likely to prefer formal appraisal practices, and less likely to prefer rewards and promotions based on individual merit compared with job seekers

who were low on collectivism. In addition, job seekers who scored high on collectivism were more likely to prefer long-term job security than individuals who scored low on collectivism. As such, the relationship between individualism and collectivism and HRM has been found at multiple levels of analysis.

Employee Motivation

The nature of motivation varies in individualistic and collectivist cultures. Most theories on motivation developed within the United States, an individualistic culture, focus on individual strivings based on personal needs (McClelland, 1967), rational calculations of possible outcomes (Vroom, 1964), and experienced psychological states (Hackman & Oldham, 1976). These perspectives highlight the importance of individuals' interests and needs for understanding goal-directed behavior. By contrast, in collectivist cultures the need to fulfill duties and obligations and to contribute to the group are central components of motivation (Kashima & Callan, 1994; Markus & Kitayama, 1991; Yu & Yang, 1994). These perspectives highlight the importance of the social context for understanding goal-directed behavior. For example, Yu and Yang (1994) argued that Chinese achievement motivation is fundamentally socially oriented, with the success of the group being a primary motivator. In an Islamic context, Abu-Saad (1998) contrasted the notion of the Protestant Work Ethic (PWE) with the Islamic Work Ethic (IWE). He found that whereas PWE includes an orientation toward personal success, the IWE also measures the importance of organizational obligations and cooperation among Islamic managers. Likewise, in the Japanese cultural context, Kashima and Callan (1994) argued that motivation in organizations is regulated through an *amae-on-gimu* exchange between supervisors and subordinates. Within this system, subordinates seek to be accepted by and dependent upon their superiors, which is referred to as *amae* (Doi, 1973). *Amae* generally refers to the love and unconditional dependence that exists between a parent and child. Within organizations, when superiors fulfill *amae,* this produces obligations (*gimu*) among subordinates to repay such favors through hard work and high performance. Thus, motivation is highly relational in the Japanese context. Not surprisingly, Matsui, Kakuyama, and Onglatco (1987) found that Japanese performed much better if they set group goals than if they set individual goals. In related research, Earley (1994) also demonstrated that Chinese managers had higher motivation if being trained in groups as opposed to being trained individually, whereas the reverse was the case for United States managers.

Another important difference between motivation in collectivist and individualistic cultures is the importance of individual choice. Much theory and research in the United States, an individualistic culture, has focused on the importance of intrinsic motivation and the importance of personal choice and control. Specifically, in his classic theory of motivation, Deci (1971, 1972) argued that having others make choices for oneself, or performing a task for external reasons, would ultimately reduce motivation. More recent evidence, however, illustrates that these notions are less applicable to people of collectivist backgrounds. Iyengar and Lepper (1999) found that European American children were much more motivated if given the chance to choose the task they were performing, whereas Asian American children were much more motivated if the task was chosen by their mothers (i.e., in-group members).

Job Attitudes

Individualism and collectivism have been found to relate to job attitudes, including organizational commitment (Wasti, 2000) and job satisfaction (Hui, Yee, & Eastman, 1995). With respect to the former, Wasti (2000) argued that current conceptualizations of commitment are laden with individualistic elements in that they focus on "cold calculation of costs and benefits." By contrast, she argued that in Turkey, a collectivist culture, continuance commitment would be laden with cultural expectations of loyalty toward the organization. In support of these notions, she found that Turkish employees' continuance commitment was predicted by generalized norms for loyalty and the approval of in-group members for staying in the organization. These findings were also replicated

when examining individual-level attributes of individualism and collectivism as predictors. For individuals high on allocentrism, norms for loyalty increased continuance commitment, whereas this relationship did not exist for individuals low on allocentrism. Thus, the nature of organizational commitment appears to take on different elements in individualistic and collectivist cultures.

In an interesting multilevel analysis, Hui and colleagues (1995) examined the relationship between individualism and collectivism and employee job satisfaction. Their results illustrated that job satisfaction was positively correlated to individualism at the societal level, yet was negatively related to individualism at the individual level within the Hong Kong cultural context. Triandis (2002) later explained this finding by arguing that at the societal level individualism is associated with affluence and mobility, making it easier for individuals to find jobs that are enjoyable. At the individual level, however, idiocentrics are likely to be highly focused on the task, to the exclusion of cultivating relationships. Triandis (2002) argued that this might cause them to be rejected by others in their organizations, thus reducing job satisfaction. Although the theoretical mechanisms of these effects still need to be tested, this study reinforces the importance of examining relationships at multiple levels of analysis, as they can reveal very different patterns of results.

Group Processes

Individualism and collectivism have been linked to a number of group processes including conformity, social loafing, cooperation, and conflict. In a series of studies, Earley (1989, 1994) illustrated that social loafing is higher in individualistic cultures, such as the United States, as compared to collectivist cultures, such as China. Later research by Earley (1993) illustrated the importance of in-group–out-group distinctions in social loafing. In particular, Chinese exhibited less social loafing if they were working with in-group members, as compared to if they were working with out-group members. By contrast, Americans' social loafing tendencies did not vary as a function of such in-group–out-group distinctions.

Other studies have linked individualism and collectivism with conformity and cooperation in groups. For example, in a meta-analysis Bond and Smith (1996) found that conformity was higher in nations that were high on collectivism, as assessed by both Hofstede (1980) and Schwartz (1994). Furthermore, numerous studies at different levels of analysis (team, individual) have illustrated that collectivism is related to cooperation. At the team level of analysis, Eby and Dobbins (1997) illustrated that team collectivist orientation was related to team cooperation, which was in turn related to team performance. Likewise, Cox, Lobel, and McLeod (1991) illustrated that groups composed of people with historically collectivist orientations (Asians, Hispanics, and African Americans) were more cooperative than groups composed of Caucasians. At the individual level of analysis, Wagner (1995) and Cox and colleagues (1991), found that collectivism was related to cooperation in groups. Similarly, Moorman and Blakely (1995) illustrated that individuals higher on collectivism (Wagner, 1995) are more likely to engage in organizational citizenship behaviors (i.e., prosocial behaviors). These studies are also consistent with Miller (1994), who found that Indians are more likely to believe that helping others is a matter of duty, whereas Americans are more likely to believe that helping others is a matter of choice. At the same time, these findings are likely moderated by whether the other group is an in-group or an out-group (Triandis, 1995).

All in all, these findings illustrate that there is an emphasis on cooperative team processes in collectivistic cultures. Later, we will return to this issue when discussing the hypothesized relationship between collectivism and team-oriented leadership behaviors as well.

Organizational Trust and Psychological Contracts

Although there has been little empirical research in this area, it is likely that the nature of psychological contracts and organizational trust varies in individualistic and collectivist cultures. Psychological contracts refer to the nature of the exchange relationship between employees and organizations. Rousseau (1995) has distinguished between transactional and relational psychological contracts within cultures. From a cross-cultural perspective it is likely that *transactional* contracts, which are characterized by short time frames and specific obligations, are more prevalent in individualistic cultures, whereas *relational* contracts, which are characterized by long-term relationships with diffuse obligations, are more prevalent in collectivist cultures.

Along similar lines, it is likely that the nature of trust between employees and organizations varies in individualistic and collectivist cultures. Trust has been described as taking on four potential forms, and these forms include shallow dependence, deep dependence, shallow interdependence and deep interdependence (Sheppard & Sherman, 1998). In individualistic cultures, trust should theoretically take the form of shallow or deep dependence. According to Sheppard and Sherman, the strength of trust in such relationships is based on the employee's belief in the discretion and integrity of the organization. If trust is betrayed and the employee's trust is shallow, the employee may simply leave the organization. If trust is betrayed and the employee's trust is deep, then the employee may look for a solution that allows him or her to remain with the organization. In such organizations, this solution may involve the establishment of a third entity to oversee and arbitrate future conflict, such as an employee's union. On the other hand, in collectivist cultures, trust should theoretically take the forms of "shallow interdependence" and "deep interdependence." The strength of trust would be a function of the level of interdependence between parties. Moreover, if trust is betrayed, individuals whose personal identities are defined, in large part, by their organizational membership are likely to experience a tremendous amount of dissonance.

Accountability

Organizations must rely on a division of labor and make members accountable for task accomplishment. However, the nature of accountability is likely to vary in individualistic and collectivist cultures. In individualistic cultures, accountability is likely to rest with specific individuals, for both organizational successes and failures. As Chen, Chen, and Meindl (1998) discuss, in these cultures cooperation is fostered if there are clear rules regarding who is responsible for specific tasks. This is likely to have symbolic manifestations within organizations as well. For example, paper trails and signature trees are likely to be used to help establish individual accountability, which in turn create sequential lines of communication.

On the other hand, accountability in collectivist cultures would be more likely to rest with groups (cf. Kashima & Callan, 1994). In these organizations cooperation would not be optimized in situations in which culpable individuals could be clearly identified (Chen et al., 1998), and written documents and long lists of signatures would rarely be used. This, in turn, would reduce organizational boundaries and the clarity of lines of communication within organizations.

Entrepreneurial Activity

Research has illustrated that there is no simple relationship between entrepreneurship and individualism and collectivism. For example, Morris, Avila, and Allen (1993) found a curvilinear relationship between individualism and collectivism and entrepreneurship across 84 industrial firms. Entrepreneurship was highest under balanced conditions of individualism and collectivism and less so in highly individualistic and highly collectivist contexts. This is also consistent with research at the individual level, which has illustrated that a combination of individualistic and collectivist traits can enhance entrepreneurial success. For example, Bhawuk and Udas (1996) argued that successful entrepreneurs must have the ability to be creative and to develop new and unique ideas, characteristics that are typically associated with individualistic orientations. On the other hand, entrepreneurs must also have the ability to gather people together, form an organization, and foster commitment and sacrifice among employees, characteristics that are typically associated with collectivist orientations. Consistent with this, Bhawuk and Udas (1996) found that successful Nepalese entrepreneurs

considered independence, individual merit, internal control, competition, and hedonism to be important. At the same time, Nepalese entrepreneurs also showed strong collectivist tendencies. The vast majority lived in extended families, lived near close friends, and believed that aging parents should live with their children and that individuals should help their relatives. Additional factor analytic results supported the notion that this sample was high on both competition and responsibility, a combination of idiocentrism and allocentrism.

Summary

Individualism and collectivism have numerous implications for organizations, including the nature of human resource management practices, motivation, job attitudes, group processes, organizational trust and accountability, and entrepreneurship. A summary of the implications of individualism and collectivism for organizations can be found in Table 16.2

IMPLICATIONS OF INDIVIDUALISM AND COLLECTIVISM FOR LEADERSHIP

In this section, we briefly review research pertaining to individualism and collectivism and its relationship to leadership. Research on this topic is generally sparse, and further, in most of the studies reported, individualism and collectivism were not directly assessed. Nevertheless, it provides an important backdrop to the GLOBE study.

Behavioral Tradition

The behavioral approach to leadership focuses on identifying the types of behaviors that are used by effective leaders. Dating back to the Ohio State University studies of leadership in the 1950s, researchers have consistently found a cluster of leadership behaviors focused tasks (labeled *initiating structure*) as well as a cluster of leadership behaviors focused relationships (labeled *consideration*). Interestingly, this taxonomy, although originating in an

Table 16.2   Higher Individualism and Collectivism for Organizations Versus Lower Individualism and Collectivism for Organizations

Organizations That Score High on Collectivism	*Organizations That Score High on Individualism*
• Members assume that they are highly interdependent with the organization and believe it is important to make personal sacrifices to fulfill their organizational obligations	• Members assume that they are independent of the organization and believe it is important to bring their unique skills and abilities to the organization
• Employees tend to develop long-term relationship with employers from recruitment to retirement	• Employees develop short-term relationships, and change companies at their own discretion
• Organizations take responsibility for employee welfare	• Organizations are primarily interested in the work that employees perform and not their personal or family welfare
• Important decisions tend to be made by groups	• Important decisions tend to be made by individuals
• Selection can focus on relational attributes of employees	• Selection focuses primarily on employees' knowledge, skills, and abilities
• Jobs are designed in groups to maximize the social and technical aspects of the job	• Jobs are designed individually to maximize autonomy
• Training is emphasized more than selection	• Selection is emphasized more than training
• Compensation and promotions are based on what is equitable for the group and on considerations of seniority and personal needs	• Compensation and promotions are based on an equity model, in which an individual is rewarded in direct relationship to his or her contribution to task success
• Motivation is socially oriented, and is based on the need to fulfill duties and obligations and to contribute to the group	• Motivation is individually oriented and is based on individual interests, needs, and capacities
• Organizational commitment is based on expectations of loyalty and in-group attitudes	• Organizational commitment is based on individuals' rational calculations of costs and benefits
• Prosocial behaviors, or organizational citizenship behaviors, are more common	• Prosocial behaviors, or organizational citizenship behaviors, are less common
• Avoidant, obliging, compromising, and accommodating conflict resolution tactics are preferred	• Direct and solution-oriented conflict resolution tactics are preferred
• Accountability for organizational successes and failures rests with groups	• Accountability for organizational successes and failures rests with individuals

individualistic culture, has now been replicated in a study in Japan (Misumi, 1985). Specifically, in his PM theory of leadership, Misumi found that effective leader behaviors in Japan were composed of two dimensions, one that was focused on the task, labeled *performance-oriented leadership* (P), and another that was focused on the maintenance of group relations, labeled *maintenance-oriented leadership* (M). Nevertheless, there are some differences in PM leadership theories in individualistic and collectivist cultures. First, the degree to which the two clusters of behaviors are seen as distinct varies across cultures. Smith, Misumi, Tayeb, Peterson, and Bond (1989) found that respondents in the United States and Britain made clearer distinctions between harmony maintenance and task accomplishment, whereas respondents in collectivist cultures perceived work group harmony to be intimately related to task accomplishment. Second, research has found that although there is a set of core P and M leadership behaviors that are enacted by leaders in both collectivist and individualistic cultures, such general functions can be fulfilled through *different* specific behaviors (Smith et al., 1989).

More specifically, behaviors linked to the M function in Britain were directed more toward the task than toward in-group maintenance, whereas M behaviors in Japan and Hong Kong had much more to do with group interaction. By contrast, in Japan and Hong Kong, distinctive P behaviors focused more on collective interactions, whereas in Britain, P behaviors were more task-centered. In addition, Smith and colleagues (1989) illustrated that in collectivist cultures M functions are best characterized by a deep concern for subordinates and by the ability to resolve personal difficulties in an indirect manner that ensures face saving (Smith et al., 1989), whereas M functions in Britain were related to work and not personal issues involving subordinates. Indeed, these findings are also consistent with research in India by Sinha (1984), who found that the most effective leader exhibits both person-oriented and production-oriented behaviors. Specifically, an effective leader in India is one who is paternalistic and provides nurturance in exchange for subordinates' task accomplishment. Interestingly, the nurturant-task style described by Sinha is similar to leader-subordinate relationships in Japan, another collectivist culture, which are characterized by *amae,* or indulgent dependence, discussed previously (Kashima & Callan, 1994; see also Ling, 1989).

In other studies within the behavioral tradition, Dorfman and his colleagues (Dorfman & Howell, 1988; Dorfman et al., 1997) found that the effects of leaders' directiveness and participativeness on performance varied across individualistic and collectivist cultures. Directive leadership had a positive impact on performance in Taiwan and in Mexico, both collectivist cultures (Hofstede, 1980). Participative leadership, on the other hand, only had positive effects in the United States, presumably because high individualism reinforces beliefs in participation. However, there is some evidence that participative leadership behaviors may be preferred to delegation in some collectivist cultures, such as Kuwait (Ali, Taqi, & Krishnan, 1997) and India (Aycan et al., 1999). For example, Aycan and colleagues (1999) found that Indian managers had stronger beliefs in the importance of employee participation, as compared to Canadian managers. At the individual level of analysis, they also found that managers who reported that the sociocultural context was high on paternalism and loyalty toward community also reported that employees within the organization had high obligations toward others and should use joint goal setting. Likewise, Ali and colleagues (1997) found that Kuwaitis, who were highly collectivist, had a strong preference for consultative and participative decision-making styles. Thus, there is inconsistency in the literature regarding the relationship between individualism and collectivism and participation. In keeping with the above notion that leader constructs may be defined differently across cultures, it is possible that participation is equally valued in both individualistic and collectivist cultures, but is manifested through different behaviors.

Cognitive Tradition

Cognitive perspectives on leadership focus on the process by which a person becomes labeled as a leader and the characteristics that are perceived to be associated with effective leadership. Within this approach, personal identities are defined, in large part, by their organizational membership; for an individual to be considered a leader, he or she must first be categorized as a leader (Dorfman, 1998; Erez & Earley, 1993; House, Wright, & Aditya, 1997; Shaw, 1990). During the cognitive categorization process, a person's attributes are compared with the attributes that potential followers believe "prototypical" leaders to have. Such prototypes are thought to reflect a culture's image of an ideal leader (Hanges, Lord, & Dickson, 2000). As such, the better the match between a person's characteristics and followers' leader prototypes, the more likely it is for the person to be considered a leader (Lord & Maher, 1991).

Although these notions are theoretically appealing, there have been very few direct empirical tests of them in the literature. Dorfman (1998) theorized that in the individualistic culture of the United States, leader prototypes reflect the cultural values of being independent, strong willed, and forceful, whereas in collectivist cultures such as Japan prototypes reflect the cultural values of interdependence, collaboration, and self-effacement. One study that did directly assess leader prototypes found support for the notion that business leader prototypes vary systematically as a function of culture (Gerstner & Day, 1994).

Charismatic Tradition

Various researchers have speculated that collectivism at the societal and organizational levels is associated with charismatic leadership. For example, Jung, Bass, and Sosik (1995) provided a conceptual argument that transformational leadership would emerge more easily and would be more effective in collectivist as compared to individualistic societal cultures because of the strong emphasis on group orientation, work centrality, and respect authority in collectivist cultures. Meindl (1995) also argued that for the work-group level the emergence of charismatic leadership would be higher in collectivist than individualistic organizational cultures. This is predicated on the notion that a readiness for charismatic leadership within work groups is a function of the degree of cohesiveness or interconnectedness of relational networks within a work group, which in turn, is a function of collectivism (see Kashima et al., 1995). In support of this, Pillai and Meindl (1998) found a significant positive correlation between work group collectivism and charismatic leadership ($r = .37, p < .001$).

Summary

Research suggests that leadership can vary in collectivist and individualistic cultures. In collectivist cultures, leadership is associated with paternalism, group maintenance activities, face saving, conformity, as well as charisma and lack of social loafing. By contrast, leadership in individualistic cultures emphasizes individual discretion, autonomy, and task accomplishment (Erez & Earley, 1993; Hofstede & Bond, 1988; Triandis, 1993). In individualist cultures there is higher susceptibility to social loafing as well. A summary of the implications of individualism and collectivism for leadership can be found in Table 16.3.

OVERVIEW OF GLOBE RESEARCH ON INDIVIDUALISM AND COLLECTIVISM

As is evident from the previous discussion, the constructs of individualism and collectivism have received much theoretical and empirical attention in the literature over the past 20 years. It is clear that the constructs have numerous economic, social, and organizational correlates; operate at multiple levels of analysis; and are often multidimensional in nature. The purposes of the GLOBE research project of 62 nations have already been reviewed in detail in Chapter 2 by House and Javidan. In this section we review and interpret the results from the GLOBE study with respect to collectivism and individualism. Before we turn to the empirical results, we will briefly introduce the measures of the constructs within this research project.

First, in keeping with a levels perspective, individualism and collectivism were assessed at both the societal and the organizational levels of analysis in the GLOBE study. Previous research on the constructs has not examined these levels simultaneously, and as such, the current research builds on previous research across different fields (e.g., cross-cultural psychology, organizational behavior). On the basis of the previous discussion we expected that societal-level individualism and collectivism would be related to organizational-level individualism and collectivism, providing evidence for cross-level effects of the constructs. Furthermore, this design enabled us to examine the joint contribution of both levels of analysis to perceptions of effective leadership. We expected that collectivism scores at both levels

Table 16.3   Implications of Individualism and Collectivism for Leadership

In Collectivistic Cultures	In Individualistic Cultures
• Task-performance (P) leadership behaviors are perceived as being intimately related to relationship-maintenance (M) behaviors	• Performance and maintenance behaviors are seen as more distinct
• Leadership behaviors associated with task functions (P) tend to focus on relational interactions and behaviors associated	• Leadership behaviors associated with relational functions (M) tend to focus more on the task than on in-group maintenance
• Effective leaders are paternalistic and nurturant	• Effective leaders are less directive and more autonomous
• Leader behaviors emphasize group maintenance activities and face saving	• Leader behaviors emphasize individual discretion and task accomplishment
• Leader prototypes reflect cultural values of interdependence, collaboration, and self-effacement	• Leader prototypes reflect cultural values of being independent, strong willed, and forceful
• Charismatic leadership is highly valued	• Charismatic leadership is less valued

of analysis would be negatively related to autonomous leadership scores, and positively related to team-oriented and charismatic leadership scores. At the same time, since individualism and collectivism are not isomorphic at the two levels of analysis, we also anticipated that there could be unique relationships between individualism–collectivism and leadership at the societal and organizational levels of analysis.

In keeping with the notion that individualism and collectivism are multidimensional, the constructs were measured with two different scales at each level of analysis. Briefly, at the societal level, measures assessed both In-Group Collectivism and Institutional Collectivism. This is consistent with Triandis and associates (Triandis et al., 1986), who empirically demonstrated that family integrity is an important factor that differentiates societies, as well with other scholars who have focused on non-kin components of collectivism (Realo et al., 1997; Rhee, Uleman, & Lee, 1996). Although we expected that these measures would be correlated, we also expected that each would measure unique aspects of the constructs (see specific items below). As such, we anticipated that the measures could have different

correlates and, moreover, that country-level rankings could vary depending on which aspect of collectivism was measured. In addition, we also anticipated that the GLOBE Individualism and Collectivism scales would correlate with previous measures of the constructs (Hofstede, 1980; Schwartz, 1994). In particular, we expected that GLOBE's In-Group Collectivism measure would be highly related to other measures because a similar measure by Triandis (Triandis et al., 1986) of family integrity had previously been related to Hofstede's (1980) rankings.

In parallel fashion, at the organizational level GLOBE measures assessed the degree of organizational In-Group pride and loyalty as well as Institutional Collectivism. The former measure is consistent with Kanungo et al. (1999), who focused on managerial assumptions of loyalty toward others as an indicator of organizational collectivism. The latter measure is consistent with more general organizational design differences expected in individualistic and collectivist organizational cultures that prioritize group over individual interests. Similar to expectations at the societal level, we expected that the two GLOBE measures of collectivism would be correlated but would measure different aspects of organizational collectivism, and would consequently have unique relationships with effective leadership.

Lastly, GLOBE measures of these constructs also made another important differentiation between collectivist *values* and collectivist *practices*. Previous research has included items that focus only on values (Schwartz, 1994), practices (Hofstede et al., 1991) or a mix of both in the same scale (Hofstede, 1980). The current research explicitly examined both values and practices at both the societal and organizational level of analysis to determine whether any important variation between the two can be captured with this distinction.

In what follows, we first describe GLOBE results for collectivism at the societal and organizational level of analysis. We then discuss the relationship of societal and organizational collectivism scales and perceptions of effective leadership attributes. Please refer to Chapter 6 by House and Hanges for a further description of the 62 nations included in this study, sample characteristics, how scales were developed, and study procedures.

GLOBE Measures

Societal-Level Measures

Institutional Collectivism: The Institutional Collectivism construct was measured through a set of four questions that were focused on the degree to which institutional practices at the societal level encourage and reward collective action. Specifically, the questions assessed whether group loyalty is emphasized at the expense of individual goals, whether the economic system emphasizes individual or collective interests, whether being accepted by other group members is important, and whether individualism or group cohesion is valued more in the society (see Tables 16.4a and 16.4c for sample items).

In-Group Collectivism: The Societal In-Group Collectivism construct was also operationalized by a set of four questions that assessed the degree to which individuals express pride, loyalty, and interdependence in their families. The items specifically measured whether children take pride in the individual accomplishments of their parents and vice versa, whether aging parents live at home with their children, and whether children live at home with their parents until they get married (see Tables 16.4b and 16.4d for sample items).

For both Institutional Collectivism and In-Group Collectivism, there were *As Is* and *Should Be* versions of the scales. The As Is scales were probed by the statement, "In this society, people are generally . . ." and assessed existing practices in societies. The Should Be scales, on the other hand, have the same content except they were probed by the statement, "In this society, people should . . ." These scales assessed societal values. Study participants responded to all items on a 7-point scale in which 1 = low collectivism (or high individualism) and 7 = high collectivism (or low individualism). It is important to note that the items in these scales were constructed by GLOBE in ways that assessed Individualism and Collectivism as opposites of the same continuum. As reviewed previously, whereas some scholars concur with the unidimensionality of the constructs at the societal level (e.g., Hofstede, 1980; Schwartz, 1994), others argue that they can be orthogonal (e.g., Triandis, 1995). Factor analyses of the scales demonstrated that they are all unidimensional.

It is also important to note that there were some differences across the practices and values scales for both Institutional and In-Group Collectivism scales. For example, the Institutional Collectivism practices scale included a unique item regarding the emphasis that is placed on being accepted in other groups that is not included in the values scale. Likewise, the Institutional Collectivism values scale included an item regarding the preference people have for individual versus team sports that was not included in the practices scale. In addition, the In-Group Collectivism practices scale focused exclusively on families, children, and parents. By contrast, the In-Group Collectivism values scale also included a focus on the value of having pride in the society as a whole. Therefore, although the scales mostly measure common elements, they also have some uniqueness and have some qualitative differences.

Table 16.4a   Societal-Level Institutional Collectivism Practices

In this society, leaders encourage group loyalty even if individual goals suffer: (reverse scored)

Strongly agree   Strongly disagree

1	2	3	4	5	6	7

The economic system in this society is designed to maximize:

Individual interests   Collective interests

1	2	3	4	5	6	7

Table 16.4b   Societal-Level In-Group Collectivism Practices

In this society, children take pride in the individual accomplishments of their parents: (reverse scored)

Strongly agree   Strongly disagree

1	2	3	4	5	6	7

In this society, parents take pride in the individual accomplishments of their children: (reverse scored)

Strongly agree   Strongly disagree

1	2	3	4	5	6	7

Table 16.4c   Societal-Level Institutional Collectivism Values

I believe that, in general, leaders should encourage group loyalty even if individual goals suffer: (reverse scored)

Strongly agree   Strongly disagree

1	2	3	4	5	6	7

I believe that the economic system in this society should be designed to maximize:

Individual interests   Collective interests

1	2	3	4	5	6	7

Table 16.4d   Societal-Level In-Group Collectivism Values

In this society, children should take pride in the individual accomplishments of their parents: (reverse scored)

Strongly agree   Strongly disagree

1	2	3	4	5	6	7

In this society, parents should take pride in the individual accomplishments of their children:

Strongly agree   Strongly disagree

1	2	3	4	5	6	7

Table 16.4e   Organizational-Level Institutional Collectivism Practices

In this organization, managers encourage group loyalty even if individual goals suffer: (reverse scored)						
Strongly agree						Strongly disagree
1	2	3	4	5	6	7
The pay and bonus system in this organization is designed to maximize:						
Individual interests						Collective interests
1	2	3	4	5	6	7

Table 16.4f   Organizational-Level In-Group Collectivism Practices

In this organization, group members take pride in the individual accomplishments of their group:						
Strongly agree						Strongly disagree
1	2	3	4	5	6	7
In this organization, group managers take pride in the individual accomplishments of group members:						
Strongly agree						Strongly disagree
1	2	3	4	5	6	7

Table 16.4g   Organizational-Level Institutional Collectivism Values

I believe that in this organization, managers *should* generally encourage group loyalty even if individual goals suffer: (reverse scored)						
Strongly agree						Strongly disagree
1	2	3	4	5	6	7
In this organization, the pay and bonus system *should* be designed to maximize:						
Individual interests						Collective interests
1	2	3	4	5	6	7

Organizational-Level Measures

Tables 16.4e, 16.4f, 16.4g, and 16.4h present the sample measures for organizational collectivism. Organizational Institutional Collectivism assessed the degree to which institutions encourage and reward collective action and the collective distribution of resources. Organizational In-Group Collectivism assessed the degree to which individuals express pride, loyalty, and cohesiveness in their organization. As stated in the introduction to this part of the volume, there were also two versions of each of these scales: measures of practices (As Is scales) and measures of values (Should Be scales).

It is important to note that there were some notable differences across the practices and values scales for organizational Institutional Collectivism. Specifically, both scales included

Table 16.4h   Organizational-Level Group Values

In this organization, group members *should* take pride in the individual accomplishments of their group:

Strongly agree   Strongly disagree

  1   2   3   4   5   6   7

In this organization, group managers *should* take pride in the individual accomplishments of group members:

Strongly agree   Strongly disagree

  1   2   3   4   5   6   7

items related to the importance of group loyalty versus individual goals, the pay and bonus system maximizing group or individual interests, and the emphasis on group cohesion versus individualism. In addition, the values version of this scale also included additional items that measure the value of achieving consensus and the value of group versus individual work in the organization. There was also some variation across the practices and values versions of the organizational In-Group Collectivism scale. Specifically, the values version included an item concerning whether outsider statements against the organization should be bothersome to members inside the organization. Thus, it is important to note that there are some qualitative differences between the scales.

GLOBE RESULTS: SOCIETAL LEVEL

Descriptive Statistics

Table 16.5a presents the summary statistics for both the practices and values versions of the societal Institutional Collectivism scale, and Table 16.5b presents summary statistics for societal In-Group Collectivism scale. These tables illustrate some interesting patterns. First, it is evident that across all cultures, values and practices scores are higher for In-Group Collectivism, as compared to Institutional Collectivism. Second, it is interesting to note that for both the In-Group Collectivism and the Institutional Collectivism scales, scores are higher for values than they are for practices.

This illustrates that respondents across societies generally want more in-group and institutional collectivism than they have. Finally, it is also interesting to note patterns for the variances of the scales. For example, it is clear that there is lower variance across cultures (or more universal agreement) for In-Group Collectivism values, as well as Institutional Collectivism practices and values. By contrast, the GLOBE results illustrate that societies are most variable on In-Group Collectivism practices.

Table 16.6 presents the correlations among all four Collectivism scales. As shown in this table, the correlation between the societal practices and values versions of the Institutional Collectivism scale is negative ($r = .61$, $p < 0.01$). This indicates that the less a society practices collectivism and emphasizes collective goals and interests, the more it values societal collectivism. Peng and Nisbett (1999) refer to this phenomenon as "deprivation-based preferences" at the individual level, wherein individuals express preferences for things that they believe they are lacking or things they have taken for granted. By contrast, there is no significant correlation between societal In-Group Collectivism for the practices and values scale, indicating that this same sentiment is not applicable to societal emphases on family pride and interdependence.

Interestingly, the table illustrates that the Institutional Collectivism practices scale is not at all correlated with either the In-Group Collectivism practices or values scale. As such, the Institutional Collectivism practices scale is highly distinct from both In-Group Collectivism scales.

Table 16.5a   Summary Statistics for Societal Institutional Collectivism

Variable	N	Minimum	Maximum	Mean	Standard Deviation
Society practices	61	3.25	5.22	4.25	0.42
Society values	61	3.83	5.65	4.72	0.49

Table 16.5b   Summary Statistics for Societal In-Group Collectivism

Variable	N	Minimum	Maximum	Mean	Standard Deviation
Society practices	61	3.53	6.36	5.13	0.73
Society values	61	4.94	6.52	5.66	0.35

Table 16.6   Correlations Between Societal Institutional and In-Group Collectivism

	Institutional Collectivism Practices	Institutional Collectivism Values	In-Group Collectivism Practices	In-Group Collectivism Values
Institutional Collectivism practices		−.61**	−.19	−.16
Institutional Collectivism values			.43**	.29*
In-Group Collectivism practices				.21
In-Group Collectivism values				

* Correlation is significant at the .05 level.

** Correlation is significant at the .01 level.

By contrast, there are significant correlations between Institutional Collectivism values and In-Group Collectivism practices ($r = .43$, $p < .01$) as well as significant correlations between Institutional Collectivism values and In-Group Collectivism values ($r = .29$; $p < .05$). These correlations suggest that the more a society values Institutional Collectivism, the more it practices and values In-Group Collectivism.

Societal Rankings

Tables 16.7a and 16.7b present the societal rankings and means for Institutional Collectivism and In-Group Collectivism practices scales.[5] In these tables, the countries are ranked, within bands, according to country means on the scales. The bands are calculated according to the formula $2 \times SED$ (standard error of

Table 16.7a   Societal Institutional Collectivism Practices Scores*

			Band				
A		**B**		**C**		**D**	
Country	*Score*	*Country*	*Score*	*Country*	*Score*	*Country*	*Score*
Sweden	5.22	Indonesia	4.54	Portugal	3.92	Greece	3.25
South Korea	5.20	Albania	4.54	Ecuador	3.90		
Japan	5.19	Poland	4.53	Iran	3.88		
Singapore	4.90	Russia	4.50	Morocco	3.87		
New Zealand	4.81	Qatar	4.50	Spain	3.85		
Denmark	4.80	Egypt	4.50	Brazil	3.83		
China	4.77	Kuwait	4.49	Colombia	3.81		
Philippines	4.65	Israel	4.46	Germany[e]	3.79		
Ireland	4.63	Netherlands	4.46	El Salvador	3.71		
Finland	4.63	South Africa[b]	4.39	Guatemala	3.70		
South Africa[a]	4.62	Canada[c]	4.38	Italy	3.68		
Zambia	4.61	India	4.38	Argentina	3.66		
Malaysia	4.61	Austria	4.30	Germany[f]	3.56		
Taiwan	4.59	Australia	4.29	Hungary	3.53		
		Kazakhstan	4.29				
		England	4.27				
		Switzerland[d]	4.22				
		U.S.	4.20				
		Nigeria	4.14				
		Hong Kong	4.13				
		Namibia	4.13				
		Slovenia	4.13				
		Zimbabwe	4.12				
		Switzerland	4.06				
		Mexico	4.06				
		Bolivia	4.04				
		Thailand	4.03				
		Georgia	4.03				
		Turkey	4.03				
		Venezuela	3.96				
		Costa Rica	3.93				
		France	3.93				

NOTES:

a South Africa (White sample)
b South Africa (Black sample)
c Canada (English-speaking)
d Switzerland (French-speaking)
e Germany (West): Former FRG
f Germany (East): Former GDR

* Higher scores indicate greater collectivism. Countries are ranked according to mean scores.
Number of cases: 61
GLOBE response bias correction procedure identified response bias in some countries for this scale (see endnotes).

difference), where *SED* is a function of the reliability of the scale of interest. As stated earlier, scores in band A are significantly higher than scores in bands B, C, or D, but within bands the mean scores are not statistically different from each other.

Tables 16.7c and 16.7d present the country rankings and means for the Institutional and

Table 16.7b   Societal In-Group Collectivism Practices Scores*

Band					
A		B		C	
Country	Score	Country	Score	Country	Score
Philippines	6.36	Costa Rica	5.32	Canada[d]	4.26
Georgia	6.19	Hong Kong	5.32	U.S.	4.25
Iran	6.03	Greece	5.27	Australia	4.17
India	5.92	Kazakhstan	5.26	England	4.08
Turkey	5.88	Hungary	5.25	Finland	4.07
Morocco	5.87	Brazil	5.18	Germany[e]	4.02
Zambia	5.84	Ireland	5.14	Switzerland	3.97
Ecuador	5.81	South Africa[a]	5.09	Switzerland[f]	3.85
China	5.80	Italy	4.94	Netherlands	3.70
Kuwait	5.80	Austria	4.85	New Zealand	3.67
Albania	5.74	Qatar	4.71	Sweden	3.66
Colombia	5.73	Israel	4.70	Denmark	3.53
Mexico	5.71	Japan	4.63		
Thailand	5.70	Namibia	4.52		
Indonesia	5.68	Germany[b]	4.52		
Egypt	5.64	South Africa[c]	4.50		
Singapore	5.64	France	4.37		
Guatemala	5.63				
Russia	5.63				
Taiwan	5.59				
Zimbabwe	5.57				
Nigeria	5.55				
South Korea	5.54				
Venezuela	5.53				
Poland	5.52				
Malaysia	5.51				
Portugal	5.51				
Argentina	5.51				
Bolivia	5.47				
Spain	5.45				
Slovenia	5.43				
El Salvador	5.35				

NOTES:

a South Africa (Black Sample)
b Germany (East): Former GDR
c South Africa (White Sample)
d Canada (English-speaking)
e Germany (West): Former FRG
f Switzerland (French-speaking)

* Higher scores indicate greater collectivism
Countries are ranked according to mean scores.
Number of cases: 61
GLOBE response bias correction procedure identified response bias in some countries for this scale (see endnotes).

In-Group Collectivism values scales.[6] In these tables, the bands are based on the GLOBE scale scores, and the countries are ranked from the country with the highest mean to the country with the lowest mean. These rankings are interpreted in more detail, after we describe the correlations of GLOBE Collectivism scales with other GLOBE scales and with other collectivism scales in the literature.

Table 16.7c   Societal Institutional Collectivism Values Scores*

Band							
A		*B*		*C*		*D*	
Country	*Score*	*Country*	*Score*	*Country*	*Score*	*Country*	*Score*
El Salvador	5.65	Nigeria	5.03	Hungary	4.50	Korea	3.90
Brazil	5.62	Morocco	5.00	Albania	4.44	Russia	3.89
Iran	5.54	Mexico	4.92	Hong Kong	4.43	Georgia	3.83
Ecuador	5.41	Zimbabwe	4.87	Australia	4.40		
Greece	5.40	Malaysia	4.87	South Africa[c]	4.38		
Venezuela	5.39	France	4.86	Namibia	4.38		
Colombia	5.38	Egypt	4.85	Slovenia	4.38		
Argentina	5.32	Germany[a]	4.82	Switzerland[d]	4.31		
Portugal	5.30	Philippines	4.78	England	4.31		
Turkey	5.26	Zambia	4.74	South Africa[e]	4.30		
Guatemala	5.23	Austria	4.73	Israel	4.27		
Spain	5.20	India	4.71	Poland	4.22		
Indonesia	5.18	Switzerland	4.69	New Zealand	4.20		
Costa Rica	5.18	Germany[b]	4.68	Denmark	4.19		
Taiwan	5.15	Ireland	4.59	Canada[f]	4.17		
Kuwait	5.15	China	4.56	U.S.	4.17		
Qatar	5.13	Singapore	4.55	Finland	4.11		
Italy	5.13	Netherlands	4.55	Kazakhstan	4.04		
Thailand	5.10			Japan	3.99		
Bolivia	5.10			Sweden	3.94		

NOTES:

a Germany (West): Former FRG
b Germany (East): Former GDR
c South Africa (White sample)
d Switzerland (French-speaking)
e South Africa (Black sample)
f Canada (English-speaking)

* Higher scores indicate more collectivism
Countries are ranked according to mean scores.
Number of cases: 61
GLOBE response bias correction procedure identified response bias in some countries for this scale (see endnotes).

Societal-Level Collectivism and Other GLOBE Culture Dimensions

As shown in Tables 16.8a and 16.8b, the four societal Collectivism scales are significantly correlated with other GLOBE dimensions. The more a society is characterized by Institutional Collectivism practices, the more it is characterized by Uncertainty Avoidance, Future Orientation, Humane Orientation, and Performance Orientation practices, and the less it is characterized by Assertiveness and Power Distance practices. On the other hand, the more a society is characterized by Institutional Collectivism practices, the more it is characterized by Assertiveness and Power Distance values and the less it is characterized by Future Orientation and Performance Orientation values. Table 16.8a also illustrates that the more a society is characterized by Institutional Collectivism values, the more it is characterized by Power Distance practices and the less it is characterized by Uncertainty Avoidance, Future Orientation and Gender Egalitarianism practices. Such societies are also characterized by more Uncertainty Avoidance, Future Orientation, and Performance Orientation values, and by less Power Distance values.

Table 16.7d   Societal In-Group Collectivism Values Scores*

Band					
A		*B*		*C*	
Country	*Score*	*Country*	*Score*	*Country*	*Score*
El Salvador	6.52	Mexico	5.95	Switzerland[c]	5.35
Colombia	6.25	Portugal	5.94	India	5.32
New Zealand	6.21	South Africa[b]	5.91	Austria	5.27
Philippines	6.18	Iran	5.86	Japan	5.26
Ecuador	6.17	Malaysia	5.85	Germany[d]	5.22
Venezuela	6.17	Zimbabwe	5.85	Albania	5.22
Argentina	6.15	Russia	5.79	Germany[e]	5.18
Guatemala	6.14	Spain	5.79	Netherlands	5.17
Costa Rica	6.08	Zambia	5.77	Brazil	5.15
Namibia	6.07	U.S.	5.77	Hong Kong	5.11
Sweden	6.04	Turkey	5.77	China	5.09
Bolivia	6.00	Thailand	5.76	South Africa[f]	4.99
Canada[a]	5.97	Israel	5.75	Switzerland	4.94
		Australia	5.75		
		Poland	5.74		
		Ireland	5.74		
		Italy	5.72		
		Slovenia	5.71		
		Morocco	5.68		
		Indonesia	5.67		
		Georgia	5.66		
		Qatar	5.60		
		Egypt	5.56		
		England	5.55		
		Hungary	5.54		
		Denmark	5.50		
		Singapore	5.50		
		Nigeria	5.48		
		Greece	5.46		
		Taiwan	5.45		
		Kazakhstan	5.44		
		Kuwait	5.43		
		France	5.42		
		Finland	5.42		
		Korea	5.41		

NOTES:

a Canada (English-speaking)
b South Africa (White sample)
c Switzerland (French-speaking)
d Germany (East): Former GDR
e Germany (West): Former FRG
f South Africa (Black sample)

* Higher scores indicate greater collectivism
Countries are ranked according to mean scores.
Number of cases: 61
GLOBE response bias correction procedure identified response bias in some countries for this scale (see endnotes).

Table 16.8a   Correlations of Societal Institutional Collectivism and Other GLOBE Societal Dimensions

GLOBE Scale	Institutional Collectivism Practices	Institutional Collectivism Values
Assertiveness practices	−.42**	
Future Orientation practices	.46**	−.29*
Gender Egalitarianism practices		−.31*
Humane Orientation practices	.43**	
Performance Orientation practices	.43**	
Power Distance practices	−.44**	.41**
Uncertainty Avoidance practices	.40**	−.32*
Assertiveness values	.37**	
Future Orientation values	−.25*	.48**
Performance Orientation values	−.39**	.44**
Power Distance values	.38**	−.31*
Uncertainty Avoidance values		.42**

Only significant correlations are displayed in the table.

** Correlation is significant at the .01 level.

* Correlation is significant at the .05 level.

With respect to In-Group Collectivism practices, Table 16.8b shows that the more a society is characterized by In-Group Collectivism practices, the more it is characterized by Humane Orientation and Power Distance practices and the less it is characterized by Uncertainty Avoidance and Future Orientation practices. In addition, the more a society is characterized by In-Group Collectivism practices, the more it is characterized by Uncertainty Avoidance, Future Orientation, and Assertiveness values and the less it characterized by Gender Egalitarianism values. Lastly, Table 16.8b illustrates that the more a society is characterized by In-Group Collectivism values, the more it is characterized by Power Distance practices and the less it is characterized by Future Orientation, Performance Orientation, and Uncertainty Avoidance practices. Likewise, the more a society is characterized by In-Group Collectivism values, the more it is characterized by Uncertainty Avoidance, Future Orientation, and Performance Orientation values.

Thus, as can be seen, the two different GLOBE measures of Collectivism are differentially related to other cultural dimensions. As Triandis (1994) notes, cultures can be seen as syndromes with interrelated dimensions. As such, one may see these results as indicative of different "Collectivism syndromes." Institutional Collectivism practices seem to be part of a cultural syndrome wherein societies are characterized by future and performance orientation, yet seek to accomplish such orientations through collective efforts, through practices which are concerned with others, and through practices which are not being assertive or power dominating. This syndrome can be seen in the rankings of societies on Institutional Collectivism practices: Cultures scoring high on this

Table 16.8b   Correlations of Societal In-Group Collectivism With Other GLOBE Societal Dimensions

GLOBE Scale	In-Group Collectivism Practices	In-Group Collectivism Values
Future Orientation practices	−.44**	−.42**
Humane Orientation practices	.30*	
Performance Orientation practices		−.36**
Power Distance practices	.55**	.33**
Uncertainty Avoidance practices	−.60**	−.45**
Assertiveness values	.28**	
Future Orientation values	.62**	.51**
Gender Egalitarianism values	−.44**	
Performance Orientation values		.57**
Uncertainty Avoidance values	.80**	.30*

Only significant correlations are displayed in the table.

** Correlation is significant at the .01 level.

* Correlation is significant at the .05 level.

included many of the Asian Dragons, which have been economically successful, yet using Confucian values as a basis for such success. In addition, some Scandinavian cultures are also characteristic of this syndrome, illustrating a combined focus on collective interests and nonassertiveness. This cultural syndrome may be reflective of a dual emphasis on collectivism and self-transcendence values found in Schwartz's circumplex of values. It may also be reflective of Triandis's notion of "horizontal collectivism" (Triandis, 1995; Triandis & Gelfand, 1998), which emphasizes collective interests in which power differences practices are not as important.

By contrast, In-Group Collectivism practices seem to be part of a cultural syndrome in which there are close ties among family members, and in which people are concerned with others, are respectful of authority, and have fewer rules. As illustrated in the previous rankings, countries that are characterized by this cultural syndrome include many Latin American and African countries, and several Asian countries. Not surprisingly based on previous culture studies, cultures that score low on this syndrome include many Western cultures, including the United States, Australia, England, Canada, Germany, and some Scandinavian cultures as well. Thus, it is clear from these results that societies such as those found in Scandinavia can score high on certain forms of collectivism (Institutional Collectivism) yet score very low on other forms of collectivism (In-Group Collectivism). It is also worth noting that this form of collectivism seems to overlap with Triandis's (1995; Triandis & Gelfand, 1998) notion of "vertical collectivism."

GLOBE scores on Collectivism values (or what *should be*) also reflect distinct cultural syndromes. Cultures characterized by high scores on Institutional Collectivism values, which feature a strong focus on collective interests, are more likely to be characterized by practices wherein there are close family ties, authority is respected, short-term focus and men tend to be dominant, and there are few rules and little structure. As can be seen in this description, this syndrome is similar to that found for societies characterized by In-Group Collectivism practices, which is consistent with correlations reported previously between these two scales ($r = .43$, $p < .01$). And, as can be seen in the rankings for this scale, societies that score high on this syndrome include numerous Latin and Central American cultures and Spain, and several Middle Eastern cultures (i.e., Kuwait and Turkey). Many of these nations have not had economic prosperity in the recent past, yet perhaps are in transition and in search of new ways to organize in the 21st century. By contrast, cultures that score low on this syndrome include many Western and Scandinavian cultures, and several Eastern European cultures (e.g., Hungary, Poland, Slovenia). Notably, it also includes several Confucian Asian cultures, such as Japan, Korea, and Hong Kong. This is perhaps reflective of a decrease in emphasis on some forms of collectivism in Confucian Asian cultures (see also Oyserman et al., 2002, for similar findings on Japan and Korea).

Finally, societies with high In-Group Collectivism value scores also tend to be characterized by practices wherein authority is respected and wherein there are few rules and little structure, more short-term orientation, and less performance orientation. As can be seen, this syndrome is somewhat similar to that found for societies characterized by Institutional Collectivism values, which is consistent with correlations between these two scales reported previously ($r = .29$, $p < .05$). Interestingly, the United States, although falling low on Institutional Collectivism values scores, is in the middle ranking on this scale, suggesting that respondents in the United States believe they should be more focused on this form of collectivism.

Correlations of GLOBE Collectivism and Hofstede and Schwartz

Table 16.9 displays the correlations among the four GLOBE societal Collectivism scores, Hofstede's (1980) individualism scores, and Schwartz's (1994) embeddedness and autonomy value scores. As can be seen, of the four GLOBE scales, In-Group Collectivism practices have the strongest correlations with these other collectivism scales.

In particular, as expected, there is a strong negative correlation between In-Group Collectivism practices and Hofstede's (1980) measure of individualism ($r = - .82$; $p < .01$). This fits with Hofstede's conceptual definition of collectivism. In addition, recall that GLOBE's societal In-Group Collectivism scale was in part derived from Triandis and colleagues' (1986) culture-level family integrity scale, and that the latter was also previously correlated with Hofstede's (1980) scores on collectivism ($r = .78$). Thus, the current results also replicate this relationship 15 years after Triandis conducted his research.

Indeed, a comparison of Hofstede's country rankings on individualism with the country rankings of GLOBE's In-Group Collectivism practices reveals that, for the most part, the same countries that were considered individualistic in Hofstede's (1980) dataset would still be classified as individualistic in the GLOBE dataset. Indeed, there is remarkable consistency among the countries that are were in the top third of Hofstede's most individualistic cultures and the countries that are in the most individualistic band in the GLOBE data (band C). These countries include the United States, Australia, Great Britain, Canada, the Netherlands, New Zealand, Denmark, and Sweden. Likewise, the countries that fell into the most collectivist third in Hofstede's dataset also tended to fall into the most collectivist band (band A) within the GLOBE dataset. This includes Venezuela, Colombia, Thailand, Portugal, Mexico, and the Philippines. Overall, these results suggest that rankings on societal individualism and collectivism have been remarkably stable over the last 30-year period.

Within this framework of similarities, there are also some interesting differences. For example, Hong Kong was in the most collectivist third in Hofstede's dataset, but was clustered in band B within the GLOBE dataset. This may be due to the rapid economic growth within this country in the past 20 years, which may have led to increased social independence, as discussed previously in this chapter. Of course,

Table 16.9 Correlations Between GLOBE's Societal Collectivism Scales and Hofstede's (1980) and Schwartz's (1994) Scales

GLOBE Scales	Hofstede's Individualism Scale	Schwartz's Embeddedness Value Scale	Schwartz's Intellectual Autonomy Value Scale	Schwartz's Affective Autonomy Value Scale
Institutional Collectivism practices	.15	.09	−.10	−.05
Institutional Collectivism values	−.55**	.14	−.13	−.25+
In-Group Collectivism practices	−.82**	.66**	−.59**	−.67**
In-Group Collectivism values	−.20	.15	−.14	−.14

** Correlation is significant at the .01 level (2-tailed).

+ Correlation is significant at the .10 level

differences in scale characteristics and samples between the two studies could also be operative, necessitating caution in interpreting such specific comparisons.

Table 16.9 also illustrates that other GLOBE scales also correlated with Hofstede's (1980) measure. Specifically, there was a significant negative correlation between Institutional Collectivism values and Hofstede's individualism scores ($r = .55, p < .01$) although this relationship is weaker than the In-Group Collectivism practices scale. Thus, according to these results, Hofstede's (1980) ranking is most similar to the ranking on GLOBE's In-Group Collectivism practices, but also shares some variance with the GLOBE Institutional Collectivism values scale.

With respect to Schwartz's (1994) value scales, Table 16.9 illustrates that GLOBE In-Group Collectivism practices is positively correlated with embeddedness ($r = .66, p < .01$) and negatively correlated with intellectual autonomy ($r =− .59, p < .01$) and affective autonomy ($r = .67, p < .01$). This too, fits with

the conceptual definition of conservatism that was offered by Schwartz (1994), which included the importance of close-knit harmonious relations in which the interests of the person are not viewed as distinct from those of the group.

In sum, these correlations reveal that of the two societal level Collectivism scales used in the GLOBE study, the In-Group Collectivism practices scale is the most highly correlated with other well-established societal-level collectivism scales in the literature. Thus, this scale received substantial convergent validity. It is interesting that the In-Group Collectivism practices scale correlates with several of Schwartz's values scales (positively with embeddedness, and negatively with intellectual and affective autonomy). Although the In-Group Collectivism values scale was also correlated with Schwartz's measure of embeddedness, it was nonsignificant. As reviewed previously, however, it is possible that there was a restriction of range of other GLOBE scales. Indeed, the In-Group Collectivism practices scale had the highest variability, which facilitated its correlation with other scales in the literature.

Based on these results, it is also evident that GLOBE's Institutional Collectivism practices scale seems to measure a different aspect of collectivism from those previously examined at the societal level of analysis. For example, as discussed in the previous section, Institutional Collectivism practices seem to be part of a cultural syndrome wherein such cultures are future focused and performance oriented yet seek to accomplish such orientations through practices that emphasize being concerned about others, and not being assertive or power dominating. This syndrome is not well captured by either Hofstede's (1980) measure or by the embeddedness versus autonomy distinction in Schwartz (1994). It may however, reflect, the combination of embeddedness and transcendence in Schwartz's theory.

Regional Differences and GLOBE Societal Collectivism

In Table 16.10a, the GLOBE countries are sorted into 10 clusters and the respective means for Institutional Collectivism practices and values are presented (see Chapter 10 by Gupta and Hanges for a discussion of the construction of clusters). Table 16.10b presents the mean scores for In-Group Collectivism practices and values for each cluster. Analyses of variance revealed that the clusters' means are statistically different for each of the four scales: Institutional Collectivism practices ($F[9, 51]$ = 6.22, $p < .01$), Institutional Collectivism values ($F[9, 51] = 9.36$, $p < .01$), In-Group Collectivism practices ($F[9, 51] = 14.98$, $p < .01$), and In-Group Collectivism values ($F[9, 51] = 6.47, p < .01$).

Table 16.10a illustrates several interesting patterns. First, the clusters with the highest Institutional Collectivism practices scores were Nordic Europe and Confucian Asia. The clusters with the lowest scores on Institutional Collectivism practices were Latin America, Latin Europe and Germanic Europe. This is consistent with the previous discussion of the country rankings. The scores for Latin America may, at first glance, seem surprising. However, it may be that since Latin American

respondents place such a strong emphasis on In-Group Collectivism (both practices and values, see below), this creates a vantage point from which societal practices are perceived as actually being too individualistic or are not to be trusted.

By contrast, the clusters with the highest Institutional Collectivism values scores were Latin America, the Middle East, and Southern Asia. On the other hand, Nordic Europe, Anglo countries, and Eastern Europe scored among the lowest on Institutional Collectivism values.

It is also interesting to note that respondents in most clusters desire more of Institutional Collectivism than they actually have (i.e., values scores are higher than practices scores). This is the case for the Middle East, Eastern Europe, Germanic Europe, Latin America, Latin Europe, Southern Asia, and Sub-Saharan Africa cultures. There may be different reasons, however, for these findings, depending on the region. For example, it may be that Germanic European respondents have a longing for more collectivism because of their focus on individualistic practices. On the other hand, respondents in the Middle East, Sub-Saharan Africa, and Latin America clusters may have higher scores on values than practices because of the fact that they are undergoing rapid cultural changes in political and economic structures (see the Annual Report, 2001, from the World Bank, for arguments along these lines). The only clusters wherein societal practices are rated higher than values are Confucian Asia, Anglo, and Nordic Europe. This illustrates that respondents in such regions express a desire for less institutional collectivism than they report having. Again, this may be due to different reasons, depending on the region. Respondents in Anglo regions, which are ruggedly individualistic, may highly devalue Institutional Collectivism but not In-Group Collectivism (see below) because of the historical distrust of collective structures and goals imposed through colonization. By contrast, respondents in Confucian Asian cultures may be less inclined to endorse institutional collectivism because of rapid changes toward individualism within the structure of societies (e.g., less focus on lifetime employment). Clearly, these

Table 16.10a   Culture Clusters and Institutional Collectivism—Practices and Values Mean Scores**

Culture Cluster	*Institutional Collectivism Practices Mean Scores*	*Institutional Collectivism Values Mean Scores*
Anglo England Ireland Australia South Africa (White sample) Canada New Zealand U.S.	4.46[b]	4.32[c]
Middle East Qatar Morocco Turkey Egypt Kuwait	4.28[b]	5.08[a]
Confucian Asia Taiwan Singapore Hong Kong South Korea China Japan	4.80[a]	4.43[b]
Eastern Europe Hungary Russia Kazakhstan Albania Poland Greece Slovenia Georgia	4.10[b]	4.34[c]
Germanic Europe Austria Switzerland Netherlands Germany (former East) Germany (former West)	4.03[c]	4.69[b]
Latin America Argentina Bolivia Brazil Colombia	3.86[c]	5.32[a]

(Continued)

Table 16.10a (Continued)

Culture Cluster	Institutional Collectivism Practices Mean Scores	Institutional Collectivism Values Mean Scores
Costa Rica Ecuador El Salvador Guatemala Mexico Venezuela		
Latin Europe Israel Italy Portugal Spain France Switzerland (French-speaking)	4.01[c]	4.84[b]
Nordic Europe Finland Sweden Denmark	4.88[a]	4.08[c]
Southern Asia India Indonesia Philippines Malaysia Thailand Iran	4.35[b]	5.03[a]
Sub-Saharan Africa Namibia Zambia Zimbabwe South Africa (Black sample) Nigeria	4.28[b]	4.66[b]

NOTE: Means with the letter superscript *a* are significantly higher than the others at $p < .05$, *b* are not significantly different from the others, and *c* are significantly lower than the others.

* Higher scores indicate more collectivism.

** Number of cases: 61.

arguments are merely speculative and need to be tested in future research, especially because it is argued that cultural practices and values change very slowly across generations (Hofstede, 2001).

Turning to the In-Group Collectivism scores, Table 16.10b also reveals some interesting patterns. First, the clusters with the highest In-Group Collectivism practices scores were Southern Asia, Middle East, Eastern Europe,

Table 16.10b   Culture Clusters and In-Group Collectivism—Practices and Values Mean Scores**

Culture Cluster	In-Group Collectivism Practices Mean Scores	In-Group Collectivism Values Mean Scores
Anglo England Ireland Australia South Africa (White sample) Canada New Zealand U.S.	4.30[c]	5.84[a]
Middle East Qatar Morocco Turkey Egypt Kuwait	5.58[a]	5.61[b]
Confucian Asia Taiwan Singapore Hong Kong South Korea China Japan	5.42[a]	5.30[c]
Eastern Europe Hungary Russia Kazakhstan Albania Poland Greece Slovenia Georgia	5.53[a]	5.57[b]
Germanic Europe Austria Switzerland Netherlands Germany (former East) Germany (former West)	4.21[c]	5.16[c]
Latin America Argentina Bolivia Brazil Colombia	5.52[a]	6.06[a]

(Continued)

Table 16.10b (Continued)

Culture Cluster	In-Group Collectivism Practices Mean Scores	In-Group Collectivism Values Mean Scores
Costa Rica Ecuador El Salvador Guatemala Mexico Venezuela		
Latin Europe Israel Italy Portugal Spain France Switzerland (French-speaking)	4.80[b]	5.66[b]
Nordic Europe Finland Sweden Denmark	3.75[c]	5.65[b]
Southern Asia India Indonesia Philippines Malaysia Thailand Iran	5.87[a]	5.77[b]
Sub-Saharan Africa Namibia Zambia Zimbabwe South Africa (Black sample) Nigeria	5.31[b]	5.63[b]

NOTE: Means with the letter superscript *a* are significantly higher than the others at $p < .05$, *b* are not significantly different from the others, and *c* are significantly lower than the others.

* Higher Scores indicate more collectivism.

** Number of cases: 61.

Latin America, and Confucian Asia. By contrast, Anglo, Germanic Europe, and Nordic Europe clusters score the lowest on In-Group Collectivism practices. As discussed previously, this scale is most highly correlated with Hofstede's (1980) rankings of nations. This is also reflected in these cluster rankings, which are similar to patterns identified by Hofstede.

Thus, even with different methods and with the passage of 30 years, the rankings on this form of collectivism remain similar.

Table 16.10b also illustrates that the clusters with the highest In-Group Collectivism values scores were Latin America and Anglo. Particularly low scores were found for Confucian Asia and Germanic Europe. This is important, as much research on the constructs has previously focused on Asian and American comparisons in which Asian respondents are seen as desiring In-Group Collectivism. However, these data illustrate that respondents in Anglo cultures actually express a desire for more of this form of collectivism than Confucian Asian cultures. Perhaps because it has historically been low in this region.

Finally, it is notable that the Anglo and the Nordic Europe clusters have large discrepancies between respondents' In-Group Collectivism values and practices. Specifically, scores for these clusters have much higher values than practices on In-Group Collectivism, which is perhaps not surprising given that both regions have been characterized as having low In-Group Collectivism in the past. Other clusters, such as Germanic Europe, also have higher scores on values than practices, although they are not as pronounced. Finally, two clusters—namely Southern Asia and Confucian Asia—have higher scores on practices than values, which may be indicative of the changes in interdependence among family members as such regions acquire more affluence (see previous discussion on the relationship between collectivism and wealth, and the Annual Report, 2001, from the World Bank).

GLOBE Measures and Other Economic and Social Indicators

In this section, we describe how Individualism–Collectivism is related to economic and social indicators. The indicators of interest have been extracted from three major databases: The World Economic Forum's Competitiveness Rankings, the United Nations Human Development Report, and the World Values Survey. Correlations between the practices and values scales of both GLOBE Institutional Collectivism and In-Group

Collectivism and these social and economic indicators were computed. The results are organized into the following categories: Economic health, success in science and technology, human condition, family and friends, achievement, political ideology, religion, and gender equality. For all of these analyses, we also report whether the relationships between Institutional and In-Group Collectivism change when controlling for national wealth (GNP per capita, based on 1998 data). As noted in Chapter 7 by Javidan and Hauser, In-Group Collectivism practices are highly negatively correlated with GNP per capita ($r = -.76$, $p < .01$), making it difficult to separate the two analytically. Nevertheless, we report both analyses below for the interested reader.

GLOBE Individualism–Collectivism and Economic Health

As discussed in previous sections, the question of whether individualism or collectivism is associated with healthier economies has been the focus of some research. Whereas some scholars have asserted that individualism leads to greater economic growth, others have suggested that collectivism is also associated with economic growth. The GLOBE findings on these issues are presented in Tables 16.11a and 16.11b.

Specifically, as discussed in Chapter 7 by Javidan and Hauser, economic health was assessed with four measures: Economic Prosperity, Public Sector Support for Prosperity, Societal Support for Competitiveness, and the Global Competitiveness Index from the World Economic Forum (1979).

Table 16.11a illustrates that societal Institutional Collectivism has some relationships with economic health. Three of the four economic indicators are significantly correlated with Institutional Collectivism scores. Institutional Collectivism practices are positively correlated with Economic Prosperity, Public Sector Support for Economic Prosperity, and Competitiveness Index. Societies reported to be practicing Institutional Collectivism tend to be more competitive and more economically prosperous. They also seem to have public sectors that are supportive of economic success.

Table 16.11a   Institutional Collectivism and Economic Health

Economic Health	Institutional Collectivism Practices	Institutional Collectivism Values
Economic prosperity	.33* N = 57	−.48** N = 57
Public sector support for prosperity	.36* N = 40	−.46** N = 40
Societal support for competitiveness	.28 N = 40	−.29 N = 40
WEF competitiveness index	.40** N = 41	−.47** N = 41

* Correlation is significant at the .05 level (2-tailed).

** Correlation is significant at the .01 level (2-tailed).

Table 16.11b   In-Group Collectivism and Economic Health

Economic Health	In-Group Collectivism Practices	In-Group Collectivism Values
Economic prosperity	−.78** N = 57	−.29* N = 57
Public sector support for prosperity	−.67** N = 40	−.27 N = 40
Societal support for competitiveness	−.14 N = 40	−.11 N = 40
WEF competitiveness index	−.45** N = 41	−.27 N = 41

* Correlation is significant at the .05 level (2-tailed).

** Correlation is significant at the .01 level (2-tailed).

As illustrated in Table 16.11a, the direction of the correlations between GLOBE Institutional Collectivism scores and these economic indicators are consistently reversed for Collectivism practices and values. Institutional Collectivism values are negatively correlated with economic prosperity, public sector support for prosperity, and competitiveness index. This is not surprising in light of the negative correlation between the values and practices scales for Institutional Collectivism (r =− .61**). We would note, however, that the correlation between Institutional Collectivism values and public support for prosperity becomes nonsignificant if GNP per capita is controlled for.

On the other hand, Table 16.11b illustrates that the relationship between In-Group Collectivism practices is negative with economic prosperity, public support for prosperity, and competitiveness index, but these relationships

Table 16.11c   Institutional Collectivism and Success in Science and Technology

Science and Technology	Institutional Collectivism Practices	Institutional Collectivism Values
Success in basic science	.39* N = 40	−.53** N = 40

* Correlation is significant at the .05 level (2-tailed).

** Correlation is significant at the .01 level (2-tailed).

Table 16.11d   In-Group Collectivism and Success in Science and Technology

Science and Technology	In-Group Collectivism Practices	In-Group Collectivism Values
Success in basic science	−.45** N = 40	−.44** N = 40

* Correlation is significant at the .05 level (2-tailed).

** Correlation is significant at the .01 level (2-tailed).

become nonsignificant after controlling for GNP per capita is controlled for. The significant relationships between In-Group Collectivism values scores and economic prosperity also become nonsignificant after controlling for GNP. Because GNP per capita and economic prosperity are positively related ($r = .91$, $p < .01$), the above findings suggest that prosperity is driven by higher GNP and not necessarily lower In-Group Collectivism.

GLOBE Individualism–Collectivism and Success in Science and Technology. We now turn to a discussion of GLOBE Individualism–Collectivism and success in science and technology, as well as the relationship between individualism–collectivism and societal attitudes toward science and research more generally. Success in basic science reflects the amount of technology transfer that occurs between corporations and universities, the ability of research to enhance economic and technological development, as well as the ability of science and technology to arouse the interest of youth.

The results in Table 16.11c show that Institutional Collectivism practices are positively related to success in basic science, whereas Institutional Collectivism values are negatively related to success in basic science. These findings suggest that in societies with high Institutional Collectivism practices scores, there is greater interest in basic science and there is also greater cooperation between academia and the business world. The greater incidence of technology transfer between universities and corporations may be due to a general societal focus on collective interests and cooperation within collectivistic societies in the interest of the betterment of the entire society.

As illustrated in Table 16.11d, both In-Group Collectivism values and practices are negatively and significantly correlated with success in basic science. However, both of these correlations become nonsignificant after controlling for GNP per capita. Thus, the positive relationship between individualism and success in basic science is likely driven by higher GNP per capita in individualistic cultures.

Table 16.11e   Institutional Collectivism and the Human Condition

Human Condition	Institutional Collectivism Practices	Institutional Collectivism Values
Societal health	.26 $N = 40$	−.33* $N = 40$
Human health	.08 $N = 56$	.06 $N = 56$
Life expectancy	.02 $N = 56$	−.13 $N = 56$
General satisfaction	.12 $N = 38$	−.01 $N = 38$
Human Development Index	.05 $N = 56$	−.19 $N = 56$

* Correlation is significant at the .05 level (2-tailed).

** Correlation is significant at the .01 level (2-tailed).

GLOBE Individualism–Collectivism and the Human Condition. In this section, the human condition refers to the general quality of life within a society and encompasses factors such as societal health, human health, life expectancy, general satisfaction, and the Human Development Index. The components of the human condition are specified in more detail in Chapter 7 by Javidan and Hauser and consist of societal health, human health, general satisfaction, and psychological health. Recall that in Chapter 7 the following hypotheses were advanced: Societies that are more collectively oriented tend to enjoy higher levels of societal health, enjoy higher levels of human health, and enjoy higher levels of human development.

As illustrated in Table 16.11e, the only significant correlation involving the human condition variables and Institutional Collectivism is the negative correlation between societal health and Institutional Collectivism values. This correlation suggests that cultures with high scores on Institutional Collectivism values experience lower societal health in terms of perceptions regarding justice, personal security, quality of life, and alcohol and drug abuse within the society.

By contrast, as illustrated in Table 16.11f, In-Group Collectivism appears to be more strongly associated with the human condition variables than Institutional Collectivism. In particular, the significant correlations involving In-Group Collectivism practices suggest that the higher the In-Group Collectivism practices, the lower the societal health, life expectancy, general satisfaction, and the Human Development Index. The findings are contrary to previously cited research by Triandis and his colleagues (Triandis et al., 1988), who found that heart-attack rates are lower in collectivistic than in individualistic cultures. However, the results are consistent with findings by Diener and colleagues (1995), who showed that individualism is positively associated with subjective well being at the societal level of analysis, as well as Hofstede's (2001) correlation of his individualism index with previous World Value Survey items on life satisfaction.

Overall, the pattern of results illustrates a negative relationship between In-Group Collectivism practices and the human condition, which is opposite from the original hypotheses presented by Javidan and Hauser in Chapter 7. One explanation for this may be that

Table 16.11f In-Group Collectivism and the Human Condition

Human Condition	In-Group Collectivism Practices	In-Group Collectivism Values
Societal health	−.60** N = 40	−.39* N = 40
Human health	−.11 N = 56	.03 N = 56
Life expectancy	−.45** N = 56	−.14 N = 56
General satisfaction	−.69** N = 38	−.06 N = 38
Human Development Index	−.56** N = 56	−.12 N = 56

* Correlation is significant at the .05 level (2-tailed).

** Correlation is significant at the .01 level (2-tailed).

many cultures with high scores on In-Group Collectivism are among the least wealthy and, therefore, have less access to medical care. Alternatively, these findings may be due to the fact that the construct of the human condition is itself partly cultural and in some cases Western. For example, an indicator of societal health in this analysis refers to "personal security and private property," which reflects a Western notion of health that may be inappropriate for evaluating societal health in collectivistic cultures. If strength of family ties were included as an indication of the human condition (as will be discussed below), then we would see that collectivist cultures fare better on other indicators. Likewise, alcohol and drug abuse in the workplace may not be a problem in many developing countries, but malaria, ailments due to the poor quality of drinking water, and the availability of hygiene facilities may be more crucial issues in these countries. As such, it may be more meaningful to look at specific health issues and collectivism rather than general indices of health.

GLOBE Individualism–Collectivism and Family and Friends. The strength of family ties in a society was indexed by items regarding the extent to which family is important in life, people are motivated to make their parents proud, and parents are supposed to make sacrifices for their children. Respect for family and friends refers to beliefs about loving and respecting one's parents unconditionally, exerting effort to live up to the expectations of friends, and living with one's parents. As can be seen in Table 16.11g, Institutional Collectivism values are positively correlated with the strength of family ties scale. Likewise, as shown in Table 16.11h, In-Group Collectivism practices and values are positively related to strength of family ties, and In-Group Collectivism practices are also correlated with respect for family and friends. Not surprisingly, this is consistent with the constructs and with previous research on the importance of family ties in many collectivist cultures (Triandis, 1995).

GLOBE Individualism–Collectivism and Achievement. This section involves correlations among collectivism, achieving results, and initiative. *Achievement* is defined in terms of the amount of freedom and control that people feel they have in the course of life, the extent to which people persevere until they are satisfied

Table 16.11g Institutional Collectivism and Family and Friends

Family and Friends	Institutional Collectivism Practices	Institutional Collectivism Values
Strength of family ties	−.29 N = 38	.52** N = 38
Respect for family and friends	.08 N = 38	.13 N = 38

* Correlation is significant at the .05 level (2-tailed).

** Correlation is significant at the .01 level (2-tailed).

Table 16.11h In-Group Collectivism and Family and Friends

Family and Friends	In-Group Collectivism Practices	In-Group Collectivism Values
Strength of family ties	.48** N = 38	.39* N = 38
Respect for family and friends	.76** N = 38	.09 N = 38

* Correlation is significant at the .05 level (2-tailed).

** Correlation is significant at the .01 level (2-tailed).

with the results of a task, and the importance that people place on doing a job that provides a sense of accomplishment. *Initiative* is a measure of the importance that people place on being able to use initiative in their jobs and on having a responsible job. As Table 16.11i shows, Institutional Collectivism values are positively correlated with Initiative. This relationship may be explained by the tendency for cultures that endorse Institutional Collectivism values to also believe that they should be more Performance Oriented, as discussed previously in the section on correlations with other GLOBE dimensions.

As shown in Table 16.11j, In-Group Collectivism values are significantly positively correlated with achieving results, although we note this correlation becomes nonsignificant after controlling for GNP per capita. This suggests that it is GNP per capita, and not collectivism, that explains achieving results. Because GNP per capita is an index of societal industrialization (and, thus, indirectly a measure of achieving results), this makes intuitive sense.

GLOBE Individualism–Collectivism and Political Ideology. In this section we explore the relationship between collectivism and six facets of political ideology. These are described in Chapter 7 by Javidan and Hauser and consist of disdain for democracy, passiveness, lack of voice, dislike for democracy, role of government, and stability. Similar to what has been found in other sections, Institutional Collectivism has fewer significant correlations with the political ideology variables than does

Table 16.11i   Institutional Collectivism and Achievement

	Institutional Collectivism Practices	*Institutional Collectivism Values*
Achieving results	.03 $N = 38$	.02 $N = 38$
Initiative	−.18 $N = 38$	.38* $N = 38$

* Correlation is significant at the .05 level (2-tailed).

** Correlation is significant at the .01 level (2-tailed).

Table 16.11j   In-Group Collectivism and Achievement

	In-Group Collectivism Practices	*In-Group Collectivism Values*
Achieving results	−.27 $N = 38$	.35* $N = 38$
Initiative	−.02 $N = 38$	.08 $N = 38$

* Correlation is significant at the .05 level (2-tailed).

** Correlation is significant at the .01 level (2-tailed).

In-Group Collectivism. The only significant correlation in Table 16.11k—the positive correlation between passiveness and Institutional Collectivism values—becomes nonsignificant after controlling for GNP.

Table 16.11l shows that In-Group Collectivism practices are positively correlated with passiveness, lack of voice, role of government, and stability, although the correlation involving stability becomes nonsignificant after controlling for GNP. The positive correlation of In-Group Collectivism practices and passiveness illustrates that the phenomena of signing petitions, boycotting, attending demonstrations, and joining unofficial strikes are less frequent in these societies. It is possible that clusters with respondents that scored high on In-Group Collectivism practices are likely to tolerate injustices because of their obligations to familial needs such as the need for a job to support the family. Likewise, having voice in governmental decisions and the community is likely to be a less salient issue in these societies, given that the focus is on more immediate in-groups and their survival.

GLOBE Individualism–Collectivism and Religion. As discussed previously, aspects of collectivism such as strong group identity have been evident in religions across the globe for centuries. In this section, we explore the relationship between Individualism–Collectivism and religiousness in modern-day societies. The components of religiousness are described in Chapter 7 by Javidan and Hauser. These components are religious devotion and religious dogma.

Table 16.11k   Institutional Collectivism and Political Ideology

Political Ideology	Institutional Collectivism Practices	Institutional Collectivism Values
Disdain for democracy	−.03 N = 26	.12 N = 26
Passiveness	−.23 N = 37	.34* N = 37
Lack of voice	.04 N = 38	.11 N = 38
Dislike for democracy	.18 N = 27	−.19 N = 27
Role of government	−.09 N = 38	.14 N = 38
Stability	.09 N = 38	−.15 N = 38

* Correlation is significant at the .05 level (2-tailed).

** Correlation is significant at the .01 level (2-tailed).

Table 16.11l   In-Group Collectivism and Political Ideology

Political Ideology	In-Group Collectivism Practices	In-Group Collectivism Values
Disdain for democracy	.32 N = 26	.31 N = 26
Passiveness	.66** N = 37	.28 N = 37
Lack of voice	.75** N = 38	.03 N = 38
Dislike for democracy	.25 N = 27	.30 N = 27
Role of government	.79** N = 38	.06 N = 38
Stability	.51** N = 38	.05 N = 38

* Correlation is significant at the .05 level (2-tailed).

** Correlation is significant at the .01 level (2-tailed).

Table 16.11m Institutional Collectivism and Religion

Religious Ideology	Institutional Collectivism Practices	Institutional Collectivism Values
Religious devotion	−.24 N = 38	.38* N = 38
Religious dogma	.11 N = 37	.22 N = 37

* Correlation is significant at the .05 level (2-tailed).

** Correlation is significant at the .01 level (2-tailed).

Table 16.11n In-Group Collectivism and Religion

Religious Ideology	In-Group Collectivism Practices	In-Group Collectivism Values
Religious devotion	.49** N = 38	.38* N = 38
Religious dogma	.49** N = 37	.35* N = 37

* Correlation is significant at the .05 level (2-tailed).

** Correlation is significant at the .01 level (2-tailed).

As seen in Table 16.11m, the only significant correlation is found between Institutional Collectivism values and religious devotion, although this positive correlation becomes nonsignificant after controlling for GNP. Table 16.11n shows that both In-Group Collectivism practices and values are significantly and positively correlated with religious devotion and religious dogma. After controlling for GNP, however, all of these correlations become nonsignificant.

GLOBE Individualism/Collectivism and Gender Equality. Tables 16.11o and 16.11p present results related to Collectivism and gender equality. Gender equality is discussed in Chapter 7 by Javidan and Hauser. As can be seen from these tables, gender equality as reported by the World Values Survey is not correlated with Institutional Collectivism. In contrast, In-Group Collectivism practices are negatively correlated with gender equality. In-group-oriented societies, such as those found in the Middle East and Southern Asia, tend to be male dominated.

Summary: Societal Collectivism

As the cumulative findings in this section reveal, the Institutional Collectivism and In-Group Collectivism scales measure different aspects of collectivism. In particular, the two scales show different patterns of correlations with other GLOBE scales and existing collectivism scales in the literature, different country and cluster rankings, and different relationships with external data. Likewise, values and practices measure different components and, indeed, are negatively related for Institutional Collectivism. Although institutional collectivism constructs have traditionally been seen as broad

Table 16.11o   Institutional Collectivism and Gender Equality

	Institutional Collectivism Practices	Institutional Collectivism Values
Gender equality	−.02 $N = 38$	−.05 $N = 38$

* Correlation is significant at the .05 level (2-tailed).

** Correlation is significant at the .01 level (2-tailed).

Table 16.11p   In-Group Collectivism and Gender Equality

	In-Group Collectivism Practices	In-Group Collectivism Values
Gender equality	−.69** $N = 38$	.05 $N = 38$

* Correlation is significant at the .05 level (2-tailed).

** Correlation is significant at the .01 level (2-tailed).

and complex (Triandis, 1995), they are often discussed as unitary in the literature. As such, GLOBE findings provide additional needed complexity that can help researchers understand and differentiate among different "syndromes" of collectivism. Next we turn to GLOBE results at the organizational level, before turning to GLOBE leadership results.

GLOBE RESULTS:
ORGANIZATIONAL LEVEL

Descriptive Statistics

Table 16.12 presents the summary statistics for the Organizational Collectivism I (Institutional Collectivism) and Organizational Collectivism II (In-Group Pride and Loyalty) practices and values scales, across all 62 cultures that participated in the GLOBE study. As with other chapters in this book, the results are separated by industry. For both Institutional and In-Group Collectivism practices, the food industry had a higher mean than the financial services and

telecommunication industries, although the differences in means were marginally significant only for the In-Group Collectivism practices ($F = 1.38$, $p > .10$ and $F = 2.87$, $p > .05$, respectively). For Institutional Collectivism values, the financial industry had a lower mean than the telecommunications industry (5.04) and the food industry (5.00), and these differences were significant ($F = 4.15$, $p < 0.05$). For In-Group Collectivism values, the financial services had a higher mean than the other two industries, but these differences were not statistically significant ($F = 1.51$, $p > .10$). As a general pattern, it is interesting to note that the food industry tends to have the most collectivist practices; in contrast, the financial industry tends to have the most Collectivism In-Group values.

Summary: Organizational Collectivism

The findings reveal that at the organizational level, both measures of Collectivism tend to be valued more than they are practiced. For both scales, the means on the Collectivism values

Table 16.12 Summary Statistics for Organizational Institutional and In-Group Collectivism for Three Industries

Variable	n	Minimum	Maximum	Mean	Standard Deviation
Financial Industry					
Institutional Collectivism practices	130	1.38	5.57	4.18	0.60
Institutional Collectivism values	130	3.83	5.83	4.85	0.41
In-Group Collectivism practices	130	2.85	5.69	4.64	0.51
In-Group Collectivism values	130	3.56	6.58	5.66	0.57
Food Industry					
Institutional Collectivism practices	91	2.17	5.20	4.31	0.50
Institutional Collectivism values	91	3.89	6.14	5.00	0.50
In-Group Collectivism practices	91	3.00	6.00	4.79	0.50
In-Group Collectivism values	91	3.57	6.41	5.52	0.58
Telecommunications Industry					
Institutional Collectivism practices	53	2.90	5.82	4.25	0.61
Institutional Collectivism values	53	3.68	6.00	5.04	0.57
In-Group Collectivism practices	53	3.48	5.56	4.62	0.54
In-Group Collectivism values	53	3.76	6.50	5.58	0.64

are consistently higher than the means for the Collectivism practices scales, and this finding is constant across all three industries (see Table 16.12).

GLOBE RESULTS: RELATIONSHIP BETWEEN SOCIETAL AND ORGANIZATIONAL PRACTICES AND SOCIETAL AND ORGANIZATIONAL VALUES

As indicated in Chapter 2, the GLOBE theoretical model postulates that societal practices and values affect organizational practices and values. For this chapter, we conducted four hierarchical linear models (HLMs) to test these hypotheses for organizational Individual–Collectivism practices and values. We tested the GLOBE hypothesis regarding the effect of societal culture on organizational culture by conducting HLM analyses in which organizational Collectivism was predicted by societal Collectivism (for both Institutional and In-Group Collectivism). These analyses supported our hypotheses in three of the four tests.

Specifically, practices for societal Institutional Collectivism have a significant and strong positive relationship with organizational Institutional Collectivism practices ($p < .01$). Unexpectedly, In-Group Collectivism practices at the societal level were not related to In-Group Collectivism practices at the organizational level. However, we found a significant and even stronger relationship between societal Collectivism values and organizational Collectivism values ($p < .01$) for both Institutional and In-Group Collectivism.

Therefore, in three of four tests, our analyses support a principal proposition in the GLOBE theoretical model (i.e., Proposition 3, Figure 2.1, Chapter 2, by House & Javidan); societal cultural values and practices affect organizational cultural values and practices.[7] This is particularly true for values. In both tests involving values, societal Institutional Collectivism values are associated with organizational Collectivism values. Thus, organizations in societies with high scores on institutional collectivist values tend to emphasize collective rewards over individual rewards. The results also indicate that the more a society values

Table 16.13   Second-Order Leadership Dimensions

Leadership Dimension:	Leader Attribute Items
Autonomous (second order) Autonomous	Individualistic, independent, autonomous, unique

Team Oriented (second order)
    Team I: Collaborative
        Team Orientation
    Team II: Team integrator
 	
    Diplomatic
    Malevolent (r)
 	
    Administratively competent
	Group-oriented, collaborative, loyal, consultative, mediator, fraternal
	Intra-group face-saver, team builder, informed, clear, integrator, coordinator, subdued (r)
	Diplomatic, worldly, win–win problem solver, effective bargainer
	Hostile, dishonest, vindictive, irritable, cynical, dependable (r), noncooperative, egotistical, and intelligent (r)
	Orderly, administratively skilled, organized, good administrator

Charismatic/Value-Based
(second order)
    Charismatic I: Visionary
 	
    Charismatic II: Inspirational
 	
    Charismatic III: Self-sacrifice
    Integrity
    Decisive
    Performance oriented
	Foresight, intellectually stimulating, future-oriented, prepared, anticipatory, plans ahead, inspirational, visionary, able to anticipate
	Enthusiastic, positive, encouraging, morale booster, motive arouser, confidence builder, dynamic, motivational
	Risk taker, self-sacrificial, convincing
	Honest, sincere, just trustworthy
	Willful, decisive, logical, intuitive
	Improvement-oriented, excellence-oriented, performance-oriented

NOTE: (r) indicates that the dimension or item is reverse scored.

In-Group Collectivism, the more organizations within that society are reported to practice organizational In-Group Collectivism.

Finally, although not illustrated in these tables, it is important to note that the societal scales for Collectivism are highly correlated across industries, demonstrating that societal scores on these scales are generalizable across industries (see Hanges & Dickson, Chapter 8, this volume, for statistical details).

GLOBE FINDINGS: INDIVIDUALISM AND COLLECTIVISM AND IMPLICIT THEORIES OF EFFECTIVE LEADERSHIP

In this last section, we present GLOBE findings that relate Individualism–Collectivism to reported effective leadership dimensions at the societal and organizational levels of analysis. On the basis of our previous review (see Table 16.3), we generally expected that societal collectivism would be negatively related to Autonomous leadership and positively related to Team-Oriented and Charismatic/Value-Based leadership. At the same time, we also expected that different forms of collectivism might have different leadership correlates. We also examined whether the effects would be found at the organizational level of analysis. The measures for the leadership attributes that were of primary interest (Autonomous leadership, Team-Oriented leadership, and Charismatic/Value-Based leadership) are presented in Table 16.13. We will also provide a discussion of the relationship between Individualism–Collectivism and other leadership attributes (i.e., Humane-Oriented, Self-Protective, and Participative leadership) for exploratory purposes (see Chapter 8 by Hanges & Dickson for specific measures of these dimensions).

Culture Cluster Rankings for Predicted Culturally Endorsed Leadership Theories

As discussed in Chapter 8, there are significant differences in values and practices for every cultural dimension among the 61 societal cultures (i.e., recall that GLOBE uses the term *societal cultures* rather than nations). Table 16.14 presents the average perceived effectiveness scores for each cluster for the three leadership dimensions. Analyses of variance were conducted to evaluate whether the differences across clusters are statistically significant. Results indicate that cluster differences are significant for Charismatic/Value-Based, Team-Oriented, and Autonomous leadership ($p < .05$). Post hoc analyses demonstrate that the Latin America cluster has a higher score for Team-Oriented leadership than all others, which, in turn, have higher scores than the Middle East. For Charismatic/Value-Based leadership, the Anglo, Latin America, and Southern Asia clusters have the highest scores and the Middle East the lowest scores. For the Autonomous dimension, the Eastern Europe cluster has the highest scores and Latin America has the lowest.

Correlation Between Societal Collectivism and Leadership Dimensions

Table 16.15 displays the correlations between the leadership dimensions and the four societal Collectivism scales. As the table illustrates, the correlations are generally consistent with theoretical expectations. The only significant correlation involving Autonomous leadership, however, was with Institutional Collectivism values, and this correlation was negative ($r = -.48$, $p < .01$) as hypothesized. This indicates that managers in those cultures that desire to emphasize collective goals and interests more than they currently do are less likely to emphasize Autonomous leadership. This relationship makes conceptual sense, as independent, individualistic, unique, and autonomous leader behaviors are incongruent with the promotion of collective interests.

Team-Oriented leadership was positively correlated with Institutional Collectivism values ($r = .26$, $p < .05$) and In-Group Collectivism practices ($r = .30$, $p < .05$) and values ($r = .37$, $p < .01$). In other words, those cultures in which respondents value collective goals and interests, and practice and value family pride and interdependence are more likely to endorse collaborative and team-integrating leader behaviors as effective behaviors.

The leader behaviors listed in Table 16.13 comprising Team-Oriented leadership are perceived to be in the service of collectivistic practices and norms. Finally, Charismatic/Value-Based leadership was positively correlated with In-Group Collectivism values ($r = .32$, $p < .05$). This relationship suggests that charismatic leadership is more highly endorsed by managers in those cultures that value family pride and interdependence. Those societies in which managers express a desire for increased family pride and interdependence are more receptive to charismatic leadership, and this finding supports hypotheses that have been advanced in the literature (e.g., Jung et al., 1995; Meindl, 1995; Pillai & Meindl, 1998) and that were discussed in previous sections. Indeed, the emergence of charismatic leadership appears to be more likely in societies with high In-Group Collectivism values, presumably because the readiness for charismatic leadership is a function of the degree of interconnectedness within workgroups, which, in turn, is assumed to be a function of societal collectivism. In the following section, we report the results of the more sophisticated HLM analyses to examine the relationships between culture and culturally endorsed leadership theories (CLTs).

Hierarchical Linear Modeling Analyses

We tested for the relationship between culture and the CLT leadership dimensions by using hierarchical linear modeling. An overview of HLM analyses and a detailed discussion of how we conducted these analyses are provided in Chapter 11 by Hanges, Dickson, and Sipe. This present chapter presents relationships between one culture dimension (Individualism and Collectivism) and the six CLTS. Competitive tests of all culture dimensions and

Table 16.14   Perceived Effectiveness Scores for Leadership Scales Based on Culture Clusters

Culture Cluster	Autonomous Leadership	Charismatic Leadership	Team-Oriented Leadership
Anglo England Ireland Australia South Africa (White sample) Canada New Zealand U.S.	3.82	6.05	5.74
Middle East Qatar Morocco Turkey Egypt Kuwait Iran	3.68	5.35	5.47
Confucian Asia Taiwan Singapore Hong Kong South Korea China Japan	4.04	5.63	5.61
Eastern Europe Hungary Russia Kazakhstan Albania Poland Greece Slovenia Georgia	4.20	5.74	5.88
Germanic Europe Austria Switzerland Netherlands Germany (Former East) Germany (Former West)	4.16	5.93	5.62
Latin America Argentina Bolivia Brazil	3.51	5.99	5.96

Culture Cluster	Autonomous Leadership	Charismatic Leadership	Team-Oriented Leadership
Colombia Costa Rica Ecuador El Salvador Guatemala Mexico Venezuela			
Latin Europe Israel Italy Portugal Spain France Switzerland (French- speaking)	3.66	5.78	5.73
Nordic Europe Finland Sweden Denmark	3.94	5.93	5.77
Southern Asia India Indonesia Philippines Malaysia Thailand Iran	3.99	5.97	5.86
Sub-Sahara Africa Namibia Zambia Zimbabwe South Africa (Black sample) Nigeria	3.63	5.79	5.70

CLTs are presented in Chapter 21 by Dorfman and colleagues.[8] In general, as Dorfman argues in Chapter 21, GLOBE expected that societal and organizational values will be more strongly related to CLT leadership dimensions than societal and organizational practices. (See Dorfman argument in Chapter 21.) As indicated previously, our notions of values and CLT leadership dimensions represent idealized concepts of how the world *Should Be* in contrast to practices, which represent the world *As Is*. As you

read through the results discussed below, it may be helpful to view Figures 16.1 and 16.2 for a visual summary. These figures, however, show only results regarding cultural values, not practices. (All HLM coefficients are presented in Table 21.10 of Chapter 21 by Dorfman et al.)

Specifically, we explored whether Collectivism values and practices were related to Team-Oriented, Autonomous, Charismatic/ Value-Based, Self-Protective, Participative,

Table 16.15   Societal Collectivism and Leadership Correlation Matrix

Leadership Dimensions	Institutional Collectivism Practices	Institutional Collectivism Values	In-Group Collectivism Practices	In-Group Collectivism Values
Autonomous leadership	.22	−.48**	−.01	−.20
Team-Oriented leadership	−.24	.26*	.30*	.37**
Charismatic leadership	−.11	.10	−.06	.32*

* Correlation is significant at the .05 level (2-tailed). $N = 61$

** Correlation is significant at the .01 level (2-tailed).

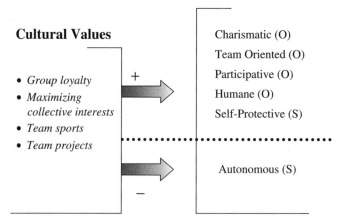

Institutional Collectivism Cultural Dimension

Leadership CLT Dimensions*

Cultural Values

- *Group loyalty*
- *Maximizing collective interests*
- *Team sports*
- *Team projects*

Charismatic (O)
Team Oriented (O)
Participative (O)
Humane (O)
Self-Protective (S)

Autonomous (S)

Figure 16.1   Institutional Collectivism Cultural Values as Drivers for CLT Leadership Dimensions

* Only statistically significant relationships for values (not practices) are shown ($p < .05$; see Table 21.10, Chapter 21 by Dorfman et al.)

CLT = Culturally endorsed leadership theory

O = Organizational level

S = Societal level

and Humane-Oriented leadership. In the following results, we first report the total amount of societal and organizational variance explained by Institutional Collectivism. We then turn to the total amount of organizational and societal variance explained by In-Group Collectivism.

HLM Results for Institutional Collectivism

- *Charismatic/Value-Based leadership.* Institutional Collectivism practices and values scores were significantly related to Charismatic/ Value-Based leadership and explained a total of

In-Group Collectivism Cultural Dimension

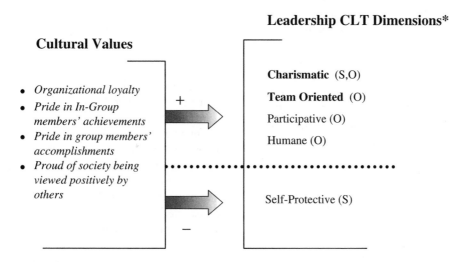

Figure 16.2 In-Group Collectivism Cultural Values as Drivers for CLT Leadership Dimensions

* Only statistically significant relationships for *values* (not Practices) are shown ($p < .05$; see Table 21.10, Chapter 21 by Dorfman et al.). The most important leadership CLT relationships are bolded (i.e., relationship is significant at both society and organization levels of analyses or highest HLM coefficient within each level of analysis). Results for Practices are described in the text.

CLT = Culturally endorsed leadership theory

O = Organizational level

S = Societal level

5.9% of the organizational and societal variance for this dimension. All of this explained variance was associated with forces operating at the organizational level. The organizational Institutional Collectivism practices scores were significantly positively related to the Charismatic/Value-Based leadership dimension ($p < .01$), as were the organizational Institutional Collectivism values scores ($p < .01$). Charismatic/Value-Based leadership is more likely to be perceived as contributing to effective leadership in organizations with high Institutional Collectivism practices and values scores.

• *Team-Oriented leadership.* Institutional Collectivism practices and values scores were significantly related to the Team-Oriented leadership dimension and explained a total of 6.6% of the organizational and societal variance for this dimension. All of the explained variance was associated with forces operating at the organizational level. The organizational Institutional Collectivism practices scores were significantly positively related ($p < .01$) to the Team-Oriented leadership dimension, as were the Organizational Institutional Collectivism values scores ($p < .01$). Team-Oriented leadership is more likely to be perceived as contributing to effective leadership in organizations with high Institutional Collectivism practices and values scores.

• *Participative leadership.* Institutional Collectivism practices and values scores were significantly related to the Participative leadership dimension and explained a total of 6.8% of the organizational and societal variance. Of the total explained variance, 13.6% was associated with forces operating at the organizational level of analysis. The remaining explained variance, 86.4%, was associated with forces operating at the societal level of analysis.

The organizational Institutional Collectivism values scores were significantly positively related ($p < .01$) to the Participative leadership dimension. Participative leadership is more likely to be perceived as contributing to effective leadership in organizations with high Institutional Collectivism values scores. The societal Institutional Collectivism practices scores were significantly negatively related ($p < .05$) to the Participative leadership dimension. Participative leadership is less likely to be perceived as contributing to effective leadership in organizations with high Institutional Collectivism practices scores.

• *Humane-Oriented leadership.* Institutional Collectivism practices and values scores were significantly related to the Humane-Oriented leadership dimension and explained a total of 4.1% of the organizational and societal variance for this dimension. All of the explained variance was associated with forces operating at the organizational level. The organizational Institutional Collectivism practices scores were significantly positively related ($p < .05$) to the Humane-Oriented leadership dimension, as were the organizational Institutional Collectivism values scores ($p < .01$). Humane-Oriented leadership is more likely to be perceived as contributing to effective leadership in organizations with high Institutional Collectivism values and practices scores.

• *Autonomous leadership.* Institutional Collectivism practices and values scores were significantly and negatively related to this dimension and explained 12.3% of the organizational and societal variance. Of this total explained variance, approximately 7.8% was associated with forces operating at the organizational level of analysis. The majority (92.2%) of the explained variance was associated with forces operating at the societal level of analysis.

The organizational Institutional Collectivism practices scores were significantly negatively related ($p < .05$) to the Autonomous leadership dimension. Autonomous leadership is less likely to be perceived as contributing to effective leadership in organizations with high Institutional Collectivism practices scores.

The societal Institutional Collectivism values scores were significantly negatively related ($p < .05$) to the Autonomous leadership dimension. Autonomous leadership is less likely to be perceived as contributing to effective leadership in societies with high Institutional Collectivism values scores.

• *Self-Protective leadership.* Institutional Collectivism practices and values scores were significantly related to this dimension and explained a total of 8.4% of the organizational and societal variance. One hundred percent of this explained variance was associated with forces operating at the societal level of analysis. The societal Institutional Collectivism values scores were significantly positively related ($p < .05$) to the Self-Protective leadership dimension. Self-Protective leadership is more likely to be perceived as contributing to effective leadership in organizations with high Institutional Collectivism values scores.

HLM Results for In-Group Collectivism

• *Charismatic/Value-Based leadership:* Collectivism II practices and values scores were significantly related to the Charismatic/Value-Based leadership dimension and explained a total of 22.1% of the organizational and societal variance for this dimension. Approximately 53.8% of this total explained variance was associated with forces operating at the organizational level of analysis. The remaining portion of the explained variance (46.2%) was associated with forces operating at the societal level of analysis.

The organizational Group Pride and Loyalty values scores were significantly positively related ($p < .01$) to the Charismatic/Value-Based leadership dimension. Charismatic/Value-Based leadership is more likely to be perceived as contributing to effective leadership in organizations with high In-Group Collectivism values scores.

The societal In-Group Collectivism values scores were significantly positively related ($p < .01$) to the Charismatic/Value-Based leadership dimension. Charismatic/Value-Based leadership is more likely to be perceived as contributing to effective leadership in societies with high In-Group Collectivism values scores.

• *Team-Oriented leadership:* Collectivism II practices and values scores were significantly related to this dimension and explained a total of 33.8% of the organizational and societal variance for this dimension. Approximately 36.8% of this total explained variance was associated with forces operating at the organizational level of analysis. The remaining portion of the explained variance (63.2%) was associated with forces operating at the societal level of analysis.

The organizational Group Pride and Loyalty values scores were significantly positively related ($p < .01$) to the Team-Oriented leadership dimension. Team-Oriented leadership is more likely to be perceived as contributing to effective leadership in organizations with high In-Group Collectivism values scores.

The societal In-Group Collectivism practices scores were significantly positively related ($p < .05$) to the Team-Oriented leadership dimension. Team-Oriented leadership is more likely to be perceived as contributing to effectiveness in societies with high In-Group Collectivism practices scores.

• *Participative leadership:* Collectivism II practices and values scores were significantly related to the Participative leadership dimension and explained a total of 28% of the organizational and societal variance. Approximately 4.6% of this total explained variance was associated with forces operating at the organizational level of analysis. The rest of the explained variance (95.4%) was associated with forces operating at the societal level of analysis.

The organizational In-Group practices scores were significantly negatively related ($p < .05$) to the Participative leadership dimension, whereas the organizational Group Pride and Loyalty values scores were significantly positively related ($p < .01$) to the Participative leadership dimension. Participative leadership is less likely to be perceived as contributing to effective leadership in organizations reported to have practices consistent with In-Group Collectivism. Participative leadership is more likely to be perceived as contributing to effective leadership in organizations with high In-Group Collectivism values scores.

The societal In-Group Collectivism practices scores were significantly negatively related ($p < .01$) to the Participative leadership dimension. Participative leadership is less likely to be perceived as contributing to effective leadership in societies with high In-Group Collectivism practices scores.

• *Humane-Oriented leadership:* Collectivism II practices and values scores were significantly related to this dimension and explained a total of 20.1% of the organizational and societal variance. Approximately 50.6% of this total explained variance was associated with forces operating at the organizational level of analysis. The remaining portion of the total explained variance (49.4%) was associated with forces operating at the societal level of analysis.

The organizational In-Group values scores were significantly positively related ($p < .01$) to the Humane-Oriented leadership dimension. Humane-Oriented leadership is more likely to be perceived as contributing to effective leadership in organizations with high In-Group Collectivism values scores.

The societal In-Group Collectivism practices scores were significantly positively related ($p < .01$) to the Humane-Oriented leadership dimension. Humane-Oriented leadership is more likely to be perceived as contributing to effective leadership in societies with high In-Group Collectivism practices scores.

• *Autonomous leadership:* Collectivism II practices and values scores were significantly related to this dimension, but they explained a total of just 0.8% of the organizational and societal variance. One hundred percent of this variance was associated with forces operating at the organizational level of analysis. The organizational Group Pride and Loyalty practices scores were significantly positively related ($p < .05$) to the Autonomous leadership dimension. Autonomous leadership is more likely to be perceived as contributing to effective leadership in organizations with high In-Group Collectivism practices scores.

- *Self-Protective leadership:* Collectivism II practices and values scores were significantly related to this dimension and explained a total of 49.2% of the organizational and societal variance. One hundred percent of this explained variance was associated with forces operating at the societal level of analysis. The societal In-Group Collectivism practices scores were significantly positively related ($p < .01$) to the Self-Protective leadership dimension, whereas the societal In-Group Collectivism values scores were significantly negatively related ($p < .05$) to the Self-Protective leadership dimension. Self-Protective leadership is more likely to be perceived as contributing to effective leadership in societies reported to have practices that conform to In-Group Collectivism, whereas Self-Protective leadership is less likely to be perceived as contributing to effective leadership in societies with high In-Group Collectivism values scores.

As with previous results, the relationship between collectivism and leadership has some commonality across different measures of collectivism, but also varies depending on the nature of collectivism being considered and the level of analysis being considered. Below we first describe the effects of collectivism that were generally found for most measures across both levels of analysis. These can be considered "strong" universal effects of collectivism and perceptions of effective leadership. We then consider effects that were unique to the societal and organizational levels of analysis, as well as those effects that even illustrated reversals across the societal and organizational levels of analysis.

Collectivism and Leadership: Strong Universals Across Type and Level

The HLM analysis illustrated that two CLTs were consistently related to collectivism across the societal and organizational levels, and generally across different scales, namely Charismatic/Value-Based and Team-Oriented leadership. As expected, those societies (and organizations) that either practice or value collectivism (Institutional or In-Group) are more likely to endorse Charismatic/Value-Based leadership as important for effective leadership, and these effects are particularly strong at the organizational level of analysis for the Institutional Collectivism scale.

These findings suggest that collectivism as a cultural pattern is related to charismatic leadership at both levels. This is consistent with previously discussed research that has been conducted at the organizational level (Pillai & Meindl, 1998), and further illustrates that these effects operate at the societal level as well. Theoretically speaking, because charisma is the power to inspire devotion and commitment for the group's goals, it is not surprising that charismatic attributes are seen as effective in collectivistic societies. Within collectivistic societies, the interdependent concept of the self, relational social exchanges, and obligations to in-groups all likely facilitate the perception that charismatic leadership is effective.

Likewise, as expected, the HLM analyses generally illustrated that across levels and types, Collectivism is positively associated with Team-Oriented leadership. These effects, interestingly, are also stronger at the organizational level for Institutional Collectivism, but stronger at the societal level for In-Group Collectivism. However, it is important to note that team leadership itself does not account for a large amount of variance in the analyses. Thus, overall, the expectation that collectivism is associated with charismatic and team leadership received support, although the former was much stronger than the latter.

Collectivism at the Societal Level: Unique Effects

The HLM results also illustrated that the perception of certain leadership dimensions is largely driven by societal Collectivism, including the CLTs of Self-Protective and Participative leadership. First, the results indicated that both Institutional Collectivism (practices and values) and In-Group Collectivism (practices) were associated with an emphasis on Self-Protective leadership, which includes status-conscious and face-saving leader behaviors. This is not surprising given the emphasis in Asian cultures (several of which scored high on both forms of GLOBE Collectivism) on face-saving as an important component of harmony regulation in groups (Kim, 1994). In other words, the interdependence that is associated with collectivism, be it in societal institutions or in the in-group, requires leaders to be effective in managing interpersonal dynamics.

We suspect that the emphasis on face-saving in both types of Collectivist cultures may be due to different reasons. For example, it may be due to the importance of respect for authority in societies that emphasize In-Group Collectivism, yet it may be due to the importance of non-assertiveness and humane orientation in societies that practice Institutional Collectivism (i.e., in Scandinavian cultures). One surprising result, however, is that the less a society values In-Group Collectivism, the more it views Self-Protective leadership as effective. As discussed previously, the In-Group Collectivism scale is associated with the syndrome in which societal practices focus on authority differentiation, and in which people believe that there should be more of a focus on family ties and concern for others. As such, the desire for such cultural elements could possibly be served by attention to face-saving. As noted above, these effects are based entirely at the societal level of analysis; Collectivism at the organizational level is not related to Self-Protective leadership.

Second, Institutional and In-Group Collectivism practices at the societal level were consistently negatively associated with Participative leadership, and the societal level accounted for the vast majority (greater than 80%) of variance in this CLT. These effects illustrate that those societies that practice Institutional or In-Group Collectivism are less likely to perceive that participativeness is an important component of effective leadership. Again, this may be for different reasons, depending on the nature of collectivism. For example, this relationship may be due to the reliance on individual authority figures in societies that emphasize In-Group Collectivism, yet it may be due to the reliance on collectivities (e.g., government, top management groups) to take care of others in societies that practice institutional collectivism. This explanation, of course, needs substantiation in future research.

DIFFERENCES IN PERCEPTIONS OF LEADERSHIP ACROSS LEVELS

As stated previously, Dorfman argues that cultural values, not practices, are more compatible with CLTs as the latter reflect desired leadership attributes. Consistent with this, not surprisingly, the results across levels are very consistent for cultural values, but less so for cultural practices. Consistent with a multilevel perspective, the data showed that Collectivism and effective leadership were not always consistent across levels and, in fact, had some notable reversals in effects, particularly for cultural practices. For example, although Participative leadership practices were negatively associated with effective leadership at the societal level, they were positively associated with effective leadership at the organizational level for In-Group Collectivism values, as well as Institutional Collectivism values.

Likewise, whereas Autonomous leadership was negatively associated with effective leadership at the societal level for Institutional Collectivism values, the results were mixed at the organizational level. For example, organizations that practice Institutional Collectivism—those organizations that focus on group over individual interests—were less likely to perceive autonomy as being associated with effective leadership. However, the more organizations practice group pride and loyalty (Collectivism II), the more likely Autonomous leadership was seen as effective. Because the latter form of collectivism focuses on having pride in individuals' accomplishment within groups, it is perhaps understandable that uniqueness and independence in leadership is also embraced in these organizations. However, it is worth noting that the amount of variance explained for this CLT is very low, thus rendering these findings not very substantial.

Overall, these analyses indicate that the extent to which the collectivistic cultural practices and values are emphasized in organizations and societies is reflected in the kind of leadership that is viewed as effective. Our findings support the argument that culture plays a role in influencing the content of leader attributes that are considered effective. Furthermore, the results were consistent with predictions regarding Collectivism values and leadership (see Figures 16.1 and 16.2). The leadership attributes that were commonly associated across both types of Collectivism values included Charismatic/Value-Based, Team-Oriented, Participative, and Humane-Oriented leadership.

CONCLUSION

In this chapter we have traced the evolution of the constructs of individualism and collectivism from ancient civilizations to early philosophers and on to modern-day science. Since the publication of the work by Hofstede in 1980, scholars have demonstrated the usefulness of the constructs at all levels, whether individual, organizational, or societal. The GLOBE project has built on these traditions and furthers our understanding of the multilevel and multidimensional nature of individualism and collectivism. Below, we briefly review several important lessons learned through this research journey.

First, the GLOBE project replicates and extends our understanding of individualism and collectivism at the societal level of analysis. Remarkably, although GLOBE data were collected 25 years after Hofstede's (1980), GLOBE's culture (i.e., nation) scores for In-Group Collectivism are very highly and inversely correlated with Hofstede's (1980) nation scores on individualism. Thus, rankings of societal culture on the constructs have, with some exceptions, been quite stable. On the one hand, this finding should not be too surprising. Cultures are complex entities that consist of interacting forces of ecology, institutions, groups, and individuals. As such, they should change quite slowly. On the other hand, given the enormous rate of change in the world in the past few decades, some have argued that we are experiencing the development of a "universal civilization" and the acceptance of shared values, beliefs, and practices around the world (see Huntington, 1996).

The GLOBE data reveal, however, that variability in values and practices of In-Group Collectivism is alive and well at the societal level despite changes in world economic and political activity. Of course, it is not possible to state that specific cultures have not changed; we can state only that the rankings of cultures with respect to collectivism have generally not changed. Nevertheless, GLOBE provides compelling evidence of the diversity of culture at the societal level when it comes to In-Group Collectivism. Furthermore, GLOBE also makes another important contribution by providing a measurement of another form of collectivism—Institutional Collectivism—and thereby moving the literature beyond an exclusive focus on In-Group Collectivism (cf. Triandis & Gelfand, 1998). In particular, GLOBE's Institutional Collectivism scale shows important societal variability that is not captured by the In-Group Collectivism scale. For example, Scandinavian nations can score high on Institutional Collectivism, yet score very low on other forms of In-Group Collectivism. Thus, project GLOBE expands the literature by further illustrating the multidimensional nature of the construct at the societal level of analysis.

Second, Project GLOBE has enriched our understanding of individualism and collectivism at the organizational level of analysis. To date, there has been little research that explicitly considers the nature of organizational collectivism. It is now clear that organizations can be reliably differentiated on different forms of collectivism, and that such constructs are qualitatively similar to those at the societal level of analysis. Further, in support of a multilevel perspective, Project GLOBE illustrates that societal-level collectivism is highly related to organizational-level collectivism. This provides compelling evidence of the cross-level effects of the constructs, a notion that has thus far been more of an assumption than an empirical fact. Project GLOBE also found support for other predictors of organizational-level collectivism, namely, the nature of the industry, which is consistent with the findings of Kanungo and his colleagues (Kanungo et al., 1999). Moreover, Project GLOBE demonstrates that organizational-level collectivism has consequences for the nature of effective leadership in predictable ways. Aside from these specific learnings, the project provides a very useful template for future multilevel cross-cultural research.

Third, project GLOBE has illustrated that culture plays an important role in influencing the attributes that are perceived to contribute to leadership effectiveness. Although there have been some studies conducted on culture and leadership, none have the scope (62 nations at societal and organizational levels) and depth (multiple dimensions of leadership) provided by the GLOBE project. The data presented clearly illustrate that societal and organizational collectivism are related to the kind of leadership that is viewed as effective. Consistent with culture theory, across both levels and across most scales, the attributes that were commonly associated with collectivism included Team-Oriented and Charismatic/ Value-Based leadership. In addition, for both types of Collectivism values, Humane-Oriented leadership was also endorsed as contributors to leadership effectiveness. The ranking of 62 nations on perceptions of effective leadership will be useful for future theory building on leadership as well as for helping to train managers who are traversing different cultures.

This research makes clear the multidimensional nature of the constructs at different levels of analysis. Collectivism varies both in terms of the institutional structures that are used to solve societal and organizational problems, as well as in the nature of family and group loyalty. It also varies in terms of both values and practices, which can result in different country rankings and different societal and organizational correlates. This complexity should be welcomed.

In conclusion, as this chapter has shown, future efforts should be made to develop theory and measurements of individualism and collectivism that are both multidimensional and multilevel, and research needs to move away from a simplistic and unitary view of the constructs. In addition to developing theory and measurements across levels, much research is needed to examine cross-level analyses of the constructs. Research is also sorely needed on the nature of culture change, again at multiple levels of analysis. Although this chapter reviewed data that were collected at one point in time, the constructs are dynamic and future research is needed to delineate the antecedents and consequences of change of different forms of individualism and collectivism. We suspect that the constructs of individualism and collectivism are unlikely to languish in the near future and that efforts to harness this theory for understanding and predicting human behavior in our global village will advance the science and practice of organizational behavior.

ENDNOTES

1. Although Triandis discusses these four attributes as separate, Bhawuk (2001) presented a theoretical framework that integrates the four defining attributes. He put concept of self, or the first defining attribute, at the center of the framework and argued that the other three defining attributes relate to how an individual interacts with *other groups* (e.g., the structure of goals), how an individual interacts with *society at large* (e.g., attitudes vs. norms), and how individuals interact with *other individuals* (e.g., relationality vs. rationality).

Specifically, according to Bhawuk (2001) the first attribute, the nature of the self, is the most central or most important defining attribute (cf. Markus & Kitayama, 1991; Triandis, 1989). The second defining attribute focuses on the relationship between self and groups of people. Depending on how people view themselves, they develop different types of affinity to groups. For example, those with an independent concept of self develop ties with other people to satisfy their self needs and may not give importance to the needs of other people (i.e., everybody takes care of his or her own needs). However, those with the interdependent concept of self develop ties with other people to satisfy the needs of the self as well as the members of the collective included in the self. This attribute characterizes what Triandis and colleagues (Triandis, 1989; Triandis, Leung, Villareal, & Clark, 1985) labeled the subordination (or lack) of individual goals to the goals of a collective. One reason for this difference between individualists and collectivists lies in their different concept of self and how they define an in-group or out-group. When a certain group of people is accepted as trustworthy, collectivists cooperate with these people, are even willing to make self-sacrifices to be part of this group, and are less likely to indulge in social loafing (Earley, 1989). However, they are likely to indulge in exploitative exchange with people who are in their out-groups (Triandis et al., 1988). Individualists, on the other hand, do not make such strong distinctions between in-groups and out-groups. Another reason for making this distinction is the collectivists' perception of a common fate with their family, kin, friends, and coworkers (Hui & Triandis, 1986; Triandis, McCusker & Hui, 1990). The reason for giving priority to the in-group goals could be the narrowness of the perceived boundary between the individual and the others or smaller social distance between the self and others.

The third defining attribute focuses on how the self is viewed vis-à-vis the larger society, or how the self interacts with the society. Those with independent concept of self do what they like to do, or what they think is good for them (i.e., they pursue their individual desires, attitudes, values, and beliefs). Because this meets the need of most of the people in a culture in which most people have an independent concept of self, the individualistic society values people doing their own thing. However, people with interdependent concept of self inherit many relationships and learn to live with these interdependencies. Part of managing the interdependencies is to develop goals that meet the needs of more than one's own self. In the process of taking care of the needs of one's in-group members, a social mechanism evolves in collectivist cultures that is driven by norms. Thus, for those with interdependent concept of self it is much easier cognitively to resort to methods that have been tried in the past for interacting with people at large. A sense of duty guides them toward social norms in both the workplace and interpersonal relationships. Individualists, on the other hand, are more concerned about their personal attitudes and values. They care much less than collectivists about what their family members have to say, let alone the extended family, friends, or neighbors. Hence, the difference between following one's own attitude versus norms of the society becomes a salient difference between individualist and collectivist cultures.

The fourth defining attribute focuses on the interpersonal relationships, or the nature of social exchange between self and others. When the self is viewed as independent, interpersonal relationships are developed to meet the need of the self to maximize the benefits to the self. Thus, social exchange is based on the principle of equal exchange, and people form new relationships to meet their changing needs based on cost-benefit analysis. Thus, individualists are rational in their social exchange. On the other hand, those with an interdependent concept of self and relationships that are inherited are likely to view their relationships as long term in nature and, therefore, are unlikely to break a relationship even if it is not cost-effective. Thus, collectivists value relationships for their own sake, and nurture them with unequal social exchanges over a long period of time.

2. Triandis (1995) illustrated that that this four-way typology articulates exceptionally well with some of the literature that has examined varieties of cultural patterns. For instance, Fiske (1992) has discussed cultural patterns that correspond to collectivism (which was referred to as communal sharing), vertical and horizontal relationships (authority ranking and equality matching, respectively), and individualism (market pricing). He also illustrated that the typology is consistent with Rokeach's (1973) analysis of political systems. He discussed political systems that highly value both equality and freedom, which correspond to horizontal individualism (social democracy; e.g., Australia, Sweden). Systems that he discussed as valuing equality but not freedom correspond to our conceptualization of horizontal collectivism (e.g., the Israeli kibbutz). Those systems that value freedom but not equality correspond to our notion of vertical individualism (e.g., competitive capitalism and market economies such as in the United States). Lastly, those societies that value neither equality nor freedom correspond to vertical collectivism (e.g., fascism or the communalism of traditional societies with strong leaders) in our conceptualization.

3. We would argue that the terms *parochial* and *professional* have unnecessary pejorative connotations. We think many people in collectivist countries will find the labels offensive because it insinuates that it is parochial not to separate work and family, and that to do so is professional.

4. Unfortunately, the terminology *allocentrism* and *idiocentrism* has not been used widely in the literature. Given this, in the rest of this discussion we use the more commonly used terms, *collectivism* and *individualism*.

5. Our response bias correction procedure identified response bias in some countries for this scale. We recomputed the predicted response bias corrected scale score for each country:

Institutional Collectivism practices: France, 4.20 (no change in band); Indonesia, 4.27 (no change in band); Morocco, 4.18 (moves from band C to band B); Philippines, 4.37 (moves from band A to band B); Qatar, 4.78 (moves from band B to band A); and Taiwan, 4.30 (moves from band A to band B).

In-Group Collectivism practices: France, 4.66 (no change in band); Morocco, 6.37 (no change in band); Qatar, 5.07 (no change in band).

For a complete discussion of this procedure and all response bias corrected scores, see Appendix B.

6. The response bias correction procedure identified a substantial amount of response bias in some countries for this scale. We recomputed the predicted response bias corrected scale score for each country:

Institutional Collectivism values: France, 5.27 (moves from band B to band A); and Morocco, 5.34 (moves from band B to band A).

In-Group Collectivism values: Ecuador, 5.81 (moves from band A to band B); France, 5.88 (no change in band); Morocco, 6.03 (moves from band B to band A); and New Zealand, 6.54 (no change in band).

For a complete discussion of this procedure and all response bias corrected scores, see Appendix B.

7. As reported in Chapter 20 by Brodbeck, Hanges, Dickson, Gupta, and Dorfman, we found that all the cultural dimensions of organizational cultural values and practices significantly differed across societies. Although important, this prior analysis did not identify the particular aspect of societal differences that was related to organizational culture. In the present chapter, we found that societal and organizational Individual–Collectivism practices were significantly related for Institutional Collectivism only (R^2 Total = 2.8%, R^2 Societal = 56.9%, $p < .01$). We found even stronger results for societal and organizational Individual–Collectivism values (R^2 Total for Institutional Collectivism = 14.2%, R^2 Societal = 70.9%, $p < .01$; R^2 Total for In-Group Collectivism = 11.1%, R^2 Societal = 52.8%, $p < .01$). As discussed in Chapter 11 by Hanges, Dickson, and Sipe, the R^2 Total considers all levels of analysis (i.e., individual, organizational, and societal) whereas the R^2 Societal isolates the societal level portion of the dependent variable and indicates the percentage of variance accounted for by the predictor at only this level. Whereas GLOBE has primarily taken the conservative approach and reported the R^2 Total in GLOBE, a number of scholars suggest that R^2 Societal provides a more accurate description of aggregated relationships. For further discussion, see the paper by Lance and James (1999).

8. Results between the single HLM and multiple HLM tests will likely differ somewhat. The differences between the results of the multiple HLMs and single HLMs are conceptually similar to the differences between a multiple regression analysis and a correlation coefficient. Table 21.10 in Chapter 21 by Dorfman et al. presents both single and multiple HLM coefficients. In addition, the relationships for all culture dimension values are summarized in Chapter 3 by Javidan, House, and Dorfman.

REFERENCES

Abu-Saad, I. (1998). Individualism and Islamic work beliefs. *Journal of Cross-Cultural Psychology, 29*(2), 377–383.

Ali, A. J., Taqi, A. A., & Krishnan, K. (1997). Individualism, collectivism, and decision styles of managers in Kuwait. *Journal of Social Psychology, 137*(5), 629–637.

Aycan, Z., Kanungo, R. N., Mendonca, M., Yu, K., Deller, J., Stahl, G., & Kurshid, A. (2000). Impact of culture on human resource management practices: A 10 country comparison. *Applied Psychology: An International Review, 49*(1), 192–221.

Aycan, Z., Kanungo, R. N., & Sinha, J. B. P. (1999). Organizational culture and human resource management practices: The model of culture fit. *Journal of Cross-Cultural Psychology, 30*(4), 501–526.

Bakan, D. (1966). *The duality of human existence.* Chicago: Rand McNally.

Bellah, R. N., Madsen, R., Sullivan, W., Swidler, A., & Tipton, S. M. (1985). *Habits of the heart: Individualism and commitment in American life.* Berkeley: University of California Press.

Barry, H., III, Child, I. L., & Bacon, M. K. (1959). A cross-cultural survey of sex differences in socialization. *Journal of Abnormal and Social Psychology, 55,* 327–332.

Berry, J. W. (1976). Sex differences in behavior and cultural complexity. *Indian Journal of Psychology, 51,* 89–97.

Berry, J. W. (1994). Ecology of individualism and collectivism. In U. Kim, H. C. Triandis, C. Kagitçibasi, S.-C. Choi, & G. Yoon (Eds.), *Individualism and collectivism: Theory, method and applications* (pp. 77–84). Thousand Oaks, CA: Sage.

Berry, J. W., Poortinga, Y. H., Segall, M. H., & Dasen, P. R. (1992). *Cross-cultural psychology: Research and applications.* New York: Cambridge University Press.

Berry, J. W., Trimble, J. E., & Olmedo, E. L. (1986). Assessment of acculturation. In W. J. Lonner & J. W. Berry (Eds.), *Field methods in cross-cultural research. Cross-cultural research and methodology series* (Vol. 8, pp. 85–110). Thousand Oaks, CA: Sage.

Bhawuk, D. P. S. (2001). Evolution of culture assimilators: Toward theory-based assimilators. *International Journal of Intercultural Relations, 25*(2), 141–163.

Bhawuk, D. P. S., & Udas, A. (1996). Entrepreneurship and collectivism: A study of Nepalese entrepreneurs. In J. Pandey, D. Sinha, & D. P. S. Bhawuk

(Eds.), *Asian contributions to cross-cultural psychology* (pp. 307–317). New Delhi: Sage.

Bhawuk D. P. S., Bechtold D. J., & Jones, W. (1998, November). *Bridging theory and practice: Application of individualism and collectivism in human resource management.* Paper presented at the Management of Human Resources Conference, Honolulu, Hawaii.

Bhawuk, D. P. S., Bechtold, D. J., & Munusami, V. (2003). *Culture and economic success: Is individualism the only way?* Manuscript in preparation.

Bierbrauer, G., Meyer, H., & Wolfradt, U. (1994). Measurement of normative and evaluative aspects in individualistic and collectivistic orientations: The cultural orientation scale (COS). In U. Kim & H. C. Triandis (Eds.), *Individualism and collectivism: Theory, method, and applications* (Cross-Cultural Research and Methodology, Vol. 18., pp. 189–199). Thousand Oaks, CA: Sage.

Bond, R., & Smith, P. B. (1996). Culture and conformity: A meta-analysis of studies using Asch's (1952b, 1956) line judgment task. *Psychological Bulletin, 119,* 111–137.

Bontempo, R., & Rivero, J. C. (1992, August). *Cultural variation in cognition: The role of self-concept in the attitude-behavior link.* Paper presented at the American Academy of Management meeting, Las Vegas, Nevada.

Brandt, V. S. (1974). Skiing cross-culturally. *Current Anthropology, 15,* 64–66.

Brodbar-Nemzer, J. (1986). Divorce and group commitment: The case of the Jews. *Journal of Marriage and the Family, 48*(2), 329–340.

Chatman, J. A., Polzer, J. T., Barsade, S. G., & Neale, M. A. (1998). Being different yet feeling similar: The influence of demographic composition and organizational culture on work processes and outcomes. *Administrative Science Quarterly, 43,* 749–780.

Chen, C. C., Chen, X.-P., & Meindl, J. R. (1998). Deciding on equity or parity: A test of situational, cultural, and individual factors. *Journal of Organizational Behavior, 19*(2), 115–129.

Chen, C. C., Meindl, J. R., & Hunt, R. G. (1997). Testing the effects of vertical and horizontal collectivism: A study of reward allocation preferences in China. *Journal of Cross-Cultural Psychology, 28,* 44–70.

Chinese Culture Connection. (1987). Chinese values and the search for culture-free dimensions of culture. *Journal of Cross-Cultural Psychology, 18*(2), 143–164.

Choi, Y.-E. (1996, August). *The self in different context: Behavioral analysis.* Paper presented at the International Congress of Psychology, Montreal.

Cox, T. H., Lobel, S. A., & McLeod, P. L. (1991). Effects of ethnic group cultural differences on cooperative and competitive behavior on a group task. *Academy of Management Journal, 34*(4), 827–847.

Davidson, A. R., Jaccard, J. J., Triandis, H. C., Morales, M. L., & Diaz-Guerrero, R. (1976). Cross-cultural model testing: Toward a solution of the etic-emic dilemma. *International Journal of Psychology, 11,* 1–13.

Dawood, N. J. (1956). *The Koran.* New York: Penguin.

Deci, E. L. (1971). Effects of externally mediated rewards on intrinsic motivation. *Journal of Personality and Social Psychology, 18*(1), 105–115.

Deci, E. L. (1972). Intrinsic motivation, extrinsic reinforcement, and inequity. *Journal of Personality and Social Psychology, 22*(1), 113–120.

Dewey, J. (1930). *Individualism old and new.* New York: Minton, Balch.

Diener, E., Diener, M., & Diener, C. (1995). Factors predicting the subjective well-being of nations. *Journal of Personality and Social Psychology, 69,* 851–864.

Doi, T. (1973). *The anatomy of dependence.* Tokyo: Kodanshi International.

Dorfman, P. W. (1998). Implications of vertical and horizontal individualism and collectivism for leadership effectiveness. In J. L. C. Cheng & R. B. Peterson (Eds.), *Advances in international comparative management* (Vol. 12, pp. 53–65). Stamford, CT: JAI.

Dorfman, P. W., & Howell, J. P. (1988). Dimensions of national culture and effective leadership patterns: Hofstede revisited. *Advances in International Comparative Management, 3,* 127–150.

Dorfman, P. W., Howell, J. P., Hibino, S., Lee, J. K., Tate, U., & Bautista, A. (1997). Leadership in Western and Asian countries: Commonalities and differences in effective leadership processes across cultures. *Leadership Quarterly, 8*(3), 233–274.

Dumont, L. (1986). *Essays on individualism.* Chicago: University of Chicago Press.

Durant, W. (1935). *Our oriental heritage.* New York: Simon & Schuster.

Durant, W. (1939). *The life of Greece.* New York: Simon & Schuster.

Durkheim, E. (1933). *The division of labor.* Chicago: Free Press.

Earley, P. C. (1989). Social loafing and collectivism: A comparison of the U.S. and the People's Republic of China. *Administrative Science Quarterly, 34,* 565–581.

Earley, P. C. (1993). East meets West meets Middle East: Further explorations of collectivist and individualist work groups. *Academy of Management Journal, 36,* 319–348.

Earley, P. C. (1994). The individual and collective self: An assessment of self-efficacy and training across cultures. *Administrative Science Quarterly, 39,* 89–117.

Earley, P. C., & Gibson, C. B. (1998). Taking stock in our progress on individualism and collectivism: 100 years of solidarity and community. *Journal of Management, 24,* 265–304.

Eby, L. T., & Dobbins, G. H. (1997). Collectivistic orientation in teams: An individual and group-level analysis. *Journal of Organizational Behavior, 18*(3), 275–295.

Encyclopedia Britannica. (1953). Vol. 12 (p. 256a).

Erez, M. (1994). Toward a model of cross-cultural industrial and organizational psychology. In H. Triandis, M. Dunnette, & L. Hough (Eds.), *Handbook of industrial and organizational psychology* (2nd ed., Vol. 4, pp. 559–607). Palo Alto, CA: Consulting Psychologists Press.

Erez, M., & Earley, P. C. (1993). *Culture, self-identity, and work.* New York: Oxford University Press.

Fiske, A. P. (1992). The four elementary forms of sociality: Framework for a unified theory of social relations. *Psychology Review, 99,* 689–723.

Freeman, M. A. (1997). Demographic correlates of individualism and collectivism: A study of social values in Sri Lanka. *Journal of Cross-Cultural Psychology, 28*(3), 321–341.

Gabriel, S., & Gardner, W. L. (1999). Are there "his" and "hers" types of interdependence? The implications of gender differences in collective versus relational interdependence for affect, behavior, and cognition. *Journal of Personality and Social Psychology, 77*(3), 642–655.

Gaines, S. O., Jr., Marelich, W. D., Bledsoe, K. L., Steers, W. N., Henderson, M. C., Granrose, C. S., et al. (1997). Links between race/ethnicity and cultural values as mediated by racial/ethnic identity and moderated by gender. *Journal of Personality and Social Psychology, 72,* 1460–1476.

Gelfand, M. J., Triandis, H. C., & Chan, K. S. (1996). Individualism versus collectivism or versus authoritarianism? *European Journal of Social Psychology, 26,* 397–410.

Georgas, J., Mylonas, K., Bafiti, T., Poortinga, Y. H., Christakopoulou, S., Kagitçibasi, C., Kwak, K., & Ataca, B. (2001). Functional relationships in the nuclear and extended family: A 16-culture study. *International Journal of Psychology, 36,* 289–300.

Gerstner, C. R., & Day, D. V. (1994). Cross-cultural comparison of leadership prototypes. *Leadership Quarterly, 5*(2), 121–134.

Griffith, S. B. (1963). *Sun Tzu: The art of war.* Oxford: Oxford University Press.

Gudykunst, W. B., Gao, G., & Franklyn-Stokes, A. (1996). Self-monitoring and concern for social appropriateness in China and England. In J. Pandey, D. Sinha, & D. P. S. Bhawuk (Eds.), *Asian contributions to cross-cultural psychology* (pp. 255–267). New Delhi: Sage.

Gudykunst, W. B., Gao, G., Schmidt, K. L. Nishida, T., Bond, M. H., Leung, K., et al. (1992). The influence of individualism-collectivism, self-monitoring, and predicted outcome value on communication in in-group and out-group relationships. *Journal of Cross-Cultural Psychology, 23,* 196–213.

Hackman, J. R., & Oldham, G. R. (1976). Motivation through the design of work: Test of a theory. *Organizational Behavior and Human Decision Processes, 16*(2), 250–279.

Hall, E. T. (1959). *The silent language.* New York: Doubleday.

Hanges, P. J., Lord, R. G., & Dickson, M. W. (2000). An information-processing perspective on leadership and culture: A case for connectionist architecture. *Applied Psychology: An International Review, 49*(1), 133–161.

Herzberg, F., Mausner, B., & Snyderman, B. B. (1959). *The motivation to work.* New York: John Wiley.

Hofstede, G. (1980). *Culture's consequences.* Beverly Hills, Sage.

Hofstede, G. (1994). Foreword. In U. Kim, H. Triandis, C. Kagitçibasi, S.-G. Choi, & G. Yoon (Eds.), *Individualism and collectivism: Theory, methods, and applications* (pp. ix–xiii). Thousand Oaks, CA: Sage.

Hofstede, G. (1997). Cultural constraints in management theories. In R. P. Vecchio (Ed.), *Leadership: Understanding the dynamics of power and influence in organizations* (pp. 465–483). Notre Dame, IN: University of Notre Dame Press.

Hofstede, G. (2001). *Culture's consequences* (2nd ed.). Thousand Oaks, CA: Sage.

Hofstede, G., & Bond, M. H. (1988). The Confucius connection: From cultural roots to economic growth. *Organizational Dynamics, 16,* 4–21.

Hofstede, G., Neuijen, B., Ohayv, D. D., & Sanders, G. (1991). Measuring organizational cultures. *Administrative Science Quarterly, 35,* 286–316.

Holtgraves, T. (1997). Styles of language use: Individual and cultural variability in conversational indirectness. *Journal of Personality and Social Psychology, 73,* 624–637.

House, R. J., Wright, N. S., & Aditya, R. N. (1997). Cross-cultural research on organizational leadership: A critical analysis and a proposed theory. In P. C. Earley & M. Erez (Eds.), *New perspectives on international industrial and organizational psychology* (pp. 535–625). San Francisco, CA: Lexington Press.

Hui, C. H. (1988). Measurement of individualism-collectivism. *Journal of Research on Personality, 22,* 17–36.

Hui, C. H., & Triandis, H. C. (1986). Individualism-collectivism: A study of cross-cultural researchers. *Journal of Cross-Cultural Psychology, 20,* 296–309.

Hui, C. H., Yee, C., & Eastman, K. L. (1995). The relationship between individualism-collectivism and job satisfaction. *Applied Psychology: An International Review, 44,* 276–282.

Huismans, S., & Schwartz, S. H. (1992). Religiosity and value priorities: A study of Protestants, Catholics, and Jews. In I. Saburo & Y. Kashima (Eds.), *Innovations in cross-cultural psychology* (pp. 237–249). Bristol, UK: Swets & Zeitlinger.

Huntington, S. P. (1996). *The clash of civilizations and the remaking of world order.* New York: Simon & Schuster.

Iyengar, S. S., & Lepper, M. R. (1999). Rethinking the value of choice: A cultural perspective on intrinsic motivation. *Journal of Personality and Social Psychology, 76,* 349–366.

Jung, D., Bass, B., & Sosik, J. (1995). Bridging leadership and culture: A theoretical consideration of transformational leadership and collectivistic cultures. *Journal of Leadership Studies, 2,* 3–18.

Kagan, D. (1966). *The ancient near east and Greece.* London: The Macmillan Group, Ltd.

Kagitçibasi, C. (1997). Individualism and collectivism. In J. W. Berry, M. H. Segall, & C. Kagitçibasi (Eds.), *Handbook of cross-cultural psychology* (2nd ed., pp. 1–50) Boston: Allyn & Bacon.

Kanungo, R. N., Aycan, Z., & Sinha, J. B. P. (1999). Organizational culture and human resource management practices: The model of culture fit. *Journal of Cross-cultural Psychology, 30*(4), 501–526.

Kanungo, R. N., & Jaeger, A. M. (1990). Introduction: The need for indigenous management in developing countries. In A. M. Jaeger & R. N. Kanungo (Eds.), *Management in developing countries* (pp. 1–23). London: Routledge.

Kashima, Y., & Callan, V. J. (1994). The Japanese workgroup. In H. C. Triandis, M. D. Dunnette, & L. M. Hough (Eds.), *Handbook of industrial and organizational psychology* (2nd ed., Vol. 4, pp. 606–649). Palo Alto, CA: Consulting Psychologists Press.

Kashima, Y. Y., & Kashima, E. M. (1998). Culture and language: The case of cultural dimensions and personal pronoun use. *Journal of Cross-Cultural Psychology, 29*(3), 461–486.

Kashima, E. S., & Kashima, Y. (1999). Negotiation of the self in interpersonal interactions: Japan-Australia comparison. In J. Adamopoulos & Y. Kashima (Eds.), *Social psychology and the cultural context* (pp. 189–202). Thousand Oaks, CA: Sage.

Kashima, Y., Yamaguchi, S., Kim, U., Choi, S.-C., Gelfand, M., & Yuki, M. (1995). Culture, gender and self: A perspective from individualism-collectivism research. *Journal of Personality and Social Psychology, 59,* 925–937.

Kateb, G. (1992). *The inner ocean: Individualism and democratic culture.* Ithaca, NY: Cornell University Press.

Kennedy, P. (1987). *The rise and fall of the great powers: Economic change and military conflict from 1500 to 2000.* New York: Random House.

Kim, U. (1994). Individualism and collectivism: Conceptual clarification and elaboration. In U. Kim, H. Triandis, C. Kagitçibasi, S.-G. Choi, & G. Yoon (Eds.), *Individualism and collectivism: Theory, methods, and applications* (pp. 19-41). Thousand Oaks, CA: Sage.

Kim, U., Triandis, H. C., Kagitçibasi, C., Choi, S.-C., & Yoon, G. (Eds.). (1994). *Individualism and collectivism: Theory, method, and applications.* Thousand Oaks, CA: Sage.

Klein, K. J., Dansereau, F., & Hall, R. J. (1994). Levels issues in theory development, data collection, and analysis. *Academy of Management Review, 19,* 195–229.

Kluckhohn, F., & Strodtbeck, F. (1961). *Variations in value orientation.* Evanston, IL: Row, Peterson.

Lance, C. E., & James, L. R. (1999). A proportional variance accounted for index for some cross-level and person-situation research designs. *Organizational Research Methods, 2,* 395–418.

Lester, D. (1996). Individualism and divorce. *Psychological Reports, 76*(1), 258.

Levine, R., Sato, S., Hashimoto, T., & Verma, J. (1995). Love and marriage in eleven cultures. *Journal of Cross-Cultural Psychology, 26*(5), 554–571.

Levine, R. V., & Norenzayan, A. (1999). The pace of life in 31 countries. *Journal of Cross-Cultural Psychology, 30,* 178–192.

Ling, W. (1989). Pattern of leadership behavior assessment in China. *Journal of Psychology in the Orient, 32*(2), 129–134.

Lord, R. G., & Maher, K. J. (1991). *Leadership and information processing: Linking perceptions and performance.* Cambridge, MA: Unwin Hyman.

Markus, H., & Kitayama, S. (1991). Culture and self: Implications for cognition, emotion and motivation. *Psychological Review, 98,* 224–253.

Markus, H. R., Kitayama, S., & Heiman, R. J. (1997). Culture and "basic" psychological principles. In E. T. Higgins & A. W. Kruglanski (Eds.), *Social psychology: Handbook of basic principles* (pp. 857–913). New York: Guilford.

Marmot, M. G., & Syme, S. L. (1976). Acculturation and coronary heart disease in Japanese-Americans. *American Journal of Epidemiology, 104*(3), 225–247.

Marshall, R. (1997). Variances in levels of individualism across two cultures and three social classes. *Journal of Cross-Cultural Psychology, 28,* 490–495.

Matsui, T., Kakuyama, T., & Onglatco, M. U. (1987). Effects of goals and feedback on performance in groups. *Journal of Applied Psychology, 72*(3), 407–415.

McClelland, D. (1967). *The achieving society.* New York: Free Press.

Mead, M. (1961). *Cooperation and competition among primitive peoples.* Boston, MA: Beacon Press.

Meindl, J. R. (1995). The romance of leadership as a follower-centric theory: A social constructionist approach. *Leadership Quarterly, 6*(3), 329–341.

Miller, J. G. (1984). Culture and the development of everyday social explanation. *Journal of Personality and Social Psychology, 46,* 961–978.

Miller, J. G. (1994). Cultural diversity in the morality of caring: Individually-oriented versus duty-oriented interpersonal codes. *Cross-Cultural Research, 28,* 3–39.

Misumi, J. (1985). *The behavioral science of leadership: An interdisciplinary Japanese research program.* Ann Arbor: University of Michigan Press.

Mobley, W. H. (1977). Intermediate linkages in the relationship between job satisfaction and employee turnover. *Journal of Applied Psychology, 62*(2), 237–240.

Moorman, R. H., & Blakely, G. L. (1995). Individualism–collectivism as an individual difference predictor of organizational citizenship behavior. *Journal of Organizational Behavior, 16*(2), 127–142.

Morris, M., Avila, R. A., & Allen, J. (1993). Individualism and the modern corporation: Implications for innovation and entrepreneurship. *Journal of Management, 19*(3), 595–612.

Muchinsky, P. M. (2000). *Psychology applied to work: An introduction to industrial and organizational psychology* (6th ed.). Belmont, CA: Wadsworth.

Oishi, S., Schimack, V., Diener, E., & Suh, E. M., (1998). The measurement of values and individualism-collectivism. *Personality and Social Psychology Bulletin, 24,* 1177–1189.

Oyserman, D. (1993). The lens of personhood: Viewing the self, and others, in a multicultural society. *Journal of Personality and Social Psychology, 65,* 993–1009.

Oyserman, D., Coon, H. M., & Kemmelmeier, M. (2002). Rethinking individualism and collectivism: Evaluation of theoretical assumptions and meta-analyses. *Psychological Bulletin, 128,* 3–72.

Parsons, T. (1949). *Essays in sociological theory; Pure and applied.* New York: Free Press.

Parsons, T., & Shils, E. A. (1951). *Toward a general theory of action.* Cambridge, MA: Harvard University Press.

Peng, K., & Nisbett, R. E. (1999). Culture, dialectics, and reasoning about contradiction. *American Psychologist, 54,* 741–754.

Pillai, R., & Meindl, J. R. (1998). Context and charisma: A "meso" level examination of the relationship of organic structure, collectivism, and crisis to charismatic leadership. *Journal of Management, 24*(5), 643–671.

Podsakoff, P. M., Dorfman, P. W., Howell, J. P., & Todor, W. D. (1986). Leader reward and punishment behaviors: A preliminary test of a culture-free style of leadership effectiveness. *Advances in International Comparative Management, 2,* 95–138.

Putnam, R. D. (2000). *Bowling alone: The collapse and revival of American community.* New York: Simon & Schuster.

Ramamoorthy, N., & Carroll, S. J. (1998). Individualism/collectivism orientations and reactions toward alternative human resource management practices. *Human Relations, 51*(5), 571–588.

Realo, A., Allik, J., & Vadi, M. (1997). The hierarchical structure of collectivism. *Journal of Research in Personality, 31*(1), 93–116.

Redfield, R. (1956). *Peasant society and culture: An anthropological approach to civilization.* Chicago: University of Chicago Press.

Redding, S. G., Norman, A., & Schlander, A. (1994). The nature of individual attachment to the organization: A review of East Asian variations. In H. C. Triandis & M. D. Dunnette (Eds.), *Handbook of industrial and organizational psychology* (2nd ed., Vol. 4, pp. 647–688). Palo Alto, CA: Consulting Psychologists Press.

Reykowski, J. (1994). Collectivism and individualism as dimensions of social change. In U. Kim, H. C. Triandis, C. Kagitçibasi, S.-C. Choi, & G. Yoon (Eds.), *Individualism and collectivism: Theory, method, and applications* (pp. 276–292). Newbury Park, CA: Sage.

Rhee, E., Uleman, J. S., & Lee, H. K. (1996). Variations in collectivism and individualism by in-group and culture: Confirmatory factor analyses. *Journal of Personality and Social Psychology, 71,* 1037–1054.

Riesman, D., Denny, R., & Glazer, N. (1950). *The lonely crowd: A study of the changing American character.* New Haven, CT: Yale University Press.

Rokeach, M. (1973). *The nature of human values.* New York: Free Press.

Rotter, J. (1966). Generalized expectancies for internal versus external control of reinforcement. *Psychological Monograph, 80*(1), 1–28.

Rousseau, D. (1995). *Psychological contracts in organizations: Understanding written and unwritten agreements.* Thousand Oaks, CA: Sage.

Schein, E. H. (1992). *Organizational culture and leadership.* San Francisco: Jossey-Bass.

Schwartz, S. H. (1992). Universals in the content and structure of values: Theoretical advances and empirical tests in 20 countries. In M. Zanna (Ed.), *Advances in experimental social psychology,* (Vol. 25, pp. 1–66). New York: Academic Press.

Schwartz, S. H. (1994). Beyond individualism and collectivism: New cultural dimensions of values. In U. Kim, H. C. Triandis, C. Kagitçibasi, S.-C. Choi, & G. Yoon (Eds.), *Individualism and collectivism: Theory, method, and applications* (pp. 85–122). Newbury Park, CA: Sage.

Schwartz, S. H., & Bilsky, W. (1990). Toward a theory of universal structure and content of values: Extensions and cross-cultural replications. *Journal of Personality and Social Psychology, 58,* 878–891.

Segall, M. H., & Kagitçibasi, C. (1997). Introduction. In J. W. Berry, M. H. Segall, & K. Kagitçibasi (Eds.), *Handbook of cross-cultural psychology* (Vol. 3, pp. xxv–xxxv). Needham, MA: Allyn & Bacon.

Shaw, J. B. (1990). A cognitive categorizations model for the study of intercultural management. *Academy of Management Review, 12,* 626–645.

Sheppard, B. H., & Sherman, D. M. (1998). The grammars of trust: A model and general implications. *Academy of Management Review, 23*(3), 422–437.

Singelis, T. M. (1994). The measurement of independent and interdependent self-construals. *Personality and Social Psychology Bulletin, 20,* 580–591.

Singelis, T. M., Triandis, H. C., Bhawuk, D. P. S., & Gelfand, M. (1995). Horizontal and vertical dimensions of individualism and collectivism: A theoretical measurement refinement. *Cross-Cultural Research, 29,* 240–275.

Sinha, D. (1988). The family scenario in a developing country and its implications for mental health: The case of India. In P. R. Dasen, J. W. Berry, & N. Sartorius (Eds.), *Health and cross-cultural psychology: Toward applications* (pp. 48–70). Newbury Park, CA: Sage.

Sinha, J. B. P. (1984). A model of effective leadership styles in India. *International Studies of Management and Organization, 14*(3), 86–98.

Sinha, J. B. P., & Verma, J. (1994). Social support as a moderator of the relationship between allocentrism and psychological well-being. In U. Kim, H. C. Triandis, K. Kagitçibasi, S.-C. Choi, & G. Yoon (Eds.), *Individualism and collectivism: Theory, methods and applications* (pp. 267–275). Thousand Oaks, CA: Sage.

Smith, P. B., & Bond, M. H. (1993). *Social psychology across cultures: Analysis and perspectives.* Hemel Hempstead, UK: Harvester/Wheatsheaf.

Smith, P. B., Dugan, S., & Trompenaars, F. (1996). National culture and the values of organizational employees. *Journal of Cross-Cultural Psychology, 27,* 231–265.

Smith, P. B., Misumi, J., Tayeb, M., Peterson, M., & Bond, M. H. (1989). On the generality of leadership style measures across cultures. *Journal of Occupational Psychology, 62, 97–109.*

Smith, P. B., & Schwartz, S. H. (1997). Values. In J. W. Berry, M. H. Segall, & K. Kagitçibasi (Eds.), *Handbook of cross-cultural psychology* (pp. 77–118). Needham, MA: Allyn & Bacon.

Streep, P. (1995). *Confucius: The wisdom.* Boston: Bullfinch.

Taylor, C. (1989). *Sources of the self: The making of the modern identity.* Cambridge, UK: Cambridge University Press.

Toennies, F. (1957). *Gemeinschaft und Gesellschaft* [Community and society]. New Brunswick, NJ: Transaction Publishing.

Trafimow, D., Triandis, H. C., & Goto, S. (1991). Some tests of the distinction between the private and collective self. *Journal of Personality and Social Psychology, 60,* 649–655.

Triandis, H. C. (1988). Collectivism v. individualism: A reconceptualization of a basic concept in cross-cultural social psychology. In G. K. Verma & C. Bagley (Eds.), *Cross-cultural studies of personality, attitudes and cognition* (pp. 60–95). London: Macmillan.

Triandis, H. C. (1989). The self and social behavior in differing cultural contexts. *Psychological Review, 96,* 506–520.

Triandis, H. C. (1990). Cross-cultural studies of individualism and collectivism. In J. Berman (Ed.), *Nebraska Symposium on Motivation, 1989* (pp. 41–133). Lincoln: University of Nebraska Press.

Triandis, H. C. (1993). Collectivism and individualism as cultural syndromes. *Cross-Cultural Research, 27,* 155–180.

Triandis, H. C. (1994). *Culture and social behavior.* New York: McGraw-Hill.

Triandis, H. C. (1995). *Individualism & collectivism.* Boulder, CO: Westview.

Triandis, H. C. (2002). Individualism and collectivism. In M. Gannon & K. Newman (Eds.) *Handbook of cross-cultural management* (pp. 16–45). New York: Lawrence Erlbaum.

Triandis, H. C., & Bhawuk, D. P. S. (1997). Culture theory and the meaning of relatedness. In P. C. Earley & M. Erez (Eds.), *New perspectives in international/organizational psychology* (pp. 13–52). New York: The New Lexington Free Press.

Triandis, H. C., Bontempo, R., Bentancourt, H., Bond, M., Leung, K., Brenes, A., et al. (1986). The measurement of the etic aspects of individualism and collectivism across cultures. *Australian Journal of Psychology, 38,* 257–267.

Triandis, H. C., Bontempo, R., Villareal, M. J., Asai, M., & Lucca, N. (1988). Individualism and collectivism: Cross-cultural perspectives on self-ingroup relationships. *Journal of Personality and Social Psychology, 54,* 323–338.

Triandis, H. C., Chan, D. K.-S., Bhawuk, D., Iwao, S., & Sinha, J. B. P. (1995). Multimethod probes of allocentrism and idiocentrism. *International Journal of Psychology, 30,* 461–480.

Triandis, H. C., Chen, X. P., & Chan, D. K.-S. (1998). Scenarios for the measurement of collectivism and individualism. *Journal of Cross-Cultural Psychology, 29,* 275–289.

Triandis, H. C., & Gelfand, M. J. (1998). Converging measurement of horizontal and vertical individualism and collectivism. *Journal of Personality and Social Psychology, 74,* 118–128.

Triandis, H. C., Leung, K., Villareal, M., & Clack, F. L. (1985). Allocentric vs. idiocentric tendencies: Convergent and discriminant validation. *Journal of Research in Personality, 19,* 395–415.

Triandis, H. C., McCusker, C., Betancourt, H., Iwao, S., Leung, K., Salazar, J. M., et al. (1993). An etic-emic analysis of individualism and collectivism. *Journal of Cross-Cultural Psychology, 24,* 366–383.

Triandis, H. C., McCusker, C., & Hui, C. H. (1990). Multimethod probes of individualism and collectivism. *Journal of Personality and Social Psychology, 74,* 118–128.

Triandis, H. C., & Vassiliou, V. A. (1972). Interpersonal influence and employee selection in two cultures. *Journal of Applied Psychology, 56,* 140–145.

Trompenaars, F. (1985). *The organization of meaning and the meaning of organization: A comparative study of the conceptions of organizational structure in different cultures.* Unpublished doctorial dissertation, Wharton School of Management, University of Pennsylvania, Philadelphia.

Trompenaars, F. (1993). *Riding the waves of culture.* London: Nicholas Brealey.

Vroom, V. H. (1964). *Work and motivation.* New York: John Wiley.

Wagner, J. A., III. (1995). Studies of individualism-collectivism: Effects on cooperation in groups. *Academy of Management Journal, 38,* 152–170.

Wagner, J. A., III, & Moch, M. K. (1986). Individualism-collectivism: Concept and measurement. *Group and Organizational Studies, 11,* 280–304.

Wasti, S. A. (2000). Organizational commitment in a collectivist culture: The case of Turkey [Abstract]. *Dissertation Abstracts International Section A: Humanities and Social Sciences, 60*(9-A), p. 3547.

Weissman, M. D., Matsumoto, D., Preston, K., Brown, B. R., & Kupperbusch, C. (1997). Context-specific measurement of individualism-collectivism on the individual level: The individualism-collectivism interpersonal assessment inventory. *Journal of Cross-Cultural Psychology, 28*(6), 743–767.

Wheeler, L., Reis, H. T., & Bond, M. H. (1989). Collectivism-individualism in everyday social life: The Middle Kingdom and the melting pot. *Journal of Personality and Social Psychology, 57,* 79–86.

World Bank Annual Report (2001). Retrieved January 9, 2004, from http:www.worldbank. org/annualreport/2001/wbar2001.htm.

World Economic Forum. (1979). *Report on international competitiveness.* Geneva, Switzerland: Author.

Yamaguchi, S. (1994). Empirical evidence on collectivism among the Japanese. In U. Kim, H. C. Triandis, C. Kagitçibasi, S.-C. Choi, & G. Yoon (Eds.), *Individualism and collectivism: Theory, method, and applications* (pp. 175–188). Newbury Park, CA: Sage.

Yu, A.-B., & Yang, K.-S. (1994). The nature of achievement motivation in collectivist societies. In U. Kim, H. C. Triandis, C. Kagitçibasi, S.-C. Choi, & G. Yoon (Eds.), *Individualism and collectivism: Theory, method, and applications* (pp. 239–250). Newbury Park: CA: Sage

Yutang, L. (1938). *The wisdom of Confucius.* New York: Modern Library.

17

POWER DISTANCE

DALE CARL

VIPIN GUPTA

MANSOUR JAVIDAN

One of the GLOBE dimensions of societal and organizational values and practices is Power Distance. Broadly speaking, this dimension reflects the extent to which a community accepts and endorses authority, power differences, and status privileges. It is an important aspect of a community's culture and has been related to a variety of behaviors in organizations and societies in the literature. This chapter will present a review of the literature relevant to cultural influences on power distance values and practices as well as the GLOBE findings on power distance. We will first explain the concept of power distance and its societal and organizational correlates, and then move on to the historical, religious, and psychological roots of power distance in societies. We will then describe the GLOBE scales used to measure the Power Distance construct at the societal and organizational levels and appraise the effects of power distance on the culturally implicit support for leadership theories at organizational and societal levels. In the last part of the chapter we will report the study of the relationships between power

distance and a variety of indicators of societal economic prosperity and the individual psychological and physical welfare of the members of the societies studied.

ROOTS OF POWER DISTANCE

The concept of power has intrigued writers throughout the centuries, from Pope Gregory VII in the 11th century CE, who attempted to extend the temporal power of the papacy; to Niccolo Machiavelli, who wrote in the 16th century about how to hold and exercise power; to numerous social scientists in the 21st century. In this section we will consider the major themes of the predominant theorists, how they have increased our understanding of both personal and position power, the needs and motivations of people who seek power, and why people might accept a position of less power relative to their perceived superiors.

Two major research streams provide substantial insights into this dimension: psychologists, who have investigated the needs, motivations, and enactment of power, and cross-cultural researchers, who have explored the existence of power distance differences across societies. We shall discuss these two research traditions separately, although their insights are interrelated in shedding light on this complex and sometimes controversial fact of human existence.

The Psychological Stream and Power

Sources of Power

One of the most fundamental questions concerning power is what gives an individual or a group influence over others? French and Raven (1959) advanced a five-category classification scheme that identified the various sources or bases of power that they believed were "especially common and important." They consist of coercive, reward, legitimate, expert, and referent power. The *coercive power* base was defined by French and Raven as being dependent on fear. It rests on the application, or threat of application, of physical harm or other unpleasant outcomes as a form of punishment for the lack of compliance. *Reward power,* at the other extreme, is based on the opposite motivation: People enact positive behaviors to obtain valuable rewards controlled by the powerful person. Rewards can be intangible, such as praise, friendliness, and acceptance, or tangible, such as increased pay, promotion, or access to information, to name a few.

Legitimate power is the power that is vested in a person as the result of his or her position within the formal hierarchy. The subordinate responds to a request or demand because the superior has the right to request it and the subordinate has the obligation to comply. Legitimate power has been referred to alternatively as "authority" and "position power" (Stogdill, 1974). This power base includes both coercive and reward power; however, as Yukl (2002) noted, the person in the position must be perceived as having a legitimate right to the position if he or she will be allowed to exert any influence. *Expert power* is the ability to influence on the basis of technical expertise, special skills, or special knowledge that are both relevant and necessary to the organization. The credibility, and hence the respect, of the

individual is enhanced through this expertise. It is based on the personal power of the individual, rather than on power emanating from the position itself. In an increasingly technological world, this source of power is becoming more important within many organizations. Finally, *referent power* refers to a subordinate's feeling of oneness with the leader and a desire to identify with, emulate, and internalize the values of the superior. This is another form of personal power (Yukl, 2002). Referent power is operationalized by showing consideration for the needs and feelings of subordinates, by expressing feelings of trust, acceptance, and concern for their welfare, and by challenging them through a personal appeal to move beyond the formal requirements of their roles (Bass, 1985; French & Raven, 1959; Hinkin & Schriesheim, 1989; House, 1977; Yukl, 2002).

Despite the implicit logic of the French and Raven typology and its wide use in power research, there have been several concerns about the lack of conceptual consistency regarding the source or origin of the influence (Hinkin & Schriesheim, 1989; Yukl, 2002).

Over the years, research has indicated several additional sources of power. First, Burt (1992) identified *structural holes,* defined as the holes in the social structure, as an important source of power. The structural holes arise if different subgroups of a society are not fully interconnected. As a result, some members gain a position of power by virtue of their ability to provide a connection among the unconnected subgroups (Burt, 1992). The unique connection provided by the members in power allows them to gain a larger share of the value of goods and services exchanged or traded among the various subgroups. Second, information generates power not on the basis of one's expertise or knowledge, but because of one's ability to rapidly and efficiently discover or obtain relevant information and to be a good listener. Third, credibility indicates the respect one commands because of repeated interaction and past behavior (Milgrom & Roberts, 1992). Through their behavior, people can accrue a reputation for themselves in society, which helps them influence the behavior of others. Fourth, visibility enhances power by making one's presence felt—people who have a pleasing, helpful, and supportive personality tend to have more resourceful networks and command more trust. Fifth, charisma produces power through infectious qualities of leadership and influence, involving a leader's aura, dynamism, and persuasiveness (Weber, 1976). In addition, research on influence behavior has indicated several influence tactics that also add to one's power (Yukl, 2002). These include rational persuasion, exchange tactics, legitimate requests, and personal appeals (including ingratiation).

Need for Power

Perhaps the most foundational treatment of the concept of power emerged from Maslow's hierarchy of needs. His pyramid presented five categories of human needs, starting at the base with physiological needs, followed by safety, social, esteem, and self-actualization. The top two needs shed some light on a person's need for power. The need for esteem included internal need factors such as self-respect and autonomy, whereas external esteem needs included factors such as growth, achieving one's potential, and self-fulfillment. Both of the categories can be viewed from the perspective of gaining individual power, free from stifling dictates or obligations from more powerful others. According to Maslow, this yearning was not simply a desire, but rather a fundamental need of mankind. Although this theory has since been discredited in the psychological community (Whaba & Bridwell, 1976), Maslow's work has been very influential over the years.

McClelland (1961, 1975) and McClelland and Burnham (1976) focused on the needs of managers within organizations. McClelland had originally determined that managers are motivated by three basic and *nonconscious* needs—the need for achievement, the need for affiliation, and the need for power. The need for achievement is the drive to excel and to strive to succeed, the need for affiliation is a desire for friendly and close interpersonal relations, and the need for power is the nonconscious desire to have an impact and to gain status. McClelland referred to the need for power (*nPow*) to distinguish it from other conceptualizations concerning desire for power. In studying 49 line managers in a large American corporation,

McClelland and Burnham determined that effective managers were characterized primarily by their need for power. This need takes two forms in organizations: first, the personalized power type, who strives for dominance and who seeks to pursue personal goals and second, the socialized power type, who seeks to further the goals of subordinate individuals, groups, and the organization. McClelland and Burnham found the latter to be the most effective form of power.

How is the need for power enacted? On the basis of a study of Harvard University undergraduates, Winter (1973) saw the need for power, or the need for "having impact," enacted in three basic ways. First, impact can be achieved through strong action, such as assaults or aggression; by giving help, advice, or assistance; by controlling someone; by persuading someone; or by trying to impress someone. Second, it can be achieved through arousing a strong emotion in someone, ranging from fear to desire. Third, it can be expressed by striving to enhance one's own personal reputation, thereby gaining status.

But in many of today's societies, in which overt expressions of power are unacceptable, how do people satisfy their need for power? McClelland (1975) tested Winter's perspectives on a group of 50 white-collar and blue-collar workers in the United States. On the basis of his research, he identified four ways in which men with a high need for power express or satisfy this need. First, they read sex and sports magazines and watch violent television programs. Second, they accumulate prestigious possessions, like a special car or valuable art objects. Third, they engage in competitive sports in which there is "man-to-man" competition such as football, baseball, tennis, and basketball. Finally, they tend to join organizations in which they can hold office and, thus, have an impact on others. Other research on power indicates that high power-motivated individuals tend to inhibit group discussion, with the result that fewer alternatives may be considered and a suboptimal decision reached (Fodor & Smith, 1982). Further, high power-motivated individuals, if their influence attempts are thwarted, exhibit more stress than low power-motivated individuals (Fodor, 1985).

In addition, the social beliefs, values, and practices of societies tend to carry over not just to the organizations, but also to a whole range of cultural landscapes, through influences on leadership patterns. One of the insights of the Charismatic/Value-Based theory of leadership (House, 1977) is that because societal culture influences people's values, the enactment, acceptance, and effectiveness of specific leader behaviors and global leader behavior patterns are also accordingly modified (Triandis, 1995). The nonconscious power motivation of American presidents, which was measured using content analysis of their inaugural addresses, was found by Winter and Stewart (1977) to be predictive of the frequency of the United States entry into war ($r = .62$, $p < .01$) and the frequency of assassination attempts on the presidents ($r = -.81$, $p < .01$). House, Spangler, and Woycke (1991) postulated that an exceptionally high need for power explains why charismatic leaders develop the persuasive skills to influence others and to gain satisfaction from leading. Consistent with this reasoning, need for power was positively related to behavioral charisma of the United States presidents.

Why would a person, who has his or her own innate need for power, willingly accept another person's power over him or her? The most obvious answer is that there are some things that we have to do to achieve need satisfaction. Staying in the organization and being subjected to the whims and dictates of a superior are often preferable to leaving the organization. There is also a conditioned human acceptance of some degree of legitimate authority. In addition, people in positions of power are often accepted because of their personal power, whether it is based on expertise or referent power (French & Raven, 1959). Many of the charismatic attributes and behaviors (Bass, 1985; House, 1977) play a role in convincing subordinates to comply because of their wish to please and to emulate the leader.

Western psychologists have also been concerned with the "dark side" of power. This concern exposes the potential harm that a powerful individual can cause among hapless subordinates or followers due to their wish to comply with the wishes of a despot. Examples in the political sphere include Adolph Hitler, Idi Amin, Augusto Pinochet, and James Jones.

McClelland (1970) provided the following emotive description of the negative reaction to unbridled power in many societies:

> It is a fine thing to be concerned about doing things well (n Achievement) or making friends (n Affiliation), but it is reprehensible to be concerned with having influenced others (n Power). The vocabulary behavioral scientists use to describe power relations is strongly negative in tone . . . one finds these people depicted as harsh, sadistic, fascist, Machiavellian, prejudiced, and neurotic. Ultimately, many claim, the concern for power leads to Nazi-type dictatorships, and the exploitation of helpless masses who have lost their freedom. Even less political terms for power than these have a distinctly negative flavor—dominance-submission, competition, zero-sum game (if I win, you lose). (p. 32)

In France, Etienne de la Boetie wrote in 1954 in his *Discours de la Servitude Voluntaire* that a tyrant has no other power than that which is given to him, and that the problem is less the tyrant than the "voluntary servitude" of his subjects (Hofstede, 1980). This historically accurate statement refers to a society's acceptance of the power that can be exerted by an influential person, which is the essence of power distance. As will be discussed in the following section on cross-cultural power distance, the acceptance of unbridled power is limited in many societies by several cultural factors. Moreover, as McClelland and Burnham (1976) proposed, leaders are more effective when they are motivated by fulfilling the needs of the organization or the concerns of subordinates. Within organizations, as opposed to political positions in some countries, there are usually checks and balances that will not allow a despotic leader to remain in place for very long.

In summary, the need for power perspective suggests that individuals vary in their motives and attitudes toward the use of power, and that power differences may be accepted if need for power is socialized or is exerted by a person of influence.

The Role of Gender Concerning the Use of Power

The discussion of the sources of power, the need for power, and the enactment of power has focused primarily on men's attitudes and behaviors. But at least half of the world's population is female. Is there a gender divide on the acceptance and enactment of power? (Please refer to Emrich, Denmark, & Den Hartog's Chapter 14, Gender Egalitarianism, for a more detailed discussion.)

We might be tempted to think of political leaders such as Margaret Thatcher and Benazir Bhutto to underscore the necessity for "successful women" to play the power game to succeed, both in politics and in business. However, this male-oriented perspective might be shallow, inaccurate, and self-serving from a female perspective.

The literature that deals with the female relationship with power is not straightforward, because it tends to blend the concepts of power with expected female managerial styles and the effectiveness of autocratic leadership. For example, Bartol and Butterfield (1976) claimed that women are evaluated more favorably than men if they use a "consideration style," whereas men were evaluated more positively than women if they used a structured approach. Haccoun, Sallay, and Haccoun (1978) determined that male, nonmanagement subordinates judged a woman using a directive management style to be less effective than a man using a similar style. Similarly, Campbell, Bommer, and Yeo (1993) concluded that gender has no impact on leadership style. Jago and Vroom (1982) noted that if stereotype gender roles are not met, women are perceived to be autocratic and are judged negatively, whereas men are assessed positively. Smith and Smits (1994) concluded that female leaders generally influence the workplace differently, despite the fact that the female and male leaders' characteristics might be similar.

Another stream of research has examined the differences in the perceptions of male versus female subordinates. Using canonical correlations, Ronk (1993) concluded that gender of the subordinate appears to play a role in the acceptance of some of the dimensions of power. There was no significant difference between the male and female students' acceptance of the use of coercive, reward, and expert power by their professors. However, there were some statistically different reactions by gender to other power dimensions. Specifically, female students rated their instructors higher than did the male students if the instructor used legitimate and referent power.

In summary, it can be concluded that women have different conceptions of power and how power should be enacted. Women tend to be more sensitive to the use of legitimate and referent power, and are expected to enact their specific role demands to be accepted positively in the society. Further, there are evidently gender stereotypes concerning the acceptance of various dimensions of power that, although declining (Bartol & Butterfield, 1976), still exist in most societies.

The Cross-Cultural Stream and Power Distance

The term *power distance* was coined by Mulder to mean "the degree of inequality in power between a less power Individual (I) and a more powerful Other (O), in which I and O belong to the same (loosely or tightly knit) social system" (Mulder, 1977, p. 90). Building on the work of Mulder and his colleagues (Mulder, 1971, 1976, 1977; Mulder, Ritsema van Eck, & De Long, 1971), Hofstede concluded that, "the basic issue involved . . . is human equality. Inequality can occur in areas such as prestige, wealth, and power; and different societies put different weights on status consistency among these areas" (Hofstede, 2001, p. 75). Following Hofstede (2001), the GLOBE project definition of Power Distance is "the degree to which members of an organization or society expect and agree that power should be shared unequally."

Inequality among various members of a society has been a concern since time immemorial. In ancient Greece in approximately 350 BCE, Plato, although appreciating a fundamental need for equality among people, endorsed a society in which an elite class would exercise leadership. Those who were educated and belonged to the upper class were moral equals given the same status as others in that class, but different from those who were laborers or who worked in nonscholarly jobs. The English philosopher Thomas Hobbes (1588–1679) maintained that individual behavior is motivated by the desire for pleasure and avoidance of displeasure. His view was that human nature is largely self-seeking, guided by "egotistical hedonism." Therefore, power was essential to protect one's person and goods. This need for power often led to insecurity and even war, which Hobbes considered an integral part of the human condition.

More recently, Beteillie (1977) maintained that inequality is "one of the central problems of every human society" (p. ix). Building on Rousseau's (1972) distinction between natural or physical inequalities and moral or political inequalities, he suggested that "society is inconceivable without conventions and rules, and that these constitute the seedbed of what may be called social as opposed to natural inequality" (p. 4). The functional necessity of unequal power through force and domination to hold societies together was a common theme among many of his French contemporaries, including Mountesque, Durkeim, Pareto, Mosca, and Michels. Dahrendorf (1969) summarized this view succinctly: "human society without inequality is not realistically possible and is therefore ruled out" (p. 42). Runciman (1969) proposed three dimensions of social inequality that are evident, to various degrees, in most cultures: class structure, power, and status.

Differences in power distance are by no means confined to Western thought. In China around 500 BCE, Confucius spoke of five hierarchical relationships, each with its norms and duties. The relationships were ruler–subject, father–son, older brother–younger brother, husband–wife, and senior friend–junior friend. In these relationships, the junior partner owed the senior respect and obedience; the senior partner, in turn, owed the junior protection, consideration, help, support, and assistance in personal and spiritual matters. Within India, occupation, geography, kinship, and other factors combined to create a complex class structure, later termed the caste system. This caste system provided each class with a degree of power legitimated and derived from one's hereditary social class.

In high power distance cultures such as France, some individuals are perceived to have a higher overall rank whose power is unquestionable and virtually unattainable by those with lower power. In low power distance countries such as Scandinavia and the Netherlands, each individual is respected and appreciated for what that person has to offer, and people expect access to upward mobility in both their class and their jobs. Within low power distance cultures, the distaste for large power differentials is often based on the beliefs that power corrupts, and that excessive power results in the abuse of power, from which people in less powerful positions have no recourse. The history of many nations will bear out these concerns, but they are not necessarily relevant in some high power distance cultures. For example, in the Buddhist religion and the Confucian philosophy, power distance implies a reciprocal arrangement that has traditionally protected the less powerful in a relationship.

Whatever our perspective on the uses and abuses of power, many of the roots of power distance, whether high or low, are historically derived and satisfy cultural expectations within societies (Cullen, 2001). It is our interpretation that the acceptance of a certain level of power distance within societies can be traced to four fundamental phenomena. These are the predominant religion or philosophy, the tradition of democratic principles of government, the existence of a strong middle class, and the proportion of immigrants in a society's population. We discuss each of these phenomena below.

The Role of Predominant Religions and Philosophies

Many of our values and beliefs are programmed at an early age by families and basic institutions, which in turn are guided by our group's religion or philosophy. The distinction is made here between a religion, which includes some relationship with one or more deities or spirits and generally with an afterlife, and a philosophy such as Confucianism, which is concerned with human interrelations and our present life. In both cases, they provide fundamental influences on a society's value systems, and they provide the basis for many of the laws, rituals, and rites to which we are exposed. As will be discussed, they also provide a foundation for our acceptance or rejection of high power distance.

The religions that will be discussed are Christianity (Catholicism and Protestantism), Islam, Hinduism, and Buddhism. Confucianism, a philosophy, will also be examined for its influences on power distance within many Eastern societies. Several historically important religions will not be considered in this chapter because of the relatively small number of adherents or their geographical dispersion. Judaism, for example, comprises only 14 million followers worldwide, with more than 7 million in the Americas, 4 million in Europe, and 3 million in Israel. Shinto is a purely native Japanese religion that has fewer than 130 million followers, most of whom also follow Confucian and Buddhist traditions. The following synopsis of the fundamental teachings of the world's most predominant religions and philosophies is intended to provide some insight into their influences with respect to the acceptance of a higher or lower degree of power distance.

Christianity. Christianity is a religion based on the belief that Jesus of Nazareth (Christ) was the son of the one God and that he is Lord and Savior of the world. Upon his death, he became part of God within the Holy Trinity. In his lifetime 2,000 years ago in Palestine, Jesus gained notoriety by challenging the establishment, both secular and religious. He argued for personal freedom, individual determination of one's fate through personal prayer, the need for meekness, and concern for all people, regardless of their status in life.

After his death, Christianity grew to an independent imperial religion by the 4th century CE. Christians now live in every part of the world, constituting a quarter of the world's population. Christians are the majority in Europe, throughout the Western Hemisphere, and in Australia and New Zealand. In Africa, the modern spread of Christianity has produced Christian majorities in many countries south of the Sahara. In Asia, only the Philippines has a Christian majority, whereas South Korea has a significant minority, approximately one third of the population.

Despite its unstructured beginnings, Christianity became more formally organized as it spread. By the 4th century CE, it was headed by five patriarchs in Alexandria, Jerusalem,

Antioch, Rome, and Constantinople. Reinforcing this hierarchy were the bishops, who in turn were responsible for the ordination and administration of lower level priests and deacons. The Catholic Church ("catholic" meaning "universal") established a synthesis of religion, culture, and governmental and social structure that was referred to as Christendom, or the domain of Christianity (Oxtoby, 1996). The power and influence of the church hierarchy became more pronounced as the result of mutual support between the Church and heads of state, with Church representatives holding increasingly powerful positions within royal courts throughout Europe. The Catholic Church eventually asserted its power even over heads of state: Pope Gregory VII, in 1075, issued a decree that the Pope could depose emperors through excommunication from the Church.

The Roman Catholic Church, whose headquarters in the Vatican in Rome is a separate state, generally reinforced the status quo within the countries where it settled. While it maintained the power and influence of its own representatives, it conditioned the common man and woman to accept his or her own fate to ensure social stability.

By the late 14th century CE, the Roman Catholic Church was facing criticism for lavish and corrupt practices, and for the Church's presumed jurisdiction over people's personal salvation. In 1517, a German monk named Martin Luther nailed a list of 95 propositions on a church door in Wittenberg, Germany, outlining injustices that he felt should be corrected in the Roman Catholic Church. His primary concerns were related to how sins should be forgiven. Rather than accepting the practice that specific sins are confessed through a priest of the Church, he argued that the divine grace of Jesus reaches out to every human being who seeks repentance individually, regardless of their merit or performance. In essence, Luther was taking priesthood off the pedestal of status and authority that it had enjoyed since the time of Constantine (Oxtoby, 1996).

The subsequent religious movement against the Roman Catholic Church was called Protestantism, based on the concept of "protesting" against many practices of the established Christian Church. Fundamentally, these sects were opposed to centralized control and hierarchy, preferring instead to allow a person to interpret and apply the lessons in the scriptures individually. The Lutheran sect, based on Luther's writings, became the predominant religion in Northern Germany and the Scandinavian countries. The other two main sects that emerged from the Protestant Reformation in the 16th century were Calvinists and Anglicans. Since that time, more than 100 Protestant sects have emerged, each based on some derivation of the basic Protestant tenet that the individual needs no one to intercede on his or her behalf with Christ and God. The Protestant religions, in general, support the concept of equality of status before God, egalitarianism of access to God, individualist assertion, and hence lower power distance before other human beings.

Roman Catholicism was carried by both missionaries and state representatives to parts of Africa, countries in Southern Asia, and to most countries in Latin America, where it continues to exert influence. Protestantism spread throughout much of northern Europe and to the English-speaking British colonies of Canada, the United States, Australia, and New Zealand. Although present-day Catholicism is more benign than in previous centuries, it still supports the status quo in many societies, and it continues to recognize women as unsuitable to hold the highest positions within the Church establishment. Consequently, societies that have been primarily Roman Catholic tend to be high in power distance, whereas Protestant societies prefer lower power distance.

Islam. Islam is an innately personal and empowering religion that is the primary religion from Northern Africa in the west to Pakistan and Bangladesh in the East, and also in Malaysia and Indonesia. Islam is the third of the historic monotheistic (one God) religions that sprung from the Middle East, following Judaism and Christianity. In many ways, it is comparable to Judaism, with which it shares many of the same prophets, with Adam as the first prophet. Its theological split from Judaism is traced to Abraham, a Jewish patriarch who was the first prophet to embrace one God. Abraham had two sons, Ishmael, his first born by a servant named Hagar, and Isaac, the second son born by his aging wife.

When Hagar was either sent away (Judaic and Christian Bibles) or escorted by Abraham (Qur'an) to settle in the valley of Makkah (present-day Mecca according to the Muslim tradition), she and Ishmael eventually ended up in present-day Saudi Arabia, where they became the progenitors of the Muslim Arabs.

The history of Islam as a formal religion started with Mohammed (also Muhammed and numerous other spellings in the West). He was born in approximately 570 CE somewhere near Makkah. While sitting in the solitude of a cave, he was confronted by the angel Jibril (Gabriel to Jews and Christians), who taught him the messages that Mohammed should preach to his people. The message was that the people should worship only one God (Allah), they should care for the orphaned, they should feed the hungry, they should assist the oppressed and destitute, and they should offer hospitality to the traveler. Although it is perhaps needless to say, his ideas were completely against the status quo. The Qur'an (Koran), the holy book of Islam, reports the reaction of the established leaders: "We found our fathers following a custom, and we shall follow in their footsteps" (Qur'an, 40:22). They did not want their hierarchical society destabilized by this latest prophet.

According to Islamic scripture, Mohammed was the last and greatest prophet from Allah. On the surface, his message was simple: Every person has equal value before Allah. Live a pure life by following the five pillars of Islam: Declaring that there is no God except Allah and that Muhammad is the Messenger of God; establishing regular worship; paying *zakat* alms in service of the poor and needy; observing the fast of Ramadan; and performing the *hajj* pilgrimage. But the Qur'an makes an important distinction between Islam and faith. Islam is outwardly an all-encompassing blend of religious, social, and legal institutions, as opposed to *Iman* (faith), which is an inner belief in God expressed through worship and moral relations with others. Thus, Islam provides a template for both religious and temporal institutions.

Islamic scholars have argued over the centuries about whether Islam actually endorses a hierarchical society. One of the basic Qur'anic principles is consultation between the leaders and the followers. However, immediately following

Muhammad's death, the institution of the caliphate was devised by the elders of the Muslims to vest both religious and temporal authority in one leader. On the basis of Muhammad's practice of asserting legal, political, and religious authority, the caliphs became his successors, similar to their former institution of Sub-Sahara chief. They were both the *imam,* or chief religious leader, and the commander of the Muslims in times of peace and war. However, after the fourth caliph, there was so much infighting among various tribes and factions that the caliphs were split into different camps, and there ceased to be just one caliph. As Islam spread across the Middle East, North Africa, Southern Europe, and into Asia, the imam held a primarily religious position at the side of what were often considered irreligious monarchical rulers. *Sunnis,* the largest Islamic group, accept this split between governance and religion, but the *Shias,* who represent one sixth of Muslims and are based primarily in Iran, believe that religion and state should be inseparable.

Islam does not endorse high power distance; on the contrary, unlike the Roman Catholic Church, Islam has no hierarchy in its network of mosques, nor are there any positions of authority within the mosques. However, what ultimately matters in the discussion of power distance is that most countries that embrace Islam as their principle religion tended historically to be highly hierarchical in nature. Because Islam is a newer religion, the traditions of supreme rulers (e.g., in Saudi Arabia, the United Arab Emirates, Kuwait, Oman, Syria, and Iraq) or elitist governments (e.g., in North Africa) have not been changed by the acceptance of Islam by the country's majority. A good example is Iran, which is a highly fundamentalist and religious Islamic state, but one in which the power distance practices continue. Within government ministries, the senior officials are normal people who dress and act like average people, but they also exert substantial power over those in lesser positions. Evidently, Islam and a high power distance culture can coexist comfortably.

Hinduism. Hinduism is the religion of more than 1 billion Hindus, most of whom live in India, but there are large populations in many other countries. Hinduism is also known as *Vaidika Dharma,* meaning "religion of the Vedas," the ancient Hindu scriptures. The Vedas teach that the soul is divine, only held in the bondage of matter; perfection will be reached when this bond bursts, providing freedom from death and misery. This bondage can fall off only through the mercy of God, and this mercy is given only to the pure; thus, purity is the condition of His mercy. The fundamental message of the Hindu religion is that it is through constant struggle to purify one's physical, mental, and spiritual body that one can realize communion with the God.

The doctrine of karma is the answer provided by Hindus to the questions of why suffering and inequalities exist in the world: Why should one person be different from another in his looks, abilities, and character? Why is one born a king and another a beggar? A just and merciful God cannot create such inequalities. The word *karma* literally means "deed" or "action," but implies the entire cycle of causative forces and their effects. According to the Law of Karma (literally "action"), every human action—in thought, word, or deed—inevitably leads to results, good or bad, depending upon the ethical quality of the action. The Law of Karma conserves the ethical effects of all actions, and conditions people's future lives according to their actions in previous lives. Karma is neither predestination nor fatalism. The past karma of an individual consists of two components: constant and variable. The past karma tends to carry over to the present birth, and some of it remains constant and beyond a person's control because it determines the person's family and the country of birth, physical characteristics, and the dominant social and religious environment. The effects of past karma remain latent in the subconscious mind of the child in the form of *samskāras* (natural habits and tendencies). By manipulating this variable part of the past karma with the use of initiative and free will, an individual can break the primal, innate barriers of past karma and realize a better present and a worthy future.

Hindu religious thought embodies a great variety of ideas, principles and practices, giving rise to various religious schools (*sampradāyas*). Each school venerates the Supreme Deity, but through the veneration of a different personal god who represents a particular aspect of the Ultimate Reality (*Brahman*). Each school has temples, guru lineages, religious leaders, pilgrimage centers, monastic communities, and sacred literature. However, all of these schools believe in the central doctrines of Hindu religion.

One of the main aspects of Indian social life associated with Hinduism is the caste system. There are four different levels within this system of class hierarchy: At the top, *brahman* (priests and guru, the spiritual teacher), then *kshatriya* (rulers and warriors who were ready to give their lives up for the safety of the masses, and so accorded a premium position), *vaishya* (merchants, artisans, and agriculturalists, who served the society through their services and earned compensation to make their living), and *shudra* (those at the unskilled and lower-income strata). Each of these categories (*varnas*) largely reflect the occupational roots of the families from which its members have descended.

The Vedas, principal Hindu scriptures, do not talk of castes in terms of ancestral lineages. However, during the post-Vedic times, amid considerable social and political chaos arising from external invasions, the caste system came to be used to maintain the social positions of the wealthy, to ensure the sharing of economic production, and to ensure an orderly society. Attempts were made to convince people that caste is a preordained and hereditary institution with divine sanction. Moreover, although the caste system is not formally a part of Hinduism, the theory of cycles of rebirth, with the possibility of birth in a higher caste, was linked to carrying out one's duties in accordance with caste rules. Thus, Hinduism was used as the vehicle to integrate religion with a highly rigid social structure.

Although the caste system was officially outlawed after India became an independent country in 1947, the practice still exists in the minds of many Hindus today. They continue to marry within, and associate with, their former caste. The poorer castes are limited in educational opportunities by their poverty and current lack of education, although attempts are being made by several private sector organizations to improve their plight. At the top of the social spectrum, the governing class is still seen as entrenched and protective of its own vestiges of power. The major conclusion to be drawn from this discussion is that within Indian and other Southern Asian societies, power distance was historically very high, and it remains very high in practice today.

Buddhism. In approximately 530 BCE, along the Ganges River in northern India, a boy named Sakyamuni was born to Queen Mahamaya and King Suddhodana. At the age of about 29 years, while on a chariot ride through the royal park, Sakyamuni saw "four great sights" that altered his perceptions of life: A sick man, an old and suffering man, a dead man, and a monk. This experience focused his thoughts on the vanity of youth, on health, and on life in general, and toward the role of religion. Sakyamuni fled the palace that night, abandoning his privileged birthright to enter into a *bodhisattva* stage of learning. After many years of study and meditation, he achieved the supreme human status of becoming the Buddha, or Enlightened One.

Without dwelling on the rich history of Buddhism, there are three major "vehicles" of Buddhism that reflect the diversity of the cultures into which this religion was introduced. Buddhists today accept what they call "the Three Jewels" of Buddhist teaching, which are the Buddha himself, his teachings, and the "Order of Disciplines" in achieving personal enlightenment. Fundamentally, followers of this religion are encouraged to progress from becoming more compassionate, to becoming more generous, to detaching from worldly desires, to becoming more focused mentally on spiritual wisdom and purity.

There are Buddhists in almost every country in Europe, Asia, and North America, and they form a high percentage of the population in Tibet and in the Southern Asian countries of Thailand, Cambodia, and Myanmar (Burma). Buddhism also has a substantial number of adherents in Vietnam, Laos, China, Korea, and Japan.

From a power distance perspective, Buddhism is somewhat fatalistic but, on the whole, neutral. It is dedicated to the concern of an individual's personal path to enlightenment, in which societal hierarchy is irrelevant. Because of the cultural overlays on this religion, it is difficult to disentangle the role of power distance within different Buddhist teachings. Included in this philosophy is the acceptance of the worldly social position into which we are born. Sakyamuni taught that a person should be judged by his or her character rather than by social status. Although rulers are accepted as a functional necessity, a good Buddhist government should provide the basic human needs for all its citizens, and the punishment of crimes should be fair and equal for all people. In the balance, it appears that the level of power distance accepted within a society would not be influenced by the Buddhist religion.

Confucianism. Unlike the religions discussed previously, Confucianism is a philosophical tradition. It was developed originally in China to deal with social order, veneration of ancestors, and transmitting the wisdom of the past to later ages. The ideology was first espoused by a man called Confucius in the Western world (552–479 BCE). "Confucius" is the Latin translation of *K'ung fu-tzu,* or "Master K'ung," who was a man named K'ung Ch'iu, from Shandong province. Little is known of his early life, except that he travelled through many Chinese feudal states seeking a ruler who would follow his advice, but he did not find such a ruler. In his later years, he devoted his time to teaching his disciples, and his teachings were not fully recorded and systemized until approximately 200 years after his death.

Although there is a religious side to Confucianism in some texts on the subject, its adherents do not, for example, have temples dedicated to Confucian gods. Rather, Confucius and subsequent scholars following his tradition provided ethical answers to the questions of life's meaning and order in society, including teachings on the virtue of humaneness (*jen*).

Confucianism addresses the "Five Relationships" that deal with the norms and duties of five pivotal relationships in society: ruler–minister, father–son (filial piety), husband–wife, elder and younger brother, and senior friend–junior friend. The responsibilities implied by these relationships emphasize a vertical hierarchy based on age and seniority. The senior person is expected to provide support and encouragement for the lower-status person, whereas the lower-status person is expected to give loyalty and respect to the senior person. This relationship extends to society at large; senior people are entitled to respect and loyalty, whereas junior people are, in turn, entitled to support.

Societies in which Confucian traditions are strong include the People's Republic of China, Taiwan, Singapore, the Koreas, and Japan. Within these cultures Confucianism formalizes the principle of high power distance, which is the essence of its message. Confucian institutions embody a very hierarchical, bureaucratic structure, with a patriarchal expectation of total loyalty and obedience. Age is accorded wisdom, an important determinant of one's status, which in turn influences the system of rewards and promotions. But Confucianism, with its stress on reciprocal obligations between senior and junior, mitigates the Western concern about the potential abuse of power by those in positions at the top of the hierarchy. The major conclusion to be drawn from this discussion is that societies that embrace Confucianism, from Chinese to Japanese, are predisposed by this philosophy to accept high power distance as a fundamental characteristic of an orderly society.

Summary. The literature suggests that the respect for experience and tradition in the Confucian and Hindu societies, and the emphasis on hereditary class roles and spiritual leaders in the Hindu, Islamic, and Roman Catholic societies, predispose members of these societies to accept strong power distance. In contrast, emphasis on individual initiative for enacting one's dream and attaining high status in the Protestant societies, make these societies less accepting of power distance. Similarly, the Buddhist societies are expected to endorse low levels of power distance due to their thrust on bridging the social castes and their emphasis on a community spirit.

Tradition of Democratic Principles of Government

Most developed countries have emerged, or are in the process of emerging, from feudalistic societies. Feudalism is a system of governing in which an upper class (nobility) has certain well-defined responsibilities to the ruler, in return for the use of land exploited with the labor of a peasantry (serfs), and whose produce was traded using the services of the merchants. Whereas early feudalism was developed mainly to allow monarchs to maintain large armies of mounted troops by giving the nobles—who "owned" the armies—land in exchange for service, classic feudalism consisted of a more political relationship between a monarch and the nobility.

The breakdown of feudalism was initiated by the landed nobility, who opposed the authoritarian rule of the monarchs. Through intrigue and war, they managed to wrestle absolute power from the king. But what made the ultimate difference in changing the power establishment was the growth of strong, town-based merchants. They became increasingly necessary to process and distribute agricultural commodities from the countryside to the cities and to far-flung trading empires, which again shifted the balance of actual power to the guardians of commerce in the towns (Blum, 1978). Commensurate with their increased importance in the economic prosperity of their societies, the merchants increased their demand for representation at the government level. In this new capitalist environment, the town merchants became the *bourgeoisie,* who could no longer be ignored.

In the West, the road to democracy was the result of protracted contests over several centuries among various interest groups that made alliances with and against each other. For example, in England the aristocracy extracted numerous concessions from the royalty during the 15th and 16th centuries, particularly concerning how taxes were raised. In Russia during the 18th century, the nobility had its obligations to the tsarist autocracy removed. In Germany, the aristocracy fought furiously to gain a voice in government rather than suffer under the dictates of the Great Elector. In France, another hotbed of political activity in the late 16th century, the establishment of the First Republic marked the end of an absolute monarchy and subsequently virtually eliminated much of the upper class. The result was an abrupt change to a more democratic society, but one that would take many years to actually fulfill its promise. Each of the movements led initially to limited democracy, and subsequently to full democratic rights for all men, and later for women.

These early efforts in European countries laid the foundation for present-day democracy.

Democracy was actually a Greek term that evolved several centuries BCE. Depending upon the theoretical school, it involved governing "by the people" or "for the people." In its early incarnations in ancient Greece, democracy was perceived as governing for the people, which was undertaken by the social elite. In today's democratic societies, the term "democracy" has several standard, but not universal, characteristics:

> As most commonly understood by social scientists today, the term democracy denotes a regime in which the authority to govern derives from the consent of the majority of the people. In practice such consent is expressed through arrangements whereby certain people acquire and exercise government power on the basis of regular, free, competitive elections by all adults, whose votes have equal value. The electoral principle of democracy is intertwined with basic liberal principles, that is, civil liberties—including freedom of speech, of association, and of participation in the contest for power—without which free elections would not be possible. (Etzioni-Halevy, 1997, p. xxiii)

Western Europe's last remaining dictatorships in Greece, Portugal, and Spain fell in the 1970s. In other parts of the world, the emergence of democracy is still going on today. In Latin America, most military dictatorships collapsed in the 1980s. A movement toward democracy is also evident in East Asia: The Philippines, South Korea, Japan, and Taiwan all have forms of democracy. Since the end of the 1980s, the former communist regimes in Eastern Europe have been forced to grapple with democracy, whereas South Africa accepted democracy in 1994 with the dismantling of apartheid and the country's first free elections.

Although there are inequalities in all democratic societies, particularly economic inequities in capitalist states, the mechanisms of democracy, such as free elections, civil liberties, and the separation of powers, serve to limit the oppressive might of the state and the power of the state's elite. Even if one believes that the masses have no real power and virtually no influence over government policies, which is the contention of most Marxist theorists, it is still evident in democracies that business, academia, the press, and trade unions have usually gained a degree of autonomy from the state. Thus, they continue to disperse centralized power to the interests that they represent.

We cannot escape from at least a brief discussion of the role of communism in this debate. Communism is a system of socialism enshrined in a draconian system of government. In some ways, it might be viewed as a form of democracy "for the people," but this is not an argument that most people are willing to accept. Like other more traditional forms of autocracy, it is a political system that perpetuates the inequalities in society, although the new heads of the governing elite have changed from the formerly disenfranchised to the newly entrenched as a result of their first-mover position within the dominant political party. This is not democracy, whether in China, North Korea, Vietnam, or Cuba. This is a form of government that strongly emphasizes the levels of status inequality.

What is most important about the role of democracy in predicting a society's level of power distance is the tradition, or comfort level gained over time, with the fundamental elements of a democratic government. We expect that, in societies that have a long experience with the democratic rights of free speech, free association, and access to the contest for governmental power sharing, there will be less power stratification and centralization.

The Role of the Middle Class

The middle class is a heterogeneous group whose members are relatively wealthy in terms of disposable and discretionary income, tend to have a higher education, and hold managerial or administrative jobs rather than positions as physical laborers. They not only believe that they are responsible for their own lives, but also that they are in the position to make substantive choices concerning their futures, including their education, their careers, and where they live.

Because of their financial security and the crucial roles that they play within their country's economy, members of the middle class demand access to decision-making bodies at all levels of government and within their organizations. Consequently, they do not accept

a large power difference between themselves and their superiors. The societies with a large middle class tend to be pluralist and embrace diversity and equal opportunity. As Hofstede (1980) explained, "in pluralist societies, new members will be more easily admitted into elites than in elite societies, because the middle groups in the pluralist society are stepping stones to the top dog ranks" (p. 96). Examples of such societies are most historically capitalist countries, including Australia and countries in Western Europe and North America.

Countries with virtually no middle class, including many in Latin America, the Arabian Gulf region, Asia, and Africa, have a class structure comprised of a small upper class and a large majority of lower-class citizens. As a result of their lack of access to decision making and their inability to make substantial changes in their future, members of the lower class are forced to accept high power distance. At the same time, members of the elite expect a large power distance, and try to reinforce the rigid class structure.

It should be noted that this stereotypical split between countries with a large, powerful middle class and those without a middle class has changed considerably in the past 20 years. As countries around the world become less agrarian, with a commensurate higher education level and access to global information, middle classes have emerged in most countries. This new class, with its expectations of mobility and power sharing, is putting considerable pressure on the ruling regimes to change the distribution of power within their societies. However, it generally takes many years to effect the transition from a high power distance to a low power distance culture, even when widespread expectations already exist for low power distance. Consequently, societies with a large, established middle class will have a lower level of power distance than societies with a newly emerging middle class.

The Role of a High Proportion of Immigrants

Immigrants leave their native countries for a variety of reasons, notably religious or political persecution, relative poverty, access to higher education, or access to higher paying jobs. The common denominator among these factors is the desire to change their position within society. When arriving in their new country, they often have no extended family as a support group, nor do they have communal obligations and strictures to uphold. Rather, they are forced to use their own initiative to succeed.

It should be noted that there is a considerable difference between countries that accept immigrants as citizens and those that allow foreign workers who cannot attain citizenship. Foreign workers cannot exert their independence, nor are they allowed to share power in any way. This is particularly evident in some countries in Western Europe, throughout the Arabian Gulf states, and in some countries in Southern Asia.

Countries that have traditionally accepted a large proportion of immigrants, notably Canada, the United States, and Australia, are highly individualist and democratic, and they have a large, mobile middle class. There are no barriers to entry into the middle class that cannot be overcome through a mixture of talent, personal initiative, contacts, and sometimes a bit of luck. Even if one enters the country as a menial laborer, the expectation is that advancement is possible and that nobody controls one's destiny. Consequently, within countries with a large proportion of immigrants, power distance, both *As is* (practices) and *Should be* (values) is expected to be very low.

Which Factor Has the Greatest Influence on Power Distance?

We have treated the four primary factors affecting a society's level of power distance as virtually distinct influences. In reality, they are often interdependent, and it is difficult to consider one aspect in isolation. However, we speculate that a society's predominant belief system and its religion or philosophy will have the most profound and enduring influence on power distance. This will then be moderated somewhat by a democratic tradition and the existence of a strong middle class, which go virtually hand in hand in the development of a society. Moreover, both factors can be expected to exert similar influence toward lowering the level of power distance. Hence, a

Roman Catholic society that is exposed to democracy and a middle class would reduce its level of power distance over time, but it would still have a higher level of power distance than a Protestant country with a democratic tradition and a large middle class. Finally, the role of a large proportion of immigrants in a given society reinforces the low power distance trend that is in all likelihood already present.

We propose one corollary: Regardless of the religion, any society that has neither a democratic tradition nor an established middle class will have a relatively high level of power distance. In our discussion of Islam, we suggested that several of the Islamic principles were fundamentally opposed to high power distance, but that both authoritarian regimes and Islam could coexist comfortably. Although this corollary does not provide an explanation, it does serve as a basis for predicting a society's relative level of power distance.

How Family Power Values Are Taught

Several studies have compared the motives for having children in a variety of countries (Darroch, Meyer, & Singarimbun, 1981; Fawcett, 1983; Kagitçibasi, 1982). They have identified two sets of values attributed to having children: Economic and psychological support. In many less-developed countries, children are seen as the source of economic support for parents in their old age. They are expected to be obedient and to take care of their parents in their old age. Iranians refer to their children as "the cane for the hand in old age." In contrast, those who are motivated by psychological support, such as Americans and Germans, dismiss such a notion, because children are expected to be autonomous after they leave the family home.

Another stream of literature reinforces the significance of indoctrinating children at an early age in cultural values, this one from the perspective of personal empowerment. McClelland (1961) set out to propose a psychological perspective on Weber's (1976) chronicle of the Protestant Reformation. Weber's hypothesis was that the Protestant values of self-reliance and hard work led to the evolution of the spirit of modern and rational capitalism. McClelland proposed a more detailed process in which Protestant values led to greater emphasis among parents on teaching their children to set high standards and to value independence. Winterbottom (1958) had shown that mothers of 8- to 11-year-old boys in families with a high need for achievement tended to set high performance expectations for their sons at an early age. Other data demonstrate that Protestant parents tend to put more emphasis on the importance of independence, knowledge, planning, and achieving (McClelland, Rindlisbacher, & de Charms, 1955; Rosen & D'Andrade, 1959). Such characteristics are perceived as necessary to succeed in low power distance societies. Also, according to Hofstede (1980), "the boss–subordinate relationship is a basic human relationship which bears fundamental resemblance to even more fundamental relationships earlier in life: that of parent and child . . . and of teacher and pupil" (p. 97).

In summary, the role of the family in learning social values is very influential. Families are pivotal in developing the values and attitudes of their children, which then serves as our primary source of reference concerning collective values and culture. Acceptance of a low or a high power distance is conditioned by families and support groups from an early age.

Summary

Above we discussed the psychological and cross-cultural perspectives on power, and their implications for the concept of power distance. Next, we review the concept of power distance as a dimension of culture.

COMPARISON OF HIGH VERSUS LOW POWER DISTANCE SOCIETIES

In this section, we review the concept of power distance based on three streams of literature: those dealing with society, organization, and leadership.

Power Distance in Societies

As noted earlier, power distance as a cultural dimension is traditionally related to the perception of social inequality. Social inequality arises if the differences in resources such as wealth, education, and physical characteristics allow people to exert social influence that is disproportionate to the social benefits generated from such influence. An unequal distribution of power per se is not equivalent to power distance, unless power is used to secure special rank or advantages. The people in more powerful positions, whether in organizations or societies, might demand that others accept their positions unquestingly. Or, they could create barriers so that the underprivileged might not develop new skills and, therefore, not move on to positions at par or even better than their positions.

Early Studies on Power Distance

Haire, Ghiselli, and Porter (1966) were the first prominent researchers to explore differences in preferences for power among different cultures, although they did not refer directly to the concept of power distance. They used a questionnaire based on a modified version of Maslow's hierarchy of needs to assess how the needs of managers from 14 countries were fulfilled in their current positions. The dimensions in their questionnaire that potentially measure some aspects of power distance across cultures were composed of autonomy and self-actualization. The items presented in their questionnaire explored the following power-related concerns:

Autonomy

–   The authority connected with management position.

–   The opportunity for independent thought and action in management positions.

Self-Actualization

–   The opportunity for personal growth and development in management positions.

–   The feeling of self-fulfillment a person gets from being in a management position.

–   The feeling of worthwhile accomplishment in management positions.

On the basis of the responses to the 11 items in their questionnaire, they were able to cluster

Table 17.1a   Haire, Ghiselli, and Porter's (1966) Standardized Scores

Haire, Ghiselli, & Porter 1966 Country Clusters	Autonomy	Self-Actualization
Nordic European	.36	.25
Latin European	−.16	.23
Anglo American	−.14	−.09
Developing	−.25	−.11
Japan	−.25	−.11

the 14 countries into five groups, which they labeled *Nordic-European* (Denmark, Germany, Norway, and Sweden), *Latin-European* (Belgium, France, Italy, and Spain), *Anglo-American* (England and the United States), *Developing* (Argentina, Chile, and India), and *Japan* (by itself). For this analysis, what is important are the different mean standardized scores that the various groups demonstrated with respect to autonomy and self-actualization. Positive values indicate greater fulfillment of need than for the average manager across all 14 countries; negative values indicate lesser fulfillment. Their results are presented in Table 17.1a.

The implications of their findings with respect to power distance are complicated. Summarily, it would appear that the Nordic-Europeans who were sampled were very content with the fulfillment of their need for power, Anglo-Americans were somewhat frustrated, and the other clusters had a higher preference for power than that experienced within their current jobs. The importance of this study is that countries can be clustered on the basis of their preference for power. Further, there are substantive differences that might be explained by the influence of the four criteria explained previously: the predominant religion or philosophy, an established tradition of democracy, the long-term existence of a middle class, and the proportion of immigrants in each country. However, we have to note that the Anglo-American societies sampled in this study appear to have a greater preference for power than our influencing factors would suggest.

The next major study of power distance was undertaken by Mulder (1977) in the Netherlands. As the societies become weaker in power distance, the underprivileged tend to reject their power dependency. Laboratory experiments in social and organizational settings in the Netherlands, a low power distance culture, have shown attempts by people to seek "power distance reduction" (Mulder, 1977). The findings indicated the following:

1. More powerful individuals attempt to maintain or to enhance the power distance from the less powerful people.

2. The greater the power distance from the less powerful person, the greater the attempts to enhance it by the power holder.

3. Less powerful individuals attempt to reduce the power distance between themselves and more powerful people.

4. The smaller the power distance from the more powerful person, the stronger the tendency to reduce it by the individuals with low power.

The above set of findings suggests a condition of quasi-equilibrium in which power holders have achieved a certain distance from those who lack power and this distance is difficult for the latter to bridge.

Hofstede's Seminal Study

Chronologically, the next major research on this construct was conducted by Geert Hofstede

(1980). Hofstede used IBM data in this ground breaking study that assessed commonalities and differences in various fundamental value constructs across cultures. Building on Mulder's work and Aston's research that identified centralization as a key attribute of organizations (Pugh, 1976), Hofstede used the IBM survey data to compute a power distance index for evaluating the degree of power distance in each country. Hofstede's power distance index was a composite measure computed using the responses to three questions:

a. How frequently, in your experience, are employees afraid to express disagreement with their managers? (mean score across respondents in a society)

1	2	3	4	5
Very Frequently			Very Seldom	

The measure was based on Patchen's (1965) index of "willingness to disagree with supervisors." Patchen's measure was correlated negatively with employee control over work goals and interest in work innovation. The theoretical base for its use at the societal level derived from Whyte (1969), who wrote, with respect to Venezuela, that in a highly stratified society where all powers are concentrated in the hands of the superior, subordinates learn that it can be dangerous to question a decision of the superior.

b. How would you describe the actual decision-making style of your boss?

To measure power distance in boss–subordinate relationships in various countries, Hofstede's questionnaires presented four alternative decision-making styles: (a) autocratic ("tells"), (b) persuasive/paternalistic ("sells"), (c) consultative ("consults") and (d) democratic (majority votes, "joins"). In 1970, the fourth category was renamed as participative ("consensus"). Hofstede noted that to understand the boss's influence on subordinate behavior, a subjective description of the boss's decision-making behavior is relevant. He found that item (b) is significantly correlated with item (a), and therefore included it as part of the power distance measure. The perceived manager question was used as a feature of the organizational "regime" (the superior's decision-making style), in contrast to a characteristic of the organizational "climate" indicated in item (a).

c. What decision-making style would you prefer your boss to have?

In contrast to the second item (b) concerning the perceived manager, item (c) deals with preferences. Hofstede noted that in societies in which superiors endorse large power distances, subordinates prefer a dependent relationship with the superiors, or go to the other extreme of counter-dependent relationship by preferring a superior who does not decide at all and instead goes by democratic majority.

Building on Mulder's (1977) and Pugh's (1976) frameworks, Hofstede maintained that his power distance index is a measure of the extent to which a society accepts the unequal distribution of power in institutional and organizational environments. According to Hofstede, members of high power distance cultures accept large differences in power among the various levels of a hierarchy, whereas members of low power cultures expect a lower level of power differential. Subordinates in high power distance cultures accept artifacts such as titles, ranks, and commensurate privileges and status, whereas those in low power distance cultures expect virtually equal treatment on the basis of their self-worth and their contributions to the organization, regardless of status, seniority, or age. In low power distance cultures, superiors still have authority, but employees are not duty-bound to be respectful or hold a sense of awe toward their superiors.

The respondents were the first-level supervisors in the sales and service offices of IBM in 41 countries and three regions. In countries with lower scores on Hofstede's power distance index there was limited dependence of subordinates on bosses and a preference for consultation. Subordinates approached and critiqued their bosses quite freely. In contrast, high power distance index was associated with significant dependence of the subordinates on bosses. The subordinates let the boss decide, whether on the basis of personal preferences or on majority vote, rather than actively discussing their point

Table 17.1b   Hofstede's Occupational-Level Power Distance Index

Category of Occupations	Number of Occupations in This Category	Power Distance Index Range		
		Minimum	Maximum	Mean
Unskilled and semiskilled workers	3	85	97	90
Clerical workers and nonprofessional salesmen	8	57	84	71
Skilled workers and technicians	6	33	90	65
Managers of the previous categories	8	22	62	42
Professional workers	8	−22	36	22
Managers of professional workers	5	−19	21	8
Total	38	−22	97	47

NOTE: Data from Hofstede (1994, p. 30).

of view. An additional analysis of power distance index in 38 occupations, using data from the United Kingdom, France, and West Germany subsamples, was also conducted. As shown in Table 17.1b, the power distance index tended to be higher in lower-skilled occupations than among professional workers such as engineers and scientists.

However, another analysis using data from four occupations in 11 countries showed that in high power distance countries, the power distance index was high across all occupations. In contrast, in low power distance countries, whereas the employees in higher skilled occupations had a low power distance index, the employees in lower skilled occupations had power distance indices similar to their counterparts in high power distance countries. These findings suggested that power distance tends to emerge in all countries, but with higher education the people in some societies are able to reduce power distance within organizations.

Hofstede (1980) also proposed that the history of power distance philosophy in countries is a function of the climate. He found that 43% of the variance in power distance index scores could be predicted from the geographical latitude (of the country's capital), an additional 8% from

population size, and a further 7% from wealth (1970 gross national product [GNP] per capita). Power distance index was lower in countries at higher latitudes where, due to colder, adverse climate, a greater social mobility had traditionally been supported, and power differences could never be stabilized as continuous technological innovations rendered older wealth bases obsolete.

The robustness of Hofstede's power distance index has been established to a fairly high degree by independent replication in several studies. Hoppe (1993) included Hofstede's original power distance questions in a survey of high-positioned alumni from an Austrian conference center. The power distance index scores of the 18 overlapping countries in Hoppe's and Hofstede's studies were significantly correlated ($r = .67$, $p < .01$). Similarly, Helmreich and Merritt (1998) surveyed commercial airline pilots in 23 countries and included Hofstede's original questions in the survey. The power distance index scores for the 21 overlapping countries were strongly correlated with the IBM scores ($r = .76$, $p < .01$). Also, Shane (1994) used Hofstede's questions in a survey of more than 6,000 employees of six organizations in 32 nations in 1991–1992. The power distance index scores were again strongly correlated with the

IBM scores ($r = 0.54, p < 0.01$) for 29 overlapping nations.

In addition, Hofstede reported a high correlation between his power distance index and scores on the following items, using Gordon's (1976) survey of interpersonal values:

1. Greater conformity: Doing what is socially correct, following regulations closely, doing what is accepted and proper, being a conformist.

2. Less independence: Not having the right to do whatever one wants to do, being free to make one's own decisions, being able to do things in one's own way.

In higher power distance countries, student samples in 17 countries endorsed the values of greater conformity ($r = .80$) and less independence ($r = .79$). The differentiation between the values of conformity and independence was less stark using managerial respondents. Thus, in countries in which high power distance is reported, the less powerful tended to endorse the values of conformity and dependence more strongly than the more powerful people.

Significant evidence also links power distance with role overload as well as lack of role ambiguity in organizations. Peterson and colleagues (1995) found that Hofstede's measure of power distance is positively correlated with the national level of role overload ($r = .42$). Later, van de Vliert and van Yperen (1996) found that, although Hofstede's power distance measure was positively correlated with the national levels of role overload ($r = .44$, $n = 20$, $p < .05$), the correlation disappeared when average temperature of the capital city was partialed out of the correlation, most likely reflecting higher power distance countries closer to the equator. Temperature was positively correlated with the role overload ($r = .56$, $n = 21$, $p < .01$), and remained significant even after controlling for the power distance. In a larger sample, Peterson and Smith (1997) again found a positive correlation between Hofstede's power distance measure and national levels of role overload ($r = .64$, $n = 26$, $p < .01$), even after controlling for the average temperature of the capital city. Further, power distance was negatively correlated with the national levels of role ambiguity ($r = -.42$,

$n = 26$, $p < .05$). These findings suggest that managers or leaders in societies in which high power distance is reported make greater demands on subordinates, but do so with clarity.

For further validation, Hofstede (2001) correlated his power distance index with several items from Inglehart's World Values Survey. In societies that scored high on Hofstede's power distance index, children were encouraged to learn the qualities of "hard work" and "obedience" at home and were not encouraged to learn the quality of "independence." In addition, Hofstede's power distance index was correlated positively with the percentages of people choosing equality to be more important than freedom. That is, the power distance index, which reflects more inequality, was negatively related with the value of inequality. Thus, Hofstede's power distance index likely does not reflect power distance values, but instead reflects power distance practices. This interpretation is supported empirically in other studies and will be reported and discussed below in the section discussing GLOBE Power Distance and Hofstede's power distance index.

Other Studies on the Construct of Power Distance

Another important study was the Chinese Culture Connection described by House and Javidan in Chapter 2. The members of the Chinese Culture Connection developed measures of Chinese cultural values (Chinese Culture Connection, 1987, p. 145). For the purpose of this discussion, power distance correlated significantly with integration ($r = -.58$) and with moral discipline ($r = .55$). In societies that practice power distance, there is less emphasis on integrating different societal groups. Also, power differences can be legitimated and sustained only if those in power maintain and enforce a sense of moral discipline. It is important to note that both integration and moral discipline correlated significantly with Hofstede's individualism index.

Are power distance and individualism really distinct dimensions? Hofstede reported a correlation of .67 between the power distance and individualism-collectivism indices. However, he concluded that they are conceptually different, because power distance refers to emotional dependence on more powerful persons, whereas individualism is concerned with personal emotional independence.

Also recall from Chapter 2 that the existence of a cultural dimension concerned with power inequalities in various societies was also explored by Schwartz (1999). Schwartz developed a 2-dimensional graph consisting of seven value domains, one of which was *hierarchy*. In this framework, power differences are expressed as a hierarchy value, which relies on "hierarchical systems of ascribed roles to insure socially responsible behavior" in which people seek "to comply with the obligations and rules attached to their roles" (Schwartz, 1999). The values typifying a hierarchical culture, that is, one that scores high on Schwartz's hierarchy measure, are social power, authority, humility, and wealth. Hierarchical cultures are deemed to be in opposition with the voluntary cooperation, maintained through egalitarianism value-oriented norms, that encourage people to feel concern for everyone's welfare by internalizing a commitment to voluntary cooperation with others. Schwartz argued that involuntary dependence on roles, enforced through some kind of authority, is at the essence of hierarchical power distance, whereas cooperativeand voluntary negotiation characterizes low power distance and egalitarianism. However, Schwartz did not provide any independent validation linking the construct of hierarchy–egalitarianism with the forced and involuntary dependence on roles.

The work by Trompenaars (1993) also offers insight on this dimension. One of the dimensions derived by Trompenaars, using factor analysis based on the theoretical formulation of Parsons and Shils (1951), was achievement–ascription, which corresponds best with Hofstede's conception of power distance. In achievement-oriented societies, each person is responsible for his or her own fate; in ascriptive societies, status is granted by who you are and power status grows automatically with age and experience.

Trompenaars determined that countries could be clustered on the basis of each of his dimensions, including achievement–ascription, which yielded results similar to those of Hofstede. Trompenaars's initial findings were extended by Trompenaars and Hampden-Turner (1998), who used a 5-point scale to measure achievement–ascription with more than 30,000 respondents. In response to the statement, "The respect a person gets is highly dependent on their family background," the highest ascribed status countries were in the Middle East (Kuwait, Saudi Arabia, Oman, and Bahrain), Southern Asia (Thailand, Hong Kong, and the Philippines), and Africa (Kenya and Burkina Faso). Austria and Serbia were also among this group. The highest achieved status countries were Nordic (Norway, Denmark, Finland, and Sweden) and Anglo (Ireland, New Zealand, the United Kingdom, the United States, Canada, and Australia).

The next study of importance, also reviewed in Chapter 2, was conducted by Smith, Dugan, and Trompenaars (1996). Achievement–ascription was measured with six items designed by Trompenaars using a 5-point Likert scale format. Completed questionnaires were returned by 8,841 respondents from 43 countries. Multidimensional scaling (MDS) solutions of dimensionality were computed in a 3-dimensional solution, two of which were labeled *conservatism–egalitarian commitment* and *utilitarian involvement—loyal involvement.* Power distance scores from Hofstede (1980) are related to both dimensions, with higher power distance associated with conservatism and loyal involvement. The first dimension of the MDS solution correlated 0.68 ($p < 0.01$) with Hofstede's power distance index and -0.81 ($p < 0.01$) with Hofstede's individualism. Smith and colleagues concluded that their first dimension has to do with the nature of one's obligations to groups and organizations, only one aspect of which is captured in Hofstede's power distance index. They maintained, "the more general terms of conservatism, ascription, and particularism cover not just hierarchy but the overall basis of one's obligations toward all other in-group members" (p. 261). Combining their first two dimensions with Hofstede's power distance index, they proposed that the highest power distance would be associated with conservatism and loyal involvement, whereas the lowest power distance would be associated with egalitarianism and utilitarian involvement.

Smith and colleagues found power distance to be one of the important constructs that can distinguish whether a society is collectively or individually oriented. In addition, there is a strong relationship between Hofstede's individualism measure and power distance as evidenced by items representing both measures in the Hofstede questionnaire loading on a single factor; power distance and individualism remained separate constructs in this study because they were hypothesized to be conceptually distinct. High power distance is associated with collectivist societies. On the whole, Smith, Dugan, and Trompenaars's study and that of Hofstede not only provide considerable validation for the construct of power distance, but they also suggest possibilities for a broader reconstruction of the dimension.

The final important cross-cultural study was conducted by Inglehart (1997), described earlier in Chapter 2 by House and Javidan. Inglehart summarized several key items from the World Values Survey into two summary factors that were used to compare fundamental cultural tendencies. One of Inglehart's factors, *traditional versus secular rational* authority reflects an emphasis on traditional authority in high power distance cultures, and on secular-rational, impersonal authority in low power distance cultures.

In addition to vindicating the centrality of the power distance construct in cross-cultural analysis, Inglehart's work also points to an intriguing relationship between power distance practices, as measured using Hofstede's power distance index, and the use of technology. In societies that rated high on Hofstede's power distance index, people tend to agree that more emphasis on the development of technology is desirable. Inglehart interpreted this item as uncritical and absolute support for technology in traditional societies. Hofstede (2001) also noted support for technology in high power distance societies as reflective of an uncritical attitude. A similar finding appears in the commercial pilot surveys of Helmreich and Merritt (1998). Using the original Hofstede IBM power distance items for their own surveys, Helmreich and Meritt reported that in high power distance cultures, pilots are both more positive about automation and more likely to use it under all circumstances.

There may be an alternative explanation. It is possible that a stronger preference for technology in high power distance cultures may have to do less with an uncritical or absolute attitude toward technology, than with the relevance of technology for reducing an arbitrary and absolute exercise of power. Hofstede (2001), however, presumes that if the "need for technology" is high, then power distance has to be lower. He observes that the high latitude societies have colder climates in which the need for technology is higher for survival, and this contributed to historically lower levels of power distance in such societies. In contrast, the low latitude societies have warmer climates, where the need for technology is weaker, and this has contributed to historically higher levels of power distance in such societies.

Contemporary organizational research (discussed below) emphasizes how information technology has allowed firms to transform from hierarchical bureaucracies to horizontal high-performance organizations in which authority is shifted to the empowered grassroots personnel because of a lower need for the top managers to spend time monitoring control issues. Such personalized authority may also be functional in defending against external threats. With the emergence of more secure conditions, governed by international laws concerning national sovereignty, efforts in high power distance societies to support the use of technology may obviate an absolute use of traditional authority, so that people are encouraged to channel their personal energy into more developmental activities. Consequently, support for technological development may facilitate the reduction of traditional power distance, not just in organizations, but in the society as a whole.

Power Distance in Organizations

Social beliefs, values, and practices within societies often tend to carry over to their organizations and their informal codes of conduct (Meyer & Rowan, 1977; Selznick, 1949). Under these situations, people often seek to defend their entrenched interests rather than to assist their clientele and higher officials. Culture also plays a major role in how dominant coalitions are formed within an organization, and how their power is balanced for furthering the overall interests of the organization. Social norms and social arrangements in the organizations are manifested in terms of the power hierarchy (Cohen, 1976), and the analysis of power dynamics can yield fundamental insights into the ontology of the organizational culture.

In general, organizations tend to mirror the culture of power distance practices and values in their society so that they can gain legitimacy and also appeal to the people from their host societies. Further, organizations often need to respond to cultures of several different societies in which they conduct business. They tend to prefer business with societies that have similar cultures of power distance and avoid societies in which a cultural gap is significant. Thus, for instance, Confucian societies that have higher power distance are reluctant investors in the Nordic nations, which tend to be highly egalitarian.

However, sometimes the organizations may seek to buffer themselves from the societal practices and values of power distance. High power distance may be favored in military-type organizations, even if the societal culture is of low power distance. Similarly, power egalitarianism may be favored in knowledge-intensive organizations, in which team-based systems and empowerment are of considerable interest.

In the contemporary learning- and knowledge-driven environment, the mantra in several Western cultures is that lower power distance is more effective in organizational settings. Power sharing, empowerment, and, hence, lower power distance is the prescribed norm. The concept of empowerment and semi-autonomous teams has proved particularly striking in the societies at the forefront of the information technology revolution (Gupta, 1998). In the United States, information technology has allowed firms to delay the monitoring and control role of middle managers, and instead assign a more learning and knowledge development role to them. In Europe, firms have used information technology to make knowledge about the inputs, outputs, and process support available to teams of employees, who are then expected to work semiautonomously on internal assignments and accomplishment of their role obligations. In Japan, technology has always been applied with creative techniques, such as *kanban* (a manufacturing strategy whereby supplies and production demands are operationally linked) and job rotation, to allow

for decentralized decision-making, learning, and corrective actions. On the whole, such power distance reduction in the organizations adds to the employee beliefs of self-efficacy and control in themselves, adds to their work satisfaction, and enhances growth and productivity (Huselid, 1995; Nadler, 1989).

The use of teams that allow some informal power sharing is one of the most prominent approaches to power distance reduction in contemporary organizations, which also allows for a more strategic and need-based intervention of authority. The team-based organization is at the core of the high performance work systems (Nadler, 1989). Team systems support job rotation and total quality management and positively influence the level and type of training offered to employees (Smith & Dowling, 2001). In a sample of 1,000 firms, Huselid (1995) maintained that the magnitude of the returns on investments in high performance work practices is substantial. One standard deviation increase in such practices was associated with $27,044 more sales, $18,641 more market value, and $3,814 more profits (all in U.S. dollars) on a per employee basis, and a 7.05% decline in employee turnover.

In summary, although some degree of power distance is implicit in the concept of hierarchy and may be essential for organizational coordination and control, substantial gains can be obtained by reducing the level of power distance within an organization. Reduced power distance can contribute to the flexibility of the organization and enhance competence building and learning. The gains from empowerment may be particularly great in high power distance cultures, in which workforces otherwise may not feel free or encouraged to make suggestions and be committed to the organizational mission. At the same time, it may be more difficult to initiate and sustain egalitarian power practices in such high power distance cultures, in which workforces have been accustomed to depend on their supervisors for direction and decision making. Unless appropriate technology and techniques are adopted that facilitate the introduction and incremental refinement of empowerment, power distance reduction may be dysfunctional. Installment of empowerment practices, when effective, will allow supervisors to focus more on strategic developmental initiatives.

Leadership and Power Distance

The use of power as a source of influence by leaders, which was studied extensively in the 20th century, particularly in the context of political or military environments, is beyond the scope of this chapter. Within the organizational leadership domain, much of the literature flows from French and Raven's (1959) typology of sources of power, which was discussed previously in this chapter. At one end of the spectrum, from a power distance perspective, is the use of coercive power, which focuses on the threat or application of punishments to enforce the leader's wishes. Organizational examples include the power to reprimand, suspend, demote, fine, or dismiss an employee. We tend to associate a domineering, autocratic leadership style with this leadership type.

Various leadership models have incorporated autocratic leadership in a dimension concerned with decision making, expressing the relative degree of participation that the subordinate is allowed (Heller & Yukl, 1969; Strauss, 1977; Tannenbaum & Schmidt, 1958; Vroom & Yetton, 1973). This continuum generally starts with autocratic decision making followed by some form of consultation, then joint decision making, and finally delegation (Yukl, 2002). Hofstede's perceived and preferred manager questions for measuring power distance index are also based on a similar typology of autocratic, paternalistic, democratic, or consultative decision-making style of the leaders.

As several prominent researchers have pointed out, most leaders use a variety of decision-making styles, either concurrently or at different times. Their decision-making style will vary with contingent factors such as the degree of formalization of the situation, external threat faced by the leader and the group, the organizational structure, sophistication of the subordinates (Heller & Yukl, 1969; Vroom & Yetton, 1973), and the degree to which the specific situational context might give the leader power, control, or influence (Fiedler, 1967).

The leader–member exchange theory proposed by Dansereau, Grean, and Haga (1975), and further developed in many iterations (e.g., Wayne & Green, 1993), addresses the role-making process between a supervisor and his or her subordinate. Accordingly, the leader's choice of whether to increase or decrease power distance may also be conditioned by specific relationships with individual subordinates. This theory questioned the concept that members of an organizational unit are homogeneous, and that a superior behaves in essentially the same way toward each of the subordinates. Instead, they considered two vertical exchange techniques that might occur: Either *supervision* or *leadership*. Under the higher power distance style of supervision, there is virtually no rapport between the leader and subordinate. Leaders will rely almost exclusively on the formal contract with subordinates to achieve organizational goals, with the organization compensating the employee through financial remuneration. In the leadership mode, which corresponds closely with lower power distance, the leader works with followers by directly influencing their behavior through techniques such as offering job latitude, allowing them to influence decision making, encouraging open and honest discussions, and demonstrating confidence in the group members.

Which type of power utilization will make a leader more effective? This would depend on how effectiveness is measured; the situational context; and the societal, industrial, and organization cultures in which a given style of leadership is assessed. On the basis of Western research, Yukl (2002) concluded that the use of coercive (autocratic) power is very unlikely to create commitment among subordinates; compliance will possibly occur if it is used in a helpful, nonpunitive way, and resistance is likely if coercion is used in a hostile and manipulative way. However, Hersey and Blanchard's (1977) situational leadership theory suggested that a leader should be very directive and autocratic in defining subordinates' roles, objectives, standards, and procedures if subordinates are very immature in relation to their task within the organization. Bass (1985), Vroom and Yetton (1973), and Yukl (2002) determined that leaders tend to be more directive and autocratic if subordinates have relatively structured tasks with low complexity, low variability, low uncertainty, and low difficulty.

However, with the growth of empowerment and team-based organizations discussed earlier, there is currently a strong trend toward

Table 17.2   Higher Power Distance Societies Versus Lower Power Distance Societies

Parameters	Higher Power Distance	Lower Power Distance
1. Social inequities	Society differentiated into classes on several criteria	Society has large middle class
2. Power bases	Power bases are stable and scarce (e.g., land ownership)	Power bases are transient and sharable (e.g., skill, knowledge)
3. Role of power	Power is seen as providing social order, relational harmony, and role stability	Power is seen as a source of corruption, coercion, and dominance
4. Social mobility	Limited upward social mobility	High upward social mobility
5. Information control	Information is localized	Information is shared
6. Governance	Different groups (e.g., women) have different involvement, and democracy does not ensure equal opportunities	All the groups enjoy equal involvement, and democracy ensures parity in opportunities and development for all
7. Indigenous orientation and independence	Strong nonnative historical influences and recent independence of the society	Strong native historical influences and long standing independence of the society
8. Civil freedom	Civil liberties are weak and public corruption high	Civil liberties are strong and public corruption low
9. Resources and capabilities	Only a few people have access to resources, skills, and capabilities, contributing to low human development and life expectancies	Mass availability of tools, resources, and capabilities for independent and entrepreneurial initiatives, as reflected in wide educational enrolment
10. Consumption	High growth rates of consumption and high need for resource coordination	Mature growth rates of consumption and high per capita purchasing power
11. Technology	Mass use of technology, which supports general power distance reduction	Need for specialized technology, adapted to each user

transformational leadership, in which the leader inspires subordinates to exert themselves to achieve the organization's goals (Bass, 1985, 1997; House, 1977; House, Wright, & Aditya, 1997). Often, effective leaders use power in a subtle manner that diminishes status differentials and avoids threats to the target person's self-esteem (Yukl, 2002). In societies that emphasize this use of power, power distance may not be perceptible in practice and therefore would not be overtly devalued. On the other hand, leaders who engage in a manipulative, domineering, and arrogant use of power tend to engender resistance (Yukl, 2002). In societies that do not promote this use of power, power distance practices would clearly be perceptible to all and the value placed on power distance would be low.

Summary

Table 17.2 summarizes the differences between higher and lower power distance cultures expected in the GLOBE Project.

Table 17.3a   Power Distance: Society Practices (As Is)

---

1. In this society, followers are expected to: (reverse scored)

Obey their leader without question						Question their leaders when in disagreement
1	2	3	4	5	6	7

2. In this society, power is: (reverse scored)

Concentrated at the top						Shared throughout the society
1	2	3	4	5	6	7

Table 17.3b   Power Distance: Society Values (Should Be)

---

1. I believe that followers *should*: (reverse scored)

Obey their leader without question						Question their leader when in disagreement
1	2	3	4	5	6	7

2. I believe that power *should be*: (reverse scored)

Concentrated at the top						Shared throughout the society
1	2	3	4	5	6	7

GLOBE's CONCEPTUALIZATION AND MEASURES OF POWER DISTANCE

In the development of the Power Distance scales, GLOBE investigators began with the theory of power distance. Following Hofstede (1980), we defined the Power Distance cultural dimension as "the degree to which members of an organization or society expect and agree that power should be shared unequally." In the GLOBE study, Power Distance is measured in terms of two constructs: *As Is* (*practices*), and *Should Be* (*values*). These measures were used to collect data relevant to Power Distance at two levels of analysis: societal level and organizational level.

Tables 17.3a and 17.3b show sample GLOBE questionnaire items for Power Distance practices and values at the societal level. Practice questions relate to the society's current practices regarding the basis of influence, concentration of

power, privileges of power, and interpersonal behaviors concerning differences in power *as is*. Essentially, they measure the extent to which a society is perceived to practice and encourage behaviors that enact power differences. A similar set of items is used to measure values in terms of responses to questionnaire items with a *should be* response format.

GLOBE Power Distance at the organizational level was measured using an isomorphic set of items, in a different set of questionnaires given to a matching set of managerial respondents. Tables 17.3c and 17.3d show sample GLOBE questionnaire items for Power Distance practices and values at the organizational level.

Thus, the GLOBE measures of Power Distance represent the degree to which a community maintains inequality among its members by stratification of individuals and groups with respect to power, authority, prestige, status, wealth, and material possessions. The critical aspects are the

Table 17.3c　　Power Distance: Organization Practices (As Is)

1. In this organization, subordinates are expected to: (reverse scored)

Obey their boss
without question

Question their
boss when in
disagreement

| 1 | 2 | 3 | 4 | 5 | 6 | 7 |

2. In this organization, a person's influence is based primarily on:

One's ability and
contribution to
the organization

The authority of
one's position

| 1 | 2 | 3 | 4 | 5 | 6 | 7 |

Table 17.3d　　Power Distance: Organization Values (Should Be)

1. In this organization, subordinates *should*: (reverse scored)

Obey their boss
without question

Question their
boss when in
disagreement

| 1 | 2 | 3 | 4 | 5 | 6 | 7 |

2. In this organization, rank and position in the hierarchy *should* have special privileges: (reverse scored)

Strongly
agree

Neither agree
nor disagree

Strongly
disagree

| 1 | 2 | 3 | 4 | 5 | 6 | 7 |

establishment and maintenance of dominance and control of the less powerful by the more powerful. To differentiate GLOBE's Power Distance and Uncertainty Avoidance cultural dimensions, items concerning standardization, rules, procedures, and other forms of formalization were reserved for the Uncertainty Avoidance construct, unless they implied the exercise of control over individuals, groups, or organizations.

GLOBE FINDINGS ON POWER DISTANCE

GLOBE society-level means of Power Distance are given in Table 17.4a for practices and Table 17.4b for values.[1] The worldwide sample is comprised of 62 societies. The societies are classified into five bands of practices scores and four bands of values scores on the basis of their aggregated means for Society As Is and Society Should Be dimensions, respectively.

We will now discuss the GLOBE findings using the grand means of reported Power Distance in societies and organizations, along with an analysis of the broad patterns of power distance in clusters of societies around the world.

Overall Findings on Societal Power Distance

Descriptive Statistics

Of all nine dimensions of societal culture practices studied in GLOBE, Power Distance practice has the greatest mean of 5.17. In contrast, of all nine dimensions of societal culture values, Power Distance value has the least mean of 2.75. Table 17.5a presents the grand mean for GLOBE's society Power Distance practices and values scales. The grand means represent the worldwide sample averages of the aggregated society scores. All GLOBE societies, except for Denmark (3.89), have Power Distance practices

Table 17.4a   Power Distance: Society Practice (As Is)*

Band							
A		*B*		*C*		*D*	
Country	*Score*	*Country*	*Score*	*Country*	*Score*	*Country*	*Score*
Morocco	5.80	Germany[b]	5.25	Qatar	4.73	Netherlands	4.11
Nigeria	5.80	Mexico	5.22	Israel	4.73	South Africa[f]	4.11
El Salvador	5.68	Georgia	5.22	Albania	4.62	Denmark	3.89
Zimbabwe	5.67	Taiwan	5.18	Bolivia	4.51		
Argentina	5.64	Indonesia	5.18				
Thailand	5.63	Malaysia	5.17				
South Korea	5.61	South Africa[c]	5.16				
Guatemala	5.60	England	5.15				
Ecuador	5.60	Ireland	5.15				
Turkey	5.57	Kuwait	5.12				
Colombia	5.56	Japan	5.11				
Hungary	5.56	Poland	5.10				
Germany[a]	5.54	China	5.04				
Russia	5.52	Singapore	4.99				
Spain	5.52	Hong Kong	4.96				
India	5.47	Austria	4.95				
Philippines	5.44	Egypt	4.92				
Portugal	5.44	Switzerland	4.90				
Iran	5.43	Finland	4.89				
Italy	5.43	New Zealand	4.89				
Greece	5.40	U.S.A.	4.88				
Venezuela	5.40	Switzerland[d]	4.86				
Slovenia	5.33	Sweden	4.85				
Brazil	5.33	Canada[e]	4.82				
Zambia	5.31	Australia	4.74				
Kazakhstan	5.31	Costa Rica	4.74				
Namibia	5.29						
France	5.28						

a Germany (East): Former GDR
b Germany (West): Former FRG
c South Africa (White sample)
d Switzerland (French-speaking)
e Canada (English-speaking)
f South Africa (Black sample)

*Higher scores indicate greater power distance.

Our response bias correction procedure identified response bias in some countries for this scale (see endnotes).

scores that exceed the midpoint of 4.0 on the scale of 1 to 7. On the other hand, in all of the societies, the Power Distance values average is less than 4.0. Power Distance is thus reported to be the least desirable, but the most prominent, feature of social practices in countries around the world. The strong perceptions of the practices of Power Distance, and the general consensus against it in value terms, are indicative of a strong existence of power structures that are universally disliked.

Correlation Between As Is (Practices) and Should Be (Values)

The literature review suggested that power has two elements: An influence and a command-oriented element. The influence element is the

Table 17.4b   Power Distance: Society Values (Should Be)*

Band									
A		B		C		D			
Country	*Score*	*Country*	*Score*	*Country*	*Score*	*Country*	*Score*	*Country*	*Score*
South Africa[a]	3.65	Hong Kong	3.24	Namibia	2.86	Hungary	2.49	Colombia	2.04
New Zealand	3.53	Egypt	3.24	Thailand	2.86	Italy	2.47		
Albania	3.52	Qatar	3.23	Japan	2.86	Netherlands	2.45		
Bolivia	3.41	Kuwait	3.17	U.S.A.	2.85	Austria	2.44		
		Kazakhstan	3.15	Mexico	2.85	Switzerland	2.44		
		Poland	3.12	Georgia	2.84	Zambia	2.43		
		Morocco	3.11	Iran	2.80	Turkey	2.41		
		China	3.10	Switzerland[b]	2.80	Greece	2.39		
		Taiwan	3.09	England	2.80	Portugal	2.38		
		Singapore	3.04	Australia	2.78	Brazil	2.35		
		Malaysia	2.97	Denmark	2.76	Guatemala	2.35		
				France	2.76	Argentina	2.33		
				Philippines	2.72	Ecuador	2.30		
				Israel	2.72	Venezuela	2.29		
				Ireland	2.71	Spain	2.26		
				Sweden	2.70	Finland	2.19		
				Canada[c]	2.70				
				Nigeria	2.69				
				Germany[d]	2.69				
				Indonesia	2.69				
				El Salvador	2.68				
				Zimbabwe	2.67				
				India	2.64				
				South Africa[e]	2.64				
				Russia	2.62				
				Costa Rica	2.58				
				Slovenia	2.57				
				South Korea	2.55				
				Germany[f]	2.54				

a South Africa (Black sample)
b Switzerland (French-speaking)
c Canada (English-speaking)
d Germany (East): Former GDR
e South Africa (White sample)
f Germany (West): Former FRG

*Higher scores indicate greater power distance.

Our response bias correction procedure identified response bias in some countries for this scale (see endnotes).

Table 17.5a   Descriptive Statistics for GLOBE Power Distance-Society

Power Distance	*N*	*Minimum*	*Maximum*	*Mean*	*Standard Deviation*
Society practices	61	3.89	5.80	5.17	0.41
Society values	61	2.04	3.65	2.75	0.35

capability of doing or accomplishing something. The command-oriented element is the possession of control or authority over others. Much of the interpretation of the concept of power distance is based on the second element of power. However, literature on power also points toward the significance of the first element. Verderber and Verderber (1992) observed, "Social power is a potential for changing attitudes, beliefs, and behaviors of others" (p. 280). Similarly, Cangemi (1992) suggested, "Power is the individual's capacity to move others, to entice others, to persuade and encourage others to attain specific goals or to engage in specific behavior; it is the capacity to influence and motivate others" (p. 499). Although these interpretations of power rely on its interpersonal character, power can also be seen from a purely functional perspective. Thus, Folger, Poole, and Stutman (1993) referred to power as "the capacity to act effectively" (p. 69).

One may hypothesize that if power operates through a personal command mode and becomes a source of distance, inequity, and lack of growth in a society, then the value of its influence would also diminish. On the other hand, if power is enacted more in a leadership, mentor, coach, or facilitator capacity, then people in power would be respected and valued.

Consistent with the dual elements of power, there exists a strong negative correlation between GLOBE societal practices and values scores of Power Distance ($r = -.43, p < .01$). In societies with high Power Distance practices scores, respondents prefer a more equitable distribution of power. In contrast, in societies with low Power Distance practices scores, respondents prefer a less equitable distribution of power. For the subset of cultures that have high scores on societal Power Distance practices (in band A, Table 17.4a), the correlation coefficient between societal practices and values of Power Distance is insignificant at 0.02 ($p > .05$). The grand mean for societal practices for this subset is 5.51, which is greater than its grand mean for societal values at 2.57 ($p < .01$). Several of the societies in this subset are from Catholic, African, and Southern Asian regions. On the other hand, the second subset of cultures with low societal practices scores on Power Distance (see bands B, C, and D in Table 17.4a), the

correlation coefficient was insignificant at -0.15 ($p > .05$). The grand mean for societal practices of Power Distance for the second subset was 4.88, which was again greater than its grand mean for societal values of Power Distance at 2.90 ($p < .01$). Several of the societies in the second subset are from Nordic-Germanic-Anglo regions, which historically had Protestant and migrant traditions. Though both subsets of societies reported Power Distance practices means exceeding the midpoint of 4.0 and Power Distance values below the midpoint of 4.0, the degree of dissatisfaction with Power Distance was greater in the subset of societies that scored high in Power Distance practices. The gap between Power Distance practices and values was 2.94 for the first higher Power Distance practices subset (Table 17.4a, band A), but only 1.99 for the second lower Power Distance practices subset (in bands B, C, and D). These findings suggest that the cultures that are perceived to have stronger practices of Power Distance tend to put greater value on equal opportunities, whereas the cultures with less strong Power Distance practices put somewhat lower value on encouraging power balances. This may also reflect that some degree of power differentiation is functional in providing incentives to aspire to gain power positions through hard work and capability development.

Overall Findings on Organizational Power Distance

An important issue of managerial relevance is the extent to which society's practices and values of power distance influence the culture of organizations. Table 17.5b shows the grand means of Power Distance practices and Power Distance values at the organizational level. The data used for this purpose were obtained from respondents from 276 organizations in which the organizational identification could be coded using the questionnaires and from which there were at least seven respondents per organization. Although there are considerable interorganizational variations in the practices and values of power distance around the world, the organizational mean for Power Distance practices equals 4.01, and for Power Distance values equals 3.56. Put differently, organizations currently have a

Table 17.5b   Descriptive Statistics for GLOBE Power Distance-Organization

Power Distance	N	Minimum	Maximum	Mean	Standard Deviation
Organization practices	276	2.01	6.07	4.01	0.67
Organization values	276	1.90	5.06	3.56	0.44

moderate degree of power hierarchy in practice (around the midpoint of 4.0), and they prefer only a small reduction in the degree of power control. The societies, on the other hand, have substantially higher power inequalities (mean = 5.17), and prefer to attain a greater degree of power equality (mean = 2.75) than that in organizations.

Is there any relationship between power distance practices and values in societies and in organizations? The answer, as may be expected from the survey of institutional and other theories conducted by Dickson, BeShears, and Gupta in Chapter 5, is yes. As an empirical test, we aggregated organizational scores of societal Power Distance practices and values using the GLOBE database. The respondents who reported higher practices of Power Distance in their societies tended to also report higher practices of Power Distance in their organizations ($r = .48$, $p < .01$, $N = 225$). Similarly, respondents who reported higher values of Power Distance in their societies, tended to also report higher values of Power Distance in their organizations ($r = .48$, $p < .01$, $N = 225$). In either case, about 25% of the variation in organizational Power Distance was accounted for by the variation in the societal Power Distance as perceived or valued by that organization's managers.

Using matched pair t tests of difference, we also found that, on average, respondents reported lower practices of Power Distance in their organizations than in their societies (mean difference = 1.17, $df = 224$, $p < .01$), but higher values of Power Distance in their organizations than in their societies (mean difference = 0.89, $df = 224$, $p < .01$).

A possible explanation for lower levels of Power Distance practices lies in the nature of organizations compared to societies. Organizations tend to have narrower goals, a narrower range of power levels, and a more limited pool of resources than societies in general. They are usually focused on producing a limited set of services and products, and executives' power over their subordinates is linked to the work environment and to the organization's goals. At the societal level, the distribution of power, income, and wealth is wider due to the society's wider range of goals, greater resources, and wider range of levers of power. Therefore, it is plausible to observe a lower average score on Power Distance in organizations than in societies.

The higher levels of desired Power Distance in organizations can also be explained by the nature of organizations compared to societies. They are focused on narrower goals and results. To achieve these goals and results they need working relationships that facilitate decision making and action. Such relationships require an arrangement between managers and employees in which decision making by higher levels is typically accepted. In accepting employment in an organization, employees offer their implicit or explicit acceptance of authority and are, therefore, more tolerant of higher levels of power distance at the organization level than at the society level, in which such an agreement or contract does not exist.

The Relationship Between Societal and Organizational Practices and Societal and Organizational Values

As indicated in Chapter 2 by House and Javidan, the GLOBE theoretical model postulates that societal practices and values affect organizational practices and values. Two hierarchical

Table 17.6   Correlation Between GLOBE and Hofstede Power Distance Measures

GLOBE Power Distance	Hofstede's PDI (2001)	Hoppe's PDI (rho)	Shane's PDI (rho)	Helmrich & Merritt's PDI (rho)
Practices	.57**	0.84**	0.18	0.83**
Values	0.03	−0.54*	0.23	−0.13
Common N	47	16	25	21

*$p < .05$. **$p < 0.01$.

PDI = Power Distance Index.

linear models (HLMs) were conducted to test these hypotheses more rigorously for organizational Power Distance practices and values. We tested the GLOBE hypothesis regarding the effect of societal culture on organizational culture by conducting HLM analyses in which organizational Power Distance was predicted by societal Power Distance. These analyses supported our hypotheses that societal Power Distance practices have a significant and strong positive relationship with organizational Power Distance practices ($p < .01$). We found a similar significant and even stronger relationship between societal Power Distance values and organizational Power Distance values ($p < .01$). Both analyses support a principal proposition in the GLOBE theoretical model (i.e., Proposition 3, Figure 2.1, Chapter 2, by House & Javidan): societal cultural values and practices affect organizational cultural values and practices.[2]

GLOBE POWER DISTANCE AND HOFSTEDE'S POWER DISTANCE INDEX

Because both GLOBE and Hofstede's measures seek to evaluate the construct of power distance, a significant correlation between the two may be expected. Hofstede (2001), in fact, holds that his measure would provide a valid comparative scoring of societies for at least the next 100 years. One can use the findings of Hofstede and GLOBE to confirm the nature of correlation between the two measures. Table 17.6 shows the correlation of GLOBE societal Power Distance practices and values with Hofstede's power distance index, using Hofstede's IBM sample and the three replication samples. Hoppe's (1993) survey was conducted in 1981–1982, Shane's (1994) survey was in 1991–1992, and Helmreich and Merritt's (1998) survey was in 1995–1997.

The GLOBE Power Distance practices measure is correlated positively with Hofstede's measure in all the four studies, and the correlation is significant in all studies except that of Shane (1994) ($r = .57**$, $r = .84**$, $r = .18$ns, $r = .83**$). On the other hand, the GLOBE Power Distance values measure is not correlated with Hofstede's power distance index for the IBM data. The same holds true for the multinational organizations surveyed by Shane (1994), and for the commercial airline pilots surveyed by Helmreich and Merritt (1998). However, for the elite sample of Hoppe's (1993) study, Hofstede's measure of power distance index is significantly and negatively correlated with the GLOBE Power Distance values measure ($r = -.54$).

In summary, it appears that Hofstede's original power distance index reflects more of societal Power Distance practices than values, at least in terms of the GLOBE measures. In fact, Hofstede (2001) also recognizes that two of the three items ("employees afraid" and "perceived managerial behavior") used to measure the power distance dimension reflect perceptions, which are likely guided more by situational factors than by personal dispositions or cultural values.

Table 17.7   Correlations of Societal Power Distance With Other Cultural Dimensions of Society

GLOBE Societal Culture Construct	Correlation With Power Distance Practices	Correlation With Power Distance Values
Uncertainty Avoidance practices	−.50**	—
Uncertainty Avoidance values	.48**	—
Future Orientation practices	−.52**	—
Future Orientation values	.60**	—
Institutional Collectivism practices	−.44**	.38**
Institutional Collectivism values	.41**	−.31*
In-Group Collectivism practices	.55**	—
In-Group Collectivism values	.33**	—
Performance Orientation practices	−.36**	.34**
Performance Orientation values	.40**	−.39**
Gender Egalitarianism practices	−.29*	—
Gender Egalitarianism values	—	−.49**
Assertiveness practices	—	—
Assertiveness values	—	.29*
Humane Orientation practices	—	.30*
Humane Orientation values	—	−.42**

* Significant at $p < .05$. **Significant at $p < .01$.

POWER DISTANCE AND OTHER GLOBE CULTURAL DIMENSIONS

Table 17.7 shows the correlation between mean societal scores of GLOBE Power Distance and the other eight GLOBE constructs of societal culture. The societal practices of Power Distance are significantly and negatively correlated with the societal practices of Uncertainty Avoidance, Future Orientation, Institutional Collectivism, Performance Orientation, and Gender Egalitarianism. Therefore egalitarian (low power distance scores) societies seem to be more future and performance oriented, more institutional collectivist, less male dominated, and more rules oriented. In contrast, societal values of GLOBE Power Distance are associated negatively with the values of Institutional Collectivism, Performance Orientation, and Gender Egalitarianism.

The power hierarchy in organizations may mirror, at least to some extent, the pattern in the society. Indeed, GLOBE Power Distance organizational practices scores were correlated significantly ($p < .01$) and negatively with Future Orientation organizational practices scores ($r = -0.34$), Performance Orientation ($r = .62$), Institutional Collectivism ($r = .27$), In-Group Collectivism ($r = .36$), Humane Orientation ($r = .39$), and Gender Egalitarianism ($r = -.17$). The correlation was significant ($p < .01$) and positive with Assertiveness organizational practices scores ($r = .23$). There was no significant correlation with Uncertainty Avoidance organizational practices scores.

In addition, GLOBE's Power Distance organizational values scores are significantly ($p < .01$) and negatively correlated with Performance Orientation organizational values

Table 17.8a   Descriptive Statistics for GLOBE Industry-Level Societal Power Distance

Variable	N	Minimum	Maximum	Mean	Standard Deviation
Finance Power Distance practices	55	3.69	5.90	5.16	0.46
Finance Power Distance values	55	2.00	3.79	2.77	0.38
Food Power Distance practices	45	4.06	5.83	5.16	0.42
Food Power Distance values	45	2.20	3.54	2.73	0.37
Telecom Power Distance practices	32	4.49	6.39	5.18	0.42
Telecom Power Distance values	32	1.40	3.70	2.72	0.50

scores ($r = .34$), Uncertainty Avoidance ($r = -.50$), and Gender Egalitarianism ($r = .56$).

In summary, the analysis of the relationship of organizational Power Distance with other dimensions of organizational culture indicates that strong hierarchical power practices are associated with an environment in which self-interest is pursued without any emotional involvement in the group. Such an environment fosters low humanism, giving rise to what may be termed as a "soulless organization."

INDUSTRY AND POWER DISTANCE

Societal Power Distance Reported in Three Industries

The GLOBE study was confined to three industries: Financial services, food processing, and telecommunications. Table 17.8a presents the summary statistics for Power Distance societal practices and values dimensions in these three industries. None of the between-industry differences in Power Distance practices and values are statistically significant ($p > .10$). Power Distance is perceived to be equally strong, and people aspire to more equitable opportunities equally strongly across all three industries. No support is found for the perspective that the industrial contingencies shape the responses of the managers, at least in regard to their assessment of power differentiation and need for equal opportunity in the society. On the other hand, the broader societal context, with its complex

historical and institutional environment and diffused principles of work design, appears to pervade the power evaluations across industries.

Table 17.8b shows the correlations among Power Distance societal practices and values in each of the three industries. First, the Power Distance practices scores in all three industries are significantly correlated (r ranging from .59 to .88, $p < .01$). The same holds true for Power Distance values scores (r ranging from .69 to .86, $p < .01$). Power Distance practices and values pervade all sectors of a society. These findings are consistent with institutional theory of organizations (Meyer & Rowan, 1977), but they do not support the view that new technological industries such as telecommunications are increasing the "digital divide" within societies. Second, Power Distance practices and values scores are significantly and negatively correlated for the finance and food sectors, mirroring the findings for the overall society-level scores. But, as may be expected for a new industry, the aspirations for Power Distance in telecommunications are independent of its own assessment of the realities of Power Distance practices, and instead possibly reflect a more ideal vision of the preferred societal culture.

Organizational Power Distance Reported in Three Industries

Table 17.9 provides summary data on Power Distance organizational practices and values in the three industries. In all three industries, mean

Table 17.8b   Correlations Among GLOBE Industry-Level Society Power Distance

	Finance Industry Score Practices	Food Industry Score Practices	Telecom Industry Score Practices	Finance Industry Score Values	Food Industry Score Values	Telecom Industry Score Values
Finance industry score practices		.87** $N = 41$	.57** $N = 30$	−.42** $N = 55$	−.44** $N = 41$	−.35 $N = 30$
Food industry score practices			.55** $N = 22$	−.44** $N = 41$	−.40** $N = 45$	−.37 $N = 21$
Telecom industry score practices				−.23 $N = 30$	−.16 $N = 22$	−.17 $N = 32$
Finance industry score values					.86** $N = 41$	.68** $N = 30$
Food industry score values						.78** $N = 22$
Overall practices	.96** $N = 55$	.93** $N = 45$	.78** $N = 32$	−.40** $N = 55$	−.41** $N = 45$	−.37* $N = 32$
Overall values	−.43** $N = 55$	−.44** $N = 45$	−.23 $N = 32$	.97** $N = 55$	.92** $N = 45$	.82** $N = 32$

* Significant at $p < .05$. ** Significant at $p < .01$

Table 17.9   Descriptive Statistics for GLOBE Industry-Level Organization Power Distance

Variable	n	Minimum	Maximum	Mean	Standard Deviation
Finance Power Distance practices	130	2.01	5.30	4.03	0.58
Finance Power Distance values	130	2.69	4.80	3.60	0.41
Food Power Distance practices	91	2.54	5.64	3.88	0.66
Food Power Distance values	91	1.90	5.06	3.58	0.50
Telecom Power Distance practices	53	2.58	6.07	4.21	0.86
Telecom Power Distance values	53	2.65	4.29	3.43	0.40

organizational practices scores are significantly higher than the mean Power Distance organizational values scores ($p < .01$). Power Distance practices scores are highest in telecommunications organizations, but these organizations also put least value on Power Distance. In the food sector, the mean score for organizational Power Distance practices is 3.88, which is less than the midpoint of 4.0. The food processing organizations appear to use more egalitarian approaches

Table 17.10a   Power Distance and Geographic Region One-Way ANOVA

Power Distance	Source of Variance	Sum of Squares	Mean Square	F	Significance
Society practices	Between groups	2.34 df = 9	0.26	1.74	.11
	Within groups	7.63 df = 51	0.15		
	Total	9.98 df = 60			
Society values	Between groups	2.07 df = 9	0.23	2.24	.03
	Within groups	5.24 df = 51	0.10		
	Total	7.31 df = 60			

not based on positional ranks, privileges, and power. In the telecommunications sector, and to a lesser extent in the financial sector, power diffusion appears to be more difficult to practice, possibly due to a more volatile and uncertain environmental situation and a consequent need to control, coordinate, and audit the actions of frontline employees.

On the whole, our analysis shows that GLOBE's Power Distance practices and values scores are similar across industries. But there do exist interindustry differences in Power Distance organizational scores. Specifically, organizational practices tend to be quite egalitarian in the food sector, where stable environment conditions are more conducive to diffusion of control. Power hierarchy practices are most pervasive in the telecommunications sector, which has an emergent and volatile environmental context subject to high costs of technology development.

GEOGRAPHICAL REGIONS AND POWER DISTANCE

Geographical Regions and Societal Power Distance

As discussed in Chapter 8 by Hanges and Dickson, there are significant differences in values and practices for every cultural dimension among the 62 societal cultures. In this section we examine the grouping of these 62 sampled societies into 10 regional clusters. An Analysis of Variance (ANOVA) test was conducted to determine if there exist cross-regional differences of Power Distance values and practices. The results for the ANOVA test are summarized in Table 17.10a. There are no significant cross-regional differences in Power Distance societal practices ($F9, 51 = 1.74, p > .10$). Recall that in Table 17.4a that the GLOBE societies fall into four bands on the basis of their Power Distance societal practices scores. Only three societies were in band D: the Netherlands, South Africa (Black sample), and Denmark. Each of these belongs to a different regional cluster: Germanic Europe, Sub-Saharan Africa, and Nordic Europe, respectively. Similarly, there were only four societies in band C (Qatar, Israel, Albania, and Bolivia) and each of these also belongs to a different regional cluster: Middle East, Latin Europe, Eastern Europe, and Latin America, respectively. The other 54 societies in the GLOBE sample are distributed across bands A and B, with no clear relationship with any regional cluster. Thus, these findings indicate a similarity among all regions in the practice of hierarchical control in their societies.

Table 17.10b   Descriptive Statistics for GLOBE Geographical Regions: Society Power Distance-Values

Geographical Region	N	Mean	Standard Deviation	Standard Error	95% Confidence Interval	
					Lower Bound	Upper Bound
Latin America	10	2.52	0.39	.10	2.31	2.72
Anglo	7	2.86	0.31	.12	2.61	3.10
Nordic Europe	3	2.55	0.31	.19	2.18	2.92
Germanic Europe	5	2.51	0.11	.14	2.23	2.80
Latin Europe	6	2.57	0.23	.13	2.30	2.83
Eastern Europe	8	2.84	0.39	.11	2.61	3.06
Confucian Asia	6	2.98	0.24	.13	2.72	3.24
Southern Asia	6	2.78	0.12	.13	2.52	3.04
Sub-Saharan Africa	5	2.86	0.47	.14	2.57	3.15
Middle East	5	3.03	0.35	.14	2.74	3.32

On the other hand, there do exist significant cross-regional differences in Power Distance societal values ($F9$, $51 = 2.24$, $p < .05$). For instance, all Confucian Asia societies were banded in B or C with respect to Power Distance societal values, whereas all Nordic Europe clusters were in C and D bands. We found that regional differences account for 28% of the variation in Power Distance societal values, whereas 72% represent idiosyncratic societal differences.

The nature of cross-regional differences for Power Distance societal values can be seen in Table 17.10b. Power Distance values are reported to be greatest for the Middle East cluster (mean = 3.03). On a scale of 1 to 7, this reflects aspirations for a modest degree of power differentiation in the society. Power Distance values are reported to be least for the Germanic Europe (mean = 2.51) and Latin America (mean = 2.52) clusters. In general, the Germanic Europe, Nordic Europe, Latin America, and Latin Europe clusters have significantly lower aspirations for societal Power Distance than do the other regions (value of contrast = .34, $t = 3.97$, $df = 51$, $p < .01$).

Put differently, in Continental Europe and Latin America, the movement toward a wider distribution of power is valued most.

Geographical Regions and Organizational Power Distance

Geographical region accounts for 21.1% of the variation in organizational Power Distance practices ($F9$, $266 = 7.90$, $p < .01$) and 51.4% of the variation in organizational Power Distance values ($F9$, $266 = 31.27$, $p < .01$). Thus, regional cluster explains half of the global differences in organizational Power Distance values, and about a fifth of the global differences in organizational Power Distance practices.

The regional pattern of organizational Power Distance practices is presented in Table 17.11. The regional scores range from 3.47 to 4.41, which is around the midpoint 4.0 on a scale of 1 to 7. We used analysis of variance contrast test to identify the clusters with significantly higher or lower scores on the organizational Power Distance practices scale. The means for organizational Power Distance practices are significantly higher in Southern Asia (contrast = .48, $p < .01$), Eastern Europe (contrast = .27, $p < .05$), Anglo (contrast = .27, $p < .05$), and Confucian Asia (contrast = .23, $p < .10$) clusters. In these clusters with high organizational Power Distance practices scores, respondents report a strong orientation toward obeying and respecting authority. In Anglo organizations, for instance, historical application of scientific management principles often resulted in a considerable gap in the skills, compensation, and power of those in higher positions, as compared with those in lower positions.

The means for organizational Power Distance practices are significantly lower in Germanic Europe (contrast =− .56, $p <.01$), Nordic Europe (contrast =− .39, $p < .01$), and Latin America (contrast =− .26, $p < .05$) clusters. In general, the Northern European and Latin American managers report practices emphasizing subordinate participation, open expression of disagreement with those in authority, and emphasis on people's potential for the organization. The literature, indeed, identifies the Northern European organizations as pioneers of the semiautonomous team systems in which autonomy and power are granted to the members of the team (see Gupta, 1998). Formal training and professional qualification of the members is emphasized, and monitoring of performance is done through information technology as opposed to formal supervision (Gupta, 1998). Consequently, greater power decentralization can be, and appears to be, practiced in these organizations.

Latin American organizations, on the other hand, are usually characterized in the literature as having low employee participation and a high deference to authority (Hofstede, 2001). GLOBE's findings are therefore surprising, but they may be capturing some recent trends in Latin America. Traditionally, power holders in Latin America often reserved key positions for their actual or adopted family members (under the Godfather system, in which power holders accept their loyal employees as godchildren). The control of power at the top has created considerable distrust and disinterest among the employees and has made it difficult for the organizations to adopt international best practices (Altschul, 2003). There may be a growing trend

in Latin American organizations to engage their employees using a variety of teamwork initiatives. In fact, as also discussed in Chapter 21 by Dorfman and colleagues, the Latin America cluster reports higher mean scores (5.96) on the effectiveness of team-oriented leadership than any other cultural cluster (contrast = .25, $p < .01$).

As shown in Table 17.11, Middle Eastern organizations stand out, compared with other clusters, as reporting the highest values of Power Distance at 4.04. Put differently, respondents from Middle Eastern organizations are most neutral in their values of Power Distance, and are open to a moderate amount of power distance. Respondents from organizations in the other clusters seem to desire a lower level of Power Distance.

Summary

For both practices and values, the Asia-Pacific region reports higher societal and organizational Power Distance. Middle Eastern organizations report highest values of Power Distance in any region, while Sub-Saharan African societies report moderate practices and values of Power Distance. In contrast, the Nordic Europe and Germanic Europe clusters report lower societal and organizational Power Distance. Although the Anglo cluster also reports strong organizational practices of Power Distance, it has low organizational and societal Power Distance values. Finally, the Latin American and Latin European clusters report lower organizational Power Distance practices, and also lower societal and organizational Power Distance values.

CLIMATIC REGIONS AND SOCIETAL POWER DISTANCE

Hofstede (2001) identified physical climate as a key factor shaping power distance of societies. He observed that in colder, nontropical climates there has been a greater need to perform and to develop technology for surviving against nature. As a result, there was a greater need for education for those of lower socioeconomic status and also for greater social mobility and development

Table 17.11   Descriptive Statistics for Geographical Regions: GLOBE Organization Power Distance
Practices and Values

Geographical Region	N	Mean	Standard Deviation	Standard Error	95% Confidence Interval	
					Lower Bound	Upper Bound
Organizational Power Distance practices						
Latin America	37	3.74	0.67	.10	3.55	3.94
Anglo	33	4.23	0.49	.11	4.02	4.43
Nordic Europe	26	3.63	0.52	.12	3.39	3.86
Germanic Europe	27	3.47	0.61	.12	3.24	3.70
Latin Europe	11	3.86	0.50	.18	3.50	4.22
Eastern Europe	36	4.22	0.56	.10	4.02	4.42
Confucian Asia	28	4.19	0.41	.12	3.96	4.41
Southern Asia	46	4.41	0.74	.09	4.23	4.59
Sub-Saharan Africa	10	4.09	0.64	.19	3.71	4.47
Middle East	22	3.93	0.75	.13	3.68	4.19
Organizational Power Distance values						
Latin America	37	3.18	0.29	.05	3.08	3.28
Anglo	33	3.31	0.27	.06	3.20	3.42
Nordic Europe	26	3.50	0.32	.06	3.38	3.62
Germanic Europe	27	3.06	0.33	.06	2.94	3.18
Latin Europe	11	3.48	0.25	.10	3.30	3.67
Eastern Europe	36	3.74	0.36	.05	3.63	3.84
Confucian Asia	28	4.00	0.36	.06	3.88	4.11
Southern Asian	46	3.77	0.28	.05	3.68	3.87
Sub-Saharan Africa	10	3.54	0.30	.10	3.35	3.74
Middle East	22	4.04	0.36	.07	3.91	4.17

of a middle class. More federal and negotiated forms of political representation resulted, and children learned the things that their parents never did, on the whole keeping the power differences very low. But in warmer, tropical, and subtropical climates there was less need for technology, and agriculture provided sufficient means for survival. As a result, there was less social mobility, and wealth and political power were concentrated in a few hands. Children were dependent on the experience and learning of their parents, and authority was not questioned.

To examine the relationship between physical climate and societal Power Distance, we rely on a more systematic classification of physical climates. In Chapter 10, Gupta and Hanges classified GLOBE societies into seven clusters of physical climates: tropical humid, tropical wet and dry (savanna), sub-tropical humid, subtropical wet and dry (Mediterranean), continental, and marine west coast (maritime). We conducted Analysis of Variance tests to examine if societal Power Distance practices and values vary across the seven physical climate clusters. Physical climate clusters accounted for 24.8% of the between-society differences in Power Distance practices ($F = 2.97, p < .05$), and only 14.7% of the between-society differences in Power Distance values ($F = 1.55, p > .10$). Further analysis revealed that only two climatic clusters differed significantly in the level of their societal Power Distance practices. Savanna climates have significantly higher practices of Power Distance (mean = 5.58, contrast = .43, $p < .01$), whereas continental climates have significantly lower practices of Power Distance (mean = 4.90, contrast = –.33, $p < .01$). We found no clear pattern among the countries in these two clusters. Neither Power Distance practices nor Power Distance values were significantly correlated with mean temperature, mean rainfall, mean humidity, or mean number of rain days. Thus, contrary to Hofstede's thesis, climate or temperature by itself does not appear to account for any overwhelming differences in practices or values of Power Distance.

POWER DISTANCE AND CULTURALLY ENDORSED LEADERSHIP

How much Power Distance is practiced and valued should be an important factor in the leadership styles endorsed in various cultures. In general, the concept of leadership itself may be supported more strongly in high power distance cultures because high power distance practices and values likely enhance the legitimacy of a leader's authority. Strong power distance may also relieve frustration among those people who would find it difficult to act on their own initiative. On the other hand, Charismatic/Value-Based and Participative leadership can prove to be quite effective in engaging the efforts of employees in egalitarian cultures. So, in low power distance cultures, Charismatic/Value-Based and Participative leadership styles may be quite effective.

Findings on the Effect of Power Distance on Culturally Endorsed Implicit Theories of Leadership

We tested for the relationship between culture and the culturally endorsed implicit theories of leadership (CLT) dimensions by using hierarchical linear modeling (HLM). As stated in Chapter 11 by Hanges, Dickson, and Sipe, HLM can be thought of as a multistep process designed to test the significance of relationships between independent and dependent variables at multiple levels of analyses. An overview of HLM analyses and a detailed discussion of how these analyses were conducted are provided in Appendix C by Hanges and colleagues. This chapter presents relationships between one culture dimension (Power Distance) and the six CLTs. Competitive tests of all culture dimensions and CLTs are presented in Chapter 21 by Dorfman and colleagues.[3] In general, we expect that societal and organizational values will be more strongly related to CLT leadership dimensions than societal and organizational practices. As indicated previously, our notions of values and CLT leadership dimensions represent idealized concepts of how the world *should be* in contrast to practices that represent the world *as is*. As you read through the results discussed below, it may be helpful to view Figure 17.1 for a visual summary. The figure, however, only shows results regarding cultural values, not practices. (All HLM coefficients are presented in Table 21.10 of Chapter 21 by Dorfman and colleagues.)

In the present analysis we examine the simultaneous predictive power of organizational and societal Power Distance values and practices on CLTs. The total amount of organizational and societal variance explained by Power Distance scales ranged from 1% to 38.6%. Power Distance was found to be a better

Power Distance Cultural Dimension

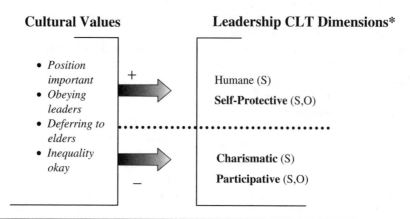

Figure 17.1   Power Distance Cultural Values as Drivers for CLT Leadership Dimensions

* Only statistically significant relationships are shown ($p < .05$; see Table 21.10, Chapter 21 by Dorfman et al.). The most important leadership CLT relationships are bolded (i.e., relationship is significant at both society and organization levels of analyses or highest HLM coefficient within each level of analysis).

CLT = Culturally endorsed leadership theory

O = Organizational level

S = Societal level

predictor for some of the CLTs (e.g., Self-Protective leadership) than for others (e.g., Autonomous leadership).

If organizational level and societal level Power Distance values and practices were considered, significant relationships were found with the following:

• *Charismatic/Value-Based leadership.* Power Distance cultural values scores were significantly related to the Charismatic/Value-Based leadership dimension and explained a total of 17.7% of organizational and societal variance for this dimension. All of this explained variance was associated with forces operating at the societal level of analysis. The societal Power Distance cultural values scores were negatively related ($p < .01$) to the Charismatic/Value-Based leadership dimension. Charismatic/Value-Based leadership is less likely to be a part of the shared leadership belief system in organizations reported to espouse Power Distance values.

• *Team-Oriented leadership.* Power Distance practices scores were significantly related to the Team-Oriented leadership dimension and explained a total of 7.5% of organizational and societal variance for this dimension. All of this variance was associated with forces operating at the societal level of analysis. The societal Power Distance cultural practices scores were positively related ($p < .05$) to the Team-Oriented leadership dimension. Team-Oriented leadership is more likely to be a part of the shared leadership belief system in organizations reported to have high Power Distance practices.

• *Participative leadership.* Power Distance cultural practices and values scores were significantly related to the Participative leadership dimension and explained a total of 29.9% of organizational and societal variance for this dimension. Approximately 5.2% of this explained variance was associated with forces operating at the organizational level of analysis. The majority of the explained variance (94.8%)

was associated with forces operating at the societal level of analysis.

The organizational Power Distance cultural values scores were negatively related ($p < .01$) to the Participative leadership dimension. Participative leadership is less likely to be a part of the shared leadership belief system in organizations reported to espouse Power Distance values.

The societal Power Distance cultural practices scores were negatively related ($p < .01$) to the Participative leadership dimension, as were the societal Power Distance cultural values scores ($p < .01$). Participative leadership is less likely to be a part of the shared leadership belief system in societies reported to have Power Distance practices, and it is less likely to be a part of the shared leadership belief systems in societies reported to espouse Power Distance values.

• *Humane-Oriented leadership.* Power Distance cultural values scores were significantly related to the Humane-Oriented leadership dimension and explained a total of 5.5% of organizational and societal variance for this dimension. All of the explained variance was associated with forces operating at the societal level of analysis. The societal Power Distance cultural values scores were positively related ($p < .05$) to the Humane-Oriented leadership dimension. Humane-Oriented leadership is more likely to be a part of the shared leadership belief system in organizations reported to espouse Power Distance values.

• *Autonomous leadership.* Power Distance cultural practices scores were significantly related to the Autonomous leadership dimension but explained a total of just 1.1% of organizational and societal variance for this dimension. All of this explained variance was associated with forces operating at the organizational level of analysis. The organizational Power Distance cultural practices scores were positively related ($p < .05$) to the Autonomous leadership dimension. Autonomous leadership is more likely to be part of a shared leadership belief system in organizations reported to have Power Distance practices.

• *Self-Protective leadership.* Power Distance cultural practices and values scores were significantly related to the Self-Protective leadership dimension and explained a total of 38.6% of organizational and societal variance for this dimension. Approximately 3.5% of this explained variance was associated with forces operating at the organizational level of analysis. The remaining portion of the explained variance (96.5%) was associated with forces operating at the societal level of analysis.

The organizational Power Distance cultural values scores ($p < .01$) were positively related to the Self-Protective leadership dimension. Self-Protective leadership is more likely to be a part of a shared leadership belief system in organizations reported to espouse Power Distance values.

The societal Power Distance cultural practices scores were positively related ($p < .01$) to the Self-Protective leadership dimension, as were the societal Power Distance cultural values scores ($p < .01$). Self-Protective leadership is more likely to be a part of the shared leadership belief system in societies reported to have Power Distance practices and Power Distance values.

In summary, Power Distance cultural values and practices were statistically significant predictors of all six CLT dimensions. In particular, if a society's Power Distance values increase, the more likely Humane-Oriented and Self-Protective leadership, and the less likely Charismatic/Value-Based and Participative leadership, are seen as effective. If a society's Power Distance practices increase, the more likely it is that Team-Oriented and Self-Protective leadership, and the less likely it is that Participative leadership, will be seen as effective. At the organizational level, if employees describe the organization as holding Power Distance values, the more likely it is that Self-Protective leadership, and the less likely that Participative leadership, will be seen as effective. Finally, if employees describe the organization as having high Power Distance practices, the more likely that Autonomous leadership will be seen as effective. The implications of these findings are discussed separately below for societal and organizational Power Distance.

Societal Power Distance and Leadership

HLM results suggest that societal Power Distance practices are associated with lower scores for Participative leadership. In the GLOBE dataset, Nordic Europe, Germanic Europe, and Anglo clusters score low on societal Power Distance practices, but have comparatively stronger scores on Participative leadership. These three clusters share Protestant reformation as a major influence. The reformed clusters profess the direct relationship of God and humans without the mediation of the Church or clerics, and thus nurtured a vision of humans as responsible persons. The institutional leadership in these clusters is thus oriented toward encouraging participation at the grassroots levels, and empowering the masses to share their ideas and express their independent perspectives in a formalized participatory forum. In contrast, societies such as Turkey score high on societal practices of Power Distance but have weak scores on the effectiveness of Participative leadership. Previous research by Kozan (1993) suggests that in Turkey it is common to use a domineering style for handling differences with subordinates, and such style is perceived to be an effective method by superiors and subordinates alike. In general, compared with other nations, Turkish managers fall toward the lower end in sharing information and objectives, participation, and internal control.

On the other hand, high societal Power Distance values are associated with stronger Self-Protective and Humane-Oriented leadership, and weaker Charismatic/Value-Based and Participative leadership. These findings possibly reflect an emphasis on authoritarian and paternalistic modes of leadership, involving harmony, face saving, benevolence, and in-group cooperation, in societies that value Power Distance. An illustrative nation from the GLOBE database is Egypt. Previous research by Leila, Yassin, and Palmer (1985) shows that Egyptian employees have a high degree of apathy, low concern for productivity, and a strong emphasis on job security. Under these conditions, Humane-Oriented and Self-Protective leadership are favored, whereas Participative and Charismatic/Value-Based leadership are likely to be very difficult to implement. From a historical perspective, General Abdel Nasser in Egypt is counted as an outstanding Egyptian leader (Bill & Leiden, 1979). Nasser and other outstanding Arab leaders share patrimonial and paternalistic orientations in which the leader retains ideological and strategic centrality for designing and administrating societal programs (Kabasakal & Bodur, 2002). In-Group Collectivism forms the basis for leadership in all the societal domains, with leaders relying on their close circle—with whom they share emotional ties—for advice and protection against being seen as autocratic and dictatorial.

Alternatively, low societal Power Distance values are associated with stronger Participative and Charismatic/Value-Based leadership, and weaker Humane-Oriented and Self-Protective leadership. These findings are indicative of a more impersonal, task-oriented focus of leadership in nonegalitarian societies—that is, societies in which power is unequally shared. Thus, for example, the Nordic Europe cluster, which strongly values equitable power in all spheres, has also been at the forefront of semi-autonomous approaches at the team level (as opposed to the leadership level). These approaches, designed to give self-managing autonomy to teams, are termed *sociotechnical work systems*. Also, if an egalitarian power distribution is expected within a society, there is fundamental distrust of any individual trying to enact a leadership role. House and colleagues (1999), for instance, noted that "The Dutch place emphasis on egalitarianism and are skeptical about the value of leadership. Terms like leader and manager carry a stigma. If a father is employed as a manager, Dutch children will not admit it to their schoolmates" (p. 171). In such cases, universal value-based orientation is critical for the leaders to enact their role of helping to preserve and promote egalitarianism.

Organizational Power Distance and Leadership

High organizational Power Distance practices are associated with stronger Autonomous leadership. In hierarchical organizational cultures, leaders may be effective only by following an independent style and making decisions on the basis of their best judgment. Illustrative nations from the GLOBE database with Autonomous leadership include former East Germany and Greece. Greece was at the center of the Eastern Orthodox theology that developed in 1054 C.E. under the influence of Islam. This split Western Christianity from the Christianity in Eastern Europe. Still, clerics continued to have an autonomous leadership role as the blessed messengers of God, helping to connect their followers with the transcendental power of God (Bakacsi, Sandor, Andras, & Viktor, 2002). The effective leaders in the Greek context are authority-principled and paternalistic, who carry a God-like sanctity and thus tend to take independent decisions within a hierarchical organization.

On the other hand, high organizational Power Distance values are associated with stronger Self-Protective leadership and weaker Participative leadership. Illustrative nations are included in the Middle East cluster, in which firms endorse hierarchical power and leadership that is Self-Protective and not very Participative. In most of the Middle Eastern organizations, societal effects have an important influence. As such, they might find it difficult to gain the trust of the populace, which is essential for the effectiveness of Participative leadership.

Summary

In summary, organizational Power Distance values have a positive association with Self-Protective leadership, and societal Power Distance values are positively related with Self-Protective and Humane-Oriented leadership. The Self-Protective leadership dimension is composed of items that reflect being status and class conscious, ritualistic, procedural, normative, secretive, evasive, indirect, self-centered, and asocial. If a society operates in a very difficult internal environment or is focused on the dependent and powerless groups, leaders may need to make autonomous and paternalistic decisions when responding to humane needs and be self-protective so that they are not made into scapegoats for political ends.

Further light is shed on the relationship between the societal values of Power Distance and Self-Protective and Humane-Oriented
leadership by prior research on the use of power. Gardner (1990), for instance, observed that

> In our democratic society we make grants of power to people for specified purposes. If for ideological or temperamental reasons they refuse to exercise the power granted, we must turn to others. To say a leader is preoccupied with power is like saying that a tennis player is preoccupied with making shots his opponent cannot return. Of course leaders are preoccupied with power! (cited in Pfeffer, 1994, p. 12)

Thus, endorsement of power distance in the society carries an implicit theory that effective leaders would be ones who make autonomous decisions, are able to protect themselves from the acts of criticism and corruption, and respond to humane considerations.

Similarly with respect to the use of power in organizations, and the effectiveness of Self-Protective leadership, Pfeffer (1994) emphasized that

> By pretending that power and influence don't exist, or at least shouldn't exist, we contribute to what I and some others (such as John Gardner) see as the major problem facing many corporations today, particularly in the United States—the almost trained or produced incapacity of anyone except the highest-level managers to take action and get things accomplished. (p. 10)

If Power Distance is valued in organizations, it thus becomes critical for the leadership to take steps for being protected from the likely criticism of arbitrary decisions and oversight, as illustrated recently, for instance, by the case of leadership in the Enron Corporation in the United States.

Leaders are presented with a different type of challenge in cultures that do not value Power Distance. Here, it is important not to appear bossy or dictatorial, but instead to delegate and recognize egalitarian and collectivist interests and to focus on the big picture rather than micromanage. Charismatic/Value-Based leadership approaches that encourage team-based engagement and participation at the grassroots level therefore become most effective.

Power Distance and Archival Data

In this section, we compare GLOBE Power Distance scores with those of other major cross-cultural and comparative studies focusing on different countries' social and economic performance. Recall that Javidan and Hauser (Chapter 7) proposed a series of hypotheses. The following are those relating to Power Distance:

Societies that are lower on Power Distance practices and values tend to

a. be more economically prosperous and competitively successful

b. enjoy higher levels of societal health

c. enjoy higher levels of human development

Societal Power Distance and Economic Health

What is the relationship between Power Distance and economic prosperity? Is there a linkage between low Power Distance practices and economic health? As explained in Chapter 7, the various elements of economic health include economic prosperity, which refers to consumption and growth; economic productivity, which refers to the lack of hostility in the labor environment and growth in productivity; government support for prosperity, reflecting the extent to which the government and the political body are supportive of economic progress; and societal support for competitiveness, which is a measure of the general social attitude toward, and support for, business competitiveness. In addition to these measures, we also examined the relationship between the GLOBE findings and the Global Competitiveness Ranking report.

Table 17.12 reports correlations of the GLOBE societal Power Distance scores with various external measures of socioeconomic health. Consistent with Hypothesis (a), societal Power Distance practices are associated with lower economic prosperity, less supportive public and social policies for business prosperity, lower national competitiveness, and less success in basic science. These findings are consistent with HLM results, which show that societal Power Distance practices are associated with Self-Protective leadership, as opposed to

Participative and Charismatic/Value-Based leadership. In societies practicing differential allocation of power, the resources and rewards are unequally allocated and, consequently, there are detrimental influences on the socioeconomic development of the nation as a whole.

Earlier Veblen (1904/1965) alluded to the corrupting influences of power by suggesting that people of wealth often seek influence over the government, which they can then turn to their own purposes so that the "Representative government means, chiefly, representation of business interests" (p. 286). He defined vested interests of the businesses as "a marketable right to get something for nothing. . . . Vested interests are immaterial wealth, intangible assets" (Veblen, 1919, p. 100). Thus, in societies in which power distance is endorsed, power holders may use power for their self-benefit and for limiting the general liberties in the society while ostensibly creating an impression of an egalitarian approach.

Strong Power Distance practices might frustrate the ability of people to pursue their ambitions and dreams, and cause even the more powerful to worry about the protection of their status and prestige in the society. Under these conditions the quality of life, organizations, and institutions will likely fail to adapt to the need for societal integration and adaptation to environmental change and would likely deteriorate.

In addition, consistent with Hypothesis (b), Power Distance societal practices are also associated with lower life expectancy and lower scores on the Human Development Index. The three critical elements of human development are long and healthy lives, a reasonable standard of living, and knowledge. Longevity is measured by life expectancy, standard of living is measured by adjusted income, and knowledge is measured by educational attainment.

The United Nations Development Programme (UNDP) uses the Human Development Index to measure human development, which is defined as "a process of enlarging people's choices, achieved by expanding human capabilities and functioning" (UNDP, 1998, p. 14). We hypothesized that countries that score lower in Power Distance tend to enjoy higher levels of human development. As reported in Table 17.12, this hypothesis is confirmed.

Table 17.12   Relationship Between Power Distance and Socioeconomic Health

Power Distance	Economic Prosperity	Societal Support for Economic Competitiveness	Public Sector Support for Prosperity	Competitiveness Index	Success in Basic Science	Life Expectancy	Human Development Index (HDI)
Society practices	−.53** n = 57	−.47** n = 40	−.65** n = 40	−.53** n = 41	−.52** n = 40	−.33** n = 56	−.36** n = 56
Society values	−.03 n = 57	.47** n = 40	.24 n = 40	.38* n = 41	.30 n = 40	−.01 n = 56	−.17 n = 56

NOTE: Each correlation remained significant, even when per capita GNP was controlled.

* Correlation is significant at the .05 level (2-tailed).

** Correlation is significant at the .01 level (2-tailed).

Societal Power Distance and Human Condition

Additional insights into the dynamics of power distance culture can be gained by looking at the correlations between GLOBE societal Power Distance scores and archival measures of the human behavior reported in Table 17.13. Consistent with Hypothesis (c), societal Power Distance practices are associated with poor societal health and poor general satisfaction. However, they are also related to respect for family and friends, most likely reflecting the formative role of family in inculcating an absolute and uncritical respect for power. Family and friends may provide some degree of protection against abuse of power. The results in the table also suggest that strong Power Distance practices are also associated with passive involvement in demonstrations and petitions, less importance on giving people a voice in the community and government decisions, stronger expected role of government in business and welfare, and lower gender equality.

However, once the per capita GNP is controlled, Power Distance practices no longer remain significantly correlated with family ties or with passiveness, lack of voice, and government roles. Thus, lower income might also be a factor supporting an authoritarian orientation of the privileged members of families and government because they play a crucial support function in times of need, which are likely to be quite frequent in lower-income societies. With enhanced incomes, support from the privileged members is not a critical survival function for other members of the community and, therefore, family and government may no longer be able to command absolute authority. None of the measures of human health are significantly correlated with societal Power Distance values.

Taken together, GLOBE's findings support the hypotheses that societal practices of power distance impede socioeconomic development and human health. However, in some societies the causality may be in the other direction: The weak socioeconomic conditions could account for higher practices of power distance because authority relationships in institutional and family domains may offer critical support and security for people under such conditions. A substantial challenge for many societies in which power distance is highly practiced, therefore, is how to respond to the preferences for lowering power distance. One solution is to seek leaders who appreciate the physical, psychological, intellectual, and knowledge potential of the people. With growing emphasis on value-based and participative approaches, leaders are in a position to successfully foster

Table 17.13   Relationship Between Power Distance and Human Condition

Power Distance	Societal Health	General Satisfaction	Strength of Family Ties	Respect for Family and Friends	Passiveness	Lack of Voice	Role of Government	Gender Equality
Society practices	−.62** n = 40	−.48** n = 38	.29 n = 38	.52** n = 38	0.36* n = 37	0.45** n = 38	0.47** n = 38	−.39* n = 38
Society values	.18 n = 40	−.11 n = 38	.00 n = 38	.21 n = 38	−.09 n = 37	.26 n = 38	.15 n = 38	−.24 n = 38

NOTE: The correlation of Power Distance practices with strength of family ties, passiveness, lack of voice, role of government, and gender equality became nonsignificant when per capita GNP was controlled.

** Correlation is significant at the .01 level (2-tailed).

* Correlation is significant at the .05 level (2-tailed).

empowerment of others. Such leaders often need to enact their power by motivating, preparing, training, and helping others to be empowered.

Using additional archival measures not discussed by Javidan and Hauser, we found that higher GLOBE Power Distance societal values predict greater corruption ($r = .36, p = 0 < .01$) and lower civil liberties ($r = .38, p < .01$). The Corruption Index is a measure published online by Transparency International, an organization that assesses perceptions of corruption in public services (www.transparency.org). The Civil Liberties Index is a measure published by Freedom House (Freedom House Surveys, 1991) that assesses freedom of demonstration, media, movement, religious institutions, and business and private organizations. We interpret these findings to mean that under conditions in which Power Distance is highly valued, corrupt behavior is legitimated as a privilege of position. Furthermore, in such societies higher status people are allowed to restrict the liberties of others.

Thus, the focus of managerial intervention in societies that practice or value power distance must also be based on the desire of people to accomplish results, not just on developing a select few into leadership positions that need to be protected. A greater sense of performance orientation would endow a self-generated sense of empowerment, contribute to a vibrant socioeconomic milieu, and facilitate a healthy devotion to family and religion that supports the development of each member of the society.

We are now in the position to examine the validity of Hofstede's thesis that power distance is associated with less affluent and highly populated low-latitude conditions. These conditions are munificent and nonthreatening to individuals or organizations in that people can live off natural resources easily. Hofstede (1980) identified power distance as one of the most critical defining attributes of societies. He supported his argument using the findings of stepwise regression that showed that external data such as the type of political system are most strongly related to the dimension of power distance, as compared with three other dimensions: individualism, masculinity, and uncertainty avoidance. Our findings show that, consistent with Hofstede's (1980), GLOBE's measure of societal Power Distance practices is negatively correlated with national wealth as measured by GNP per capita ($r = .40, p < .01, N = 62$), and with latitude ($-.28, p < .05, N = 62$). Despite the fact that in Chapter 7 Javidan and Hauser caution against controlling for GNP, to be consistent with Hofstede we followed his practice of partialing out GNP per capita. Our analysis showed that latitude did not explain any incremental correlation with the societal practices of Power Distance; thus our analysis did not support Hofstede's position. We might note that

GLOBE's measure of societal Power Distance values showed no significant correlation with either GNP per capita or latitude.

Summary and Conclusions

In Project GLOBE, the construct of Power Distance primarily refers to the perceived or desired magnitude of Power Distance practices and values as reported by middle-level managers. However, the generalizability of the GLOBE findings beyond the perception of middle managers as well as the correlations with the unobtrusive measures scale scores reflect much of the broader culture in which the middle management informants are embedded.

Our findings suggest that power distance is a cultural dimension that is relevant for both Eastern and Western societies. Within the high power distance cultures of the East, the stable distribution of power is expected to bring order to the society and to allow unambiguous allocation of roles and rigid structure of relationships. One element of high power distance is clearly dysfunctional as it preempts the society from questioning, learning, and adapting as there is little opportunity for debate and voicing of divergent views. Asking questions may be interpreted or regarded as criticizing and blaming, and therefore may be prohibited. In contrast, within the low power distance cultures of the West, the flexible distribution of power is expected to facilitate entrepreneurial innovation, to allow broader participation in education, and to constrain the abuse of power and corruption. There are, however, significant variations in the practice and preference of power distance in both Eastern and Western societies, which indicates that the dominant expectations in these regions are largely historically derived. Moreover, the enhanced use of technology is likely to reduce the arbitrary use of authority and expedite the spread of democratic values, thereby empowering women and the underprivileged classes.

Traditionally, Catholic societies tended to have a culture of strong power distance. This was despite the fact that Jesus Christ had founded the Catholic tenets on premises that challenged the extant power structures in the contemporary Judaist and Roman environment.

Subsequently, Protestantism became prominent in the West, which shifted the power from the church and the priests directly to the hands of the people, and thereby fostered lower Power Distance practices in these societies.

GLOBE findings indicate that strong practices of Power Distance are associated with higher levels of male domination in societies. In this chapter we have demonstrated that organizations reflect the culture (practices and values) in the society in which they are embedded, and this is certainly true with respect to Power Distance values and practices. On the whole, the GLOBE sample of societies shows that Power Distance is the most strongly practiced, yet most strongly despised, dimension of societal cultures. The GLOBE societal Power Distance practices mean is 5.16 on a scale of 1 to 7, and is the highest among all nine dimensions of societal practices studied in GLOBE. Similarly, GLOBE's societal Power Distance values mean is 2.74 on a scale of 1 to 7, which is the lowest mean among all nine dimensions of social values studied in GLOBE. Managers in all cultures reported that their societies practice Power Distance more strongly than they believe they should.

Although there are significant cross-societal (i.e., 62 societal cultures) differences in societal and organizational Power Distance values and practices, there are no significant cross-regional differences in societal practices of GLOBE Power Distance. The regions, however, do differ in terms of values of societal Power Distance. In general, the Germanic Europe, Nordic Europe, Latin America, and Latin Europe clusters have lower aspirations for societal Power Distance than do the other regions. Across regions, the aspirations for egalitarian power distribution are stronger in the societal context than in the organizational context. In addition, we found significant cross-regional differences in value aspirations of GLOBE organizational Power Distance, as well as organizational Power Distance practices.

Power Distance values have a significant influence on culturally endorsed leadership. Power Distance values are positively correlated with Self-Protective and Humane leadership and negatively correlated with Charismatic/Value Based and Participative leadership dimensions. Societies that value a high level of Power Distance expect leaders to be caring and benevolent while being conscious of status and privilege. At the same time people in these societies do not expect the leaders to allow for participation or to be accountable for results. Leaders in such societies are treated with such a level of deference and respect that they are not expected to be performance oriented or visionary.

ENDNOTES

1. Our response bias correction procedure identified response bias in some countries for this scale. We recomputed the predicted response bias corrected scale score for each country. Response bias corrected scores are

Practices: Ecuador, 5.29 (no change in band); France, 5.68 (no change in band); Morocco, 6.14 (no change in band); and Qatar, 5.05 (moves from band C to band B).

Values: Finland, 2.46 (no change in band); Indonesia, 2.38 (moves from band C to band D); Namibia, 2.59 (no change in band); and Taiwan, 2.77 (moves from band B to band C).

For a complete discussion of this procedure and all response bias corrected scores, see Appendix B.

2. As reported in Chapter 20 by Brodbeck, Hanges, Dickson, Gupta, and Dorfman, we found that all the cultural dimensions of organizational cultural values and practices significantly differed across societies. Although important, this prior analysis did not identify the particular aspect of societal differences that was related to organizational culture. In the present chapter, we found that societal and organizational Power Distance practices were significantly related (R^2 Total = 2.4%, R^2 Societal = 30.9%, $p < .01$). We found even stronger results for societal and organizational Power Distance values (R^2 Total = 6.2%, R^2 Societal = 32.7%, $p < .01$). As discussed in Chapter 11 by Hanges, Dickson, and Sipe, the R^2 Total considers all levels of analysis (i.e., individual, organizational, and societal) whereas the R^2 Societal isolates the societal level portion of the dependent variable and indicates the percentage of variance accounted for by the predictor at only this level. Whereas we have primarily taken the conservative approach and reported the R^2 Total in GLOBE, a number of scholars suggest that R^2 Societal provides a more accurate description of aggregated relationships. For further discussion, see the paper by Lance and James (1999).

3. Results between the single HLM and multiple HLM tests will likely differ somewhat. The differences between the results of the multiple HLMs and single HLMs are conceptually similar to the differences between a multiple regression analysis and a correlation coefficient. Table 21.10 in Chapter 21 by Dorfman and colleagues presents both single and multiple HLM coefficients. In addition, the relationships for all culture dimension values are summarized in Chapter 3 by Javidan and House.

REFERENCES

Altschul, C. (2003). Sense-making in change interventions: Lessons from the Argentine context. In V. Gupta (Ed.), *Transformative organization: A global perspective* (pp. 361–372). New Delhi: Sage.

Bakacsi, G., Sandor, T., Andras, K., & Viktor, I. (2002). Eastern European cluster: Tradition and transition. *Journal of World Business, 37,* 69–80.

Bartol, K., & Butterfield, D. (1976). Sex effects in evaluating leaders. *Journal of Applied Psychology, 61,* 446–454.

Bass, B. M. (1985). *Leadership and performance beyond expectations.* New York: Free Press.

Bass, B. M. (1997). Does the transactional-transformational leadership paradigm transcend organizational and national boundaries? *American Psychologist, 52*(2), 130–139.

Beteille, A. (1977). *Inequality among men.* Oxford, UK: Blackwell.

Bill, J. A., & Leiden, C. (1979). *Politics in the Middle East.* Boston: Little, Brown.

Blum, J. (1978). *End of the old order in rural Europe.* Princeton, NJ: Princeton University Press.

Burt, R. S. (1992). *Structural holes: The social structure of competition.* Boston: Harvard University Press.

Campbell, D. J., Bommer, W., & Yeo, E. (1993). Perceptions of appropriate leadership style: Participation versus consultation across two cultures. *Asia Pacific Journal of Management, 10*(1), 1–19.

Cangemi, J. (1992). Some observations of successful leaders, and their use of power and authority. *Education, 112,* 499–505.

Chinese Culture Connection. (1987). Chinese values and the search for culture-free dimensions of culture. *Journal of Cross-Cultural Psychology, 18*(2), 143–164.

Cohen, A. (1976). *Two-dimensional man.* Berkeley: University of California Press.

Cullen, J. B. (2001). *Multinational management: A strategic approach* (2nd ed.). Cincinnati, OH: South-Western Thomson Learning.

Dahrendorf, R. (1969). On the origin of inequality among men. In A. Beteille (Ed.), *Social inequality: Selected readings* (pp. 16–44). Baltimore, MD: Penguin.

Dansereau, F., Grean, G., & Haga, W. J. (1975). A vertical dyad linkage approach to leadership within formal organizations: A longitudinal investigation of the role making process. *Organizational Behavior and Human Performance, 13,* 46–78.

Darroch, R. K., Meyer, P. A., & Singarimbun, M. (1981). *Two are not enough: The value of children to Javanese and Sudanese parents* (Vol. 60-D). Honolulu: East-West Center Publishers.

Etzioni-Halevy, E. (1997). *Classes and elites in democracy and democratization* (Vol. 23). New York: Garland.

Fawcett, J. T. (1983). Perceptions of the value of children: Satisfactions and costs. In R. A. Bulatao, R. D. Lee, P. E. Hollerbach, & J. Bongarrts (Eds.), *Determinants of fertility in developing countries* (Vol. I, pp. 429–457). Washington, DC: National Assembly Press.

Fiedler, F. E. (1967). *A contingency theory of leadership effectiveness.* New York: McGraw-Hill.

Fodor, E. M. (1985). The power motive, group conflict, and physiological arousal. *Journal of Personality and Social Psychology, 49,* 1408–1415.

Fodor, E. M., & Smith, T. (1982). The power motive as an influence on group decision making. *Journal of Personality and Social Psychology, 42,* 178–185.

Folger, J., Poole, M., & Stutman, R. (1993). *Working through conflict.* New York: HarperCollins.

Freedom House Surveys. (1991). In M. J. I. Sullivan (Ed.), *Measuring global values: The ranking of 162 countries.* New York: Greenwood.

French, J. R. P., & Raven, B. (1959). The bases of social power. In D. Cartwright & A. Zander (Eds.), *Group dynamics* (3rd ed., pp. 259–269). New York: Harper & Row.

Gardner, J. W. (1990). *On leadership.* New York: Free Press.

Gordon, L. V. (1976). *Survey of interpersonal values: Revised manual.* Chicago: Science Research Associates.

Gupta, V. (1998). *A dynamic model of technological growth: Diffusion of Japanese investment networks overseas.* Philadelphia: Wharton School of the University of Pennsylvania.

Haccoun, D. M., Sallay, G., & Haccoun, R. R. (1978). Sex differences in "appropriateness" of supervisory styles: Non-management view. *Journal of Applied Psychology, 63,* 124–127.

Haire, M., Ghiselli, E. E., & Porter, L. W. (1966). *Managerial thinking: An international study.* New York: John Wiley.

Heller, F., & Yukl, G. A. (1969). Participation, managerial decision making, and situational variables. *Organizational Behavior and Human Performance, 4,* 227–241.

Helmreich, R. L., & Merritt, A. C. (1998). *Culture at work in aviation and medicine: National, organizational and professional influences.* Aldershot, UK: Ashgate.

Hersey, P., & Blanchard, K. H. (1977). *Management of organizational behavior* (3rd ed.). Englewood Cliffs, NJ: Prentice Hall.

Hinkin, T. R., & Schriesheim, C. A. (1989). Development and application of new scales to measure the French and Raven (1959) bases of social power. *Journal of Applied Psychology, 74*(4), 561–567.

Hofstede, G. (1980). *Culture's consequences: International differences in work related values.* Newbury Park, CA: Sage.

Hofstede, G. (1994). *Cultures and organizations: Intercultural cooperation and its importance for survival.* London: HarperCollins.

Hofstede, G. (2001). *Culture's consequences: Comparing values, behaviors, institutions and organizations across nations* (2nd ed.). Thousand Oaks, CA: Sage.

Hoppe, M. H. (1993). The effects of national culture on the theory and practice of managing R&D professionals abroad. *R&D Management, 23*(4), 313–325.

House, R. J. (1977). A 1976 theory of charismatic leadership. In J. G. Hunt & L. L. Larson (Eds.), *Leadership: The cutting edge* (pp. 189–207). Carbondale: Southern Illinois University Press.

House, R. J., Hanges, P. J., Ruiz-Quintanilla, S. A., Dorfman, P. W., Javidan, M., Dickson, M. W., Gupta, V., et al. (1999). Cultural influences on leadership and organizations: Project GLOBE. In W. H. Mobley, M. J. Gessner, & V. Arnold (Eds.), *Advances in global leadership* (pp. 171–233). Stamford, CT: JAI.

House, R. J., Spangler, W. D., & Woycke, J. (1991). Personality and charisma in the U.S. presidency:

A psychological theory of leader effectiveness. *Administrative Science Quarterly, 36,* 364–396.

House, R. J., Wright, N., & Aditya, R. N. (1997). Cross-cultural research on organizational leadership: A critical analysis and a proposed theory. In P. C. Earley & M. Erez (Eds.), *New perspectives on international/organizational psychology* (pp. 535–625). San Francisco: New Lexington Press.

Huselid, M. A. (1995). The impact of human resource management practices on turnover, productivity and corporate financial performance. *Academy of Management Journal, 38*(3), 635–672.

Inglehart, R. (1997). *Modernization and postmodernization: Cultural, economic and political change in 43 societies.* Princeton, NJ: Princeton University Press.

Jago, A., & Vroom, V. (1982). Sex differences in the incidences and evaluation of participative leader behavior. *Journal of Applied Psychology, 67,* 776–783.

Kabasakal, H., & Bodur, M. (2002). Arabic cluster: A bridge between East and West. *Journal of World Business, 37,* 40–54.

Kagitçibasi, C. (1982). *The changing value of children in Turkey* (Vol. 60-E). Honolulu: East-West Center Publishers.

Kozan, M. K. (1993). Cultural and industrialization level influences on leadership attitudes for Turkish managers. *International Studies of Management & Organization, 23*(3), 7–17.

Lance, C. E., & James, L. R. (1999). A proportional variance accounted for index for some cross-level and person-situation research designs. *Organizational Research Methods, 2,* 395–418.

Leila, A., Yassin, E., & Palmer, M. (1985). Apathy, values, incentives and developments: The case of the Egyptian bureaucracy. *Middle East Journal, 39,* 341–361.

McClelland, D. (1970). The two faces of power. *Journal of International Affairs, 24*(1), 29–47.

McClelland, D. C. (1961). *The achieving society.* Princeton, NJ: D. Van Nostrand.

McClelland, D. C. (1975). *Power: The inner experience.* New York: Free Press.

McClelland, D. C., & Burnham, D. H. (1976, March–April). Power is the great motivator. *Harvard Business Review,* 100–110.

McClelland, D. C., Rindlisbacher, A., & de Charms, R. C. (1955). Religious and other sources of parental attitudes toward independence training.

In D. C. McClelland (Ed.), *Studies in motivation* (pp. 389– 397). New York: Appleton-Century-Crofts.

Meyer, J. W., & Rowan, B. (1977). Institutionalized organizations: Formal structure as myth and ceremony. *American Journal of Sociology, 83,* 340–363.

Milgrom, P. R., & Roberts, J. (1992). *Economics, organization, and management.* Englewood Cliffs, NJ: Prentice Hall.

Mulder, M. (1971). Power equalization through participation. *Administrative Science Quarterly, 16,* 31–38.

Mulder, M. (1976). Reduction of power distance in practice: The power distance reduction theory and its applications. In G. Hofstede & M. S. Kassem (Eds.), *European contributions to organizational theory.* Assen, The Netherlands: Van Gorcum.

Mulder, M. (1977). *The daily power game.* Leydem, The Netherlands: Martinus Nijhoff.

Mulder, M., Ritsema van Eck, J. R., & De Long, R. D. (1971). An organization in crisis and non-crisis situations. *Human Relations, 24,* 19–41.

Nadler, D. A. (1989, Fall). Organizational architectures for the corporation of the future. *Benchmark,* 12–13.

Oxtoby, W. G. (1996). The Christian tradition. In W. G. Oxtoby (Ed.), *World religions, Western traditions* (pp. 198–350). Toronto, Canada: Oxford University Press.

Parsons, T., & Shils, E. A. (1951). *Toward a general theory of action.* Cambridge, MA: Harvard University Press.

Patchen, M. (1965). *Some questionnaire measures of employee motivation and morale.* Ann Arbor: University of Michigan, Institute for Social Research, Survey Research Center.

Peterson, M. F., & Smith, P. B. (1997). Does national culture or ambient temperature explain cross-national differences in role stress? No sweat! *Academy of Management Journal, 40,* 930–946.

Peterson, M. F., Smith, P. B., Akande, A., Ayestaran, S., Bochner, S., Callan, V., et al. (1995). Role conflict, ambiguity, and overload: A 21-nation study. *Academy of Management Journal, 38*(2), 429–452.

Pfeffer, J. (1997). Understanding power in organizations. In M. L. Tushman & P. Anderson (Eds.), *Managing strategic innovation and change* (pp. 217–232). New York: Oxford University Press.

Pfeffer, J. (1994). Managing with power: *Politics and influence in organizations.* Boston, MA: Harvard Business School Press.

Pugh, D. S. (1976). The "Aston" approach to the study of organizations. In G. Hofstede & M. S. Kassem (Eds.), *European contributions to organization theory* (pp. 62–78). Assen, The Netherlands: Van Gorcum.

Ronk, L. A. (1993, May). Gender gaps within management. *Nursing Management, 24*, 65–67.

Rosen, B. C., & D'Andrade, R. G. (1959). The psychosocial origins of achievement motivation. *Sociometry, 22,* 185–218.

Rousseau, J. J. (1972). *Du contrat social* [From the social contract]. Oxford, UK: Clarendon.

Runciman, W. G. (1969). The three dimensions of social inequality. In A. Beteille (Ed.), *Social inequality: Selected readings* (pp. 45–63). Middlesex, UK: Penguin.

Schwartz, S. H. (1999). A theory of cultural values and some implications for work. *Applied Psychology: An International Review, 48*(1), 23–47.

Selznick, P. (1949). *TVA and the grassroots.* Berkeley: University of California Press.

Shane, S. (1994). Cultural values and the championing process. *Entrepreneurship Theory & Practice, 18*(4), 25–41.

Smith, A., & Dowling, P. J. (2001). Analyzing firm training: Five propositions for future research. *Human Resource Development Quarterly, 12*(2), 147–167.

Smith, P. A., & Smits, S. J. (1994, February). The feminization of leadership. *Training and Development,* pp. 43–46.

Smith, P. B., Dugan, S., & Trompenaars, F. (1996). National culture and the values of organizational employees: A dimensional analysis across 43 nations. *Journal of Cross-Cultural Psychology, 27*(2), 231–264.

Stogdill, R. M. (1974). *Handbook of leadership: A survey of the literature.* New York: Free Press.

Strauss, G. (1977). Managerial practices. In J. R. Hackman & J. L. Suttle (Eds.), *Improving life at work* (pp. 297–362). Santa Monica, CA: Goodyear.

Tannenbaum, R., & Schmidt, W. H. (1958, March–April). How to choose a leadership pattern. *Harvard Business Review, 36*, 95–101.

Triandis, H. C. (1995). *Individualism and collectivism.* Boulder, CO: Westview.

Trompenaars, F. (1993). *Riding the waves of culture.* London: Nicholas Brealey.

Trompenaars, F., & Hampden-Turner, C. (1998). *Riding the waves of culture: Understanding diversity in global business* (2nd ed.). New York: McGraw-Hill.

United Nations Development Programme. (1998). *Human development report.* Geneva: UNDP.

van de Vliert, E., & Van Yperen, N. W. (1996). Why cross-national differences in role overload? Don't overlook ambient temperature! *Academy of Management Journal, 39,* 986–1004.

Veblen, T. (1919). *The vested interests and the common man.* New York: B. W. Huebschy.

Veblen, T. (1965). *The theory of business enterprise.* NY: Sentry Press. (Original work published 1904)

Verderber, R. F., & Verderber, K. S. (1992). *Inter-act—using interpersonal communication skills.* Belmont, CA: Wadsworth.

Vroom, V. H., & Yetton, P. W. (1973). *Leadership and decision-making.* Pittsburgh, PA: University of Pittsburgh Press.

Wayne, S. J., & Green, S. A. (1993). The effects of leader-member exchange on employee citizenship and impression management. *Human Relations, 46*(12), 1431–1441.

Weber, M. (1976). *The Protestant ethic and spirit of capitalism.* London: George Allen & Unwin.

Whaba, M., & Bridwell, L. (1976). Maslow reconsidered: A review of research on the need hierarchy theory. *Organizational Behavior and Human Performance, 15,* 212–240.

Whyte, W. F. (1969). Culture and work. In R. A. Webber (Ed.), *Culture and management* (pp. 30–39). Homewood, IL: Irwin.

Winter, D. G. (1973). *The power motive.* New York: Free Press.

Winter, D. G., & Stewart, A. J. (1977). Content analysis as a technique for assessing political leaders. In M. G. Hermann (Ed.), *A psychological examination of political leaders* (pp. 27–61). New York: Free Press.

Winterbottom, M. R. (1958). The relation of need for achievement to learning experiences in independence and mastery. In J. W. Atkinson (Ed.), *Motives in fantasy, action and society* (pp. 453–478). Princeton, NJ: Van Nostrand.

Yukl, G. A. (2002). *Leadership in organizations* (5th ed.). Upper Saddle River, NJ: Prentice Hall.

18

HUMANE ORIENTATION IN SOCIETIES, ORGANIZATIONS, AND LEADER ATTRIBUTES

HAYAT KABASAKAL

MUZAFFER BODUR

T his chapter begins with a discussion of the historical, religious, psychological, and sociological roots of the concept of humane orientation. Within this first section we also explore the relationship of the concept of humane orientation to the role of government and economic development. In the second part we define GLOBE's construct of Humane Orientation and relate it to prior cross-cultural studies on the concept of humane orientation. The third part of this chapter describes GLOBE's measures of Humane Orientation, and the fourth part presents GLOBE's findings and explains the correlations between the country scores for Humane Orientation and other GLOBE culture dimensions. In the fifth and sixth sections of the chapter we discuss and interpret GLOBE's findings. We also explore the relationship between GLOBE's findings and

other economic and social indicators, and other institutional and societal forces and practices, such as political systems, modernization, family values, human rights, and country demographics. Then we explain the industry-specific findings on Humane Orientation. In the seventh part of the chapter we explore the relationship between societal values and practices and organizational values and practices. In the eighth part we present and discuss Humane Orientation as a leadership attribute. In the ninth and tenth parts of the chapter we interpret the relationship between societal humane orientation and leadership characteristics and present hierarchical linear models (HLMs) using GLOBE's Humane Orientation cultural dimension to predict culturally endorsed implicit leadership theory dimensions (CLTs). We conclude with a summary of findings.

AUTHORS' NOTE: The authors wish to thank Idil Evcimen, Fahri Karakas, Aslihan Nasir, and Murat Sahtiyanci for their help and assistance.

Literature on the Concept of Humane Orientation

Descriptions of ideas and values and prescriptions for behavior associated with the dimension of culture referred to in Project GLOBE as Humane Orientation have existed since ancient times. These ideas and values can be found in the writings of the classic Greek philosophers as well as in the teachings of many of the major religions of the world. Aristotle's ideal of friendship represents his moral philosophy. Embedded in Aristotle's ideology is the concept that "a person becomes a friend when he is loved and returns that love, and this is recognized by both people in question" (Price, 1989, p. 132). Plato's theories in *Phaedrus* (Ferrari, 1987) and *Symposium* (Dover, 1980) define love as an intimate relationship with another here on earth as well as in Platonic heaven. According to Plato, it is possible to love someone without feeling affectionate. In Socrates's ideology, winning a friend is above all else a fulfillment of a fundamental human need and desire.

Religion and Humane Orientation

There is no doubt that religion is one of the means for understanding why people behave as they do. Religious institutions have been perceived to play significant roles as intermediaries between human beings and God. In the religions of Judaism, Christianity, and Islam the world is perceived as containing good and evil as objective entities. God grants the capability to be good, and evil is associated with the devil. However, Hardy (1988) notes that, "This type of binary, objectifying thought is alien to the religions of further east. Objectively, there is only the world with its inbuilt rhythm and structure. As long as, subjectively, man harmonizes himself with this rhythm, he does what is 'good'" (p. 6). In some religions of the East, goodness is not associated with God; as discussed below, in these religions, in fact, there is no monotheistic God.

Because in Judaism, Christianity, and Islam God is associated with ultimate "goodness," orders from God include specific duties and prohibitions that are associated with goodness and humanitarian behaviors. Some of the Laws of God require humane-oriented behaviors and doing good to others, like alms giving. Other laws require individuals to refrain themselves from directly causing harm to others, such as homicide or theft. Still other laws require individuals to refrain from sensual enjoyment and hedonistic activities, such as adultery, consumption of alcohol, eating (fasting), or being lustful.

In some religions of Asia, such as Buddhism and Taoism, there is no God that gives orders in the direction of goodness. Religion spells out how to harmonize oneself with the universal rhythm; through achieving harmony with this cosmic rhythm an individual does what is "good." Harmony with nature can be possible with purification of oneself of the desire of material possessions and selfish enjoyment. Refraining from sensual enjoyment and hedonistic activities are the guide to goodness, as partly perceived in the religions of the West.

Social Norms, Practices, Dominant Motivation Bases, and Humane Orientation

According to culture theory (Triandis, 1995) values of altruism, benevolence, kindness, love, and generosity are salient as motivating factors guiding people's behavior in societies characterized by a strong humane orientation. In these societies, the need for belongingness and affiliation, rather than self-fulfillment, pleasure, material possessions, and power, are likely to be the dominant motivating bases.

According to Schwartz (1992), the central norms of a society can be categorized based on the polar dimensions of self-transcendence and self-enhancement. In his conceptualization, the dimension of self-transcendence has two facets: universalism and benevolence. Universalism emphasizes values of understanding, tolerance, and protection of all people, including strangers, and nature. Benevolence is the preservation and enhancement of people with whom one has a close relationship. Benevolence includes providing social and financial support to intimate friends, sharing time with them, and helping them solve their problems. These attributes strongly connote humane orientation. On the other hand, self-enhancement involves promoting self-interest and self-gratification, and can be interpreted as being less humane oriented.

Hofstede (1980, 2001) identifies toughness and tenderness as a component of his masculinity versus femininity dimension, as measured with his MAS Index. On the other hand, he uses this dimension to refer to the distribution of emotional roles between genders, asserting that his MAS Index also measures materialistic orientation and success striving. Although the index includes and is confounded by several cultural variables, it is similar to GLOBE's Humane Orientation dimension in that cultures that score low on the MAS Index are considered to be as relationship oriented as in high humane-oriented societies.

Paternalism, a form of benevolence, is also a dimension of social norms that differentiate cultures from each other (James, Chen, & Cropanzano, 1996; Kanungo & Aycan, 1997). In paternalistic societies, people in authority are expected to act like a parent and take care of subordinates' and employees' families. Eastern cultures, such as China, India, Turkey, Pakistan, and Taiwan, and most Latin-American societies demonstrate more paternalistic values. In societies that score low in paternalism, there is a limited interest in workers' problems, which is restricted to job-related issues.

In societies that lack formal welfare institutions, where resources are very unevenly distributed and where political power is often unstable, a system of patronage based on relationships of family and friends emerges to fulfill some needs of individuals (Wolf, 1966). Organizations in these societies tend to choose employees on the basis of the individual's relationship to the employer or patron, rather than the organization's needs or the skills of the individual (Kiray, 1997; Ong, 1987).

Family Practices, Norms, and Humane Orientation

Many studies conducted in English-speaking cultures point to the influence of family relations on children's well-being. There is strong evidence that parental attention and warmth produce high self-esteem (Adams & Jones, 1983; Hoelter & Harper, 1987; Peterson & Kellam, 1977). A cross-cultural study conducted in seven countries and eight communities—Canberra, Brisbane, Winnipeg, Phoenix, Berlin, Hong Kong, Taipei, and Osaka—achieved similar findings of the importance of family for the development of children's personalities (Scott, Scott, & McCabe, 1991). In all the communities that were included in the study, children's self-esteem was associated positively with family harmony and parental nurturance, and children's hostility was correlated with parental punitiveness. There was general uniformity over cultures in magnitudes of correlations. These findings indicate that there would be more psychologically healthy individuals in societies that promote parental nurturance and minimize punitiveness in the family.

The associated cross-cultural comparisons reflect the influence of societal context on perception of social support. In societies located in North America and Europe where child-rearing norms emphasize autonomy rather than close control, children perceive close parental supervision as rejection and lack of love.

One of the few cross-cultural studies of families was conducted in the mid-1970s in Indonesia, Germany, Korea, the Philippines, Singapore, Taiwan, Thailand, Turkey, and the United States (Bulatao, 1979; Darroch, Meyer, & Singarimbun, 1981; Fawcett, 1983; Hoffman, 1987; Kagitçibasi, 1982a, 1982b, 1982c). This study attempted to find the motives for having children and the kinds of value attributed to children in these societies. Cross-cultural comparisons indicated the presence of two types of values that are attributed to children: Economic and psychological. Economic value of children refers to a child physically helping the family and serving as a guarantee of positive treatment in the old age of parents. In developing societies, to serve the purpose of economic value, obedience rather than autonomy is valued in children as a desirable trait. An autonomous child may place self-interest above the interests of the family; consequently, autonomy in children is discouraged. In developing countries, particularly in the rural areas, the normal way of life is such that children take care of their parents and provide material help in their old age.

In some developed countries, such as Japan, close parental control continues to be perceived as a sign of attention, acceptance, and affection because of the persistence of traditional values, even if there is no economic necessity for children to take care of aging parents. Interdependence among family members continues even without economic necessity. In Japan, and most Western, developed countries, children are viewed as sources of psychological satisfaction rather than economic security. In these societies children provide psychological value to their parents and are regarded as sources of pleasure, friendship, and companionship.

Human Rights, Discrimination, and Humane Orientation

Human rights are recognized by almost all nations. Moreover, half of the world's states have accepted legal obligations to enforce "these rights by becoming parties to the International Human Rights Covenants and almost all the other nations have either signed but not yet ratified the Covenants or otherwise expressed approval of and commitment to their content" (Donelly, 1989, p. 2).

The Universal Declaration of Human Rights, as adopted by the United Nations General Assembly in 1948, covers a wide range of issues including the right to life (i.e., protection from infliction of death), rationality, recognition before law, protection against torture, protection against discrimination on such bases as race and sex, and the right to education and to participate in the cultural life of the community. These standards reflect what are considered the minimum conditions for a dignified life.

Prior to the creation of capitalist market economies and modern nation states, the problems that human rights seek to address, in particular violations of human dignity as Donnelly (1989) points out, either did not exist or were not widely perceived as crucial social problems.

Multicultural societies and communities that stand for the freedom and equality of all people rest upon mutual respect for intellectual and cultural differences. Failing to recognize or respect the particular identities of different cultural groups is under severe criticism, especially in liberal democracies in which commitment to the principle of equal representation is the highest, especially with regard to the rights and needs of members of specific cultural groups.

Collective and communistic societies are communal, status-based, and governed according to tradition. As Donnelly (1989) describes, there is generally no notion of autonomous individuals in such societies, and censorship is sometimes practiced (Wolf, 1994).

The Role of Government and Humane Orientation

In many industrialized nations, a welfare state replaces informal and family relationships that are needed for the survival of members of society. According to Briggs (1961), a welfare state is one in which organizational power is used through politics and administration to modify the market forces so that individuals and families are guaranteed a minimum income irrespective of the market value of their property. Jessop (1991) views such an effort by the state as narrowing the extent of insecurity and ensuring that all citizens are offered a certain range of social services to meet contingencies such as illness, old age, and unemployment.

Esping-Anderson (1985) discusses three forms of welfare state in a typology, namely the social democratic model, the conservative model, and the liberal model. Among the three types of welfare states, the social democratic model is argued to be more humanely oriented in the sense that the personal worth of all individuals is honored by the recognition of universal welfare rights and the concept of social citizenship prevails. Financing comes from general taxation and there is a commitment to egalitarian distribution of resources and high standards of public provision. This type of welfare state is best illustrated in Scandinavian countries such as Sweden and Norway where the working class is unionized.

In the conservative model, there are differentiated welfare rights that are linked to occupation and status, and social welfare does not have egalitarian aims. Austria, Germany, France, Italy, and Belgium in Europe, and Japan in East Asia have this type of a welfare state. Finally, in the liberal model, limited welfare rights are provided to individuals by the state, and state expenditures are made only for the benefits that are means-tested. Britain, the United States, Canada, and Australia depict this type of a welfare state.

In general, states in all societies have been attributed a positive role in intervening to correct market failures, such as shortages in capital, foreign exchange, or some other inputs. Neoclassical development theory proposes that the ideal role of the state is to provide property rights and basic infrastructural services. As best demonstrated by the Japanese experience, the state plays a positive and socially constructive role in the development process by maintaining a mixture of autonomy and cooperation. Thus, the state performs more of a strategic role for sustaining long-term social reforms by disengaging from the intervening role in favor of facilitating organizational links that connect business interests to the state through such practices as privatization of state enterprises. Theoretically, as a result, direct public provisions are reduced, and profit-making investments and joint business–state ventures are encouraged.

The equal opportunities policy perspective in European social protection systems calls for the need to integrate child care into the system as a social risk just like the risk of growing old. As described by Brouwer and Wierda (1998), the basic feature of this scenario is that both women and men are able to fulfill child care responsibilities by combining paid labor tasks and unpaid care tasks in their "private" time. In this model, social security rights are not individualized but "familized."

With the internationalization of capital that came with world market integration, production was decentralized to exploit locational advantages in sourcing. New technologies in telecommunication and computer-aided manufacturing systems generated more flexibility in adapting to consumer demand by specialization. As mobility of white-collar workers increased, a need for flexibility in labor markets also became apparent. Consequently, recruitment rules and wage rates started to require more heterogeneity.

When flexibility is viewed as a central part of international economic modernization, states often choose a neo-liberal model to restructure their economy. As put forth by Hirsch (1991), when a neo-liberal model is adopted, the state is reoriented to revitalize the market by promoting small business, reforming environmental protection measures, and by liberation of wage and working conditions such as short-time working arrangements and a reserve labor force. Under these circumstances, the states' role turned into promoting flexibility to compensate for deficiencies in the market and making compliance with state measures voluntary through "third sector" forces (Jessop, 1991).

In general, in the more economically developed nations of the world, the state takes on the role of at least a minimum standard of guaranteeing well-being of members of societies. In low humane-oriented societies, which are economically more developed, the state is actively involved in social protection, providing business incentives, and improving working conditions.

Participation of children under age 15 in the workforce differs from country to country. Rates increase with age and are higher for boys in the case of wage work or work in the household enterprise, whereas girls participate more in domestic activities (International Labor Organization, 1992).

According to a study by Grootaert and Kanbur (1995), in less-developed countries the variables of larger household size, low parent income and landholdings, and failure in educational systems play a significant role as determinants of child labor. Developing countries, such as India and Egypt, are implementing policies to reduce child labor; however, the welfare states of the developed countries have introduced more radical measures to attack the child labor problem.

In addition to their more controlling character, most European governments take a more supportive role toward organizations in comparison to the United States by use of vocational training conducted in cooperation with state agencies (Pieper, 1990), allocation of a fairly high percentage of gross domestic product to public expenditure on labor market programs, retraining, and job transition support for the unemployed (Brewster, 1995).

Economics and Humane Orientation

In less-developed societies, individuals rather than governments are expected to offer both material and psychological support. Privileged members of these societies are expected to share their money, material possessions, and other resources. When people are living through difficult times, such as death, illness, or financial problems, friends, neighbors, and family members spend time with them, bring cooked food, and visit them often.

Table 18.1 summarizes major connotations and variations of the humane orientation construct at the societal level, on the basis of the above literature review of societal practices and country-specific manifestations of humane orientation.

COMPARISON OF HIGH VERSUS LOW HUMANE ORIENTATION SOCIETIES

GLOBE's concept of the Humane Orientation cultural dimension is defined as the degree to which an organization or society encourages and rewards individuals for being fair, altruistic, friendly, generous, caring, and kind to others (House et al., 1999). This dimension is manifested in the way people treat one another and in the social programs institutionalized within each society. Research indicates that the way in which people treat one another, in the terms defined above, varies by culture.

The GLOBE study implicitly relates quality of life and social relations. Other studies have explicitly associated quality of life and resources, both tangible and intangible. In 1970, national studies measuring the level of welfare in societies were conducted in all Scandinavian countries including Sweden, Denmark, Norway, and Finland (Allardt, 1993; Erikson, 1993). The Scandinavian approach assumed that one's standard of living is associated with the resources by which individuals can master and control their lives. Resources were defined to include money, possessions, knowledge, mental and physical energy, security, recreation, and political resources, as well as social relations. Allardt (1993) notes that it was agreed that an emphasis on resources to the exclusion of social support would in practice lead to a one-sided focus on material conditions.

A general finding in the Scandinavian study was that the amount and strength of social relations were not correlated with material possessions. However, we might speculate the lack of correlation is a statistical finding that applies to a normal Scandinavian. "As soon as material conditions markedly deteriorate

solidarity and love relationships are also likely to suffer" (Allardt, 1993, p. 91). Although this is the only study relating humane social relationships to quality of life, we speculate that it is likely that this finding represents a universal relationship between these two variables.

Social Support and Stress

In a review of research on social support, Güngör (1997) identified five basic sources of social support: (a) instrumental support, which involves material, financial, and service support; (b) social companionship, which is spending leisure time together; (c) emotional support based on extending empathy and love; (d) esteem support whereby the individual is accepted together with problems and deficiencies; and (e) informational support, which involves supplying relevant information and the necessary skills to cope with problems. Güngör (1997) concluded that all types of social support from supervisors, peers, subordinates, family members, and friends contribute to psychological and physical health.

Social support has a positive effect on individual well-being by alleviating the negative effects of stress (Maslach & Jackson, 1984; Russell, Altmaier, & Van Velzen, 1987). Social support can directly enhance well-being because it satisfies important human needs such as security, social contact, approval, belonging, and affection. In addition, social support moderates the relationship between stressors and burnout through the use of adaptive coping strategies (Cordes & Dougherty, 1993).

Overview of Prior Cross-Cultural Studies on the Concept of Humane Orientation

As described in the review of large sample cross-cultural studies in Chapter 2 by House and Javidan, Schwartz and Bilsky (1987) derived and confirmed seven distinctive motivational domains of values that they claim to be universal. These motivational domains were derived from a literature review of needs, social motives, institutional demands, and functional requirements of social groups. One of the domains is labeled the *prosocial domain*. This positive social requirement is expressed in

Table 18.1   Higher Humane Orientation Societies Versus Lower Humane Orientation Societies

High Humane Orientation Societies	Low Humane Orientation Societies
Others are important (i.e. family, friends, community, strangers).	Self-interest is important.
Fewer psychological and pathological problems.	More psychological and pathological problems.
Values of altruism, benevolence, kindness, love, and generosity have high priority.	Values of pleasure, comfort, self-enjoyment have high priority.
Need for belonging and affiliation motivate people.	Power and material possessions motivate people.
Personal and family relationships induce protection for the individuals.	Welfare state guarantees social and economic protection of individuals.
Close circle receives material, financial, and social support; concern extends to all people and nature.	Lack of support for others; predominance of self-enhancement.
Members of society are responsible for promoting well-being of others: The state is not actively involved.	State provides social and economic support for individuals' well-being.
The state supports the private sector and maintains a balance between public and private domains.	The state sponsors public provisions and sectors.
Public policymakers establish sanctions against child labor practices.	Public policymakers consider child labor practices as a somewhat less-important issue.
Members of society are urged to be sensitive to all forms of racial discrimination.	Members of society are not sensitive to all forms of racial discrimination.
People are expected to promote paternalistic norms and patronage relationships.	Formal welfare institutions replace paternalistic norms and patronage relationships.
People are urged to provide social support to each other.	People are expected to solve personal problems on their own.
The children of less-developed societies are expected to give material support to their parents in their old age.	The children of more-developed societies are not expected to give material support to their parents in their old age.
The children of less-developed societies can participate in the labor force to help out their families.	The children of more developed societies are not expected to participate in labor force to help out their families.
Children should be obedient.	Children should be autonomous.
Parents should closely control their children.	Family members are independent.

such values as altruism, benevolence, kindness, or love. To test the structure of the values, the researchers asked a sample of Israeli teachers ($N = 455$) and German college students ($N = 331$) to rank the 36 Rokeach values in order of importance. Schwartz and Bilsky (1987) found

that a value preference for promoting other's welfare (prosocial) contradicts both valuing personal success (achievement) and valuing one's own pleasure and comfort (enjoyment).

Schwartz and Bilsky (1990) further confirmed the universality of the seven distinct motivational

Table 18.2a   Sample Questions: Humane Orientation: Society Practices (As Is)

1. In this society, people are generally: (reverse scored)							
Very concerned about others					Not at all concerned about others		
1	2	3	4	5	6	7	
2. In this society, people are generally: (reverse scored)							
very sensitive toward others					Not at all sensitive toward others		
1	2	3	4	5	6	7	

types of values with data from Australia, Finland, Hong Kong, Spain, and the United States. Moreover, the opposition between pro-social and achievement values held across all seven samples, indicating that the value conflict between the two motivational domains is likely to be universal.

In another cross-cultural study using factor analysis conducted in 12 nations (Bigoness & Blakely, 1996), responses of 567 managers yielded four factors in which the first factor included the values of forgiving, helpful, loving, and cheerful, corresponding to the humane orientation construct. However, compared with the other three value dimensions, managers ranked humane orientation as least important in directing their lives, providing an interesting insight into the values of managers as an occupational group.

Schwartz (1992) developed an instrument that represented the basic universal human values, with a procedure that avoided a Western imposed bias. Data were collected from 44,000 schoolteachers and university students in 54 countries. Results showed that value types are organized in two bipolar dimensions, one being the self-transcendence (universalism and benevolence) and the other the self-enhancement (power and achievement) dimension, discussed in an earlier section. The duality between self-transcendence and self-enhancement reflects the opposition between humane orientation and task concerns. At the same time, however, humane orientation was confirmed as a basic value that is prevalent in all of the regions of the world.

In a cross cultural study of Canada, the United States, Romania, Turkey, China,

Pakistan, and India, Kanungo and Aycan (1997) included *paternalism* as one of the four sociocultural dimensions of societies. Paternalism was assessed with statements such as "In our society, the ideal boss is like a parent," and "People in authority in our society should take care of their subordinates as they would take care of their children." Eastern cultures were found to carry significantly more paternalistic values compared with Western countries. Thus, paternalism might reflect a different form of humane orientation that is dominant in Eastern societies.

GLOBE MEASURES OF HUMANE ORIENTATION

Five questionnaire items in the GLOBE study were used to operationalize the societal Humane Orientation construct: Being concerned, sensitive toward others, friendly, tolerant of mistakes, and generous. Chapter 8 by Hanges and Dickson describes the development, validation, and format of the items. Tables 18.2a and 18.2b show sample questionnaire items that are used for the societal Humane Orientation construct.

As stated in the introduction to this section, the organizational *As Is* (practices) questions are designed to measure the respondents' assessment of the extent to which an organization engages in Humane Orientation practices. The *Should Be* (values) questions measure the values of respondents regarding how humane-orientated they would like their organizations to be. Tables 18.3a and 18.3b show sample questions that measure the organizational Humane Orientation practices and values, respectively.

Table 18.2b   Sample Questions: Humane Orientation: Society Values (Should Be)

1. In this society, people *should be* encouraged to be: (reverse scored)

Very concerned about others					Not at all concerned about others	
1	2	3	4	5	6	7

2. In this society, people *should be* encouraged to be: (reverse scored)

Very sensitive toward others					Not at all sensitive toward others	
1	2	3	4	5	6	7

Table 18.3a   Sample Questions: Humane Orientation: Organization Practices (As Is)

1. In this organization, people are generally: (reverse scored)

Very concerned about others					Not at all concerned about others	
1	2	3	4	5	6	7

2. In this organization, people are generally: (reverse scored)

Very sensitive toward others					Not at all sensitive toward others	
1	2	3	4	5	6	7

Table 18.3b   Sample Questions: Humane Orientation: Organization Values (Should Be)

1. In this organization, people *should be* encouraged to be: (reverse scored)

Very concerned about others					Not at all concerned about others	
1	2	3	4	5	6	7

2. In this organization, people *should be* encouraged to be: (reverse scored)

Very sensitive toward others					Not at all sensitive toward others	
1	2	3	4	5	6	7

GLOBE FINDINGS: HUMANE ORIENTATION

Table 18.4a presents the summary statistics for societal Humane Orientation practices and values dimensions, whereas Tables 18.4b and 18.4c present the mean scores for 61 cultures for the two dimensions.[1] As seen in Table 18.4a, society practices scores for Humane Orientation has an average rating of 4.09 with a range of 3.18 to 5.23. The society average values score for Humane Orientation is 5.42 with a range of 4.49 to 6.09.

As seen in Table 18.4b, four bands of societies emerged when societal Humane Orientation practices mean scores for each society were examined. Societies in band A have

Table 18.4a Summary Statistics for Humane Orientation at the Societal Level

Variable	N	Minimum	Maximum	Mean	Standard Deviation
Society practices	61	3.18	5.23	4.09	0.47
Society values	61	4.49	6.09	5.42	0.25

Table 18.4b Humane Orientation Scores: Society Practices*

Band							
A		B		C		D	
Country	Score	Country	Score	Country	Score	Country	Score
Zambia	5.23	Indonesia	4.69	U.S.	4.17	Italy	3.63
Philippines	5.12	Ecuador	4.65	Taiwan	4.11	Poland	3.61
Ireland	4.96	Albania	4.64	Sweden	4.10	Switzerland	3.60
Malaysia	4.87	India	4.57	Nigeria	4.10	South Africa[d]	3.49
Thailand	4.81	Kuwait	4.52	Israel	4.10	Singapore	3.49
Egypt	4.73	Canada[a]	4.49	Bolivia	4.05	Germany[e]	3.40
		Zimbabwe	4.45	Kazakhstan	3.99	France	3.40
		Denmark	4.44	Argentina	3.99	Hungary	3.35
		Qatar	4.42	Mexico	3.98	Greece	3.34
		Costa Rica	4.39	Finland	3.96	Spain	3.32
		China	4.36	Namibia	3.96	Germany[f]	3.18
		South Africa[b]	4.34	Turkey	3.94		
		New Zealand	4.32	Russia	3.94		
		Japan	4.30	Switzerland[c]	3.93		
		Australia	4.28	Portugal	3.91		
		Venezuela	4.25	Hong Kong	3.90		
		Iran	4.23	Guatemala	3.89		
		Morocco	4.19	Netherlands	3.86		
		Georgia	4.18	South Korea	3.81		
				Slovenia	3.79		
				Austria	3.72		
				Colombia	3.72		
				England	3.72		
				El Salvador	3.71		
				Brazil	3.66		

a Canada (English-speaking)
b South Africa (Black sample)
c Switzerland (French-speaking)
d South Africa (White sample)
e Germany (East): Former GDR
f Germany (West): Former FRG

* Higher scores indicate greater humane orientation. Our response bias correction procedure identified response bias in some countries for this scale (see endnotes).

Table 18.4c   Humane Orientation: Society Values (Should Be)*

				Band					
A		*B*		*C*		*D*			
Country	*Score*	*Country*	*Score*	*Country*	*Score*	*Country*	*Score*	*Country*	*Score*
Nigeria	6.09	Spain	5.69	Philippines	5.36	Costa Rica	4.99	New Zealand	4.49
Finland	5.81	Brazil	5.68	Albania	5.34				
Singapore	5.79	France	5.67	Hong Kong	5.32				
Austria	5.76	South Africa[a]	5.65	China	5.32				
		Sweden	5.65	Portugal	5.31				
		Canada[b]	5.64	Venezuela	5.31				
		Switzerland[c]	5.62	Qatar	5.30				
		Kazakhstan	5.62	Poland	5.30				
		Israel	5.62	India	5.28				
		Iran	5.61	Taiwan	5.26				
		Colombia	5.61	Ecuador	5.26				
		Georgia	5.60	Guatemala	5.26				
		South Korea	5.60	Slovenia	5.25				
		Russia	5.59	Greece	5.23				
		Italy	5.58	Netherlands	5.20				
		Australia	5.58	Zimbabwe	5.19				
		Argentina	5.58	Egypt	5.17				
		Switzerland	5.54	Indonesia	5.16				
		Zambia	5.53	Mexico	5.10				
		U.S.	5.53	South Africa[f]	5.07				
		Turkey	5.52	Bolivia	5.07				
		Malaysia	5.51	Kuwait	5.06				
		Morocco	5.51	Thailand	5.01				
		Hungary	5.48						
		Ireland	5.47						
		Germany[d]	5.46						
		El Salvador	5.46						
		Denmark	5.45						
		Germany[e]	5.44						
		England	5.43						
		Japan	5.41						
		Namibia	5.40						

a South Africa (White sample)
b Canada (English-speaking)
c Switzerland (French-speaking)
d Germany (West): Former FRG
e Germany (East): Former GDR
f South Africa (Black sample)

* Higher scores indicate greater humane orientation. Our response bias correction procedure identified response bias in some countries for this scale (see endnotes).

the highest scores on the construct, followed by bands B, C, and D. On the other hand, Table 18.4c shows that societal Humane Orientation values scores for each society are grouped primarily into three bands, namely A, B, and C, with one society each in bands D and E. Similarly, higher scores in each cluster reflect more Humane Orientation values.

The Correlation Between Overall Values and Practices Scores

In general, there is a modest negative correlation between societal practices and values scores ($r = -.32$, $p < .05$). Societal practices scores increase as values scores decrease. Those societies with lower Humane Orientation practices aspire to higher humane orientation in their societies. In societies in which humane orientation practices are relatively low, members of society express a desire to reach higher humane orientation relationships. It is interesting to note that the four highest-rated countries with respect to Humane Orientation values measures (band A: Nigeria, Finland, Singapore, Austria) are all in the C and D bands of the Humane Orientation practices measures, illustrating the negative relationship between societal practices and values in Humane Orientation.

As indicated in Chapter 2, the GLOBE theoretical model postulates that societal practices and values affect organizational practices and values. Two hierarchical linear models (HLMs) were conducted to test these hypotheses for organizational Humane Orientation practices and values. We tested the GLOBE hypothesis regarding the effect of societal culture on organizational culture by conducting HLM analyses in which organizational Humane Orientation was predicted by societal Humane Orientation. These analyses supported our hypotheses that societal Humane Orientation practices have a significant and strong positive relationship with organizational Humane Orientation practices ($p < .01$). We found a trend between societal Humane Orientation values and organizational Humane Orientation values ($p < .10$). Both analyses support a principal proposition in the GLOBE theoretical model (i.e., Proposition 3, Figure 2.1, Chapter 2, by House & Javidan); societal cultural values and practices affect organizational cultural values and practices.[2]

Societal Humane Orientation and Other GLOBE Culture Dimensions

Table 18.5 shows the correlations between the societal Humane Orientation dimension and the other GLOBE societal constructs. Societal Humane Orientation practices are correlated at a statistically significant level with the GLOBE societal practices scores of Institutional Collectivism ($r = .43$, $p < .01$), In-Group Collectivism ($r = .30$, $p < .05$), Performance Orientation ($r = .25$, $p < .05$), and Assertiveness ($r = -.42$, $p < .01$) scales and with the GLOBE societal *values* of Assertiveness ($r = .45$, $p < .01$), Gender Egalitarianism ($r = -.39$,

$p < 01$), Future Orientation ($r = .26$, $p < .05$), Power Distance ($r = .30$, $p < .05$), and Uncertainty Avoidance ($r = .29$, $p < .05$). These findings point out that as the humane orientation practices of a society increase, it tends to have more collectivist, performance-oriented, and nonassertive practices. Many of the humane practices found in societies at the same time reflect practices aimed at maximizing collective interests and achievement in a supportive, nonassertive way. These data show that social support and solidarity go hand in hand with promoting collective interests in a supportive manner in societies across the globe. In addition, those societies that have more humane-oriented practices value assertiveness, masculinity, power distance, future orientation, and avoiding uncertainty to a greater extent. The negative relationship of Humane Orientation practices with the values of Gender Egalitarianism, and the positive relationship with the values of Assertiveness, remained significant even when we controlled for the Humane Orientation values, suggesting that the results are not just a reflection of the negative relationships between Humane Orientation values and practices. A possible explanation lies in the emphasis on paternalistic behaviors, associated with men, and with an assertive protection of the rights of the members in many societies that practice humane orientation.

When the relationship between the societal Humane Orientation values and the other GLOBE societal constructs is considered, it is found that there is a significant negative correlation between the Humane Orientation values and the values of Power Distance ($r = .42$, $p < .01$), and a significant positive correlation with assertive practices ($r = .35$, $p < .01$). These findings show societies that value humane orientation seek to reduce power distance and use rather assertive practices, possibly to fight against injustice.

HUMANE ORIENTATION AND OTHER ECONOMIC AND SOCIAL INDICATORS

In understanding the conceptual foundations for antecedents to humane orientation, a multidisciplinary perspective is required. In this section,

Table 18.5 Correlations of Humane Orientation as a Societal Construct with Other GLOBE Societal Dimensions

GLOBE Societal Culture Construct	Correlation With Humane Orientation Practices	Correlation With Humane Orientation Values
Assertiveness practices	−.42**	.35**
Assertiveness values	.45**	—
Institutional Collectivism practices	.43**	—
In-Group Collectivism practices	.30*	—
Performance Orientation practices	.25*	—
Gender Egalitarianism values	−.39**	—
Future Orientation values	.26*	—
Power Distance values	.30*	−.42**
Uncertainty Avoidance values	.29*	—

NOTE: Only statistically significant relationships are shown.

* $p < .05$.

** $p < .01$.

we analyze the relationship between the GLOBE Humane Orientation construct and other major cross-cultural data in various disciplines. As explained in Chapter 7 by Javidan and Hauser, four major ongoing reports produce the relevant data: the IMD's Global Competitiveness Ranking, the United Nations Development Program's Human Development Report, and the World Values Survey. In addition, 1995 U.S. census data and data from other cross-cultural research were used to compare and contrast GLOBE Humane Orientation scores with other indicators of the human condition.

Political Systems and Humane Orientation

Two alternative political ideologies, liberal and socialist, claim to create a humane-oriented society (Macpherson, 1966). The liberal ideology concentrates on rationality, self-interest, and property rights. The socialist ideology focuses on eliminating the exploitation of labor by preventing concentration of means of production in the hands of a few. As such, the socialist ideology is more concerned with individual welfare maximization and freedom. It

considers the capitalist system inhumane in the sense that there is alienation and detachment of mechanical workers from workplace decisions.

The political ideology of a society influences the belief about distribution fairness among its members. Deutsch (1975) identified three basic norms concerning distribution fairness: Equity norm, equality norm, and need norm. The equity norm is expected to produce high average group productivity. The equality norm leads to the best group harmony and stability. The need norm is the most humanistic and most helpful to individual well-being and personal development (Kaicheng, 1998).

In Marxism the norm of allocation of resources according to needs is regarded as ideal although unrealistic because of the requirement for material wealth in the society. Because of the difficulties in achieving distributive justice based on the need norm, the Chinese perspective is based on egalitarianism. Kaicheng (1998) and Mao (1929) pointed out that egalitarianism is an illusion of peasants and small proprietors and even under socialism there can be no absolute equality. After Deng Xiaoping took control of China in the 1970s, he implemented a series of policies to increase the participation of China in the international arena. As a result of these globalization patterns, preferences of Chinese managers shifted to equity-based and highly differentiated distributive patterns (Meindl, Yu, & Lu, 1987).

The GLOBE findings revealed a positive correlation between GLOBE Humane Orientation practices scores and the extent of liberal thinking in society, as measured in the World Values Survey using respondent self-placements of their beliefs as left versus right ($r = .54$, $n = 37$, $p < .01$). This finding implies that the more humane oriented a society is, the more right-wing and less socialist its political ideology. It could be argued that socialist political systems are preferred in low humane-oriented societies in order to provide more formal and organized support systems for the people in need and to fill the existing gap in helping behavior and solidarity. However, left versus right political ideology and Humane Orientation values were not correlated at a statistically significant level ($r = .20$, $p < .10$).

Urbanization

Parallel with the modernization trends, there is some support for the "urban unhelpfulness" prediction. A cross-cultural study in England and the Sudan (Yousif & Korte, 1995) and previous findings by Korte (1980) show that helpfulness toward relatives and friends are unaffected by the urban–nonurban variable, whereas helpfulness toward neighbors and strangers decreases with urbanization.

The correlations of societal Humane Orientation practices scores with percentage of inhabitants living in urban settings ($r = - .37$, $n = 56$, $p < .01$) and percentage of labor force in agriculture ($r = .43$, $n = 56$, $p < .01$) as taken from the Human Development Report support the urban unhelpfulness proposition. As percentages of inhabitants living in rural settings and labor force in agriculture increase, humane orientation practices increase. However, no statistically significant correlations were found between Humane Orientation values and either measure of urbanization. Table 18.6 summarizes the relationship between societal Humane Orientation and modernization measures.

The Human Condition

Correlations between both the GLOBE Humane Orientation practice and value dimensions and the human condition indices such as societal health, human health, and general satisfaction, are found not to be statistically significant. However, supporting the modernization hypothesis, life expectancy ($r = .35$, $n = 56$, $p < .01$) and the Human Development Index ($r = .38$, $n = 56$, $p < .01$) are found to be negatively correlated with the GLOBE Humane Orientation practices dimension. These findings imply that societies that have relatively lower standing in terms of life expectancy and human development have higher Humane Orientation practices scores. Humane Orientation practices scores are found to be negatively correlated with total population with access to safe water ($r = .34$, $n = 56$, $p < .05$), birth-to-death rate ($r = .84$, $n = 56$, $p < .01$), and adult literacy rate ($r = - .26$, $n = 56$, $p < .05$) also. Similarly, Humane Orientation practices decrease as infant mortality rate ($r = .33$, $n = 56$, $p < .05$) and maternal mortality rate ($r = .34$, $n = 56$, $p < .05$) decrease. In general, as human condition in a society gets worse, Humane Orientation practices scores increase. However, no such relationships were found with the Humane Orientation values. Table 18.6 shows the relationship between Humane Orientation practices and the human condition variables.

However, neither societal Humane Orientation practices nor values dimensions showed significant correlation ($p > .10$) with the psychological health measure of Javidan and Hauser in Chapter 7.

Economic Health

Cross-national research based on INTERPOL data supports the Durkheimian-modernization hypothesis that homicide and theft rates increase with economic development (Ortega, Corzine, Burnett, & Poyer, 1992). In societies in which economic development is relatively low, there is a need for more solidarity and help among members of society and thus there is more social control. With increasing modernization, the necessity for prosocial behavior decreases and the accompanying social control among members of the society breaks down.

Correlations between the GLOBE Humane Orientation practices dimension and economic health indices such as economic prosperity, public sector support for economic prosperity, societal support for economic competitiveness, and overall competitiveness ranking are not found to be statistically significant. However, as seen in Table 18.6, Humane Orientation practices scores are negatively correlated with gross national product (GNP) per capita ($r = .36, n = 54, p < .01$). These results suggest that more industrially wealthy countries have less Humane Orientation practices in general. On the other hand, no relationship has been found between Humane Orientation values and economic health indicators.

The Gini coefficient of a country (a measure of income inequality) is not related to societal practices and values Humane Orientation scores. Although economic development is correlated with Humane Orientation, distribution of income within the country has no relation to it.

Behavioral norms in highly humane oriented, collectivist, and economically less-developed societies have some overlap. This overlap can be expected based on the statistically significant correlation between GLOBE societal Humane Orientation practices with the GLOBE societal practices of Institutional Collectivism ($r = .43$, $p < .01$), In-Group Collectivism ($r = .30, p < .05$), and with GNP per capita ($r = .36, p < .01$). In highly humane-oriented societies, the central behavioral norms include helping others and being generous and friendly. Further, the Humane Orientation practices dimension was negatively correlated with alcohol consumption per capita ($r = .45, p < .05$).

In sum, in humane-oriented cultures, members of society are expected to provide material and financial help, spend time together, extend empathy and love, and share information that is required to solve problems effectively. In cultures reported in the GLOBE survey as having highly humane-oriented practices, if individuals have a problem they are expected to ask for help and others are expected to offer help. On the other hand, in societies reporting low levels of humane orientation, individuals are expected to be more self-centered and promote self-enjoyment and self-interests.

Family Values and Humane Orientation

Based on the World Values Survey, no significant correlation between Humane Orientation practices and strength of family ties ($r = .16, n = 38$, $p > .10$) is found.

With an attempt to scrutinize whether or not there is a relationship between attributing an economic value to children and GLOBE societal Humane Orientation scores, Spearman rank order correlations were conducted between the two constructs for eight countries that appeared in both the GLOBE and the Value of Children datasets (Kagitçibasi, 1996). Results show that there is a positive and statistically significant relationship between Humane Orientation practices of a society and economic value attributed to children ($r_s = .81, p < .01$). Societies that have relatively more helping behavior among their members tend to perceive children as an economic value to a greater extent. On the other hand, partial correlation analysis, which holds GNP per capita constant, yields an insignificant relationship between GLOBE societal Humane Orientation practices and economic value attributed to children. Whereas there seems to be no relationship between Humane Orientation and economic value attributed to children if economic development is held constant, there is a statistically significant negative correlation between GNP per capita and economic value attributed to children ($r_s = -.919, p < .01$). Societies that have a lower level of economic development tend to be both more humane and attribute more economic value to children.

Our data show that Humane Orientation practices in societies increase as economic development decreases. The negative correlation between GLOBE Humane Orientation practices and GNP per capita is still found to be statistically significant after the effect of GLOBE Institutional Collectivism is controlled for by partial correlation analysis ($r = -.50, n = 58, p < .01$), but the significance attenuates greatly after the effect of GLOBE In-Group Collectivism is controlled ($r = -.22, n = 58, p < .10$). It seems there is a higher need for solidarity and help within the family and members of societies in less-developed countries, which increases Humane Orientation practices at the societal level.

Table 18.6   Relationship Between Societal Humane Orientation Practices and Modernization Measures*

Modernization Measures	Humane Orientation Societal Practices
Urbanization	
Percentage of inhabitants living in urban settings	−.37**
Percentage of labor force in agriculture	.43**
Human condition	
Life expectancy	−.35**
Human Development Index	−.37**
Total population with access to safe water	−.34*
Birth-to-death rate	−.84**
Life expectancy at birth	−.33*
Adult literacy rate	−.26*
Infant mortality rate	.33*
Maternal mortality rate	.34*
Economic health	
Gross national product per capita	−.36**

NOTE: Data for each variable are for year 1998.

$N = 54$.

Thus, economic development, economic value of children, expectations of obedience from children, and Humane Orientation seem to be related to each other.

Human Rights and Humane Orientation

The GLOBE societal Humane Orientation values dimension is found to be correlated with the number of years a society has been a member of the International Convention on the Elimination of All Forms of Racial Discrimination ($r = .34$, $p = .018$). Those countries that aspire to higher levels of Humane Orientation seem to have longer membership in this convention. On the other hand, such societal indicators as membership in "Convention Against Torture and Other Cruel, Inhuman, or Degrading Treatment or Punishment" and "Convention on the Rights of the Child" are not correlated with the GLOBE societal Humane Orientation scores. Data for membership statistics were obtained from *The United Nations and Human Rights, 1945–1995* (1995). Further, societal Humane Orientation values score was found to be negatively correlated with prisoners per 100,000 people ($r = .56$, $p < .05$), as given in the Human Development Report (United Nations Development Program, 1998). The societies that are reported to value more Humane Orientation are less likely to keep a significant proportion of their population in prison.

In summary, if GLOBE's Humane Orientation findings are compared with the findings from secondary data, those societies that scored higher in Humane Orientation practices have lower life expectancy, score lower on the Human Development Index, are less developed economically, and have lower preference for left-wing political ideology. In addition, those societies that score higher in Humane Orientation values are less inclined to imprison people and are against societal discrimination.

HUMANE ORIENTATION AND COUNTRY DEMOGRAPHICS

Physical Conditions, Climate, and Humane Orientation

Parallel with the modernization hypothesis, in societies in which physical conditions and climate create difficulties for survival there is likely to be a greater need for helping and solidarity among members of society.

GLOBE countries were categorized by climate into seven groups: tropical humid, tropical wet and dry (savanna), desert, subtropical humid, subtropical wet and dry (Mediterranean), marine west coast (maritime), and continental. These groups are discussed in detail in Chapter 10 by Gupta and Hanges. One-way ANOVA tests were conducted to determine if there exist climatic differences in the practices and values of societal Humane Orientation. There is modest evidence of climatic differences in the societal practices $F6, 54 = 2.18, p < .10$), and no evidence of climatic differences in the societal values ($F6, 54 = 0.81, p > .10$) of Humane Orientation. Climatic differences account for 20% of the variation in societal Humane Orientation practices scores, whereas 80% represent idiosyncratic societal differences. Thus, climate has a moderate influence on the observed societal differences in Humane Orientation practices.

We used Analysis of Variance contrast tests to identify the climates that are reported to have significantly different levels of Humane Orientation practices. Only one climatic region was found to be significant: Societies in tropical humid climates tend to score higher for societal Humane Orientation practices in general (contrast $= 0.39, p < .05$). In tropical humid regions, the air is like that in a very hot sauna, and the humidity causes a lot of perspiration and makes people tire quite easily. Thus, there is some support for our conjecture that societies with climates that create hardship for survival (e.g., tropical humid) have significantly higher Humane Orientation practices. Table 18.7 shows the mean scores for Humane Orientation practices across climates.

Under exceptionally stressful times, when physical conditions deteriorate markedly, support among members of a unit may diminish in many nonindustrial societies of tropical humid climates. For instance, Shalinsky and Glascock (1988) observe that when the Yanomamo of northern Brazil perceive a societal threat, they may decide to kill expendable persons to stabilize their conditions. These societies clearly distinguish between the killing of infants and the aged and killing a fully developed human. The latter is considered homicide and society severely punishes those who execute a homicide. Infanticide concerns only the family, especially the mother, and not any larger unit of society. These societies perceive benefit to the mother and the family from infanticide and killing the aged.

On the other hand, Shalinsky and Glascock (1988) point to beliefs and practices in modern Western society that are parallel to the killing of infants and the aged in nonindustrial societies: (a) the beliefs and practices regarding abortion and (b) active support of the suffering aged person's right to die, and, at least in the United States, shunting off the decrepit aged to nursing homes with extremely poor conditions and few humanitarian practices.

Humane Orientation and Region

As discussed in Chapter 8 by Hanges and Dickson, there are significant differences in values and practices for every cultural dimension among the 62 societal cultures (i.e., recall that we use the term societal cultures rather than nations). As reported in Chapter 10 by Gupta and Hanges, societies were grouped into 10 cultural clusters: (a) Eastern Europe, (b) Latin America, (c) Latin Europe, (d) Confucian Asia, (e) Nordic Europe, (f) Anglo, (g) Sub-Saharan Africa, (h) Southern Asia, (i) Germanic Europe, and (j) the Middle East. One-way ANOVA tests showed that there exist significant cross-regional differences in the societal practices ($F9, 51 = 5.06, p < .01$), but not in societal

Table 18.7   Climate and Societal Humane Orientation Scores

		Societal Humane Orientation Practices	
Climate	N	Mean	SD
Tropical humid	8	4.44	0.56
Tropical wet and dry (savanna)	7	4.35	0.53
Desert	11	4.15	0.34
Subtropical humid	5	3.94	0.18
Mediterranean	7	3.83	0.47
Marine west coast (maritime)	10	3.88	0.55
Continental	13	4.02	0.33

values ($F9$, $51 = 0.91$, $p > .10$) of Humane Orientation. Regional differences (country clusters) account for 47% of the variation in societal Humane Orientation practices scores, whereas 53% represent idiosyncratic societal differences. In other words, there is substantial regional differentiation among societies with respect to practices of humane orientation.

Table 18.8 illustrates the averages for each country cluster on Humane Orientation practices scores. We used Analysis of Variance contrast tests to identify the clusters with significantly higher or lower practices of Humane Orientation. The Humane Orientatio practices score is significantly higher in the Southern Asia cluster (mean = 4.71; contrast = 0.68, $p < .01$), followed by Sub-Saharan Africa (mean = 4.42, contrast = 0.35, $p < .05$). The Humane Orientation practices score is significantly lower in Germanic Europe (mean = 3.55 contrast = 0.60, $p < .01$), followed by Latin Europe (mean = 3.71, contrast = 0.43, $p < .01$).

Gupta, Surie, Javidan, and Chhokar (2002) observe that a group-oriented humane approach is the hallmark of Southern Asian societies and involves a delicate, nonassertive balancing of power versus performance. They illustrate the humane orientation of Southern Asian societies using the example of the Philippines. In rural Philippine, neighbors commonly offer to help if a person is constructing a house. Filipinos love helping not just one another, but also other people. Gratitude is a prized trait in Filipino society and any help is valued as a debt of honor. Most Germanic societies, on the other hand, tend to view humane orientation in rather rational terms, often overburdened with formal procedures such as those related to the condition of labor.

Technology and Market Development and Humane Orientation

The argument that development and industrialization have produced processes that lead to universal attitudes about work finds some support in the literature (Harbison & Myers, 1959; Kerr, Dunlop, Harbison, & Myers, 1960; Ronen, 1986). According to the convergence argument, industrialization affects all organizations the same way, and one outcome of economic development and technological advancement is to produce organizational cultures that are similar and independent of national culture.

Organizations of industrialized Western countries in the 20th century had predominantly Taylorist or Fordist processes and structures. The aim of the Taylorist-Fordist paradigm was to limit the arbitrariness of the supervisors and employees on the shop floor by tying work rhythm to the pace of the assembly line. This paradigm created a uniform mode of control over the labor process, which is heavily

Table 18.8   Regional Clusters and Societal Humane Orientation Practices Mean Scores**

Region (Cultural Clusters)	N	Societal Humane Orientation Practices	
		Mean	SD
Latin America	10	4.03	0.32
Anglo	7	4.20	0.49
Nordic Europe	3	4.17	0.25
Germanic Europe	5	3.55	0.27
Latin Europe	6	3.71	0.32
Eastern Europe	8	3.85	0.44
Confucian Asia	6	3.99	0.33
Southern Asia	6	4.71	0.30
Sub-Saharan Africa	5	4.42	0.49
Middle East	5	4.36	0.30

criticized for its low humane orientation: Forced pace and work pressure, physical strain, and psychological stress on workers (Friedman, 1974; Widick, 1976).

In the early 1980s, in response to the pressures of global competition, the advantages of the Taylorist-Fordist control forms were increasingly questioned. Leibenstein (1987) introduced the concept of "X-inefficiency" to describe the phenomenon of many incomprehensible inefficiencies in traditional mass production facilities. There is a tendency toward a relative increase in skilled laborers and more flexible forms of work design in high-technology areas in the postindustrial societies. Jürgens (1991) studied 17 assembly plants at three automobile companies in the United States, Great Britain, and the Federal Republic of Germany. His results showed differing configurations of departure from the traditional Tayloristic-Fordist mode of work related to strategic choices based on the demands for adaptation recognized in the early 1980s (p. 240). Further, he found that the technological and human resource strategies chosen were strongly influenced by the national context,

including the national institutions governing labor policy.

Table 18.9 presents the summary statistics for societal Humane Orientation practices and values dimensions in three industries: financial services, food processing, and telecommunications. As seen in Table 18.9, societal practices and values scores for Humane Orientation in the finance industry have an average rating of 4.04 and 5.43, respectively. For the food industry, Humane Orientation practices score has an average value of 4.07, and the mean values score is 5.42. In the case of telecommunication sector, mean Humane Orientation practices and values scores are 4.14 and 5.41, respectively.

Table 18.10 shows the correlations among societal Humane Orientation practices and values for finance, food, and telecommunication industries. The Humane Orientation values in the telecommunication industry correlate significantly with the Humane Orientation values in the finance ($r = .48$, $p < .01$) and the food sectors ($r = .72$, $p < .01$). Furthermore, the Humane Orientation practices in the telecommunications industry correlate significantly with the Humane

Table 18.9   Summary Statistics for Societal Humane Orientation for Three Industries

Variable	n	Minimum	Maximum	Mean	Standard Deviation
Finance Humane Orientation practices	55	3.15	5.24	4.04	0.49
Finance Humane Orientation values	55	4.59	6.12	5.43	0.26
Food Humane Orientation practices	45	3.23	5.23	4.07	0.47
Food Humane Orientation values	45	4.61	6.14	5.42	0.32
Telecommunication Humane Orientation practices	32	2.95	6.24	4.14	0.65
Telecommunication Humane Orientation values	32	4.02	5.99	5.41	0.42

Table 18.10   Correlations of Societal Humane Orientation for Three Industries

	Finance Industry Score Practices	Food Industry Score Practices	Telecom Industry Score Practices	Finance Industry Score Values	Food Industry Score Values	Telecom Industry Score Values
Finance industry score practices		.76** $N = 41$	.54** $N = 30$	−.16 $N = 55$	−.35* $N = 41$	−.16 $N = 30$
Food industry score practices			.59** $N = 22$	−.34* $N = 41$	−.30* $N = 45$	−.49* $N = 22$
Telecommunication industry score practices				.12 $N = 30$	−.14 $N = 22$	−.46** $N = 32$
Finance industry score values					.59** $N = 41$	.48** $N = 30$
Food industry score values						.72** $N = 22$

* $p < .05$.

** $p < .01$.

Orientation practices in the finance sector ($r = .54$, $p < .01$) and practices in the food sector ($r = .59$, $p < .01$). In addition, Humane Orientation practices in the food sector correlate significantly and negatively with Humane Orientation values in all three sectors. Societal Humane Orientation values and practices are found to be modestly similar among the three industries, indicating a significant societal effect; however, the societal effect is not so strong that it eliminates an industry effect.

HUMANE ORIENTATION AS A DIMENSION OF ORGANIZATIONAL CULTURE

The Nordic Model provides a pioneering example of workplace reform and restructuring that attempts to address the problems of Taylorism-Fordism (Elam & Börjeson, 1991). In the late 1960s, the Nordic economies were experiencing a structural crisis, mainly because of increasing competitive forces in the international market and standard wage rates forced on employers regardless of varying profitability and ability to pay (Martin, 1984). Nordic Europeans sought alternatives to replace the Taylorist paradigm, which labor perceived as inhumane, and improve their competitive position in the international markets.

Severe levels of dissatisfaction with work on the part of well-educated young Nordic people resulted in widespread absenteeism, tardiness, turnover, and strikes in workplaces, indicating that private Nordic firms rather than the unions, the politicians, or the academics (Elam & Börjeson, 1991) were most active in seeking new ways of working that encouraged individual involvement and growth of team spirit. In many cases, codetermination agreements were signed, which incorporated demands for a more humane workplace in Nordic Europe.

Jürgens (1991) further concludes that in the process of dissolution of Taylorist-Fordist control system two models emerge: The German model (or the Nordic-German model) of skilled worker-oriented labor regulation, and the Japanese model of group-oriented labor regulation. The German model focuses on the technical aspect of skilled work, the concept of profession, and increased responsibility and self-regulation in carrying out the task.

The Japanese model likewise focuses on skilled labor, but in its ideal form the Japanese worker was self-regulated under the pressure of the assembly line and the machine pace. Further, the Japanese system emphasizes societal context and cultural means to reinforce the importance of group solidarity and support in Japanese organizations. According to Jürgens (1991), American companies were more inclined to adapt the Japanese concepts of group support than the German emphasis on technical expertise and professional ethic in the de-Taylorization process.

Bureaucratic Versus Organic Organizations and Organization Design

An ideally rational organization, in the Weberian sense, is an organization performing its tasks with maximum efficiency. The complexity and size of modern administrative tasks make the bureaucratic type of organization the most efficient, if compared with feudal or patrimonial organizations. According to Marx, bureaucracy is the instrument of the capitalist class and a means of exploitation.

In bureaucratic organizations, human resource practices are standardized and aim at the efficient running of the organization. On the other hand, dominant paternalistic values in a society lead to practices in which concern for employees' families and obligation to one's community override systematic application of human resource practices.

Rather than the standard rules and regulations of a bureaucratic system, organizations in paternalistic cultures make exceptions for employees on the basis of their needs, and managers and supervisors show concern for workers' personal problems. In paternalistic cultures, patronage relationships emerge as a form of providing informal support, whereas in nonpaternalistic cultures mentoring relationships between more experienced and younger employees may replace the patronage relationship as a means of providing informal support. According to Kanungo and Aycan (1997), in paternalistic societies managers believe that employees by nature seek more supervisory guidance. Hence, jobs are designed in a way that does not give much autonomy to employees.

Employee Relations

The concept of human resource management (HRM) was developed initially on the basis of American practices in the 1960s and 1970s. Central to the notion of HRM as currently accepted in the literature is the notion of organizational independence and autonomy, which may not be prevalent in many parts of the world. In highly humane-oriented societies, organizations are relatively autonomous in their employee relations, whereas in the relatively low humane-oriented societies there is greater control of organizations in their HRM practices.

The European system is characterized by the significant role of *social partners* in the employment relationship (Sparrow & Hiltrop, 1994). These influences include the role of trade unions in the setting of HRM policies, collective bargaining at the state and regional levels, and direct codetermination at the company level. In many European countries union recognition for collective bargaining is required by law.

Relationships to Stakeholders

In the relatively low humane-oriented societies such as the European countries, human social life is not viewed as an economic transaction but rather from the sociological perspective, and there is lower emphasis on contractual sale of labor by employees (Schneider & Barsoux, 1997; Sparrow & Hiltrop, 1994). From this perspective, organizations are not expected to make a profit without fulfilling social responsibility and giving serious consideration to all stakeholders, not only the shareholders. Compared with the United States and Japan, in Europe there is greater influence of trade unions and the state on the business system.

In the more humane-oriented societies of the world, satisfying shareholders and making a profit is the primary focus of organizations. Making profits is a legitimate goal that is shared in organizations. Although social responsibility is left to the initiative of senior managers and owners, some organizations apply the charity and stewardship principles and corporate social responsiveness (Frederick, 1987).

Manufacturing Strategy

Advanced technology highlighted the need for flexible manufacturing systems such as just-in-time and computer-aided processes. Post-Taylorist and post-Fordist manufacturing processes and ideas integrated the skilled labor and greater autonomy required by these systems, relieving workers from the physical and psychological strains of machine-paced mass production systems. In this way they create more humane organizational workplaces. Ironically, although the societies of Western Europe score relatively low on the dimension of Humane Orientation, these humane organizational structures are prevalent there.

Table 18.11 summarizes the major connotations and variations of the Humane Orientation dimension at the organizational level. It particularly addresses technology and development, economic context, organizational design, trust versus control, relationships to stakeholders, manufacturing strategies, HRM practices, employee relations, and societal culture.

Table 18.12 summarizes organizational Humane Orientation for three industrial sectors. Organizational Humane Orientation practices are weakest in the financial services sector, in which economic logic is expected to dominate more strongly, than in the food and telecommunications sectors. The same is true with respect to organizational Humane Orientation values also, though the inter-industry differences here are much smaller.

To analyze whether organizational Humane Orientation practices and values differ on the basis of region (i.e., cultural clusters), an analysis of variance test was used. There are significant between-region differences in organizational Humane Orientation practices ($F9, 264 = 4.39, p < .01$); cultural region accounts for 13% of the between-organization differences in Humane Orientation practices. Similarly, there are significant between-region differences in organizational Humane Orientation values ($F9, 264 = 4.59, p < .01$); cultural region accounts for 13.5% of the between-organization differences in Humane Orientation values.

In addition, a series of one-way analyses of variance were conducted for each industry. Table 18.13 shows the regional breakdown of organizational Humane Orientation scores for the three industries. There exist strong statistically significant differences in organizational Humane Orientation practices across regions in the financial services industry ($F9, 120 = 2.90, p < .01$, eta sq = 0.18) and telecommunications industry ($F8, 44 = 3.00, p < .01$, eta sq = 0.35), and weak differences in the food industry ($F9, 81 = 1.73, p < .10$, eta sq = 0.16).

When practices are investigated, there are two cultural clusters with significantly higher Humane Orientation scores in their organizations: Sub-Saharan Africa (mean = 4.83, contrast = .38, $p < .01$), followed by Nordic Europe (mean = 4.72, contrast = .22, $p < .05$). Similarly, there are two cultural clusters with significantly lower scores for Humane Orientation in their organizations: Latin Europe (mean = 4.15, contrast =– 38, $p < .01$), followed by Eastern Europe (mean = 4.21, contrast = .31, $p < .01$).

In the case of organizational values also, one-way analysis of variance revealed statistically

Table 18.11   Summary of Major Connotations and Variations of the Humane Orientation Differences in Terms of Organizational Practices and Values

High Humane-Orientation Organizations	Low Humane-Orientation Organizations
Informal relationships.	Formal relationships.
Social control based on shared values and norms.	Social control based on bureaucratic practices.
Practices reflect individualized considerations.	Practices reflect standardized considerations.
Mentoring and patronage support.	Supervisory support.
Organizations are trusted more and are autonomous in human resource practices.	Organizations are controlled by legislation and unionization.
Organizations are relatively autonomous in their employee relations.	Organizations are restricted in their employee relations by the concept of *social* partners.
Less influence of trade unions and the state on the business system.	Greater influence of trade unions and the state on the business system.
Higher emphasis on contractual sale of labor.	Lower emphasis on contractual sale of labor.
Shareholder's approach.	Stakeholders' approach.
Primary focus is on profits.	Primary focus is on social responsibility.
Organizational members prefer to work with others to get jobs done.	Organizational members prefer to be left alone to get jobs done.

Table 18.12   Summary Statistics for Organizational Humane Orientation for Three Industries

Variable	N	Minimum	Maximum	Mean	Standard Deviation
Finance Humane Orientation practices	130	2.83	5.77	4.45	0.51
Finance Humane Orientation values	130	3.71	5.93	4.97	0.39
Food Humane Orientation practices	91	3.06	5.63	4.52	0.43
Food Humane Orientation values	91	3.96	5.91	4.99	0.37
Telecommunication Humane Orientation practices	53	3.53	5.46	4.51	0.43
Telecommunication Humane Orientation values	53	4.03	5.88	5.00	0.44

NOTE: N = number of organizations. Only identifiable organizations with at least 7 respondents are included in the analysis.

Table 18.13   Regional Breakdown of Organizational Humane Orientation Based on Industry

Regions (Country Clusters)	Finance		Food		Telecommunications	
	Practices	*Values*	*Practices*	*Values*	*Practices*	*Values*
Eastern Europe	4.28	4.72	4.11	4.77	4.18	4.89
Latin America	4.31	5.02	4.65	4.98	4.48	5.08
Latin Europe	4.00	5.10	4.27	5.02	4.27	5.27
Confucian Asia	4.69	5.01	4.63	4.97	4.45	4.93
Nordic Europe	4.68	5.12	4.52	5.33	4.93	5.42
Anglo	4.38	4.97	4.65	4.89	4.31	5.13
Sub-Saharan Africa	5.09	5.18	4.44	5.33	—	—
Southern Asia	4.51	5.15	4.65	5.13	4.77	4.61
Germanic Europe	4.36	4.73	4.54	4.78	4.72	5.06
Middle East	4.34	4.81	4.44	4.85	4.54	4.89

NOTE: Only organizations with at least 7 respondents are included in the analysis.

significant differences in Humane Orientation across regions in the financial services sector ($F9, 120 = 2.69, p < .01$, eta sq $= 0.17$), telecommunications industries ($F8, 44 = 2.35, p < .05$, eta sq $= 0.30$), as well as food industries ($F9, 81 = 2.70, p < .01$, eta sq $= 0.23$).

The cultural clusters with significantly higher organizational Humane Orientation values scores are Nordic Europe (mean $= 5.36$, contrast $= .27, p < .01$), followed by Sub-Saharan Africa (mean $= 5.24$, contrast $= 0.26, p < .05$), whereas Eastern Europe (mean $= 4.78$, contrast $= .25, p < .01$), followed by Germanic Europe (mean $= 4.81$, contrast $=- .22, p < .01$) and Middle East (mean $= 4.83$, contrast $=- .19$, $p < .05$) have the significantly lower scores.

In summary, Nordic European and Sub-Saharan African organizations stand out in the GLOBE sample as having significantly higher scores for practices as well as values for Humane Orientation. On the other hand, Eastern European and Germanic European organizations stand out as having significantly lower scores for Humane Orientation practices as well as

values. Latin European organizations also report low Humane Orientation practices scores, whereas the Germanic European and Middle Eastern organizations scored low in Humane Orientation values.

HUMANE ORIENTATION AS A LEADERSHIP CHARACTERISTIC

Various studies have shown that satisfaction of belongingness and social needs can be achieved with considerate leadership. Although there are no empirical leadership studies that we know of that specifically use humane orientation as a leadership behavior, there are other leadership constructs that come close. Much of the early research that reflects aspects of humane orientation leadership behaviors was conducted by Ohio State University researchers in the United States. Ohio State researchers found that subordinates perceived their supervisors' behavior primarily in terms of two broadly defined categories, which are labeled *consideration* and *initiating structure* (Fleishman, 1953; Halpin & Winer, 1957; Hempill & Coons, 1957). A second major research program on humane-oriented leadership behavior was carried out by researchers at the University of Michigan at the same time as the Ohio State leadership studies (Katz, Maccoby, & Morse, 1950; Katz & Kahn, 1952; Katz, Maccoby, Gurin, & Floor, 1951). Three types of leadership behaviors influence effectiveness of leaders: task-orientation, relation-orientation, and participative leadership (Likert, 1961, 1967). Relation-oriented behaviors correspond to consideration behaviors that were used in the Ohio State studies.

Perhaps one of the most robust research findings in the field of leadership is the relationship between supportive or considerate leadership behaviors and employee satisfaction with supervisors (Yukl, 2002). Fisher and Edwards's (1988) meta-analysis of studies found that the correlation between supervisors' consideration with overall job satisfaction of subordinates and satisfaction with supervisor to be very high. Schriesheim (1982) found that consideration by itself accounted for most of the influence on the satisfaction of employees; initiating structure added only 2%–4% to satisfaction after the effects of consideration were controlled in a multiple regression analysis. A meta-analysis by Wofford and Liska (1993) also supports the overall importance of supportive–considerate leadership. However, it is important to note that most studies used in meta-analyses were based on *male* United States samples.

Overview of Prior Cross-Cultural Studies on Humanely Oriented Leadership

Findings derived from a 30-year research endeavor conducted in Japan indicate two factors of leadership behavior as similar to the Ohio State and Michigan studies of the United States (Misumi & Peterson, 1985). These studies, which were conducted in Japan, were formulated around the performance-maintenance (PM) theory of leadership. The consideration measures used in field studies in the United States were quite similar to the maintenance measures used in Japan.

In a study of five countries in the Asian-Pacific Basin—Japan, South Korea, Taiwan,

Mexico, and the United States—Dorfman and colleagues (1997) found supportive leadership led to subordinate satisfaction in all samples. The universality of leader supportiveness should not be surprising, because a leader demonstrates supportiveness through a humane concern for followers. The effects of supportive leadership were strongest in Mexico and Japan. Interestingly, supportive leadership influenced job performance only in Mexico.

From the above review, it appears that humane orientation of leaders through considerate and supportive actions is a culturally generalizable phenomenon. That is, across all cultures reviewed in the above studies, leaders can be compared in terms of the degree to which they enact humane behaviors toward subordinates and followers of leaders. This, however, does not imply that societies value humane orientation to the same degree.

Image of Leaders

Various studies conducted across countries show that business leaders often do not have an image reflecting a humane orientation. In a 12-country study, Bass and his associates (Bass, Burger, Doktor, & Barrett, 1979) asked managers to judge the importance of *generosity* as a requirement for lower, middle, and top management. In general, generosity was judged to be of low importance. The faster climbing managers were less rejecting of generosity as an important trait compared with managers with low rate of advancement. In almost all countries, managers were less rejecting of generosity in top management than in middle and lower management levels. These results indicate that more successful managers seemed to attribute more importance to being generous and that top management was more associated with generosity compared with lower management levels.

According to an eight-country cross-cultural comparison of leadership prototypes conducted by Gerstner and Day (1994), leaders are not perceived to have highly humane-oriented traits. Subjects in this study were chosen from American, Chinese, French, German, Honduran, Indian, Japanese, and Taiwanese students enrolled in a graduate program at an American university. They were presented with a questionnaire consisting of 59 attributes relevant to leadership. The list of traits included items such as caring, concerned, and generous, which clearly can be considered to be humane oriented traits. For each attribute, subjects were asked to assign a prototypicality rating for a business leader by indicating the extent to which an attribute fits their image of a business leader. In none of the countries were attributes related to humane orientation rated as highly prototypical of business leaders. This finding reinforces the notion that in many countries from different parts of the world, business leadership is not strongly associated with highly humane oriented attributes.

Although leaders in general do not have a highly humane-oriented image, those in the more humane-oriented societies give more priority to the pursuit of ideals rather than promoting self. Bass and his associates (1979) compared the life goals of managers from 12 countries. One of the life goals was *duty,* which was operationalized by "dedication to the pursuit of ultimate values, ideals, and principles." This variable was found to have a positive Spearman rank order correlation of .45 with the societal Humane Orientation practices scores. The goal of duty seems to be an important correlate of societal humane orientation.

Country-Specific Manifestations of Societal Humane Orientation With Respect to Humane-Oriented Leader Behaviors

In a study conducted by Gebert and Steinkamp (1991), considerate leadership in the paternalistic societies of Nigeria and Taiwan was measured as *patriarchal care-taking* which was operationalized as taking care of the welfare of the workers' families, which sometimes meant hiring an employee's family member despite the fact that performance on the job is not economically necessary or the person is not qualified for the job. In both the Taiwanese and the Nigerian samples, production orientation and patriarchal caretaking were not correlated at a statistically significant level.

Similar to Taiwan and Nigeria, patriarchal leadership is frequently observed in Turkey, which has a paternalistic culture (Kabasakal & Bodur, 1998). For example, a Turkish company

owner escorted the son of his employee to England for medical care because the family did not speak English. As a consequence, this employee would not leave the organization in the future even for better salary or promotion opportunities.

In some societies, patronage relationships may be common in family businesses that fear losing their skilled labor to competitors: The owners of such businesses may be inclined to develop personal links of obligation with members of their organization. A study conducted among cotton spinners in Hong Kong showed that benevolent paternalism was the only way to retain workers (Wong Siu-lun, 1986).

In a cross-cultural study conducted by Smith and his colleagues (Smith, Misumi, Tayeb, Peterson, & Bond, 1989) in Britain, the United States, Japan, and Hong Kong, specific manifestations of maintenance or performance behaviors were considered and some specific behaviors were found to be common in the four countries. For example, in all countries, a maintenance-oriented supervisor was perceived as one who responds sympathetically when told about a team member's personal difficulties, spends time discussing subordinates' careers and plans, and is more likely to accept suggestions for work improvements.

In the United States, high performance (P) and high maintenance (M) behaviors were distinctively differentiated. High M behaviors meant not being task-concerned most of the time, not talking about immediate work problems, and not showing disapproval of tardiness. Maintenance behaviors also included not meeting socially outside work.

Contrary to the Western countries, in Hong Kong and Japan high M leadership behaviors included discussing a subordinate's personal difficulties with others in their absence and talking about work problems with the subordinates themselves. In Hong Kong other distinctive M behaviors included spending time together socially at work and after hours, whereas in Japan meeting socially after hours was characteristic of a high P behavior. In Japan, high M leadership included teaching new job skills and sending written notes. On the other hand, there was much overlap between characteristics of

Table 18.14   Major Implications of Variations in Societal Humane Orientation for Humane-Oriented Leadership

High Humane Orientation Societies	Low Humane Orientation Societies
More consideration and maintenance-oriented leadership.	Less consideration and maintenance-oriented leadership.
More benevolence exhibited in leadership.	Less benevolence exhibited in leadership.
Individualized consideration.	Standardized relationships.
Duty orientation as a life-goal has high priority.	Duty orientation as a life-goal has low priority.
Generous and compassionate leader attributes contribute to leader effectiveness.	Generosity and being compassionate do not contribute to leader effectiveness.
Holistic concern for the followers.	Limited concern for the followers.
Maintenance behaviors involve less task orientation and consultation.	Maintenance behaviors involve more task orientation and consultation.
Relationships with subordinates are more informal and personal.	Relationships with subordinates are more formal and impersonal.

maintenance and performance functions in the Japanese case: Similar to high M supervisors, high P leadership behaviors included teaching new job skills and discussing difficulties in the person's absence.

The separation between the task and maintenance functions was most distinctive in the United States case. In other cultures, task-oriented behaviors indicating consideration or considerate behaviors were used to facilitate task orientation. On the other hand, the British supervisors who exhibited strong M behaviors demonstrated more task-centered and consultative behaviors compared with the other three countries. This finding fits the relatively low ranking of Britain in terms of Humane Orientation societal practices scores. For example, high M-oriented supervisors in Britain demonstrated or used equipment, consulted widely about necessary changes, expected suggestions for work improvements from subordinates, and responded positively to new suggestions. Thus, it can be proposed that in the less humane-oriented societies, maintenance-oriented leadership behaviors would involve more task orientation and consultation that is geared toward improving the task. Table 18.14 presents the major implications of variation in the societal Humane Orientation dimension for leadership.

Measures

As explained in Chapter 21 by Dorfman, Hanges, and Brodbeck, one of the six second-order leadership factors identified in the GLOBE study is Humane-Oriented leadership. Respondents indicated on a 7-point scale the degree to which attributes such as being generous and compassionate contribute to or hinder effective leadership, where 7 = contributes greatly to outstanding leadership and 1 = greatly inhibits outstanding leadership.

Findings

Table 18.15a presents the summary statistics for perceived effectiveness of Humane-Oriented

Table 18.15a   Summary Statistics for Humane Oriented Leadership Dimension

Humane-Oriented Leadership	Mean	Standard Deviation	Minimum	Maximum	Valid n
Overall	4.89	0.40	3.82	5.75	61
Finance industry	4.88	0.43	3.81	5.68	56
Food industry	4.87	0.41	3.76	5.89	45
Telecommunication industry	4.95	0.45	4.15	5.95	32

Table 18.15b   Intercorrelations Among Humane Oriented Leadership Scores in Three Industries

Humane-Oriented Leadership	Finance Industry Score Leadership	Food Industry Score Leadership	Telecommunication Industry Score Leadership
Finance industry		.86** $N = 42$	.67** $N = 30$
Food industry			.82** $N = 22$
Telecommunication industry			

** Relationship is significant at $p < .01$.

leadership. Humane-Oriented leadership has an average rating of 4.89 with a range of 3.82 to 5.75. On the average, Humane-Oriented leadership is perceived to slightly contribute to outstanding leadership. Table 18.15a also shows the Humane-Oriented leadership scores for the three industries. As seen in this table, average ratings for Humane-Oriented leadership scores in the finance, food, and telecommunications industries are 4.88, 4.87, and 4.95. Table 18.15b presents the intercorrelations among the Humane-Oriented leadership scores for the three industries. The highly statistically significant correlations among the three industries show that perceptions of the effectiveness of Humane-Oriented leadership in the three industries are similar.

THE RELATIONSHIP BETWEEN HUMANE ORIENTATION AS A SOCIETAL DIMENSION AND THE HUMANE-ORIENTED LEADERSHIP DIMENSION

Humane-Oriented Leadership and Region (Cultural Clusters)

Humane-Oriented leader behaviors are perceived to be most significantly effective in the Southern Asia cluster (mean = 5.38, contrast = .57, $p < .01$), followed by the Sub-Saharan Africa cluster (mean = 5.16, contrast = .33, $p < .05$). This finding is in line with the high Humane Orientation societal practices scores of these two regions as discussed earlier. Perhaps

Table 18.16   Perceived Effectiveness Scores for Humane-Oriented Leadership Based on Regions (Cultural Clusters)

Region (Cultural Cluster)	Mean	Standard Deviation
Eastern Europe	4.76	0.53
Latin America	4.85	0.18
Latin Europe	4.45	0.33
Confucian Asia	5.04	0.26
Nordic Europe	4.42	0.27
Anglo	5.08	0.19
Sub-Saharan Africa	5.16	0.25
Southern Asia	5.38	0.24
Germanic Europe	4.71	0.19
Middle East	4.80	0.45

NOTE: Higher scores indicate more humane-oriented leadership.
N = 61.

those societies with high Humane Orientation practices scores, like Southern Asia and Sub-Saharan Africa, would endorse Humane Oriented leadership more. The regions with significantly lower scores are Nordic Europe (mean = 4.42, contrast =– .49, $p < .05$) and Latin Europe (mean = 4.45, contrast =– .46, $p < .01$). Table 18.16 presents the effectiveness scores for Humane-Oriented leadership on the basis of clusters.

Societal Humane Orientation and Humane-Oriented Leadership

Although leaders make a difference by being different from their followers, at the same time their behaviors are shaped by dominant values in their societies (House, Wright, & Aditya, 1997). Love, friendship, concern, and care are universal values that are shared in all societies across the globe, although the emphasis given to them and how care and concern are manifested might vary across cultures. Societies included in the GLOBE study indicated a strong desire for more Humane Orientation in their cultures. The mean score for the Humane Orientation societal values dimension was 5.42 and the range was 4.49 to

6.09. The mean score for the Humane-Oriented leadership dimension was 4.89 and the range was 3.82 to 5.75. The findings regarding the perceived effectiveness of Humane-Oriented leadership show that, in general, humane-oriented traits are perceived to contribute slightly to outstanding leadership; however, there are clear differences among societal cultures and clusters regarding this leadership dimension.

INTERPRETATION OF HLMs USING HUMANE ORIENTATION TO PREDICT CULTURALLY ENDORSED LEADERSHIP

This chapter presents relationships between one culture dimension (Humane Orientation) and the six culturally endorsed leadership theories (CLTs). Competitive tests of all culture dimensions and CLTs are presented in Chapter 21 by Dorfman and colleagues.[3] In general, we expect that societal and organizational values will be more strongly related to CLT leadership dimensions than societal and organizational practices. As indicated previously, our notions of values and CLT leadership dimensions represent idealized concepts of how the world *Should Be* in

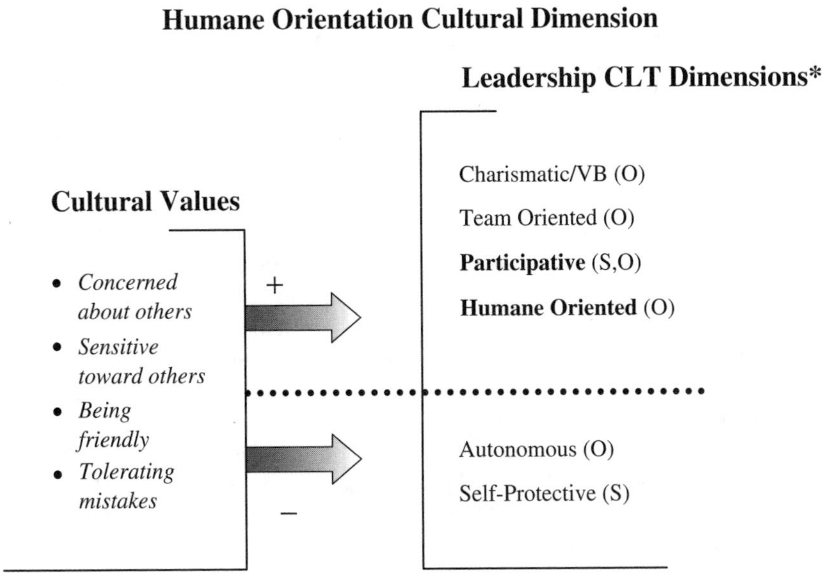

Humane Orientation Cultural Dimension

Figure 18.1 Humane Orientation Cultural Values as Drivers for CLT Leadership Dimensions

* Only statistically significant relationships are shown ($p < .05$; see Table 21.10, Chapter 21 by Dorfman et al.). The most important leadership CLT relationships are bolded (i.e., relationship is significant at both society and organization levels of analyses or highest HLM coefficient within each level of analysis).

VB = Value-Based

O = Organizational level

S = Societal level

contrast to practices, which represent the world *As Is*. As described earlier in this volume, culture is believed to have its effect on the content of CLTs at multiple levels of analysis. Leader attributes perceived to be effective might be a function of (a) societal cultural practices, (b) societal cultural values, (c) organizational cultural practices, and (d) organizational cultural values. In the present chapter we discuss the results of statistical analyses examining the extent to which the cultural dimension of Humane Orientation has an effect on CLTs. Specifically, we examine the extent to which the content of CLTs varies as a function of Humane Orientation values and practices in societies and organizations within societies. As you read through the results discussed below, it may be helpful to view Figure 18.1 for a visual summary. The figure, however, shows only results regarding cultural values, not practices. (All HLM coefficients are presented in Table 21.10 of Chapter 21 by Dorfman et al.)

We tested for the relationship between culture and the CLT leadership dimensions by using hierarchical linear modeling (HLM). HLM is a multistep process designed to test the significance of relationships between independent and dependent variables at multiple levels of analyses. An overview of HLM analyses and a detailed discussion of how these analyses were conducted is provided in Chapter 11 by Hanges, Dickson, and Sipe. In the next section, we report the HLM results exploring the relationship between organizational and societal culture and the content of CLT leadership dimensions.

HLM Analysis: Organizational and Societal Variation

In the present analysis we examine the association of organizational and societal Humane Orientation values and practices with the six GLOBE CLT dimensions. The total amount of organizational and societal variance explained by Humane Orientation ranged from 4.1% to 27.6%. Humane Orientation was found to be a better predictor for some of the CLTs (e.g., Humane-Oriented leadership) than for others (e.g., Autonomous leadership).

When organizational level and societal level Humane Orientation values and practices were considered, significant relationships were found with the following CLTs:

• *Charismatic/Value-Based leadership.* Humane Orientation cultural values scores were significantly related to the Charismatic/ Value-Based leadership dimension and explained a total of 5.6% of organizational and societal variance for this dimension. All of the explained variance was associated with forces operating at the organizational level of analysis; only the organizational Humane Orientation cultural values scores were positively related ($p < .01$) to the Charismatic/Value-Based leadership dimension. Charismatic/Value-Based leadership is more likely to be a part of the shared leadership belief system in organizations reported to espouse Humane Orientation values.

• *Team-Oriented leadership.* Humane Orientation practices and values scores were significantly related to the Team-Oriented leadership dimension and explained a total of 12.2% of the organizational and societal variance for this dimension. All of this variance was associated with forces operating at the organizational level of analysis. The organizational Humane Orientation cultural practices scores were negatively related ($p < .01$) to the Team-Oriented leadership dimension, whereas the organizational Humane Orientation cultural values scores were positively related ($p < .01$) to the Team-Oriented leadership dimension. Team-Oriented leadership is less likely to be a part of the shared leadership belief system in organizations reported to have Humane Orientation practices, but more likely to be in the leadership belief systems of organizations reported to espouse Humane Orientation values.

• *Participative leadership.* Humane Orientation cultural values scores were significantly related to the Participative leadership dimension and explained a total of 19.3% of the organizational and societal variance for this dimension. Of the total explained variance, approximately 16.8% was associated with forces operating at the organizational level of analysis. The majority of the explained variance (83.2%) was associated with forces operating at the societal level of analysis.

The organizational Humane Orientation cultural values scores were positively related ($p < .01$) to the Participative leadership dimension. Participative leadership is more likely to be a part of the shared leadership belief system in organizations reported to espouse Humane Orientation values.

The societal Humane Orientation cultural values scores were positively related ($p < .01$) to the Participative leadership dimension. Participative leadership is more likely to be a part of the shared leadership belief system in societies reported to espouse Humane Orientation values.

• *Humane-Oriented leadership.* Humane Orientation cultural practices and values scores were significantly related to the Humane-Oriented leadership dimension and explained a total of 27.6% of organizational and societal variance for this dimension. Of the total explained variance, approximately 70.9% was associated with forces operating at the organizational level of analysis. The remaining portion of the explained variance (29.1%) was associated with forces operating at the societal level of analysis.

The organizational Humane Orientation cultural practices scores were negatively related ($p < .01$) to the Humane-Oriented leadership dimension, but the organizational Humane Orientation cultural values scores were positively related ($p < .01$) to the Humane-Oriented leadership dimension. Humane-Oriented leadership is less likely to be a part of the shared leadership belief system in organizations reported to have Humane Orientation practices. This finding may suggest that if organizational practices are highly humane, the need for humane-oriented leadership is less. Finally, Humane-Oriented leadership is more likely to be in the shared leadership belief systems of organizations reported to espouse Humane Orientation values.

The societal Humane Orientation cultural practices scores were positively related ($p < .01$)

to the Humane-Oriented leadership dimension. Humane-Oriented leadership is more likely to be a part of the shared leadership belief systems in societies reported to have Humane Orientation practices.

• *Autonomous leadership.* Humane Orientation cultural practices and values scores were significantly related to the Autonomous leadership dimension and explained a total of 4.1% of the variance for this dimension. All of this explained variance was associated with forces operating at the organizational level of analysis.

The organizational Humane Orientation cultural practices scores were positively related ($p < .05$) to the Autonomous leadership dimension, but the organizational Humane Orientation cultural values scores were negatively related ($p < .01$) to the Autonomous leadership dimension. Autonomous leadership is more likely to be a part of a shared leadership belief system in organizations reported to have Humane Orientation practices, but is less likely to be part of the shared leadership belief system in organizations reported to espouse Humane Orientation values.

• *Self-Protective leadership.* Humane Orientation cultural values scores were significantly related to the Self-Protective leadership dimension and explained a total of 21.4% of the organizational and societal variance for this dimension. All of this explained variance was associated with forces operating at the societal level of analysis.

The societal Humane Orientation cultural values scores were negatively related ($p < .01$) to the Self-Protective leadership dimension. Self-Protective leadership is less likely to be a part of a shared leadership belief system in societies reported to espouse Humane Orientation values.

Interpretation

Overall, our analyses indicate that Humane Orientation affects culturally endorsed leadership attributes at multiple levels. If the joint effect of organizational and societal culture is considered, organizational values and practices had a stronger impact on the evaluations of leadership attributes compared with the impact of societal culture values and practices. Although to a lesser degree than organizational culture,

societal Humane Orientation had an impact on correlations for different leadership attributes. The higher the society's scores on Humane Orientation values, the higher the rating of Participative leadership as a desired attribute and the lower the rating of Self-Protective leadership. The more Humane Orientation is practiced in a society, the higher the likelihood of evaluating Humane-Oriented leadership as effective. Differences among organizations regarding how much Humane Orientation is valued and practiced relate significantly to all of the leadership dimensions except Self-Protective leadership. The more organizations value Humane Orientation and the less they practice it, the more likely it is that Humane-Oriented, Team-Oriented, Charismatic/Value-Based, and Participative leadership would be favored, and the less likely Autonomous leadership would be rated as effective by the members of that organization. With few exceptions, organizational Humane Orientation values are more strongly related to the perceived effectiveness of CLT dimensions in comparison to organizational practices or societal values or practices.

SUMMARY AND CONCLUSIONS

Conceptual foundations of the humane orientation construct are based on an interdisciplinary perspective. This perspective includes a combination of organization studies, psychology, economics, philosophy, history, anthropology, political science, and theology. Humane orientation is operationalized as the degree of concern, sensitivity, friendship, tolerance, and support that is extended to others at the societal, organizational, and leadership levels. Highly humane-oriented behaviors include care, nurturance, and help to others, whereas low humane orientation involves promoting self-interest and lack of consideration. Humane orientation of societies is closely related to the economic, physical, and psychological well-being of their members. Different societies, organizations, and leaders place varying emphasis on the breadth of support that is extended to others.

As revealed by the GLOBE study results, less Humane Orientation is observed in societies that are economically developed, modern, and urbanized. Furthermore, in societies in which physical conditions and climate create difficulties for well-being, there is higher Humane Orientation. Statistical analysis between GLOBE societal Humane Orientation scores and physical climate indicates that in countries where there are difficult climatic conditions, there is higher solidarity and help among the citizens. On the other hand, if preindustrial societies go through exceptionally stressful conditions, Humane Orientation decreases.

At the organizational level, Humane Orientation increases with advanced technology. Post-Taylorist and post-Fordist production systems grant more autonomy to workers and alleviate them from physical and psychological pressures of machine-paced production processes.

Societal culture influences the reported effectiveness of Humane-Oriented leader behaviors as found by GLOBE data analysis. Higher Humane Orientation practices at the societal level are associated with higher endorsement of Humane-Oriented leadership. In the more paternalistic societies leaders act as patrons, whereas in the nonpaternalistic cultures they serve as mentors and manifestations of Humane-Oriented leader behaviors.

Several connotations of the Humane Orientation dimension can be drawn for societies, organizations, and leaders. The major connotations for society are related to social norms, practices, and dominant motivation bases, family, and role of government. In highly humane-oriented societies, central norms and values are altruism, benevolence, kindness, love, and generosity that also have high priority as dominant motivating factors. Family, friends, and others in the close circle as well as strangers are important, and relations with these parties induce protection for the individuals in highly humane societies.

In paternalistic societies, people in authority are expected to provide social support by taking care of subordinates' and employees' problems. As far as family practices are concerned, in some strongly humane-oriented societies, parents closely control their children and expect them to be obedient and to participate in the labor force to help their families.

In addition, societies investigated by the GLOBE study demonstrated different levels of Humane Orientation based on geographic regions, where Southern Asia and Sub-Saharan Africa attained the highest, and Germanic Europe and Latin Europe the lowest, Humane Orientation practices scores, respectively.

For organizations, connotations and variations of societal Humane Orientation cover bureaucratic versus organic designs, employee relations, and relationships to stakeholders. In highly humane-oriented societies social control is based on shared values and norms, practices reflect individualized consideration, and informal relationships provide development opportunities to employees. On the other hand, in the less humane-oriented societies, social control is based on bureaucratic practices; formal relationships and standardized consideration such as formalized procedures are common. Furthermore, in the less humane-oriented societies, organizations are trusted less by their members, and mechanisms of control are established by legislation, unionization, and state interventions. In highly humane-oriented societies, organizations are relatively autonomous in their employee relations, and trade unions and the state have less influence on the business system.

Connotations of Humane Orientation for leaders indicate the presence of some themes that are common across countries. In the high humane-oriented societies, leaders are more consideration and maintenance oriented. Individualized consideration is reported more often in the highly humane-oriented cultures. As long as leaders are considerate and humane oriented, they are granted high influence and are allowed to exercise power and task orientation at work. The image of a leader in more humane-oriented societies is portrayed as giving priority to the pursuit of ideals. Thus, the life goal of "duty" on the part of leaders is important in high humane-oriented societies.

A statistical analysis of the GLOBE data shows that, in societies with high Humane Orientation scores, generosity and compassion are the attributes that contribute to leader effectiveness. Furthermore, perceived effectiveness of Humane-Oriented leadership differs with respect to regions of societies investigated by the GLOBE study. The clusters reporting Humane-Oriented leader behaviors to be most effective are Southern Asia and Sub-Saharan Africa; the least Humane-Oriented clusters are Latin Europe and Nordic Europe. In societies scoring high in Humane Orientation, leaders have a holistic concern for followers, and relations to subordinates are informal and personal. If the joint effect of organizational and societal culture is considered, societal values and practices had a weaker impact on the evaluations of leadership attributes compared with organizational culture. If the influence of societal culture is considered, the more a society values Humane Orientation, the higher the members of that society rate Participative leadership as a desired attribute and the lower they rate Self-Protective leadership. As Humane Orientation practices in a society increase, the likelihood of evaluating Humane-Oriented leadership as an effective attribute increases.

Humane Orientation values and practices in organizations relate significantly to all of the leadership dimensions. In general, the less organizations practice Humane Orientation and the more they value it, the more likely it is that Humane-Oriented, Team-Oriented, Charismatic/Value-Based, and Participative leadership are perceived as outstanding attributes, and the less likely Autonomous leadership is rated as outstanding by the members of that organization. This overall finding likely reflects dissatisfaction with the current state of affairs in organizations that do not use humane orientation practices as a way of organizational life.

Our study, on the basis of a through literature review of secondary data and the original GLOBE data, presents several generalizations about Humane Orientation at the societal, organizational, and leadership levels. First, Humane Orientation at the societal level seems to increase under more difficult economic, physical, and climatic conditions. Help and generosity among members of society become the necessary norms for life survival and well being. As a result of social solidarity, the human condition in the form of psychological and physical health improves in highly humane-oriented societies. Second, because the norms regarding solidarity and helping behavior are less endorsed in less humane-oriented societies, the state more often and more strongly intervenes to protect and give social support and security to its members. Third, in the less humane-oriented societies, the state intervenes

in the control of organizations by promoting legislation, unionization, and codetermination in employee relations and human resource practices. In the more humane-oriented societies, organizations are granted more trust and power and are more autonomous in their relations to employees and other institutions. Fourth, organizations reflect the culture (practices and values) in the society in which they are embedded. Humane societies foster humane organizations. Fifth, Humane-Orientation practices in a society influence perceived effectiveness of Humane-Oriented leader behaviors. The more societies practice humaneness, the more Humane-Oriented leader behaviors are perceived to be effective. Finally, leaders in the less humane-oriented cultures are more formal and impersonal in their relationships to their followers because the organizations in which they operate are more controlled by formalized policies, procedures, unionization, and legislation.

The Humane Orientation construct has implications for the new international scene. In response to trends in globalization and regionalism, companies operating in world markets need to understand the level of humane orientation that exists in various cultures. In practices of multinational corporations, strategic alliances, and joint ventures, the construct may influence negotiations, employee relations, human resource practices, and leader behaviors. Clusters of world markets based on humane orientation may reveal strategic guidelines for firms entering into different countries. Thus, Humane Orientation as a construct becomes a valuable analytical dimension for international business as well as for organization theories.

ENDNOTES

1. Our response bias correction procedure identified response bias in some countries for this scale. We recomputed the predicted response bias corrected scale score for each country. Response bias corrected scores are:

Practices: Morocco, 4.52 (no change in band); Qatar, 4.79 (moves from band B to band A); and Taiwan, 3.82 (no change in band).

Values: France, 5.91 (moves from band B to band A); New Zealand, 4.85 (moves from band E to band

D; furthermore, this move eliminates band E); and Nigeria, 5.71 (moves from band A to band B).

For a complete discussion of this procedure and all response bias corrected scores, see Appendix B.

2. As reported in Chapter 20 by Brodbeck, Hanges, Dickson, Gupta, and Dorfman, we found that all the cultural dimensions of organizational cultural values and practices significantly differed across societies. Although important, this prior analysis did not identify the particular aspect of societal differences that was related to organizational culture. In the present chapter, we found that societal and organizational Humane Orientation practices were significantly related (R^2 Total = 2.7%, R^2 Societal = 37.0%, $p < .01$). We also found a trend between societal and organizational Humane Orientation values (R^2 Total = 0.8%, R^2 Societal = 10.5%, $p < .10$). As discussed in Chapter 11 by Hanges, Dickson, and Sipe, the R^2 Total considers all levels of analysis (i.e., individual, organizational, and societal) whereas the R^2 Societal isolates the societal-level portion of the dependent variable and indicates the percentage of variance accounted for by the predictor at only this level. Although we have primarily taken the conservative approach and reported the R^2 Total in GLOBE, several scholars suggest that R^2 Societal provides a more accurate description of aggregated relationships. For further discussion, see the paper by Lance and James (1999).

3. Results between the single HLM and multiple HLM tests will likely differ somewhat. The differences between the results of the multiple HLMs and single HLMs are conceptually similar to the differences between a multiple regression analysis and a correlation coefficient. Table 21.10 in Chapter 21 by Dorfman et al. presents both single and multiple HLM coefficients. In addition, the relationships for all culture dimension values are summarized in Chapter 3 by Javidan and House.

REFERENCES

Adams, G. R., & Jones, R. M. (1983). Female adolescents' identity development: Age comparisons and perceived child-rearing experiences. *Developmental Psychology, 19,* 249–256.

Allardt, E. (1993). Having, loving, being: An alternative to the Swedish model of welfare research. In M. C. Nussbaum & A. Sen (Eds.), *The quality of life* (pp. 88–94). Oxford, UK: Clarendon.

Bass, B. M., Burger, P. C., Doktor, R., & Barrett, G. V. (1979). *Assessment of managers.* New York: Free Press.

Bigoness, W. J., & Blakely, G. L. (1996). A cross-national study of managerial values. *Journal of International Business Studies, 27*(4), 739–753.

Brewster, C. (1995). Towards a "European" model of human resource management. *Journal of International Business Studies, 26*(1), 1–23.

Briggs, A. (1961). The welfare state in historical perspective. *Archives Europeennes de Sociologie, 2,* 221–258.

Brouwer, I., & Wierda, E. (1998). The combination model: Child care and part time labour supply of men in the Dutch welfare state. In J. J. Schippers, J. J. Siegers, & J. de Jong-Gierveld (Eds.), *Child care and female labour supply in the Netherlands: Facts, analyses, policies.* Amsterdam: Thela Thesis.

Bulatao, R. A. (1979). *On the nature of the transition in the value of children* (Publication No. 60-A). Honolulu: East-West Center.

Cordes, C., & Dougherty, T. (1993). A review and an integration of research on job burnout. *Academy of Management Review, 18,* 621–656.

Darroch, R. K., Meyer, P. A., & Singarimbun, M. (1981). *Two are not enough: The value of children to Javanese and Sundanese parents* (Publication No. 60-D). Honolulu: East-West Center.

Deutsch, M. (1975). Equity, equality, and need: What determines which values will be used as the basis of distributive justice? *Journal of Social Issues, 31,* 137-149.

Donnelly, J. (1989). *Universal human rights in theory and practice.* Ithaca, NY: Cornell University Press.

Dorfman, P. W., Howell, J. P., Hibino, S., Lee, J. K., Tate, U., & Bautista, A. (1997). Leadership in Western and Asian countries: Commonalities and differences in effective leadership processes across cultures. *Leadership Quarterly, 8*(3), 233–274.

Dover, K. J. (1980). *Plato: Symposium.* New York: Cambridge University Press.

Elam, M., & Börjeson, M. (1991). Workplace reform and the stabilization of flexible production in Sweden. In B. Jessop, K. Nielsen, H. Kastendiek, & O. K. Pedersen (Eds.), *The politics of flexibility* (pp. 314-337). Cheltenham, UK: Edward Elgar.

Erikson, R. (1993). Descriptions of inequality: The Swedish approach to welfare research. In

M. C. Nussbaum & A. Sen (Eds.), *The quality of life* (pp. 67–83). Oxford, UK: Clarendon.

Esping-Andersen, G. (1985). *Politics against markets. The social democratic road to power.* Princeton, NJ: Princeton University Press.

Fawcett, J. T. (1983). Perceptions of the value of children: Satisfactions and costs. In R. A. Bulatao, R. D. Lee, P. E. Hollerbach, & J. Bongaarts (Eds.), *Determinants of fertility in developing countries* (Vol. 1, pp. 367-369). Washington DC: National Assembly Press.

Ferrari, G. R. F. (1987). *Listening to the cicadas: A study of Plato's Phaedrus.* New York: Cambridge University Press.

Fisher, B. M., & Edwards, J. E. (1988). Consideration, initiating structure and their relationships with leader effectiveness: A meta-analysis. In *Best paper proceedings* (pp. 201–205). Anaheim, CA: Academy of Management.

Fleishman, E. A. (1953). The description of supervisory behavior. *Personnel Psychology, 37,* 1–6.

Frederick, W. C. (1987). Corporate social responsibility and business ethics. In S. P. Sethi & C. M. Falbe (Eds.), *Business and society* (pp. 142–161). Lexington, MA: Lexington Books.

Friedman, G. (1974). *Industrial society: The emergence of the human problems of automation.* Toronto: Ayer.

Gebert, D., & Steinkamp, T. (1991). Leadership style and economic success in Nigeria and Taiwan. *Management International Review, 31,* 161–171.

Gerstner, C. R., & Day, D. V. (1994). Cross-cultural comparison of leadership prototypes. *Leadership Quarterly, 5*(2), 121–134.

Grootaert, C., & Kanbur, R. (1995). Child labor: An economic perspective. *International Labor Review, 134*(2), 187–203.

Güngör, S. (1997). *Effects of job stressors and social support on burnout in a Turkish sample.* Unpublished master's thesis, Bogaziçi University, Istanbul, Turkey.

Gupta, V., Surie, G., Javidan, M., & Chhokar, J. (2002). Southern Asia cluster: Where the old meets the new? *Journal of World Business, 37,* 16–27.

Halpin, A. W., & Winer, B. J. (1957). A factorial study of the leader behavior descriptions. In R. M. Stogdill & A. E. Coons (Eds.), *Leader behavior: Its description and measurement.* Columbus: Ohio State University, Bureau of Business Research.

Harbison, F., & Myers, C. A. (1959). *Management in the industrial world: An international study.* New York: McGraw-Hill.

Hardy, F. (Ed.). (1988). *The religions of Asia.* London: Routledge.

Hempill, J. K., & Coons, A. E. (1957). Development of the leader behavior description questionnaire. In R. M. Stogdill & A. E. Coons (Eds.), *Leader behavior: Its description and measurement.* Columbus: Ohio State University, Bureau of Business Research.

Hirsch, J. (1991). From the Fordist to the Post Fordist state. In B. Jessop H. Kastendiek, K. Nielsen, & O. K. Pedersen, (Eds.), *The politics of flexibility: Restructuring state and industry in Britain, Germany, and Scandinavia* (pp. 67–81). Cheltenham, UK: Edward Elgar.

Hoelter, J., & Harper, L. (1987). Structural and interpersonal family influences on adolescent self-conception. *Journal of Marriage and the Family, 49,* 129–137.

Hoffman, L. W. (1987). The value of children to parents and child rearing patterns. In C. Kagitçibasi (Ed.), *Growth and progress in cross-cultural psychology* (pp. 159-170. Lisse, The Netherlands: Swetz and Zeitlinger.

Hofstede, G. (1980). *Culture's consequences: International differences in work-related values.* Beverly Hills, CA: Sage.

Hofstede, G. (2001). *Culture's consequences: Comparing values, behaviors, institutions, and organizations across nations* (2nd ed.). Thousand Oaks, CA: Sage.

House, R. J., Hanges, P. J., Ruiz-Quintanilla, S. A., Dorfman, P. W., Javidan, M., Dickson, M. W., Gupta, V., et al. (1999). Cultural influences on leadership and organizations: Project GLOBE. In W. H. Mobley, M. J. Gessner, & V. Arnold (Eds.), *Advances in global leadership* (pp. 171–233). Stamford, CT: JAI.

House, R. J., Wright, N., & Aditya, R. N. (1997). Cross-cultural research on organizational leadership: A critical analysis and a proposed theory. In P. C. Earley & M. Erez (Eds.). *New perspectives on international/organizational psychology* (pp. 535–625). San Francisco: New Lexington Press.

International Labor Organization. (1992). *World labour report 1992.* Geneva: Author.

James, K., Chen, D. L., & Cropanzano, R. (1996). Culture and leadership among Taiwanese and

U.S. workers: Do values influence leadership ideals? In M. N. Ruderman, M. W. Hughes-James, & S. E. Jackson (Eds.), *Selected research on work team diversity* (pp. 33–52). Greensboro, NC: Center for Creative Leadership.

Jessop, B. (1991). The welfare state in the transition from Fordism to post-Fordism. In B. Jessop, H. Kastendiek, K. Nielsen, & O. K. Pedersen, (Eds.), *The politics of flexibility: Restructuring state and industry in Britain, Germany, and Scandinavia* (pp. 82–105). Cheltenham, UK: Edward Elgar.

Jürgens, U. (1991). Departures from Taylorism and Fordism: New forms of work in the automobile industry. In B. Jessop, K. Nielsen, H. Kastendiek, & O. K. Pedersen (Eds.), *The politics of flexibility: Restructuring state and industry in Britain, Germany, and Scandinavia* (pp. 233–247). Cheltenham, UK: Edward Elgar.

Kabasakal, H., & Bodur, M. (1998). *Leadership and culture in Turkey: A multifaceted phenomena.* Unpublished manuscript.

Kagitçibasi, C. (1982a). *The changing value of children in Turkey* (Publication No. 60-E). Honolulu: East-West Center.

Kagitçibasi, C. (1982b). Sex roles, value of children and fertility in Turkey. In Ç. Kagitçibasi (Ed.), *Sex roles, family and community in Turkey* (pp. 151-180). Bloomington: Indiana University Press.

Kagitçibasi, C. (1982c). Old-age security value of children and development. *Journal of Cross-Cultural Psychology, 13,* 29–42.

Kagitçibasi, C. (1996). *Insan, aile, kültür* [Person, family, culture]. Istanbul: Remzi Kitabevi.

Kaicheng, Y. (1998). Chinese employees' perceptions of distributive fairness. In A. M. Francesco & B. A. Gold (Eds.), *International organizational behavior* (pp. 302-313). Englewood Cliffs, NJ: Prentice Hall.

Kanungo, R. N., & Aycan, Z. (1997, June 11–14). *Organizational culture and human resource practices from a cross-cultural perspective.* Paper presented at the annual meeting of the Canadian Psychological Association, Toronto.

Katz, D., & Kahn, R. L. (1952). Some recent findings in human relations research. In E. Swanson, T. Newcomb, & E. Hartley (Eds.), *Readings in social psychology.* New York: Holt, Rinehart & Winston.

Katz, D., Maccoby, N., Gurin, G., & Floor, L. (1951). *Productivity, supervision, and morale among railroad workers.* Ann Arbor: University of Michigan, Survey Research Center.

Katz, D., Maccoby, N., & Morse, N. C. (1950). *Productivity, supervision, and morale in an office situation.* Ann Arbor: University of Michigan, Institute for Social Research.

Kerr, C., Dunlop, J. T., Harbison, F., & Myers, C. A. (1960). *Industrialism and industrial man.* Cambridge, MA: Harvard University Press.

Kiray, M. (1997). Abandonment of the land and transformation to urban life. In *Human development report: Turkey.* Ankara, Turkey: The United Nations Development Programme.

Korte, C. (1980). Urban-nonurban differences in social behavior and social psychological models of urban impact. *Journal of Social Issues, 36,* 29–51.

Lance, C. E., & James, L. R. (1999). A proportional variance accounted for index for some cross-level and person-situation research designs. *Organizational Research Methods, 2,* 395–418.

Leibenstein, H. (1987). *Inside the firm: The inefficiencies of hierarchy.* Cambridge, UK: Cambridge University Press.

Likert, R. (1961). *New patterns of management.* New York: McGraw-Hill.

Likert, R. (1967). *The human organization: Its management and value.* New York: McGraw-Hill.

Macpherson, C. B. (1966). *The real world of democracy.* New York: Oxford University Press.

Mao, Z. (1929). On correcting mistaken ideas in the party. *Selected works of Mao Zedong* (Vol. 1, 1st ed.). Beijing: Foreign Language Press.

Martin, A. (1984). The erosion of the Swedish model. In P. Gourevitch (Ed.), *Unions and economic crisis: Britain, West Germany and Sweden.* London: Allen and Unwin.

Maslach, C., & Jackson, S. E. (1984). Burnout in organizational settings. In S. Oskamp (Ed.), *Applied social psychology annual: Applications in organizational settings* (Vol. 5, pp. 133–153). Beverly Hills, CA: Sage.

Meindl, J. R., Yu, K. C., & Lu, J. (1987). Distributive justice in the workplace: Preliminary data on managerial preferences in the PRC. In J. B. Beak (Ed.), *Proceedings of the International Conference on Personnel and Human Resources Management,* Hong Kong.

Misumi, J., & Peterson, M. F. (1985). The performance-maintenance (PM) theory of leadership:

Review of a Japanese research program. *Administrative Science Quarterly, 30,* 198–223.

Ong, A. (1987). *Spirits of resistance and capitalist discipline.* New York: State University of New York Press.

Ortega, S., Corzine, J., Burnett, C., & Poyer, T. (1992). Modernization, age structure, and regional context: A cross-national study of crime. *Sociological Spectrum, 12,* 257–277.

Peterson, A., & Kellam, S. (1977). Measurement of the psychological well-being of adolescents: The psychometric properties and assessment procedures of how I feel. *Journal of Youth and Adolescence, 6,* 229–247.

Pieper, R. (Ed.). (1990). *Human resource management: An international comparison.* Berlin: Walter de Gruyter.

Price, A. W. (1989). *Love and friendship in Plato and Aristotle.* Oxford, UK: Clarendon.

Ronen, S. (1986). *Comparative and multinational management.* New York: John Wiley.

Russell, D. W., Altmaier, E., & Van Velzen, D. (1987). Job-related stress, social support, and burnout among classroom teachers. *Journal of Applied Psychology, 72,* 269–174.

Schneider, S. C., & Barsoux, J. L. (1997). *Managing across cultures.* London: Prentice Hall.

Schriesheim, C. A. (1982). The great high consideration-high initiating structure leadership myth: Evidence on its generalizability. *Journal of Social Psychology, 116,* 221–228.

Schwartz, S. H. (1992). Universals in the structure and content of values: Theoretical advances and empirical tests in 20 countries. In M. P. Zanna (Ed.), *Advances in experimental social psychology* (Vol. 25, pp. 1–65). Orlando, FL: Academic Press.

Schwartz, S. H., & Bilsky, W. (1987). Toward a universal psychological structure of human values. *Journal of Personality and Social Psychology, 53*(3), 550–562.

Schwartz, S. H., & Bilsky, W. (1990). Toward a theory of the universal content and structure of values: Extensions and cross-cultural replications. *Journal of Personality and Social Psychology, 58*(5), 878–891.

Scott, W. A., Scott, R., & McCabe, M. (1991). Family relationships and children's personality:

A cross-cultural, cross-source comparison. *British Journal of Social Psychology, 30,* 1–20.

Shalinsky, A., & Glascock, A. (1988). Killing infants and the aged in nonindustrial societies: Removing the liminal. *Social Science Journal, 25*(3), 277–287.

Smith, P. B., Misumi, J., Tayeb, M., Peterson, M., & Bond, M. (1989) On the generality of leadership style measures across cultures. *Journal of Occupational Psychology, 62,* 97–109.

Sparrow, P., & Hiltrop, J. M. (1994). *European human resource management in transition.* London: Prentice Hall International.

Triandis, H. C. (1995). *Individualism and collectivism.* Boulder, CO: Westview.

The United Nations and human rights 1945–1995. (1995). New York: United Nations Blue Book Series, Vol. 7.

United Nations Development Program. (1998). *Human development report 1998.* New York: Oxford University Press.

Widick, B. J. (Ed.). (1976). *Auto works and its discontents. Policy studies in employment and welfare* (Vol. 25). Baltimore, MD: Bks Demand UMI.

Wofford, J. C., & Liska, L. Z. (1993). Path-goal theories of leadership: A meta-analysis. *Journal of Management, 19*(4), 857–876.

Wolf, E. R. (1966). Kinship, friendship, and patron-client relations in complex societies. In M. Banton (Ed.), *The social anthropology of complex societies* (p. 1–22). New York: Frederick A. Praeger.

Wolf, S. (1994). Comment. In A. Gutman (Ed.), *Multiculturalism: Examining the politics of recognition* (pp. 75–103). Princeton, NJ: Princeton University Press.

Wong Siu-lun. (1986). Modernization and Chinese culture in Hong Kong. *China Quarterly, 106,* 306–325.

Yousif, Y., & Korte, C. (1995). Urbanization, culture, and helpfulness: Cross-cultural studies in England and the Sudan. *Journal of Cross-Cultural Psychology, 26*(5), 474–489.

Yukl, G. A. (2002). *Leadership in organizations* (5th ed.) Upper Saddle River, NJ: Prentice Hall.

19

Uncertainty Avoidance

Mary Sully de Luque

Mansour Javidan

The concept of uncertainty avoidance has been widely discussed in the natural and social science literature, and has been operationalized and interpreted in many related ways (Hofstede, 2001). Uncertainty avoidance involves the extent to which ambiguous situations are threatening to individuals, to which rules and order are preferred, and to which uncertainty is tolerated in a society. The notion of uncertainty avoidance has been examined extensively at the individual level, as well as in organizations and societal cultures. The GLOBE research is focused at the organization and societal levels, reported from a sample of middle manager survey respondents. In this chapter, we provide a brief introduction of the uncertainty avoidance construct and a review of the disciplinary research conducted over the past few decades. We then discuss the correlates of the construct at the individual, organizational, and societal levels of analysis. In the second part of the chapter, we describe results of the 62-society study of GLOBE'S Uncertainty

Avoidance cultural dimension construct. We provide rankings of societies on GLOBE's measures of Uncertainty Avoidance, discuss relationships of GLOBE's measures with other measures that exist in the literature, and describe several important societal correlates of GLOBE's measures. Finally, we discuss the relationship of GLOBE's measures of Uncertainty Avoidance with reports of effective leadership at different levels of analysis.

Uncertainty exists, of this we are certain. Moreover, it seems the closer scholars are to explaining uncertainty, the more it exists. The concept of uncertainty has been examined through the disciplines of philosophy, math, and physics, as well as many of the social sciences (Inlis, 2000). In quantum mechanics, the notion of uncertainty relations (e.g., Hansen, 1972) suggests that humans are held to the fundamental uncertainties of our universe. In the second law of thermodynamics, it is posited that as a system becomes more entropic, the system experiences simultaneous change (Rossini,

AUTHORS' NOTE: The authors are indebted to Robert House for his painstaking review and detailed comments on previous drafts of this chapter. The authors gratefully acknowledge the dedicated assistance provided by Narda Quigley, Danielle Rizk, Tom Spies, Melanie Morris, Jana Heard, Chris Morgan, Robin Broyles, Arul Rajendran, Chad Law, and James Louis at various times during the preparation of this chapter.

1950). Similarly, assessing the limits of logic, Godel's incompleteness theorem claims that a variety of statements about natural numbers, although true, may be not be provable and thus would be considered "undecidable" (Dawson, 1999). Ultimately, even Einstein found the deterministic laws of the universe to be cloaked in mystery (Clark, 1984).

Many scholars consider it a fundamental need to reduce uncertainty in our lives, to explain our world, and establish predictability (Berger & Calabrese, 1975). More recently, several scholars suggest that certainty or true predictability are illusions, perpetuated by misguided Western thought, which advocates the control of nature (Bradac, 2001). Influenced by Zen Buddhism, this stream of thought suggests that we live in an earthly impermanence and we show naïveté in trying to go beyond our reality. Whether the world is fundamentally predictable or essentially waiting to be predicted, however, the notion that uncertainty exists remains. Perhaps conceptualizing uncertainty and certainty on a continuum, instead of as an either–or proposition, is more useful (Clampitt & de Koch, 2002). On the continuum, there are degrees of uncertainty, and the degree to which people accept uncertainty depicts their tolerance level. The effects of organizational and societal influences on a broader cultural continuum are the focus of the research that follows.

CONCEPT OF UNCERTAINTY AVOIDANCE

As defined by GLOBE, Uncertainty Avoidance refers to the extent to which members of collectives seek orderliness, consistency, structure, formalized procedures, and laws to cover situations in their daily lives. Known by many labels, the study of uncertainty avoidance has been researched throughout many social science disciplines for decades. Originally used by Cyert and March (1963) as an organizational phenomenon, Hofstede's (1980) publication, *Culture's Consequences,* brought the term *uncertainty avoidance* to prominence in explaining the behavior of societies. Discussing the relationship between uncertainty avoidance and one of its many correlates, Hofstede (1980) states that the concept represents "a national syndrome

that relates to neuroticism, anxiety, stress, uncertainty avoidance, or whatever we want to call it, that differentiates among modern nations and affected IBM employees [his original sample] as much as anyone else" (p. 156). There may be distinctions among these various terms; however, the terms appear to be of the same class of concepts (Clampitt & de Koch, 2002). The focus of this section is on identifying commonalities and interrelationships between these concepts and uncertainty avoidance. We will discuss some of the early origins of the notion of uncertainty and its influence on the construct of uncertainty avoidance.

Uncertainty Avoidance at the Individual Level

Tolerance for Ambiguity

Humans cognitively possess some varying level of uncertainty avoidance. Frenkel-Brunswik (1949), in one of the earliest known citations of ambiguity tolerance, described a study that assessed respondents' attitudes regarding ethnic prejudice, in which ambiguity tolerance was noted as a personality variable related to social orientation. Research in ambiguity and uncertainty may have been hastened by psychologists' interest in the study of authoritarianism, which was prompted by the need to understand the origins of World War II (Adorno, Frenkel-Brunswick, Levinson, & Sanford, 1950). Defining the concept, Frenkel-Brunswik (1949) posited, "ambiguity tolerance generalizes to the entire emotional and cognitive functioning of the individual, characterizing cognitive style, belief and attitude systems, interpersonal and social functioning, and problem solving behavior" (Furnham & Ribchester, 1995, p. 180). According to one of the more noted researchers on the subject, being intolerant of ambiguity does not necessitate an increase of rules. More accurately, an increase in rules is a function of being intolerant of ambiguity (Budner, 1962).

As mentioned earlier, although not fully synonymous, intolerance of ambiguity (an individual cognitive state) and uncertainty avoidance (a behavioral phenomenon) are concepts that are likely to be positively related (Furnham & Ribchester, 1995). Determining ambiguity intolerance has been the focus of many researchers (Budner, 1962; Norton, 1975; Rydell & Rosen, 1966) as well as cognitive tests (Bochner, 1965; Kreitler, Maguen, & Kreitler, 1975).

Anxiety, Stress, and Neuroticism

The notion of anxiety and stress is a common theme in uncertainty and ambiguity research. In one compelling study, tolerance of ambiguity demonstrated a close association to anxieties (Furnham, 1994). Studies linking anxiety and stress at the psychological level have been prolific, with many connecting stress to personality dimensions of neurotic anxiety, extraversion, flexibility, and security (Kahn, Wolfe, Quinn, Snoek, & Rosenthal, 1964). Differences in the effects of uncertainty were reported from a psychological survey in five countries (Tannenbaum, Kavcic, Rosner, Vianello, & Wieser, 1974), including such effects as depression, resentment, and low self-esteem. In another study, the relationship of the individual-level personality test, the Eysenck Personality Questionnaire (Eysenck & Eysenck, 1975), was correlated with various medical-related indexes across 37 countries (Lynn & Martin, 1995). The researchers found the national-level norms differed along the three personality dimensions,[1] with an especially strong relationship noted between Hofstede's (2001, p. 156) uncertainty avoidance and *neuroticism versus emotional stability*. This supports analyses at the ecological level that have shown uncertainty avoidance to be strongly related with national neuroticism–anxiety and stress levels (Hofstede, 1980, 2001).

The recent focus on positive psychology (Seligman 1999; Seligman & Csikszentmihalyi, 2000; see also Aspinwall & Staudinger, 2003, and Snyder & Lopez, 2002) has elicited research on a wide variety of constructs in the social sciences. One such topic is the notion of subjective well-being (SWB), commonly defined as people's cognitive and affective assessment of their lives (Diener, 2000). Subjective well-being has been suggested as a societal-level manifestation (Arrindell et al., 1997; Hofstede, 1980, 2001; Schyns, 1998) related to uncertainty avoidance (Arrindell et al., 1997), neuroticism (Steel & Ones, 2002), and happiness (Diener, Diener, & Diener, 1995). Aggregated individual measures of uncertainty avoidance showed a significant relationship with subjective well-being (Arrindell et al., 1997), with low uncertainty avoidance related to high levels of subjective well-being. Further, Steel and Ones (2002) found that aggregated personality traits explain variance in subjective well-being, with neuroticism–stress accounting for substantial variance in national subjective well-being clearly above other factors such as national wealth.

Feedback Seeking

In organizational research, uncertainty is a notable issue and is an implicit reason for disseminating feedback (Kluger & DeNisi, 1996). Uncertainty is a pivotal catalyst in feedback-seeking behavior (Ashford & Cummings, 1983); if individuals experience uncertainty, they will be motivated to enact an information search (Ashford, 1986; Morrison, 2002). Individuals less tolerant of ambiguity have been shown to be more likely to seek feedback than those more tolerant of ambiguity (Bennett, Herold, & Ashford, 1990), especially in high uncertainty situations (Ashford & Cummings, 1985). Tolerance for ambiguity was shown to moderate feedback-seeking behaviors and uncertainty regarding an individual's role contingencies (Ashford & Cummings, 1985). Research shows that in order to manage uncertainty, individuals will engage in strategies for seeking feedback from a variety of sources (superiors, peers, subordinates), either through asking questions (inquiry) or observing (monitoring).

Over the past two decades research on feedback seeking behavior has focused on three motives (Ashford, Blatt, & VandeWalle, in press): instrumental motive for achieving goals (Brown, Ganesan, & Challagalla, 2001; Renn & Fedor, 2001), ego-based motive for ego protection, and image-based motive for protecting and enhancing one's image in the organization (Bailey, Chen, & Dou, 1997; Heine et al., 2001). These motives may be affected by the context in which feedback seeking takes place; in a context filled with uncertainty, the instrumental motive for seeking feedback may dominate (Ashford et al., in press). The situations that encourage the instrumental motive are exemplified by contextual uncertainty (Ashford & Cummings, 1985), change (Ashford, 1988), and novelty (Callister, Kramer, & Turban, 1999; Morrison, 1993; Wanberg & Kammeyer-Mueller, 2000). In uncertain situations, people seek feedback more frequently if feedback has particularly high instrumental value. This is especially true in situations such as new job or organization entry (Ashford, 1986; Ashford & Cummings, 1985; Brett, Feldman, & Weingart, 1990; Callister et al., 1999; Miller & Jablin, 1991; Morrison, 1993). Further, information seeking has been associated specifically with uncertainty avoidance across cultures (Earley, 1997; Sully de Luque & Sommer, 2000).

Communication

In communication, uncertainty has been a focus of study. The phenomenon of uncertainty has been associated with uncertainty reduction theory (Berger & Bradac, 1982; Berger & Calabrese, 1975), problematic integration theory (Babrow, 1992) and uncertainty management theory (Babrow, Hines, & Kasch, 2000; Ford, Babrow, & Stohl, 1996). Additionally, Festinger (1957) alludes to the concept of uncertainty in his work on cognitive dissonance. Uncertainty reduction has been found to be a common element in interpersonal relationships, and has been found to vary (Gudykunst, 1983; Gudykunst, Nishida, & Schmidt, 1989) across cultures (Hall, 1976; Nakane, 1974). Uncertainty has been described as a cognitive experience, with predictive uncertainty being related to the estimation of others' feelings, attitudes, and behaviors (Berger & Calabrese, 1975). Anxiety is the emotional equivalent of uncertainty, and it is derived from feeling worried, uncomfortable, or apprehensive (Gudykunst & Nishida, 2001). Avoidance is a behavioral effect of anxiety (Stephan & Stephan, 1985), and there is a reciprocal positive relationship suggested between these concepts (Demerath, 1993; Turner, 1988). Anxiety/uncertainty management theory proposes that communication effectiveness is influenced by individuals' capacity to manage uncertainty and anxiety (Gudykunst, 1988, 1995), and Hofstede (2001) recognizes its relationship with uncertainty avoidance.

Levels of analysis issues become particularly salient when examining a construct studied so thoroughly at the individual level (Judge & Bono, 2001), such as the research on individual-level uncertainty avoidance differences across cultures (Basabe et al., 2002; Gudykunst & Nishida, 2001). Urging the use of subjective well-being (SWB) as a national-level index, Diener (2000) states that great progress has been made in deciphering the components, the underpinnings, and the cultural influences of SWB. Methodological refinements are now used in the study of individual-level constructs such as SWB, which allow its use as a national indicator. Steel and Ones (2002) convincingly argue that aggregated data in applied psychology research commonly show that constructs of personality can have robust relationships, with stronger correlations found at the national level than at the individual level. A similar argument has been advanced for mood and emotion contagion in work teams (Kelly & Barsade, 2001). The effects may be greater at the group level than at the individual level.

Uncertainty Avoidance as an Organizational Phenomenon

Cyert and March (1963, p. 116) originally coined the term *uncertainty avoidance,* to refer to an organizational phenomenon, one of the four major relational concepts in their behavioral theory of the firm. Addressing Gordon's (1948) observation of a wide discrepancy between organizations' reaction to uncertainty and theoretical predictions in economic theory, Cyert and March (1963) posited that organizations adopt procedures that minimize the need for predicting uncertain events in the future (pp. 13, 102).

Uncertainty avoidance may occur within various levels of the organization. To illustrate, Beatty and Gordon (1988) have used the term uncertainty avoidance to describe a human barrier to the successful implementation of Computer Aided Design/Computer Aided Manufacturing (CAD/CAM) systems in manufacturing firms. In this context, uncertainty avoidance refers to an individual phenomenon at various levels in the organization. At senior levels of management in the organization, especially where technical expertise on proposed implementation of new projects is lacking, there may be a reluctance to take on new projects with uncertain outcomes. At the same time, in the middle management levels, uncertainties relating to the mastery of new tools and ways of doing work (on which managers may be evaluated) constitutes a barrier to new projects such as CAD/CAM.

Feedback

Short-term feedback is one proactive method that organizations use to avoid the uncertainty associated with outcomes (Ilgen, Fisher, & Taylor, 1979; Kluger & DeNisi, 1996). Acceptance and enforcement of standardized decision rules also serve the same purpose. Internal biases in organizations (such as sales departments' estimates of sales) serve to increase pressure on the firm to develop decision heuristics, or "rules of thumb." Organizational rules are suggested as a way of maintaining a stable environment given that the behavior of organizational members may be unpredictable (Perrow, 1972).

Short-term reactions to short-term feedback, in Cyert and March's behavioral theory of the firm, help to explain how organizations avoid the problem of correctly predicting future events. For instance, production decisions are usually dictated by daily and weekly feedback from inventory and sales departments rather than by long-term sales forecasts. In a similar vein, in the behavioral theory of the firm (Cyert & March, 1963), the strategy of negotiated environments helps to eliminate uncertainties. This is in contrast to the classical models of oligopoly in which firms make predictions about the behavior of the environment, such as competition, consumer behavior, and supplier dynamics. Control over the environment is a more proactive way of dealing with uncertainty than is prediction of the environment. The establishment of customary practices in an industry acts as a control on competitive behavior. Examples of such practices include product pricing, codes of ethics, and budgeting. Product pricing on the basis of industry-established conventions ensures predictability and stabilization of consumer demand. Fair business practice codes in an industry regulate the behavior of organizations in competing with one another and

in their relationships with the market. Internal budgeting and planning procedures (in contrast to sales plans and forecasts) act as contracts within the organization among the various departments so that the uncertainty of the immediate environment of a division of the organization can be controlled (McNally, 1980).

Planning

The relationship between planning and organizational success, especially in small business development, has been related to uncertainty management (Nakata & Sivakumar, 1996). The literature on small firm success assumes that to reduce uncertainty, planning is a central factor (Ryans, 1997), although the support for this has been equivocal. Although some studies have shown no relationship between planning and success (Lumpkin, Shrader, & Hills, 1998), others have shown that thorough planning, in the initial stages of creating a small-scale business, is associated with organizational success (Ackelsberg & Arlow, 1985; Bracket, Keats, & Pearson, 1988).

Planning is thought to control uncertainty within the organization, yet the connection between planning and return on investment can be tenuous. In a study assessing formal planning in small business environments, relationships were revealed between formal planning and the growth rate of sales, although no relationships were found on return on equity or return on assets (Lyle, Baird, Orns, & Kuratko, 1995). Although the focus and findings of this research have been multifaceted, a primary issue in internal planning is the management of uncertainty.

Innovation

The uncertainty created by the introduction of innovative activities has been the implicit focus of research in organizations. In conventional organizations, innovation is frequently difficult to develop because employees usually want to hold to established procedures on which past organizational legitimacy has been based (Dimaggio & Powell, 1983). Indeed, employees often rely on the traditional hierarchical organization if they are presented with information that challenges their norms and beliefs (Williamson,

1975), even if this approach is inefficient in a changing environment (Venkataraman, Shane, McGrath, & MacMillan, 1993). Innovation tends to introduce unanticipated changes for the employees and cause uncertainty that may lead to resistance to innovation (Shane, Venkataraman, & MacMillan, 1995; Van de Ven, 1986).

The GLOBE research has furthered insight into the topic of uncertainty avoidance. Specifically, GLOBE developed scales to evaluate uncertainty avoidance at the organizational level of analysis, using organizational referents in its measures. In addition, GLOBE research specifically examined the association between organizational and societal uncertainty avoidance, extending the understanding of the multilevel complexity of the construct.

Uncertainty Avoidance as a Dimension of National Culture

Initially interpreting the concept of uncertainty avoidance as explaining organizational occurrences, Hofstede (1980)[2] used it to describe how people in societies accept uncertainty in everyday life. Through this reconceptualization, uncertainty avoidance shifted from being viewed as a behavioral organization-level variable in Cyert and March's (1963) theory to being thought of as a societal value orientation.

People in societies create coping mechanisms to handle the anxiety produced by excessive uncertainty (Hofstede, 2001). All individuals are affected by anxiety in different ways, depending on their psychological, physical, spiritual and philosophical dispositions. Hofstede (2001) notes that the primary mechanisms through which societies cope with uncertainty are technology, law, and religion. He convincingly presents the roles of the three mechanisms by stating, "Technology has helped us to defend ourselves against uncertainties caused by nature; law, to defend against uncertainties in the behavior of others; religion, to accept the uncertainties we cannot defend ourselves against" (Hofstede, 2001, p. 146). The simplicity of these mechanisms is translated into a complexity of practices in societies and organizations.

In societies, uncertainty-reducing technologies may take the form of a service such as product warranties, insurance policies or investment markets and plans. Technologies developed to handle uncertainty may include medical devices, security systems, and even military armament or capital goods industries, such as machinery and transport equipment. Laws are enacted in societies to cope with uncertainty by providing both informal and formal rules to guide behavior. The legal system in a society sets forth guidelines for managing the consequences when laws are not followed. Uncertainties that exist outside technological and legal resolutions are often coped with through religion, often in the form of rites and rituals. Hofstede (2001) argues rituals serve the function of allowing societal members to carry on with their lives while confronting intolerable levels of anxiety. Often revealing a philosophical understanding of the nature of existence, religion imparts a sense of acceptance of uncertainties.

Technology, rules, policies, and rituals are all means used by organizations to deal with uncertainty. Organizations confront uncertainty in their environments, through the behavior of both employees and stakeholders, as well as the external agencies with which the organizations interact (Hofstede, 2001). Rules and regulations serve to bring about more predictable behavior. Hofstede (2001) notes that there are both good and bad rules: Good rules lead to desired outcomes and concur with peoples' values; bad rules are formed when there are value differences between those who generate the rules and those who follow them. Organizational rituals include events such as business meetings, which have both acceptable and proscribed behaviors, as well as management training programs, which are often initiation rites for potential organizational leaders. Many additional uncertainty-avoiding rituals may be observed in organizations, Hofstede (2001) notes, including "the writing and filing of memos and reports, accounting, planning and control systems, computer simulations, and the nomination of experts as persons who are beyond uncertainty" (p. 148). At the national cultural level, Hofstede (2001) suggests that traditionalism and ethnocentrism, intolerance of differing opinions, inflexibility and dogmatism, tendencies toward racism, and prejudice are associated with the norm for intolerance for ambiguity, which he measures through the uncertainty avoidance index (p. 146).

Tight and Loose Cultures

Closely related to uncertainty avoidance are the concepts of *tight* and *loose cultures,* as originally suggested by Pelto (1968). This construct encompasses such things as rules and norms that exist in and are enforced by a society (Witkin & Berry, 1975). Tight cultures are characterized by many rules supervising actions, and individuals are expected to conform to standard practices (Triandis, 1989). Deviation from rules is discouraged, whereas durability, permanence, and solidarity-norms are encouraged. In such societies, there are significant formal information systems incorporated into organizational structures (Earley, 1997). In societies characterized as having a loose culture, a wide range of alternative channels exist through which norms are relayed. Organization formality is less developed and values such as stability, solidarity, and duration are not accentuated (Earley, 1997). The tight-loose culture nomenclature may be another way of expressing fundamental differences across cultures in uncertainty avoidance, as the terms seem very closely related.

Time-orientation

Cyert and March's (1963) and Hofstede's (1980) concepts of uncertainty avoidance have different implications for time orientation in organizational and societal behavior, respectively. At the organizational level, high levels of uncertainty avoidance would lead to a greater focus on short-term performance. The national culture dimension of uncertainty avoidance, in contrast, is associated with long-term orientation in organizational practices (Zhao, 2000). In traditionally high uncertainty avoidance societies, the focus is on long-term rather than short-run results in organizations. These results may take time to develop and are often fostered through the nurturing of relationships.

Summary

The origins of uncertainty avoidance, or its many related terms, cross many levels of analysis. Addressing levels of analysis in cross-cultural research, scholars suggest that with a multilevel perspective each cultural dimension may be discernible through indicators at the societal, organizational, group, and individual levels (Lytle, Brett, Barsness, Tinsley, & Janssens, 1995). These levels are considered to be interrelated, interacting through such structures as organizations, norms, beliefs, and institutions (Kim, Triandis, Kagitçibasi, Choi, & Yoon, 1994). Discussing uncertainty avoidance, Hofstede (2001) notes that the concept is associated with a wide scope of psychological characteristics generally related to shared cultural logic, but not always obvious at the individual level (p. 159). Much research assessing uncertainty avoidance has been conducted at various levels and then extrapolated to other levels, committing both an ecological fallacy (Robinson, 1950; Thorndike, 1939) and reductionism (Le Vine, 1973; Walsh, 1995). As a consequence, there are many misnomers resulting from research extrapolated to levels of analysis other than from the level at which data are gathered, but undeniably the concept of uncertainty has implications at all levels of analysis. Focusing on societal contexts, Hofstede (1994) argues that he is interested in how personalities develop within different countries, not the comparison of different personalities. Throughout his book on organizational- and societal-level culture,[3] Hofstede (2001) used aggregated individual-level sample examples to illustrate his arguments, having proposed that some aspects of cultural values may be effectively examined at various levels of analysis. Ultimately, in cross-cultural research the use of individual-level analysis, organizational-level analysis, or culture-level analysis depends on the research question that is being asked (Smith & Schwartz, 1997).

CORRELATES OF UNCERTAINTY AVOIDANCE

Operationalizing Uncertainty Avoidance

The preceding arguments provide a depiction of uncertainty avoidance as originally introduced by social science researchers, as formulated by Cyert and March (1963) and as reclassified by Hofstede (1980). The societal uncertainty avoidance norm as conceptualized and operationalized by Hofstede is developed from survey items originally proposed to measure organization-level or individual-level constructs (Hofstede, 1980, 2001). As a composite of three items, the uncertainty avoidance scale showed great variability across countries. From this, the index for uncertainty avoidance (UAI) was calculated through responses to these three items (Hofstede, 1980, 2001), labeled as *stress, rule orientation,* and *employment stability,* respectively. Stemming from the conceptual link of mean level of anxiety in a country, Hofstede accounted for the correlation among these three scores. According to Hofstede, high scores on the UAI represent higher levels of uncertainty avoidance.

The first question in the UAI scale asked respondents to rate their agreement with the statement that rules should never be broken, even if it is in the best interests of the company to do so. Higher rule orientation (agreement with the statement) aggregated at the societal level raised the UAI. The second item asked respondents to estimate the amount of time they planned to stay in the employment of their company. The longer they planned to stay, the higher their desire for employment stability, and the higher their presumed uncertainty avoidance. The percentage of respondents planning to spend more than 5 years in their present company contributed directly to the societal UAI. The third item asked respondents to indicate how often they felt nervous or tense at work. The higher this frequency was reported at the societal level, the higher the UAI. Revisiting the construct two decades later, Hofstede (2001, p. 148) distinguished uncertainty avoidance from risk avoidance.

Some features of Hofstede's UAI measure are noteworthy. The item in his measure that targeted employment longevity may be a function of not only the respondent's desire for employment stability, but also of the amount of time already spent in the company and forecasts of employment stability. Thus, a person who has spent 10 years in the company at the time of survey who answers that she plans to move on within the next couple of years would serve to lower the UAI; another employee who has been in the company for less than a year who responds that he plans to continue in the company for another 10 years would raise the UAI. Yet, according to Hofstede, they are both operationally in the same category with regard to

their tolerance for uncertainty. The UAI may also possibly reflect labor market opportunities or collective orientation of the society (see Chapter 16 by Gelfand, Bhawuk, Nishii, & Bechtold).

Even with the employment stability question limitations, it is possible for two countries to obtain the same UAI scores through very different profiles. Rule orientation, for instance, may be preferred for reasons other than coping with uncertainty. In a country whose dominant religion ensures a philosophical approach to managing uncertainty, respondents may have very low stress levels even though they are rule oriented. Again, in certain societies a mean higher rate of national or occupational employment security and longer average tenure on jobs is likely to be associated with making individuals feel fairly secure and, consequently, less stressed in their jobs, although this state of affairs is by no means indicative of how they would react if their jobs were not secure. These profiles are compensatory so that, ultimately, their UAI scores will be similar.

The relationship between anxiety and rule orientation was proposed initially by Van Gunsteren (1976). Through this, it is suggested that when anxiety levels are high, people experience more stress. Through the formulation of rules and structure, stress and anxiety are often managed, enhancing the sense of security. Hofstede (2001) notes that the research suggesting that anxiety is a construct with societal-level implications has been rigorous and compelling, as outlined earlier in this chapter. In assessing societal shifts in stress levels, Hofstede (2001) states that shifts toward higher stress have occurred in both high and low UAI cultures (p. 182). However, these significant worldwide shifts did not occur for either high or low UAI cultures on the other questions (rule orientation and employment stability). Thus Hofstede (2001) acknowledges that using the UAI composite measure as an index for longitudinal culture change is not advisable. This admission, together with importance of the "stress" component shift and the remarkable association between stress–anxiety measures and UAI, creates the impression that UAI may be a more likely measure of stress than an overarching measure of uncertainty avoidance.

In spite of explicit acknowledgment of the constraints under which the uncertainty avoidance items came to constitute UAI (Hofstede, 1984, 2001), scholars have made few attempts to probe deeper into the construct as a cultural dimension until the GLOBE study and the subsequent revision of the UAI measure in the values survey module (VSM 94; Hofstede, 2001, p. 186).[4] However, several scholars have noted the limitations of the UAI in measuring societal culture (for further discussion, see Fernandez, Carlson, Stepina, & Nicholson, 1997; Hansen, 2001; Tayeb, 1994). Arguing in favor of the contribution that an ethnographic approach can make to the clarification of constructs in cross-cultural organizational research, d'Iribarne (1997) highlights two major limitations in Hofstede's measures: the issue of neutrality of items and the question of interpretation. Neutrality refers to the fact that two cultures may have the same level of the attribute—in this case the UAI score—but may manifest different ways of coping with uncertainty within the framework of their cultures. The question of interpretation is a concern voiced by many cross-cultural researchers. For instance, d'Iribarne (1997) explains how the French take the letter of the rule less seriously than do Americans. This would lead to differences in responses to the item in Hofstede's survey that deals with rule breaking (rule orientation). As a result, France ranks high in Hofstede's UAI, whereas the United States ranks low, in contrast to what d'Iribarne finds in the two cultures. The French presumably express strong agreement with the statement that rules should not be broken— except that the qualifiers to the statement are taken for granted. Americans, on the other hand, are more likely not to assume qualifying conditions unless explicitly stated in the item.

More recently, Hofstede (2001) does allow for estimating reliability estimates for his Uncertainty Avoidance scale. He then justifies the validity of the construct by the strong correlations he finds with other measures, interpreting these in ways consistent with the construct definition. Many correlations can be interpreted in two or more ways by using culturally specific manifestations as examples. In the GLOBE study, we argue that constructs first need to be of good quality, supported by rigorous methodology. As a result of rigorous, theory-driven research, we may have more assurance of the

validity of the measures. The fact that Hofstede suggests that the employment stability question may be unique to his sample is an example of this. Recognizing the limitations of his measures, Hofstede (1984, 2001) acknowledges the restricted scope of his uncertainty avoidance measure: the choice of items for UAI was restricted to the items available in archived data, from surveys used for a different purpose. Thus, the authors here suggest the items have questionable face validity. Further, findings related to UAI may reflect the competitive hypothesis that UAI is more a measure of stress than it is of Uncertainty Avoidance values or practices.

As evidenced by the confluence of literature from a variety of disciplines, uncertainty has an influence in societies. In Project GLOBE, Uncertainty Avoidance was defined in terms of a tendency toward orderliness and consistency, structured lifestyles, clear specification of social expectations, and rules and laws to regulate uncertain situations. In addition, built into the GLOBE design was a validation study based on an independent unobtrusive measure of societal-level practices, and independently collected data reported by Inglehart (1997) to measure societal-level values (see Chapter 9 by Gupta, Sully de Luque, & House).

Uncertainty Avoidance Correlates in Large-Scale Studies and Meta-Analysis of Hofstede

The impact of the Hofstede (1980) study on the concept of uncertainty avoidance is substantial and the contribution is notable. Business textbooks often include a discussion of the dimensions of culture put forth in his seminal work. Hofstede (2001) notes that in 140 further studies comparing from 5 to 39 countries, one or more of the four (later five) dimensions were found to be correlated with his original rankings.

Assessing the replications and applications of the Hofstede study, Søndergaard (1994) conducted an analysis of published and unpublished work spanning the years 1980–1993. He found four distinctive means through which Hofstede's work was being applied: citations, reviews, empirical replications, and as a paradigm.[5] At the time of his analysis, 61 replications had been conducted.[6] Among studies that found full confirmation with all of Hofstede's (1980) dimensions (Hoppe, 1990; Punnett & Withaney, 1988; Shackleton & Ali, 1990), the Hoppe study was the first broad-based attempt to replicate the Hofstede results. This study of 19 countries[7], using an elite sample from the Salzburg Seminar Alumni Study (SSAS), revealed a high degree of agreement between the UAI scores of the SSAS respondents and the scores of Hofstede UAI respondents ($r = .64$, $p < .01$; rho $= .63$, $p < .01$).[8] However, this comparison of the two studies also revealed that Hoppe's power distance index (PDI) was more strongly related to the Hofstede UAI than to the Hofstede PDI ($r = .71$, $p < .01$; rho $= .81$, $p < .001$). It is important to note that Hofstede's PDI and UAI were highly correlated ($r = .78$, $p < .001$; rho $= .75$, $p < .001$), while Hoppe's PDI and UAI were also highly related ($r = .65$, $p < .01$; rho $= .81$, $p < .001$). As a consequence of this multicollinearity, comparison of UAI and PDI is problematic. Speculating on these results, Hofstede (2001) notes that the higher educational level of the Salzburg alumni "implied less rule orientation and less employment stability" (p. 154), which led to discrepant findings. Indeed, the Hoppe (1990) study played an important role in Hofstede's second version of his value survey module (VSM 94).

Helmreich and Merritt (1998) conducted a large-scale study of commercial airline pilots that included the original three UAI questions used by Hofstede (1980). During the years 1993 and 1997, the researchers surveyed 15,000 commercial airline pilots across 23 companies from 36 countries. They reported a significant relationship between the commercial airlines pilot respondents and the Hofstede (1980) respondents from IBM ($r = .49$, $p < .05$; rho $= .47$, $p < .05$). Interestingly, the airline pilots' PDI scores also correlated with the IBM UAI scores ($r = .46$, $p < .05$; rho $= .50$, $p < .05$). Whereas the IBM respondents shared a mutual employer but came from different professions, the commercial airline pilots had a common profession but not a common employer. Hofstede (2001) notes that the three uncertainty avoidance questions carried different implications for the pilot respondents, who shared the same profession, than they did for the IBM respondents, who had a common employer.

The Søndergaard (1994) review included several studies reflecting partial replications of

country rankings of the Hofstede dimensions (Ashkanini, 1984; Chew & Putti, 1993; Chow, Shields, & Chan, 1991; Dunphy & Shi, 1986; Fidalgo, 1993; Forss, 1989; Huo & Randall, 1991; Maldonado, 1983; Pooyam, 1984; Punnett & Whitaney, 1988; Westwood & Everett, 1987; Yeh, 1988). Although many studies confirmed Hofstede's rankings, confirmation was not found for uncertainty avoidance in several other attempted replications (Fidalgo, 1993; Pooyan, 1984; Punnett & Withaney, 1988). Often, political and environmental factors were cited as reasons for these discrepancies. Of the scores of studies conducted based on the Hofstede findings, Lowe (1996) was one of few researchers to use a population of respondents similar to the respondents in the Hofstede study. Interestingly, Lowe (1996) found similar ranking of all of the dimensions *except* for uncertainty avoidance.

The most frequent use of the Hofstede (1980) dimensions is as a paradigm for describing country differences (Søndergaard, 1994). In other words, the original four Hofstede dimensions are used to categorize and rationalize (often in a speculative way) the influence of culture on the dependent variable of interest to the researchers. Decades after the original Hofstede study, these dimensions are quite often used as paradigmatic reference points for research across disciplines. Many scholars have cautioned researchers about taking these dimensions, and the countries' placement on these dimensions, as taken-for-granted assumptions (Baskerville, 2003; Tayeb, 1994).

Correlates of Uncertainty Avoidance and Individual-Level Phenomena

In a study examining country-level medical statistics, Lynn and Hampson (1975) found the notion of neuroticism–anxiety as the primary factor (explaining 57% of the variance) of a factor analysis conducted for 18 developed countries (p. 125). Collected in 1960, their data show a strong correlation of neuroticism–anxiety factor scores with Hofstede's UAI and related stress scores (rho $= 73$, $p < .01$), and this relationship was quite compelling for the neuroticism–anxiety construct. Hofstede's UAI also rank-correlated at .71 ($p < .05$) with Millendorfer's stress rankings across 12 countries (Millendorfer, 1976). In a later study assessing national normative scores on the EPQ personality inventory, the personality dimension "neuroticism versus emotional stability" was correlated significantly (rho = .44, $p < .05$) with Hofstede's UAI across the 25 countries common for each sample (Lynne & Martin, 1995). As such, greater tendency to avoid uncertainty, as measured by the Hofstede UAI scale, appears strongly related to higher levels of neuroticism and stress. Supporting this, Arrindell and colleagues (1997) found that uncertainty avoidance is more predictive of happiness (inverse of stress–neuroticism) than wealth ($t = -1.38$, $p < .10$, one-tailed).

Hofstede examined McClelland's (1961) article, which used data obtained in 1925, to assess need for achievement (nAch), need for affiliation (nAff), and need for power (nP). He found across 22 countries a strong negative correlation between uncertainty avoidance and nAch (rho $= -.64$, $p < .01$), suggesting that societies low in tolerance for uncertainty tended to be less achievement oriented. This relationship is consistent with the idea that willingness to take risks may be a prerequisite to extraordinary levels of achievement. Thus, willingness to take risks may also be negatively related to one's level of anxiety.

In another study, a survey of consumption patterns and attitudes was conducted measuring younger and older generations (*Reader's Digest*, 1970). Hofstede (1980, p. 128) found a strong negative correlation (rho $= -.77, p < .01$) across 15 countries between favorable attitudes toward the younger generation and the UAI. Consistent with this result, Hofstede also found that ages of leaders in 11 European countries correlated strongly with the UAI (rho = .75, $p < .05$) (de Bettignies & Evans, 1977).

Hofstede also examined Least Preferred Coworkers (LPC) (Fiedler, 1967) scores of managers from 16 countries attending a course at International Management Development Institute in Switzerland IMEDE. He found a correlation of $-.44$ ($p < .10$) between LPC and UAI, consistent with the notion that high LPC scores could be a reflection of greater tolerance for uncertainty. Analyzing data from another study of managers in 19 countries (Haire, Ghiselli, & Porter, 1966), he found that in countries characterized by high uncertainty avoidance there exists a stronger preference for group decisions and consultative management (interpreted as reducing risk for the individual decision maker) and a tendency toward McGregor's (1960) theory X, involving less optimism about people's capabilities and ambitions.

Assessing the effect of uncertainty and anxiety on perceived effectiveness of communication across relationships and cultures, stranger and close-friend relationships have been specifically examined in the U.S. and Japan[9] (Gudykunst & Nishida, 2001) at the individual level.[10] The results show a moderate connection between anxiety and uncertainty with perceived communication effectiveness, across both close-friend and stranger relationships. For perceived communication effectiveness in the United States, anxiety had a substantially greater effect than uncertainty (reverse scored) ($r = -.59$, $p < .001$) for stranger interaction, whereas uncertainty had a greater effect than anxiety ($r = .73, p < .001$) for close-friend interaction. In Japan, anxiety had a greater effect than uncertainty on perceived communication effectiveness in both stranger ($r = .54, p < .001$) and friend ($r = .56, p < .001$) interactions.

Among the characteristics of uncertainty avoiding societies in Hofstede's analysis are higher anxiety levels in the population, higher job stress, more resistance to change, higher average age in higher-level jobs, fear of failure, less risk taking, lower ambition for individual advancement, preference for clear requirements and instructions, strong values against breaking rules, lower tolerance for ambiguity in perceiving others, and lower readiness to compromise (for details see Hofstede, 1984, pp. 132–133). All of these associations between the UAI countries' scores, with the exception of higher average age in higher-level jobs, are consistent with higher levels of stress. Given that one of Hofstede's items concerned level of stress, these findings are consistent with the notion that the UAI index may be a more specific measure of stress rather than a general measure of uncertainty avoidance. This competitive hypothesis remains to be tested.

Correlates of Uncertainty Avoidance and Organizational-Level Phenomena

The uncertainty avoidance norm has been examined conceptually and empirically in relation to several behavioral and economic variables. In new product development, for example, Nakata and Sivakumar (1996) conceptually examined the relationship between national culture and new product development. According to the authors, low levels of uncertainty avoidance will be conducive to new product development, especially in the initiation phase, through higher risk taking and minimal planning or controls. On the other hand, high levels of uncertainty avoidance will not be conducive to new product development but will favor the implementation stage through risk aversion and tight controls.

In view of the differences of society scores on this dimension over the course of time, it is informative to reexamine the data in these studies in relation to the GLOBE rankings, as is done later in this chapter. However, other theoretical and empirical studies with interesting implications for further theoretical development are described below.

Trust. In uncertainty avoidant societies, the desire to establish rules allows predictability of behavior (Kale & McIntyre, 1991; Singh, 1990), which, in turn, has implications for trust in both the organization and society. Following this, it has been theoretically posited that people in low uncertainty avoidant societies, having less regard for stability and permanence in relationships, would be less willing to trust other people and institutions than those from high uncertainty avoidance societies (Doney, Cannon, & Mullen, 1998). On the other hand, high uncertainty avoidance societies such as China may be less trusting due to strong in-group collectivism, which results in a lack of trust outside the family and in-group (Fukuyama, 1995). Societies exhibiting low trust may give a higher level of importance to interpersonal trust (Fukuyama, 1995; Reeder, 1987), thus avoiding uncertainty. A study assessing difference between Chinese and American salespeople and supervisor trust found that process control was related to supervisee trust in China but not in the United States. This strengthens the assumption that in higher uncertainty avoidance societies, such as China, process control is perceived as more nurturing and supportive among salespeople than in lower uncertainty avoidant societies, such as the United States (Atuahene-Gima & Li, 2002).

Participation. Studying national differences in the way managers in organizations interpreted worker participation, Stohl (1993) observed an interesting, though nonsignificant, correlation ($r = .49, p > 0.10$) between the societal scores on interpretation of the term and the Hofstede rankings of these countries on uncertainty avoidance. The insignificant p value is likely due to the small sample ($n = 5$). Stohl observed that in countries with relatively high UAI scores, such as France, managers tended to focus more on formal or structural interpretations of the term worker participation. In contrast, in countries with relatively low UAI scores, such as Denmark, the emphasis was on informal and interpersonal aspects: They stressed informal actions and believed that participation is not something to be mandated, but to be allowed to evolve out of the daily interactions between managers and workers.

Organization Roles. In organizations, uncertainties arising from a variety of sources can serve to cause stress at work. Peterson, Smith, and colleagues (1995) examined three such sources of stress (role ambiguity, role conflict, and role overload) in 21 countries. Although none were statistically significant, these researchers found correlations of $-.25$, $-.20$ and $-.34$ between Hofstede's UAI and role ambiguity, conflict, and overload, respectively. Again, the small sample size may explain the lack of significant relationships.

Work Commitment. Hypothesizing that countries high in uncertainty avoidance would exhibit higher work commitment scores (because Hofstede believed that people in these countries prefer to stay with a single employer for longer periods and tend to be more loyal to their employers), Randall (1993) reviewed the cross-cultural literature on work commitment. Contrary to expectations, she observed that countries scoring low on Hofstede's (1980) UAI had relatively high work commitment scores. In this case, most of the studies in her review came from 1987 or later, so the two measures in her correlation are spaced more than a decade apart.

Selection Practices. Use of low-risk recruiting practices such as employee referrals, internal recruitment, or internships and apprenticeships may be considered credible low-risk practices preferred in high uncertainty avoidance cultures (Jeanquart-Barone & Peluchette, 1999). Thus, choice of selection techniques such as assessment centers' structured interviews that are designed to reduce uncertainty (Dessler, 1993) may be favored in societies high on uncertainty avoidance. In a study comparing U.S. and German firms, Jeanquart-Barone and Peluchette (1999) found that German firms reported a greater use of internal recruiting than did U.S. firms for blue-collar ($t = 1.77, p < .05$) and white-collar ($t = 2.46, p < .01$) employees. For both blue- and white-collar employees, German firms were also more likely than U.S. firms to hire their apprentices and interns ($t = 2.32, p < .05$). At the white-collar level, German firms used internships and apprenticeships significantly more than did United States firms ($t = 2.54, p < .01$), and German firms were found to invest a higher percentage of their total budget on training than did firms in the United States ($t = 2.36, p < .01$). Finally, the authors reported that for white-collar recruitment, the German firms used more structured interviews ($X_2 = 11.57, p < .001$) and assessment centers ($X_2 = 3.86, p < .05$) than did U.S. firms.

Ryan, McFarland, Baron, and Page (1999) examined the influence of national culture on personnel selection practices using responses from 959 organizations, mostly from developed countries. The authors found evidence for an association between the societal norm of uncertainty avoidance and a number of organizational selection practices. The selection practices concerned number of verification methods used, frequency of verification, and number of interviews. For the cultural dimension scores, they adopted the indices reported by Hofstede (1984; cited in Ryan et al., 1999, p. 365). Hofstede's UAI correlated negatively with the number of verification methods used ($r = .72, p < .01$) as well as with extent of verification (frequency; $r = -.61, p < .01$), and positively with the number of interviews ($r = .57, p < .05$). They found significant corresponding correlations of $-.80, -.71$, and $.37$ ($N = 959$) with number of verification methods used, frequency of verification, and number of interviews, respectively.

These results suggest that the less the tolerance for uncertainty, the lower the number of verification methods used, and the fewer the extent of verification. They also suggest that reported uncertainty avoidance cultures tend to rely on interpersonal methods of investigation rather than on formal methods.

Accounting Practices. Studies in the field of accounting have revealed that accounting systems differ among the various parts of the world. Gray (1988) has offered a theoretical model of cultural influences on accounting practices. From a review of the literature, Gray (1988) identified four value dimensions in accounting: professionalism versus statutory control, uniformity versus flexibility, conservatism versus optimism, and secrecy versus transparency. From this theoretical platform, Gray advanced four propositions involving Hofstede's dimensions of national culture. With regard to uncertainty avoidance, Gray proposed that societies high in this dimension will have greater preference for statutory controls as opposed to individual professionalism, have greater uniformity in procedures across companies, be more conservative in their measurement of accounting and finance variables, and have more stringent confidentiality and disclosure policies.

Gray's (1988) theoretical postulations were operationalized and tested by Salter and Niswander (1995). They collected data from 29 countries, involving all major stock markets and comprising more than 84% of the 1989 global domestic product and more than 97% of the 1990 stock market capitalization. Their sample contained a variety of cultures in terms of language, geographical location, colonial antecedents, and economic development. A total of nine dependent variables representing Gray's accounting value dimensions were developed for their ordinary least squares regression analyses.

Consistent with Gray's (1988) first proposition, the investigators found that uncertainty avoidance (as measured by Hofstede's UAI) was significantly negatively related to both practice and structure of subdivisions of professionalism. On the other hand, uncertainty avoiding countries tend to have more prescriptive legal and statutory requirements regarding accounting procedures.[11] With regard to the second proposition, one of the measures assessing uniformity of procedures, that is "the extent to which a country's legal system is code-law based" (legal uniformity), was significantly positively related to Hofstede's UAI. The other measure of uniformity, assessing the actual extent to which uniformity is achieved in practice (effective uniformity), revealed a significant negative relationship to Hofstede's UAI. The first measure of uniformity was also significantly negatively related to Hofstede's masculinity scale and the second was significantly positively related. In reconciling these results, the researchers argue that the second uniformity measure is vulnerable to the comprehensiveness of rules dictating the legal accounting procedures, a characteristic of many societies high in uncertainty avoidance. Therefore, in situations where no rules exist, decisions are left to the individual accountant, giving the impression of flexibility when in fact it is simply a failure of the high masculinity system. Thus, the negative relationship must be seen as ambiguous rather than unequivocally valid.

With respect to the third proposition of Gray (1988), Salter and Niswander (1995) had two measures of conservatism. The first measure, assessing the "aggressive conservatism designed to reduce income whenever possible," failed to reveal any significant relationship. The second (labeled pessimism), addressing a generally conservative approach, revealed a significant positive relationship to the UAI, suggesting that more uncertainty avoidance societies tend to be more conservative. Finally, the fourth proposition was supported by both of their measures of secrecy—informative annual reports and extent of disclosure of accounting practices (both reverse coded)—with a relatively strong relationship.

In an interesting extension of Gray's (1988) theory, Salter and Niswander (1994) posited the influence of two economic, as opposed to cultural, factors: The state of development of a nation's capital markets and the country's marginal tax rate. They hypothesized that the more developed a country's capital market, the higher would be the extent of professionalism and effective uniformity, and the lower would be the

degree of legal uniformity, pessimism (one of their measures of conservatism), and secrecy. Higher marginal tax rates would achieve the opposite effect on professionalism, legal uniformity, conservatism, and secrecy. They found support for the hypothesized relationships between market capitalization and professionalism, legal uniformity, conservatism, and secrecy. With regard to marginal tax rates, they found support for the hypothesized relationships to professionalism and conservatism. These results, which extend the original hypotheses, highlight the influences of factors other than cultural in the accounting value dimensions theorized by Gray (1988). Overall, Gray's hypothesized association between accounting values and the uncertainty avoidance construct of culture are supported, with the exception of one measure of uniformity.

Following up on Salter and Niswander's (1995) study, Zarzeski (1996) modeled the influence of several organizational variables (sales, debt ratio, and size of the firm) followed by Hofstede's measures of uncertainty avoidance, individualism, masculinity, and power distance on accounting disclosure practices, using data from published sources in seven industrialized countries. In a regression model that accounted for 48% of the variance in disclosure, Hofstede's UAI yielded a negative beta coefficient of $-.18$, ($p < .001$), coming in fourth after debt ratio, firm size, and individualism. This negative relationship between uncertainty avoidance and disclosure lends further support for Gray's hypothesis regarding secrecy.

One must remember, however, that accounting firms, like other firms, also have global operations. Soeters and Schreuder (1988) found significant differences based on cultural characteristics between three Dutch accounting firms and three international Big Eight accounting firms operating in the Netherlands. These differences were particularly noticeable in uncertainty avoidance. The authors, however, are careful to point out that these differences are probably due to a process of self-selection rather than socialization of employees resulting in any internalization of other societal cultural values by the Dutch. Whatever the case, the implication is that data collection from accounting firms should be sensitized to potential biases in international accounting practices.

To conclude this section, several issues should be noted. As operationalized by Hofstede, uncertainty avoidance across countries was uncorrelated across occupations. However, among the individual items comprising the societal dimension, mean levels of the uncertainty avoidance index across occupations were correlated with the educational levels of occupations, with higher-educated occupations tending to show fewer uncertainty avoidance practices (Hofstede, 1984, p. 121). Stress levels were related primarily to hierarchical levels across occupations, with managers showing more stress than nonmanagers. Employment stability was positively related to age, negatively related to educational level, and negatively related to the proportion of women in the occupation. Because many of these relationships were unrelated to uncertainty avoidance at the occupational level, Hofstede rejected the idea of creating an occupational uncertainty avoidance index from these items and reserved them for country-level analyses. Unfortunately, as with his other scales, Hofstede did not provide any information concerning the internal consistency of the items or the interrater agreement of the respondents within each country.

Correlates of Uncertainty Avoidance and Societal-Level Phenomena

Innovation. New products invention is fundamentally an outcome of individual and group effort (Kanter, 1982, 1988). An environment conducive to innovation, however, may be a contingency of organizational and national culture (Shapero & Sokol, 1982). As such, tolerance of uncertainty in a society may create an environment more encouraging of innovation in research and development. Theorizing that uncertainty-avoiding societies will be less innovative than societies more tolerant of uncertainty, Shane (1993) examined the relationship between Hofstede's national culture dimensions and rates of innovation. For the years 1975 and 1980,[12] innovation rates were assessed through per capita numbers of trademarks approved, controlling for differences in trademark regulations at the national level.[13] Shane (1993) found that Hofstede's uncertainty avoidance index (UAI) was predictive of number

of trademarks granted in worldwide markets for the years 1975 and 1980. These results corroborate the argument that societies more tolerant of uncertainty, measured by Hofstede's UAI, report higher rates of innovation than societies less tolerant of uncertainty.[14]

Examining product innovation, Nakata and Sivakumar (1996) argue that mechanisms beneficial for developing new products depend on the *stage* of new product development. High uncertainty avoidance societies, with their reliance on structures and tendency toward strong planning, may be helpful for the implementation stage. However in lower uncertainty avoidance societies, risk taking (which is important for idea generation) and nonstandardized procedures (which make greater use of problem solving) may be more beneficial at the initiation stage (Nakata & Sivakumar, 1996).

Perception of Risk. Given the increasing globalization of commerce, an important area for scrutiny that has emerged in cross-cultural research is negotiation. Perceptions and valuations of various dimensions of negotiation are especially germane to the study of societal culture. For instance, Yates and colleagues (1989) observed differences among cultures on the calibration of probability judgments of future uncertainty events, concluding that these constitute a definite source of problems in international negotiation.

Bontempo, Bottom, and Weber (1997) examined cross-cultural differences in the perception of risk. Specifically, they hypothesized that the valuation of losses and gains will be differentially influenced by cultural norms of uncertainty avoidance. In a different study, Weber and Hsee (1998) found that Chinese respondents engage in more risky choices than do Americans or other Western respondents. Research on risk preference (e.g., Weber & Milliman, 1997) has shown that people may choose a riskier option either because they have a positive attitude toward risk or, as happens more frequently, because they perceive the chosen option to be less risky. This fact complicates the interpretation of risk-choice behavior. However, Bontempo and colleagues (1997) administered monetary lottery options to undergraduate samples at large universities in the United States, the Netherlands, Hong Kong, and Taiwan. Their findings are interesting: Whereas positive outcomes dampened perceptions of risk to a greater degree among the two Western samples than it did for Taiwan (Hong Kong being intermediate), negative outcomes were more complex in their effects. The Western samples were more influenced by the probability of a loss; Hong Kong and Taiwan, on the other hand, were influenced more by the magnitude of the loss. Bontempo and colleagues (1997) found that the direction and interpretation of the cultural differences in their results were consistent with Hofstede's UAI.

Innovation Championing Strategies. Whereas uncertainty avoidance can be theoretically associated with the societal level variable of innovation per se, the championing of innovation is an organization-level variable that may also be theoretically linked with national culture. Shane (1994) investigated the association between national culture, using Hofstede's measures, and national preference for innovation-championing strategies. Shane conducted a study of 24 national offices with a financial services company, surveying 937 managers engaged in accounting and consulting, to assess this phenomenon.

The study of champions in the promotion of innovations in organizations has gained momentum since the sixties (Schon, 1963). Broadly, champions are defined as people who go beyond formally assigned roles in organizations to promote a product or venture (Chakrabarti, 1974; Shane, 1994). Of six innovation-championing strategies addressed by Shane (1994), persuasion and autonomy are relevant to the present discussion. Through the strategy of persuasion, the champion rationally presents the value of innovation through quantitative approaches. Thus, the champion convinces managers of the need for change through such notions as cost–benefit analysis, budgets, presentation models, and financial projections (Howell & Higgins, 1991). Societies with higher levels of uncertainty avoidance are thought to prefer champions who acquire backing for new ideas through formal mechanisms such as plans and forecasts.

Through the strategy of autonomy, the champion "protects" the innovator from the constraining rules, policy, systems, and any other form of interference by the organization. These champions have been found to manage this through two methods. In one approach, the champion creates a greater level of autonomy for the innovator, who is then free to develop and suggest creative solutions (Burgelman, 1983; Howell & Higgins, 1990; Schon, 1963). In another approach, the autonomy champion encourages the innovator to create ideas that work well within the strategy and culture of the organization. The champion develops an environment compatible with the innovator's norms, procedure, and rules.

Shane (1994) found that uncertainty avoidance was significantly related to a proclivity for champions who go against rules, procedures, and norms of the organization (rho $=-$ .35, $p < .05$).[15] This implies that in higher uncertainty-avoiding societies, the preferred champion strategies are those that operate within the procedures, rules, and norms of the organization. In similar research, Shane and colleagues (1995) examined the influence of national culture on innovation championing strategy preferences. This study of 1,228 individuals in 30 countries who were members of four organizations[16] found that Hofstede's UAI scales were significantly negatively related to autonomy from organizational norms and procedures when controlling for demographic difference ($t = 3.96, p < .001$), organizational differences ($t = 3.23, p < .001$), and economic differences ($t =- 3.28, p < .001$). Shane and colleagues (1995) state that "the more uncertainty accepting a society is, the more people in it prefer champions to overcome organizational inertia to innovation by violating organizational norms, rules and procedures" (p. 945). In societies reporting high UAI scores, employees in organizations preferred innovation champions who followed budgetary processes, justifying their decision on the basis of financial rationale.

This is not to say that innovators in high uncertainty avoidance cultures would not achieve as much as in low uncertainty avoidance cultures. As Hofstede (1984) points out, there is some evidence (e.g., Inkson, Schwitter, Pheysey, & Hickson, 1970; Kohn, 1971) that working with the structure of rules and procedures within a culture can actually promote

Table 19.1   Higher Uncertainty Avoidance Societies Versus Lower Uncertainty Avoidance Societies

Societies That Score Higher on Uncertainty Avoidance Tend to:	*Societies That Score Lower on Uncertainty Avoidance Tend to:*
• Have a tendency toward formalizing their interactions with others	• Have a tendency to be more informal in their interactions with others
• Document agreements in legal contracts	• Rely on the word of others they trust rather than contractual arrangements
• Be orderly, keeping meticulous records, documenting conclusions drawn in meetings	• Be less concerned with orderliness and the maintenance of records, often do not document the conclusions drawn in meetings
• Rely on formalized policies and procedures, establishing and following rules, verifying communications in writing	• Rely on informal interactions and informal norms rather than formalized policies, procedures and rules
• Take more moderate calculated risks	• Be less calculating when taking risks
• Inhibit new product development but facilitate the implementation stage through risk aversion and tight controls	• Facilitate the new product development especially in the initiation phase, through higher risk taking and minimal planning or controls
• Show stronger resistance to change	• Show less resistance to change
• Show stronger desire to establish rules allowing predictability of behavior	• Show less desire to establish rules to dictate behavior
• Show less tolerance for breaking rules	• Show more tolerance for breaking rules

innovation. It is possible that people in more formalized organizations can be more intellectually flexible than their counterparts in less formalized ones.

Summary

In this overview of the literature on uncertainty avoidance, we have discussed the construct from three perspectives: (a) as individual phenomena, (b) as organizational-level phenomena, and (c) as societal-level phenomena. On the basis of the above analysis, Table 19.1 provides a summary comparison in terms of "typical" strong versus weak uncertainty avoidance orientation. This table is neither inclusive nor exhaustive of uncertainty avoidance attributes. It should be noted that cultures do not exactly fit into these categories; however, to delineate better the concept of uncertainty avoidance we present extreme stereotype cases in Table 19.1. This table is intended to be used as a guide,

showing cultural attributes that tend to cluster together; thus societies may be expected to have a mixture of the extreme attributes presented.

GLOBE RESEARCH ON UNCERTAINTY AVOIDANCE

As stated in the scale development chapter by Hanges and Dickson (Chapter 8) and above in this chapter, Uncertainty Avoidance was measured separately at the societal and organizational levels in the GLOBE study. Further, both practices and values were assessed at each level; thus, there were four different scales to measure Uncertainty Avoidance. From an initial pool of items, four basic items were used to measure current practices at both societal and organizational levels, with appropriate modifications in wording for the corresponding organization-level items. The item composition

Table 19.2   Uncertainty Avoidance: Society Practices (As Is)

1. In this society, orderliness and consistency are stressed, even at the expense of experimentation and innovation. (reverse scored)

Strongly agree			Neither agree nor disagree			Strongly disagree
1	2	3	4	5	6	7

2. In this society, societal requirements and instructions are spelled out in detail so citizens know what they are expected to do. (reverse scored)

Strongly agree			Neither agree nor disagree			Strongly disagree
1	2	3	4	5	6	7

Table 19.3   Uncertainty Avoidance: Society Values (Should Be)

1. I believe that orderliness and consistency *should be* stressed, even at the expense of experimentation and innovation. (reverse scored)

Strongly agree			Neither agree nor disagree			Strongly disagree
1	2	3	4	5	6	7

2. I believe that societal requirements and instructions *should be* spelled out in detail so citizens know what they are expected to do.

Strongly agree			Neither agree nor disagree			Strongly disagree
1	2	3	4	5	6	7

was determined in each case by the psychometric analyses reported in Chapter 8.

Four items measured current GLOBE-defined Uncertainty Avoidance practices at the societal level. Two sample items are shown in Table 19.2. The questions address the extent to which life is structured, predictable, orderly, and consistent, and rules and regulations to regulate societal practices are emphasized. Table 19.4 shows sample questionnaire items designed to measure existing organizational practices with regard to Uncertainty Avoidance. Three of the items in this scale are isomorphic; the corresponding societal scale may be seen in Table 19.3. Tables 19.4 and 19.5 show the items that are isomorphic with those in the practices scales for societal and organizational Uncertainty Avoidance, respectively, with regard to values. The items were coded so that strong agreement with the statements resulted in a high Uncertainty Avoidance scale of scores. Details of scale validation are provided in Chapter 8.

The manifestation of Uncertainty Avoidance in values systems, as well as in current practices, underlies the rationale for two separate measures of this construct in the GLOBE project. In the following sections, the findings from the GLOBE study are presented and set against the backdrop of other empirical evidence from cross-cultural research. Uncertainty Avoidance is examined as an aspect of practices and values at both societal and organizational levels and the implications of this cultural dimension for organizational leadership are explored.

Table 19.4   Uncertainty Avoidance: Organization Practices (As Is)

---

1. In this organization, orderliness and consistency are stressed, even at the expense of experimentation and innovation. (reverse scored)

Strongly agree			Neither agree nor disagree			Strongly disagree
1	2	3	4	5	6	7

2. In this organization, job requirements and instructions are spelled out in detail so employees know what they are expected to do. (reverse scored)

Strongly agree			Neither agree nor disagree			Strongly disagree
1	2	3	4	5	6	7

Table 19.5   Uncertainty Avoidance: Organization Values (Should Be)

---

1. In this organization, orderliness and consistency *should be* stressed, even at the expense of experimentation and innovation. (reverse scored)

Strongly agree			Neither agree nor disagree			Strongly disagree
1	2	3	4	5	6	7

2. In this organization, job requirements and instructions *should be* spelled out in detail so employees know what they are expected to do. (reverse scored)

Strongly agree			Neither agree nor disagree			Strongly disagree
1	2	3	4	5	6	7

Overall Scores on Uncertainty Avoidance

Table 19.6 shows the grand means of GLOBE societal practices and societal values scales for Uncertainty Avoidance across all GLOBE societies. The average of societal Uncertainty Avoidance practices across 61 countries is 4.16, and the range is 2.88 to 5.37. The mean value falls near the midpoint of 4.0 on a scale of 1 to 7. The average of societal Uncertainty Avoidance values, across 61 countries, is slightly higher at 4.62, with a range of 3.16 to 5.16.

Unobtrusive measures of the GLOBE scales Uncertainty Avoidance were gleaned from a separate content analysis and were compared to the GLOBE Uncertainty Avoidance societal practices measure. The unobtrusive index of Uncertainty Avoidance correlates .60 ($p < .01$) with the GLOBE Uncertainty Avoidance practices scale (see Chapter 9 by Gupta, Sully de Luque, and House). Through the use of independent measures to validate the GLOBE societal-level scales for Uncertainty Avoidance, we strengthened the argument that the GLOBE measures are meaningful indicators of the constructs they were expected to measure.

Country Rankings

The GLOBE ordering of the scores of individual societies on Uncertainty Avoidance ratings is shown in Tables 19.7. Table 19.7 shows practices (As Is) scores with societies rank-ordered from highest to lowest in the GLOBE Uncertainty Avoidance cultural dimension.[17]

Table 19.6   Grand Mean for GLOBE Societal Uncertainty Avoidance

Variable	Mean	Standard Deviation	Minimum	Maximum	Valid N
Uncertainty Avoidance practices	4.16	0.60	2.88	5.37	61
Uncertainty Avoidance values	4.62	0.61	3.16	5.61	61

N = 61 cultures.

The scores ranged from 2.88 (Russia) to 5.37 (Switzerland). Also shown are country groupings, ranked similarly in descending order of scale values. Society groupings were carried out using two statistical procedures: Scheffe's post hoc test, and the standard error of difference banding procedure (see Chapter 8, by Hanges & Dickson). The two results were very similar; the grouping shown here represents the somewhat clearer results from the second procedure. The groups' ranks imply that countries shown within a band were not meaningfully different in their scale mean scores, but were significantly different from countries of a different band. Table 19.8 gives societal values (Should Be) scores, with societies rank-ordered from highest to lowest in the GLOBE Uncertainty Avoidance cultural dimension.[18] The scores range from 3.16 (Switzerland) to 5.61 (Thailand).

The Correlation Between Overall Practices and Values Scores

The Pearson correlation between GLOBE societal Uncertainty Avoidance practices and GLOBE societal Uncertainty Avoidance values was negative ($r = -.62$, $p < .01$) across the 61 GLOBE cultures used in the analysis. The grand mean for societal practices was 4.16, whereas for societal values it was 4.62, suggesting that the societies reflect Uncertainty Avoidance more in their values than in their practices (difference statistically significant $t(60) = 3.30$, $p < .01$). These findings suggest that cultures reported in the GLOBE survey as having strong Uncertainty Avoidance values have weaker Uncertainty Avoidance practices, with only a few exceptions. In contrast, the cultures reporting

Uncertainty Avoidance only modestly in their values tend to exhibit this cultural characteristic rather strongly in their practices. There is an exception to this that is notable. GLOBE respondents from China reported highest band on both values and practices of Uncertainty Avoidance, as reported in Tables 19.7 and 19.8.

An examination of Table 19.7 shows that most of the countries with high reported uncertainty avoidance practices are technologically developed and those with low reported practices are technologically developing countries. Table 19.8 shows that the opposite is true with regard to values.

Technology seems to be the underlying element of distinction between the two groups. All things considered, it appears that the difference between the practices and values scores is a reflection of the current national level of uncertainty caused by unresolved issues. For developing nations, the positive difference would imply that members of these societies perceive themselves as being on the road to, but not quite accomplished in, reducing the uncertainties in their lives. As they acquire more sophisticated technologies, over the long term, this difference between their practices and values scores may grow smaller. For most of the developed nations, however, the negative difference would imply that members of these societies see excessive structure in their environment, leading perhaps to boredom and a resulting desire to have *less* structure in their lives. In the workplace, we may see this in the use of such things as flextime. Employees in Germany and Switzerland have embraced flextime (see Hofstede, 2001, p. 168). The respondents in the GLOBE surveys from both of these countries ranked very low in Uncertainty Avoidance

Table 19.7   Uncertainty Avoidance: Society Practices (As Is)*

Band							
A		B		C		D	
Country	Score	Country	Score	Country	Score	Country	Score
Switzerland	5.37	Netherlands	4.70	Japan	4.07	Venezuela	3.44
Sweden	5.32	England	4.65	Egypt	4.06	Greece	3.39
Singapore	5.31	South Africa[d]	4.59	Israel	4.01	Bolivia	3.35
Denmark	5.22	Canada[e]	4.58	Qatar	3.99	Guatemala	3.30
Germany[a]	5.22	Albania	4.57	Spain	3.97	Hungary	3.12
Austria	5.16	France	4.43	Thailand	3.93	Russia	2.88
Germany[b]	5.16	Australia	4.39	Portugal	3.91		
Finland	5.02	Taiwan	4.34	Philippines	3.89		
Switzerland[c]	4.98	Hong Kong	4.32	Costa Rica	3.82		
China	4.94	Ireland	4.30	Italy	3.79		
Malaysia	4.78	Nigeria	4.29	Slovenia	3.78		
New Zealand	4.75	Kuwait	4.21	Ecuador	3.68		
		Namibia	4.20	Iran	3.67		
		Mexico	4.18	Kazakhstan	3.66		
		Indonesia	4.17	Morocco	3.65		
		Zimbabwe	4.15	Argntina	3.65		
		India	4.15	Turkey	3.63		
		U.S.	4.15	Poland	3.62		
		Zambia	4.10	El Salvador	3.62		
		South Africa[f]	4.09	Brazil	3.60		
				Colombia	3.57		
				South Korea	3.55		
				Georgia	3.50		

a Germany (West): Former FRG
b Germany (East): Former GDR
c Switzerland (French-speaking)
d South Africa (Black sample)
e Canada (English-speaking)
f South Africa (White sample)

* Higher scores indicate greater uncertainty avoidance.
Our response bias correction procedure identified response bias in some countries for this scale (see endnotes).

values, indicating their desire for more flexible schedules. In the leisure market, we see the emergence of sporting activities that test the limits of human endurance, abilities, and skills, serving to enhance the uncertainty of outcomes for individuals within industrialized societies.

Overall Scores and Industry Scores

Each culture in the GLOBE study sampled up to three industries: Financial services, food processing, and telecommunications. Table 19.9 shows the correlations among industries on both societal values and practices scores across cultures.

As can be seen from the table, there is much correspondence among industries in the reported societal Uncertainty Avoidance scores for both the current practices and values dimensions.

Correlation With Other GLOBE Society Culture Dimensions

In this section we review the relationships between managerial responses to the GLOBE societal-level Uncertainty Avoidance practices scale and responses to other scales. The correlations of societal Uncertainty Avoidance practices

Table 19.8   Uncertainty Avoidance: Society Values (Should Be)*

Band									
A		*B*		*C*		*D*		*E*	
Country	*Score*	*Country*	*Score*	*Country*	*Score*	*Country*	*Score*	*Country*	*Score*
Thailand	5.61	Slovenia	4.99	Kazakhstan	4.42	Switzerland[d]	3.83	Netherlands	3.24
Nigeria	5.60	Brazil	4.99	Israel	4.38	Denmark	3.82	Switzerland	3.16
Albania	5.37	Colombia	4.98	Japan	4.33	Canada[e]	3.75		
Iran	5.36	Malaysia	4.88	France	4.26	Austria	3.66		
Egypt	5.36	Guatemala	4.88	Singapore	4.22	Sweden	3.60		
El Salvador	5.32	Qatar	4.82	England	4.11	Germany[f]	3.32		
Morocco	5.32	South Africa[a]	4.79	New Zealand	4.10				
Taiwan	5.31	Kuwait	4.77	Ireland	4.02				
China	5.28	Spain	4.76	U.S.	4.00				
Venezuela	5.26	Zimbabwe	4.73	Australia	3.98				
Mexico	5.26	India	4.73	Germany[c]	3.94				
Georgia	5.24	Poland	4.71	Finland	3.85				
Indonesia	5.23	Bolivia	4.70						
Ecuador	5.16	Turkey	4.67						
Philippines	5.14	Zambia	4.67						
Namibia	5.13	South Korea	4.67						
Greece	5.09	South Africa[b]	4.67						
Russia	5.07	Hungary	4.66						
		Argentina	4.66						
		Hong Kong	4.63						
		Costa Rica	4.58						
		Italy	4.47						
		Portugal	4.43						

a South Africa (Black sample)
b South Africa (White sample)
c Germany (East): Former GDR
d Switzerland (French-speaking)
e Canada (English-speaking)
f Germany (West): Former FRG

* Higher scores indicate greater uncertainty avoidance.
Our response bias correction procedure identified response bias in some countries for this scale (see endnotes).

and values scores with the other eight dimensions of culture assessed in the GLOBE program are presented in Table 19.10.

Uncertainty Avoidance
Practices and Other GLOBE Dimensions

Respondents to the GLOBE questionnaire show that Uncertainty Avoidance practices are positively correlated with the practices of Future Orientation, Institutional Collectivism, and Performance Orientation; these same practices are negatively correlated with Power Distance and In-Group Collectivism. These relationships suggest that, in societies scoring high on

GLOBE Uncertainty Avoidance practices, uncertainties are reduced through institutional collectives; however, with less reliance on in-group collective practices. This tendency toward collective institution interests helps manage technology and information, as well as skills and knowledge. The managing of uncertainty and risk creates an outlook that promotes long-term thinking. This in turn allows societies to focus on performance, with less of an inclination for societal power differential status. In addition, Uncertainty Avoidance practices scores are inversely correlated with values scores for Future Orientation and both Institutional and In-Group Collectivism. Many

Table 19.9   Correlation Between Industries on Uncertainty Avoidance Societal Values and Practices Scores Across Cultures

Uncertainty Avoidance	Food	Telecommunications
Values		
Finance	.84**	.90**
	(41)	(30)
Food		.77**
		(22)
Practices		
Finance	.94**	.78**
	(41)	(30)
Food		.82**
		(22)

NOTE: Figures in parentheses denote number of societies included in the analysis.

** Correlations significant at $p < .01$.

Table 19.10   Correlations of Societal Uncertainty Avoidance With Other Societal Cultural Dimensions

GLOBE Societal Culture Construct	Correlation With Uncertainty Avoidance Practices	Correlation With Uncertainty Avoidance Values
Future Orientation practices	.76**	−.53**
Future Orientation values	−.57**	.67**
Power Distance practices	−.50**	.48**
Power Distance values	—	—
Institutional Collectivism practices	.40**	—
Institutional Collectivism values	−.32*	.42**
In-Group Collectivism practices	−.60**	.80**
In-Group Collectivism values	−.45**	.30*
Performance Orientation practices	.58**	—
Performance Orientation values	—	—
Gender Egalitarianism practices	—	—
Gender Egalitarianism values	—	−.55**
Assertiveness practices	—	—
Assertiveness values	—	—
Humane Orientation practices	—	.29*
Humane Orientation values	—	—

$N = 61$

* Significant at $p < .05$.

** Significant at $p < .01$.

societies *practicing* uncertainty avoidance seem more assured that their collectives are handling uncertainty, thus they *value* more flexibility and are more open to change.

Uncertainty Avoidance
Values and Other GLOBE Dimensions

Respondents to the GLOBE questionnaire show that Uncertainty Avoidance values are positively correlated with the values of Future Orientation and both Institutional and In-Group Collectivism; these same values of Uncertainty Avoidance are negatively correlated with Gender Egalitarianism. We speculate that if societies desire more management of uncertainty, members may be motivated to look to institutional and in-group collectives to accomplish this. As a desire for uncertainty management increases, women may play a part within the group and institutional collective, but only through more traditional female roles. In societies desiring more management of uncertainty, members may be encouraged to use such techniques as long-term planning, which in turn leads to better management of technology and information. In addition, Uncertainty Avoidance values scores are positively related to Power Distance, In-Group Collectivism, and Humane Orientation practices and inversely related to practices scores for Future Orientation. Members of many societies *valuing* uncertainty avoidance may prefer more of a stratified distribution of power within the society and the societal group to which they belong, relying on such structures (practices) to fulfill the desires (values) of managing uncertainty. Further, societies *valuing* uncertainty avoidance tend to favor caring and generous *practices* within these collectives. However, societies hoping to manage uncertainty do not tend to favor techniques such as scenario planning to accomplish the reduction of uncertainty.

Interestingly, several societies' rankings on the GLOBE scores do not vary between practices and values: China, where members practice and value the strong avoidance of uncertainty, tends to practice strong Institutional and In-Group Collectivism, yet tends to be only modestly Future Oriented. It seems the institutional and in-group collective practices combine with an overall strong preference for managing uncertainty to create a secure environment. For example, in a study comparing the United States with China, text analysis revealed that achieving mutual understanding, mutual benefit, and mutual trust, and long-term cooperation is important in reaching agreement on business standards if negotiating in China (Zhao, 2000). In a study of Hong Kong-based small companies conducting business in China, researchers reported that social meetings in restaurants and sending gifts were the two most common ways of relationship building (*guanxi*), and that these relationships were essential for business success (Leung & Yeung, 1995). This development of trust in relationships reduces the uncertainty in the society. A common saying from the philosophy of Confucius, which is the foundation of much of the Chinese society, dictates that sons should obey their fathers, and wives should obey husbands. Another common saying is that the middle road is best. By conforming to this philosophy, society members maintain harmony and respect for structures of the state, which in turn reduces ambiguity and allows predictability in the society. These examples illustrate the importance of managing certainties through values and practices in a society.

The Relationship of
Collectivism and Power
Distance to Uncertainty Avoidance

The dimensions of national culture proposed by Hofstede (1980) were framed on the basis of relative theoretical and empirical independence. A possible association between uncertainty avoidance and individualism–collectivism is worth mentioning. On a logical basis, one may speculate on collectivism as an uncertainty avoidance mechanism. The old adage "united we stand, divided we fall" would help explain why a society may emphasize collective values to overcome the uncertainties associated with threats to its existence. The empirical correlation of Hofstede's (1984, p. 213) UAI with individualism ($r = .35$, $p < .05$, across 40 countries) supports this line of reasoning. The GLOBE study affords separate examination of Uncertainty Avoidance practices and values. The correlation between GLOBE Uncertainty Avoidance practices and Institutional Collectivism practices ($r = .40$, $p < .01$, across 61 cultures) supports the conceptual relationship expressed above. GLOBE Uncertainty Avoidance values correlate $-.19$ with GLOBE Institutional Collectivism practices, which was nonsignificant.

In like manner, it may be that the cultural dimension referred to as Power Distance is also an outcome of Uncertainty Avoidance. What Lebas and Weigenstein (1986) observed with respect to organizations may also be extended to societies. Groups or individuals derive power and status partly from the uncertainty inherent in the environment. The greater the uncertainties faced by that society, the greater the need to reduce them. Under such circumstances, the greater is the power of those who control that environment and the greater the public's acceptance of their authority. However, the actual reduction of uncertainties in society is rarely achieved by any single individual, but through an organization of forces and the creation of structure and systems. Once these are in place, the perceived need for leadership may be diminished. These arguments suggest a complex theoretical relationship between power distance and uncertainty avoidance. In the GLOBE data, a strong negative correlation between GLOBE Uncertainty Avoidance practices and Power Distance values ($r =- .50$, $p < .01$, across 61 cultures) suggests that highly organized and structured societies no longer endorse power hierarchies in their current practices. That the acceptance of power hierarchies may be associated with a concurrent need for the incorporation of structure, orderliness, and consistency is borne out by a strong positive correlation between Power Distance practices and Uncertainty Avoidance values ($r = .48$, $p < .01$, across 61 cultures).

COMPARISON OF GLOBE FINDINGS WITH PREVIOUS STUDIES

It is interesting to compare the GLOBE findings with other cross-cultural studies that have investigated the same or similar variables. The most well-known study based on questionnaire data similar to the GLOBE study was conducted by Hofstede (1980, 2001). Other studies that have produced comparable data are by Schwartz (1999) and Inglehart and Baker (2000).

Relation to Hofstede's Rankings

It should be noted that there are inherent difficulties comparing the GLOBE rankings with those obtained by Hofstede (1980). As outlined earlier in this chapter, Hofstede's uncertainty avoidance scale had three items measuring one ecological variable (employment stability) and two individual-level variables (rule orientation and stress) aggregated to the societal level. In contrast, the GLOBE measure used four items measuring individual-level variables on a 7-point scale and emphasized consistency–orderliness, structured lifestyles, explicit specification of societal requirements, and societal regulations. Further, the GLOBE items formed two distinct measures—one reflecting respondents' perceptions of current societal practices and the other reflecting values. In contrast, one of Hofstede's items measured a value orientation (rule orientation), the second assessed an expectation of future outcome (the amount of time a respondent expected to remain with the firm), and a third expressed an outcome (the experience of stress). The scores on these three items were formed into a composite index so that separation of values from practices for the purpose of a clear comparison becomes impossible (see Hanges Appendix A).

Therefore, a comparison of rankings from the two studies is not easily interpretable. That said, the GLOBE Uncertainty Avoidance practices scores exhibit the following correlations with Hofstede's UAI: $r = .62$, rho $= .60$, $p < .01$. At first glance, this significant negative correlation may seem unexpected; however, it is consistent with the overall GLOBE finding that cultural practices are negatively correlated with cultural values scales. The GLOBE Uncertainty Avoidance values scores have the following correlations with Hofstede's UAI: $r = .35$, rho $= .36$, $p < .05$. This indicates a moderate positive relationship between Hofstede UAI and GLOBE societal level values scores. Although modestly related, these comparisons indicate that Hofstede's measure of uncertainty avoidance is not the same as that measured in the GLOBE study.

Results from a variety of studies may serve to highlight these differences. In a qualitative study of Demark and France regarding their tendency toward rule orientation, Schramm-Nielsen (2000) found disparities with the Hofstede findings. Contrary to expectations, the French respondents did not report that they refrain from bending or breaking company rules; the Danish respondents were not averse to structuring activities, and unlike the French, were more likely to actually obey the rules.

As stated above, the Hofstede UAI scale has questionable face validity and can be interpreted as a variety of outcomes, whereas the GLOBE Uncertainty Avoidance scales have face validity in, and were validated against, unobtrusive and outcropping measures (see Chapter 9, by Gupta, Sully de Luque, & House) and within the context of a nomological net (see Chapter 8, by Hanges and Dickson).

An important deviation from the Hofstede data (1984, 2001) should be highlighted because of the extant research that has been conducted on the basis of his ranking. GLOBE respondents from the country of Japan reported Uncertainty Avoidance scores in the lower half of Uncertainty Avoidance practices, and moderate levels of Uncertainty Avoidance values. Hofstede reported the Japanese society to rank among the highest of his sample on UAI.[19] GLOBE respondents from Japan reported significantly lower scores for both *practices* and *values* than did respondents from the United States, quite contrary to the Hofstede rankings. It should be recognized that in Japan the concepts of ambiguity and uncertainty do not necessarily have undesirable connotations, as they do in the United States (Pascale & Athos, 1983).

Indeed, many cross-cultural researchers who include Japan in their sample assume Japan to be a high uncertainty avoidance society in accordance with the Hofstede (1980) paradigm. When confronted with contrary results, much discussion usually follows as to why Japan was not found to be a high uncertainty avoidant culture. For example, in a study comparing planning and control practices in Japan and the United States, no differences were found in planning time horizons between the two societies, although it was predicted that Japanese companies would engage in significantly higher long-term planning than would United States companies, given the assumption that Japan was a higher uncertainty avoidant society (Ueno & Sekaran, 1992). GLOBE respondents' scores from Japan and the United States were not significantly different on societal practices, and Japanese respondents ranked lower than American respondents on societal values.

The Schwartz Study

Schwartz (1999) identified three fundamental values relating to all cultures: (a) autonomy versus embeddedness, (b) mastery versus harmony, and (c) hierarchy versus egalitarianism. The concept most salient for Uncertainty Avoidance is autonomy versus embeddedness.

In autonomous cultures, individuals are perceived as autonomous, bounded entities, finding meaning in life by appreciating their uniqueness. Two types of autonomy are distinguished in Schwartz's framework. Intellectual autonomy is realized as individuals are encouraged to follow their own ideas and intellectual directions, with an emphasis on creativity, curiosity, and broadmindedness. Affective autonomy is realized as people are encouraged to find positive experiences for themselves, with an emphasis on variety, excitement, and pleasure in life. Conversely, in embedded cultures people are perceived as compelled by the collectivity, finding life's meaning through participating in the group and identifying with its goals. Respect for tradition, social order, obedience, and family security are some of the values emphasized.

Cultures embedded in relationships generally encourage social order for security. On the other hand, autonomous cultures tend to encourage contractual types of behavior that are less based on social order (see Granovetter, 1985). Indeed, as reported in Table 19.11, Schwartz's autonomy-embedded scale ($r = .42, p < .01$) is positively related with GLOBE's Uncertainty Avoidance practices scale and negatively related to the Uncertainty Avoidance values scale ($r = .73, p < .01$). Further, GLOBE's Uncertainty Avoidance practices correlate positively with affective and intellectual autonomy ($r = .44, p < .01$ and .30, $p < .05$) and negatively with Schwartz's embeddedness scale ($r = .41, p < .01$). GLOBE's Uncertainty Avoidance values scale is correlated

Table 19.11   GLOBE Uncertainty Avoidance and Schwartz's measures

Schwartz Scales	GLOBE Uncertainty Avoidance Society Practices	GLOBE Uncertainty Avoidance Society Values
Autonomy-embedded	.42**	−.73**
Embeddedness	−.41**	.74**
Intellectual autonomy	.30**	−.61**
Affective autonomy	.44**	−.67**

NOTE: We thank Shalom Schwartz and Lilach Sagiv for providing the above correlations.

$N = 48$.

* Correlation significant at $p < .05$.

** Correlation significant at $p < .01$.

negatively with affective and intellectual autonomy ($r = .67, p < .01$ and $−.61, p < .01$) and positively with Schwartz's embeddedness scale ($r = .74$, $p < 0.01$). As such, Uncertainty Avoidance society values scores share the belief in social order and security engaging in long-term interaction inherent in embeddedness, as opposed to behavior based on more contractual relationships associated with autonomy. However, the Uncertainty Avoidance society practices scores share the importance of behavior based on more contractual relationships.

The Inglehart and Baker Study

The World Values Survey evaluates more than 70 societies and includes responses across societies covering a range of economic, political, and cultural issues, from approximately 350 questions on human values (Inglehart, Basanez, & Moreno, 1998). In the World Values Surveys, two dimensions surface along which cultures appear to be differentiated (Inglehart & Baker, 2000, p. 21). The first, termed *survival versus self-expression values*, indicates the changes associated with the prosperous conditions created in advanced industrial societies. This dimension is revealed through the increase of the knowledge and service sectors, reflected in the concepts of postmodernization. The second dimension, termed *traditional versus*

secular-rational authority, is connected with early industrialization and the ascendancy of the working class and reflects the process of modernization. Prominent in preindustrial and premodern societies, a traditional worldview reflects an emphasis on obedience to traditional authority, particularly deference to God that goes with deference to the family and nation. Conversely, a secular worldview is prominent in industrial and modern societies, where authority is legitimated by rational-legal norms, emphasizing economic accumulation and individual achievement. According to Inglehart and Baker (2000), the societal development process is associated with an increased probability of a shift first from traditional to secular rational authority, and second from survival to self-expression values.

As reported in Table 19.12, the GLOBE societal Uncertainty Avoidance practices scale is positively and significantly correlated with both the traditional–secular rational authority scale ($r = .55$, $p < .01$) and the survival–self-expression scale ($r = .78, p < .01$). Respondents in societies that report higher Uncertainty Avoidance practices scores are more likely to encourage traditional behavior emphasizing hard work and self-denial, which will be reflected in the survival scale. In contrast, the GLOBE societal Uncertainty Avoidance values scale is negatively and significantly correlated

Table 19.12   GLOBE Uncertainty Avoidance and Inglehart's Modernization and Postmodernization
Dimensions

Inglehart and Baker Scales	GLOBE Uncertainty Avoidance Society Practices	GLOBE Uncertainty Avoidance Society Values
Traditional secular rational authority	.55** N = 36	−.54** N = 36
Survival self-expression	.78** N = 37	−.88** N = 37

** Correlation is significant at $p < .01$.

to both the traditional–secular rational authority scale ($r = .54, p < .01$) and the survival–self-expression scale ($r = .88, p < .01$). In societies that rely on traditional authority and survival values, the respondents are less likely to endorse the value of Uncertainty Avoidance.

ECONOMIC AND SOCIAL CORRELATES OF GLOBE UNCERTAINTY AVOIDANCE

The country rankings for GLOBE's Uncertainty Avoidance cultural dimension were next examined in relation to a number of economic and societal variables culled by Javidan and Hauser (see Chapter 7) from the following secondary sources of published data: The World Values Survey and the United Nations' Human Development Report for a number of social and economic factors; and the World Economic Forum's Competitiveness rankings. In addition, three variables relating to economic activity and the human condition have been examined with the help of secondary data compiled for the statistical profile of the GLOBE sample. Recall that Javidan and Hauser advanced the following hypotheses:

8.   Societies that are high on uncertainty avoidance tend to:

8.1 Enjoy a healthier state of mind

8.2 Enjoy stronger scientific progress

8.3 Have governments that support economic activities

Uncertainty Avoidance and Economic Health

The economic variables available from the four published sources together address the extent to which a country has developed the means to overcome the uncertainties in the environment. A detailed description of the factors examined in this section is available in Chapter 7. To avoid repetition, only the implications of the results of correlational analyses are discussed here.

The correlations obtained with several economic indicators are shown in Table 19.13. (The 1998 World Economic Forum Competitiveness index has been analyzed again as a ranking instead of an index.) The results indicate that countries whose respondents perceive their society as relatively higher on Uncertainty Avoidance practices are currently among the more prosperous in terms of consumption and growth. They also enjoy more government support for economic development, backed up by societal support as well. They are, not surprisingly, more competitive in the global marketplace. We have already seen how managers in countries with relatively high uncertainty avoiding practices tend to desire less regulation, so the negative correlations with uncertainty values is not surprising either.

Economic Prosperity. Both GLOBE Uncertainty Avoidance practices and values revealed high correlations with economic prosperity. Across 57 cultures common to the external and the GLOBE datasets, the correlation of .60 ($p < .01$) with GLOBE Uncertainty Avoidance practices scale scores was positive, indicating the higher the level of Uncertainty Avoidance practices in a society, the more its economic prosperity. In practical terms, a society that currently has formalization of social expectations and a high degree of orderliness enjoys more telephone lines, cellular phones, personal computers, and fax machines per 1,000 inhabitants. However, equally interesting is the even greater *negative* correlation with GLOBE Uncertainty Avoidance values ($r = .80, p < .01$), indicating that the higher a society's level of economic prosperity, the less that society endorsed the value of Uncertainty Avoidance. These results would suggest that prosperous societies do not value the very factors that seem to have benefited them. On the other hand, in poor nations, characterized by low levels of rule orientation, people recognize the value of rules.

Government Support for Economic Prosperity. In Chapter 7, Javidan and Hauser proposed three hypotheses around uncertainty avoidance. One of these, Hypothesis 8.3, stipulated that countries that are high on uncertainty avoidance tend to have governments that support economic activities. Our results confirm this hypothesis. We found that the extent to which a society has high Uncertainty Avoidance practices is highly correlated with governmental support for economic development of the country ($r = .74, p < .01$). This indicates that in uncertainty-avoiding societies, the public sector is able to function without much political interference and there is relatively less bribery and corruption. In such societies, technological development is not constrained by lack or insufficiency of financial resources and is not restricted by the legal environment. In addition, the prevalence of competition laws discourages unfair business practices, economic literacy is high, and industrial relations are generally productive rather than hostile.

Societal Support for Economic Competitiveness. The prevalence of rules and regulations, orderliness, and structure in a society, as measured by the GLOBE Uncertainty Avoidance practices scales, is positively related to the extent to which its political and social systems are adapted to long-term competitiveness in world markets, the extent to which its labor regulations are flexible, the extent to which infrastructure development and maintenance is planned and financed, and the extent to which the values of hard work and innovation support competitiveness. Across 40 cultures, the correlation is .44 ($p < .01$) between societal support for economic competitiveness and GLOBE Uncertainty Avoidance practices. The correlation with GLOBE Uncertainty Avoidance values ($r = -.24$) is not statistically significant.

World Competitiveness. Across 40 cultures common to both data sets, GLOBE Uncertainty Avoidance practices correlated .60 ($p < .01$) with the competitiveness index (for details see chapter 7 by Javidan & Hauser), signifying that more formalized and structured economies are more competitive in the global environment. The corresponding correlations of GLOBE Uncertainty Avoidance values are $-.49$ ($p < .01$) with the World Competitiveness Index. That the direction of relationship with practices rankings is the opposite of that with values is consistent with our earlier observed negative correlation between GLOBE Uncertainty Avoidance practices and values.

Uncertainty Avoidance and the Human Condition

The correlations of GLOBE Uncertainty Avoidance with a number of variables relating to societal well-being are reproduced in Table 19.14.

Societal Health. In uncertainty-avoiding societies, we may expect to find, in relative terms, fair administration of the justice system, personal security and protection of private property, higher quality of life, and relatively fewer problems posed by alcoholism and drug abuse in the work place. The correlation across 40 cultures was .76 ($p < .01$) with GLOBE Uncertainty Avoidance practices, and $-.74$ ($p < .01$) with GLOBE Uncertainty Avoidance values. However, these societies do not necessarily enjoy a high level of physical well-being, as reflected by the low correlations with the variable "human health."

Life Expectancy. Across 56 cultures common to both datasets, life expectancy was negatively associated with GLOBE Uncertainty Avoidance values ($r = .44, p < .01$), and positively correlated ($r = .28, p < .05$) with GLOBE Uncertainty

Table 19.13   Relationship of Uncertainty Avoidance Scores and Economic Variables

Economic Variables	N	Correlation With	
		Uncertainty Avoidance Practices	*Uncertainty Avoidance Values*
Economic prosperity	57	.60**	−.80**
Government support for prosperity	40	.74**	−.75**
Societal support for competitiveness	40	.44**	−.24
World Competitiveness Index, WEF 1998	41	.60**	−.49**

WEF = World Economic Forum

* Significant at $p < .05$ two tailed.

** Significant at $p < .01$ two tailed.

Avoidance practices. Predictably, then, we may expect to find a longer average life span in countries where Uncertainty Avoidance practices are experienced and Uncertainty Avoidance values are not endorsed. However, the driving force behind this correlation is probably the availability of advanced medical technologies and health services in the economically developed countries, which also rank lower on Uncertainty Avoidance values.

General Satisfaction. In Chapter 7, Javidan and Hauser proposed the hypothesis (Hypothesis 8.1) that societies that are high on uncertainty avoidance tend to enjoy a greater general satisfaction. This measure, which consists of items on people's general feelings about themselves, their health, their lives, and their countries, correlated .63 ($p < .01$) with GLOBE Uncertainty Avoidance practices. These results suggest that people in presently rule-oriented cultures enjoy a better general satisfaction, confirming the earlier hypothesis.

Human Development Index. For the composite index of human development, there is a modest but significant positive correlation ($r = .28$, $p < .05$) with GLOBE Uncertainty Avoidance practices, and a large negative correlation ($r = −.59$, $p < .01$) with GLOBE Uncertainty Avoidance values, across 56 cultures. Recall that the Human Development Index was made

up of the following items: Life expectancy, knowledge, and standard of living. In general, therefore, societies with greater uncertainty avoiding mechanisms tended to enjoy higher qualities of life and human development.

Civil Liberties Index. This variable measures the extent to which members of a society enjoy freedom in several areas, with higher values indicating less liberty for individuals. A moderate negative correlation between GLOBE Uncertainty Avoidance practices and this index ($r = −.36$, $p < .01$) supports the notion that in societies characterized by a high degree of orderliness, consistency, and structure, there is greater assurance of individual liberty. However, the reason that one may not expect a stronger correlation is that democratic cultures characterized by lower levels of rule orientation may, nevertheless, have a high level of civil liberties. In societies that have a low level of civil liberties, the people are desirous of more structure and social order, as evidenced by a strong positive correlation of civil liberties index with GLOBE Uncertainty Avoidance values ($r = .64$, $p < .01$).

Similar results are found using the World Values Survey findings (Inglehart et al., 1998). As reported in Table 19.15, rule-oriented societies that scored higher on Uncertainty Avoidance tend to have a higher regard for democratic systems ($r = −.51$, $p < .01$), individual

Table 19.14   Relationship Between Uncertainty Avoidance and Human Condition

Uncertainty Avoidance	Societal Health	Human Health	Life Expectancy	General Satisfaction	Human Development Index (HDI)	Civil Liberties
Society practices	.76** n = 40	.13 n = 56	.28* n = 56	.63** n = 38	.28* n = 56	−.36** n = 57
Society values	−.74** n = 40	−.12 n = 56	−.44** n = 56	−.66* n = 38	−.59** n = 56	.64** n = 57

** Correlation is significant at the .01 level (2-tailed).

* Correlation is significant at the .05 level (2-tailed).

Table 19.15   Relationship Between Uncertainty Avoidance and Political Ideology

Uncertainty Avoidance	Disdain for Democracy	Passiveness	Lack of Voice	Dislike of Democracy	Role of Government	Stability
Society practices	−.51** n = 26	−.52** n = 37	−.53** n = 38	−.49** n = 27	−.62** n = 38	−.29 n = 38
Society values	.40* n = 26	.60** n = 37	.75** n = 38	.38* n = 27	.81** n = 38	.56** n = 38

* Correlation is significant at the .05 level (2-tailed).

** Correlation is significant at the .01 level (2-tailed).

involvement in the political system ($r = -.52$, $p < .01$), greater voice for people in the running of the country ($p = -.53$, $p < .01$), a greater admiration for democracy ($r = -.49, p < .01$), and a less-active role for the government ($r = -.62$, $p < .01$). The negative signs are due to the way these scales are measured (see Chapter 7, Javidan & Hauser). In contrast, regarding Uncertainty Avoidance values, respondents in societies in the GLOBE sample reported to desire more order have less of a regard for democracy ($r = .40, p < .05$), are more passive ($r = .60, p < .01$), have little voice in the running of the country ($r = .75, p < .01$), dislike democracy ($r = .38, p < .05$), and aspire to more rules and structure, a more active government ($r = .81$, $p < .01$), and more stability ($r = .56, p < .01$) in their communities.

In sum, as far as the human condition is concerned, societies whose respondents perceive their society as formalized and orderly (i.e., scoring high in GLOBE Uncertainty Avoidance practices) are those that also enjoy a high quality of life and relative safety and security. Life expectancy in these societies tends to be somewhat higher. People in these societies are generally more satisfied and happy. The Human Development Index, which includes measures of life expectancy, adult literacy, and standard of living, yields correlations with GLOBE Uncertainty Avoidance that are consistent with the other results in the table.

Uncertainty Avoidance With Science and Technology

Perhaps in no other realm of human endeavor would we expect uncertainty avoidance, defined in terms of formalization and structure, to be more influential than in the

Table 19.16   Relationship Between Uncertainty Avoidance and Scientific Progress

Science and Technology	Uncertainty Avoidance Practices	Uncertainty Avoidance Values
Success with basic science	0.59** N = 40	−.58** N = 40

* Correlation is significant at the .05 level (2-tailed).

** Correlation is significant at the .01 level (2-tailed).

conduct and progress of science and technology. In Chapter 7, Javidan and Hauser hypothesized (Hypothesis 8.2) that societies that are high on uncertainty avoidance tend to enjoy stronger scientific progress. Our findings confirm this hypothesis. As Table 19.16 shows, societies that are reported to have high Uncertainty Avoidance practices also tend to be successful in basic science research. Across 40 cultures common to both datasets, the correlation between progress of science and technology is .59 ($p < .01$) with reported Uncertainty Avoidance practices. In formalized and orderly cultures, therefore, one may also find more company–university cooperation, more emphasis on basic science and research, and more interest among youth regarding science and technology issues. There was a strong negative relationship between GLOBE Uncertainty Avoidance values and science and technology ($r = .58, p < .01$).

Uncertainty Avoidance With Religion

The theoretical role of religion, viewed by Hofstede (1980) as a coping mechanism for uncertainty avoidance was touched on earlier in this chapter. Several sources provide data for investigation of the empirical relation between these constructs. It is generally expected that people in cultures low in uncertainty avoidance would exhibit a lesser degree of religious involvement to the extent that they do not need to use religion to help them cope spiritually or practically with the uncertainties in life.

The empirical evidence is not unequivocal. At the societal level, overall indices of religiosity show that predominantly Catholic countries returned the highest GLOBE Uncertainty Avoidance practices scores, and Protestant cultures the lowest (Verweij, Ester, & Nauta, 1997). Because empirical studies of religious practices are based primarily on church attendance, only Christian countries have been targeted for investigation. Across 16 countries, Verweij and colleagues (1997) found a high correlation ($r = .77$, $p < .05$) between the percentage of Catholics in a country and Hofstede's UAI. However, across the 12 countries common to the GLOBE and Verweij and colleagues' (1997) datasets, the percentage of regular church attendance (defined as one or more times per week) correlated $-.69$ ($p < .05$) with GLOBE Uncertainty Avoidance practices scores, and .34 (nonsignificant) with Uncertainty Avoidance values scores—implying a lower rate of church attendance in societies with high Uncertainty Avoidance practices and possibly a high rate of church attendance in cultures with high Uncertainty Avoidance values. Verweij and colleagues (1997) had also constructed a religious orientation index derived from a factor score. This index correlated $-.73$ ($p < .05$) with reported GLOBE Uncertainty Avoidance practices scores and .37 (nonsignificant) with the GLOBE Uncertainty Avoidance values scores, consistent with the relationships found with church attendance. The findings conveyed here show a negative relationship between reported GLOBE Uncertainty Avoidance practices and degree of religiosity in a society, which is contrary to the conventional wisdom and Hofstede's supposition.

Further supportive evidence is provided by GLOBE's measures of religiousness. In Chapter 7, Javidan and Hauser developed a scale of religious devotion and a scale of religious dogma. Table 19.17 shows the correlations between these scales and GLOBE measures of Uncertainty Avoidance. As can be seen from this table, GLOBE Uncertainty Avoidance practices scores are negatively correlated with degree of religious devotion ($r = .42, p < .01$) and degree of religious dogma ($r = .33$, $p < .05$). Societies that are reported to have high Uncertainty Avoidance practices attach a lower level of importance to religion, and less frequently attend religious services. On the other hand, societies reported to value (aspire toward) more rules in their lives tend to attach a greater significance to religion, attend religious services more frequently, and have stronger beliefs in heaven and hell, indicating a greater value of religious devotion ($r = .43, p < .01$) and religious dogma ($r = .48, p < .01$).

To summarize, it appears that the relationship between Uncertainty Avoidance and religion is more complicated than that envisioned by Hofstede and presumed in the literature. Those societies that are reported to have procedures and practices in place to reduce uncertainties in peoples' lives do not necessarily need religion to create further structure and certainty. Only respondents in societies reporting deficient processes and procedures, as well as those desiring a higher level of structure and clarity in their lives, need religion to fill the gap.

In addition to the findings presented in this chapter, it is very likely that many aspects of cultures are culture-specific and, thus, are not likely to be reflected in the findings reported in this chapter or others. An illustrative case pertains to the association between uncertainty avoidance and religion, which has been posed as a coping mechanism of societies (Hofstede, 1984, p. 111). The GLOBE data described here suggest that religiosity, or the extent of religious beliefs in a society, has a complex relationship with the level of Uncertainty Avoidance in that society. Hofstede (2001) has discussed (pp. 176–177) and summarized (p. 181) the association between type of religion and his UAI. The issues run deeper than these simplistic explanations, however.

First, there are countries that are almost entirely of a single religious persuasion (e.g., Pakistan, Iraq), while at the other extreme there are highly secular states (e.g., India, the United States). Religions, although possessing many common fundamental tenets, differ in their prescriptions for social order. Whereas all religions by definition promote the acceptance of uncertainty by the very acknowledgment of a higher power, different religions impose different degrees of restriction or prescription for personal and social behavior.

Still, it would be difficult to make a statement about a society's tolerance of uncertainty from religious faith per se. Practically every major religion has different sects that have emerged through differences in the interpretation of religious texts. Thus Hinduism, one of the oldest religions in existence, has seen different phases in its own following: In the reactionary birth of Buddhism when the practice of Hinduism became too ritualistic, and in the birth of the Sikh faith as a militant response to the perceived threat of Islam against the passive stance of Hinduism. Similar undercurrents may be observed in the Western world in the emergence of Christianity from the Jewish faith, in the Catholic and Protestant persuasions, and in the scores of divisions that have occurred in these faiths. There exists no extensive or intensive study of the relation between different faiths and the extent to which they incorporate the tolerance or avoidance of uncertainty, although we can speculate on their emergence as a historical response to uncertainties in the social milieu of the times.

Uncertainty Avoidance and Financial Transactions

The relationship between GLOBE Uncertainty Avoidance scores and cash holding was examined using data on 14 developed nations published by Humphrey, Pulley, and Vesala (1996). It was hypothesized that societies exhibiting a preference for high uncertainty avoidance would have high cash holdings. The practice of holding cash reserves is proposed to reduce uncertainty in high uncertainty avoidance societies (Humphrey et al., 1996). Across the 12 countries common to both datasets, the correlation between Uncertainty Avoidance practices scores and cash holdings per capita is .07 ($p > .10$, two-tailed). The corresponding correlation with Uncertainty Avoidance values scores is $-.27$ ($p > .10$, two-tailed). Of the

Table 19.17   Relationship of Uncertainty Avoidance Scores and Religious Orientation

Religious Orientation	Uncertainty Avoidance Practices	Uncertainty Avoidance Values
Religious devotion	−.42** N = 38	.43** N = 38
Religious dogma	−.33* N = 37	.48** N = 37

** Significant at $p < .01$, two-tailed.

* Significant at $p < .05$, two-tailed.

12 countries analyzed, all but 2 countries are among the 16 developed countries that scored lowest on Uncertainty Avoidance values. If these two countries (Italy and Japan) are excluded from the analysis, the correlations spiral to .55 ($p < .10$, two-tailed) between cash holdings and Uncertainty Avoidance practices scores, and −.80 ($p < .01$, two-tailed) between cash holdings and Uncertainty Avoidance values scores.

Correlations with the number of noncash transactions per capita are consistent with the results for cash holdings. As cash holdings decrease, we may expect the number of noncash transactions to go up. As expected on the basis of cash-holding correlations, the number of non-cash transactions varies as an inverse function of the GLOBE Uncertainty Avoidance practices scores ($r = .78, p < .01$) and as a direct function of GLOBE Uncertainty Avoidance values scores ($r = .43, p > .10$, two-tailed). Among the developed nations (with the exception of Japan and Italy), a higher GLOBE Uncertainty Avoidance values orientation is associated with lower cash holdings and higher noncash transactions.

UNCERTAINTY AVOIDANCE REGIONAL CLUSTERS

As discussed in Chapter 8 by Hanges and Dickson, there are significant differences in values and practices for every cultural dimension among the 61 societies (i.e., recall that we use the term societal cultures rather than nations). Societies in the GLOBE sample were clustered into 10 geographical regions (details of these clusters are discussed in Chapter 10 by Gupta & Hanges). Analysis of variance tests (Table 19.18) were conducted to determine if cross-regional differences exist in the practices and values of societal Uncertainty Avoidance as measured by the GLOBE scales. There exist significant cross-regional differences in Uncertainty Avoidance societal practices ($F9, 51 = 11.75, p < .01$) as well as in societal values ($F9, 51 = 17.36, p < .01$). Further analysis showed that regional differences account for 68% of the variation in GLOBE societal Uncertainty Avoidance practices scores, whereas 32% represented idiosyncratic societal differences. With respect to GLOBE societal Uncertainty Avoidance values, 75% of the variation was explained by regional differences, whereas 25% represented unique societal differences. In other words, there is substantial within-region commonality among societies within clusters with respect to Uncertainty Avoidance as well as smaller nontrivial differences.

Table 19.18 shows the mean and standard deviation of societal GLOBE Uncertainty Avoidance practices and values scores in each of the regions. It can be seen that Southern Asia, Middle East, Sub-Saharan Africa, Eastern Europe, and Latin America scored relatively high on GLOBE Uncertainty Avoidance values measures, whereas Northern European and Anglo societies scored relatively low. Nordic Europe and Germanic Europe scored highest in Uncertainty Avoidance societal practices. Eastern Europe, Latin America, and Middle East cultures, on the other hand, scored less than the midpoint of 4.0 on GLOBE Uncertainty Avoidance practices.

Uncertainty Avoidance and Climatic Differences

The GLOBE sample of societies is grouped into seven categories of climates (see Chapter 10 by Gupta & Hanges). Analysis of Variance tests suggest significant climatic differences for Uncertainty Avoidance societal practices ($F6$, $54 = 4.41$, $p < .01$) as well as for societal values ($F6$, $54 = 10.72$, $p < .01$). Further analysis (not shown) showed that climatic differences account for 33% of the variation in societal Uncertainty Avoidance practices scores, whereas 67% represented idiosyncratic societal differences. With respect to GLOBE societal Uncertainty Avoidance values scores, 54% of the variation was explained by climatic differences, whereas 46% represented unique societal differences. In other words, climatic differences have a considerably stronger effect on reported societal Uncertainty Avoidance values than on practices.

Table 19.19 provides grand mean scores for GLOBE societal Uncertainty Avoidance practices and values across each of the climatic categories. The GLOBE Uncertainty Avoidance practices scores for tropical wet and dry (savanna), subtropical humid, and subtropical wet and dry (Mediterranean) climate regions average to less than the midpoint of the GLOBE scale (i.e., 4.0). The reported practices are distinctively strong in the maritime climate region (marine west coast). In contrast, reported Uncertainty Avoidance values are distinctively strong in tropical wet and dry climate; the average of GLOBE Uncertainty Avoidance values scores is less than the midpoint of 4.0 for the temperate marine west coast climate region. To summarize, temperate climates (especially maritime, but also continental) tend to have strong Uncertainty Avoidance practices, but do not value Uncertainty Avoidance. The opposite is true for the nontemperate wet and dry climates, especially in the tropics, but also extending even to the subtropics.

Table 19.18   Uncertainty Avoidance Scores by Geographic Region

Geographic Region	N	Society Practices		Society Values	
		Mean	Standard Deviation	Mean	Standard Deviation
Nordic Europe Finland Sweden Denmark	3	5.19	0.16	3.76	0.13
Eastern Europe Albania Kazakhstan Hungary Poland Russia Slovenia Greece Georgia	8	3.56	0.50	4.94	0.32
Latin America Argentina Bolivia Brazil Colombia Costa Rica Ecuador El Salvador	10	3.62	0.25	4.98	0.27

Geographic Region	N	Society Practices		Society Values	
		Mean	Standard Deviation	Mean	Standard Deviation

Guatemala
   Mexico
   Venezuela					

Middle East
   Egypt
   Kuwait
   Morocco
   Qatar
   Turkey
	5	3.91	0.26	4.99	0.33

Latin Europe
   Italy
   Portugal
   Spain
   France
   Switzerland
     (French-speaking)
   Israel
	6	4.18	0.45	4.36	0.31

Germanic Europe
   Austria
   Germany (Former West)
   Germany (Former East)
   The Netherlands
   Switzerland
	5	5.12	0.25	3.46	0.33

Sub-Saharan Africa
   Namibia
   Nigeria
   South Africa (Black sample)
   Zambia
   Zimbabwe
	5	4.27	0.20	4.99	0.39

Confucian Asia
   Taiwan
   Singapore
   Hong Kong
   South Korea
   China
   Japan
	6	4.42	0.62	4.74	0.46

Southern Asia
   India
   Indonesia
   Malaysia
   Philippines
   Thailand
   Iran
	6	4.10	0.38	5.16	0.32

Anglo
   Australia
   Canada
   New Zealand
   U.S.
   South Africa (White sample)
   England
   Ireland
	7	4.42	0.25	4.09	0.28

GLOBE FINDINGS ON ORGANIZATIONAL UNCERTAINTY AVOIDANCE

The cultural norm of uncertainty avoidance has implications for organizational research and development practices as well. For instance, high societal scores on Hofstede's UAI have been associated with promoting innovations in the marketplace (Shane, 1995; Shane et al., 1995). In other words, the more uncertainty avoiding a society is in its national character (as measured by Hofstede's UAI), the more its people prefer champions to enact organizational rules, norms, and policy when promoting innovation. This finding is consistent with the notion of societal uncertainty avoidance as a component (Nakata & Sivakumar, 1996) of organizational uncertainty avoidance. The major organizational practices associated with uncertainty avoidance in the literature are discussed below.

Table 19.19   Climate and Uncertainty Avoidance

Climate	N	Society Practices		Society Values	
		Mean	Standard Deviation	Mean	Standard Deviation

Tropical Humid
  Costa Rica
  Ecuador
  Colombia
  Philippines
  Singapore
  Indonesia
  Malaysia
  India
	8	4.17	0.59	4.86	0.34

Tropical Wet and Dry
  El Salvador
  Venezuela
  Guatemala
  Thailand
  Nigeria
  Zambia
  Zimbabwe
	7	3.83	0.38	5.15	0.39

Desert
  Egypt
  Israel
  Kazakhstan
  Kuwait
  Namibia
  Turkey
  Qatar
  Iran
  South Africa
    (White sample)
  South Africa
    (Black sample)
  Mexico
	11	4.02	0.29	4.87	0.35

Table 19.19 (Continued)

Climate	N	Society Practices		Society Values	
		Mean	Standard Deviation	Mean	Standard Deviation
Subtropical Wet and Dry Albania Greece Italy Portugal Slovenia Spain Morocco	7	3.87	0.36	4.92	0.38
Subtropical Humid Bolivia Brazil Argentina Hong Kong Taiwan	5	3.85	0.45	4.86	0.29
Marine West Coast Denmark France Germany (East and West) Ireland New Zealand Netherlands Switzerland (French–speaking) Switzerland United Kingdom	10	4.88	0.36	3.78	0.40
Continental Austria Finland Hungary Japan Korea Sweden Poland Georgia Canada U.S. Russia China Australia	13	4.18	0.80	4.37	0.61

Uncertainty Avoidance and Selection Practices

The influence of national culture on personnel selection was examined by Ryan et al. (1999). Selection practices such as verification methods, number of interviews, and frequency of verification were studied. Among the seven aspects of background verification, across the 15 countries with 20 or more firms in the Ryan and colleagues' data sample, "requesting written documentation" had the strongest correlation with GLOBE societal Uncertainty Avoidance as reflected by current practices in the GLOBE ranking of countries ($r = .54$, $p < .05$, rho $= .44$, $p > .10$). Curiously, checking for criminal records yielded a moderate negative correlation with Uncertainty Avoidance current practices ($r = -.34$, $p > .10$, rho $= -.50$, $p < .10$). It may be that criminal backgrounds are more rare and, therefore, less of an issue in highly uncertainty-avoiding cultures.

Uncertainty Avoidance and Championing Strategies

Shane (1994) hypothesized and observed a negative relationship between Hofstede's (1980) UAI and a preference for autonomy (Spearman's rho $= -.32$, $p < .05$, $n = 24$). The GLOBE values rankings (of countries common to both studies) supported this relationship (Spearman's rho $= -.31$, $n = 18$, $p < .10$) to much the same extent. Predictably, the GLOBE current practices rankings correlated positively ($r = .24$, $p > .10$) with preference for autonomy. Although the comparison of Shane and GLOBE scores was not statistically significant, the relationships are worth noting.

Another innovation championing strategy that we hypothesized as relevant to Uncertainty Avoidance is monitoring. It has been proposed that some degree of control exercised over the innovation process will help a team achieve its goals (e.g., Sathe, 1988). Among the monitoring processes advocated is the approval of funds on a periodical basis in installments rather than in entirety at one time. Monitoring can be seen as an attempt to reduce uncertainty of outcomes at least in part by minimizing the losses on bad investments. Shane (1994) did not hypothesize a relationship between UAI scores and monitoring.[20] Had he done so, he would have found a rather large rank correlation of .47 ($p < .05$) with Hofstede's UAI,[21] consistent with the notion that people in high uncertainty avoidance cultures prefer monitoring as an innovation championing strategy. Shane's (1994) rankings on monitoring correlate .38 ($p > .10$) with the GLOBE values rankings and $-.43$ ($p < .10$) with current practices rankings. These are consistent with our hypothesized relationships, although further research is needed to verify this association better.

UNCERTAINTY AVOIDANCE AND FORMALIZATION

In his work on the influence of national cultures on corporate cultures, Trompenaars (1994) asked respondents to choose between four possible descriptions of their company. The descriptions were keyed, respectively, to reflect the power priority of the "family" type organizational culture, the role dominance of the "Eiffel Tower" culture, the task orientation of the "guided missile" culture, and the person orientation of the "incubator" culture. He obtained results from 12 countries, mapped along two dimensions: degree of centralization and degree of formalization. As the time of data collection in this study coincides with GLOBE's, the GLOBE Uncertainty Avoidance practices scores can be rank-correlated with the ranking of countries on the two organizational culture dimensions. Across the 11 countries common to both datasets, GLOBE Uncertainty Avoidance practices scores rank-correlated .40 ($p > .10$) with the degree of formalization and $-.26$ ($p > .10$) with the degree of centralization.[22] Cyert and March (1963) posited that organizations adopt procedures that minimize the need for predicting uncertain events in the future. We theorize that in countries with high levels of uncertainty avoidance, we may expect to find a high degree of formalization and *de*centralization.

The Relationship Between Societal and Organizational Practices and Societal and Organizational Values

As indicated in Chapter 2 (House & Javidan, this volume), the GLOBE theoretical model postulates that societal practices and values affect organizational practices and values. Two hierarchical linear models (HLMs) were conducted to test these hypotheses for organizational Uncertainty Avoidance practices and values. We tested the GLOBE hypothesis regarding the effect of societal culture on organizational culture by conducting HLM analyses in which societal Uncertainty Avoidance

Table 19.20   HLM Regression of GLOBE Societal Culture Dimensions on Organizational Uncertainty Avoidance Practices

Predictors	Organizational Uncertainty Avoidance R²	Change in Organizational Uncertainty Avoidance R²	Predictor Significant .05 level
Societal practices (block) • Power Distance • In-Group Collectivism	.22		
Societal Uncertainty Avoidance practices	.26	.04	Yes
Societal Uncertainty Avoidance values	.33	.07	Yes

Table 19.21   HLM Regression of GLOBE Societal Culture Dimensions on Organizational Uncertainty Avoidance Values

Predictors	Organizational Uncertainty Avoidance R²	Change in Organizational Uncertainty Avoidance R²	Predictor Significant .05 level
Societal values (block) • Power Distance • Future Orientation	.37		
Societal Uncertainty Avoidance values	.61	.24	Yes
Societal Uncertainty Avoidance practices	.61	.00	No

predicted organizational Uncertainty Avoidance. As shown in Table 19.20 and Table 19.21, societal Uncertainty Avoidance practices did have a significant and strong positive relationship with organizational Uncertainty Avoidance practices ($p < .05$). We also found a strong relationship between societal Uncertainty Avoidance values and organizational Uncertainty Avoidance values ($p < .01$). Therefore, this analysis supports a principal proposition in the GLOBE theoretical model (i.e., Proposition 3, Figure 2.1, Chapter 2, by House and Javidan): societal cultural values

and practices affect organizational cultural values and practices.[23]

HLM Analysis: Uncertainty Avoidance and Leadership CLTs

This chapter presents relationships between one culture dimension (Uncertainty Avoidance) and the six culturally endorsed leadership dimensions. Competitive tests of all culture dimensions and GLOBE dimensions are presented in Chapter 21 by Dorfman and

Uncertainty Avoidance Cultural Dimension

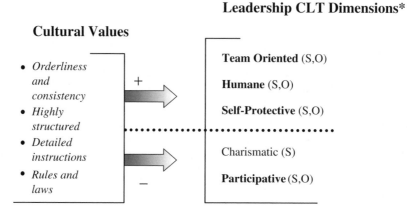

Figure 19.1   Uncertainty Avoidance Cultural Values as Drivers for CLT Leadership Dimensions

* Only statistically significant relationships are shown (see Table 21.10, Chapter 21 by Dorfman et al.). Relationship significant at $p < .05$. The most important leadership CLT relationships are bolded (i.e., relationship is significant at both society and organizational levels of analyses or highest HLM coefficient within each level of analysis).

O = Organizational level

S = Societal level

coauthors.[24] In general, we expect that societal and organizational values will be more strongly related to CLT leadership dimensions than societal and organizational practices. As indicated previously, our notions of values and CLT leadership dimensions represent idealized reports of how the world *Should Be* in contrast to practices that represent the world *As Is*. As you read through the results discussed below, it may be helpful to view Figure 19.1 for a visual summary. The figure, however, only shows results regarding cultural values, not practices. (Dorfman et al. present all HLM coefficients in Table 21.10 of Chapter 21.)

Here we discuss the results of statistical analyses examining the extent to which Uncertainty Avoidance, as measured by GLOBE practices and values scales, has an effect on each of the dimensions. Specifically, we examine the extent to which the content of GLOBE dimensions varies as a function of GLOBE Uncertainty Avoidance values and practices in societies and in organizations within societies. We tested for the relationship between culture and the CLT leadership dimensions by using

Hierarchical Linear Modeling (HLM). An overview of HLM analyses and a detailed discussion of how we conducted these analyses, as well as how to interpret the R^2 information in HLM, is provided in Chapter 11 by Hanges, Dickson, and Sipe.

The total amount of organizational and societal variance explained by Uncertainty Avoidance values and practices ranges from 0.3% to 69.3%. Uncertainty Avoidance was found to be the most predictive of Self-Protective and least predictive of Autonomous CLT leadership dimensions.

If organizational-level and societal-level Uncertainty Avoidance values and practices were considered, significant relationships were found with the following:

- *Charismatic/Value-Based leadership.* Uncertainty Avoidance cultural values were significantly related to this CLT dimension and explained a total of 5.3% of the organizational and societal variance for this dimension. All of this explained variance was associated with forces operating at the societal level of analysis.

The societal Uncertainty Avoidance cultural values scale was negatively related ($p < .05$) to this CLT dimension. Charismatic/Value-Based leadership is less likely to be a part of the shared leadership belief system in societies reported to espouse Uncertainty Avoidance values.

• *Team-Oriented leadership.* Uncertainty Avoidance practices and values were significantly related to this CLT dimension and explained a total of 25.2% of the organizational and societal variance for this dimension. Approximately 15.6% of this explained variance was associated with forces operating at the organizational level of analysis. The remaining portion of the explained variance (84.4%) was associated with forces operating at the societal level of analysis.

The organizational Uncertainty Avoidance cultural practices scale was negatively related ($p < .05$) to this CLT dimension, whereas the organizational Uncertainty Avoidance cultural values scale was positively related ($p < .01$) to this CLT dimension. Team-Oriented leadership is less likely to be a part of the shared leadership belief system in organizations reported to have Uncertainty Avoidance practices, but it is more likely to be a part of the shared leadership belief system in organizations reported to espouse Uncertainty Avoidance values.

The societal Uncertainty Avoidance cultural practices scale was negatively related ($p < .05$) to this CLT dimension, whereas the societal Uncertainty Avoidance cultural values scale was positively related ($p < .05$) to this CLT dimension. Team-Oriented leadership is less likely to be a part of the shared leadership belief system in societies reported to have Uncertainty Avoidance practices, but it is more likely in societies reported to espouse Uncertainty Avoidance values.

• *Participative leadership.* Uncertainty Avoidance cultural practices and values were significantly related to this CLT dimension and explained a total of 33.8% of the organizational and societal variance for this dimension. Approximately 5.5% of this explained variance was associated with forces operating at the organizational level of analysis. The majority of the explained variance (94.5%) was associated with forces operating at the societal level of analysis.

The organizational Uncertainty Avoidance cultural practices scale was negatively related ($p < .05$) to this CLT dimension, as was the organizational Uncertainty Avoidance cultural values scale ($p < .01$). Participative leadership is less likely to be a part of the shared leadership belief system in organizations reported to have Uncertainty Avoidance practices and it is less likely to be a part of the shared leadership belief system in organizations reported to espouse Uncertainty Avoidance values.

The societal Uncertainty Avoidance cultural values scale was negatively related ($p < .01$) to this CLT dimension. Participative leadership is less likely to be a part of the shared leadership belief system in societies reported to espouse Uncertainty Avoidance values.

• *Humane-Oriented leadership.* Uncertainty Avoidance cultural practices and values were significantly related to this CLT dimension and explained a total of 20.9% of the organizational and societal variance for this dimension. Approximately 32.2% of this explained variance was associated with forces operating at the organizational level of analysis. The remaining portion of the explained variance (67.8%) was associated with forces operating at the societal level of analysis.

The organizational Uncertainty Avoidance cultural practices scale was negatively related ($p < .05$) to this CLT dimension, whereas the organizational Uncertainty Avoidance cultural values scale was positively related ($p < .01$) to this CLT dimension. Humane-Oriented leadership is less likely to be a part of the shared leadership belief system in organizations reported to have Uncertainty Avoidance practices, but it is more likely to be a part of the shared leadership belief system in organizations reported to espouse Uncertainty Avoidance values.

The societal Uncertainty Avoidance cultural values scale was positively related ($p < .01$) to this CLT dimension. Humane-Oriented leadership is more likely to be a part of the shared leadership belief system in societies reported to espouse Uncertainty Avoidance values.

• *Autonomous leadership.* Uncertainty Avoidance cultural practices were significantly related to this CLT dimension but explained a total of just 0.3% of the organizational and societal variance for this dimension. All of this explained variance was associated with forces operating at the organizational level of analysis. The organizational Uncertainty Avoidance cultural practices scale was positively related ($p < .05$) to this CLT dimension. Autonomous leadership is more likely to be a part of a shared leadership belief system in organizations reported to have Uncertainty Avoidance practices.

• *Self-Protective leadership.* Uncertainty Avoidance cultural practices and values were significantly related to this CLT dimension and explained a total of 69.3% of the organizational and societal variance for this dimension. Approximately 8.3% of this explained variance was associated with forces operating at the organizational level of analysis. The remaining portion of the explained variance (91.7%) was associated with forces operating at the societal level of analysis.

Both the organizational Uncertainty Avoidance cultural practices scale ($p < .05$) and the organizational Uncertainty Avoidance cultural values scale ($p < .01$) were positively related to this CLT dimension. Self-Protective leadership is more likely to be a part of a shared leadership belief system in organizations reported to have Uncertainty Avoidance practices and it is more likely to be a part of the shared leadership belief system in organizations reported to espouse Uncertainty Avoidance values.

The societal Uncertainty Avoidance cultural practices scale was positively related ($p < .05$) to this CLT dimension, as was the societal Uncertainty Avoidance cultural values scale ($p < .01$). Self-Protective leadership is more likely to be a part of the shared leadership belief system in societies reported to have Uncertainty Avoidance practices and it is more likely to be a part of the shared leadership belief system in societies reported to espouse Uncertainty Avoidance values.

Overall, these analyses indicated that Uncertainty Avoidance cultural practices and values were associated with all six CLT dimensions. However, in general, the influence of Uncertainty Avoidance culture was stronger and more consistently found at the societal than the organizational level of analysis. The analyses showed that both societies and organizations valuing Uncertainty Avoidance desired leaders who were more team oriented and humane. For humane leadership, people valuing greater Uncertainty Avoidance prefer leaders that are more compassionate and supportive. Chapter 8 by Hanges and Dickson provides support for this association. They argue that societies practicing uncertainty avoidance also provide more welfare consideration, reflecting more humane-oriented leadership.

We should also note that many of these relationships with the CLT dimensions, particularly the relationship between Participative and Self-Protective leadership with higher Uncertainty Avoidance, make intuitive sense. Participation creates a certain amount of uncertainty and, conversely, societies and organizations less tolerant of uncertainty would be less likely to endorse participative leadership. In addition, self-protective leadership should increase as situations become more uncertain and less predictable.

SUMMARY AND CONCLUSION

This chapter began by tracing the evolution of uncertainty avoidance as a construct from its beginnings in the social sciences and organizational behavior (Cyert & March, 1963) to its conceptualization as a dimension of national culture by Hofstede (1980). Cross-cultural research on uncertainty avoidance since Hofstede's (1980) seminal publication has largely made use of his scale. The GLOBE study represents the first rigorous attempt to operationalize the construct from theoretical underpinnings since Hofstede's work. The GLOBE scales, in addition to overcoming some of the limitations of Hofstede's measures, also distinguished between practices and values at the societal and organizational levels of analyses. In the GLOBE project, Uncertainty Avoidance was defined in terms of the tendency toward orderliness, consistency, structure, and regulation in society.

The empirical results of the GLOBE study provide some insight into the construct of

Uncertainty Avoidance. In this chapter we have demonstrated that organizations reflect the culture (values, but not practices) in the society in which they are embedded. The notion that organizational values are reflected in the society is consistent with Hofstede's (2001) thesis regarding uncertainty avoidance as a value. A negative association between GLOBE Uncertainty Avoidance practices and values at the societal level suggests that the desire for order and structure may be strongly influenced by the extent of order and structure present in society. Notably, whereas the industrialized nations ranked high in GLOBE Uncertainty Avoidance practices and low in values, the reverse is the case with the developing nations. GLOBE Uncertainty Avoidance scores are highly correlated among the three industries from which data were obtained: food processing, finance, and telecommunications industries. This indicates a high level of consistency among industries within a societal culture.

A review of the prior research on this cultural dimension in relation to GLOBE data described in this chapter suggests that uncertainty avoidance may be related to several societal, economic, and organizational variables. Specifically, Uncertainty Avoidance practices and values, as measured by the GLOBE scales, were found to be related to innovation, perceptions of risk, per capita cash holdings, and growth, among other variables. The data suggest that societies with high scores for GLOBE Uncertainty Avoidance practices tend to have a higher level of economic prosperity and enjoy more civil liberties, a higher level of competitiveness in the global market, greater security, higher life expectancy, and greater general satisfaction. Higher Uncertainty Avoidance practices were also related to more emphasis on basic science and research.

At the organizational level, uncertainty avoidance has implications for organizational variables such as selection practices. The above review of the literature suggests that uncertainty-avoiding societies may have a relatively high degree of formalization and decentralization in organizational structure. It is plausible that appropriate uncertainty avoidance practices make it possible for decentralization of operations rather than management by personal control.

Finally, uncertainty avoidance has implications for which leadership styles are seen as most effective in society. A series of hierarchical linear modeling procedures performed to examine the influence of Uncertainty Avoidance on implicit leadership theories at the individual, organizational, and societal levels of analysis showed that cultural dimensions differently influence each of six leadership styles: Higher Uncertainty Avoidance values were associated with higher Team-Oriented, Humane-Oriented, and Self-Protective leadership CLT dimensions; and higher Uncertainty Avoidance values were associated with lower Participative and Charismatic/Value- Based leadership CLT dimensions.

In conclusion, the GLOBE study offers further insights into the construct of Uncertainty Avoidance and its relationship to societal, organizational, and leadership variables. The distinction between Uncertainty Avoidance values and practices scores is brought into sharp focus through a negative correlation between the scores. Uncertainty Avoidance, as measured in the GLOBE study, also has conceptual and empirical links to Power Distance, Individualism, and other dimensions of national culture.

ENDNOTES

1. The three personality dimensions for the EPQ are *neuroticism versus emotional stability, extraversion versus introversion,* and *psychoticism versus ego control.*

2. Hofstede (1984) also distinguished the intolerance of ambiguity as an attitudinal component of the authoritarian personality from the intolerance of ambiguity as a cultural norm. The first is presumably an aspect of power distance, the second of uncertainty avoidance.

3. The Hofstede (1980) model does not address the individual level of analysis. However, Hofstede, Bond, and Luk (1993) suggest that some aspects of cultural values could be effectively studied at differing levels of analysis, although these manifestations will not be the same at the various levels of analysis.

4. On the basis of research conducted into the 1980s and 1990s using value survey modules (VSM) developed by Hofstede, a new set of measures was developed (VSM 94). The uncertainty avoidance

measure was amended such that the employment longevity question was removed, replaced by two additional questions: "One can be a good manager without having precise answers to most questions that subordinates may raise about their work" and "Competition between employees usually does more harm than good." Unfortunately, no psychometric properties were made available justifying the selection and inclusion of these items as measures of uncertainty avoidance.

5. Using the Hofstede dimensions as a paradigm is practiced whenever the dimensions, or the Hofstede country rankings on which the dimensions are based, are used as a theoretical framework external to their original setting.

6. Twenty-eight replications examined matched populations with paired sets of a minimum of two separate populations; 16 studies examined single populations; 13 studies made use of research designs and measures different from Hofstede (1980).

7. The Hoppe study had 18 countries in common with the Hofstede sample.

8. The average Salzburg alumni score was 32.9 points lower on UAI than the Hofstede sample of IBM employees.

9. To measure uncertainty, the authors modified measures developed by Gudykunst and Nishida (1986), to measure anxiety they used measures developed by Stephan and Stephan (1985), and to assess perceived effectiveness of communication the authors developed original measures (see Gudykunst, & Chua, Nishida, 1986).

10. There was also a significant multivariate main effect for culture, and significant univariate effects for anxiety, uncertainty, and effectiveness for relationship and culture.

11. The authors do not provide correlation values; only the p values associated with each relationship and the model fit estimates.

12. These years were carefully selected to closely match the time period of the data collection of Hofstede (1980).

13. This control was achieved by taking national rates of innovation as per capita numbers of trademarks granted in the United States and world markets to nationals from the 33 countries under study.

14. Shane did not provide correlations of the independent and dependent variable, thus a more detailed discussion is precluded.

15. Reliable measures for the championing strategy of persuasion could not be created for this study, thus the relationship between uncertainty avoidance

and persuasion based on financial measures could not be tested.

16. The four companies were a life and property insurance company, a financial services firm, a petrochemical firm, and a consumer electronics firm.

17. Our response bias correction procedure identified response bias in some countries for this scale. We recomputed the predicted response bias corrected scale score for each country:

Practices: Indonesia, 3.92 (moves from band B to band C); Morocco, 3.95 (no change in band); Qatar, 4.26 (moves from band C to band B); and Taiwan, 4.04 (moves from band B to band C).

For a complete discussion of this procedure and all response bias corrected scores, see Appendix B.

18. Our response bias correction procedure identified response bias in some countries for this scale. We recomputed the predicted response bias corrected scale score for each country:

Values: France, 4.65 (moves from band C to band B) and Morocco, 5.77 (no change in band).

For a complete discussion of this procedure and all response bias corrected scores, see Appendix B.

19. Controlling for age, Hofstede reported Japan to be highest on UAI.

20. In a later study involving 30 countries, Shane et al. (1995) again missed an opportunity to investigate this influential variable in connection with uncertainty avoidance.

21. This correlation was obtained by ranking the country mean scores on monitoring.

22. With the sample size of 11 nations, however, none of the correlations are statistically significant, but the relationship is worth noting.

23. As reported in Chapter 20 by Brodbeck, Hanges, Dickson, Gupta, and Dorfman, we found that all the cultural dimensions of organizational cultural values and practices significantly differed across societies. Although important, this prior analysis did not identify the particular aspect of societal differences that was related to organizational culture. In the present chapter, we found that societal and organizational Uncertainty Avoidance practices were not significantly related ($p > .05$). In contrast, we found strong results for societal and organizational Uncertainty Avoidance values (R^2 Total = 23.1%, R^2 Societal = 84.5%, $p < .01$). As discussed in Chapter 11 by Hanges, Dickson, and Sipe, the R^2 Total considers all levels of analysis (i.e., individual, organizational, and societal), whereas the R^2 Societal isolates the societal-level portion of the dependent variable and

indicates the percentage of variance accounted for by the predictor at only this level. Whereas we have primarily taken the conservative approach and reported the R^2 Total in GLOBE, several scholars suggest that R^2 Societal provides a more accurate description of aggregated relationships. For further discussion, see the paper by Lance and James (1999).

24. Results between the single HLM and multiple HLM tests will likely differ somewhat. The differences between the results of the multiple HLMs and single HLMs are conceptually similar to the differences between a multiple regression analysis and a correlation coefficient. Table 21.10 in Chapter 21 by Dorfman et al. presents both single and multiple HLM coefficients. In addition, the relationships for all culture dimension values are summarized in Chapter 3 (Javidan & House).

REFERENCES

Ackelsberg, R., & Arlow, P. (1985). Small businesses do plan and it pays off. *Long Range Planning, 18*(5), 61–67.

Adler, N. J. (1991). *International dimensions of organizational behavior.* Boston: Plus Kent.

Adorno, T. W., Frenkel-Brunswick, E., Levinson, D. J., & Sanford, R. N. (1950). *The authoritarian personality.* New York: Harper.

Arrindell, W. A., Hatzichristou, C., Wensink, J., Rosenberg, E., van Twillert, B., Stedema, J., & Meiijer, D. (1997). Dimensions of national culture as predictors of cross-national differences in subjective well-being. *Personality and Individual Differences, 23*(1), 37–53.

Ashford, S. J. (1986). Feedback-seeking in individual adaptation: A resource perspective. *Academy of Management Journal, 29*, 465–487.

Ashford, S. J. (1988). Individual strategies for coping with stress during organizational transitions. *Journal of Applied Behavioral Science, 24*, 19–36.

Ashford, S. J., Blatt, R., & VandeWalle, D. (in press). Reflections on the looking glass: A review of research on feedback-seeking behavior in organizations. *Journal of Management.*

Ashford, S. J., & Cummings, L. L. (1983). Feedback as an individual resource: Personal strategies of creating information. *Organizational Behavior and Human Performance, 32*, 370–398.

Ashford, S. J., & Cummings, L. L. (1985). Proactive feedback seeking: The instrumental use of the information environment. *Journal of Occupational Psychology, 58*, 67–97.

Ashkanini, M. G. A. (1984). *A cross-cultural perspective on work related values.* Unpublished doctoral dissertation, International University, San Diego.

Aspinwall, L., & Staudinger, U. (2003). *A psychology of human strengths: Fundamental questions and future directions for a positive psychology.* Washington, DC: American Psychological Association.

Atuahene-Gima, K., & Li, H. (2002). When does trust matter? Antecedents and contingent effects of supervisee trust on performance in selling new products in China and the United States. *Journal of Marketing, 66*(3), 61–81.

Babrow, A. S. (1992). Communication and problematic integration: Understanding diverging probability and value, ambiguity, ambivalence, and impossibility. *Communication Theory, 2*, 95–130.

Babrow, A. S., Hines, S. C., & Kasch, C. R. (2000). Managing uncertainty in illness explanation: An application of problematic integration theory. In B. Whaley (Ed.), *Explaining illness: Research, theory, and strategies* (pp. 41–67). Hillsdale, NJ: Lawrence Erlbaum.

Bailey, J. B., Chen, C. C., & Dou, S.-G. (1997). Conceptions of self and performance-related feedback in the U.S., Japan, and China. *Journal of International Business Studies, 28*, 605–625.

Basabe, N., Paez, D., Valencia, J., Gonzalez, J. L., Rime, B., & Diener, E. (2002). Cultural dimensions, socioeconomic development, climate, and emotional hedonic level. *Cognition and Emotion, 16*(1), 103–125.

Baskerville, R. F. (2003). Hofstede never studied culture. *Accounting, Organizations and Society, 28*, 1–14.

Beatty, C. A., & Gordon, J. R. M. (1988). Barriers to the implementation of CAD/CAM systems. *Sloan Management Review, 29*(4), 25–33.

Bennett, N., Herold, D. M., & Ashford, S. J. (1990). The effects of tolerance for ambiguity on feedback-seeking behavior. *Journal of Occupational Psychology, 63*, 343–348

Berger, C. R., & Bradac, J. J. (1982). *Language and social knowledge: Uncertainty in interpersonal relations.* London: Edward Arnold.

Berger, C. R., & Calabrese, R. J. (1975). Some explorations in initial interaction and beyond: Toward a developmental theory of interpersonal communication. *Human Communication Research, 1,* 99–112.

Bochner, S. (1965). Defining intolerance of ambiguity. *Psychological Record, 15,* 393–400.

Bontempo, R. N., Bottom, W. P., & Weber, E. U. (1997). Cross-cultural differences in risk perception: A model-based approach. *Risk Analysis, 17*(4), 479–488.

Bracket, J. S., Keats, B. W., & Pearson, J. N. (1988). Planning and financial performance among small firms in a growth industry. *Strategic Management Journal, 9,* 591–603.

Bradac, J. J. (2001). Theory comparison: Uncertainty reduction, problematic integration, uncertainty management, and other curious constructs. *Journal of Communication, 51*(3), 456–476.

Brett, J. M., Feldman, D. C., & Weingart, L. R. (1990). Feedback-seeking behavior of new hires and job changers. *Journal of Management, 16,* 737–149.

Brown, S. P., Ganesan, S., & Challagalla, G. (2001). Self-efficacy as a moderator of information-seeking effectiveness. *Journal of Applied Psychology, 86,* 1043–1051.

Budner, S. (1962). Intolerance of ambiguity as a personality variable. *Journal of Personality, 30,* 29–59.

Burgelman, R. (1983). A process model of internal corporate venturing in the major diversified firm. *Administrative Science Quarterly, 28,* 223–244.

Callister, R. R., Kramer, M. W., & Turban, D. B. (1999). Feedback seeking following career transitions. *Academy of Management Journal, 42,* 429–438.

Chakrabarti, A. (1974). The role of champion in product innovation. *California Management Review, 17*(2), 58–62.

Chew, I. K. H., & Putti, J. (1993). *A comparative study of work-related values of Singaporean and Japanese managers in Singapore* (Working Paper). Nanyang Technological University, Singapore.

Chow, C. W., Shields, M. D., & Chan, Y. K. (1991). The effects of management controls and national culture on manufacturing performance. *Accounting, Organizations and Society,* 209–226.

Clampitt, P. G., & de Koch, R. J. (2002). *The essence of leadership* (2nd ed.). New York: M. E. Sharpe.

Clark, R. W. (1984). *Einstein: The life and times.* New York: Avon Books.

Cyert, R. M., & March, J. G. (1963). *A behavioral theory of the firm.* Englewood Cliffs, NJ: Prentice Hall.

Dawson, J. W. (1999, June). Godel and the limits of logic. *Scientific American,* pp. 76–81.

de Bettignies, H. C., & Evans, P. L. (1977). The cultural dimension of top executives' careers: A comparative analysis. In T. D. Weinshall (Ed.), *Culture and management.* Harmondsworth, UK: Penguin.

Demerath, L. (1993). Knowledge-based affect. *Social Psychology Quarterly, 56,* 136–147.

Dessler, G. (1993). Value-based hiring builds commitment. *Workforce, 72*(11), 98–101.

Diener, E. (2000). Subjective well-being: The science of happiness and a proposal for a national index. *American Psychologist, 55*(1), 34–43.

Diener, E., Diener, M., & Diener, C. (1995). Factors predicting the subjective well-being of nations. *Journal of Personality and Social Psychology, 69*(5), 851–864.

Dimaggio, P. J., & Powell, W. (1983). The iron cage revisited: Institutional isomorphism and collective rationality in organizational fields. *American Sociological Review, 48,* 147–160.

d'Iribarne, P. (1997). The usefulness of an ethnographic approach to the international comparison of organizations. *International Studies of Management and Organization, 26*(4), 30–47.

Doney, P. M., Cannon, J. P., & Mullen, M. R. (1998). Understanding the influence of national culture on the development of trust. *Academy of Management Review, 23*(3), 601–620.

Dunphy, D., & Shi, J. (1986). *A comparison of enterprise management in Japan and the People's Republic of China* (Working Paper 86/016). Australian Graduate School of Management, The University of Sydney and The University of New South Wales.

Earley, P. C. (1997). *Face, harmony and social structure.* New York: Oxford University Press.

Eysenck, H. J., & Eysenck, M. (1975). *Manual of the Eysenck Personality Questionnaire.* London: Hodder and Stoughton.

Fernandez, D. R., Carlson, D. S., Stepina, L. P., & Nicholson, J. D. (1997). Hofstede's country classification 25 years later. *Journal of Social Psychology, 137*(1), 43–54.

Festinger, L. (1957). *A theory of cognitive dissonance.* Palo Alto, CA: Stanford University Press.

Fidalgo, A. J. S. C. (1993). *Comparative study in work-related values between Portuguese managers using the value survey module (VSM) designed by Hofstede (1980).* Unpublished masters thesis, Fairleigh Dickinson University, Teaneck, NJ.

Fiedler, F. (1967). *A theory of leadership effectiveness.* New York: McGraw-Hill.

Ford, L. A., Babrow, A. S., & Stohl, C. (1996). Social support and the management of uncertainty: An application of problematic integration theory. *Communication Monographs, 63,* 189–207.

Forss, K. (1989). *Comparative management in public administration, a pilot study of values and attitudes in two organizations.* The Central Bureau of Statistics, The National Institute for Civil Service Training and Development and the National Tax Board.

Frenkel-Brunswik, E. (1949). Personality theory and perception. In R. Blake & G. Ramsey (Eds.), *Perception: An approach to personality* (pp. 356-419). New York: Oxford University Press.

Fukuyama, F. (1995). *Trust: The social virtues and the creation of prosperity.* New York: Free Press.

Furnham, A. (1994). A content, correlational and factor analytic study of four tolerance of ambiguity questionnaires. *Personality and Individual Differences, 16,* 403–410.

Furnham, A., & Ribchester, T. (1995). Tolerance of ambiguity: A review of the concept, its measurement and applications. *Current Psychology, 14,* 179–199.

Gordon, R. A. (1948). Short-period price determination. *American Economic Review, 38,* 265–288.

Granovetter, M. (1985, November). Economic action and social structure: The problem of embeddedness. *American Journal of Sociology, 91,* 481–510.

Gray, S. J. (1988). Towards a theory of cultural influence on the development of accounting systems internationally. *Abacus, 24*(1), 1–15.

Gudykunst, W. B. (1983). Uncertainty reduction and predictability of behavior in low- and high context cultures. *Communication Quarterly, 33,* 236–251.

Gudykunst, W. B. (1988). Uncertainty and anxiety. In Y. Y. Kim & W. B. Gudykunst (Eds.), *Theories in intercultural communication* (pp. 123–156). Newbury Park, CA: Sage.

Gudykunst, W. B. (1995). Anxiety/uncertainty management (AUM) theory: Current status. In R. Wiseman (Ed.), *Intercultural communication theory* (pp. 8–58). Thousand Oaks, CA: Sage.

Gudykunst, W. B., & Nishida, T. (2001). Anxiety, uncertainty, and perceived effectiveness of communication across relationships and cultures. *International Journal of Intercultural Relations, 25,* 55–71.

Gudykunst, W. B., Nishida, T., Chua, W. (1986). Uncertainty reduction in Japanese-North American dyads. *Communication Research Reports, 3,* 39–46.

Gudykunst, W. B., Nishida, T., & Schmidt, K. (1989). Cultural, relational, and personality influences on uncertainty reduction processes. *Western Journal of Speech Communication, 51,* 256–278.

Haire, M., Ghiselli, E. E., & Porter, L. W. (1966). *Managerial thinking: An international study.* New York: John Wiley.

Hall, E. T. (1976). *Beyond culture.* New York: Doubleday.

Hansen, J. (2001, August). *Culture's quantitative consequences: A meta analysis of the effect size of Hofstede's culture dimensions in international management.* Paper presented at the Academy of Management meetings in Washington, DC.

Hansen, N. R. (1972). The philosophical implications of quantum mechanics. In P. Edwards (Ed.), *The encyclopedia of philosophy* (Vol. 7, pp. 41–49). New York: Macmillan.

Heine, S. J., Kitayama, S., Lehman, D. R., Takata, T., Ide, E., et al. (2001). Divergent consequences of success and failure in Japan and North America: An investigation of self-improving motivations and malleable selves. *Journal of Personality and Social Psychology, 81,* 599–615.

Helmreich, R. L., & Merritt, A. C. (1998). *Culture at work in aviation and medicine: National, organizational and professional influences.* Aldershot, UK: Ashgate.

Hofstede, G. (1980). *Culture's consequences.* London: Sage.

Hofstede, G. (1984). *Culture's consequences: International differences in work-related values.* Beverly Hills, CA: Sage.

Hofstede, G. (1994). *Uncommon sense about organizations: Cases, studies, and field observations.* Thousand Oaks, CA: Sage.

Hofstede, G. (2001). *Culture's consequences: Comparing values, behaviors, institutions, and organizations across nations.* Thousand Oaks, CA: Sage.

Hofstede, G., Bond, M. H., and Luk, C.-L. (1993). Individual perceptions of organizational cultures: A methodological treatise on levels of analysis. *Organization Studies, 14*(4), 483–503.

Hoppe, M. H. (1990). *A comparative study of country elites: International differences in work-related values and learning and their implications for management training and development.* Unpublished doctoral thesis, University of North Carolina at Chapel Hill.

Howell, J., & Higgins, C. (1990). Champions of technological innovation. *Administrative Science Quarterly, 35,* 317–341.

Howell, J., & Higgins, C. (1991). Champions of change: Identifying, understanding, and supporting champions' technological innovations. *Organizational Dynamics , 10*(1), 40–55.

Humphrey, D. B., Pulley, L. B., & Vesala, J. M. (1996). Cash, paper, and electronic payments: A cross-country analysis. *Journal of Money, Credit, and Banking, 28*(4), 914–939.

Huo, P. Y., & Randall, D. M. (1991). Exploring subcultural differences in Hofstede's value survey: The case of the Chinese. *Asia Pacific Journal of Management, 8*(2), 159–173.

Ilgen, D. R., Fisher, C. D., & Taylor, M. S. (1979). Consequences of individual feedback on behavior in organizations. *Journal of Applied Psychology, 64,* 349–371.

Inglehart, R. (1997). *Modernization and postmodernization: Cultural, economic and political change in 43 societies.* Princeton, NJ: Princeton University Press.

Inglehart, R., & Baker, W. E. (2000). Modernization, cultural change, and the persistence of traditional values, *American Sociological Review, 65*(1), 19–51.

Inglehart, R., Basanez, M., & Moreno, A. (1998). *Human values and beliefs: A cross-cultural sourcebook.* Ann Arbor: University of Michigan Press.

Inkson, J. H. K., Schwitter, J. P., Pheysey, D. C., & Hickson, D. J. (1970). A comparison of organization structure and managerial roles: Ohio, U.S.A., and the Midlands, UK. *Journal of Management Studies, 7,* 347–363.

Inlis, I. R. (2000). The central role of uncertainty reduction in determining behaviour. *Behaviour, 137,* 1567–1599.

Jeanquart-Barone, S., & Peluchette, J. L. V. (1999). Examining the impact of the cultural dimension of uncertainty avoidance on staffing decisions: A look at U.S. and German firms. *Cross Cultural Management, 6*(3), 3–12.

Judge, T., & Bono, J. E. (2001). Relationship of core self-evaluation traits—self-esteem, generalized self-efficacy, locus of control, and emotional stability—with job satisfaction and job performance: A meta-analysis. *Journal of Applied Psychology, 86,* 80–92.

Kahn, R. L., Wolfe, D. M., Quinn, R. P., Snoek, J. D., & Rosenthal, R. A. (1964). *Organizational stress: Studies in role conflict and role ambiguity.* New York: John Wiley.

Kale, S. H., & McIntyre, R. P. (1991). Distribution channel relationships in diverse cultures. *International Marketing Review , 8*(3), 31–45.

Kanter, R. (1982). *The change masters.* New York: Simon and Schuster.

Kanter, R. (1988). When a thousand flowers bloom: Structural, collective, and social conditions for innovation in organizations. In L. Cummings & B. Staw (Eds.), *Research in organizational behavior* (Vol. 10, pp. 169–211). Greenwich, CT: JAI.

Kelly, J. R., & Barsade, S. G. (2001). Mood and emotions in small groups and work teams. *Organizational Behavior & Human Decision Processes, 86,* 99–130.

Kim, U., Triandis, H. C., Kagitçibasi, C., Choi, S.-C., & Yoon, G. (1994). Introduction. In U. Kim, H. C. Triandis, C. Kagitçibasi, S.-C. Choi, & G. Yoon (Eds.), *Individualism and collectivism: Theory, method, and applications* (pp. 1-16). Thousand Oaks, CA: Sage.

Kluger, A. N., & DeNisi, A. (1996). The effects of feedback interventions on performance: A historical review, a meta-analysis, and a preliminary feedback intervention theory. *Psychological Bulletin, 119,* 254–284.

Kohn, M. L. (1971). Bureaucratic man: A portrait and an interpretation. *American Sociological Review, 36,* 461–474.

Kreitler, S., Maguen, T., & Kreitler, H. (1975). The three faces of intolerance of ambiguity. *Archiv Für Psychologie, 127,* 238–250.

Lance, C. E., & James, L. R. (1999). A proportional variance accounted for index for some cross-level and person-situation research designs. *Organizational Research Methods, 2,* 395–418.

Lebas, M., & Weigenstein, J. (1986). Management control: The roles of rules, markets, and culture. *Journal of Management Studies, 23,* 259–273.

Leung, T., & Yeung, L. L. (1995). Negotiation in the People's Republic of China: Results of a survey of small businesses in Hong Kong. *Journal of Small Business Management, 33*(1), 70–77.

Le Vine, R. A. (1973). *Culture, behavior and personality: An introduction to the comparative study of psychosocial adaptation.* Chicago: AVC.

Lowe, S. (1996). Hermes revisited: A replication of Hofstede's study in Hong Kong and the UK. *Asia Pacific Business Review , 2*(3), 101–119.

Lumpkin, G. T., Shrader, R. C., & Hills, G. E. (1998). Does formal business planning enhance the performance of new ventures? In P. S. Reynolds, W. D. Bygrave, N. M. Carter, S. Manigart, C. M. Mason, G. D. Meyer, & K. G. Shaver (Eds.), *Frontiers of entrepreneurship research* (pp. 180-189). Wellesley, MA: Babson College Press.

Lyle, M. A., Baird, L. S., Orns, B., & Kuratko, D. E. (1995). Formalized planning in small business: Increasing strategic choice. *Journal of Small Business Management, 33*(1), 38–50.

Lynn, R., & Hampson, S. L. (1975). National difference in extraversion and neuroticism. *British Journal of Social and Clinical Psychology, 14,* 223–240.

Lynn, R., & Hampson, S. L. (1977). Fluctuations in national levels of neuroticism and extraversion, 1935-1970. *British Journal of Social and Clinical Psychology, 16,* 131–137.

Lynn, R., & Martin, T. (1995). National differences for 39 nations in extraversion, neuroticism, psychoticism and economic, demographic and other correlates. *Personality and Individual Differences, 19,* 403–406.

Lytle, A. L., Brett, J. M., Barsness, Z. I., Tinsley, C. H., & Janssens, M. (1995). A paradigm for confirmatory cross-cultural research in organization behavior. In *Research in organizational behavior* (Vol. 17, pp. 167–214). Greenwich, CT: JAI.

Maldonado, E. M. (1983). *Mexican-American participation in law enforcement in California: Law enforcement: the impact of cultural related value differences.* Unpublished doctoral thesis, Claremont Graduate School, Claremont, CA.

McClelland, D. C. (1961). *The achieving society.* Princeton, NJ: Van Nostrand Reinhold.

McGregor, D. (1960). *The human side of enterprise.* New York: McGraw-Hill.

McNally, G. M. (1980). Responsibility accounting and organizational control: Some perspectives and prospects. *Journal of Business Finance and Accounting , 7*(2), 165–181.

Millendorfer, J. (1976). *Mechanisms of socio-psychological development.* Vienna: Studiengruppe für Internationale Analysen.

Miller, V. D., & Jablin, F. M. (1991). Information seeking during organizational entry: Influences, tactics, and a model of the process. *Academy of Management Review, 16,* 92–120.

Morrison, E. W. (1993). Newcomer information seeking: Exploring types, modes, sources, and outcomes. *Academy of Management Journal, 36,* 557–589.

Morrison, E. W. (2002). Information seeking with organizations. *Human Communication Research, 28,* 229–242.

Nakane, C. (1974). The social system reflected in interpersonal communication. In J. Condon & M. Saito (Eds.), *Intercultural encounters with Japan* (124–131). Tokyo: Simul Press.

Nakata, C., & Sivakumar, K. (1996). National culture and new product development: An integrative review. *Journal of Marketing, 60,* 61–72.

Norton, R. (1975). Measurement of ambiguity tolerance. *Journal of Personality Assessment, 39,* 607–619.

Pascale, R. T., & Athos, A. G. (1983). *The art of Japanese management.* New York: Penguin.

Pelto, P. J. (1968, April). The difference between "tight" and "loose" societies. *Trans-Action,* 37–40.

Perrow, C. (1972). *Complex organizations: A critical essay.* Glenview, IL: Scott, Foresman.

Peterson, M. F., Smith, P. B. Akande, A., Ayestaran, S., Bochner, S., Callan, V., Cho, N., et al. (1995). Role conflict, ambiguity, and overload: A 21-nation study. *Academy of Management Journal, 38*(2), 429–452.

Pooyam, A. (1984). *Acculturation, acculturative stress and their relationships to both work and non-work outcomes.* Unpublished doctoral dissertation, Management Science, University of Texas at Dallas.

Punnett, B. J., & Withaney, S. (1988). *Testing the validity of Hofstede's value indices.* Unpublished paper, University of Windsor, Ontario, Canada.

Randall, D. M. (1993). Cross-cultural research on organizational commitment: A review and application of Hofstede's Values Survey Module. *Journal of Business Research, 26*(1), 91–110.

Reader's Digest. (1970). *A survey of Europe today.* London: Author.

Reeder, J. A. (1987). When west meets east: Cultural aspects of doing business in Asia. *Business Horizons, 30,* 69–74.

Renn, R. W., & Fedor, D. B. (2001). Development and field test of a feedback seeking, self-efficacy, and goal setting model of work performance. *Journal of Management, 27,* 563–583.

Robinson, W. S. (1950). Ecological correlations and the behavior of individuals. *American Sociological Review, 15,* 351–357.

Rossini, F. D. (1950). *Chemical thermodynamics.* New York: John Wiley.

Ryan, A. M., McFarland, L., Baron, H., & Page, R. (1999). An international look at section practices: Nation and culture as explanations for variability in practice. *Personnel Psychology, 52,* 359–391.

Ryans, C. C. (1997). Resources: Writing a business plan. *Journal of Small Business Management, 35*(2), 95–98.

Rydell, S., & Rosen, E. (1966). Measurement and some correlates of need cognition. *Psychological Reports, 19,* 139–165.

Salter, S. B., & Niswander, F. (1995, Second Quarter). Cultural influence on the development of accounting systems internationally: A test of Gray's [1988] theory. *Journal of International Business Studies,* 379–397.

Sathe, V. (1988). Fostering entrepreneurship in the large diversified firm. *Organizational Dynamics, 7*(2), 20–32.

Schon, D. (1963). Champions for radical new inventions. *Harvard Business Review, 41,* 77–86.

Schramm-Nielsen, J. (2000). How to interpret uncertainty avoidance scores: A comparison study of Danish and French firms. *Cross Cultural Management, 7*(4), 3–11.

Schwartz, S. H. (1999). A theory of cultural values and some implications for work. *Applied Psychology: An International Review, 48,* 23–47.

Schyns, P. (1998). Crossnational differences in happiness: Economic and cultural factors explored. *Social Indicators Research, 43,* 3–26.

Seligman, M., & Csikszentmihalyi, M. (2000). Positive psychology. *American Psychologist, 55,* 5–14.

Seligman, M. E. P. (1999). The president's address. *American Psychologist, 54,* 559–562.

Shackleton, V. J., & Ali, A. H. (1990). Work-related values of managers: A test of the Hofstede model. *Journal of Cross-Cultural Psychology, 21*(1), 109–118.

Shane, S. (1993). Cultural influences on national rates of innovation. *Journal of Business Venturing, 8,* 59–73.

Shane, S. (1994). Cultural values and the championing process. *Entrepreneurship Theory and Practice, 18*(4), 25–41.

Shane, S. (1995). Uncertainty avoidance and the preference for innovation championing roles. *Journal of International Business Studies, 26,* 47–68.

Shane, S., Venkataraman, S., & MacMillan, I. (1995). Cultural differences in innovation championing strategies. *Journal of Management, 21*(5), 931–952.

Shapero, A., & Sokol, L. (1982). The social dimensions of entrepreneurship. In C. Kent, D. Sexton, & K. Vesper (Eds.), *Encyclopedia of entrepreneurship* (pp. 72–90). Englewood Cliffs, NJ: Prentice Hall.

Singh, J. P. (1990). Managerial culture and work-related values in India. *Organization Studies, 11*(1), 75–101.

Smith, P. B., & Schwartz, S. H. (1997). Values. In J. W. Berry, M. H. Segall, & K. Kagitçibasi (Eds.), *Handbook of cross-cultural psychology* (Vol. 3, 77–118). Needham, MA: Allyn & Bacon.

Snyder, C. R., & Lopez, S. J. (2002). *Handbook of positive psychology.* New York: Oxford University Press.

Soeters, J. L., & Schreuder, H. (1988). The interaction between national and organizational cultures in accounting firms. *Accounting, Organizations and Society, 13,* 75–85.

Søndergaard, M. (1994). Hofstede's consequences: A study of reviews, citations and replications. *Organization Studies, 15,* 447–456.

Steel, P., & Ones, D. S. (2002). Personality and happiness: A national-level analysis. *Journal of Personality and Social Psychology, 83,* 767–781.

Stephan, W., & Stephan, C. (1985). Intergroup anxiety. *Journal of Social Issues, 41,* 157–166.

Stohl, C. (1993). European managers' interpretations of participation: A semantic network analysis. *Human Communications Research, 20*(1), 97–117.

Sully de Luque, M. F., & Sommer, S. M. (2000). The impact of culture on feedback seeking behavior: An integrated model and propositions. *Academy of Management Review, 25,* 829–849.

Tannenbaum, A. S., Kavcic, B., Rosner, M., Vianello, M., & Wieser, G. (1974). *Hierarchy in organizations*. San Francisco: Jossey-Bass.

Tayeb, M. (1994). Organizations and national culture: Methodology considered. *Organization Studies, 15*(3), 429–446.

Thorndike, E. L. (1939). On the fallacy of imputing the correlations found for groups to the individuals or smaller groups composing them. *American Journal of Psychology, 3,* 122–124.

Triandis, H. C. (1989). The self and social behavior in differing cultural contexts. *Psychological Review, 96,* 506–520.

Trompenaars, F. (1994). *Riding the waves of culture.* New York: Irwin.

Turner, J. H. (1988). *A theory of social interaction.* Palo Alto, CA: Stanford University Press.

Ueno, S., & Sekaran, U. (1992). The influence of culture on budget control practices in the USA and Japan: An empirical study. *Journal of International Business Studies, 23*(4), 659–674.

Van de Ven, A. (1986). Central problems in the management of innovation. *Management Science, 32*(5), 590–607.

van Gunsteren, H. R. (1976). *The quest for control: A critique of the rational-central-rule approach in public affairs.* London: Wiley.

Venkataraman, S., Shane, S., McGrath, R., & MacMillan, I. (1993). Some central tensions in the management of corporate venturing. In S. Birley & I. MacMillan (Eds.), *Entrepreneurship research: Global perspectives* (pp. 177–199). Amsterdam: Elsevier Science.

Verweij, J., Ester, P., & Nauta, R. (1997). Secularization as an economic and cultural phenomenon: A cross-national analysis. *Journal for the Scientific Study of Religion, 36*(2), 309–324.

Walsh, T. (1995). *Biosociology: An emerging paradigm.* Westport, CT: Praeger.

Wanberg, C. R., & Kammeyer-Mueller, J. D. (2000). Predictors and outcomes of proactivity in the socialization process. *Journal of Applied Psychology, 85,* 373–385.

Weber, E. U., & Hsee, C. (1998). Cross-cultural differences in risk perception, but cross-cultural similarities in attitudes toward perceived risk. *Management Science, 44,* 1205–1218.

Weber, E. U., & Milliman, R. A. (1997). Perceived risk attitudes: Relating risk perception to risky choice. *Management Science, 43,* 123–145.

Westwood, R. G., & Everett, J. E. (1987). Culture's consequences: A methodology for comparative management studies in Southeast Asia. *Asia Pacific Journal of Management, 4*(3), 187–202.

Williamson, O. (1975). *Markets and hierarchies.* New York: Free Press.

Witkin, H. A., & Berry, J. W. (1975). Psychological differentiation in cross-cultural perspective. *Journal of Cross-Cultural Psychology, 6,* 4–87.

Yates, J. F., Zhu, Y., Ronis, D. L., Wang, D. F., Shinotsuka, H., & Masanao, T. (1989). Probability judgment accuracy: China, Japan, and the United States. *Organizational Behavior and Human Decision Processes, 43,* 145–171.

Yeh, R. (1988, August). Values of American, Japanese and Taiwanese managers in Taiwan: A test of Hofstede' framework. In *Best Paper Proceedings* at the annual meeting of the Academy of Management Annual Meetings, Anaheim, CA.

Zarzeski, M. T. (1996). Spontaneous harmonization effects of culture and market forces on accounting disclosure practices. *Accounting Horizons, 10*(1), 18–37.

Zhao, J. J. (2000). The Chinese approach to international business negotiation. *Journal of Business Communication, 37,* 209–237.

20

SOCIETAL CULTURE AND INDUSTRIAL SECTOR INFLUENCES ON ORGANIZATIONAL CULTURE

FELIX C. BRODBECK

PAUL J. HANGES

MARCUS W. DICKSON

VIPIN GUPTA

PETER W. DORFMAN

A major premise of the GLOBE study is that organizational cultural practices are influenced by factors external to the organization itself. As indicated in the GLOBE conceptual model, societal culture is predicted to affect the cultures of the organizations embedded within these societies. In addition to societal culture, the basic nature of industry also influences organizational practices. Many authors observe that the industrial sector to which an organization belongs and the common kinds of pressures encountered by organizations, such as the rate of technological change and the general level of environmental turbulence, affect organizational cultural practices (e.g., Chatman & Jehn, 1994; Gordon, 1991; Phillips, 1994).

The purpose of the present chapter is to explore the extent to which there are unique and interactive effects of societal system and industry sector on organizational cultural practices (See Chapter 5 by Dickson, BeShears, & Gupta for theoretical background).

As described in Chapter 8 by Hanges and Dickson, we developed separate cultural practices and cultural values scales at both the organizational and societal level of analysis. We sampled multiple middle managers from organizations. The middle managers were randomly assigned and asked to complete one of two versions of the GLOBE survey. Although both versions asked about effective leadership characteristics and behaviors, only Form Alpha asked about organizational cultural practices and values and only

Form Beta asked about societal cultural practices and values[1]. Multiple organizations from one or more of three different industries (finance, food processing, telecommunications) were sampled from the 62 different cultures.

In the next section, we will discuss the rationale for choosing the three specific industries sampled in GLOBE. In particular, we will discuss the range of environmental pressures experienced by organizations in these different industries to indicate why we expect sufficient variation in these types of industries to expect an effect on organizational cultural practices.

INDUSTRY SECTORS AND
ORGANIZATIONAL CULTURAL PRACTICES

The GLOBE data were sampled from the telecommunications, food processing, and financial services industrial sectors. We selected these three industries because we believed that they were present in most, if not all, countries in the world, and because we believed that these industries systematically differed from one another. In this section, we provide brief descriptions of these industrial sectors. We obtained this information by reviewing electronic databases such as the Standard & Poor's industry surveys or the Economist Intelligence Unit's industry reports.

The telecommunication industrial sector is relatively new in comparison to the financial and food services industrial sectors. Although the telecommunication industrial sector initially embraced bureaucratic cultural practices and values, major transformations of this industrial sector started in the 1980s. For example, the British Telecommunication Company was privatized during this decade and the AT&T monopoly was broken up in the United States. The telecommunication industrial sector was among the fastest growing sectors in the 1990s.

The food-processing industry, in contrast, is one of the oldest industrial sectors. This sector is currently facing new market challenges, such as customer preferences for fresher, organic, ready-to-eat, and ecologically friendly food. The processed food industry is among the least sensitive to the general economic turbulence. Though people often tend to shift their consumption patterns in times of economic downturn, overall demand appears to be stable in this industry. In fact, the processed food sector is frequently considered a safe haven for global investors in times of slower economic growth.

Finally, with regard to the financial services industry, the dismantling of regulatory barriers separating banking, insurance, and securities segments has facilitated development of a global capital market. Over the years, commercial paper and corporate bonds have substituted bank loans, while mutual funds and securities have replaced some bank deposits. There has also been competition from outside each industry. Although automotive and aerospace firms have had their own financial service subsidiaries for a long time, as have retailers and several consumer electronic firms offering credit facilities, telecommunication and utility firms have also begun offering payment and other services through their distribution networks and customer relationships. The result is growth of financial service companies that offer a whole range of services, combining financial services production with distribution networks and brand names (Clasessens, Glaessner, & Klingebiel, 2000).

The financial services firms are intermediaries who seek to profit from exposing themselves to risks and not matching assets and liabilities on a one-to-one basis. The financial services industry therefore is quite sensitive to economic fluctuations. Demand for these services tend to peak during the early phases of economic upturn, when interest rates are low. As economic growth proceeds, organizations that fall outside of the financial services sector tend to provide sources of financing to consumers, thereby decreasing demand for the services of traditional financial services industry organizations. Consequently, there is much emphasis on international diversification of portfolios, which makes the industry more sensitive to economic crises in any part of the world, and less sensitive to the societal factors.

In summary, there are differences in the environments experienced by these three industries. The food services industry experiences a more stable environment, the telecommunications industry has experienced a more turbulent environment since the 1980s, and the financial services industry is quite sensitive to environmental pressures. Indeed, consistent with this perspective, Harvey (personal communication with Vipin Gupta, July 27th, 2001) has examined the volatility of these three industries worldwide. He found that the global financial services industrial sector is the most volatile of our three industries. The food services industrial sector has been relatively stable for a long time. Finally, Harvey has documented that the telecommunications industry experienced a dramatic change worldwide after the 1980s. As documented by Harvey's research, these three industries have experienced different environments over their histories and the organizational cultural practices seen in these industries probably differ as a result.

HYPOTHESES

We propose and test three potential relationships between industrial sectors and societal cultures. The first hypothesis is concerned with the effects of societal systems on organizational cultures. The simple fact that most people live the majority of their lives within a single culture makes it highly likely that the normative prescriptions and behavioral expectations of that culture would be reflected in the organizations in which they function. Given that there is a long tradition in the management literature of viewing organizations as "open systems influenced by the environment" (Katz & Kahn, 1966; Lee & Barnett, 1997, p. 398), societal culture should be a major source of influence on organizational systems. Further, the founder of an organization, along with other influential organizational leaders, probably has a major influence on the practices, policies, and culture of an organization (Schneider, 1987; Schneider, Goldstein, & Smith, 1995). It is likely that these leaders try to develop organizational practices and policies that appear to be sensible and strategic for their organization.

Although there is variation in the extent to which any given individual shares a society's cultural values and beliefs, cultural immersion theory as well as cognitive researchers (e.g., Hanges, Lord, & Dickson, 2000) have argued that societal culture influences the beliefs of individuals regarding what is sensible or strategic within a particular society. Values of

founders and other organizational leaders are thus differentially influenced by the larger society's values, and these founders and leaders have differential effects on the organizations they create and lead. Thus, an effect of a value at the societal level on the analogous value at the organizational level is mediated by the values of founders. Resource dependency theory and institutional theory also suggest that coercive isomorphism (based on political and legal pressures), mimetic isomorphism (based on modeling other successful organizations), and normative isomorphism (based on rules and norms) all operate to influence organizations through the society in which they are embedded. Further, the international business literature suggests that organizations compete in a globalizing world on the basis of their home-base advantages. On the basis of this discussion, we suggest the following hypothesis on the significance of home-based societal factors in the practices of the organizations:

Hypothesis 1: The societal system has a significant effect on organizational cultural practices

The second hypothesis is concerned with a common industry sector effect on organizational cultural practices. There is evidence that organizational practices respond to the industry-related contextual contingencies. For example, Kerr, Dunlop, Harbison, and Charles (1960) and Hickson, Hinings, McMillan, and Schwitter (1974) indicate that technology and machines directly influence how people perform their work, regardless of nationality, and constrain organization design choices. In addition, several theoretical mechanisms suggest that industry might have a direct effect on organizational culture. Resource dependency theory, for example, suggests that organizations attempt to control the resources that are necessary to them (Pfeffer, 1981; Pfeffer & Salancik, 1978). The commonality of the perception of necessary resources by organizational leaders in the same industry probably reduces the range of practices in these organizations as these leaders attempt to maintain their organization's technological and operational efficiency as well as achieve social legitimacy for their organization (Abernathy & Chua, 1996).

Further, institutional theory takes into consideration the larger institutional environment, which consists of the elaboration of rules, practices, symbols, beliefs, and normative requirements to which individual organizations must conform to receive support and legitimacy (DiMaggio & Powell, 1983; Meyer & Rowan, 1991). In an attempt to achieve legitimacy and support, institutional theory suggests that organizations mimic other organizations in their industry (DiMaggio & Powell, 1983). Finally, so called "value added networks" within industries link organizations into collectives. Such collectives tend to increase the similarity of member organizations' strategic profiles (Abrahamson & Fombrun, 1994) and thus foster the development of industry-specific interorganizational macrocultures, such as beliefs that are shared by managers across organizations. An industrial culture, therefore, emerges because of the similarity in practices by organizations within a given industry. More generally, in global industries, one would expect a shared industry-wide practice to emerge as a result of bench-marking, and of common and converging technical imperatives, needs of customers, and regulatory standards. Given this review, we advance the following hypothesis on the existence of some global element in the industries sampled:

Hypothesis 2: The industrial sector has a significant main effect on organizational cultural practices

The third, and final, hypothesis is concerned with a society by industry interaction. Sufficient evidence indicates that industrial sector effects are often mediated and shaped by societal cultures. For instance, the regulatory environment tends to differ across societies, as is the case with financial services as well as telecommunications industry. Empirical evidence of this interaction was provided in a study by Mason and Finegold (1997). These authors compared the organizational practices of eight biscuit manufacturing factories in Germany and the United States. After controlling for size of plant, the productivity of these factories was equivalent even though the organizations in Germany appeared to be characterized as adopting sociotechnical systems principles whereas in the United States, the factories were using practices based on scientific management principles. The German workers, who were vocationally qualified and experienced, underwent extensive on-the-job training and were given responsibility for multiple baking operations within semi-autonomous, three-person teams. In contrast, the U.S. firms used standardized production procedures that were supported by a greater use of automated or dedicated production equipment. The contrast between both systems is clear: The American experts relied on work principles consistent with scientific management, and the Germans on work principles consistent with sociotechnical systems.

In addition, a simple imitation of worldwide industry practices is not competitively advantageous for any organization existing within a particular society. The administrative heritage of the society plays an important role in the adaptation of industrywide practices by any organization (Bartlett & Ghoshal, 1990). Such society-specific adaptation of the industrywide practices can help firms gain robust home-based advantage in specific industry sectors and be differentiated from the competing organizations in other societies. Further, given the significance of the societal systems, one might observe the emergence of local industry clusters, as opposed to global industry clusters. In the local industry clusters, the organizations within a specific industry may learn from one another and develop similar organizational culture practices. Thus, we have the following third hypothesis that postulates the existence of such local industry clusters:

Hypothesis 3: There is a significant industry sector-by-societal system interaction effect on organizational cultural practices

What factor drives the development of a convergent organizational practice within a local industry cluster? We suggest that societal culture values play an important role in this process. For instance, if the value of uncertainty avoidance is prominent in a society, then the organizations may converge in adopting some practices that respond to this common societal value. The degree to which the organizations converge in responding to the common societal values may, however, vary by industry. The costs of leveraging societal culture values for developing organizational practices may vary by industry; the costs may be lower in relatively localized industries such as telecom, and be higher in relatively global industries such as financial services. Similarly, the benefits may also be lower in relatively global industries such as financial services, and greater in more local industries such as telecommunications. One may expect that the isomorphic societal values will be particularly salient in shaping the convergent organizational practices within each local industry cluster. Therefore, we propose the following additional hypothesis:

Hypothesis 4: The industry sector-by-societal culture interaction effect on organizational culture practices will be a function of the isomorphic societal culture values

METHOD

The Dependent Variable: Organizational Cultural Practices

All of the hypotheses advanced in this chapter were tested using the GLOBE organizational cultural practices scales as the dependent variable. Specifically, the following nine GLOBE organizational cultural practice scales were used: (a) Uncertainty Avoidance, (b) Power Distance, (c) Institutional Collectivism, (d) In-Group Collectivism, (e) Gender Egalitarianism, (f) Assertiveness, (g) Future Orientation, (h) Performance Orientation, and (i) Humane Orientation.

The Independent Variables

For Hypotheses 1–3, we operationalized societal system and industry sector using a fixed-effects ANOVA model, with a hierarchical design (Kirk, 1995). The fixed-effects model estimates the percentage of commonality in variation within societies or within industries.

For Hypothesis 4 we used isomorphic societal culture value scales. As reported in Chapter 8, by Hanges and Dickson, isomorphic scales for the nine societal culture value dimensions are also included in the GLOBE program.

Sample and Procedures

We used three criteria to get a reasonably reliable and representative sample of organizations from the GLOBE database. First, we limited the organizational-level data to cases with responses from a minimum of seven respondents per organization. Second, data sets with less than two organizations per industry per country were excluded. This criterion helped us separate variance due to organizational differences from industry-level effects. Third, data sets from countries with only one industry sampled were also excluded. This last criterion enabled us to separate variance due to society from variance due to industry. After applying these three criteria, the final data set for this analysis consisted of 3,859 midlevel managers from 208 organizations within 27 societies and 3 industries. There were 92 financial organizations, 73 organizations from the food industry, and 43 organizations from the telecommunications industry (see Table 20.1). The average number of respondents per organization was 18.6 ($SD = 18.1$, with a minimum of 7 and a maximum of 148). All organizations were middle- to large-sized companies operating mainly within their respective society. Multinational organizations were not included in the GLOBE database to ensure that the respondents represented their culture and not other cultures. More details about the GLOBE sample and procedures for data gathering are described in Chapter 6, by House and Hanges.

ANALYSIS

We used an analysis of variance (ANOVA) model, using a hierarchical design, to estimate the amount of variance operating at each level of analysis (i.e., society, industry, and society by industry) on the GLOBE organizational cultural practices scales (Hypotheses 1–3). By using an ANOVA of a hierarchical design, we treated organizations as nested within societies and individuals as nested within organizations (Kirk, 1995). In addition, we relied on a series of hierarchical linear modeling (HLM) analyses to formally test our hypotheses concerning the effect of isomorphic societal culture values on the GLOBE organizational cultural practice

Table 20.1   Sample of Organizations by Society and Industry

Society	Finance	Food	Telecommunication	Total
Argentina	4	3		7
Australia	4		3	7
Brazil		5	4	9
Canada (English)		3	3	6
China	3	3		6
Egypt	3	5		8
England	4	2		6
Finland	3	2	2	7
Georgia	4		3	7
Germany (West)	4	4	2	10
Greece	4		3	7
Hungary	2	3		5
India	4	5		9
Italy	4	3		7
Netherlands	3	3		6
Philliplines	3	3		6
Poland	2	2		4
Singapore	5	2		7
Slovenia	3	2	3	8
South Africa (Black sample)	5	3		8
South Korea	3	3	3	9
Sweden	4	6	4	14
Switzerland		3	3	6
Taiwan	3		3	6
Thailand	5	5	5	15
Turkey	7	3		10
USA	3	3	2	8
Total	**92**	**73**	**43**	**208**

NOTES:

N = number of organizations per industry.

Data sets with less than two organizations per industry per country were excluded.

Data sets from countries with only one industry sampled were excluded.

Average number of respondents per organization = 18.6 (minimum 7; maximum 148).

scales (Hypothesis 4). A detailed description of HLM analyses of GLOBE data is presented in Chapter 11, by Hanges, Dickson, and Sipe.

RESULTS

Societal Effects on Organizational Culture

Our first hypothesis concerned whether societal systems affect organizational cultural practices. As shown in Table 20.2, we found that societal systems had a significant effect on all nine organizational cultural practice dimensions. If considering variance for each dependent variable (e.g., GLOBE Power Distance organizational practices scale $\eta_{(org)} = 37\%$) that occurs only at the organizational level ($\eta^2_{(org)}$ in Table 20.2), societal systems accounted for 21% to 47% of this variance. Consistent with Hypothesis 1 and the original GLOBE conceptual model, societal-level differences have a substantial impact on the cultural practices of organizations. The relationship between societal and

Table 20.2   Results for Analyses of Variance With the GLOBE Organizational Culture Practices ("As Is") Scales as the Dependent Variable

Organizational Cultural Practices	Society		Industry		Society * Industry	
Dimensions	*Significant?*	η^2 *(org)*	*Significant?*	η^2 *(org)*	*Significant?*	η^2 *(org)*
Assertiveness	Yes	.45	No	.00	Yes	.19
Institutional Collectivism	Yes	.22	No	.00	No	.09
In-Group Collectivism	Yes	.21	No	.00	No	.07
Future Orientation	Yes	.47	No	.06	No	.06
Gender Egalitarianism	Yes	.36	Yes	.11	Yes	.28
Humane Orientation	Yes	.24	No	.00	No	.10
Performance Orientation	Yes	.26	No	.00	No	.11
Power Distance	Yes	.37	No	.00	Yes	.42
Uncertainty Avoidance	Yes	.36	No	.03	Yes	.17

NOTE: η^2 is an estimator of the amount of variance in the dependent variable accounted for by a particular factor. The significance level used for these analyses was the traditional $p < .05$ level.

organizational practices is described further in each of the culture dimension chapters (Chapters 12–19, this volume).

Industry Effects on Organizational Culture

We examined the significance of the industry sector in the ANOVA model to assess whether there was a main effect of industry on organizational cultural practices. As shown in Table 20.2, only one organizational cultural practice dimension showed a significant main effect for industry (Gender Egalitarianism scale, $p < .05$). This main effect is a result of organizational cultural practices being more male-oriented in the telecommunications industry (mean = 2.55) than in either the financial industry (i.e., mean = 3.34) or the food industry (i.e., mean = 3.36).[2] The industry main effect for organizational gender egalitarianism cultural practices accounted for 11% of the organizational-level variance.

Overall, however, with the exception of the results for gender egalitarianism, our results did not support Hypothesis 2. As can be seen in Table 20.2, the industry effect on organizational culture ranged from 0% to 11% of the dependent variable.

Society by Industry Interaction Effects on Organizational Culture

Although we found little support for a main effect due to worldwide industry sector, it is possible that the effect of industry is local in nature. Thus, we explored whether there is a society by industry interaction in our data.

Our results show that industry type interacted with societal system on four organizational culture practice dimensions. As shown in Table 20.2, there was a significant industry by society interaction for the GLOBE organizational culture practices scales of Assertiveness, Gender Egalitarianism, Power Distance, and Uncertainty Avoidance. The percentage of variance accounted for by the industry–society interactions, as shown in Table 20.2, ranged from 6% to 42% for these four dimensions. Overall, these results partially support Hypothesis 3. Industry interacted with societal system to affect four of the nine organizational cultural practices.

ANALYZING INDUSTRY-BY-SOCIETY INTERACTIONS ON ORGANIZATIONAL CULTURAL PRACTICES: THE EFFECTS OF ISOMORPHIC SOCIETAL CULTURE VALUES

Next we examined Hypothesis 4—that the observed societal system-by-industry sector interaction on the organizational cultural practice dimensions can be accounted for by the isomorphic (i.e., same) societal culture value dimensions. Put differently, isomorphic societal culture values define how the organizations develop convergent cultural practices within specific industries. We test this hypothesis for the four dimensions of organizational cultural practices on which there was a significant industry by society interaction. As noted above, these dimensions are Assertiveness, Gender Egalitarianism, Power Distance, and Uncertainty Avoidance.

HLM analysis showed that isomorphic societal culture values are able to account for the society by industry interaction effect on three of these four dimensions. Specifically, isomorphic societal culture values explain how the organizations within specific industries develop convergent cultural practices of Uncertainty Avoidance, Assertiveness, and Gender Egalitarianism.

Figure 20.1 shows the interaction between societal Uncertainty Avoidance culture values and industry on the organizational Uncertainty Avoidance cultural practices. This interaction comes about because there does exist some industry-specific convergence in organizational Uncertainty Avoidance practices on account of industry-specific effects of societal Uncertainty Avoidance values. In particular, industry-specific convergence in organizational Uncertainty Avoidance practices on account of isomorphic societal values is most evident in the case of the telecommunications industry and is least evident in the case of the financial services industry.

Figure 20.2 shows the interaction between societal Assertiveness cultural values and industry on organizational Assertiveness cultural practices. Once again, industry-specific convergence in organizational Assertiveness cultural practices is not evident in the financial services industry but is remarkable for the telecommunications industry.

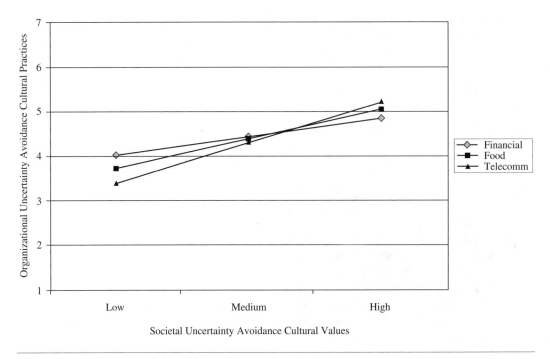

Figure 20.1   Society and Industry Interaction on GLOBE Organizational Uncertainty Avoidence Cultural Practices

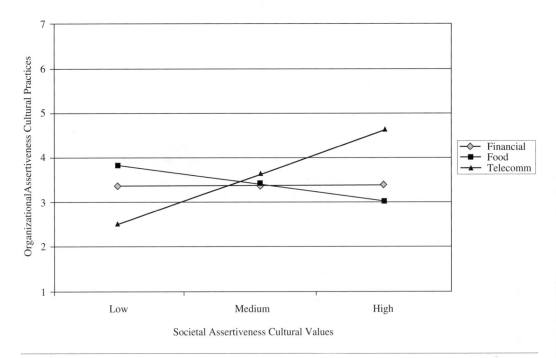

Figure 20.2   Society and Industry Interaction on GLOBE Organizational Assertiveness Cultural Practices

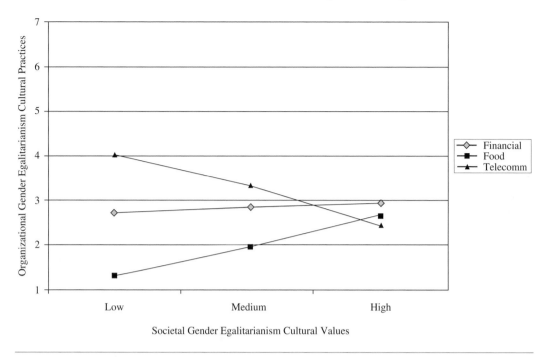

Figure 20.3   Society and Industry Interaction on GLOBE Organizational Gender Egalitarianism Cultural Practices

Figure 20.3 shows the interaction between societal Gender Egalitarianism cultural values and industry on organizational Gender Egalitarianism cultural practices. Once again, industry-specific convergence in organizational Gender Egalitarianism cultural practices is not evident in the financial services industry but exists for the telecommunications and food industries.

Though the societal Power Distance values and industry interaction effect on organizational Power Distance cultural practices was not significant, we decided to investigate if any non-isomorphic societal culture value dimension might explain the industry–society interaction effect on organizational Power Distance culture practices. The most appropriate nonisomorphic societal culture value dimension influencing organizational Power Distance practices is probably Uncertainty Avoidance. Hofstede (2001) holds that organizational cultures are influenced strongly by the interaction between power distance and uncertainty avoidance. Also, in Chapter 9, Gupta, de Luque, and House suggest that the GLOBE Uncertainty Avoidance cultural practice scale is strongly related to the

use of technology, with greater information, communication, transportation, safety, and health technology indicating investments in security, comfort, and resolution of uncertainty, all of which are likely to have a strong influence on the power in organizations.

Indeed, our results indicated that societal-level Uncertainty Avoidance cultural values captured the industry by society interaction on organizational Power Distance culture practices. Figure 20.4 shows the Uncertainty Avoidance societal cultural values by industry interaction for the organizational Power Distance cultural practices. As can be seen in this figure, industry plays an important role in the positive association of organizational Power Distances practices and societal Uncertainty Avoidance values. The association is particularly strong with respect to the telecommunication and food industries, but not with the finance industries.

In summary, we found support for our cultural value interpretation that lies behind the interaction between industry and societal effects as it affects organizational practices. Taken

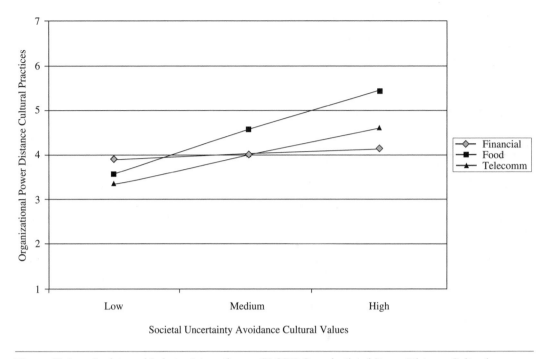

Figure 20.4   Society and Industry Interaction on GLOBE Organizational Power Distance Cultural
Practices

together, the organizations in the financial industrial sector do not appear to have industry-specific local organizational practices, whereas the organizations in the food and, particularly, the telecommunications industrial sectors are more likely to have industry-specific organizational practices for four of the nine GLOBE dimensions. Further, the industry-specific convergent local organizational practices are associated with isomorphic societal culture values for three of the practice dimensions (Uncertainty Avoidance, Gender Egalitarianism, and Assertiveness) and with Uncertainty Avoidance societal culture value for the fourth practice dimension (Power Distance). It is possible that a greater emphasis on the global market norms in the financial industrial sector is responsible for these results. These norms, in turn, probably make the organizations in the financial industrial sector less sensitive to developing a local industry-specific practice culture. It is also possible that the local industry-specific practice innovations of the financial services organizations more rapidly diffuse to the local organizations in other industries.

The financial services sector is very closely involved with all the other industries, and so its practice innovations could rapidly gain cross-industry acceptance. Such a process will not show up as an interaction-effect of society and industry, but instead will show up as shared society effects on organizational practices of all the industries in a society.

DISCUSSION

Our findings can be summarized succinctly. First, organizational cultural practices differ among the societal systems investigated regardless of industrial sector. This means that the societal system is an important influence on organizational culture practices irrespective of industry. Second, we found almost no industry-sector effects on organizational practices across societies. Although this may appear surprising given the literature suggesting likely industry effects, it is explained by the third major finding regarding the interaction of societies and industries. For our sample of industries, we did find society-specific differences in the organizational practices of the three industries.

The few and weak industry effects on organizational culture across societies strongly suggest that the major force shaping organizational practices is rooted in societal-level systems rather than industry-specific work systems. We did, however, find societal system by industry interactions (moderate to high in effect size) for four of the nine organizational cultural practice dimensions investigated. This interaction supports the paramount role of societal cultural variables as influencing organizational practices, either directly or indirectly.

We also found evidence that indirect effects of societal system on organizational culture practices are influenced by cultural values. Three of the four society-by-industry interaction effects on organizational cultural practice dimensions (on Uncertainty Avoidance, on Gender Egalitarianism, and on Assertiveness) were explained by isomorphic societal cultural values. The fourth interaction effect (on Power Distance) was explained by Uncertainty Avoidance societal cultural value. In other words, issues of how to deal with uncertainty played a key role in determining organizational power distance differences among industries within societies. In societies with high scores on the GLOBE Uncertainty Avoidance values scale, respondents in both food and telecommunications organizations tended to report higher levels of organizational power distance cultural practices than respondents from these industries in societies with lower scores on the GLOBE Uncertainty Avoidance scale. Furthermore, the industry-specific power distance practices of the telecommunications industry organizations were most sensitive to the uncertainty avoidance values of the broader society, whereas those of the financial industry organizations were least sensitive to the uncertainty avoidance norms of the broader society. Similar results were obtained for the effects of isomorphic societal value dimensions.

These findings may suggest that the more pervasive an industry is (finance being highly pervasive), the more likely should this industry's organizations' cultures be shared with other industries in the society. Indeed, interlinkages among various industries within a society could

explain the strong and significant influences of the societal system on all organizational culture practices.

Finally, we would like to highlight some limitations of the current study, and directions for further research. First, there may be considerable variability among common characteristics for distinguishing industries within societies, such as technology, growth rate, governmental regulations, national economic systems, traditional strength of labor unions, or status of an organization as a national monopoly. The effects of such differences on industry characteristics and on organizational culture have been demonstrated in empirical studies that were conducted in singular societies (e.g., Chatman & Jehn, 1994; Dansereau & Alutto, 1990; Phillips, 1994). There is a need to examine the effects of these differences in a larger cross-cultural sample, like the one used here.

Second, the three industries' profiles may also vary considerably across societies depending on the degree of modernization, economic growth, gross national product, or more generally on the political and economic systems. For an example, differences in product market concentration among food, finance, and telecommunication may be a consequence of differences among societies. At the time of data gathering for GLOBE, in some societies (e.g., the United States), finance, food, and telecommunication industries all consisted of privately owned companies with a high number and variability of competitors. In other societies (e.g., Germany, Austria), one state monopolist dominated the telecommunication industry or private companies were entering the very recently opened market, whereas finance and food were always fully private. Thus, aspects in organizational culture that relate to product market concentration should be more different between telecommunication and the other two industries within Germany than within the United States. Similar interaction effects are to be expected for other industry characteristics, for example, differential customer demands between industries, as documented in the change from reliability to novelty for the AT&T monopolist in telecommunication in the United States. Similarly, different societal expectations—for example, the preeminence of property rights versus human rights like safety and health issues—should have profound effects on the food industry, but not so much on the finance and telecommunications industries. These and similar social changes that have taken place in most Western modernized societies are currently taking place in others and have not yet begun in many other societies. In this respect the GLOBE database warrants further research: for example, for particular sets of countries and industries that differ meaningfully in the above-mentioned characteristics, particular hypotheses about societal culture by industry interactions can be investigated.

Third, an important explanation for the lack of industrial sector main effects in the GLOBE study might be due to the organizational cultural practice dimensions studied in Project GLOBE. That is, we deliberately developed organizational cultural practice scales that were isomorphic to our societal cultural practice dimensions. This decision probably influenced the size of the relationships we found between organizational and societal practices. Clearly, it is reasonable to expect that organizations reflect the societies in which they are embedded. We did not create or measure organizational variables that are likely to be particularly salient to organizational members from one industrial sector over the others. For instance, the food services industrial sector might be less concerned with innovation of services in comparison to organizations in the financial or telecommunication sectors. Stronger support for an industrial sector main effect might have been obtained if the organizational cultural practices scales focused on the practices that were important for distinguishing one industrial sector from another.

COMPARING EFFECT SIZES: SOCIETY, INDUSTRY, AND SOCIETY-BY-INDUSTRY INTERACTIONS

Although not part of any formal hypothesis, we initially thought about the relative influence of the three effects specified in our three hypotheses—societal culture, industry culture, and the interaction between the two. Which should be

most important and which least important? Thus, across a multination, multi-industry sample of organizations such as the GLOBE sample, we expect society main effects on organizational culture across all industries to be stronger than industry main effects across all societies. Furthermore, as adaptation to industrial conditions tends to be contingent on society factors, as was demonstrated in earlier discussion of the study of biscuit manufacturing factories in Germany and the U.S. (Mason & Finegold, 1997), one might also expect stronger society-by-industry interaction effects than industry effects alone across societies.

The interaction effect, however, is not likely to overpower the pervasive effect of societal culture. Unfortunately, significance tests of the magnitude of the explained variance for variables at these different levels of analysis are not available. However, we can examine the average amount of variance accounted for by each main effect, and the interaction effects, to assess whether these magnitudes were consistent with our hypotheses.

Thus, we predicted that the strongest influence on organizational practices would be societal differences, followed by the industry by society interactions, and then the main effect due to industry. Although we could not formally test this assertion, results reported in Table 20.2 provide indirect support. Specifically, the level of organizational-level variance (for all nine scales together) accounted for by society was 49% (9% of explained total variance within and between organizations) followed by 29% organizational level variance for the industry by society interaction (4% of explained total variance within and between organizations), and 4% organizational-level variance for the industry main effect (1% of explained total variance within and between organizations). Therefore, the results are consistent with our predictions regarding relative effect sizes.

CONCLUSION

The GLOBE results presented here, unique in their broad coverage of societies from all regions in the world, support the thesis that societal system has the most significant and strongest effects on all organizational culture dimensions measured, whereas industry only weakly influences some of the measured aspects of organizational cultures across all societies.

The strong society system effects found in this chapter suggest that the organizational design and competitive advantage of firms tend to be strongly influenced by their domestic home base. This is particularly true for the organizations in culture-sensitive industries such as food processing, and for those in locally regulated industries such as telecommunication at the time of data gathering. For the firms in the financial services industry, in which industrial domain is strongly interlinked with the rest of the industries, an industry-specific isomorphic adaptation of organizational practices to the societal values may not be appropriate to attain or maintain an effective competitive advantage. Still, the firms may develop practice innovations that they share with all the industries locally, as is indicated by strong society effects for firms in all three sampled industries. Thus, there are more or less degrees of freedom for the alignment of an organization's cultural practices with societal conditions, depending on specific industry demands facing the organization under consideration.

ENDNOTES

1. The use of different middle managers in the completion of the organizational culture questions and the societal culture questions is critical for the GLOBE study. Any findings connecting society culture to organizational cultural practices cannot be attributed to same-source biases because different people completed the different scales.

2. As indicated earlier, the analyses reported in this chapter are based on a subset of the GLOBE data. Specifically, the 208 organizations used in these analyses were identified because these observations were collected in a way that we could separate organizational-, industry-, and societal-level effects from one another. The means reported in this chapter are not comparable with the results reported in the dimension chapters because they used the larger sample of 276 organizations.

REFERENCES

Abernathy, M. A., & Chua, W. F. (1996). A field study of control system "redesign": The impact of institutional processes on strategic choice. *Contemporary Accounting Research, 13,* 569–595.

Abrahamsen, E., & Fombrun, C. J. (1994). Macrocultures: Determinants and consequences. *Academy of Management Review, 19*(4), 728–755.

Bartlett, C. A., & Ghoshal S. (1990). *Managing across borders: The transnational solution.* Boston: Harvard Business School Press.

Chatman, J. A., & Jehn, K. A. (1994). Assessing the relationships between industry characteristics and organizational culture: How different can you be? *Academy of Management Journal, 37*(3), 522–553.

Clasessens, S., Glaessner, T., & Klingebiel, D. (2000). *Electronic finance: Reshaping the financial landscape around the world* (Financial Sector Discussion Paper). Washington, DC: World Bank.

Dansereau, F., & Alutto, J. A. (1990). Level-of-analysis issues in climate and culture research. In B. Schneider (Ed.), *Organizational climate and culture* (pp. 193–236). San Francisco: Jossey-Bass.

DiMaggio, P. J., & Powell, W. W. (1983). The iron cage revisited: Institutional isomorphism and collective rationality in organizational fields. *American Sociological Review, 48,* 147–160.

Gordon, G. G. (1991). Industry determinants of organizational culture. *Academy of Management Review, 16*(2), 396–415.

Hanges, P. J., Lord, R. G., & Dickson, M. W. (2000). An information processing perspective on leadership and culture: A case for connectionist architecture. *Applied Psychology: An International Review, 49,* 133–161.

Hickson, D. J., Hinings, C. R., McMillan, C. J., & Schwitter, J. P. (1974). The culture-free context of organizational structure. *Sociology, 8,* 59–80.

Hofstede, G. (2001). *Culture's consequences: Comparing values, behaviors, institutions, and organizations across nations.* Thousand Oaks, CA: Sage.

Katz, D., & Kahn, R. L. (1966). *The social psychology of organizations.* New York: John Wiley.

Kerr, C., Dunlop, J. T., Harbison, F. H., & Charles, A. M. (1960). *Industrialism and industrial man.* Cambridge, MA: Harvard University Press.

Kirk, R. E. (1995). *Experimental design: Procedures for the behavioral sciences.* San Francisco, CA: Brooks/Cole.

Lee, M., & Barnett, G. A. (1997). A symbols-and-meaning approach to the organizational cultures of banks in the United States, Japan, and Taiwan. *Communication Research, 24*(4), 394–412.

Mason, G., & Finegold, D. (1997, October). Productivity, machinery and skills in the United States and Western Europe. *National Institute of Economic Review, 162,* 85–98.

Meyer, J. W., & Rowan, B. (1991). Institutional organizations: Formal structure as myth and ceremony. In W. W. Powell & P. J. DiMaggio (Eds.), *The new institutionalism in organizational analysis* (pp. 41–62). Chicago: University of Chicago Press.

Pfeffer, J. (1981). *Power in organizations.* Marshfield, MA: Pitman.

Pfeffer, J., & Salancik, G. R. (1978). *The external control of organizations: A resource dependency perspective.* New York: Harper & Row.

Phillips, M. E. (1994). Industry-mindsets: Exploring the cultures of two macro-organizational settings. *Organization Science, 5*(3), 384–402.

Schneider, B. (1987). The people make the place. *Personnel Psychology, 14,* 437–453.

Schneider, B., Goldstein, H. W., & Smith, D. B. (1995). The ASA framework: An update. *Personnel Psychology, 48,* 747–773.

21

LEADERSHIP AND CULTURAL VARIATION

The Identification of Culturally Endorsed Leadership Profiles

PETER W. DORFMAN

PAUL J. HANGES

FELIX C. BRODBECK

In this chapter we discuss implicit leadership theory (ILT) and extend ILT from a focus on individual-level differences in beliefs about effective leaders to a culture-level theory that focuses on the beliefs about effective leaders shared by members of an organization or society. According to ILT, individuals hold a set of beliefs about the kinds of attributes, personality characteristics, skills, and behaviors that contribute to or impede outstanding leadership. These belief systems, variously referred to as prototypes, cognitive categories, mental models, schemas, and stereotypes in the broader social cognitive literature, are assumed to affect the extent to which an individual accepts and responds to others as leaders (Lord & Maher, 1991).

We extend ILT to the cultural level of analysis by arguing that the structure and content of these belief systems will be shared among individuals in common cultures. We refer to this shared cultural level analog of individual implicit leadership theory (ILT) as *culturally endorsed implicit leadership theory (CLT)*. Hanges and Dickson in Chapter 8 provide convincing evidence that people within cultural groups agree in their beliefs about leadership such that there are statistically significant differences among cultures in leadership beliefs. This agreement within cultural groups validates the aggregation of individual ratings to the organizational and societal level of analysis. Therefore, the focus of this chapter is the testing, validation, and cross-cultural implications

AUTHORS' NOTE: The first author would like to acknowledge the help provided by Jon Howell and Renée Brown. Jon's perceptive feedback and encouragement along with Renée's excellent copyediting improved this chapter immeasurably.

of CLT—a major focus of GLOBE Phase 2 research. Later in the chapter we represent the leadership beliefs shared by people of a common culture by a set of *CLT leadership profiles* developed for specific cultures and clusters of cultures. This CLT profile construct directly corresponds to the shared mental models concept discussed in the team literature and is the cultural analog of the schema or prototype construct discussed in the individual-level social cognition literature.

After introducing culturally endorsed leadership theory, the remainder of the chapter presents evidence regarding major objectives of Project GLOBE. Specifically, one objective was to empirically identify leadership attributes that are universally perceived as contributors to or inhibitors of outstanding leadership. A second objective, discussed by Hanges and Dickson in Chapter 8, was to develop a set of scaled leadership dimensions composed of these leadership attributes. Project GLOBE has identified six such "global" leadership dimensions. We use these dimensions to differentiate cultures in terms of the content of their CLT profiles. A third objective of the GLOBE project was to determine whether the grouping of societies into 10 empirically determined cultural clusters, as discussed by Gupta and Hanges in Chapter 10, would result in meaningful differences in the CLT leadership profiles. Lastly, as part of validating the GLOBE model in Chapter 2, a fourth objective was to link the content of CLT profiles to measures of organizational and societal culture. This was accomplished by conducting analyses using the nine GLOBE cultural dimensions to predict the six CLT leadership dimensions. Whereas the previous cultural dimension chapters (12–19) present evidence separately relating each of the nine cultural dimensions to the six CLT leadership dimensions, this chapter provides a competitive comparison *among* the nine culture dimensions to find the most important dimensions affecting the content of the six CLT leadership profiles.

Implicit Leadership Theory: Conceptual Underpinnings

Whereas academics have had difficulty developing a consensus regarding the definition and conceptualization of leadership, lay people do not seem to struggle with this term nearly as much. Most individuals have their own ideas about the nature of leaders and leadership, and have little trouble indicating who they believe are leaders in business, government, or other domains, and why. These naive or idiosyncratic individualized leadership theories have been studied under the rubrics "implicit leadership theory," "leader categorization theory" (Lord, Foti, & DeVader, 1984) or, more generally, "social cognition theory applied to leadership." According to these researchers, individuals have certain beliefs about the attributes and behaviors of leaders. These belief systems help individuals quickly process and interpret new social information as well as aid recall and anticipate others' behavior. Thus, ILT suggests that these belief systems allow individuals to efficiently distinguish leaders from others. By knowing the content of an individual's leadership belief system, it is believed that one could predict whether that individual would perceive another individual as an effective or ineffective leader, or even a moral or evil leader (House et al., 1999; Lord & Maher, 1991).

A major assertion of ILT is that leadership is in the "eye of the beholder." That is, leadership is a social label given to individuals if either (a) their personality, attributes, and behaviors sufficiently match the observer's beliefs about leaders or (b) the observer attributes group success or failure to the activities of perceived leaders (Lord & Maher, 1991). Although there is ongoing debate as to many aspects of implicit leadership theory such as likely (antecedent) factors involved in the development of leadership belief systems (Keller, 1999), precise memory mechanisms involved (Hanges, Lord, & Dickson, 2000), and consequences of holding particular belief systems (Hains, Hogg, & Duck, 1997; Nye & Forsyth, 1991), implicit leadership theory in general is widely regarded as a valid perspective (Yukl, 2002).

We believe that integrating ILT with cross-cultural research will be synergistic for both literatures. As Dickson, Hanges, and Lord (2001) have argued, truly integrating these two academic disciplines highlights certain issues that were previously overlooked. For example, although ILT postulates that leader perceptions are a function of the overlap between an observer's leadership belief systems and the attributes of the person being rated, it is not known whether all attributes in a person's leadership belief system are equally important. Is it more important for a leader to exhibit behavior consistent with culture-specific expectations, or for a leader to exhibit behavior consistent with universally held leadership expectations? In other words, we know little about the effect of leadership that violates culturally endorsed norms. The present results from GLOBE are useful for specifying the content of CLT profiles for a variety of cultures. Later phases of GLOBE will explore the consequences of violating culturally endorsed norms.

Conceptual Extension of Implicit Leadership Theory to Culturally Endorsed Implicit Leadership Theory

Even though most of the social cognitive literature focuses on the information processing of individuals, there has been some recent discussion of the tendency for people within teams, groups, or cultures to develop commonalities in the content of their leadership beliefs. For example, in the team literature the concept of "team mental models" has more recently been identified as an important construct. Klimoski and Mohammed (1994) defined team mental models as the team members' organized understanding and mental representation of knowledge or beliefs about key elements of the team's environment. Not surprisingly, team effectiveness is believed to be partly a function of the extent to which team members share their conceptualizations of key task and situational requirements (Duncan et al., 1996). It is believed that team performance is enhanced if there is greater commonality among the mental models of team members because team members can process information faster with fewer errors of interpretation, resulting in increased coordination among team members (Mohammed & Dumville, 2001; Mohammed, Klimoski, & Rentsch, 2000). As predicted, Rentsch and Klimoski (2001) found that several antecedents such as similar demography and team experience led to team member

agreement concerning beliefs about task requirements that in turn are related to team effectiveness. Since effective leadership is generally critical for team success, a shared team mental model of effective leaders is also likely to emerge among team members.

On the basis of the organizational culture literature (e.g., Schein, 1992), it can be argued that organizational members, like team members, share mental models and implicit theories about the functioning and leadership of organizations. This is exactly what Bass (1990) argued when he indicated that most people of the same culture hold a common set of beliefs about the attributes of a typical leader. The commonality in the leadership belief systems of organizational members probably results from repeated exposure to common organizational policies, practices, and procedures (e.g., organizational reward systems, common task requirements) that were in place partially because of the founder's beliefs and values (Kraiger & Wenzel, 1997). In addition to the beliefs about leaders shared by team or organizational members, researchers have argued that enduring, pervasive cultural values can also influence shared conceptions of members of nations concerning effective leadership (e.g., Hanges et al., 2000).

In this chapter, the hypothesis that organizational and societal cultures are associated with culturally endorsed leadership belief systems is tested and confirmed. To the extent that cultural influences are important and enduring, there should be important differences in the CLT profiles endorsed in various cultures. For instance, it is likely that individualistic values espoused in societies such as the United States would result in a strongly shared belief that rugged individualists are effective leaders, whereas more group-oriented leaders should be viewed as effective in collectivistic societies. Thus, what is different in our approach to implicit leadership theory is that we not only invoke the notion of shared beliefs about leaders as theoretical and practical perspectives ascribing how individuals within a culture view leaders and leadership, we test the differences in the content of these CLT profiles among cultures. The empirical formulation and testing of culturally relevant CLT profiles has never been done before.[1]

Research Findings for Cross-Cultural Differences in CLT Profiles

Shaw (1990) suggested that much of the cross-national literature indicating differences in managerial beliefs, values, and styles can be interpreted as showing culturally influenced differences in leader belief systems. Specifically, Shaw (1990) theorized that cultural values would affect the content, structure, and automaticity of leadership prototypes. What evidence exists to confirm Shaw's hypotheses about the influence of culture on leadership belief systems? A study by O'Connell, Lord, and O'Connell (1990) found that culture plays a strong role in influencing the content of leader attributes and behaviors perceived as desirable and effective by individuals in that culture. Their study specifically examined the similarities and differences between Japanese and American conceptions of useful leadership attributes. For the Japanese, the personality traits and behaviors of being fair, flexible, a good listener, outgoing, and responsible were highly rated for leadership effectiveness in many domains such as business, media, and education. For Americans, personality traits and behaviors of intelligence, honesty, understanding, verbal skills, and determination were strongly endorsed as facilitating leader effectiveness in numerous domains. A study by Gerstner and Day (1994) also provided evidence that ratings of effective leadership attributes and behaviors vary across cultures. University students from eight nations identified the fit among 59 attributes (previously developed from Lord et al., 1984), and each student's image of a business leader. As expected, attributes that were seen as most characteristic of business leaders varied across cultures—no single trait was rated in the top 5 as being most prototypical across all eight cultures. In summary, these two studies confirm Shaw's prediction regarding the influence of culture on the content of leadership belief systems.

Studies by O'Neill and Hanges (2001) and Hanges and colleagues (2001) provide support for Shaw's prediction that culture affects the structure of leadership belief systems (i.e., the interconnections among attributes). In these studies, participants rated the similarity of 15 leadership attributes that earlier work by GLOBE researchers (i.e., Den Hartog et al., 1999; House et al., 1999) had shown were universally endorsed as attributes of effective leadership. Thus, by limiting responses to these 15 attributes, the content of the leadership belief systems under investigation in these studies was held constant. Using the Pathfinder computer algorithm, differences in the structure of participants' leadership belief systems were identified. Consistent with Shaw's prediction, cultural values were found to meaningfully relate to the centrality (i.e., importance) of leadership attributes in these belief systems. Thus, these studies provide empirical support for Shaw's culture-leadership belief system prediction. It should be recognized that although these four studies have supported Shaw's (1990) hypothesis at the individual level of analysis, these studies were restricted in size, scope, and sample selection and limited a priori theorizing such that their theoretical significance and generalizability are limited beyond the specific cultures sampled.

Two studies published as part of Project GLOBE further attest to the existence and importance of CLT profiles. Den Hartog and colleagues (1999) presented evidence that attributes of charismatic–transformational leadership are universally endorsed as contributing to outstanding leadership. These results will be briefly reviewed in this chapter. In addition, Den Hartog and colleagues also provided evidence that the content of leadership belief systems varies by hierarchical levels within an organization: The belief systems held by top managers and CEOs differed from those held by supervisors. Using a European culture subset of the GLOBE data, Brodbeck and colleagues (2000) presented convincing evidence that clusters of European cultures sharing similar cultural values also share similar CLT profiles. The research designs and results of these two studies deserve a complete reading. In this chapter we expand these concepts to provide a more complete picture of the usefulness of implicit leadership theory. We do this by showing how CLT leadership dimensions and composite CLT profiles vary as a function of the nine GLOBE cultural dimensions and differences among the 10 GLOBE culture clusters. Further, we integrate cultural information presented in earlier chapters and suggest practical applications and implications of our results to the theory and practice of global leadership.

The GLOBE Conceptual Model and CLT Hypotheses

A diagram of the GLOBE integrated leadership theory was presented and discussed in Figure 2.1, Chapter 2, by House and Javidan. Recall that a central theoretical proposition of this theory is that societal culture influences the kind of leadership found to be acceptable and effective in that society. The integrated theory consists of many relationships and hypotheses specified in the system diagram in Figure 2.1. For purposes of this chapter, Relationships 5 and 6 in the figure are critical. Societal and organizational cultural values and practices influence the process by which people come to share common beliefs about leaders. Over time, members of cultures develop leadership prototypes as part of the normal socialization process that occurs with respect to both societal and organizational cultures. We argue that the GLOBE CLT profiles are culturally defined prototypes and elucidate important differences between societal cultures. Research evidence will be presented that supports this assertion. The complete research methodology is presented in Part III of this book.

Leadership questionnaire items in Project GLOBE consisted of 112 behavioral and attribute descriptors that were hypothesized to either facilitate or impede outstanding leadership. Items were rated on a 7-point scale that ranged from a low of 1 (this behavior or characteristic greatly inhibits a person from being an outstanding leader) to a high of 7 (this behavior or characteristic contributes greatly to a person being an outstanding leader). Items reflecting both organizational and societal cultures were also a major aspect of GLOBE Phase 2. We obtained responses to approximately 17,000 questionnaires from middle managers of 951 organizations in 62 nations.

The following four hypotheses concern how leadership attributes regarded as critical for effective leadership are influenced by specific cultures.

The hypotheses progress from considering the potential universality of specific individual leadership attributes (Hypothesis 1) to the potential for developing profiles of leadership attributes for separate cultures and clusters of cultures (Hypotheses 2a and 2b). That is, while the level of analysis remains at the cultural level, it is extended in Hypotheses 2a and 2b from separate cultures to groupings of cultures that we label societal *clusters*. Hypotheses 3 and 4 consider how nine societal and organizational cultural dimensions are related to the six global CLT leadership dimensions identified previously in Chapter 8 by Hanges and Dickson. The strength of specific cultural dimensions (e.g., Individualism–Collectivism) influencing CLT dimensions (e.g., Participative leadership) is examined in this chapter by determining the unique contribution of each cultural dimension to a specific CLT leadership dimension.

Hypothesis 1: Two leadership characteristics—Charismatic/Value-Based leader behavior and leader integrity— will be universally perceived as leading to effective leadership

We expected the Charismatic/Value-Based leader behavior to be universally endorsed because the visions articulated by, and the integrity enacted by, value-based leaders stress values that have universal appeal (House, Wright, & Aditya, 1997). Charismatic/Value-Based leaders articulate and emphasize end-values such as dignity, peace, order, beauty, and freedom. End-values are intrinsically motivating, self-sufficient, and need not be linked to other values. They are not exchangeable for other values and have universal appeal (Rokeach, 1973). Thus, the end-values stressed by Charismatic/Value-Based leaders are likely to be universally accepted and endorsed; consequently, their visions are also likely congruent with the values stressed in the culture (House & Aditya, 1997). Similarly, we expected leader integrity to be universally endorsed because integrity is an end-value that is also universally held in all cultures (Rokeach, 1973).

We recognize that aspects of Hypothesis 1, particularly with respect to the universal endorsement of charismatic leadership, may be controversial. Bass (1997) argued that transformational leadership, a form of Charismatic/Value-Based leadership, is universally acceptable and effective. In contrast, it may be argued that some cultures may more highly value leaders who can find pragmatic accommodations with all influential parties. In such cultures, value-based leadership may be far less important than the ability to achieve pragmatic results regardless of the means by which such results are attained.

Whether it is supported or not, the test of Hypothesis 1 is of both theoretical and practical interest. Failure to support this hypothesis would result in identifying specific cultures in which Charismatic/Value-Based leadership is and is not endorsed. Thus, the issue of universal endorsement of leadership dimensions, by necessity, needs to be answered on the basis of empirical evidence. The test of Hypothesis 1 is intended to clarify this issue.

Although not part of the formal Hypothesis 1, we were intrigued by the possibility that certain "negative attributes" might be universally perceived as inhibitors to effective leadership. The universal refutation of leader attributes, specifically those such as *autocratic* and *malevolent* that have negative connotations at least in Anglo cultures, is an empirical question worthy of investigation. Borrowing from the work of Schwartz (1992) and others, we should not be surprised to find people of all cultures reject attributes that embody negative values. At a minimum, the opposite of positive end-values suggested by Rokeach (1973), such as dishonesty and deceit, should be universally rejected. Most interestingly from the cross-cultural perspective would be the identification of characteristics that are perceived to be facilitators or inhibitors depending on culture—thus identifying them as culturally contingent attributes. We made no predictions as to which attributes might fall into this latter group. Nonetheless, the discovery of universally endorsed, universally refuted, and culture-specific leadership dimensions would be of major importance to the development of cross-cultural leadership theory. This knowledge should also be practically important to individuals whose work involves cross-cultural interaction.

Hypothesis 2a: Leadership CLT profiles, which are in essence profiles of prototypical leader behaviors and attributes, can be developed for each societal culture. These indicate which aspects of leadership are perceived to contribute to or impede outstanding leadership within that culture

Hypothesis 2b: Societal CLT profiles can be aggregated into culture cluster CLT profiles indicating which aspects of leadership (found in Hypothesis 2a) are perceived to contribute to outstanding leadership for societal clusters

Recall that data regarding the grouping of leadership attributes into common dimensions was addressed in Chapter 8 by Hanges and Dickson. A brief review is included here as a necessary precursor to understanding Hypotheses 2a and 2b. In Chapter 8, Hanges and Dickson describe how leadership attributes were statistically grouped into 21 first-order factors (henceforth called *primary* leadership dimensions) that were then consolidated into 6 second-order factors (henceforth called *global* leadership dimensions). The *global* moniker reflects (a) participation of GLOBE colleagues from around the world to generate the hundreds of attributes originally thought to contribute to, or inhibit, outstanding leadership; (b) the factor and Q sort analytical techniques that provide evidence that the final composition of factor attributes is comparable across all GLOBE cultures; and (c) the intent to develop measures differentiating all GLOBE societal cultures regarding attributes that are perceived by more than 17,000 managers to influence outstanding leadership. These global CLT leadership dimensions are labeled:

1. Charismatic/Value-Based leadership,

2. Team Oriented leadership,

3. Participative leadership,

4. Humane Oriented leadership,

5. Autonomous leadership, and

6. Self-Protective leadership.

Table 21.1 shows the 6 *global* CLT leadership dimensions along with the 21 *primary* or first-order leadership dimensions. These dimensions are summary indices of the characteristics, skills, and abilities culturally perceived to contribute to, or inhibit outstanding leadership. They can be thought of as being somewhat similar to what laypersons refer to as leadership styles and are defined as follows:

Charismatic/Value-Based. A broadly defined leadership dimension that reflects the ability to inspire, to motivate, and to expect high performance outcomes from others on the basis of firmly held core values. This GLOBE CLT Charismatic/Value-Based leadership dimension includes six primary leadership subscales labeled (a) *visionary,* (b) *inspirational,* (c) *self-sacrifice,* (d) *integrity,* (e) *decisive,* and (f) *performance oriented.*

Team Oriented. A leadership dimension that emphasizes effective team building and implementation of a common purpose or goal among team members. This GLOBE CLT Team-Oriented leadership dimension includes five primary leadership subscales labeled (a) *collaborative team orientation,* (b) *team integrator,* (c) *diplomatic,* (d) *malevolent* (reverse scored), and (e) *administratively competent.*

Participative. A leadership dimension that reflects the degree to which managers involve others in making and implementing decisions. The GLOBE CLT Participative leadership dimension includes two primary leadership subscales labeled (a) *autocratic* (reverse scored) and (b) *non participative* (reverse scored).

Humane Oriented. A leadership dimension that reflects supportive and considerate leadership but also includes compassion and generosity. The GLOBE CLT Humane Oriented leadership dimension includes two primary leadership subscales labeled (a) *modesty* and (b) *humane oriented.*

Autonomous. This newly defined leadership dimension has not previously appeared in the literature. This dimension refers to independent and individualistic leadership. The GLOBE

CLT Autonomous leadership dimension includes a single primary leadership subscale labeled *autonomous.*

Self-Protective. From a Western perspective, this newly defined leadership dimension focuses on ensuring the safety and security of the individual or group member. The GLOBE CLT Self-Protective leadership dimension includes five primary leadership subscales labeled (a) *self-centered,* (b) *status conscious,* (c) *conflict inducer,* (d) *face saver,* and (e) *procedural.*

Given the information presented earlier in this chapter, GLOBE researchers hypothesized that it would be possible to construct profiles of leadership dimensions based on individuals' questionnaire responses aggregated to the culture and culture cluster levels. These aggregated responses would indicate the extent to which certain leader attributes and leadership dimensions are perceived to contribute to effective leadership among cultures and clusters.[2]

Hypothesis 3: There will be positive relationships between CLT dimensions and societal culture dimensions that are conceptually similar or clearly related on theoretical grounds

The rationale for this hypothesis is that cultural dimensions would influence the legitimacy and acceptance of leader behaviors. More specifically, we believe that culture would influence the kinds of attributes and behaviors considered to be effective. For GLOBE, this *cultural influence hypothesis* (Triandis, 1995) posits that culture will have a pervasive influence on values, expectations, and behaviors and would, therefore, influence the content of the CLT profiles. For instance, because charismatic leaders motivate followers to achieve high levels of performance, we expect that societies that promote high societal expectations for performance would likewise believe in the efficacy of charismatic leaders and the CLTs profiles associated with such leaders. In sum, predicting and finding significant relationships between specific cultural dimensions (e.g., Performance Orientation) and conceptually

Table 21.1   Global Culturally Endorsed Implicit Leadership (CLT) Dimensions

1. *Charismatic/Value-Based,* 4.5–6.5
   Charismatic 1: Visionary
   Charismatic 2: Inspirational
   Charismatic 3: Self-sacrifice
   Integrity
   Decisive
   Performance oriented
 	
3. *Self-Protective,* 2.5–4.6
   Self-centered
   Status conscious
   Conflict inducer
   Face saver
   Procedural
 	
5. *Humane Oriented,* 3.8–5.6
   Modesty
   Humane oriented
	2. *Team Oriented,* 4.7–6.2
	   Team 1: Collaborative team orientation
	   Team 2: Team integrator
	   Diplomatic
	   Malevolent (reverse scored)
	   Administratively competent
	
	4. *Participative,* 4.5–6.1
	   Autocratic (reverse scored)
	   Nonparticipative (reverse scored)
	
	6. *Autonomous,* 2.3–4.7
	   Autonomous

NOTE: The numbered, italicized topics are global CLT leadership dimensions. They consist of primary CLT leadership subscales. The only exception is dimension 6 (Autonomous), which consists of a single subscale of four questionnaire items. It is considered both a specific subscale and global dimension. Numbers represent mean values for the 62 societal cultures on a 7-point scale ranging from 1 (*greatly inhibits*) to 7 (*contributes greatly to*) outstanding leadership.

relevant CLT leadership dimensions (e.g., Charismatic/Value-Based) constitutes a test of the cultural influence hypothesis. Because we also expect that national culture would also influence organizational values and practices, we form the following hypothesis.

Hypothesis 4: There will be positive relationships between organizational culture dimensions and CLT leadership dimensions that are conceptually similar or related on theoretical grounds

We believe that in addition to the effect of societal culture, organizational cultural values and practices will influence the expectation that certain leadership attributes lead to effective leadership. For instance, organizational cultures that stress performance orientation should hold in high regard leaders with high expectations of their followers. Determining the relationships between organizational culture dimensions and conceptually relevant CLT leadership dimensions constitutes a test of this *organizational influence*

hypothesis. Note that Hypothesis 4 concerns organizational influence and associated levels of analyses, whereas Hypothesis 3 concerns societal influence and levels of analyses.

We present our results in the following order. First, we provide evidence related to Hypothesis 1—specific attributes that are universally seen as facilitators or inhibitors of effective leadership, or as inhibitors in some cultures and facilitators in other cultures. We then present results related to Hypotheses 2a and 2b. For Hypothesis 2a, we investigate whether respondents from 62 different cultures differ from each other in terms of CLT leadership dimensions that enhance effective leadership. The focus of Hypothesis 2b was whether clustering societies into the 10 culture categories (reported by Gupta and Hanges in Chapter 10) results in differences in CLT profiles for these clusters. Finally, we summarize the hierarchical linear modeling (HLM) evidence that addresses Hypotheses 3 (societal influence on CLT leadership dimensions) and 4 (organizational influence on CLT leadership dimensions).

Table 21.2   Universal Positive Leader Attributes

Leader Attribute Questionnaire Items	Corresponding Primary Leadership Dimensions
Trustworthy	Integrity
Just	Integrity
Honest	Integrity
Foresight	Charisma 1: Visionary
Plans ahead	Charisma 1: Visionary
Encouraging	Charisma 2: Inspirational
Positive	Charisma 2: Inspirational
Dynamic	Charisma 2: Inspirational
Motive arouser	Charisma 2: Inspirational
Confidence builder	Charisma 2: Inspirational
Motivational	Charisma 2: Inspirational
Dependable	Malevolent (reverse score)
Intelligent	Malevolent (reverse score)
Decisive	Decisiveness
Effective bargainer	Diplomatic
Win–win problem solver	Diplomatic
Administrative skilled	Administratively competent
Communicative	Team 2: Team Integrator
Informed	Team 2: Team Integrator
Coordinator	Team 2: Team Integrator
Team builder	Team 2: Team Integrator
Excellence oriented	Performance oriented

RESULTS

Hypothesis 1: Universal Facilitators, Inhibitors, and Culturally Contingent Attributes of Effective Leadership

Hypothesis 1 states that leadership attributes comprising the Charismatic/Value-Based leadership dimension will be universally endorsed as contributing to outstanding leadership. The global Charismatic/Value-Based leadership dimension had culture scores ranging from 4.5 to 6.5 on the 7-point response scale, indicating positive endorsement by all cultures. We established the following criteria for items listed in the GLOBE questionnaire to be considered universally endorsed as attributes (within each dimension) contributing to outstanding leadership: (a) 95% of the societal averages for an attribute had to exceed a mean of 5 on a 7-point scale, and (b) the worldwide grand mean score

for that attribute (considering all 62 cultures together) had to exceed 6 on a 7-point scale. The results of this analysis are presented in Table 21.2.

Universal Facilitators of Leadership Effectiveness.
The following is a partial list of leadership attributes (with each corresponding primary leadership dimension in parentheses) universally endorsed by respondents in the GLOBE sample to contribute to effective leadership (see Table 21.2 for the complete listing):

- Being trustworthy, just, and honest (integrity)
- Having foresight and planning ahead (charismatic–visionary)
- Being positive, dynamic, encouraging, motivating, and building confidence (charismatic–inspirational)
- Being communicative, informed, a coordinator, and team integrator (team builder).

Table 21.3   Universal Negative Leader Attributes

Questionnaire Attributes	Corresponding Primary Leadership Dimensions
Loner	Self-protective
Asocial	Self-protective
Noncooperative	Malevolent
Irritable	Malevolent
Nonexplicit	Face saver
Egocentric*	
Ruthless*	
Dictatorial	Autocratic

* These items did not load on any factor.

The *visionary* and *inspirational* leadership dimensions are critical aspects of Charismatic/Value-Based leadership (Yukl, 2002) and contain the most number of attributes universally perceived as contributors to effective leadership (see Table 21.2). However, attributes comprising the *self-sacrificial* dimension (e.g., risk taking) of Charismatic/Value-Based leadership were not universally endorsed. Please note that three of the positively endorsed items concerned aspects of integrity. In addition, most of the other universal positively endorsed attributes, which did not relate to the Charismatic/Value-Based leadership dimension, were found in the Team-Oriented dimension (see Table 21.2). The portrait of a leader who is universally viewed as effective is clear: The person should possess the highest levels of integrity and engage in Charismatic/Value-Based behaviors while building effective teams. These questionnaire results strongly support the hypothesis that *charismatic–visionary* and *charismatic–inspirational* attributes of the Charismatic/Value-Based leadership dimension are universally endorsed as contributing to outstanding leadership.

Universal Impediments to Leadership Effectiveness. Our criteria for specific attributes to be universally considered as impediments to effective leadership required that (a) the attribute or item grand mean for all cultures be less than 3 on a 7-point scale and (b) 95%

of culture scores on the item be less than 3 on a 7-point scale.

These combined criteria would indicate that the attribute is universally perceived as inhibiting outstanding leadership. Results are presented in Table 21.3, which shows that many attributes in the primary CLT dimensions labeled *self-protective* and *malevolent* are universally viewed as impediments to effective leadership by the GLOBE international sample of middle managers.

Culturally Contingent Endorsement of Leader Attributes. Most interesting, from a cross-cultural viewpoint, were attributes that in some cultures are considered to enhance outstanding leadership and in other cultures are considered to impede outstanding leadership. We present in Table 21.4 those aggregated attributes (questionnaire responses) that yielded scores above and below the scale midpoint of 4, contingent on culture-specific responses aggregated to the societal level of analysis. Many of these attributes fell into the *self-centered* and *individualistic* leadership dimensions (see Table 21.4). For instance, although the attribute *individualistic* had a grand culture mean of 3.11 (slightly inhibits outstanding leadership), individual culture scores ranged from a low of 1.67 (somewhat inhibits) to a high of 5.10 (slightly contributes). Similarly, the attribute *status conscious* ranged in value from a low of 1.92 (somewhat inhibits) to a high of 5.77 (moderately contributes). Even more

Table 21.4   Culturally Contingent CLT Items

Anticipatory (3.84–6.51)	Intuitive (3.72–6.47)
Ambitious (2.85–6.73)*	Logical (3.89–6.58)
Autonomous (1.63–5.17)	Micromanager (1.60–5.00)
Cautious (2.17–5.78)	Orderly (3.81–6.34)
Class conscious (2.53–6.09)	Procedural (3.03–6.10)
Compassionate (2.69–5.56)	Provocateur (1.38–6.00)*
Cunning (1.26–6.38)*	Risk taker (2.14–5.96)
Domineering (1.60–5.14)	Ruler (1.66–5.20)
Elitist (1.61–5.00)	Self-effacing (1.85–5.23)
Enthusiastic (3.72–6.44)	Self-sacrificial (3.00–5.96)
Evasive (1.52–5.67)	Sensitive (1.96–6.35)*
Formal (2.12–5.43)	Sincere (3.99–6.55)
Habitual (1.93–5.38)	Status-conscious (1.92–5.77)
Independent (1.67–5.32)	Subdued (1.32–6.18)
Indirect (2.16–4.86)	Unique (3.47–6.06)
Individualistic (1.67–5.10)	Willful (3.06–6.48)
Intragroup competitor (3.00–6.49)	Worldly (3.48–6.18)
Intragroup conflict avoider (1.84–5.69)	

NOTE: CLT = culturally endorsed implicit leadership theory. Numbers represent minimum and maximum values for the 62 societal cultures on a 7-point scale ranging from 1 (*greatly inhibits*) to 7 (*contributes greatly to*) outstanding leadership.

* These items did not load on any factor.

striking was the *risk taker* attribute, a component of the primary CLT dimension labeled *Charismatic III: Self-Sacrificial,* which, in turn, is part of the Charismatic/Value-Based global CLT dimension. The risk taker attribute ranges in value from 2.14 (somewhat inhibits) to 5.96 (contributes somewhat).

Summary of Hypothesis 1: CLT Results. For GLOBE, an initial question concerned whether the six global CLT leadership dimensions would be viewed positively or negatively. Given the prior research on charismatic leadership, summarized by House et al. (1997) among others (Dorfman, 1996; Yukl, 2002), it should not be surprising that one GLOBE hypothesis was that attributes comprising the Charismatic/Value-Based leadership dimension would be universally endorsed. This hypothesis is strongly supported for charismatic–visionary

and charismatic–inspirational attributes, but not for charismatic–self-sacrificial. Team-Oriented leadership is strongly correlated with Charismatic/Value-Based leadership, and attributes comprising this dimension are also universally endorsed. Humane–Oriented and Participative leadership dimensions are generally viewed positively, but significant variability exists across cultures. The remaining CLT dimensions of Self-Protective and Autonomous leadership are generally viewed as neutral or negative but still vary significantly by culture.

Hypotheses 2a and 2b: CLT Dimensions Associated With GLOBE Societal Cultures and Societal Clusters

For each culture we developed a profile that reported the extent to which the six CLT leadership dimensions were believed to contribute to

Table 21.5   Leadership CLT Scores for Societal Clusters

Societal Cluster	CLT Leadership Dimensions					
	Charismatic/ Value-Based	Team Oriented	Participative	Humane Oriented	Autonomous	Self-Protective
Eastern Europe	5.74	5.88	5.08	4.76	4.20	3.67
Latin America	5.99	5.96	5.42	4.85	3.51	3.62
Latin Europe	5.78	5.73	5.37	4.45	3.66	3.19
Confucian Asia	5.63	5.61	4.99	5.04	4.04	3.72
Nordic Europe	5.93	5.77	5.75	4.42	3.94	2.72
Anglo	6.05	5.74	5.73	5.08	3.82	3.08
Sub-Saharan Africa	5.79	5.70	5.31	5.16	3.63	3.55
Southern Asia	5.97	5.86	5.06	5.38	3.99	3.83
Germanic Europe	5.93	5.62	5.86	4.71	4.16	3.03
Middle East	5.35	5.47	4.97	4.80	3.68	3.79

NOTE: CLT leadership scores are absolute scores aggregated to the cluster level.

effective leadership.[3] For each culture we also used both *absolute* measures obtained directly from the raw score questionnaire data, and a *relative* measure constructed from the former to further illustrate similarities and differences among cultures. Both measures are described in the following sections.

Absolute Measure

Recall that the scores for each CLT leadership dimension (such as Team Oriented) could range from 1 (greatly inhibits outstanding leadership) to 7 (contributes greatly outstanding leadership). A profile can be developed and presented in graph form indicating aggregated responses of informants in a specific culture on each of the six CLT leadership dimensions. As indicated previously, we called the profile of the CLT leadership dimensions for each cluster the *cluster culturally endorsed leadership profile* (cluster CLT profile). This cluster CLT profile is our best quantitative summary of the content of the leadership belief system shared by members in each of these clusters. For practical reasons, we present graphs representing the CLT profiles for the 10 clusters as opposed to graphs presenting findings for all 62 cultures.

Table 21.5 presents absolute scores for all 10 clusters. Analysis of Variance (ANOVA) was used to determine if the cultures and clusters differed with respect to the CLT leadership dimensions reported to be contributors to effective leadership. Results indicate that cultures (i.e., 62 societal cultures) and clusters (i.e., 10 groups consisting of the 62 societal cultures) differed with respect to all six CLT leadership dimensions ($p < .01$).

Relative Measure

In addition to the absolute measure described above, we calculated a relative measure that controlled for some of the potential cultural response biases that could influence our leadership survey results. As discussed in Chapters 4 and 8, cultural values can bias the questionnaire responses of individuals. For example, a general acquiescence response bias occurs if respondents use a general positive or negative response set. In this case, the responses would be positively or negatively skewed, assuming the "true" responses are different from the actual responses. Second, research has shown that there are societal-wide differences in individuals' responses to closed-ended items in Likert-type scales, either exclusively using or not using end points, or only midpoints, of the scale (Dorfman, 2004; Triandis, 1994). A third problem concerns the rating of concepts that may not be exactly comparable due to differences in meaning created during language translation. These response biases can cause difficulty if comparing cultures using questionnaire items.

As discussed in Chapter 8, we went to extraordinary lengths when designing the GLOBE project and questionnaire to minimize response bias. To give one example, after obtaining the data we used a statistical procedure to check on the actual amount of response bias in our results by creating a response bias corrected measure. This procedure is described in detail in Chapter 8 by Hanges and Dickson and is advocated by cross-cultural researchers (van de Vijver & Leung, 1997). Whereas one might use this measure as simply a check on bias, in this chapter we will use the response bias corrected measure as an integral part of the analysis strategy. We are going to refer to this measure hereafter as the *relative measure* because of a unique property attributed to this procedure. These relative CLT scores indicate the relative importance of each CLT leadership dimension *within* a person, culture, or culture cluster.[4] Computing relative scores is critical because they are an important check on the accuracy and validity of the absolute scores. Recall that the latter are problematic if interpreting questionnaire responses, particularly if indicating differences among cultures or clusters. That is, this procedure not only removed the cultural response biases, but it also had the advantage of illustrating the differences among the cultures and the clusters. It is analogous to using a microscope. It sensitized us to meaningful differences within each cluster as to the relative importance of each CLT leadership dimension. We also used this relative measure to compare the relative importance of each CLT dimension *among* cultures.[5]

We should note that in most cases, the relative CLT measures confirmed the significant differences among the clusters with respect to using the original (i.e., absolute) scores. As a caveat, both the relative and absolute measures should be viewed in tandem to provide an accurate portrait of the CLT leadership dimensions important for each cluster. Also, we should point out that the correlation between the absolute and relative measures is close to perfect—above .90 for all of the CLT leadership dimensions. Furthermore, using the relative measure along with the absolute measure guards against the possibility that our results are tainted by response biases, and specifically lends credibility to the validity of our ranking cultures on CLT leadership dimensions.

Although the concept of standardization used to create the relative measure is simple, the mechanics are more complex (fully described in Chapter 8). First, we conducted a "within-person" standardization procedure and aggregated those responses to the culture level and then to the cluster level. Responses to all items in each respondent's questionnaire were standardized around the person's average response score and standard deviation. To illustrate, think of two people who respond exactly the same to all questions but with one significant difference. One person always responds to items using the extreme positive end of the scale, whereas the other is more conservative and responds positively, but more toward the midpoint of the scale. Assume that the leadership attribute *integrity* is the most important leadership attribute to each respondent. Although the mean score for this attribute will vary between these two people because of their acquiescence response bias, their standard scores will not (assuming equal variance around each mean score).

After computing the relative scores, we assessed whether cultures and clusters differed with respect to both absolute and relative CLT measures. As expected, all Analysis of Variance (ANOVA) results were significant using either culture or cluster as the independent variable and CLT leadership dimension scores as the dependent variable (for both absolute and relative scores, $p < .01$). These tests confirmed the differences among clusters using both measures. For ease of presenting and communicating the results, cluster data are shown in several formats. Figures 21.1–21.10 show the absolute CLT scores for each cluster in a graphic form. The graphs enable us to compare the importance of various CLT dimensions within each cluster. Table 21.5 presents the absolute scores for each

Table 21.6   Ranking of Societal Clusters Using Absolute CLT Scores

Charismatic/ Value-Based	Team Oriented	Participative	Humane Oriented	Autonomous	Self-Protective
higher	*higher*	*higher*	*higher*	*higher*	*higher*
Anglo L. America Southern Asia Germanic E. Nordic E.	L. America	Germanic E. Nordic E. Anglo	Southern Asia Sub-Sahara A. Anglo	E. Europe[a] Germanic E. Confucian A. Southern Asia Nordic E. Anglo Middle East L. Europe	Southern Asia Middle East Confucian A. E. Europe
Sub-Sahara A. L. Europe E. Europe Confucian A.	E. Europe Southern Asia Nordic E. Anglo Sub-Sahara A. Germanic E. Confucian A.	L. America L. Europe Sub-Sahara A.	Confucian A. L. America Middle East E. Europe Germanic E.	Sub-Sahara A. L. America	L. America Sub-Sahara A. L. Europe
Middle East	Middle East	E. Europe Southern Asia Confucian A. Middle East	L. Europe Nordic E.		Anglo Germanic E. Nordic E.
lower	*lower*	*lower*	*lower*	*lower*	*lower*
Charismatic/ Value-Based	Team Oriented	Participative	Humane Oriented	Autonomous	Self-Protective

NOTE: The placement of each societal cluster indicates the relative rank of this cluster compared with other clusters with regard to the size of the absolute scores on this dimension. For example, the Anglo cluster is the highest in rank for Charismatic/Value-Based leadership, indicating that this leader dimension had the highest score (absolute measure) compared with other clusters. Using the Tukey HSD analysis, clusters in the top band are significantly different from those in the bottom band. The clusters in the middle band are placed between these extremes for heuristic purposes. Societal clusters within each block are not significantly different from each other.

a Societal clusters in this column are ranked in order; however, there are no significant differences among them.

of the 10 clusters in a format that enables us to compare the CLT dimension scores across clusters. Finally, three additional tables indicate the rank, from high to low, of each cluster with regard to the CLT dimension scores. Table 21.6 ranks each cluster using absolute scores. Table 21.7 ranks the clusters using relative scores, and Table 21.8 summarizes the cluster rankings.

An example should help clarify this "two-step look" using both absolute and relative scores for the six CLT leadership dimensions. By examining the societal cluster *Anglo,* which

includes the United States, we note from Table 21.5 and Figure 21.6 that the Anglo cluster has high absolute scores for Charismatic/Value-Based, Team-Oriented, and Participative CLTs, and a moderately high score for the Humane-Oriented CLT. The Autonomous CLT score indicates that this factor is about neutral (mean score = 3.82, which is slightly below the midpoint of the scale). The Self-Protective leadership score is low (mean = 3.08), indicating that this factor is perceived to inhibit effective leadership. Examining the ranking of clusters

Table 21.7   Ranking of Societal Clusters Using Relative (i.e., Standardized) CLT Scores

Charismatic/ Value-Based	Team Oriented	Participative	Humane Oriented	Autonomous	Self-Protective
higher	*higher*	*higher*	*higher*	*higher*	*higher*
Anglo Germanic E. Nordic E. Southern Asia L. Europe L. America	Southern Asia[a] E. Europe Confucian A. L. America Sub-Sahara A. L. Europe Nordic E.	Germanic E. Anglo Nordic E.	Southern Asia Anglo Sub-Sahara A. Confucian A.	Germanic E.[b] E. Europe Confucian A. Nordic E. Southern Asia Anglo Middle East	Middle East Confucian A. Southern Asia E. Europe L. America
Confucian A. Sub-Sahara A. E. Europe	Anglo Middle East Germanic E.	L. Europe L. America Sub-Sahara A.	Germanic E. Middle East L. America E. Europe	L. Europe Sub-Sahara A. L. America	Sub-Sahara A. L. Europe
Middle East		Southern Asia E. Europe Confucian A. Middle East	Nordic E. L. Europe		Anglo Germanic E. Nordic E.
lower	*lower*	*lower*	*lower*	*lower*	*lower*
Charismatic/ Value-Based	Team Oriented	Participative	Humane Oriented	Autonomous	Self-Protective

NOTE: The placement of each societal cluster below a leadership dimension indicates the relative importance of this dimension compared with the other leadership dimensions within a particular societal cluster. For example, the Anglo cluster is the highest in rank for Charismatic/Value-Based leadership, indicating that this leader dimension was extremely important (relative measure) in comparison to the other five leadership dimensions within the Anglo cluster. The size of the relative score for each societal cluster is thus compared to the size of the relative scores for other societal clusters. Using the Tukey HSD analysis, clusters in the top band are significantly different from those in the bottom band. The clusters in the middle band are placed between these extremes for heuristic purposes. Societal clusters within each block are not significantly different from each other.

a, b Societal clusters in these columns are ranked in order; however, there are no significant differences among them in each column.

for the absolute scores (Table 21.6), it is apparent that the Anglo cluster is among the highest ranks for Charismatic/Value-Based, Participative, and Humane-Oriented CLT leadership dimensions, but among the lowest for Self-Protective.

Now let's examine the same six CLT leadership dimensions using the relative scores (see Table 21.7). Recall that each relative score contrasts the importance of a global leadership dimension in each cluster by comparing it to other leadership dimensions within that same cluster. Table 21.6 allows us to make and

present two comparisons simultaneously. The first comparison shows the strength of each CLT leadership dimension compared with the other CLT dimensions within the same *cluster.* Recall that this is an ipsative measure. The second comparison shows how each CLT leadership dimension's relative score compares with other relative scores from other clusters. By examining Table 21.7, note that the Anglo cluster has the highest ranking for Charismatic/Value-Based leadership. This cluster is also highly ranked for Participative and Humane-Oriented CLT dimensions. Furthermore, the Anglo cluster is ranked

Table 21.8   Summary of Societal Cluster Rankings for CLT Leadership Dimensions

Societal Cluster	CLT Leadership Dimensions					
	Charismatic/ Value-Based	Team Oriented	Participative	Humane Oriented	Autonomous	Self-Protective
Eastern Europe	M	M	L	M	H/H	H
Latin America	H	**H**	M	M	L	M/H
Latin Europe	M/H	M	M	L	L	M
Confucian Asia	M	M/H	L	M/H	M	H
Nordic Europe	H	M	H	**L**	M	L
Anglo	**H**	M	H	H	M	L
Sub-Saharan Africa	M	M	M	H	L	M
Southern Asia	H	M/H	L	**H**	M	H/H
Germanic Europe	H	M/L	**H**	M	H/H	L
Middle East	**L**	**L**	**L**	M	M	H/H

NOTE: For letters separated by a "/", the first letter indicates rank with respect to the absolute score, second letter with respect to relative score.

H = high rank; M = medium rank; L = low rank.

H or **L** (bold) indicates **H**ighest or **L**owest cluster score for a specific CLT dimension.

about average on the Autonomous CLT dimension, but somewhat lower on the Team Oriented dimension and among the lowest on the Self-Protective CLT dimension. Taken together, this presents a compelling image of facilitating and inhibiting leadership characteristics for the Anglo cluster relative to the hierarchy of the other clusters in each of the CLT leadership dimensions. The Anglo cluster strongly endorses Charismatic/Value-Based leadership qualities along with Humane-Oriented and Participative leadership. However, Anglo respondents report that Self-Protective leadership is an impediment to effective leadership and the Autonomy CLT dimension is about average relative to other societal clusters.

Ten Societal Clusters and Associated CLT Profiles

We will now examine each cluster and identify its distinguishing CLT leadership dimension characteristics with respect to culturally endorsed leadership profiles at the cluster level.[6] Although we will not discuss the profiles for each of the 62 societal Cultures considered independently of their cluster, these CLT scores are presented in Appendix 21.1.

Eastern Europe Cluster. This cluster includes Albania, Georgia, Greece, Hungary, Kazakhstan, Poland, Russia, and Slovenia. In examining Table 21.5 and Figure 21.1 (absolute scores), note that the Charismatic/Value-Based and Team-Oriented CLT leadership dimensions are reported to be the most important dimensions for effective leadership. Participative leadership is viewed positively, as is Humane-Oriented leadership, but not as important as the first two CLT leadership dimensions. Autonomous leadership is viewed in a neutral to slightly positive manner, whereas Self-Protective leadership is slightly negative. Table 21.6 provides a ranking of country clusters using the absolute CLT scores. The Eastern Europe cluster has the highest rank of all clusters for Autonomous leadership. It is among the lowest grouping of clusters for Participative leadership, and is among the highest clusters for Self-Protective leadership.

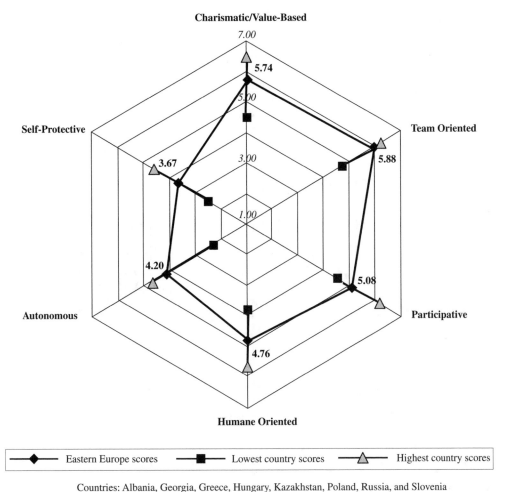

Figure 21.1   Eastern Europe Leadership Scores in Cultural Space

Examining the relative CLT scores in Table 21.7 provides a view that compliments the findings with the absolute scores presented above. Supporting the findings with the absolute scores, the most noteworthy result is that in comparison to other clusters, the Eastern Europe cluster is ranked as one of the lowest clusters for Participative leadership and one of the highest clusters for Self-Protective leadership. Similar to the rank obtained using absolute scores, this cluster has the second highest rank for Autonomous leadership. Thus, ranking the clusters using relative CLT scores reinforces the information provided by the absolute scores. Both absolute and relative findings for the 10 culture clusters and six CLT leadership dimensions are summarized in Table 21.8.

These rankings indicate that a leadership exemplar for the Eastern Europe cluster would be one who is somewhat Charismatic/Value-Based, Team-Oriented, and Humane-Oriented, but is his or her own person, does not particularly believe in the effectiveness of Participative leadership, and is not reluctant to engage in Self-Protective behaviors if necessary.

Latin America Cluster. The Latin America cluster includes the largest number of cultures in the GLOBE sample (Argentina, Bolivia, Brazil, Colombia, Costa Rica, Ecuador, El Salvador, Guatemala, Mexico, and Venezuela). In examining Table 21.5 and Figure 21.2 (absolute scores), we note that the CLT leadership dimensions contributing the most to outstanding leadership

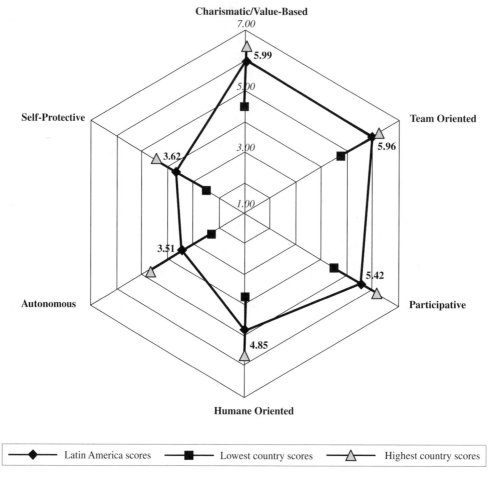

Figure 21.2   Latin America Leadership Scores in Cultural Space

include Charismatic/Value-Based and Team-Oriented leadership, followed by the Participative and Humane-Oriented CLT dimensions. Autonomous and Self-Protective leadership are viewed as slightly inhibiting outstanding leadership. Ranked by absolute CLT scores in Table 21.6, the Latin America cluster has the highest rank for the Team-Oriented CLT leadership dimension, the second highest rank for Charismatic/Value-Based leadership, and ranks lowest with respect to the Autonomous CLT leadership dimension. It occupies the middle ranks for the remaining CLT leadership dimensions.

The ranking of clusters using relative CLT scores (Table 21.7) is very similar, but not identical to the ranking using absolute scores

(Table 21.6). The Latin America cluster moves from the middle block of clusters with respect to the Self-Protective CLT dimension (absolute scores) to the highest block of clusters (relative scores). It remains among the highest ranked clusters for Charismatic/Value-Based leadership, and its Team-Oriented leadership scores keep it among the top three ranks after removing potential response bias. As might be expected given the high Team-Oriented CLT score, Autonomous leadership was rated lowest using relative scores, supporting the low rank for absolute scores. The Latin America cluster rankings for Participative and Humane-Oriented leadership remain about average in comparison to other clusters. A

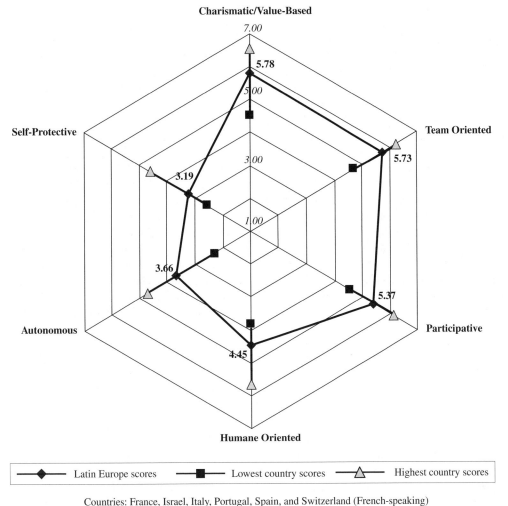

Figure 21.3 Latin Europe Leadership Scores in Cultural Space

summary of CLT leadership dimension findings is presented in Table 21.8.

For the Latin America cluster, an exemplar of effective leadership would be a person who practices Charismatic/Value-Based and Team-Oriented leadership, and would not be adverse to some elements of Self-Protective leadership. Independent action would not be endorsed. Participative and Humane-Oriented leadership behaviors would be viewed favorably, but not to the highest level as in other clusters.

Latin Europe Cluster. France, Israel, Italy, Portugal, Spain, and Switzerland (French-speaking) are included in this cluster. By

examining Table 21.5 and Figure 21.3, we note that the CLT leadership dimensions viewed as most contributing to outstanding leadership include Charismatic/Value-Based and Team-Oriented leadership. Participative leadership is viewed positively but is not as important as the first two dimensions. Humane-Oriented leadership is viewed as slightly positive, whereas Autonomous leadership is viewed as slightly negative and Self-Protective is viewed negatively. By examining the rankings using absolute scores in Table 21.6, note that the Latin Europe cluster is in the middle rank for all CLT leadership dimensions except the Humane-Oriented and Autonomous CLT dimensions, in which it ranks among the lowest scoring clusters.

As with the other clusters, differences between the Latin Europe cluster and others are further revealed by examining the relative CLT scores in Table 21.7. When comparing relative CLT scores with those of other clusters, it is noteworthy that the Latin Europe cluster is ranked similarly to the Latin America cluster, but with a few differences. One difference occurs with respect to the Self-Protective CLT leadership dimension. In the Latin Europe cluster, Self-Protective leadership is viewed as more of an impediment to effective leadership than in the Latin America cluster. This is true for both the absolute and relative scores. Another interesting contrast is reflected in the Humane-Oriented CLT dimension. The Latin Europe cluster occupies the lowest band for the Humane-Oriented CLT in contrast to the Latin America cluster, which is found in the middle band (for both absolute and relative scores).

In sum, by integrating all CLT leadership dimension results for the Latin Europe cluster (see Table 21.8), an exemplar of an effective leader would be a person who endorses Charismatic/Value-Based and Team-Oriented leadership. Autonomous action would not be endorsed and Humane-Oriented behaviors would not play a particularly important role. Although Participative leadership would be viewed favorably, the Latin Europe cluster would not be noted for it.

Confucian Asia Cluster. The Confucian Asia cluster includes China, Hong Kong, Japan, Singapore, South Korea, and Taiwan. In examining Table 21.5 and Figure 21.4, we note that the CLTs contributing to outstanding leadership include Charismatic/Value-Based and Team-Oriented leadership, even though the latter is not scored particularly high. Humane-Oriented leadership is viewed favorably, but it is not as important as the first two CLT dimensions. Although Participative leadership is also viewed positively, it is about equal to the lowest-scoring clusters. In fact, the Confucian Asia and Southern Asia clusters share the interesting characteristic that they are the only two clusters in which the Participative CLT score is less than the Humane-Oriented CLT score for effective leadership. This finding likely reflects the role

of the paternalistic but autocratic father in families. Autonomous leadership is viewed neutrally, and Self-Protective leadership is seen as a slight impediment to effective leadership. In examining the rankings in Table 21.6, note that the Confucian Asia cluster is ranked low with respect to Participative and high with respect to Self-Protective leadership dimensions.

The relative ranking of clusters (Table 21.7) reveals that the Confucian Asia cluster is characterized by relatively high scores for Self-Protective, Team-Oriented, and Humane-Oriented leadership. Again, what is striking is the very low relative ranking for Participative leadership. Thus, we find a high level of agreement between the relative and absolute measures for several CLT dimensions. For instance, the absolute CLT scores for Participative leadership rank the Confucian Asia cluster as one of the lowest of all clusters; it is also ranked low on the basis of relative CLT measures. Although the absolute scores indicate that Self-Protective leadership is approximately neutral as a contributor to effective leadership (mean = 3.72), it is among the highest scores in all the clusters. However, the relative measure shows more relevance for the Team-Oriented and Humane-Oriented CLT dimensions than does the absolute measure. In addition, the Confucian Asia cluster is among the highest ranks for Self-Protective leadership along with the Southern Asia and Middle East clusters. We can account for the relatively high Self-Protective scores by examining specific scores for the 21 first-order leadership factors (also called the primary leadership factors, which, are not shown here), where it is apparent that modesty and face saving are viewed positively for the Confucian Asia cluster, as might be expected for the collective cultures in the Far East (Bond & Hwang, 1986). Finally, as will be apparent when discussing the Southern Asia cluster later in this section, the Confucian Asia and Southern Asia CLT dimension rankings are very similar to each other with regard to effective leadership (see Table 21.8).

An example of effective leadership for the Confucian Asia cluster would include Charismatic/Value-Based and perhaps Team-Oriented leadership. Self-Protective actions are viewed less negatively than in other

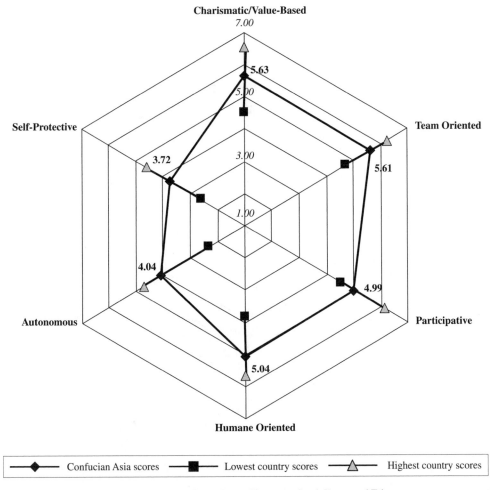

Figure 21.4   Confucian Asia Leadership Scores in Cultural Space

cultures. Participative leadership would not be expected.

Nordic Europe Cluster. Cultures included in this cluster are Denmark, Finland, and Sweden. In examining Figure 21.5 and Table 21.5 (absolute scores), we note that the Charismatic/Value-Based, Team-Oriented, and Participative CLT leadership dimensions are reported as contributing most to outstanding leadership. In fact, the Participative score is as high as the Team-Oriented score. The Humane-Oriented CLT dimension score is slightly positive, but lowest among the clusters. Autonomous leadership is viewed as neutral but the Self-Protective CLT

dimension is viewed extremely negatively. In fact, the Self-Protective score is the most negative (i.e., lowest score) for all clusters. The ranking of clusters in Table 21.6 indicates that the Nordic Europe cluster is among the highest ranks for the Participative and Charismatic/Value-Based CLT leadership dimensions and among the lowest ranks for Humane-Oriented and Self-Protective leadership.

By examining the relative scores in Table 21.7, it is apparent that the Nordic Europe cluster is characterized by its extremely low ranking for Self-Protective leadership. Being self-centered, status conscious, face saving, and inducing conflict are attributes seen as

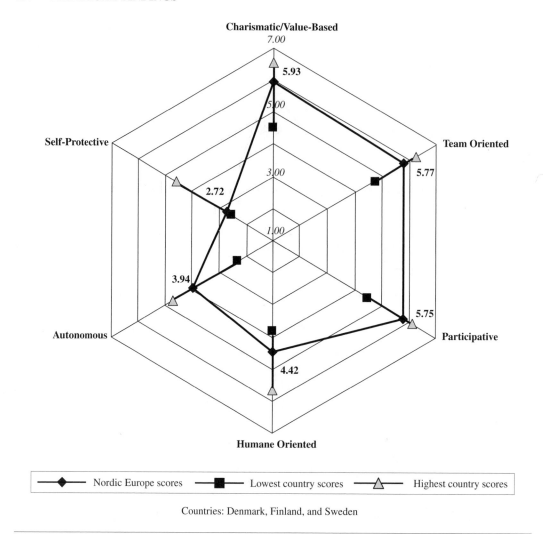

Figure 21.5   Nordic Europe Leadership Scores in Cultural Space

extremely inhibiting to effective leadership. The Participative CLT rank is among the highest, as might be expected for this cluster. Interestingly, the Humane-Oriented leadership score is among the lowest of all clusters. This finding may be surprising, especially because this cluster's score on the Humane Orientation cultural values score is the highest of all clusters. This paradox probably reflects specific attributes related to effective leadership and does not reflect a general nonendorsement of humane values.

In sum, by examining all CLT leadership dimension findings together (Table 21.8), the effective Nordic Europe leadership style would contain elements of Charismatic/Value-Based and Team-Oriented leadership. However, in contrast to most other cluster profiles, it would be particularly noted for high Participative leadership and low Humane-Oriented and Self-Protective attributes.

Anglo Cluster. The Anglo cluster includes Australia, Canada (English-speaking), Ireland, New Zealand, South Africa (White sample), the United Kingdom, and the United States. In examining Table 21.5 and Figure 21.6 (absolute scores), we note that the CLT leadership dimensions viewed as contributing to outstanding leadership include Charismatic/Value-Based and Team-Oriented leadership. The Charismatic/Value-Based score is the highest for all clusters. Participative leadership is viewed positively and

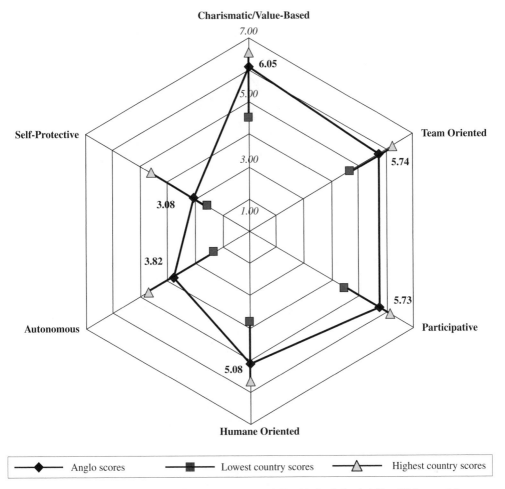

Figure 21.6   Anglo Leadership Scores in Cultural Space

has a score equal to that of the Team-Oriented CLT. (This is relatively unusual in our data and only occurs within the Anglo, Nordic Europe, and Germanic Europe clusters; the last is the only cluster in which the Participative dimension is valued more than Team Oriented.) Humane-Oriented leadership is considered a facilitator of effective leadership, and Self-Protective leadership is considered an impediment. In examining the ranking of clusters in Table 21.6, note that the Team-Oriented CLT dimension score is about average in comparison to other clusters, Humane-Oriented leadership is viewed positively and is among the top ranking, and Self-Protective leadership is among the lowest ranking.

Differences between the Anglo cluster and others can also be seen by examining the relative CLT scores in Table 21.7. When comparing relative CLT scores with those of other clusters, note that those for Charismatic/Value-Based, Participative, and Humane-Oriented leadership are very high in the hierarchy of scores for the Anglo cluster. Surprisingly, the Team-Oriented CLT dimension score is among the lower end of the ranks for the clusters (using the relative measure), likely reflecting the strong individualistic characteristic represented in the Anglo cluster. This cluster is ranked very low on Self-Protective leadership, indicating that status conscious, face saving,

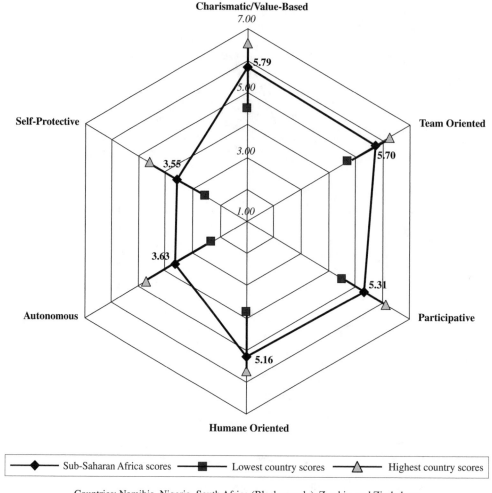

Figure 21.7 Sub-Saharan Africa Leadership Scores in Cultural Space

and self-centered attributes strongly inhibit effective leadership. The Autonomous CLT dimension score is about average in comparison to other cluster rankings.

Thus, to summarize this cluster (see Table 21.8), an exemplar of effective Anglo leadership includes high Charismatic/Value-Based elements with high levels of Participative leadership enacted in a Humane-Oriented manner. Team-Oriented is valued, but not ranked among the highest CLT dimension. Self-Protective actions would be viewed very negatively.

Sub-Saharan Africa Cluster. Namibia, Nigeria, South Africa (Black sample), Zambia, and

Zimbabwe are included in this cluster. The absolute scores for the Sub-Saharan Africa cluster (see Figure 21.7) are not particularly striking with the exception of the high score for the Humane-Oriented CLT leadership dimension and relatively low score for the Autonomous CLT dimension (see Table 21.5). The Humane-Oriented score was the second highest for all clusters, as seen in Table 21.6. Similar to other clusters, Charismatic/Value-Based, Team-Oriented, and Participative leadership are viewed as positive contributors to outstanding leadership. The Autonomous and Self-Protective CLT dimensions are slightly negative, and therefore seen as slightly impeding effective leadership.

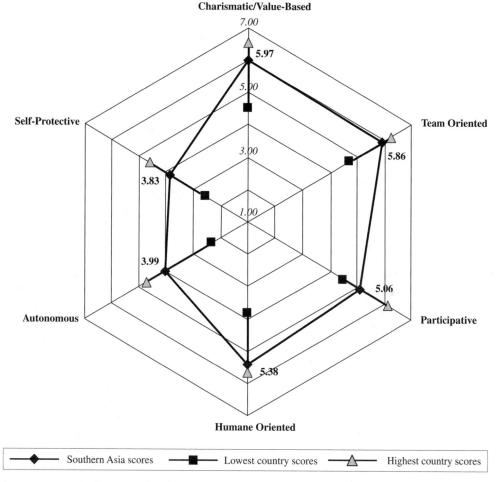

Figure 21.8   Southern Asia Leadership Scores in Cultural Space

Examining the relative CLT leadership dimension scores confirms the importance of the Humane-Oriented CLT dimension as contributing to effective leadership. The Sub-Saharan Africa cluster ranks among the highest cultures with respect to this CLT leadership dimension (Table 21.7), is among the lowest ranking with respect to the Autonomous CLT dimension, and is generally about average rank with respect to the other CLT dimensions.

Thus, findings for the absolute and relative CLT measures are in concert and do not lead to many distinguishing characteristics for the Sub-Saharan Africa cluster leadership profile. As with other clusters, an effective CLT prototype would exhibit Charismatic/Value-Based, Team-Oriented,

Participative, and Humane-Oriented leadership elements, and would be noted for a relatively high endorsement of Humane-Oriented characteristics (see Table 21.8).

Southern Asia Cluster. India, Indonesia, Iran, Malaysia, the Philippines, and Thailand form the cultures in this cluster. In examining Table 21.5 and Figure 21.8 (absolute scores), we note that the CLT leadership dimensions viewed as contributing most to outstanding leadership include Charismatic/Value-Based and Team-Oriented leadership. Participative leadership is viewed positively, as is Humane Oriented, but not as importantly as the first two CLT leadership dimensions. The Humane-Oriented leadership score, however, is the highest score for all clusters. Autonomous leadership is reported to be a neutral factor. Self-Protective leadership is viewed as slightly negative to almost neutral and is, therefore, less negative than indicated in all other clusters. The absolute score for the Self-Protective CLT dimension is the highest of all clusters and similar to the Middle East and Confucian Asia clusters. The ranking of clusters presented in Table 21.6 places the Southern Asia cluster among the highest ranks for Charismatic/Value-Based, Humane-Oriented, and Self-Protective leadership dimensions.

Examining the relative CLT scores in Table 21.7 also reveals differences between this cluster and others. When comparing relative CLT leadership dimension scores with those of other clusters, Team-Oriented leadership is very high in the hierarchy for this cluster as is the Humane-Oriented CLT dimension, but Participative leadership is not. The Southern Asia cluster is also in the highest group for the Self-Protective CLT, which also supports the finding for the absolute scores. Overall, considering both measures (Table 21.8), one may note the close correspondence between the CLT leadership dimension profile for the Southern Asia cluster and the Confucian Asia cluster profiles. Both profiles are characterized by high Team-Oriented, Humane-Oriented, and Self-Protective CLT dimensions, and relatively low Participative leadership. Charismatic/Value-Based leadership is higher in importance for the Southern Asia cluster than for the Confucian Asia cluster as reflected in both the relative and absolute scores.

The profile of an effective Southern Asia leader would be a person who exhibits Charismatic/Value-Based, Team-Oriented, and Humane-Oriented leadership attributes. The person would be relatively high on Self-Protective behaviors, and would not be noted for high levels of Participative leadership.

Germanic Europe Cluster. The Germanic Europe cluster includes Austria, Germany (former GDR–East), Germany (former FRG–West), the Netherlands, and Switzerland. In examining the CLT leadership dimensions in Table 21.5 and Figure 21.9 (absolute scores), we note that Charismatic/Value-Based and Team-Oriented leadership are reported to be very important

in contributing to outstanding leadership. Participative leadership is viewed positively; this is the only cluster in which the Participative CLT score exceeded that of the Team-Oriented CLT score. It is almost identical in importance to Charismatic/Value-Based leadership. The Autonomous CLT dimension is viewed in a neutral manner but Self-Protective leadership is viewed negatively. The relative ranking of clusters (Table 21.6) places the Germanic Europe cluster in the highest rank for Participative leadership and among the lowest for Self-Protective leadership.

Examining the relative CLT scores in Table 21.7 further reveals differences between the Germanic Europe cluster and others. When comparing this cluster's relative CLT scores with those of other clusters, the Germanic Europe cluster profile is striking in its pattern of leadership dimensions thought favorable for effective leadership. The Charismatic/Value-Based, Participative, and Autonomous CLTs score highly in the leadership hierarchy for this cluster. The Self-Protective CLT dimension is one of the most undesirable leadership dimensions in the hierarchy for this cluster in comparison to other clusters' rankings. Note that Charismatic/Value-Based leadership is about equal in importance to that given for the Anglo cluster. Most striking is that the Participative CLT dimension is scored highest for all clusters for both absolute and relative measures.

According to this CLT profile (Table 21.8), people in the Germanic Europe cluster would seek out Charismatic/Value-Based leaders who believe in Participative leadership but who also support independent thinking yet reject elements of Self-Protectiveness.

Middle East Cluster. This cluster includes Egypt, Kuwait, Morocco, Qatar, and Turkey. There are a number of striking differences in comparison to other clusters. Using the absolute scores given in Table 21.5, Table 21.6, and Figure 21.10, we note that although the CLT leadership dimensions viewed as contributing to outstanding leadership include Charismatic/Value-Based and Team-Oriented leadership, these dimensions have the lowest scores and ranks relative to those for all other clusters. Participative leadership is viewed positively,

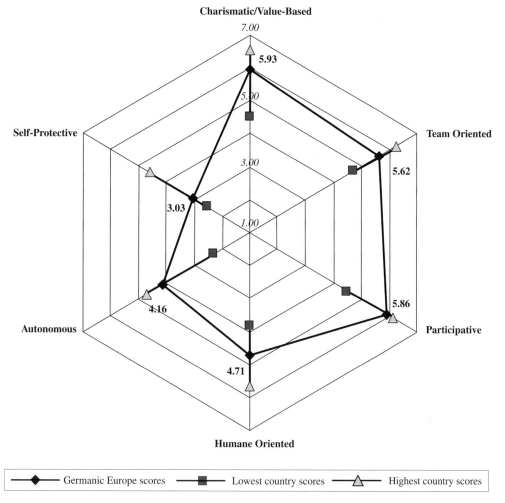

Figure 21.9   Germanic Europe Leadership Scores in Cultural Space

but again scores low compared with other clusters' absolute score and ranks. Humane-Oriented leadership is perceived positively, but only about equally to other cluster scores. The Self-Protective CLT dimension is viewed as an almost neutral factor; however, it has the second-highest score and rank of all clusters.

The relative CLT scores paint a picture that is consistent with the absolute scores described above. When comparing these relative CLT leadership scores with other clusters' scores, almost all Middle East CLT scores rank at the low end of the leadership comparisons. The exception is the Self-Protective CLT dimension,

in which the Middle East cluster has the highest relative CLT score. Thus, the relative scores support the findings with regard to absolute scores. This similarity is pointed out particularly for this cluster given the very low absolute scores. The possibility of response biases affecting the findings is always a possibility whenever absolute scores are used to compare cultural data.

Clearly, this CLT profile is the most unusual among all 10 clusters. Two explanations, although speculative, come to mind. First, Middle Easterners may not require the same amount of leadership from their leaders as do other clusters. However, this is unlikely, which

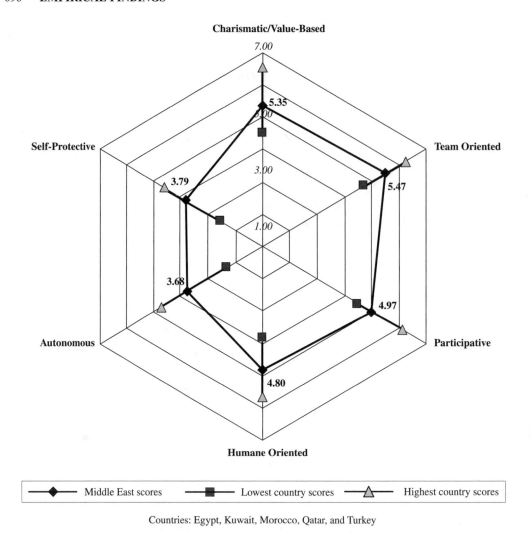

Charismatic/Value-Based

7.00

5.35

3.00

1.00

Self-Protective

3.79

3.68

Autonomous

Team Oriented

5.47

4.97

Participative

4.80

Humane Oriented

◆—— Middle East scores   ■—— Lowest country scores   △—— Highest country scores

Countries: Egypt, Kuwait, Morocco, Qatar, and Turkey

Figure 21.10   Middle East Leadership Scores in Cultural Space

leads to the alternative explanation that critical leadership attributes for this cluster were not part of the GLOBE attribute list. This alternative explanation gains credence from the findings of GLOBE researchers who administered a version of the research instrument in the Middle East containing additional leadership attributes not found in the final GLOBE-administered questionnaire (Dastmalchian, Javidan, & Alam, 2001). Somewhat fortuitously, factor analyses of their data indicated leadership dimensions similar to the six GLOBE dimensions, but in addition there were several more that may help explain the enigma of the Middle East CLT

profile. These additional leadership dimensions were labeled *familial, humble,* and *faithful*. It is likely that the pervasive influence of the Islamic religion is a key to understanding the Arab world, and presumably leadership in the Arab world (Hagan, 1995).

We believe that for an accurate portrayal of the Middle East cluster, it is particularly important to consider both the relative and absolute measures simultaneously (Tables 21.6, 21.7, and 21.8). That is, even with lower absolute and relative CLT scores for most of the leadership dimensions, an effective leader still exhibits Charismatic/Value-Based and Team-Oriented

Table 21.9   Amount of Variance Accounted for in CLTs by Societal Culture and Societal Cluster

CLT Leadership Factor	Societal Culture	Societal Cluster	Percent Overlap
Charismatic/Value-Based	.204[a]	.067	.328
Team Oriented	.145	.044	.303
Self-Protective	.355	.250	.704
Participative	.212	.115	.542
Humane Oriented	.182	.083	.456
Autonomous	.135	.041	.304

NOTE: All ANOVAs using societal cultures and societal clusters as independent variables were significant at $p < .001$ for each of the six CLT leadership dimensions.

a Numbers are eta squares that reflect amount of variance accounted for.

leadership dimensions as well as Participative and Humane-Oriented leadership, but not nearly to the extent indicated for other clusters. As pointed out in previous culture dimension chapters, Middle East respondents expect a visionary and future-oriented leader to direct followers to embrace a more performance-oriented culture. In addition to the culture-common findings, we see culture-unique elements of a more traditional leadership profile in the Middle East countries that include the endorsement of leadership attributes such as familial, humble, faithful, self-protective, and considerate.

Summary of Hypotheses 2a and 2b: Culturally Endorsed Implicit Leadership Theory and Future Research.

The previously described results support the belief that clusters can be viewed as coherent entities of cultures. Each cluster is characterized by a specific CLT configuration of leadership dimensions that vary in importance. Further, the concept of shared mental models is a useful theoretical mechanism by which cultures and clusters develop CLTs. We also found that cultures and clusters capture differing amounts of variability in CLT leadership dimensions depending on the specific CLT profile in question, with more variance accounted for by individual cultures than combined clusters (see Table 21.9). We realize that not only is there considerable variability among cultures, there also is variability among individuals within each society and that the clusters mask some of this variability.

However, given that clusters vary in leadership profiles, which implies that differences among cultures and individuals within cultures do not overwhelm cluster differences, we are justified in thinking of clusters as viable entities that reveal interesting leadership prototypes across the world.

Our findings raise several important questions for future research. For instance, if CLT leadership dimensions are differentially endorsed among nations or cultures as contributors to effective leadership (as indicated by our analyses), are these CLT leadership dimensions equally compelling and influential? Do the behaviors of leaders typically reflect the CLT profiles of their cultures? If the CLT profiles of the cultures are not enacted by the leader, will the leader be less accepted? Less effective? Project GLOBE Phase 3, which is currently under way, was designed to answer these questions. Even for CLT leadership dimensions found to be equally influential among cultures, results from GLOBE country-specific studies (to be published in 2004) along with considerable cross-cultural research suggest we should expect considerable variability in how managerial leadership is actually enacted across cultures. Researchers are also likely to investigate the mechanisms by which psychological and sociological processes link the six CLT leadership dimensions to dominant cultural values. One neglected area of inquiry in cross-cultural studies concerns the degree of variability within societies. For GLOBE, this issue might be captured by the question, "Are CLT leadership dimensions more rigidly set for homogeneous societies, such as

Japan, than for culturally diverse societies, such as the United States?"

We also have a great deal to learn about gender differences across cultures. In the Gender Egalitarian chapter (14) by Emrich and coauthors, we demonstrated statistically significant, but not substantial, gender differences with Charismatic/Value-Based, Participative, Team-Oriented, and Self-Protective leadership CLT dimensions, but not with Autonomous or Humane-Oriented leadership CLTs. Female managers rated the first three leadership CLT dimensions higher than did the male managers for contributing to outstanding leadership, and Self-Protective leadership as more inhibiting to outstanding leadership than did male managers. Gender differences were more apparent in certain cultures than in others, indicated by a significant gender-by-nation (i.e., societal culture) interaction for all but the Humane-Oriented leadership CLT dimension. For instance, gender differences for the Team-Oriented CLT were much smaller in the United States than in Hong Kong or Guatemala. A dissertation by Paris (2003) explores the antecedent cultural mechanisms that lead to these gender differences: Gender differences were moderated by the level of gender egalitarianism in the culture and were minimized in gender egalitarian cultures. Yet, we know very little about gender differences with respect to the effectiveness of these leadership dimensions among nations. Clearly the wealth of information provided by this phase of Project GLOBE research raises interesting questions regarding gender differences.

Hypotheses 3 and 4: Linking Leadership and Culture—Results of Hierarchical Linear Modeling

As just described, evidence indicates that CLT leadership dimensions are associated with cultures and clusters in unique combinations. These findings are consistent with the hypothesis that cultural differences strongly influence important ways in which people think about leaders, as well as the societal norms concerning the status, influence, and privileges granted to leaders. However, to use a culturally based explanation for these results instead of a nation-based explanation, it is necessary to determine the link between culture and leadership. This link was stated in Hypotheses 3 and 4. A critical issue concerns the strength of the relationships between culture and CLT leadership dimensions.

Hypothesis 3 asserts that there will be significant positive relationships between *societal* cultural dimensions (e.g., Individualism and Collectivism) and conceptually related CLT leadership dimensions (e.g., Team Oriented). Hypothesis 4 asserts there will be significant positive relationships between *organizational* culture dimensions and conceptually related CLT leadership dimensions. The second column in Table 21.10 shows our predictions concerning the relationships between the nine GLOBE-specific cultural dimensions and the six CLT leadership dimensions. These predictions were generated by examining each cultural dimension and CLT leadership dimension scale and identifying the conceptual similarities or likely causal relationships among them. For example, the perceived effectiveness of the Charismatic/Value-Based leadership dimension was expected to be associated with the Performance Orientation cultural dimension, because high performance expectations and goal attainment are defining characteristics of charismatic/value-based leaders and performance-oriented cultures.

We tested Hypotheses 3 and 4 using hierarchical linear modeling (HLM), a procedure (discussed by Hanges, Dickson, & Sipe in Chapter 11) that identifies the total amount of variance in a dependent variable that is accounted for by forces at the individual, organizational, industrial, and societal levels. This procedure also allows us to determine the amount of variance accounted for at each of these levels of analysis considered independently. That is, GLOBE research is primarily concerned with how cultural values and practices influence CLT profiles at the organizational and societal levels. Because GLOBE is focused on shared leadership belief systems, the individual level of analysis is not of direct concern for the present chapter. There are four critical points to keep in mind while discussing these results.

First, the total amount of CLT leadership dimension variance accounted for is a joint function of forces at the individual-, organizational-, industrial-, and societal-level cultural values. However, this chapter is mostly concerned with

(Text continues on page 701)

Table 21.10 A Priori Hypotheses and Results Predicting CLT Leadership Style From Societal and Organizational Culture

		HLM Tests							
		Single Culture Dimension				*Multiple Culture Dimension*			
CLT Leadership Dimension	*Predicted & Actual Culture Dimensions*	*Societal*		*Organizational*		*Societal*		*Organizational*	
		Value	*Practice*	*Value*	*Practice*	*Value*	*Practice*	*Value*	*Practice*
Charismatic/ Value-Based	**Performance Orientation**	.48**		.60**				.42**	
	Future Orientation			.42**				.17**	
	Humane Orientation			.37**				.17**	
	Institutional Collectivism			.35**	.11**				
	In-Group Collectivism	.41*		.69**		.25*		.26**	
	Assertiveness◊			− .18**					−.15**
	Gender Egalitarianism	.41**				.36**			
	Power Distance	−.57**							
	Uncertainty Avoidance	−.20*							
Team Oriented	**Institutional Collectivism**			.20**	.13**				.12**
	In-Group Collectivism		.17**	.47**				.18**	
	Humane Orientation			.35**	−.10*			.13**	−.12**
	Assertiveness◊			− .14**	−.16**				−.15**
	Uncertainty Avoidance*	.12*	−.12*	.17**	−.06*	.19**		.14**	−.07**
	Performance Orientation			.31**				.15*	
	Future Orientation		−.15*	.28**				.13**	
	Gender Egalitarianism				.10**				.07**
	Power Distance		.23*						
Participative	**Assertiveness◊**			−.13**	−.14*			‡ **	
	Power Distance◊	−.85**	−.35*	−.32**					
	Humane Orientation	.62*		.32**			.21**		
	Uncertainty◊ Avoidance◊	−.49**		−.13**	−.08*	−.23**		⊕ **	

(Continued)

Table 21.10 (Continued)

		HLM Tests							
CLT Leadership Dimension	Predicted & Actual Culture Dimensions	Single Culture Dimension				Multiple Culture Dimension			
		Societal		Organizational		Societal		Organizational	
		Value	Practice	Value	Practice	Value	Practice	Value	Practice
	Institutional Collectivism		−.49*	.20**					
	In-Group Collectivism	ß **	ß **		−.08*				
	Performance Orientation	.47**		.25**				.24**	
	Future Orientation			.14*	−.07*				
	Gender Egalitarianism	.65**		.21**		.44**		.15**	
Humane Oriented	**Humane Orientation**		.33**	.56**	−.15**			.47**	−.11**
	Gender Egalitarianism				.12**				
	Institutional Collectivism			.22**	.11**				
	In-Group Collectivism		.20**	.52**					
	Performance Orientation		.33**	.25**			.40**	.13**	
	Assertiveness	.23*		.27**	.20**				.22**
	Future Orientation	.35		.27**				.12**	
	Power Distance	−.34*							
	Uncertainty Avoidance	.32**		.23**	−.10*	.29**		.20**	
Autonomous	**Institutional Collectivism ◊**	−.35*			−.11*	−.34**		−.16**	
	In-Group Collectivism ◊				.13*				
	Performance Orientation			.19**				.24**	
	Assertiveness			.23**	.14*				.20**
	Future Orientation								
	Humane Orientation			−.29**	.11*				
	Power Distance				.10**				
	Uncertainty Avoidance				.08*				.12**

		HLM Tests							
CLT Leadership Dimension	**Predicted & Actual Culture** Dimensions	Single Culture Dimension				Multiple Culture Dimension			
		Societal		Organizational		Societal		Organizational	
		Value	Practice	Value	Practice	Value	Practice	Value	Practice
Self-Protective	**Humane Orientation**	◊ *							
	Power Distance	.87**	.48**	.25**		.29**		.10*	
	Uncertainty Avoidance	.63**	.16**	.26**	.04**	.53**		.26**	
	Institutional Collectivism	.38**							
	In-Group Collectivism	◊ 30*	.45**			−.25			
	Performance Orientation			◊ 11**				◊ 12**	
	Future Oriented	.40*		.27**				.12**	
	Gender Egalitarianism	◊ 62**		◊ 20**					

NOTE: Numbers in each column are unstandardized HLM coefficients. Predicted dimensions are noted in bold. Dimensions followed by "◊" are hypothesized to be inversely related to leadership factors.

* $p < .05$.

** $p < .01$.

the total CLT variance and the variance accounted for by forces at the organizational and societal levels.

Second, the following HLM results reflect *competitive* tests among the nine cultural dimensions, showing the specific efficacy of a cultural dimension in relation to the other cultural dimensions in predicting CLT leadership dimension scores. We will refer to the competitive tests as the multiple HLM tests because multiple culture dimensions are included in the analysis. Please refer to the individual culture dimension chapters (Chapters 12–19) for a discussion of the single HLM tests related to CLT leadership dimensions. In a sense, this competitive multiple-HLM procedure is analogous to a multiple-regression procedure using several independent variables, but with the addition of multiple levels of analysis. However, readers are provided a complete picture of all HLM analyses in Table 21.10, which shows both the

single and multiple HLM results. The results may differ somewhat depending on which perspective is used—noncompetitive or competitive tests. It is for this reason that Figures 21.11 to 21.16 differ from those in the individual dimension chapters (12–19) as well as from the figures in the Nontechnical Summary (Chapter 3).

Third, results of HLMs based on multiple dimensions of culture indicated that endorsement of CLT dimensions is most associated with the cultural or organizational *values* orientation (*Should Be* questionnaire responses), and less so with cultural or organizational *practices* (*As Is* questionnaire responses). This makes sense given that values reflect an idealized state of what should be and, therefore, ought to correspond to individuals' implicit beliefs regarding idealized leadership attributes. Thus, we are much more confident that the cultural dimension values are more important than practices—they are more conceptually and theoretically related to CLT

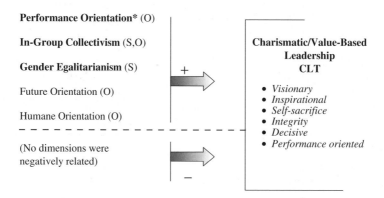

Figure 21.11   Cultural Value Drivers of the Charismatic/Value-Based CLT Leadership Dimension

* Only statistically significant relationships are shown. The most important cultural dimensions for this leadership CLT are bolded (i.e., relationship is significant at both society and organization levels of analyses or highest HLM coefficient within each level of analysis).

CLT = culturally endorsed leadership theory

O = Organizational level

S = Societal level

dimensions. We should also note, that sometimes the interpretation of results regarding cultural dimension practices is problematic, an issue we will return to in detail in the final chapter of the book.

Fourth, a priori hypotheses were developed to reflect what we anticipate will be the relationship between each leadership CLT style and varying societal and organizational culture dimensions. For instance, we predicted that members of performance-oriented organizations would positively assess Charismatic/Value-Based skills and behaviors as contributing to effective leadership. These predicted relationships are shown in bold in Table 21.10.

In the following discussion, statistically significant relationships between the nine societal and organizational culture dimensions and the six CLT leadership dimensions are organized around each of the CLT leadership dimensions. Figures 21.11–21.16 show a summary of significant relationships between GLOBE-defined cultural values and the CLT leadership dimensions.

Charismatic/Value-Based Leadership

Multiple Culture Dimension HLM Tests. A major finding for this critical leadership dimension was the large influence of Performance Orientation cultural values as the most important cultural dimension predicting Charismatic/Value-Based leadership at the organizational level of analysis. This finding supports our original prediction that the Performance Orientation cultural values scale should be significantly and strongly related to the endorsement of Charismatic/Value-Based leadership (see Table 21.10 and Figure 21.11). The Performance Orientation cultural value dimension includes societal characteristics related to improving and rewarding performance, being innovative, and setting challenging goals. These characteristics mirror the skills and behaviors often exhibited by charismatic leaders, who demand high standards of performance, are intolerant of the status quo, use innovative means to achieve a desirable mission and vision of the organization, and challenge people to excel (Howell & Costley, 2001).

A second major finding, certainly less expected than the first regarding Performance Orientation, was that In-Group Collectivism values (Collectivism II) is an important predictor of Charismatic/Value-Based leadership for both societal and organizational levels of analysis. Other cultural values positively related to this CLT include Gender Egalitarianism, Future Orientation, and Humane Orientation dimensions. Assertiveness practices were seen as an impediment to effective leadership; however our discussion throughout this section concentrates on cultural values.[7]

Cultures Endorsing Charismatic/Value-Based Leadership. Respondents in societies report that Charismatic/Value-Based behaviors contribute to effective leadership: It is universally perceived as important, yet there is variability among cultures. The Charismatic/Value-Based leadership scale values reported by a culture were best predicted by the levels of Performance Orientation and In-Group Collectivism cultural values. Absolute and relative CLT scores yield interesting similarities and differences among findings for Charismatic/Value-Based leadership. The mean of absolute CLT scores for all cultures exceeds 5.00, an important element of identifying this as a universally endorsed CLT leadership dimension. In addition, all clusters except Confucian Asia and Middle East have mean absolute scores above 5.70 for this leadership dimension; however, clusters do differ somewhat regarding the importance of this CLT dimension in contributing to effective leadership (see Tables 21.6, 21.7, and 21.8).

When considering the CLT scores, clusters such as the Anglo cluster particularly endorse Charismatic/Value-Based attributes as contributing to effective leadership. In fact, more than half of the clusters have high scores for this CLT dimension. Members of societies and organizations who value performance improvement and have ambitious goals that demand excellence are more likely to accept and expect leaders who enact value-based charismatic leader behaviors. It should be stressed, however, that the GLOBE view of charismatic leadership is not synonymous with the notions portrayed in the popular press—being flamboyant, glib, and attractive. Instead, we empirically found this leadership style to embody performance-oriented skills and behaviors, and to be composed of visionary, inspirational, self-sacrificial, integrity-based, and decisive attributes. This important leadership style can be demonstrated in several ways as described in the Den Hartog and colleagues (1999) article. The forthcoming GLOBE book consisting of country-specific chapters will further describe how certain leadership behaviors, including Charismatic/Value-Based leadership, are enacted differently among cultures. The compelling results for this CLT dimension should allow us to expect that members of organizations and societies reporting high performance-oriented, collectivist (in-group), and gender egalitarian values are likely to have leadership prototypes that particularly emphasize Charismatic/Value-Based leadership attributes.

Team-Oriented Leadership

Multiple Culture Dimension HLM Tests. As predicted, the In-Group Collectivism and Humane Orientation cultural value dimensions were significantly and positively related to the endorsement of the Team-Oriented CLT dimension as contributors to effective leadership at the organizational level of analysis (Table 21.10 and Figure 21.12). We also found that Performance Orientation and Future Orientation values were significant predictors at the organizational level. Unexpectedly, Uncertainty Avoidance values were particularly important as they were significant at both the societal and organizational levels of analysis. Although a number of cultural dimension practices were also related to this leadership dimension, the interpretation of these results is more problematic. We are much more confident that the cultural dimension values are more important than practices—they are more conceptually and theoretically related to CLT dimensions.[8]

Cultures Endorsing Team-Oriented Leadership. This CLT leadership dimension is universally perceived to be important in enhancing effective leadership. All cultures had absolute scores exceeding 5.00, and most exceeded 5.60. However, when examining the results using both absolute and relative CLT measures, the Southern Asia, Confucian Asia, Eastern Europe, and Latin

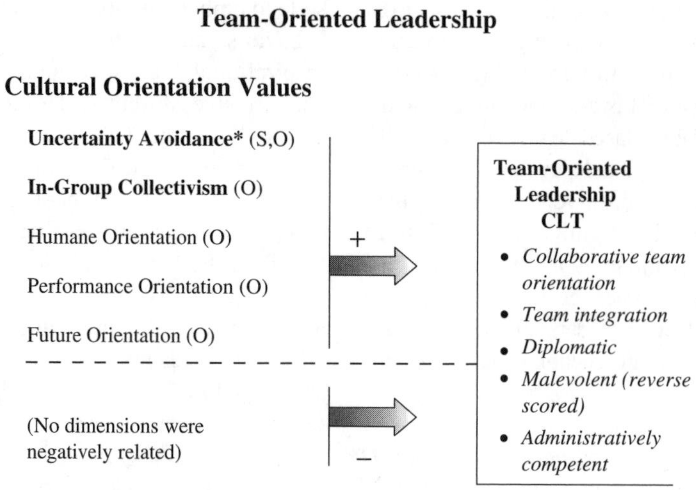

Team-Oriented Leadership

Cultural Orientation Values

Uncertainty Avoidance* (S,O)

In-Group Collectivism (O)

Humane Orientation (O)

Performance Orientation (O)

Future Orientation (O)

(No dimensions were
negatively related)

+

−

**Team-Oriented
Leadership
CLT**

- *Collaborative team
  orientation*
- *Team integration*
- *Diplomatic*
- *Malevolent (reverse
  scored)*
- *Administratively
  competent*

Figure 21.12   Cultural Value Drivers of the Team Oriented CLT Leadership Dimension

* Only statistically significant relationships are shown. The most important cultural dimensions for this leadership CLT are bolded (i.e., relationship is significant at both society and organization levels of analyses or highest HLM coefficient within each level of analysis).

CLT = culturally endorsed leadership theory

O = Organizational level

S = Societal level

America clusters report Team-Oriented leadership to be particularly critical for effective leadership. HLM tests reveal that the In-Group Collectivism and Uncertainty Avoidance cultural values are the most important in predicting this CLT dimension. Organizations that value the expression of pride, loyalty, and interdependence will include the Team-Oriented CLT as part of the prototypical CLT leadership dimensions for effective leadership. In addition, the more the society and organization report valuing the reduction of uncertainty, the more they report endorsing team-oriented leadership. Members of societies and organizations who have collectivist (in-group) values and who want to reduce uncertainty are likely to have leadership prototypes that emphasize team-oriented leadership attributes.

Participative Leadership

Multiple Culture Dimension HLM Tests. We predicted that several cultural value dimensions should relate to the endorsement and, conversely, the nonendorsement, of Participative leadership. Our expectations were that Power Distance,

Uncertainty Avoidance, and Assertiveness cultural value dimensions should have negative relationships with the Participative CLT leadership dimension. The Humane Orientation cultural dimension was predicted to have a positive relationship with Participative leadership. For the most part, our predictions were supported with the single dimension tests as documented in the individual culture dimension chapters (12-19). The findings are a little more complex when examining the statistical results of the multiple-dimension HLM analysis (see Table 21.10 and Figure 21.13).

As predicted, Uncertainty Avoidance and Assertiveness were negatively related to Participation. Unexpectedly, the Power Distance value dimension was not significant for the multiple dimension HLM tests; however, it had a strong negative relationship with the Participative CLT in the single dimension HLM tests (see Chapter 17, by Carl, Gupta, & Javidan). Gender Egalitarianism turned out to be a strong, yet unexpected predictor of Participative leadership. Performance Orientation was also important as a positive predictor. Overall, the results

Participative Leadership

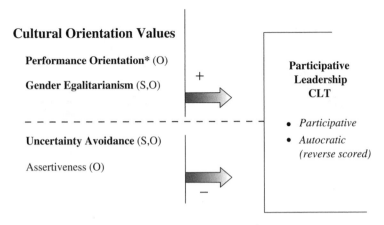

Figure 21.13   Cultural Value Drivers of the Participative CLT Leadership Dimension

* Only statistically significant relationships are shown. The most important cultural dimensions for this leadership CLT are bolded (i.e., relationship is significant at both society and organization levels of analyses or highest HLM coefficient within each level of analysis).

CLT = culturally endorsed leadership theory

O = Organizational level

S = Societal level

are very strong considering the summary picture of cultural values leading to Participative leadership. Clearly, the two most important cultural variables positively related to Participative leadership were Performance Orientation and Gender Egalitarianism, in which the most important cultural value negatively related was Uncertainty Avoidance. (Because the Power Distance single HLM results were so compelling, they are included as a relevant negative predictor in the Nontechnical Summary.)[9]

Cultures Endorsing Participative Leadership. Overall, Participative leadership was viewed favorably by respondents from all cultures, but their endorsement of the Participative CLT leadership dimension as contributing to effective leadership also varied considerably among cultures. The Germanic Europe, Anglo, and Nordic Europe clusters reported in the GLOBE survey were particularly supportive of Participative leadership. There was complete consensus between the absolute and relative scores for this leadership dimension. Given the popularity of Participative leadership in the Western and European leadership literature, this

confirms preconceived notions about these cultures (Bass, 1990). To sum up, members of societies reporting high performance oriented and gender egalitarian values who also have a high tolerance for uncertainty will likely have Participative leader attributes as part of their effective CLT leadership prototype.

Humane-Oriented Leadership

Multiple Culture Dimension HLM Tests. One obvious prediction was that the Humane-Oriented CLT leadership dimension should be related to the endorsement of the Humane Orientation cultural dimension values. We also predicted that Gender Egalitarianism values would be related to Humane Oriented leadership. The former, but not the latter, prediction proved to be true: Humane Orientation cultural values were a strong predictor of Humane-Oriented leadership for organizations. Gender Egalitarianism values were not. We also found that Performance Orientation, Future Orientation, and Uncertainty Avoidance were all positively related to Humane Oriented leadership (see Table 21.10 and Figure 21.14).[10]

Humane-Oriented Leadership

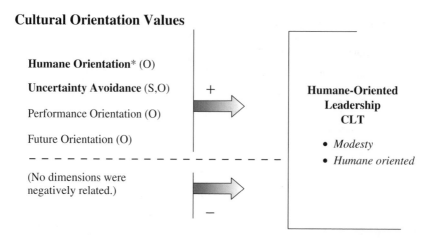

Figure 21.14   Cultural Value Drivers of the Humane-Oriented CLT Leadership Dimension

* Only statistically significant relationships are shown. The most important cultural dimensions for this leadership CLT are bolded (i.e., relationship is significant at both society and organization levels of analyses or highest HLM coefficient within each level of analysis).

CLT = culturally endorsed leadership theory

O = Organizational level

S = Societal level

Cultures Endorsing Humane-Oriented Leadership. As a group, all clusters report this CLT leadership dimension as slightly positive in contributing to effective leadership, yet the ranking indicates that four clusters may be singled out. Aggregated responses in the Southern Asia, Anglo, Sub-Saharan Africa, and Confucian Asia clusters particularly endorse this characteristic as enhancing effective leadership.

As expected, the most important cultural dimension predicting the Humane-Oriented leadership dimension is the Humane Orientation cultural dimension. These societies and organizations are reported to value attributes such as concern, sensitivity, friendship, tolerance, and support for others that are extended at the societal and organizational levels. Obviously, the Humane Orientation of societies is closely related to an overall concern about the well-being of their members. This, in turn, contributes to the endorsement of the Humane-Oriented leadership dimension leading to effective leadership. Examining the two strongest cultural dimensions predictors, we should expect that members of societies and organizations that value humane orientation and reductions in uncertainty will likely have CLT leadership prototypes that emphasize humane attributes.

Autonomous Leadership

Multiple Culture Dimension HLM Tests. Two cultural dimensions were related to Autonomous leadership. As predicted, collectivism values (specifically Institutional Collectivism) were negatively related to the Autonomous leadership CLT at both the societal and organizational levels of analysis. In addition, Performance Orientation values were positively related to Autonomous leadership (see Table 21.10 and Figure 21.15).[11]

Cultures Endorsing Autonomous Leadership. Autonomous leadership attributes were generally viewed within each cluster as being neutral to slightly negative with respect to contributing to or impeding effective leadership. The

Autonomous Leadership

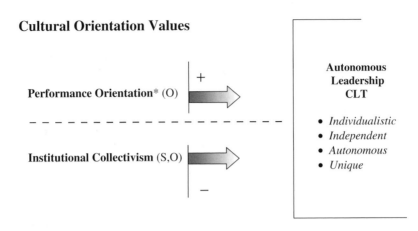

Figure 21.15 Cultural Value Drivers of the Autonomous CLT Leadership Dimension

* Only statistically significant relationships are shown. The most important cultural dimensions for this leadership CLT are bolded (i.e., relationship is significant at both society and organization levels of analyses or highest HLM coefficient within each level of analysis).

CLT = culturally endorsed leadership theory

O = Organizational level

S = Societal level

absolute and relative scores converge in portraying the Sub-Saharan Africa, Middle East, Latin Europe, and Latin America clusters as rejecting the Autonomous CLT as a contributor to effective leadership. In contrast, the Eastern Europe and Germanic Europe clusters were the two highest-ranking clusters for this CLT. In sum, members of societies and organizations with high performance-oriented and individualistic values will likely have autonomous attributes as part of their effective CLT leadership prototype.

Self-Protective Leadership

Multiple Culture Dimension HLM Tests. HLM results supported most predictions related to Self-Protective leadership. Power Distance and Uncertainty Avoidance values were strong positive predictors of this CLT, whereas In-Group Collectivism and Performance Orientation values were negatively related to this CLT (see Table 21.10 and Figure 21.16). The high power distance values and practices of Asian societies

are often associated with face saving and status consciousness, both of which are elements of the self-protective leadership dimension. In addition, being self-protective is one means to reduce uncertainty.[12]

Cultures Endorsing Self-Protective Leadership. Almost all cluster respondents viewed the Self-Protective CLT dimension as an impediment to effective leadership—some strikingly so as reflected by the low absolute and relative scores for the Anglo, Germanic Europe, and Nordic Europe clusters, yet the Confucian Asia and Southern Asia clusters viewed Self-Protective leadership in an almost neutral manner (with some attributes of this factor being viewed positively, such as face saving). Richard Brislin (personal communication, 2000) suggested that the concept for Asian cultures actually reflects "group-protective" rather than "self-protective" elements and, therefore, would be viewed more positively in the Confucian Asia and Southern Asia clusters. We expect that Self-Protective leadership attributes

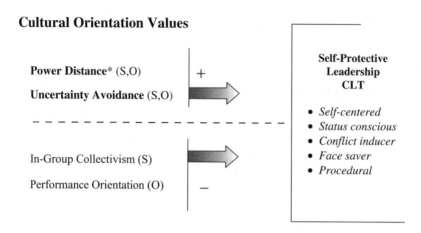

Figure 21.16   Cultural Value Drivers of the Self-Protective CLT Leadership Dimension

* Only statistically significant relationships are shown. The most important cultural dimensions for this leadership CLT are bolded (i.e., relationship is significant at both society and organization levels of analyses and/or highest HLM coefficient within each level of analysis).

CLT = culturally endorsed leadership theory

O = Organizational level

S = Societal level

would be part of an effective leadership prototype of members of organizations and societies valuing high power distance and reductions in uncertainty.

Summary of Hypotheses 3 and 4

Hypotheses 3 and 4 are generally supported with respect to the relationships between societal culture dimensions and endorsement of all six CLT leadership dimensions. Overall, our findings show that GLOBE-defined societal and organizational cultural values have significant influence on the content of CLT profiles; societal and organizational cultural practices generally do not. As an additional issue, recall that Hypothesis 3 concerns relationships between societal culture and CLT leadership dimensions whereas Hypothesis 4 concerns the relationships between organizational culture and CLT leadership dimensions. Although we have not made an a priori assertion of the relative predictive power of societal versus organizational values (Hypothesis 3 vs. Hypothesis 4),

we clearly found that organizational values were more frequently predictive of leadership CLTs than societal values (see Figures 21.11–21.16). A likely explanation for this is that the questionnaire asked respondents to think about outstanding leadership in their organization or industry, therefore providing a strong organizational frame of reference in the minds of respondents. Organizational leadership and culture should be more immediate, tangible, and salient in the minds of respondents than societal leadership and culture. The reason for this approach was our intention to focus on business leadership and not on leadership in other endeavors, such as religious or political leadership.

MANAGERIAL IMPLICATIONS

The rapid development of regional and global economic integration of nations through entities such as the North American Free Trade Agreement (NAFTA), the European Union (EU), and the World Trade Organization

(WTO) has created a need for culturally knowledgeable managers who can work in multicultural environments. Project GLOBE findings should be of particular value to managerial leaders in multinational companies that are affected by globalization. These companies are increasing the number of their expatriate managerial leaders throughout the world (Cullen, 2002). Managers placed in cross-cultural situations face problems associated not only with rapid change in their industries, but also those associated with multicultural misunderstandings. Although a thorough comprehension of cultural values and behaviors will not guarantee organizational success, it should provide managers with an initial awareness and understanding of critical aspects of effective leadership within a specific culture.

Before discussing specific management practices and how these relate to GLOBE findings, it may be useful to reflect on the process of cultural change and the stability of cultural values. After all, if cultural values change as quickly as organizations and industries change, why be concerned with particular cultural values if globalization eventually leads to a "one-world managerial culture"? Stated another way, if cultural convergence is assured through modern industrialization, globally effective and ineffective management practices will inevitably surface. Although this argument has some merit, a contrasting position of cultural stability with enduring cultural patterns is more likely. Historians and social psychologists note the fundamentally stable nature of the values and beliefs of citizens in various countries (Inkeles, 1981; Smith & Bond, 1993). The Project GLOBE results presented in this book, along with research findings from other large-scale studies (see House et al.'s 1997 review of Hofstede's [1980, 2001] and others' seminal research projects) lead us to reject the culture convergence hypothesis, particularly in its most extreme deterministic form. Although we acknowledge that global communication, technical innovation, and industrialization can create a milieu for cultural change, a convergence of cultural values is by no means assured. In fact, cultural differences among societies may be exacerbated as they adapt to modernization

while simultaneously striving to preserve their cultural heritage. The stability and continuing significance of societal values have important implications for organizations and managers. As Smith (1997) points out, "Euromanagers" who want to bridge cultural gaps in Europe must consider the full range of cultural variability within contemporary Europe. Global managers who want to work effectively across continents and cultures still require specific cultural information to lead successfully. The knowledge of core cultural values and associated leadership profiles can help managers enact effective management practices.

We suggest that knowledge of culturally endorsed implicit leadership profiles (CLT profiles) should be useful for organizations to select, counsel, and train individuals who will work with members of other cultures. For example, once adapted to the individual level of analysis, GLOBE results will assist in designing expatriate personnel assessment and selection tools. Organizations may select expatriate managers partly on the basis of how strongly their values, belief systems, and leadership concepts overlap with those predominantly held in the host culture. The selection process may use a simple match such as having participative leaders selected for cultures that endorse participative leadership. Alternatively, it may use sophisticated statistical procedures such as profile analysis and discriminant function analysis using data from a host of differing cultural dimensions. A similar matching process may be used for leaders who manage culturally diverse work teams. For instance, military and civilian service members who enforce UN-mandated peacekeeping operations should find it useful to understand indigenous cultural dimensions and their effective leadership profiles to lead and function successfully within a foreign population. It seems that this information would be especially helpful to them because they act not only in the cultural context of their member nation, but also have the extra burden of a military culture to uphold. Nonetheless, empirical validation will be necessary to demonstrate the usefulness of this type of selection tool for intercultural managerial effectiveness.

Selecting the right manager to become an expatriate is merely the first step in improving the success rate for expatriate managers. Selection is not a substitute for cross-cultural training or developing mutual respect for differences in conducting collaborative work (cf. Smith, 1997). GLOBE findings can be used for informing and training managers about leadership behaviors and organizational practices that are viewed as acceptable and effective and those that are viewed as unacceptable and ineffective in foreign cultures. The particular leadership styles and attributes that were shown to be universal, and those shown to be culturally specific, should be used as a starting point. Consider participative leadership, which is generally viewed across cultures as a positive leadership style; nevertheless, there is considerable variability among cultures in its endorsement. Participative leadership is reported to be a particularly effective leadership style for the Anglo, Nordic Europe, and Germanic Europe clusters, but is much less so for the Eastern Europe, Southern Asia, Confucian Asia, and Middle East clusters. Even for cultures that endorse participative leadership, the manner in which it is effectively enacted will likely differ in day-to-day managerial situations (Smith & Peterson, 1994). Because of these culture-specific variations, it would be useful to develop a range of situations likely to generate cross-cultural misunderstanding in leader–follower relationships involving delegation, consultation, and normal, everyday decision making. In a future publication covering culture-specific chapters, this additional handbook will provide valuable detailed information regarding effective leadership actions consistent with cultural norms.

GLOBE findings are relevant to the critical issue of how much prior training, coaching, and actual experience in the host society is necessary to ensure effective cross-cultural leadership. We believe that the question of amount will depend on the magnitude of differences among the cultures. The cultural proximity between an organization and a potential host culture should determine the amount and type of training materials and methods for cross-cultural management preparations. Ordering cultures according to the GLOBE CLT leadership dimensions may be useful for developing a range of training situations likely to generate cross-cultural fit or misfit in leader–follower relationships. For example, respondents in Germany and Spain report two different concepts related to the CLT dimension *integrity* (honest, sincere, just, trustworthy). In line with the Germanic Europe leadership prototype, a German manager favors a more autonomous and interpersonally direct approach, an approach that will likely collide with the expectations of Latin European managers, who favor a team integrative and interpersonally less-direct approach. Thus, in situations with inherent conflict between individual and group interests, it is most likely that dissent will occur if particular leadership prototype misfits become salient. It should be possible to translate potential leader prototype misfits into training scenarios relating to real-world situations. GLOBE results would lead us to predict problems; conversely, if leadership profiles match cultural requirements, fewer problems will likely occur.

For the development of cross-cultural training, GLOBE delivers empirically grounded information for any combination of target countries. Whereas this chapter concerns the six global leadership dimensions, in the future all 21 primary (first-order) leadership dimensions consisting of more than 100 leadership attributes can be analyzed and transformed into diagnostic training situations. We suggest that understanding culturally endorsed differences in leadership concepts is a first step managers can take to adjust their leadership behavior to that required in a host society. Knowledge about particular cultural variations in leadership prototypes should help expatriate managers to more accurately anticipate potential problems in cross-cultural business interactions. More broadly speaking, knowledge of cultural and organizational norms and practices can inform meaningful prescriptions for cross-cultural strategy and policy formulation, organizational improvement interventions, human resource management practices, the design of organizational structures and incentive and control systems, and a multitude of business and management issues.

CONCLUSIONS

A common question permeates the cross-cultural management literature: Does culture influence leadership, and, if so, why and how? The Project GLOBE findings presented in this chapter clearly indicate that although there are commonalities across societies, culture influences leadership in several ways. We broadened the concept of individualized implicit leadership theories (ILT) into a cultural-level theory labeled culturally endorsed implicit leadership theory (CLT). We hypothesized and demonstrated that members of cultures share a common frame of reference regarding effective leadership. A leadership CLT profile was developed for each of 10 culture clusters using six global leadership CLT dimensions. These culturally endorsed leadership profiles highlight elements of leadership perceived to be culturally common as well as those that are culturally unique. We also determined the extent to which specific leadership attributes and behaviors are universally endorsed as contributing to effective leadership, in contrast to those that are culturally contingent.

When examining the content of the leadership profiles for the 10 clusters, an interesting worldwide view of leadership emerges. In many instances, the cluster-ranked CLT leadership dimensions present an enigma; they highlight commonalities among cultures by illustrating their universal endorsement of some leadership attributes and global CLT leadership dimensions while simultaneously highlighting meaningful differences indicated in the findings of cultural specificity for other leadership attributes and CLT dimensions. Because leadership attributes from the Charismatic/Value-Based and Team-Oriented leadership dimensions were universally seen as positive, we expected that these two leadership dimensions would be positively perceived among all 10 clusters. They are. However, we were surprised that, for these two leadership CLT dimension, the least variability among culture clusters shown by both the range and R^2 was found with the Team-Oriented CLT, not the Charismatic/Value-Based CLT leadership dimension (see Tables 21.5 and 21.9).

Humane-Oriented leadership was reported among culture clusters to be somewhat of a contributor to effective leadership, but not nearly as important as the Charismatic/Value-Based or the Team-Oriented CLT leadership dimensions. Autonomous leadership was often reported among the 10 clusters to be about neutral regarding its contribution to effective leadership, but for some of the 62 cultures (in the 10 clusters) it was reported to be a contributing factor and in others an inhibiting one.

For the two remaining CLT leadership dimensions, there was considerable variation among cultures and culture clusters. Whereas the Self-Protective CLT dimension was usually perceived to be an inhibitor of effective leadership, it was less so for the Middle East, Confucian Asia, and Southern Asia clusters, which were also all reported to be high Power Distance cultures. Participative leadership was reported to contribute to effective leadership for all culture clusters; however, considerable variation exists. The Germanic Europe, Anglo, and Nordic Europe clusters were particularly attuned to Participative leadership according to GLOBE results, whereas the Middle East, Eastern Europe, Confucian Asia, and Southern Asia clusters were not.

Additional evidence linking culture to beliefs about effective leadership is most intriguing. Our findings show that both societal and organizational culture values have significant links to beliefs about effective leadership. Not only have we demonstrated significant relationships between GLOBE cultural and leadership dimensions (as discussed in Chapters 12–19), through HLM statistical analysis we also determined the most important relationships (see Figures 21.11–21.16).

A major finding was the large influence of the Performance Orientation cultural dimension as the most important predictor of the Charismatic/Value-Based leadership dimension. Societies and organizations that value excellence, superior performance, performance improvement, and innovation will likely seek leaders who exemplify Charismatic/Value-Based qualities, and such leaders are likely to be effective. In-Group Collectivism values (Collectivism II) and Gender Egalitarianism were also important predictors of Charismatic/ Value-Based leadership. Other cultural values positively related to this CLT dimension include the Future Orientation and Humane Orientation dimensions. These findings in their totality suggest that if an organization wishes to enhance charismatic/value-based leadership, they might consider developing an organizational or societal culture that is more performance oriented, organizational collectivistic, gender egalitarian, humane, and future oriented.

Team-Oriented leadership was best predicted by In-Group Collectivism values and Uncertainty Avoidance values. The results regarding In-Group Collectivism were expected, given the conceptual overlap between the two constructs; collaborative team orientation would be expected in organizations that value pride, loyalty, and cohesiveness in their organizations. Less expected was the importance of Uncertainty Avoidance— the more the society and organization values the reduction of uncertainty, the more they report to endorse team-oriented leadership. Humane-oriented, performance–oriented, and future-oriented organizations would also likely seek team-oriented leaders.

Several societal and organizational values were found to relate to the endorsement and, conversely, rejection of Participative leadership. From the positive side, two dimensions stand out in importance: Performance Orientation and Gender Egalitarianism. The most important negative cultural value was Uncertainty Avoidance. Assertiveness and Power Distance were also negatively related to the Participative CLT. Thus, organizational members from high power distance and assertive organizations, and organizations that are intolerant of uncertainty, are not likely to use participative leadership effectively. Conversely, organizational members from gender egalitarian and performance-oriented organizations are likely to use participative leadership.

As might be expected, the most important cultural dimension predicting the effectiveness of Humane-Oriented leadership is the Humane Orientation cultural dimension. Members of humane organizations value attributes such as concern, sensitivity, friendship, tolerance, and support for others. Obviously, Humane

Orientation of societies is closely related to the overall concern about the well-being of their members. This, in turn, contributes to the endorsement of Humane-Oriented leadership dimension values leading to effective leadership. Less anticipated was the large influence of the Uncertainty Avoidance cultural dimension as an important predictor of a societal inclination toward Humane-Oriented leadership. Similar to the endorsement of Team-Oriented leadership, higher levels of Uncertainty Avoidance are associated with the endorsement of humane leadership.

Finally, we also found cultural dimensions that were related to the two neutral-to-negatively perceived CLTs. Two cultural dimensions were related to Autonomous leadership. As predicted, Institutional Collectivism values were negatively related to the Autonomous leadership at both societal and organizational levels of analysis. In addition, Performance Orientation values were positively related to Autonomous leadership. Regarding Self-Protective leadership, a general impediment to effectiveness for all clusters, Power Distance and Uncertainty Avoidance were strong positive predictors of this leadership dimension. In contrast, In-Group Collectivism and Performance Orientation were negatively related to it.

To summarize, the leadership profiles identified in the GLOBE studies should be useful in a very practical sense. Foremost, the societal and organizational values help delineate culture-specific boundaries of acceptable, effective leader behaviors and practices. Leaders who are aware of a culture's values and practices can make conscious, educated decisions regarding their leadership practices and likely effects on the day-to-day operations and crisis management within an organization. Acknowledgment and explanation from a leader to his followers that a customary cultural practice will be breached, and why, can help avoid or diminish problems and complications. We also suggest that knowledge of culturally endorsed implicit leadership profiles of the 10 culture clusters should be useful for selecting, counseling, and training individuals who work in intercultural environments.

Appendix 21.1   Leadership CLT Scores for Societal Cultures

Culture Cluster	Country	CLT Leadership Dimensions					
		Charismatic/ Value-Based	*Team Oriented*	*Participative*	*Humane Oriented*	*Autonomous*	*Self-Protective*
Eastern Europe	Albania	5.79	5.94	4.50	5.24	3.98	4.62
	Georgia	5.65	5.85	4.88	5.61	4.57	3.89
	Greece	6.01	6.12	5.81	5.16	3.98	3.49
	Hungary	5.91	5.91	5.22	4.73	3.23	3.24
	Kazakhstan	5.54	5.73	5.10	4.26	4.58	3.35
	Poland	5.67	5.98	5.04	4.56	4.34	3.52
	Russia	5.66	5.63	4.67	4.08	4.63	3.69
	Slovenia	5.69	5.91	5.42	4.44	4.28	3.61
Latin America	Argentina	5.98	5.99	5.89	4.70	4.55	3.45
	Bolivia	6.01	6.10	5.29	4.56	3.92	3.83
	Brazil	6.00	6.17	6.06	4.84	2.27	3.49
	Colombia	6.04	6.07	5.51	5.05	3.34	3.37
	Costa Rica	5.95	5.81	5.54	4.99	3.46	3.55
	Ecuador	6.46	6.21	5.51	5.13	3.53	3.62
	El Salvador	6.08	5.95	5.40	4.69	3.47	3.43
	Guatemala	6.00	5.94	5.45	5.00	3.37	3.77
	Mexico	5.66	5.74	4.64	4.72	3.86	3.86
	Venezuela	5.72	5.62	4.88	4.85	3.39	3.81
Latin Europe	France	4.93	5.11	5.90	3.82	3.32	2.81
	Israel	6.23	5.91	4.96	4.68	4.26	3.64
	Italy	5.98	5.87	5.47	4.38	3.62	3.25
	Portugal	5.75	5.92	5.48	4.62	3.19	3.10
	Spain	5.90	5.93	5.11	4.66	3.54	3.38
	Switzerland[a]	5.90	5.62	5.30	4.55	4.02	2.94
Confucian Asia	China	5.56	5.57	5.04	5.19	4.07	3.80
	Hong Kong	5.66	5.58	4.86	4.89	4.38	3.67
	Japan	5.49	5.56	5.07	4.68	3.67	3.60
	Korea, South	5.53	5.52	4.92	4.87	4.21	3.67
	Singapore	5.95	5.76	5.30	5.24	3.87	3.31
	Taiwan	5.58	5.69	4.73	5.35	4.01	4.28
Nordic Europe	Denmark	6.00	5.70	5.80	4.23	3.79	2.81
	Finland	5.94	5.85	5.91	4.30	4.08	2.55
	Sweden	5.84	5.75	5.54	4.73	3.97	2.81
Anglo	Australia	6.09	5.81	5.71	5.10	3.95	3.05
	Canada[b]	6.15	5.84	6.09	5.20	3.65	2.96
	Ireland	6.08	5.81	5.64	5.06	3.95	3.00
	New Zealand	5.87	5.44	5.50	4.78	3.77	3.19
	South Africa[c]	5.99	5.80	5.62	5.33	3.74	3.19
	United Kingdom	6.01	5.71	5.57	4.90	3.92	3.04
	United States	6.12	5.80	5.93	5.21	3.75	3.15

(Continued)

Appendix 21.1 (Continued)

Culture Cluster	Country	CLT Leadership Dimensions					
		Charismatic/ Value-Based	Team Oriented	Participative	Humane Oriented	Autonomous	Self-Protective
Sub-Saharan Africa	Namibia	5.99	5.81	5.48	5.10	3.77	3.36
	Nigeria	5.76	5.65	5.18	5.49	3.62	3.89
	South Africa[d]	5.16	5.23	5.04	4.79	3.94	3.62
	Zambia	5.92	5.86	5.29	5.27	3.43	3.66
	Zimbabwe	6.11	5.97	5.57	5.18	3.37	3.20
Southern Asia	India	5.85	5.72	4.99	5.26	3.85	3.77
	Indonesia	6.15	5.92	4.60	5.43	4.19	4.12
	Iran	5.81	5.90	4.97	5.75	3.85	4.34
	Malaysia	5.89	5.80	5.12	5.24	4.03	3.49
	Philippines	6.33	6.06	5.40	5.53	3.75	3.32
	Thailand	5.78	5.76	5.29	5.09	4.28	3.91
Germanic Europe	Austria	6.02	5.74	6.00	4.93	4.47	3.07
	Germany East[e]	5.84	5.49	5.88	4.44	4.30	2.96
	Germany West[f]	5.87	5.51	5.70	4.60	4.35	3.32
	Netherlands	5.98	5.75	5.75	4.82	3.53	2.87
	Switzerland	5.93	5.61	5.94	4.76	4.13	2.92
Middle East	Egypt	5.57	5.55	4.69	5.15	4.49	4.21
	Kuwait	5.90	5.89	5.03	5.21	3.39	4.02
	Morocco	4.81	5.15	5.32	4.10	3.34	3.26
	Qatar	4.51	4.74	4.75	4.66	3.38	3.91
	Turkey	5.95	6.01	5.09	4.90	3.83	3.57

a Switzerland (French-speaking)
b Canada (English-speaking)
c South Africa (White sample)
d South Africa (Black sample)
e Germany (East): Former GDR
f Germany (West): Former FRG

CLT leadership scores in this table are absolute scores aggregated to the societal level.

ENDNOTES

1. The reader might wonder why we did not use a more common term such as *stereotype* to refer to the concept of a shared leadership belief system. Stereotypes share some elements common to the construct of shared belief systems particularly if stereotypes are defined as socially shared prototypes or schema. But the term stereotype often carries extra linguistic meaning such as belief systems related to prejudice and inappropriate perceptions of an identifiable group. Hence we prefer to use the concept of CLT profiles to refer to the leadership belief systems that people of a society share and that influences their acceptance of and reaction to leaders. In short, we hypothesize that CLT profiles exist, and that they are a product of the interaction of individual experiences and cultural values and act as a mechanism by which culture influences leadership processes. We expect that in all cultures people are accepted as leaders on the basis of the degree of fit, or congruence, between the leader behaviors they enact and the belief systems held by the attributers.

2. Before presenting the next Hypothesis, we should comment on a very important potential problem in any cross-cultural research endeavor—that of committing the "ecological fallacy" error. The error occurs if we assume isomorphic relationships between

variables across differing levels of analysis, such as assuming that characteristics or relationships that exist at the societal level apply to the individual level. Conversely, the reverse ecological fallacy is said to occur if we assume that relationships at the individual level reflect relationships at the societal level. What applies for individuals may or may not apply for groups. We argue, however, that both ecological fallacy problems can be minimized by paying careful attention to the level of analysis issue as was discussed in detail in Chapter 8. Further, GLOBE researchers were specific in phrasing culture questions to explicitly refer to organizational and societal entities, in contrast to phrasing questions with individuals as referents. Further, GLOBE responses represent organizational and societal level measures that are more than simple aggregations of individual responses. Regarding CLT profiles, it seems sensible to expect that if individuals indicate that certain characteristics lead to effective leadership, an aggregation of responses to the societal level is appropriate given sufficient generalizability or "sameness" of responses within that society. The same should hold true for societal clusters. Evidence supporting these assertions is presented throughout the chapter.

3. Recall that for three nations it was important to differentiate societal cultures within each nation: East and West Germany, White and Black samples in South Africa, and Germanic and French Switzerland constitute separate samples.

4. An interesting outcome of the standardization procedure is that our newly created measure is an *ipsative* measure that has a particularly important quality. It allows us to see how important a specific CLT leadership dimension is, such as Charismatic/Value-Based leadership, in comparison to the hierarchy of leadership dimensions for that same person. Similarly, by aggregating to the societal level, we determine how important a specific CLT leadership dimension is for the society in comparison to the hierarchy of leadership dimensions within that society. The rationale for using this standardization process is that even for CLT dimensions that are universally endorsed such as Charismatic/Value-Based leadership, some societal cultures may endorse this leadership style more strongly than others in relation to the other CLT leadership dimensions. Thus, this second procedure using standardized scores constitutes a *relative* metric, rather than an *absolute* metric. We believe these types of comparisons will reveal useful differences among societal cultures.

Nevertheless, we will discuss results using both; the relative metric has the heuristic advantage of revealing differences among societal clusters. The specific mechanics used to compute the relative CLT measure are presented in Chapter 8.

Because the standardizing procedure maximizes the differences among societal clusters, we need to remain cognizant of the "absolute" scores that are taken directly from the responses in the questionnaire. There *are* leadership attributes that are seen as universal facilitators and universal inhibitors to effective leadership. Our standardized procedure focuses on relative comparisons. We feel both are necessary to get a true picture of leadership processes across cultures. The descriptions for each culture cluster use both the absolute (raw scores) and the relative (standardized scores) to achieve the most meaningful interpretation of qualities important for outstanding leadership.

5. At first glance one might incorrectly conclude that because this relative measure is by definition an ipsative measure, reporting high scores on one CLT leadership dimension automatically creates lower scores on the other CLTs. However, recall that we used the entire domain of constructs and items when creating our ipsative scores (i.e., we used both the leadership items as well as the items assessing the various cultural dimensions). Thus, all the ipsatively scored CLT items do not necessarily sum to zero. Although the possibility still exists that high scores on one CLT leadership dimension affected the standing on the other dimensions, it is incorrect to conclude that this automatically occurred. In fact, we have confidence in the validity of the relative CLT scores given similar, but not identical, results for the absolute and relative CLT measures.

6. It is important to discuss the validity of thinking of societal cultures and societal clusters as having "shared mental models" of leadership. Although culture is a macro variable, there is evidence that the responses to the GLOBE scales can be meaningfully aggregated to the macro level (i.e., societal level). Similarly, we argue that individual schemas of leadership can be aggregated to yield shared mental models for a societal culture and for the societal cluster. To consider the validity of our shared mental model construct for the CLT data, we might ask and answer the following questions: First, do societal cultures differ with respect to each of the six CLT leadership dimensions reported as contributing to effective leadership? Second, do societal clusters differ with

respect to each of the six CLT dimensions? Obviously, it would be fruitless to examine differences among clusters for those CLT dimensions that do not vary among societal cultures. Third, what percentage of the variance in CLT leadership dimensions is accounted for by societal cultures? The result will answer the question of whether societal cultures are meaningfully different with respect to differences among cultures. Fourth, what percentage of the variance in CLT leadership dimensions do societal clusters account for? In this case, we are investigating the importance of societal clusters in contrast to the question that reflects the importance of individual societal cultures. Fifth, what is the amount of overlap between information provided by the societal cultures in contrast to the societal clusters? The latter question speaks to the issue of whether the societal clusters capture the variance in leadership dimensions that are accounted for by societal differences.

To answer the above questions, we conducted a series of one-way Analysis of Variance (ANOVA) statistical tests using societal codes and societal cluster codes as the between-subject factors on the original individual respondent data (i.e., original data). Our results provide strong evidence that the concept of shared mental models of leadership is affected by societal culture. It is clear from examining Table 21.9 that all leadership CLTs are predicted by using societal cultures and societal clusters as independent variables. In addition, the amount of variance accounted for, as indicated by eta squares, varies by leadership dimension. Also, eta-squared statistics speak to the issue of the actual amount of influence of societal cultures in contrast to societal clusters, and overlap of societal cultures versus societal clusters. Results indicate that societal culture differences account for the most variance in the Self-Protective CLT and the least variance in the Autonomous CLT. The specific order in terms of variance accounted for by societal culture is: Self-Protective leadership followed by Participative, Charismatic/Value-Based, Humane-Oriented, Team-Oriented, and Autonomous leadership.

As indicated in the previous paragraph, when examining how the CLTs vary according to societal clusters, each CLT leadership dimension is impacted significantly by this between-groups societal-cluster factor. The total variance accounted for, however, is less than when considering the effect of societal cultures. This is to be expected because information is lost when the societal data are collapsed into societal

cluster data. However, the order of impact on specific CLT leadership dimensions is roughly the same, with a large amount of variance being captured for the Self-Protective CLT and the least for the Team-Oriented and Autonomous CLT dimensions. Lastly, the third column of Table 21.9 indicates the overlap in explained variance by the clusters as compared to the societal cultures. The size of the overlap indicates that societal *clusters* capture almost all of the information distinguishing societal *cultures* for Self-Protective leadership, but not for the Team-Oriented or Autonomous CLTs. This result suggests that societal clusters can provide a very handy shortcut, or summary, for societal cultures within the cluster for the Self-Protective CLT dimension, but less so for Team-Oriented or Autonomous CLTs.

7. The five cultural dimension values and practices (see Figure 21.11) explain a total of 14% of the variance for the Charismatic Value-Based CLT leadership dimension. Approximately 47.5% of this total explained variance was associated with forces operating at the organizational level of analysis. The remaining portion of the explained variance (52.5%) was associated with forces operating at the societal level of analysis. It should be noted that the total variance accounted for gives a very conservative impression of the impact of the culture variables because individual variation in the dependent variable (CLT) has not been removed. Because GLOBE hypotheses have been conceptualized at the culture level of analysis, individual variation is considered measurement error. Therefore we also followed the procedure discussed by Hanges et al. in Chapter 11 to provide explained variance estimates separately at the organizational or societal level of analysis. The organizational R^2 for the Charismatic/Value-Based CLT was 48.2% and the societal R^2 was 44.5%. See Chapter 11 by Hanges et al. for a detailed discussion of this level-specific R^2. These percentages correspond to the traditional regression R^2 done at each level of analysis separately.

8. The five cultural dimension values and practices (see Figure 21.12) explain a total of 13.1% of the variance for the Team-Oriented CLT leadership dimension. Approximately 65.5% of this total explained variance was associated with forces operating at the organizational level of analysis. The remaining portion of the explained variance (34.5%) was associated with forces operating at the societal level of analysis. The organizational R^2 for the Team-Oriented CLT was 54.2% and the societal R^2 was

34.7%. See Chapter 11 by Hanges et al. for a detailed discussion of this level-specific R^2. These percentages correspond to the traditional regression R^2 done at each level of analysis separately.

9. The four cultural dimension values and practices (see Figure 21.13) explain a total of 15.5% of the variance for the Participative CLT leadership dimension. Approximately 13.1% of this total explained variance was associated with forces operating at the organizational level of analysis. The remaining portion of the explained variance (86.9%) was associated with forces operating at the societal level of analysis. The organizational R^2 for the Participative CLT was 39.6% and the societal R^2 was 54.3%. See Chapter 11 by Hanges et al. for a detailed discussion of this level-specific R^2. These percentages correspond to the traditional regression R^2 done at each level of analysis separately.

10. The four significant cultural dimension values and practices (see Figure 21.14) explain a total of 12.7% of the variance for the Humane-Oriented CLT leadership dimension. Approximately 45.2% of this total explained variance was associated with forces operating at the organizational level of analysis. The remaining portion of the explained variance (54.8%) was associated with forces operating at the societal level of analysis. The organizational R^2 for the Humane-Oriented CLT was 51.3% and the societal R^2 was 60.5%. See Chapter 11 by Hanges et al. for a detailed discussion of this level-specific R^2. These percentages correspond to the traditional regression R^2 done at each level of analysis separately.

11. The two cultural dimension values and practices (see Figure 21.15) explain a total of 3.9% of the variance for the Autonomous CLT Leadership Dimension. Approximately 37.2% of this total explained variance was associated with forces operating at the organizational level of analysis. The remaining portion of the explained variance (62.8%) was associated with forces operating at the societal level of analysis. The organizational R^2 for the Autonomous CLT was 30.4% and the societal R^2 was 18.0%. See Chapter 11 by Hanges et al., for a detailed discussion of this level-specific R^2. These percentages correspond to the traditional regression R^2 done at each level of analysis separately.

12. The four cultural dimension values (see Figure 21.16) explain a total of 33.1% of the variance for the Self-Protective CLT Leadership dimension. Approximately 8.2% of this total explained variance was associated with forces operating at the organizational level of analysis. The remaining portion of the explained variance (91.8%) was associated with forces operating at the societal level of analysis. The organizational R^2 for the Self-Protective CLT was 51.2% and the societal R^2 was 82.2%. See Chapter 11 by Hanges et al. for a detailed discussion of this level-specific R^2. These percentages correspond to the traditional regression R^2 done at each level of analysis separately.

References

Bass, B. M. (1990). *Bass and Stogdill's handbook of leadership: Theory, research, and managerial applications* (3rd ed.). New York: Free Press.

Bass, B. M. (1997). Does the transactional-transformational leadership paradigm transcend organizational and national boundaries? *American Psychologist, 52*(2), 130–139.

Bond, M., & Hwang, K. K. (1986). The social psychology of the Chinese people. In M. H. Bond (Ed.), *The psychology of the Chinese people* (pp. 213–266). Hong Kong: Oxford University Press.

Brodbeck, F. C., Frese, M., Akerblom, S., Audia, G., Bakacsi, G., Bendova, H., et al. (2000). Cultural variation of leadership prototypes across 22 European countries. *Journal of Occupational and Organizational Psychology, 73,*1–29.

Cullen, J. B. (2002). *Multinational management: A strategic approach* (2nd ed.). Cincinnati, OH: South-Western Thomson Learning.

Dastmalchian, A., Javidan, M., & Alam, K. (2001). Effective leadership and culture in Iran: An empirical study. *Applied Psychology: An International Review, 50*(4), 532–551.

Den Hartog, D., House, R. J., Hanges, P. J., Ruiz-Quintanilla, S. A., Dorfman, P. W., & GLOBE Associates. (1999). Culture specific and cross culturally generalizable implicit leadership theories: Are attributes of charismatic/transformational leadership universally endorsed? *Leadership Quarterly, 10*(12), 219–256.

Dickson, M. W., Hanges, P. J., & Lord, R. G. (2001). Trends, developments and gaps in cross-cultural research on leadership. In W. H. Mobley & M. W. McCall (Eds.), *Advances in global leadership* (Vol. 2, pp. 75–100). Oxford, UK: Elsevier Science.

Dorfman, P. W. (1996). International and cross-cultural leadership research. In B. J. Punnett & O. Shenkar (Eds.), *Handbook for international management research* (pp. 267–349). Oxford, UK: Blackwell.

Dorfman, P. W. (2004). International and cross-cultural leadership research. In B. J. Punnett & O. Shenkar (Eds.), *Handbook for international management research* (2nd ed., pp. 265–355). Ann Arbor: University of Michigan Press.

Duncan, P. C., Rouse, W. B., Johnston, J. H., Cannon-Bowers, J. A., Salas, E., & Burns, J. J. (1996). Training teams working in complex systems: A mental model-based approach. *Human/Technology Interaction in Complex Systems, 8,* 173–231.

Gerstner, C. R., & Day, D. V. (1994). Cross-cultural comparison of leadership prototypes. *Leadership Quarterly, 5*(2), 121–134.

Hagan, C. M. (1995). *Comparative management: Africa, the Middle East, and India* (Working Paper). Boca Raton: Florida Atlantic University Press.

Hains, S. C., Hogg, M. A., & Duck, J. M. (1997). Self-categorization and leadership: Effects of group prototypicality and leader stereotypicality. *Personality and Social Psychology Bulletin, 23*(10), 1087–1099.

Hanges, P. J., Higgins, M., Dyer, N. G., Smith-Major, V., Dorfman, P. W., Brodbeck, F. C., et al. (2001, April). *Influence of cultural values on leadership schema structure.* Paper presented at the 16th Annual Society of Industrial and Organizational Psychology Conference, San Diego, CA.

Hanges, P. J., Lord, R. G., & Dickson, M. W. (2000). An information processing perspective on leadership and culture: A case for connectionist architecture. *Applied Psychology: An International Review, 49,* 133–161.

Hofstede, G. (1980). *Culture's consequences: International differences in work-related values.* London: Sage.

Hofstede, G. (2001). *Culture's consequences: Comparing values, behaviors, institutions, and organizations across nations.* Thousand Oaks, CA: Sage.

House, R. J., & Aditya, R. N. (1997). The social scientific study of leadership: Quo vadis? *Journal of Management, 23*(3), 409–473.

House, R. J., Hanges, P. J., Ruiz-Quintanilla, S. A., Dorfman, P. W., Javidan, M., Dickson, M.,

Gupta, V., et al. (1999). Cultural influences on leadership and organizations: Project GLOBE. In W. F. Mobley, M. J. Gessner, & V. Arnold (Eds.), *Advances in global leadership* (Vol. 1, pp. 171–233). Stamford, CT: JAI.

House, R. J., Wright, N. S., & Aditya, R. N. (1997). Cross-cultural research on organizational leadership: A critical analysis and a proposed theory. In P. C. Earley & M. Erez (Eds.), *New perspectives in international industrial/organizational psychology* (pp. 535–625). San Francisco: New Lexington Press.

Howell, J. P., & Costley, D. L. (2001). *Understanding behaviors for effective leadership.* Upper Saddle River, NJ: Prentice Hall.

Inkeles, A. (1981). Convergence and divergence in industrial societies. In M. O. Attir, B. Holzner, & Z. Suda (Eds.), *Directions of change: Modernization theory, research and realities* (pp. 3–38). Boulder, CO: Westview.

Keller, T. (1999). Images of the familiar: Individual differences and implicit leadership theories. *Leadership Quarterly, 10*(4), 589–607.

Klimoski, R., & Mohammed, S. (1994). Team mental model: Construct or metaphor? *Journal of Management, 20,* 403–437.

Kraiger, K., & Wenzel, L. H. (1997). Conceptual development and empirical evaluation of measures of shared mental models as indicators of team effectiveness. In M. T. Brannick, E. Salas, & C. Prince (Eds.), *Team performance assessment and measurement* (pp. 63–84). Mahwah, NJ: Lawrence Erlbaum.

Lord, R. G., Foti, R. J., & DeVader, C. L. (1984). A test of leadership categorization theory: Internal structure, information processing, and leadership perceptions. *Organizational Behavior and Human Performance, 34,* 343–378.

Lord, R. G., & Maher, K. J. (1991). *Leadership and information processing: Linking perceptions and performance* (Vol. 1). Cambridge, MA: Unwin Hyman.

Mohammed, S., & Dumville, B. (2001). Team mental models in a team knowledge framework: Expanding theory and measurement across disciplinary boundaries. *Journal of Organizational Behavior, 22*(2), 80–106.

Mohammed, S., Klimoski, R., & Rentsch, J. R. (2000). The measurement of team mental models: We have no shared schema. *Organizational Research Methods, 3*(2), 123–165.

Nye, J. L., & Forsyth, D. R. (1991). The effects of prototype-based biases on leadership appraisals: A test of leadership categorization theory. *Small Group Research, 22*(3), 360–379.

O'Connell, M. S., Lord, R. G., & O'Connell, M. K. (1990, August). *Differences in Japanese and American leadership prototypes: Implications for cross-cultural training.* Paper presented at the meeting of the Academy of Management, San Francisco.

O'Neill, O. A., & Hanges, P. J. (2001). *Individual values and the structure of leadership schemas: Verification of a connectionist network* (Working Paper). University of Maryland, College Park.

Paris, L. (2003). *The effect of gender and culture on implicit leadership theories: A cross-cultural study.* Unpublished doctoral dissertation, New Mexico State University, Las Cruces.

Rentsch, J. R., & Klimoski, R. (2001). Why do "great minds" think alike? Antecedents of team member schema agreement. *Journal of Organizational Behavior, 22*(2), 107–120.

Rokeach, M. (1973). *The nature of human values.* New York: Free Press.

Schein, E. H. (1992). *Organizational culture and leadership: A dynamic view* (2nd ed.). San Francisco: Jossey-Bass.

Schwartz, S. H. (1992). Universals in the content and structure of values: Theoretical advances and empirical tests in 20 countries. In M. P. Zanna (Ed.), *Advances in experimental social psychology* (Vol. 25, pp. 1–66). New York: Academic Press.

Shaw, J. B. (1990). A cognitive categorization model for the study of intercultural management. *Academy of Management Review, 15*(4), 626–645.

Smith, P. B. (1997). Cross-cultural leadership: A path to the goal? In P. C. Earley & M. Erez (Eds.), *New perspectives on international industrial/organizational psychology* (pp. 626–639). San Francisco: New Lexington Press.

Smith, P. B., & Bond, M. H. (1993). *Social psychology across cultures: Analysis and perspectives.* London: Harvester Wheatsheaf.

Smith, P. B., & Peterson, M. K. (1994 July). *Leadership as event-management: A cross-cultural survey based upon middle managers from 25 nations.* Paper presented at the Cross-Cultural Studies of Event Management at the International Congress of Applied Psychology, Madrid, Spain.

Triandis, H. C. (1994). Cross cultural industrial and organizational psychology. In H. C. Triandis, M. D. Dunette, & L. M. Hough (Eds.), *Handbook of industrial and organizational psychology* (2nd ed., Vol. 4, pp. 103–172). Palo Alto, CA: Consulting Psychologists.

Triandis, H. C. (1995). *Individualism and collectivism.* Boulder, CO: Westview.

van de Vijver, F., & Leung, K. (1997). *Methods and data analysis for cross-cultural research.* Thousand Oaks, CA: Sage.

Yukl, G. A. (2002). *Leadership in organizations* (5th ed.). Upper Saddle River, NJ: Prentice Hall.

PART V

CONCLUSION

22

Conclusions and Future Directions

Mansour Javidan

Robert J. House

Peter W. Dorfman

Vipin Gupta

Paul J. Hanges

Mary Sully de Luque

G LOBE is a worldwide organization of scholars who conceptualized, operationalized, and validated a cross-level theory of the relationship between culture and societal, organizational, and leadership effectiveness. A group of 170 social scientists and management scholars representing 62 cultures and all continents of the world have been working together for a decade to advance the field of cross-cultural research. Many scholars dedicated much of their time to help GLOBE achieve its aims. In his Foreword to this book, Harry Triandis calls GLOBE "the Manhattan Project of the study of the relationship of culture to conceptions of leadership" resulting in "thousands of doctoral dissertations in the future." Mark Chadwin, the Senior Fellow at The Weissman Center for International Business at Baruch College, has called GLOBE "the single most important piece of cross-cultural research in a quarter of a century." Others have called it "the most ambitious study of global leadership" (Morrison, 2000).

This book is a key product of this collective cross-cultural effort. An important feature of the book is that it is itself a collective effort. More than 20 scholars have worked for more than 5 years on its various chapters. Many chapters, especially those on cultural dimensions, have undergone at least five major revisions and numerous drafts. But the book is not an edited book; our goal was to produce a seamless book written by many authors. Although managing the process in this way entailed many complexities and extended the timeline for completion, we felt that it was the only viable way to report our work.

The preceding chapters have provided substantial information on what we set out to do and what we have found. We have found answers to many questions. This volume is filled with a wide variety of findings, some confirming conventional wisdom and others questioning it, but like any other research project our work has also led to many new questions. Although we have advanced the current state of knowledge on several fronts, we have uncovered many new and puzzling questions that require additional research. In this chapter, we provide a brief summary of GLOBE's main theoretical and methodological contributions and present a series of new questions to help direct future research on the important issues of cross-cultural management.

Main Features of GLOBE's Theoretical Framework

GLOBE developed an integrated and cross-level theory of the relationship between cultural values and practices and leadership, organizational, and societal effectiveness. The theory is based on the integration of four important theoretical perspectives: The implicit leadership theory expanded to the cultural level, the strategic contingency theory, McClelland's achievement theory of human motivation, and Hofstede's culture theory. We have extended the current knowledge base by a more comprehensive conceptualization of cultural dimensions and by introducing new dimensions. We further conceptualized and measured culture in terms of practices and values. At the organizational level, we introduced nine new dimensions of organizational culture.

Main Features of GLOBE's Methodological Framework

The instruments developed by GLOBE researchers are based on the existing literature but they are truly cross-cultural in the sense that the country co-investigators (CCIs) are either natives of their cultures or are very knowledgeable about them. They participated in the process

of instrument design from the beginning. The scales were designed to independently measure cultural practices and values using a sound theoretical basis, and items were developed and validated against exacting standards. The instruments used isomorphic structures at the societal and organizational levels of culture. We found high degrees of interrater agreement within cultures and a high degree of discrimination across societies. The levels of interitem consistency were well above conventional standards. Two independent pilot tests produced sound psychometric properties.

We developed new methods for identifying and controlling for response bias and built nomological nets to test the construct validity of the scales. Multilevel confirmatory factor analysis was used to confirm the internal consistency and cross-cultural viability of the culture and leadership scales. Contextual analysis was also performed to verify that the aggregated phenomena were operating at the appropriate organizational and societal levels. In essence, we addressed the reverse ecological fallacy error by showing that the GLOBE measures operate at higher levels than simply an aggregation of the individual responses. We further validated cultural value scales against outcropping measures and used unobtrusive measures to validate cultural practice scales. The validation of the GLOBE societal-level practices and values scales using independently collected, unobtrusive, and outcropping measures data, as well as the relationships with other variables as theoretically predicted, all attest to the validity of the GLOBE societal variables and indicate that the findings reflect the societies in which middle managers work rather than the cultures of middle managers alone.

To avoid common source bias, two forms of the survey were developed and administered to two different groups of respondents. Form Alpha contained items measuring leadership effectiveness and organizational culture. Form Beta contained items measuring leadership effectiveness and societal culture. When analyzing the relationship between leadership and culture, we correlated the responses from one group on leadership with those from another group on culture, thus preventing common source bias.

In total, more than 17,000 managers from 951 organizations that disclosed their identity in three industries participated in our surveys. Employees of local offices of multinational firms were excluded to avoid cultural contamination. These industries were selected in a poll of the CCIs and because they exist in all countries. At the same time, the three industries face different industry contingencies. The telecommunications industry is more severely regulated than the food industry and tends to be more dynamic. The finance industry entails a set of universal rules that go beyond individual countries to ensure global consistency.

Previous cross-cultural scholars have used samples such as first-line supervisors in marketing and service occupations (Hofstede, 1980), school students and teachers (Schwartz, 1999), and the general population (Inglehart, Basanez, & Moreno, 1998) for developing cultural-level constructs. Our findings suggest that middle-level managers are also an appropriate group for studying cultural constructs. The responses of the middle-level managers appear to be both reliable (high within-culture response consistency, and high between-culture response variation) and valid (strong predictive relationship with convergent constructs, and weak secondary relationship with divergent constructs).

The CCIs collected the data in their respective countries in a culturally sensitive way and, to the extent possible, sampled the dominant cultures in their countries. Furthermore, we developed a theoretically driven comprehensive database of information regarding economic prosperity and the human condition in GLOBE countries.

Our findings, based on a pilot study in Phase 1 of the GLOBE study, suggested that the *average* number of respondents needed for a cross-cultural construct of a target reliability of 0.85 is 45 (see Chapter 8, by Hanges & Dickson). In Phase 2, the number of respondents on the societal culture scale ranged from 13 (El Salvador) to 300 (Iran) and as many as 895 respondents in Sweden. Eight societies were able to sample fewer than 45 respondents for the societal culture constructs. Our estimates of societal culture scales for even these societies appear to be in the true ballpark. There is little evidence of response bias in the scores of these societies (see Appendix B, this volume). Further, these societies could be grouped into their predicted clusters on the basis of their cultural scores (see Chapter 10, by Gupta & Hanges). One possible explanation for the difference between Phase 1 and Phase 2 results about the required number of respondents may be the quality of scales. On the basis of the feedback received in Phase 1 consisting of two pilot studies, we made significant improvements in leadership as well as societal culture scales, as discussed in Chapter 8 by Hanges and Dickson. Therefore, it is likely that high quality scale measures may reduce the number of respondents needed to obtain accurate estimates of the cultural-level constructs.

We further show that it is appropriate to generalize about the national-level cultural constructs on the basis of a single sample of individuals, even in highly diverse nations where multiple subcultures coexist. We studied subcultures in three nations: South Africa, Germany, and Switzerland. In other countries, we studied only one sample in each nation. In the societies in which the subcultures were studied, our results indicated predictable patterns of societal-cultural constructs (see Chapter 10, by Gupta & Hanges). In South Africa, the Black sample belonged to the Sub-Saharan Africa cluster, whereas the White sample belonged to the Anglo cluster. In Germany, both former East and former West German samples were part of the Germanic Europe cluster. Finally, in Switzerland, the French-speaking subculture was part of the Latin Europe cluster, whereas the German-speaking sub-culture belonged to the Germanic Europe cluster. Our findings affirm the significance of sampling and studying subcultures. At the same time, our findings also suggest that by sampling from a dominant subculture within each society, one may indeed be able to predict several national-level behaviors (see Chapter 9, by Gupta, Sully de Luque, & House).

Last, but not least, we show that it is appropriate to use the survey data for measuring cultural-level practices, values, and implicit leadership effectiveness constructs. Our findings indicate that survey data yield reliable and valid estimates of cultural-level constructs, provided the survey is based on a sound research design and a rigorous measurement instrument. To add rigor to our instrument, we used Q-sort methodology to confirm that at least 80% of the respondents across societies associate the cultural items with respective constructs. In addition, we requested the country co-investigators to evaluate each cultural item, and to report if the item carries the attributed meaning in their society and language. These "item evaluation" reports yielded some surprising findings. An item "begging is banned in the city centers" was indicated by most respondents to be an indicator of the Humane Orientation construct. However, in some societies, the respondents held that the item connotes a high Humane Orientation, because their society provides institutional mechanisms, such as nongovernment organizations, for rehabilitating beggars as a result of the ban. In other societies, the respondents held that the item connotes a low Humane Orientation because it prevents the poor people from seeking support from others and may even encourage a higher crime rate. Because the item did not carry a common meaning across cultures, it had to be deleted from the survey to allow for cross-cultural comparability of the scores on the Humane Orientation scale.

GLOBE's Major
Empirical Contributions

GLOBE country culture scores are reported using a banding technique to improve the interpretation of country rankings. We have identified the universally desirable cultural dimensions like performance orientation and the universally undesirable dimensions like power distance. We used the existing literature to develop a conceptual clustering of societies and empirically validated them. The clusters are the first empirical attempt to use a holistic approach to understand and verify cultural differences across societies. We now have cluster scores on cultural values, practices, and implicit leadership theories.

Our findings will help enhance the theoretical development of the cross-cultural field. We have identified 21 primary and 6 global leadership dimensions. From these, we created endorsed leadership profiles across the 10 culture clusters, which, in turn, follow from the development of our culturally implicit leadership theory (CLT). We have also identified universally desirable, universally undesirable, and

culturally contingent attributes of leadership. Hierarchical linear modeling (HLM) was used to explore the relationships at different levels of analysis using alternate data sources in a way that eliminates common source bias. Our findings show the relationships among cultural dimensions, organizational practices, and culturally endorsed (i.e., CLT) leadership dimensions. They also show the relationship between cultural dimensions and measures of societal achievement such as economic prosperity and human condition.

In terms of the relationship between leadership and culture, we have identified the cultural dimensions that can best predict CLT dimensions and assessed the differential strength of association between each cultural dimension in relation to each CLT dimension. We have also determined the differential explanatory power of the organizational-level culture versus societal-level culture in terms of outstanding leadership.

In terms of the linkage between societal and organizational culture, we show a strong relationship between the two—organizations mirror societies from which they originate. Most important, the analysis demonstrating this fact eliminated potential common source bias. Although we showed the interactive effects of society and industry on organizational culture, organizational cultures seem to be more of a reflection of their societal context rather than their industry context. In fact, the industry context seems to have limited, if any, influence on the assessment of societal-level cultural dimensions, organizational-level cultural dimensions, and leadership attributes.

Our findings also show that the difference between the cultural value score and cultural practice score for each dimension is larger at the societal level than at the organizational level, perhaps pointing to the broader range of variables involved at the society level than at the organizational level. It also leads to the conclusion that changing culture is likely to be easier at the organizational level than at the societal level.

We further showed the differential association between various cultural dimensions and measures of societal achievement and confirmed a clear cultural underpinning to the way societies generate and distribute wealth and take care of their people. As a result, any decision or action to change the way governments operate or the way societies allocate their resources has to take into consideration the cultural issues and their implications.

FUTURE DIRECTIONS

The wealth of findings provided in this book sets the stage for a more sophisticated and complex set of questions. Our enhanced knowledge about societal practices and values, organizational practices and values, leadership attributes, and societal accomplishments enables us to pursue even more complicated questions. In his Foreword to the book, Triandis wrote that "Thousands of doctoral dissertations in the future will start with these findings." In this section, we intend to speed up this process by posing a series of questions to help direct and energize further research on important issues in cross-cultural management.

Culture and Leadership

To begin with, Phase 3 of GLOBE, which is currently under way, is focused on several important leadership questions. Although GLOBE findings so far have shown the various attributes of leadership, they have not identified the behavioral manifestations of such attributes. For example, it is clear that integrity is a universally desirable attribute. But does it mean the same thing to a Chinese as it does to an American? How do people in different cultures conceptualize, perceive, and exhibit behavior that reflects integrity? What specific behaviors comprise high integrity leadership, and do they have the same function and impact across cultures? Can a leader's integrity be adequately measured across cultures with a single survey instrument? Related to this, we need to understand the nonverbal and emotional manifestations of the CLT leadership dimensions. In what ways other than visible behavior do leaders connect to others in their organizations? And to what extent are these nuances, nonverbal behaviors, and emotional expressions universal or culturally contingent?

Phase 3 research will delve deeper into the relationship between the behavior of chief executive officers (CEOs) and the culturally implicit leadership theory (CLT). It will study the extent to which CEO behavior conforms to CLTs. It will also examine the consequences of CEO behaviors that violate CLTs. In this book, we have shown that culturally implicit leadership theories are shaped by societal and organizational cultures. Our explanation was that leaders grow up in their cultures and build their worldview on the basis of their own learning and development. Furthermore, they have to motivate and energize employees who are also culturally conditioned. But what if leaders violate societal cultural norms or leadership expectations represented by a culture's CLT profile? Under what conditions do they violate these norms? Can they violate the norms and succeed? Which norms are more critical for leaders—The societal norms or the CLTs? Can they violate one and not the other? Although these are important academic questions, they do have significant managerial implications. For instance, several GLOBE countries are reported to score low on the Performance Orientation cultural dimension. Suppose a corporation from a high performance-oriented culture decides to start an operation in a low performance-oriented country. What kind of a business-unit leader should they assign to this new position? If they assign an executive with high performance orientation, he or she will be in violation of the local norms and CLTs. How good are the new leader's chances of success? If a local person with low performance orientation is appointed, can he or she succeed in achieving the company's goals? He or she may be in tune with the local employees and ensure peace and stability, but can he or she deliver results? GLOBE Phase 3 is designed to address these questions.

Another issue relating to leadership CLTs is the potential confounding effect of unexpected contingencies that will likely pressure the leader to operate outside his or her comfort level. Presumably, leaders enact CLTs because they have learned that acting according to CLTs is desirable and rewarded in their cultures. For example, a leader in a society in which the CLT emphasizes team orientation has learned over time to be a team player. But a typical leader faces a variety of situations and challenges, each with its own contingencies. For example, there may be urgent challenges to attend to—teams may be ineffective and slow to respond, or reductions in personnel due to poor economic conditions could have a detrimental effect on team spirit. What should a team-oriented leader do in such a situation? It is important to understand the interactions between societal norms, CLTs, and situation-based contingencies. How does a leader reconcile the broader cultural and CLT prescriptions with the narrower and shorter-term situation-based contingencies? Which one ends up shaping the leader's actions and decisions? And why?

There are several other important issues that need attention. For example, our leadership profiles are based on factor analyses of the leadership items that were included in the instruments. Although we were meticulous in the design of the leadership instrument, we make no claim that it is all encompassing and exhaustive. There are other aspects of leadership that could be included in the leadership model. For instance, we have learned that family and religion play a bigger role for leaders in Arab countries than for those in other societies. As another example, we had fewer leadership attribute items related to Participative leadership than was desirable. Additional leadership items regarding differing aspects of participation (e.g., consultation vs. delegation) would clarify the distinctions that likely exist among cultures regarding this leadership dimension.

Another major finding of GLOBE is that there are indeed universal attributes of leadership. GLOBE's theoretical model postulated that each culture develops its own culturally implicit theory (CLT) of leadership. We empirically verified a significant relationship between culture and leadership. The implication of this assertion is that to the extent that cultures are different, their CLTs will be different. At the same time, we have also shown a set of leadership attributes that are universally desirable and universally undesirable. Many reasons have been suggested for the universality of leadership attributes. Common technological imperatives (Woodward, 1958), common industrial logic (Adler, Doktor, & Redding, 1986), and globalization of institutions and practices have all been suggested as drivers of common management practices and processes (Child & Tayeb, 1983). Others have suggested that some leadership dimensions such as charismatic leadership may satisfy universal and basic human needs, such as the need for achievement, that go beyond cultural boundaries (Fyans, Salili, Maehr, & Desai, 1983; Javidan & Carl, in press; McClelland, 1961).

Another possible driver of universality may lie in ethical values. Several authors have argued that some types of leadership, namely transformational leadership, are rooted in strong ethical values (Bass & Steidlmeier, 1999; Kanungo, 2001; Kanungo & Mendonca, 1996; Mendonca, 2001). Mendonca (2001) speculated that "good moral character is the essence of every human being" (p. 270) and transformational leadership provides the opportunity to "fully realize the unique and unrepeatable potential that is in each person" (p. 270).

On the basis of these assertions, Javidan and Carl (in press) have proposed that

> the . . . reason for commonality of charismatic leadership across cultures may be due to its moral and ethical foundations. It is plausible that charismatic leadership is embedded in a universal implicit theory of leadership because of the human desire for autonomy and a sense of self-control.

On the other hand, a desire for autonomy and self-control may reflect societal norms found in high individualistic and low collectivistic societies.

Although the various explanations and speculations for universal attributes of leadership are all plausible, none are empirically verified. It is important to test the various competing arguments and propositions and reach a clear and definite conclusion on the drivers of universality in leadership. Furthermore, if it is true that universal needs drive universal leadership attributes, then a related question concerns the interaction between universal and cultural drivers of leadership. How do they interact? Which one is more important? Under what conditions?

Measuring Cultures

Thus far the discussion has been centered on the generalizations we could make about societal culture and its influence on organizational culture and practices, and on implicit leadership theories prevalent in the culture. To the extent that the measuring instruments contain items that are not behavior specific, we minimize the risk of nonequivalence of measures across the cultures studied. Even so, we must recognize the fact that two cultures with the same levels of a cultural dimension may exhibit different behaviors associated with that dimension. This aspect is well expounded by d'Iribarne (1997). Culture-specific behaviors are difficult to interpret from outside a culture, except in terms of the outside observer's culture. There is a distinction between "knowing" a culture and "internalizing" a culture: the former belongs to the realm of rational thought, the latter to subjective experience. Although GLOBE provides a profile of cultural dimensions for each society, it does not present a behavioral profile. Further research is required to build an in-depth understanding of how people actually function and manifest different cultural attributes.

The current cross-cultural literature, influenced by Hofstede's (1980) seminal work, has been focusing on cultures as a collection of cultural dimensions. Much has been written about the various dimensions and their implications. GLOBE has introduced several new cultural dimensions and has studied each dimension individually. It is easy to suggest that no particular set of cultural dimensions is all encompassing or exhaustive. There are of course new dimensions that researchers could study. Cultures are obviously very complex multidimensional phenomena that extend beyond any particular box of categories. But an even more important issue, and one that has received little attention in the literature, is the gestalt of cultures. Our cross-cultural understanding will be substantially enhanced by taking a holistic view of cultures. Cultures are not a set of independent self-standing dimensions, but instead are formed as a confluence of cultural attributes. It is of course easier to study each dimension independently, as various researchers, including GLOBE, have done. But such an approach leaves many questions unanswered. How do different cultural dimensions interact? What is the relative importance of each dimension in understanding each culture? A country like Iran is distinguished by its strong in-group collectivism and power distance (Javidan & Dastmalchian, in press). What roles do the other dimensions play in such a setting? Although these are important

academic questions, they also have significant managerial implications. The current cross-cultural literature advises managers on what to do in high power distance cultures or in high collectivist cultures. What is the advice for high power distance *and* high collectivist cultures? Is it different from the advice for high power distance and high performance-oriented cultures? In other words, which cultural dimensions, if any, should be attended to most in different cultures? What is the impact of different bundles of cultural dimensions? Which combination of cultural dimensions should be studied in each culture? In short, although the current literature informs us about different cultural strands, it fails to shed light on the cultural fabric. The GLOBE findings presented in this book should help pave the way for new thinking and analysis to move us in this direction.

One final point about measuring cultures is the GLOBE finding that there is a negative correlation between cultural values and practices in seven out of nine cultural dimensions. As a typical example, cultures with high *values* on a dimension are likely to exhibit low *practices* (e.g., as seen with the Performance Orientation scores). This is contrary to the conventional wisdom in the literature. Much of the writing on culture suggests implicitly or explicitly that cultural practices are driven by cultural values and that there is a linear and positive relationship between them (Hofstede, 1980; Schein, 1992).

One potential explanation for our findings is that they are an artifact of the questionnaire design. Perhaps the simple act of asking the respondents about "as is" and "should be" cultural items triggers this type of response because people usually want more than they have, particularly if the element is positive (e.g., pay). However, the "as is" and "should be" items were physically separated on the questionnaire. But even if they were not, it is not clear why the relationship should be negative rather than positive. In general, it is unclear as to whether a high or low level of any dimension is necessarily desirable.

Another possible explanation is that the way GLOBE conceptualized the construct of cultural values is different from the literature and is not appropriate. Schwartz (personal communication, August 4, 2003), for instance suggested that respondents might be able to accurately report their own values, but inaccurately report a society's values. We have addressed this issue by showing that GLOBE scales have strong external and internal validity, they are validated by other independent measures of cultural values, and they relate in meaningful ways to leadership dimensions and aspects of societies.

A third explanation, and one that we would subscribe to, is that the relationship between values and practices is nonlinear and more complex than initially assumed. GLOBE is the first rigorous attempt to empirically measure and verify the relationship between cultural values and practices and it shows counterintuitive results. The extant view is that people behave in a particular way because they hold particular views on how things should be. Our findings show that the opposite relationship may be at work; people may hold views on what *should be* based on what they observe in action. For instance, in the case of Future Orientation, with very few exceptions, all societies have higher values scores than practices scores—societies report a desire for a more future oriented society. The negative correlation between practices and values occurs because for societies with higher practices scores, the difference between values and practices scores (i.e., the increment) is much smaller than it is for those with low practices scores. This can be seen by comparing Tables 13.5 and 13.6 which show societal level scores on the GLOBE Future Orientation practices and values scales, respectively. Singapore respondents report the highest practice score of 5.07 and their value score is only slightly higher (i.e., 5.51). Russian respondents, on the other hand, reported the lowest practice score of 2.88 but their value score was dramatically higher (i.e., 5.41).

It is important to recognize, however, that the direction of people's reaction to what *should be* compared to what is may be dimension specific. For example, if one considers another culture dimension, namely Uncertainty Avoidance, the more societal uncertainty avoiding practices reported by respondents, the less uncertainty avoiding values were reported. This can be seen by comparing the Uncertainty Avoidance cultural practices and values scores in Tables 20.7 and 20.8. As shown in these tables, respondents

in Switzerland, Sweden, and Denmark report some of the highest practice scores and the lowest value scores on this dimension.

In short, our findings point to the need for a more complex understanding of this relationship which views it as dynamic and double directional rather than static and uni-directional. What exacerbates the situation is that our findings show that attributes of societal success are strongly related to cultural practices, but attributes of outstanding leadership are strongly related to cultural values. Unless we can better understand the relationship between cultural practices and values, we are unable to explain this complex situation and have little to offer to leaders who are trying to improve their societies' well being.

Cross-Cultural Contact

An important reason for the interest in understanding cultures is the increasing rate of contact among cultures. Today, people and organizations from different cultures come into regular contact as customers, competitors, partners, and suppliers. As a result, there is an academic and practical need to understand what happens when cultures connect. The current literature typically examines each culture in isolation from others but reaches conclusions about cultural contact. For example, the field of cross-border mergers is populated by studies that measure cultural distance and reach conclusions on whether it is functional or dysfunctional (Conn & Connell, 1990; Datta & Puia, 1995; Doukas & Travlos, 1988; Morosini, Shane, & Singh, 1998). The typical approach to measuring cross-cultural differences is to calculate the mathematical difference on Hofstede's country scores. Despite somewhat conflicting findings, the conventional wisdom is that cultural distance is dysfunctional and leads to failure of cross-border mergers.

It is important to consider the possibility that cultural contact between two or more separate cultures entails unique dynamics that go beyond these objective measures of each culture. Objective measures of each culture may not be sufficient to understand what happens during the contact. What is probably important is not how a culture is objectively measured but how it is subjectively perceived by those from another culture. Furthermore, in cross-cultural settings in which more than two cultures are represented, should we study cultural difference as a dyadic phenomenon or as a complex web of multilateral issues? For example, do Germans and Austrians behave the same toward each other if Americans are present? Do they behave the same if the French are present? Do people from the Middle Eastern countries behave the same with and without the presence of Europeans?

Another related issue is the relative and differential effect of cultural dimensions. When two cultures come in contact, which cultural dimensions are key in that relationship? Are they all important or are some more important than others? Under what conditions? Unless we can understand this, we are unable to conceptualize cross-cultural contact and its implications. We also need to study the direction of cultural distance. The existing literature assumes symmetry in cultural difference. This is an important and not necessarily logical assumption. There may in fact be asymmetry in such relationships. The German and Russian cultures are different on many dimensions. Can we reach the same conclusions in a German–Russian corporate acquisition when the German firm is the acquirer and when it is the acquiree?

In addition, there is a clear need to study the consequences of cross-cultural differences. New research needs to study the conditions under which cross-cultural differences can be positive or negative. Furthermore, we know little of how to deal with these consequences. The current writing on this topic is based mostly on anecdotes and limited case studies. Given the increasing globalization of markets, it seems obvious that there is both a theoretical and practical need for rigorous research in this area. A related issue is the role of leadership. We have shown in this book that societies can have similar leadership CLT profiles. It is not clear whether similar CLT profiles necessarily mean that leadership styles can easily be transported between the two cultures. Although this is an intuitively obvious and appealing conclusion, it needs empirical verification.

In the previous paragraphs, we have attempted to raise new and interesting questions

to help improve the state of knowledge in this important field. We used our collective experience over the past decade to generate these thoughts. It is now up to the readers to take up the action. We look forward to the upcoming work in this area.

REFERENCES

Adler, N. J., Doktor, R., & Redding, S. G. (1986). From the Atlantic to the Pacific century: Cross-cultural management reviewed. *1986 Yearly Review of Management of the Journal of Management, 12*(2), 295–318.

Bass, B., & Steidlmeier, P. (1999). Ethics, character, and authentic transformational leadership behavior. *Leadership Quarterly, 10,* 181–217.

Child, J. D., & Tayeb, M. (1983, Winter). Theoretical perspectives in cross-national research. *International Studies of Management and Organization, 32*–70.

Conn, R., & Connell, F. (1990). International mergers: Returns to U.S. and British firms. *Journal of Finance and Accounting, 17*(5) 689–711.

Datta, D. K., & Puia, G. (1995). Cross-border acquisitions: An examination of the influence of relatedness and cultural fit on shareholder value creation in U.S. acquiring firms. *Management International Review, 35,* 337–359.

D'Iribarne, P. (1997). The usefulness of an ethnographic approach to the international comparison of organizations. *International Studies of Management and Organization, 26*(4), 30–47.

Doukas, J., & Travlos, N. G. (1988). The effects of corporate multi-nationalism on shareholders' wealth: Evidence from international acquisitions. *Journal of Finance, 43*(5), 161–175.

Fyans, L. J., Jr., Salili, F., Maehr, M. L., & Desai, K. A. (1983). A cross-cultural exploration into the meaning of achievement. *Journal of Personality and Social Psychology, 44*(5), 1000–1013.

Hofstede, G. (1980). *Culture's consequences: International differences in work-related values.* Beverly Hills, CA: Sage.

Inglehart, R., Basanez, M., & Moreno, A. (1998). *Human values and beliefs: A cross-cultural sourcebook.* Ann Arbor: University of Michigan Press.

Javidan, M., & Dastmalchian, A. (in press.). Culture and leadership in Iran: The land of individual achievers, strong families, and powerful elite. *Academy of Management Executive.*

Javidan, M., & Carl, D. (in press.). East meets West: Searching for the etic in leadership. *Journal of Management Studies.*

Kanungo, R. N. (2001). Ethical values of transactional and transformational leaders. *Canadian Journal of Administrative Sciences, 18*(4), 257–265.

Kanungo, R. N., & Mendonca, M. (1996). *Ethical dimensions of leadership.* Thousand Oaks, CA: Sage.

McClelland, D. C. (1961). *The achieving society.* Princeton, NJ: D. Van Nostrand.

Mendonca, M. (2001). Preparing for ethical leadership in organizations. *Canadian Journal of Administrative Sciences, 18*(4), 266–276.

Morosini, P., Shane, S., & Singh, H. (1998). National cultural distance and cross-border acquisition performance. *Journal of International Business Studies, 29*(1), 137–158.

Morrison, A. J. (2000). Developing a global leadership model. *Human Resource Management Journal, 39*(2 & 3), 117–131.

Schein, E. (1992). *Organizational culture and leadership* (2nd ed.). San Francisco: Jossey-Bass.

Schwartz, S. H. (1999). A theory of cultural values and some implications for work. *Applied Psychology: An International Review, 48,* 23–47.

Woodward, J. (1958). *Management and technology.* London: HMSO.

APPENDIX A

SOCIETAL-LEVEL CORRELATIONS AMONG GLOBE SOCIETAL CULTURE SCALES

PAUL J. HANGES

Table A.1 Correlations Among GLOBE Cultural Dimension Practice (As Is) Scales at the Societal Level of Analysis

	Assertiveness	Institutional Collectivism	In-Group Collectivism	Future Orientation	Gender Egalitarianism	Humane Orientation	Performance Orientation	Power Distance
Institutional Collectivism	-.42*							
In-Group Collectivism	.08	-.19						
Future Orientation	.07	-.46*	-.44*					
Gender Egalitarianism	-.08	-.01	-.20	-.06				
Humane Orientation	-.42*	.43*	.30*	.07	-.15			
Performance Orientation	.06	.43*	-.11	.63*	-.31*	.25*		
Power Distance	.16	-.44*	.55*	-.52*	-.29*	-.15	-.36*	
Uncertainty Avoidance	-.07	.40*	-.60*	.76*	-.06	.00	.58*	-.50*

* Indicates that the correlation was statistically significant ($p < .05$). These correlations are based on $N = 61$ societies.

Table A.2 Correlations Among GLOBE Cultural Dimension Values (Should Be) Scales at the Societal Level of Analysis

	Assertiveness	Institutional Collectivism	In-Group Collectivism	Future Orientation	Gender Egalitarianism	Humane Orientation	Performance Orientation	Power Distance
Institutional Collectivism	−.21							
In-Group Collectivism	.01	.29*						
Future Orientation	.09	.48*	.51*					
Gender Egalitarianism	−.28*	−.04	.13	−.36*				
Humane Orientation	−.11	−.14	−.15	−.12	.21			
Performance Orientation	−.02	.44*	.57*	.41*	.22	.06		
Power Distance	.29*	−.31*	−.22	−.06	−.49*	−.42*	−.39*	
Uncertainty Avoidance	.20	.42*	.30*	.67*	−.55*	−.18	.15	.17

* Indicates that the correlation was statistically significant ($p < .05$). These correlations are based on $N = 61$ societies.

Table A.3 Correlations Among GLOBE Cultural Dimension Practices (As Is) and Cultural Values (Should Be) Scales at the Societal Level of Analysis

	Assertiveness	Collectivism 1: Institutional	Collectivism 2: In-Group	Future Orientation	Gender Egalitarianism	Humane Orientation	Performance Orientation	Power Distance	Uncertainty Avoidance
Assertiveness	-.26*	.12	-.24	.09	.18	.35*	-.01	-.11	.04
Institutional Collectivism	.37*	-.61*	-.16	-.25*	-.25*	-.01	-.39*	.38*	-.19
In-Group Collectivism	.28*	.43*	.21	.62*	-.44*	-.09	.12	.02	.80*
Future Orientation	.17	-.30*	-.42*	-.41*	.19	.22	-.23	.12	-.53*
Gender Egalitarianism	-.01	-.31*	.16	-.24	.32*	-.01	.02	.10	-.06
Humane Orientation	.45*	-.02	.20	.26*	-.39*	-.32*	.00	.30*	.29*
Performance Orientation	.37*	-.22	-.36*	-.24	-.11	-.06	-.28*	.34*	-.24
Power Distance	-.05	.41*	.33*	.60*	-.08	.21	.40*	-.43*	.48*
Uncertainty Avoidance	.07	-.32*	-.45*	-.57*	.12	.11	-.14	.19	-.62*

* Indicates that the correlation was statistically significant ($p < .05$). These correlations are based on $N = 61$ societies.

APPENDIX B

RESPONSE BIAS CORRECTION PROCEDURE USED IN GLOBE

PAUL J. HANGES

Cross-cultural researchers have noted a tendency for people from different cultures to respond in characteristic ways when completing questionnaires (Triandis, 1994). For example, in Asian cultures, people tend to avoid the extreme ends of a scale (to avoid diverging from the group) whereas in Mediterranean cultures, people tend to avoid the midpoint of a scale (to avoid appearing non-committal; Hui & Triandis, 1989; Stening & Everett, 1984). The presence of these culturally based response patterns is believed to bias subsequent cross-cultural comparisons based on self-report data because these patterns are not a function of the intended construct of interest. Thus, cross-cultural researchers have argued that interpretation of the rank order of cultures based on average uncorrected scale scores is problematic. These researchers argue that some correction is needed to minimize the influence of this bias.

A statistical standardization correction procedure has been developed that is used in the cross-cultural literature to remove response biases from questionnaire data. The classic procedure is described in Triandis's (1995) *Handbook of Industrial and Organizational Psychology* chapter. First, each respondent's mean and standard deviation are computed across all items in a survey. If the survey measures a large range of constructs, these means and standard deviations lose any construct-specific meaning and reflect an individual's response biases. Next, the item responses for each individual are corrected by subtracting that individual's average response from all of his or her actual item responses and dividing this difference by his or her standard deviation. These "corrected" scale scores are then aggregated to the society level of analysis and are believed to be response biased corrected self-reports of societal-level cultural constructs.

Although useful, there are several limitations of this statistical correction procedure. One limitation with the current correction procedure is that although it is apparently successful in removing cultural response bias, the values of the corrected scales are no longer interpretable. More specifically, if participants use a 7-point rating scale to respond to a series of items tapping a particular construct, the meaning of the average responses produced by these participants is directly interpretable simply by referring back to the adjectives anchoring the original rating scale. However, the corrected scores are no longer directly interpretable because the correction procedure creates scores that are not bound to the original 7-point scale. Indeed, the aggregated corrected scale values frequently include negative values. Thus, interpretation of the aggregated corrected score by referring to the original response scale is impossible.

Another limitation with the current correction procedure is that it only provides a global indication of whether cultural response bias is present in the data. Currently, cross-cultural researchers correlate the corrected scale scores with the original (i.e., "uncorrected") scores. If the magnitude of the correlations between these two scores is large, the data are declared to be relatively free from response bias. However, if the correlations are small, then the data appear to have problems with response bias, and conclusions drawn from the survey data are suspect. Although useful, this omnibus assessment of response bias does not provide for the possibility that the cultural response bias found in the data might be attributable to a few societies rather than the entire sample. Thus, it would be useful to have a procedure that identifies potentially response bias contaminated observations.

One final limitation of the current response bias procedure is that it produces *ipsative* scores. In other words, the corrected scores reflect the average response to a scale relative to how all individuals in a society rate all of the scales. There is a long history in the psychometric literature about the difficulty of using ipsative scores to make between-group comparisons.

In this appendix, I describe a modification of the traditional cultural response statistical correction procedure that addresses these aforementioned limitations. This modified procedure not only addresses the first aforementioned limitation by rescaling the corrected values to make them directly interpretable, but it also enables the use of well-established diagnostic tools that address the second aforementioned limitation. Specifically, by using simple regression analysis to predict the uncorrected scale scores from the corrected scale scores, the corrected scores can be rescaled into the original 7-point scale. Further, one can use residual analysis to identify data points that are outliers in this regression analysis (Draper & Smith, 1981). Residual analysis can be used to identify countries with substantial degrees of response bias.

Use of Corrected GLOBE Scale Scores: Modification of Existing Procedure

To provide the reader with a better understanding of the modification that was developed and used for the GLOBE procedure, Table B.1 shows the societal level *Uncertainty Avoidance cultural practices* scores for some of the societies in the GLOBE database. The uncorrected and corrected average scores (using the traditional correction procedure) for these societies are shown in this table. The zero-order correlation for the entire dataset between these two scores was .98. As can be seen in this table, the original scale scores are directly interpretable and range from 2.88 to 5.37. The corrected scores range are ipsative scores ranging from −.72 to +.56. Thus, they are not directly interpretable because they are no longer on the 1 to 7 anchored rating scale. All that is known is that relative level of support for uncertainty avoidance cultural practices in a particular society compared with how people in that society rated the other cultural and CLT scales.

The first modification that was made to the traditional procedure was to use regression analysis to rescale these corrected scores back onto the original 7-point anchored scale. Specifically, we performed a simple ordinary least squares regression analysis using the corrected Uncertainty Avoidance cultural practices scores to predict the uncorrected Uncertainty Avoidance cultural practices scores. The obtained regression equation was significant and the unstandardized predicted values from this equation are shown in Table B.1 under the column labeled *Regression Predicted Scores*.[1] As can be seen from this table, the regression predicted scores are back on the original 7-point anchored scale. Because only a single predictor was used in this regression analysis, these "regression-predicted" values are simply an isomorphic transformation of the corrected scores (i.e., there is a perfect positive correlation between the corrected and the regression-predicted scale scores). Thus, the unstandardized regression predicted values represent our best estimate of what the society Uncertainty Avoidance cultural practices averages would have been if the respondents were not influenced by cultural-response bias. Thus, by performing this extra step, the first limitation of the traditional correction procedure is addressed. The magnitude of the corrected scale scores can now be directly interpreted.

The second modification to the traditional response bias correction procedure was the use of well-established diagnostic tests to identify societies whose scale scores exhibit substantial response bias. The last column in Table B.1, labeled *Studentized Residuals,* basically compares the difference (i.e., residual) between the uncorrected and the regression-predicted Uncertainty Avoidance cultural practices scales and assesses whether the discrepancy between these two is substantial enough for a particular society's data to be considered an outlier. Basically, these studentized residuals are *t* values. If the absolute value of the *t* value is greater than 2, the data point is considered a potential outlier (i.e., the difference between the uncorrected and the regression-predicted score is larger than would have been expected by chance).

Examining the studentized residuals column in Table B.1 identifies four countries that are potential outliers (i.e., Taiwan, Morocco, Qatar, and Indonesia) for this scale. In other words, the response bias correction procedure substantially changed the scale scores for these four societies. These four societies can be interpreted as exhibiting substantially more response bias than the other societies for this scale. Another interpretation is that the rank order of these four societies significantly changes after correction for response bias.[2]

APPLICATION OF THE MODIFIED CULTURAL RESPONSE BIAS CORRECTION PROCEDURE

We used this modified correction procedure on the GLOBE culture data and discovered some interesting insights into our data. Table B.2 shows the regression-based response bias corrected scores for all of the GLOBE societal culture scales, and Table B.3 shows the societies that were identified as outliers for each of the 18 societal culture scales. As can be seen, only a few societies are listed as outliers for a particular rating scale. As discussed in Chapter 8 by Hanges and Dickson (this volume), this is consistent with the conclusions obtained by applying the traditional response-bias correction procedure. Overall, very little evidence for response bias was present in our data.

Table B.1   Societal Means for Uncertainty Avoidance Cultural Practices Scale Scores and Response Bias Corrected Values

Society	Uncorrected Scores	Corrected Scores	Regression Predicted Scores	Studentized Residual
Switzerland	5.37	0.56	5.42	−0.41
Sweden	5.32	0.52	5.36	−0.31
Germany (Former West)	5.22	0.52	5.35	−1.12
Denmark	5.22	0.5	5.32	−0.81
Germany (Former East)	5.16	0.43	5.19	−0.27
Singapore	5.31	0.41	5.16	1.19
Finland	5.02	0.39	5.11	−0.80
Austria	5.16	0.38	5.10	0.47
Switzerland (French-speaking)	4.98	0.35	5.05	−0.50
New Zealand	4.75	0.25	4.86	−0.89
China	4.94	0.22	4.81	1.03
Netherlands	4.70	0.22	4.81	−0.93
England	4.65	0.16	4.70	−0.38
France	4.43	0.14	4.66	−1.79
South Africa (Black sample)	4.59	0.13	4.64	−0.33
Malaysia	4.78	0.1	4.59	1.47
Canada (English-speaking)	4.58	0.07	4.54	0.30
Albania	4.62	0.02	4.45	1.31
Australia	4.39	0	4.40	−0.12
Qatar	**3.99**	**−0.08**	**4.26**	**−2.15**
Ireland	4.3	−0.09	4.25	0.42
Hong Kong	4.32	−0.13	4.17	1.15
U.S.	4.15	−0.14	4.15	0.01
Nigeria	4.29	−0.15	4.14	1.16
Zimbabwe	4.15	−0.16	4.12	0.27
Namibia	4.2	−0.17	4.09	0.83
Japan	4.07	−0.18	4.07	−0.01
South Africa (White sample)	4.09	−0.19	4.06	0.25
Mexico	4.18	−0.19	4.06	0.96

Society	Uncorrected Scores	Corrected Scores	Regression Predicted Scores	Studentized Residual
Taiwan	**4.34**	**−0.2**	**4.04**	**2.35**
India	4.15	−0.21	4.02	1.02
Kuwait	4.21	−0.21	4.02	1.50
Egypt	4.06	−0.24	3.97	0.69
Israel	4.01	−0.24	3.97	0.30
Portugal	3.91	−0.25	3.96	−0.38
Morocco	**3.65**	**−0.25**	**3.95**	**−2.34**
Spain	3.97	−0.25	3.95	0.16
Zambia	4.10	−0.27	3.92	1.43
Indonesia	**4.17**	**−0.27**	**3.92**	**1.97**
Italy	3.79	−0.31	3.85	−0.51
Costa Rica	3.82	−0.31	3.84	−0.12
Thailand	3.93	−0.34	3.79	1.10
Kazakhstan	3.66	−0.36	3.76	−0.81
Slovenia	3.78	−0.36	3.76	0.19
Brazil	3.6	−0.37	3.74	−1.09
Poland	3.62	−0.38	3.71	−0.72
El Salvador	3.62	−0.39	3.69	−0.63
Philippines	3.89	−0.39	3.69	1.57
Turkey	3.63	−0.40	3.67	−0.34
Ecuador	3.68	−0.43	3.63	0.38
Argentina	3.65	−0.43	3.63	0.14
Colombia	3.57	−0.43	3.62	−0.41
Venezuela	3.44	−0.47	3.55	−0.89
Georgia	3.50	−0.48	3.54	−0.31
South Korea	3.55	−0.49	3.52	0.25
Greece	3.39	−0.49	3.52	−1.02
Guatemala	3.3	−0.53	3.44	−1.08
Bolivia	3.35	−0.6	3.32	0.25
Hungary	3.12	−0.63	3.26	−1.18
Russia	2.88	−0.72	3.09	−1.69

Table B.2 Response Bias Corrected Scores for Societal Cultural Scales

	Assertiveness	Institutional Collectivism	In-Group Collectivism	Future Orientation	Gender Egalitarianism	Humane Orientation	Performance Orientation	Power Distance	Uncertainty Avoidance
Country									
Albania	4.57	4.28	5.51	3.69	3.48	4.40	4.57	4.44	4.45
Argentina	4.18	3.66	5.51	3.10	3.44	3.94	3.63	5.56	3.63
Australia	4.29	4.31	4.14	4.09	3.41	4.32	4.37	4.81	4.40
Austria	4.59	4.34	4.89	4.47	3.18	3.77	4.47	5.00	5.10
Bolivia	3.78	3.96	5.44	3.55	3.45	3.99	3.57	4.46	3.32
Brazil	4.25	3.94	5.16	3.90	3.44	3.76	4.11	5.24	3.74
Canada (English-speaking)	4.09	4.36	4.22	4.40	3.66	4.51	4.46	4.85	4.54
China	3.77	4.67	5.86	3.68	3.03	4.29	4.37	5.02	4.81
Colombia	4.16	3.84	5.59	3.35	3.64	3.72	3.93	5.37	3.62
Costa Rica	3.83	3.95	5.26	3.64	3.56	4.38	4.10	4.70	3.84
Denmark	4.04	4.93	3.63	4.59	4.02	4.67	4.40	4.14	5.32
Ecuador	3.98	3.82	5.55	3.66	3.09	4.45	4.06	5.29	3.63
Egypt	3.91	4.36	5.49	3.80	2.90	4.60	4.15	4.76	3.97
El Salvador	4.49	3.74	5.22	3.73	3.23	3.69	3.72	5.56	3.69
England	4.23	4.31	4.08	4.31	3.67	3.74	4.16	5.26	4.70
Finland	4.05	4.77	4.23	4.39	3.55	4.19	4.02	5.08	5.11
France	4.44	4.20	4.66	3.74	3.81	3.60	4.43	5.68	4.66
Georgia	4.15	4.03	6.18	3.45	3.52	4.17	3.85	5.15	3.54
Germany (former East)	4.77	3.67	4.59	4.04	3.17	3.45	4.16	5.70	5.19

Regression Predicted Scores for Societal Cultural Practices Scales

Country	Assertiveness	Institutional Collectivism	In-Group Collectivism	Future Orientation	Gender Egalitarianism	Humane Orientation	Performance Orientation	Power Distance	Uncertainty Avoidance
Germany (former West)	4.66	3.97	4.16	4.41	3.25	3.30	4.42	5.48	5.35
Greece	4.55	3.41	5.28	3.53	3.53	3.44	3.34	5.35	3.52
Guatemala	3.96	3.78	5.54	3.35	3.14	3.91	3.85	5.47	3.44
Hong Kong	4.53	4.03	5.33	3.88	3.26	3.72	4.69	4.94	4.17
Hungary	4.71	3.63	5.31	3.31	4.02	3.39	3.50	5.57	3.26
India	3.70	4.25	5.81	4.04	2.89	4.45	4.11	5.29	4.02
Indonesia	3.70	4.27	5.50	3.61	3.04	4.47	4.14	4.93	3.92
Ireland	3.93	4.57	5.12	3.93	3.19	4.96	4.30	5.13	4.25
Israel	4.19	4.40	4.63	3.82	3.21	4.07	4.03	4.71	3.97
Italy	4.12	3.75	4.99	3.34	3.30	3.66	3.66	5.45	3.85
Japan	3.69	5.23	4.72	4.29	3.17	4.34	4.22	5.23	4.07
Kazakhstan	4.51	4.38	5.50	3.72	3.87	4.15	3.72	5.40	3.76
Kuwait	3.56	4.32	5.70	3.18	2.59	4.44	3.79	4.97	4.02
Malaysia	3.77	4.45	5.47	4.39	3.31	4.76	4.16	5.09	4.59
Mexico	4.31	3.95	5.62	3.75	3.50	3.84	3.97	5.07	4.06
Morocco	4.72	4.18	6.37	3.50	3.08	4.52	4.31	6.14	3.95
Namibia	3.81	4.02	4.39	3.32	3.69	3.83	3.52	5.29	4.09
Netherlands	4.46	4.62	3.79	4.72	3.62	4.02	4.46	4.32	4.81
New Zealand	3.53	4.96	3.58	3.46	3.18	4.43	4.86	5.12	4.86
Nigeria	4.53	4.00	5.34	3.95	3.04	3.96	3.79	5.53	4.14

(Continued)

743

Table B.2 (Continued)

		Regression Predicted Scores for Societal Cultural Practices Scales							
Country	Assertiveness	Institutional Collectivism	In-Group Collectivism	Future Orientation	Gender Egalitarianism	Humane Orientation	Performance Orientation	Power Distance	Uncertainty Avoidance
Philippines	3.85	4.37	6.14	3.92	3.42	4.88	4.21	5.15	3.69
Poland	4.11	4.51	5.55	3.23	3.94	3.67	3.96	5.09	3.71
Portugal	3.75	4.02	5.64	3.77	3.69	3.96	3.65	5.50	3.96
Qatar	4.39	4.78	5.07	4.08	3.86	4.79	3.76	5.05	4.26
Russia	3.86	4.57	5.83	3.06	4.07	4.04	3.53	5.61	3.09
Singapore	4.06	4.77	5.66	4.88	3.52	3.29	4.81	4.92	5.16
Slovenia	4.01	4.09	5.49	3.56	3.84	3.75	3.62	5.32	3.76
South Africa (Black sample)	4.43	4.47	5.18	4.66	3.78	4.46	4.72	4.31	4.64
South Africa (White sample)	4.49	4.54	4.42	4.08	3.25	3.45	4.07	5.10	4.06
South Korea	4.36	5.20	5.71	3.90	2.45	3.73	4.53	5.69	3.52
Spain	4.39	3.87	5.53	3.52	3.06	3.29	4.00	5.53	3.95
Sweden	3.41	5.26	3.46	4.37	3.72	4.09	3.67	4.94	5.36
Switzerland	4.58	4.20	4.04	4.80	3.12	3.73	5.04	5.05	5.42
Switzerland French-speaking	3.61	4.31	3.82	4.36	3.46	3.98	4.36	5.00	5.05
Taiwan	3.70	4.30	5.45	3.65	2.92	3.82	4.27	5.00	4.04
Thailand	3.58	3.88	5.72	3.27	3.26	4.87	3.84	5.62	3.79
Turkey	4.42	4.02	5.79	3.74	3.02	3.92	3.82	5.43	3.67
U.S.	4.50	4.21	4.22	4.13	3.36	4.18	4.45	4.92	4.15
Venezuela	4.26	3.96	5.41	3.43	3.60	4.19	3.41	5.22	3.55
Zambia	4.00	4.41	5.72	3.55	2.88	5.12	4.01	5.23	3.92
Zimbabwe	4.04	4.08	5.53	3.76	3.09	4.38	4.20	5.54	4.12

Regression Predicted Scores for Societal Cultural Values Scales

Country	Assertiveness	Institutional Collectivism	In-Group Collectivism	Future Orientation	Gender Egalitarianism	Humane Orientation	Performance Orientation	Power Distance	Uncertainty Avoidance
Albania	4.39	4.30	4.98	5.17	4.04	5.16	5.47	3.47	5.17
Argentina	3.18	5.29	6.07	5.73	4.89	5.50	6.28	2.30	4.62
Australia	3.83	4.47	5.82	5.21	5.02	5.60	5.99	2.77	3.99
Austria	2.85	4.78	5.32	5.15	4.83	5.68	6.12	2.52	3.65
Bolivia	3.68	5.03	5.91	5.56	4.65	5.11	5.98	3.31	4.64
Brazil	3.06	5.57	5.17	5.60	4.91	5.52	5.98	2.59	5.00
Canada (English-speaking)	4.15	4.20	5.94	5.34	5.04	5.58	6.13	2.73	3.73
China	5.52	4.52	5.12	4.70	3.73	5.34	5.72	3.01	5.34
Colombia	3.45	5.27	5.99	5.52	4.85	5.43	6.15	2.21	4.92
Costa Rica	4.04	5.14	5.94	5.10	4.59	5.08	5.78	2.66	4.58
Denmark	3.59	4.41	5.71	4.49	5.20	5.59	5.82	2.96	4.01
Ecuador	3.57	5.19	5.81	5.62	4.42	5.13	5.95	2.36	4.95
Egypt	3.22	4.72	5.39	5.60	3.34	5.13	5.71	3.20	5.24
El Salvador	3.67	5.60	6.28	5.89	4.66	5.38	6.37	2.76	5.27
England	3.76	4.39	5.66	5.15	5.20	5.52	6.03	2.82	4.17
Finland	3.91	4.34	5.60	5.24	4.47	5.80	6.23	2.46	4.04
France	3.57	5.27	5.88	5.35	4.71	5.91	6.10	2.96	4.65
Georgia	4.29	3.79	5.58	5.45	3.83	5.48	5.63	2.86	5.23
Germany (former East)	3.24	4.86	5.38	5.36	4.97	5.56	6.24	2.74	4.02
Germany (former West)	3.21	5.07	5.46	5.06	5.06	5.63	6.27	2.66	3.38

(Continued)

Table B.2 (Continued)

Regression Predicted Scores for Societal Cultural Values Scales

Country	Assertiveness	Institutional Collectivism	In-Group Collectivism	Future Orientation	Gender Egalitarianism	Humane Orientation	Performance Orientation	Power Distance	Uncertainty Avoidance
Greece	3.05	5.41	5.47	5.17	4.84	5.28	5.79	2.57	5.16
Guatemala	3.65	5.16	5.95	5.78	4.49	5.24	5.96	2.49	4.85
Hong Kong	4.80	4.35	5.11	5.52	4.27	5.38	5.71	3.00	4.52
Hungary	3.42	4.57	5.58	5.74	4.65	5.48	5.97	2.59	4.74
India	4.65	4.59	5.22	5.43	4.40	5.20	5.87	2.58	4.58
Indonesia	4.50	4.96	5.46	5.48	3.71	5.06	5.54	2.38	5.04
Ireland	4.00	4.55	5.72	5.18	5.07	5.45	5.99	2.66	3.94
Israel	3.74	4.25	5.69	5.17	4.66	5.51	5.71	2.72	4.34
Italy	3.87	5.20	5.76	6.01	4.88	5.57	6.11	2.51	4.52
Japan	5.84	4.01	5.44	5.42	4.41	5.53	5.37	2.76	4.40
Kazakhstan	3.88	4.16	5.62	5.22	4.85	5.66	5.57	3.19	4.52
Kuwait	3.61	5.04	5.32	5.62	3.50	5.06	5.89	3.02	4.65
Malaysia	4.73	4.78	5.77	5.84	3.72	5.43	5.96	2.75	4.81
Mexico	3.67	4.77	5.78	5.74	4.57	5.10	6.00	2.75	5.18
Morocco	3.68	5.34	6.03	6.33	4.07	5.73	6.12	3.30	5.77
Namibia	3.76	4.26	6.13	6.30	4.20	5.47	6.52	2.59	5.19
Netherlands	3.13	4.76	5.39	5.24	5.10	5.41	5.71	2.61	3.34
New Zealand	3.52	4.31	6.54	5.90	4.32	4.85	6.24	3.56	4.17
Nigeria	3.14	4.86	5.31	5.80	4.16	5.71	5.99	2.66	5.45
Philippines	4.93	4.55	5.86	5.66	4.36	5.19	6.00	2.54	4.92

Regression Predicted Scores for Societal Cultural Values Scales

Country	Assertiveness	Institutional Collectivism	In-Group Collectivism	Future Orientation	Gender Egalitarianism	Humane Orientation	Performance Orientation	Power Distance	Uncertainty Avoidance
Poland	3.95	4.24	5.69	5.17	4.53	5.32	6.06	3.19	4.75
Portugal	3.61	5.40	5.97	5.50	5.12	5.40	6.41	2.45	4.50
Qatar	3.72	5.10	5.55	5.92	3.49	5.31	5.94	3.18	4.82
Russia	2.90	4.01	5.90	5.60	4.34	5.62	5.68	2.73	5.26
Singapore	4.28	4.42	5.46	5.46	4.43	5.66	5.70	2.84	4.08
Slovenia	4.61	4.36	5.71	5.43	4.78	5.31	6.41	2.50	5.03
South Africa (Black sample)	3.97	4.46	5.14	5.25	4.43	5.23	5.09	3.80	4.92
South Africa (White sample)	3.65	4.36	5.82	5.59	4.54	5.53	6.13	2.67	4.65
South Korea	3.69	3.84	5.50	5.83	4.23	5.61	5.41	2.39	4.74
Spain	4.01	5.25	5.82	5.66	4.82	5.63	5.85	2.23	4.80
Sweden	3.49	3.91	6.25	4.96	5.19	5.72	6.01	2.49	3.45
Switzerland	3.31	4.87	5.16	4.93	5.01	5.63	6.00	2.54	3.20
Switzerland French-speaking	3.83	4.42	5.54	4.89	4.77	5.68	6.17	2.80	3.84
Taiwan	2.91	4.95	5.30	4.94	3.88	5.15	5.58	2.77	5.14
Thailand	3.43	5.08	5.73	6.26	4.12	5.05	5.76	2.74	5.71
Turkey	2.68	5.18	5.63	5.71	4.46	5.40	5.34	2.52	4.61
U.S.	4.36	4.20	5.79	5.34	5.03	5.51	6.14	2.88	3.99
Venezuela	3.34	5.28	5.92	5.61	4.70	5.24	6.11	2.43	5.19
Zambia	4.24	4.55	5.64	5.76	4.27	5.37	6.08	2.37	4.45
Zimbabwe	4.60	4.84	5.74	6.01	4.40	5.20	6.33	2.65	4.68

Table B.3   Societies Identified as Outliers Separated by Societal Culture Scale

Societal Cultural Practices (As Is) Scales	
Cultural Dimension	*Outliers*
Assertiveness	• Qatar • France • Nigeria
Institutional Collectivism	• Taiwan • Indonesia • Qatar • Morocco • France • Philippines
In-Group Collectivism	• Qatar • Morocco • France
Future Orientation	• Taiwan • Qatar • France
Gender Egalitarianism	• Taiwan • Morocco
Humane Orientation	• Taiwan • Qatar • Morocco
Performance Orientation	• Taiwan • Qatar • Morocco • France
Power Distance	• Qatar • Morocco • France
Uncertainty Avoidance	• Taiwan • Qatar • Morocco
Societal Cultural Values (Should Be) Scales	
Cultural Dimension	*Outliers*
Assertiveness	• Taiwan • Morocco • Japan
Institutional Collectivism	• Morocco • France
In-Group Collectivism	• Ecuador • Morocco • France

Societal Cultural Values (Should Be) Scales (continued)	
Cultural Dimension	*Outliers*
Future Orientation	• Ecuador • Morocco • France • New Zealand
Humane Orientation	• France • Nigeria • New Zealand
Gender Egalitarianism	• Morocco • France
Performance Orientation	• Ecuador • Morocco • France
Power Distance	• Taiwan • Indonesia
Uncertainty Avoidance	• Morocco • France

Table B.4 Frequency for Society to be Identified as Outlier in Response Bias Regression Procedure

Country	*Frequency*	*Percentage*
Ecuador	3	17
France	13	72
Indonesia	2	11
Japan	1	6
Morocco	14	78
New Zealand	2	11
Nigeria	2	11
Philippines	1	6
Qatar	8	44
Taiwan	8	44

Table B.4 summarizes these findings by indicating the percentage of times that a particular society was identified as an outlier. As can be seen from this table, most societies identified as outliers by this regression-based correction procedure were only identified as such for one or two culture scales. However, a few societies (i.e., France, Morocco, Qatar, and Taiwan) were repeatedly identified as outliers. The observed frequency of these societies being classified as outliers across the 18 societal cultural scales is substantially greater than what would be expected by chance, and so these results suggest that the data from these societies might be exhibiting substantial levels of cultural response bias. It is the societies that are repeatedly identified as outliers that are of concern and, once identified, researchers need to seek confirmatory evidence from their research notes, discussions with individuals who collected the data, or from some other source that confirms that respondents in these societies were overly sensitive to cultural response bias before taking any action with regard to these observations (e.g., discarding data from these societies).

It is worth repeating that researchers should not automatically discard data from societies identified as problematic. Outlier status cannot be unambiguously attributed to cultural response bias. Rather, outlier status could indicate that some novel but theoretically meaningful process is occurring in these identified societies. The history of science has several cases of research progress being slowed by adopting the practice of automatically excluding outliers. For example, the measurements indicating existence of the hole in the ozone layer were initially thought to be outliers and so they were automatically discarded. This oversight delayed the discovery of this environmental problem by several years (Berthouex & Brown, 1994). Thus, labeling an observation as an outlier should activate researchers to seek additional information that provides possible explanations for the outlier status of the observation rather than activate researchers to automatically reject parts of their data.

In the GLOBE project, we spoke to the country co-investigators of these four outlier societies and learned that although they experienced some unique data collection problems, there was no clear-cut confirmatory evidence of rampant response bias. Thus, we followed the protocol outlined above and kept these observations in the analyses. However, it should be noted that we did explore whether our conclusions would have substantially differed if these countries were excluded. No substantial or systematic changes in conclusions were noted when we reran our HLM analyses excluding these four societies or when we reran the HLM analyses using the response-bias corrected scores instead of the raw scores.

In summary, I developed a new protocol that modifies the traditional cultural response statistical correction procedure used in the cross-cultural literature. This regression-based correction procedure addresses several limitations of the traditional approach. First, it rescales the corrected values so that they are directly interpretable. Second, it enables use of well-established diagnostic tools that can identify specific observations that appear to be problematic.

ENDNOTE

1. It should be noted that data from the Czech Republic was not included in this analysis. Prior application of this regression-based procedure revealed that the Czech Republic data exhibited substantial and pervasive response bias. Once the Czech Republic was removed from these analyses, the results reported in this appendix were obtained.

2. A simple test confirms this last interpretation of the regression modification. If the reader compares the rank order of the societies using the uncorrected scales to the rank order of the societies using the regression-predicted scores, it will be discovered that the four countries identified as outliers in Table B.1 are the four countries with the largest change in their rank ordering. The outlier analysis identifies the societies that change their rank ordering the most after controlling for response bias.

REFERENCES

Berthouex, P. M., & Brown, L. C. (1994). *Statistics for environmental engineers.* London: CRC Press.

Draper, N. R., & Smith, H. (1981). *Applied regression analysis* (2nd ed). New York: John Wiley.

Hui, C. C., & Triandis, H. C. (1989). Effects of culture and response format on extreme response style. *Journal of Cross-Cultural Psychology, 20,* 296–309.

Stening, B. W., & Everett, J. E. (1984). Response styles in a cross-cultural managerial study. *Journal of Social Psychology, 122,* 151–156.

Triandis, H. C. (1994). Cross-cultural industrial and organizational psychology. In H. C. Triandis, M. D. Dunnette, & L. M. Hough (Eds.), *Handbook of industrial and organizational psychology* (2nd ed., Vol. 4, pp. 103–172). Palo Alto, CA: Consulting Psychologists Press.

Appendix C

Evidence for Contextual Effects

Paul J. Hanges

Mina T. Sipe

Ellen G. Godfrey

As discussed by Hanges, Dickson, and Sipe in Chapter 11, we conducted several hierarchical linear model (HLM) analyses to test our hypotheses regarding the relationship among organizational culture, societal culture, and the six culturally endorsed leadership theory (CLT) dimensions. The results of these analyses are discussed in the culture dimension chapters, the organizational culture chapter, and the CLT cluster chapter (i.e., Chapters 12–21). In this appendix, we discuss the results of additional HLM analyses conducted to demonstrate that the organizational-level relationships reported in these aforementioned chapters are truly a function of organizational-level covariation and not simply a function of individual-level biases. Even though we used HLMs to test the GLOBE hypotheses about the relationships between organizational culture and the six CLTs, individual-level covariation could have biased our findings because the same individuals provided both the CLT dimensions scores and the organizational culture scores in these analyses. The analyses reported in this appendix will demonstrate that the obtained organizational culture and CLT relationships reported in the body of this book go beyond individual-level biases and are a function of forces operating at the organizational level of analysis.

There are several statistical methods[1] that have been developed to evaluate the level of covariation influencing statistical relationships. In particular, WABA 2 (Within and Between Analysis; Dansereau & Yammarino, 2000) and contextual analyses (Bliese, 2000) are two statistical procedures specifically developed to disentangle the level of covariation influencing statistical relationships. We used the latter statistical procedure to ascertain whether our organizational-level results were due to organizational-level or individual-level covariation.

We conducted our contextual analysis in the following way. For each cultural dimension, we performed an HLM analysis in which we entered the group-mean centered organizational cultural practices and values scales at the individual level (HLM Step 1) and then entered the averages of these scales at the organizational level (HLM Step 2). The dependent variables used in these analyses were the six CLT dimension scales. The magnitude of the HLM coefficient for a particular scale at the individual level of analysis is compared with the magnitude of the HLM coefficient for that same scale at the organizational level of analysis. A chi-square test is used to determine if the magnitude of these coefficients differ significantly (Bryk & Raudenbush, 1992). Evidence that organizational level covariation was affecting the culture–CLT relationship (i.e., a context effect) is obtained when (a) the organizational-level HLM coefficient was significantly different from zero and (b) the organizational-level HLM coefficient was significantly different from its individual-level counterpart.

We used only the data from Form Alpha of the GLOBE questionnaire for these analyses because they require estimation of both individual- and organizational-level HLM coefficients. Further, as discussed in Chapter 11 by Hanges and colleagues, our sample was reduced by including only organizations that had seven or more respondents.

Chi-square analyses of organizational cultural practices and values across the six CLT dimensions resulted in a total of 12 tests of significance for each organizational culture scale. The results of these analyses are shown in Table C.1. For each organizational culture scale, the context effect was considered strong if 50% or more of its chi-square tests were significant (i.e., at least 6 out of the 12 tests) and weak if 25 % or less of its chi-square tests were significant. For example, when examining the relationships of the Power Distance organizational culture scale with the CLT dimensions, 75% of the chi-square tests were significant, indicating strong evidence for covariation at the organizational level.

As seen in Table C.1, there is evidence of strong contextual effects for most of our organizational culture scales. Therefore, consistent with expectations, the relationship between the organizational culture scales and the higher order CLT dimensions does appear to operate at the organizational level of analysis.

Table C.1 Results of Contextual HLM Analysis for the Relationship Between Organizational Culture Scales and the Higher-Order CLT Dimensions

Strong evidence for organizational level-effects:		
	Power Distance	
Dependent Variables: CLTs	Practices (As Is)	Values (Should Be)
Charismatic/Value-Based leadership	Context effect	Context effect
Team-Oriented leadership	Context effect	Context effect
Participative leadership		Context effect
Self-Protective leadership		Context effect
Autonomous leadership	Context effect	
Humane-Oriented leadership	Context effect	Context effect

Strong evidence for organizational level-effects:		
	Uncertainty Avoidance	
Dependent Variables: CLTs	Practices (As Is)	Values (Should Be)
Charismatic/Value-Based leadership	Context effect	
Team-Oriented leadership	Context effect	Context effect
Participative leadership	Context effect	Context effect
Self-Protective leadership	Context effect	Context effect
Autonomous leadership	Context effect	
Humane-Oriented leadership		Context effect

Medium evidence for organizational-level effects:		
	Collectivism 1	
Dependent Variables: CLTs	Practices (As Is)	Values (Should Be)
Charismatic/Value-Based leadership		
Team Oriented leadership		Context effect
Participative leadership	Context effect	
Self-Protective leadership	Context effect	Context effect
Autonomous leadership		
Humane-Oriented Leadership		Context effect

Strong evidence for organizational level-effects:		
	Collectivism 2	
Dependent Variables: CLTs	Practices (As Is)	Values (Should Be)
Charismatic/Value-Based leadership		Context effect
Team-Oriented leadership		Context effect
Participative leadership	Context effect	Context effect
Self-Protective leadership	Context effect	Context effect
Autonomous leadership		Context effect
Humane-Oriented leadership		Context effect

Strong evidence for organizational level-effects:

	Gender Egalitarianism	
Dependent Variables: CLTs	Practices (As Is)	Values (Should Be)
Charismatic/Value-Based leadership	Context effect	Context effect
Team-Oriented leadership	Context effect	Context effect
Participative leadership	Context effect	Context effect
Self-Protective leadership		Context effect
Autonomous leadership		Context effect
Humane-Oriented leadership	Context effect	Context effect

Weak evidence for organizational-level effects:

	Assertiveness	
Dependent Variables: CLTs	Practices (As Is)	Values (Should Be)
Charismatic/Value-Based leadership		
Team-Oriented leadership	Context effect	
Participative leadership		
Self-Protective leadership	Context effect	
Autonomous leadership	Context effect	
Humane-Oriented leadership		Context effect

Strong evidence for organizational-level effects:

	Humane Orientation	
Dependent Variables: CLTs	Practices (As Is)	Values (Should Be)
Charismatic/Value-Based leadership	Context effect	Context effect
Team-Oriented leadership	Context effect	Context effect
Participative leadership	Context effect	
Self-Protective leadership	Context effect	
Autonomous leadership	Context effect	Context effect
Humane-Oriented leadership		Context effect

Strong evidence for organizational level-effects:		
	Performance Orientation	
Dependent Variables: CLTs	Practices (As Is)	Values (Should Be)
Charismatic/Value-Based leadership	Context effect	Context effect
Team-Oriented leadership	Context effect	Context effect
Participative leadership		Context effect
Self-Protective leadership	Context effect	Context effect
Autonomous leadership		
Humane-Oriented leadership	Context effect	

Strong evidence for organizational level-effects:		
	Future Orientation	
Dependent Variables: CLTs	Practices (As Is)	Values (Should Be)
Charismatic/Value-Based leadership		Context effect
Team-Oriented leadership	Context effect	Context effect
Participative leadership		Context effect
Self-Protective leadership		
Autonomous leadership	Context effect	Context effect
Humane-Oriented leadership	Context effect	Context effect

ENDNOTE

1. Elimination of individual-level covariation from the organizational-level relationships could have been handled empirically by having one set of respondents complete the organizational culture items and a different set of respondents complete the CLT questions. Indeed, this is the method used in the HLM analyses reported in Chapters 12–21 to ensure that any obtained societal-level culture–CLT relationships were a function of societal-level covariation.

REFERENCES

Bliese, P. D. (2000). Within-group agreement, non-independence, and reliability: Implications for data aggregation and analysis. In K. J. Klein & S. W. J. Kozlowski (Eds.), *Multilevel theory, research, and methods in organizations: Foundations, extensions, and new directions* (pp. 349–381). San Francisco, CA: Jossey-Bass.

Bryk, A. S., & Raudenbush, S. W. (1992). *Hierarchical linear models for social and behavioral research: Applications and data analysis methods.* Newbury Park, CA: Sage.

Dansereau, F., & Yammarino, F. J. (2000). Within and between analysis: The variant paradigm as an underlying approach to theory building and testing. In K. J. Klein & S. W. J. Kozlowski (Eds.), *Multilevel theory, research, and methods in organizations: Foundations, extensions, and new directions* (pp. 425–466). San Francisco, CA: Jossey-Bass.

APPENDIX D

Confidence Interval Estimation of Correlations

PAUL J. HANGES

I n this book we reported whether the correlations between variables were statistically significant. For example, we indicated if particular cultural practices and culturally endorsed leadership theory dimensions were related to each other. Essentially, these statistical tests indicate whether relationships are significantly different from zero, which then allows us to reject the possibility that variables are completely unrelated. Although providing information about the statistical significance of a correlation is useful, statisticians have argued that confidence intervals provide more useful information about the nature of the relationship between two variables (e.g., Cohen, 1994; Schmidt, 1996; Schmidt & Hunter, 1997). A confidence interval is basically a range of values that have a known probability of containing the population correlation. For example, if 50 people were surveyed and the correlation between two variables was found to be 0.40, the 95% confidence interval for this relationship would be .14 to .61. In other words, the best estimate of the relationship between these two variables is that the correlation is between .14 and .61. Similar to statistical significance tests, confidence intervals that do not include zero indicate that the possibility that two variables are completely unrelated can be rejected. However, unlike significance tests, confidence intervals data provide information about the level of precision that a particular study provides in estimating the relationship between two variables. Assuming that the error rate of a confidence interval is held constant, the smaller confidence intervals (e.g., .30 to .37) provide more precision in the estimation of some relationship than do larger confidence intervals (e.g., .10 to .57).

Although we believe that providing confidence intervals for each relationship throughout the book would have been useful, unfortunately the volume of results is overwhelming and prevented us from reporting confidence intervals for all findings. Instead, the table provided in this appendix will provide an approximation of confidence intervals that one might expect given the size of the correlations and sample size. Specifically, Table D.1 provides 95% confidence intervals for a representative sample of correlations. For example, this table shows that if the correlation between two variables

Table D.1   Confidence Intervals for a Representative Sample of Correlations

Sample Size	Obtained Correlation				
	.10	.20	.30	.40	.50
25	−.31 to .48	−.21 to .55	−.11 to .62	.01 to .69	.13 to .75
30	−.27 to .44	−.17 to .52	−.07 to .60	.05 to .66	.17 to .73
35	−.24 to .42	−.14 to .50	−.04 to .58	.08 to .65	.20 to .71
40	−.22 to .40	−.12 to .48	−.01 to .56	.10 to .63	.22 to .70
45	−.20 to .38	−.10 to .47	.01 to .55	.12 to .62	.24 to .69
50	−.18 to .37	−.08 to .45	.02 to .53	.14 to .61	.26 to .68
55	−.17 to .36	−.07 to .44	.04 to .52	.15 to .60	.27 to .68
60	−.16 to .35	−.06 to .43	.05 to .51	.16 to .59	.28 to .67
65	−.15 to .34	−.05 to .42	.06 to .51	.17 to .59	.29 to .66

is reported to be .30 and if this correlation was based on 45 observations, the 95% confidence interval for the relationship between these two variables would be .01 to .55. We hope that this table will provide the reader with a feel for the magnitude of the confidence intervals that would have been reported in our study.

REFERENCES

Cohen, J. (1994). The earth is round ($p < .05$). *American Psychologist, 49,* 997–1003.

Schmidt, F. L. (1996). Statistical significance testing and cumulative knowledge in psychology: Implications for the training of researchers. *Psychological Methods,1,* 115–129.

Schmidt, F. L., & Hunter, J. E. (1997). Eight common but false objections to the discontinuation of significance testing in the analysis of research data. In L. L. Harlow, S. A. Mulaik, & J. H. Steiger (Eds.), *What if there were no significance tests?* (pp. 37–64). Mahwah, NJ: Lawrence Erlbaum.

AUTHOR INDEX

SUBJECT INDEX

About the Editors

Robert J. House received his PhD degree in management from the Ohio State University, June 1960. He was appointed the Joseph Frank Bernstein Professor Endowed Chair of Organization Studies at the Wharton School of the University of Pennsylvania in 1988. He has published 130 journal articles. In total, his articles have been reprinted in approximately 50 anthologies of readings in management and organizational behavior. He received the Award for Distinguished Scholarly Contribution to Management, and four awards for outstanding publications. The awards were conferred by the Academy of Management and the Canadian Association of Administrative Sciences. He has also authored two papers that are Scientific Citations Classics.

He is a Fellow of the Academy of Management, American Psychological Association, and Society for Industrial/Organizational Psychology. He has served as chairperson of the Academy of Management Division of Organizational Behavior (1972–1973) and President of the Administrative Science Association of Canada (1985–1986).

He was the Principal Investigator of the Global Leadership and Organizational Behavior Effectiveness Research Program (GLOBE) from 1993 through 2003. In this capacity he visited universities in 38 countries. He has also been a visiting scholar or visiting professor at 14 universities, most of which are in Europe or Asia.

His major research interests are the role of personality traits and motives as they relate to effective leadership and organizational performance, power, and personality in organizations, leadership, and the implications of cross-cultural variation for effective leadership and organizational performance.

Paul J. Hanges is an Associate Professor of Industrial–Organizational Psychology and Chair of the I/O Area at the University of Maryland. He received his PhD in industrial–organizational psychology from the University of Akron and has been a faculty member at the University of Maryland since 1986. His research interests center around topics in social cognition, cross-cultural leadership, research methodology, and personnel selection. The majority of his work has focused on understanding factors affecting social perceptions (e.g., leadership) and the factors (e.g., societal culture, gender stereotypes, personality) that cause these perceptions to stabilize or change over time. He has developed a dynamic measure of perception and explored the utility of various mathematical models (e.g., catastrophe analysis, neural network analysis) to model changes in leadership ratings over time. His methodology work has dealt with such topics as multilevel statistical modeling, range restriction, and test banding methodology. He joined the GLOBE project in 1993 and became a coprincipal investigator. His work has appeared in such journals as *Applied Psychological Measurement, Applied Psychology:*

An International Review, Educational and Psychological Measurement, Human Performance, Journal of Applied Psychology, Leadership Quarterly, and *Psychology Bulletin.* He is currently on the editorial board of *Organizational Research Methods* and the *Journal of Applied Psychology,* and he is one of the associate editors of the Quantitative Methods section of *Leadership Quarterly.*

Mansour Javidan, is Professor of Strategic Management and Chairman of the Strategy and Global Management Area at Haskayne School of Business, University of Calgary, Canada. He received his MBA and PhD degrees from the Carlson School at the University of Minnesota. His interests are in the areas of strategic management, cross-cultural leadership, and mergers and acquisitions.

His publications have appeared in such journals as *Strategic Management Journal, Academy of Management Executive, Long Range Planning, Journal of Management Studies, Organizational Dynamics, Journal of Applied Behavioural Sciences, Public Administration Review, Human Relations, Journal of World Business, Journal of Organizational Change Management, Leadership Quarterly, Applied Psychology: An International Review,* and *Canadian Journal of Administrative Sciences.* He has received several Best Paper awards and citations of excellence.

He is on the Board of Directors of GLOBE (Global Leadership and Organizational Behavior Effectiveness) and hosted the first GLOBE research conference in Calgary in 1993. He was the cochair of the Mergers and Acquistions Summit, 2002 and is the coeditor of an upcoming book on mergers and acquisitions.

He has designed and taught a variety of executive development courses and workshops in 20 countries. During 1997–2000 he was on leave from the university to work with the CEO of a multibillion-dollar energy company, helping him develop new directions and strategies, and facilitate strategic and cultural change. He was directly involved in a $15 billion merger, at the time the largest in Canada.

He is the Country Close-up editor of the *Academy of Management Executive.* He was recently elected a Fellow of the Pan Pacific Business Association and was named in Lexington's 2001–2002 Millennium Edition of the North American *Who's Who Registry.*

Peter W. Dorfman is a full Professor and the Department Head of the Department of Management, New Mexico State University. His master's and PhD degrees are from the University of Maryland. His articles on leadership, cross-cultural management, and employee discrimination have appeared in the *Journal of Applied Psychology, Academy of Management Journal, Academy of Management Review, Journal of Management, Advances in International Comparative Management,* and *Advances in Global Leadership,* among others. His current research involves investigating the impact of cultural influences on managerial behavior and leadership styles. He has been a coprincipal investigator of the decade-long Global Leadership and Organizational Behavioral Effectiveness (GLOBE) Research Project. As part of GLOBE, he has been a country co-investigator for Mexico, a member of the GLOBE coordinating team for overall coordination of the project, and is now an executive committee member.

Vipin Gupta is an Assistant Professor and International Research Scholar at Seidman School of Business, Grand Valley State University, Michigan. Earlier he was at Fordham University (1997–2003). He has a PhD (1998) and a 5-year post-doctorate fellowship (1999–2003) from the Wharton School. He was a gold medalist at the postgraduate program of the Indian Institute of Management—Ahmedabad (1988–1990). He has been a Japan Foundation Fellow, a visiting researcher at the University of Tokyo (1994–1995), and a member of the Japanese Multinational Enterprise Study

Group. He is the Director of the Globe India Development Center, a network of business schools participating in the CEO study of the GLOBE program in different states of India. He has offered invited programs in about 20 business schools spread across all regions of India, and has also been an invited speaker in several nations. He has received several research grants, including from the National Science Foundation and Marsh and McLennan Companies.

His work has appeared in such journals as *Journal of Business Venturing, Research in Organizational Behavior, Asia-Pacific Journal of Management, Multinational Business Review, Journal of World Business, Journal of Academy of Business and Economics, Journal of Case Studies, and Advances in Global Leadership.* He has edited books: *Creating Performing Organizations: International Perspectives for Indian Management* (2002, Sage) and *Transformative Organizations: A Global Perspective* (2003, Sage). He has authored a textbook on *Strategic Management and Business Policy* (2004, Oxford). His research includes management, leadership, and entrepreneurship in different cultures of the world; research methodology and mathematical modeling for cultural effects, technological growth, and performance measures; and study of national systems, with special reference to Japan, China, and India.

ABOUT THE CONTRIBUTORS

Neal Ashkanasy is Professor of Management in the University of Queensland Business School. He has a PhD (1989) in social and organizational psychology from the University of Queensland, and has research interests in leadership, organizational culture, and business ethics. Since 1995, he has been the Australian Country Co-Investigator for GLOBE. In more recent years, however, his research has focused on the role of emotions in organizational life. He has published his work in journals such as the *Academy of Management Review,* the *Academy of Management Executive,* the *Journal of Management,* and the *Journal of Organizational Behavior,* and has edited three books: *The Handbook of Organizational Culture and Climate* (Sage), *Emotions in the Workplace: Theory, Research, and Practice*; and *Managing Emotions in the Workplace.* He is a past Chair of the Managerial and Organizational Cognition Division of the Academy of Management.

David J. Bechtold is a PhD candidate at the University of Hawaii at Manoa in the International Management program and is also the Director of Project Management at the Pacific Health Research Institute. He has co-authored papers on the effects of culture on group decision making, leadership, and creativity. His research interests include the attributes associated with the success of leadership in internationl settings and the impact of culture on organizational effectiveness and creativity.

Renee S. BeShears is a doctoral student in the industrial–organizational psychology program at Wayne State University. Her research interests include leadership, organizational culture and change, and executive-level selection. She has a master's degree in clinical psychology and a bachelor's degree in psychology from Wayne State University as well.

Dharm P. S. Bhawuk, a citizen of Nepal, is a Professor of Management and Culture and Community Psychology, University of Hawaii at Manoa. He received his PhD in organizational behavior from the University of Illinois at Urbana-Champaign. His research interests include cross-cultural training, individualism and collectivism, inter-cultural sensitivity, diversity in the workplace, indigenous psychology and management, culture and quality, culture and entrepreneurship, and political behavior in the workplace. He has published several papers in the *Journal of Cross-Cultural Psychology, International Journal of Intercultural Relations, Applied Psychology: An International Review, International Journal of Psychology, Cross-Cultural Research, Indian Psychological Review, Delhi Business Review,* and *Journal of Management.* He has also published a number of book chapters and is a coeditor of the book *Asian Contributions to Cross-Cultural Psychology* (1996, Sage).

He has received many awards and honors including the Distinguished Scholar Award, Management Department, College of Business Administration (2000), the Best Paper Award from the International Division of the Academy of Management (1996), the Distinguished Service Award from the East West Center (1989), and the Lum Yip Kee Outstanding MBA Student Award from the College of Business Administration, University of Hawaii (1990). He is a Founding Fellow of the International Academy of Intercultural Research.

Muzaffer Bodur is a Professor of Marketing at the Management Department of Bogaziçi University in Istanbul, Turkey. She received her doctor of business administration from Indiana University in 1977 and acted as a Visiting Assistant Professor at George Mason University upon graduation. In 1979 she joined Bogaziçi University faculty where she teaches a global marketing management course to MBA students and research methods courses to doctoral students. She has organized training programs and seminars for executives and has served as the department head.

She is a member of the Academy of International Business and the Consortium for International Marketing Research . Currently, she is the editor of *Bogaziçi Journal: Review of Social, Economic and Administrative Studies* and serves on the editorial board of *Journal of International Marketing.* She has visited Uppsala University of Sweden and Odense University of Denmark to teach international marketing courses and conducted cross-cultural research on the implications of business culture for internationalization of firms. Her publications focus on marketing strategies of multinational firms in emerging markets; export marketing management; expatriate managers; and consumer satisfaction, dissatisfaction, and complaining behavior with services and intangible product.

Felix C. Brodbeck holds a doctoral degree from the University of Giessen, and a Post-Doctorate (Doctor Habilitated) from the University of Munich. He is a Professor of Organizational and Social Psychology and Head of the Department of Work and Organisational Psychology at Aston Business School, Aston University, Birmingham, England. He is a member of the coordination team of the GLOBE Program. He has written or edited six books and authored more than 70 scholarly articles in the fields of leadership, cross-cultural psychology, social psychology, group performance and group decision making, team climate and effectiveness, innovation, human–computer interaction, and applied research methods in organizations. His repertoire of experience and practice comprises experimental, applied, and field research; development of theory and practical tools; as well as executive training and business consulting in the above areas and human resource management in general.

Dale Carl is an Associate Professor in the School of Business Management at Ryerson University in Toronto, Canada. He has a BA degree in history, an MBA in international business, and a PhD in international business and strategy from the University of Calgary. He was a diplomat in the Canadian Foreign Service, with postings in Pakistan, Norway, the United States, and Iraq. Subsequently, he lived in Dubai, working in the private sector, with a territory that included the Middle East and East Africa. His research interest is comparative cross-cultural leadership. He has coauthored papers titled "Motivational Consequences of Charismatic Leadership: An Empirical Investigation," "East Meets West: Exploring Charismatic Leadership Among Canadian and Iranian Executives," and "Universality of Charismatic Leadership: A Multi-County Study."

Deanne N. Den Hartog holds a master of science and a doctoral degree in organizational psychology from the Free University in Amsterdam, the Netherlands. She is currently a full professor of Organizational Psychology at the School of Economics and Business of the Erasmus University in Rotterdam, the Netherlands. Her research has focused on cross-cultural and transformational leadership processes. Other research interests include team reflexivity and effectiveness as well as human resource management. She has published on these topics in a variety of journals (e.g., *Leadership Quarterly, Journal of Organizational Behavior*) as well as in chapters in international volumes and two Dutch books.

Florence L. Denmark, PhD, is the Robert Scott Pace Distinguished Research Professor at Pace University in New York, where she served as Chair of the Psychology Department for 13 years. A social psychologist who received her doctorate from the University of Pennsylvania, she has published extensively in the psychology of women and gender. She served as the 88th president of the American Psychological Association (APA) in 1980. She is a fellow of 12 APA Divisions and served as a president of APA Divisions 1, 35, and 52. In addition, she was president of the International Council of Psychologists, Eastern Psychological Association, New York State Psychological Association, and Psi Chi. She was also a vice president of the New York Academy of Sciences. She has four honorary doctorates and is the recipient of many awards, including APA's Distinguished Contributions to Education and Training, Public Interest and the Advancement of International Psychology. She is currently an APA nongovernmental organization representative to the United Nations and continues to teach graduate courses at Pace University.

Marcus W. Dickson is Associate Professor of Industrial–Organizational Psychology and Chair of the I/O Area at Wayne State University in Detroit, Michigan. He was a charter member of GLOBE, a member of the GLOBE Coordinating Team for 6 years, and he served as Co-Principal Investigator on that project for 2 years. He received his PhD in industrial–organizational psychology from the University of Maryland in 1997. His research interests include leadership and leadership development, cross-cultural organizational culture analysis, organizational climate (especially ethical climate and climate for innovation), and computer-mediated communication in organizations. He currently serves as a member of the editorial board of the *Journal of Organizational Behavior,* and his work has appeared in *Journal of Applied Psychology, Leadership Quarterly, Applied Psychology: An International Review, Organizational Behavior and Human Decision Processes, Annual Review of Psychology,* and *Handbook of Organizational Culture and Climate,* among others.

Cynthia G. Emrich is an Associate Professor at The School of Business, The College of William and Mary. Her current research interests include leader communication, image, and firm performance as well as gender stereotyping and discrimination in organizations. Recent publications include "Images in Words: Presidential Rhetoric, Charisma, and Greatness" with H. H. Brower, J. M. Feldman, and H. Garland (*Administrative Science Quarterly*), "Thinking Outside the Box by Looking Inside the Box" with R. G. Lord (*Leadership Quarterly*), and "Context Effects in Leadership Perception" (*Personality and Social Psychology Bulletin*). She earned her PhD in psychology from Rice University.

Michele J. Gelfand is an Associate Professor of Organizational Psychology at the University of Maryland. Her research focuses on negotiation, diversity, and cross-cultural theory and methodology. She is the author of more than 30 articles and chapters, which have been published in outlets such as *Journal of Applied Psychology, Journal of Personality and Social Psychology, Journal of Experimental Social*

Psychology, and *Organizational Behavior and Human Decision Processes.* She received the Ernest J. McCormick Award from the Society for Industrial and Organizational Psychology, the L. L. Cummings Scholars Award from the Organizational Behavior division of the Academy, the Best Article of the Year Award from the International Association for Conflict Management, and the Dorothy Harlow award for the Best Paper at the Academy of Management. Along with Jeanne Brett, she edited a book titled *Negotiation: Theoretical Advances and Cross-Cultural Perspectives* (in press). She has received two grants from the National Science Foundation, and serves on the boards of the *Journal of Applied Psychology, Personnel Psychology, International Journal of Cross-Cultural Management,* and is Associate Editor of *Applied Psychology: An International Review.*

Ellen G. Godfrey received her bachelor's degree in psychology from Wake Forest University in 1998 and her master's degree in industrial–organizational psychology from the University of Maryland in 2000. She is currently a doctoral candidate in the industrial–organizational psychology program at the University of Maryland. Her research interests include motivation for seeking developmental opportunities, gender differences on organizational citizenship behaviors, metaphors for negotiation, and reactions to performance appraisal. In addition to her dissertation, she has been working as a Manager of Organization Effectiveness for Campbell Soup Company since 2001. In this role, she focuses on in-class and online training initiatives, individual development, performance improvement, 360-degree feedback, leadership assessment, and culture change.

Markus Hauser holds a PhD in organizational behavior and strategic management from the University of Zurich. He completed a postdoctoral fellowship at the Wharton School, where he worked closely with Robert House on the GLOBE study. He has published in areas such as leadership, organizational culture and change, innovation, strategic management, and sales and marketing related topics. In addition to his academic accomplishments, he is a cofounder of Adpilot, New York, a company that provides services to optimize advertising, pricing, and promotion strategies for Fortune 500 companies. For several years, he also consulted for global pharmaceutical companies on strategic sales and marketing issues. In this capacity, he supported several product launches in areas such as regulatory environment, product definition, pricing, launch investment strategy. For in-line products, he devised promotion and sales force optimization strategies, positioning, and targeting programs.

Hayat Kabasakal is Professor of Management and Organization Studies at the Management Department of Bogaziçi University, Istanbul, Turkey. She received her PhD in 1984 in strategic management and organizational behavior from the University of Minnesota. In 1984 she joined the Bogaziçi University faculty, where she teaches management and organizational behavior courses to undergraduate, MBA, executive MBA, and doctoral students. She has served as the Associate Dean of the Faculty of Administrative Sciences and Department Head of the Management Department. She is currently the codirector of the Center for Disaster Management.

Her research interests center on organizational behavior, with a focus on leadership, culture, and gender in organizations. She has published in *Journal of Strategic Management, Organizational Behavior Teaching Review, Journal of Applied Psychology: An International Journal, Journal of World Business, International Journal of Social Economics,* and *Bogaziçi Journal: Review of Social, Economic and Administrative Studies.* She is a member of Academy of Management, Turkish Faculty Members' Association, and GLOBE Foundation. She has served as the editor of

Bogaziçi Journal: Review of Social, Economic and Administrative Studies and on the editorial boards of several international and national journals focusing on management and organizational studies.

Melinda S. Mayfield is a Compensation Analyst in Human Resources Strategy at Cerner Corporation in Kansas City, Missouri, and was a PhD candidate in organizational behavior at the Krannert Graduate School of Management at Purdue University at the time this research was conducted. She earned an MBA in human resources management from the University of Missouri-Columbia, and a BS in economics and business administration from William Jewell College in Liberty, Missouri.

Lisa Hisae Nishii is currently an Assistant Professor in the Departments of Human Resource Studies and International and Comparative Labor in the School of Industrial and Labor Relations at Cornell University, where she is also a member of the faculty of the East Asian Program. Born and reared in Tokyo, Japan, her research reflects a personal interest in cross-cultural issues involving Japan, in addition to cross-cultural management issues more generally. Her other areas of research include diversity in the workplace and strategic human resource management. She received her BA in economics from Wellesley College and her PhD in industrial–organizational psychology from the University of Maryland, where she worked closely with Michele Gelfand to publish numerous articles having to do with culture, conflict and negotiation, and gender issues in organizations.

Mina T. Sipe is a doctoral candidate in industrial–organizational psychology at the University of Maryland. Her primary research interests are leadership development and follower reactions, organizational culture and service quality, and group and team processes. She is also interested in the application of hierarchical linear modeling to group and organizational research. She has worked on applied projects ranging from improving service quality and organizational synergy, understanding the relationship between managerial personality and team service quality, and gender bias in a performance appraisal context. Prior to entering graduate school, she was involved in stress research at the Boston Veterans Administration, National Center for Post-Traumatic Stress Disorder.

Mary Sully de Luque is an Assistant Professor of Management at Thunderbird, the American Graduate School of International Management and a Research Fellow in the Garvin Center for Cultures and Languages. Before joining Thunderbird, she spent 3 years as a Senior Fellow in the Wharton School at the University of Pennsylvania, working with the GLOBE project. She earned her bachelors degree in organizational communication at Creighton University and holds a PhD in organizational behavior from the University of Nebraska, College of Business Administration.

Her research interests include the influences of culture on leadership, feedback processes in the work environment, and human resource management. She is currently cofacilitating the GLOBE Phase 3 Project, which is a multicountry study of entrepreneur and nonentrepreneur leadership effectiveness. She has presented her work at numerous conferences and has published in top academic journals. Prior to finishing her formal education, she worked as an aide for two United States Senators.

Edwin Trevor-Roberts holds a Bachelor of Business Management degree with honors from the University of Queensland Business School and has been actively involved in the GLOBE project since 1998, coauthoring several articles and book chapters on leadership and culture. His research interests now focus on careers and he is currently completing his doctoral degree in this field. He is also a Career Consultant and Business

Development Manager for Trevor-Roberts Associates, a Career Consulting firm. He shares responsibility for the management of the organization and has been integral in the development and launch of several innovative career services. Prior to this he held positions in a variety of industries including the banking and online services sectors. He has been involved in several successful start-ups such as an Internet business solutions firm and a human resource contracting firm.

He is an advocate of youth development, being a past president of the Brisbane West Rotaract Club, and a member of the International Young Professionals Foundation. He represented Australia at the 2002 Asia-Pacific Economic Cooperation Young Leaders Forum.

Harry C. Triandis is Professor Emeritus of Psychology at the University of Illinois. His 1958 PhD is from Cornell University in Ithaca, New York. He is the author of numerous books, including *Attitudes and Attitude Change* (1971), which became a citation classic. His *Analysis of Subjective Culture* (1972) included extensive empirical work done in Greece with Vasso Vassilious, and resulted in an honorary degree from the University of Athens in 1987. In addition, he published *Interpersonal Behavior* (1977), *Variations in Black and White: Perceptions of the Social Environment* (1976), *Culture and Social Behavior* (1994), and *Individualism and Collectivism* (1995). He was the general editor of the six-volume *Handbook of Cross-Cultural Psychology* and coeditor (with Dunnette & Hough) of Volume 4 of the *Handbook of Industrial and Organizational Psychology* (1994).

He was Chairman and Secretary General of the Society of Experimental Social Psychology (1972–1974); President of the International Association of Cross-Cultural Psychology (1976), the Interamerican Society of Psychology (1987–1989), and the International Association of Applied Psychology (1990–1994), as well as of Divisions 8 and 9 of the American Psychological Association. His other honors include Fellow of the Center for International Studies (Cornell University, 1968–1969), Guggenheim Fellow (1972–1973), Center for Advanced Studies of the University of Illinois (1972–1980), the Interamerican Society of Psychology Award (1981), Fellow of the American Association for the Advancement of Science (1984), Distinguished Fulbright Professor to India (1983), the Klineberg Award (1984), and the American Psychological Association's Distinguished Contributions to International Psychology.